We recently lost our beloved pet "Bear," who was not only our best and dearest friend but also the "Vice President of Sunshine" here at Atlantic Publishing. He did not receive a salary but worked tirelessly 24 hours a day to please his parents. Bear was a rescue dog that turned around and showered myself, my wife Sherri, his grandparents Jean, Bob and Nancy and every person and animal he met (maybe not rabbits) with friendship and love. He made a lot of people smile every day.

We wanted you to know that a portion of the profits of this book will be donated to The Humane Society of the United States.

–Douglas & Sherri Brown

REMEMBERING A FRIEND

The human-animal bond is as old as human history. We cherish our animal companions for their unconditional affection and acceptance. We feel a thrill when we glimpse wild creatures in their natural habitat or in our own backyard.

Unfortunately, the human-animal bond has at times been weakened. Humans have exploited some animal species to the point of extinction.

The Humane Society of the United States makes a difference in the lives of animals here at home and worldwide. The HSUS is dedicated to creating a world where our relationship with animals is guided by compassion. We seek a truly humane society in which animals are respected for their intrinsic value, and where the human-animal bond is strong.

Want to help animals? We have plenty of suggestions. Adopt a pet from a local shelter, join The Humane Society and be a part of our work to help companion animals and wildlife. You will be funding our educational, legislative, investigative and outreach projects in the U.S. and across the globe.

Or perhaps you'd like to make a memorial donation in honor of a pet, friend or relative? You can through our Kindred Spirits program. And if you'd like to contribute in a more structured way, our Planned Giving Office has suggestions about estate planning, annuities, and even gifts of stock that avoid capital gains taxes. Maybe you have land that you would like to preserve as a lasting habitat for wildlife. Our Wildlife Land Trust can help you. Perhaps the land you want to share is a backyard—that's enough. Our Urban Wildlife Sanctuary Program will show you how to create a habitat for your wild neighbors.

So you see, it's easy to help animals. And The HSUS is here to help.

THE HUMANE SOCIETY OF THE UNITED STATES ©

The Humane Society of the United States
2100 L Street NW
Washington, DC 20037
202-452-1100
www.hsus.org

TABLE OF CONTENTS

CHAPTER 2
BASICS OF BUYING
OR LEASING A RESTAURANT

CHAPTER 3
CREATING A SUCCESSFUL
BUSINESS PLAN

CHAPTER 4
STEPS TO SECURE FINANCING

CHAPTER 5
HOW TO ANALYZE AND INVEST IN A RESTAURANT FRANCHISE

CHAPTER 6
EFFECTIVE RESTAURANT LAYOUT & REMODELING

CHAPTER 7
BASIC COST CONTROL
FOR RESTAURANTS

CHAPTER 8
PROFITABLE MENU PLANNING

CHAPTER 9
DIETARY AND NUTRITIONAL GUIDELINES

CHAPTER 10
CHOOSE THE PROPER EQUIPMENT

CHAPTER 11   PURCHASING

CHAPTER 12
INVENTORY, RECEIVING,
AND STORAGE

CHAPTER 13
FOOD BUYING TECHNIQUES

CHAPTER 14
FOOD COST CONTROLS

CHAPTER 15
SUCCESSFUL KITCHEN MANAGEMENT AND CONTROL PROCEDURES

CHAPTER 16
ESSENTIALS OF FOOD SAFETY, HACCP, AND SANITATION

CHAPTER 17
SAFETY AND RISK MANAGEMENT

CHAPTER 18
SUCCESSFUL BAR LAYOUT, SET UP, AND LOCATION

CHAPTER 19
BAR SERVICE, PRECAUTIONS, AND LEGALITIES

CHAPTER 20
SUCCESSFUL WINE MANAGEMENT

CHAPTER 21
MANAGEMENT OF OPERATIONAL COSTS AND SUPPLIES

CHAPTER 22
COMPUTERS AND FOOD SERVICE OPERATIONS

CHAPTER 23
MANAGING THE DINING ROOM AND WAITSTAFF

CHAPTER 24
INCREASE ORDER AMOUNT AND YOUR BOTTOM LINE

CHAPTER 25
FINDING, RECRUITING, AND HIRING GREAT EMPLOYEES

CHAPTER 26
TRAINING EMPLOYEES

CHAPTER 27
HANDLING EMPLOYEES TIPS

CHAPTER 28
MOTIVATE YOUR EMPLOYEES

CHAPTER 29
DAILY LEADERSHIP
AND TEAMBUILDING

CHAPTER 30
CONTROL LABOR COST
WITHOUT SACRIFICING
SERVICE OR QUALITY

CHAPTER 31
PUBLIC RELATIONS FOR YOUR RESTAURANT

CHAPTER 35
INTERNAL BOOKKEEPING

CHAPTER 36
SUCCESSFUL BUDGETING AND
PROFIT PLANNING

CHAPTER 37
HOW TO PREPARE THE MONTHLY
AUDIT AND COST PROJECTIONS

CHAPTER 38
PERFORM AN INTERNAL AUDIT ON RESTAURANT AND BAR OPERATIONS

CHAPTER 39
BASICS OF SELLING A RESTAURANT

ADDITIONAL MATERIALS

ACKNOWLEDGEMENTS

Many people helped to make this new edition of *The Restaurant Manager's Handbook* possible. Some were inspirational and some provided valuable information, while others provided editorial talent, encouragement and support. Without the assistance of the individuals listed below, this book would never have become a reality. I sincerely thank all these fine people and organizations:

- Sherri Lyn Brown
- Bruce & Vonda Brown
- James & Karen Haven
- Ed Manley; IFSEA
- Hal & Charlanne Brown
- Dr. Joseph E. Gelety
- Richard Meade, CPA
- Angela C. Adams
- Meghan MacDonald
- Tracie Kendziora
- Ed Fleming
- Dianna Podmoroff
- Jessica Hudson
- B.J. Granberg
- Amanda Miron
- National Restaurant Association
- The Internal Revenue Service
- Ocala Public Library
- Central Florida Community College & Library
- Gizmo Graphics Web Design **www.gizwebs.com**

- Halowell & Jean E. Brown
- Shri L. Henkel
- Kim Hendrickson
- Robert Baker
- Lynn & Jim Durante
- Robert M. & Nancy Frazier
- Meg Buchner
- Christina Mohammed
- Whitney Roach
- Vickie Taylor
- Sharon Fullen
- Lynda Andrews
- Cheryl Lewis
- Lora Arduser
- Mr. Ed Larson; Superior Products
- The Small Business Administration
- The U.S. Department Of Labor
- University of Florida Library

*Special thanks to Shri L. Henkel for assistance in compiling this edition. Shri has 21 years of business management and 15 years of marketing experience. For more information about her work, visit her fiction Web site at **www.nikkileigh.com** or her business Web site **www.sandcconsulting.com**.*

INTRODUCTION

In the year 2006 there were over 60,000 new or newly opened restaurants started in the USA. A longitudinal study of restaurants in Ohio found the failure rate for restaurants was 57 to 61 percent for a three year period (1996-1999) The highest failure rate was noted during the first year when about 26 percent of the restaurants failed. About 19 percent failed in the second year and 14 percent in the third year. Cumulative failure rate for the three-year period (1996-99) was 59 percent. Among franchised chains, the failure rate was 57 percent over the three years and among independent restaurants, the rate was 4 percent higher – 61 percent. Countless others are losing money and on the verge of closing. These are, of course, only the failures actually reported. Although the reasons for these unfortunate statistics are many and varied, they can be pinpointed to one main fact; there hasn't been any comprehensive source of information about the subject of restaurant management to guide the prospective restaurateur prior to the publication of this book.

Virtually everyone, at one time or another, has been tempted to run, or at least considered running, his or her own restaurant. This may be due to a number of reasons. Perhaps the prospective restaurateur is accomplished in the kitchen, or so his spouse and friends tell him. Perhaps the motivation was derived from an unfortunate experience at a local restaurant, and the "I can do this much better" syndrome has set in. Or, perhaps he feels his town could use a "good seafood restaurant". The reasons for starting a restaurant are varied. However, most have one factor in common: they end in financial disaster due to a lack of pertinent knowledge about setting up, operating and managing a financially successful restaurant.

Americans enjoy eating out, and the pace of development of the modern lifestyle indicates that they will continue to eat out more in the future. Higher economic levels, more mobility and more women in the workforce will all lead to a continuing growth in the industry in the next decade. A preview of the 2007 Restaurant Industry Forecast available from the National Restaurant Association indicates the nation's The nation's 935,000 restaurants should hit $537 billion in sales in 2007, according to the NRA's 2007 Restaurant Industry Forecast. Restaurant-industry sales are forecast to advance 5% in 2007 and equal 4% of the U.S. gross domestic product. The overall economic impact of the restaurant industry is expected to exceed $1.3 trillion in 2007, including sales in related industries such as agriculture, transportation and manufacturing.

Food service continues to lead other industries, such as housing, auto making and electronics, in total sales. The food service industry continues to gain a greater share of all food dollars spent in America. Four out of five — consumers agree that going out to a restaurant is a better way to use their leisure time than cooking and cleaning up. The average household expenditure for food away from home in 2005 was $2,634, or $1,054 per person. Average unit sales in 2004 were $795,000 at full-service restaurants and $671,000 at limited-service restaurants.

As these figures clearly show, there is room for entry into the restaurant marketplace. Profits, however, can only be realized from the application of modern management procedures. Food service is a complex business. The preparation and the serving of food entails warehousing, manufacturing and retailing. It is one of the few retail trades where the product is manufactured, sold and consumed on the premises. Properly armed with the right information and entrepreneurial drive, you will find the restaurant business can be very rewarding both financially and through a sense of personal achievement.

This manual and companion CD-ROM will arm you with the right information. Keep it on your desk for constant reference. The many valuable forms contained in this work are all available on the CD-ROM. There is no other publication as comprehensive as Fourth Edition of *The Restaurant Manager's Handbook*. This book truly is appropriately titled.

Good reading and good luck!

Sincerely,

Douglas R. Brown

AUTHOR BIOGRAPHY

Douglas R. Brown is a best-selling author in the area of food service management, having worked for both national chains and independent restaurants, as well as providing consulting services. He is the author of several new books and numerous articles on food service management. In 1982 he established Atlantic Publishing Group, Inc., and today the company is the leader in providing training materials including books, videos, posters, tools and software to the food service industry. Visit **www.atlantic-pub.com** to view a complete selection of products.

CHAPTER

1

SUCCESSFUL
PRE-OPENING ACTIVITIES
FOR A RESTAURANT VENTURE

The purpose of this chapter is to list and describe the activities fundamental to opening a restaurant. Each restaurant offers its own unique, challenging problems. The following chapter will make the prospective restaurateur aware of all the pre-opening procedures that must be completed for any restaurant.

Before engaging in any business activity seek the guidance of a lawyer. You will have many legal questions and will need legal counseling during the opening period. The services of a local accountant or CPA should also be retained. The accountant will be instrumental in setting up the business and can provide financial advice to inform your decision making. The most important task to prepare for is writing the formal business plan, which will be your road map for success. We will discuss Business Plans in full detail in Chapter 3.

TYPES OF BUSINESS ORGANIZATIONS

When organizing a new business, decide on the structure of the business. Factors influencing your business organization decision include:

- Legal restrictions
- Type of business operation
- Capital needs
- Tax advantages or disadvantages

- Liabilities assumed
- Earnings distribution
- Number of employees
- Length of business operation

The advantages and disadvantages of sole proprietorship, partnership, corporation, and the new hybrid Limited Liability Company are listed on the next page.

SOLE PROPRIETORSHIP

Sole Proprietorship is the easiest, least costly way of starting a business. It can be formed by finding a location and opening the door for business. There are fees to obtain a business name registration, a fictitious name certificate, and other necessary licenses. Attorney's fees for starting the business will be less than those of the other business forms because less preparation of documents is required and the owner has absolute authority over all business decisions.

PARTNERSHIP

There are several types of partnerships. The two most common types are general and limited. A general partnership can be formed by an oral agreement between two or more persons, but a legal partnership agreement drawn up by an attorney is strongly recommended. Legal fees for drawing up a partnership agreement are higher than those for a sole proprietorship but may be lower than incorporating. A partnership agreement will be helpful in solving any disputes. However, partners are responsible for the other partner's business actions as well as their own.

A partnership agreement should include the following:

- Type of business
- Amount of equity invested by each partner
- Division of profit or loss
- Partners' compensation
- Distribution of assets on dissolution
- Duration of partnership
- Provisions for changes or dissolving the partnership
- Dispute settlement clause
- Restrictions of authority and expenditures
- Settlement in case of death or incapacitation

CORPORATION

A business may incorporate without an attorney, but legal advice is strongly recommended. The corporate structure is the most complex and costly to organize. Control depends on stock ownership. Persons with the largest stock ownership, not the total number of shareholders, control the corporation. With control of 51 percent of stock shares, a person or group is able to make policy decisions. Control is exercised through regular board of directors' meetings and annual stockholders' meetings. Records must be kept to document decisions made by the board of directors. Small, closely held corporations can operate more informally, but record keeping cannot be eliminated entirely. Officers of a corporation answer to stockholders for improper actions. Liability is generally limited to stock ownership, except where fraud is involved. You may want to incorporate as a "C" or "S" corporation, the most common types of incorporation. The C Corporation is the most complex and must comply with many government regulations on a continual basis. In most states the S Corporation can choose to comply with the same regulations or elect those most suitable to its purpose.

LIMITED LIABILITY COMPANY (LLC)

LLCs are relatively new and lack standardization among the states. The LLC is not a corporation but offers many of the same advantages. Many small business owners and entrepreneurs prefer LLCs because they combine the limited liability protection of a corporation with the "pass through" taxation of a sole proprietorship or partnership.

- LLCs have additional advantages over corporations.

- LLCs allow greater flexibility in management and business organization.

- LLCs do not have the ownership restrictions of S Corporations, making them ideal business structures for foreign investors.

- LLCs accomplish these aims without the IRS's restrictions for an S Corporation.

LLCs are now available in all 50 states and Washington, D.C. If you have other questions regarding LLCs, be sure to speak with a qualified legal and/or financial advisor.

BUSINESS ENTITY COMPARISON CHART			
Issue	Sole Proprietorship	General Partnership	Limited Partnership
Number of owners	One	Unlimited (at least two)	Unlimited, must have at least one general partner and one limited partner
Liability	Unlimited personal liability	Joint and several unlimited personal liability	Limited liability only if limited partners do not participate in management; unlimited liability for general partner
Federal income tax	Taxed at individual level	No tax at partnership level	No tax at limited partnership level
Management	By sole proprietor	By all partners	By general partners only to prevent limited partners from losing limited liability
Transferability of interest	Unrestricted—sale or transfer of business assets	Determined by partnership agreement	Determined by limited partnership agreement
Duration	As long as proprietor lives and operates	Indefinite, but may have to terminate earlier on occurrence of certain events (death, bankruptcy) to qualify as partnership for tax purposes	Indefinite, but may have to terminate earlier on occurrence of certain events (death, bankruptcy of a general partner) to qualify as partnership for tax purposes

BUSINESS ENTITY COMPARISON CHART 2

Issue	Joint Venture	"C" Corporation	"S" Corporation
Number of owners	Unlimited (at least two)	Unlimited	Up to 75 individuals; no corporate, trust (with certain exceptions), or nonresident alien shareholders
Liability	Joint and several unlimited personal liability	Limited liability for shareholders even with shareholder participation in management	Limited liability for shareholders even with shareholder participation in management
Federal Income Tax	No tax at partnership level by joint venturers	Taxed on both corporate and shareholder level (double taxation)	Generally not taxed at the corporate level
Management	Determined by joint venture agreement	By board of directors or shareholders	By board of directors or shareholders
Transferability of interests		No restriction but subject to securities law and shareholders' agreement	No restriction but subject to securities law and shareholders' agreement
Duration	Indefinite, but may have to terminate earlier on occurrence of certain events (death, bankruptcy) to qualify as partnership for tax purposes	Perpetual	Perpetual

BUSINESS ENTITY COMPARISON CHART 3		
Issue	Limited Liability Company	"C" Corporation
Number of owners	Unlimited (but at least two in certain states)	Unlimited (but at least two)
Liability	Limited liability for members even with their management participation	No personal liability of partners for debts of the partnership or the malfeasance or malpractice of other partners
Federal income taxes	Not taxed at the company level; taxed as a partnership (no entity level of taxation)	Not taxed at the partnership level
Management	By member or a manager	By all partners
Transferability of interest	By statute other members must consent or no right to participate in management	Determined by limited liability partnership agreement
Duration	Maximum of 30 years, but may have to terminate earlier on occurrence of certain events in order to quality as partnership for tax purposes	Indefinite, but may have to terminate earlier on occurrence of certain events (death, bankruptcy) to quality as partnership for tax purposes

ELECTING THE RESTAURANT SITE LOCATION

After finding a likely area for the restaurant, obtain as many facts as you can about the area: How many restaurants like yours are there? Can you find out something about their sales volume? Since restaurants attract primarily local inhabitants, what is the population of the area? Is the population trend increasing, stationary, or declining? Are the people native-born, mixed, or foreign? What do they do for a living? Are they predominantly laborers, clerks, executives, or retired persons? Are they all ages or principally old, middle-aged, or young? To help you gauge their buying power, find out the average sales price and rental rates for homes in the area, the average real estate taxes for homes, the number of telephones, number of automobiles, and, if the figure is available, the per capita income. Zoning ordinances, parking availability, transportation facilities and natural barriers—such as hills and bridges—are important in considering the location of the restaurant.

Possible sources for this information are the Chamber of Commerce, trade associations, real estate companies, local newspapers, banks, city officials, and personal observations. The United States Census Bureau may have developed census tract information for the area you are considering. A census tract is a small, permanently established geographical area within a large city and its environs. The Census Bureau provides population and housing characteristics for each tract; their Web site is located at **www.census.gov**. This information is valuable in measuring your market or service potential. Use the score sheet on the following page to help determine the best location.

SCORE SHEET ON SITES

Grade each factor: "A" for excellent, "B" for good, "C" for fair, and "D" for poor.

Factor	Grade	Factor	Grade
1. Centrally located to reach the market		10. Taxation burden	
2. Merchandise or raw materials available readily		11. Quality of police and fire protection	
3. Nearby competition situation		12. Housing availability for employees	
4. Transportation availability and rates		13. Environmental factors (schools, cultural, community activities, enterprise of business people)	
5. Quality of available employees			
6. Prevailing rates of employee wages		14. Physical suitability of building	
7. Parking facilities		15. Type and cost of lease	
8. Adequacy of utilities (sewer, water, power, gas)		16. Proven for future expansion	
9. Traffic flow		17. Estimate of overall quality of site in 10 years	

NATIONAL RESEARCH

You will need national research if you plan to open a business in a different area of the country than your own. These are some resources to evaluate different areas:

According to *Forbes Magazine*, the nine best metro areas to start a business in 2005 were:

- Boise, Idaho
- Washington, DC
- Huntsville, Alabama
- Norfolk, Virginia
- Madison, Wisconsin
- Raleigh-Durham, North Carolina
- Albuquerque, New Mexico
- Fayetteville, Arkansas
- Atlanta, Georgia

The ten best small metro areas were:

- Sioux Falls, South Dakota
- State College, Pennsylvania
- Bismarck, North Dakota
- Lincoln, Nebraska
- Iowa City, Iowa
- Rochester, Minnesota
- Fargo, North Dakota
- Rapid City, South Dakota
- Las Cruces, New Mexico
- Bloomington, Indiana

MARKET AREA RESEARCH

"Market" is one way of referring to a city or a metropolitan statistical area (MSA). MSA is a term used in census research. Decide on a target city for your business. Start looking at various parts of the city. Focus on the parts that would be good for your business.

- **Trade area research.** Trade area refers to the area from which most of your customers will come.

- **Site research.** After you have narrowed down your choices, it is time to look at the sites. Take pictures, make notes, and evaluate the various sites to determine which is best for your restaurant.

POPULATION AND DEMOGRAPHICS

Population and demographics are factors to consider in choosing your location. Places to obtain the details you need include: the United States Census Bureau (**www.census.gov**) which can supply important information and statistics about the restaurant industry.

Demographics to evaluate include:

- Population density
- Age groups
- Employment statistics
- Personal income
- Ethnic populations

A favorite source for information is the local Chamber of Commerce. To contact a Chamber in another area, go to **www.chamberofcommerce.com**. You can get in touch with the state restaurant association and peers will assist you with economic and lifestyle patterns for your business research.

Your library and online sources can provide valuable information. There are research librarians who can help you. Some books you should check are:

- *Demographics USA* (ZIP edition). Find out the market statistics in different areas of the United States.

- *Lifestyle Market Analyst.* Standard Rate & Data Service—look under "gourmet cooking/ fine foods" and cross-reference market, lifestyle, and consumer.

STANDARD & POOR'S INDUSTRY SURVEYS

For additional data and statistics, visit the following sites online:

- **http://quickfacts.census.gov/qfd/index.html**

- **http://www.searchbug.com/sitemap.aspx**

- **www.melissadata.com/Lookups/index.htm**

- **The American Community Survey**—provides additional information from the supplemental census survey. This information includes demographics by county and metropolitan statistical areas (MSAs). An MSA is an area with at least one major city and includes the county or counties located within the MSA. This survey is replacing the Census Bureau's long survey. It provides full demographic information for communities each year, not every 10 years.

- **Censtats** – **http://censtats.census.gov/** provides economic and demographic information that you can compare by county. Information is updated every two years.

- **County Business Patterns** – Economic information is reported by industry, and the statistics are updated each year. Statistics include the number of establishments, employment, and payroll for more than 40,000 zip codes across the country. Metro Business Patterns provides the same data for MSAs.

- **American FactFinder** – **http://factfinder.census.gov** lets you evaluate all sorts of U.S. census data.

SITE RESEARCH

You can use the following list to evaluate a potential business site:

- Downtown area
- Business district
- Colleges/universities
- Religious schools
- Hospitals
- Beaches/Ocean
- State parks
- Rivers
- Nature preserves
- Hotels
- Historical district
- Government offices
- Technical schools
- Military bases
- Major highway
- Lakes
- Sports arenas
- Mountains
- Zoos
- Shopping

Evaluate these specifics about any location you are considering:

- How many similar restaurants are located in the area?
- Find sales volume. (Check business licenses for previous year.)
- Are there colleges or student housing in the area?
- Is there a high number of working mothers in the area?
- What is the population of the immediate area?
- Is the population increasing, stationary, or declining?
- Are the residents of all ages or old, middle-aged, or young?
- What is the average sales price and rental rates for area homes?
- What is the per capita income?
- Find the average family size.
- Is the building/location suitable for a food service establishment?

COMPETITION

Never underestimate the value of knowing your competition. Make a list of the other restaurants in your market. Which ones target the same population that you will? Find out what they are selling and their prices.

Take a detailed look at your competition when you narrow down your choices. The information you want can be hard to find. The best way to find information about your competition may be a visit to their establishments. Be creative. Other sources of information on competition include the following ideas:

- **Telephone book.** Will give you the number and location of your competitors.

- **Chambers of Commerce.** They have lists of local businesses. Verify whether it is a complete list, not just Chamber members.

- **Local newspapers.** Study the local advertisements and help wanted ads. There could also be a weekly entertainment section with information about local restaurants, their prices, and menus.

- **National Restaurant Association.** They provide by state the number of establishments, projected sales, and the number of employees. This can be found at **www.restaurant.org/research/state/index.cfm**.

SCOUTING THE COMPETITION

Mark the proposed location on a street map. You can determine how far to research, depending on how far you believe people will travel for your products.

Once you determine your target area, visit every business that serves items that are similar to the menu you plan to feature. Sample items from those businesses that have similar menus or serve your target customer. If they have menus you can take, grab one. Be critical and answer the following questions:

- What did and did not work for you in their restaurant?
- Do they serve your target customer?
- If not, who do they serve?
- Do their customers seem to like the surroundings?
- How busy are they at peak times?
- What kind of presentation do they have for their menu items?
- How is the food?
- What does the plate presentation look like?
- Do they offer anything unique?
- What is their seating capacity?
- What is the atmosphere?
- When are their busy periods?

GOVERNMENT LAWS, REGULATIONS, AND LICENSES

STATE REGISTRATION

Contact the Secretary of State's Office as early as possible and discuss your plans for opening a new business. All states have different regulations. This office will be able to describe all of the state's legal requirements and direct you to local and county offices for further registration. There is generally a fee required for registering a new business; most often it is less than $100. The city, county, or state agency will run a check to make certain no other businesses are currently using your business name. You may be required to file and publish a fictitious name statement in a newspaper of general circulation in the area. You must renew this fictitious name periodically to protect it legally.

Should your state have an income tax on wages, request from the State Department of Labor or Taxation all pertinent information, such as required forms, tax tables, and tax guides. Also contact the State Department of Employee Compensation for their regulations and filing procedures.

CITY BUSINESS LICENSE

Contact the city business department. Almost all cities and counties require a permit to operate a business. Your application will be checked by the zoning board to ensure the business conforms to all local regulations. Purchasing an existing restaurant will eliminate most of these clearances.

SALES TAX

Contact the state revenue or taxation agency concerning registry and collection procedures. Each state has its own methods of taxation on the sale of food products. States that require collection on food and beverage sales also require an advance deposit or bond to be posted against future collectable taxes. The state revenue agency may waive the deposit and accept instead a surety bond from your insurance company. Sales tax is collected only on the retail price paid by the end user. Thus purchasing raw food products to produce menu items will not require sales tax on the wholesale amount. However, you must present the wholesaler with your sales tax permit or number when placing orders and sign a tax release card for their files. A thorough investigation into your state's requirements is a must.

Certain counties or cities may also assess a sales tax in addition to the state sales tax. This issue needs to be thoroughly researched, as a future audit could present you with a considerable tax liability.

HEALTH DEPARTMENT LICENSE

The health department should be contacted as early as possible. A personal visit to discuss your plans and their needs is in order. Show cooperation and compliance from the very beginning. The health department can close your facility until you comply with its regulations. A restaurant shut down by the health department can be ruined if the closure becomes public knowledge. Prior to opening day, the health department will inspect the restaurant. If the facilities pass inspection, they will issue the license allowing the restaurant to open. The cost of the license is usually less than $50. Should they find faults in your facility, you must have them corrected before they will issue a license.

Every year, the health department will make unannounced inspections of the restaurant. An examination form will be completed outlining their findings. You must have all violations rectified before their next inspection.

Many health inspections are brought about by customer complaints. The health department will investigate every call they receive. Depending upon the number of calls and the similarity of the complaints, a pattern may develop. They will then trace the health problem to its source. Usually the problem is a result of mishandling food by a member of the staff, or the problem can sometimes be traced to your supplier.

Although the health department can seem like a terrific nuisance, they really are on your side. Cooperation between both sides will resolve all the restaurant's health problems and make it a safe environment. Many states have laws requiring that the manager   and in some states the entire staff   attend and pass an approved health and sanitation program.

Check with your state restaurant association. A list of all associations is located in the back of this book. The most common approved program is the ServSafe program developed by the NRA Educational Foundation. Materials may be purchased at **www.atlantic-pub.com** or by calling 800-814-1132. The ServSafe products, including instructor guides, answer sheets, instructor slides, manager training, food safety CD-ROMs, and instructor tool kits are available in English and Spanish.

FIRE DEPARTMENT PERMIT

An occupational permit from the fire department will be required before opening. Contact the fire department as early as possible, preferably in person, for their regulations and rules. Fire inspectors will check exhaust hoods, fire exits, extinguisher placements, and the hood and sprinkler systems. Many city fire departments do not permit the use of open-flame candles, flaming foods, or flaming liquor in the building. It is best to ask in advance. Based on the size of the building, the local and national fire codes, and the number of exits, the fire inspectors will establish a "capacity number" of people permitted in the building at one time. Follow their guidelines strictly, even if this means turning away customers because you have reached capacity.

BUILDING AND CONSTRUCTION PERMIT

If you plan on renovating the restaurant, you may need a local building permit, Permits are generally issued from the local building and zoning board. The fee is around $100, or it may be based on a percentage of the total cost of the project. You need to show the building inspector your blueprints or plans to determine if a permit is required. If so, he will inspect your plans ensuring that they meet all the local and federal ordinances and codes. After the plans are approved a building permit will be issued. The building inspector will make periodic inspections of your work at various stages to ensure that construction conforms to the approved plans.

SIGN PERMITS

Many city governments are instituting sign ordinances and restrictions. These ordinances restrict the sign's size, type, location, lighting, and proximity of the sign to the business. Owners or managers of a shopping mall or shopping center may also restrict the use and placement of signs.

STATE LIQUOR LICENSE

A state liquor license requires extensive investigation because of its complexity. Many states do not allow the sale of liquor in restaurants; others allow only beer and wine. Certain states vary the restrictions on sales of alcoholic beverages by county. A license to sell liquor in some states may cost a few hundred dollars; in others a license can cost upwards of $100,000. Several states are on quota systems and licenses are not even available. Sometimes the decision to allow liquor sales is up to the county. Conduct a thorough investigation concerning your particular state, possibly with your lawyer. After you obtain a license, it is imperative that you adhere to its laws and regulations. Most states have so many laws regarding the sale of liquor that they fill an entire book.

Make certain all employees are thoroughly familiar with the liquor laws. Carefully train new employees; test them if necessary. Constantly reiterate the laws. Employees will become lax if they are not reminded often of this big responsibility.

FEDERAL IDENTIFICATION NUMBER

All employers, partnerships, and corporations must have a Federal Identification Number. This number will be used to identify the business on all tax forms and other licenses. To obtain a federal identification number, fill out Form 55-4, obtainable from the IRS. There is no charge. Also request the following publications, or download them via the Internet at **www.irs.gov**:

1. Publication #15, circular *"Employer's Tax Guide."*

2. Several copies of Form W-4, *"Employer Withholding Allowance Certificate."* Each new employee must fill out one of these forms.

3. Publication 334, *"Tax Guide for Small Businesses."*

4. Request free copies of *"All about O.S.H.A."* and *"O.S.H.A. Handbook for Small Businesses."* Depending on the number of employees you have, you will be subject to certain regulations from this agency. Their address is: O.S.H.A., U.S. Department of Labor, Washington, D.C. 20210, **http://osha.gov**.

5. Request a free copy of *"Handy Reference Guide to the Fair Labor Act."* Contact: Department of Labor, Washington, D.C. 20210, **www.dol.gov.**

INTERNAL REVENUE REGISTRATION

In conjunction with the liquor license, you need to obtain tax stamps from the IRS. Call the local IRS office and have them send you application Form 11 or check the Web site at **www.irs.gov**. Based on the restaurant information you supply on the form, the IRS will assess a fee. This application makes the IRS aware that you are engaging in the retail sale of liquor.

OPENING THE RESTAURANT BANK ACCOUNT

If you received your financing through a local commercial bank, it is suggested you also use this bank for your business account if it fills all your needs.

Choose a bank that will provide you with these services:

- Night deposits.

- All credit card services (if you will be accepting credit cards).

- Change service (coins, small bills).

- A line of credit to certain suppliers.

- Nearby location for daily transactions.

It is very important that you get to know all the bank personnel on a first-name basis, particularly the manager. You will be in the bank every day. Make an effort to meet them and introduce yourself. Their assistance in obtaining future loans and gaining credit references will be valuable. We suggest using a smaller bank. Your account will mean more to it than to a larger bank.

Take time to shop around for the bank that will serve you best. When you go into a prospective bank, ask to see the bank manager; tell him of your plans and needs. All banks specialize in certain services. Look at transaction charges and all other service charges. Compare handling charges on charge card deposits. A small percent of thousands of dollars over a couple of years adds up to a great deal of money. Look at the whole picture very carefully. After you have selected a bank, you should order:

- Checks
- Deposit book
- Coin wrappers for all change

- Deposit slips
- Night deposit bags and keys
- Small bank envelopes

INSURANCE

Liability protection is of the utmost concern. Product liability is also desirable, as the consumption of food and beverages always presents a hazard. Described in this section are all the different types of insurance coverage applicable to all types of restaurants. By no means is it recommended that you obtain all this insurance. You would probably be over insured if you did. Determine with your agent which insurance coverage should be in place. Any policy should contain a basic business plan of fire/theft/liability/Workers' Compensation.

FIRE INSURANCE

Covers the buildings and all permanent fixtures belonging to and constituting a part of the structures. Coverage usually includes machinery used in building services such as air-conditioning systems, boilers, and elevators. Personal property may also be covered.

REPLACEMENT COST ENDORSEMENT

Provides for full reimbursement for the actual cost of repair or replacement of an insured building.

EXTENDED COVERAGE ENDORSEMENT

Covers property for the same amount as the fire policy against damage caused by wind, hail, explosion, riot, aircraft, vehicles, and smoke.

GLASS INSURANCE

Covers replacement of show windows, glass counters, mirrors, and structural interior glass broken accidentally or maliciously.

SPRINKLER DAMAGE

Insures against all direct loss to buildings or contents as a result of leakage, freezing, or breaking of sprinkler installations.

VANDALISM

Covers loss or damage caused by vandalism or malicious mischief.

FLOOD INSURANCE

Flood insurance is written in areas declared eligible by the Federal Insurance Administration. Federally subsidized flood insurance is available under the National Flood Insurance Program.

EARTHQUAKE INSURANCE

Covers losses caused by earthquakes.

CONTENTS AND PERSONAL PROPERTY DAMAGE

- General property form
- Boiler and machinery insurance
- Extended coverage endorsement
- Vandalism
- Business interruption (use and occupancy)
- Replacement cost endorsement
- Improvements and betterments insurance
- Direct damage insurance
- Consequential damage endorsement

BUSINESS OPERATIONS INSURANCE

- Valuable papers
- Transportation policy
- Time element
- Electrical signs
- Motor truck cargo owners
- Business interruption

- General liability
- Product liability
- Contractual liability
- Owner's protective liability
- Personal injury vehicle
- Fidelity bonds
- License bonds
- Business legal expense
- Life insurance
- Partnership
- Key man insurance
- Comprehensive general liability
- Major medical
- Earnings insurance
- Extra expense
- Rental value insurance
- Lease hold interest
- Umbrella liability
- Crime
- Liquor liability
- Fiduciary liability
- Group life insurance
- Travel/Accident
- Health insurance
- Dishonesty, destruction and disappearance
- Endorsement extending period of indemnity

WORKERS' COMPENSATION INSURANCE

Workers' Compensation Insurance covers loss due to statutory liability as a result of personal injury or death suffered by an employee in the course of employment. This insurance coverage pays all medical treatment and costs plus a percentage of the employee's salary due to missed time resulting from the injury. Workers' Compensation Insurance is highly regulated by both state and federal agencies, particularly O.S.H.A. Be certain to obtain all the information that pertains to your particular state. Workers' Compensation Insurance is mandatory in most states.

ORGANIZING THE PRE-OPENING ACTIVITIES

Opening a restaurant or any business is a great test of anyone's organizational and managerial abilities. It is imperative that you communicate well with your key personnel. The best way to do this is to use the form at the end of this chapter. Keep track of the assignments that need to be completed, who is handling the assignment, and when they must be completed. Allow plenty of time for assignments and projects to be accomplished. Even the simplest task may uncover a web of tangles and delays. Delegate responsibilities whenever possible, but above all stay organized. Maintain a collected composure and deal with people and problems on a level and consistent basis, and you will be off to a great start.

FIRST PRIORITY ITEMS

Suggested items that must be completed well ahead of opening date are:

1. List the restaurant's name and number in the phone book and yellow pages.

2. Order and install an employee time clock or appropriate software.

3. Allow shipping and lead time for:

- China, tables, chairs, settings

- Silverware

- Equipment

- Drop safe for office

- Printing: menus, stationery, business cards, matches, and napkins

4   Develop a list of all construction projects to include who is completing them, when they will be completed, and a list of materials needed.

5. Set up a large calendar on the wall with deadlines, when deliveries will be expected, construction projects finished, equipment installed, meetings, and the opening date.

6. Contact the art galleries or artists' groups in your area. They may be able to supply you with artwork to be displayed in the restaurant on a consignment basis.

PRE-OPENING PROMOTION

Described below are some pre-opening promotional ideas. There is a definite distinction between promotion and advertising. Promotion involves creating an interest in a new project usually at little or no cost. As soon as possible, put up the new restaurant sign or a temporary sign explaining the name of the new restaurant, type of restaurant, hours of operation, and the opening date. People are interested in what is occurring in their neighborhood; give them something to talk about.

1. **Meet with the advertising representatives of the local papers.** Determine advertising costs and look into getting a news story published describing the restaurant.

2. **Have plenty of the restaurant's matches and business cards** on hand: they are a great source of publicity.

3. **Join the Better Business Bureau and the local Chamber of Commerce.** Besides lending credibility to your organization, they can supply you with good free publicity.

4. **When you place your employment ad in the classified section always list the type of restaurant and location.** This inexpensive classified advertising will help spread the word. Many people in the restaurant industry also love to find new restaurants to try out.

INITIALLY CONTACTING PURVEYOR AND SUPPLIERS

Six to eight weeks before the scheduled opening date, contact all the local suppliers and meet with their sales representatives. Have the kitchen and bar managers present if possible. These companies will be supplying the restaurant with its raw materials. Make certain each sales representative understands that quality products are your top consideration. Competition is fierce among sales representatives and suppliers. Let each know you are considering all companies equally. Never become locked into using one purveyor only. Shop around and always be willing to talk with new sales representatives. Consider these points when choosing a purveyor:

1. Quality of products. Accept nothing but A-1.

2. Reliability.

3. Delivery days. All deliveries should arrive at a designated time.

4. Is the salesperson really interested in your business?

5. Does he seem to believe in what he sells?

6. Terms in billing (interest, credit).

7. Is the company local   for emergencies?

8. From the first meeting with the sales representative you should obtain:

   • Credit applications to be filled out and returned.

   • Product lists or catalogs describing all the products.

   • References of the restaurants they are currently servicing in the area. Check them out!

You should supply them with a list of the products you will be purchasing with estimates of the amount of each item you will be using every week.

Emphasize to the sales representative that price is certainly an important consideration, but not your only one when selecting a supplier. Point out to the sales representative the other concerns you have about using their company. Indicate that you intend to compare prices among the various companies but would not switch suppliers due to a one-time price undercutting. Loyalty is important to sales representatives; they need to expect that order from you each week, but at the same time let them know they must be on their toes and earn your business.

Most companies offer a discount to restaurants once they purchase a certain number of cases. Keep this in mind when comparing prices and suppliers. Choosing a supplier is often a difficult task with so many variable factors to consider. Begin to analyze these problems in terms of the overall picture, and your purchasing decisions will become consistently more accurate.

PAYROLL

Before the opening date, you will need personnel to assemble chairs, do odd painting, hang pictures, and do anything required. Many of these temporary employees may be used for various jobs in the restaurant after opening. The time clock should certainly be used during this period for better control. Overtime must be carefully monitored, and if possible, avoided. Managing employees and payroll will require a great deal of organization between assignments and scheduling.

Many of these jobs will be boring and tedious. Compensate these employees well for their efforts. Giving them a free lunch or dinner will be appreciated. These small tokens on your behalf will be returned in gratitude many times over the small cost incurred.

In most restaurants the internal bookkeeper calculates and prepares the payroll. I recommend the use of Quickbooks or Peachtree computer software for payroll processing. Quickbooks will be very useful in other parts of your business. The Web site is **www.quickbooks.com**, Peachtree is **www.peachtree.com**.

You may prefer to use a computerized payroll service or your accountant. All computerized payroll service companies operate in a similar manner. The bookkeeper totals the number of hours each employee worked for the pay period from the time cards. This information is transmitted to the computer company via telephone. or as part of your service, it may be picked up from your office.

Using the rate and number of hours worked, the computer calculates the gross pay, overtime, social security, federal and state taxes, other miscellaneous deductions, and the net check amount. Based upon this information, each check will be printed along with a corresponding stub. The checks are verified and returned, often within 24 hours.

Payroll checks are issued from a special checking account that will be set up with your bank. This account enables you to transfer only the exact funds needed for the payroll as a safety measure. The service will also provide a report detailing the amounts withheld from each check, allowing you to prepare the IRS Form 941, "*Employers Federal Quarterly Tax Return.*" Use the information on Form 941 to compute your quarterly state unemployment compensation form. Annually the service will also prepare a W-2 form for each employee who received wages during the year.

PUBLIC UTILITIES

Notify public utility companies of your opening date. Allow plenty of lead time for completion. Do not lose valuable time because the utilities are not hooked up yet. Some of these companies may require a deposit before they will issue service. Every company and city has different policies, so be sure to investigate yours.

PHONE COMPANY

You will need a minimum of two phone lines for the restaurant for taking reservations. Remember a fax line. Do not lose customers because they cannot get through. You should have two phones in the offices, one or two extensions at the entrance area, one or two extensions in the bar, and a public pay phone. The phones in the entrance and bar areas should not have long distance to prevent misuse by customers and employees. Place local emergency numbers at all phones.

You will need an intercom, handheld radio or paging system throughout the restaurant to speak from your position to key areas. Discuss with your local phone company business office your needs and their options. A music intercom/paging system is also available; see the discussion in the section on music.

GAS AND ELECTRIC COMPANIES

All major equipment requires hookups that can only be completed by trained technicians of the gas or utility company or authorized representatives. These technicians should be contacted as early as possible to evaluate the work required. In many cases they will need to schedule the work several weeks ahead of time.

Many gas and electric companies have service contracts to purchase. If available, it is highly recommended that you purchase them. Equipment that is maintained to the manufacturer's specifications will last longer and operate more efficiently. Calibration of kitchen ovens is a must in any service contract. It is critical that all ovens register true temperatures for consistent cooking results. Most ovens need to be calibrated monthly.

Set up a loose-leaf binder containing all the information and maintenance schedules for your equipment. Include all warranties, brochures, equipment schematics, operating instructions, maintenance schedules, part lists, order forms, past service records, manufacturers' phone numbers, and a chart showing which circuit breaker operates each piece of equipment. Ensure that this manual is kept up to date. Become aware of your equipment's needs and act accordingly. Train your employees in the proper use of all equipment, and it will serve the restaurant for many years.

WATER

Water composition is different throughout the country. Water that has been subjected to chemical treatment may contain a high level of chlorine. Water taken directly from the water table will contain any number of minerals depending upon the geological makeup of the soil it came from. Different types of water give different results when used in cooking.

Chemical particles in the water can have a bad effect on fresh-brewed coffee, food, recipes, and cocktails. Several companies market filtering devices that attach directly to the water lines. Filters need only be connected to the water lines that are used for drinking and cooking. Filtering devices are usually tube shaped canisters containing charcoal or special filtering paper. Discuss your particular situation with the state Department of Natural Resources and the sales representative for your coffee supplier.

SERVICE PERSONNEL NEEDED

LOCKSMITH

A registered or certified locksmith must be contacted to change the locks when you occupy the building. Keys should be issued on a "need to have" basis. Only employees who need access to a locked area to perform their jobs should have keys to that lock. The locksmith can set door locks so that certain keys may open some doors but not others. Only the owner and manager should have a master key to open every door. Each key will have its own identification number and "Do Not Duplicate" stamped on it. Should there be a security breach, you can easily see who had access to that particular area. The restaurant should be entirely re-keyed when key-holding personnel leave or someone loses keys. Safe combinations should be changed periodically by the locksmith.

On the next page is an example of a key system chart. In the example, the key code corresponds to a particular key that only opens doors with a similar letter. By determining who should have access to an area, you will be able to develop a good, security system. It is important that only the manager has a key to the liquor, wine, or china storage areas.

KEY SYSTEM CHART

Key System Chart Area	Key Code	Issued To (Employee)
Front Door	A	#2
Back Door	A	#2
Food Storage (Dry)	B	#6
Freezer	B	#6
Walk-Ins	B	#6
Reach-In	B	#6
Liquor Storage	**	Manager Only
Wine Storage	**	Manager Only
Bar Area	C	#3, 4
China Storage	**	Manager Only
Cleaning Supplies	D	#2, 3, 5, 6
Offices	E	#2, 3, 6, 7
Safe Combination	-	#7

** Manager Master Key   Janitors – 5   Dining Room Manager – 2   Kitchen Director – 6
Bar Manager – 3   Bookkeeper – 7   Bartenders – 4

FIRE AND INTRUSION ALARMS

Every restaurant should have two separate alarm systems: a system for fire, smoke, and heat detection and one for intrusion and holdup.

The fire detection system consists of smoke monitors and heat sensors, strategically placed throughout the building. This system must be audible for evacuations and directly connected to either the fire department or a private company with 24-hour monitoring service. In newer buildings the sensors also activate the sprinkler system. Most cities and states also require restaurants to install a hood system in the kitchen areas. This consists of a sprinkler-type system situated above equipment with an exposed cooking surface or flame. The system may be operated automatically or manually. When released, a chemical foam is immediately sprayed over the area. This foam is particularly effective in stopping grease fires. Once activated, the system will automatically shut off the gas or electric service to the equipment. To regain service the company that installed the system must reset it. Ask the local fire department for their recommendations for a reputable fire and safety service company.

An intrusion alarm system is recommended for any restaurant. Begin this search by contacting the police department. They will recommend companies. Ask them for a survey and proposal for the building and your needs.

The security system should contain magnetic contact switches on the main doors, windows, internal doors, and other places of entry such as trapdoors and roof hatches. Do not overlook the air conditioner vents. The interior of the building should be monitored by strategically placed motion detectors that are zoned so that if one fails, the entire system will continue to function. The safe area must be monitored. The locking-type holdup buttons, which may only be released with a key, are an excellent option and should be placed in the cashier, bar, and office areas. Alarm companies can also provide video monitors.

Another recommended option is temperature monitoring for the freezers and walk-ins. Have temperature-sensitive devices installed in these areas. If the temperature rises to a certain level, an alarm is triggered at the monitoring station. The operator may then call the restaurant manager or dispatch the refrigeration repairman. Some of these security service companies also provide guard service in the lounge area and escort service to the bank. These companies must be bonded, licensed, and insured.

The installation of an alarm system in the restaurant is a necessity. It will increase property value. A 24-hour monitored system may save 5 to 10 percent on insurance premiums.

DISHWARE CHEMICAL COMPANY

Contact all the dishwasher chemical suppliers in the area and meet with their representatives. Several of these companies maintain large research staffs that are developing innovative chemicals and devices that conserve the machine's energy and chemical usage, reducing your overall operational cost. Their field service people will monitor the entire system ensuring the machine and staff are working together for maximum efficiency. A local company supplying the chemicals and service as a sideline cannot possibly maintain the service offered by these national companies. Clean dishes and silverware are an absolute necessity for a restaurant.

KNIFE SHARPENER

A knife sharpening service is a must for any restaurant. Sharp knives are essential. A service contract guarantees that all knives and blades of cutting and slicing machines will be sharpened on a regular basis. In between servicing, the staff may keep the blades honed on a sharpening oil stone or ceramic sharpening sword.

SANITATION SERVICE

In most counties, a private business must provide its own garbage pickup. A restaurant of any size has a great deal of waste. A sanitation service company is required to maintain a proper health environment. Receive quotes from all the sanitation companies in the area. Prices may vary considerably depending on who purchases the dumpsters. You may wish to get the advice from your health department for the selection. Any service contract should contain provisions for the following:

- Dumpsters with locking tops
- Periodic steam cleaning of the dumpsters
- Fly pesticide sprayed on the inside of the dumpster
- Number of days for pickup
- Extra pickups for holidays and weekends

Some restaurant waste may be used by manufacturers in the area. Soap manufacturers will be interested in purchasing all the meat and fat scraps for a few cents a pound. Pig farmers may buy all the food scraps. Buyers will provide special containers to store the products. Scrap glass from empty liquor bottles may also be sold or donated to the local recycling or ecology project.

PARKING LOT MAINTENANCE

Parking lots will need periodic maintenance other than the daily duty of light sweeping and trash pickup. Painting new lines for the parking spaces should be done annually. Blacktop surfaces will also require a sealant to stop water from seeping into it. Winter climates will require snow removal, salting, and sanding of the lot. Most of these services may be purchased under contract.

PLUMBER

A local plumber will be needed to handle any miscellaneous work and emergencies that come up. The plumber must have 24-hour emergency service. Make every effort to retain the plumber that did the original work on the building. He will be familiar with the plumbing.

Due to the large amount of grease that goes through the restaurant's plumbing, clogs and backups will be a major problem. Extra-wide pipes should be fitted to the dishwasher and sink drains. Grease will collect in the elbows and fittings along the plumbing lines. When cold water is put through the drain the grease will solidify, closing the pipe. A plumber will need an electric snake and the necessary acids to remove the clog. For everyday use, a hand snake and plunger should always be on hand in the kitchen.

ELECTRICIAN

Retain the original electrician who worked on the building, if possible. An electrician will be needed when equipment is moved or installed. The electrician should check out and label all the circuits and breakers in the building and should also be on 24-hour emergency service.

REFRIGERATION SERVICE

The most important consideration when choosing a refrigeration company is the response time to emergencies. At any given time the refrigeration systems and freezer could go out, resulting in the loss of thousands of dollars in food. Make certain any prospective company understands this crucial point.

Situations arise where the refrigeration units cannot be brought back to work in time, usually because of a broken part that must be replaced. There are solutions to prevent food loss. Contact your purveyors. They have large refrigeration units you may be able to use to store the food temporarily. Call the tractor trailer companies in the area: they may have an empty refrigeration truck that could be rented for storage.

A fully loaded freezer generally stays cold enough to keep foods frozen for two days if the cabinet is not opened. In a cabinet with less than half a load, food may not stay frozen for more than a day.

If normal operation cannot be resumed before the food starts to thaw, use dry ice. If 125 pounds of dry ice is placed in a half-loaded 10-cubic-foot cabinet soon after power loss, it will maintain a temperature below freezing for two to three days. In a fully loaded cabinet, sub-freezing temperature will be maintained for three to four days.

Place dry ice on cardboard or small boards on top of the packages and do not open the freezer again except to put in more dry ice. Monitor the temperature with an accurate thermometer.

EXTERMINATOR

Exterminators must be licensed professionals with references. Consult the health department for recommendations. Exterminators can eliminate any pest-control problems: rats, cockroaches, ants, termites, and flies. Have several companies come in to appraise the cost. They are experts and can read the "telltale" signs that might be missed. Take their suggestions. This is not an area to cut corners or try to do yourself. It will not pay in the long run.

PLANT MAINTENANCE

If the restaurant has large expensive botanicals, you may need a maintenance company. A professional plant-care person can provide all the necessary services to protect these investments: watering, pruning, transplanting, and arranging. Contact companies in the area and get their opinions, quotes, and references. Make sure the company you hire is aware that they are working in an environment where toxic sprays may only be used with the approval of the health department.

OUTSIDE LANDSCAPING

You may want the exterior areas of the restaurant professionally designed and landscaped. An appealing exterior is as important as the interior. You may have little room to work with, but a landscaper can put together a design that can be very appealing. Contact local landscapers and get their opinions, designs, quotes, and references.

FLORIST

If you have fresh cut flowers, you need to contact a local florist. Each week the florist will set aside a selection of cut flowers of your choice. Many restaurants use only a single flower or rose in a long-stem vase. Should you decide to do this, make sure there is a large supply of backup flowers. Some customers will take them home when they leave. Adding fresh water with a little dissolved sugar, or a chemical provided by the florist to the vases every day will keep the flowers fresh looking for a week or more.

EXHAUST HOOD CLEANING SERVICE

Contact a company that specializes in exhaust hood and ventilation system cleaning. They should appraise and inspect the whole ventilation system before opening day. Depending upon the amount and type of cooking performed, they will recommend a service that will keep the system free from grease and carbon buildup. Usually twice-a-year cleaning is required. Without this service, the exhaust hoods and vents will become saturated with grease, causing a dangerous fire hazard. All that would be necessary to ignite a fire would be a hot spark landing on the grease-saturated hood. Most of these companies also offer grease and fat (deep fryer oil) removal.

HEATING AND AIR-CONDITIONING

You will need a company that can respond 24 hours a day at a moment's notice. Losing the heating system in the winter or the air conditioning in the summer will force the restaurant to close. Make certain the company is reliable with many references. Heating and air-conditioning systems need regular service and preventative maintenance to ensure they function at maximum efficiency. Energy and money will be wasted if the system is not operating correctly. A service contract should be developed with these companies to ensure the machines are being serviced to the manufacturer's schedule. Keep the contract and all additional information in the equipment manual.

JANITORIAL AND MAINTENANCE SERVICE

Depending on the size and operating hours of the restaurant, it is recommended that you use a professional cleaning company. Restaurant cleanliness should not be left to an amateur responsible.

The cleaning service usually arrives after closing time. It will clean and maintain the areas previously agreed on in the service contract. Its work is guaranteed. Never will a customer enter the restaurant and see a dirty fork left on the floor from the night before.

Cleanliness also has an important effect upon the employees. A spotless restaurant will create the environment for positive employee work habits. They will become more organized and neater in their jobs. The maintenance service company selected must have impeccable references. The company should be insured against liability and employee pilferage. Employees should be bonded. You will need to give the owner of the company her own keys to the entrance, maintenance closets, security system, and possibly the office, for cleaning. It must be made very clear that food and liquor are completely off limits to maintenance employees.

Some important factors to consider when choosing a maintenance company:

- Can they assist with cleaning prior to opening?
- Will they submit a bid as you request?
- What are the hours they will be in the restaurant?
- Who buys the soaps and chemicals?
- Will they consent to a trial period?
- How will you communicate to discuss problems?
- Will they provide references from other restaurants?
- Are they aware that no toxic chemicals are allowed in the kitchen?
- How long have they been in business?
- Will they lock all doors once their employees are inside.

BASIC MAINTENANCE FUNCTIONS

The following are some basic maintenance functions any service contract should contain.

This outline is basic. The actual contract must contain specific items that must be cleaned and when. You and the maintenance company's supervisor should have a check-off list of everything that must be completed each night. The following morning, walk through the restaurant spot-checking from the check-off sheet that all items have been completed as prescribed. Notify the supervisor immediately of any unsatisfactory work. At first, it may take a great deal of communication to get the desired results. After operating a few months, it will run smoothly.

Items to be cleaned daily:

1. All floors washed and treated.

2. Entire restaurant vacuumed.

3. Windowsills, woodwork, pictures, chairs, tables dusted.

4. Outside area—swept and picked up.

5. Public bathrooms cleaned, sanitized, and deodorized; supplies replaced: toilet paper, soap, napkins, and tampons.

6. Trash containers emptied and sterilized.

7. All sinks and floor drains cleaned.

8. Maintenance room cleaned and organized.

Weekly services:

1. All windows cleaned inside and out.

2. All chairs and woodwork polished.

3. Decorative floors stripped, waxed, and polished.

Annually:

1. All carpets steam cleaned.

Be specific in your instructions about all these areas.

Some manufacturers include detailed instructions for cleaning their product. Special cleaners must be used on some equipment. Improperly cleaning a piece of equipment can ruin it forever. Keep all of this information in a loose-leaf binder in the office. The cleaning supervisor should have access to this manual and must be thoroughly familiar with its contents.

OTHER SERVICES AND SYSTEMS

CIGARETTE MACHINES/CIGARS/ELECTRONIC GAMES

Cigarette, cigars, and electronic games can provide a small additional source of revenue for the restaurant with little or no investment if they are pertinent to the restaurant's environment. Cigarette and cigars are provided as a service to customers and should always be available; electronic games are not a necessity and should be used only if they are compatible with the restaurant's atmosphere. Distributors for all of these products may be found online or in the yellow pages of most city directories.

Depending on the type of clientele and the image of the establishment, you might look into the leasing of electronic games. There are numerous types of games available. You may choose from the more traditional games, like the pinball machine, or from an array of computerized video games. Some of these games have become extremely popular and can contribute a good sum of additional revenue. Most companies lease the machines to the restaurant under various terms of agreement. Service to the games should be included in any contract. Many of these companies can also provide TVs, wide-picture screens, and movies with projection equipment.

Before contracting for any of these electronic games or video equipment, carefully consider the pros and cons. Keep in mind that you are primarily in the restaurant business—the last thing you want to do is turn away any of your regular restaurant customers. If the restaurant's atmosphere is right, these games can bring in substantial additional income.

COFFEE EQUIPMENT

All major coffee distributors offer the same basic plan to restaurants: they will provide all the equipment necessary for coffee service including brewing machines, filters, pots, maintenance, and installation of all equipment. All that is required of you is to sign a contract stating that you will buy their coffee exclusively. The price of all the equipment and maintenance is included in the price of the coffee.

As an alternative, you can buy all your own equipment and pay to have someone install and maintain it, enabling you to purchase coffee from any company at reduced prices. Because doing so is costly, it is recommended that restaurants use the coffee distributor contract method.

There are many different coffee blends available. Coffee is an extremely important part of any dining experience: get the finest and most popular blend available. Have the restaurant employees try the different blends under consideration in a blind tasting.

When negotiating with the coffee salespeople, inform them that you want brand new equipment. They are competing for your business, but once you sign the contract you will be locked in to it. Use this leverage while you have it.

Place the coffee machines in the main and service bars. Various specialty teas, sugar packets, and sugar substitute packages may also be purchased from these distributors, and for an additional charge your restaurant's name and logo can be imprinted on the outside of each packet.

SODA AND DRAFT BEER SYSTEMS

Soda and draft beer systems may be contracted for in the same manner as coffee. National brand soda and beer distributors will connect all the hoses, valves, taps, and guns needed to operate the bar, usually at no cost. You will be obligated to sign a contract stating you will purchase their products exclusively. The price of the system is passed on to you as you purchase soda canisters and kegs of beer. The distributor will also provide promotional material such as wall plaques, neon lights, and drink coasters.

These systems occasionally break down; maintain at least two cases of each type of soda in bottles or cans and three to four cases of beer in the storeroom. Draught beer and soda lines must be flushed out every week. The cost of this service is usually borne by the restaurant. You may do this yourself, and many people do; however, it is recommended that you use the services of professionals who have the proper equipment to do the job thoroughly. Soda and beer is no better than the lines they flow through. Distributors can recommend a service.

ICE CREAM FREEZERS/MILK DISPENSERS

These companies allow you to use their equipment when you guarantee to purchase their product exclusively. Ice cream freezers, milk dispensers, and other kitchen equipment are available. Their sales representative will have all the information about the equipment.

These arrangements are beneficial for small restaurants with limited capital. Whatever your financial situation, do a thorough investigation into the terms of the service contract. In some cases, the price of the product may be so high you are better off purchasing equipment. You should always compare competitive prices of the products after several months of operation. The free equipment may not justify the total cost of the product. Should you decide to sign the contract and use the free equipment, remember that you may be locked in for a long time. Be sure to request new equipment from the sales representative.

All the freezers and dispensers that are left in the open should be locked for better control. Small ice cream freezers are also available for use in the bar should you serve ice cream cocktails.

LINEN SERVICE

When tablecloths and napkins are used on the tables, a linen service will be needed to clean and press them. Tablecloths and napkins are an integral part of the table setting. They must be spotless and wrinkle free. A poorly folded or soiled tablecloth will leave a lasting negative impression on the customer. In choosing a linen service, you must look at your restaurant's available capital and sales volume. These factors will determine which option is the most economical for the establishment.

A linen service will provide tablecloths, napkins, uniforms, and bar towels; it will pick up dirty linen and leave a sufficient supply of clean ready-to-use items. Generally, there are two parts to this service: the use of the linen and cleaning. You may also be charged for linen that is torn or soiled from misuse. Many medium to large restaurants purchase their own linen from their food-service supplier, and the linen company would then be used to clean the used linen.

It is advantageous to purchase all your own linen if you have the capital. Remember to budget for new linen.

Many large-volume restaurants install their own laundry systems. Under the right circumstances restaurants can save a great deal of money. Go with an experienced company for washers and dryers. A complete in-house laundry system costs several thousand dollars to set up. The system will easily recoup the initial investment. A big development in the in-house laundry market came a few years ago with the introduction of Visa material. Visa requires no ironing or pressing when washed and dried. The material is ideal for tablecloths and napkins. Its disadvantages compared to conventional material is that water tends to bead on it rather than to be absorb into it, and the napkins are smoother and more likely to slide off one's lap than conventional cloth.

When ordering tablecloths and napkins, figure six times the number of seats and tables for napkins and tablecloths. You will need one set for the initial setting; two to three more sets for changing during the evening; and one to two sets will be at the cleaners or in the laundry room.

MUSIC

Music is a very important part of any dining experience. The least expensive way to provide a music system for the restaurant is to set it up yourself. Contact a local stereo dealer. After examining the acoustics in the building, he will be able to suggest a system that will meet your needs. Take care to camouflage the speakers. Place the cassette or CD deck in an area where an employee is stationed, such as the bar or cashier stand. The speakers should have individual volume controls for each area. Long-playing cassettes with the type of music that suits the restaurant's atmosphere should be used. Never use a radio station.

There are systems available that use special CD players, long-playing tapes, or multiple CD changers that play for several hours and then start all again without pausing. The entire system in many cases may be leased and combined with a paging system.

Live music is usually in a bar and lounge area because most customers do not mind waiting for a table in the lounge with entertainment. Live music will draw diners looking for music or after-dinner dancing. Some restaurant managers add a cover charge or a drink minimum for people who come for the live entertainment only.

An average band will cost upwards of $1,000 for three or four nights. However, if they blend in well and attract customers, the expense may be recovered through increased food and liquor sales. Live entertainment can be a great source of word of mouth publicity.

MUSIC LICENSING

If you are interested in playing recorded music in the restaurant you will need permission. Although most people buy a tape or CD thinking it becomes their property, there is a distinction in the law between owning a CD and owning the songs on the CD. There is also a difference between a private performance of copyrighted music and a public performance. When you buy a tape or CD, the purchase price covers only your private listening use, similar to the "home" use of "home videos." When you play these tapes or CDs in your restaurant it becomes a public performance. Songwriters, composers, and music publishers have the exclusive right of public performance of their musical works under U.S. copyright law. There are some distinctions in the law if the performance is by means of public communication on TV or radio. Transmissions within establishments of a certain size that use a limited number of speakers or TVs must not extend to another room, and there must be no admission charge.

There are two licensing agencies in the United States, BMI and ASCAP. You can contact ASCAP at 800-95-ASCAP or **www.ascap.com** and BMI at 212-586-2000 or **www.bmi.com/home.asp.** Contact both BMI and ASCAP to ensure your compliance.

HOW MUCH CHINA AND SILVERWARE TO ORDER

The following chart is based on an average dining room in a moderately priced restaurant. To compute your needs for place settings, multiply the number indicated by the number of seats in the restaurant. Keep in mind that all dishwashers and machines work at different speeds. Use this chart as a guide in ordering.

This chart will provide a basic outline to indicate what will be required in an average dinner restaurant. Not maintaining enough stock will slow up service. Too much stock will cause you to store it in the restaurant, tying up cash. Figures will need to be adjusted depending on the menu and how many uses you have for the same piece of china or silverware.

Bar glasses are diversified and it is difficult to estimate the usage of each. If you have a mechanical dishwasher in the bar area, you will not require as much stemware.

CHINA AND SILVERWARE TO ORDER		
China	**Flatware**	**Glasses**
Dinner plate............2	Teaspoon 5	Water glass............3
Bread plate 3	Soup spoon............1	Wineglass 1
Salad bowl............2	Tablespoon............½	
Soup bowl............2	Iced-tea spoon............½	
Sauce dish............1½	Fork............3	
Dessert plate............2	Salad fork 2	
Cup/Mug............3	Oyster fork 1	
Saucer............3	Knife 2	
	Steak knife............1	

If you are interested in a specialized food service business, you might consider any of these books from Atlantic Publishing **www.atlantic-pub.com**.

- *How to Open a Financially Successful Bakery*
- *How to Open a Financially Successful Bed and Breakfast*
- *How to Open a Financially Successful Coffee, Espresso & Tea Shop*
- *How to Open a Financially Successful Pizza and Sub Restaurant*
- *How to Open a Financially Successful Specialty Retail and Gourmet Foods*

Additional details are available for these titles at **www.atlantic-pub.com/entreneurship.htm**

 # WORKSHEETS

The following worksheets, provided courtesy of the Small Business Administration, will help the restaurant manager to estimate start-up costs and expenses.

HOW MUCH MONEY DO YOU NEED?

When using the chart on the next page, keep in mind that not every category applies to all businesses. Estimate monthly amount.

ESTIMATED START-UP FUNDS NEEDED	
Expense Category	**Projected Cost**
Salary of Owner-Manager (if applicable)	
All Other Salaries and Wages	
Rent	
Advertising	
Delivery Expenses	
Supplies	
Telephone	
Utilities	
Insurance	
Taxes, Including Social Security	
Interest	
Maintenance (Facilities/Equipment)	
Legal and Other Professional Fees	
Dues/Subscriptions	
Leases (Equipment/Furniture/Etc.)	
Inventory Purchases	
Miscellaneous	
One-Time Start-Up Costs	
Fixtures/Equipment/Furniture	
Remodeling	
Installation of Fixtures/Equipment/Furniture	
Starting Inventory	
Deposits with Public Utilities	
Legal and Other Professional Fees	
Licenses and Permits	
Advertising and Promotion for Opening	
Accounts Receivable	
Cash Reserve/Operating Capital	
Other	
TOTAL	

Item	If you plan pay to pay cash in full, enter the full amount below and in the last column.	If you are going to pay by installments, fill out the columns below. Enter in the last column your down payment plus at least one installment			Estimate of he cash you need for furniture, fixtures & equipment.
		Price	Down Payment	Amount of Each Installment	
Counters					
Storage Shelves					
Display Stands, Shelves, Tables					
Cash Register					
Safe					
Window Display Fixtures					
Special Lighting					
Outside Sign					
Delivery Equipment					
Other (list)					

GOING INTO BUSINESS

Determine what will be involved in each method

Factors	Start From Scratch	Existing Business	Franchise
Time			
Availability			
Time Before Opening			
Financial			
Cost			
Available Financing			
Investors			
Personal Worth			
Total Indebtedness			
Break-even Point			
Royalties & Fees			
Purchasing Restrictions			
Current Profitability			
Intangibles			
Goodwill			
Historical Recognition			
Known vs. Unknown (obstacles to success or existing profitability)			
Reputation			
Convenience			
Exclusivity			
Assets			
Location			
Facility			
Equipment			

GOING INTO BUSINESS

Determine what will be involved in each method

Factors	Start From Scratch	Existing Business	Franchise
Existing Staff			
Customer Base			
Owner			
Independence			
Business Experience			
Food Service Experience			
Restaurant Experience			
Management Experience			
Owner Expectations			
Outside Expectations			
Training			
Support			
Market Share			
Marketing Support			
Product Mix			
Competition			
Customer Needs			
Other (your personal list)			

A

accounting, financial services

advertising

air cleaners, purifiers

air conditioning, heating equipment

air curtains

air pollution control systems

air purification, dust collection

air screens, air curtains for entranceways

alcoholic beverages

aluminum foil

animated displays

antiques

apparel

appetizers

appliances: food service machines

aprons

aquariums/lobster tanks

architects/engineers

art

artificial flowers, plants

ashtrays, stands

associations, trade

ATMs—automated teller machines

attorney

audiovisual equipment

awards, plaques, certificates

awnings, canopies, poles

B

badges

bags and covers

bains marie

baked goods

bakers' equipment and supplies

baking ingredients

baking supplies

balers

balloons

banners and flags

banquet service equipment

bar codes and product codes

bar equipment and supplies

barbecue pits, machines

bars, liquor service

bars, portable and folding bases, legs, tables, and booths

baskets, bread and rolls

bathroom accessories and baby changing stations

batter: doughnut, pancake, and waffle

beer, ale

beer brewing equipment

beer service equipment

beverage service equipment

beverage, coffee servers

beverages, concentrated fruit

beverages, nonalcoholic

beverages: beer/ale/wine

beverages, carbonated and noncarbonated

beverages: liquors/liqueurs

bibs: adult and child

binders

bins, ingredient

bins, silverware

bins, storage

biscuits, fancy and soda

blackboards

blenders

bookkeeping systems

books, educational and technical

books, reservation

booths, chairs, tables bases and legs

bowls: mixing, salad, and serving

brass fittings and tubing

bread and rolls

bread specialties

bread sticks

breading machines

breadings and batters: seafood and poultry

brochures and postcards

broilers, electric and gas

broilers, infrared

broilers, charcoal and conveyor

broilers, electric and gas

brooms

brushes, cleaning

buffalo products

buffet products: chafers, fuel

buildings, modular

bulletin boards. changeable letters

butchers equipment and supplies

butter, margarine, and cooking oils

C

cabinets: food warming and conveying

cabinets: miscellaneous

cafeteria equipment

cakes and cake decorations; cookies and pastries

can openers: electric and hand-operated

candelabra and candle holders

candies, chocolates, and confectioneries

candle light, nonflammable

candle warmers for food and beverages

candles and tapers

canned foods: fish, fruits and vegetables, meat and poultry

canopies

canopies: ventilation

cappuccino coffee equipment

carbon dioxide

carbonators

carbonic gas/bulk

carpet sweepers

carpets and rugs

carriers, food and beverage, insulated

carts, espresso and coffee

carts, food-service

carts, transport

carts, storage and serving

cash register supplies: tape, ribbon

cash registers and control systems

casters

catalogs and directories

catering supplies and banquet service equipment

catering trucks/delivery trucks

ceilings: acoustical, tin, wood

ceramic dinnerware

ceramics

cereals, ready-to-serve and uncooked

chafing dishes

chairs, folding or stacking

chairs, infant

chairs, restaurant

chairs, upholstered

check recovery services

children's favors and party supplies

children's rides and amusements

chillers

china, table

Chinese foods

chocolate

choppers: electric for food and meat

chopping blocks

cigars, cigarettes, tobacco products display and storage systems

citrus products, citrus syrups

cleaners for grills, griddles, pans

cleaners, hand

cleaners, multipurpose

cleaners, ovens

cleaners, rug and upholstery

cleaners, window

cleaning equipment, materials, services and supplies

cleaning systems, pressurized

cleaning: exhaust maintenance

clocks, electric

coasters, beverage

coat and hat checking equipment

cocktail mixes

cocktail stirrers

cocoa

coffee

coffee-brewers, glass and filters

coffee mills

coffee urns and makers

coin sorters and handling equipment

cold plates

communication systems, services

compactors, waste

computer aided design (cad) systems

computer furniture

computer software: accounting administrative, hospitality

computer software: hospitality,and cost control

computer supplies

computerized food service systems

computerized restaurant management systems

computerized systems, wireless

computers/internet

concession equipment and supplies

condiments and condiment holders

confectionery and chocolate products

connectors: gas/water/steam

construction: materials/ renovation

consulting services

containers, food

containers, microwave

containers, oven proof paperboard

containers: aluminum, plastic and glass

conveyors and subveyors

conveyors, belt

cookies

cooking computers or timers

cooking equipment, electric, and gas

cooking equipment, induction

cooking equipment, outdoor

cooking heat/warmers

cooking wines and marinades

cookware, induction

cookware: pots, pans, and microwave

coolers, beverage

copperware

costumes

cotton candy machines

counters and tabletops

counters, cafeteria

covers, rack

crackers

creamers

credit cards: card processing/ authorization

crepe-making machines

croutons

crushers, can and bottle, electric

cups: disposable, portion, thermal

custom-built kitchen equipment

cutlery: chef's equipment and supplies

cutlery, disposable

cutlery, silver-plated and stainless steel

cutters, food

cutting boards

D

dairy substitutes

dance floors, portable

decaffeinated beverages

decor and display materials

decorations: holiday, party favors, balloons,

degreasers and non-slip treatment products

deli products

deodorizers

designers/decorators

dessert products

dicers, hand-operated

dicers, vegetable-cutting, power

dietetic foods

dinnerware, china, stainless steel, plastic or disposable

dinnerware, heat resistant, glass

dinnerware, metal

disco equipment

dish tables

dishwashers: equipment and supplies

dishwashing compounds

disinfectants and cleaning supplies

dispensers for concentrates

dispensers, carbonated beverage

dispensers, condiment

dispensers: controls and timers

dispensers, cup

dispensers, custom

dispensers, French fries

dispensers, glove

dispensers, ice

dispensers, ice cream

dispensers: liquor, beer and wine

dispensers, malted milk

dispensers, napkins

dispensers, noncarbonated beverage dispensers

dispensers, salad dressing

dispensers: self-leveling for dishes and trays

dispensers, snack

dispensers, soap and detergent

dispensers, straw

dispensers, toilet paper

dispensers, water   hot and/or cold

dispensers, whipped cream

dispensers, wine

dispensers: liquids, beverages, cream/milk, syrup, and dressings

display cases

display cases, heated

display cases, refrigerated

distributor, food and beverage

distributor: food, equipment

doilies: paper or plastic

doors: cold storage and freezer doors: hinged, revolving and swinging

dough dividers/rounders

dough: prepared, frozen and canned

doughnut machines

doughnut mix

drain cleaners/line maintenance

draperies, curtains, and hangings

draperies, stage

drapery and curtain hardware

dressings, salad

drive-thru service equipment

drug testing service

dry grocery items: staples

dry ice

dryers, clothes

dryers, dish/tray

E

eggs/egg products, egg substitutes, boilers, and timers

electric utility services/energy conservation

electronic data capture

electronic funds transfer

embroidered apparel

employee benefit services

employee scheduling and services

employment agencies services

enclosures, patio and pool

energy conservation equipment

energy cost analysts

entertainment, sports-themed

entertainment systems

entrees, fresh and frozen

environmental products

equipment, cook/chill

equipment, dish handling

equipment, drain cleaning

equipment, food forming

equipment, front office

equipment, heating   boilers, furnaces, radiators

equipment, hot-chocolate making

equipment, leasing

equipment, marinade

equipment, preventive maintenance programs

equipment, repairs/parts/ installation

equipment, rug cleaning

equipment, sales and service

equipment, under-bar

equipment, upholstery cleaning and shampooing

espresso coffee and coffee equipment

ethnic foods

executive recruiters, hospitality industry

exhaust fans

exhaust maintenance, cleaning

extractors, fruit juice

extracts, flavoring

F

fabrics

fabrics, fire resistant

fans, electric and ventilating

fats and oils, cooking

fats and oils: equipment systems and supplies

faucets

filters, air-conditioning

filters: coffee makers

filters, cooking oil

filters, exhaust systems

filters, grease extracting

filters, water

financial services

financial consultants

financial: tax and legal planning

fire alarm systems

fire protection systems: extinguishers/suppression/ sales/service

first-aid equipment and supplies

fish: canned, fresh, frozen, pre-portioned, and smoked

flagpoles, flags and accessories

flatware carts and trays for storage and dispensing

flatware, disposable

flatware, recovery machines

flatware: silver/gold plated, stainless and disposable

floor cleaning and maintenance equipment

floor drain treatment

flooring tile, vitrified or ceramic

flooring: floor treatments, non-slip preparations and coating

flour and flour sifters

flowers, foliage and plants

food containers, aluminum, plastic,and glass

food covers

food, dehydrated

food delivery and catering equipment

food equipment,Serviceand parts

food: frozen   cooked/precooked

food photography

food portioning equipment

food processors: grinders and slicers,electric and manual

food products: deli/ethnic, import/export

food products: prepared, canned or frozen

food reproduction and replication/props

food safety training

food thawing device

food waste disposers

food, processed

footwear

forms: business

fountain syrups and flavors

fountains, beverage

fountains, ornamental and display

franchise consultants

freezers/refrigeration equipment, service, and parts

freezers, portable

frequent dining programs/ clubs

frozen breakfast food

frozen cocktail machines

frozen food reconstitutor

fruit juices: canned,

concentrated, fresh, frozen

fruit syrups

fruits and vegetables: candied, brandied, pickled

fruits and vegetables: canned, fresh, frozen

fryers, convection

fryers, deep fat and pressure

fryers, oilless

fuel: synthetic/alternative

furniture design

furniture, health care

furniture: fiberglass, metal, plastic, upholstered and wood

furniture: lawn, garden, patio, and casual

furniture: portable/folding

G

games

garbage can liners

garbage containers: metal, plastic or concrete; waste receptacles and compactors

gas, propane

gas: service/supplier, and natural

gelatin

gelato

gift basket packaging

glass replacement service

glass, washers

glass, beveled and tempered

glass, decorative

glassware chiller and froster

glassware, service

glazes

gloves: cloth or synthetic

gourmet foods

gravy mix or base

grease exhaust systems: cleaning and maintenance

grease traps: cleaning, maintenance, elimina tion and analysis

griddles and grills

groceries

guest checks

guest questionnaires, comment

cards, and boxes

guest services

H

HAACP training

hand dryers

hand trucks

handicapped: aids and accessories

hangers, clothes

health foods

healthcare products and equipment

heat lamps

heaters, water

heaters, patio and indoor

herbs

high chairs

hors d'oeuvres

hoses: flexible gas connectors

hot chocolate mix

hot dog grills/cookers

hot food tables

hot plates, electric and gas

hotel amenities

I

ice bins, buckets, carts, and containers

ice cream

ice cream cabinets

ice cream dishes

ice cream freezers

ice cream makers and soft serve machines

ice cream, toppings, syrups and cones

ice crushers, cubers, and shavers

ice machine repairs, service, and maintenance

ice makers, bins, dispensers, crushers, and cubers

ice transport systems

ice, equipment and supplies

incentive programs

information service

infrared ovens, ranges, and

broilers
insect traps
insecticides
inserts, steam table
insulation materials: hot and cold
insurance
interior decor/ interior design
international marketer/ distributor: food equipment inventory control equipment
inventory systems: equipment and supplies
investigative services

J

janitorial: cleaning/sanitizing
janitorial supplies
Japanese foods
juice fountains
juicers/extractors

K

kettles, steam
key and lock systems
key tags
kitchen accessories
kitchen fabrication
kitchen layout and design
knife sharpeners
kosher food/products

L

ladles
laminated plastic for counters.
laminating services and products
lamps: floor, table, electric, battery, candle, infrared and oil
lampshades
laundry equipment and supplies
laundry machinery
lawn care services
led message displays
legal services

legumes
lighting fixtures
lighting systems, emergency
lighting, fluorescent, neon
lights: flood, spot
linen products
linen products, rental
liquor substitutes
liquor supplies, liqueurs
lobster tanks
lockers
locks

M

machines: soft ice, cream, milk shake
magazines, newspapers
management services
management systems
marinades
markers, chalks, and crayons
marketing materials and services
marketing research
marketing: promotional items, public relations
matches/matchbooks
mats, floor
mats, rubber, composition
mayonnaise
meat analogs
meat cookers
meatball machines
meats: fresh, frozen, canned, pre-portioned, processed
menu accessories
menu covers and holders
menu display
menu planning, development
menu price changers
menus, menu boards
menu card systems
mesquite wood
metal polish
metal work, kitchen equipment
Mexican foods
microwave accessories
microwave food

microwave ovens and cookware
mini bars
mints: hospitality and printed
mirrors, murals, and wall decorations
mixers, drink
mixers, food   electric
mixes, cocktail
mixes, food
mixes: prepared
flour/dough
mobile restaurants
money counters
mops and mopping equipment
motivational incentives, employee contests, and games
muffin depositor
murals and wall decorations
mushrooms
music and sound systems
music licensing: organizations and copyright law
music systems
music videos
musical instruments
name badges/tags

N

napkin rings
napkins, disposable
napkins, fabric
nondairy creamers
nutrition services and information
nuts

O

office machines
office supplies
oils, cooking
olives
on-line services
onion rings
onions, dehydrated
ordering systems
organizers: calendars,

notebooks and seating charts

ovens and ranges: cooking equipment, parts and service

ovens, baking and roasting

ovens, brick

ovens, combination convection/ steam

ovens: convection, conveyor, infrared, low temperature, microwave, quartz, vapor and wood burning

ovenware: china or glass

P

packaging and wrap: foil, plastic and paper

packaging materials: wrapping

packaging, take-out

paging systems and employee call systems

paint markers or strippers

pan liners and coatings

paneling and partitions, acoustical

paper goods and disposable tabletop items

parking lot maintenance

partitions or walls, movable

pasta cookers

pasta making equipment/ machines

pasta: fresh, frozen, flavored, homemade, and processed

pastry products

pates

payroll companies

payroll processing services

peanut butter

peppermills

personnel services: recruitment, leasing, and consultants

pest control services and products

photographic services and equipment

pickles and pickled products

pie fillings

pie making machines

pies, baked and frozen

pitchers

pizza equipment and supplies

pizza products

place mats

plants, flowers, and greenery

plastic signs

plasticware, disposable and nondisposable

plasticware, disposable, molded

plates, disposable

platforms and risers, portable

platters

playground equipment

plumbing fixtures and equipment

point-of-sale equipment materials and supplies

polishes and waxes, floor

popcorn equipment

portable toilets and sanitation

posters and poster systems

pot and pan washing equipment

potato products

potatoes, processed

pots and pans

poultry information

poultry: fresh, frozen canned and pre-portioned

powders, fry-kettle

precooked frozen food

pre-portioned foods: jam, cheese, salt, pepper

pre-portioned meat, fish, and poultry

pre-washing machines

premiums and incentives

pressure cookers

pressure fryers

pretzels

printing and design

printing forms, notices

produce: fruits, vegetables

property management systems

public address systems

public cold storage

pushcarts

R

racks, coat and hat

racks, dish and glass

racks, dishwashing

racks, drying

racks, luggage

racks, shelving, storage

railings: brass, chrome, stainless steel, wood

ramekins

ranges, electric and gas

real estate: analysis, brokerage, and financing

recipe card indexers

recipes: new ideas

recycling containers, equipment and services

refinishing services: tableware

refrigeration equipment: display

refrigeration equipment: reach-in

refrigeration equipment: repair and service

refrigeration equipment: walk-ins, relishes, chutneys

rendering services

rental: supplies and equipment

rentals and leasing: cars, and trucks

rentals and leasing party supplies

reservation services training

restaurant consultants

restoration

rice/rice products

room service products

rotisseries

S

safes and vaults

safety products

salad dressings

salad dryers

salad oils

salads and salad bars: equipment and supplies

sandwich and salad units, refrigerated

sandwiches

sanitation equipment and supplies

sauces and sauce bases

saws, meat cutting   power

scales, food

schools and educational services

scouring pads

seafood and seafood products

seafood steaming equipment

seasonings and spices

seating systems: charts and wait lists

seating, auditorium and theater

seating, food court

secret shopper service

security equipment systems and services

septic tank cleaning, repairs and maintenance

serving dishes

sharpening services: knives and equipment

shelf liners

shellfish tools/mesh

steaming bags

shelving, plastic

shelving, steel and wood

shortening

shower curtains

signs, changeable letter

signs, electrical and electronic

signs, painted

signs, tabletop

signs, wooden

signs: engraved, led, and neon

silver burnishers, cleaners, and compounds

silver plating

sinks, kitchen

sinks, under-bar

slicers, food   electric

slicers, mechanical/hand-operated

slush machines

snack bar units

snack foods: candies, chips and nuts

sneeze guards

soap, toilet

soaps: detergents and cleaning compounds

soda fountain supplies

soda fountains and equipment

soft serve equipment and products

sorbet

sound systems

soups: condensed, dehydrated and ready- to-serve

soups, frozen

soups and soup bases

souvenirs, novelties and party favors

specialty foods

stages, mobile and fold-ing; dance floors

stainless steel stanchions and decorative rope

staples

starch, cooking

steam cleaning services

steam cookers

steam tables

sterilizers

stirrers: wood or plastic

straws, sipping

strip doors

sugar and sugar products

supplies: electronic machines paper, rolls, and ribbon

sweetening products

syrups and toppings

systems, intercom

T

table covers, disposable

table padding

table toys and table games

table: skirting, linens, napkins

tables, bakers' tables, banquet room and folding tables and counters

tables, kitchen

tables, outdoor

tables, pedestal

tables, room service

tables: hot/cold food, serving and folding

tableware, disposable

takeout service/delivery service

tea making and dispensing equipment

tea and iced tea

technical research

telecommunication services

telephone, pay

telephone systems, sales and service

television, closed circuit

television, satellite

tenderizers

tents and canopies

testing and evaluation services: safety and sanitation

textured vegetable protein product

theme party supplies

thermo delivery pouches

thermometers

thermoware

tiling

tilting skillets

time keeping equipment and supplies

time recorders

tissues, disposable

toasters, automatic   gas or electric

tobacco products

toilet paper

toilet seat covers

tomato products

tools: garnishing, ice carving

toothpicks and party picks

toppings

tortilla press

tortilla products

touch screens

towels: cotton or linen

towels, paper

trade publications

training videos

training materials

tray covers

tray stands
tray washers
trays, baking
trays, foam
trays, paper
trays, plastic
trays, restaurant
trays: storage, serving and display
trucks for folding tables, chairs
trucks, delivery
trucks, dish and food
trucks, laundry, and linen supply

U

umbrellas, aluminum, outdoor
uniform emblems: imprinted or embroidered
uniforms: clothing
uniforms: hats and caps
uniforms: protective apparel
upholstery cleaners
utensils, cooking/kitchen
utility, analysis, control and distributions

V

vacuum cleaner
vacuum-packed/vacuum-sealed bags and pouches
vegetable cutters and peelers
vegetable juice

vehicles, maintenance
vehicles, personnel
vending machines
vending products
vending vehicles
ventilating systems, kitchen ventilators and ventilating equipment
vinegars
visitor guides, maps

W

waffle irons and cone makers
waffles
wait staff call system
walk-in coolers and freezers
wall covering
wall panels, tile
wallboard
wall cleaners and maintenance
walls, movable
warehousing
warmers, beverage
warmers, dish/plate
warmers, food
warmers, electric
wash cloths
waste disposal systems
waste grease collection
waste reduction equipment and services
waste reduction
waste disposal

wastebaskets and receptacles
water conditioner and softener equipment and supplies
water machines: heating and cooling
water purification/filtration
water vacuums/brooms
water, bottled
water, mineral
water and water dispensers
whipping equipment: cream, sour cream and toppings
whipping equipment: accessories
wholesale club
windows
wine accessories
wine cellar
wine consultants and distributors
wine service equipment
wines
wipes
wire accessories
woks, electric and nonelectric
woodenware, bowls and kitchen utensils
work tables, kitchen
wraps: lemon, stem

Y

yogurt equipment
yogurt: frozen, fresh, and soft-serve

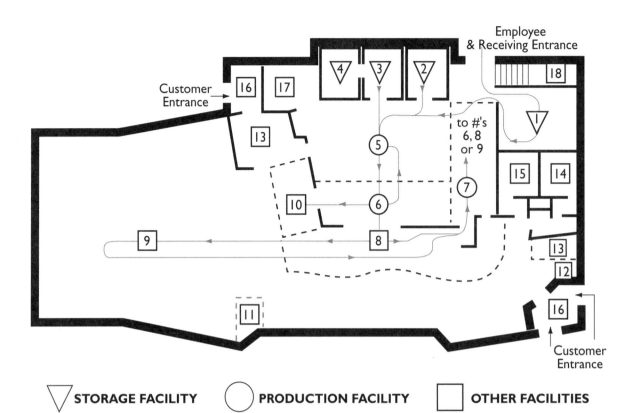

▽ **STORAGE FACILITY**   ◯ **PRODUCTION FACILITY**   ☐ **OTHER FACILITIES**

1. Storeroom
2. Dairy and vegetable walk-in cooler
3. Meat walk-in cooler
4. Walk-in freezer
5. Combination meat and vegetable preparation, salad preparation and pot and pan washing area
6. Meat and vegetable cooking area
7. Dish room

8. Dining room counter
9. Dining room
10. Takeout area
11. Waiters' station
12. Cashier
13. Customer lounge (two)
14. Men's restroom
15. Women's restroom

16. Customer entry and exit (two)
17. Manager's office
18. Employee lockers, equipment room and miscellaneous storage located in basement

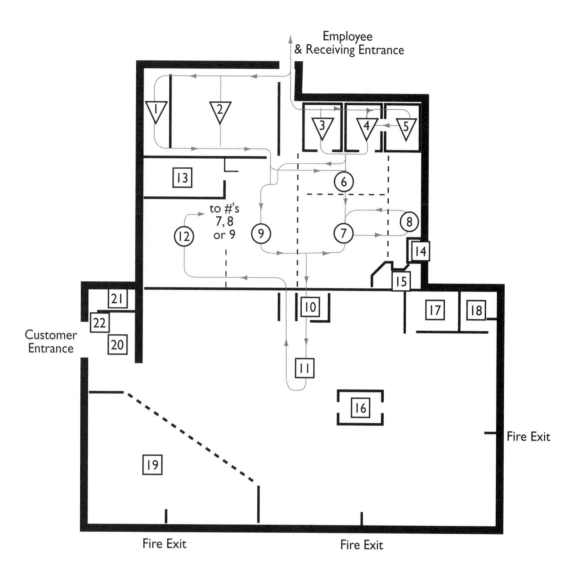

▽ **STORAGE FACILITY**   ◯ **PRODUCTION FACILITY**   ☐ **OTHER FACILITIES**

1. Liquor storage	9. Salad preparation	16. Waiters' station
2. Storeroom	10. Checker/cashier's station	17. Women's restroom
3. Dairy and vegetable walk-in cooler	11. Dining room	18. Men's restroom
4. Meat walk-in cooler	12. Dish room	19. Cocktail lounge
5. Walk-in freezer	13. Employee dining	20. Customer lounge
6. Meat and vegetable preparation	14. Janitor's closet	21. Checkroom
7. Meat and vegetable cooking	15. Chef's office	22. Reservation station
8. Pot and pan washing		

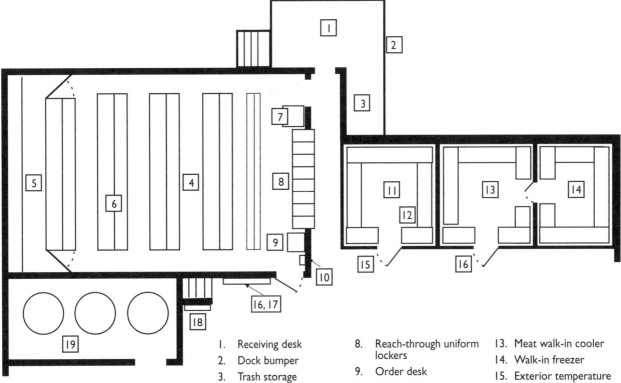

1. Receiving desk
2. Dock bumper
3. Trash storage
4. Storeroom
5. Liquor storage
6. Shelving (eleven)
7. Platform scale
8. Reach-through uniform lockers
9. Order desk
10. Wall telephone
11. Dairy and vegetable walk-in cooler
12. Mobile racks (fourteen)
13. Meat walk-in cooler
14. Walk-in freezer
15. Exterior temperature gauges (three)
16. Time clock
17. Time card racks (two)
18. Bulletin board
19. Employee dining

CHAPTER

BASICS OF BUYING
OR LEASING A RESTAURANT

T he real estate property of a restaurant can be its most valuable feature. In many cases the land is a bigger attraction to the buyer than the business itself. Conversely, restaurants may be bought and sold without the property being part of the operation.

The restaurant owner may lease its property from a landlord who has no involvement in the business itself. "Real estate" is a reversion asset, which means it is expected to retain most or all of its value, regardless of whether the business on it is successful. The value of real estate is one of the major assets that needs to be calculated when determining a food-service operation's value. There are three procedures for determining the value of a restaurant: market approach, cost approach, and income approach.

DETERMINING THE RESTAURANT'S VALUE

MARKET APPROACH

The market approach is based on the idea of substitution. The value of a property is determined by comparing it to like pieces of property in similar areas. Since these comparable properties are not exactly the same as the property you are trying to value, you will need to make adjustments to place an accurate market value. Determining these adjustments is a subjective process at best, and at worst it is impossible because owners of similar properties are unlikely to tell you the details of their businesses. For these reasons the market approach is generally not used to estimate the value of a restaurant's real estate. However, if you are selling land only, the market approach can be an accurate determiner of value, since there are considerably fewer adjustments to make.

COST APPROACH

The cost approach is based on the idea of replacement. The property is valued on what it would cost to replace it completely. To determine this value you must add the replacement costs of all the assets in your establishment. Obtain purchase prices for new equipment and assets that exactly match your existing ones. With equipment that is no longer made, add the price of a new piece of equipment. Include all taxes, freight, and installation in your quotes, and factor in depreciation. The cost approach is not widely used to estimate the value of a restaurant's real estate but is used by insurance companies for processing claims.

INCOME APPROACH

The income approach is preferred because the basis of its valuation is the anticipated income to be derived from the property, so that the real estate value is the present value of the estimated future net income, plus the present value of the estimated profit to be earned when the property is sold. Investors are concerned with the amount of income they can earn while using a property's assets, not with what it would cost to replace those assets.

There are other approaches to value as well. If your property was recently assessed for tax purposes, the assessed value may be a useful estimate to you, even if the valuation does not match current market conditions. The book value approach is based on the initial purchase price for the property, minus accrued depreciation. This value will no doubt have very little to do with current market conditions, but it can be useful if you want to compute a low estimate of value for other reasons. The underwriter approach is used by lenders to determine the amount of loan proceeds an income property can support. This amount is determined by multiplying the debt-service-coverage ratio, DSC, (the amount of income available for debt service, divided by the annual amount of debt-service payment demanded by the lender) by the loan constant, then dividing this sum by the annual income available for debt service.

You may use several valuation procedures to determine the most likely sales price because establishments may have separate aspects of business that can be valued separately. A bar may have its real property as well as its tavern license. The real estate may be valued through the income approach and the license through the market approach.

HE VALUE OF OTHER ASSETS

A restaurant's assets are often broken down into three categories: real estate, other reversion assets, and the business. A reversion asset is one that retains its value regardless of the success or failure of the business. These are assets like the real estate, equipment, inventories, receivables, prepaid expenses (deposits, taxes, advertising), lease-hold interest, antiques, licenses, franchises, and exclusive distributorships like lottery ticket sales. These assets keep their value even if a business goes under, and they can be sold at market value. Therefore, it is in an owner's best interest to own as many reversion assets as possible, because these assets increase the business's value to sellers.

The business itself consists of everything the owner wishes to sell: furniture, fixtures, equipment, and leasehold improvements. It may also include tax credits, favorable operating expenses, customer lists, and name recognition. The price for a food-service business is usually 40 to 70 percent of the operation's 12-month food-and-beverage sales volume. The seller usually sets the sale price at the high end of this percentage, and the prospective buyer sets it at the low end.

Setting a sales price is not, of course, a straightforward process, and there are many other factors that need to be considered. Here are a few:

- **Profitability.** The most common way to determine profitability is to examine the net operating income figure. If it is average in the market, the sales price equals 50 percent of the previous 12 months' food-and-beverage sales. The net income should be compared to the industry standard and the regional standard for that type of operation.

- **Leasehold terms and conditions.** The term remaining on the property lease and the monthly payment will affect the sales price greatly. Buyers normally want five-year leases, and a seller should be prepared to assign the existing lease or help in negotiating a new lease with the landlord. Buyers who cannot get a minimum five-year lease are usually not interested in buying a restaurant unless it is very profitable or priced very low. In addition to a five-year lease, most buyers also need a reasonable monthly payment and a reasonable common area maintenance payment, not exceeding 6 percent to 8 percent of the monthly food-and-beverage sales.

- **Track record.** Businesses need to show acceptable track records to entice buyers. The business must be at least a year old. The track record will be used to project the business's future prospects. A business dependent on the work of highly skilled employees, such as a well-known chef, makes the business more difficult to expand and more expensive to operate, affecting price.

- **Other income.** Most restaurants do not earn much other income, usually less than 2 percent, but there may be rebates; interest on bank deposits; vending machines; and salvage from aluminum, grease, and cardboard. All of these can make an impact, particularly vending machines, and need to be taken into consideration when valuing a restaurant.

- **Below-market financing.** When a restaurant is sold, the buyer puts up a small down payment and the seller then carries back the remainder of the sales price at favorable terms. Seller financing is usually below market, and the buyer avoids the fees associated with bank loans.

- **Personal goodwill.** If a restaurant's business depends on the personal relationships between staff and management who will not be staying, the sales price will probably decrease.

- **Franchise affiliation.** If a restaurant is part of a franchise, the sale price will increase significantly, truer of the larger national franchises than the regional ones.

- **Number of buyers and sellers.** A seller should plan to market his business when there are as many potential buyers as possible meaning early spring and summer, especially if it is a tourist business, or after legislation limiting construction has passed, or taxes are lowered.

- **Contingent liabilities.** Contingent liabilities reduce a restaurant's net income. These may be coupons issued by the previous owner, dining club memberships, or pension plans that eat into the net profit margin. If a buyer cannot eliminate these expenses, they most likely represent a negative value that should be factored into the offering price.

- **Grandfather clauses.** New owners are expected to meet fire, health, and safety codes that the previous owner may have been able to avoid because of being "grandfathered in" when the regulations were passed. Grandfather clauses usually expire when a business changes hands. The seller or buyer may need to bring the building up to code. If the buyer may ask that the expense be deducted from the sale price. If the cost is very high, it could affect the salability of the business altogether.

OODWILL

The IRS determines goodwill as the amount of money paid for a restaurant in excess of the current book value of the physical assets. Most investors look at excess earnings as attributable to positive goodwill and deficient earnings to negative goodwill.

To compute the goodwill value, the restaurant's income statement from the past 12 months must be reconstructed. The idea is to develop a financial statement that reflects what could have happened if a wise and knowledgeable restaurateur had been running the business. The best model to use for this process is the National Restaurant Association's Annual Restaurant Industry Operations Report, which itemizes in detail the following income and expense areas:

- Food sales
- Other income
- Payroll
- Direct operating expenses
- Advertising and promotion
- Administrative and general
- Occupation costs
- Depreciation

- Beverage sales
- Cost of sales
- Employee benefits
- Music and entertainment
- Utilities
- Maintenance and repairs
- Interest expense

Sales volume is most critical because the sales price is tied into the previous 12 months' net food-and-beverage sales volume. The sales volume is important because a seller will have to adhere to the figure supported in the sales reports. Buyers generally are not interested in hearing about phantom buried income or optimistic forecasts of future sales. In some cases net sales increase is good, but usually a buyer will not allow a seller to profit from something the seller did not create.

To arrive at a credible goodwill value, a seller needs to work with the existing income/expense figures and only make changes that can be supported. In most cases sales volume figures cannot be supported, but expense adjustments can as they include the expenses owners usually list on their tax returns, travel, cars, supplies, and unwarranted employee benefits that are unrelated to the business. The flip side is that a seller may increase payroll and benefits if they are artificially low because the owner took salaries directly from profits.

A buyer may be willing to pay for goodwill, but a seller should expect the buyer to downplay its value to lower the sale price as much as possible. A few other complications with goodwill can arise:

- **There is a difference between personal goodwill and goodwill attributable to the**

business itself. Unless the appropriate staff has agreed to stay on, personal goodwill is not transferable to the next owner. It is up to the buyer to distinguish between transferable goodwill and goodwill that vanishes with the previous owner.

- **Sellers must be able to convince the buyer that the excess net income that is positive goodwill will not decrease after the business changes hands.** It is in the sellers' interest to prove that positive goodwill is due to something like a great location and to point out that the new owner should generally operate according to established standards and practices that generated or supported that positive goodwill.

- **The IRS does not allow the buyer to depreciate goodwill.** In most cases a buyer will assign the value of the goodwill to a non-competition agreement with the seller, and thereby be able to rescue the goodwill amount in a tax shelter.

- **If the restaurant is less than one year old, it is very difficult to project a stabilized annual net income.** Reasonable estimates are the best thing here. A buyer will not want to talk about goodwill unless the numbers are based on reasonable projections of revenues and expenses.

- **If a restaurant has negative goodwill, the seller is in the difficult position of making a convincing argument that the buyer should purchase a marginally profitable business.** The best argument here is to point out the existing reversion assets that are part of the sale price. If there are no reversion assets, it is very difficult to point out the potential of future earnings without questioning why the seller did not capitalize on that potential. Pointing out the elimination of excessive start-up costs by purchasing an already running business is the only option. This option only works if there is a reasonable expectation the business's net income will improve significantly.

- **It can be difficult for restaurateurs to receive fair compensation for their investment.** Judges and arbitrators usually do not consider goodwill   only the book value of tangible assets.

TERMS, CONDITIONS, AND PRICE

Generally, sellers will determine likely sales price, terms, and conditions, and then pad them somewhat to create room for negotiation and compromise. Sellers should prepare a pragmatic and well documented solicitation and then search for buyers who will appreciate these considerations.

Anticipating every potential problem that may arise during negotiations will put sellers in a good position to offer solutions to a buyer's objections. It is a good idea for a seller to hire an attorney, accountant, or business broker when preparing a preferred sales price, terms, and conditions. Savvy buyers and sellers also incorporate their transaction costs   brokerage fees, lawyers   into the price asked or offered. In most cases there are higher transaction fees for the seller. It is a good practice for the seller to enumerate all the assets that are included in the sale of the restaurant. Doing so will garner respect from potential buyers, and it may give the seller an advantage during initial negotiations.

TERMS

The terms of sale are the procedures used by the buyer to pay the seller. A buyer is willing to accept a proposed sales price if the seller will accept the buyer's terms. Sellers receive a minimal down payment and the remainder of the purchase price over a three- to five-year period. "All cash" offers are rare, and seller financing is usually necessary to attract buyers. It is in the seller's interest to receive a large down payment because it signifies the buyer's commitment. Sellers are also more likely to grant favorable terms to a buyer making a substantial down payment because the financial risk is lessened.

Sometimes buyers will want to pay with property or corporate stock instead of cash, a good move from a tax perspective; however, stock can decrease in value, and usually the stock used for this type of deal cannot be sold for a year or more, often only in small amounts.

Seller financing is the most desirable aspect of the investment in a restaurant, and buyers want to assume favorable loans. Sellers offering favorable terms must be sure they receive adequate compensation in the form of a higher sales price. Seller financing is negotiable, but the marketplace suggests typical loan amounts and terms. The loan payments should not be tied into sales volume or any other performance measures, because the seller does not want to suffer if a new owner drives the business under. The only instance where loan payments should be tied into performance measures is in an "earn-out agreement," where the premium part of the sales price is contingent on its future performance.

CONDITIONS

There are several conditions the seller and buyer will attach to sales contracts. Sometimes they are separate agreements, but most of the time they are part of the sales contract. The following lists are the conditions of greatest concern to a seller:

- **Conclusion of sale.** Sellers want to finish the transaction as fast as possible because delays give buyers time to second-guess.

- **Buyer access.** Sellers want minimal contact with the buyer while waiting for the transaction to close, and they do not want the buyer spending time with the restaurant staff. It is good for a seller to provide assistance for the ownership transition, but it should only be after the buyer has taken possession of the business.

- **Guarantees.** Sellers usually have to guarantee the condition of assets. Sometimes sellers have to guarantee that buyers can assume some of the restaurant's current contracts. Sellers should never guarantee things they do not have total control over. Imprecise language should also be avoided here. If the seller is making guarantees, buying the relevant insurance to back up these claims is prudent.

- **Indemnification.** Sellers will want to be compensated if a buyer backs out of the deal. Sellers should also be protected for expenses paid to fix code violations or for legal expenses if the seller needs to sue the buyer to uphold an agreement.

- **Escrow agent.** Independent escrow agents are usually hired to supervise transactions. They see that all terms and conditions are met and afterwards ownership can be transferred. The seller should insist that the buyer agree to an independent third-party escrow agent, ensuring the myriad details of this transaction are handled efficiently and legally.

- **Legal requirements.** Seller and buyer must agree to comply with all pertinent laws and statutes. Escrow agents ensure that all current creditors are notified of the restaurant's sale and that all legal requirements are met, ensuring that the buyer can begin with a clean slate without any of the seller's responsibilities to creditors.

- **Buyer's credit history.** Before agreeing to seller financing, the seller must investigate the buyer's credit history. It is standard for buyers to give personal financial statements, resumes, references, and permission to run a credit report. Serious buyers have no problem submitting this information because doing so assures the seller's respect.

- **Security for seller financing.** Many deals go bad because buyer and seller cannot agree on financing. If a seller agrees to hold paper, the buyer must sign a promissory note and security agreement. The note represents the buyer's promise to pay. The security agreement is the collateral pledged to secure the loan. If the seller is the only lender, a clause should be added that requires his approval before the new owner can obtain additional financing. The promissory note should contain a default provision that the lender can foreclose if loan payments are not met in addition to other specific provisions pertinent to the business, such as a provision that the seller can foreclose if the new owner does not maintain a required balance sheet or does not produce previously agreed upon menu items.

- **Assumable loans and leases.** Buyers will want to assume any contract that calls for below-market payments. Sellers should do everything possible to ensure a favorable transition because many deals rest on buyers' being able to assume outstanding contracts.

- **Life and disability insurance.** If the seller carries the paper, the buyer should be required to purchase the appropriate insurance naming the seller as beneficiary. If the buyer refuses to purchase this insurance, the seller should do so. If the new owner dies or becomes ill without insurance, the previous owner would lose his investment.

- **Collection of receivables.** It is reasonable for the owner to receive a modest fee for the collection of receivables. This fee can be for business booked prior to the change of ownership.

- **Inventory sale.** This sale is usually handled at the close of escrow. Physical inventory of all food, beverages, and supplies should be taken by an independent service and a separate bill of sale prepared for the price agreed upon.

- **Non-compete clause.** This clause is quite common in the sale of an ongoing business, because the new owner does not want the seller to open up a competing business nearby. Smart sellers make sure the agreement covers only the same type of food operation; therefore, if they are selling a pizza parlor, they are not prohibited from opening a five-star bistro.

- **Repurchase agreement.** Sellers often include agreements that grant them the option to buy the restaurant back within a certain time. This agreement usually notes the purchase price and terms of the sale. If the restaurant becomes incredibly valuable all of a sudden, the former owner can buy it back or sell the repurchase agreement to someone else.

- **Employment contract.** If a seller agrees to remain as an employee of the new restaurant, a very specific contract should be drafted. Most sellers have no interest in these contracts and just want out. Offering to stay on may increase the potential of selling the restaurant.

- **Consulting contract.** This contract may be a more acceptable type of employment, giving the new owner a tax-deductible expense without burdening the former owner.

- **Conditions not met.** Often buyers cannot meet every sales condition. Sellers can use this agreement as a way to cancel the deal. However, the seller should also reserve the right to proceed with the sale even if certain conditions are not met.

DETERMINING PRICE FROM A BUYER'S PERSPECTIVE

Potential buyers must do a thorough financial analysis of the restaurant, carefully studying its current profitability to determine its potential capacity for generating revenue. Because there is a very close relationship between a restaurant's current profitability and its likely sales price, the buyer should examine this income very carefully. Understandably, sellers are not eager to divulge their financial records to buyers. However, if a seller is forthcoming with this information it can signal the buyer that he has nothing to hide.

The buyer should hire an accountant to assist in this financial analysis. An accountant's analysis will help determine whether the deal meets the buyer's investment requirements. Buyers should also hire other specialists to work with contracts, unemployment compensation, insurance, and banking. If the buyer qualifies, Small Business Development Centers (SBDC) throughout the country offer free consulting services to businesses with fewer than 500 employees.

Buyers should complete a rough market and competition survey before performing a financial evaluation. Doing so ensures familiarity with the restaurant's location and helps when calculating estimated future revenues and expenses. If the buyer is unfamiliar with the area, an independent consulting service can be hired to provide a useful survey.

A seller expects a written offer with price, terms, conditions, and an earnest money deposit before allowing a potential buyer to review confidential financial information. It must be agreed that the buyer can withdraw after reviewing the financial records. The earnest deposit is at risk unless the right to retract the offer is in place. When reviewing the sellers' financial records, buyers should expect that an independent CPA has never audited them because auditing is a costly process that most small businesses cannot afford.

The buyer needs to reconstruct historical financial statements as they would have been had the buyer been operating the business. This reconstruction is usually done from the previous year's statement and is time-consuming. If it contains errors, the estimate of the restaurant's sales price may be inaccurate. Sellers tend to overestimate customer counts and check averages and underestimate utilities and other expenses. The inexperienced buyer should be wary when evaluating these numbers and may want to hire professional counsel.

Be aware that sellers include only the financial details they initially want to reveal. These numbers are optimistic. The typical listing agreement contains the asking price, financing possibilities, current sales volume, current expenses, age, and size of the restaurant. Buyers should evaluate this information carefully, giving attention to the apparent net cash flow before spending time and money on a detailed analysis.

During this analysis, note that the typical restaurant purchase will not appear to generate enough money to provide sufficient cash flow, give the buyer an appropriate salary, and ensure a return on the initial investment. As a buyer, do not be put off too quickly. Solid analysis often reveals that a change in ownership can considerably enhance a restaurant's profitability.

The buyer's analysis should examine all relevant tax filings to determine the most likely annual sales volume that the restaurant will generate. Profit figures included in these filings will be used to determine an accurate sales price. Payroll costs will be used to predict future personnel and payroll requirements and minimal tax liabilities. Personnel records are crucial in determining whether there have been any Department of Labor judgments against the current owner or if there are any pending judgments that could impede the transfer of ownership. Meet with a DOL representative to find out whether the restaurant is currently under investigation.

Cost of food, beverages, and supplies are a restaurant's biggest expense. The buyer should take a random sample of canceled invoices and check their consistency with the cost of goods sold and direct operating expenses (supplies) listed on the current income statement. If these numbers match, the buyer has a good idea of what product and supply expenses the restaurant will incur if no organizational and operational changes are made. The canceled invoices are also a good test of the current owner's purchasing skills. If invoices show higher prices than those of competing suppliers, the buyer can expect to decrease those expenses.

Most lenders require a cash budget prepared by buyers. This budget will point out the operation's daily cash requirements and the times of year when short-term money must be borrowed to cover brief shortages.

Buyers should analyze balance sheets and income statements carefully. Balance sheets can reveal the anxiety level of a seller and indicate the current management's abilities. If ability is in question, it could predict greater earnings under sound management. Income statements are used by the buyer to determine whether the restaurant could have satisfied salary demands and provided a return on the initial investment, had it been under the buyer's management for the previous 12 months. Most sellers require a pro forma income statement for the coming year as part of the loan application process. Because a buyer is basing the offer on current income but purchasing the operation's future revenue-making ability, this income statement is the most critical tasks the buyer will perform.

INITIAL INVESTMENT

Buyers must estimate as accurately as possible the total initial investment needed. An appealing aspect of purchasing an existing restaurant is that many start-up costs are avoided. Here are a number of start-up costs to be aware of:

- **Investigation costs.** Buyers must be willing to spend time and money to examine opportunities available. Typical buyers want to begin running their new establishment as soon as possible and do not want to be bothered with extensive analyses. By contrast, restaurant developers or chain-restaurant companies spend time and effort before investing in a property. Many investors falsely believe that once initial development work is complete, start-up costs are eliminated. While they are reduced considerably, the costs still exist, and wise investors calculate them in their analysis.

- **Down payment.** Standard down payment is around a quarter of the sales price. Buyers who offer this down payment usually can expect the seller to provide below-market financing for the remainder of the sales price. The down payment can affect the sales price, and in many cases sellers will accept a lower sales price with a larger down payment and vice versa.

- **Transaction costs.** Escrow agents will prorate insurance, payroll, vacation pay, license renewal fees, and advertising costs on the close-of-escrow date. The buyer will have a debit balance that the escrow agent will transfer to the seller. Fees paid to the escrow company and for creating documents needed to close the transaction constitute the closing costs.

- **Working capital.** Buyers must budget for sufficient supplies to run the restaurant.

- **Deposits.** Most creditors require cash deposits as assurance they will be paid for their products and services. Utility, telephone, sales-tax, payroll-tax, and lease deposits must be set aside.

- **Licenses and permits.** Most restaurants must have retail, health, and government permits. All required operating licenses and permits should be budgeted for as start-up expenses.

- **Legal fees.** Competent legal advice is a very good idea for buyers. Escrow agents should not be counted on to draw papers correctly and to make sure that the interests of various parties have been represented. An attorney for the buyer should look out for the buyer's interests solely.

- **Renovations and utensils.** There may be building code violations to rectify or large renovations necessary to bring the restaurant into a competitive position. It may also be necessary to purchase new china, glass, silver, and utensils to replace worn older ones.

- **Advertising.** Promoting an opening or reopening, rebuilding, and promotional discounts or other incentives are good ways to build patronage for a new establishment.

- **Fictitious name registration.** If the name of a restaurant is fictitious, the name must be registered at the local courthouse or County Recorder's Office.

- **Loan fees.** Buyers who are not acquiring seller financing will accrue loan fees from the lending parties.

- **Equity fees.** Buyers who want to sell common stock to a few investors will incur attorney, document preparation, and registration fees.

- **Insurance.** A lender will require a borrower to have appropriate life and disability insurance and that the lender be named sole beneficiary.

- **Franchise fees.** Buyers acquiring an existing franchise will be required to pay the franchiser a transfer-of-ownership fee for the costs of evaluating the prospective owner. It is paid in up front in cash before the new franchise begins operations.

- **Distributorship fees.** Buyers who assume exclusive distributorship licenses or who want to discontinue a current license agreement may incur costs similar to franchise fees. Exclusive distributorships are usually granted to individuals, but some are given to business locations, and in this instance a buyer can assume the license with little out-of-pocket expense.

- **Pre-opening labor.** This expense is greatly minimized by purchasing an existing operation. Buyers usually plan to make some personnel changes, and a portion of current staff members should be expected to leave during the change of management.

- **Accounting fees.** Fees for assistance in the evaluation of a restaurant purchase need to be budgeted.

- **Other consulting fees.** A restaurant owner's primary consultants are an attorney and an accountant, but others are graphic artists, labor-relations specialists, and computer consultants.

- **Other prepaid expenses.** When new owners take over an existing business, it is common for creditors to demand a form of prepayment.

- **Sales taxes.** Property may be subject to a transfer tax, and non-food supplies are often subject to sales tax.

- **Locksmith.** Most buyers will change all the locks on a restaurant after the sale is final.

- **Security.** A buyer will transfer the current security service or else contract for a new one.

- **Contingency.** Successful restaurateurs suggest having a contingency fund large enough for the first six months' operating expenses. Among other things, it is often necessary to over-hire and over-schedule employees before an effective sales distribution pattern emerges, so that operators incur higher expenses during the first six months of operation. Financing options appears in more detail in Chapter 4.

LEASING AS AN OPTION TO GET STARTED

LEASE AND THE START-UP OWNER

There are a number of potential problems attendant to leases. As a restaurant owner who is looking to lease space where the current owner is considering moving to a new location, you want to do the following:

- **Check any current leases before you begin searching for a new one.** If you are already leasing space for your restaurant and are looking to change locations, be sure to check the lease you already have before looking for a new one so that you time your new lease to avoid double rent payments. Start looking several months in advance. You do not want to wait until your current lease ends before beginning your search because your landlord might require you to sign a new lease to stay put. Plan to start a new lease close to the termination date of your current lease.

- **Check out subletting options.** If your current lease gives you the option to sublet the property, you may actually be able to hold on to the current property and sublet it for a profit. This profit, in turn, can be used to help pay the expenses on your new, better restaurant location. Have your attorney check the fine details before making a decision.

- **Ask about a buyout.** If you cannot or do not want to sublet the property and must leave before your current lease expires, ask your landlord about a buyout amount. The buyout is a negotiated or set amount of money that the landlord will take to let you out of your lease. It should be a smaller amount than you would pay for the remaining time on your lease.

- **Consider signing a long-term lease.** When shopping around for new space, you should plan to sign a long-term lease that will protect the new landlord and you; most landlords will be open to the idea. A long-term lease is a smart option.

- **Make your list; check it twice.** You decide to opt for a lease; now make a list of "wants" and "needs." When buying a restaurant, you are actually paying for its future profitability. Will this location still be good for you five years from now? Make sure all your interior and exterior needs are on the list. What about security, the neighborhood, pending road construction, and parking? Make sure your list covers everything.

- **Try to have the landlord pay the broker's fees as part of the lease agreement.** Many landlords will pick up the tab for the broker's fees even if you hired the broker. If you come down to two properties that you like, check out the landlord's position on broker's fees. If one will pay the fee while the other will not, that point may make your decision easier.

ASK YOURSELF THE QUESTION "WHY LEASE?"

Before disrupting and moving your business to a totally new location, ask yourself why you are making this move. Some reasons are not valid in light of losses incurred during the move.

Consider the following possibilities:

- **Constant change is not good for your business.** Bear in mind that if you sign short-term leases, you will be moving several times   not good for business. People who enjoy your eatery will come for the familiarity as well as the food. They do not want changes every year, so neither should you.

- **Talk to your customers.** If you really feel you must move your restaurant, consider talking with some of your regular customers about it. If moving to a particular area would cause you to lose half your current customers, it would not be worth the change.

- **Put your cash into your restaurant instead.** Moving a restaurant is expensive and time consuming. If you are distracted from your work every few years to look for space, your business will suffer.

- **Ask your landlord for help.** Sometimes your reasons for leaving involve things that your landlord can change. Some concerns may even be covered in your current lease. If the building needs updating, your landlord may be responsible for maintenance of the building. Check your lease and talk to your landlord. Chances are he would rather put out a little cash in some paint than to begin the lease process again.

- **Ask your landlord for more space.** If you have outgrown your current location, your landlord may be able to help. If there is an adjacent space available, you may be able to add this square footage to your current location. Some lease agreements may give you first option on the space. Check the possibilities before you pick up and move somewhere else.

USING A LEASE BROKER

Make sure you hire a commercial broker who specializes in commercial leases. Find a broker who works with commercial leases every day. Consider the following:

- **Check out references before you retain a broker.** Find out whether other clients of this broker were satisfied. The best question to ask is this: "Would you use this broker again?"

- **Have everything in writing.** If you hire a broker with less than pure motives, avoid problems by having the broker sign a very detailed contract that covers all obligations to you. Have your attorney look over the contract before you present it to the broker.

- **"Listing brokers."** In the same way that some brokers are paid by the buyer in a restaurant-buy situation, brokers can also used by the landlord in a lease situation. These brokers are called listing brokers because the landlord has listed the property with the broker. Restaurant owners who are looking for property should beware of listing brokers because they work for the landlord.

- **Hire your own broker.** Rather than working through a broker who is representing the landlord's interests, it is better to hire your own broker. True, it will add some expense to the whole lease process, but you will have the confidence of knowing that the broker's loyalties are with you.

- **Stay away from dual agents.** Some states allow brokers to work for both the landlord and the tenant in which case the broker agrees to be neutral. This situation is good in the sense that you know the broker will not be working against you. It is not good because he cannot give you professional advice. If you are going to use a broker, you might as well get all the professional benefits that go with a broker's service. Skip the dual agent agreement. It is not in your best interest.

WHAT ARE THE BENEFITS OF HIRING A BROKER?

Now that you know the kinds of brokers to hire, examine the benefits of hiring a broker who is working to find your perfect restaurant space.

- **A broker will save you time.** A broker who knows the geographic area you work in can save you time by weeding out lease spaces and showing you only the places that fit your business plan.

- **Brokers will do the legwork.** A broker who is working for you will take care of details, freeing you to focus on your business. The broker contacts all professionals needed, such as property inspectors and space planners, as well as gathering other operating data for you.

- **Acts as your negotiator.** Many details are involved in a restaurant lease. Make sure your broker acts as your negotiator.

- **Explains the lease to you.** A business lease can be a lengthy and detailed legal contract. Your broker has the expertise to explain the lease to you in terms you can understand. If you do not understand something, ask your broker before you sign.

GETTING YOURSELF READY TO LEASE

Just as there are preparatory steps to take when you plan to buy a restaurant, you must also position yourself to get a good lease. If you are a landlord who is looking to lease your restaurant space, you will want to secure the best possible tenant. Bear in mind the following issues:

- **Get your financial records in order.** The landlord will want to know that your business generates enough income to pay the rent on his lease space. You will need to be prepared to show the landlord current and historical financial records including bank statements. Do not make him have to ask for them; have them organized and ready.

- **Clean up your credit report.** If your personal credit has any blemishes, you want to clean them up. Obtain a copy of your credit report and begin working to improve it up today. The three major credit reporting agencies include:

    Equifax — **www.equifax.com** 800-685-1111

    Experian — **www.experian.com** 888-397-3742

    Trans Union — **www.transunion.com** 800-888-4213

- **Have a copy of your credit report handy.** Make it easy for the landlord to get the information he needs to expedite this lease.

- **Add a letter of reference to your file.** While you are setting up a file, go ahead and acquire a letter of reference from your current and past landlords. It always puts a landlord at ease to see a reference from someone in his position.

- **Keep a list of past landlords and their phone numbers in your file.** A landlord will want to know where you have leased in the past and how to get in touch with those landlords. Have that information available when asked.

- **Business tax returns.** You need to have copies of the restaurant's tax returns for the last two or three years available. Add them to your file.

- **Personal tax returns.** Your tax returns will also come under scrutiny. When copying the restaurant's tax returns, do not forget to include your personal returns.

- **Put a copy of your business plan in the file for good measure.** Be sure to include the plan in your file. It helps the landlord understand your vision and long-term plans.

- **If you've got it, flaunt it.** A landlord is always looking for lessors who will bring goods or services to other tenants in the same building, shopping center, or area. As a restaurant owner, you are in a strong position, so flaunt it. It really does not matter who leases the spaces in the shopping center around you. Everyone needs to eat!

THE POWER OF WORDS

Words can get us into trouble in every situation imaginable. When dealing with real estate issues, our words are especially powerful. Think carefully about the words you use with regard to lease letters of intent as well as during the lease negotiating process.

- **Weigh the pros and cons of writing a letter of intent.** A letter of intent is composed after you and a landlord decide to form a working relationship that benefits both of you. A letter of intent puts into writing the ideas and terms that the two of you agree to, at least in theory. It can be written by you and your lawyer or by the landlord.

- **A letter of intent can be seen as legally binding.** Although a letter of intent can be positive and beneficial in that it can set the stage for smooth negotiations, it can be very negative if it is seen as binding: You do not want to be bound to anything yet. If you choose to write the letter yourself, make sure your attorney reviews it before you give it to the landlord. If your attorney writes it for you, read it carefully.

- **Avoid any language that says you have agreed to something.** You may want to confirm that the landlord remembers what he or she has agreed to, but make sure you avoid phrases like "We agreed to" and "As we agreed on in our conversation."

- **Read letters of intent from the landlord/attorney carefully.** Go through any letter from the landlord carefully. If there is language implying an agreement, take action to ensure that everyone knows that you have not yet agreed to any specific terms. Send a letter of your own to that effect. State that you do not feel that a letter of intent is appropriate at this time and that, for the time being, you prefer to continue with further informal negotiations. Make sure your language states that you have not agreed to anything and avoid being confrontational.

- **Make sure you can change terms in any lease.** Sometimes a letter of intent will specify that the landlord/attorney will draft the lease. Do not agree to anything that says the landlord will draft the lease. You want to be able to add and delete from any lease until you are comfortable with its contents and language.

- **Never let yourself get boxed in.** It is advisable that an attorney or experienced broker help you through this process. What seems like nothing to you might be a costly, legally binding statement.

- **Talk to other restaurant owners who lease their property.** Find out details about their personal lease situations. They may have stumbled upon problems with lease wordings or sections that they did not see before they signed. Sharing their information with you before you sign might save you headaches later.

- **Talk to other restaurant and business owners who lease from this particular landlord.** Other business owners may share with you important facts about this particular landlord to prevent problems.

- **Go over every single point in the lease with your lawyer.** It should go without saying that you need a lawyer when leasing space for your restaurant.

- **Talk to your lawyer early on in the process.** Do not wait until the night before you are to meet with the landlord to select a lawyer. Many new restaurant owners want to do the entire preliminary work on a lease themselves and just have a lawyer glance at it and say it is fine right before signing, but that is inadvisable. Involve your lawyer early in the process.

CHANGING THE FACE OF YOUR SPACE

It is unlikely that you will find a property and building that appears exactly as you would like it to look. Before you lease anything, be very clear on who will be responsible for alterations and improvements to the property. Investigate the following:

- **First, get any agreements about alterations and improvements written into the lease.** Make sure the language is clear enough that you will not have to prove your case at a later date. It should be self-explanatory.

- **Keeping what belongs to you.** Trade fixtures are additions to the leased building that you have purchased and have used as a part of your business. If you have added anything to the structure that has become an integral part of the building or would damage the premises to remove, the landlord can force you to leave it when you terminate your lease. Although there are some exceptions to this rule, the only way to protect your property is to write a very detailed clause about trade fixtures. Be sure to consult a lawyer.

- **Consider drafting a separate agreement regarding alterations and improvements.** Although it may be possible to add all alterations to the lease if extensive changes to the property are required, you may want to consider drafting a separate document to cover these changes.

- **Do not take anything labeled "as is."** If a lease agreement lists the building or space in these terms, you need to be wary. "As is" indicates the landlord knows about problems with the structure. He is likely trying to have you pay the costs of those repairs. You would be accepting the property in an unlawful state, meaning it would be your financial responsibility to bring it up to standards.

- **Make sure franchise requirements are covered in the lease.** If your restaurant is a franchise, keep in mind that the franchiser will have very specific requirements on how your restaurant must look. Some franchisers even have their franchises laid out down to where filing cabinets will go. You must make sure that the requirements that bind you are covered in your lease agreement as well. I will discuss restaurant layout, design and remodeling in more detail in Chapter 6.

CLEARLY DEFINE WHO DOES WHAT

Make sure that "who is responsible for what" is very clearly defined in the lease agreement. Even if conversations have been very clear, commit everything to writing to avoid unexpected expenses.

- **You should expect the landlord to pay for all capital improvements.** Capital improvements are those that will forever change the property and increase its market value. Because the landlord would benefit from such improvements long after you are gone, she should incur the cost of such a change.

- **You should expect to pay for all non-capital improvements.** There will be alterations and improvements that you make solely for your restaurant, which no future tenant would benefit from or want. These are called non-capital improvements and you will be expected to cover their cost.

- **Planning for the cost of insurance is a smart move.** Many landlords require that you carry several different types of insurance including liability. Even if the landlord does not require it, insurance is a smart move. It is highly recommended that a restaurant owner carry workers' compensation and liability as well as other kinds of insurance policies. Talk to your insurance agent and attorney about the minimum amount of insurance you should carry.

- **The landlord should pay for any structural work done on a new building.** If the place you are leasing is brand new and construction is going on when you sign the lease, make sure that you do not pay for part of normal construction. The landlord pays the cost of constructing his building. Do not let him slip some of these costs in as disguised alterations.

- **Consider adding a "liquidated damages" clause to your lease.** When a landlord is late in completing alterations and improvements, causing your opening date to be pushed back, you should be entitled to compensation. You must make sure that your choice of compensation is included in your lease agreement. The liquidated damages clause defines a specific, predetermined sum of money to be paid to you if the landlord is late. There are some variations and some risks as well. Consult your attorney about what is right for your individual situation.

- **Another franchise concern.** If you are legally bound by a franchiser to open your restaurant on a specified date, you should ensure that the landlord is legally bound to that date also, especially if the landlord is responsible for some or all of the improvements or alterations to the property. If a landlord causes you to miss a date specified by the franchise, you should have the legal compensation already named in writing.

- **Plan for the future. Improvements may be needed in the future in the form of maintenance and repairs.** Be sure that you and the landlord come to some kind of agreement regarding whose responsibility maintenance and repairs will be. Have these agreements included in writing as part of the lease agreement.

UNDERSTANDING YOUR LEASE AGREEMENT

In the lease agreement you sign, there will be numerous sections or clauses. Some of them are as simple as the names of the people entering into the agreement and the amount of rent that will be paid. The following list is some of the common clauses that you may see in your lease agreement.

- **Alterations and Repairs.** If alterations and improvements are significant, you may want to draft a separate document to outline all of the details in this section.

- **Term.** The clause defines the actual term of the contract. It will define when the lease begins and when it ends. Make sure you understand when you will begin paying rent, especially if repairs or construction is unfinished.

- **Parking.** A restaurant should always have adequate parking. If your food is awesome, but parking is a major issue, customers may choose an eatery where parking is easier. Make sure adequate parking is outlined in detail in the lease agreement.

- **Insurance.** Always check with your attorney and your insurance agent, as it may be wise to take out more insurance than your landlord requires.

- **Utilities.** This clause should explain how the utility cost is figured and whether the landlord is responsible for any of these costs.

- **Subletting.** This clause defines whether you are allowed to sublet the space you are leasing. If you believe you may desire to sublet in the future, you may push for the right to do so as a provision in the lease.

- **Condemnation.** This clause explains your rights should the building you are leasing be condemned by local, state, or federal government agencies. You may think this could never happen, but make sure this clause is intact and protects you in the event of condemnation.

- **Defaults and Remedies.** The consequences if either you or the landlord defaults on the lease agreement should be covered in this section. Read it carefully and make sure the penalty for a landlord's defaulting is enough to cover your losses in such an incident.

- **Destruction.** This part explains what will happen to your lease agreement if part or all of the building is destroyed. If you live in an area that is prone to floods, tornadoes, hurricanes, earthquakes, or other devastating natural events, you will want coverage in writing.

- **Deposit.** This section lists the deposit(s) required by the landlord.

- **Hold Over.** If you get to the end of your lease and decide not to leave, this section will cover all the details of what happens next.

- **Use of Premises.** Read this section very carefully. It defines the parameters of how you can use your rented space, and you must make certain that the restrictions listed here do not interfere with the operation of your business. If the lease states that no alcoholic beverages may be sold on the premises, yet your bar tab is a large portion of your income, you must renegotiate this issue before signing the lease.

- **Taxes.** This section defines, in detail, taxes due with regard to the property and who pays them.

- **Ongoing Maintenance and Repairs.** If you sign a long-term lease, repairs and maintenance are inevitable. It is vital that they are laid out ahead of time, including who will be financially responsible for them.

- **Options.** If you outgrow your current space, an options clause can prove to be very important. It can cover everything from an option to buy down to an option to expand. Make sure it is worded to your advantage now.

- **Guaranty.** Some landlords may request that you have a guarantor who will agree to cover financial obligations should you falter. If the landlord requires a guarantor, the guarantor must sign the lease.

- **Dispute Resolution.** This section outlines how disputes between you and the landlord will be resolved. This section is set up with the intention of keeping disputes out of the courtroom.

LEASE VERSUS OWN

Leasing a building involves less expense up front. There may be certain tax advantages to leasing, and if the time comes to move, it is easier to do so, avoiding a costly selling process. If you decide to go for a commercial lease, look at the following:

- **Length of lease.** Many commercial leases run for 5 or 10 years rather than one year.

- **Rent and rent increase.** Investigate whether the rent includes insurance, property taxes, and maintenance costs (called a gross lease), or whether you will be charged for these items separately (called a net lease).

- **The security deposit and conditions for its return.**

- **The square footage of the space you are renting.**

- **How improvements and modifications will be handled.** Who, for example, will pay for them?

- **Who will maintain and repair the premises?**

- **Is there an option to renew the lease or possibly expand the space at a later date?**

- **How the lease may be terminated, including notice requirements and penalties for early termination.**

- **Whether disputes must be mediated or arbitrated as an alternative to court.**

- **Commercial leases are different from residential leases in that they do not fall under most consumer protection laws.** There are no caps on security deposits or rules protecting a tenant's privacy. Commercial leases are customized to the landlord's needs, but they can also be subject to much more negotiation between business owners and the landlord as well. Because there is no standard format, be sure to read each lease agreement you consider. Unlike residential leases where breaking the lease simply forfeits the security deposit, commercial leases are contracts. If you break such a contract, more than your security deposit is at stake.

- **Think before you enter into a lease agreement and make sure it fits your business needs now and in the future.** Consider where you think your business will be in the future if you are entering into a long-term lease agreement. Make sure the lease covers your ability to make the necessary modifications your building may need now or five years down the road.

- **Make sure you are allowed to put up a sign.** If you are leasing in a large commercial complex, make sure the lease includes some competition safeguards for you. You do not want to open your coffee shop and see the landlord rent the space next door to another coffee shop two months later.

- **Consider engaging a leasing broker to help you locate business leases.** Leasing brokers work much the same way as real estate brokers, doing a lot of the legwork for a fee.

- **Have a lawyer review any lease before you sign it.**

VARIOUS SITE CONSIDERATIONS BEFORE BUYING OR LEASING

FRANCHISE

If you are uncertain as to the type of operation you want to own, you may want to look into franchise opportunities. A franchise allows you to buy an existing business with an existing system in place for a fee. For a fee which can run several thousand dollars, you get the right to use the company's name and the franchiser assists in setting up and running your business. The franchiser may find a location and provide training and marketing advice. Consider the following:

- **By buying a franchise, you can limit up front costs in buying a business, but bear in mind that you are also required to give up some control** because you will be obligated to follow the franchiser's rules.

- **If you are opening a restaurant because you love to be creative, a franchise is not the best option for you.** If you know little about the restaurant industry and you are simply looking for a business, it may be a good option.

- **Many of the costs you incur taking on a franchise are similar to those you incur opening an independent business:** rental or purchase, equipment, operating, and insurance. You may also incur these fees: grand opening, royalties, and advertising.

- **The Web site www.franchiseopportunities.com can link you to franchise opportunities across the country.** Check your local paper as well; franchise opportunities are often listed in the classified section.

FRANCHISER CONTROL

Because all franchises are operating under the same name, the franchiser will want to have some control and be sure that the customer is getting a consistent product and service at every location. Some controls franchisers may have in place include:

- **Site approval**

- **Site design or appearance standards**

- **Periodic renovations or seasonal design changes**

- Restrictions on goods and services offered for sale

- Pre-approved signs

- Employee uniforms

- Fixed advertisements

- Particular accounting or bookkeeping procedures

- Purchasing supplies from approved suppliers only

- Limiting your business to a specific territory

- **Franchise contracts are for a limited time, usually 15 to 20 years.** When that time is up, you are not guaranteed renewal on your franchise license.

- **Franchise advice.** To help you evaluate whether owning a franchise is right for you, the Federal Trade Commission has a booklet and online information regarding purchasing a franchise business. You can reach them at 877-FTC-HELP or **www.ftc.gov**.

- **Several states also regulate the sale of franchises.** Check with your state division of securities or office of the attorney general for more information.

EXISTING OPERATIONS

There are also numerous opportunities for buying existing operations. Points to consider include:

- **Buying an existing operation requires less capital at the start.** When someone sells an existing operation, the transaction includes all the equipment.

- **You need to be careful if you are considering buying an existing operation that it is not failing.** Take a look at the company's financial records over the past several years to get an indication of its financial health. While you may be able to breathe some life back into the business, do not expect miracles.

- **Be on site for a few days and see what happens at the operation to make sure the location is a good one for your operation.**

- **Find existing operations for sale in the classified section of newspapers.** Try trade publications.

NEW BUILDINGS VERSUS EXISTING BUILDINGS

There are pros and cons to both new and existing buildings. Review the differences carefully to determine what will work best for your restaurant.

- **New buildings.** The good thing about new buildings is that you should not have to carry out lengthy renovations, remodeling, or updating before you can start operating.

- **New buildings will also be up to code.**

- **If you are buying a site to build a structure, you may find this Web address useful: www.CMDFirstSource.com/means/index.asp.** After registering as a user, you can enter information on the type of structure you want to build, the gross square feet you need and the ZIP code. The program will provide you with an itemized cost estimate. You can find a database for building codes for most major cities on this Web site.

- **Existing buildings.** Older buildings often have more character than new buildings.

- **You may also be able to benefit from a tax break with some older buildings.** Since 1976 there have been provisions in the federal tax code to benefit taxpayers who own historic commercial buildings. These buildings are structures that are listed on the National Register of Historic Places or are in national historic districts or local historic districts or are national historic landmarks. This tax credit has gone a long way toward helping cities revitalize historic areas. Currently the tax benefit to the owner is a 20 percent tax credit. For further information on this tax credit, visit the Internal Revenue Service's Web site at **www.irs.gov**, or write to Federal Historic Preservation Tax Incentives, Heritage Preservation Services (2255), National Park Service, 1849 C St. NW, Washington, D.C. 20240. They can be reached by e-mail at hpsinfo@nps.gov or by phone at 202-343-9594.

LOCATION REQUIREMENTS

Consider whether you want the restaurant to be a freestanding structure or part of a strip mall or shopping center. Will tourists be a significant part of your business? You may want to consider locating in a theme/historical shopping area. Here are some additional considerations:

- **Freestanding location.** Freestanding locations have their good and bad points. If you are located in such a facility, you may not have the benefit of business created by nearby stores; however, you have more flexibility with how you use your space. You also have greater scope for expansion compared with operations in a mall or part of a strip mall. Further, you do not have to worry about regulations that might govern what type of sign you can use, and you do not have to share your parking spaces.

- **If you choose to be part of a shopping area, you are likely to attract customers from the other business areas,** although there may be more competition in such an area, compared to a freestanding location.

- **Consider whether to locate in the urban center or the suburbs of the community.** If your customer profile reveals that your customers are business people, obviously you want to be located in a business district.

STRIP MALL LOCATIONS

If you decide to locate in a strip mall, there are three positions your restaurant can be in:

- Detached from the other buildings

- Attached to the other stores in the strip mall

- At one end of a line of attached buildings.

Here are some tips for choosing the best strip mall location for your operation:

- **Freestanding.** In general, the freestanding building may be the best and most visible option.

- **Attached.** Of all the attached premises, the ones at the ends produce more sales than those in the middle. Usually, one end of the strip mall has higher visibility.

- Many lessors will have restrictions on signage, so that you may not be able to differentiate yourself with your restaurant's sign. There may be other ways to distinguish your restaurant, depending on your lease agreement. Put tables outside or a sandwich board listing specials. Consider using piped-out music to attract customers, or put one of your servers on the sidewalk with samples.

- If your restaurant is located in the center, you may have greater visibility due to the architecture of the building. Be sure to pay attention to any anchor stores in a mall. You will have higher visibility located next to such buildings.

- If you decide to locate in a strip mall location, pay attention to other shopping venues in the area. Generally, where there is one strip mall, there is another. Be sure that you are not locating your restaurant in a secondary location. Pay attention to how visible your location will be to passersby. Can they pick you out of all the other storefronts?

- Find out from the owner if there are plans to build in front of your strip mall, thus obscuring your future visibility.

- Think about where you want to take your operation in the future. If you are planning to expand in five years, a strip mall location may not be the best choice because it could limit, or eliminate, your expansion plans.

SHOPPING MALL LOCATIONS

If you decide to look at shopping mall locations, you will also want to do your homework. Visit the mall and find out what stores are already there and what new stores are planned. Investigate the potential:

- **Square footage.** Find out about available square footage and the going rates.

- **Pay attention to peak shopping hours.** Note the customer mix.

- **Location of major stores.** As in the strip mall location, make a note of where the larger stores, such as department stores, are located. A location near one of these gives you an advantage.

- **Stay away from dead end corridors.** Customers tend to avoid exploring in a mall if they do not see much activity down the corridor.

- **Consider locating your restaurant in a food court.** Operations in food courts are typically small, so you may have to serve a limited menu because of the space and equipment constraints, affecting your sales and ability to make profits.

FACILITY REQUIREMENTS

You need to think about space and design requirements for your site. Break up the operation between front of the house and back of the house and figure out what you need in both areas:

- **According to facility experts, dining will take up the majority of your space, followed by kitchen and prep space and then by storage space.** Space breaks down as follows:

    o   40 percent to 60 percent of total facility for dining space

    o   About 30 percent for kitchen

    o   About 12 percent for actual food preparation with the remainder being production space allocated to dishwashing, trash, and receiving

    o   Storage and administrative office fill the remainder

- **Design consultant.** If you are starting from scratch, you may want to engage the services of an architect or restaurant design consultant.

- **How much room do you need for dining?** Your sales forecast information can provide you with some information on how much dining space you will need. Let's say your sales forecast tells you that you have the potential to make $20,000 a week serving 800 people. You plan to be open six days a week and you estimate you can turn your tables once a night, so you need to be able to fit about 70 patrons at a time. (800 people/6 days = 133.33 people; 133.33 people/2 table turns = 66.66) For dining you will need about 15-18 square feet per customer per table. Therefore, you will need approximately 1,300 square feet for dining. Remember, this square footage does not take into consideration the bar, lobby, hostess area, coatroom, or restrooms.

- **If you have a bar you should have one bar seat for every three dining seats.** Allow 2 square feet for bar stools and chairs and about 10 square feet per customer at a table.

EXAMPLE OF SPACE REQUIREMENTS

Here are the typical space requirements for several types of food service operations:

- **Pizzeria.** For the production area in a neighborhood pizzeria, there must be room for a steam table, a cold food table, pizza ovens, sandwich ovens, and a fryer. If it is a carryout establishment, a counter and cash register are necessary for the front area; a dine-in pizzeria requires a dining area, customer restrooms, possibly a jukebox, and a place for coats. Most pizzerias do not have a large seating area because they are designed primarily as carryout and home-delivery operations. They require between 800 and 1,500 square feet. For a larger facility with a dining area, about 2,500 to 4,000 square feet is necessary.

- **Sandwich shop.** Between 500 and 3,000 square feet.

- **Coffeehouse.** Between 800 and 3,000 square feet.

- **Bakery.** If your customers do not eat on site, 1,000 to 1,500 square feet; if they do, 3,000 square feet.

SITE CHARACTERISTICS

In a restaurant, the site may determine whether you can draw in the customers. Here are some considerations when choosing a site:

- **Visibility.** How easy is it for the customer to see the location? Maximum visibility is at the far corner of a main road intersecting a secondary road.

- **Try to avoid dead end and one-way streets.**

- **Parking.** The Urban Land Institute **www.uli.org** and International Council of Shopping Centers **www.icsc.org** lists standard ratios of parking needed for shopping centers. They suggest that there should be at least 2.2 square feet of parking for every square foot of shopping center space. For supermarkets they suggest at least three square feet of parking for every square foot of supermarket space. In areas with little parking or areas with higher crime rates, you may want to consider using valet parking. A level parking lot increases visibility and easy entry/exit in cold weather, and traffic lights may pose a hazard.

- **Accessibility.** How easy is it for your customers to get to the location from their homes or businesses during the times you expect the most customers?

- **Retail synergy.** How does the presence or absence of other retailers affect consumer traffic? Synergism means increased business because of proximity to other businesses. If yours is a French restaurant and there are a steak house, a Japanese restaurant, a furniture store and a shopping mall on the same block, you will see increased sales because of the increased exposure you are gaining to potential customers. Fast food restaurants seem to be an exception to the synergism rule; the fact that another fast food restaurant is nearby does not appear to impact sales negatively.

- **Security.** How safe is the location? Check with the local police department to see what types of problems are going on in the neighborhood. Be sure to make your specific site safe with outside lighting.

SITE VISIT

Now that you have made a list of the site characteristics that are important for your operation, take this list with you when you conduct site visits at your potential locations. Make a worksheet you can use to compare the sites on which you are focusing.

Take a look at the following examples:

LOCATION ANALYSIS CHART

Address: 3217 Jefferson, Cincinnati, OH 45219

	VISIBILITY	PARKING	INGRESS	ACCESS	SYNERGY	SECURITY
Excellent		✓				✓
Good	✓					
Average				✓	✓	
Poor			✓			

Comments: Building is new, looks like little remodeling to be done.

Address: 316 Ludlow, Cincinnati, OH 45220

	VISIBILITY	PARKING	INGRESS	ACCESS	SYNERGY	SECURITY
Excellent		✓			✓	
Good	✓					
Average			✓	✓		✓
Poor						

Comments: Building was a flower shop, will need remodeling.

Address: 16 Corry St., Cincinnati, OH 45219

	VISIBILITY	PARKING	INGRESS	ACCESS	SYNERGY	SECURITY
Excellent	✓				✓	✓
Good			✓			
Average				✓		
Poor		✓				

Comments: Seller flexible on price due to poor parking situation.

LOCATION COMPARISON CHART

	3217 JEFFERSON	316 LUDLOW,	16 CORRY ST.
VISIBILITY	Good	Good	Excellent
PARKING	Excellent	Excellent	Poor
INGRESS	Poor	Average	Good
ACCESS	Average	Average	Average
SYNERGY	Average	Excellent	Excellent
SECURITY	Excellent	Average	Excellent

- **Enter this information into a database or spreadsheet application.** Doing so enables you to compare pros and cons easily.

- **No site will be 100 percent perfect.** At this point you have some decisions to make. In the example above, none is a perfect choice but of the three sites, 316 Ludlow will probably be best. Using the information gathered from the site visits described in the previous chapter, investigate further:

- **Compare cost per square footage.** You can obtain square footage measurements from your realtor, the multiple listing services, and the county auditor's Web page.

Let's set up another table for square foot measurements and cost:

SQUARE FOOT MEASUREMENTS AND COST			
	3217 JEFFERSON	**316 LUDLOW,**	**16 CORRY ST.**
SELLING PRICE	$85,000	$120,000	$175,000
SQUARE FEET	2,400	3,000	3,800
COST PER SQUARE FOOT	$35.82	$40.00	$46.05

- **Check with your realtor about the average cost per square foot in the area** and compare this with your table so that you do not overpay!

If you do not have access to the building you are interested in, you can still find out size and required improvements.

- **Sanborn Fire Insurance Maps** were created for insurance underwriters who used them to determine risks and establish premiums. Today, these maps are used by researchers into history, urban geography, architectural changes, and preservation. You can also check with your local library or historical society. These maps can provide you with information on building size and layout and are helpful if you are looking at locations where you do not have access to the building to do any measuring for yourself.

- **Auditors' Web site.** Many county auditors have Web sites that you can use to look up information about specific properties. By searching the address, you can obtain information about building size, price of the sale, former owners, and improvements. Most of them include information on commercial buildings as well as residential ones.

- **Neighborhood.** Take a look at the neighborhood of the proposed location. How old is it? Is the neighborhood in decline or is there new construction going on? Notice if there are many vacant lots and properties for sale. Are there parks, schools, businesses, hospitals, places of entertainment such as movie theaters or ballparks? All of these factors can be a detriment or a plus to you depending upon your chosen type of operation.

- **Demographics.** Just as with your larger search, neighborhood demographics are an important research tool. Who lives and works in your neighborhood? Are there enough people in the neighborhood who fit your customer profile to make your restaurant profitable?

RAFFIC COUNT

One of the considerations in selecting the location is the traffic count, which is available from the state or local government and may be found online.

TRAFFICE COUNT CHART	
Address:	
HOUR ENDING	**NUMBER OF CARS**
7 a.m.	
8 a.m.	
9 a.m.	
10 a.m.	
11 a.m.	
12 p.m.	
1 p.m.	
2 p.m.	
3 p.m.	
4 p.m.	
5 p.m.	
6 p.m.	
7 p.m.	
8 p.m.	
9 p.m.	
10 p.m.	
11 p.m.	
12 a.m.	

COMPETITION

Here are some tips for sizing up the competition:

- **Count the number of competing restaurants by checking online.** Make a mental or actual map of their locations. Visit them and take note of their pluses and minuses.

- **Categorize competitors.** Place each competitor in one of two categories: direct or indirect competition. The direct competitors' category refers to restaurants with the same concept. Indirect competitors are all the other restaurants.

- **The proximity factor.** Your bottom line may be adversely affected if the competition is close to your location.

- **Other factors.** If the competition offers a unique dining concept and attracts customers simply for its unparalleled menu, your menu is critical.

- **Take a look at this example of the competition.** The establishments in the next chart represent all the restaurants in your trade area. By creating a database with this information, you can compare your direct and indirect competition. The information will help you determine the size of facility that you need and the weekly sales income you can expect from your new establishment.

- **Optimum space.** You can see from the table that your direct competitors are using 750 and 8,000 square feet of space. It is safe to assume you will need a facility in a similar size range. If you anticipate higher sales like Pablito's or even one of your indirect competitors, look for a larger building.

A Competition Comparison Chart is on the next page.

For additional information, check *The Food Service Professional Guide to Buying & Selling a Restaurant Business (Item # FS2-01)* and *The Food Service Professional Guide to Restaurant Site Location (Item # FS1-01)*. Both books are available from Atlantic Publishing **www.atlantic-pub.com**.

COMPETITION COMPARISON CHART				
NAME	DIRECT/ INDIRECT	LOCATION	SIZE (SQ FEET)	WEEKLY SALES
Pablito's	D	5th & Market St.	8,000	$30,000
Bob's Steakhouse	I	1600 Blue Street	7,500	$25,000
Joe's Surf and Turf	I	14688 HWY 35	8,000	$15,000
Vincent's Pizza	D	6th & Main Street	750	$5,500
Silas' Slow Cooked BBQ	I	7th & May Blvd	1,000	$8,500
Spaghetti Shop	I	829 August Lane	1,050	$10,000

CHAPTER

CREATING A
SUCCESSFUL BUSINESS PLAN

As you begin exploring the possibilities of opening a new restaurant or enhancing your current business, many ideas, emotions, and dreams are bouncing around in your head. Should you do this or would that be better? So many things to think about, where do you start? The answers are within the entrepreneur's best guide and decision-making tool —your business plan.

I do not know too many people who are excited about the prospect of writing their business plan. It requires you to do extensive research, ask many questions, calculate current and future financial pictures, and do some real soul searching. Nevertheless, the benefits are worth the effort. Once you get everything down on paper, I am confident you will be glad you invested the time to think through the "good, bad, and the ugly" so that you can be prepared to handle a multitude of business situations. If your personal future and business success is not worth the time and effort it takes to write your business plan—then perhaps you should rethink whether you are ready to be a restaurant owner.

A business plan is a document where you:

1. Describe your new or existing business.

2. Define your customers' needs and your ability to meet them.

3. Explore competitor strengths and weaknesses to outperform them.

4. Address possible stumbling blocks to success.

5. Establish yourself and your team as capable businesspeople and food artists.

6. Detail marketing strategies to capture your share of the market.

7. Set benchmarks and goals for launching, developing, and profit making.

8. Provide financial projections and returns on investment.

9. Ask for money to support your success.

10. Tell investors and lenders what is in it for them.

In this chapter I will discuss how to compile the information you need for a business plan. Are you still panicked about writing a business plan? Remember that your plan is a collection of information and ideas based upon your knowledge, expertise, background, and faith at that time. Your plan is not a rigid set of rules to live by, but a powerful living guide. As you move through each stage of your business development, you will learn new facts and gain additional experience that may alter your path and goals.

WHY DO I NEED A PLAN?

You need a business plan to explore your business ideas, determine their viability, and secure money to make your ideas happen. Most people concentrate on the last reason—to get money. Their plan is then written solely to attract outside investors or satisfy lender requirements. If you are writing your plan primarily for them, you are at risk of slanting the truth and overlooking other areas that will benefit you.

HOW YOU CAN BENEFIT

Researching and writing your business plan offers multiple benefits for new and experienced restaurant owners. The process of developing the plan helps you solidify your desires and set your professional goals.

Writing your plan will:

1. **Clarify your vision.** Instead of just saying, "I'd like to own a restaurant," you will be creating a Technicolor version of your cozy little Italian deli or your sleek and sophisticated restaurant featuring live jazz.

2. **Prove your potential.** You will prove to yourself and others that your community needs another steak house or tearoom. You may even discover that your idea is not a viable one. Too much competition, wrong location, inadequate customer base, or insufficient customer demand are all reasons to stop and reassess your ideas.

3. **Look at obstacles.** Every business venture will have obstacles. By looking at potential problems and outlining solutions, you will prepare yourself. Not all problem/solution scenarios will make it into your plan, but you will uncover many of them as you research your business prospects, vendors, lenders, and employees.

4. **Determine your business's viability.** Are your goals exceptionally high? Is the idea too trendy? Will it have sufficient lifespan to repay lenders? Will investors be attracted to the idea?

5. **Project your success.** Will your restaurant provide you with the personal and financial rewards you are seeking? Can you physically or emotionally deal with the workload? Do you have sufficient experience to make it happen?

6. **Secure ample capital.** By projecting your cash flow and working capital needs, you will have a better understanding of how much money you have coming through the door every day to pay vendors, lenders, and employees. Before you invest your whole nest egg or borrow money, you must decide if you will have enough money (from every possible source) to keep you afloat until profits roll in. Insufficient capitalization is a primary reason why new businesses fail.

GREAT RISKS, GREAT REWARDS

As an entrepreneur, you are the one with the greatest investment and the most at risk. Your financial future, emotional and physical health, and reputation are on the line. Sure, investors and lenders have a risk — that is why they ask for ownership rights or charge interest. A well-researched business plan looks at and analyzes various risk factors. No one likes to think about failing, but truthfully, the success rate for new restaurants is not exceptionally high. The better prepared you are, the more likely you will be one of the successful ones.

Everyone focuses on the process of writing the plan. How do I convince the lender to grant the loan? What if my writing skills are not the best? I will address these issues in later chapters. Right now, I want you to concentrate on research. Corporations invest millions on research before launching a new sales division or product line. Your diligence in researching your customer demographics, competitors, equipment purchases, menu choices, and more is just as important. It is your key to determining whether your dream can be successful.

NO PROFITS, NO REASON

Sometimes business owners discover after months of research and number crunching that their idea has insufficient profit potential. As you look at all the variables, create sales and expense reports, and set budgets, you must be proving that you will be profitable within a reasonable time. These profit points also must be worth your time and effort. It is not just earning money that counts, but is it enough to finance your growth, pay your employees fairly, provide a quality product, and have enough to live on?

If your plan tells you that your idea is not a profit-maker, it will have been time well spent. Saving yourself from potential financial ruin, long-term debt, and stress is an invaluable lesson.

WHO SHOULD REVIEW YOUR BUSINESS PLAN

Your business plan should be reviewed by your accountant and legal counsel, who should have been consulted on specific sections of the plan. Their comments can be invaluable for catching confusing passages or fine-tuning ideas.

Your banker should be the next person to assist you. In some smaller communities, businesspeople will have a personal relationship with a local bank. Even if you are not seeking a loan, a business specialist banker has experience in reviewing business plans and can give you feedback.

OTHER OUTSIDE ADVISORS AND CONSULTANTS

You may find other people in your community who can provide you with advice, recommendations, and a critique of your plan. Your local university or community college may have a business development advisor on staff. SCORE, a volunteer program manned by retired businesspeople, provides no- or low-cost counseling aimed at helping businesspeople succeed. You can find more information on SCORE at **www.score.org**.

WHO WILL USE YOUR BUSINESS PLAN

Investors (family, friends, outside professionals) will need a full version of your business plan to review its profitability potential. Lenders (bank, credit union, government, family/ friends) will also need a full version to determine your ability to repay loans. Both will be looking at your idea along with your financial projections.

Your insurance agent may want to see sections of your plan to help determine your business insurance needs such as liability, auto, fire, casualty, theft, and life.

Your real estate broker may want to see sections of your plan to help you locate the right property (land or land and building) for your new restaurant. Your architect or builder/ contractor may also want to review parts of your plan as they begin designing a new building, planning renovations, or specifying remodeling projects. Other designers (landscape, interior, kitchen, lighting, sound) may also benefit from seeing your vision.

CONFIDENTIALITY/NON-DISCLOSURE AGREEMENTS

The information you gather and report in your business plan is confidential. While it may not be top secret, it is in your best interest to have interested parties sign a non-disclosure agreement before reviewing your plan. A non-disclosure agreement outlines that the information is proprietary and confidential and not to be shared, copied, distributed, or discussed with unauthorized parties. This agreement can be verbal or written. Should a violation of the agreement occur, a written agreement is your best bet. Investors may be hesitant to sign a non-disclosure agreement; however, terms can be negotiated. Your attorney can assist you with an appropriate agreement for your situation and advise you on when to use it.

Please be aware that bankers, lenders, and venture capitalists are professionals bound to confidentiality. Requiring a non-disclosure agreement (and/or contract clause) may be considered insulting so be careful when requiring a signed agreement.

WHAT INTERESTED PARTIES SHOULD FIND IN YOUR PLAN

Everyone who reads your business plan will be looking for something different based upon his or her needs. The messages within your plan can play an important roll in selling your concept; these are the soul of your business and can affect how people respond to your requests for support. Even bankers, who want to see strong financials, are looking for a gut reaction that tells them you are worth the investment.

YOUR FAMILY

Your first support group should be your family members. You will have a network of people interested in your success. In addition, family members are a common source of start-up capital. Your family should see why your dream is important to you and how they can take an active role in its success.

YOUR PARTNERS

Whether you have a silent or active partnership arrangement, everyone should share the vision expressed in the plan. You will not be detailing assigned duties, but general responsibilities based upon experience and skills will be outlined. If you have partners, you will be writing the plan together. You may co-author each section or only work on specific sections that require your expertise. If partners are assigned sections to research and write, be certain that the writing style and "voice" remain consistent throughout to avoid confusing the reader. You may also use your business plan to help you secure a partner. Perhaps you are a talented chef looking for a partner with more front-of-the-house experience or you are a great restaurant manager searching for a partner with outstanding culinary talents.

Partner(s) should see a healthy partnership, a mutual respect, and their value to the business in your restaurant's business plan. Their role in the business should provide them with more than money — it should fulfill their entrepreneurial dreams also.

YOUR LENDER

Anyone who gives you money in exchange for periodic payments and interest is a lender. Lenders can be a family member or friend, bank, private organization or government agency.

FAMILY MEMBERS AND FRIENDS

Borrowing from family members and friends can be an excellent way to finance your business launch or growth. While you may not have a lengthy loan application, you should treat these loans just as seriously as you would a bank loan.

Have your attorney draw up an appropriate contract for all parties to sign. Creating a financial relationship with family and friends can have more than financial risks. Everyone must separate the business arrangement from personal interactions. You should also consider what might happen if you are unable to repay the loan according to its terms or should your business fail. Even if everyone shakes hands and agrees to the lender/borrower terms, people just cannot seem to separate their personal feelings when it comes to doing business with family and friends.

BANKERS

Your banker may be an advocate for your business. Additional business banking services may also be available to you just for the asking. In the age of ATMs and Web-based banks, many have lost touch with the value of a bank professional. Even major national bank conglomerates offer business services through a specific department. Regional and state banks use their individualized business banking services as a way to set themselves apart from the national banks. Shop around for a small-business banker and meet him face to face.

This relationship can prove to be invaluable and costs you nothing more than your time. Secured loans use real property (business or personally owned) or other tangible assets as collateral. There are other types of collateral such as community economic development, personal goodwill, or just your potential for success.

Bankers should see that your business will have ample capital and resources for continuous operation over several months (and maybe even more than a year) and sufficient profits to pay back your loan on time.

PRIVATE ORGANIZATIONS

Depending upon your community's economic needs, you may qualify for financial support in the way of low-interest loans or grants (essentially a financial gift) through privately funded organizations and associations. These funds are typically used to stimulate economic development in high-risk communities or economic parity for woman and minorities. Check your local business development agency to see if they have a list of private loans and grant programs.

Philanthropic organizations should see that you, your community, and your restaurant meet their criteria for economic support. They will consider your ability to repay your loan. If you are applying for a grant, they will look at your potential for success, contribution to the community (creating jobs, paying taxes, rejuvenating neighborhoods), and need.

GOVERNMENT AGENCIES

Have you ever seen the guy in the loud suit with question marks shouting on TV about the millions to be had from government agencies for whatever purposes you can dream up? The fact is there actually are national, state and county agencies that can provide you with loans and grants.

The federal government, through the Small Business Administration, is a major supporter of small businesses. The SBA does not directly loan you money; their role is to underwrite small business loans through local banks. You will need to meet all SBA loan requirements along with the bank's.

Publicly funded grants operate similarly to privately funded ones and are targeted at people and communities that need economic stimulus. Government agencies should see that your business would be capable of repaying loans. Grant applications will be reviewed for their ability to satisfy the grant program's mission.

YOUR INVESTORS

Any person or business who gives you money in exchange for a share of ownership is an investor. Investors can be a family member or friend, an angel investor, or a venture capitalist.

Investors typically come into play when you are unable to obtain a conventional loan. Where as a lender might be charging 9.5 percent interest and has no stake in your business, investors will want to own a percentage of your restaurant. Ownership equals a greater risk, so this money will cost you more. You will not only have a financial relationship, you may also be entering into a partnership. While your investor(s) may not actually help you run your restaurant, they will have expectations and needs that you will have to meet.

Investors should see that your business has an excellent profit potential. They will be looking at your numbers first. A plan that does not demonstrate an ample return on their investment may not be worth their time. They will also want to see that you and your team have the ability to start and operate a successful restaurant.

YOUR EMPLOYEES

Key personnel such as head chefs, master bakers, and managers not only serve your customers, they also serve you. Their energy, enthusiasm, expertise, and input are the foundation of your business. If you have an existing business, involve your staff in the development or updating of your business plan. You may not feel comfortable sharing specific aspects of your financial plan; however, involving your staff in researching, developing, and writing portions of the plan can be a wise decision. Not only can you tap into their skills and expertise, you also empower them to think creatively and to own the idea. This ownership mentality is invaluable in making your goals and creating a successful restaurant.

Your employees should see how they can make a difference, what your mutual goals are, and how you will actively support them. Your plan can also establish success benchmarks, business guidelines, and employee performance standards.

YOUR SUPPLIERS

As a new business, establishing yourself with vendors can be arduous. Even existing businesses have failed to develop strong business partnerships with their suppliers only to discover that there is little or no goodwill to trade upon. You may find it advantageous to share sections of your business plan with select vendors. While companies do not base your established credit line on projections and owner bios, you may find partners who will extend you courtesies and considerations that you had not even considered. Solid companies want to build long-term relationships with trusted customers. Sharing your vision and potential may be a way to start that relationship.

Your suppliers should see the fiscal wisdom of your endeavor and see the payoff (in long-term business with increasing purchase volume). Select vendors may learn how you intend to use equipment/services and how working with you can prove profitable for everyone.

WHO SHOULD WRITE YOUR BUSINESS PLAN?

As I have emphasized already, the person who gains the most wisdom from the research and writing of the business plan is you. By writing the plan yourself (or with the help of business partners or key employees), you will be able to document your ideas, ensure that the research is appropriate and accurate, and gain a better understanding of the financial aspects of operating your restaurant. Your business plan should incorporate your dreams and passions — no one else is better suited to that task.

BUT I ONLY WANT TO BE A RESTAURATEUR

The analysis skills used in developing your business plan are the same ones you will use to become a successful restaurant owner. There is no better time than now — before you become consumed with daily business needs — to learn all about your community and competitors, practice reading and interpreting financial reports, calculate your break-even numbers, and create a realistic, I-can-be-successful-with-this budget. Once you aggressively begin your launch, you will need to make quick decisions based upon solid research. When your doors open, having this information gives you a solid foundation to successfully handle the difficulties that are inevitable in any business.

If you are hesitant about your own research and writing skills, there are plenty of resources to guide you, along with experts to review and fine-tune your finished plan. There are books, software programs, support consultants, classes and seminars designed to help you with the gathering and writing process. When I say "do-it-yourself," I am referring to you being the primary developer of your business plan, but that does not mean outside support is discouraged. Remember, you are already getting outside expert advice as you read this book.

If, after reading this book, you still feel uncertain about writing your own business plan, there are other sources for business plan advice and training.

WEB-BASED ADVICE

The Web is brimming with information on writing business plans. You can become overwhelmed with all the free advice online. To make it easier, I have created a list of some of the best sites.

BUSINESS PLAN CLASSES

You can take classes or attend seminars online, via the telephone, at your local community college, or through your state's small-business or economic development agency.

Local business plan writing classes for entrepreneurs are an excellent time and money investment. You will learn plenty of other skills that you will find helpful as a restaurant owner. You will have peers to network with and classes often feature local experts (bankers, accountants, lawyers, etc.) who also offer one-on-one counseling.

LOCAL CLASSES

You will find business plan writing classes and seminars by contacting:

- **SCORE, www.score.org,** for local classes.
- **NxLevel, www.nxlevel.org,** for local nonprofit programs and classes.
- **Your community college's** or university's school of business.
- **Your city's chamber of commerce** or state's small-business development agency.
- **Local economic development nonprofit organizations.**
- **Your business banker** or accountant.
- **Your state and/or national restaurant and food service associations.**
- **Local newspapers** (and their Web sites)

ONLINE CLASSES

You can attend a class at your convenience on the Web. Here are a few available sources:

- Writing Trainers—www.writingtrainers.com

- Web Campus—www.webcampus.stevens.edu

- **Small Biz Lending** and **SBA—https://www.smallbizlending.com/resources/workshop/sba.htm,** slideshow class

TELECLASSES

A teleclass is where you call a specific phone number and punch in an assigned code. You are then connected with the lecturer and other attendees. You will have to pay any long-distance fees in addition to the tuition. Here are a few available sources.

- **Career Masters Institute www.cminstitute.com/EntreprenurialEagles.html**—a variety of business teleclasses

- **Parker Associates www.asparker.com/freecoaching.html**—free teleclass

SOFTWARE-SPECIFIC CLASSES

When reviewing and choosing business plan software, check out online tutorials and/or third-party consultants to guide you with specific business plan software packages. These classes should not be for software technical support, but how to write your plan using the tools provided.

SOFTWARE PROGRAMS

There are several business plan software programs designed to help you gather your thoughts and write a standardized plan for restaurant operators. Others will provide you with text ideas and a boilerplate format. Beware that cutting and pasting canned text will result in an ordinary plan with little individuality.

RITING ALTERNATIVES

Technically all you need is a basic word processor, a calculator, and a printer to turn out a professional-looking business plan. With this book and a few online reference sites, you may be able to write your own business plan from scratch. Not everyone feels comfortable with the process and the financial data and projections typically trip up most new entrepreneurs. That is where business plan software can come to your rescue.

The interactive nature of business planning software can help you through the entire process and make it a very wise investment. Software templates with a fill-in-the-blanks format and sample business plans can stimulate ideas and help you get over a frightening blank page. Most commercial products offer sample plans for restaurants and other food service businesses. A few have specific tools for launching a new restaurant or for seeking improvement capital for existing restaurants.

SEARCHING FOR A BUSINESS PLAN WRITER

Before you begin the search process, you need to be able to tell potential candidates what you want, when you want it, and what data and information you can give them to work with. Writers may actually interview you. Others will have complex forms that you will complete. The better prepared you are, the better results you will get.

HIRING A BUSINESS PLAN WRITER

As an experienced business plan writer, I personally understand why people come to me; however, I also know the value of writing your own plan as I have written plans for my own business ventures. You might consider the services of a restaurant consultant for writing your plan and/or conducting a feasibility study to determine the potential for your business venture.

Here is what you should look for in a business plan writer. A well-qualified business plan writer will have:

- **Writing experience.** Review sample business plans, along with other business writing. It takes a specific talent to be able to write insightful and compelling business documents. Remember, your plan is 1) a sales piece to sell your idea, 2) a plan of action, and 3) a set of realistic and attainable goals.

- **Research experience.** Unlike writing a work of fiction, you will need facts and analysis to support your ideas. Can your business plan writer handle a portion of this for you? Does he know what types of research are needed to create a customized plan?

- **Listening abilities.** Your plan is a reflection of your dreams and desires. Never hire someone who does not listen carefully to what you have to say.

- **Questions.** Does he ask lots of in-depth questions or just want you to fill out a short form to work from? The more he knows about you, your business proposal, and your concept, the better your finished plan will be.

- **A business background.** Does he or she have a business background that will provide an understanding of what it takes to be a successful businessperson? Business training can be a plus.

- **Strong references.** Word-of-mouth is the best way to find any service provider. Ask other businesspeople for a referral. If that is not possible, ask for a list of references that you can contact personally.

WHAT IT WILL COST YOU

Paying for a comprehensive plan can be costly with pricing based upon the research required, length of plan, turnaround time, and financial reports to be generated. There is no typical plan fee because a custom plan will have a custom price. You can expect to pay $1,200 to $10,000 for a top-notch professional business plan. Pricing variables are also based on your intended use, local prevailing rates, and the expertise of the plan writer.

Paying $150 to $300 for a plan will provide you with a boilerplate project that covers just the basics. Outside investors and lenders see these often and will not give you any bonus points for this type of professionally written plan. Be aware that your pay-and-go plan may be a poor investment.

Above the basic plan level, you will receive more personalized service and some advice. Review what is included with any quote along with any built-in review and revision procedures. Once you sign off and accept your plan, additional work will mean additional costs.

You will be required to pay a deposit, periodic payments (for projects running more than a month), and the balance upon completion.

TELL THEM WHAT YOU NEED

When interviewing potential business plan writers (also known as business plan consultants), the first thing you should do is clarify who does what. Will you have to provide them with all background research on customers, competitors, economic situations, and financial reports? If the writer is not local, who will gather community-specific information? Does the writer have restaurant plan experience? You will save time and money if you do some basic research (for example, read this entire book) on what you need in and from your business plan.

TELL THEM WHAT YOU WANT

Write down some specifics. Create a list of purposes and determine who will be reviewing your finished plan. Develop your elevator speech describing your future or current business. Do not be afraid to share your passion; if you bore your prospective plan writers with the facts, they may never catch the spirit. A business plan is a business document but it is also a sales piece— you will be selling investors, lenders, and others on your concept and ability to be profitable.

Your goal is to be able to say to prospective business plan writers "I need..." Even if your chosen plan-writing expert directs you differently, you will have a place to start the exploration.

TELL THEM WHEN YOU NEED IT

Writers will need to have an approximate completion date to provide you with a quote. If your time frame is flexible, you will not be paying any rush charges. However, do not let it drag on or you will lose your momentum and frustrate your consultant.

TELL THEM WHAT RESOURCES YOU HAVE

Will you be providing all the supporting data? Do you have research that you have already completed? Do you have an accountant who will help with the financials? Is there an attorney to advise and review your business structure? Do you have a business plan that you have used in the past? What else can you provide the writer so he can deliver what you want and need?

WRITE A REQUEST FOR PROPOSAL (RFP)

In choosing a business plan writer, you must be able to tell each prospective consultant your requirements. The more specific you can be, the more accurate the quotes will be. A good way to accomplish that is with a written Request for Proposal (also known as an RFP).

An RFP describes the task (service/product) to be provided, outlines the scope of the need, establishes what qualifications are required, and asks consultants to bid. Having a set of rules from which to work will help consultants give you an accurate quote. In addition, you will know that each bid is based upon the same criteria so you do not have to factor in variables when comparing pricing and services to be provided.

IF I COULD ONLY WRITE AN RFP

RFPs can be quite report-like; however, a basic outline clearly defining your needs and expectations can be quite adequate for quoting purposes. Quotes will be based upon your specifications so provide as much information as possible; be accurate and have a clear set of expectations. You will need a brief RFP if you want to search for business plan writers through various consultant and business service Web sites such as Guru, **www.guru.com,** or E-lance, **www.elance.com**. Many of these sites are free to businesses seeking assistance.

CONTRACTS AND AGREEMENTS

Your business plan writer should have a standard consulting contract that you will read carefully and sign. The contract should be reviewed by your attorney prior to signing. The contract should be a work-for-hire agreement where you own all copyrights to the complete plan including all original research, artwork, diagrams, and charts. The contract should also prevent the writer from using your name or any part of your plan for advertising or marketing purposes without your written permission. You may also want to include a non-disclosure agreement.

The contract will also outline periodic payments and what constitutes completed and accepted. You will want to watch for errors and omissions and do not sign off on anything that is not correct to the best of your knowledge. You will be accepting the plan as accurate and presenting the facts as true to investors and lenders.

CONFIDENTIALITY/NON-DISCLOSURE CLAUSES

You may be sharing confidential ideas and information with a stranger. A confidentiality (also known as non-disclosure) clause can be especially important if you are hiring someone locally where there is a greater chance that competitive restaurateurs would use the same expert.

WHAT DOES A GOOD BUSINESS PLAN CONTAIN?

A good business plan contains dreams and ideas backed by facts and figures in a fairly standardized format. The standardized format makes it easier for lenders and investors (who look at hundreds and even thousands of business plans every month) to scan for specific information efficiently. Lenders may even just skim your plan and assign it to a lower-level employee who will read it thoroughly

Investors, with more demanding criteria for funding, may not actually read your plan at all.

They will be checking specific sections for the potential return on their investment. Your financial reports and projections will provide them with enough information to either reject your request, refer the plan to a subordinate for full follow-up, or read it in full.

STANDARD BUSINESS PLAN FORMAT

There are specific sections that must be included in your business plan; however, the format can be varied to explain your business thoroughly. You may find sample plans with different titles, but the information will closely match the plan format outlined below.

I. **Executive Summary**

II. **Background Information**
    a. Personal Information
        i. Personal Skills and Expertise
        ii. Personal Financial Capability

III. **Business Concept**
    a. Mission Statement
    b. Business Goals and Objective
    c. General Description of Business

IV. **Description of Products and Services**
    a. Features of Products/Services
    b. Benefits to Customers
    c. Future Products/Services

V. **Management Structure and Organization**
    a. Legal Form
    b. Ownership
    c. Management and Personnel

VI. **Marketing**
    a. Industry Description
        i. Food Trends
        ii. Industry Future
    b. Marketing
        i. Customer Profile
        ii. Market Size
        iii. Market Potential
    c. Competition
        i. Direct and Indirect
        ii. Evaluation
    d. Marketing Strategies
        i. Marketing Positioning
        ii. Business Location
        iii. Pricing
        iv. Customer Service
        v. Advertising
        vi. Promotion

VII. Financial Data
    a. Investment Required for Start Up
        i. Start-Up Costs/Needs
        ii. Loan Applications
        iii Capital Equipment and Supply List
    b   Income Projections (Profit and Loss Statements)
        i. Three Year Summary
        ii. Detail by Month, First Year
        iii.Detail by Quarters, Second and Third Years
        iv.Assumptions Upon Which Projections Are Based
    c. Cash Flow Projections
        i. Sales and Expenses Estimates
        ii. Monthly Cash Flow Projections
    d. Summary of Financial Needs

VIII. Conclusion
    a. Feasibility Statement

IX. Support Documents
    a. Copies of Personal Financial Documents
    b. Copies of Franchise Contracts
    c. Copies of Lease Agreements
    d. Copies of Licenses
    e. Copies of Legal Documents
    f. Copies of Resumés
    g Copies of Letters of Intent

Your plan will require some research to prove that your new restaurant concept or expansion has merit. You might want to get out a pad and pen to jot down notes on how you will complete each of the plan sections. Following the plan outline, I will define unfamiliar terms and provide you with some thought-provoking ideas to explore that need to be conveyed section-by-section.

COVER PAGE

You will need to include your legal business name, assumed business name (also known as "doing business as" or "DBA"), owner name(s), contact address, phone, fax, and e-mail information.

TABLE OF CONTENTS
This is the last page you will write for your plan.

EXECUTIVE SUMMARY

Your executive summary is an abbreviated version of your entire plan, written to catch the attention of your most important audience. Often busy lenders or investors will not read beyond the executive summary and your financial projections; therefore, it is imperative that your executive summary is a strong distillation of your research and plans for success. You will write this critical section after you have completed your plan.

BACKGROUND INFORMATION

PERSONAL RESOURCES

The background section covers the personal assets — skills, expertise, financial, and other personal resources — that all owners bring to the table. Like a résumé that gets you a dream job, this section will help you secure your dream business. The first half of this section should detail the work history, education, skills, and talents that you and your partners will rely on to become successful restaurant owners. Outline the food service-specific creative talents and work experience of each owner.

This information is presented to assure lenders and investors that you have what it takes to manage your restaurant and deliver profits. If the food service experience of your ownership team is not exceptionally strong, emphasize your accumulated business skills. You will have an opportunity in subsequent sections to discuss the talent and expertise you will be hiring to fill any gaps in your background.

FINANCIAL RESOURCES

Your financial resources will be of great consideration to lenders and investors. Start by creating a personal financial statement listing your assets and liabilities to determine your net worth. Your net worth (and especially assets that can be easily converted to cash) will be of great interest to franchisers, as many have minimum net worth requirements. Bankers want to know what you will require as earnings from your business. Insufficient business (or other financial resources) earnings can undermine your ability to repay loans or become profitable.

Your financial contributions to launching a new business or expanding a current one are also of great interest. Ideas without personal funding are considered high-risk investments. Remember that finding money to fund 100 percent of your dream is virtually impossible. Lenders and investors will not be interested in a plan that requires their funds to be the only money at risk. As a new entrepreneur with no business assets, you will be asked to use your personal assets as loan collateral.

If you are turned down for outside funding because of a lack of personal finances, take your plan and transform it into a goal for yourself. Determine the percent of start-up and operating expenses you will need to have in hand before you can present your plan again to investors and lenders.

BUSINESS CONCEPT

MISSION STATEMENT

Also known as a statement of purpose, your mission statement is similar to the objective section of a résumé. This statement should capture the reasons why you personally want to be in business, what you want to accomplish with your business, who your business serves, and what your company is (or will be).

Mission statements are hard to write. They are more honest than an advertisement, more personal than a sales pitch, and a bit touchy-feely.

1. **Start with your elevator pitch.** Some experts believe that your mission statement should be very brief and easy to remember. Keep it as short as possible and never more than three or four sentences.

2. **Write clearly and concisely** for people who are not in the food service industry.

3. **Do not brag;** just be straightforward and realistic.

4. **Do not go overboard with superlatives,** such as unequalled service or fabulous food.

5. **Think about what you want your customers to receive** from dining at your restaurant. For example:

   • You want them to be physically and emotionally satisfied.

   • You want them to experience the pleasures of quality food.

   • You want them to have fun.

6. **Read *Creating Mission Statements for Smaller Groups*** by Beverly Goldberg ($3.95 PDF download at **www.amazon.com**).

7. **Look at sample statements of purpose** for creative stimulus, but do not take one as your own as it simply will not capture the essence of your plan's message.

BUSINESS GOALS AND OBJECTIVES

Your business goals and objectives will cover your short-term (within one year) and long-term (two to five years) expectations as a business and entrepreneur. Think of goals as your dreams with a deadline and your objectives as the way you will achieve those goals. Your goals are typically measured in dollars or other tangible results.

Common restaurant goals are:

• Sales volume.

• Number of customers.

• Number of future employees.

• Expansion (additional stores or larger restaurant facility).

• Hours the owner(s) work.

• Profit levels.

• Cash flow.

Objectives are the steps you will take to achieve these goals. These are measurable activities that answer the queries of who, what, how, why, and when.

• **Who** = Management team

• **What** = Increase customer returns

• **How** = Weekly customer service training

• **Why** = Happier customers equals repeat customers

• **When** = Three-month review and assessment

Your first goal — the launch of your new restaurant — is detailed on the next page.

BUSINESS GOALS	
Short Term Goal	**Long Term Goal**
Goal #1 — Official restaurant opening date of November 5.	Goal #5 — Open second restaurant in local suburb in year three.
• Hire general manager to assist with overseeing complete renovation of leased building. • Hire general contractor with restaurant remodeling experience. • Obtain $50,000 capital equipment loan.	• Cash reserves of $150,000 to be set aside for expansion funding. • Set monthly savings goals to raise additional $150,000 in eight months. • Create training/mentoring program for assistant manager to be responsible for outfitting and starting second restaurant.

Start by creating three to five short-term goals and outline how you will achieve these. Be realistic and use your financial projections to benchmark and support your ability to reach each goal. Your objectives should be doable for a busy restaurant owner. It is okay to dream, but the purpose here is to set business and personal goals that are attainable and—go beyond the normal daily requirements of being in business for yourself.

GENERAL DESCRIPTION OF BUSINESS

Your business description is an expanded paragraph that details what your business does. Start again with your elevator pitch (see Introduction). It includes descriptions of the products (food, beverage, other) that you will offer, your concept (theme, formal/ informal), your service style (dine-in, take-out), along with any other pertinent information that enables the reader to visualize your food service establishment. Your description can also include your legal business structure (corporation, partnership, sole proprietorship) and fiscal year (annual or other date). Your restaurant name — your brand name — will be revealed here.

Below are two examples of business descriptions for food service establishments.

BUSINESS DESCRIPTION SAMPLES
Example #1: Arden Meadows
Arden Meadows will be a seasonal café, located next to Lake Arden, featuring BBQ and American cuisine. Customers will be seasonal visitors to the 250-square-mile Lake Arden public-use region including the Mt. Ray National Park (U.S. Forest Service-operated camping facilities). Operating from May 15 through September 30, the café while have an informal sunflower theme and outdoor dining areas. Picnic-style take-out and sit-down service will be available. An adjoining full-service bar operated by the Big Beer Company will provide Arden Meadows' customers with alcoholic beverages. Arden Meadows will be owned and operated by partners Jim Sweet and Fred Anderson as a Nevada limited liability corporation with a November 1 to October 31 accounting period.

Example #2: Fargo

Fargo is a family friendly steak house with a historical Wild West theme located at the Smithridge Mall in Irvine, California, near Interstate 5. Open seven days a week, Fargo serves Southern California tourists and residents with family oriented entertainment, including line dancing servers and classic country and western music. The menu features cowboy-style meals served family style in a rustic atmosphere including glass jars for mugs and tin plates as chargers. Owned and operated by the husband and wife partnership of Norman and Betty Paul, Fargo has shown a 35 percent annual pretax profit for the past six calendar years.

Your business description is your creation. You will not need to do any specific research to write this section. Look at sample business plans for other ideas on how to tell your story so a stranger would immediately know what your restaurant is like.

DESCRIPTION OF PRODUCTS/SERVICES

Restaurants sell products — foods and beverages — and they sell services. For example, your business could offer a 20-minute pizza delivery service, custom off-site catering, or banquets. A good way to define what you will sell and what services you offer is to create a list of features (what you offer customers) and add the benefits your customers will receive from each feature. Benefits are the what's-in-it-for-me part of marketing your products and services.

Here are a few examples of the features and benefits that a café/bakery might offer to their customers.

SAMPLE FEATURES & BENEFITS	
Feature	**Benefit**
Staff arrives very early for first shift.	Customers have plenty of time to stop by before work. Convenient time for local manufacturing plant workers on first shift.
Fresh baked bagels, muffins, and bread.	Convenient, great-tasting breakfast items for dine-in and take-out.
Custom decorated cakes.	Easy to stop by and order a special occasion cake. Place order during breakfast and pick up after work.
Fresh coffee with any purchase.	Save money eating here.
Delivery service.	No one has to leave a business meeting or luncheon to feed guests.

Lists are a great way to get ideas on paper. Your lists can be a single word or an entire thought to explain the topic. Grab that notepad and let your mind go to create lists from which to write your product/service description section.

- **List 1: To help you develop your niche** — what you do best and promote most—create another list that answers the question, what makes your products and/or services unique or special?

- **List 2: How do you differ from your competitors?** Are you higher priced? Do you offer take-out? Open longer? Write down every difference you can think of.

- **List 3: What special resources do you have going for you?** This can be anything from name recognition within your community to outstanding chef awards to a patent or trademark.

- **List 4: How will you produce your product/service?** Will everything be made in-house? What special equipment will be required?

- **List 5: Are there any obstacles or negatives associated with your products?** Need an air quality permit for a charbroiler? Is your menu too foreign for your community? Will you need to rely on hard-to-locate items? Are there limited vendors capable of supplying you?

- **List 6: What products/services are in your future?** Will you be able to respond to food trends? Will your customers want you to?

FROM YOUR LISTS TO YOUR PLAN

The free-form nature of creating lists should reveal some good ideas and some great ones; concentrate on the great ones in your plan. Your first subsection is to describe in detail your products and services. You do not have to include recipes, but a sample menu is an appropriate support document.

Do not dismiss the off-the-wall ideas that appear on your lists. Some of the world's greatest innovations came to life because someone let their imagination soar.

Discuss specific ingredients, preparation and serving methods. Tell the reader how these set you apart from competitors, why they are desired by customers, and your profit potential. Good marketing focuses on the benefits to the customers and your plan should do likewise. No matter how excited about a specific product you are, unless it connects with patrons, it is not a winner.

Your service (dining style, service levels, etc.) is also a critical part of your offerings and a way to set your business apart from the competition. Discuss how these affect the product quality, your customer needs, and profitability. Do not forget to tie your service style/methods into your customer demographics. For example: If you have a café serving a tourist area at a lake, your take-out window conveniently situated for docked boats is a real asset.

MANAGEMENT STRUCTURE AND ORGANIZATION

The legal form of your business is important to the operation, tax structure, and many other elements of the business operation. These were discussed in detail in Chapter 1.

The structure and organization will impact ownership percentages and participation requirements. After you review the information in Chapter 1, discuss the advantages and disadvantages with your accountant and/or attorney. They can offer advice on the best form for your business to protect yourself from personal financial risks and for the greatest tax benefits.

A business may incorporate without an attorney, but legal advice is highly recommended.

YOUR MANAGEMENT TEAM

Managing a business requires more than just the desire to be your own boss. It demands dedication, persistence, the capacity to make wise decisions, and the ability to manage both employees and finances. Your management plan, along with your marketing and financial management sections, is your business foundation.

People are your greatest business resources and most valuable asset. To maximize your human resources, take a good look at the talents you possess and what skills you lack. Your job now is to hire personnel that can supply your missing skills.

Look at what you do best and how that can best serve your business. Even if you can create a profit and loss statement or design a Web page, you need to consider if this time is well spent. Until there are more than 24 hours in a day, you will need to invest your time in activities that earn money first. If you are the creative talent in the kitchen, do not be afraid to hire someone to handle the operational and support duties. Learn how to train people for advancement and delegate duties. Entrepreneurs often like to do it themselves or feel they are the only one who can do it; this style is a self-limited managerial style. Share the duties and responsibilities and you will have rewards to share.

Your management plan should answer questions such as:

- How does your background/business experience help you in this business?

- What are your weaknesses and how can you compensate for them?

- Who will be on the management team?

- What are management's strengths/weaknesses? (Although you will not write directly about the weak spots in your team, they will be noticed by business professionals. Explain the missing skills before someone can question your team's ability.)

- What are their duties?

- Are these duties clearly defined?

- If a franchise, what type of assistance can you expect from the franchiser? Will this assistance be ongoing?

- What are your current personnel needs?

- What are your plans for hiring and training personnel?

- What salaries, benefits, vacations, and holidays will you offer?

- If a franchise, will these issues be covered in the management package the franchiser will provide?

- How will you attract quality employees?

- How can you keep employees happy and productive?

- What benefits, if any, can you afford at this point?

If a franchise, the operating procedures, manuals, and materials devised by the franchiser should be included in this section of the business plan. If they are too bulky, simply list them by title and refer the reader to their location. Lenders will consider the strength of the franchiser as part of your management capabilities. Study these documents carefully when writing your business plan and be sure to incorporate the important highlights. The franchiser should assist you with management training and ongoing management support.

YOUR KEY PERSONNEL

As the owner/operator of a small hot dog stand, you will probably hold all the key positions in your company — owner, employee, accountant, personnel director. If your business is a solo operation, you will be telling the reader what makes you capable of filling these roles.

If your food service establishment is significantly larger, you will have a variety of key personnel to share the responsibility of daily operations, decision-making, and supervision of people and things. Here is where you will discuss the skills and expertise your key personnel bring to your business. For example, if you want to feature rich, elaborate European-style pastries, then your pastry chef's talents and experience are of great importance.

Key personnel in your restaurant could be:

- Operations Manager
- Maitre d'
- Partner
- Wine Steward
- Banquet Manager
- Human Resources Manager
- Head Chef
- Bookkeeper
- Pastry Chef
- Catering Salesperson
- Head Bartender

OUTSIDE SUPPORT

An owner or manager need not handle all of the restaurant's fiscal and managerial responsibilities. Outside consultants and advisors are a great way to enhance your management resources. Your accountant, lawyer, insurance broker, ad agency, PR firm, remodeling contractor, food service consultants, real estate broker, restaurant equipment salesperson, and suppliers can all add depth to your management capabilities.

MANAGEMENT PHILOSOPHY

Your management style indicates how you make decisions, how you delegate, and how you interact with personnel. Do not say, "I am an easy boss to get along with;" talk about your team-building philosophy or other work ethics that support your mission statement.

ORGANIZATIONAL CHART

Depending upon the size of your organization, you can either include a chart or just describe who will be reporting to whom. Organizational or flow charts can be created using the Chart/ Diagram functions of Microsoft Word. Charts and diagrams can also be created in PowerPoint and Excel.

THE NEXT THREE BIG SECTIONS

The next three sections of your plan — Marketing, Financial Data, and Feasibility Study — are the most detailed and complex. The marketing section is a plan within a plan. Marketing plans can be created separately for internal purposes instead of a full business plan. The information provided in your financial section shows your ability to pay for your business requirements and make a profit. Your feasibility study is your report on the ability to accomplish your restaurant's economic goals. I will discuss this later in this chapter.

COMING TO A CONCLUSION

Your conclusion is not just the end of your written business plan. It is a recap of the points you have made that prove your plan to be viable and profitable. Your conclusion is also your opportunity to ask for what you want and tell them why.

> *I am seeking an additional $50,000 in loans to complete the renovation of the historical Adams building. This sum represents 15 percent of the funds needed for this project and would provide Provencal with six additional tables.*

SUPPORT DOCUMENTS

This section includes various personal financial documents, legal documents and other items that support your statements within the plan. Examples are listed below. You may have other documents that you feel will give your lender or investor additional information of importance.

- Personal tax returns of the principals (owners) for the last three years.

- Business tax returns for the last three years (if you are already operational).

- Personal financial statements for each principal detailing your assets and liabilities.

- Copy of franchise contracts and documents supplied by the franchiser (if applicable).

- Copy of proposed lease or purchase agreement for building space and/or land.

- Copy of licenses and other legal documents.

- Copies of résumés of all principals.

- Copies of résumés of key employees.

- Copies of letters of intent from suppliers, etc.

Note: Never attach originals unless they can be easily reproduced.

WRITING A FEASIBILITY ANALYSIS

Feasibility is the likelihood that something can be carried out or achieved. A feasibility study covers the physical, emotional, financial, and market needs of your business idea and answers the big question: Should I start (or expand) a food service business? Many aspects of a feasibility study and analysis overlap with your business plan; however, they have different functions. Your feasibility study is your confirmation that your idea has sufficient merit to create your business plan — with the emphasis on planning. Think of a feasibility analysis as an exploration of your ideas and your business plan as a plan for action.

Your restaurant's study is a critical decision-making tool for you, your partners, and your lender. The analysis can be a financial lifesaver allowing you to revise your vision and improve its potential for success before you invest your financial future.

After reading this chapter, you may decide that your first step should be to conduct a feasibility study, as much of the information gathered for the feasibility analysis can be used to write your formal business plan.

Start by reading over your plan, looking at your projected numbers, and examining your self-determination. Before putting anything on paper in this section, you will need to determine if your restaurant idea is financially, physically, and emotionally achievable in the real world. It is important to be honest with yourself; slanting the outcome towards profitability means that you are not facing business realities — not all ideas are money makers and not everyone is cut out to be an entrepreneur.

- Can it be profitable?

- Will people come?

- Do I have the desire to be successful?

- Am I willing to work hard for little pay?

- Do I have sufficient financial resources to sustain my family and business until I become profitable?

If the answers to these questions are yes, you are ready to create your written feasibility analysis.

PREPARING YOUR ANALYSIS

Your analysis must be based upon thorough research and fact-based assumptions. As you research the categories below, think about the questions people will ask you before deciding to loan you money, invest in your ideas, become a partner, or accept a job.

Your feasibility analysis should give you a clear picture of your:

- **Needs** — Must-haves that are the foundation of your concept and success.

- **Wants** — Desirable elements that will make life easier, increase profits, or save money.

- **Wishes** — Features that you would love to have but are not important to your launch or short- term ability to grow

Your analysis will cover your:

- **Concept** — Your theme, service style, menu, customer needs, and competition.

- **Location** — Its convenience, accessibility, visibility, and proximity to your customer base.

- **Execution** — How you will make it real.

- **Financing Needs** — What will it cost to start or grow a profitable restaurant?

CONCEPT ANALYSIS

In reviewing the potential of your concept, you will be asking and answering a variety of quantitative questions. Are the numbers there to support your idea? Is your community struggling economically? Do dining trends support your growth assumptions?

In analyzing the feasibility of your concept, you will be reviewing food service industry statistics, local economic conditions, community growth potential, customer demographics, and consumer patterns.

Look at the data you have gathered to determine:

- **The meals people eat when dining out.** Do potential patrons only eat breakfast out on weekends? Are competitors busiest during lunch hours? Are locals interested in lingering after work?

- **Traffic patterns around your location.** Are there natural commuting patterns that go past your restaurant? Are you located in a destination spot that will bring people to your door? Is there easy access or must they do a U-turn to get to you?

- **The economic health of your community.** Everyone needs to eat, but dining out is a discretionary activity directly affected by economic ups and downs. Is your community growing? Are businesses shutting down?

- **Seasonal conditions.** Do you have a seasonal population fluctuation? Are you near a tourist destination? Will people be interested in heavy, comfort food during your long, hot summer months?

- **Spending history and patterns.** Are locals spending their dining-out dollars at fast-food joints or upscale dinner houses? Can your potential customers afford your offerings?

The key question to answer is, "Does my restaurant concept fit with what I know about my community, customers, and competitors?" For example, if you are located in a bedroom community where people drive by on their way out of town and never stop for breakfast, would a pancake house be a wise venture?

GOING INTO BUSINESS CHECKLIST			
(This form can be used to tally pluses and minuses or to make comments.)			
FACTORS	**FROM SCRATCH**	**BUY EXISTING BUSINESS**	**FRANCHISE**
TIME			
Availability			
Launch Time (planning to opening)			

GOING INTO BUSINESS CHECKLIST

(This form can be used to tally pluses and minuses or to make comments.)

FACTORS	FROM SCRATCH	BUY EXISTING BUSINESS	FRANCHISE
FINANCIAL			
Cost			
Available Financing			
Investors			
Personal Worth Requirements			
Total Indebtedness			
Break-Even Point			
Royalties & Fees			
Purchasing Restrictions			
Current Profitability			
INTANGIBLES			
Goodwill			
Historical Recognition			
Known vs. Unknown (obstacles to success or existing profitability)			
Reputation			
Convenience			
Exclusivity			

GOING INTO BUSINESS CHECKLIST

(This form can be used to tally pluses and minuses or to make comments.)

FACTORS	FROM SCRATCH	BUY EXISTING BUSINESS	FRANCHISE
ASSETS			
Location			
Facility			
Equipment			
Existing Staff			
Customer Base			
OWNER			
Independence			
Business Experience			
Food Service Experience			
Management Experience			
Owner Expectations			
Outside Expectations			
Training			
Support			

GOING INTO BUSINESS CHECKLIST			
(This form can be used to tally pluses and minuses or to make comments.)			
FACTORS	FROM SCRATCH	BUY EXISTING BUSINESS	FRANCHISE
MARKET SHARE			
Marketing Support			
Product Mix			
Competition			
Customer Needs			
OTHER			

THE MARKETING PLAN

The marketing plan is the first additional plan that needs to be created. We will discuss the marketing plan, the management plan, and the financial plan throughout the remainder of this chapter.

Marketing plays a vital role in successful business ventures. How well you market your business will ultimately determine your degree of success or failure. The key element of a successful marketing plan is to know your customers — their likes, dislikes, and expectations. By identifying these factors, you can develop a marketing strategy that will allow you to arouse and fulfill their needs.

Identify your customers by their age, sex, income/educational level, and residence. At first, target only those customers who are more likely to purchase your product or service. As your customer base expands, you need to consider modifying the marketing plan to include other customers.

Develop a marketing plan for your business by answering these questions. (Potential franchise owners will have to use the marketing strategy the franchisor has developed.) Your marketing plan should be included in your business plan and contain answers to the questions outlined below.

- Who are your customers? Define your target market(s).

- Are your markets growing? Steady? Declining?

- Is your market share growing? Steady? Declining?

- If a franchise, how is your market segmented?

- Are your markets large enough to expand?

- How will you attract, hold, and increase your market share? If a franchise, will the franchisor provide assistance in this area? How will you promote your sales?

- What pricing strategy have you devised?

COMPETITION

Competition is a way of life. We compete for jobs, promotions, scholarships, in sports, and in almost every aspect of our lives. Nations compete for the consumer in the global marketplace, as do individual business owners. Advances in technology can send the profit margins of a successful business into a tailspin causing them to plummet overnight or within a few hours. When considering these and other factors, we can conclude that business is a highly competitive, volatile arena. Because of this volatility and competitiveness, it is important to know your competitors. Questions like these can help you:

- Who are your five nearest direct competitors?

- Who are your indirect competitors?

- How is their business: Steady? Increasing? Decreasing?

- What have you learned from their operations? From their advertising?

- What are their strengths and weaknesses?

- How does their menu or service differ from yours?

Start a file on each of your competitors. Keep manila envelopes of their advertising and promotional materials and their pricing strategy techniques. Review these files periodically, determining when and how often they advertise, sponsor promotions and offer sales. Study the copy used in the advertising and promotional materials and their sales strategy. For example, is their copy short? Descriptive? Catchy? How much do they reduce prices for sales? Using this technique can help you better understand your competitors and how they operate their businesses.

PRICING AND SALES

Your pricing strategy is another marketing technique to improve your overall competitiveness. Get a feel for the pricing strategy your competitors are using. That way you can determine if your prices are in line with competitors in your market area and if they are in line with industry averages. Some of the pricing considerations are:

- Menu cost and pricing
- Pricing below competition
- Price lining
- Service components
- Labor costs
- Competitive position
- Pricing above competition
- Multiple pricing
- Material costs
- Overhead costs

The keys to success are having a well-planned strategy, establishing your policies, and constantly monitoring prices and operating costs to ensure profits. Even in a franchise where the franchisor provides operational procedures and materials, it is a good policy to keep abreast of the changes in the marketplace because these changes can affect your competitiveness and profit margins.

ADVERTISING AND PUBLIC RELATIONS

How you advertise and promote your restaurant may make or break your business. Having a good product or service and not advertising and promoting it is like not having a business at all. Many business owners operate under the mistaken concept that the business will promote itself and channel money that should be used for advertising and promotions in other areas of the business. Advertising and promotions are the lifeline of a business and should be treated as such. I have devoted a whole chapter to marketing and promoting your restaurant.

Devise a plan that uses advertising and networking as a means to promote your business. Develop short, descriptive copy (text material) that clearly identifies your goods or services, its location, and price. Use catchy phrases to arouse the interest of your readers, listeners, or viewers. In the case of a franchise, the franchisor will provide advertising and promotional materials as part of the franchise package; you may need approval to use any materials that you and your staff develop. As a courtesy, allow the franchisor the opportunity to review, comment on and, if required, approve these materials before using them. Make sure the advertisements you create are consistent with the image the franchisor is trying to project. Remember the more care and attention you devote to your marketing program, the more successful your business will be.

THE MANAGEMENT PLAN

Managing a business requires more than just the desire to be your own boss. It demands dedication, persistence, the ability to make decisions, and the ability to manage both employees and finances. Your management plan, along with your marketing and financial management plans, sets the foundation for and facilitates the success of your business.

People are a business's most valuable resources. You will discover that employees and staff play an important role in the total operation of your business. It is imperative that you know the skills you do and do not possess. You will have to hire personnel to supply the skills that you lack, making them part of the team. Keep them informed of, and get their feedback regarding, changes. Employees have ideas that can lead to new market areas, innovations to existing products or services, or new product lines or services that can improve your overall competitiveness. Your management plan should answer these questions:

- How does your background/business experience help you in this business?

- What are your weaknesses and how can you compensate for them?

- Who will be on the management team?

- What are their strengths/weaknesses?

- What are their duties?

- Are these duties clearly defined?

- If a franchise, what type of assistance can you expect from the franchisor?

- Will this assistance be ongoing?

- What are your current personnel needs?

- What are your plans for hiring and training personnel?

- What salaries, benefits, vacations and holidays will you offer? If a franchise, are these issues covered in the management package the franchisor will provide?

- What benefits, if any, can you afford at this point?

If a franchise, the operating procedures, manuals, and materials devised by the franchisor should be included in this section of the business plan. Study these documents carefully when writing your business plan and be sure to incorporate this material.

The franchisor should assist you with managing your franchise. Take advantage of her expertise and develop a management plan that will ensure the success of your franchise and satisfy the needs and expectations of employees, as well as those of the franchisor.

THE FINANCIAL PLAN

Sound financial management is one of the best ways for your business to remain profitable and solvent. How well finances are managed is the cornerstone of every successful business venture. Each year thousands of businesses fail because of poor financial management. As a business owner, identify and implement policies that will lead to and ensure that you will meet your financial obligations.

To effectively manage your finances, plan a sound, realistic budget by determining the actual money needed to open your business (start-up costs) and the amount needed to keep it open (operating costs). The first step to building a sound financial plan is to devise a start-up budget. Your start-up budget will include such one-time-only costs as major equipment, utility deposits, and down payments.

START-UP BUDGET

The start-up budget should allow for these expenses:

- Personnel (costs prior to opening)
- Occupancy
- Equipment
- Supplies
- Salaries/Wages
- Income
- Payroll expenses

- Legal/Professional fees
- Licenses/Permits
- Insurance
- Advertising/Promotions
- Accounting
- Utilities

OPERATING BUDGET

An operating budget is prepared when you are ready to open for business. The operating budget will reflect your priorities in spending your money, the expenses you will incur, and meeting those expenses (income). Your operating budget should include money to cover the first three to six months of operation. It should allow for the following expenses:

- Personnel
- Rent
- Loan payments
- Legal/Accounting
- Supplies
- Salaries/Wages
- Taxes
- Dues/Subscriptions/Membership Fees

- Insurance
- Depreciation
- Advertising/Promotions
- Miscellaneous expenses
- Payroll expenses
- Utilities
- Repairs/Maintenance

The financial section of your business plan should include any loan applications you have filed, a capital equipment and supply list, balance sheet, break-even analysis, pro-forma income projections (profit and loss statement), and pro-forma cash flow. The income statement and cash-flow projections should include a three-year summary, detail by month for the first year, and detail by quarter for the second and third years.

The accounting system and the inventory control system that you will be using are generally addressed in this section of the business plan. Have your financial advisor develop these systems and assist you in developing this section of your business plan. If a franchise, the franchisor may stipulate in the franchise contract the type of accounting and inventory systems you may use. She should have a system already intact for you to adopt. You will need a thorough understanding of each segment and how it operates.

The following questions will help determine the start-up capital you will need to purchase and open a franchise.

- How much money do you have?

- How much money will you need to purchase the franchise?

- How much money will you need for start-up?

- How much money will you need to stay in business?

Other questions that you will need to consider are:

- What type of accounting system will you use? Is it a single entry or dual entry system?

- What will your sales and profit goals for the coming year be? If a franchise, will the franchisor set your sales and profit goals? Or will she expect you to reach and retain a certain sales level and profit margin?

- What financial projections will you need to include in your business plan?

- What kind of inventory control system will you use?

Your plan should include an explanation of all projections. Unless you are thoroughly familiar with financial statements, get help in preparing your cash-flow and income statements and your balance sheet. Your aim is not to become a financial wizard, but to understand the financial tools well enough to gain their benefits. Your accountant or financial advisor can help you accomplish this goal.

For additional business plan information, I recommend *Opening a Restaurant or Other Food Business Starter Kit: How to Prepare a Restaurant Business Plan and Feasibility Study (Item # ORF-02)* and *How to Write a Great Business Plan for Your Small Business in 60 Minutes or Less (Item # GBP-01)*. Both titles are available from Atlantic Publishing, **www.atlantic-pub.com,** and each book has an accompanying CD-ROM with forms and a sample business plan.

CHAPTER

STEPS TO SECURE FINANCING

I f only it were this easy: Business Idea + Money = Success. Many businesses, large and small, have discovered they cannot buy their way to the top. It takes more than an influx of cash to launch and grow a business. There are few "do-overs" when it comes to seeking financing.

You have only one chance with a potential investor. You may only have ten minutes to tell your story, show your profit potential, "close the deal," and secure the money you need for your business.

DID YOU KNOW?

- A small business is any independent business with 500 or fewer employees.

- As of 2003, 5.7 million small businesses have at least one employee.

- As of 2003, 17 million small businesses are sole proprietorships.

- Fifty-three percent of small businesses are home-based.

- Women own at least 50 percent of some 10.6 million firms.

- The number of minority-owned firms is growing four times faster than all other U.S. firms.

- Of all employers, 99.7 percent are small businesses.

- Sixty to 80 percent of all new jobs (net) over the past ten years were created by small businesses.

- Eighty-two percent of small businesses use some form of credit for financing.

- Approximately 95 percent of new small businesses rely on personal financing (savings, second mortgages, and family or friend support).

MONEY, MONEY, MONEY

Angel investors invested an estimated $22.5 billion in 48,000 companies in 2004. Venture capital firms estimate that they invest between $3 and $5 billion annually. The Small Business Administration (SBA) guarantees more than $10 billion in loans every year.

Borrowing wisely is important — even if it is from your own piggy bank. Initial financing may be a loan from Mom, but how you approach this business relationship and use the funds is just as important as borrowing from a bank. In the next section I will discuss the various types of personal financing and tips on how to make each work for you.

For the 5 percent of entrepreneurs who will rely on formal "outside" financing, remember that every new business starts with some type of personal financing. Investors and lenders expect you to be financially invested in your dream.

Whether it is a few hundred dollars or thousands of dollars needed to launch your new business, there is money available to people with sound business skills and a solid business plan.

LEARNING YOUR MONEY FORMULA

BE PREPARED

The most common mistakes made by beginning entrepreneurs result from lack of preparation. All of the enthusiasm in the world cannot make up for a failure to research when seeking capital. Before you fill out a loan application or contact an investor be prepared — in your head, heart, and on paper. Create your "elevator pitch."

DEVELOP AN ELEVATOR PITCH

Imagine you are alone in an elevator with a rich investor. Here is your chance to pitch your idea. Can you capture his attention, sell him on your idea, and intrigue his entrepreneurial spirit before you reach the twenty-second floor?

Your elevator pitch is a brief description that neatly sums up your business concept. It is not a lifeless declaration "I want to start a Chinese restaurant." It is a statement that captures the excitement and potential of your idea—"I'm starting a trendy restaurant featuring exquisite dinners from every region of China. I have hired a chef from a popular New York establishment and renowned restaurant designer Barbara Lazaroff is working with us."

Your elevator pitch is also useful in helping you focus on your goals. You will find several ways to build upon your elevator pitch throughout the book.

KNOW YOUR INVESTORS

Understanding the current market, as well as anticipating and addressing the needs and concerns of typical investors, is necessary when creating a business plan. Entrepreneurs need to show that their business will be capable of generating a steady flow of revenue with profits on the horizon.

Show that your team is competent and familiar with the target industry. Otherwise, the risk may seem too great to investors. Many investors rely on the "bet on the jockey, not on the horse" philosophy (investing based on the person in charge).

FOCUS YOUR SEARCH

Focus your search on the sources most likely to deliver. Otherwise, you risk spending countless hours preparing deals that are destined never to materialize or to collapse at the last minute.

PLAN AHEAD

Predicting how long it takes to close a financing deal can be difficult. Misjudging this time can have devastating effects on your business. Planning ahead for secondary, or backup, financing can keep your business from stumbling.

If the capital is needed and the deal still is not closed, be prepared to have your prospects vanish. After all, customers are on a tight schedule too. The best time to raise money is before you need it, not when you need it.

BE FLEXIBLE

A good, solid business plan is a necessity, but entrepreneurs that are too attached to their plans tend to fail. There are several reasons for this:

- **The market is always changing.** If a business cannot adapt to the market, it will struggle to create revenue. Any sign of stubbornness or inflexibility is sure to send investors running toward an investment headed up by someone who can deal with change.

- **Your assumptions are just that.** As you set about creating a plan, you base statements and ideas on assumptions that may turn out to be inaccurate. Although time and effort are put into creating projections, remember that they are only educated guesses of projected sales. If sales fall short of these projections, the consequences can be disastrous.

- **Consumer demands and trends change.** The need for your product may pass or be filled by another vendor, if too much time is spent in development. You need a real product to have real customers, not a product in development.

REMEMBER TO MIND THE STORE

Sometimes entrepreneurs spend too much time searching for capital. Neglecting the day-to-day operations of the business can leave others with little reason to invest. If your are not spending the money you have earned effectively, you might as well not be raising it.

BUILD A STRONG TEAM

Investors pay attention to your management team; it is the infrastructure of your company.

Investors want to see that you have strong personnel resources. Investors know that it takes more than one person to make a company succeed. If potential investors have no confidence in your team, they will have no confidence in you.

WRITE A LEAN AND MEAN BUSINESS PLAN

Investors do not have time to read a business plan that resembles a novel. Keep it short and concise without sacrificing essential information. Keep an abridged version or a synopsis of your plan handy in case an investor wants just the meat of it. I discussed how to write a business plan in detail in Chapter 3.

OWNERSHIP VERSUS CONTROL

A founder may hold only a small percentage of the business ownership and retain a large percentage of its control. It works the other way around as well. Or investors can negotiate deals, especially with desperate businesses that have fallen on hard times in which they take over a substantial portion of the control without investing much capital.

STAY ON THE RIGHT SIDE OF THE LAW

No legitimate businessperson intends to break the law; however, taking shortcuts and being ignorant of laws regulating your business can derail even the most well-intentioned entrepreneur. Business law and regulations can be overwhelmingly complex and confusing. Unfortunately, ignorance of these laws does not absolve one from any wrongdoing.

Learn as much as you can about the laws in the following areas:

- **Employer-employee laws** — Liability, overtime regulations, and workplace safety.

- **Protection of ideas** — Copyright laws, patents, and trade secret regulations.

- **Contractual law** — What voids a contract.

- **Securities** — Know the regulations that govern how you raise capital.

- **Industry-specific government regulations** — Trade regulations, interstate commerce, and other local, state, or federal laws.

- **Environmental laws** — Use of natural resources, pollution, waste, and ecological-impact laws.

HIRE A LAWYER

Having a corporate attorney is critical for starting a business. Although these specialists are expensive, they have experience in the key areas of employee negotiations, intellectual property rights, setting up stock-option plans, and state and federal tax laws.

Legal errors can be costly. This investment allows you to concentrate on other aspects of the business. Too many entrepreneurs believe they do not need a lawyer. Competent legal counsel may not seem affordable, but ignorance can collapse your business.

CREATE STRONG AGREEMENTS

When writing a contract, make sure your interests are protected and leave yourself some options. Stay flexible, but be certain that all agreements are in writing and reviewed by your business attorney.

KEEP GOOD CORPORATE RECORDS

Keeping track of every meeting and transaction is essential to protecting your company. Poor recordkeeping can cause serious problems with the IRS, resulting in serious problems raising future capital. Keep records of these commonly overlooked items:

- Board meeting minutes
- Stock issuance
- Shareholders' meeting minutes
- Stock transfers

WRITE GOOD EMPLOYEE POLICIES

Poor documentation and enforcement of employee policies are lawsuits waiting to happen. Although it is necessary to establish a good rapport with employees, do not let their standards fall below your own, putting your company at risk. Set clear policies on Internet use, discrimination, sexual harassment, employee safety, and drug use and enforce them. Your attorney can advise you on specific issues that your employee handbook must address.

Be sure that your employees understand that they are "at will" employees — you can terminate them at any moment without your business being held liable.

DEFINE PARTNERSHIP AGREEMENTS

Partners in a business must share the drive and will to succeed. Define in writing what is expected of each partner. The following points should be addressed in a partnership agreement:

- The amount of capital each partner is expected to contribute.

- A plan of action if the business needs more capital (Where is it going to come from? Are the partners expected to dig deeper into their own pockets?).

- A clear outline of each partner's responsibilities, workload, and time commitment to the business's operations.

- A plan of action in case a partner dies or decides to leave the business.

PROTECT YOURSELF

Consider the risk of your personal assets. In many states, general partnerships hold the partners jointly liable for outstanding debts, meaning all of your personal assets are at risk if the business encounters a problem. Starting as a corporation or other limited liability entity can help you avoid liability issues.

SECURE YOUR INTELLECTUAL PROPERTY

Intellectual property issues are as important in low-tech industries as they are in the world of software and computers.

Employees should always be required to sign confidentiality agreements. All company logos and trademarks should be registered, vital documents should be copyrighted, and, if applicable, products patented.

Protecting trade secrets is also important. The future of your business relies on it. Place copyright notices on all documentation and have potential investors sign nondisclosure agreements when meeting with you.

RESOLVE CONFLICTS WISELY

In the event of a legal dispute, leave litigation as the last resort. First, attempt to resolve conflicts through mediation, arbitration, and settlement. Although settling may seem like giving up, it is often more cost effective and less time consuming than litigation. Because time and money are at the heart of any business, it is important not to be stubborn; standing on principle could hurt the business.

CAPITAL BUDGETING

Raising capital arbitrarily is no way to run a business. Before looking for capital, determine how much working and investment capital you actually need. The process of identifying and prioritizing the capital investments that increase the value of your business is known as capital budgeting. This process depends on restrictions and priorities.

RESTRICTIONS

Choices are restricted because you can only raise so much capital and still service your debts and deliver investor returns. Figure out exactly the money coming in and going out and if any can be set aside for investments.

PRIORITIES

Ranking your projects according to which adds the most value to your business can help evaluate where the money is going. Those projects that add the most value get more investment money.

Maintaining steady cash flow and investments in expansion to add sales to that cash flow is the heart of capital budgeting. Instead of paying off debt, the debt is paid down slowly in order to keep funds for expansion projects available.

Paying off debt over time will cost more, but only in terms of the debt itself. If the business uses its cash flow to expand and sales increase, the amount of capital that is generated from that might outweigh the fact that servicing the debt requires monthly interest payments.

There are three primary methods for ranking projects and their value to the company:

- **The Payback Method** — A simple method that ignores future possible cash outflows and does not use discounted cash flow (DCF) analysis. This method rates projects on how quickly they will be able to pay for themselves.

- **The IRR Method** — Projects are ranked through this method by the investor's rate of return (IRR). This method takes into account cash flow structures by measuring the hurdle rate or the opportunity cost of investment capital, which is manifest as the appropriate interest rate or rate of return.

- **The Net Present Value Method** — Net present value (NPV) uses DCF analysis to rank projects by their current worth to the company from an opportunity standpoint. The IRR and NPV methods are used far more than the payback method because most businesses think in terms of cash flow. Without adequate cash flow, the owner knows the company is vulnerable to all sorts of unpleasant situations, including the inability to pay suppliers or falling behind in the industry due to lack of expansion.

THE MONEY IS OUT THERE

Lending money to businesses is the foundation of the banking industry. Venture capitalists do nothing but invest in people and ideas. At every level, our economy depends upon borrowing and investing. Even in a down economy, there is money available to start a new venture or to grow a healthy business. If your idea has merit and you can establish a plan, you may have better luck during slow investment periods. During economic booms, investors are bombarded with business opportunities. When few dollars are available to invest, the marginal proposals are quickly dismissed.

SIX WAYS TO FINANCE A BUSINESS

- **Give it** — The primary source for business financing is ownership contribution.

- **Borrow it** — Commercial, government, or private loans range from small business seed money to multimillion dollar open lines of credit.

- **Sell it** — Selling a part of your company to investors can provide needed capital, but sharing ownership has its drawbacks.

- **Earn it** — Saving requires long-range planning and wise money management, but it is the most economical way to finance growth.

- **Pledge it** — Private or public business development grants are available based upon your ability and willingness to "give back" to the community.

- **Share it** — Find an upline sponsor (coach), employer, business, or individual who will subsidize your idea with the goal of enhancing their financial picture.

Money comes from four types of potential "investors," each with her own motivations:

- **Owners** — You and your partners are motivated by dreams, desires, and needs. These can often cloud your decision-making abilities.

- **Private parties** — Family and friends may be motivated primarily by friendship (profits are an added bonus), but it is serious when you enter into a business relationship.

- **Commercial profit-making entities** — Banks, venture capitalists, and angel investors are seeking profits (interest, ownership) and personal gain (bonuses, recognition, achievement).

- **Nonprofit entities** — Government agencies and charitable foundations have missions to enhance lives and communities through economic growth and development. They are motivated to "do good," but that does not mean they overlook good business practices.

BEFORE YOU SEARCH

You must know what you need the money for, how much you need, what you can afford to "pay" for the money, and what you are willing to sacrifice for it. Chapter 8, "Debt Financing Versus Equity Financing," in *How to Get the Financing for Your New Small Business* from Atlantic Publishing, **www.atlantic-pub.com**, will help you make these determinations.

EXPLORING THE OPTIONS

Examining your business and discovering your entrepreneurial style are the first steps in finding the funding that matches your company's needs. When the need for money arises, entrepreneurs can become consumed by raising capital. Their judgment becomes clouded and their decision-making ability compromised. The cliché "the end justifies the means" is not always true. Your first step in exploring your financing options is to determine what you are willing to sacrifice.

WHAT WILL YOU DO TO FINANCE YOUR DREAM?

Here are a few exploratory questions to help determine your comfort level with various methods of acquiring startup or expansion financing.

- Am I willing to make personal sacrifices? No new car, renting a less expensive apartment, eliminating your daily latte?

- Can I emotionally handle the risk and debt incurred starting a business?

- Do I have a strong vision and can I see myself as successful?

- Am I willing to share the profits with a silent partner?

- Will I resent paying a partner who does not work as hard as I do?

- Is my idea (and future success) more important than my need to control the business?

- Will I be able to tolerate "interfering" investors?

- Am I open to unsolicited advice from investors?

- Is my idea strong enough to support partners?

- Can I afford the interest rate?

- What are the risks in paying "too much" for a loan?

- Will I have the ability to repay the debt on time?

- Am I ignoring warning signals (about people, situations, and risk)?

- Should I stop and regroup before proceeding?

- Is my business plan ready to go?

AVAILABLE FINANCING SOURCES

The overview below outlines the types of financing available to businesses. Making the decision to start or expand a small business opens up a variety of considerations and options. Many burgeoning companies spend far too much time chasing down funds from sources that do not mesh with their business. Making the right deal with the right investors or lenders provides you with the opportunity to grow in a manageable and hospitable environment. Making the wrong deal with the wrong investors can cause serious problems down the road, setting you up for conflicts and even potential failure.

GIVE IT — YOUR PERSONAL INVESTMENT

Investors and lenders will expect you to provide a significant amount of the capital necessary to launch or expand your business. When an entrepreneur puts assets on the line, it sends the message that he is committed to making the company a success, making it easier to acquire supplemental funding from outside sources. (There are a few exceptions, such as seed money programs created to assist economically disadvantaged at-risk individuals.)

INVESTING YOUR MONEY

Nearly 80 percent of entrepreneurs rely on personal savings to begin a new enterprise. Using personal savings secures the entrepreneur's control and ownership of the business. Because it is your money, no debt is incurred and future profits are not shared with investors.

Converting personal assets to business use is the same as giving your business cash. Not only will you avoid purchasing these items, but you will also be able to depreciate them. Your accountant will set up the conversion and depreciation schedules. For many people, their greatest personal asset is their home.

Lines of credit, refinancing, and home equity loans are often used. Raising cash this way can be risky. Personal credit cards, signature loans, and loans against insurance policies and retirement accounts are other common ways of raising start-up capital.

HOME EQUITY LOANS

You will need to know the equity you have in your home. For less than $500, an appraiser or real estate agent can locate home sale comparisons for you to use as an estimate.

If you own your home outright, you can refinance without staking all of the equity you have in your home, leaving room for future refinancing should something go wrong. If you own 20 percent or less in equity, by no means should you ever consider borrowing against that. The funds you gain will be minimal and the second lender will not hesitate to foreclose should trouble arise. The best way to determine feasibility is by following these steps:

1. Get your home appraised; if the value has gone up, you may own more equity than you think.

2. Figure out exactly how much you still owe on your mortgage.

3. Take the appraisal valuation and subtract your debt to determine the amount of equity.

4. Figure out your percentage by dividing your equity amount by the valuation amount. If it is less than 50 percent, you should find a different source of capital for your business.

5. If your equity is more than 50 percent, you may be in business. Now is the time to get loan quotes.

6. Figure out how your business plan will be affected by this cash infusion and make projections for how long it will take for the loan to be paid off.

Pay down the principal balance of the debt in order to get out of debt faster and regain the equity on your home.

LEVERAGING YOUR CREDIT

Leveraging your personal credit worthiness is another way to support your business. A new business has no established credit. Your signed personal guarantee will help establish credit for your business. Ask your attorney about personal liability issues for all business debts. Protecting your personal credit and financial health is a key reason to incorporate.

BORROW IT — LOANS TO REPAY

Borrowing can save your business or act as a noose around your company's neck. When looking at various types of loans, consider such issues as collateral required, interest rates, and repayment terms.

LOANS FROM FAMILY AND FRIENDS

Asking for help from those closest to you can be another smart move when looking for capital. Since you already have a relationship with friends and family, there are no questions of trust and a willingness to help already exists.

Interest-free or low-interest loans from relatives or friends can help a start-up business gain important supplemental capital without having to take out a bank loan or give up control and profits to investors. You may even have an angel investor in the family.

LOANS FROM COMMERCIAL LENDERS

A bank loan is the typical source of outside funding for businesses. In fact, Small Business Administration (SBA) and state government loans are actually bank loans in which the government agency provides financial support and underwriting.

Having a sound business proposal is the key element to obtaining a loan from a bank, credit union, or commercial lender. The lender will factor in personal credit history, outstanding debt, and past business performance when reviewing a loan application for a new business.

LINES OF CREDIT

A tempting source of short-term small borrowing for small businesses are micro loans. These alternative loans are often safer with lower interest rates. They can help fill the gap between expenditures incurred while manufacturing and delivering and the time it takes customers to pay in full. Lines of credit are useful for making sure payroll is met.

SELL IT — SHARED OWNERSHIP

Investors are a type of owner, which means you must be willing to "sell" a portion of your business and future profits. Some investors are active participants in daily operations, while others offer guidance and support through board meetings. Still others prefer to let you do it all while they reap the rewards.

FRIENDS

Friends can also be a great source of investment money. Unless your friend is a professional investor, you will be able to negotiate a fair and less costly investment agreement. The trust factor works here as it does when borrowing money from family. When considering these investors, ask yourself five questions:

1. Will this person panic about money after investing?

2. Does this person understand the risks and benefits?

3. Will this person want to take control or become a nuisance?

4. Would a failure ruin your relationship?

5. Does this person bring something to the table, besides cash, that can benefit my company and me?

ANGEL INVESTORS

Angel investors are wealthy individuals, or small groups, who help launch small businesses by providing capital. These investors, who expect returns in seven years or so, look for businesses they believe are going to fill a gap in the current market.

Angel investors tend to be successful entrepreneurs who want to stimulate unique business concepts and product ideas. They often specialize in investing in specific industries, so finding the right angel for your business is important.

These investors are experienced businesspeople who will notice if your business plan is filled with unrealistic projections and expectations.

Angel investors think long term and are willing to take risks beyond those of a traditional lender. Typically, they receive an equity share or partial ownership of the company in exchange for their funding.

Venture Capital Firms

Like angels, these investor firms help small businesses expand by exchanging capital for equity or partial ownership. The difference between an angel investor and a venture capitalist is the source of the money — angels invest their own money while venture capitalists invest other people's money.

Venture capitalists follow more stringent investment guidelines and are not as "emotionally" involved in your success.

They want to invest significant funds (rarely less than $5 million) in high-growth industries. They look to cash out in three to five years.

Venture capitalists play an active role in your company management, such as a board position. Expect these investors to have their own agenda that may not complement your business vision and direction.

EARN IT — CREATIVE WAYS TO RAISE CASH

Some entrepreneurs have discovered nontraditional ways to launch or expand a business. Networking with other entrepreneurs and local established businesses is an excellent way to find creative solutions to financing your company. Here are some creative ways other entrepreneurs have used to earn cash and discounts.

Saving

Trimming costs, taking advantage of banking discounts and rebates, and starting a business savings plan should have first priority. Make regular deposits to start your future.

Bartering

The world's oldest economic system is a great way to pay for products and services your company needs. The Web has made connecting with other interested parties easy and has introduced bartering programs in which a series of barters can be put into play to earn bartering points.

Buying Groups

These groups maximize vendor/supplier discounts and reduce costs for entrepreneurs needing everything from office supplies to raw materials. Some are free; others have a membership fee.

Rebate Programs, Co-op and Marketing Funds, Support Freebies

These vendor-sponsored programs can be used to reduce your inventory costs, pay for advertising expenses, train employees, improve productivity, and decrease turnaround times.

Competitive Awards

There are local, state, and national "contests" where companies compete for financial and support awards based on inventions, technological advances, excellent customer service, and hiring practices.

EMPLOYEE OWNERSHIP PROGRAMS

Earn the money you need to launch a franchise. Domino's Pizza rose to the second largest pizza chain by assisting employees in owning their own franchise store.

PLEDGE IT — GOOD FOR YOU AND YOUR COMMUNITY

There are private organizations and public agencies that help businesses in exchange for their "giving back" to the community. Their helping hand can come in the form of one of the following:

- Direct grants that require no financial repayment.

- Grants that are repaid from future revenues; zero repayment should your business fail.

- Economic development programs that are designed to maximize your business's financial impact on the community.

- Location grants that offer a financial incentive to locate or move your business to provide economic stimulus to a community, city, or state.

- "Soft" loans that offer less stringent qualifications and "softer" terms and conditions. These can be no-interest or low-interest loans.

- Tax cuts, deferrals, and deductions that lower your business, personal, or property taxes.

- Subsidies that pay for a portion of the cost of approved products or services. Your repayment is made by actively promoting your use of these goods/services.

- Technology grants and support that transfers technology rights and sharing information that may be worth millions to a fledgling company.

- Support in the form of free advice and access to resources that saves you consulting fees and improves your chances for success.

Your repayment could come in the form of being located in an economically depressed area, hiring special needs or high-risk employees, volunteering within your community, or mentoring others. The financial benefits for your company and your community can be substantial. In addition, being a good citizen never hurts your company's brand and community image.

SHARE IT — WIN-WIN SITUATIONS

Beyond every successful business is an assortment of people and companies that financially share your success. It is a simple concept — if you sell more hot dogs at your corner stand, the bakery that supplies the buns sells more too. Who in your personal or business life could benefit from your entrepreneurial success? Who might subsidize your idea in exchange?

FACTORING ACCOUNTS RECEIVABLE

Factoring companies exist to buy a small business's accounts receivable, immediately releasing anywhere from 50 to 80 percent of the value of those receivables directly to the business. The remaining balance is relinquished once the receivables are collected, with the factor's help, and the factor takes 1 to 5 percent off the top. Factoring is an expensive way to obtain cash, but can work effectively for businesses that do not qualify for any other forms of financing. Beware of missed repayment deadlines and escalating fees; they can keep you stuck in the factoring cycle for daily working capital.

OTHER FINANCING OPTIONS

There are still many different financing options that may be right for your business. Creatively raising capital is what running a business is all about. Very few businesses receive their capital from a single source and those that do usually are not around for long.

The best approach to raising capital is a diverse set of funding sources, each tailored to a specific need of the business. Each type of funding has different benefits and drawbacks, as well as different turnaround times and amounts of paperwork. Here are some alternatives to traditional sources of funding:

- Customer financing
- Credit card financing
- Leasing versus buying

- Purchase order financing
- Strategic alliances/mergers
- Employee stock ownership plans (ESOPs)

Weigh the positives and negatives before determining what alternative funding sources are right for your company. Taking the first source of capital that presents itself can be damaging to your company in the long run.

These funding sources are usually considered supplemental to traditional sources of financing. They are business practices that should be considered to keep your business in good financial shape. Having multiple sources of funding is the best way to finance a venture.

CUSTOMER FINANCING

Businesses recognize that they need one another to survive and this recognition often leads to alliances and teamwork. When one business can help another, and in doing so, help itself, it makes sense to form a good relationship.

Perhaps your company needs a new piece of equipment that will help you serve the needs of your largest customer. Ask that customer for the money to buy the equipment and, in return, fill their orders for free, paying them with credit instead of cash.

This arrangement worked well for American Design, a Seattle ad-specialty manufacturer. They received $30,000 from one of their largest customers to buy a new embroidery machine to be paid back with credit. According to the founder, the deal was fast and easy.

One thing to watch for, though, are the demands the lending company will place on your business. You must specify that they can only have so much product a month or they might order more than you can produce, without infusing any cash into the business.

A standard customer financing agreement has a minimum payback period of six months, depending on the size of the loan. Make sure you specify a minimum payback period that your business can handle.

PURCHASE ORDER FINANCING

Some small banks will extend lines of credit to local companies with whom they have good relationships, based on that company's contracts or purchase orders. This type of financing is primarily used for solving issues of cash flow. Purchase order financing can help float a business through a busy season, enabling the business to maintain its inventory to generate higher sales.

Purchase order financing allows the company to take on larger orders. The money that ordinarily comes in after the fact is borrowed from a lender and used to help finance the order itself. This financing can help a business grow quickly, providing it stays current with its accounts receivables.

The financing rates on this type of credit line are often high, so entrepreneurs should exercise caution when entering into such an arrangement. When Chelsea Marketing and Sales began purchase order financing in 1991, they eventually had to take out a second line of credit in order to pay for the first. They did manage to retain all of their equity. It was difficult and complicated, but it worked and the company grew to more than $13 million in sales in a short period of time.

CREDIT CARD FINANCING

When used carefully, credit cards can supply supplemental or emergency cash flow. The "buy now, pay later" philosophy is one that can work well for businesses that may not have the capital needed to pay bills but expect to soon.

Many businesses will try to finance their entire operation using personal and business credit cards. It is not recommended. The interest rates are high, and once you have reached your limit and you no longer have adequate cash flow, you could be out of business. Using a personal credit card to fund a business is in direct violation of the consumer-cardholder agreement. Although it is a breach of contract, thousands of companies do it.

Get a business credit card account. Once your business has established itself, you will notice that credit card offers are coming in by the score. Banks that would never give a small business a loan for $100,000 will extend a $100,000 credit line to the same small business. The interest rates are much higher, anywhere from 11 to 25 percent. The rates are rarely fixed and, if you fall behind on payments, they rise immediately.

Still, these interest costs are often lower than the bank's loan fees, driving many businesses to use credit cards in lieu of bank loans. This extends the time it takes to pay off the credit card and saves money by swapping balances with another card with a better interest rate.

Credit cards should be used primarily for fast capital that will be repaid in a short amount of time. The longer it takes you to pay off the existing balance, the more the money you borrowed costs you.

Brents Sportswear, while attempting an expansion overseas in the fall of 1996, saw cash flow begin to steadily diminish. The founders, thinking cash-flow loss was temporary, used cash advances of \$150,000 on their credit cards to make payroll. The company did not recover, as the owners had hoped. They were unable to pay even the minimum on the balance. The founders' credit was not completely ruined. Soon after filing for bankruptcy, they were receiving pre-approved credit card offers, claiming that they could help rebuild their now-ailing credit.

On the other side of the coin is a West Coast manufacturer who has figured out how to use credit cards in an effective way. The founder got his suppliers to agree to charge his purchases the day after his card statement closed. Although typical billing cycles are 30 days, this founder was able to extend this period considerably by asking a small favor of his supplier. Because he spends nearly \$1 million on that card every year, his Frequent Flier miles pay for all of his business travel.

Credit cards can work both ways for companies. When handled correctly, they can supply a great deal of emergency and short-term funding, sometimes less expensively and more easily than other sources of capital. Using them incorrectly not only can cause the business to suffer, but the founder's personal credit history also may be irreparably damaged.

To sum up, the good points of credit cards include:

- They are easy to obtain.
- Lines of credit can be as high as \$100,000.
- They are accepted almost everywhere.
- The money is immediately available for emergencies.
- Incentive programs, such as Frequent Flier miles, can save money on other expenses.
- There is little paperwork and no extensive forms to complete.

The bad points include:

- The interest rates can be as high as 25 percent.
- Interest rates are not locked and will rise considerably if you fail to make minimum monthly payments.
- Many cards have hidden fees, making them more expensive.
- Mismanagement of cards can ruin your personal credit.
- Having to make monthly payments on cards combined with other loans can cause huge cash flow problems for your business, forcing it into a cycle of debt.

MERGERS/STRATEGIC ALLIANCES

Merging with a larger company can be wise if the business considering the merger feels choked by competition or wishes to shift gears and gain capital for a new venture. Many mergers often lead to the founders of the small business either being bought out or being reduced to a minor decision-making role.

Mergers with similar-sized businesses may be a better decision. Combining resources and brain power along with complementary products, skills, and specialties to create a new partnership can be a solution for smaller businesses and increase their competitive advantage against major industry players.

A business in need of capital can ally with a larger business, supplier, or customer that has an interest in its technologies. Often some kind of value is exchanged. The larger company may demand exclusive rights to proprietary products, equipment, or ideas; a long-term purchasing agreement or set pricing from a supplier; specific distribution rights of products in certain locations; or special discount programs.

A strategic alliance can be a win-win situation. There are such risks as being bought out by a larger company, restricting future growth, damaging other business relationships, or potentially violating laws regarding free trade, price setting, or fair competition.

EMPLOYEE STOCK OWNERSHIP PLANS

For mature businesses that have confidence in their cash flow and earnings potential, Employee Stock Ownership Plans (ESOPs) are a great way to provide internal funding. Employees become investors in the company, which improves morale and drive to succeed.

Once the ESOP is established, it borrows money from a bank or other financial institution in order to buy stock from the company. The stock is purchased from the treasury or the owners and is used as collateral for the bank loan.

The business then uses the money from the sale of the stock for whatever purposes it needs. In exchange, it services the bank loan through tax-deductible contributions to the ESOP.

The lender makes out well too, as half of the interest on the loan is tax deductible. The ESOP is very attractive to many businesses, because it can be a win-win-win situation: the lender gets a tax break, the company gets funding, and the employees get to invest.

 LEASING VERSUS BUYING

Leasing can work far better than buying with borrowed money for many small businesses. A major advantage to leasing equipment is that leasing allows you to have up-to-date equipment, avoiding costly replacement as items grow obsolete. Also, leasing is usually less expensive than servicing a bank loan, allowing young businesses to conserve capital.

Businesses spend hundreds of billions of dollars a year leasing equipment. More than 80 percent of all businesses lease at least some portion of the equipment or property that they use.

A lease takes the form of a contract. Your business (the lessee) makes payments of a specific amount to the lessor over the course of the lease. How much is paid and how often are determined by the value of the equipment and its accompanying service agreement.

The two major areas of leasing for businesses are:

1. **Equipment leasing** in which businesses can lease everything from furniture to manufacturing equipment to fleets of vehicles.

2. **Real estate leasing** provides storage space, offices, retail space, parking, and warehouses. Also popular is the "sale and lease-back" method of real estate leasing, in which a company sells space to someone in order to gain capital and then leases it back from them.

DIFFERENCES IN LEASE TYPES

There are two primary lease types: the operating lease and the capital lease.

THE OPERATING LEASE

Operating leases require smaller monthly payments than standard bank loans. At the end of the lease term, the equipment or property is not fully paid for, leaving what is known as "residual value."

Once the lease term is complete, the lessee has the option of purchasing the equipment at the residual value, walking away, or renewing the lease based on the residual value. This purchase option is standard on an operating lease.

The lessor is responsible for all of the maintenance and service on the equipment. These service costs are factored into the monthly payments on the lease. Most operating leases come with this kind of service contract. The lessee reserves the right to terminate the lease at any time, even before the end of the lease term.

THE CAPITAL LEASE

The payments on a capital lease are larger than those on an operating lease because the equipment is paid off in full by the end of the lease term. The lessee does not receive any tax benefits, such as depreciation, associated with owning the equipment. Capital lease payments are comparable to those of a standard term loan. This type of lease is far less common for businesses that wish to conserve cash by leasing instead of buying.

DECIDING WHETHER TO LEASE OR BUY

Although leasing does have its advantages, so does outright ownership. Whichever is going to be less expensive in the long run should not be the only factor in making the decision. Here are some additional items to consider:

LEASING VS. BUYING	
Leasing	**Buying**
• Smaller periodic payments	• Ownership
• Service contract	• Resale value
• Noncommittal	• Tax savings on depreciation and interest
• Smaller down payment	• Usually less expensive in the long run
• Option to buy	• No restrictions on use of equipment
• Protects from owning obsolete equipment	• No penalties for termination of lease or
• Increases company flexibility	misuse of equipment
• Helps cash flow	
• More equipment can be obtained at once	
• Preserves capital	
• Improves credit	
• Counts as an expense, not as a debt, so leverage stays low	

Consider your company's leverage and how much debt it has assumed. Leasing helps keep leverage low by preventing you from having to borrow to purchase equipment.

If you want your business to grow quickly, leasing will provide the opportunity to have more equipment available, which means the capacity to fill more orders, including large orders that other firms in your industry might not be able to handle.

One reason to lease instead of buy is to ensure your business is using up-to-date equipment. Technology is advancing at an unprecedented rate and purchasing computers can be a big mistake, as they may be obsolete before you finish paying for them.

INVESTING IN YOUR DREAM

Whether you want to start a home-based business or build a 100-employee manufacturing plant, you will be your company's initial investor. In launching a new business, your personal financial history plays a critical role in obtaining credit, avoiding deposit fees, and outfitting your company. Although business experts advise against signing personal guarantees, it may be the only option until your business is credit-worthy.

All entrepreneurs dream of easy, low-interest loans, plentiful investors, and parents who ask, "How much do you need?" The truth is most small business start-ups are self-financed. Ninety-five percent of small business financing comes from personal resources, which means you need to look for every dime you can muster. The first place to start is with your credit.

YOUR PERSONAL FINANCIAL HEALTH

Often after losing one's job, returning to the workforce from an extended absence, or tiring of being underemployed, an employee begins to consider starting his own business. Each of these situations may have created financial issues that need to be repaired. Improving your personal credit score will help you leverage your creditworthiness and underwrite your business venture.

The first step is to obtain a copy of your credit history and Fair Isaac Corporation (FICO) score from the three largest credit reporting agencies — Experian, TransUnion, and Equifax. The federal Fair Credit Reporting Act (FCRA) requires these agencies to provide you with a free report every 12 months. For complete information, visit **www.ftc.gov/bcp/conline/pubs/credit/freereports.htm.**

FICO is a scoring system in which your debt-to-income ratio, total indebtedness, and other credit factors are reduced to a numerical credit score. The higher the score, the better your credit rating and the more likely you will be to repay a loan. A strong FICO score means less potential risk for the lender and lower interest rates for you. To learn what your score means, visit FICO at **www.MyFICO.com**. Check the reports for accuracy. Credit issuers use the FICO score to assess your credit worthiness and income-to-debt ratio.

FIX IT

Upon reviewing your credit reports (be certain to obtain a detailed report, not just a FICO credit score), look for discrepancies and errors. Errors, which can range from a simple clerical error to a serious case of identity theft, are common. It is up to the individual to dispute them. Each credit bureau has its own procedure for disputing financial activity; you may have to file multiple disputes for the same creditor error.

If you received your credit report through the mail, information will be provided on how to request an investigation of a disputed listing. Investigations can also be filed online. Check the credit bureau's Web site for complete instructions.

You will have to write a letter (or complete an online form) explaining why you believe a listing to be incorrect. If you have paperwork supporting your claim, send a copy along with your letter. Your letter should be sent via certified mail with a return receipt requested to prove mailing and receipt. Online claims typically are assigned an identifying number.

You may also want to contact the creditor in writing, requesting a resolution to the error before filing a credit bureau investigation claim. If you do not receive a resolution within 30 days, start the credit bureau investigation procedure. Sometimes getting even obvious mistakes corrected can be difficult. Be diligent and clearly document your case.

CLEAN IT UP YOURSELF

There are legitimate nonprofit credit counseling services available. Contact them as a last resort. Their methods can get the bill collectors off your back and repay everyone, but using a credit counselor can negatively affect your credit score. If you determine you need credit counseling, contact the National Foundation for Credit Counseling, **www.nfcc.org**, for a legitimate referral. Do not pay anyone who promises to clean up your credit. The process is a do-it-yourself job.

IMPROVE YOUR CREDIT SCORE

Even if your credit score is low because of valid credit problems, making some changes can boost your score. There is no fast way to improve your credit.

- **Contact your creditors about removing poor notations.** If you have cleaned up your act, some creditors may be willing to remove older unfavorable entries. Keep your tone friendly and firm. If you are unsuccessful with the customer service person, ask to speak with a supervisor. Keep a log of your conversations. It takes time for changes to appear on your credit report, so it may benefit you to ask for a letter of confirmation.

- **Look for errors** such as business obligations (which were not personally secured) mixed in with your personal data. Also watch for accounts that are not yours.

- **Do not close accounts in an effort to raise your credit score;** doing so has the opposite effect.

- **If you do cancel accounts, keep the oldest one open to give you a longer history.**

- **If you have credit cards close to being "maxed out," transfer balances to reduce the percentage of used versus available credit.** The amount of "available" credit on a card is a plus for you.

- **Try "rapid rescoring."** In this process, legitimate corrections and credit card payoffs are updated quickly with the credit bureau for a fee. You cannot do this process by yourself; you will need to find a lender who is a customer of a rapid rescoring service to handle this process on your behalf. The fee can run as much as $75 for every account that needs to be adjusted; however, these adjustments can make the difference in obtaining a lower interest rate.

CREATE AN ASSET LIST

Anything of value that can be converted to cash is an asset. If you earnestly want to raise money to start a business, look at every potential source for cash. Converting assets to cash means selling them for the best price you can get. Thanks to the Web and such sites as eBay, Yahoo auctions, and Half.com, selling personal possessions has never been easier.

Start compiling your personal asset list, but remember that cashing in insurance policies, bonds, and other investments is risky.

ASSET LIST		
Asset Category	**Items with Potential Value**	**Converting to Cash**
Cash	Savings and checking	Not required
College funds	College savings	Beware; raiding college funds can be too "easy" and are difficult to replace
Investments	Stocks, bonds, mutual funds, etc.	
Retirement	401k, pension plans, Roth IRA, IRA	Beware; may trigger federal and state tax penalties and income taxes
Insurance	Life insurance	
Home(s)	Home, rental property, vacation homes	
Vehicles	Recreation vehicles/property	
Antiques and collectibles	Artwork, coins, stamps, sports memorabilia, books	eBay, consignment shops
Personal possessions	Household goods, clothing, electronics, etc.	Garage sale, consignment shops, classified ads, eBay

OTHER ASSETS

Other Ways to Raise (or Save) Cash

- Collect on outstanding debts owed to you.

- Ask for deposit refunds from utilities.

- Take advantage of all early-pay or cash discounts.

- Whenever possible, avoid delivery or shipping charges.

- Join a co-op or buying group.

- Open wholesale accounts and ask for commercial discounts.

- Negotiate long-term customer discounts based upon future purchases.

For some home businesses, a successful garage sale may be enough to pay for the necessary business licenses, equipment, and business cards to get you started.

BARTERING

Although bartering is still a taxable activity based on value exchanges, it can be an excellent way to obtain what you need now, allowing you to deal with tax implications later. Your accountant can advise you on how bartered transactions are taxed.

Bartering can be done on an informal basis directly between you and local suppliers or through a barter exchange. Barter exchanges have an advantage in that you can earn "points" that can be spent with other exchange members.

Say you sell computer printers and need some photography for a brochure. Through the exchange you find someone who needs a printer. The exchange is made and you receive 1,000 barter points that you spend with a local commercial photographer. The commercial photographer uses the 1,000 barter points you "paid" him to obtain the business cards he needs and has points left for another need.

When bartering, be specific about what you have to offer and what you seek. Agree on the value of each item traded. When exploring bartering, be aware that "over-bartering" can adversely affect your cash flow.

NEITHER A LENDER OR A BUYER BE

These wise words from William Shakespeare offer sound fiscal advice, but the bard was actually referring to the personal problems borrowing can create: "For loan oft loses both itself and friend."

To make your entrepreneurial dreams come true, you may have to visit the Bank of Mom and Dad. Universally, more than half of all start-up capital comes from family and friends. In fact, experts believe family or friend loans and investments easily exceed all monies invested by venture capitalists.

Family or friend financing can be through a loan, a gift, or an investment. The following will explore each and help you avoid potential pitfalls.

SHOULD YOU ASK?

The following are some things you should think about before you ask your family or a friend to help finance your business venture.

- **Is there money available?** Not all families are open and honest about their financial status, so money may not be available for lending.

- **Do you feel "entitled?"** Money can cloud your judgment, trigger "entitlement" issues, and create animosity, particularly among siblings.

- **Can they afford to "lose" the money?** Should your business fail, will they be at financial risk?

- **Will you treat them as a creditor?** When cash gets tight, will you let payments slide because they will "understand" better than the bank?

- **Could you lose a friend or alienate a relative?** If you are unable to repay the debt or if the investment does not yield what you promised, will it affect your relationship?

- **Is it a loan, a gift, or an inheritance "payout?"** Be clear and formalize the transaction. A written "statement of gift" or contract will clarify the transaction. If it is a loan, you want to be able to deduct the interest. If it is a gift, you will need to meet IRS regulations to avoid additional taxes.

- **Can you protect their investment?** Unless your relative is a professional investor or banker, he or she probably is not appropriately cautious about assessing the risk. Likewise, accepting money from people you care about increases your responsibility to accept and spend it wisely.

KNOW HOW MUCH YOU NEED

When seeking financial support, determine how much you need, when you need it, and when you can repay it. Inadequate financing and poor cash flow increases your family's or friend's financial risk. As you review your plan and assess your potential for success, factor in the personal costs of losing their investment or gift.

BORROWING FROM FAMILY OR FRIENDS

Borrowing from relatives or friends can be the easiest (and sometimes the only) way to accumulate enough seed money for your new business venture. Whether you need $1,000 or $100,000, it is in everyone's best interest to follow sound business practices when borrowing from acquaintances. It is tempting to be lax and forget to sign a contract or not set an appropriate repayment schedule. Borrowing money on a handshake can create problems for you later on. You should negotiate fair loan terms and sign a formal loan document.

DEDUCT THE INTEREST AS A BUSINESS EXPENSE

A contract or promissory note is your proof to the IRS that the loan is a legitimate business loan and not a personal loan where interest is not tax-deductible.

THE IRS

The IRS has regulations regarding gifts and loans. For this financial change to be considered a loan you will need to:

- Have an enforceable agreement such as a promissory note.

- Pay an appropriate interest rate. Low- or no-interest loans may be classified as gifts, thus triggering gift taxation rules.

- Have a reasonable repayment schedule. Loans with no repayment schedules also may be deemed as gifts.

- The lender must include interest paid as other income.

LOAN AGREEMENTS

Your loan agreement can be a verbal commitment; however, getting it in writing is a much smarter way to do business. If you are uncertain what necessary elements should be outlined in the note, seek legal advice.

PROMISSORY NOTES

A promissory note is a written promise to repay a set amount within a set period plus a specific amount of interest. It does not need to be notarized to be valid and can be completed by both parties. For smaller dollar amounts with simple terms, a do-it-yourself promissory note may be all you need. You and the lender will sign one original, which is kept by the lender. Once you repay the note, the original is returned to the borrower.

You can find fill-in-the-blank promissory notes at your local stationery or office supply store, as part of business form software packages, or free online at Internet Legal Research Group, **www.ilrg.com/forms/promisry.html.**

For larger sums and more complicated repayment terms and conditions, you should have an attorney prepare the note. It is also in your best interest to have an attorney review any loan agreement prepared by the other party.

Circle Lending, **www.circlelending.com**, is an online resource for financial transactions between family and friends. For a fee, this service will prepare and administer (accept payments) your promissory notes for a fee.

ASKING FOR A LOAN

Here are ten guidelines to help you obtain financial support from family and friends. Remember that this support is a business transaction based on your personal pledge of repayment; failing to honor your commitments can end friendships and divide families.

- **Start by explaining your idea using your "elevator pitch"** and ask if they might be interested in providing some financial support.

- **Make an appointment** for an appropriate time to talk and share your business plan.

- **Provide a copy of your complete business plan** to be read later.

- **Be prepared to discuss your commitment and intentions.** Assure them that you are entering this arrangement with a signed note and consider this a business deal.

- **Do not let your excitement improperly color your presentation.** It is easy to get overly excited and overstate the potential for success when you are talking to friends or family members. You want them to enter into this arrangement knowing all the facts.

- **Make a full disclosure.** When presenting yourself and your business plan to a professional lender or investor, you will do everything you can to present your case positively and honestly. It is wise when dealing with a friend or family member to be as open and honest as possible. You want the money, but you do not want them to make a poor financial decision.

- **Understand that borrowing from family and friends always comes with hidden strings.** Your personal connection opens the door to unsolicited advice, unspoken expectations, and disappointments. However, it can also be a wise investment with ample rewards for everyone.

- **Schedule a time to return to discuss your plan** along with repayment terms and potential investment earnings. Return with a promissory note outlining all details. Encourage them to have their attorney review the document before signing.

- **Do not make assumptions that a friend or relative will overlook a late payment** or that the loan will "disappear" should your business fail.

- **If this arrangement is an early payout of a trust or inheritance, see your attorney** and your accountant regarding tax and inheritance implications.

Thanks for the Gift

Depending upon your family circumstances, your proposal to borrow money for your business may be answered with, "How about if we give you the money?" Often parents and other relatives continue to feel a sense of responsibility for the well-being of their adult children; others simply enjoy sharing the wealth and helping you realize your dreams. Few gifts, however, are without strings.

Some strings may be hidden or implied ones that parents can attach. Will the money be spent wisely? Do you really need that much? How about we give you the money and you can hire your younger sister too? You know your family dynamics — what strings might make this gift unacceptable for you?

Keep in mind that there are federal tax laws regarding financial gifts and some states have gift taxes. Gift taxes occur when you transfer any property (including money) to another without expecting something of at least equal value in return. If your mother deeds you a piece of property to build your business, it is considered a gift.

The IRS works from the viewpoint that all gifts are taxable with exceptions, such as:

- The gift is less than the annual exclusion amount (in 2005, this is $11,000 per giver, so your mother and father together could give you $22,000 before it becomes taxable).

- The gift is from a spouse.

- The gift is to a qualified political or charitable organization.

- The gift pays for tuition or medical expenses.

For gifts worth more than the annual exclusion, refer to IRS Publication 950, Introduction to Estate and Gift Taxes. Your investment counselor, attorney, or CPA should be consulted regarding taxable gifts. These gifts are not tax-deductible for the giver.

MONEY FROM TRUSTS AND INHERITANCES

There are many different types of living trusts through which family assets are administered, each with its own set of stipulations. Before withdrawing funds from these, speak with your financial adviser as to potential penalties and tax obligations.

Usually an inheritance is willed after the death of a loved one. However, like living trusts, inheritance trusts are set up to administer assets that will be passed on at death. These assets are not passed on to individuals but to the trust. If the funds are coming from a family member's inheritance trust, the administering trustee will outline the proper procedure or changes required for an early distribution.

YOUR LOAN PROPOSAL

Loans are about trust and risk. Lenders want to trust that the loan will be repaid and to risk as little as possible. Your loan request should be a reasonable amount and you should document how the money will be spent and that you will meet the scheduled payments.

The loan proposal acts as your ambassador. Even if a lender believes in you, agrees your business is worth the risk, and is impressed by your business savvy, other decision-makers in the organization may not agree. Ultimately, it comes down to your loan proposal.

MORE THAN AN APPLICATION

You have probably obtained a mortgage, car loan, or credit card, so you are familiar with loan applications. Commercial lenders will have a standard loan application form that you will complete and SBA-backed loans usually have a complete application package. A few lines on a form cannot tell the story of why you should be granted the loan. Many lenders allow you to provide additional documentation that supports your ability to repay the debt, explains potential problems, and builds confidence in your business concept.

A good proposal will contain everything the lender needs to know in order to be convinced that you are a competent entrepreneur, that your business is capable of growth, and that you are not a high credit risk. Be complete, neat, and organized.

Many loan proposals are immediately rejected simply because they are messy. Most lenders refuse to sift through disorganized paperwork. It reflects poorly on your business and indicates a potential management problem.

ESSENTIAL COMPONENTS OF A LOAN PROPOSAL

Including a full business plan with your proposal is a good way for lenders to get to know your business. Of course, the plan should be modified to suit the needs of the lenders, as opposed to the needs of investors.

LOAN REQUEST SUMMARY

- No longer than two to four pages.

- The amount you hope to borrow.

- How the money will be used.

- Type of loan applied for (line of credit, term loan, etc.).

- Repayment schedule and source of repayment.

- Collateral offered.

- Financial performance summaries: past, present, and projected.

FINANCIAL STATEMENTS

The type of financial statements you must provide depends on the stage of growth in which your business is in.

FINANCIAL STATEMENTS BY BUSINESS TYPE		
Start-up Businesses	**Established Small Businesses**	**Larger Businesses**
1. Projected balance sheets and income statements for the next three years.	1. Historical balance sheets and income statements from the past three years.	1. Historical balance sheets and income statements from the past three to five years.
2. Owners' personal financial statements.	2. Projections for the next three years.	2. Projections for the next three to five years.
3. Social Security numbers for checking owners' credit reports.	3. CPA-audited financial statement or tax returns, depending on the lender's needs.	3. CPA-audited financial statement, assuring that your financial statements conform to GAAP (generally accepted accounting principles) standards.
4. Detailed information about the collateral pledged.	4. Owners' personal financial statements.	4. Owners' personal financial statements.

Make sure your projected balance sheets, income statements, and cash flow projections are achievable. The lender will often condition the loan based on calculations from your projections, so do not think you will not be held to them. Break down the projections for the first year by month. Projections for following years may be broken down quarterly.

Summarize key points for the lender on a separate summary page. Also include a page of explanations for anything in your financial statements that might be misinterpreted. This page will prevent the lender from making any false assumptions about the status of your business. Clarify — up front — anything you think might be misinterpreted.

You may also include the following:

- Collateral value summary.

- Appraisals of property.

- Inventory value summary.

- Accounts receivable and payable summaries will help the lender determine how long it takes customers to pay you and how long it takes you to pay suppliers.

Researching your lender's specific financing guidelines and providing the necessary information in an organized and efficient manner expedites the loan process.

YOUR FINANCIAL STATEMENTS

Keeping track of a business's accounts can be a complicated endeavor, which is why most businesses keep an accountant on staff or use an accounting firm. When doing business, every transaction needs to be documented, tracked, and organized, making it much easier to compile financial statements at the end of the month, quarter, or year.

The four most common types of financial statements and their components are income statement, statement of capital, balance sheet and cash flow statement. See the chart below for the components and applications of each type.

FINANCIAL STATEMENTS TYPES AND COMPONENTS		
Type	Components	Applications
The Income Statement	1. Categorized revenues from a single business period. 2. Categorized expenses from a single business period. 3. Difference from revenues and expenses indicating net income or net loss.	1. Represents bottom line. 2. Indicates where money is being spent. 3. Indicates where money is coming from.
Statement of Capital	1. Owner's capital account (how much of the business he owns). 2. Net income or net loss from a single business period (as derived from income statement). 3. Change in owner's capital account based on net income or net loss (any net income becomes the owner's).	1. Helps owner to decide whether to reinvest net income, keep some profit as personal income, or withdraw completely. 2. Indicates to owner whether or not his personal stake is at risk.
The Balance Sheet	1. Listing of all current assets (everything a business owns). 2. Listing of all current liabilities (everything a business owes to creditors). 3. Value of owner's capital account. 4. Company's financial condition (liabilities + owner's equity = assets).	1. Indicates a company's financial condition at a specific moment in time, as opposed to a full business period. 2. Helps owner get a clear picture of assets and liabilities.
Cash Flow Statement	1. Categorized list of all sources of income for business (sales of assets, revenues, financing, etc.). 2. Categorized list of ways income is used (purchases, debt repayment, operating losses, etc.).	1. Indicates whether business's cash flow is increasing or decreasing. 2. Helps owner monitor possible cash flow problems.

Financial statements are like a heart monitor for business. Without them, it would be impossible to recognize downward trends or to know when to enact countermeasures to reverse these trends. Work with an accountant to make sure you understand these documents. Otherwise, you may not notice the early warning signs of an impending disaster.

Having accurate financial documents also can help you gain financing, as these statements are often included in your business plan or loan proposal. Investors and bankers are going to feel more comfortable about investing in a business that keeps track of its money in an organized and communicable way.

After you have completed your business plan, you will know your current and future financial needs. Once you have determined how much money is needed at each stage, look for sources of financing.

No matter how much capital you need to launch a new business, your personal financial resources are the first place to look. Investors and lenders will not come on board unless you have made a significant financial commitment.

 OW TO WRITE A LOAN PROPOSAL

Approval of your loan request depends on how well you present yourself, your business, and your financial needs to a lender. Lenders want to make loans, but they must make loans they know will be repaid. The best way to improve your chances of obtaining a loan is to prepare a written proposal.

COMPONENTS OF A WELL-WRITTEN LOAN PROPOSAL

GENERAL INFORMATION

1. **Business name, names of principals, Social Security number for each principal, and the business address.**

2. **Purpose of the loan** — Exactly what the loan will be used for and why it is needed.

3. **Amount required** — The exact amount you need to achieve your purpose.

BUSINESS DESCRIPTION

1. **History and nature of the business,** including details of what kind of business it is, its age, number of employees, and current business assets.

2. **Ownership structure,** detailing the company's legal form.

MANAGEMENT PROFILE

1. **Develop a short statement on each principal in your business.** Provide background, education, experience, skills, and accomplishments.

MARKET INFORMATION

1. **Clearly define your company's products as well as your markets.**

2. **Identify your competition** and explain how your business competes in the marketplace.

3. **Profile your customers** and explain how your business can satisfy their needs.

FINANCIAL INFORMATION

1. **Financial statements** — Balance sheets and income statements for the past three years. If you are starting out, provide a projected balance sheet and income statement.

2. **Personal financial statements** on yourself and other principal owners of the business.

3. **Collateral you would be willing to pledge** as security for the loan.

HOW YOUR LOAN REQUEST WILL BE REVIEWED

When reviewing a loan request, the lender is primarily concerned about repayment. To help determine this ability, many loan officers will order a copy of your business credit report from a credit reporting agency. Work with these agencies to help them present an accurate picture of your business.

Using the credit report and the information you have provided, the lending officer will consider the following issues:

- Have you invested savings or personal equity in your business totaling at least 25 to 50 percent of the loan you are requesting? A lender or investor will not finance 100 percent of your business.

- Do you have a sound record of creditworthiness as indicated by your credit report, work history, and letters of recommendation?

- Do you have sufficient experience and training to operate a successful business?

- Have you prepared a loan proposal and business plan that demonstrate your understanding of and commitment to the success of the business?

- Does the business have sufficient cash flow to make the monthly payments?

There are many other ways to get financing for your business. For this information and much more, I recommend *How to Get the Financing for Your Small Business (Item # HGF-01)* from Atlantic Publishing, **www.atlantic-pub.com**. I covered some of the information from that book within this chapter, but there is much more to learn and the book contains extensive resource listings for financing options and procedures on how to acquire less conventional financing.

CHAPTER

How to Analyze and Invest In a Restaurant Franchise

If you are considering opening a franchise restaurant, this chapter will be invaluable in giving you details about the ins and outs of franchising. The information can help you make an informed decision about whether franchising is for you.

Choosing the Right Franchise

You are interested in buying a franchise, but how do you know which franchise is right for you? Which franchise will suit your individual knowledge, skills, goals, and preferred level of involvement? By choosing the right franchise, your chances of success increase substantially— most failed franchises result from a buyer not doing sufficient research to find the franchise that suits him best. This chapter will help you decide how to choose the perfect franchise and will tell you where to find the information essential to making your choice.

Franchises Are Not Independent Businesses

The first thing any franchisee must realize is that a franchise is not an independent business. Franchising is not for you if you are the type of person who needs exacting control over your business. Do not forget: When you purchase a franchise, you are simply providing the capital to enable another person's dream, idea, or product to enter the marketplace. Why? Because it has already proven its worth — it works.

Most independent businesses fail within three years of their launch. A large amount of capital, time, energy, and personal sacrifice is needed to make an independent business succeed.

If you have a big, new idea for a product or service that you are sure consumers cannot live without, perhaps establishing an independent business is the way to go.

There are many resources available to help you decide whether your business idea is worth pursuing.

- **Check out the Service Corps of Retired Executives (SCORE www.score.org).** The Corps partners with the U.S. Small Business Administration (SBA) **www.sbaonline. sba.gov** and offers the advice and counseling of retired business executives to those thinking about starting an independent business. SCORE can help with financial planning, creating and following a business plan, and other issues that are critical to starting a business.

- **The Small Business Development Center (SBDC) www.sbaonline.sba.gov/sbdc** is another organization affiliated with the SBA. The SBDC has 63 of its own centers across the nation, as well as more than 1,100 offices within local schools, colleges, and chambers of commerce. Your local SBDC can provide you with technical and management assistance for your independent business.

Before establishing an independent business, you should do extensive market research on your idea. Is it appealing to consumers? Will it have a market? Have SCORE and an SBDC review your findings and point out any weaknesses. Also, be sure that your idea is economically feasible. Will your costs (rent, inventory, taxes, fees, payroll, insurance, legal fees) be covered by your revenue? Is your product pricing fair? Do you have a supportive and reliable bank? Once again, use SCORE and an SBDC to be sure your financial calculations make sense.

BECOMING A FRANCHISEE

Establishing an independent business may seem like a lot of work. It does hold a great amount of risk. If you do not have a unique product in mind and you want to build upon the proven success, reputation, and customer base of an established product or service, then franchising is your answer. Unlike independent businesses, decisions are made for you by experienced industry professionals. Your name, trademark, and product line are known, trusted, and recognizable from day one.

Going this route, you still have a large decision to make — which franchise is right for you? Which franchise will keep you interested, will make proper use of your skills and knowledge, and will bring you profit in the end? You have a number of options as you begin to gather the information to choose the right franchise.

You may want to consider visiting a franchise broker. Brokers have low fees and can match you to a franchise based on your education, skills, and psychological attributes. Brokers match you based upon a small list of available franchises. Brokers are paid by franchisers to market their businesses. That means brokers will not suggest all possible options, but only those businesses with which they are in partnership. To find the perfect franchise, narrowing your options by visiting a broker is not your best bet.

I suggest gathering your own information to make the most informed choice. A number of resources exist that can help you remain organized during the information-gathering stage. Keep detailed records of names, databases, and Web sites. Be sure to record which information goes with which franchise or industry. Such detailed analyses will prove invaluable when the time comes to make your final selection.

Begin your information gathering by making a list of questions. Write these questions down and do not stop gathering information until you have a satisfactory answer to every one. Try to find the overlap in your questions and answers. How do the questions and answers interact? Such observations can provide you with even deeper insight.

What kinds of questions should you be asking? Consider your personal needs or expectations, company and product longevity, competition, and modernization. Research the company's past financial records and its relationship with other companies. Research where the market and technology are heading and assess the company's products and services in that light. Has the company stayed up to date with current trends? Are there any upcoming introductions of new products or services that might threaten the company's own products and services? How would the company respond? Is the company expanding? Is it focused? What kinds of services and support does it offer its franchisees? Is the labor attractive? Would you be able to offer competitive pay rates?

The answers to your questions can be found on the Internet, in franchise and business directories, in books and magazines, and at trade shows.

INTERNET

As with all Internet research, be careful of your sources. You should check the individual Web sites of the companies you are considering taking a franchise with.

DIRECTORIES

A number of franchise directories are available to assist you. Directories are the best place to begin the information gathering process.

- **Franchise Opportunities Guide www.franchise.org.** Published bi-yearly by the International Franchise Association (IFA), this guide contains essential information such as the names and contact information of franchisers, suppliers, and legal consultants specializing in the franchise industry. It also includes franchise statistics and articles of interest to the franchisee. You can order the guide through the IFA at 800-543-1038 or on the IFA Web site for $17.

- **Franchise Update Publications www.franchise-update.com.** This organization publishes a number of guides, including Executive's Guide to Franchise Opportunities, Food Service Guide to Franchise Opportunities, Guide to Multiple-Unit Franchise Opportunities, and Franchise Update Magazine. These are essential publications. For information about ordering them, go to the Web site or call 800-289-4232.

- **Bond's Franchise Guide www.worldfranchising.com.** This guide covers both the United States and Canada and includes contact information for more than 1,000 franchisers. It costs $29.95 and can be purchased at 800-841-0873 or via the Web site. World Franchising also publishes a number of helpful books.

- **Franchise Annual www.infonews.com.** This guide also publishes franchiser contact information, along with brief business descriptions and fees. The guide is available online and can be purchased for $44.95 or by calling 716-754-4669.

- **Franchise Handbook www.franchise1.com.** This handbook is published quarterly and contains information about companies offering current franchise opportunities. The handbook contains relevant articles and success stories. You can subscribe to it for $29.95 a year at 800-272-0246 or via the Web site.

- **International Herald Tribune International Franchise Guide www.franchiseint1. com.** This annual publication, printed by Source Book Publications, contains information on international franchising. It can be purchased for $29.95 at 510-839-5471 or from the Web site.

CONSUMER BUSINESS PUBLICATIONS

There are a number of business publications and newspapers you should consult for information that is useful to the future and current franchisee:

- *Inc.*, **www.inc.com**

- *Entrepreneur*, **www.entrepreneurmag.com**

- *Franchise Times*, **www.franchisetimes.com**

- *Franchising World*, **www.franchise.org**

- *Franchise Update*, **www.franchise-update.com**

- *USA Today*, **www.usatoday.com**

- *The Wall Street Journal*, **www.wsj.com**

- *The New York Times*, **www.nytimes.com**

TRADE SHOWS AND EXPOSITIONS

Franchise trade shows may be the best source for information. They offer the opportunity to meet face to face with prospective franchisers. You should leave a trade show with brochures, pamphlets, and other great tools for answering the questions you wrote down at the beginning of the information-gathering stage.

The world's largest trade show, the International Franchise Expo, is sponsored by the IFA and is held annually in Washington, D.C. This gathering includes hundreds of organizations offering franchises to interested individuals and includes classes for an extra fee. It is well worth a visit. Information can be obtained from the IFA at 1501 K Street NW, Suite 350, Washington, D.C. 20005, **www.franchise.org**, or 202-628-8000.

Additional smaller shows are held every year. Your local SBDC might hold low-fee seminars of interest to you. Regional trade shows are held throughout the year and could include franchise opportunities specific to the needs and market of your region. Check the Internet for these.

Keep the following things in mind when visiting a trade show.

- **Make sure you are dealing with a franchise and not some other kind of business opportunity.** Many companies at trade shows offer "multi-level marketing plans" or other such business plans. These are not franchises. The best way to ensure that you are looking at a true franchise is to ask for a copy of the company's Uniform Franchise Offering Circular, or UFOC. These circulars, which must conform to FTC regulations, ensure that the company is offering a true franchise. They contain a wealth of relevant and important information about the franchise opportunity. You may be asked to sign for the circular and to provide your contact information. That is acceptable. Taking a UFOC and reviewing it does not mean you are under any obligation to buy a franchise. Companies are required to abide by a ten-day "cooling off period" before selling a franchise, giving the prospective franchisee and franchiser time to reconsider and clear up any mistakes. By providing your contact information, the company can ensure that you purchase your franchise legally. Franchises cannot be purchased legally at a trade show.

- **Have a plan before you walk into the trade show.** Take the time to look at the show directory before the event and know which franchises you want to examine. Structure and organization are your most important allies. Have any specific questions about your chosen franchises ready beforehand.

BUYING AN EXISTING FRANCHISE

Often companies provide a list of existing franchise locations that are available either from a current franchisee or from the company directly. Such locations provide the benefit of being already established, with a presence in the community and an existing customer base. These locations already have trained employees and many may be willing to stay through the change in management. Taking over such a location can save you months of preparation and allow you to bypass such time-consuming steps as finding a location, negotiating a lease, and hiring.

Before you purchase an existing location, be sure to research its history. Some owners might be planning a retirement, looking for a new occupation, or have other such innocuous reasons for "getting out." It is possible that the location is suffering and the owner is looking to "unload" on another buyer. Do not count on the existing owner to provide you with all the information you need to make an educated choice. Use all the resources at your disposal to discover what you need to know about a location's history. Check media sources, public records, and available financial data. Is the owner legally obligated to share any franchise information? If so, it would be good information to have and would be useful to you.

If you find that a location's history is not favorable, you need to be able to determine the cause of any failures. Sometimes a new owner with energy and foresight is all that is needed to bring new life to a beleaguered franchise. However, location problems, competition problems, or other such issues may be harder to overcome.

Purchasing an existing franchise will cut down on advertising, hiring, and other costs associated with opening a new location. However, you will likely have to pay a transfer fee (a fixed fee or a percentage), in addition to legal fees. Be sure to pay close attention to the terms of the new franchise contract. Some owners may sell you only the remainder of their own contract rather than a new, full-term contract. If you are interested in finding existing franchises that are up for sale, take a look at the Business Resale Network Web site: **www.br-network.com**.

STARTING NEW

If you would rather purchase a franchise and open a new location, odds are that you will not be entirely on your own. The help you may receive in this endeavor will vary from company to company. While the franchiser will often help you to locate an appropriate property, sign a lease, advertise, and hire help, be sure of the quality of the assistance you will receive before agreeing to the purchase.

Getting to know the franchiser and its other franchisees in person is a good step to take in deciding if the franchiser will provide you with the aid you need as you begin your business venture. Take a trip to company headquarters — it is well worth the expense. Talk to the staff, evaluate the premises, and decide if the company is well-run. If it is not well-run and if there are disgruntled staff members at headquarters, chances are that franchisees are also unhappy. Take any invitations to tour premises and other outlets, but also take the initiative to visit some outlets unexpectedly. If you are touring with other interested franchisees, make yourself known and share information.

Ask current franchise owners if they have received satisfactory aid from the parent company. Ask about any problems they have encountered and how the problems were solved, as well as how much capital was required for them to set up their franchise and how long it took for them to begin realizing a profit.

You should expect a quality company to want to get to know you as well. Good, responsible companies will only want to sell franchises to responsible franchisees. If a company takes your check without any kind of interviewing or examination of your background, how interested are they in the success of their company and how interested will they be in you and your personal success after that check is cashed?

If you are satisfied, begin to search for the right site to establish your new location. Consider such things as demographics, traffic patterns, crime, zoning, future construction projects, and competition in the immediate area. Interview pedestrians or other local business owners to get an idea if your franchise will be welcome and successful in the neighborhood.

Stay organized, stay focused, and use all the resources available to you. Choose the right franchise and take intelligent initial steps, and your chances of success will increase dramatically.

OING YOUR RESEARCH

When it comes time for the nitty gritty of research, organization and preparedness are key. You will be inundated with material during your search for information. This chapter will help you to tackle the stacks of paper you are likely to collect.

INTERNET RESEARCH

The Internet is beneficial in that it allows companies and individuals to publish and disseminate information freely. This open use can also be a hindrance because the quality of information on the Internet varies widely. Despite this fact, the Internet is going to be your primary tool as you collect preliminary and background information.

If you were to go to "Google" and enter the word "franchise," you would find more than 60 million results. Internet research is most useful if you focus your search on companies, products, or services in which you have an interest. The Internet is only a starting point, a means to gather contact numbers and general information. In the end, you will need to make phone calls, attend interviews, and "get out there" to gather information to make an intelligent decision.

SEPARATE THE GOOD, THE BAD, AND THE UGLY

For effective Internet research results, you need to learn how to sort the useful from the worthless. It is helpful to be on the lookout for certain characteristics that are very common among untrustworthy or illegitimate franchising sites. This section will give you some useful tips.

- **Look for disclosure information.** While many companies will provide UFOCs in electronic versions on the Internet, you should be aware that the federal government has yet to make these electronic versions legal. A franchiser who delivers these documents in electronic form is not abiding by FTC regulations and should not be trusted. If a Web site with such UFOCs provides a disclaimer stating that electronic documents cannot be used to buy or sell a franchise, you can be more confident that the company is legitimate and trustworthy.

- **Check for the quality of grammar and spelling on a site.** Poor spelling and grammar are often a sign that something is amiss. Professional, legitimate companies will post only well-written information on their Web sites.

- **Avoid doing business with companies that have "hype" on their sites.** A good company can sell itself with facts, figures, and other concrete indications of success. A company that tries to sell itself with overblown statements and self-accolades has nothing substantial to say.

- **Avoid sites with overly aggressive marketing.** As in the previous tip, a truly successful company will be able to sell itself with facts rather than aggressive sales tactics or intimidation.

- **Avoid dealing with a company that does not provide full financial details at the outset.** You should be able to browse estimated setup costs, fees, cash flows, and other such financial information freely. Companies that hide this information probably have even more to hide.

STARTING POINTS

I would like to recommend a few starting points to those who have no idea where to begin. While my list is in no way exhaustive, it contains great sites with trustworthy information.

Franchises are heavily regulated by state and national governments, so governmental Web sites often contain a large amount of useful and trustworthy information. I suggest you begin with the Federal Trade Commission **www.ftc.gov.** The FTC plays a large part in the regulation of franchises and disseminates a great deal of information for franchisees. Here you can find laws, legal actions, investigations, and proceedings against faulty franchisers.

I recommend these sites: *Entrepreneur* magazine at **www.entrepreneurmag.com; www.franchise.com;** the IFA at **www.franchise.org; www.franchisesolutions.com;** and **www.franchiseopportunties.com**.

STAYING ORGANIZED

Print out the information you find on the Internet. You will probably get a massive amount of printed material at franchise expositions. Rather than creating slipshod piles around your home or office, you will be best served by systematically organizing these materials.

Prepare to organize your materials even before you begin collecting them. Visit your local office supply store and purchase an affordable filing system, along with hanging folders, tab folders, and labels. As you begin to gather information, create a separate file folder for each company you correspond with. Within each company folder, create subfolders for such categories as correspondence (letters sent and received, contact information, memos, faxes, and business cards); promotional items (brochures, glossies, and other printed information); legal items (UFOCs and contracts); and operational items. This last category, which will come into play once you have made a deal with a franchiser, will include items concerning operational specifics such as potential locations, suppliers, and employees. Additional categories can be created according to your own needs, but the above categories (at minimum) are suggested for careful organization of your materials. Such a filing system will be a great help as you attempt to locate specific information quickly.

Even after you have purchased a franchise, keep the information you have filed. You never can tell what might happen in the future and having your self-created database at your fingertips will be a blessing should you change your mind about your purchase.

TERRITORIAL STRATEGIES

If you own a franchise with territorial concerns, your franchiser will have set up territorial rules and limitations for you. You should be aware of how territorial conditions are arranged and understand how they are formed by your franchiser. Three considerations must be taken into account: 1) whether multi-unit franchising is an option, 2) how territories should be made up, and 3) whether franchisees should be allowed to expand their existing territories.

MULTI-UNIT FRANCHISING

A franchiser needs to decide whether one or multiple units will be made available for sale to a single franchisee. Multi-unit franchising can take one of three forms, which are outlined and described below.

MASTER FRANCHISING

In this system the franchiser sells a master franchisee the right to recruit and train other franchisees in exchange for royalty payments or a portion of the franchise fees collected from these additional franchisees. This arrangement is great for the growth of the franchise system in that it reduces the franchiser's overhead by cutting down on permanent headquarters staff and reduces conflict caused by excessive market growth. In addition, master franchising makes buyback easier by reducing the number of people with whom the franchiser must deal during the buyback of a unit.

When knowledge of a particular market or locale is needed, master franchising is great because the franchiser is able to work with someone established in that market. This knowledge is beneficial when a franchiser is looking to expand internationally, as the master franchiser will be familiar with local customs and currency and able to judge the worthiness of potential franchisees in that region or country.

Master franchising does have its drawbacks. New franchisees lose some of their incentive for success because they do not hold an exclusive contract. Second, master franchising makes quality control much more difficult. In addition, the selection of a single bad franchisee can inflict serious damage on the system as a whole.

AREA DEVELOPMENT

In this system a franchisee is given the right to a large area with the potential to host more than one outlet. The area is thus given to the franchisee for development. This system puts a stop to the piggybacking of individually owned franchises in a single area on one another's advertising efforts and reduces the total number of franchisees to manage. In addition, this system requires less training and development on the part of the franchiser, as not every newly opened outlet needs guidance, information, and starting materials.

The franchiser loses some incentives in starting such a system. Individual franchisees realize increased power over the franchiser.

SUBFRANCHISING

In this system the franchiser permits certain franchisees to sell new franchises and become subfranchisers who are responsible for training and development and entitled to collect royalties from the subfranchisees.

This system is great for quicker growth and requires fewer employees at headquarters. However, conflicts between the franchiser and subfranchisers may arise over such issues as the schedule of system development and the ability of subfranchisers to recruit new franchisees in a time frame desired by the franchiser. In addition, the franchiser loses some power because subfranchisers have a great deal more power than regular franchisees. Also, choosing new subfranchisers is difficult given the relatively small number of people with enough capital to become a subfranchiser.

TERRITORY DIVISIONS

Exclusivity is an important feature of territory formation. Although guaranteeing exclusive territory rights to franchisees usually results in a reduced amount of market saturation, it is still a great strategy to use for certain products or for new franchise systems. Statistics have shown that of the 170 new franchise systems begun in the 1990s, 91 percent of the surviving systems use exclusive territories.

As suggested by the concept of area development, exclusive territories cut down on the practice of some franchises, exploiting the advertising efforts of other franchises in the same area. In addition, franchisees with exclusive territory rights need not worry about excessive competition from other franchisees or the franchiser.

Exclusive territories are generally small. The franchiser wants to offer the benefits of exclusive territories without diminishing market saturation to such a degree that the franchise system as a whole suffers. Without enough franchises in the marketplace, competing franchises will gain a better position. Territories must be small enough to allow healthy competition while also sheltering franchisees against encroachment. Territories can be allotted based on population, wealth, or other demographic factors—not on an equality of geographic size.

RIGHT TO EXPAND

Whether or not franchisees have the right to expand their territories is a final factor that must be weighed and considered by a franchiser. Allowing expansion has many benefits. It gives franchisees a greater incentive to succeed and conform to the franchise system's strategies and rules, making franchisees much easier to monitor. The incentive lies in the fact that most expansions are permitted based upon the success level of the franchisee. In addition, allowing franchisees to expand cuts costs for the franchiser because it costs less to expand than to open a new outlet. From the perspective of the franchisee, expansion eliminates fears of encroachment and makes saturation problems disappear because they are in control of all outlets within their territory.

EXPANDING YOUR OPERATIONS

For you, owning one franchise might be enough. On the other hand, you might be the kind of person who wants to own and run more than one outlet. In this chapter, you will find the information and guidance to help you determine whether you are cut out for multiple franchise ownership — legally, financially, and personally. I will also discuss the negative and positive aspects of owning more than one franchise.

CHECKING YOUR FRANCHISE AGREEMENT: CAN YOU BUY ANOTHER FRANCHISE?

Before you can own multiple units, you need to make sure that multi-unit ownership is permissible. If multi-unit ownership is an option, learn all you can about the restrictions governing it. You want to remain in compliance with your agreement at all times. This information might be included in the UFOC. If it is not, a simple query to your franchiser will provide all the information you need. Make sure to ask about franchise fees and royalties for multiple units. Fees will probably be lower for expansion units than for the original unit, but double check to be sure.

Transfers might be permitted, but your agreement may state that the franchiser has the right to reject proposed transfers. If your current location is not functioning up to the franchiser's standards, a rejection is possible. In addition, the franchiser may have the right of first refusal for any franchise that comes onto the market.

UNDERSTANDING YOUR PURCHASE OPTIONS

If there are no restrictions on the establishment of an additional franchise, you will need to decide where, when, and how to set up shop. You will need to evaluate sites for your new franchise in the same way you did for your original franchise, considering traffic, demographics, lease terms, competition, and building costs.

BUYING AN EXISTING FRANCHISE

You might have your eye on a neighbor's business. Even if it seems as though the franchise is happy and successful, she might be ready to leave the business for any number of reasons. You will never know until you inquire. Communication with your fellow franchisees could alert you to businesses that will soon be for sale or that could be for sale if you express an interest.

You should learn about the sales status of existing franchises from your franchiser. Once they know about your plans to expand, they could suggest an existing franchise for you to take over or you can ask them about any that might be up for sale. Your franchiser might even sponsor an active resale network. They would rather see existing franchises taken over by willing owners than see them close completely.

The location you find to take over should be close enough to your original location that you can easily keep tabs on both, but far enough away to avoid competition with your current location. Figure out why the current owners are willing to sell. If they are selling for personal reasons, that is one thing, but if they are selling because there are problems with the store, you will need to address those problems and determine whether they can be solved.

Insist on seeing the performance statistics. Ask either your franchiser or the franchisee for operating figures and results. You should be able to analyze these numbers and decide whether the business will be profitable for you.

When considering the purchase of an existing franchise, you should answer the following questions:

- **Does the current location meet the franchise system's standards?** One of the benefits of buying an existing franchise is that the equipment should already be there and the building itself should be ready to go. If the location is not quite up to par, weigh the expenses of improvements against the expense of building a new location and go from there.

- **How profitable is the existing franchise?** Can any problems be solved?

- **Does the original franchise contract have enough years remaining** on it to allow you to amortize your additional costs?

- **Has the franchiser assigned the location good reviews in the past?**

- **What are the current employees like?** Will they be willing to continue working at the location after a transfer of ownership? Can you resolve any current labor conflicts? Are the managers reliable and trustworthy? Will the managers at your current location be willing to transfer, if necessary?

- **What does the public think about the location?** If the public's opinion is low, can steps be taken to regain trust and customers? Do current demographics of the area still match your target-customer profile or has the demographic landscape changed with time?

- **What are the terms of the current lease** and do they meet your interests?

- **Are there existing legal problems** that could affect you in the future?

- **Does the location pass all standards you would set for a new location?**

RETRO-FRANCHISING

Through retro-franchising you have the opportunity to buy a location directly from your franchiser. Many franchisers own and operate their own locations; some of these were set up for the long-term and others were set up with the intention of selling them to franchisees at a later date. Your franchiser may be willing to sell you a company-owned location for a number of reasons — to cut losses, expand markets, increase capital, or simply because the location was created just for that purpose.

At times a franchiser has an opportunity to purchase space that will serve as a great location in the future. For example, a new subway station might be built with room for a restaurant and a restaurant franchiser might purchase that slot with the intention of finding someone to run the location at a later date. These could present great opportunities for you, although many of these locations are nontraditional.

Franchisers take into account the concept of "critical mass" when considering whether to sell a location to a franchisee. Critical mass is simply the number of units deemed necessary to infiltrate a market area. Critical mass allows efficient advertising and increases brand recognition within these markets. Also, when an area reaches critical mass, the franchiser is able to provide better support for existing franchises by sending field agents out to more units at a lower total cost. Your franchiser may be willing to sell you a location to get closer to critical mass in a given market.

Retro-franchising is a great option because you will acquire a store that is already running and is up to standards. Franchisers will sometimes sell these units at a discounted price. My only caution to you is to beware of "churning," a practice in which a franchiser will sell a location to a franchisee and then take it back with the intention of selling again, knowing that every franchisee is destined to fail at that location due to unavoidable problems. Check the history of any location you are considering retro-franchising.

CONVERTING A COMPETITOR'S LOCATION

If you would like to take over an existing establishment but cannot find any opportunities in your desired market within your own franchise system, you might want to consider taking over a competitor's location. If you find a suitable location that meets your needs and is up for sale, you can expand your business and reduce your competition in one move.

Independent mom-and-pop businesses are finding it more difficult to compete with franchises in the same market. If you ask around, you might be able to purchase a location from one of these independents. Since you are operating in the same industry, you will benefit from an existing customer pool and, while employees will need to be trained, they may be willing to stay and work for you.

Taking over a competitor's location will entail substantial remodeling. Zoning issues should not come into play. You will need to hire a contractor to complete any restructuring and you might need to invest in equipment that meets your franchise system's standards. It costs less to remodel than to build a new location.

In certain situations, such as when extensive plumbing, electrical, or structural changes are required, it might be easier and cheaper to build a new location. You should check with your franchiser's development department to determine the costs of each move.

You will also need to check with a lawyer to go over the franchise agreements of your franchiser and the franchiser of the original owner, if applicable. The original franchisee might have signed an agreement preventing the selling of the location to a competitor. You should also make sure that by purchasing the new location you are not violating the territorial rights of another franchisee within your system.

STARTING FROM SCRATCH

Do not forget that if you cannot locate a suitable existing location, you always have the option of starting from scratch and repeating the steps you took to select and prepare your first location.

BUYING MULTIPLE UNITS

While some franchisees decide to expand after experiencing success with their first business, you might have purchased your franchise with the intent to expand right from the beginning. You are not alone. Many franchisees are part of an investor group looking to open up multiple locations and get an inside edge on a market. Some of these groups could even be larger and more powerful than the franchiser. After the purchase of a handful of units you will probably find that you need to establish your own management facilities to coordinate the management of all your units. You might also need to establish training centers in order to accommodate the constant influx of new employees. Managers will have greater responsibility and will need training similar to that provided to the franchisees.

ACQUIRING AN AREA

If you have your sights set on multiple ownership from the beginning, you should find out if your franchiser offers the right to develop an area. You can purchase this right and it will permit you to expand within a certain territory at an established rate (a certain number of units in a certain amount of time). Some franchise systems only allow expansion along this model. This way, the franchise systems minimize management and training needs, while simultaneously growing. Alternatively, your franchiser might offer area development expansion only within large, core markets; in smaller markets, your franchiser might only sell to individual franchisees who want to own one business.

Before you purchase area development rights, consider the following: 1) how many stores would you like to own?, 2) what is your financial situation and will you be able to support your desired number of units?, 3) will the area being offered for development be able to support your desired number of units?, and 4) what costs or savings will you see based on your decision to develop an area as opposed to over-purchasing additional units when they become available?

Do not enter into an area development agreement without substantial funds. You can expect to pay a huge up-front fee or a fee per franchise. Either way, the cost to you will most likely be large. You will, at the very least, be expected to pay the full franchise fee for the first unit along with a large percentage up-front deposit for each additional expected unit, with the remainder of the fee due upon the opening of each unit.

Keep in mind that if you do not end up opening the additional units, for whatever reason, you cannot necessarily expect your deposit back from the franchiser. You will also be expected to keep up with set development schedules. You should check on your franchiser's default policy before investing in area development.

While financial policies are often in place, many franchisers will adapt their responses to late development according to individual circumstances. A fee could be assessed or you might be granted a grace period. The franchiser will likely evaluate your degree of commitment to the project before determining the consequences of your default.

REVIEWING YOUR PERSONAL AND BUSINESS RESOURCES

After reading this chapter you might find yourself contemplating becoming a multi-unit owner. You need to perform some serious and honest personal and financial reflection before making any multi-unit commitments. When you add units, the entire structure and functioning of your business changes. You will find yourself operating on an entirely different scale. A good first bit of advice is to get your ideas, plans, and tactics out on paper. Often, the numbers, notes, and options you jot down will help you to visualize your situation more clearly and will help you to make the right decision.

TAKE SOME TIME FOR PERSONAL REFLECTION

Along with multiple ownership comes more frequent and required relationships. Ask yourself if you are ready to be in charge of a large team.

Your responsibilities will increase dramatically. If you are currently struggling to get through the day — opening, operating, and closing up your business, while also maintaining a healthy personal life — then multiple ownership is not for you.

Imagine needing to manage the daily operations of two, three, or even 20 units! Alternatively, imagine managing the number of people it will take to oversee daily operations. If your personal life is too demanding, then multiple ownership is not right for you.

Since you cannot be everywhere at once, you will need to hire and manage reliable employees so that you can delegate authority. At the start of this new venture, you will focus on the new units, but eventually you will need to address the issues of all units. You will need to be able to entrust individual unit managers with many responsibilities.

You will need the organizational skills necessary to set up staff training and administration centers if you plan to operate more than a handful of units. These centers will need competent clerical, legal, and financial personnel.

Remember that the desire to expand is not enough. You must be personally capable of the expansion as well.

TAKE A HARD LOOK AT YOUR BUSINESS AND FINANCES

Before expanding, look at the current state of your finances and the health of your business. You did a lot of preparation before purchasing your first franchise unit. Did you prepare well? Did you make the right decisions? Before you purchase your next unit, think about the following.

- **Are your employees ready to meet the demands an expansion will require?** Look at your management. As a single store owner, you might be the general manager, with shift managers overseeing your employees directly. If you purchase additional units, you will need to manage all of the units as a whole and give more responsibility to your shift managers. Are they able to become general managers? Are your other employees ready for new responsibility and can you trust all your employees to operate the store without your constant presence?

- **Before you invest time and money into expansion, take a look at the competitor landscape.** If you are having problems keeping up with your competitors and want to expand to get a leg up, make sure they do not also have expansion plans. It would be a bad move to expand only to be shut down by a similar move by the competition.

- **How will expansion affect your customer base?** Will the loss of a personal touch be felt by loyal customers or will expansion fit the needs of more customers in other ways?

- **Do you have the finances to expand?** What fees and other costs will you be expected to pay in addition to the funds needed to open the new unit?

CRUNCHING THE NUMBERS

Whatever you do, you do not want the opening of a new unit to damage the success of a current unit. Examine your financial picture to ensure that no damage will happen. Use your up-to-date balance sheets, investment portfolios, budgets, profit-and-loss statements, and cash flow analyses to make sure there are current sources of funding for the new unit. You might be able to make the numbers work by seeking out additional financing, perhaps even from your franchiser. Do not overburden yourself with debt to the point that both units suffer. Rates or loan policies may have changed since you took out the loan for your original unit. Costs of construction, licensure, or real estate may also have changed. Changing franchise agreements can make your start-up costs higher than they were originally, despite the possibility of a reduced franchise fee for multiple ownership. Make sure you do your calculations based on current rates.

Do not forget that with more units to stock and maintain you will be purchasing more supplies. You may be able to get supplies at better cost through volume purchasing. Financial burdens as well as blessings should be taken into account when determining if you are financially ready to expand.

Finally, it is highly recommended that you turn to your legal, financial, and marketing professionals before committing to any expansion plans. They may provide you with insights that you missed during your own review. They may also be able to provide you with useful tips and advice. Discuss any plans with your franchiser's development staff as well.

THE PROS AND CONS OF MULTIPLE OWNERSHIP

If you find yourself looking in the mirror in the morning thinking what a great guy or gal you are for being such a success; if your bank, franchiser, accountant, employees, and community all love you and congratulate you on a job well done; if you are planning to kick back and enjoy that dream vacation to Maui; if you are even planning on cashing in by opening more units—STOP! Do not think that your success as an individual franchise owner will carry over to multiple franchises. Multiple ownership has its pros and cons. I discuss these in this section. Weigh them carefully.

PROS

Opening more units can bring you more money. You will be building equity in your businesses and in any real estate you purchase for your businesses. More units can mean cheaper costs in terms of supplies and employee benefits. You can receive better rates when you apply for loans and other financing.

Additional units also make the cost of marketing more palatable. You might have difficulty justifying the high cost of radio or television advertising for one unit, but when you are paying to promote multiple units, the advantages easily outweigh the costs. More media exposure means more customers.

The larger your operations within a particular market, the more qualified employees you will attract. You will have the capability to offer more career development opportunities and employees will have an easier time imagining such opportunities. You will no longer need to turn away as many qualified applicants because you will have more positions to fill. You will also be able to transfer staff from unit to unit, as need dictates, within the same market, allowing you and your employees much greater flexibility.

If pricing is not determined by your franchiser, you will be able to standardize pricing on identical products within your market (as opposed to having customers notice price differences between individually owned franchise units within the same area), leading to greater customer satisfaction by cutting down on confusion.

CONS

If you are not personally and financially prepared, opening multiple units can ruin your successful original unit. You will need the leadership, management skills, and capital to run multiple businesses. For some the old saying, "If it ain't broke, don't fix it," might apply. If you are not ready to expand and you do it anyway, you could ruin a good thing.

Your success as a multi-unit owner may cause you to discover problems and flaws with the organization and practices of the franchise system and you may be tempted to institute your own changes within your units — but you cannot. You must remember that no matter how large you grow, you are still a franchisee and there are still rules to follow. You can easily turn these negatives into positives with the right thinking and the right approach.

FRANCHISING ADVANTAGES AND DISADVANTAGES

If you have a business you are thinking of franchising, this section is important. In it we will discuss the advantages and disadvantages of the franchise model. You should use this section to help decide whether franchising your own business is a step you should take.

When you own a business, one of the most important decisions you will need to make is how to organize management. Sole proprietorships give you all the control and changes can be implemented in the blink of an eye. However, you may lack the range of talent that larger management systems can provide.

Large corporations have the necessary talent, but change is difficult and takes time. Pyramid-shaped organizations function well at the top, but at the bottom levels you will often find that the organization is no longer in touch with its customer base. The lesson learned? No matter what organization you use for your company, it will have advantages and disadvantages. The key is to decide which organization is best suited to your company and which will give you the advantages you most need within your industry. One of the methods of organization to consider is franchising. It too has advantages and disadvantages.

ADVANTAGES

There are four basic advantages to the franchise model:

1. You take on a relatively low amount of risk for your financial returns.

2. Each store will realize better incentives for success.

3. You will be able to attract better management talent.

4. You will experience an increased rate of growth over other models.

I discuss each of these benefits in the following sections.

Low Risk for Financial Returns

In franchising you are distributing risk among the various franchisees rather than holding all the cards in your own hand. Any failed expansions or failed efforts for improvement are funded from the franchisees' pockets, not yours. You, as the franchiser, will also be able to assume more risk than otherwise possible. If you owned each outlet, you would want to have a very high chance of success at a particular location before paying to build a unit there. By franchising, this risk is partly assumed by the franchisee and thus locations that are less than optimal can be developed for potential use.

Better Incentives for Success At The Unit Level

The best way to understand this benefit is to imagine the differences in managerial style between two managers, one corporate, one a franchisee. Imagine that Manager A works at a company-owned store with about $800,000 in sales per year. Manager A receives a salary of $55,000 plus the possibility of a bonus, which is based upon his sales and his ability to operate under budget. Most years, he does not get a bonus. Manager B, on the other hand, is a franchisee. Her store also does around $800,000 in sales annually.

Rather than earning a set salary, Manager B takes the profit of the store minus expenses and royalty payments. At the end of the year she ends up taking home about the same amount as Manager A: $55,000.

Suppose both managers learn about a new food handling technique which, if implemented properly, will cut costs by about $10,000. The only cost to them will be about ten hours of their time, required to train employees in this new procedure. If the managers decide to undertake the training, Manager A, because of his bonus, will earn an extra $2,000, while Manager B will take home the extra $10,000 she saved in expenses.

In addition, Manager A will get the added personal profit (the bonus) in the first year only (the new operating costs become his baseline in following years). Manager B, on the other hand, will appreciate the $10,000 profit every year to follow as part of her personal take. Imagine if Manager A gets no bonus for cutting costs — he would have no incentive to spend ten hours of his time trying to save the company $10,000 a year.

Put simply, owners have more of a stake in a business than employees. In company-owned stores, managers are just employees after all. In a franchise, on the other hand, the manager is often the owner and will have a much greater interest in cutting costs, increasing sales, and seeing the business succeed and turn a profit.

ATTRACT BETTER MANAGEMENT TALENT

Why can a franchiser attract better management talent than ordinary corporations? Quite simply, because franchising requires a large financial investment on the part of the franchisee.

Investing in a franchise can cost hundreds of thousands of dollars. Most people able to finance such an investment will be responsible and hard-working and have business savvy. Anyone who makes that kind of investment will have more of an incentive to see the investment pay off.

While corporate positions typically have flat salaries, franchise managers see profit based upon their own hard work and efforts. Profit based upon effort is more appealing to managers with expertise and know-how because they are aware of their work ethic and ability to get results.

MORE RAPID GROWTH

A lack of capital will decrease growth and an excess of capital will allow more rapid expansion. In the franchise system, capital comes from individual franchisees rather than from the parent company. The franchise system is unique in that, during times of growth, the franchiser will see more capital arriving from royalty payments and franchise fees, while the cost of setting up new units is borne mostly by franchisees. The advantages to the franchiser are enormous and are the primary reason why the franchising system was developed in the first place.

If your company is relatively new, it might be more difficult for you to secure funding for expansion from a bank or other source. Without an extensive track record, banks will be hesitant to loan you large sums of money, even assuming that the market for your product is good. Franchising is a great solution to this problem as the money needed for expansion is supplied by franchisees. Franchisees are usually more willing to invest in a new company— they have the time and incentive to do the extensive research needed to determine whether the business is bound for success or failure. Banks do a more cursory examination when they determine investment risk.

DISADVANTAGES

There are four major disadvantages to franchising. They are as follows:

1. Your goals as a franchiser might differ from the goals of your franchisees.

2. Large franchise systems resist change.

3. Your returns as a franchiser will tend to be lower than if you owned all the units directly.

4. You will see higher costs of doing business.

These are discussed in more detail in the following sections.

DIFFERENT GOALS

While the primary goal of a franchisee is to realize maximum profit (which will increase personal earnings), franchisers are more interested in increasing sales, which will increase their revenue because of higher royalty payments. These goals involve different sales strategies. Franchisees will be looking for business that will decrease costs and time, while franchisers will want more business at every turn.

Coupon promotions started by the franchiser illustrate this conflict well. Coupons that offer products for free or at reduced prices draw in customers. While the franchiser will benefit from coupons because more products are being sold, increasing royalty payments, the franchisee will not see profit from free or reduced-price products, which will decrease their bottom line.

Conflict often arises during expansions. Franchisers want new stores to open because they receive large franchise fees and more royalty payments. Franchisees see additional properties close by as threats — new stores can draw customers away from their own stores.

While it is in the franchiser's best interest to keep franchisees happy and franchised units doing well, there is always a give and take between franchiser and franchisee. This give and take can complicate the running of your business.

RESISTANCE TO CHANGE

A franchise system is comprised of dozens or even hundreds of owners with individual agendas and goals. Trying to introduce change into the system can be difficult. The franchiser wants to avoid coercion at all costs. Trying to win mass approval for a change is not an easy task. The franchiser must be aware of legal issues preventing the preferential treatment of one franchisee over another. While regular corporations can change processes or products at one or more stores for experimental purposes, the franchiser cannot make such changes without consent from the franchisee. Any change to be implemented must be negotiated and renegotiated with each and every contracted franchisee, resulting in high costs for very small changes.

As a franchiser, you may not be in touch with the market trends that trigger changes necessary to keep up with changing times. Most change in corporations is in response to shifts in the market or consumer trends; these corporations actively collect data to spot such shifts. In the franchise model, this data would have to be collected from franchisees. Collecting such data would be expensive, time-consuming, and not directly profitable to the franchisee. As a result, the franchiser can expect poor analyses, if any.

Because of the high unit-level costs of introducing new products and services, franchisees are often reluctant to sell new products until the products have a proven track record. Franchisees have to spend time and money in training, signage, promotion, and inventory to introduce a new product. They will be unwilling to do so if they are not confident that the product will be a success.

LOWER RETURNS

In setting up a franchise system you will be faced with a number of high costs. The first such cost is setting up the system itself. Because of the necessary legal and financial advice, the cost of training materials, brochures, UFOCs, and start-up resources for each potential franchise, setting up the system can cost hundreds of thousands of dollars.

While the capital necessary to expand will be lower, profits generated at the unit level will revert to the franchisee. Research suggests that, on average, the franchiser can expect to see $1 per every $3 of profit at the unit level. The other $2 goes into the pocket of the franchisee. In addition, technological changes that will improve efficiency at the unit level will tend to benefit the franchisee and not the franchiser. The only thing that will benefit the franchiser is increased sales (because they result in higher royalties).

HIGHER COSTS OF DOING BUSINESS

There are several costs associated with the franchise model that are an inherent part of the model and cannot be avoided. These costs are due to the nature of the relationship of franchise units to one another.

There is the "free rider" problem. The costs of a negative action by one unit are borne by all units and the cost of a positive action is borne by one member but benefits all members. If one unit of a well-known franchise is sued for discrimination, the negative publicity generated by that unit's actions will tend to reduce sales across the same system. If one unit of a well-known franchise pays for a large billboard advertisement, other units in the area benefit from the advertisement without paying a dime in advertising fees. Such a free rider situation can have profound effects on all units and can add costs otherwise unexpected at the unit level. It can also lead to hostility between unit owners. The free rider phenomenon can be partly overcome if the franchiser imposes quality and service requirements on the franchisees. Creating a list of approved vendors also helps. These actions also incur costs to the franchiser.

Another example of the higher costs of doing business involves protecting confidential information. Reflect on your business for a moment: Do you have any trade secrets, secret recipes, or intellectual property that must be protected from common knowledge for your business to succeed? If so, you will have to pay substantially to protect these secrets. You will have to entrust some amount of knowledge to your franchisees, but for full protection you will need to employ the aid of professionals who can set up elaborate ways to protect your information. You will need to hire legal professionals to create nondisclosure agreements and the like. Costs for these protections are particularly galling because there is no guarantee that your efforts will protect confidential information, and yet, they are necessary costs.

FRANCHISING AND THE LAW

Franchise systems are legally regulated. If you are thinking of franchising your business, you must be aware of the various legal obligations by which you, as a franchiser, will need to abide. In this chapter we will outline some important legal issues. Franchise regulations will be discussed according to both state and federal laws and some pros and cons of operating within various state frameworks will be analyzed.

FEDERAL LAW

Franchisers are required by the Federal Trade Commission to provide certain information to prospective franchisees, including details of the history, operations, and governing principles of the company. This information is contained in the UFOC and must be provided at least ten days in advance of any signing. However, franchisers selling to overseas franchisees or to franchisees meeting the criteria of "sophistication" do not need to provide this document. The FTC has created a standard UFOC template, which it provides to franchisers. This table lists items required for disclosure in a UFOC document.

ITEMS REQUIRED FOR DISCLOSURE IN A UFOC
1.   The franchiser and predecessors
2.   Business experience of persons affiliated with the franchiser
3.   Litigation history
4.   Bankruptcy history
5.   Initial fee
6.   Other fees
7.   Initial investment
8.   Restrictions of franchisee sourcing
9.   Franchisee's obligations
10. Financing
11. Franchiser's obligations
12. Territory
13. Trademarks and service marks
14. Patents and copyrights
15. Obligation of the franchisee to participate in the business
16. Restrictions on franchisee sale of goods and services
17. Renewal and termination
18. Arrangements with public figures
19. Earnings claims
20. Statistics on system
21. Audited financial statements
22. Contracts
23. Acknowledgment of receipt
Compliance with the UFOC requires an audited financial statement, driving up franchise expenses significantly because of hiring both the auditing firm and an experienced franchise attorney. Furthermore, if you make claims about franchisee earnings from your outlets, you need to provide additional disclosure about those earnings.

STATE LAW

State laws often govern two key aspects of franchising. First, state regulations may dictate what can and cannot be done by franchisers to sell franchises and may include restrictions concerning registration of the company and the provision of information to potential franchisees. Second, state laws may govern the relationship between franchisers and franchisees, including issues such as the termination of a franchise agreement.

Not every state has franchise laws; some states only have laws governing the first aspect of franchising and some only the second. There are large differences between franchise laws from state to state. Consult a legal professional about state laws. It is important to be acquainted with your own state's laws, as well as the laws of the states in which you have operating franchises.

REGISTRATION STATES

In states requiring the registration of franchised companies, franchisers must furnish state regulatory agencies with a UFOC before starting any franchising activity. In most states you can provide the same version as you gave the FTC; California, Indiana, Maryland, Minnesota, Rhode Island, South Dakota, Virginia, and the District of Columbia require different versions. Registration states also require you to file annual, sometimes quarterly, reports containing specific information. Recently, registration has been simplified by an electronic registration system that allows franchisers to register with all registration states simultaneously.

Why do states require registration? First, the theory is that if they are required to register, franchisers will be more likely to provide accurate information to franchisees. Second, franchisees are afforded some level of protection through the registration process: Fees might be required to be put into an escrow account; bonds could be issued protecting franchisees from an under-capitalization of the franchiser; and any performance claims made by the franchiser to attract potential franchisees can be more easily verified.

As a franchiser, you must document any changes made to your franchise system and you must provide updated versions of your UFOC to registration states. Things that must be documented include changes to your fee schedule, franchisee obligations, or the legal structure of the company; updated financial information; or any programs added or modified concerning your interaction with franchisees. It is in your interest to minimize negotiations with franchisees and to offer standardized agreements to all franchisees to avoid re-filing the UFOC frequently.

Because of the large regulatory burden, you may decide to avoid operating in registration states altogether, as do almost 50 percent of existing franchised organizations. By operating in registration states, however, you receive a number of benefits. Some estimates show that the oversight system provided by registration states has made companies operating in registration states 22 percent more successful on average. Also, franchisee confidence is bolstered by your willingness to comply with state regulations; they take it as a sign you are on the up-and-up. Finally, the larger your company, the cheaper it is to operate in registration states; conversely, the larger your company, the more expensive operating outside of registration states becomes.

RELATIONSHIP STATES

Relationship laws are typically put into place to protect franchisees. The laws make sure that franchisers provide an acceptable reason for contract breaches such as termination.

Relationship laws give franchisees a way to fight any contract breaches by the franchiser. Such protections also raise franchiser costs, causing many of them to demand higher royalty payments from units located within relationship states.

Franchisees will be more willing to take on a unit with your franchise if you operate in relationship states. Relationship laws simply make franchisees more comfortable in their investment. At the same time, relationship laws make getting rid of ineffective or problem franchisees difficult. This table lists states with different relationship provisions.

STATES WITH DIFFERENT RELATIONSHIP PROVISIONS	
States That Require Cause for Termination	States That Allow Cure in Termination
Arkansas	Arkansas
California	California
Connecticut	Hawaii
Delaware	Illinois
Hawaii	Michigan
Illinois	Minnesota
Indiana	Washington
Michigan	Wisconsin
Minnesota	
Nebraska	
New Jersey	
Virginia	
Washington	
Wisconsin	

FRANCHISER CERTIFICATION

Getting your franchise certified will win you respect and trust from potential franchisees. Through winning contests or being ranked by media outlets, you will gain recognition and much-desired notice. Recognition by any reputable medium, be it a magazine, newspaper, or some other organization, will benefit your company more than you can imagine.

You should apply for membership in important trade associations such as the International Franchise Association. Membership is not a given: Only about 600 of 2,500 existing franchises are members. To be a member, you must be able to demonstrate higher than normal standards, that you have no legal violations on record, and that you operate in compliance with all state and federal regulations. Membership is a sign of quality, reliability, and profitability.

EFFECTIVE RESTAURANT LAYOUT & REMODELING

PUBLIC AREAS IN YOUR RESTAURANT

What will your customers think when they drive by your restaurant? Will they notice trash in the parking lot or will their attention go to the bushes and flowers that line the sidewalk leading to your door? Once they get inside, they will scan the waiting area, counters, and dining room. These areas must be:

- **Attractive** — Is the appearance of your shop appealing?

- **Clean** — The majority of your customers will never see inside your kitchen, so they draw conclusions from what they can see.

- **Efficient** — Your staff must be well-trained to offer good customer service.

- **Organized** — An organized staff and work space allow you to offer quicker service while you maintain a high level of quality and service.

- **Inviting** — Most restaurants have a welcoming combination of sights, smells, and personality which can draw people to your shop and encourage them to return.

Some of the large restaurant chains are working to offer an upscale design. When food is served in an upscale environment, the restaurant can place a higher value on their food. Upscale design is just another way to set yourself apart from your competition.

OUTDOOR AREAS

The exterior of your restaurant is the first thing people see. What do they see? Is it appealing enough to make them venture inside? These are some considerations for the exterior of your restaurant:

- **Review zoning regulations** for possible restrictions to your present plans and future expansion.

- **Place all plants, trees, and decorations in a way that hide unattractive views**, shelter customers from the wind, and soften noise levels, especially if you offer outdoor seating.

- **Provide ample lighting** to prevent accidents.

- **You can add gas heaters, fireplaces, and fire pits for chilly nights.**

- **Attractive umbrellas can fill several needs.** They can protect customers from the sun or unexpected rain. Awnings or patio covers may be a more conducive possibility for your restaurant.

- **Use tables and seating that are easy to clean and safe.** They also need to endure the weather in your area.

PARKING

Can your shop be seen from the street? When customers park, ensure there is sufficient signage to help them find the door. Make it obvious how to get inside. Ensure that customers have easy access to your entrance. Check local laws and ADA requirements for accessibility by disabled customers.

FIRST IMPRESSIONS

You want a front door that welcomes customers into your restaurant. The same is true for the exterior of your shop. Does it grab their attention and draw them to your door? It should. One important thing is sufficient lighting. Consider these possibilities when you walk to your front door:

- **What is the first thing that catches your attention?**

- **Does it look clean and well-maintained?**

- **Is the appearance comfortable and inviting?**

- **Do you see trash and debris or overflowing, ugly trash cans?**

- **Can approaching customers smell fresh pizza or bread baking?**

- **Can the counterperson be heard over the "cooking noises?"**

Does the appearance send a consistent message of quality and concern for your customers? If not, make some changes to give that feeling. Ensure that people are assigned to keep all public areas clean throughout the day.

WINDOW DISPLAYS

There are many ways to dress your windows. A word of caution: Do not overdo the window dressing. Make it inviting, but not overwhelming. You can do amazing things with some fabric, a few tools, and your creativity. It is also good to change the windows from time to time. Simple changes can be effective. You can use bright colors that work with your décor, nice props, and signage.

Window ledges can be spruced up and fabric can be used in many appealing ways. Secure items on your shelves or ledges or create a small rail or barrier that does not hide your decorations. Be sure to work with the theme you picked for your restaurant.

Another concern that I kept in mind with window displays was the safety of the store and the team. There were a series of thefts in the area and my store was on a dark side street. Everyone's safety was a concern, so I left areas of the windows open to ensure a clear view of the parking area and the street.

There is no sense in placing so many signs on your windows that you give a potential robber the upper hand. Place signs and ads, but be sure you can still keep an eye on the exterior of the shop.

USE SOME GREENERY

Plants can be used in a variety of ways both inside and outside. They add life to your restaurant. Outdoor plants add an attractive and welcome environment and can be used to hide unattractive elements. You can also use them to lead the customer to your door. Interior plants filter the air and provide oxygen. When incorporating plants into your interior design, remember that they require light, moisture, and accessibility. The following are some plant décor and landscaping hints for those without a green thumb:

- **Hire a plant maintenance or landscape firm** to keep everything trimmed, fed, and looking fresh. Dead or spindly plants and yellowed leaves lying about are unappetizing signals to guests. Rotate indoor plants regularly. Make certain the plants look good year-round or can be inexpensively replaced with seasonally suitable choices.

- **Go faux.** Sometimes silk plants are a better choice. Use only high quality artificial plants and work within your existing color scheme, using colors that are natural. Unusual colors will stand out and look phony.

- **Portable gardens can be created** with pots, planters, hanging baskets, barrels, or antique or unusual kitchen items. These can be filled with plants and moved around the restaurant.

- **Unfriendly plants should not be used in your shop.** These include foul smelling and prickly plants. Some plants have poisonous leaves or berries and should not be used.

- **Put plants in the right place.** Remember light and watering needs. Consider the full grown size of the plants. Vines should be directed away from seating and customer service areas.

- **Add non-plant elements.** Attractive tiles, fishponds, flags, sculpture, fountains, dry creek beds, ambient lighting, and birdbaths can decorate parking lots, entries, and waiting areas.

- **Select the right plant for the space.** Use full-spectrum lights for healthier indoor plants. Have plant shelves installed with drains and incorporate hanging plants using a retracting or track system.

- **Place water faucets (interior and exterior) near areas that will have trees and large plants** that require lots of water. Include plants that create "fresh air" to purify indoor air. To learn more about healthy air plants, read the section on indoor air quality, "The Air We Breathe."

YOUR RESTROOMS

Your restrooms are a small part of your business, but they are important. They need to be sufficient for your shop capacity and must be clean. Verify plumbing and health department requirements. The ADA requires handicapped accessible restrooms. Insufficient restrooms can delay your opening and cause issues with the health department. Consider these factors when you design your restrooms:

- **Remember your customers' physical needs.** You can offer sinks, hand towels, or dryers at levels for adults, children, and handicapped customers. The ADA can offer advice at 800-514-0301.

- **Choose lasting materials that do not show dirt and tolerate strong cleaners.** Ceramic tile is great, but the grout may become discolored.

- **Avoid unisex rooms.** You may have no choice, but if feasible you should provide separate women's and men's restrooms. Some individuals may feel uncomfortable in a unisex restroom and it could keep them from your restaurant. Separate restrooms are critical in a dine-in restaurant.

- **Provide separate staff restrooms.**

COUNTERTOP DISPLAYS

Generate interest in your specialties or temporary specials with countertop displays. These are also great for impulse purchases like appetizers and desserts. It is important to keep it simple. Too many signs and displays are too busy and do not influence the customer in a positive way.

Use a variety of signs or cardboard displays to promote various items. If there are displays you use often, you might upgrade them with glass units, bowls, or special stands. These can help you sell more add-on items when the orders are being processed. They are a great way to increase your ticket prices.

FRONT WORK AREAS

There are setups that make it impossible to do all prep work in a closed kitchen. I ate at a Carabba's in North Carolina and they had cooks lining two walls of a dining room. Here are some additional things that are needed in your front work areas:

- Display prepared food.
- Packaged food for travel.
- Order taking areas.
- Ring up on cash register or enter sales in computer.
- Areas to prepare food and drink items.
- Finish and pack food items.
- Storage items, forks, knives, spoons, and cash in the till.

Suggestions for the layout of your front work areas:

- Find an attractive and functional layout.
- Maintain a clean and orderly work environment visible to customers.
- Have rollers on all carts and trash cans.
- Be sure to offer adequate lighting and avoid glare on customers.
- Use non-slip flooring and mats.
- Install drains in the floor and use vinyl baseboards to eliminate scuffs. Equipment on casters is easier to rearrange.
- Work areas should be laid out to avoid stooping, reaching, and lifting.
- Handle "wet" and "dry" tasks in different areas to avoid damage, electrical problems, and food contamination.
- Have hand sinks handy for workers.
- Plan to have sufficient counter space to store deliveries, to pass food items to servers, and to talk with servers.

SHELVING

Your staff needs adequate storage areas to work efficiently. There are tools, equipment, and food items that need to be handy. Makelines can be a huge help. These store the food in a refrigerated setting and there is room to store additional food and supplies underneath. There are many sizes and varieties, depending on what you offer. Keep these areas clean and they can be within customer view. Many customers enjoy watching their pizzas and subs being made.

You can keep cleaning supplies and cash registers out of view, but handy for your employees. The work area needs to look good, but must be functional.

DEDICATED WORK AREAS

There are work areas in your restaurant other than the kitchen and the public area. How will you handle the space and supplies needed for delivery? Your food and supply storage area can take up considerable space in your restaurant.

DELIVERY AREAS

It is best to have a back door for all deliveries. A back door gives you a separate point of access for the supplies to be delivered, especially during peak hours. You need information from any perspective vendors. Some specific questions may be:

- What method do they use to package heavy bulk items?

- Do they leave racked goods?

- Do they drop items inside the door?

- Will they move heavy bags of flour to storage areas?

Set up an effective delivery and storage area. Here are some tips:

- **Provide gloves** and heavy-lifting belts for your employees.

- **Check-in can be handled quicker with a computer in the delivery area.** Compare packing slips with orders, then accept, and sign off on the delivery. But, you can also do check-ins with a clipboard and copies of orders.

- **Have an established procedure to accept deliveries** and train all staff members. There will be written damaged-goods and return policies, which should be stored in the binder to support employee training.

These procedures will help employees catch ordering and shipping errors:

- **Note all visibly damaged merchandise on packing slips** or bills of lading or refuse the item. Your action depends on the vendor's recommendations.

- **Note any hidden damage on the packing slip**; advise management immediately and file a claim.

- **Inspect all items for damage,** signs of pests, excess debris, or mishandling.

- **Note overages or shortages on the packing slips** or bills of lading.

- **Sanitize hands and remove soiled aprons** to avoid potential contamination.

- **Take complaints to vendor's customer service department** or your sales representative.

LAST BUT NOT LEAST — YOUR OFFICE

You should have an office at the restaurant, even if you do bookkeeping at home. It need not be big and showy, but it needs to be centrally located and organized. Have sufficient lighting, file cabinets, shelves, a desk, and two chairs; the second chair is for meetings. When you arrange your office, consider these things:

- Be organized, so others can find files and paperwork in your absence.

- Store confidential and personnel documents in locked file cabinets.

- Have copies of Policy and Procedural Manuals available for employees.

As a business owner, you will be spending a good deal of time in your office. Be sure to make it comfortable — physically and emotionally. Your office is like every other area of the store. Organization is a key to making your restaurant run smoothly and profitably.

THE BEST SEATS IN THE HOUSE

The best seats in the house are now in full view of all the action. Special "chef's tables" or "kitchen tables" have become a trendy part of the fine-dining experience. Savvy food-lovers wait months for these coveted tables in Commander's Palace (New Orleans) or the Biltmore Hotel (Los Angeles). Even more casual chains such as Buca di Beppo (Minneapolis-based) have 50 units with highly profitable chef's tables. A National Restaurant Association 2000 industry study discovered four out of ten adults expressed an interest in display cooking — where food prep becomes entertainment. You can capture this audience by bringing a select few into the chef's domain. Bring your customers into your kitchen.

- **Safety.** Remember that diners need to be safely escorted and seated away from potential hazards. Check local health regulations regarding table placement. Some communities may require a low wall to separate the table from active work areas.

- **Create an entertaining, voyeuristic environment.** The heat, noise, and chaos are part of the charm — to a degree. Tune into your target customer's expectations. Place the table with a direct view of the cooking areas and away from the dish room. An elevated booth can alter the perspective so diners are looking slightly down. Choose roomy seating for six to eight. Couples can be grouped together to create a social event.

- **Go totally upscale with a glass-enclosed air-conditioned balcony** with a sound system (to regulate kitchen noise).

- **No room for a chef's table?** Perhaps you can incorporate a tour of the kitchen.

Commander's Palace asks all diners if they would like to leave through the kitchen to see the action. People relish the experience and even wait in line to go down a small back staircase.

WAITING

- **Decide on whether you will include exterior seating.** Know your target audience to determine whether long lines are a sign of a great hot spot or a signal that customers should go elsewhere for a quick meal.

- **Look for exterior seating materials that are easy to clean,** drain well, stay reasonably cool to the touch and will not snag or stain clothes or shed slivers.

- **Select chairs, benches, or low "walls" that can be secured for stability** and reflect your interior style.

MOOD SETTING

- **Introduce diners to your theme in bold strokes** with playground equipment, oversized decorative sculptures, dramatic color schemes, and fantasy environments.

- **Help differentiate your restaurant** from the monochromatic industrial looks of malls, strip centers, and office buildings. Transform your entry with colorful awnings, fresh flower boxes, window displays, attractive murals, and signs.

- **Add music,** piped through exterior speakers, to set the mood and stimulate appetites.

- **Post menus and add "daily special" signage.** These are great marketing tools to reinforce the decision to wait for a table or lure in potential customers passing by.

- **Greet customers with positive smells.** Fill your landscape with colorful and fragrant flowers, place freshly baked goods near exterior vents, and use pleasant-smelling cleaning products in entry ways.

MAY I TAKE YOUR COAT?

An entryway can be as grand as a hotel lobby or merely a hallway. No matter how much open space you have available just inside the front door, use it wisely. Entry areas need functional and decorative features that make the waiting process less stressful and seem shorter.

Your waiting area can include:

- **Comfortable seating with controlled temperatures.** Try not to freeze or bake customers every time the door opens.

- **Child activities.** Entertain the children with indoor play areas, arcade games, and other activities. Offer small trinkets.

- **Signs that give seating and serving instructions.** For example: "Please Seat Yourself," "Our Hostess Will Seat You," and "Our Sumptuous Buffet Starts Here." Make sure that the host/hostess and cashier stations are clearly defined.

- **Traffic-control features.** Construct a well-placed wall, movable barriers, signs, and railings. Also, pay phones, local publications, and vending machines must be located in a convenient position.

- **Menus.** Introduce "daily special" bulletin boards and displays. Have menus posted or hand them out. How about a decorative raw food display (e.g. whole salmons, fresh bread, or imported cheeses)? Display your desserts in the dining room. Offer a take-out service.

- **Retail items for sale.** Have a house specialty, stuffed animal mascot, or after-dinner treat.

- **Décor as entertainment.** Introduce décor features that entertain, such as fish tanks, jukeboxes, or local memorabilia.

- **Coat rooms.** Encourage your staff to assist customers with their coats. Whether your coat room is a walk-in closet or a formal affair with an attendant, do your best to provide a sense of security and have an organized way to "file and retrieve" checked items. Restrict access whenever possible. Tag check-in items and hand out corresponding chips or receipts. Provide ample airflow to keep dampness, cigarette/cigar smoke, and other smells from transferring. Use good-quality hangers to protect fragile sweaters, expensive furs, and heavyweight coats.

DINING ALFRESCO

Outdoor dining can be a great way to expand seating areas, stimulate appetites, take advantage of natural views, and entice others to join in for a good time. When considering an outdoor dining area, be certain to:

- **Review zoning regulations.** Check for possible restrictions, such as serving alcohol outdoors.

- **Look at the environment during morning, noon, and evening hours.** Note whether ambient lighting from streetlights and nearby buildings is overly bright. Is the air quality good? Does the noise level make conversation difficult? Are there any other undesirable conditions that cannot be controlled, such as wind or unpleasant smells?

- **Watch the sun during daylight hours to determine overly sunny and shadowy areas.** Is the heat during lunchtime excessive? Are customers blinded by direct or reflective glare off tabletops, walk surfaces, and nearby windows?

- **Consider whether food can be served quickly and easily in an alfresco setting.** Compute the distance from the kitchen. Create a flowchart to determine whether traffic patterns could create problems for servers carrying full trays.

Outwit environmental conditions and extend the outdoor dining season:

- **Strategically place plants, trees, and decorative accents to obscure unattractive views,** shelter customers from the wind, and soften noise levels.

- **Play soft music to reduce traffic sounds** and create a more intimate environment.

- **Provide ample and well-placed lighting** to read menus and ward off slip-and-fall injuries, without forsaking the desired atmosphere.

- **Warm chilly evenings with portable gas heaters,** fireplaces, and fire pits.

- **Include a well-outfitted "wait station"** to help reduce trips to a distant kitchen, keep beverages hot and cold, and shorten customer-request response times.

- **Tame Mother Nature and protect customers from sunburns** or sudden showers with well-secured umbrellas, patio covers, pergolas, and awnings.

- **Control the environment.** Install trap fencing, low walls, shrubbery, or other attractive barriers that direct people back through your main doorway. Physical barriers may also be a requirement when serving alcohol outdoors and can foil "dine and dash" events.

COLORS THAT COMPLEMENT

Moods often dictate the type of food customers seek out and where they eat it. Creating the right mood means using proper design elements and more subtle factors that affect humans psychologically.

COLORS AND MOODS

Scientists have proven that people are affected by the colors surrounding them. Why not incorporate one or two to create the right mood for your restaurant?

- **Yellow.** Sunlight, cheerful, vitality. Many designers believe every room should have a dash of yellow. Stay away from greenish yellows.

- **Red.** Intensity, passion, stimulates appetites. Use boldly or as an accent.

- **Blue.** Cool, clean, and refreshing. Blue should be used away from food, as it is not complementary.

- **Green.** Well-being, nature, fresh, and light. Be aware that it can also make people and food look off-color.

- **Gold.** Wealth and power. Warms up other colors and brightens dark wood.

- **Neutrals**. Masculine — darker browns. Feminine — lighter terra cotta shades. Rosy hues make food and people more attractive, rarely go out of style, and provide a background for bold color accents.

- **White.** Clean, fresh, and new. Can be a good foundation color, but beware — it can also signal institutional, bland, ordinary. Can create glare and eyestrain and be hard to maintain.

- **Black.** Death and mourning. However, used properly, black can add elegance and style. Black and white is a classic look. Avoid as a background color unless you are creating a nightclub or are using unique colored lighting. Do not forget that black can show finger and foot prints and can be difficult to keep looking clean.

THE ANCIENT ART OF FENG SHUI

Feng Shui (say fung shway) is the Chinese art form dealing with the proper placement of buildings and the elements within and how they can positively and negatively affect human behavior and fortunes. Whether you are an ardent believer or merely curious, Feng Shui offers some sound design principles.

AREAS FENG SHUI ADDRESSES

- **Seating.** It is considered bad Feng Shui to have your back to an entryway because enemies could surprise you. The design translation: Sitting with your back to the door makes you feel uncomfortable.

- **Mirrors.** Should reflect beautiful views (not glimpses of hallways and storage areas).

- **Colors.** Colors should be used in specific areas of the building to create specific positive influences, actions, and fortunes.

- **Activities.** All buildings are divided into areas where specific activities should take place. For example, your office should be placed in the building's money area.

- **Organization.** Clutter causes distress and chaos. Busy restaurants can benefit from the organizational aspects of Feng Shui.

Hire a Feng Shui advisor to bring customers (and good luck and money) into your restaurant. Try **www.fengshuidirectory.com** to find a local consultant. Or pick up a couple of books. Review the principles, which work for home or business. Popular author Lillian Too has written over 50 Feng Shui books and **Amazon.com** lists over 400 books on the subject.

You can also visit the World of Feng Shui online magazine at **www.wofs.com** or Feng Shui Times at **www.fengshuitimes.com.** Ask your architect and design consultants about this "hot" design topic. Many tradition-based creative professionals are adding Feng Shui to their skills.

COMMISSIONING ARTISTS

Finding the right artwork for your restaurant may mean that you have to commission an artist to create the perfect piece. Hiring an artist is not like hiring any other professional. What constitutes "art" is in the eye of the beholder and can frequently be difficult to define. Working closely with an artist during the conceptualization stage is critical. You or your interior decorator may choose to commission visual art such as a mural, an oil painting, a kinetic sculpture, a fountain, a stained glass window, photographs, metalwork, woodcarvings, ceramics, or glassware. Musical artists can also be commissioned to create customized background music or create original compositions. Bear in mind the following:

- **Discussion.** Discuss your concept in detail, including size, installation requirements, budget, and production timetable. Allow the artist to maintain the creative spirit. When commissioning a project, remember, overly coordinated mass-produced art is not your goal.

- **Review the artist's portfolio.** Examples of the artist's work can stimulate ideas and eliminate things that you do not like. Choose the right artist for the project. Artistic style and experience, along with your personal chemistry, are important.

- **Preview.** Ask whether initial sketches, models, or other preliminary design work can be previewed before expensive materials are purchased or too much time passes.

- **Your target audience.** Communicate your restaurant's theme, design notes, ideal customer profile, and other information that can give the artist more background and stimuli from which to draw.

- **Invest in good frames, target lighting, and proper display areas.** Showcase the artist's efforts for maximum effect.

- **Develop relationships with local artists** where featured artwork is rotated regularly to give your public areas fresh new looks. These relationships can be a great cost-effective way to help the artists and your business. Tasteful signage should be provided with details about the artist and subject matter.

MUSIC TO STIMULATE, SOOTHE, AND WOO

Whether you want to mask kitchen noises, create a romantic environment, or stimulate appetites, music can enhance your restaurant's bottom line. Properly selected background music builds upon your restaurant theme and brand and helps draw in specific customers. Like many restaurant features, it is best to incorporate music system needs in the early budgeting and design stages. The following offer some useful ideas for adding musical enhancements to your restaurant:

- **Hire a commercial music system specialist.** Ask him to assess your building's acoustics, develop a properly balanced system, and block irritating noises.

- **Select a system that meets your budget and customer quality expectations.** Installed commercial music systems range from $0.75 to $10 per square foot (pricing information from JBL Pro at **www.jblpro.com**). Discriminating adults will have higher standards than preteens.

- **Ask about upgradeability and volume capabilities** (loud = distortion free; soft = full tones). Explore options; e.g., would an "off-the-shelf" or custom system be more appropriate?

- **Paging.** Incorporate your paging needs to ensure staff and patrons can clearly hear pages and announcements without sacrificing music quality.

- **Check out your cable or satellite TV provider for commercial music options.** You may not need to set up a separate system. Digital Music Express, DMX, at

www.dmxmusic.com, offers over 100 CD-quality music channels through 800+ cable TV providers and direct satellite systems.

- **Remember the fees.** Businesses are legally required to pay music-licensing fees. Companies like Award-Winning Music at **www.royaltyfreemusic.com** can supply royalty-free music and eliminate this fee.

- **Create a sound-positive music niche away from dining room traffic lanes for piano or harp soloists.** Provide adjustable mood and spotlights and build in conveniently located electrical outlets and music system plug-ins. The flooring and substructure should be able to handle heavy instruments (up to 1,000 pounds for a grand piano). Have your designer incorporate background speakers to avoid the ugly "black box" look.

Do not overlook music in the kitchen and staff areas. Music is proven to enhance productivity and reduce stress. Just make certain that it does not overwhelm normal voice-level conversation or conflict with your dining room ambiance.

LET THERE BE LIGHT

Lighting is more than a chandelier here and a lamp there. Well-designed lighting creates a mood, enhances décor, makes it easier and safer to work, and makes diners and their food look better. When considering how to light your dining area, there are some things you will have to bear in mind. Take a long, hard look at your establishment. Consider these factors:

- **Level of natural light** and seasonal changes that affect it.

- **Activities within the room** — work areas, walkways, tables, waiting areas.

- **Ambiance you wish to create** — bright and stimulating or soft and romantic.

- **Artistic and creative uses** — the use of light and shadows to accent attractive features or mask "ugly" areas.

- **Lighting effects.** These can be obtained through wall sconces, fiber optics, chandeliers, track lighting, table lamps, directional spotlights, and even candles. Incorporate indirect lighting. Well-placed wall sconces add light without the glare.

- **Install dimmers to adjust your lighting levels by the time of day.** Lunchtime lighting should be brighter than evening lighting. Do not mistake a dim room for an elegant or romantic room. Dining is a social experience and good lighting should enhance that.

- **Use color-accurate table lighting to enhance the taste of food.** The sense of taste is affected by what the eyes see. Table lighting should softly accent the food, the china, and the diners.

- **Choose lighting that enhances a color scheme.** Incandescent lighting has a warmer, yellow-orange cast; fluorescent lighting produces a blue-green cast, which is a real appetite deadener. Halogen lights are closest to true white light.

- **Explore full-spectrum lighting** (which reportedly makes people feel healthier) for work areas and plant displays.

- **Create a balance within the room.** Overly bright areas next to dim rooms are a distraction and create eye-adjustment problems.

- **Invest in automation for complex lighting systems.** Companies like Lutron Electronics, 800-523-9466, **www.lutron.com**, offer a variety of preset lighting control systems.

- **Hire a lighting designer.** This lighting expert can help you upgrade existing lighting for appearance and energy savings or design a completely new look. Alternatively, visit GE Lighting online at **www.gelighting.com/na/business_lighting/lighting_applications/restaurant/index.htm** for design ideas, product selection, and energy audits.

CEILINGS

Ceilings are often overlooked when designing and decorating a restaurant. Diners actually do notice attractive colors, artistic displays, and great lighting along with all the dust, cobwebs, stains, and ugly ceiling materials. Attractive and clean ceilings tell customers that you value cleanliness throughout your restaurant. Here are some things you should know about choosing ceiling materials, designing unique ceilings, and maintaining ceilings:

- **Look for sound-deadening materials.** Your choice must be easy to clean and easy to secure tightly to beams, sheetrock, or suspension hardware.

- **Use moisture-proof, mildew-resistant materials.** Materials on ceilings in high-moisture areas (food prep, dishwashing, and restroom areas) must meet your local sanitary standards.

- **Transform ceilings with wallpaper, wood paneling, fabric, or other suspended treatments.** Just be certain that all materials are flame-resistant and meet code.

- **Use exposed beams, pipes, and vents as great color accents and high-tech art pieces**. Make certain paint and other treatments are fireproof and heat-resistant for heating and steam pipes and waterproof for water pipes.

- **Reflect more light and make the room feel larger with lighter-colored ceilings.** Remember, lighter-colored ceilings will also show venting-related dirt stains. Your local health department may require light ceilings in work areas to aid inspectors.

- **Make certain your HVAC is properly vented and well maintained to eliminate ceiling stains.** Lack of maintenance is not just unsightly; it also wastes electricity.

- **Natural light.** Incorporate skylights, light tubes, and windows to bring in more natural light. Make certain these can be easily cleaned at least once a quarter.

- **Think of your ceiling as another wall to be decorated.** Tin ceilings, "faux" painting techniques, mirrors, posters, faux beams, decorative molding, and fabric are all potential ways to add drama, carry out a theme, or enhance a peaceful environment. Search for unique ceiling materials from architectural salvage yards.

Covering Your Floors

Although people might not gush about your flooring, it certainly influences their overall impressions of your restaurant and your restaurant's atmosphere. In a busy environment with heavy foot traffic, flooring choices have lasting consequences and can overwhelm your construction or renovation budget. Here are a few facts you should consider when selecting flooring materials:

- **Hard-wearing.** Choose commercial grade whenever possible as anticipated usage and lifespan are typically much greater. Research commercial flooring, including hardwood flooring, at Floor You at **www.flooryou.com**. Select materials for public areas that:
  - Will not show scuff marks.
  - Can handle chairs or equipment being dragged or wheeled over them.
  - Will not be dented by high heels.
  - Have a medium-colored pattern to hide crumbs, and dirt between cleanings.

- **Warranties.** Check all manufacturers' warranties for coverage in commercial environments.

- **Compare hardwood flooring with modern vinyl or acrylic-infused look-alikes.** Remember, wood can be sanded and refinished easily, while the look-alike would need to be replaced. Select the more expensive strip vinyl flooring for a longer life expectancy. The ability to replace small damaged areas is an added benefit.

- **Ask your architect about the ways that concrete can be used in commercial buildings.** New processes and color techniques make concrete an attractive and durable choice.

- **Explore more unusual flooring such as cork and bamboo.** These green products have unique looks and are great high-traffic choices.

- **Avoid dark, high-gloss flooring,** which can appear wavy and magnify any substructure imperfections.

Make certain all flooring is:

- Easy to maintain.
- Durable and stain-resistant.
- Slip-resistant in wet and dry conditions.
- Code approved for food prep areas.

Seating

You will be profitable if you have enough seats or can turn them quickly enough. This means creating an environment where people can find a seat when they want it, rest comfortably, and have ample elbowroom — and will leave when you want them to. Your goal in choosing your dining room seating is to balance beauty, functionality, and psychological factors. Your seating choices add decorative elements to the room, dictate the traffic/work flow, and signal diners to the upcoming experience. Proper seating can help your wait staff serve patrons more quickly and efficiently.

When choosing seating, remember to choose chairs that:

- **Are easy to move, stack, and store.**

- **Provide plenty of elbow room** and remember left-handed customers.

- **Do not overlook solo diners.** Have plenty of suitable deuces (tables for two) in good locations and have a communal table for those craving some company.

- **Select chairs that are of appropriate height in relationship to the table.** Is the legroom sufficient without making shorter adult diners feel like children? Supply sturdy chairs for larger folks and booths where shorter customers can easily reach their plates.

- **Durability.** Purchase sturdy, stable seating that can handle the wear-and-tear of a busy restaurant.

- **Consider your customers.** Opt for swivels, wheels, glider pads, and other enhancements to make sitting down easier. Or customize wooden chairs with chair pads. Remember, elderly and handicapped patrons may need roomier access.

- **Supply high chairs** that can slide close to tables and booster seats that fit your chairs and/or benches.

- **Do not forget that you may want to use your chairs for alfresco dining options.** Choose materials that will not tarnish when exposed to the sun.

- **Hire a restaurant consultant with experience in seating design and layout.** She can help you calculate the profit potential of your seating. Profit potential is critical when expanding your seating to ensure that the ROI is significant enough to offset your costs.

There are a multitude of options available to you when choosing your seating. Following are a few excellent resources.

Art Marble Furniture brings a unique elegance to your non-commercial facility. Their granite top tables are affordable, durable, and lightweight. They offer a beautiful choice for your dining room. Check the selection of chairs and stools that were designed to complement granite top tables at **www.artmarblefurniture.com** or by calling 866-400-1688.

Art Marble Furniture dining options

Gasser Chair Company offers a variety of chair options. They were the first to design a unique style of aluminum framed seating specifically for the hospitality industry. The second generation of the Gasser family is still guided by the founders' principles and proudly continues the tradition of introducing new ideas and innovations. Visit their Web site at **www.gasserchair.com** or call 330-759-2234, fax 330-759-9844, or e-mail **sales@gasserchair.com**.

Royal Industries offers a wide variety of table and chair options. They

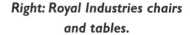

Above: booth from Gasser Chair Company.

Right: Royal Industries chairs and tables.

also offer highchairs, children's chairs, and booster seats. For the full line of products, please visit **www.royalindustriesinc.com/source/furniture.php** or contact Royal Industries at 800-782-1200 or fax 800-321-3295.

SELECTING TABLES

Unless you are a drive-up-only establishment, your guests will need a table to gather around. The following offer some practical tips on table selection:

- **Determine whether your tables will be visible or covered.** You will save on less attractive, yet practical, surfaces if tablecloths hide them.

- **Choose light-colored tabletops if you are using white or pale tablecloths.**

- **Confirm that tabletop surfaces are waterproof.** Sealants or a glass top can be added to less durable surfaces.

- **Look for self-leveling legs/bases to compensate for uneven flooring.** There is a solution for wobbly tables, and you can find it at **www.tableshox.com.** Wobbly tables are the number one customer complaint. Call 800-457-6454.

- **Think of your tables as decorative opportunities.** Unusual legs, eye-popping colors, and creative mosaics can be incorporated. Paper items (old calendars, cocktail napkins) can be displayed under urethane sealer or a glass top.

- **Review your customer makeup and mix and match tables.** Factor in guests with books, newspapers, and briefcases and solo diners preferring larger tables.

TABLE SIZES	
Number of Guests	Size
1 – 2 guests (2-top)	24-in. by 30-in. square
3 – 4 guests (4-top)	36-in. by 36-in. square
3 – 4 guests (4-top)	30-in. by 48-in. rectangle
3 – 4 guests (4-top).	42-in. round.
5 – 6 guests	2-top and 4-top joined
5 – 6 guests.	48-in. or 54-in. round
7 – 8 guests	Joined two 4-tops
7 – 8 guests	72-in. round

- **Purchase tables with uniform heights and widths for easier grouping and chair compatibility.** Purchase tops and bases separately for additional flexibility and easier storage.

- **Consider your customers' sizes.** Larger customers may feel cramped at smaller tables. Likewise, oversized booths can make it hard for shorter customers to sit within reach of drinks or condiments.

TABLES FOR DISABLED CUSTOMERS

- **Purchase tables 27-inches high by 30-inches wide by 19-inches deep.**

- **Examine booth ends for support legs that will not interfere with wheelchairs.**

- **Set up a typical table setting for your restaurant to compute accurate table size.** An average place setting is 24-inches wide. Do not forget to allow for trays in self-service situations.

- **Select booths with freestanding tables.** You will be able to shift these to accommodate smaller or larger guests.

- **Add a lazy Susan to large round tables** for condiments and family-style dining.

SEATING AS DÉCOR

From '50s retro vinyl to high-tech banquettes to wing back chairs, the seats you offer your customers should reflect your dining room design or theme. Your food service style has a direct impact on the type of eating and sitting surfaces that you provide. Here are some popular choices for seating, based on your service style. Choose the type of seating that will compliment your décor. Consider which category is most appropriate for your establishment.

- **Fast-food.** For outdoors, choose picnic-table-style seating with benches and cover umbrellas. For indoors, choose counters with stools for diners, bench-table combinations, booths, and banquettes. Take-out? Choose chairs for waiting only. Focus on hard-surface seating (concrete, molded plastic, vinyl) that can handle heavy traffic, cleans easily, and encourages quick turns.

- **Cafeteria/buffet.** Seating geared at easy access. Freestanding tables and chairs with ample walk space. Tables and carpets designed for heavy traffic and easy cleaning.

- **Sit-down.** A combination of seating could be provided to accommodate diners who prefer the privacy of a booth or the visibility of a centrally located table. Understanding your ideal customer will help you choose which a customer would most likely prefer.

- **Family restaurants.** There is plenty to choose from when it comes to family-style restaurants. Just be certain to select sizes and materials suitable for busy kids.

- **Formal dining.** Formal restaurants will typically include more soft surfaces, which are considered more luxurious. Colors will be more muted and elegant.

YOUR PROFIT CENTER

Filling and turning seats is your primary profit center. Ample capacity means greater profit potential. Your seating can directly affect your pocketbook, from the initial purchase to the room layout to upkeep. You need to accommodate sufficient customers on an hourly, weekly, and monthly basis to pay for overhead and food and post a profit. Turning tables quickly is critical in high-volume, low-margin operations. Here are some profit-motive suggestions you should consider:

- **Compute your average check size.** Figure out if extra seats mean greater profits. For example, bulky barrel-shaped chairs fit your décor but require more space. Smaller seating allows you to serve ten more people for lunch. If your average ticket is $12, you take in an extra $120 per lunch shift and over $2,500 extra per month.

- **Figure out how many customers you will need to seat during peak times.** Work at minimizing wait times and increasing your potential to serve more people per hour with ample seating.

- **Do not make it too comfortable.** If your goal is quick turnover, use more rigid seating to subtly discourage lingering.

- **Help your servers.** Table layout can affect the speed in which diners are served. If faster service is your goal, make certain servers are not battling your table placement.

- **Help your bus person.** Do not use fussy tablecloths and napkins and make certain surfaces can be cleaned quickly and efficiently.

SEATING AS WORK (AND PLAY) AREAS

Consider the ergonomics of your chosen seating and dining area layout. For more information on how customers and staff interact with physical objects, read the section on ergonomics.

Here are some practical ideas you should consider that will enhance the dining experience and improve server performance.

Determine the activities your customers and staff will be doing at the table.

- **Will salads or desserts be prepared and served tableside?**

- **Will diners wish to use their laptops for business, read the morning paper, or feed small children?**

- **Will diners be cooking or preparing their own food? Dipping bread into a fondue pot or assembling a taco?**

- **Will people want a view of your stage or other focal point?**

- **Review how well servers can reach each diner.** Will they be forced to hoist heavy bowls or drink trays over a patron's head? Does a maze exist or will food come directly from the kitchen?

- **Make certain staff can rearrange tables quickly and easily to accommodate the party's size.** Can you quickly create a cozy table for 2 or seating for 15?

- **Allow for tabletop accessories** (napkins, salt, and pepper) and marketing items (dessert or drink specials). Can the table accommodate oversized place mats, plates, or glassware? Will silverware for multi-course presentations be well displayed?

ACTING AS YOUR OWN DECORATOR

Many entrepreneurs enjoy the creative process of decorating with or without professional help. Some projects are not large enough to warrant the services of an interior design consultant. Perhaps you are simply seeking concept ideas. The following are some valuable national resources for restaurant décor:

DECORATING RESOURCES	
Décor Item	**Source**
Limited to your imagination	eBay (auction site) **www.ebay.com**
Antique architectural elements	Architectural Antiques **www.archantiques.com**
Antique lighting	Antique Lighting **www.antique-lighting.com**
Restoration/decorative hardware	Crown City Hardware **www.crowncityhardware.com** • 800-950-1047
Plastic food replicas, and menu-oriented displays	Fax Food **www.faxfoods.com** • 800-929-1189
Antique hardware	Liz's Antique Hardware **www.lahardware.com**
Sports décor	Sports Expressions **www.sportsexpressions.com** • 480-596-1913

DECORATING RESOURCES

Décor Item	Source
Posters, vintage food ads	Bare Walls • 800-455-3955 **www.barewalls.com/indexes/b2brest.html**
Vintage neon, and signs	Roadhouse Relics **www.roadhouserelics.com** • 512-442-NEON
Everything from rugs to columns	Interior Mall **www.interiormall.com** • 800-590-5844
Giclee canvas, framed art	Ariel of France **www.arieloffrance.com**
Robots	Robot Factory **www.robotfactory.com**
Celtic pub items	ARE Restaurant Equipment **www.amer-rest-equip.com** Celtic Dragon Pub Co. **www.celticdragonpubco.com**
Fiberglass mounted fish	King Sailfish Mounts **www.kingsailfish.com**
Antique cash registers & drug store memorabilia	National Brass **www.nationalbrass.com**
Celebrity memorabilia	Startifacts **www.startifacts.com**
Neon	Neonetics **www.neonetics.com**
Cowboy and Mexican	El Paso Saddle Blanket **www.elpasosaddleblanket.com**
"Tiffany" lamps	Meyda **www.meyda.com**
Animated displays	Characters Unlimited **www.charactersunlimitedinc.com** • 702-294-0563

A few suggestions for sourcing innovative decorative items:

- **Architectural salvage yards** — old gates, wrought iron fencing, arches, pillars, signs, windows.

- **Flea markets and antique stores.** Find lots of ideas for trash-to-treasure, such as collectable glassware to integrate with your fine china, old food advertising, and old kitchen items.

- **Aquarium stores.** Integrating fresh- or salt-water fish can make a colorful addition.

- **Garden shops** — fountains, live plants. Bring outdoor garden items like arbors, lattices, and seed packages inside.

- **Craft stores** — artificial plants, decoupage, and glass 110 etchings.

- **Paint supply** — faux painting supplies and techniques. Paint is a versatile and inexpensive decorative tool.

- **Kitchen shops, home décor stores.** Walk up and down the aisles looking for new and creative ways to incorporate ordinary items into your décor.

THE SMALLEST ROOM IN THE HOUSE

Restrooms may be the smallest rooms in the house but they are important for guests. An ample, clean restroom speaks loudly about how you value cleanliness and are considerate of guests' needs. Here are some practical and creative ideas on designing and decorating restrooms:

- **Locate them with easy access.** Depending upon your plumbing layout, restrooms can be up front, so guests can enter before moving into the dining room or tucked back out of view. For their children's safety, many parents would prefer restroom entrances that are visible from the dining area.

- **Remember your customers' physical needs.** Provide sinks, dryers, and dispensers at levels appropriate for children and wheelchair-bound patrons. For ADA advice, call the U.S. Department of Justice at 800-514-0301.

- **Plan on ample restroom capacity.**

- **Small restaurants (up to 50 seats) should allot at least a 35- to 40-square-foot area for one toilet and a washbasin.**

- **Create a room that reflects the front-of-the-house.** The more elegant the restaurant, the more spacious and elegant the restroom.

- **Select materials that wear well,** will not show dirt, and can handle strong cleaners. Ceramic tile is great but be aware of grout discoloration.

- **More automated is better.** People dislike touching bathroom surfaces and automation conserves water and electricity.

Make your female customers happy with:

- **Extra square footage and more stalls.** Women expect more privacy and have to deal with more carry-in items (purses, strollers) and small children.

- **Adequate and flattering lighting and mirrors** by which to touch up makeup and hair.

- **A separate, clean nursing area with comfortable seating.** Would you like to eat in a typical washroom?

- **Staff facilities.** Provide separate facilities for staff if possible.

FRONT-OF-THE-HOUSE SUPPORT STATIONS

Realistically, not all food prep and service work can be accomplished behind closed doors. To do so would exhaust your wait staff unnecessarily, slow down your service, and create a workflow nightmare in the back-of-the house.

WORK STATIONS

Depending upon your restaurant layout and service methods, some workstations could have multiple functions. Here are some different types of workstations you might need in the front-of-the-house:

- **Reception**. Meet and greet, take reservations, assign customers to servers.

- **Computerization.** Point-of-sale ordering centers, item availability, and inventory control.

- **Cashiering.** Ring up and accept payments, process credit cards, sell retail items.

- **Food service.** Beverage centers, salad prep area, dessert service.

- **Dinnerware and utensil storage.** Storage for place settings, additional napkins, specialty utensils.

SUPPORT STATIONS

Here are some helpful suggestions on designing and implementing front-of-the-house support stations:

- **Make them attractive.** Support stations can be camouflaged with decorative panels and plants or designed to be a part of the "show."

- **Cleanliness and orderliness are required** when service personnel prepare food in full view of guests. Hide all the extra equipment and supplies behind doors.

- **Build in floor drains**, use scuff-resistant baseboards, and add casters to equipment that must be moved for cleaning.

- **Reduce lifting and carrying with mobile carts and rolling waste receptacles.**

- **Use properly aimed task lighting** to avoid glare while allowing staff full visibility of the work surface.

- **Use anti-fatigue mats and non-slip flooring.**

- **Design work areas to minimize stooping, reaching, and lifting.**

- **Run computer network, phone, and electrical wiring to each workstation.**

- **Incorporate hand and/or utility sinks wherever possible to save steps and promote cleanliness.**

- **Provide ample counter space below pass-throughs to add garnishes, verify orders, and fill trays.**

- **Consider including a small (and quiet) under-counter glass washer for thorough cleanup of critical tools and utensils.**

STREAMLINE YOUR BACK-OF-THE-HOUSE

The "show" may be up front – but its driving force is behind the swinging doors. A well-designed and properly outfitted back-of-the-house combines three elements: ergonomics, efficiency, and economy:

ERGONOMICS

Create a worker-friendly environment that protects your employees and improves attitudes. Ask yourself the following questions about each piece of equipment:

- Are the control knobs, levels, on/off switches, or other critical components placed within easy reach?

- Can shorter or left-handed employees safely use it?

- Are people walking through a maze of equipment and worktables?

- Is the height accurate for sitting, standing, or reaching?

- Can people easily move the object to use or clean it?

- Can a different layout, material, or design make it easier on the operator's body?

- Can a piece of equipment or better tool reduce repetitive stress injuries?

EFFICIENCY

Efficiency translates directly into time and time is money. When selecting tools, fixtures and equipment, and establishing layouts, you should always weigh the ability to produce more or save more against the initial cost. A more efficient dishwasher might cost more initially; however, the ROI translates into reduced waits for clean dishes, lower dependence on employees, and fewer plates to purchase. Ask yourself the following questions before making any kitchen design or purchasing decisions:

- **Does the item make a task easier or reduce labor costs?**

- **Can one piece of equipment be used for multiple types of tasks?** How about a mixer with grinder or slicer attachments?

- **Are the features easy to use?** Will people abandon the "time-saving" features because they do not understand them or get frustrated when operating them?

- **Does it improve serving times or the quality of your service?** It could be a computerized ordering system or direct access to finishing and holding areas.

ECONOMY

Whether upgrading or outfitting a new back-of-the-house, it is rare that you will have an unlimited budget. Economically sound decisions can improve your profit potential and save you thousands over the life of your business. Overspending takes money out of your pocket that you never recover. When considering the financial impact of designs, tools, fixtures, and equipment, do not forget to:

- **Compare lifetime costs.** Factor in costs for energy, maintenance, cleaning, and consumables (filters, ink cartridges, specialty paper). Factor in labor savings through reduced overtime or fewer employees.

- **Consider upgrade capabilities and costs** should you need something bigger, better, faster, harder.

- **Review trade-in allowances, potential rebates, low-interest loans, and special offerings** by utility companies, manufacturers, and distributors.

- **Save steps whenever possible.** There is a direct correlation between the economy of movement and productivity. Shaving even a few seconds off service times can increase your profit margin and make customers happier.

FIXTURES AND EQUIPMENT

Outfitting your kitchen and public areas requires purchasing a variety of fixtures and equipment used to prepare, store, and display raw and finished products. Fixtures such as glass display cases and miscellaneous "non-cooking" equipment, such as carts and racks, can quickly eat up your budget. Unless the fixture is a moneymaker (such as a retail display case), do not go overboard. Here are some resources and practical tips on purchasing fixtures and equipment for your restaurant:

Shop online directories for local and regional suppliers:

- Power Sourcing: **www.powersourcing.com/se/restaurantfixturesequipment.htm**

- Foodservice Central: **www.foodservicecentral.com**

- Foodservice.com: **www.foodservice.com**

- Restaurant Operator: **www.restaurantoperator.com**

- FoodServiceSearch.com: **www.foodservicesearch.com**

- SEFA (Supply and Equipment Foodservice Alliance): **www.sefa.com**

- Food Service Equipment Reports Magazine: **www.fermag.com**

- Business.com (search engine): **www.business.com/directory/food_and_beverage/ restaurants_and_foodservice/equipment_and_supplies.**

ITCHEN DESIGN

Poorly designed kitchens and equipment are a major complaint of chefs and assistants. Poor planning decreases productivity, increases wait times, contributes to employee turnover, and distracts busy workers. Whether you are a chef-owner or just share the vision of a talented chef, your attention to food quality and prompt service relies on the efficiency of a properly outfitted kitchen. Good kitchen design is an art and a science. Here is where an experienced consultant comes in handy – to balance space limitations, safety issues, food prep needs, and budgets without sacrificing food quality, productivity, and your staff's sanity.

- **Your menu directly affects your kitchen design.** Take a look at the suggestions outlined in the section "What's on the Menu?" before you make any design decisions. What you will serve (raw ingredients and prepared foods) and how you will serve it determine your needs for prep, assembly, storage, and serving.

- **Workflow.** There are several different workflow patterns that can be used to create a balance between passive storage and active work areas.

You will need areas to accommodate for:

- **Hot and cold foods** — prep and assembly

- **Beverage** — dispensing and storage

- **Storage** — food and non-food items

- **Sanitation** — ware washing and front-of-the-house cleaning equipment and supplies

- **Receiving** — off-loading space and inventory systems

YOUR CHEF'S OFFICE

Here are some suggestions on how you might make your kitchen layout work for your chef and support staff:

- **Break your kitchen activities into self-contained workstations.** Make sure that ingredients, tools, equipment, supplies, and preserving storage are within easy reach.

- **Create work triangles.** Triangle or diamond layouts give quick access to prep tables, sinks, and cooking equipment. Straight-line layouts work best for assembly line-style prep and cooking where more than one person participates.

- **Draw out traffic maps.** Minimize unnecessary steps and crisscrossing paths.

- **Locate your cooking and final prep areas closest to the dining room.** Keep food temperatures accurate.

- **Consider placing your volume or batch cooking areas towards the back of the kitchen** and your to-order needs nearest the dining room. Production that requires little tending should not take up high-activity space.

- **Isolate dishwashing tasks.** The noises and chemical smell should not mingle with your dining room ambiance.

- **Allow for ample open space.** People need to pass, carts need to be rolled, shelving moved, large buckets wheeled, and trays lifted.

- **Coordinate placement of all equipment that requires venting to share a single ventilation system** and reduce costs. Check your local code requirements on ventilation of heat- and moisture-producing equipment.

- **Include plenty of waste receptacles.** Divide by type of waste if you will be implementing recycling programs. Check with your waste management company on local requirements for segregating glass, metal, and paper.

- **Design kitchens with multiple sets of "in" and "out" doors.** Examples: doors that go directly from the dining area to the dish room (bypassing food prep); doors from the bar to the dish room, ice machine, and/or barware and liquor storage.

- **Ask your staff.** Take advantage of their daily experiences and enhance their work areas during a kitchen renovation.

PLENTY OF STORAGE

No one complains about too much storage. Ample storage allows for storing costly perishables, organizing unwieldy linens and fragile dishes, buying in quantity, and warehousing seasonal décor. Well-designed storage creates a safer work environment, encourages productivity, decreases clutter, and saves you money. Increase productivity by creating three types of storage:

TYPES OF STORAGE		
Active	**Backup**	**Long-term**
Accessed repeatedly throughout the day. Locate this type of storage closest to the active work area.	Refill (bulk) items for active areas and items used occasionally during a typical week. Locate further away from the active work area but where easily accessible.	Nonperishable, special-use and seasonal items. Use out-of-reach, back-of-the-building areas, under stairs, and other less-accessible locations.

Here are some practical ideas on creating useful storage areas.

- **Protect employees from injury.** Place heavy items close to waist height. Provide sturdy step stools, ladders, and rolling carts. Except in rarely accessed areas, keep shelving shallow enough for easy reach. See the section "Creating Environments that Work with People."

- **Make storage cabinets in public areas attractive.** Make them a part of the décor. Use materials that clean easily.

- **Recapture additional space.** Clear out (toss, sell, or trade in) fixtures, equipment, or tools that have not been used in the past 18-24 months.

- **Storage between deliveries.** Develop a list of dry and perishable foods that must be on hand to serve your average number of meals between deliveries. You will need enough space to store a two- to four-week supply of dry foods and one week or less of perishable foods.

- **Review your purchases.** Reassess purchases from a storage perspective. Base your review on availability (delivery frequency) and packaging (quantity and type). Remember, special order items, infrequent deliveries, and high-usage products require greater storage capacity.

- **Create separate (but convenient) storage for chemical cleaners and other hazardous materials.** Check your local regulations regarding hazardous materials storage.

- **Evaluate all storage for potential cross-contamination issues.**

- **Incorporate easily movable or "sectional" storage whenever possible to maximize layout flexibility.**

TORAGE

You will need various storage locations. These include raw ingredients, finished products, refrigerated areas, and dry storage, along with equipment and supply storage. Sometimes you should have short-term storage. I did this on unusually high volume weeks, when I ordered substantially more supplies and assigned someone to move supplies to the usual storage area as items were used. Take a close look at your menu and the necessary supplies in order to determine how to arrange your storage areas.

DRY STORAGE

Establish your dry storage area near your delivery door. Be sure there is enough access to move items in and out without difficulty. Any shelving needs to be at least six inches off the floor to avoid posts.

WASTE AND RECYCLING

The way you dispose of your waste products is important. Here are some tips to help you manage your waste and lower disposal costs.

- **A waste disposal unit.** Stainless steel systems with automatic reversal controls are best. Buy a unit with enough horsepower and rotor size to handle your food waste. Review expected lifespan when comparing units.

- **Build a recycling center.** Include recycling equipment in your rear storage area layout.

- **Arrange for grease/meat waste rendering companies for pickup.**

- **Use sorting bins and convenient waste receptacles.** Install color-coded recycling containers on wheels for easy use.

- **Plan for large quantities of paper, cardboard, plastics, glass, metal cans, and food waste.**

- **Cardboard balers can pay for themselves through reduced hauling costs.**

- **A commercial-grade trash compactor.** You will have some trash even if you have an aggressive recycling program. A compactor can pay for itself by saving you bin use and hauling fees.

- **Discussions with local recycling companies and government waste management agencies.** Recycling companies can handle grease/oil waste and pick up glass and cardboard. Some companies specialize in food service waste. Your city or county can help you develop waste-reduction programs.

WORKING (AND RESTING) BEHIND THE SCENES

The kitchen is not the only area where work has to be accomplished in order to run a successful restaurant. Think about the various non-food activities that your restaurant will perform: accounting, personnel, receiving and storing, and other business functions. Here are some ideas for creating suitable support areas:

- **Office space.** Designate an area where cash can be counted, deposits made, checks written, employees interviewed, and records stored. Figure out which tasks will be handled in this area before determining the amount of space required, the location, and equipment needs.

- **Non-food storage areas.** Allocate a specific area for the handling of replacement china, flatware, and tabletop accessories, along with seasonal decorations and catering/banquet/meeting equipment such as podiums and audiovisual equipment. Also, wood-burning fireplaces and ovens require significant space for wood storage.

- **Receiving area.** Create space for a designated "receiving area." It allows employees to count and inspect inbound shipments with minimum disruption. It is also easier in an open space to break down bulk items for quick and effective storage. Restaurants that provide delivery services or offer outside catering may also require a staging area.

EMPLOYEE REST AREAS

A rest area for employees should consist of something more than a back step. Creating an employee-only area is a great way to tell your team how important they are to you and your operation. Some physical benefits you can provide for your employees include:

- **A place to rest their tired feet**, have a peaceful meal, and take a shower or catch a quick nap before the next major rush.

- **Lockers** to secure their personal items and decorate with family pictures.

- **Employee-only lavatories** outfitted with personal necessities and medical supplies.

- **A communication center** with telephone for local calls, a daily paper, phone books, and a bulletin board.

- **Break rooms** that can also handle new employee orientation, training sessions, and other internal meetings.

CONSTRUCTION & RENOVATION

SELECTING THE PERFECT SITE

Selecting land for custom ground-up construction, "build to suit" locations, and leased space is a complex decision. It is a blend of technical issues (flooding potential), market research (too many competitors), financial requirements (costly excavation), and governmental restrictions (liquor licensing). Also, consider the following issues:

- **Feasibility study.** If your budget can handle a feasibility study (figure $5,000 or more), experienced analysts can help take the guesswork out of the process. This process can be cost prohibitive for many small-restaurant owners. Ask your other consultants and construction professionals to share their concerns and advice.

Tips and warning signals when selecting bare land, "build to suit," and leased space:

- **Find an experienced commercial real estate broker.**

- **Obtain free site selection resources** and Location Strategies newsletters at **www.locationstrategies.com**.

- **Find a location with the appropriate zoning.** Walk away from locations that require variances.

- **Check on the land's history.** Is the land a reclaimed dump site or marsh? Are mosquitoes or flies a problem in the area? Was it under water during the 100-year flood?

- **Determine if the elevation creates problems.** The view may be great, but will bad weather make the driveway impassable? Low elevations may create drainage and sewage problems. Are there accessibility issues for elderly or disabled customers?

- **Review the FEMA National Flood Insurance Web site at www.fema.gov/nfip.** Every area of the country has been carefully mapped out for potential flooding and national flood insurance eligibility.

- **Select a well-shaped lot.** Is there ample room for parking? Can delivery and garbage trucks get to your back door? Is the frontage sufficient to be seen by potential customers driving by?

- **Beware of short-term leases.** You may prefer a shorter commitment, but you could be putting your restaurant in jeopardy and be forced to move or pay escalated rent.

- **Look at the traffic.** Will customers cross busy traffic lanes? Is there direct access? Are there freeway off-ramps or will the world pass you by at 65 miles per hour?

- **Verify that utilities are available and adequate** for a busy restaurant before you put down any money. Your commercial real estate broker and local utility companies can verify this.

- **Read the "Location, Location, Location" section for more information.**

BUILDING PERMITS AND CODES

Most construction and remodeling projects will require several different permits. These permits and inspections are to assure the public that your facility complies with the community's accepted standards for personal and environmental health and safety. Your architect, restaurant consultant, and contractor should be diligent in their code compliance. Lack of attention can cost you time and money. Below are tips on handling permit and code issues that a typical restaurant will encounter:

- **Zoning.** Whether you purchase land or lease a building, your location must be zoned for food service activities, including liquor licenses, music venues, retail sales, and "after-hours" operations. Zone regulations will also affect signs, awnings, outdoor dining, parking, and noise levels. Exceptions can be made, but it is best to find the location that most closely meets your needs without variances.

- **Covenants and restrictions.** Neighborhoods, malls, and building complexes all may have covenants and restrictions that govern your business activities. Your real estate broker can assist you with these during lease or purchasing negotiations. Do not forget to inform your project manager and design team of these regulations.

- **Franchisee or licensee requirements.** Franchises and licensed concept companies are exacting in their requirements — many of which directly affect your construction and design efforts.

- **Building codes.** Your local building codes are adopted to protect the public. Compliance is mandatory and can sometimes be subjective, based upon an inspector's experience. Building codes control your design, construction methods, and materials used. Equipment and fixtures, such as exhaust systems, ventilation, lighting, and sanitation equipment, are all areas that must be "code approved."

- **Plumbing, mechanical, and electrical codes.** These specific construction industries are generally overseen by separate permit requirements and inspection procedures.

- **Health department regulations.** No other public service department so directly impacts your food service business. Complex (and occasionally arcane) rules and regulations require diligent attention. These complexities are a prime reason why your architects, consultants, and contractors should have extensive local experience in restaurant development.

- **Americans with Disabilities Act.** The ADA defines accessibility and traffic-pattern requirements for people with disabilities. Most public facilities must meet these regulations.

TRANSFORMING BUILDINGS INTO RESTAURANTS

Over the past several decades, restaurateurs have been transforming warehouses, historical buildings, classic homes and churches, antique train stations, defunct banks, abandoned gas stations, and old theaters into dining establishments. Economic declines, corporate mergers, and neighborhood shifts have created an ample supply of vacant buildings, one of which, with some imagination and resources, can become the restaurant of your dreams. The functional requirements of preparing and serving food have their own set of challenges and, when coupled with converting untraditional locations, may present you with significant renovation costs. However, the rewards can be more than worth the effort and cost. If you have not considered renovating an untraditional building, you might ponder some of the following suggestions:

- **Consider bank buildings.** Mergers and acquisitions have created hundreds of vacant bank and savings-and-loans branches with great locations and plenty of parking.

- **Need a drive-up window?** Gas stations typically have ample space for window service and parking.

- **Renovating abandoned property can be time consuming and costly.** So why do it? Love of a community.

- **Research government-backed reclamation projects.** Downtown redevelopment programs can underwrite a portion of your renovation costs, offer low-cost loans, and provide you with great marketing resources. Grants may also be available in areas designated as economic-stimulus areas.

- **Contact state and private historical organizations, civic groups, and preservation societies.** Learn about redevelopment districts and properties suitable for preservation.

- **Create a coalition of business owners.** Pool resources for revitalizing a building or city block.

- **Ask about financial incentives for converting underutilized buildings.** These can be license and permit waivers, tax abatements, and financing subsidies.

NEW CONSTRUCTION TIMELINE

Just how long will it take from concept through construction to your grand opening? New construction timelines are filled with pitfalls and unforeseen obstacles and sometimes things even come in under schedule. A typical new construction project will take two years or more. Concept development, market research, and financing can take a year. Acquiring land, licenses, architectural plans, and blueprints will take another eight to ten months. The contractor bidding process can eat up two to four months. Restaurant equipment can take six to eight weeks for delivery. Custom furniture may be backlogged for eight to 12 weeks. You will also need to plan for construction delays due to lack of materials and laborers. Here are some guidelines to help your project stay on track:

- **Be thorough when completing paperwork.** Loan documents, zoning variances, permits, and licenses must be fully completed and accurate. When in doubt, ask before submitting. Government agencies are not typically prepared to expedite resubmitted paperwork.

- **Introduce yourself to your future neighbors when zoning issues are a concern.** Meet with key businesses, residents, and influential parties to build support. Gather supporters at public zoning meetings.

- **Use contractors and suppliers with reputations for timeliness.** Include completion-bonus clauses in contracts. Select a project team leader. Meet regularly.

- **Create a project management system.** Purchase an oversized expanding briefcase-style folder to keep important documents, notes, and follow-up schedules. Keep this folder close to answer questions and locate information quickly.

- **Plan ahead.** Do not rush to start construction. Poor planning creates inevitable changes that delay schedules. These changes are rarely competitively bid (remember you have people waiting) and can quickly escalate your project costs.

- **Empower people to make decisions.** Set parameters on decisions that your team members can make. Establish responsibilities and let people know whom they can go to for an answer.

PEN FOR BUSINESS DURING A RENOVATION

Should you close the doors to remodel or hope that the customers do not notice the sawdust in the soup? Deciding whether or not to keep the doors open during a major renovation can be complicated. As a restaurateur, you must evaluate the immediate financial impact of empty seats and weigh the long-term effects of a closure. In some highly competitive markets, closing for even a few weeks could translate into an unrecoverable or costly decline in business. The following suggestions will help you weigh the pros and cons and cope with the process:

- **Speak with your contractor about your concerns.** Whenever possible, review, and adapt the work schedule to your slow periods. "After-hours" or tight scheduling may cost more, but compare that to potential lost revenue.

- **Have your contractor detail the construction methods** to understand just how dusty, dirty, smelly, or noisy your restaurant will be. A less-disruptive alternative method may be available. Compare cost versus convenience factors.

- **Establish a contract with stiff penalties for not meeting deadlines** to keep inconvenience and/or closure dates to a minimum.

- **Compute the cost of being closed** for X number of days and weigh that against the project requirements, reduced payroll costs, minimized inconvenience, and potential customer exodus.

- **Cleaning up.** Write into your contract that all subcontractors and laborers will be responsible for daily cleanup, trash hauling, and removal/disposal of all old materials and equipment.

- **Trust the experts.** Seek the advice and support of your contractor, designer, architect, and restaurant consultant. They should be able to offer some creative solutions based on their direct experience.

- **Understand the situation and make the most of it.** Some renovations simply cannot be done in your spare time; they require 100 percent of your facility and pocketbook.

Develop a "Closed for a New Look" plan to announce your closure and reopening. Take active steps to not be forgotten by your regulars and the community.

- **Close your restaurant during activities involving hazardous or "irritating" materials**, such as fiberglass insulation, lead paint or asbestos removal, and pest-control procedures.

WORKING IN A CONSTRUCTION ZONE

Many redecorating and some renovation projects can be handled without a temporary closure. With some good communication and careful planning, your customers can be given a sneak preview of what is to come without being too inconvenienced. Here are some helpful hints:

- **Post regular updates for employees along with some "sales talk" to help them speak with customers** about the hammering in back.

- **Attach a personal note to your menu thanking customers for their patience during construction.**

- **Post humorous "Work in Progress" signs** and photos at the door or a display with architectural renderings.

- **Pass out "Re-Grand Opening" coupons** and celebratory invitations.

- **If wait times are extended, have a mini cocktail party in your waiting area.** Pass out wine samples, simple appetizers, or freshly baked cookies. Use custom-printed napkins announcing your upcoming reopening celebration.

- **Avoid "smelly" activities during meal times.** Painting and sewer renovations are best handled during periods when customers are sparse.

- **Consider eliminating just one meal service.** Calculate your least profitable hours and schedule work then. Clearly post your "new" hours in advance.

- **Break the project down by area as opposed to task.** Instead of paneling the entire dining room at lunchtime, speak with your renovation team about dividing the project area into smaller areas. Dividing the project will increase your overall project cost, but customers will still be able to dine with minimal disturbance.

- **Route customers away from work areas.** Alter traffic patterns with freestanding signs, paintings on easels, or decorative ropes. Rent these from party/catering-supply houses.

- **Police the work area throughout the day for potential safety issues.** Never put your staff or customers at risk.

- **Seal off work areas with heavyweight plastic sheeting.** Dust and debris are minimized and work areas less distracting.

- **Rent whole-room fans.** Draw dust and odors away from diners.

REATING ENVIRONMENTS THAT WORK WITH PEOPLE

Ergonomics is the physical interaction of humans with spaces and objects during activities. A prep area that requires workers to stretch repeatedly across to reach ingredients and a broiler unit that only very tall workers can safely use are examples of "poor" ergonomics. Proper ergonomics in a restaurant can positively affect your employees' physical well-being, productivity, and attitude. Ergonomically correct seating can also enhance your diners' experience. Here are some valuable tips to help you "engineer" your restaurant to work well with people. Additional in-depth information can be found in sections covering specific issues such as lighting, equipment, workflow, and traffic patterns.

- **Temporary workstations.** Create mini work stations where all necessary food, utensils, and prep space are close at hand.

- **Streamline.** Eliminate excessive bending, lifting, and reaching while encouraging proper prep and storage procedures.

- **Seating.** Provide stools or chairs to give backs and feet a rest if the work being done does not require standing.

- **Make certain your tools and equipment were not designed only for men.** Although more and more women are donning toques, tools and equipment have not necessarily been redesigned to accommodate their shorter frames, or other physical characteristics.

- **Ladders.** Provide stable, heavy-duty work ladders for accessing top shelves and deep storage units.

- **Left-handed staff.** Purchase a supply of important tools and utensils for left-handed employees.

- **Avoid congestion.** Arrange seating to minimize steps and reduce cross-traffic patterns.

- **Clientele comfort.** Make a point of minimizing your guests' exposure to glare, drafts, and noisy areas.

- **Access.** Create easy entrances and exits.

- **Interaction.** Think about how employees, customers, and vendors will interact with your facility. Do the physical environment, fixtures, and equipment make it easier or more difficult to do a job or enjoy a meal?

- **Movable fixtures.** Choose fixtures that can be easily moved when needed.

ILL YOU HAVE ENOUGH DINING SPACE?

Space is frequently at a premium in public areas. So just how much space should you allow for eating, serving, and other activities? What works in a crowded coffee shop will not meet the expectations of an elegant dinner house. Understanding your customers' expectations and their needs will help you to allocate your precious space. The following are some useful guidelines and tips that can be used to determine dining room layout and spacing:

- **Factor in your customers' needs.** Young people can tolerate being placed close together, while less mobile, older patrons may have walkers and canes to deal with.

- **Mixing up your table sizes and seating types can help you direct traffic patterns** through a room.

- **Consider using round tables**, which can accommodate more people and allow for easier access. However, they can be harder to place in a room and cannot be used along walls.

- **Check out the views from every table.** Try to avoid work stations, bathrooms, halls, and other less-than attractive sights.

- **Build in flexibility.** You need to be able to handle crowds and small parties.

- **Set aside sufficient work areas within the dining room.**

- **Wheelchair access.** Allow at least 32 inches of aisle space and a table height of 27-inches high by 30-inches wide by 19-inches deep.

Recommended standard spacing allowances:

- **At least 18 inches between backs of chairs** to avoid chair bumping and for servers and guests to pass.

- **At least 24 inches for service aisles.** Thirty-six inches is optimum.

- **At least 48 inches for main aisles.**

- **At least 18 inches from the chair back to the table edge.**

- **About 12 inches from the seat cushion to the underside of the table** for leg room.

RECOMMENDED DINING ROOM SPACE ALLOWANCE PER SEAT	
Service Type	Square Feet Required per Seat
Banquet (minimum)	10 to 11
Buffet	12 to 18
Family Style	13 to 16
Fast Food	10 to 14
Tableside (minimum)	11 to 14
Tableside (upscale)	15 to 18
Counter	18 to 20

TRAFFIC AND WORKFLOW

A well-designed restaurant makes it faster and easier to serve meals. Improper workflow and poor traffic patterns mean thousands of wasted steps and movements every day. Analyzing your layout and equipment needs from the viewpoint of the user will increase productivity, decrease employee stress and injuries, and improve your customer service. Here are some areas of traffic within your restaurant and how you might eliminate excess steps and waiting, while increasing productivity:

- **Restrooms.** Place restrooms at the front of the restaurant to minimize traffic around the kitchen.

- **Hire a traffic/workflow expert.** A food service consultant specializing in traffic analysis and workflow streamlining can help you maximize your space while improving employee productivity.

- **Listen to your staff.** Service personnel, chefs, and assistants with hands-on experience can help you create layouts that will not tire them, will help them to respond quicker, and will improve morale.

- **Counter service.** Compare customer feelings on waiting versus service processes. With single lines, counter people typically handle specific tasks: order taking, assembly, or cash handling. Multiple line service requires more registers and each server handles all responsibilities. A single winding line is perceived to be a longer wait; however, throughput (actual customers served) is almost equal. Both line styles have similar space requirements.

- **Self-service/cafeteria location.** Centrally locate salad/dessert bars and cafeteria lines with ample walk space on all four sides whenever possible. Duplicate offerings on each side to minimize reaching and maximize the number of customers served per hour.

- **Maneuverability.** Estimate counter width at 14 feet: four feet for a customer aisle, one foot for a tray slide, two feet for counter width, four and a half feet for counter workers, and two and a half feet for back bar. Make sure that trays, bins, and service carts can fit between aisles and counter sides.

- **Use a single counter for the simplest customer traffic pattern.** Physical barriers can be used to create a directional flow and eliminate line disruption.

Position food stations to minimize cross-traffic:

- **Desserts should be placed first in self-service venues** if these are not included in all-you-can eat pricing.

- **Hot items and made-to-order foods should be positioned just prior to the beverages.**

- **Drinks should be the last food item before cashiers** and/or seating to avoid potential spills.

MORE WORKFLOW ADVICE

Seeing where every table and workstation is placed in relationship to each other and how they relate to the active prep areas and the kitchen will help you to eliminate unnecessary steps, cross-traffic, and backtracking. Consider the following:

- **Table service.** Diagram the room. Some design engineers can create helpful 3-D illustrations detailing the number of steps between tables and work areas.

- **Party areas.** Place banquet and large party areas closest to the kitchen to improve service and food delivery times.

Review outside access to and serviceability of exterior dining areas:

- **Eliminate** stepping down through a doorway.

- **Include** a fully stocked work area to avoid extra trips inside.

Enhance communication to reduce steps and speed service:

- **Centrally located or multiple-station POS equipment.** Even more efficient, handheld order-entry systems allow the wait staff to move directly to the next customer.

- **Vibrating pagers and two-way radios to signal** that tables are cleared or meals are ready.

BACK-OF-THE-HOUSE

Too many people, too little space, too much work to get done in too short a time. Sounds like a busy restaurant. Good traffic patterns and workflow make it easier for your chef and support staff to be productive. Consider the following:

- **Add traffic aisles.** Thirty inches is the minimum to allow traffic to move around the kitchen without interfering with active workspace. Be certain that aisles are wide enough for mobile carts. Heavy-traffic areas or aisles with workers on each side may require 48 inches or more.

- **Access.** Add extra doors for direct bar access.

- **Streamline procedures.** Implement a straight-line workflow for products such as sandwiches.

- **Maximize workspace.** Place single-purpose equipment next to the active workspace and shared equipment between two work centers.

Install separated kitchen access doors:

- **Separate doors should be two feet apart.**

- **Doors should only swing one way** with large, clear, unbreakable windows in each.

- **Clearly mark doors** — IN or OUT — on each side.

- **Doors should be at least 42-inches wide.**

- **If separate doors are not possible, use double-swinging doors** (at least 84-inches).

You'll find diagrams of the layout and flowchart of a typical family-type restaurant, occasional-type restaurant and layout for receiving, storage and employee dining areas at the end of chapter one.

BASIC COST CONTROL
FOR RESTAURANTS

This chapter will introduce you to the basic cost control concepts that will be developed in detail throughout the rest of this book. This chapter is being introduced now so that prior to developing the menu and menu items you can start to visualize the entire control process.

COST CONTROLS ARE CRUCIAL

Throughout the entire food-service industry, operating expenses are up and income is down. After taxes and expenses, restaurants that make money, according to the National Restaurant Association, have bottom lines at 0.5–3.0 percent of sales. This tiny percentage is the difference between being profitable and going under and it drives home the importance of controlling your costs.

A lot can be done to control costs and it begins with planning. Cost control is about numbers. It is about collecting, organizing, interpreting, and comparing the numbers that impact your bottom line. This job cannot be delegated because these numbers are your controls. They are what tell you the real story of what is going on in your restaurant. Some operators may need outside assistance in interpreting these numbers such as an accountant or food service consultant.

Understanding this story and its implications on your bottom line comes only with constant review and the resulting familiarity with the relationships between these numbers and the workings of the business. This story may seem like drudgery, but it is your key to understanding the meaning behind your numbers. Once you have mastered the numbers they will tell you the story behind your labor productivity, portion control, purchase prices, marketing promotions, new menu items, and competitive strategy. This knowledge will free you to run the most profitable operation you can.

According to government statistics, a restaurant investor has a one in 20 chance of getting his money back in five years. Furthermore, the consensus of many successful restaurateurs is that 80 percent of the success of a restaurant is determined before it opens. You must prepare. Part of that preparation is integrating an ongoing cost control program into your business.

This program can be doubly important if you are fortunate enough to start out doing great business. High profits can hide many inefficiencies that will surely expose themselves during times of low sales. Too many people become cost-control converts only after suffering losses. The primary purpose of cost controls is to maximize profits, not minimize losses. Controlling costs works — all the time — because it focuses on getting the most value from the least cost in every aspect of your operation. By keeping costs under control you can charge less than the competition or make more money from charging the same price.

These are huge operating freedoms and opportunities that are afforded you if you know what you are spending and control that spending. Most of the waste that occurs in restaurants cannot be detected by the naked eye. It takes records and reports to tell you the size of the inefficiencies taking place.

Cost control is not accounting or bookkeeping: These are the information-gathering tools of cost control. Cost control can be defined by explaining its purposes:

- To provide management with information needed for making day-to-day operations decisions.

- To monitor department and individual efficiency.

- To inform management of expenses being incurred and incomes received and whether they fall within standards and budgets.

- To prevent fraud and theft.

- To provide the ground for the business's goals (not for discovering where it has been).

- To emphasize prevention, not correction.

- To maximize profits, not minimize losses.

This idea of prevention versus correction is fundamental. Prevention occurs through advanced planning. Your primary job is not to put out fires, it is to prevent them — and to maximize profits in the process.

The larger the distance between an owner or manager and the actual restaurant, the greater the need for effective cost control records. Cost control is how franchisers keep their eyes on thousands of units across the world. Many managers of individual operations assume that since they are on the premises during operating hours, a detailed system of cost control is unnecessary. Tiny family operations often see controls the same way and view any device for theft prevention as a sign of distrust towards their staff. The main purpose of cost control is to provide information to management about daily operations. Prevention of theft is a secondary function. Cost controls are about knowing where you are going. Most waste and inefficiencies cannot be seen; they need to be understood through the numbers.

Understanding those numbers means interpreting them. To do this effectively you need to understand the difference between control and reduction. Control is achieved through the assembly and interpretation of data and ratios on your revenue and expenses.

Reduction is the actual action taken to bring costs within your predetermined standards. Effective cost control starts at the top of an organization. Management must establish, support, and enforce its standards and procedures.

There are ten primary areas that are central to any food and beverage operation and are therefore crucial elements of cost control records:

- **Purchasing.** Your inventory system is the critical component of purchasing. Before placing an order with a supplier you need to know what you have on hand and how much will be used. Allow for a cushion of inventory so you do not run out between deliveries. Once purchasing has been standardized, the manager simply orders from your suppliers. Records show supplier, prices, unit of purchase, and product specifications. This information needs to be kept on paper.

- **Receiving.** Receiving is how you verify that everything you ordered has arrived. Check for correct brands, grades, varieties, quantities, and correct prices. Incorrect receivables need to be noted and either returned or credited to your account. Products purchased by weight or count need to be checked.

- **Storage.** All food is stored until it is used. Doing so in an orderly fashion ensures easy inventory. Doing so properly, with regard to temperature, ventilation, and freedom from contamination, ensures food products remain in optimum condition until they are used. Expensive items need to be guarded from theft.

- **Issuing.** Procedures for removing inventory from storage are part of the cost control process. Head chefs and bartenders have authority to take or "issue" stock from storage to the appropriate place. To know your food and beverage costs you need to know a) your beginning inventory, b) how much was sold, and c) your ending inventory. Without this data you cannot determine accurate sales figures.

- **Rough preparation.** How your staff minimizes waste during the preliminary processing of inventory is critical.

- **Preparation for service.** Roughly prepared ingredients are finished off prior to plating. The quality and care with which preparation is done determines the amount of waste generated in preparation of standard recipes.

- **Portioning/Transfer.** Food can be lost through over portioning. Final preparation should be monitored regularly to ensure quality and quantity standards are being adhered to. Portioning is such a crucial element to cost control that management must be assigned to monitor order times, portions, presentation, and food quality with an eagle eye.

- **Order taking/Guest check.** Every item sold or issued from the kitchen needs to be recorded by paper check or computer. It needs to be impossible for anyone to get food or drinks without having them entered into the system. No verbal orders for food or beverages should be accepted by or from anybody — including management and owners.

- **Cash receipts.** Monitoring sales is crucial to cost controls. Under-/overcharging, falsification of tips, and lost checks must be investigated after every shift. Sales information from each meal period must be compiled to build a historical financial record. This record helps you forecast the future.

- **Bank deposits/Accounts payable.** Proper auditing of bank deposits and charge slips must be conducted.

Cost control is an ongoing process that must be part of the basic moment-to-moment breathing of your business. A continuous appraisal of this process is equally integral to the functioning of your restaurant. There are five key elements to an effective cost control strategy:

1. Planning in advance.

2. Procedures and devices that aid the control process.

3. Implementation of your cost control program.

4. Employee compliance.

5. Management's ongoing enforcement and reassessment.

Furthermore, your program should be assessed with the following questions:

1. Do your cost controls provide relevant information?

2. Is the information timely?

3. Is it easily assembled, organized, and interpreted?

4. Are the benefits and savings greater than the cost of the controls?

This last point is especially important. When the expense of the controls exceeds the savings, that is waste, not control. Spending $30,000 on a computer system that will save you $5,000 in waste is ineffective.

Standards are key to any cost control program. Predetermined points of comparison must be set, against which you will measure your actual results. The difference between planned resources and resources actually used is the variance. Management can then monitor for negative or positive variances between standards and actual performance and will know where specifically to make corrections. These five steps illustrate the uses of standards:

1. Performance standards should be established for all individuals and departments.

2. Individuals must see it as the responsibility of each to prevent waste and inefficiency.

3. Adherence — or lack of adherence — to standards must be monitored.

4. Actual performance must be compared against established standards.

5. When deviations from standards are discovered, appropriate action must be taken.

Your job is to make sure standards are adhered to. Is your staff using measuring scoops and ladles and sized bowls, glasses, and cups, weighing portions individually, portioning by count, and pre-portioning? These are all useful tools to make sure standards are met and your cost control program implemented effectively.

 OST RATIOS

Owners and managers need to be on the same page in terms of the meaning and calculation of the many ratios used to analyze food, beverage, and labor costs. It is important to understand how your ratios are being calculated, so you can get a true indication of the cost or profit activity in your restaurant. Numerous cost control software programs are available with built-in formulas for calculating ratios and percentages. The Uniform System of Accounts for Restaurants (USAR), published by the National Restaurant Association, is an essential guide for restaurant accounting. It establishes a common industry language that allows you to compare ratios and percentages across industry lines. The goal of this comparison is to create financial statements that are management tools, not just IRS reports. Cost control is not just the calculation of these numbers. It is the interpretation of them and the appropriate (re)actions taken to bring your numbers within set standards.

FOOD COST PERCENTAGE

This basic ratio is often misinterpreted because it can be calculated so many ways. It is food cost divided by food sales. Whether your food cost is determined by food sold or consumed is a crucial difference. For your food cost percentage to be accurate, a month-end inventory must be taken. Without this figure your food cost statement is inaccurate and therefore useless. Your inventory will vary month to month — even in the most stable environment — because months end on different days of the week.

Distinguishing between food sold and consumed is important because all food consumed is not sold. Food consumed includes all food used, sold, wasted, stolen, or given away to customers and employees. Food not sold is determined by subtracting all food bought at full price from the total food consumed.

Maximum allowable food cost percentage (MFC) is the most food can cost and still return your profit goal. If, at the end of the month, your food cost percentage is over your maximum allowable percentage, you will not meet your profit expectations. Below is how you calculate MFC:

1. **Write your dollar amounts of labor costs and overhead expenses and exclude food costs.** Refer to past accounting periods and yearly averages to get realistic cost estimates.

2. **Add your monthly profit goal as either a dollar amount or a percentage of sales.**

3. **Convert dollar values of expenses to percentages by dividing by food sales for the periods used for expenses.** Generally, do not use your highest or lowest sales figures for calculating your operating expenses. Subtract the total of the percentages from 100 percent. The remainder is your maximum allowable food cost percentage (MFC). For example:

100 – [Monthly Expenses (– Food Costs) + Profit Goal x 100] = % MFC Monthly Food Sales

Actual food cost percentage (AFC) is the percentage you are actually operating at. It is calculated by dividing food cost by food sales. If you are deducting employee meals from your income statement, then you are calculating cost of food sold. If there is no deduction of employee meals — which is true for most operations — then the food cost you are reading is food consumed. Food consumed is always a higher cost than food sold and, if inventory is not being taken, the food cost on your income statement is just an estimate based on purchases and is not accurate.

Potential food cost percentage (PFC) is also called your theoretical food cost. PFC is the lowest your food cost can be because it assumes that all food consumed is sold and that there is no waste whatsoever. It is found by multiplying the number sold of each menu item by the ideal recipe cost.

Standard food cost (SFC) is how you adjust for the unrealistically low PFC. This percentage includes unavoidable waste, employee meals, etc. This food cost percentage is compared to the AFC and is the standard management must meet.

Prime food cost includes the cost of direct labor with the food cost. Prime food cost is labor incurred because the item is made from scratch — baking pies and bread, trimming steaks. When the food cost is determined for these items, the cost of the labor needed to prepare them is added. So prime cost is food cost plus necessary direct labor. This costing method is applied to every menu item needing extensive direct labor before it is served to the customer. Indirect labor cannot be attributed to any particular menu item and is therefore overhead. Prime cost is the total cost of food and beverages sold, payroll, and employee benefits costs.

Beverage cost ratio is calculated when alcoholic beverages are sold. It is determined by dividing costs by sales — calculated the same way as food consumed. A single beverage ratio cannot be standardized because the percentage will vary depending on the mix of hard alcohol, wine, and beer. Spirits run a lower cost percentage than wine and beer and, as such, it is recommended that alcoholic beverages be split into their three categories. Beverage sales do not include coffee, tea, milk, or juice, which are usually considered food. Wherever you include soft drinks, know that it will reduce the food cost, since the ratio of cost to selling price is so low.

Check average is not just total food and beverage sales divided by customers served. It is important to see how this figure compares to the check average you need to meet your daily sales goals. If you are coming in under what you need, you should look at your prices. Check average should be determined by each meal period, especially when different menus are served for each meal. Standards need to be set on how customers who order only a drink and no food are counted.

Seat turnover is how many times you can fill a chair during a meal period with another customer. Restaurants with low check averages need high seat turnover. Inventory turnover is calculated by dividing cost of food consumed by your average inventory (beginning inventory plus your ending inventory, divided by two).

Ratio of food to beverage sales is the ratio of their percentages of your total sales. In restaurants with a higher percentage of beverage sales than food sales, profits are generally higher because there is a greater profit margin on beverages.

Sales mix is the number of each menu item sold. Sales mix is crucial to cost analysis because each item impacts food cost differently. If your Wendy's does a huge breakfast business and the one down the street does a big lunch, your food costs are going to be different than theirs.

Break-even point (BEP) is simply when sales equal expenses, period. Businesses can operate forever at breakeven if there are no investors looking for a return on their money.

Contribution margin is your gross profit. It is what remains after all expenses have been subtracted from 100 percent net.

Closing point is when the cost of being open for a given time period is more expensive than revenue earned. If it cost you $2,000 to open today, and you only made $1,800, your closing point expense will be $200.

CONTROLLING FOOD COSTS

In order to control food costs effectively, there are four things you need to do:

1. Forecast how much and what you are going to sell.

2. Purchase and prepare according to these forecasts.

3 Portion effectively.

4. Control waste and theft.

To do these effectively, you must have standards to which you rigorously adhere. Here are two main standards that will help you sustain quality, consistency, and low cost:

- **Standardized recipes.** Since the recipe is the basis for determining the cost of a menu item, standard recipes will assure consistent quality and cost. Standardized recipes include ingredients, preparation methods, yield, equipment used, and plate presentation.

- **Standardized purchase specifications.** These are detailed descriptions of the ingredients used in your standardized recipes. Quality and price of all ingredients are known and agreed upon before purchases are made, making the recipe's cost consistent from unit to unit and week to week.

YIELD COSTS

Once you have standardized recipes in place, you can determine the per plate cost of every dish. You need to know what the basic ingredients cost and the edible yield of those ingredients for each dish. There are a number of necessary terms for this process:

- **As-Purchased (AP) Weight.** The weight of the product as delivered, including bones and trim.

- **Edible Portion (EP) Weight.** The amount of weight or volume that is available to be portioned after carving or cooking.

- **Waste.** The amount of usable product that is lost due to processing, cooking, or portioning, as well as usable by-products that have no salable value.

- **Usable Trim.** Processing by-products that can be sold as other menu items. These recover a portion or all of their cost.

- **Yield.** The net weight or volume of food after processing but before portioning.

- **Standard Yield.** The yield generated by standardized recipes and portioning procedures—how much usable product there is after processing and cooking.

- **Standard Portion.** The size of the portion according to the standardized recipe and also the basis for determining the cost of the plated portion.

- **Convenience Foods.** Items where at least a portion of the preparation labor is done before delivery. These can include precut chicken or ready-made dough.

These factors allow you to calculate plate costs. The food cost of convenience foods is higher than if you made them from scratch, but once you factor in labor, necessary equipment, inventories of ingredients, more complicated purchasing and storage, you may find that these foods offer considerable savings.

To cost convenience foods you simply count, weigh, or measure the portion size and determine how many portions there are. Then divide the number of servable portions into the as-purchased price. Even with their pre-preparation, a small allowance for normal waste must be factored in, often as little as 2 percent per yield.

Costing items from scratch is a little more complex. Most menu items require processing that causes shrinkage of some kind. As a result, if the weight or volume of the cooked product is less than the as-purchased (AP) weight, the edible portion (EP) cost will be higher than the AP price. It is a simple addition of the labor involved and the amount of saleable product being reduced. Through this process, your buyer uses yields to determine quantities to purchase and your chef discovers optimum quantities to order that result in the highest yield and the least waste.

MENU SALES MIX

The menu is where you begin to design a restaurant. If you have a specific menu idea, your restaurant's location must be carefully planned to ensure customer traffic will support your concept. If you already have the location, design your menu around the customers you want to attract.

Once your concept is decided, your equipment and kitchen space requirements should be designed around the recipes on your menu. Once a kitchen has been built, there is of course some flexibility to menu changes, but new pieces of equipment may be impossible to add without high costs or renovations. To design right, you need to visualize delivery, processing, preparation, presentation, and washing. To do so you must be intimately familiar with each menu item.

When shopping for equipment, choose based on the best equipment for your needs, not price. Decide if you need a small fryer or an industrial one, two ovens or five, and then which specific brands meet your needs. Decide what pots, pans, dishes, and utensils you like before you begin to find the best price.

THE MENU ITSELF

Your menu should not just be a list of the dishes you sell; it should positively affect the revenue and operational efficiency of your restaurant. Start by selecting dishes that reflect your customer's preferences and emphasize what your staff does well. Attempting to cater to everyone generally has you doing nothing particularly well and does not distinguish your restaurant. Your menu should be a major communicator of the concept and personality of your restaurant, as well as an important cost control.

A well-designed menu creates an accurate image of the restaurant in a customer's head, even before she has been inside. It also directs her attention to certain selections and increases the chances of them being ordered. Your menu also determines, depending upon its complexity and sophistication, how detailed your cost control system needs to be.

An effective menu does five key things:

1. Emphasizes what customers want and what you do best.

2. Is an effective communication, merchandising, and cost control tool.

3. Obtains the necessary check average for sales and profits.

4. Uses staff and equipment efficiently.

5. Makes forecasting sales more consistent and accurate for purchasing, preparation, and scheduling.

The design of your menu will directly affect whether or not it achieves these goals. Plan to have a menu that works for you. Certain practices can influence the choices your guests make. Instead of randomly placing items on the menu, single out and emphasize the items you want to sell. These will generally be dishes with low food cost and high profits that are easy to prepare. Once you have chosen these dishes, use design — print style, paper color, and graphic design — to direct the reader's attention to these items. In general, a customer's eye will fall to the middle of the page first. Design elements used to draw a reader's eye to another part of the menu can be effective as well. Customers remember the first and last things they read more than anything else, so drawing their eyes to specific items is also important.

Once you have an effective menu design, analyzing your sales mix to determine the impact each item has on sales, costs, and profits is an important practice. If you have costs and waste under control, looking at your menu sales mix can help you further reduce costs and boost profits. You will find that some items need to be promoted more aggressively, while others need to be dropped altogether. Classifying your menu items is necessary for making those decisions. Here are some suggested classifications:

- **Primes.** These are popular items that are low in food cost and high in profit. Have them stand out on your menu.

- **Standards.** Items with high food costs and high profit margins. You can possibly raise the price on this item and push it as a signature.

- **Sleepers.** Slow selling low food cost items with low profit margins. Work to increase the likelihood that these will be seen and ordered through more prominent menu display, featuring on menu boards, and lowered prices.

- **Problems.** High in food cost and low in profits. If you can, raise the price and lower production cost. If you cannot, hide them on the menu. If sales do not pick up, get rid of them altogether.

PRICING

Pricing is an important aspect of your revenues and customer counts. Prices that are too high will drive customers away and prices that are too low will kill your profits. But pricing is not the simple matter of an appropriate markup over cost; it combines other factors as well.

Price can either be market driven or demand driven. Market-driven prices must be responsive to your competitor's prices. Common dishes that you and the place down the road sell or new menu items that have not met a demand need to be priced competitively. Opposite to these are demand-driven items, which customers ask for and where demand exceeds your supply. You have a short-term monopoly on these items and therefore price is driven up until demand slows or competitors begin to sell similar items.

However you determine your price, the actual marking up of items is an interesting process. A combination of methods is usually a good idea, since each menu item is different. Two basic theories are: a) charge as much as you can and b) charge as little as you can. Each has its pluses and minuses. Obviously, if you charge as much as you can, you increase the chance of greater profits. Charging the lowest price you can gives customers a great sense of value but lowers your profit margin per item.

Prices are generally determined by competition and demand. Your prices must be in line with the category customers put you in. Burrito joints do not price like a five-star restaurant and vice versa. Both would lose their customer base if they did. You want your customers to know your image and that your prices fit into that picture.

Here are four ways to determine prices:

1. **Competitive pricing.** Simply based on meeting or beating your competition's prices, which is an ineffective method, since it assumes diners are making their choice on price alone, and not food quality, ambiance, or service.

2. **Intuitive pricing.** With this method, you do not want to take the time to find out what your competition is charging, so you are charging based on what you feel guests are willing to pay. If your sense of the value of your product is good, then it works. Otherwise, it can be problematic.

3. **Psychological pricing.** Price is more of a factor to lower-income customers who go to lower priced restaurants. If they do not know an item is good, they assume it is if it is expensive. If you change your prices, remember the order in which buyers see them also affects their perceptions. If an item was initially more expensive, it will be viewed as a bargain and vice versa.

4. **Trial-and-error pricing.** Based on customer reactions to prices. It is not practical in terms of determining your overall prices, but can be effective with individual items to bring them closer to the price a customer is willing to pay or to distinguish them from similar menu items with a higher or lower food cost.

There are still other factors that help determine prices. Whether customers view you as a leader or a follower can make a big difference on how they view your prices. If people think of you as the best seafood restaurant in the area, they will pay a little more to eat with you. Service also determines people's sense of value when the difference in actual food quality between you and the competition is negligible. If your customers order at a counter and bus their own tables, this lack of service cost needs to be reflected in your prices. Also, in a competitive market, providing great service can be a factor that puts you in a leadership position and allows you to charge a higher price. Your location, ambience, customer base, product presentation, and desired check average all factor into what you feel you can charge and what you need to charge in order to make a profit.

FINANCIAL ANALYSIS

To make profits, you need to plan for profits. Many restaurants offering great food, atmosphere, and service still go out of business. They fail to manage the financial aspects of the business. Poor cost control management will be fatal to your business. Good financial management is about interpreting financial statements and reports, not simply preparing them.

A few distinctions need to be made in order to understand the language now being used. Financial accounting is for external groups to assess taxes and the status of your establishment. Managerial accounting provides information to internal users that becomes the basis for managing day-to-day operations. This data is very specific, emphasizes departmental operations, and uses non-financial data like customer counts, menu sales mix, and labor hours. These internal reports break down revenues and expenses by department, day, and meal period so they can be easily interpreted, exposing areas that need attention. Daily and weekly reports must be made and analyzed in order to determine emerging trends.

INTERNAL CONTROLS

It is estimated that about five cents on every dollar spent in U.S. restaurants is lost to theft. Clearly established and followed controls can lessen this percentage. Begin by separating duties and recording every transaction. If these basic systems are in place, then workers know that each step of the way they will be held responsible for shrinkage.

Management Information Systems (MISs) are common tools for accumulating, analyzing, and reporting data. They help establish proper rules for consistent and prompt reporting and set up efficient flows of paperwork and data collection. In short, their goal is to prevent fraud on all levels. While no system is perfect, a good MIS will show where fraud or loss is occurring, allowing you to remedy the situation.

In most restaurants the majority of theft occurs at the bar. In tightly run establishments cash is more likely to be taken by management than hourly workers because managers and some wait staff as well as bartenders have access to it and know the system well.

Hourly workers tend to steal products, not cash, because that is what they can get their hands on. Keeping food away from the back door and notifying your employees when you are aware of theft and are investigating can have a deterring effect.

The key to statistical control is entering transactions into the system, electronically or by hand. If food or beverages can be consumed without being entered into the system, your system is flawed and control is compromised. Five other cost control concepts are crucial to your control system:

1. **Documentation** of tasks, activities, and transactions must be required.

2 **Supervision** and review of employees by management intimately familiar with set performance standards.

3. **Splitting of duties** so no single person is involved in all parts of the task cycle.

---

4. **Timeliness.** All tasks must be done within set time guidelines, comparisons then made at established control points, and reports made at scheduled times to detect problems.

5. **Cost-benefit relationships.** Cost of procedures used to benefits gained must exceed the cost of implementing the controls.

The basic control procedure is an independent verification at a control point during and after the completion of a task. Often done through written or electronic reports. This verification determines if the person performing the task has the authority to do so and if the quantity of product or cash and performance results meet set standards.

Point-of-sale systems are also crucial for reducing loss. If your servers simply cannot obtain any food or beverage without a hard-copy check or without entering the sale electronically, you have eliminated most of their opportunity to steal. Many electronic systems are available in the industry and once initial training and intimidation are overcome, they can seriously reduce the amount of theft and shrinkage in your restaurant.

These systems also allow you to instantly see which items are selling best at different times of the day, enabling you to order more efficiently and keep inventory to a minimum. They also allow you to automatically subtract from inventory all the ingredients used in the items you sold. These can be invaluable tools for tracking employee productivity, initiating promotions and contests, and generating weekly, daily, by-meal, or hourly sales reports. Point-of-sale systems collect invaluable data for you to interpret.

PURCHASING AND ORDERING

What exactly is the difference? Purchasing is setting the policy on which suppliers, brands, grades, and varieties of products will be ordered. These are your standardized purchase specifications; the specifics of how items are delivered, paid for, and returned are negotiated between management and distributors. Purchasing is what you order and from whom. Ordering is the act of contacting the suppliers and notifying them of the quantity you require, a simpler, lower-level task.

Once menus have been created that meet your customers' satisfaction and your profit needs, a purchasing program designed to assure your profit margins can be developed. An efficient purchasing program incorporates:

- **Standard purchase specifications**; based on

- **Standardized recipes**; resulting in

- **Standardized yields**; that, with portion control, allow for

- **Accurate costs** based on portions actually served.

Once these criteria are met, to order the necessary supplies, your operator needs to be able to predict how much will be needed to maintain purchase specifications, follow standard recipes, and enforce portioning standards. When these are done well, optimum quantities can be kept on hand.

Buying also has its own distinctions. Open, or informal, buying is face-to-face or by over-the-phone contact and uses largely oral negotiations and purchase specifics. Formal buying terms are put in writing and payment invoices are stated as conditions for price quotes and customer-service commitments. Its customer service is possibly the most important aspect of the supplier you choose because good sales representatives know their products, have an understanding of your needs, and offer helpful suggestions.

INVENTORY

Ordering effectively is impossible unless you know your inventory. Before an order is placed, counts of stock should be made. Many software programs are able to determine order quantities directly from sales reports, but without this kind of system you must inventory what you have on hand before ordering. The taking of inventory must be streamlined because it must be done as frequently as you order. It must not be an unpleasant, late-night debacle that is done only rarely and only when it has to be. Whether your inventory system is by hand or computer, its purpose is to accomplish the following:

- Provide records of what you need.
- Provide records of product specifications.
- Provide records of suppliers.
- Provide records of prices and unit of purchase.
- Provide a record of product use levels.
- Facilitate efficient ordering.
- Increase the accuracy of inventory.
- Facilitate the inventory process.
- Make it easy to detect variance levels in inventory.

With such a system, the records generated and kept are extensive and valuable. You will have records of what you purchased, product specifications, your primary and alternative suppliers, price, and unit of purchase. Equally important, reports will indicate the usage level of the product between deliveries. These statistics allow for month-to-month comparisons to be made between units in a multi-unit operation.

LABOR PRODUCTIVITY

Labor costs and turnover are serious concerns in today's restaurant market. Increasing labor costs cannot be offset by continuously higher prices without turning customers away. Maximizing worker productivity so few can do more has become a key challenge to the restaurateur. It is especially true since the food-service industry continues to be an entry-level arena for the unskilled and uneducated. Qualified applicants are still few in the restaurant industry.

A few of the causes of high labor costs and low productivity are poor layout and design of your operation, lack of labor saving equipment, poor scheduling, and no regular detailed system to collect and analyze payroll data. The following are some suggested ways management can improve these areas for greater efficiency:

- **Scheduling.** The key to controlling labor costs is not a low average hourly wage, but proper scheduling of productive employees. Place your best servers and cooks where you need them most. Know the strengths and weaknesses of your employees. Staggering the arrival and departure of employees is a good way to follow the volume of expected customers and minimize labor costs during slow times.

- **On-call scheduling.** When your forecasted customer counts are inaccurate, scheduled labor must be adjusted up or down to meet productivity standards. Employees simply wait at home to be called if they are needed for work. If they do not receive a call by a certain time, they know they are not needed. Employees prefer this procedure to coming in only to be sent home, especially tipped staff who do not want to work when business is slow.

- **On-break schedules.** When you cannot send someone home, you can put him on a 30-minute break and give him a meal. The 30 minutes is deducted from his timecard and you can take a credit for the cost of the meal against the minimum wage.

BEVERAGE CONTROLS

Pricing of beverages is not just a cost-markup exercise. The markup of alcohol in restaurants is lower than in bars where liquor makes up the majority of sales. Prices reflect the uniqueness of an operation and the overhead operating costs. To monitor your liquor costs accurately, you need to record the sales of each type of beverage separately. Separate keys for wine, beer and spirits on your register or a point-of-sale system need to be used. Unless an electronic system is used a detailed sales mix is difficult to obtain.

Your alcoholic beverage purchaser or buyer is responsible for ensuring adequate amounts of required spirits are on hand. Unlike food and supplies, they are not required to shop around for the best deal for the following reasons:

- Specific brands are only sold by specific dealers.

- Wholesaling of alcohol is state regulated and controlled.

- Prices are published in monthly journals and there is little change from month to month.

- Only quantity discounts are available.

- Purchase is done by brand name.

Purchasing and ordering alcohol is therefore much simpler than purchasing and ordering food, but the need to inventory correctly is no less crucial. Alcohol needs to be guarded and inventoried more rigorously because of its cost, ease of theft, and possible abuses. Liquor inventory should be kept locked in different storerooms, cages, or walk-ins than other inventory. Only authorized individuals should have access to these areas and requisitions must be filled out to record withdrawals.

I recommend replenishing your stock by trading stamped empty bottles for stamped full bottles. These prevent bartenders from bringing their own bottles in and selling them. It is virtually impossible to detect without marked bottles because there will be no inventory shortages. If you have drops in sales levels of $50 to $100 in one night, it is a sign of phantom bottles in your inventory.

Inventories need to be audited to ensure your liquor is actually in the storeroom and deliveries need to be checked for accuracy. It is recommended that a purchase order — and not the driver's invoice — be used to verify deliveries. Controls for determining dispensing costs, recording sales, and accounting for consumed beverages can be done three different ways:

1. **Automated systems that dispense and count.** These range from mechanical dispensers attached to each bottle to magnetic pourers that can only be activated by the register. These systems are exact, reduce spillage, and cannot give free drinks. Basically, liquor cannot be dispensed without being put into the system.

2. **Ounce or drink controls.** Requires establishing standard glassware and recipes; recording each drink sold; determining costs of each drink; comparing actual use levels to potential consumption levels; and comparing actual drink cost percent to potential cost percent.

3. **Par stock or bottle control.** A matter of keeping the maximum amount of each type of liquor behind the bar, then turning in all empty bottles for full ones. No full bottles are given without an empty one coming in. A standard sales value per bottle is determined based on the drinks it makes. A sales value is determined from consumption and compared to actual sales for variances. If less was sold than consumed, investigate.

Standards at the bar are as important as in the kitchen. Regular inventory also needs to be done to watch for fraud and theft and management needs to be expected to meet set standards. Whenever there is a managerial shift change, you must verify inventory to make sure that numbers reported are actual and have not been adjusted to meet costs.

COMPUTERIZED INVENTORY CONTROLS

There are a number of computerized systems available that can help with this process. To follow are some examples:

• **AccuBar** is an excellent example of a computerized inventory system. Customers report a 50 to 80 percent time savings when using the AccuBar system. It's easy to learn: most users are up and running within 30 minutes. The patented technology eliminates the need to estimate levels; simply tap the fluid level on the bottle outline. Once you tap the bottle outline, data entry is complete. There is no further human intervention. Since no data entry or third party is involved, reports are generated immediately. It also provides a running perpetual inventory. Transfers between locations and returns of defective items are also covered. AccuBar also helps gauge which items aren't selling, allowing you to consider stocking something else that might bring a better return. AccuBar also recommends what needs to be ordered from each supplier based on current perpetual, par, and reorder points. The order is totally customizable. When a shipment arrives, simply scan the items; any discrepancy from what was ordered is caught immediately. AccuBar can also track food, glassware, china, and other essentials.

- **The Accardis Liquor Inventory System** is another option to save time and money and eliminate over-pouring and theft. Since 1987, Accardis Systems has been controlling liquor inventory costs. Accardis was the originator of scanning and weighing bottles to control inventory. The alcohol inventory

Cyclops Falcon Inventory System Overview: First, identify the product by scanning the bar codes or using the find key. Next, weigh open bottles. Quantities are automatically sent to CYCLOPS with precise electronic accuracy. Third, enter quantity. Use the keypad to enter full unit quantities or to estimate open bottles if scale not used. Finally, generate reports and download data to a PC via the Falcon Docking Cradle.

system has proven to be fast and accurate. It will lower your costs while increasing your profits. Most clients recover the cost of the liquor inventory system in only a few months. The Cyclops Falcon scans and weighs liquor bottles electronically and then downloads the data to the PACER 4.0 for Windows software. Pacer prints out all the management reports on a station-by-station basis. The liquor inventory system also tracks all purchases and requisitions and can be used for liquor, beer, wine, supplies, hats, T-shirts, etc. Cyclops Falcon gives the user complete control of beverages at a fraction of the cost of most other systems. For more information, contact Accardis Systems, Inc., 20061 Doolittle Street, Montgomery Village, MD 20886. Call 800-852-1992 or visit **www.accardis.com**.

CONTROLLING POURING

You want to give your bartender the tools needed to create drinks according to your specifications. By eliminating over-pour and spillage, bar owners and managers save money on every bottle served. If your bartender over-pours just $\frac{1}{8}$ ounce per drink, your loss could be up to four drinks per bottle.

Liquor-control systems (LCS). Use of technologically advanced portion-control systems is becoming increasingly commonplace in today's drinks industry. LCSs are particularly effective at controlling liquor costs. They can also virtually eliminate employee theft. LCSs are marketed on the basis of a typical return on investment within 12 months. The following suppliers offer LCSs:

- Berg Company, **www.berg-controls.com,** 608-221-4281

- AzBar, **www.azbaramerica.com**, 214-361-2422

- Bristol BM, **www.bristolnf.com/liquor.htm**, 709-722-6669

- Easybar Beverage Management Systems, **www.easybar.com**, 503-624-6744

- Precision Pours, **www.precisionpours.com**, 800-549-4491

- **Easybar Beverage Management Systems (www.easybar. com)** has multiple solutions for beverage portion control. The Easybar CLCSII is a fully computerized beverage-dispensing system that controls beverage pour sizes, improves bartender speed, and ensures perfectly portioned drinks and cocktails. This system also prevents product loss by eliminating over-pouring, spillage, breakage, and theft. It accounts for all beverages dispensed through the system and boosts receipts by lowering costs and  increasing accountability. Also available is the Easypour Controlled Spout System. This offers control for drinks that are dispensed directly from a bottle. The controlled pour spouts allow only preset portions to be dispensed and will not allow drinks to be dispensed without being recorded. Easybar's Cocktail Station creates cocktails at the touch of a button. The cocktail tower can dispense up to 48 liquors plus any combination of 10 juices or sodas. It mixes cocktails of up to five ingredients, and ingredients dispense simultaneously to cut pour time. All ingredients dispense in accurate portions every time.

- **Precision Pours (www.precisionpours.com)** manufacturers measured liquor pours, gravity-feed portion control systems, and bar accessories. By eliminating over-pour and spillage with the Precision Pour™ 3 Ball Liquor Pour, users save money on every bottle served. The Precision Pour™ 3 Ball Liquor Pour allows bartenders to pour liquor with one hand while mixing with the other, speeding up drink production. Also, since there is no need to use a messy shot glass, additional time is saved on cleanup. It also strictly regulates alcohol. A drink that is too strong will likely reduce the number of drinks customers will order and discourage repeat business. Your customers want their favorite drinks to taste like their favorite drinks. Pour them a stiff one and you're not doing them any favor. Under-pour and you're likely to rile them. With the Precision Pour™  3 Ball Liquor Pour, you'll get the same great taste every time, no matter who's pouring. The Precision Pour™ 3-Ball Liquor Pour features:

  - A new third ball bearing to guarantee accuracy.

  - A primer ring surrounding the ball bearing to ensure no sticking, even with cordials.

  - A bottom made from a solid piece of surgical plastic guarantees that the ball bearings cannot fall out into your bottles.

  - A new cork that will fit all your liter bottles including Absolute, Crown Royal, and Jack Daniels.

FREE POURING

Another alternative for controlling the amount of liquor is to use the free pour. In the free pour, the bartender uses liquor pour spouts or shot glasses to measure liquor amounts. The liquor is measured and then mixed into the drink. Bar management does lose control of the amount poured in this system since the bartender is the one controlling the pours, but this is not a problem if you trust your bartender to pour the amounts you have designated for each drink. The advantages of free pouring include more showmanship and personality to each drink, which many customers prefer, and less expensive setup of materials needed. The free-pour system does rely more on a dependable and skilled bartender, however.

Modern technology has influenced free pouring as well. BarVision combines free pouring with wireless liquor inventory control. It allows you to track liquor inventory usage automatically in real-time. Every pour is transmitted to BarVision by a wireless liquor pour spout. Every empty liquor bottle is reconciled automatically—eliminating the need for manual inventory procedures. BarVision reports provide extensive flexibility,

BarVision gives the illusion of free pouring with wireless liquor pour spout that allows you to track liquor inventory usage automatically in real time.

whether you need a usage summary for a quick grasp on your open liquor inventory or a journal detail for reconciling your POS/register receipts. It does not require extensive wiring or hardware installation.

Here's how it works:

1. Bartenders free-pour drinks.

2. The pour spouts transmit data about the pours to the receiver.

3. BarVision "talks" to the receiver and keeps a journal.

4. Managers print reports from BarVision's journal.

For more information, visit **www.barvision.com** or call 480-222-6000.

CHAPTER

PROFITABLE MENU PLANNING

The prosperity of any restaurant is directly attributable to its menu. A restaurant is the culmination of food, atmosphere, and service. Many restaurants can thrive without a fanciful atmosphere or quality service, but none can survive without exceptional food.

The restaurant manager must examine his restaurant's atmosphere and clientele carefully. Based upon these observations he can then design a menu that will be effective. The objective of this chapter is to present you with complete guidelines for planning a successful and profitable menu. It would be impractical in these pages to list specific examples of potential menu items. There are many excellent cookbooks that describe menu and recipe ideas in detail. The following sections will illustrate a basic outline, from which you can plan your own exclusive menu. Each of the procedures described plays an integral part in developing your cost control system. The procedures and systems will unfold as the book progresses. Some of these procedures may be adapted for your own particular needs. The underlying, fundamental purpose of each cannot be altered or else management will be in danger of losing control over the restaurant's costs.

MENU STYLE

Menu style describes how much or how little variety the menu offers. Do you serve a limited or expansive menu? Kitchen size and labor cost control may influence whether or not you offer a limited menu. Menus with more options do have a broader appeal. Limited-limited menus are generally offered by fast food operations. These menus allow them to keep production simple and maintain a tight rein on food and labor costs.

Extensive-limited menus are offered by restaurants that serve three meals a day, such as coffee shops. While they offer more items, they limit the number of ways these items are prepared. Specialty restaurants (TGI Friday's, Ruby Tuesday, and ethnic restaurants) have limited-extensive menus. By preparing and combining the same ingredients in different ways, these establishments are able to offer many more choices but still control inventory and costs. Fine dining restaurants offer extensive-extensive menus. These establishments offer a great variety of choices in items prepared and methods of preparation.

There are advantages to both the limited menu and extensive menu styles:

MENU STYLES	
Limited	**Extensive**
• You need less equipment and less kitchen space.	• You can appeal to a broader customer base.
• Food prep is simplified and can be speedy.	• New customers will be intrigued.
• You need fewer and less skilled kitchen employees.	• Regulars will return more often because they have a greater number of options to choose from.
• Purchasing your inventory is easier and less time-consuming.	• The menu can be more responsive to customer taste.
• Space needed for inventory is lessened.	• The menu is more flexible.
• Cost controls and quality control are simpler.	• You can charge higher prices for specialty items.
• Operating costs are lower.	
• Table turnover can be increased because transaction time is quicker.	

How many menu items should you offer? You want to provide the customer with variety, but not at the expense of your ability to control inventory and cost, nor by over-taxing your production or serving staffs. Research has shown that 60 to 75 percent of menu items sold are the same eight to 12 items, regardless of the number of choices offered. It is probably wise to offer somewhere between 18 and 24 options.

FORMATTING YOUR MENU

After you have defined your establishment's goals and determined the style of your menu, you must decide what items will go on your menu. This decision can be done in a four-step process:

1. **You must decide what menu groups you will offer.** Groups are appetizers, entrees, soups, and desserts.

2. **Decide what categories to offer within these groups.** For entree choices, for example, you could offer the following categories: beef, poultry, seafood, pork, lamb, veal, and vegetarian. Decide how many dishes you will offer in each category. You may have four beef dishes, three seafood entrees, two poultry, and two vegetarian.

3. **After deciding the groups and categories that will go on your menu, you need to decide on the specifics of the dish.** Will you be serving ground, cubed, solid, roast, baked, grilled, broiled, or fried?

4. **Finally, you must decide on the dish itself.** If you are offering three beef entrees, you may choose to serve two solid beef dishes and one ground. Your actual menu items may be a strip steak, a filet mignon, and a hamburger.

While it may sound like an onerous task, by keeping these four steps in mind you will be able to maintain variety in your menu and control cost factors.

DEVELOPING THE MENU SELECTIONS

All menu items selected must fit into the physical workings of the restaurant. The menu should be finalized prior to designing, selecting equipment for, and laying out the kitchen to maximize efficiency of time, labor, and equipment. The design and layout of the kitchen and work areas must meet the needs of the menu. If it does not, the entire operation will become slow, disorganized, and inefficient. Inefficiency can only result in a drop in employee morale and in the restaurant's profit margin.

Just as the kitchen must meet the demands of the menu, the personnel employed to prepare the menu items must be selected to fit into the design of the kitchen. Careful consideration must be given to the number and type of employees needed. Is the menu simple enough for inexperienced workers to prepare or are the skills of a professional chef needed? Will the food be prepared ahead of time or upon receipt of the order? When will these employees be needed and for how long? Will there be enough room in the kitchen for everyone to work at the same time? Who will supervise them?

Planning the restaurant menu is a lot more than merely selecting menu items that are enjoyed and demanded by the restaurant's clientele. Menu planning includes arranging equipment, personnel, and food products into an efficient unit that will be affordable and in demand by the public. Successful, growing restaurants have accomplished this blending.

Most restaurants employ a separate cooking and preparation staff. The largest restaurants may employ upwards of 30 employees for each staff. Each staff may then be divided into smaller departments. The preparation staff may be divided into baking, meat cutting, and cold food preparation and the cooking staff may be divided into broiling, frying, and carving. Smaller restaurants assign combinations of these responsibilities to a few employees on each staff. The smallest restaurant may employ one individual who arrives several hours prior to opening to prepare all of the food items and then performs a cook's duties. Having separate preparation and cooking staffs is the most efficient method for producing a large number of consistent products at the least expense. This method, used in most establishments, will be the method described and referred to in this book.

Constant communication between the preparation and cooking staff is required for success. These groups of employees will be working toward the same end—at different times. An entree incorrectly prepared by the preparation staff will destroy the normal procession and organization in the kitchen, sending repercussions throughout the restaurant. The cooking staff are dependent upon the products that the preparation staff readies for them. Management's responsibility under this arrangement is increased, as it must provide the necessary communication between the two groups for each to operate effectively. The benefits derived under this system—such as consistent final products, lower labor costs, lower food costs, and an overall increase in the organization and efficiency of the kitchen—far outweigh any disadvantages.

The major points to consider when selecting menu items:

- **The menu item must be of superior quality.**

- **The raw materials used in preparing the item must be readily available** year-round at a relatively stable price.

- **The menu item must be affordable** and demanded by your clientele.

- **The menu item must be acceptable** to the preparation and cooking staff system you use.

- **The raw materials used in preparing the menu item must be easily portioned** by weight.

- **All menu items must have consistent cooking results.**

- **All menu items must have a long shelf life.** Food items prepared ahead of time and not utilized may not be sold for as long as 36 hours.

- **All menu items must have similar cooking times** (approximately eight to 15 minutes), as any entree requiring a longer cooking time will not be completed when other orders are ready to serve.

- **The storage facilities must accommodate the raw materials** used in preparing the menu items.

- **Menu items should be creative and not readily available in other restaurants.**

LIMITING THE MENU

Begin to develop the menu by compiling those recipes and ideas that meet the requirements set forth in the previous section. Consider only the items that are compatible with the restaurant's atmosphere, décor, and anticipated clientele. Based upon these guidelines, you should have little trouble compiling a considerable list of acceptable choices. The trick is to limit the menu to only those items for which the kitchen is equipped and organized and that the staff can easily execute — while still allowing for an interesting menu with plenty of varied selections.

All too often, a new restaurant will list numerous menu selections simply to round out the menu or offer token items that are on almost every menu. New restaurants should move toward specializing and serving only those menu items that they can prepare better than the other establishments in the area. It is simply not justifiable to create a diversified menu for the sake of offering a multitude of items. Specialization in the restaurant business is the key to building a solid reputation. Word of mouth is the most effective form of advertising available to the restaurant manager. Develop the menu with only those items for which you have the trained staff and equipment to properly prepare and serve. A successful menu is one that is honed to build a reputation for excellence.

Limiting the menu will create many advantages for the entire restaurant. The kitchen staff will become more experienced and skilled at preparing each item, as there will be a smaller selection for customers to choose from. The wait staff can then concentrate on promoting and recommending those items that the restaurant specializes in. From an administrative standpoint, a smaller menu will be easier to control.

Purchasing will center on only a few major food products; thus, the buyer may utilize his large purchasing power to obtain price breaks, discounts, and above-average service. Side dishes and desserts must meet all of the same qualifications as the entrees. The number and kinds of side dishes and desserts should be limited only to those items which are exceptional and slightly out of the ordinary, so they may be promoted as house specialties as well.

Always try to include some menu selections that are produced in the local area. Maine lobster, Cajun cooking, Texas beef, Gulf shrimp, key lime pie, and San Francisco sourdough bread are some examples. The tourist trade is an important source of revenue for most restaurants. Many establishments depend on it. With a little promotion, tourist trade can be an important new avenue for sales.

Once the menu is finalized, it is necessary for management to become thoroughly familiar with every aspect of each menu item. Extensive experimentation in the kitchen will be needed to discover the precise recipe ingredients, amounts, and preparation procedures. Take the time to find out everything there is to know about the menu items.

Determine where the raw products come from, which is the best type or brand to purchase, and how the kitchen staff can best handle and store the products. How do other restaurants in the area serve similar dishes?

The rule for developing a portion size is to use the largest portion feasible but charge accordingly. It is far better to serve too much food than too little. The crucial element, which must be constantly reinforced, is that every menu item — entrees, side dishes, and some desserts — must be a specific weight and size. Portion control is the basis for the restaurant's entire cost control program. Its importance cannot be overstated.

Portion-controlling all food items is an effective way to control food costs, but it also serves another important function. It maintains consistency in the final product. Once the precise recipe is developed, the completed menu item should look and taste exactly the same regardless of who prepared it. A dinner presented to a customer on Tuesday must be exactly the same as it was on Saturday night.

Portions may have a variance of up to, but not exceeding, half an ounce. Thus, if the set portion size for a steak is 12.5-ounces, the steak may range from 12 to 13 ounces. Any amount over 13 ounces must be trimmed. A light steak should be utilized for something else. Although a half ounce variance may seem like a small amount, in actuality it will add up very quickly. Many restaurants allow a variance of only ½ of an ounce!

Since portion-controlling is such a vital kitchen function, purchase the best scales available. A good digital ounce scale will cost upwards of $200. However, this investment will be recouped many times over from the food cost savings it will provide. Purchase at least two ounce-graduated scales for the kitchen and always keep a third available in reserve.

One floor-type pound scale with at least a 150-pound capacity will be needed. This scale will be used to verify deliveries and raw yields. All scales should have a temperature-compensating device. Maintain these scales per the manufacturer's instructions; clean them periodically and oil when necessary and they will provide years of service. To ensure the accuracy of the scales test them periodically with an item of known weight. Most good scales come with a calibration kit.

For practical reasons some food items, such as dressings, sauces, and butter, are portioned by weight. However, they should still be portion-controlled by using proper-size spoons and ladles. Soups and condiments must be placed in proper-size serving containers. At each work area of the kitchen, place a chart listing the portion sizes and other portion control practices. All employees must use the measuring cups and spoons and the recipe manual when following recipes. The basis for the food cost program you are developing is based upon the knowledge that every item has a precise portion size. Management has the responsibility to ensure that these standards are being practiced and adhered to.

TRUTH AND ACCURACY IN THE MENU

Careful consideration must be taken when writing the final menu to ensure its complete accuracy. Few restaurant managers would purposely deceive their customers, as the restaurant would only suffer in the long run. You must become aware of the unintentional inaccuracies you may have in the menu and the governmental regulations regarding them.

Due to the actions of a few unscrupulous restaurant operators in recent years, a crack-down on the whole food-service industry has been declared by certain regulatory agencies. All states have one or more laws that basically say that any organization selling a product must not misrepresent the product in any manner with intent to deceive. Many states have specific "truth in menu" legislation.

Every statement made, whether it be orally by the waitress or written in the menu description, must be completely accurate. For example, "fresh bay scallops" must never be frozen; they must be bay (not sea or ocean) scallops. "Real maple syrup" must be 100 percent real maple syrup. "Imported baby spring lamb" must be imported, baby, spring lamb. Words and descriptions to watch are: fresh, real, imported, baby, 100 percent, B-B-Q or barbeque, pure, natural, and homemade. The description printed on the menu must be exactly the product you are serving.

You may be wondering how you can possibly write an enticing menu and yet still remain within the boundaries of the law. The trick is to be creative in writing the descriptions. State precisely what the product is, but modify the sentences to make the product sound enticing. Creative printing and the use of artwork will boost the appeal of the menu. The following is an example of how to dress up the most fundamental menu item—Salad—and yet still describe exactly the products for sale.

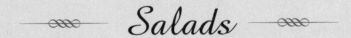

Salads

Spinach Salad
Fresh spinach with bacon, egg and mushrooms.

Green Salad
Crisp green lettuce with tomatoes, onions, cucumbers and sprouts.

Garden Salad
The above green salad served with a greater variety of fresh vegetables.

Fresh Fruit Salad
A variety of fresh fruits in season served on a bed of crisp greens and topped with our yogurt dressing.

Choice of Dressings
Our own recipes made daily
- Danish Blue
- Italian
- 1000 Island
- Creamy Cucumber

Many restaurants, to limit liability, will print a disclaimer. A disclaimer is a statement that what you have printed is accurate to the best of your knowledge and that the restaurant cannot be held responsible for any actions beyond its immediate control. Here is one type of disclaimer:

Due to the inclement weather this week, local Bay Scallops were not harvested. However, we were able to import some frozen Sea Scallops from Nova Scotia. These scallops are equal or superior to our regular fare.

Some restaurants print a general disclaimer at the bottom of the menu:

We serve only the finest food available. However, at certain times during the year we may not be able to obtain the exact product desired; therefore, we may substitute a similar product that will be equal or superior to the original item. Should this be the case your waiter/waitress will inform you of the substitution.

Carefully analyze your menu for possible misrepresentations. Self-regulation in the food industry is the key to maintaining the high standards and reputation it enjoys. You will find a copy of the Accuracy in Menu Checklist at the end of this chapter.

NUTRITIONAL CLAIMS ON MENUS

If you want to include menu items that are marketed as healthy (i.e., heart-healthy, low-fat, reduced-fat, cholesterol-free), make sure you have the nutritional information for these items readily accessible. Items described as "fresh" are included in this category.

Since 1997 restaurants have been included in the FDA's nutrition labeling laws. Any restaurant that uses health or nutrient-content claims on its menu must comply with these regulations. The FDA defines "restaurant" as "a place that serves food ready for consumption, including typical sit-down and carryout venues as well as institutional food service, delicatessens, and catering operations" (*Restaurants USA*, October 1996). If you use a symbol to designate these dishes, such as a heart shape, the regulations still apply.

The FDA regulations state that if you make health/nutrition claims on your menu you must be able to demonstrate there is a reasonable basis for making them. There is some flexibility in how restaurants may support the claim, but they must be able to show customers and officials that their claims are consistent with the claims established under the Nutrition Labeling and Education Act.

Some establishments are beginning to list ingredients and "nutritional facts" labels on the menu for the convenience of their customers. Such a label indicates the item's value in calories, total fat, cholesterol, sodium, carbohydrates, and protein. Some states now require food purchased for take-out to be labeled in this manner. If your restaurant manufactures a product (your famous salad dressing, salsa, or tomato sauce) for off-site consumption you may need to comply with the "nutritional facts" laws applied to packaged food. There are several software programs available that will perform these calculations for you and print labels. Please review these programs at **www.atlantic-pub.com**.

If you decide to include these items on your menu, you must decide on the best way to communicate the nutrition information to your customer. Here are some things to consider:

• **Information should be correct and clear.**

- **You may not need to include all the nutritional information on the menu; you may only need to have it available.** Many of the fast-food chains simply list this information on a poster in a public area in the restaurant. Depending on your menu format, you may not want to clutter the space with this information. If you find that your typical customer is requesting this information, it may be better to include it on the menu.

MENU SIZE AND COVER

The menu cover should reflect your restaurant's image as well as its identity. It can include graphics (the restaurant's logo) and copy. If your restaurant is in a historic building, you may want to include a drawing or photo of the building on your cover. If you are operating a family restaurant that has been in existence for generations, you may want to put a paragraph or two of copy about your family's history or food philosophy. The cover is the first step in the menu's role as a communication tool and it is the first place on paper you can communicate your identity to the customer. The menu is the only item that the customer is guaranteed to pay attention to when she walks into your establishment.

According to the National Restaurant Association, the ideal menu dimensions are 9 inches wide by 12 inches tall. Other sizes can work as well and the number of items on the menu will partially determine the menu size. The menu size should be manageable for the customers. They are often maneuvering in a limited space that includes water and wine glasses, candles, table tents, and flowers.

The cover should be of some durable material; part of its function is to protect interior pages. It can be leather, vinyl, laminated paper, or plastic. Your establishment's identity will help you choose the appropriate cover material. A fine-dining restaurant would not use plastic sleeves, but for a mid-price family restaurant plastic-sleeve menu covers would be appropriate. The cover's color should also be chosen with care. The color should tie into the theme and décor of your restaurant; but remember, color does have a psychological impact, so you will want colors that will evoke pleasant images and feelings. Bear in mind that the more colors you use for your menu, the more expensive the printing process becomes.

You may want to include general information on the cover, such as your hours of operation, address, telephone number, the forms of payment you accept, and any special services you provide. While your regular customers may not need this information, new customers will appreciate it and will make it easier for them to return if they know when you are open and how to find you again.

MENU DESIGN SOFTWARE

With the advent of the personal computer there have been a few menu design software programs developed in recent years. The software is generally very easy to use, having built-in templates and artwork. Your finalized menu can be printed out on a laser printer. Color, artwork, and graphics may be added.

Table tents and other promotional devices can also be utilized. The initial cost of the software will be easily recouped as you save in design and printing costs. You will have complete control over the design process. Changes can be made instantly. Daily menus can be created, which is a great way to accommodate special purchases that may have been made. The ability to generate new menus allows for instant price changes to reflect market conditions. One such software program is Menu Pro™. An extensive demonstration of the software may be found at **www.atlantic-pub.com** or by calling 800-814-1132 for information.

COPYRIGHTING THE MENU

Prior to printing the menu you would be wise to obtain a copyright. Copyrighting the menu protects it from being reproduced in any form without your written permission. A copyright would be extremely important if you were to prepare original artwork or write the menu in an interesting and novel way. Obtaining a copyright is a very simple procedure.

One of the pages of the menu, preferably the first or second, must contain the copyright registration. This notice must include the following three elements:

1. The name of the copyright owner.

2   The year of publication.

3. The symbol © and/or the word "Copyright" e.g., COPYRIGHT 2003 ABC Restaurant Corporation.

The Copyright Application Form TX may be found at the end of this chapter or at the Web site **www.loc.gov/copyright**. The registration process normally takes about four weeks and currently costs $45.

PRINTING THE MENU

Creatively printing the menu will have a marked effect upon the marketing of your offerings. The menus in restaurants across the country are probably more diverse than the food itself. Menus range from freehand writing on a white piece of 8½" x 11" paper to menus printed on boards, tables, walls, and bottles to menus spoken verbally. The menu can be turned into a promotional vehicle for your restaurant; it is a crucial internal marketing tool. It is the way you communicate to your customer your objectives and identity. Your menu design will directly impact guest-check averages, so it can help you achieve your profit goals. A well-designed menu can attract a customer's attention to specific items and increase the chances that the customer will purchase those items. If you put an item in a box on the menu, the customer's eye will be drawn to this area of the menu.

Regardless of how creatively the menu is utilized, it should be typeset and printed either by a professional or with a professional menu software. Using an unusual type style will dress up any menu. Discuss the possibilities with your local printer or graphics-art person or contact a company specializing in menu production, such as **www.mega-designs.com**. Artwork should be used; use the restaurant's logo if nothing else. Your local printer may have an artist on staff or know of some freelancers in the area who can help. You can also find professional freelancers specializing in menus at **www.elance.com**. Listed are some of the various types of printing styles and sizes available.

VARIOUS PRINTING STYLES AND SIZES FOR MENU PREPARATION

Gill Sans	**Gill Sans Bold**	*Gill Sans Italic*
Branding Iron	University	*Amaze*
Giovanni Book	**Giovanni Bold**	**Giovanni Black**
COPPERPLATE GOTHIC BOLD	COPPERPLATE GOTHIC LIGHT	*Brush*
Helios	OLD ENGLISH	*Nuptial Script*
Brophy Script	**Antique Olive Medium**	Antique Olive
Park Avenue	**Impact**	Optim
Futura Book	*Futura Book Italic*	**Futura Condensed**

8 pt   10 pt   12 pt   18 pt   24 pt   28 pt

36 pt   48 pt   60 pt

Why reinvent the wheel? Atlantic Publishing has several books dedicated to menu design. There are at least four books that contain nothing but sample menus in four colors from other restaurants around the country. These menus, many of which are award winners from the National Restaurant Association's Annual Menu Contest, will give you some great ideas. You can find these resources at **www.atlantic-pub.com**.

RECIPE AND PROCEDURE MANUAL

Your Recipe and Procedure Manual will contain all the restaurant's recipes, preparation procedures, handling instructions, and ordering specifications. This manual, if properly used, will ensure perfection and consistency every time the menu item is prepared. The Recipe and Procedure Manual must be available to the kitchen personnel at all times. Recipes should never be prepared from memory. The employee, without constant reinforcement from the manual, will tend to forget the exact proportions and may even leave an entire ingredient out of the recipe. For this reason and to ensure consistency, the Recipe and Procedure Manual should be open and in front of anyone

RECIPE AND PROCEDURE MANUAL SAMPLE

MENU ITEM: Baked Haddock

INGREDIENTS	PORTION/AMOUNT	CURRENT COST
Haddock	12.5 oz.	5.25
Lemon Juice	¼ tsp.	0.05
Bread Crumbs	½ tsp.	0.10
Butter	½ tsp.	0.14
Garlic Salt	¼ tsp.	0.02
Salt & Pepper	¼ tsp.	0.01
Tartar Sauce	0.5 oz.	0.05
Garnishes:		0.10
Parsley		
Tomato Wedge		
Lemon Slices	¼ lemon	0.06
Salad Bar		1.85
Misc. Expense		0.55
TOTAL COST		**$8.18**

PREPARATION PROCEDURE	Remove skin and bones. Cut into 12.5 oz. portion. Place on aluminum foil; fold aluminum foil tightly around fish. Sprinkle with lemon juice and cover with slices. Lightly cover with bread crumbs.
COOKING PROCEDURE	Bake in oven at 350° for 10–13 minutes. Fish is done when flaked with fork.
ORDERING INFORMATION	Use only fresh North Atlantic Haddock.
PRESENTATION	Remove aluminum foil. Place on #10 dinner plate. Arrange tartar sauce and garnishes (tomato wedge, lemon slices and parsley).
ADDITIONAL COMMENTS	Fish must be served hot. Fast service required.

The example Recipe and Procedure Manual page shows the type of information this manual should contain. A separate page will be necessary for all entrees, side dishes, desserts, dressings, and sauces. In the example, the "Current Cost" column may be omitted if you do not wish the employees to know the recipe's food costs. The inclusion of this information will increase your employees' awareness of the amount of "money" they are handling and responsible for every day. Under "Additional Comments" list all the accompaniments that a customer might request when ordering dinner. For example, if the entree is a steak dinner, the customer may request A.1. Steak Sauce, L&P Sauce, Tabasco sauce, or ketchup. These are items you will need to have available.

ORDERING MANUAL

The ordering manual contains all of the products that need to be reordered. You will find an example of an ordering manual page Food Ordering Form at the end of this chapter. The completed Recipe and Procedure Manual will list all of the food items you will need to order. Transfer these food items onto the order forms in alphabetical order. It is a good idea to group similar food items together, such as dry goods, seafood, poultry, dairy products, produce, and so forth.

PROJECTING MENU COSTS

To accurately assess the price to charge for a menu item, you must know the exact food cost of that item. You will need the completed Recipe and Procedure Manual and the current price lists from your purveyors. From your sales representative obtain projections on the average yearly prices for the major food items you order, such as meat products, seafood products, poultry, dairy, and produce.

Using the Recipe and Procedure Manual and the current price lists and price projections, compute the cost of each recipe item and place the amount in the column under current cost. Round all the amounts off to the nearest cent. Should estimates need to be given, it is better to figure a little high in order to cover yourself. Should your restaurant have a salad bar, estimate the average cost you expect for each customer. Allow yourself 25 cents per person over your estimate to cover everything.

The "Miscellaneous" column covers all the condiments and accompaniments not listed. Enter into this column approximately 5 percent of the total entree cost to cover these expenses. Adjust accordingly for each entree. If coffee, dessert, or any side orders are included in the price of an entrée, add a larger percentage to the total miscellaneous cost. Once open and operating you will be able to fix an average cost per customer for all miscellaneous costs and for the salad bar.

When computing the portion costs for items such as meat, fish, and poultry, you must consider the waste from cutting and trimming into the cost. The amount of usable portions you get when you are finished trimming or cutting a piece of food is the yield.

TO COMPUTE THE YIELD PERCENTAGE:

1. Compute the gross starting weight in ounces.

2. Compute the net ending weight (yield) in ounces.

3. Divide the net yield (in ounces) by the gross starting weight (in ounces). The resulting figure is the yield percentage.

TO COMPUTE THE ACTUAL PORTION OF A PRODUCT

1. Divide the price per pound by the average yield percentage to get the actual price per pound after waste.

2. Divide the actual price per pound by 16 to get the actual price per ounce.

3. Multiply the actual price per ounce by the average portion size; this figure is the actual portion cost.

Total all the current costs for each item. This figure is the estimated total portion cost.

This cost figure is not completely accurate because of the large number of variable factors used in the computations. This figure is an educated estimate from which you may accurately set your menu prices. The costs listed here are food costs only; no other costs (labor, paper products, plates) are factored in at this point.

PROJECTING THE ACTUAL AVERAGE COST PER CUSTOMER

Once set up and operating, it will be relatively easy to compute the actual average cost per customer. The actual average cost per customer should be projected once every month. Doing so ensures that the estimates used in computing the menu costs are accurate. Restaurants offering a buffet service or "all you can eat" specials must project their actual average cost per customer at least once a month, or better yet, biweekly.

Keep a list of all the food items you do not charge for during a specific test period and their prices. You can develop this list from the invoices, which detail daily purchases. Add into this figure the dollar amount of food you have on hand at the beginning of the test period that you are not directly charging for. At the end of the test period subtract the amount on hand from the total. Divide the total cost by the number of customers served during that period. This figure is the average actual cost per customer. Use it in projecting menu costs in place of any estimates you have made with this figure.

PROJECTING MENU PRICES

Projecting menu prices is a complex procedure because of the number of factors that must be considered. In order to operate profitably most restaurants must achieve and maintain their food cost of sales at 25 to 40 percent. The food cost percentage is the total food cost divided by the total food sales for a given period. If the total food sales for a given period was $100,000 and the total food cost was $40,000 for that same period, the kitchen would be operating at a food cost of sales of 40 percent. One percentage point in this example would be worth $1,000.

Computing what you must charge for each entree item is relatively easy. You will need the estimated total portion costs from the preceding section. The total portion cost (food cost) divided by the menu price (food sales) must equal a food cost percentage of between 0.25 (25 percent) and 0.40 (40 percent).

Portion Costs ÷ Menu Price x 100 = 25–40%

Simply plug different menu prices into the formula until you reach the desired food cost percentage.

The complications result when you have determined the price you must charge in order to

---

make the desired profit. Some of the prices you need to charge would be simply too high. No one would ever purchase the item at that price. What you must do in these cases is balance out the menu with high and low food cost items. The average cost of the menu must then be in the food-cost-percentage range desired. Poultry and seafood entrees will have a lower food cost percentage than meat entrees. Try to promote these lower food cost items to offset the higher ones.

Find out what other restaurants in the area are charging for similar dishes. Your clientele will dictate what the market will bear. The restaurant manager must set menu prices based on what customers will spend and what he must charge in order to make the desired profit margin.

Appetizers, side orders, beverages, and desserts can be priced at a very low food cost percentage. These items will contribute to a large percentage of your food sales and will lower your overall food cost percentage. Some restaurant managers, realizing this important point, have set up promotional contests awarding prizes or money to the waiter or waitress who sells the largest percentage of side orders. These contests can be very effective if the wait staff do not "hard sell" the items, but rather suggest the accompaniments to their customers.

Maintaining the food cost percentage is critical to maintaining your profit level. The food cost percentage does not tell the entire story. You must also be interested in getting the largest guest checks possible to bring the largest percentage of gross profit to your bottom line. For example, which would you rather sell:

- An item that sells for $5 and has a food cost of 35 percent (a gross profit of $3.25) or

- An item that sells for $10 and has a food cost of 50 percent (a gross profit of $5.00)?

Here is an example of a higher-food-cost-percentage item actually bringing a higher gross profit. Consider this important point when pricing out the menu!

The baked haddock dinner detailed above has a total food cost of $8.18, so if you were to charge $17.95 you would have a food cost percentage of 45.6 percent. Should the percentage be too high or the retail price too high you can reduce the portion size and the retail price. Some establishments may charge separately for the salad bar or side item. Should the retail price be lower than current market conditions or competing restaurants you can match the higher price and run a lower food cost on this entree to balance out higher food cost entree items, such as a prime rib dinner.

If you are not reaching your food cost goals or are not getting as high a check average as you would like, it may be because of your menu design. Not all items on your menu can be low cost and high profit. Your menu is likely a mix. Your menu design may be emphasizing high food cost or low profit items. Fixing the menu will help decrease food cost and increase profits. If you sell too many high cost items, your food cost will go up, because many of these (such as beef and seafood) have a high cost as well. If you sell too many low cost items, your check averages and gross profits will decline. Keep these facts in mind when designing your menu; you want to have a sales mix of both these types of items.

THE BEGINNING INVENTORY

The beginning inventory is the total dollar value of supplies on hand when the restaurant opens. This figure represents the starting point from which you can then compute individual costs. Each category — food, liquor, wine, and operational supplies — has its own beginning inventory figure.

A cost for each of these categories will be determined every month. To determine the cost for each area, simply add the beginning inventory value with the total purchases of that category for the month. Inventory the amount left at the end of the month and subtract it from total of the beginning inventory and purchases. The percentage of cost is the total cost divided by the total sales. The important thing here is to compute an accurate beginning inventory figure for your starting point.

Computing the beginning inventory is a simple calculation. If you are purchasing all new food products, simply total all your food purchases prior to opening day. This figure will be the beginning inventory.

If you are opening an existing restaurant and will be using some of the old supplies, first take an inventory of the old supplies. (See inventory procedures in Chapter 12.) Add the dollar value of these supplies with all your new food purchases prior to opening day. From the food order sheets, enter onto the inventory form all food items in alphabetical order. An example of an Inventory Form may be found at the end of the chapter.

Under the "Size" heading list the unit size of the product in your inventory. If two different sizes of the same product are used, list the item twice. For example, ketchup may be listed in the bulk, gallon size and in the individual service-bottle size. When extending a price for each unit it will be imperative that the cost corresponds to the appropriate size. The cost column, too, will be described in a later chapter.

The important consideration at this point is that all the food items you will be using are listed. All entrees, side orders, desserts, condiments, beverages — every food item in any form — must be on the inventory sheets in order for you to project an accurate food cost. The inventory pages will be used later to calculate the dollar amount of unused stock at the end of the month. Leave at least a half-page blank on the last inventory sheet for any food items that may have been left out. You can write the additional items in as you inventory them.

Each category — food, liquor, wine, and operational supplies — will have its own inventory pages. You are concentrating on food now so that you will have all the information you need at this point.

ACCURACY IN MENU CHECKLIST

Determine the accuracy of your own menu by using this checklist
and answering the sample questions.

QUANTITY REPRESENTATION

YES   NO

—— ——   1. When merchandising steaks by weight, do I use the generally accepted practice of referring to the steak's weight prior to cooking?

—— ——   2. Are my double martinis really twice the size of a single drink?

—— ——   3. Are my breaded shrimp at least 50% shrimp, as government regulations require?

—— ——   4. Is my "3-egg omelette" really made with three eggs?

—— ——   5. Are my "jumbo" eggs really "jumbo," the nationally recognized egg size, or are they actually "large?"

—— ——   6. When I say "choice sirloin of beef" do I really refer to "USDA Choice Grade Sirloin of Beef," as I've implied?

—— ——   7. Do I realize that it's OK to use the words "prime rib" to describe a cut of beef (i.e., the "primal" ribs: 6th to 12th ribs), but when I combine this term with "USDA" (USDA Prime Ribs), I'm implying a *grade* of beef, not a *cut* of beef?

—— ——   8. Do I realize that "ground beef" is just what the name implies—ground beef with no extra fat (the fat limit is 30%), water, extenders or binders?

—— ——   9. Do I understand that terms like "Prime," "Grade A," "Good," "No. 1," "Choice," "Fancy," "Grade AA" and "Extra Standard" are all descriptions of grades as set by federal and state standards?

PRICE REPRESENTATION

—— ——   10. If my pricing structure includes a cover charge, service charge or gratuity, have I brought these items to my customers' attention?

—— ——   11. Do I clearly define any restrictions regarding the use of coupons or premium promotions?

—— ——   12. If extra charges are made for special requests like "all white meat" or "no-ice drinks," are these charges clearly stated at time of ordering?

YES   NO

——— ———   13. Are my house brands really manufactured to my own specifications, even if they are prepared off premises?

——— ———   14. Am I careful when advertising brand names that the brand advertised is always the brand sold?

——— ———   15. When substitutions are necessary for whatever reason (non-delivery, availability, price, etc.), do I realize these substitutions must be reflected on my menu?

Some such substitutions:

- Maple syrup and maple-flavored syrup
- Baked ham and boiled ham
- Chopped veal cutlets and shaped veal patties
- Ice milk and ice cream
- Fresh eggs and powdered eggs
- Picnic-style pork shoulder and ham
- Milk and skim milk
- Pure jams and pectin jams
- Whipped cream and whipped topping
- Turkey and chicken
- Hereford beef and Black Angus beef
- Peanut oil and corn oil
- Beef liver and calf's liver
- Cream and half-and-half
- Cream and nondairy creamer
- Butter and margarine
- Ground beef and ground sirloin of beef
- Capon and chicken
- Standard ice cream and French-style ice cream
- Cod and haddock
- Noodles and egg noodles
- White-meat tuna and light-meat tuna
- Haddock and pollack
- Flounder and sole
- Cheese food and processed cheese
- Cream sauce and nondairy cream sauce
- Bonita and tuna fish
- Roquefort cheese and blue cheese
- Tenderloin tips and diced beef
- Mayonnaise and salad dressing

YES   NO

—— ——   16. Can I back up the following descriptions with package labels, invoices or other supplier-produced documentation to prove point of origin?
- Lake Superior Whitefish
- Maine Lobster
- Puget Sound Sockeye Salmon
- Gulf Shrimp
- Smithfield Ham
- Idaho Potatoes
- Imported Swiss Cheese
- Bay Scallops
- Florida Orange Juice
- Wisconsin Cheese

—— ——   17. Do I realize that it is all right to use the following terminology in the generic sense to describe a method of preparation or service?
- New England Clam Chowder
- Irish Stew
- French Fries
- Russian Service
- Swiss Cheese
- Country Fried Steak
- French Dip
- German Potato Salad
- Manhattan Clam Chowder
- Russian Dressing
- Country Ham
- Danish Pastries
- English Muffins
- French Toast
- Denver Sandwich
- Swiss Steak
- French Service
- Florida Fresh Juice

—— ——   18. Do I use the term "fresh juice" only for a juice without additives and prepared from the original fruit within 12 hours of sale?

MERCHANDISING TERMS

—— ——   19. Instead of using the term "homemade," do I use more accurate terminology, like "home-style," "homemade-style," "made on the premises" or "our own?"

—— ——   20. If I use any of the following terms, am I sure I can substantiate them?
- Fresh Daily
- Flown In Daily
- Center-Cut Ham
- Aged Steaks
- Slept in Chesapeake Bay
- Corn-Fed Porkers
- Finest Quality
- Black Angus Beef
- Low Calorie
- Fresh-Roasted
- Kosher Meat
- Own Special Sauce
- Milk-Fed Chicken

MEANS OF PRESERVATION

YES   NO

——   ——   21. Am I careful not to misrepresent canned orange juice as frozen or canned applesauce as homemade?

——   ——   22. Do I use food preserved by the commonly accepted means: canned, chilled, bottled, frozen and dehydrated?

——   ——   23. Am I always absolutely accurate in the terminology used to describe the method by which the food is prepared?

Some preparation methods:

- Charcoal-Broiled
- Barbecued
- Broiled
- Fried in Butter

- Deep Fried
- Baked
- Roasted
- Prepared from Scratch

- Sauteed
- Smoked
- Poached

VERBAL AND VISUAL REPRESENTATION

——   ——   24. Do my menus, wall placard or other advertising materials containing pictorial representations always portray the actual product with true accuracy?

——   ——   25. For instance, am I careful not to:

A. Use mushroom pieces in a sauce when the picture depicts mushroom caps?

B. Use sliced strawberries on a shortcake when the picture depicts whole strawberries?

C. Use four shrimps when the picture shows five?

D. Use a plain bun when the photo depicts a sesame-topped bun?

E. Let my waiter/waitress offer "butter or sour cream" when, in actuality, I'm using imitation sour cream or margarine?

F. Let my waiter/waitress tell a customer, "The pies are baked in our own kitchen," when in fact they purchased pre-baked, institutional pies?

DIETARY OR NUTRITIONAL CLAIMS

——   ——   26. Am I sure I never risk the public's health by misrepresenting the dietary or nutritional content of a food?

——   ——   27. Do "salt-free" and "sugar-free" mean just that?

——   ——   28. Can I substantiate with specific data any special nutrition claims or claims of "low calories?"

NOTE: If you cannot answer "yes" to all these questions, it is time to revise your menu to avoid misrepresentations and potential customer misconceptions about your food.

INVENTORY FORM

Item	Size	Date				Total	Cost	Extension
							TOTAL	

FOOD ORDERING FORM

Item	Build to Amount	On Hand									

For best results, fill in the form on-screen and then print it.

Form TX
For a Nondramatic Literary Work
UNITED STATES COPYRIGHT OFFICE

REGISTRATION NUMBER

TX	TXU

EFFECTIVE DATE OF REGISTRATION

Month	Day	Year

DO NOT WRITE ABOVE THIS LINE. IF YOU NEED MORE SPACE, USE A SEPARATE CONTINUATION SHEET.

1

TITLE OF THIS WORK ▼

PREVIOUS OR ALTERNATIVE TITLES ▼

PUBLICATION AS A CONTRIBUTION If this work was published as a contribution to a periodical, serial, or collection, give information about the collective work in which the contribution appeared.   Title of Collective Work ▼

If published in a periodical or serial give: Volume ▼   Number ▼   Issue Date ▼   On Pages ▼

2

a

NAME OF AUTHOR ▼

DATES OF BIRTH AND DEATH
Year Born ▼   Year Died ▼

Was this contribution to the work a "work made for hire"?
☐ Yes
☐ No

AUTHOR'S NATIONALITY OR DOMICILE
Name of Country
OR { Citizen of ▶ _____
Domiciled in ▶ _____

WAS THIS AUTHOR'S CONTRIBUTION TO THE WORK
Anonymous?   ☐ Yes ☐ No
Pseudonymous? ☐ Yes ☐ No
If the answer to either of these questions is "Yes," see detailed instructions.

NATURE OF AUTHORSHIP Briefly describe nature of material created by this author in which copyright is claimed. ▼

NOTE

Under the law, the "author" of a "work made for hire" is generally the employer, not the employee (see instructions). For any part of this work that was "made for hire" check "Yes" in the space provided, give the employer (or other person for whom the work was prepared) as "Author" of that part, and leave the space for dates of birth and death blank.

b

NAME OF AUTHOR ▼

DATES OF BIRTH AND DEATH
Year Born ▼   Year Died ▼

Was this contribution to the work a "work made for hire"?
☐ Yes
☐ No

AUTHOR'S NATIONALITY OR DOMICILE
Name of Country
OR { Citizen of ▶ _____
Domiciled in ▶ _____

WAS THIS AUTHOR'S CONTRIBUTION TO THE WORK
Anonymous?   ☐ Yes ☐ No
Pseudonymous? ☐ Yes ☐ No
If the answer to either of these questions is "Yes," see detailed instructions.

NATURE OF AUTHORSHIP Briefly describe nature of material created by this author in which copyright is claimed. ▼

c

NAME OF AUTHOR ▼

DATES OF BIRTH AND DEATH
Year Born ▼   Year Died ▼

Was this contribution to the work a "work made for hire"?
☐ Yes
☐ No

AUTHOR'S NATIONALITY OR DOMICILE
Name of Country
OR { Citizen of ▶ _____
Domiciled in ▶ _____

WAS THIS AUTHOR'S CONTRIBUTION TO THE WORK
Anonymous?   ☐ Yes ☐ No
Pseudonymous? ☐ Yes ☐ No
If the answer to either of these questions is "Yes," see detailed instructions.

NATURE OF AUTHORSHIP Briefly describe nature of material created by this author in which copyright is claimed. ▼

3

a YEAR IN WHICH CREATION OF THIS WORK WAS COMPLETED   This information must be given in all cases.
_____ ◀ Year

b DATE AND NATION OF FIRST PUBLICATION OF THIS PARTICULAR WORK
Complete this information ONLY if this work has been published.
Month ▶ _____ Day ▶ _____ Year ▶ _____
_____ ◀ Nation

4

See instructions before completing this space.

COPYRIGHT CLAIMANT(S) Name and address must be given even if the claimant is the same as the author given in space 2. ▼

TRANSFER If the claimant(s) named here in space 4 is (are) different from the author(s) named in space 2, give a brief statement of how the claimant(s) obtained ownership of the copyright. ▼

DO NOT WRITE HERE OFFICE USE ONLY

APPLICATION RECEIVED

ONE DEPOSIT RECEIVED

TWO DEPOSITS RECEIVED

FUNDS RECEIVED

MORE ON BACK ▶ • Complete all applicable spaces (numbers 5-9) on the reverse side of this page.
• See detailed instructions.   • Sign the form at line 8.

DO NOT WRITE HERE
Page 1 of _____ pages

DO NOT WRITE ABOVE THIS LINE. IF YOU NEED MORE SPACE, USE A SEPARATE CONTINUATION SHEET.

PREVIOUS REGISTRATION Has registration for this work, or for an earlier version of this work, already been made in the Copyright Office?

☐ Yes ☐ No If your answer is "Yes," why is another registration being sought? (Check appropriate box.) ▼

a. ☐ This is the first published edition of a work previously registered in unpublished form.

b. ☐ This is the first application submitted by this author as copyright claimant.

c. ☐ This is a changed version of the work, as shown by space 6 on this application.

If your answer is "Yes," give: Previous Registration Number ▶   Year of Registration ▶

5

DERIVATIVE WORK OR COMPILATION

Preexisting Material Identify any preexisting work or works that this work is based on or incorporates. ▼

Material Added to This Work Give a brief, general statement of the material that has been added to this work and in which copyright is claimed. ▼

a
6
b

See instructions before completing this space.

DEPOSIT ACCOUNT If the registration fee is to be charged to a Deposit Account established in the Copyright Office, give name and number of Account.

Name ▼   Account Number ▼

CORRESPONDENCE Give name and address to which correspondence about this application should be sent. Name/Address/Apt/City/State/Zip ▼

Area code and daytime telephone number ▶   Fax number ▶

Email ▶

a
7
b

CERTIFICATION* I, the undersigned, hereby certify that I am the

Check only one ▶

☐ author
☐ other copyright claimant
☐ owner of exclusive right(s)
☐ authorized agent of _____

of the work identified in this application and that the statements made by me in this application are correct to the best of my knowledge.

Name of author or other copyright claimant, or owner of exclusive right(s) ▲

8

Typed or printed name and date ▼ If this application gives a date of publication in space 3, do not sign and submit it before that date.

Date▶

Handwritten signature ▼

Certificate will be mailed in window envelope to this address:

Name ▼

Number/Street/Apt ▼

City/State/Zip ▼

YOU MUST:
• Complete all necessary spaces
• Sign your application in space 8
SEND ALL 3 ELEMENTS IN THE SAME PACKAGE:
1. Application form
2. Nonrefundable filing fee in check or money order payable to *Register of Copyrights*
3. Deposit material
MAIL TO:
Library of Congress
Copyright Office
101 Independence Avenue SE
Washington, DC 20559-6222

9

*17 USC §506(e): Any person who knowingly makes a false representation of a material fact in the application for copyright registration provided for by section 409, or in any written statement filed in connection with the application, shall be fined not more than $2,500.

Form TX – Full Rev: 11/2006 Print: 11/2006 — 30,000 Printed on recycled paper   U.S. Government Printing Office: 2006-xx-xxx/60,xxx

Short Form TX
For a Nondramatic Literary Work
UNITED STATES COPYRIGHT OFFICE

REGISTRATION NUMBER

| TX | TXU |

Effective Date of Registration

Application Received

Examined By

Deposit Received
One | Two

Correspondence ☐   Fee Received

TYPE OR PRINT IN BLACK INK. DO NOT WRITE ABOVE THIS LINE.

Title of This Work: Alternative title or title of larger work in which this work was published:	**1**	
Name and Address of Author and Owner of the Copyright: Nationality or domicile: Phone, fax, and email:	**2**	Phone ( ) Fax ( ) Email
Year of Creation:	**3**	
***If work has been published,* Date and Nation of Publication:**	**4**	a. Date _____ _____ _____ *(Month, day, and year all required)* Month Day Year b. Nation
Type of Authorship in This Work: Check all that this author created.	**5**	☐ Text (includes fiction, nonfiction, poetry, computer programs, etc.) ☐ Illustrations ☐ Photographs ☐ Compilation of terms or data
Signature: Registration cannot be completed without a signature.	**6**	*I certify that the statements made by me in this application are correct to the best of my knowledge.* * Check one: ☐ Author ☐ Authorized agent **X** _____
Name and Address of Person to Contact for Rights and Permissions: Phone, fax, and email:	**7**	☐ Check here if same as #2 above. Phone ( ) Fax ( ) Email

OPTIONAL

| **8**

Certificate will be mailed in window envelope to this address: | Name ▼

Number/Street/Apt ▼

City/State/Zip ▼ | Complete this space only if you currently hold a Deposit Account in the Copyright Office. | **9** Deposit account #_____
Name _____
_____
_____
_____
_____
DO NOT WRITE HERE   Page 1 of _____ pages |

CHAPTER

DIETARY AND
NUTRITIONAL GUIDELINES

Each restaurant needs to determine its standards of operation. In many cases, the federal, state, and local government will dictate how high the standard should be. All restaurants should have an obligation to provide nutritious meals for their patrons. One way to illustrate the quality expected is to include a color picture of each menu item on the recipe card. It is also a good policy to inform employees of the quality procedures for each food item. A few simple steps can help the quality process:

- Always provide quality products and ingredients.

- The items must be processed in a timely manner to enhance the quality of the final product.

- Test the final product for flavor and temperature.

- Continue working with employees to improve the quality of each menu item.

- Consider feedback you receive from patrons in your evaluation.

When reviewing feedback from employees or customers always consider the negatives and positives. Did it take too long to receive the item? Was the item the correct temperature when it was served? Was the item cooked sufficiently but not overcooked? Was there too much or too little seasoning? The answers to these questions can be an equipment problem, a recipe issue, or an employee mistake. Whatever factor caused the problem, it is your responsibility to find an acceptable solution.

TEST PANEL

Sometimes product and service evaluation can be done in-house. At other times, it is better to bring people in from outside your restaurant to make the critical evaluations. You need to pick the panel carefully.

- Do they have food-service experience?
- Are they able to distinguish individual flavors and qualities?

For taste-testing, non-smokers are preferred. A judge could stop smoking two or three hours before your taste test and be able to regain the ability to distinguish differences to give you useful in-put. When you schedule a taste test, the best time of day is an hour before lunch or an hour before dinner.

Get this critical information from the panel: appearance, color, flavor, smell, taste, and texture. You want feedback regarding the four tastes: bitter, salty, sour, and sweet. Taste and smell determine the flavor.

Let us use a banana as an example of the color of your food items. Before a banana is ripe, it is green; when it is ready to eat, it is yellow; and when it is too ripe, it is black. Many foods have a different appearance depending on the stage of the food. Keep this thought in mind when you serve menu items. Does the color of the food entice the patron or discourage them?

The texture of your food items is important: Foods may be stringy, smooth, tender, tough, crisp, mushy, or hard. Appearance includes more than just how the food looks. It can include the presentation of the food. Is the serving skimpy looking? Ask yourself whether the portion fits the container or should you find a different way to serve the item? A qualified taste test panel can provide this information and much more. The example below outlines taste panel guidelines.

TASTE PANEL GUIDELINES	
Guidelines and Number of Participants	Assign at least 10 people (and no more than 25) to be responsible for all taste test panels. The tasting should take place in a well-lighted, quiet room, separate from the food production. Participants must meet requirements as set forth below.
Test Timing	Tests should be conducted in the mid-morning (between 10:00 a.m. and 11:00 a.m.) or mid-afternoon (between 2:00 p.m. and 3:00 p.m.).
Qualifications of Participants	• Test panel participants must be trained food professionals. • Test panel participants should represent as many age ranges as possible. • Test panel participants must be nonsmokers. • Test panel participants should not have a cold or any illness that may impair their ability to taste food.
Materials Needed	Each test panel participants should have: • A writing utensil and rating cards for each sample. The cards should have the general product name only and be stacked in the order of testing. • New utensils and a napkin should be provided for each taste sample. • Glass of water. A sip of water should be taken between samples to rinse the mouth. • Sufficient food for the test panel participant enable the tester to consume 3 normal bites. • Liquids should be presented in clear glasses sufficient for 3 sips.
Comparison Samples	There should be no more than 3 different items for paired comparisons. Paired products should be at/near identical temperatures.
Acceptability Rating Test	There should be no more than 5 different items for an acceptability rating test.

TASTE PANEL GUIDELINES	
Food Temperature	All temperatures should be at or near serving temperature.
Tasting Guidelines	Test panel participants should note: • Appearance. Overall appearance as well as color, form on the plate and on the utensil. • Taste. Food should have contact with each oral taste center. • Texture. Compare texture to recognized standards.
Recording Results	Test panel participants should note feedback on each individual rating card. Additional comments should be written based on the tasting guidelines. It is preferred that the test panel participants not discuss the food offerings during the testing process.
Tabulation	A separate individual will be responsible for tallying and ranking the results of the test panel. Feedback will be given to each panel participant.

INTERNAL QUALITY CONTROL

Here are 10 steps to set up a self-evaluation process:

1. Assign a staff member to monitor and evaluate procedures.

2. Determine the scope of service in the restaurant.

3. Identify the most important parts of your service.

4. Determine indicators used to monitor your service.

5. Set up a series of plateaus to evaluate service. What will be the "trigger points" that more evaluation and possible changes are needed?

6. Collect important data as it relates to each plateau to identify problems in a reasonable time.

7. When you reach each plateau, are there new ways to improve?

8. Take all necessary action to provide better service.

9. Is your existing plan effective? If not, how can it be improved?

10. All relevant staff members need to be notified of these findings and the steps being taken to improve service.

Your employees need to be trained to implement quality control standards. An easy way is to test the first food that is prepared each day. Some things to check include:

• Are hot and cold foods served at the correct temperature?

• Does the food look fresh and appealing?

• Is each item presented properly?

• Are there various colors, flavors, and textures in the items being served?

If you answered yes to each question, you are doing a good job. If not, the appropriate corrections should be made. This little test can be done before each meal or periodically if you get good results. Include your staff members in the evaluation process and help them learn to develop a better product. Each time you get positive or negative feedback from customers, share this information with your staff, especially when your restaurant is being praised.

It is also possible that changes should be made based on the feedback you receive. These changes can include types of food, staff scheduling, and the equipment you use. Some simple changes that can make a difference are steaming items instead of boiling, preparing smaller quantities to maintain, or change the temperature where specific items will be served.

Using different equipment will change your recipe requirements and the final product. Changing the preparation method and the equipment used can make a big difference in your menu items. Another possibility is scheduling your food preparation. Something that can fix this problem is to prepare items with similar preparation and cooking time. Your standardized recipes should include this information and it needs to be considered when planning your menu items. This consideration is especially important when food is being served at improper temperature and you need to find a solution.

Consider these questions:

- Does your staff use warmed dinnerware for hot foods and chilled dinnerware for cold foods?

- When food is placed in the steam table, is it the proper temperature?

- Is there a draft near your steam table? If so, consider moving it.

- How long does it take your staff to serve the customers?

Your patrons can help you monitor the quality of the food you serve. Some restaurants ask their patrons to complete questionnaires periodically, it is a wonderful way to encourage feedback on the items you offer and the quality of your service. There are several ways to approach this evaluation, such as individual cards placed on the dining room tables or you can use a printed questionnaire handed to your customers. Below is an example I have seen used by various facilities. Keep in mind that your customers are taking their time to give you valuable insights and you should only pursue it if you plan to review their feedback and act on it.

BASIC COMMENT CARD	
Please rate your meal on a scale from 1 to 5 with 5 being excellent.	Additional Comments:
Overall Quality of Meal ❑ 1 ❑ 2 ❑ 3 ❑ 4 ❑ 5	
Appetizer Quality ❑ 1 ❑ 2 ❑ 3 ❑ 4 ❑ 5	
Salad Quality ❑ 1 ❑ 2 ❑ 3 ❑ 4 ❑ 5	
Entree Quality ❑ 1 ❑ 2 ❑ 3 ❑ 4 ❑ 5	
Vegetable Quality ❑ 1 ❑ 2 ❑ 3 ❑ 4 ❑ 5	
Dessert Quality ❑ 1 ❑ 2 ❑ 3 ❑ 4 ❑ 5	
Name (optional):	*Date:*

This is a flow chart that shows how you can gain feedback and how to implement it in the facility.

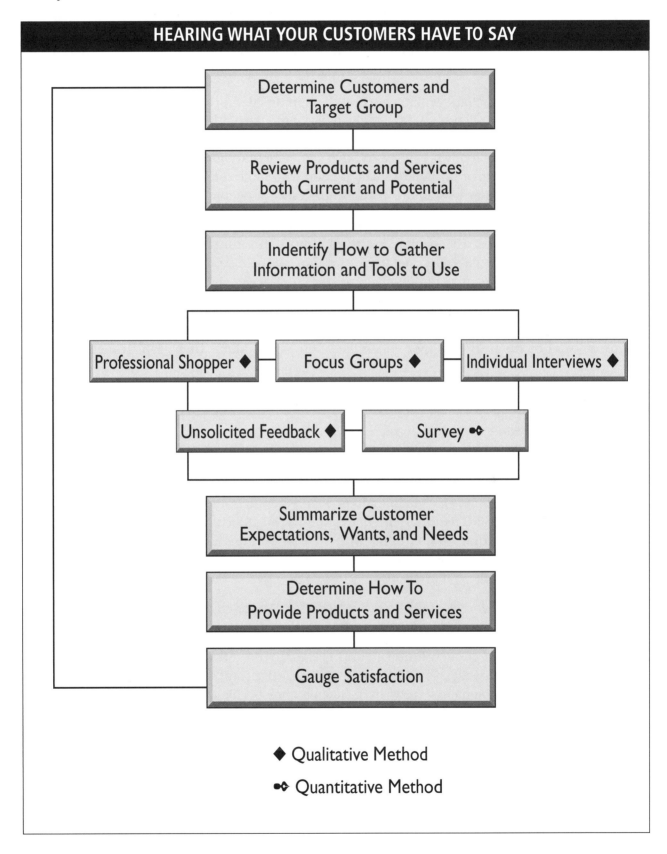

HEARING WHAT YOUR CUSTOMERS HAVE TO SAY

Determine Customers and Target Group

Review Products and Services both Current and Potential

Indentify How to Gather Information and Tools to Use

Professional Shopper ◆ | Focus Groups ◆ | Individual Interviews ◆

Unsolicited Feedback ◆ | Survey ●◆

Summarize Customer Expectations, Wants, and Needs

Determine How To Provide Products and Services

Gauge Satisfaction

◆ Qualitative Method

●◆ Quantitative Method

TOOLS TO GAIN FEEDBACK

Here are some details on each feedback tool that you can use. Which seems appropriate for your restaurant?

Focus groups can be helpful when you are developing new products or procedures. Some funding is available for in-depth studies. Make a list of the particular information you would like to find out during the focus group discussion. The best focus groups include a variety of people who are in your target market. It is good to have someone take notes to review later or you can record the group on video or audio tape. The person who moderates the group needs to remain unbiased and should know how to draw information out of people in a helpful manner.

Individual interviews or discussions will give you honest feedback without your subjects being influenced by their peers. The person asking the questions must not influence the answers. There is an art to asking the right questions and this will be discussed in the next section. The questions need to be prepared in advance and the interviewer needs to be familiar with them before an interview starts. This interview is another situation where you can tape and review at a later time.

A professional or mystery shopper gets a list of questions about their visit. It includes:

* Interior appearance
* Exterior appearance
* Cleanliness
* Quality of the service
* Promptness
* Cost
* Quality of the food

These are only some of the things they ask, but it gives the restaurant a good overview of how they are doing. When people are chosen to do mystery shopping, they need good communication skills and they need to be detail-oriented to supply the information you need. All mystery shopping organizations that I am familiar with reimburse the shopper for the meal, although they set a maximum cost. Some also pay a commission, but this is less common when the full cost of the meal is repaid.

Surveys use carefully planned questions and carefully selected participants. In any survey, choose a large enough sample of people to get accurate information.

Unsolicited feedback is given voluntarily and is usually the first source of feedback you get. Whenever someone approaches you with positive or negative feedback, take the time to consider their comments. If the comments are written, keep a copy on file or make your own notes from the information they shared. These comments could be divided into separate files for easier reference in the future.

The following forms are a good way to get feedback from customers about your facility. The forms ask a series of questions and have an area for people to offer comments or for you to note what was done in response to the comments you receive.

EVALUATING RESTAURANT IMPRESSIONS

Food is not the only consideration important to customers. Service, staff, variety, sanitation and convenience are also important factors. This evaluation checklist for operations covers basic principles essential to customer service. The focus is not productivity or efficiency, but the impressions our customers get.

You may want to have numerous people complete this checklist to get a random sampling of answers including supervisors, employees and customers. Tabulate the results and provide feedback to employees. The results will help create opportunities for meaningful in-services and retraining.

QUESTION	YES	NO
1. Are the hours convenient for customers? COMMENTS:		
2. Do customers frequently wait outside the entrance for you to open? COMMENTS:		
3. Are the hours clearly posted? COMMENTS:		
4. Is the first impression positive conveying a neat, clean, and organized environment? COMMENTS:		
5. Is the food service area clearly marked and easily accessible? COMMENTS:		
6. Is the lighting in the food service area sufficiently bright? COMMENTS:		
7. Are daily specials clearly posted and prices listed? COMMENTS:		
8. Are prices clearly posted for all other items? COMMENTS:		
9. Are portions consistent for all items? COMMENTS:		
10. Is the decor pleasing? COMMENTS:		
11. If there are self-service areas, are they clean, maintained and well stocked? COMMENTS:		
12. Are spills in any area immediately cleaned up? COMMENTS:		
13. Are all self-service areas arranged in order of use to decrease cross-traffic? COMMENTS:		
14. Is the overall traffic flow of the food service efficient? COMMENTS:		

Question	Yes	No
15. Is the hot food attractively served and portioned? COMMENTS:		
16. Is the temperature of the hot food pleasing (not too hot or cold)? COMMENTS:		
17. Are employees serving food pleasant and helpful? COMMENTS:		
18. Is the food service timed so that customers do not have to wait to long? COMMENTS:		
19. Are there enough cashiers that customers do not have to wait to long to pay? Or does the server handle check service and payment in a prompt manner? COMMENTS:		
20. Is the food priced competitively with other local operations? COMMENTS:		
21. Are service utensils clean, not bent and presented in an attractive manner? COMMENTS:		
22. Do the dishes match and are in good condition (no chips and fully glazed)? COMMENTS:		
23. Does the silverware match and is it clean and in good condition? COMMENTS:		
24. Are the trays (if used) clean and dry? COMMENTS:		
25. Is an employee available to assist children or disabled customers? COMMENTS:		
26. Does the dining area appear clean overall? COMMENTS:		
27. Are tables bussed and cleaned in a timely manner? COMMENTS:		
28. Are the tables, chairs and other furnishings in good condition? COMMENTS:		
29. Are the floors clean? COMMENTS:		
30. Are all signs up-to-date, neat, clean, and relevant? COMMENTS:		

MEAL SURVEY

Our Management and Staff are proud and pleased to serve you. We welcome your comments and suggestions so we may finds ways to improve our service. Please let us know how we rate.

	Excellent	Good	Fair	Poor
Overall acceptance of food				
Value for dollar spent				
Service				
Cleanliness				

Please list what you liked most about our food service:

1.

2.

3.

4.

Please list what you liked least about our food service:

1.

2.

3.

4.

If you would like the opportunity to discuss suggestions with the Manager, please fill in the information below:

Name:

RESTAURANT SURVEY

Date:

Meal:	Breakfast ❑	Lunch ❑	Dinner ❑	Other ❑

Time you arrived? *(choose one time only)*

1. Before 8:00 a.m. ❑		8. 12:16 p.m. - 12:30 p.m. ❑	
2. 8:00 a.m. - 9:00 a.m. ❑		9. 12:31 p.m. - 1:00 p.m. ❑	
3. 9:01 a.m. - 10:00 a.m. ❑		10. 1:01 p.m. - 2:00 p.m. ❑	
4. 10:01 a.m. - 11:00 a.m. ❑		11. 2:01 p.m. - 4:00 p.m. ❑	
5. 11:01 a.m. - 11:30 a.m. ❑		12. 4:01 p.m. - 5:00 p.m. ❑	
6. 11:31 a.m. - Noon ❑		13. 5:01 p.m. - 6:00 p.m. ❑	
7. 12:01 p.m. - 12:15 p.m. ❑		14. 6:01 p.m. - 7:00 p.m. ❑	

FOOD	Excellent	Good	Less than Satisfactory	Don't Know N/A
1. Food quality				
Beverages	❑	❑	❑	❑
Hot entrees	❑	❑	❑	❑
Grill items	❑	❑	❑	❑
Salad bar	❑	❑	❑	❑
Sandwich bar	❑	❑	❑	❑
Desserts	❑	❑	❑	❑
2. Variety of food available	❑	❑	❑	❑
3. Temperature of food *(hot/cold)*	❑	❑	❑	❑
4. Size of portion served	❑	❑	❑	❑

Please list any food items you would like to be added to the menu selection:

_____

_____

_____

_____

_____

_____

_____

Are the prices of the items fair and reasonable?
❑ Yes
❑ No

RESTAURANT SURVEY

SERVICES AND FACILITIES	Excellent	Good	Less than Satisfactory	Don't Know N/A
1. Speed of food service	❑	❑	❑	❑
2. Speed of payment/cashier	❑	❑	❑	❑
3. Facility cleanliness	❑	❑	❑	❑
4. Atmosphere of dining area (appearance/decor/furniture)	❑	❑	❑	❑
5. Courtesy of staff	❑	❑	❑	❑

Generally, how responsive do you feel we are to suggestions or recommendations for changes made by employees? Would you say the our staff is:

❑ Very responsive ❑ Somewhat responsive
❑ Not responsive at all ❑ Not Sure

Overall, what is your opinion of the service you just received? Would you say:

❑ Excellent ❑ Good
❑ Less than satisfactory ❑ Don't know

Comments:

_____
_____
_____
_____
_____
_____
_____
_____
_____
_____
_____
_____
_____
_____
_____
_____
_____
_____
_____
_____

Optional:

Name_____

TIPS TO ASK THE RIGHT QUESTIONS

There is an art to asking the right questions. Here are some tips to help:

- **Ask about one specific thing with each question.** Asking about multiple things in one question distorts the answer.

- **Use clear, easy, simple words.** You are much more likely to get a useful and accurate answer.

- **Do not ask a question that can be answered with a "yes" or "no."** When you ask this sort of question the only answer you will get is either "yes" or "no" which is of limited benefit. In-depth answers are much more useful and are volunteered when the question begins with "how" or "when" or "where" rather than "Did you...?" or "Do you...?" or "Will you...?"

- **Give the person unbiased choices, illustrated with a scale of one to five.** If you gave choices (extremely good, good, fair and bad), you have balanced the scales unfairly in your favor. If you include extremely good and very good, then you need to include extremely bad and very bad.

If you decide to use interviews, you need to choose who will talk to these people. You could speak with your patrons personally or have a trusted staff member who communicates well do the interviews. Some people will simply check good or excellent on your surveys. Others will give solid feedback that can be valuable at your facility. The individuals who gave honest information will be watching to see when these changes will be implemented.

Another interesting way to see whether your customers like the items you prepare is to conduct a plate-waste study. A plate-waste study can be done by your bus staff or dishwashing staff. It will tell you whether customers are finishing their meals and which items are not being eaten. A plate-waste study should include at least 20 plates. The more plates you evaluate, the more detailed information you will gather. If your study shows certain items are not eaten, it might be good to consider deleting them from your menu or it might be good to change the recipe or preparation method that you are using. The study could also provide additional information which includes:

- Are you serving the correct food items?

- Should you change the preparation methods?

- Is the food served at the proper temperatures?

- Is your menu item selection adequate?

- Are you preparing the right quantity of food?

Quality improvement and quality assurance are two different approaches that offer some differences. This chart will show how they vary in different situations.

QUALITY IMPROVEMENT & QUALITY ASSURANCE

Category	Quality Improvement	Quality Assurance
Commitment	Stress the importance of quality to staff members at all levels.	Not stressed as a major component.
Focus	Gather input about process and products to find areas to improve. Must organize your approach.	Structure your approach along with being appropriate, minimize risk, and ensure clinical performance.
Mass Inspection	Eliminate mass inspections.	Encourage broad-based inspections.
Measure and Improve	Use a cycle to improve the processes that you use.	Identify opportunities to improve your service and care.
Orientation	Understand the need to improve. Be proactive about improvement. Always keep customer in mind.	Monitor and measure to find areas that need improvement. Be reactive when you find problems.
Problem solving	Measure quality in the unit. Cross-functioning teams.	Use multi-disciplinary committees to ensure quality throughout units.
Quality Cost	Emphasize with improvement.	Not emphasized with assurance.
Requirements	Defined by customers.	Defined by provider.
Responsibility	Everyone is responsible.	Management determines responsibility.
Standards	Standards are the starting point. Develop standards internally.	The standards are your goals. Use standards developed by others.
Statistical Method	Sophisticated method.	Rudimentary method.
Structure	Use existing structure.	Use separate assurance structure.

Each element focuses on a different segment of your facility. The quality improvement or assurance details show what is most important and how the program could be implemented in the facility. The approach you use should be based on the specific requirements of your facility.

PERATING PROCEDURES

A thorough evaluation of operating procedures is necessary to develop a strategic long-term plan to provide quality for your customers. The importance should not be underestimated. Here are a few key steps to help you get started with the evaluation:

- Set goals for your department.

- Keep these goals in accord with the purpose of the facility.

- Develop a plan to attain these goals.

- Develop operating procedures to help you attain these goals.

- Create a plan to implement these procedures.

- Evaluate your effectiveness and make any necessary changes.

Some key points to consider when you develop your plan are:

- Do you have adequate resources to implement your program?

- Will your plan cause other problems in the facility?

- Can you find ways to improve the quality of your food production and delivery systems?

- What quality is a major factor in all department operations including: purchasing, receiving, storage, and processing?

- Do you recruit the best personnel to maintain quality?

Sometimes more information is needed to make an effective plan. One example is the difference between knowing the restaurant budget and simply being told to minimize expenses. The additional information can make a difference in how people do their job. It helps them to know where and when to minimize expenses to stay within the budget. Either way, to maintain expenses certain criteria must be met, such as:

- Are your meal plans nutritious?

- Are personal and professional goals being met?

- Does the restaurant follow sanitary practices?

Thorough investigations and evaluations are necessary to find the answers to these questions.

CONDUCT A SELF REVIEW

It can be effective to prepare for inspections or evaluations by reviewing your procedures and policies to be sure they met the criteria and that you are doing the best possible job for your clients. So, what are some ways to check and evaluate your operation to make adequate improvements?

One simple way to start is by making a checklist of each thing that should be done in the restaurant on a daily, weekly, or monthly basis. The list will help you to identify areas that need some additional focus. You may wonder how you would develop such a checklist. The checklist would be a great topic for a departmental meeting. All staff members can offer suggestions on areas that need improvement. You could assign several people to make concise lists of their responsibilities and then have a second or third person review the list to make sure it is complete. Once the lists are complete the manager should check them and add any additional points that were missed.

Many reference books include checklists and you will find 18 at the end of this chapter. If the checklists here are not exactly what you need, feel free to make changes as necessary for your specific facility. The procedure manual for your facility should offer additional information for creating your checklists.

After your checklist is finished, what should you do with it? The list should be used weekly or monthly to verify that acceptable standards are being met in the facility. If there are substantial problems, you may wish to use the lists more often. In a short time you should be able to implement substantial changes by improving your procedures. You may need more than one checklist. Remember to make multiple copies that can be used when training new employees or to retrain employees. It could be included with the annual employee evaluation that we will discuss in a later chapter.

Major changes will take time, but you do not want to drag your feet in starting the necessary changes in a restaurant. After problems are identified, you can have two or three members find ways to revise your procedures. It is a good idea for the manager to try these new procedures before they are implemented throughout the restaurant.

Staff members will need time to become familiar with the new procedures. When you feel comfortable that your employees are implementing the changes properly, it would be good to re-evaluate. Re-evaluation will help you verify that the changes are successful. If you feel the changes are not working, you should evaluate more quickly to find any new problems.

After all procedure changes are made, document them in your training manual. Any time you change these documents, they need to be updated, signed, and issued to all employees to eliminate potential confusion among staff members. If any job descriptions need to be revised, it should be done at the same time and added to the procedure manual.

EXTERNAL QUALITY CONTROL

Government agencies and private associations evaluate services in various facilities. Any dietary manager who has implemented the reviews and suggestions mentioned earlier should not have a problem meeting the requirements in these evaluations.

FOOD SAFETY INSPECTIONS

There are many ways to prepare for an inspection and I will include some tips, suggestions, and checklists for you to study and use as you see fit. We talked earlier about doing self-inspections in your facility. Food safety is another area where those inspections would be beneficial.

For a mock inspection, visit **www.metrokc.gov/health/foodsfty/mockinspection.htm**. This web site walks you through the steps of an inspection, although the specific details may vary in your area. However, it will give you an idea of the things that take place.

The City of Denver's Web site offers all sorts of valuable information at **www.denvergov. org/eh/search.asp?mode=sample**. On this page you will find specific information about the following topics:

FOOD SAFETY VIOLATIONS	
Type 1 Violations	**Type 2 Violations**
1. Food Service	9. Food Labeling and Protection
2. Personnel	10. Improper Equipment Design and Construction
3. Temperature Control	11. Testing Devices
4. Sanitization Rinse	12. Improper Cleaning of Equipment and Utensils
5. Water/Sewage/Plumbing Systems	13. Utensils – Single Service Articles
6. Hand Washing and Toilet Facilities	14. Physical Facilities
7. Pest Control	15. Other Operations
8. Toxic Items	

This site offers more information on each of these headings and various subheadings. But you can also learn why each element of this list is significant to public health. I would highly recommend that you take a look at this information to gain additional insights into many of the things discussed in this chapter.

Food Safety and Inspection Service (FSIS) is the public health agency in the U.S. Department of Agriculture which ensures the nation's commercial supply of meat, poultry, and egg products is safe, wholesome, and correctly labeled and packaged. You can visit them at **www.fsis.usda.gov**. There is also a wealth of safety information at: **www.fsis.usda.gov/Food_Safety_Education/ index.asp**. You can subscribe to their Food Safety Newsletter for up-to-date information. This newsletter reports on new food safety educational programs and materials and emerging science concerning food safety risks. The newsletter is distributed up to four times a year. This publication is free for print subscribers. Electronic copies may be downloaded from the Web site. E-mail fsis.outreach@usda.gov. Or subscribe online at: **www.fsis.usda.gov/news_&_ events/food_safety_educator_subscription/index.as**p.

HOW TO PREPARE FOR AN INSPECTION

Inspections can be traumatic for food service managers if you do not maintain the proper environment and procedures each day. This section will include some tips to help you prepare for these inspections and to alleviate some of the stress associated with inspections. They are a necessary part of the business, so it is better to be prepared for them. You can download an inspection form at **www.metrokc.gov/health/foodsfty/inspectionform.pdf** This form will help you set up and maintain a daily sanitation schedule, a wonderful way to establish sanitary practices for your facility. There are additional forms and checklists at the end of this chapter.

An online step by step inspection can help you see what will be checked and to be better prepared. Your inspection may be different, but this is an example of some of the things you should expect: **www.metrokc.gov/health/foodsfty/mockinspection.htm**

PREPARING FOR AN INSPECTION

Here are some things you need to do to prepare for an inspection:

- **Use a form similar to the local health department's** for your self inspections.

- **View the facility from the inspectors viewpoint,** not your own.

- **Begin your self-inspection from the outside** and work your way through the entire facility.

- **Immediately after your inspection, hold a brief meeting with your staff members** to review the problems you found.

- **Several priorities in your inspection should include: food temperatures in storage, preparation, serving, reheating, food type awareness, and proper hand washing techniques.**

- **You cannot emphasize the importance of hand washing too much.** Hang posters and reminders for staff members in the kitchen and restrooms.

- **Any managers should be trained to keep up-to-date about the latest food safety information and techniques.**

- **Stay current about the local health code and requirements.**

THE VISIT

- **Be prepared** and eliminate the possibility of panic.

- **When inspectors arrive, ask to see their credentials.**

- **If you are unsure about their credentials, call the health department to verify their identity.**

- **Never refuse to allow inspectors to do an inspection.** They can get an inspection warrant if needed, but the resulting inspection will be more thorough if these measures are needed. Refusing to allow an inspection will cause unneeded animosity with the inspector who is there to help you make the facility better and safer.

- **Follow the inspector and make notes about any problems.** Make the effort to fix any problems while the inspector is there. Show you are willing to make the needed changes.

- **Never offer food or other items to the inspector.** They could be viewed as a bribe to influence the inspector.

- **Sign the report after the inspection is complete.** Your signature does not indicate your agreement with the details but merely that you received a copy of the report.

- **Ask inspectors to explain any findings to you and your staff members.** They can also offer suggestions on how to make necessary improvements. Remember that even the cleanest food service facilities can have health department citations.

THE VIOLATIONS

- **Fix any small problems before inspectors leave your facility** to show your willingness to make improvements.

- **Ask for an additional explanation if you have questions or need clarification.**

- **You have the right to appeal any findings**, but keep your thoughts to yourself until after the inspector leaves.

Visit **www.denvergov.org/eh/search.asp?mode=sample** to get information about each violation and additional information which may explain the public health significance for each violation. Categories include:

- Food Source
- Temperature Control
- Water/Sewage/Plumbing Systems
- Pest Control
- Food Labeling and Protection
- Testing Devices
- Utensils – Single Service Articles
- Other Operations

- Personnel
- Sanitization Rinse
- Hand Washing and Toilet Facilities
- Toxic Items
- Equipment Design and Construction
- Cleaning of Equipment and Utensils
- Physical Facilities

For additional information about HACCP and safe food handling practices, you should see *HACCP & Sanitation in Restaurants and Food Service Operations: A Practical Guide Based on the USDA Food Code* (Item # HSR-02) from Atlantic Publishing, **www.atlantic-pub.com**.

IMPROVE DIETARY SERVICES

Effective managers conduct in-house reviews periodically. The frequency depends on how often reviews are required. They can also be done whenever you see problems.

After the problems are identified, your first priority is to resolve them. We all know people who are comfortable in their job and like to do things a certain way, but that may not be best for the restaurant when the routine needs to be changed. Many times we hear people say all they do is put out fires all day. Your job as a manager is to prepare for problems, review the situations, and find ways to improve them. With proper planning most "fires" can be eliminated.

In the beginning, there may be a number of problems that need be addressed. You can delegate some projects to others in the restaurant. When this is not possible, the manager needs to determine the worst problems and list them by priority. The worst problem should be handled first. In some cases, one solution can fix more than one problem. A common pitfall is to throw out the existing procedures instead of finding ways to improve on current practices. It is much easier for restaurant employees to adjust the way they do things instead of starting over from scratch. Help your employees make changes easier by involving them in the planning stages. How a manager handles these problems reveals his management abilities.

After the changes have been determined, they must be evaluated. Any staff members who will be involved in proposed changes should be notified as early as possible. The manager needs to explain the changes, why they are needed, and may even need to defend the changes. Remember the staff that performs these jobs each day can offer valuable insights and suggestions about proposals.

CONSIDER FOOD ALLERGIES

Food intolerances are becoming more common and the most common is lactose intolerance, which is the inability to digest significant amounts of lactose, the major sugar found in milk. Many foods contain lactose, not just milk and cream. People who are lactose intolerant need to read the labels for all foods before they eat including bread, cereal, instant potatoes, most baked goods, soup, margarine, lunch meats, salad dressing, biscuits, cookies, pancakes, and even candy.

Food allergies have a great impact on food service. As a food service worker, you should know the signs of food allergies or intolerances. For instance, if you see people taking antacids or other medicine for indigestion without getting relief, it could be food allergies and intolerances.

The following chart illustrates some food allergies or intolerances symptoms:

FOOD ALLERGIES OR INTOLERANCES SYMPTOMS	
Symptom	**Definition**
Abdominal Cramps:	Pain in the belly.
Belching:	Air which passes through your digestive tract and out of your mouth.
Bloating:	Tight abdomen caused by gas.
Diarrhea:	Loose, watery, frequent stools; chronic if it lasts more than a month.
Weight Loss:	Eating less because of illness brought on by certain foods.
Slow Growth:	Poor or unusually slow weight or height increase in children.
Floating Stools:	If the body doesn't digest and absorb fats, some of the fat leaves the body through the stools.
Foul Smelling Stools:	Stools' odor is worse than usual and is caused by diet.
Rumbling Stomach:	This can happen 30 minutes to two hours after eating. The severity depends on how much of the offending foods were eaten and how much is left in the intestinal tract.

Food allergies can be serious and life-threatening. Eight food groups cause allergic reactions including peanuts and other nuts, fish, shellfish, wheat, milk, soy, and eggs. A couple of unusual ingredients are aspartame, food colorings, and additives and these are only the tip of the allergy and intolerance iceberg.

It is advisable to ensure that the ingredient information is available to your customers. You can list these ingredients specifically on your menu or have your server communicate these details to customers. It is also helpful if your employees understand the serious nature of food allergies and this should help them assist customers who have food allergy problems.

Allergies are more prevalent than most people realize. Even a small amount of an offending food can cause a person to become nauseous, vomit, develop hives, have trouble breathing, and suffer anaphylaxis. It is critical that special order requests be taken seriously and that allergens are mentioned in person or on your menu.

You can obtain more information about food allergies from the International Food Information Council at 202-296-6540 or **www.ific.org**.

ADDITIONAL FOOD ALLERGIES & ASTHMA
AN EXCERPT FROM INTERNATIONAL FOOD INFORMATION COUNCIL
BACKGROUNDER, NOVEMBER 2006 www.ific.org/food/allergy/index.cfm

While allergy to pollen or other environmental sources typically causes a lot of discomfort during spring, summer, and fall, food allergy is one condition that knows no season. According to recent studies, approximately 11 million Americans—two percent of adults and six to eight percent of children under the age of three—have a true food allergy.

People tend to diagnose themselves, believing they have allergic reactions to certain foods or food ingredients. Unfortunately, self-diagnosis of food allergy often leads to unnecessary food restrictions, nutrient deficiencies, and misdiagnosis of potential life-threatening medical conditions other than food allergy. Therefore, experts urge people to see a board-certified allergist for proper diagnosis.

WHAT IS A FOOD ALLERGY?

A food allergy is an adverse reaction to a food or food component that involves the body's immune system. A true allergic reaction to a food involves three primary components: 1) contact with a food allergen (reaction-provoking substance, virtually always a protein); 2) immunoglobulin E (IgE-an antibody in the immune system that reacts with allergens); and 3) mast cells (tissue cells) and basophils (blood cells), which when connected to IgE antibodies release histamine or other substances causing allergic symptoms.

The body's immune system recognizes an allergen in a food as foreign and produces antibodies to halt the "invasion." As the battle rages, symptoms appear throughout the body. The most common reaction sites are the mouth (swelling of the lips), digestive tract (stomach cramps, vomiting, diarrhea), skin (hives, rashes, or eczema), and the airways (wheezing or breathing problems).

Allergic reactions to food are rare and can be caused by any food. The most common food allergens, known as the "Big 8," are fish, shellfish, milk, egg, soy, wheat, peanuts, and tree nuts such as walnuts, cashews, etc. Symptoms of a food allergy are highly individual and usually begin within minutes to a few hours after eating the offending food. People with true, confirmed food allergies must avoid the offending food altogether.

There are numerous misconceptions regarding allergy to food additives, preservatives, and ingredients. Although some additives and preservatives have been shown to trigger asthma or hives in certain people, these reactions are not the same as those reactions observed with food allergies. These reactions do not involve the immune system and therefore are examples of food intolerance or idiosyncrasy rather than food allergy. Most people consume a wide variety of food additives and ingredients daily, with only a very small number having been associated with adverse reactions.

There are also some adverse reactions to foods that involve the body's metabolism but not the immune system. These reactions are known as food intolerance. Examples of food intolerance are food poisoning or the inability to properly digest certain food components, such as lactose or milk sugar. This latter condition is commonly known as lactose intolerance.

Life-threatening Reactions

Many allergic reactions to food are relatively mild. However, a small percentage of food-allergic individuals experience severe, life-threatening reactions, called anaphylaxis. Anaphylaxis is a rare but potentially fatal condition in which several different parts of the body experience foodallergic reactions simultaneously, causing hives, swelling of the throat, and difficulty breathing. It is the most severe allergic reaction.

Symptoms usually appear rapidly, sometimes within minutes of exposure to the allergen. Because they can be life-threatening, immediate medical attention is necessary when an anaphylactic reaction occurs. Standard emergency treatment often includes an injection of epinephrine (adrenaline) to open up the airways and blood vessels.

ASTHMA AND FOOD

What is Asthma?

Asthma, a chronic medical condition, affects more than 17 million Americans (three to four percent of the population). Asthma results when triggers (or irritants) cause swelling of the tissues to the air passages of the lungs, making it difficult to breathe. Typical symptoms of asthma include wheezing, coughing, and shortness of breath.

Can Foods Trigger Asthma?

Only a few. For years it has been suspected that foods or food ingredients may cause or exacerbate symptoms in those with asthma. After many years of scientific and clinical investigation, there are very few confirmed food triggers of asthma. Sulfites and sulfiting agents in foods (found in dried fruits, prepared potatoes, wine, bottled lemon or lime juice, and shrimp), and diagnosed food allergens (such as milk, eggs, peanuts, tree nuts, soy, wheat, fish, and shellfish) have been found to trigger asthma. Many food ingredients such as food dyes and colors, food preservatives like BHA and BHT, monosodium glutamate, aspartame, and nitrite, have not been conclusively linked to asthma.

What Can Individuals with Asthma Do to Prevent a Food-Triggered Asthma Attack?

The best way to avoid food-induced asthma is to eliminate or avoid the offending food or food ingredient from the diet or from the environment. Reading ingredient information on food labels and knowing where food triggers of asthma are found are the best defenses against a food-induced asthma attack. The main objectives of an asthmatic's care and treatment are to stay healthy, to remain symptom free, to enjoy food, to exercise, to use medications properly, and to follow the care plan developed between the physician and patient.

DAILY EQUIPMENT CLEANING CHART

ITEM	CLEANING TASK	WHEN
Beverage dispensers	Wipe spills and splashes Take apart, clean and sanitize dispenser spouts Clean drain tray	Upon each occurrence Daily Once per shift
Breath guards	Wipe spills and splashes Clean and sanitize all surfaces	Upon each occurrence Once per shift
Can openers	Clean and sanitize	After every use, and once per shift 7/8
Carts, food transport equipment	Wipe spills and splashes Clean and sanitize shelves and racks	Upon each occurrence Daily, after use
Coffee and tea machines	Wipe spills and splashes Rinse baskets, urns and pots Take apart, clean and sanitize spray heads and spouts	Upon each occurrence After each use Daily
Deep fryer	Clean outside surfaces Clean and filter grease	Once per shift Once per shift
Dishwashing machines	Take apart and clean Clean doors, gaskets and surfaces	On a regular basis to remove build-up and ensure clean water Daily
Floors	Wipe spills Sweep Damp mop Sanitize and scrub	Upon each occurrence As needed After each shift Daily
Frozen dessert machines	Wipe spills and splashes Clean drain tray Take apart, clean and sanitize parts, interior surfaces and dispenser spouts	Upon each occurrence Once per shift Daily
Grill, griddle, broiler	Clean and brush grill surfaces Clean surrounding surfaces and grease tray Clean cooking surfaces and backsplash	As needed, or once per shift Once per shift Daily
Hot holding	Wipe spills Clean interior surfaces and racks Clean exterior surfaces	Upon each occurrence Daily Daily

DAILY EQUIPMENT CLEANING CHART

ITEM	CLEANING TASK	WHEN
Ice machine	Clean doors, gaskets and exterior surfaces	Daily
Microwave	Wipe spills Clean and sanitize interior surfaces Clean and sanitize fan shield and tray Clean outside surfaces	Upon each occurrence Once per shift Daily Daily
Mixers, slicers, and food processors	Take apart, clean and sanitize parts, surfaces and work tables	After each use, or between each food item change
Ovens	Wipe spills	Upon each occurrence
Range	Wipe spills Clean and sanitize work surfaces	Upon each occurrence Once per shift
Reach-in refrigerators and freezers	Wipe spills Clean outside, doors and gaskets	Upon each occurrence Daily
Scales	Clean and sanitize weighing tray Clean and sanitize exposed surfaces	After each use Daily
Sinks	Clean and sanitize sink interior Clean exterior surfaces and back splash	After each use Daily, at closing
Steam tables	Drain water and clean wells Clean outside and surrounding surfaces	Once per shift Once per shift
Steamer	Wipe spills Clean and sanitize interior surfaces and racks Clean exterior surfaces	Upon each occurrence Daily Daily
Walk-in refrigerators and freezers	Wipe spills Sweep and damp mop (freezer, sweep only) Clean door surfaces and gaskets Scrub floors	Upon each occurrence Once per shift Daily Daily (except freezer)
Walls	Splashes Wash walls in prep and cooking areas	Upon each occurrence Daily, at closing
Work tables	Clean and sanitize tops and shelves	After each use and after

WEEKLY AND MONTHLY EQUIPMENT CLEANING CHART

WEEKLY CLEANING	
ITEM	**CLEANING TASK**
Carts and transport equipment	Thoroughly clean and sanitize supports and exterior
Coffee and tea machines	Clean and brush urn, pots and baskets using cleaner specified by manufacturer
Deep fryer	Boil out fryers
Ovens	Clean interior surfaces and racks
Range	Take apart burners, and empty and sanitize catch trays
Reach-in refrigerators	Empty, clean and sanitize
Sinks	Clean legs and supports
Steam tables	De-lime
Walk-in refrigeration and freezer units	Wipe clean and sanitize walls
Work tables	Clean legs and supports; empty, clean and sanitize drawers

MONTHLY CLEANING	
ITEM	**CLEANING TASK**
Ice machine	Drain ice, clean and sanitize interior surfaces Flush ice-making unit Defrost and clean
Reach-in freezers	Empty, clean and sanitize
Reach-in refrigeration and freezer units	Defrost
Steamer	De-lime
Walk-in refrigeration and freezer units	Clean fans Empty, clean racks, walls, floors and corners Defrost freezer

DAILY FACILITIES CLEANING CHART

ITEM	CLEANING TASK	WHEN
Carpets	Vacuum	Daily
Chairs	Clean and sanitize seat	After each use
Dining tables	Clean and sanitize	After each use
Display cabinets	Clean and sanitize surfaces	Once per shift
Drains	Scrub covers	Daily
Dry storage areas	Sweep and mop floors	Daily
Employee areas	Clean and sanitize tables Sweep and mop, if applicable	After each use used for eating Once per shift
Floors	Wipe spills Sweep Damp mop Scrub	Upon each occurrence As needed, or between meals Once per shift Daily
Garbage cans	Scrub clean and sanitize cans with hot water or steam and detergent	After emptying, or at closing
Hoods	Clean walls and exposed surfaces of hoods Clean removable filters	Daily Daily
Office areas	Sweep and mop, if applicable Clean work surfaces	Daily Daily
Self-service beverage areas	Wipe spills and splashes Clean and sanitize surfaces	Upon each occurrence Once per shift
Self-service condiment areas	Wipe spills and splashes Clean and sanitize surfaces Take apart, clean and sanitize dispensers	Upon each occurrence Once per shift Daily
Upholstery	Vacuum or brush clean	Daily
Walls	Splashes Wash	As soon as possible Daily (in kitchen and cooking areas)

WEEKLY & MONTHLY FACILITIES CLEANING CHART

WEEKLY CLEANING	
ITEM	**CLEANING TASK**
Chairs	Clean chair backs, rails and legs
Dining tables	Clean table bases
Display cabinets	Clean cabinet interior
Drains	Flush drains with disinfectant
Dry storage areas	Clean shelves, scrub floors, baseboards and corners
Employee areas	Clean employee lockers and storage areas
Fans	Clean fan guards
Floors	Scrub baseboards and corners
HVAC system	Clean air intake and output ducts
Walls	Wash all walls
MONTHLY CLEANING	
ITEM	**CLEANING TASK**
Carpets	Steam clean and shampoo, bi-monthly
Ceilings	Wash
Floors	Strip and reseal twice per year
Grease traps	Remove grease and clean
Hoods	Clean and degrease hood system, bi-monthly
HVAC system	Check filters
Light fixtures	Clean shields and fixtures
Upholstery	Steam clean or shampoo, bi-monthly
Walls	Wash all walls

THE RESTAURANT MANAGER'S HANDBOOK

GENERAL FOOD SAFETY & SANITATION CHECKLIST

Check each item when completed.

EMPLOYEES

○ Employees have a designated area for storing all personal items, which is separate from food preparation areas.

○ An area is designated for non-food items such as for recipes and non-food tools.

○ Employees practice proper hand-washing between tasks, at a designated handwashing sink, with soap and single-use paper towels.

○ Employees preparing food wear clean uniforms or aprons.

○ Hair restraints are worn and no jewelry is allowed (except a wedding band). No false nails or nail polish is allowed.

○ Employees do not eat, drink, smoke or chew gum in the food preparation areas.

○ Employees with any illness are sent home. Any cuts, wounds or abrasions are bandaged and gloves are worn over the bandage.

RECEIVING FOOD

○ Receiving trucks meet standards of cleanliness and food safety storage.

○ Food is received by designated employee and checked for acceptable condition, date and temperature.

○ Once food is received, it is noted on invoice and put away immediately.

○ Any damaged or open item will not be accepted including dented or rusted cans.

○ Food is covered, labeled and stored, using the "first in, first out" system.

○ Cross-contamination is avoided by storing raw meats and un-rinsed vegetables away from ready-to-eat food.

FOOD

○ Food is thawed properly in the refrigerator or under running water.

○ Bulk food receptacles are clean and clearly labeled. Scoops with handles are used and stored separately.

○ Ice scoops are not stored in ice.

○ Cross-contamination is not possible between foods and food contact surfaces or staff and chemicals.

○ If possible, pasteurized eggs are used rather than raw eggs.

○ Food is cooked or reheated to the proper temperature (above 165°F).

○ Food is cooled in quick-chill manner such as in a shallow pan in ice or on the top shelf of the walk-in freezer.

○ Potentially hazardous foods are prepared according to safety standards.

EQUIPMENT

○ Freezer and refrigerators: Record area/temperature readings

Freezer 1 _____ / _____

Freezer 2 _____ / _____

Refer 1 _____ / _____

Refer 2 _____ / _____

Refer 3 _____ / _____

○ Equipment is cleaned and maintained according to a set schedule per manufacturer's specifications.

○ Hand sinks are easily accessible, clean and in good condition.

○ Towels that are in use for wiping are replaced every 4 hours. They are stored in sanitizer solution (200ppm) in labeled buckets.

○ Refrigerators are stocked to allow adequate air circulation. Water should not be pooled on bottom shelf, and condensers should be clear and visible.

○ Thermometers are available for all cold-holding equipment. Every thermometer is accessible, in good repair and calibrated regularly (ice water 32°F; boiling water 212°F).

○ The gaskets are clean and in excellent condition.

○ Preparation equipment is clean and well-maintained including range, deep fat fryer, oven, grill and broiler. Equipment with small parts are in good condition without cracks or leaks.

○ The ice machine is sanitized, clean and free from rust, mildew, scale and deposits. The water filters are properly tagged.

○ Beverage machines are cleaned and sanitized daily, including soda gun and holster, and soft drink nozzles are cleaned inside.

○ Glass mats are cleaned/sanitized daily.

○ Equipment not in use and spare parts are stored in separate area and cannot contaminate food or harbor pests.

DISHWASHING

○ Employees wash their hands at hand-wash sinks, regularly using proper handwashing techniques.

○ A three-compartment sink is used with separate compartments for pre-scrape, wash and rinse.

○ The three-compartment sink uses the correct temperature water and sanitizer @ _____ (200ppm).

○ Clean utensils are stored properly (upside down) and away from contamination and dirty utensils.

FACILITY

○ The plumbing is in good condition with no leaking pipes, slow drains or leaking faucets. Pipes are 2 inches above drains.

○ All fixtures, walls, ceilings and ventilation are clean and in good repair.

○ Floors are clean and in good condition, and floor mats are pressure-cleaned regularly.

○ Lighting is adequate and shatter-proof.

○ Break areas and wash stations are clean and free from clutter.

○ Maintenance is done regularly and repairs made in a timely manner.

RESTROOMS

○ Sinks are clean and stocked with soap and single-use paper towels. Hot water is at or above 110°F.

○ Handwashing signs are posted.

○ The facilities have adequate supplies and are disinfected, clean and in good repair.

CHEMICAL STORAGE

○ Chemicals are labeled, stored in designated areas (away from food), with material safety data sheets (MSDS).

FIRE & SAFETY

○ Fire extinguishers are available, charged, tagged and mounted, and employees have been instructed how to use them properly.

○ Extension cords are not used.

○ CO_2 tanks are stored upright and secured.

○ Bulletin boards with tacks or pins are not used in food preparation, washing or storage areas.

PEST CONTROL

○ There is no evidence of insects, rodents or birds (such as droppings).

○ The building is pest-proof, with sealed doors, working fly fans and no exterior holes or cracks.

○ Traps are tamper-proof and secured.

○ The pest-control operator manual has pesticide lists, map of traps and emergency contacts list.

GARBAGE & REFUSE

○ The dumpsters are clean and the lids are closed.

○ The outside premises are clean, free from trash and debris.

○ The grease bin and surrounding area is maintained and clean.

○ The recycle bins and surrounding area is maintained and clean.

○ When washing or degreasing trash cans, food bins or other equipment, wastewater does not run into storm drains.

○ Garbage and waste food cans have plastic liners, and are pressure-cleaned and disinfected.

GENERAL

○ Employees have been properly trained in food protection and Hazcom procedures. All training is documented.

○ Health permits are current and prominently posted.

○ A food-safety-certified manager is on the premises at all times.

○ Water quality is checked annually and reports are on file.

○ Cleaning tools such as mops and brooms are stored separately from food, dishes and utensils.

○ The mop sink is easily accessible and clean, with hot and cold water. Mop heads are air-dried upside down and clean.

DATE: SUPERVISOR:

NOTES/COMMENTS:

GENERAL KITCHEN SANITATION COMPLIANCE CHECKLIST

FOOD PRODUCTION AREA

☐ Equipment, appliances, walls and screens are clean in food service area.

☐ Food preparation equipment is cleaned and sanitized after every use. This would include choppers, mixers and can openers.

☐ Frozen food is thawed using the proper thawing procedures.

☐ Cutting boards are sanitized properly after each use and when alternating between raw and cooked foods.

☐ Prior to preparation, fruits and vegetables are thoroughly washed.

☐ Foods are cooked properly and internal temperatures checked.

☐ Foods that are potentially hazardous are held at the correct temperature. Hot foods at 140°F or above; cold foods at 41°F or below. Frozen food must be at or below 0°F at all times.

☐ Steam tables or food warmers are used properly and not used to reheat or prepare food.

☐ Food service employees do not touch cooked food with bare hands.

☐ The food preparation area is not used by employees for smoking or eating. All beverage containers and cups are covered and contain some type of drinking straw.

☐ Employees who are ill are sent home or restricted to activities where he or she does not come into contact with food.

☐ Employees are wearing hair restraints.

☐ Employees wash their hands thoroughly after using the bathroom, after coughing or sneezing, after handling garbage, or after any activity that could cause food contamination.

☐ The kitchen has an easily accessible, clean sink specifically for handwashing with soap and disposable towels. A sign with proper handwashing procedures is posted near the sink.

☐ Lighting has covers or bulbs that will not shatter.

☐ In holding areas, food temperatures are checked regularly with a clean, sanitized thermometer.

☐ Uncovered glassware and dishes of food items are not stacked.

CHEMICAL & NON-FOOD STORAGE

☐ Dirty water is discarded after use. All mops, brooms and cleaning equipment are cleaned and put away.

☐ The storage area is easily accessible, and clean with no refuse or food residue.

☐ Toxic materials are in the proper container and clearly labeled.

DISHWASHING AREA

☐ A high-temperature dishwashing machine is used, with wash-cycle water temperatures over 140°F, and rinse-cycle water temperatures over 160°F.

☐ A low-temperature dishwashing machine is used with a chemical agent. Manufacturer's specifications are adhered to for proper temperature and chemical concentration.

☐ For manual washing, a three-compartment sink is used. The sink has a bleach sanitizing solution or iodine, and chemical strips are used to verify the sanitizing solution's strength.

☐ Glassware and dishes are not stacked while wet.

☐ Glassware or dishes that are cracked or chipped are immediately discarded.

☐ Clean dishes, glassware, utensils and pots and pans do not have any food residue.

REFRIGERATORS & FREEZERS

☐ Shallow containers are used for cooked foods in the refrigerator.

☐ Air can circulate freely throughout the freezer or refrigerator. Food should not be stored too closely.

☐ Freezers and refrigerators are clean and free from debris.

☐ Freezers are at a temperature of 0°F or lower. Refrigerators are at a temperature of 41°F or lower.

☐ Any frozen food with freezer burn or spoilage is immediately discarded.

☐ Frozen foods are stored in their original container, or are properly packaged, labeled and dated, using the "first in, first out" method.

☐ Proper storage order is observed with prepared foods on the top shelves.

☐ Raw items, meat and eggs are stored below thawed or cooked foods.

☐ Refrigerated foods are well-wrapped, labeled and dated, using the "first in, first out" method.

☐ Seven days is the maximum holding time for refrigerated leftovers. At 45°F, food can only be held for four days.

TRASH & REFUSE AREA

☐ Trash receptacles do not leak and are clean and in good condition.

☐ Exterior dumpsters and all trash receptacles are securely covered.

FOOD TRANSPORTATION

☐ Service trays are used once and then thoroughly washed and sanitized.

☐ Carts used to transport food are clean and well-maintained.

☐ Dairy items or eggs are transported in a cart at 41°F or lower. If coolers are used, they are packed with ice.

DRY FOOD STORAGE

☐ Storage and food handling areas are clean with no insects or rodent droppings.

☐ Food packages are tightly sealed.

☐ Labeled, clean containers are used for dry bulk food items.

☐ Unprotected or exposed water or sewer lines are not in or near food storage areas.

☐ Food is stored on shelves at least 4 inches from the floor for proper cleaning.

☐ The food storage shelves are clean and well-organized without debris or empty boxes.

☐ Foods are properly dated and shelved, using the "first in, first out" method.

☐ Dented cans are discarded.

☐ All shelving units are at least 4 inches from walls, so rodents, bugs and other pests cannot nest between walls and shelves.

☐ Food items have a separate storage area from cleaning agents, pesticides and other toxic substances.

COMPREHENSIVE FOOD FACILITY COMPLIANCE CHECKLIST

Circle Yes or No for every applicable item.

 RECEIVING

Y   N   1. Food is received only from previously approved vendors.

Y   N   2. Food deliveries are inspected immediately for proper condition and temperature, with potentially hazardous foods delivered at a temperature of 41°F.

Y   N   3. Frozen foods delivered in frozen state with no evidence of thawing or refreezing.

Y   N   4. Raw or frozen clams, mussels, scallops and oysters have a temperature below 45°F and are properly labeled, with labels maintained on site for at least 90 days.

Y   N   5. Deliveries are rejected if the food is not at the proper temperature or in unacceptable condition.

Y   N   6. Food is promptly placed in proper storage locations, with refrigerated and frozen foods stored immediately.

 STORAGE

Y   N   1 All food is stored away from chemicals, vermin, insects, etc., and cannot be contaminated.

Y   N   2. All food is properly labeled using the "first in, first out" system, including prepackaged and bulk foods.

Y   N   3. Shelving for food storage is at least 6 inches from floor and walls.

Y   N   4. Items to be returned and damaged goods are stored separately.

Y   N   5. Proper layering is used in refrigerated storage, with raw meat and fish stored below and away from ready-to-eat foods (produce, vegetables, beverages).

Y   N   6. All food in storage is properly covered and sealed.

Y   N   7. Contaminated food is promptly discarded.

COMPREHENSIVE FOOD FACILITY COMPLIANCE CHECKLIST

Circle Yes or No for every applicable item.

 PREPARATION

Y   N   1. Frozen foods thawed properly using an acceptable method:

In a refrigerator.

In a microwave.

Under cold, running water.

As part of the cooking process.

Y   N   2. Hot foods (which can be potentially hazardous) are cooled quickly by the following methods before placement in a refrigerator or freezer:

With a rapid, cool stirring device.

Stirring while in an ice bath.

In a blast chiller.

Adding ice to the food.

In shallow, iced pans.

Separating food into smaller portions.

Y   N   3. Separate sinks are available and used only for food preparation activities—not hand-washing or janitorial use.

Y   N   4. Potentially hazardous foods do not have sulfite added.

Y   N   5. Potentially hazardous foods are cooked thoroughly with proper internal temperatures:

Poultry–165°F (comminuted poultry, game birds, stuffed meats, stuffed pasta and reheated foods).

Beef–155°F (ground beef, other comminuted meats and foods containing comminuted meat).

Pork–155°F.

Eggs–145°F (food containing raw eggs and other cooked, potentially hazardous food).

 SERVING

Y   N   1. All prepackaged foods are labeled properly with name, list of ingredients, net weight and name and address of manufacturer.

Y   N   2. Any food returned from customers uneaten is discarded (not reused or reserved).

Y   N   3. Food and utensils in self-service areas, such as salad bars, buffets, snack counters and beverage dispensers, are protected from contamination by customers (e.g., sneezing, coughing and handling).

Y   N   4. Bare hands are not used for food service and serving utensils, such as spoons, tongs and ladles, are provided.

COMPREHENSIVE FOOD FACILITY COMPLIANCE CHECKLIST

Circle Yes or No for every applicable item.

 TEMPERATURES

Y N 1. Hot, potentially hazardous foods kept at or above 140°F.

Y N 2. Cold, potentially hazardous foods kept at or below 41°F.

Y N 3. The danger zone for potentially hazardous foods is 42°–140°F. When cooling or reheating foods, the time spent in this temperature range is kept to a minimum.

Y N 4. Properly calibrated thermometers are visible in the warmest part of each refrigeration and freezer unit.

Y N 5. If serving potentially hazardous food, a metal probe-type thermometer is used to check temperature prior to service.

Y N 6. Thermometers are sanitized before and after each use.

Y N 7. Thermometers are calibrated regularly.

Y N 8. While in use, tongs, scoops, spoons, ladles or other serving utensils for potentially hazardous foods are kept at or below 41°F or above 140°F, or in a dipper well that has clean water continually provided.

 DISHWASHING

Y N 1. Plates, glasses and silverware are sanitized by mechanical dishwasher according to manufacturer specifications. If manually washed, they are sanitized by one of the following methods: 100ppm chlorine for 30 seconds; 25ppm iodine for 60 seconds; 200ppm quaternary ammonium for 60 seconds; or 180°F water for 30 seconds.

Y N 2. All mechanical dishwashers are provided with dual integral drain boards.

Y N 3. During operation of dish machines, the correct temperature is maintained as well as proper amounts of sanitizer and chemicals.

Y N 4. When sanitizing utensils, a test strip or thermometer is used to check effectiveness.

Y N 5. A three-compartment (preferred) or two-compartment sink is available for utensil washing.

Y N 6. All compartments can fully submerge the largest utensil in use.

Y N 7. Utensils are maintained and clean.

Y N 8. Utensils used in the kitchen or for serving are regularly cleaned and sanitized.

Y N 9. Only commercial-grade utensils that are certified by an American National Standards Institute (ANSI)-accredited program are used.

Y N 10. Utensils are stored away from any possible contamination including dirt, rodents, insects and chemicals.

Y N 11. Single-use customer utensils are used only once and disposed.

COMPREHENSIVE FOOD FACILITY COMPLIANCE CHECKLIST

Circle Yes or No for every applicable item.

RESTROOMS

- Y N 1 Restroom facilities are provided for employees.
- Y N 2. Restroom facilities are provided for customers.
- Y N 3. Toilet stalls have self-closing, locking doors.
- Y N 4. Restroom facilities are not used for storage of food, utensils, equipment or supplies.
- Y N 5. Restroom facilities have adequate supplies such as toilet paper, single-use sanitary towels (or air dryer) and sanitizing hand cleanser.
- Y N 6. A handwashing sink has pressurized hot and cold water.
- Y N 7. Restroom facilities have adequate ventilation.

HANDWASHING

- Y N 1. A separate handwashing sink is located in, or adjacent to, restrooms and kitchens.
- Y N 2. The handwashing sink has adequate supplies including single-service sanitary towels (or air dryers) and sanitizing hand cleanser.
- Y N 3. The handwashing sink has pressurized hot and cold water.
- Y N 4. The handwashing sink is easily accessible at all times.
- Y N 5. A separate handwashing sink is used exclusively for handwashing in food prep areas and is conveniently located.

CHEMICALS & CLEANING

- Y N 1. Chemicals are labeled properly.
- Y N 2. Chemicals are not stored in food preparation area.
- Y N 3. The only pesticides used have been specifically approved for food facility usage.
- Y N 4. All chemicals, pesticides and hazardous materials are used properly. Employees have access to MSDS information on all chemicals.
- Y N 5. Cleaning supplies and equipment are stored in a separate area away from food preparation, food storage, dishwashing and utensil storage areas.
- Y N 6. A separate janitorial sink has hot and cold water with a back-flow prevention device.
- Y N 7. All mops, buckets, brooms and other cleaning equipment is kept away from food and utensils.

COMPREHENSIVE FOOD FACILITY COMPLIANCE CHECKLIST

 LIGHTING

Y N 1. In food preparation and utensil cleaning areas, lighting has a minimum intensity of 20 foot candles (fc).

Y N 2. In dining and other areas, lighting has a minimum intensity of 10 fc, but intensity of at least 20 fc available during cleaning operations.

Y N 3. Food preparation, food storage and utensil cleaning areas have shatterproof light covers installed and are in good repair.

 PEST INFESTATION

Y N 1. Rodents, insects and other vermin are not in the building.

Y N 2. Building does not have cracks or openings where rodents and insects can enter, and any droppings and dead insects are cleaned up.

Y N 3. All building entrances have air curtains or tight-fitting, self-closing doors. All windows are protected by screens.

Y N 4. Any fumigation or pest control is done by a licensed pest control operator.

 GARBAGE

Y N 1. Garbage is removed frequently and proper facilities are provided for disposal and storage.

Y N 2. Garbage containers have tight-fitting lids, do not leak and are rodent-proof.

Y N 3. Before being placed in the dumpster, all garbage is in securely fastened plastic bags.

 SIGNAGE

Y N 1. Restrooms have handwashing signs posted and clearly visible.

Y N 2. Handwashing sinks have signage with proper handwashing procedures posted and clearly visible.

Y N 3. "No smoking" signs are clearly visible throughout the facility, especially in food preparation, food storage, utensil cleaning and utensil storage areas.

Y N 4. A Choking First Aid poster is visible and readily accessible to employees (in facilities with sit-down dining).

COMPREHENSIVE FOOD FACILITY COMPLIANCE CHECKLIST

Circle Yes or No for every applicable item.

 EMPLOYEES

Y N 1. Employees wear clean uniforms or approved clothing.

Y N 2. Employees only use tobacco products in designated areas, away from food preparation, storage and service.

Y N 3. Employees wash hands thoroughly and frequently. Hands are washed after engaging in any activity that may cause contamination including working between raw food and ready-to-eat foods, after coughing or sneezing, after touching soiled equipment or utensils and after using restrooms.

Y N 4. Ill employees are sent home or do not come to work.

Y N 5. Employees practice safe food-handling procedures and have been trained in food safety.

Y N 6. Employees check temperatures of potentially hazardous foods during storage, preparation and serving. Employees also check utensil-cleaning chemical levels, water temperatures and water pressures.

Y N 7. A separate employee changing area is provided, apart from toilets, food storage, food preparation, utensil cleaning and utensil storage areas.

 PLUMBING

Y N 1. Water supply has been tested and comes from an approved source.

Y N 2. Adequate amounts of hot and cold water are available.

Y N 3. Sewage and wastewater is disposed properly into a sewer or septic system.

Y N 4. All equipment that discharges waste, such as prep sinks, steam tables, salad bars, ice machines, ice storage bins, beverage machines, display cases or refrigeration/freezer units, have a floor sink or funnel drain provided for indirect waste drainage.

Y N 5. Receptacles for indirect waste are accessible and cleaned regularly.

Y N 6. Plumbing is clean, in good repair and operating properly.

Y N 7. A licensed company cleans out grease interceptors and septic tanks regularly.

COMPREHENSIVE FOOD FACILITY COMPLIANCE CHECKLIST

Circle Yes or No for every applicable item.

 FACILITY

Y N 1. Facility is fully enclosed, clean and well-maintained.

Y N 2. The building meets all applicable building and fire codes.

Y N 3. Exterior premises is clean and well-maintained.

Y N 4. All equipment is clean, well-maintained and meets applicable ANSI-accredited certification program standards.

Y N 5. No unused, out-dated or broken equipment is on the premises.

Y N 6. Cooking equipment and high-temperature dish machines have ventilation and exhaust systems installed over areas of operation.

Y N 7. In food preparation and storage areas, flooring is level, non-skid, durable, non-absorbent and easily cleaned.

Y N 8. In janitorial facilities, restrooms and employee changing areas flooring is smooth, non-skid, durable, non-absorbent and easily cleaned.

Y N 9. In food preparation, food storage areas, janitorial facilities, restrooms and employee changing areas, walls and ceilings are smooth, durable, non-absorbent and easily cleaned.

Y N 10. The health department has approved all construction, remodeling and new equipment installation prior to work.

Y N 11. All soiled linens are held in a clean container, and a linen storage area is provided.

Y N 12. Tobacco permit is valid, up to date and posted in a prominent location (if applicable).

Y N 13. Health permit is valid, up to date and posted in a prominent location.

COMPREHENSIVE SANITATION COMPLIANCE CHECKLIST

DATE: _____ TIME: _____ EMPLOYEE(S): _____

JANITORIAL ROOM		
Is it clean and neat?	Yes	No
Are buckets empty and stored upside down?	Yes	No
Are there rodent or insect droppings visible?	Yes	No
Are all toxic materials (including pesticides) in their original containers and clearly labeled?	Yes	No

Notes or Concerns:

DISHWASHING AREA	MAIN KITCHEN	AUX KITCHEN
Wash cycle temperature	_____ °F	_____ °F
Rinse cycle temperature	_____ °F	_____ °F
Are there any obstructions or contaminants in the jets and nozzles (such as food particles)?	Yes No	Yes No
Is the dishwashing equipment cleaned daily to remove food particles, chemicals and debris?	Yes No	Yes No
Is the proper amount or level of detergent and/or sanitizer being used consistently in the wash cycle?	Yes No	Yes No
Do separate employees remove and store clean tableware?	Yes No	Yes No
Do dishwashing employees practice proper handwashing between handling soiled tableware and sanitized ware?	Yes No	Yes No
Do employees pre-scrape and flush dishes and utensils prior to washing?	Yes No	Yes No
Once dishes and utensils are cleaned and sanitized, are they stored in a clean, dry location (off the floor)?	Yes No	Yes No
Are utensils and tableware toweled properly?	Yes No	Yes No

Notes or Concerns:

COMPREHENSIVE SANITATION COMPLIANCE CHECKLIST

SERVICES AREA	MAIN KITCHEN	AUX KITCHEN
Are floors, tables and chairs clean and dry in the dining area?	Yes No	Yes No
Is the floor being swept or cleaned while food is being served or when customers are eating?	Yes No	Yes No
Is the temperature correct in the dining area for customer comfort?	Yes No	Yes No
Does the dining area have any unpleasant odors?	Yes No	Yes No
Are the dishes and silverware clean, sanitized and stored correctly to prevent contamination?	Yes No	Yes No
Are condiment containers clean and in good repair?	Yes No	Yes No
Are menus clean and in good repair, without food marks or stains?	Yes No	Yes No
Are food warmers or steam tables used to re-heat prepared foods?	Yes No	Yes No
Is food being held in the hot-holding equipment at or above 140°F?	Yes No	Yes No
Is cold food being held at 41°F or lower?	Yes No	Yes No
Are cold- and hot-holding cabinets equipped with thermometers?	Yes No	Yes No
Are tongs or other serving utensils available and used to pick up rolls, bread, butter pats, ice or other food to be served?	Yes No	Yes No
Are tableware towels clean, dry and only used for wiping food spills?	Yes No	Yes No
Are servers wearing proper uniforms that are clean and in good condition?	Yes No	Yes No
Do servers show any signs of illness, such as coughing or wiping their noses?	Yes No	Yes No
Do servers handle drinking glasses and silverware properly, without touching glass tops or silverware blades?	Yes No	Yes No

Notes or Concerns:

COMPREHENSIVE SANITATION COMPLIANCE CHECKLIST

PERSONAL SANITATION	MAIN KITCHEN	AUX KITCHEN
Are all employees involved with food handling properly dressed in clean uniforms or attire?	Yes No	Yes No
Are employees wearing jewelry other than a wedding band?	Yes No	Yes No
Are employees wearing hair restraints?	Yes No	Yes No
Do employees have a noticeable odor (such as strong perfume or body odor)?	Yes No	Yes No
Do employees have properly groomed hands, without fingernail polish and with short, clean fingernails?	Yes No	Yes No
If employees have any wounds, are they properly covered and free of infection?	Yes No	Yes No
Do employees show any signs of illness, such as sneezing or coughing?	Yes No	Yes No
Do employees scratch their head, face or body?	Yes No	Yes No
Are employees seen eating in food preparation or serving areas?	Yes No	Yes No

Notes or Concerns:

GENERAL SANITATION	MAIN KITCHEN	AUX KITCHEN
Are cleaning supplies and chemicals stored separately from the food preparation and service areas?	Yes No	Yes No
Is prepared food held correctly (at the correct temperature and in the proper containers?	Yes No	Yes No
Are clean, sanitary towels available?	Yes No	Yes No
Are frozen foods thawed correctly, either in the refrigerator, under cold, running water or thawed during the cooking process?	Yes No	Yes No
Is a separate sink available for food preparation that is not used for handwashing or cleaning?	Yes No	Yes No
Is preparation equipment cleaned and sanitized between and after each use, or at the end of the day?	Yes No	Yes No
Are equipment and utensils not in use clean?	Yes No	Yes No
Is food stored in coolers and freezers covered and spaced correctly to allow air circulation?	Yes No	Yes No

COMPREHENSIVE SANITATION COMPLIANCE CHECKLIST

GENERAL SANITATION	MAIN KITCHEN	AUX KITCHEN
Are all dishes, pots, pans and other utensils stored correctly to prevent contamination?	Yes No	Yes No
Are cutting boards cleaned and sanitized after each use?	Yes No	Yes No
Are cutting boards in good condition and used only for specific types of food preparation to avoid cross-contamination?	Yes No	Yes No

Notes or Concerns:

DRY STORAGE	MAIN KITCHEN	AUX KITCHEN
Is the food storage area enclosed, dry and free from dampness?	Yes No	Yes No
Are food supplies labeled, dated and stored to ensure "first in, first out" use?	Yes No	Yes No
Is food stored separately from non-food supplies?	Yes No	Yes No
Is there any evidence of insects or rodent droppings in the storage areas?	Yes No	Yes No
Is the food storage area clean and free of dust, empty food cartons and other debris (including shelves and floor)?	Yes No	Yes No
Are shelves at least 4 inches away from walls and floors?	Yes No	Yes No
Is the area underneath the shelves easily accessible for cleaning?	Yes No	Yes No

Notes or Concerns:

COMPREHENSIVE SANITATION COMPLIANCE CHECKLIST

WALK-IN FREEZERS	MAIN KITCHEN	AUX KITCHEN
Temperature	_____ °F	_____ °F
Are shelves and floor clean and free of empty cartons or debris?	Yes No	Yes No
Are all foods properly stored and covered?	Yes No	Yes No
Are food supplies labeled, dated and stored to ensure "first in, first out" use?	Yes No	Yes No
Can air circulate freely around stored food?	Yes No	Yes No
Does freezer need defrosting?	Yes No	Yes No

Notes or Concerns:

WALK-IN REFRIGERATORS	MAIN KITCHEN	AUX KITCHEN
Temperature	_____ °F	_____ °F
Are refrigerators clean, with no mold or offensive odors?	Yes No	Yes No
Can air circulate freely around stored food?	Yes No	Yes No
Is food stored on the the floor of the refrigerators?	Yes No	Yes No
Are foods labeled, dated and stored to ensure "first in, first out" use?		
Are large-quantity containers used for storing cooked foods (ground meat, dressing or gravy)?		
Are all containers clearly labeled with date and food item?		
Is spoiled or outdated food promptly discarded?		
Are proper storage techniques used, with cooked food on the top and raw meats or poultry on the bottom shelves?		
Are shelves at least 6 inches from the floor to allow cleaning underneath?		
Are cooked foods stored in clean, sanitized, covered containers (not their original cartons)?		

Notes or Concerns:

Cold Food Production

Date: **Employee:**

❑ YES   ❑ NO   1. Before food preparation, are all equipment and utensils cleaned and sanitized (including work surfaces)?

❑ YES   ❑ NO   2. Are all utensils and containers cleaned and sanitized prior to use?

❑ YES   ❑ NO   3. Are potentially hazardous ingredients (including tuna fish and mayonnaise) refrigerated at least 24 hours before use?

❑ YES   ❑ NO   4. Are all fruits and vegetables properly washed prior to use?

❑ YES   ❑ NO   5. Before handling food, do employees wash hands properly with soap and water?

❑ YES   ❑ NO   6. Is prepared food properly covered, labeled and refrigerated, and taken directly to the serving line?

❑ YES   ❑ NO   7. Do all workstations have ready access to sanitizer solution?

❑ YES   ❑ NO   8. After each use, are work areas cleaned and sanitized?

❑ YES   ❑ NO   9. While preparing food, are employees wearing disposable gloves?

❑ YES   ❑ NO   10. Are all sinks in the food preparation area sanitized after each use?

❑ YES   ❑ NO   11. Are handwashing sinks easily accessible and stocked with hand soap from a proper dispenser and single-use paper towels?

❑ YES   ❑ NO   12. At the end of each day, is all food production equipment cleaned and sanitized?

Action Plan: **Completed By:**   **Comments:**

Supervisor:

Hot Food Production

Date:	Employee:

❑ YES ❑ NO   1.   Before and after food preparation, are all equipment and utensils cleaned and sanitized (including work surfaces)?

❑ YES ❑ NO   2.   Are frozen foods thawed correctly, either in the refrigerator, under cold, running water or thawed during the cooking process?

❑ YES ❑ NO   3.   Are potentially hazardous foods cooked thoroughly with proper internal temperatures: poultry, 165°F; beef, 155°F; pork, 155°F; and eggs, 145°F?

❑ YES ❑ NO   4.   Are hot, potentially hazardous foods cooled quickly by one of the following methods: with a rapid, cool stirring device, stirring while in an ice bath, in a blast chiller, by adding ice to the food, in shallow, iced pans or by separating food into smaller portions?

❑ YES ❑ NO   5.   Are leftovers heated to 165°F?

❑ YES ❑ NO   6.   Are sinks used for food preparation cleaned and sanitized between each use?

❑ YES ❑ NO   7.   Are handwashing sinks accessible and properly stocked with single-use towels and soap dispensers so employees can wash hands before food preparation?

❑ YES ❑ NO   8.   Are spills wiped up immediately?

❑ YES ❑ NO   9.   Are floors kept clean with regular sweeping and mopping?

❑ YES ❑ NO   10.   Does every workstation have easy access to sanitizing solution?

Action Plan:	Completed By:	Comments:
	Supervisor:	

Line Serving Areas

Date: **Employee:**

❑ YES   ❑ NO   1.   Do all refrigerators have properly calibrated thermometers and maintain a temperature of 41°F or below?

❑ YES   ❑ NO   2.   Are all deli or line items refrigerated until placement on the deli bar?

❑ YES   ❑ NO   3.   Are all items held at 45°F while on the deli bar?

❑ YES   ❑ NO   4.   Are properly calibrated thermometers used regularly to check product temperatures?

❑ YES   ❑ NO   5.   Are floors kept clean with regular sweeping and mopping?

❑ YES   ❑ NO   6.   At the end of each day, is all the deli bar equipment cleaned and sanitized?

❑ YES   ❑ NO   7.   Does every workstation have easy access to sanitizing solution?

Action Plan: **Completed By:**   **Comments:**

Supervisor:

Line Service/Hot Foods

Date:	Employee:

❑ YES ❑ NO 1. Do all refrigerators have properly calibrated thermometers and maintain a temperature of 41°F or below?

❑ YES ❑ NO 2. Are refrigerated items stored properly, with cooked or ready-to-eat items above raw products?

❑ YES ❑ NO 3. Are all refrigerated products stored in properly covered containers and labeled?

❑ YES ❑ NO 4. Is raw meat refrigerated prior to cooking?

❑ YES ❑ NO 5. Is the grill clean, in good working order and properly maintained?

❑ YES ❑ NO 6. Is the steam table clean and in good working condition?

❑ YES ❑ NO 7. Are all hot, cooked foods held at 140°F or higher?

❑ YES ❑ NO 8. Do soup kettles have a temperature of 140°F or higher?

❑ YES ❑ NO 9. Are properly calibrated thermometers used to take frequent temperature checks?

❑ YES ❑ NO 10. Are spills wiped up immediately?

❑ YES ❑ NO 11. Are floors mopped and swept on a regular basis?

Action Plan:	Completed By:	Comments:
	Supervisor:	

Restrooms

Date:	Employee:

❑ YES ❑ NO 1. Are restrooms clean and odor-free?

❑ YES ❑ NO 2. Are restrooms well-ventilated?

❑ YES ❑ NO 3. Do toilet stalls have self-closing, locking doors?

❑ YES ❑ NO 4. Are soap and towel dispensers well-stocked and working properly?

❑ YES ❑ NO 5. Does the sink(s) and have faucets with pressurized hot and cold water?

❑ YES ❑ NO 6. Are the trash containers cleaned and emptied on a regular basis?

❑ YES ❑ NO 7. Is the restroom used for storage of food, utensils, equipment or supplies?

Action Plan:	Completed By:	Comments:
	Supervisor:	

INDIVIDUAL SANITATION CHECKLISTS

Dry Storage

Date:		Employee:

❑ YES ❑ NO 1. Are all food goods stacked neatly, labeled and in proper containers?

❑ YES ❑ NO 2. Are all storage shelves or racks at least 6 inches off the floor?

❑ YES ❑ NO 3. Are shelves and storage area clean, free of dust, empty cartons and other debris?

❑ YES ❑ NO 4. Is storage area swept daily?

❑ YES ❑ NO 5. Are food items rotated properly using the "first in, first out" system?

❑ YES ❑ NO 6. Is temperature of the dry storage area regulated (between 60°F and 70°F) and ventilated to avoid dampness?

❑ YES ❑ NO 7. Is the storage area large enough for ease of use?

❑ YES ❑ NO 8. Is the storage area inspected for evidence of rodents and insects on a regular basis?

❑ YES ❑ NO 9. Are food supplies stored separately from chemicals, cleaners and pesticides?

❑ YES ❑ NO 10. Are water or sewer lines located in a separate area away from food storage?

❑ YES ❑ NO 11. Is contaminated or spoiled food promptly discarded?

❑ YES ❑ NO 12. Is the storage area well-lit?

Action Plan:	Completed By:	Comments:
	Supervisor:	

312　THE RESTAURANT MANAGER'S HANDBOOK

Dishroom/Pot & Pan Areas

Date:	Employee:

❏ YES ❏ NO   1. Are the dishroom floors cleaned and sanitized on a regular basis?

❏ YES ❏ NO   2. Are sinks cleaned and sanitized before use?

❏ YES ❏ NO   3. Are sanitizing chemicals used according to specifications and at the proper strength?

❏ YES ❏ NO   4. Is a three-compartment sink utilized for dishwashing?

❏ YES ❏ NO   5. Before washing, all are dishware, utensils, pots and pans scraped and flushed?

❏ YES ❏ NO   6. Are dishes and utensils immersed for at least 30 seconds in hot water that is at or above 170°F?

❏ YES ❏ NO   7. Are sanitizer concentrations checked using test strips?

❏ YES ❏ NO   8. Is a sanitation log book kept of test results?

❏ YES ❏ NO   9. Are all dishware, pots and pans air-dried?

❏ YES ❏ NO   10. Are all dishware, pots and pans stored in the proper manner, free from splashes and contamination?

❏ YES ❏ NO   11. If used, is the dish machine in good working order?

❏ YES ❏ NO   12. Is the final rinse temperature of the dish machine at or greater than 180°F?

❏ YES ❏ NO   13. Is the dish machine cleaned daily at the end of its use?

❏ YES ❏ NO   14. Are the detergent levels of the dish machine checked regularly?

Action Plan:	Completed By:	Comments:
	Supervisor:	

Refrigerator & Freezer Storage

Date:	Employee:

❏ YES ❏ NO 1. Is the interior temperature of the refrigerators 41°F or lower?

❏ YES ❏ NO 2. Are all refrigerators and freezers equipped with interior and exterior thermometers?

❏ YES ❏ NO 3. Are the interior and exterior thermometers of the refrigerators and freezers calibrated regularly?

❏ YES ❏ NO 4. Are refrigerators cleaned on a regular basis (including coils, grills and compressor area) and free of mold and odors?

❏ YES ❏ NO 5. Is shelving at least 6 inches from the floor and free from dust or other debris?

❏ YES ❏ NO 6. Are foods and products covered, dated and properly spaced to provide adequate air circulation?

❏ YES ❏ NO 7. Are foods stored to allow "first in, first out" usage?

❏ YES ❏ NO 8. Are raw meats stored on the bottom shelves, away from cooked or prepared food?

❏ YES ❏ NO 9. Are all spills cleaned up immediately?

❏ YES ❏ NO 10. Are cooked foods labeled and stored in clean, sanitized, covered containers?

❏ YES ❏ NO 11. Is the temperature of freezer units 0°F or lower?

❏ YES ❏ NO 12. Are products in the freezer stored above floor level?

❏ YES ❏ NO 13. Are all frozen foods wrapped and covered to avoid freezer burn?

❏ YES ❏ NO 14. Are freezers clean, in good working condition and defrosted on a regular basis?

Action Plan:	Completed By:	Comments:
	Supervisor:	

Garbage/Refuse Storage & Disposal Areas

Date: **Employee:**

❏ YES   ❏ NO   1.   Is the garbage area clean and well-maintained with no spilled liquids, food materials or debris?

❏ YES   ❏ NO   2.   Are garbage and refuse containers durable and easily cleaned?

❏ YES   ❏ NO   3.   Is garbage area cleaned regularly and are containers washed?

❏ YES   ❏ NO   4.   Are garbage and refuse containers insect- and rodent-proof with tight-fitting lids?

❏ YES   ❏ NO   5.   Are garbage and refuse materials disposed of on a regular basis, so there is no overflow or odors?

❏ YES   ❏ NO   6.   Are there any visible rodents or rodent droppings?

❏ YES   ❏ NO   7.   Is there any evidence of insect infestation?

❏ YES   ❏ NO   8.   Are dumpsters maintained and in good working condition?

❏ YES   ❏ NO   9.   Are hot water and detergents available to properly wash garbage containers?

❏ YES   ❏ NO   10. Are refrigerated garbage rooms or boxes clean and in proper condition?

Action Plan: **Completed By:**   **Comments:**

Supervisor:

Cold Beverage Areas

Date: **Employee:**

❏ YES   ❏ NO   1. Are reach-in refrigerators used for storing cold beverages at a temperature of 41°F or lower?

❏ YES   ❏ NO   2. Are all beverage hoses and nozzles maintained in a sanitary manner and cleaned regularly?

❏ YES   ❏ NO   3. Are beverage dispensers maintained in a sanitary manner and cleaned regularly?

❏ YES   ❏ NO   4. Are drinking cups, lids and straws easily accessible and stored in an orderly and sanitary manner?

❏ YES   ❏ NO   5. Are ice machines cleaned and sanitized regularly?

❏ YES   ❏ NO   6. Is the top of the ice machine free of obstructions and not being used as a storage area?

❏ YES   ❏ NO   7. Are ice scoops being used in a sanitary manner and placed on a clean surface when not in use?

❏ YES   ❏ NO   8. Are the storage cabinets under cold beverage dispensers clean, organized and inspected regularly?

Action Plan: **Completed By:**   **Comments:**

Supervisor:

KITCHEN SANITATION SCHEDULE DAILY TASKS

DATE: _____

BATHROOM MIRRORS

WHEN: Once per shift   **HOW:** As needed
CLEANSER: Glass cleaner

PERSON RESPONSIBLE: _____
INITIAL UPON COMPLETION: _____

BATHROOM SUPPLIES

WHEN: Once per shift
HOW: Hand soap, paper towels, toilet paper

PERSON RESPONSIBLE: _____
INITIAL UPON COMPLETION: _____

BATHROOM FIXTURES AND SURFACES (other than floor, tiles and mirror)

WHEN: Daily
HOW: Spray, rinse and wipe
CLEANSER: Bathroom cleaner with disposable towel

PERSON RESPONSIBLE: _____
INITIAL UPON COMPLETION: _____

CONDIMENT CONTAINERS

WHEN: Daily   **HOW:** Wash, rinse, sanitize
CLEANSER: Dish machine

PERSON RESPONSIBLE: _____
INITIAL UPON COMPLETION: _____

COOLING RACKS

WHEN: Daily
HOW: Wipe clean of food debris   **CLEANSER:**
Water and sanitizer 200ppm with in-use wiping cloth

PERSON RESPONSIBLE: _____
INITIAL UPON COMPLETION: _____

COUNTERS/SHELVES (FRONT)

WHEN: End of shift   **HOW:** Wash, rinse, sanitize
CLEANSER: Cleanser, fresh water and sanitizer 200ppm

PERSON RESPONSIBLE: _____
INITIAL UPON COMPLETION: _____

COUNTERS/SHELVES (COOLER)

WHEN: End of shift   **HOW:** Wash, rinse, sanitize
CLEANSER: Cleanser, fresh water and sanitizer 200ppm

PERSON RESPONSIBLE: _____
INITIAL UPON COMPLETION: _____

COUNTERS (DELIVERY)

WHEN: End of shift   **HOW:** Wash, rinse, sanitize
CLEANSER: Cleanser, fresh water and sanitizer 200ppm

PERSON RESPONSIBLE: _____
INITIAL UPON COMPLETION: _____

COUNTERS (PREP)

WHEN: Between uses   **HOW:** Wash, rinse, sanitize
CLEANSER: Cleanser, fresh water and sanitizer 200ppm

PERSON RESPONSIBLE: _____
INITIAL UPON COMPLETION: _____

DISH RACKS

WHEN: Daily   **HOW:** Wash, rinse, sanitize
CLEANSER: Cleanser, fresh water and sanitizer 200ppm

PERSON RESPONSIBLE: _____
INITIAL UPON COMPLETION: _____

DOORS (FRONT ENTRY)

WHEN: As needed   **HOW:** Spot clean glass;
CLEANSER: Glass cleaner wipe clean other surfaces
PERSON RESPONSIBLE: _____
INITIAL UPON COMPLETION: _____

DRAIN COVERS

WHEN: Daily
HOW: Clear debris; wash, rinse, sanitize
CLEANSER: Dish machine

PERSON RESPONSIBLE: _____
INITIAL UPON COMPLETION: _____

DRY STORAGE AREAS

WHEN: Daily   **HOW:** Sweep/mop
CLEANSER: Approved sanitizer

PERSON RESPONSIBLE: _____
INITIAL UPON COMPLETION: _____

KITCHEN SANITATION SCHEDULE DAILY TASKS

FLOORS

WHEN: Daily/as needed   **HOW:** Sweep/mop
CLEANSER: Approved sanitizer

PERSON RESPONSIBLE: _____
INITIAL UPON COMPLETION: _____

FREEZERS

WHEN: Daily
HOW: Sweep/mop if walk-in;   wipe exterior
CLEANSER: Approved sanitizer

PERSON RESPONSIBLE: _____
INITIAL UPON COMPLETION: _____

HANDWASHING SINK

WHEN: Every 4 hours
HOW: Wash, rinse, sanitize
CLEANSER: Cleanser, fresh water and sanitizer 200ppm

PERSON RESPONSIBLE: _____
INITIAL UPON COMPLETION: _____

HOOD FILTERS

WHEN: Every other p.m., end of shift
HOW: Soak in degreaser, spray
CLEANSER: Non-caustic degreaser clean with fresh water, air dry

PERSON RESPONSIBLE: _____
INITIAL UPON COMPLETION: _____

HOOD GREASE PANS

WHEN: Bi-weekly
HOW: Empty into grease bin; run through dishwasher
CLEANSER: Dish machine:
PERSON RESPONSIBLE: _____
INITIAL UPON COMPLETION: _____

ICE CARRIERS

WHEN: Every 4 hours
HOW: Wash, rinse, sanitize run through dishwasher
CLEANSER: Dish machine
PERSON RESPONSIBLE: _____
INITIAL UPON COMPLETION: _____

ICE CREAM DIPPER WELL

WHEN: Daily
HOW: Wash, rinse, sanitize
CLEANSER: Cleanser, fresh water and sanitizer 200ppm

PERSON RESPONSIBLE: _____
INITIAL UPON COMPLETION: _____

KNIFE HOLDERS

WHEN: Every 4 hours
HOW: Wash, rinse, sanitize
CLEANSER: Cleanser, fresh water and sanitizer 200ppm

PERSON RESPONSIBLE: _____
INITIAL UPON COMPLETION: _____

MIXER BASE/EXTERIOR

WHEN: Daily
HOW: Wash, rinse, sanitize
CLEANSER: Cleanser, fresh water and sanitizer 200ppm

PERSON RESPONSIBLE: _____
INITIAL UPON COMPLETION: _____

MOPS/BRUSHES

WHEN: Daily
HOW: Wash, rinse and sanitize in mop sink; hang upside down to drip dry over sink
CLEANSER: Cleanser, fresh water and sanitizer 200ppm

PERSON RESPONSIBLE: _____
INITIAL UPON COMPLETION: _____

PIZZA OVEN

WHEN: Throughout shift
HOW: Wipe interior with clean, moist towel **CLEANSER:** Water only

PERSON RESPONSIBLE: _____
INITIAL UPON COMPLETION: _____

PREMISES EXTERIOR

WHEN: Daily
HOW: Sweep entire areas of debris/trash
CLEANSER: Water spray if needed

PERSON RESPONSIBLE: _____
INITIAL UPON COMPLETION: _____

KITCHEN SANITATION SCHEDULE DAILY TASKS

PREPARATION AREAS

WHEN: Each use
HOW: Wash, rinse, sanitize
CLEANSER: Cleanser, fresh water and sanitizer 200ppm

PERSON RESPONSIBLE: _____

INITIAL UPON COMPLETION: _____

REACH-IN HANDLES

WHEN: Daily
HOW: Wipe exterior with moist cloth
CLEANSER: Sanitizer bucket at 200ppm

PERSON RESPONSIBLE: _____

INITIAL UPON COMPLETION: _____

REACH-INS AND WELLS

WHEN: Daily   **HOW:** Wash, rinse, sanitize
CLEANSER: Cleanser, fresh water and sanitizer 200ppm

PERSON RESPONSIBLE: _____

INITIAL UPON COMPLETION: _____

ROTISSERIE:
HOLDING DRAWERS, EXTERIOR

WHEN: Daily
HOW: Wash, rinse, sanitize, buff exterior
CLEANSER: Cleanser, fresh water and sanitizer 200ppm
PERSON RESPONSIBLE: _____
INITIAL UPON COMPLETION: _____

SCALES

WHEN: Between each use, and every 4 hours
HOW: Wash, rinse, sanitize
CLEANSER: Cleanser, fresh water and sanitizer 200ppm
PERSON RESPONSIBLE: _____
INITIAL UPON COMPLETION: _____

SLICERS AND STAND

WHEN: Between each use (Stand: Daily)
HOW: Wash, rinse, sanitize
CLEANSER: Cleanser, fresh water and sanitizer 200ppm
PERSON RESPONSIBLE: _____
INITIAL UPON COMPLETION: _____

STORAGE BINS

WHEN: Daily
HOW: Wipe exterior with moist cloth
CLEANSER: Sanitizer at 200ppm

PERSON RESPONSIBLE: _____

INITIAL UPON COMPLETION: _____

THREE-COMPARTMENT SINK

WHEN: Daily or between use
HOW: Wash, rinse, sanitize
CLEANSER: Cleanser, fresh water and sanitizer 200ppm

PERSON RESPONSIBLE: _____

INITIAL UPON COMPLETION: _____

TRASH RECEPTACLES

WHEN: Daily
HOW: Wipe exterior with disposable cloth
CLEANSER: Water and sanitizer 200ppm

PERSON RESPONSIBLE: _____

INITIAL UPON COMPLETION: _____

UTENSILS (IN-USE)

WHEN: Every 4 hours or between products
HOW: Wash, rinse, sanitize
CLEANSER: Dish machine

PERSON RESPONSIBLE: _____

INITIAL UPON COMPLETION: _____

WALK-IN

WHEN: Daily
HOW: Sweep and clean floor
CLEANSER: Tile cleaner

PERSON RESPONSIBLE: _____

INITIAL UPON COMPLETION: _____

WIPING CLOTHS (IN-USE)

WHEN: Every 4 hours
HOW: Put in designated container to launder

PERSON RESPONSIBLE: _____

INITIAL UPON COMPLETION: _____

MANAGER SELF-INSPECTION CHECKLIST

DATE _____ OBSERVER _____

PERSONAL DRESS AND HYGIENE	
Employees wear proper uniform including proper shoes.	❏ YES ❏ NO
Hair restraint is worn.	❏ YES ❏ NO
Fingernails are short, unpolished and clean.	❏ YES ❏ NO
Jewelry is limited to watch, simple earrings and plain ring.	❏ YES ❏ NO
Hands are washed or gloves are changed at critical points.	❏ YES ❏ NO
Open sores, cuts, splints or bandages on hands are completely covered while handling food.	❏ YES ❏ NO
Hands are washed thoroughly using proper hand-washing techniques at critical points.	❏ YES ❏ NO
Smoking is observed only in designated areas away from preparation, service, storage and warewashing areas.	❏ YES ❏ NO
Eating, drinking and chewing gum are observed only in designated areas away from work areas.	❏ YES ❏ NO
Employees take appropriate action when coughing or sneezing.	❏ YES ❏ NO
Disposable tissues are used and disposed of when coughing/blowing nose.	❏ YES ❏ NO
Corrective Actions:	

LARGE EQUIPMENT	
Food slicer is clean to sight and touch.	❏ YES ❏ NO
Food slicer is sanitized between uses when used with potentially hazardous foods.	❏ YES ❏ NO
All other pieces of equipment are clean to sight and touch — equipment on serving lines, storage shelves, cabinets, ovens, ranges, fryers and steam equipment.	❏ YES ❏ NO
Exhaust hood and filters are clean.	❏ YES ❏ NO
Corrective Actions:	

REFRIGERATOR, FREEZER AND MILK COOLER		
Thermometer is conspicuous and accurate.	❏ YES	❏ NO
Temperature is accurate for piece of equipment.	❏ YES	❏ NO
Food is stored 6 inches off floor in walk-ins.	❏ YES	❏ NO
Unit is clean.	❏ YES	❏ NO
Proper chilling procedures have been practiced.	❏ YES	❏ NO
All food is properly wrapped, labeled and dated.	❏ YES	❏ NO
FIFO (First In, First Out) inventory is being practiced.	❏ YES	❏ NO
Corrective Actions:		

FOOD STORAGE AND DRY STORAGE		
Temperature is between 50° F and 70° F.	❏ YES	❏ NO
All food and paper supplies are 6 to 8 inches off the floor.	❏ YES	❏ NO
All food is labeled with name and delivery date.	❏ YES	❏ NO
FIFO (First In, First Out) inventory is being practiced.	❏ YES	❏ NO
There are no bulging or leaking canned goods in storage.	❏ YES	❏ NO
Food is protected from contamination.	❏ YES	❏ NO
All surfaces and floors are clean.	❏ YES	❏ NO
Chemicals are stored away from food and other food-related supplies.	❏ YES	❏ NO
Corrective Actions:		

MANAGER SELF-INSPECTION CHECKLIST

HOT HOLDING		
Unit is clean.	❏ YES ❏ NO
Food is heated to 165° F before placing in hot holding.	❏ YES ❏ NO
Temperature of food being held is above 140° F.	❏ YES ❏ NO
Food is protected from contamination.	❏ YES ❏ NO

Corrective Actions:

FOOD HANDLING		
Frozen food is thawed under refrigeration or in cold running water.	❏ YES ❏ NO
Food is not allowed to be in the "temperature danger zone" for more than 4 hours.	❏ YES ❏ NO
Food is tasted using proper method.	❏ YES ❏ NO
Food is not allowed to become cross-contaminated.	❏ YES ❏ NO
Food is handled with utensils, clean-gloved hands or clean hands.	❏ YES ❏ NO
Utensils are handled to avoid touching parts that will be in direct contact with food.	❏ YES ❏ NO
Reusable towels are used only for sanitizing equipment surfaces and not for drying hands, utensils, floor, etc.	❏ YES ❏ NO

Corrective Actions:

MANAGER SELF-INSPECTION CHECKLIST

UTENSILS AND EQUIPMENT	
All small equipment and utensils, including cutting boards, are sanitized between uses.	❑ YES ❑ NO
Small equipment and utensils are air dried.	❑ YES ❑ NO
Work surfaces are clean to sight and touch.	❑ YES ❑ NO
Work surfaces are sanitized between uses.	❑ YES ❑ NO
Thermometers are washed and sanitized between each use.	❑ YES ❑ NO
Can opener is clean to sight and touch.	❑ YES ❑ NO
Drawers and racks are clean.	❑ YES ❑ NO
Small equipment is inverted, covered or otherwise protected from dust and contamination when stored.	❑ YES ❑ NO

Corrective Actions:

CLEANING AND SANITIZING	
Three-compartment sink is used.	❑ YES ❑ NO
Three-compartment sink is properly set up for warewashing (wash, rinse, sanitize).	❑ YES ❑ NO
Chlorine test kit or thermometer is used to check sanitizing process.	❑ YES ❑ NO
The water temperatures are accurate.	❑ YES ❑ NO
If heat-sanitizing, the utensils are allowed to remain immersed in 170° F water for 30 seconds.	❑ YES ❑ NO
If using chemical sanitizer, it is the proper dilution.	❑ YES ❑ NO
The water is clean and free of grease and food particles.	❑ YES ❑ NO
The utensils are allowed to air dry.	❑ YES ❑ NO
Wiping clothes are stored in sanitizing solution while in use.	❑ YES ❑ NO

Corrective Actions:

GARBAGE STORAGE AND DISPOSAL	
Kitchen garbage cans are clean.	❑ YES ❑ NO
Garbage cans are emptied as necessary.	❑ YES ❑ NO
Boxes and containers are removed from site.	❑ YES ❑ NO
Loading dock and are around dumpster are clean.	❑ YES ❑ NO
Dumpster is closed.	❑ YES ❑ NO

Corrective Actions:

PEST CONTROL	
Screen on open windows and doors are in good repair.	❑ YES ❑ NO
No evidence of pests is present	❑ YES ❑ NO

Corrective Actions:

CHAPTER

CHOOSE THE PROPER EQUIPMENT

THE RIGHT EQUIPMENT FOR THE JOB

The excitement of getting new equipment, coupled with the legitimate desire to have the right tools, can be a stumbling block for unseasoned restaurant owners. Overspending or going heavily into debt for restaurant equipment puts a new business in a financial "hole" that is not easy to overcome. Selecting poor quality or inadequate equipment can cost you significantly more in the long run than investing in the best piece of equipment for the job. To help you choose the right equipment, tools, and utensils for food preparation, storage, dispensing, and cleanup, you will first need to consider the following issues:

- **How will I know what type of equipment I need?** Thumb through food service equipment catalogs. Look for capacity figures, energy ratings, materials used, and construction methods.

- **Hire an equipment specialist.** An experienced consultant is invaluable in equipment purchasing. He can handle the research, calculate life cycle costs, determine suitability, and negotiate pricing on your behalf. Look for a food facilities designer in your area. Equipment dealers and manufacturers also have consultants to assist you. Beware of potential biases though; these people are ultimately salespeople.

- **Match equipment to your immediate needs.** Over-equipping your kitchen is a poor use of resources. Since growth is not guaranteed and needs frequently change, do not over plan for the future. It is better to use and depreciate equipment fully than to take a loss on resale or trade.

- **Visit the Food service Equipment Reports' site at www.fermag.com** for evaluations, manufacturer resources, and buyer's guides.

ESTABLISH BASIC EQUIPMENT NEEDS

Review your menu offerings, food service style, and projected number of guests in order to establish basic equipment needs and capacities:

- Determine whether you need a dedicated piece of equipment or a multifunction unit.

- Calculate capacity requirements.

- Will you be able to deliver enough hot fries during lunch?

- Will you need to purchase extra dishes or a faster dishwasher?

- Compare purchasing prepared/preprocessed products against the cost of the necessary equipment, raw materials, and labor costs to prepare your own.

MAKING WISE EQUIPMENT PURCHASES

Restaurant needs differ. But getting the best value for every dollar spent is a universal concern. Here are some helpful suggestions to ensure you get the necessary quality, service, and performance out of your equipment:

- **Seek out recommendations.** Unfortunately, there is no Consumer Reports for restaurateurs. But asking peers, used equipment dealers, industry association members, and food service equipment specialists can help you learn about desired features, life expectancies, and brand names to consider or avoid.

- **Contact your local gas and/or electric utility company.** Many utility companies have fully outfitted test kitchens where they promote gas or electric equipment from major manufacturers. Ask about available rebates and promotional programs.

- **Do not overlook custom-built equipment.** To get the quality, service, and performance you need, the solution may be custom-built, which can be the best choice when: looks are important; you have unique specifications; or your usage exceeds the capacity of stock equipment.

- **Comparison shop.** Have your consultant or equipment dealer give you "good, better, best" recommendations. Compare features, operation costs, and life expectancies.

- **Establish substitution rules.** Sometimes the equipment you select is not available due to excessive lead times, product discontinuation, or unforeseen price increases. Carefully examine substitutions for suitability.

COMMERCIAL-GRADE MATERIALS/CONSTRUCTION

- **Choose high-grade stainless steel with welded joints.**

- **Choose equipment doors that open away from the nearest worktable** to facilitate removal of hot and heavy pans.

- **Verify that the gauge of steel used is as quoted.** The smaller the number, the thicker the steel.

- **Do not have equipment delivered until you are ready to install it.** Or you risk dents and dings. Dust can irreparably damage fragile equipment.

WHICH QUALITY LEVEL?

Should I invest in the top brand on the market or purchase a serviceable low-end model? Who would not want the latest and greatest in restaurant, office, and business equipment? However, investing wisely and within your budget are both key contributors toward your long-term success. Ask yourself the following decision-making questions:

- Does it fit within my budget?

- Would a smaller model save precious space?

- Will my food or service quality improve with this equipment?

- What is the ROI? For specialty equipment: Will I sell enough products or attract enough new customers to pay for it?

- Will it save energy costs, reduce overhead, or make employees more productive?

- Is it the most productive and energy-efficient equipment for the job?

- Is it difficult or expensive to operate daily?

- Will it be on display where looks are important?

- Does it meet sanitation, plumbing, or building code requirements?

- What type of routine maintenance does it require?

- Is local service available and affordable?

- Is an economical service or maintenance contract available?

- Is the lifespan greater than the payment or lease terms?

- What is the resale value if I need to sell or trade up?

- Are there trade-in/trade-up programs available?

EQUIPMENT BUDGETING

The number one question asked is, "How much should I spend?" Quality and pricing levels vary so widely that there is no easy answer. Successful restaurateurs tend to spend no more than they actually need. Consider the following:

- **Fit for purpose.** For some light-duty equipment, a less expensive, yet highly serviceable, brand may be the best choice. Alternatively, heavy use may require the best quality manufactured.

- **Keeping within budget.** Develop an equipment/fixture/tool wish list. Divide your list into three priority categories: "Cannot Live Without," "Would Make Life Easier," and "Wouldn't It Be Great." Allocate your budget primarily to the first category. This is the equipment that makes you money. Review the items in category two for potential time and money savings. Be very objective about items in category three. Will the $14,000 espresso machine make a difference in your bottom line? Analyze your second and third category items for their potential return on investment.

- **Repayment.** Do not forget that all your equipment has to be paid for — eventually. Ask yourself how long it will take to pay for itself. Will it make you money or just make you look or feel better? Or is leasing a wise alternative?

- **Review every decision from your CPA's viewpoint.** Buying cooking equipment can be like getting a new toy. Do not let your excitement or a salesperson's pitch eat up your budget.

- **Work closely with a food service consultant or do your own research.** Compare features and benefits to your acquisition and maintenance costs. Compare cost-per-year figures.

- **Negotiate for a better price.** Start by asking for 50 percent off the list price. Depending upon the equipment and the dealer's purchasing power, there is almost always some negotiation room.

- **Shop with major restaurant supply houses first.** Factory discounts to volume distributors could give you some additional negotiating room that is not available with smaller suppliers.

- **Ask about last years' models.** Incentives may be available on older or overstocked models.

- **Check the Web for discounts.** Search under "restaurant equipment." Commercial equipment is frequently shipped directly from the manufacturer, so freight costs from a distant supplier may not be a factor. Ask whether they charge sales tax. This is a "gray" area for online purchases and some states have no sales tax on restaurant equipment.

EQUIPMENT LEASING

For some restaurateurs, leasing can be a way to extend your available capital. Leasing is 100 percent financing. Depending on your lease, you may receive better tax benefits and lower monthly payments while preserving your working capital and borrowing capabilities. To help you determine which financing method suits your needs, here are some helpful ideas and resources:

- **Do not think of leasing as easy money.** The true cost of leased equipment can be greater than the purchase price. You are paying "interest" even when you lease.

- **Avoid personal guarantees if possible.** If you sign it, you are liable even if your restaurant closes or the equipment does not last.

- **Educate yourself about leasing before shopping for a leasing company.** Leasing companies pull credit reports. Too many inquiries can negatively impact your credit report. Remain open-minded, however, and ask about used equipment leasing. It can be a cost-effective way to obtain top-quality equipment at reduced rates.

- **Confirm who is responsible for service and maintenance.** The manufacturer's warranty is extended to the lessee. You are responsible for keeping the equipment in good working order and resalable condition.

- **Compare your total annual lease costs to your annual depreciation benefits.** Restaurant equipment has a seven-year depreciation rate as compared to that of a 36- to 60-month typical lease.

- **Do not lease items with a short life** or items that are fully deductible in the purchase year, such as flatware, glassware, or dinnerware.

- **Be aware of leases with no or low buy-out provisions.** The IRS may classify it as a purchase agreement, subject to depreciation rules, instead of a 100 percent expense.

- **Insurance.** Make certain your insurance covers leased equipment adequately for fire, theft, or other losses.

- **Get the fair-market-value information in writing.** Equipment with unrealistic residual values can have excessive buyouts. Check the used market for comparison figures.

- **Read the lease before signing.** A lease is a legal contract. You may even want your lawyer to review the fine print.

- **Estimate your monthly payments** and learn more about how leasing works from GE Leasing Solutions at **www.geleasingsolutions.com**.

EQUIPMENT RENTAL

Renting may be the solution for high-tech office needs, special occasions, and for equipment with high maintenance costs, rapid obsolescence, and low resale value. Renting, unlike leasing, is a straight month to month agreement with no potential ownership benefits, in which the rental company is responsible for service and maintenance. Some rentals are tied to the purchase of consumables, such as soft drinks, coffee, tea, detergents, or printer ink. Before embarking upon equipment rental:

- **Understand the terms before signing the rental agreement.** The agreement should clearly detail the cancellation terms, who maintains ownership (important in communities where equipment is taxed), your maintenance/service responsibilities, and the guaranteed level of service (will they repair it quickly?).

- **Watch out for the fine print and hidden costs.** Are you obliged to use only the rental company's supplies and consumables? Are you overpaying for these? Is there an accompanying minimum purchase requirement? Are the "extras" too costly? Are you prohibited from using the competition's products?

- **Check close to home when renting.** Seek out local party stores, restaurant supply houses, catering supply specialists, and Auto-Chlor Systems (a 60-year-old national dishwashing service).

- **Check your Yellow Pages.** Investigate such categories as office décor, computer systems, linens, restaurant equipment, telephones, and dishwashing equipment. Below are some additional ideas and resources for renting décor, equipment, and supplies.

Consider renting:

- Indoor plants and aquariums
- Portable refrigeration units
- Seasonal décor.
- Commercial dishwashers
- Beverage dispensers
- Serving equipment (carts, warmers)

Other reasons to consider renting:

- Your need is temporary.

- You would like to "test drive" before buying.

- You want to change the décor regularly.

- You would like to add something — a saltwater aquarium, for example, that requires regular expert care or rotating to look fresh.

- You do not want the maintenance hassles.

- You do not want the commitment of a lease.

- You do not want another capital expenditure.

SHOULD I BUY USED EQUIPMENT/FIXTURES?

Buying used restaurant equipment and fixtures can be a very wise decision. Just like those of a used car, equipment depreciation rates are greatest during the first year or two. Because of the unfortunately high failure rate in the restaurant business, there is always plenty of "almost new" equipment available. Explore the following possibilities:

- **Before searching for a used piece of equipment, shop for new.** It will give you a benchmark of features, quality levels among manufacturers, and pricing. A used Mercedes is a safer investment than a used Yugo; in restaurant equipment you should focus on top manufacturers with a reputation for quality.

- **Ask about the repair history of the make and model.** Institutional equipment typically has a long projected lifespan. Your dealer will probably have personal experience with the equipment.

- **Learn the terms "reconditioned" and "rebuilt."** "Reconditioned equipment" is cleaned, with worn/ broken parts replaced, and a short dealer warranty, priced at 40-50 percent of new. "Rebuilt equipment" is totally dismantled and rebuilt, with a longer dealer warranty. It should provide performance equal to the manufacturer's specs and is priced at 50-70 percent of new.

- **Verify the equipment's age and history.** Use manufacturer's serial numbers and service records to check age and care. Do not rely on an "only driven on Sundays by Grandma" story.

- **Ask the used equipment supplier about their trade-in policy.** Some suppliers will give you above-average trade-in values when you return to purchase a new version.

- **Online.** Shop for used equipment online (auction and direct-purchase sites), at bankruptcy auctions, and from new equipment dealers and food equipment groups.

- **Ask if they have demo models available.** Trade-show, showroom, and test kitchen models can have a few "miles" on them and reduced, "scratch 'n dent" prices.

- **Save time by buying used.** Manufacturer's lead and delivery times on new equipment can be lengthy.

ITEMS YOU SHOULD NOT NOT BUY

- **Cosmetically damaged equipment** or fixtures that will be visible to customers.

- **Anything with moderate rust** (except restorable cast iron).

- **"Married" equipment** (where the legs from one model have been attached erroneously to another model).

- **Foreign-made equipment** that was not made specifically for the U.S. market. Unknown electrical conversions can be a problem.

EQUIPMENT SUPPLIES

Your local restaurant equipment supply house is an obvious choice when shopping for commercial food service equipment. Here are some other sales outlets, suppliers, and resources that you might consider when researching and shopping:

- **Food service equipment representative groups.** These sales organizations represent a variety of manufacturers. Some only sell to distributors; others will sell direct.

- **Utility companies.** Your local gas or electric company may have a test kitchen outfitted by major manufacturers. You can "test drive" equipment, comparison shop, and meet with factory reps here.

- **Web-based distributors.** Dozens of distributors have gone national with Web sites, such as:

  Restaurant Equipment World at **www.restaurantequipment.net**.

  Independent Restaurant Equipment at **www.foodequipment.com.**

  Global Restaurant Equipment at **www.globalrestaurantequip.com.**

- **Procurement specialists.** Companies like ecFood at **www.ecfood.com** provide purchasing support. Many food service consultants also offer this specialty.

- **Auctions.** Local auction houses regularly liquidate the tangible assets of defunct commercial kitchens; however, only the Web offers 24/7 shopping and unsurpassed availability. Online auctions have become increasingly popular and offer vast "supplies" of all types of office and food service equipment and fixtures.

Some sites also post local auction activities:

- eBay at **www.ebay.com** and eBay Canada at **www.ebay.ca**

- Charyn Auctions at **www.charynauctions.com**

- Restaurant Auction at **www.restaurantauction.com**

- Able Auctions at **www.ableauctions.com**

- Check the Internet Auction directory at **www.internetauctionlist.com** for current online activity

EQUIPMENT SPECIFIC TIPS

Here are some purchasing tips on common heavy-use equipment:

- **Fryers.** Look for an insulated fry vat to reduce heat loss and idle energy use. Purchase units with solid-state temperature controls for precise temperatures. Investigate built-in filter systems to decrease oil costs and improve safety.

- **Water heaters.** Install quick-recovery booster water heaters for specific high-temperature needs. Insulate water heaters and all exposed pipes.

- **Ovens.** Visit your local test kitchen to compare standard ovens and convection ovens. Select programmable ovens for consistent quality of standard food offerings and reduced labor costs.

- **Pasta cookers.** Select the most energy-efficient model available, as boiling water is costly. Look for units with easy "idle" adjustments.

- **Broilers.** Be aware of costly and extensive venting requirements in some communities. Compare separate units (cheese melters and salamanders) to combination oven/broiler units.

- **Griddles.** Choose the right griddle for your menu: smooth or grooved. Investigate manufacturers that offer combo smooth/grooved griddles. Select the best quality steel plate you can afford for better energy efficiency.

- **Ranges.** Consider 30 kBtu/h open gas burners that produce more flame/flare for display kitchens. Explore induction cooking for quick-response cooktops. Caveat: flat-bottomed cookware is required for proper contact with the cooktop surface.

- **Braising pans.** Install a versatile braising pan (tilting skillet) to boil pasta, fry bacon, or braise meat. This unit can be a cost-effective solution for busy kitchens.

- **Refrigerators.** Look for the EPA's Energy Star label for solid-door refrigerator/freezer units with an energy-savings payback of less than one and half years. To maximize a perishable's life, add separate units based on temperature needs. Some fruits and vegetables like it warmer and moister than dairy products. Make certain all walk-in units have safety systems to guard against accidental lock-ins.

- **Blast chiller.** Refrigeration units are engineered to store already-cool food. For added food safety, a blast chiller should be installed to reduce food temperatures in 120 minutes or less.

- **Ice machines.** Buy ample capacity. You will need about two pounds of ice per dining room customer, three pounds in bars, and about ½ to ⅔ the drink's weight in ice for self-service and take-out beverage units. Be certain that your ice machines/bins are not located near any heat source. Include a floor drain for maintenance and cleaning and provide nonskid rubber mats for safety.

- **Beverage dispensers.** Select longer levers or button operations for self-service soft drink units to minimize potential sanitation problems when customers refill. Look for units with removable tubes that can be cleaned easily and thoroughly.

- **Espresso machines.** Thoroughly research these, as this equipment can be difficult to maintain and repair. Since many units are made in Europe, ask how long the U.S. distributor has carried the product and source a local repairperson before purchasing.

- **Mixers.** Select a mobile mixer to share among workstations. Be certain the mixer has ample horsepower for your task (mixing pizza, cookie, or other heavy dough). Choose non-reactive stainless steel bowls for longer use. Add a timer to avoid over-processing.

There are a great number of items you need to run a successful restaurant. Some are obvious: commercial stove and refrigeration unit; and others not so obvious: cutting boards and scales. In addition to equipment, you need to meet certain facility requirements and this part of the book is designed to be a general guideline for the things you will need to get started in the restaurant business.

KITCHEN AND SERVICE EQUIPMENT

A restaurant designer or consultant may be brought in to analyze your setup. In order to design the most efficient system possible, this person will need to know everything about your equipment, staff, menu, preparation procedures, and sales. This is why it might be advantageous to contact one of these individuals after you have been operating for a while and have made all necessary changes. However, a designer certainly would be valuable in the initial planning stage. The savings derived from the increase in productivity and in employee morale created by your new setup will offset the cost of this consultant.

Kitchens will be based on how and where food products are received, stored, prepared, served, cleaned up, and disposed of. A basic kitchen will need the following:

- **Separate work surfaces** for food-contact and non-food-contact areas.

- **Work sinks** for preparation and cleanup.

- **Enough cutting surfaces** to prevent cross-contamination.

- **Storage** for utensils and small equipment, cooking equipment, food products that have been prepared for service and unused food products.

- Adequate **refrigeration** and **freezer** storage.

- **Garbage** facilities.

You may need to make some adjustments before you begin. If you are starting fresh, here are some considerations to keep in mind when designing and building:

- **The type of operation.** Will you have large or small restaurant events? What type of food will you be preparing?

- **Type of menu** and food service you will offer.

- **How food is received.** This is probably the most important area in your entire installation. In general, you will need a counter scale with a 500-pound capacity, a portion scale, space for inspecting incoming products, a stand-up desk or shelf for checking packing slips, and a heavy-duty hand truck for moving goods.

- **Where will food be stored?**

- **How often food is received?**

- **Types and amounts of ingredients that need to be stored.** How much cold and dry storage will you need? The dry storage should be dry, well ventilated, and maintained at a temperature between 55 and 60 degrees Fahrenheit. A thermometer should be placed in a prominent position to prevent temperatures fluctuating outside this range. Dry storage shelves ought to be at least six inches off the floor and should be convenient for FIFO rotation. Avoid high stacking of cereal, flour, and sugar. For expensive foods and equipment, a lockable valuable-items cabinet should be available. Depending on the size of your operation, you may need one or several refrigerated storage areas. Keep in mind, however, that unnecessarily large refrigerators and freezers waste energy, thus increasing operating costs. Greater refrigerated storage requirements may be justified when extra delivery charges are incurred for small quantities.

- **Anticipated volume of work.**

- **Access.** Avoid establishing a kitchen in a building where you must use an elevator, either to enter the kitchen or to pass from one department to another.

- **Lighting.** Install adequate lighting (both gas and 220-volt electric). Maximize on natural lighting

- **Ventilation.** Organize kitchen layout so as to make the most of natural ventilation. Also, take the extra precaution of placing ovens, ranges, and steam kettles so that the mechanical exhaust units above them can operate at peak efficiency. Exhaust hoods above cooking areas should include automatic fire-fighting equipment.

- **Open space.** The placement of equipment should allow for sufficient aisle space. For a commissary-style operation, you will need extra space for counting, organizing, packing, storing, and shipping.

Before you design your kitchen and choose equipment, be sure to find out whether the location and layout meet with local zoning laws. Check the zoning laws and the local board of health to determine what type of permit you need to set up a commercial kitchen. What are the restrictions regarding hours of operation? Is the parking space adequate for deliveries from vendors or for your employees? Also, check out whether there are waste and septic systems in place.

MAJOR EQUIPMENT

Every year new pieces of equipment, large and small, expensive and inexpensive, are introduced that will save time, labor, and energy. Aside from saving additional labor costs, new mechanization will reduce product handling, eliminate work drudgery, and make each task — as well as the overall job — more enjoyable for the employee.

The large initial capital expenditure for new equipment can usually be financed over several years through either the manufacturer or distributor. The total cost may be depreciated over several years and written off as a business tax-deductible expense. Heavy kitchen equipment is expensive and should last a long time.

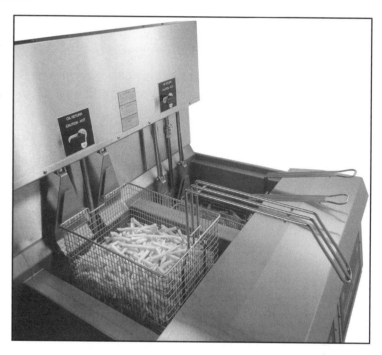

Henny Penny Open Fryer

Henny Penny is a manufacturer of food service equipment including pressure fryers, open fryers, rotisseries, heated merchandisers, island merchandisers, display counter warmers, SmartHold humidified holding cabinets, heated holding cabinets for floor or countertop, bun warmers, SmartCooking Systems™, combis, blast chillers/freezers, and breading systems. Do your homework to guarantee that you get what you really need, not just what the salesperson wants to sell you. Visit **www. hennypenny.com** for more information or call 800-417-8417.

Henny Penny's SmartCombi™

It is quite possible to manage without a range for a long time. One low-cost solution is to be licensed as a "cold" kitchen. You could also start with a half-sized convection oven, which can handle three large turkeys. Convection ovens are light, portable and very convenient. But with the SmartCooking System™ from Henny Penny cooking a complete menu is simple. Press the SmartCooking Control™ key and select the type of food. It cooks everything from roasts to fish to casseroles to pies, literally at the touch of a button. For even greater control, simply press the moist heat or dry heat mode keys and set time, temperature, and special functions.

Alto Shaam Restaurant Equipment offers a large selection of equipment for your restaurant. These include ovens, warming compartments, fryers, and much more. The full line can be seen at **www.altoshaam.com** or you can call them at 800-558-8744. Pictured at right is the Alto-Shaam Combitherm® Model 10•18ESi flash-steam combination oven/steamer.

RANGES AND OVENS

Commercial kitchens generally favor gas stoves, which may be expensive, but they can be purchased at second-hand stores or auctions.

If you are buying a regular commercial oven, you can purchase a range oven combination or there are stackable ovens. Stack ovens are good because you can buy one at a time and add as your business increases. They also take up less floor space.

Flat-top stoves are useful because you can fit any size pan on the burners. They come with four or six burners in the standards sizes. These stoves provide fast, high heat needed for items like omelets and for sautéing.

Griddle stoves are good for quickly sautéing small amounts of food, such as diced onions that you are going to put in another dish. These stoves can also be used to keep foods warm and as a griddle for items such as French toast and pancakes. .

The Blodgett Oven Company is the leading manufacturer of commercial ovens. Many businesses rely on the Blodgett name. The company's ovens come in various sizes and configurations. Your choice depends on the volume of business you do. To see a complete selection of Blodgett's combi ovens, visit **www.blodgett.com** or call 800-331-5842 or 802-860-3700.

Blodgett Deck Oven

One of the latest trends in ovens is induction cooking. The induction cooktop is becoming increasingly popular. They come in a variety of forms, from full-sized ranges to portable hot plates. They cook food quickly, are easy to use, and easy to clean. Induction cooktops can be used with any type of food, and will cook as thoroughly and evenly as any electric or gas range. Induction cooking can be used with any type of cookware from frying pans to woks. However, it only works when used with magnetic-based materials, such as iron and steel, that will allow an induced current to flow within them.

Combi ovens are also known as steamers. These ovens combine the browning capacity of a regular oven with convection steam cooking, keeping meats moist, and preventing cooking loss. They also cook 30 to 40 percent faster than conventional convection ovens. Roasting in combi mode reduces shrinkage 20 to 30 percent (and food cost), yielding a juicier product. Shellfish cook rapidly in steam mode without washing out flavors or dealing with heavy stockpots. Hot-air mode operates as a normal convection oven for baking cookies, cakes, and flaky pastries. High-sugar recipes are less likely to scorch when using combi mode. Breads, pastries, and other yeast-raised products bake up higher and lighter with combi mode.

Baker's Pride's mission is to be the leading supplier of quality bake ovens, char broilers, conveyor ovens, and convection ovens for the food service industry. They are committed to providing leadership and innovation by delivering value-added benefits to customers through excellence in communication, problem solving, on-time delivery, and world-class, worldwide after-sales service. Visit their Web site at **www.bakerspride. com**, call 914-576-0200, fax 914-576-0605, or 800-431-2745 U.S. and Canada, or e-mail **sales@bakerspride.com**.

Baker's Pride SuperDeck Series Gas Deck Oven

Other oven options include:

- **Deck ovens.** These horizontal ovens can be used for baking and roasting and usually have one shelf each.

- **Rotating ovens** have rotating shelves and are used as high-production ovens.

- **Conveyor ovens** are useful for fast, continuous production such as pizzas or steaks for large parties.

- **Roll-in ovens** are constructed so you can roll racks of food directly into the oven. These are great ovens for large events. Roll-in ovens designed for baking have steam injectors and some come equipped with automatic thermostats to keep the food at a desired temperature.

- **Low-temperature ovens** cook at a temperature so that a hood is not required. Like the combi oven, meat cooked in a low-temperature oven stays moist and shrinkage is minimal.

Amana's Commercial Division offers an oven that cooks 12 times faster than a conventional oven. Visit **www.amanacommercial.com**. This page explains the benefits of the Amana Veloci compared to a conventional oven. The infrared radiant element works with the direct air flow to enhance browning, toasting, and crisping. Contact Amana at 866-426-2621 or fax 319-622-8589.

Restaurant shows and food service magazines are the best places to look for the announcement and review of new equipment. You can also visit manufacturer's Web sites or other sites that let you compare brands and prices, such as:

- **www.amanacommerical.com**
- **www.ckitchen.com**
- **www.bevles.com**
- **www.restaurantequipment.net**
- **www.blodgett.com**

- **www.hennypenny.com**
- **www.abestkitchen.com**
- **www.horizonfoodequipment.com**
- **www.hatcocorp.com**

- www.business.com/directory/food_and_beverage/restaurants
- www.business.com/directory/foodservice/equipment
- www.business.com/directory/supplies/cooking
- www.business.com/directory/baking/ovens

GRILLS, SMOKERS, AND ROTISSERIES

Grills provide a cooking source that gives food an attractive appearance. The grill marks on steaks or vegetables add to a winning plate presentation. For most restaurants, grills are used to mark food and to pre-cook it. Then the food is finished in the oven.

You can find gas, charcoal, and electric grills. While charcoal grills are seldom used in restaurant kitchens, you may want to add this or a wood stove if you are serving dishes that require a particular smoked flavor or if you are thinking of creating a signature dish. Gas grills have lava stones. The fat dripping onto the stones gives flavor to the meat.

If you will be catering specialty items, such as barbecue, you may be interested in a grill or rotisseries. There are numerous types and many manufacturers to choose from. Check out:

Big John Grills & Rotisseries has designed, manufactured, packaged, and distributed outdoor cooking equipment for over 42 years. The extensive product line includes gas grills, portable gas grills, smokers, roasters, portable griddles, steam tables, gas towables, utility stoves, smokers, portable fryers, countertop fryers, ovens, and ranges, as well as countertop griddles, broilers, and fryers. The E-Z Way Roaster is a product of Big John Grills & Rotisseries. You simply open the hood, place a pig inside, fill the smoking trough with wood chips, start the fuel-efficient 80,000 Btu gas burner, and walk away. Come back hours later to enjoy a delicious pig pickin' party. The entire process of preparing a moist, tender, flavorful pig roast is that easy. For full information, visit **www.bigjohngrills.com** or call 800-326-9575.

The E-Z Way Roaster, a product of Big John Grills & Rotisseries.

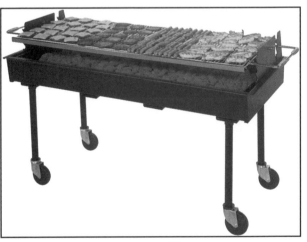

Belson's PORTA-GRILL® I Commercial Barbecue Grill.

Belson's PORTA-GRILL® I Commercial Barbecue Grill is a charcoal-fired model big enough to feed large gatherings, yet light enough to be transported without a trailer. It has casters for short trips and removable legs for long trips. With a sanitary nickel-plated cooking grate made from round steel bars, it easily adjusts to four different cooking heights. The patented flip-back grill feature allows for easy charcoal servicing and cleaning. For more information, **www.belson.com/grills.htm** or call 800-323-5664.

Holstein Manufacturing offers custom-built products and has numerous products popular with the catering and special events industry including a six-foot towable barbecue grill, a corn roaster, a deep-fat fryer, and portable concession trailer. For more information, visit **www.holsteinmfg.com** or call 800-368-4342.

Cookshack offers state-of-the-art electric smoker ovens, such as the SmartSmoker with electronic controls, pre-programmed for brisket, ribs, and chicken. It is available in four sizes and eight models to fit your needs. For more information, visit **www.cookshack.com** or call 800-423-0698.

REFRIGERATORS AND FREEZERS

At least one separate refrigerator and one large freezer are essential. As for their size, double the minimum capacity needed for your refrigerator to keep food for a good-sized event. Do not forget that you need space for usable leftovers as well. In addition, you will need refrigerated space for deliveries such as dairy items, salads, vegetables, meats, fish, and poultry. In general, a large commercial refrigerator will accommodate all these requirements. Problems can develop, however. It is a good idea to have a second freezer and refrigerator available for emergencies.

Walk-in freezers and refrigerators are used by most larger operations. These allow plenty of room to roll in carts of food as well as providing shelf space. You will also want smaller reach-in refrigeration to store small items and you might want to consider mobile refrigerators for transporting food.

Leer Limited Partnership manufactures stock and custom walk-in coolers and freezers. They offer standard nominal sizes to special configurations. Visit **www.leerlp.com** to see their product line.

U.S. Cooler manufactures premium walk-in coolers, freezers, and combination units at competitive prices. These are used for all types of cold storage. These can be constructed to suit your needs and will arrive at your shop pre-assembled to ensure a quality product. Check the Web site for the various configurations that are available. Each accessory that you need can be

U.S. Cooler walk-in cooler

purchased from U.S. Cooler to accentuate your walk-in cooler. These can include: outside ramp, rain roofs, strip curtains, shelving, glass doors, and many others. U.S. Cooler utilizes the latest technology to manufacture walk-in coolers and freezers which can be purchased from a dealer or an online discount dealer. For more information, visit **www.uscooler.com** or call 800-521-2665.

DISHWASHERS

Dishwashing is the "Rodney Dangerfield" of the kitchen. It gets no respect. What other restaurant activity is a major health concern, takes up so much space, costs so much, and is only noticed when you do not do it right? Whether you serve meals in paper bags or on fine china, you will have to wash something. Proper sanitation depends on a washing system that protects your customers while being efficient and cost-effective. Whether your establishment requires only a multi-sink configuration or you need the performance of a conveyor system, dishwashing decisions are important.

Sanitation occurs when water, chemicals, and heat are properly combined. Your basic needs in dishwashing are: waste removal, washing, sanitizing, rinsing, and drying. Do not overlook the following:

- **Make certain your water pressure is ample** to operate your chosen commercial dishwasher. Poor water pressure may slow cycle times, inhibit automatic settings, and not meet sanitation standards.

- **Calculate your water hardness.** Rinse aids may not be sufficiently effective without a separate water softener.

- **Review your hot water capacity and recovery times.** You will need consistent temperatures of 150 degrees Fahrenheit and above depending on your usage and your machine's capabilities.

- **Research low-temp dishwashing units that use chemicals to sanitize and require lower water temperatures.** Check with manufacturers such as Auto-Chlor Systems, Hobart, and Champion for their recommended units.

- **Invest in a hot water booster.** Check with your local utility company regarding subsidies and rebates on select equipment.

- **Minimize cross-contamination, noise, and unsavory smells.** Position dishwashing away from food prep and dining areas whenever possible.

- **Determine what you need to wash and when.** Will quick turnaround of expensive stemware require a separate glasswasher? Will you require a large storage area for soiled utensils or pots that are only handled after the rush is over? Will you have uniquely shaped equipment that will require soaking?

- **Consider what you will need to wash off.** Lipstick stains on stemware? Grease on plastic?

- **Install a small under-counter glasswasher in lounge/bar areas and front-of-the-house workstations.** Also, install a low-flow (1.6 gpm) pre-rinse nozzle at your dishwashing station and save up to $100 a month in energy, water, and sewer costs.

- **Non-automated washing.** In smaller operations or those with limited dish- or warewashing needs, a multi-sink configuration that complies with local regulations may be all you need. Be certain to:

  - **Add ample counters and drain racks.** Local codes dictate widths and lengths.

  - **Separate dirty and clean dishware** to avoid contamination.

  - **Install a detergent dispenser** to reduce waste.

  - **Maintain a consistent and high-enough water temperature** by placing sinks near a dedicated water heater.

COMMERCIAL DISHWASHERS

Consider a commercial dishwasher with more than two racks. It saves time when storing glasses on dishwasher trays. Heat generated by dishwashers can be a problem. Solve the problem by installing a condenser over the dishwasher. Choose a dishwashing system that is engineered to meet your kitchen's requirements. Base your decision on such factors as the space available, layout, traffic flow, amount and type of food soil, and the hardness of the water.

Select the right dishwasher for the job. There are under-counter, standing (door), and conveyor models. Some are designed to handle a variety of dishware and larger pots; others are best suited to glassware and small items. In choosing the right dishwasher, ask about:

- **Capacity.** Consider the average number of place settings per hour. Estimate 90 to 110 settings per hour for a small- to medium-sized restaurant.

- **Water use.** Different manufacturers and models have different water needs. Compare gallons per load, water pressure, and minimum temperatures. Some store and recirculate clean rinse water to minimize water waste.

- **Cycle times.** Time needed to wash and dry a load can range from 90 seconds to three minutes.

- **Dry method.** Can water spots or streaks be minimized? Will it require chemical rinse aids and/or water softeners?

- **Footprint.** Do you have enough space? Compare overall size to work capacity.

- **Openings and racks.** Can racks slide through easily? Do the doors open easily? Do you need a straight or corner configuration?

- **Ventilation.** Will additional ventilation be necessary?

- **Accessories.** How costly are additional racks?

- **Detergent requirements.** Compare the cost of recommended consumables (detergents, rinse aids).

- **Research equipment rental/chemical purchase programs.** The supplier owns and maintains the equipment. You pay a rental fee and purchase the supplier's chemicals. Auto-Chlor Systems, a well-known national supplier, can be found in your local Yellow Pages.

- **Create ample, convenient, and secure storage** (with no potential cross-contamination) for chemical dishwashing agents. Rental/supply programs with monthly service require less chemical inventory.

- **Add a three-compartment sink in your dish room.** This is really useful for bulky or unusually shaped utensils and equipment components and as a backup for your commercial unit.

- **Stains.** Ask how specific stains or food residues, such as lipstick, eggs and grease, are removed.

WASHER AND DRYER

There will be aprons, towels, napkins, and uniforms to clean regularly. Invest in a robust washer and dryer from the start. Choose a large-capacity, heavy-duty model.

SMALL EQUIPMENT

You should analyze a number of factors in order to determine your small-equipment needs. The number of guests that you intend to serve as well as the type of menu items are factors in what equipment you should purchase. For example, if you sell cold canapés, you will need to invest in rolling racks and refrigerated storage; if you sell deep-fried hors d'oeuvres, you could store the raw product in plastic containers. Although the type of equipment needed is very specific to your type of operation, the following section contains a basic overview of what most operations will need.

There are a variety of sources for small equipment. It is a good idea to compare various sources for price and quality. Small equipment can also be very personal. Many chefs have a preferred brand or manufacturer.

Browne-Halco is a prime supplier of small equipment in the United States. They offer in excess of 3,000 smallwares products. Browne-Halco's objective is to provide food service operators with high-quality and cost-efficient smallwares products. For further details and to view the Browne-Halco product line, visit **www.halco.com**.

Franklin Machine Products is another leading supplier of parts and accessories for the food service industry. Their annual catalog is over 1,000 pages and offers an enormous selection of products. For further details and to view the FMP product line, visit **www.FMPonline.com**.

BRAISING PANS AND TILT KETTLES

These pans come in many sizes and can be used for soups, stocks, stews, and even frying. They should have a water spigot for cleaning and a deep trough on the floor to catch any liquid when the pan is titled. These are used in large commercial kitchens. Smaller restaurant operations will probably not have the space.

Blodgett has long been recognized as a manufacturer of premium equipment for the food service industry. Available in electric or gas, Blodgett's braising pans have four different tilting mechanisms from which to choose: tabletop or floor model, manual, gearbox, power, or hydraulic tilt. For the choices that are available, check the web site at **www.blodgett.com** or call 800-331-5842 or 802-860-3700.

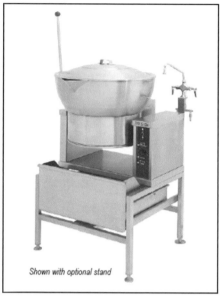

Shown with optional stand

Blodett's Electric Tabletop Tilting Round Braising Pan.

SLICER

A slicer should have a large blade, control handle, heavy body to prevent sliding when used, and a safety on/off switch.

SALAMANDER

This handy device is used as an overhead heat source to brown food. The Blodgett Infrared Salamander Broilers broil in half the time with a third less gas than ordinary broilers. The burners reach operating temperature in just 90 seconds and their intense infrared energy quickly heats the food, not the surrounding air. The broiling grid adjusts to five heights, and rolls out for easy access. See **www.blodgett.com** for more details or call 800-331-5842.

Blodgett's Infrared Salamander Broiler.

STEAM KETTLES

Steam kettles are surrounded by jackets that have steam injected into them to heat the kettle. This piece of equipment is available in a variety of sizes from 5 gallons to 100 gallons. Like tilt frying pans, these should have a facet and a trough for draining.

Direct-steam kettles are available in a variety of sizes (from 6 to 100 gallons) for connection to an outside steam source, such as the Blodgett steam boiler cabinets.

Blodgett's Gas Quad-Leg Stationary Kettle.

POTS AND PANS

The type, number, and size of pots and pans you will need is highly dependant on the menu you offer. Make sure to purchase plenty of hotel pans, half-hotel pans, sheet pans, and half-sheet pans. You will find a multitude of uses for these — cooking a chicken stew to baking cookies, transporting individual appetizers, and using them as shelves in cambros.

Following are some sources for pots and pans:

Regal Ware Food Service, a division of Regal Ware WorldwideTM, specializes in providing top-quality beverage and food preparation products to the food service industry. Visit **www.regalwarefood-service.com** or 262-626-2121 for information.

*Elegance Stainless Steel Cookware
by Regal Ware.*

*Elegance Stainless Steel Cookware
by Regal Ware.*

Sitram Cookware has, for more than 40 years, has supplied chefs across Europe with a comprehensive range of heavy-duty cookware. Sitram's success is the result of the heavy copper bottom sandwiched between two layers of stainless steel. Copper is a good conductor of heat and guarantees fast, uniform heat distribution. Extremely durable, the cookware is also impervious to acidic foods: It will not pit, discolor, or alter the flavors of foods. It is dishwasher safe and carries a lifetime limited warranty. Visit **www.sitramcookware.com** or call 800-515-8585 for more information.

Sitram's Catering (Inox) Collection.

Polar Ware Company a wide selection of food preparation, serving, and storage products—from heavy-duty mixing bowls to kitchen utensils and storage canisters. They also offer a wide variety of stainless steel and tri-ply stainless steel stock pots and matching covers. The aluminum cookware line is manufactured using deep draw techniques perfected by Polar Ware. Visit **www.polarware.com** or call 800-237-3655 for more information.

Polar Ware Aluminum Cookware.

Browne-Halco offers an extensive line of high-quality cookware that is both durable and reliable. Eagleware® Cookware is their premier line of professional aluminum cookware. It features a thick bottom construction for even heat distribution as well as a heavy top with a smooth rim. The beadless rim eliminates food traps and makes cleaning easier. Other product lines include Futura Stainless Steel Professional Cookware and Thermalloy Aluminum Cookware. To view the online catalog, visit **www.halco.com** or call 888-289-1005 for more information.

Eagleware Professional Aluminum Sauce Pans from Browne-Halco.

Eagleware Teflon Aluminum Roast Pan from Browne-Halco.

FOOD PROCESSING EQUIPMENT

Depending on your menus, you may want to consider purchasing the following items to use for food prep:

- Meat grinder
- Hand-held mixers
- Immersion blender
- Food processor
- Stand mixers
- Vacuum machine for vacuum packing food

KNIVES

Invest in the best chef's knife (sometimes called a French knife), carving knife (slicer), large serrated knife, and several smaller paring knives that the budget will allow. Complete the collection with a knife sharpener and a sharpening stone. For special purposes, you may also need a boner and a fillet knife. Learn how to sharpen and hone your knives. Hone them regularly and sharpen them about once a year.

CUTTING BOARDS

Have at least two small and two large cutting boards. Look for HDP (plastic) cutting boards as opposed to wooden ones, as any odor or stain on polyethylene boards can easily be removed with a chlorine soak. .

When using cutting boards, be aware of the possibility of contamination, especially with raw foods. Colored cutting boards are an ingenious way to avoid contamination. Each board is for a specific food item. Available from DayMark Safety Systems, the durable construction provides superior heat, chemical and warp resistance in commercial dishwashers. Tough surface won't dull knives and prevents unsafe cut-grooving where dirt and bacteria can hide The color coded cutting boards help protect against cross contamination in the work place. For more information call 800-847-0101 or visit **www.daymarksafety.com**.

SCALES

Have at least three scales: one so sensitive that it can weigh a cinnamon stick accurately; one less accurate that can weigh anything from three to ten pounds; and a third larger scale that can weigh at least 25 pounds. They should also be used to help you accurately measure portions.

6" Portion-Control Scale from Browne-Halco.

THERMOMETERS

Thermometers are critical to food safety. You will need to check temperature frequently to make sure you are preparing and holding food properly. There are a wide variety of thermometers available. Visit **www.atlantic-pub.com** to see a complete selection specifically for food service.

Browne-Halco offers a wide selection of cookware and bakeware accessories. These products are invaluable in your recipe preparation. Some of the items are shown below and the full line of products can be seen at **www.halco.com** or you can call 888-289-1005.

FOOD WHIP

For delicate operations or desserts, whipped creams, and sauces that need to be prepared at the last minute, you may want to have a food whip on hand. iSi NorthAmerica makes a variety of whippers. For information, visit **www.isinorthamerica.com/foodservice** or call 800-447-2426.

The ThermaTwin Infrared Thermometer, available from Atlantic Publishing.

EQUIPMENT FOR SERVING FOOD

If you are a smaller operation or are considering catering or special events, you may want to leave the china to the rental companies. It takes up a lot of storage space and is very heavy to move from location to location. When providing off-site catering, many of the locations you use may also have their own china sets, so you may not need to rent or buy; be sure to check when doing your pre-event work. Or consider disposable options.

If you do purchase china, at a minimum you should purchase the following types of dishes:

iSi Cream and Food Whipper.

- Service plates
- Dinner plates
- Bread plates
- Luncheon plates
- Salad plates
- Soup bowls
- Cups and saucers

- Relish trays
- Platters
- Ramekins
- Ashtrays
- Sherbet/ice cream cups
- Dessert plates

How much of these you buy depends on the size of your restaurant, the foods you plan to offer, or any special events you will handle. You may also want to consider:

- Champagne buckets and stands
- Creamer and sugar sets
- Display trays

- Compotes (footed candy/nut dishes)
- Salt and pepper sets

FLATWARE

Depending on the volume of work you do and the types of events you cater, you may want to consider renting rather than buying flatware. If you do purchase flatware, you will want it to be an attractive pattern. Open stock designs are the least expensive to purchase. You basic flatware needs will be:

- Dinner fork
- Salad fork
- Fish fork
- Dessert fork
- Dinner knife

- Butter spreader
- Steak knife
- Soup spoon
- Teaspoon
- Iced tea spoon

You will also need serving pieces such as:

- Salad tongs
- Large serving forks

- Large serving spoon
- Cake knife and server

Browne-Halco carries many different lines of flatware suited to different tastes and budgets. Below are a few options. To view their online catalog, visit **www.halco.com** or call 888-289-1005 for more information.

Celine Pattern Flatware.

Dominion Pattern Flatware.

Elegance Pattern Flatware.

GLASSWARE

Glassware, like china and flatware, can either be purchased or rented. Dining room glasses should include:

- Fruit juice glass (5 ounces)
- General beverage glass (9 ounces)

- Water tumbler (8 to10 ounces)
- Iced tea glass (12 ounces)

If you serve alcohol, you will also need:

- Wineglasses (red and white)
- On-the-rocks glasses

- Beer mugs or glasses

COFFEE SERVICE

You want to purchase a good coffee urn. They typically come in 35-cup and 85-cup models. You can also purchase attractive serving containers for your servers to take around the dining room. The following are some coffee service manufacturers and options:

Regal Ware Food Service offers a variety of commercial coffeemakers including stainless steel and aluminum. They also offer vacuum-insulated thermal carafes and vacuum-insulated airpots. Visit **www.regalwarefoodservice.com** or call 262-626-2121 for more information.

Regal Ware 101 Cup Black Satin Aluminum Coffee Urn.

Regal Ware 1.5 Liter, 2 Liter and 1 Liter Stainless Steel Thermal Carafes.

Regal Ware 2.2 Liter, 2.5 Liter and 3 Liter Stainless Steel Lever Air Pot.

The Gravity Flow Beverage Dispensers by Zojirushi provide an ideal way to keep coffee hot and fresh-tasting while using the force of gravity for quick and easy serving. These dispensers minimize the coffee's contact with air; the freshly brewed taste is sealed in. They also provide exceptional heat retention to ensure the coffee remains hot until served. Products include the Steel Lined Thermal Coffee Server, the Satellite Coffee Servers, and the Gravity Pot® (Coffee Thermal Gravity Pots®, Stainless Server). To learn more about the entire collection of serving products by Zojirushi, call 800-733-6270 or visit **www.zojirushi.com**.

Zojirushi's Stainless Steel Lined Thermal Gravity Pot® and Satellite Coffee Server.

ASTORIA espresso and cappuccino coffee machines by General Espresso Equipment are available in a variety of commercial lines. The Astoria JADA Super Automatic is the most productive espresso and cappuccino machine in the world. Two independent brewing groups can dispense four espresso servings simultaneously. The JADA is controlled by an advanced user-friendly micro-processor system with easy-to-read, easy-to-operate touch pads and an illuminated electronic functions display. The Astoria Sibilla is available in one, two, or three brewing heads (groups) with six programmable/volumetric portion selections and an override semiautomatic button. It can produce up to 240 espresso servings per hour. For more information, visit **www.espressobrewer.com** or call 336-393-0224.

TRAYS & PLATTERS

You will need trays for all sorts of tasks in your business. Make sure to have a ready supply of waiter trays (22" x 22"), kitchen trays (15" x 20"), and bar trays (12" x 14" with a cork surface). In addition to trays, you will need serving platters. These can be used directly for service on a buffet or carried by wait staff. Stock a variety of sizes or look into renting platters for larger occasions. Browne-Halco carries stainless steel oval serving platters that range in size from 14" x 9" to 26" x 18." Round platters are also available.

Browne-Halco carries stainless steel oval serving platter

BUSBOXES

These are used to carry dirty dishware from the dining room to the back kitchen area for washing. They are usually made of plastic and measure 12" x 18" to 18" x 24".

TABLES

You can never have too much work space when preparing food. For off-site events, purchase stainless steel worktables that have shelves to store equipment. Make sure tables are placed close to electrical outlets so you can use slicers, mixers, blenders, etc. You may also want to purchase mobile worktables.

EQUIPMENT FOR CATERING AND SPECIAL EVENTS

Depending on your menu and the locations you cater, you may find the need to cook some things on-site. If you do, make sure this equipment is portable. Some items that many caterers find useful to include in the pantry are:

- Electric frying pan
- Hot plate

- Small microwave
- Crock pot

PORTABLE COOKING AND HOLDING EQUIPMENT

CHAFING DISHES AND STEAM PANS

You will also want to invest in two or three chafing dishes or steam pans to use for buffet services. These dishes are used on buffets to keep dishes hot. They usually are silver pans with a cover that sit in a stand. A heat source is placed under the dish to keep food items warm during service. They are generally available in 2-, 4-, and 8-quart sizes. There are a variety of chafers available and range from utilitarian to artistic display pieces. Following are some options:

Browne-Halco offers a full line of chafers and buffet servingware. Below are a few options. To view their online catalog, visit **www.halco.com** or call 888-289-1005 for more information.

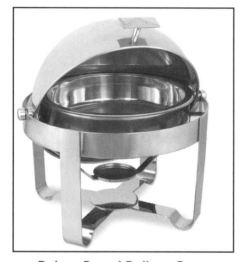

Deluxe Round Rolltop Cover.

Economy Chafer.

Polar Ware Company has a wide selection of chafers, components, accessories, and serving utensils. Below are a few options. Visit **www.polarware.com** or call 800-237-3655 for more information.

Horizon Gold Chafer.

Sierra Chafer.

WARMERS

In addition to steam pans and chafers, there are other types of warmers available, usually specific to certain types of foods. If you cater numerous soup and sandwich luncheons, you may want to look into a soup warmer.

Micom Soup Warmer is a free-standing appliance with five keep-warm temperature settings. This warmer keeps soup at the perfect serving temperature. It also works for keeping chili, nacho cheese dip, and other items hot and ready to serve. It also features a dry-type keep-warm operation that requires no water for keeping the inner pan warm.

Select the desired temperature setting and the unit's direct thermal sensor system will automatically regulate the heating elements around the inner pan to ensure the selected temperature is maintained. It has a two-gallon capacity and the stainless steel inner pan can be used directly on a stovetop burner to prepare soups of many varieties — this eliminates the need to use and clean an extra stockpot when preparing soup. For more information on the Micom Soup Warmer and other products by Zojirushi, call (800) 733-6270 or visit **www.zojirushi.com**.

COOLING EQUIPMENT

Many dishes need to be held and served cold. There are a variety of products that make this simple:

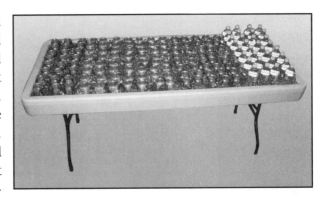

The Party Table from Chillin' Products can be placed in any convenient location, loaded with 75 pounds of ice, and filled with food and drink. It features rugged yet lightweight construction and has a durable, easy-to-clean, one-piece, FDA-approved, polyethylene top. The bottom is tapered with a centrally located drain. It is easy to transport and store. The steel legs are collapsible. For more information visit **www.chillinproducts.com** or call 866-932-4455.

The patented Satellite Cooling System is the chef-designed innovative solution for food safety, presentation, and mobility. It solves the problem of how to keep buffet appetizers, entrées, and desserts cold at a consistent, regulated temperature while maintaining a fresh, attractive appearance. It eliminates ice and decreases labor costs and food waste. The Satellite Cooling System is NSF approved, can be set up virtually anywhere, and is completely mobile. For more information, visit **www.satellitecool.com** or call 888-356-2665.

EQUIPMENT TO TRANSPORT FOOD

Caterers need equipment to use for transporting food. On-site caterers will need to get food from the kitchen to event rooms that may be on the other end of the building and off-site caterers often will need to transport food across town. This equipment will be useful if your restaurant does catering, special events, or other serving outside your restaurant.

CARRYING CASE

Make sure you have carrying cases for all your equipment needs:

- Glass boxes for glassware such as wineglasses, iced tea glasses, and water tumblers.

- Boxes for your chafing dishes.

- Plastic containers for flatware, linens, kitchen utensils, serving utensils, and pitchers.

- Boxes and packing material for any platters you take.

- Boxes for china and coffee cups.

You can find a wide selection of food transport items at **www.cambro.com.**

Wes-Pak offers pop-up food service carriers, which are an affordable alternative. Perfect for one-time, temporary use, no assembly is required. The Pop-Up Carriers are quick and easy to load. They are lightweight yet durable and, with their leak-proof liners, these carriers are great for cooling drinks and storing ice and they handle hot food pans with ease. Once the food is unloaded, disposal is easy — simply flatten them with a quick push and place them in the recycling bin. No assembly, no retrieval, no cleaning necessary. For more information, visit **www.wespakinc.com** or call 800-493-7725.

TRUCK AND VAN

You will need at least one vehicle for transporting food and supplies to the event location. Buy a professional-looking and practical vehicle. Larger operations, however, will need refrigerated trucks. Determine first which truck size is the best for you (no matter what amount you anticipate carrying, your vehicle is always too small). Vans, for example, are practical and very economical for off-premise caterers that rent tables and chairs for events, instead of supplying them themselves. Trucks, on the other hand, are expensive and you may find it is more cost-effective to rent them.

You may decide to have a self-contained refrigeration unit with a built-in generator or a refrigeration unit that can be plugged into an outside power source. As for the arrangement inside, you should have a set of fixed shelves for small- to medium-sized items and plenty of floor space for large equipment. Make sure that the shelves are sturdy and have a barrier of several inches to prevent slippage during transportation.

If you do not own a large vehicle, check into renting one. Compare rates when you call and make sure the rental company knows you are a business. If you do use rental vehicles, make sure to include the cost in your estimates.

HOLDING OVEN

During transportation and set up, a holding oven is usually required to keep food hot. These are used to keep dinner rolls, roasts, turkeys, chicken breasts, and all other hot food at the right temperature when you are transporting to the site.

ICE CHESTS

It is also a good idea to invest in some large ice chests. You will have drinks, fruit, vegetables, and dairy products you will want to keep cool during transport.

ROLLING RACKS

If you are an on-premise caterer or working a large event, rolling racks can hold a lot of food in a small space. These racks can hold sheet trays of prepared foods or raw foods that can then be placed in the oven to cook.

KITCHEN GRIPS AND MITTS

You will need these when transporting hot dishes. It is a good idea to invest in quality mitts with a good grip. You do not want to have food loss due to dropping and spilling.

Duncan Industries produces a full line of hand safety products including oven mitts and hot pads. They are designed to increase safety, hygiene, and sanitation in your kitchen and catering operation. They repel water, steam, and liquids and provide maximum protection from painful steam burns caused by wet protection equipment. Textured crosscut fabric provides a safer grip and increased control in busy operations. They are dishwasher safe and stain resistant. They are also sub-zero safe, so you can handle freezer foods, even dry ice. For more information, visit **www.kitchengrips.com** or call 800-785-4449.

DayMark Safety Systems also offers a complete line of oven mitts and burn protection gloves which offer protection in temperatures up to 900°F. For more information call 800-847-0101 or visit **www.daymarksafety.com**.

DayMark's BurnGuard® Oven Mitt

CELL PHONES

Cell phones are great investments. Sending cell phones with your crew to event sites lets them stay in contact with you if things go wrong or if they forget something and need to send someone back. It is also a good safety measure in case the crew has vehicle trouble along the way.

DISPOSABLE EQUIPMENT

Disposable equipment, such as cutlery or containers can be very usable for catering. It is also helpful to have on hands for customers that want to take portions of their meal home or to-go orders. Here area few options:

WNA Comet, **www.wna.biz**, manufacturers a variety of disposable products that are versatile and attractive. These timesaving products can help achieve a high-class look. Following is a summary of some of their product lines:

- **Reflections**™ cutlery has a look that takes disposable cutlery to a new level of sophistication. Reflections has the same shine and silver-sparkle as stainless steel cutlery, giving consumers a unique, formal alternative to white or black disposable cutlery. Available in a spoon, knife or fork, Reflections single-use silverware is the only solution addressing both the need for a formal presentation and the high costs associated with renting or owning permanent flatware. Caterers estimate that loss and accidental disposal result in the need to replace 15 to 30 percent of permanent flatware annually. A 600-unit case of Reflections™ has the same average cost of 11 permanent flatware settings. In addition, for the cost of renting just one stainless flatware setting, Reflections provides at least 5 settings.

Above: Reflections cutlery.
Below: Masterpeice dinnerware

- **Masterpiece**™ **dinnerware** combines the expensive appearance of painted china with the convenience of a premium, heavyweight disposable. Offered in two standard designs and a holiday print, Masterpiece is a distinct upscale line that enhances food presentation and distinguishes with impeccable style and grace. The Premiere stock pattern is simple sophistication printed gold on ivory, while the Bordeaux stock design is a more contemporary burgundy imprint on white. With Masterpiece dinnerware, breakage, cleanup costs, washing and

transportation expenses are all eliminated. The Masterpiece dinnerware is perfect for caterers who specialize in event or corporate catering and food service management companies that specialize in stadium and arena skybox catering, restaurants, country clubs, and hotels and resorts with pool patios.

- **Classicware's**® timeless elegance captures the look of fine china, adding a touch of class to any occasion. A heavyweight yet disposable design in clear, black or white makes this attractive dinnerware a durable alternative to china, paper and foam products. Offering four plate sizes, 10-ounce bowl, serving bowl, trays, utensils, and a wide variety of drinkware, Classicware completes any occasion. The graceful curve of the Classic Crystal drinkware complements the scalloped edge of Classicware dinnerware to deliver a stunning presentation equivalent to fine crystal and china. Fluted tumblers and stemware create the impression and sparkle of fine-cut crystal. Conveniently, Classicware single-service drinkware eliminates glassware breakage worries.

- **Classicware**® **beverage products.** One-Piece Wine Glass and One-Piece Champagne Flute capture the timeless elegance of fine-cut crystal and combine it with the convenience of single-service. With single-service plasticware you eliminate glass breakage worries and reduce labor costs for cleanup, washing and return transportation. Plus, the one-piece construction saves over $4 (per 100 count case) in costly assembly labor versus two-piece disposables. The Classicware One-Piece Wineglass and One-Piece Champagne Flute, with their sophisticated designs, can be used in place of crystal when a disposable product is more practical. The Classic Crystal™ 50-Ounce Pitcher is perfect for any cold beverage, from water to carbonated drinks, sangria to beer, and iced fruit drinks to margaritas. The sleek clean lines of the pitcher silhouette are accented by a crystal-cut design that offers the elegance of glass or crystal combined with the convenience of single-service.

Above: Classicware beverage products
Below: CaterLine products

- **CaterLine**®. From rigid platters and bowls to compartment trays to serving utensils, CaterLine products offer versatile beauty in strong, durable designs. This servingware is designed for strength and will not bend or buckle under even the heaviest loads. Sophisticated shapes of round, rectangle, oval, triangle and square are offered in assorted sizes and colors allowing caterers to differentiate themselves by mixing shaped trays and bowls for a truly unique display. To fully complete any presentation, CaterLine® brings you strong, disposable serving utensils

that reduce the costs to clean and replace lost permanentware and allows "drop and go" convenience. Offering a utensil for any occasion, CaterLine truly delivers the whole catering presentation.

- **CaterLine® Pack n' Serve.** Ease the transition from preparation to presentation with CaterLine Pack n' Serve bowls, which combine the convenience and value of a disposable bowl to transport food with an upscale look that allows you to utilize the same product for display. The subtle fluting on the bowls and lids enhances the food presentation and package appearance. These bowls are available in clear and black with clear dome lids. Bowls are offered in sizes from 24 to 320 ounces. The bowls offer superior sidewall strength and leak-resistant lids that seal in freshness. In addition to the ample-size tabs on both the lid and bowl to facilitate openings and closings, Pack n' Serve bowls stack for stability during transport. Each size bowl nests into the lid of not only that size, but also the next size up.

Sabert Nova Plus Platter

Sabert Corporation, **www.sabert.com**, also offers a wide variety of disposable products. Sabert's elegant product styling makes food look great. All platters, bowls and utensils are available in an extensive selection of styles and sizes. All products are food service tested for superior performance and designed with food service operators' needs in mind. Sabert's product solutions incorporate superior resistance to cracking and crushing since they are manufactured from the same tough materials used in beverage packaging.

Sabert knows that people eat with their eyes first and its product solutions are designed to be easy on the eyes. From the crystal clarity of the lids to the array of sophisticated colors, customers will be impressed. Like clarity and color, design is important when you are trying to turn a good first impression into a lasting one.

Following is a summary of Sabert's product line:

- **The Queen Ann Collections.** A traditional design with a touch of royal formality.

- **The Europa Gold Collections.** Designed to convey a sense of European charm and panache.

- **The Mulberry Hill Collections.** A chic and contemporary motif with unpretentious sophistication.

- **The Seashell Collections.** Designed to evoke an air of fresh refinement, the distinctive curved contour is perfect for the tasteful serving of condiments.

- **The Nova Plus Collection.** An exotic jet-black color is emphasized by an embossed, swirl pattern that dresses up any special event.

- **Round and Oval Platters.** Classic simplicity just right for any occasion.

Genpak is another manufacturer and supplier of food service packaging. Their Quality to Go®

Line features snack, sandwich and dinner foam hinged containers, foam bases with clear lids, foam and plastic serving bowls with lids, clear hinged containers, paper cones and soufflé cups, foam serving trays, and several lines of foam, laminated foam and plastic dinnerware. Visit **www.genpak.com** to view and order samples or call 518-798-9511 for more information.

For the environmentally conscious, Biocorp, Inc., **www.biocorpaavc.com**, offers biodegradable and compostable bags, liners and food service ware. Their extensive line of cost-effective, quality products makes organic recycling feasible. Biocorp has developed an exciting line of food service ware including plates, cups, bowls, lunch boxes and cutlery.

Genpak products

ADDITIONAL EQUIPMENT

EMPLOYEE UNIFORMS

How you and your employees present themselves can be as important as the food presentation. If you wear uniforms, make sure they are clean and neat. Have aprons available for staff. Many linen rental companies will supply items such as jackets for cooks and waiters. Or you may want to invest in chef's coats and hats. Following are some sources:

Dickies Chef. Since 1922, Dickies has stood for the quality, toughness, and pride that embodies the spirit of the American worker. Dickies and Selecta Corp, LLC are proud to present the Chef Collection. It offers a wide selection of shirts, coats, pants, aprons, and hats with the same quality and durability of the Dickies brand. To view the collection online, visit **www.dickieschef.com** or call 866-262-6288 to order a catalog.

Aprons, Etc. If you are looking for an apron, smock, or vest with your logo printed on it, Aprons, Etc. is an excellent source. They have a huge selection of fabrics, colors, and styles from which to choose. They also supply restaurant, chef, wait staff, and bar apparel. Visit **www.apronsetc.com** to view the collection online and find a distributor in your area.

Left: detail of one of Dickies Chef's Coats
Right: Skull Cap, Chef's Coat, and Pants.

PAPER GOODS

If you cater informal events, you will want to have a supply of paper plates and napkins and plastic cups and flatware. You can purchase these items in bulk at stores such as Gordon's Food Service or Sam's Club.

You will also want a supply of various sizes of doilies for dessert and appetizer trays, as well as paper cocktail napkins for bar service.

Left: Tuxedo-Style Apron
Right: Chef's Hats and Attire from Aprons, Etc.

SMALL STUFF

Make sure your crews always go out with the following items:

- Dish towels
- Plastic storage bags
- Garbage bags
- First-aid kit

You should be sure to have a comprehensive first aid kit in a prominent location in your facility. DayMark's patented first aid cabinet is stocked with OSHA compliant first aid products for those accidents that typically occur in the food service industry such as burns, cuts, sticks, and common workplace injuries. With the high risk of accidents in the food service industry, it's always challenging to maintain a first aid program that's both cost effective and up-to-date

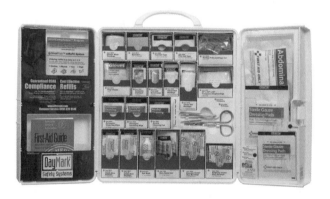

on current safety regulations. This process is easy and cost effective with the only first aid program with guaranteed OSHA compliance. For more information call 800-847-0101 or visit **www.daymarksafety.com**.

LOGOS

If you want to have your logo inscribed on your china and glassware, be discreet; you do not want to appear to be advertising. Offer individual house drinks and special desserts in large footed hurricane glasses, or oversized parfait glasses, etched or imprinted with your business name.

DECORATIVE ITEMS

Ranging from tiny to huge, you can find inexpensive baskets from various sources. In addition, you will need attractive candle holders, vases, and other décorative table pieces. Start a collection of special items for specific events. Let the client think that the preparation was designed personally for them. Check out:

• **Floralytes, Submersible Floralytes and LED Candles.** Enhance any atmosphere with battery-operated lighting. Perfect for affairs with low lighting to create an elegant touch. For more information, visit **www.chillinproducts.com**.

• **Gourmet Display, www.gourmetdisplay.com**, offers a wide variety of presentation products including beverage housings, pastry cases, cubes and staircases, ice carving pedestals, juice dispensers, ornamental iron, tiers, epic edge trays, riser rim mirror trays, serving stone trays, and acrylic and mirror trays. An example is pictured at right.

ADDITIONAL RESOURCES TO FIND EQUIPMENT

Now that you know what you need for your operation, how do you find it? I have listed many manufacturers in this chapter from which you can purchase directly. There are also many other avenues to try when searching for equipment. Make sure you are creative when looking for the larger items; you are likely to save some money.

• **Restaurant equipment stores are a good place to start.** Make sure to check the Yellow Pages for second-hand stores. It may also be worth a trip to the National Restaurant Show held each May in Chicago. Major areas of focus include food, beverage, equipment, apparel, furnishings, and design. You can get information about the show from the National Restaurant Association.

• **Retail stores such as Homegoods and T.J. Maxx are a good option for china and hotel-quality pans.** These types of stores are often hit or miss, but, if you can find what you are looking for, the price is usually right.

• **Networking is also a way to find equipment.** Talk to friends in the business.

• **Restaurant equipment auctions are a good place to look for the large and small items.** You can find everything from ovens to rolling racks to boxes of flatware. Since these are usually going-out-of-business sales, the prices tend to be pretty attractive.

• **www.chefscatalog.com and www.chefswear.com.** These are not the most cost-effective sources for equipment and uniforms, but they are convenient.

• **Institution sales.** Some colleges make their old equipment available to the public at dirt-cheap prices. The items for sale can include desks, fluorescent lighting, industrial fryers, and steam tables. Call around to your area colleges and universities to see if such a program exists.

Equipment is an area where you do not want to scrimp. Spend the money up front for quality items and avoid the hassle and expense of having to replace pieces only months later.

CHAPTER

PURCHASING

There are number of purposes for the food laws in the United States including: to monitor nutritional food used, to maintain and design proper procedures, to protect quality and quantity of basic foods, to keep producers, processors, and distributors honest and to offer informative and accurate labeling for consumers.

STEPS IN THE PROCUREMENT PROCESS

What are the steps in the food service procurement process? We will discuss each element in more detail, but this list will provide an overview.

ASSESSING YOUR NEEDS

- Determine menu items to be served.

- Use standardized recipes to guarantee consistent items.

- Use input from evaluation team.

- Gather input and feedback from your staff.

PROJECT SALES FIGURES

- What are the purchasing methods to be used?

- What is the size of the facility?

- What is your purchasing volume?

- How often do you need deliveries?

- Where are your potential vendors located?

- How much storage space is available?
- How many staff members do you have and what are their skills?

VENDOR LIST
- Who is your primary vendor?
- Who will supply other items your primary vendor does not offer?
- Determine and maintain your inventory system.
- Which items can be "just in time" items?
- Establish your perpetual inventory.
- Monitor your physical inventory.
- What is the dollar value of your inventory?
- How often will items be delivered?

ORDER QUANTITIES
- Project menu items and quantities.
- Determine standardized portions.
- Which supplies will be needed?
- What food items do you have in stock?

BIDS AND PRICES
- Establish food item specifications.
- Find best prices, quality, and service for each item.

PLACING ORDERS
- Price.
- Quantity.
- Method to pay.
- Submit orders to appropriate people and places.

RECEIVE FOOD AND SUPPLIES
- Receive the minimum number of orders.
- Verify delivery is accurate.
- Handle any returns or problems.

STORE ORDERS
- Store food using appropriate methods for each type of food.

ISSUE ITEMS

Let us start with purchasing and receiving. Purchasing is how food service managers obtain wholesome, safe ingredients for their menu items and the additional supplies needed for the operation of the restaurant. To satisfy your customers and offer a quality product, the items need to be available when needed. Quality depends on the standards in place. To maintain costs, these items need to be purchased at the lowest possible prices while still maintaining acceptable quality. Here are some considerations:

- **Vendors are responsible for the safety of their food.** You must choose vendors carefully.

- **Federal and state governments monitor your suppliers to see that they use the HAACP system** and train all employees in safe sanitation practices. HAACP will be discussed in full detail in Chapter 16.

- **Delivery Trucks**. Trucks used by vendors should have sufficient refrigeration and freezer capabilities. Food items should be packaged in leak proof, durable packaging. These quality standards should be stated in your purchase agreement with the vendor. You can also ask to see their most recent health and sanitation reports. Let the vendor know that you will inspect the cleanliness of their trucks periodically. It is much easier to make your position clear in the beginning instead of waiting until there are problems.

- **Delivery Schedule**. Quality vendors will work with you concerning deliveries and are usually willing to adjust their schedule around your busy times.

- **Inventory System**. You must have a good inventory system in place. I will discuss inventory procedures in Chapter 12 along with storage practices. The amount of food you need is based on sales history, sales projections, and your proposed menus. It is impossible to place an accurate and effective order before you inventory your items on hand. Have your menus in place before you make your order. A delivery "cushion" is important so that you do not run out of food and supplies before your next delivery. Over time and after reviewing the sales histories, you can determine a reasonable "cushion" without food expiring before it can be used. Any surplus will also tie up cash flow unnecessarily. After your purchasing is established, you can simply print a copy of your order list and fill in the blanks. Your order forms can include supplier names, prices, and unit sizes for each item, for example.

PURCHASING OR ORDERING?

Is there a difference between purchasing and ordering? Purchasing includes establishing policies to cover any possible measure or description of items being bought. After these parameters are determined, your individual orders will be simplified. The facility management negotiates terms and prices with the proposed distributors. Here are the basics of your purchasing program that need to be established:

- **Purchasing Program.** Your purchasing program includes what you will buy and which vendor you will use to provide the best quality for the best prices. To create an efficient purchasing program, you need standard purchase specifications based on your standardized recipes, standardized recipe yields, and portion controls. Each of these considerations will enable you to have accurate costs based on the portions served in the facility. The amounts you purchase need to be accurate. When you order too much, portioning suffers and you have excess spoilage, waste, and theft. Purchasing too little will raise your food costs as you may need to make costly substitutions.

- **Procedures.** Your procedures should include written specifications for each product that you buy from reliable and honest vendors.

Each of these elements is necessary to ensure a certain level of quality and standardization for your customers. A good purchasing program does these three things:

1. Allows you to acquire the items you need at the agreed upon prices.

2. Exercises control over your inventory and costs.

3. Determines procedures to guarantee the quality at the best prices.

You need to decide whether you will do the purchasing yourself or if it will be assigned to another team member. The prices must be kept up-to-date. Prices change frequently and you need the current prices to project and maintain food costs accurately.

It is a good idea to check prices with various vendors periodically. Some vendors will offer lower prices for a short time, but over time they are more expensive. If you find another vendor with lower prices, you can offer your current vendor a chance to give you an updated price quote.

ORDERING TIPS

It is impossible to place orders effectively until you understand the items in your inventory list. You need to be familiar with each item and inventory counts need to be established. Par levels and projected sales amounts need to be determined. It makes it much easier to compile an accurate order. You need to:

- Create a list of specific items needed.

- Create a vendor contact list.

- Add prices of items on your inventory list.

- Determine a simpler way to place your orders.

After you determine par levels, the Par Order Sheet or Par Amount Requisition may be helpful. It will enable you to identify quickly where your inventory is short and help you create an accurate food order. Or if you prefer to keep track of items more closely, the Daily Inventory Order Sheet and Miscellaneous Order Sheet may be more helpful. You can find examples of these forms at the end of this chapter.

Several things need to be kept in mind when you place orders. Consider each of these factors before you complete your order and inventory.

- **Inventory Amount.** Over-stocking means you have additional items to count and less control of the items in your inventory.

- **Perishables.** Meat, produce, and seafood have a shelf life of two or three days. Keep your orders tight when the shelf life is that short.

- **Tie Up Cash.** When you order too much, money is tied up.

- **Food Usage Controls.** It is human nature to serve greater portions when there is too much food available. It seems easier to control usage when you have less food available.

- **Turnover.** Your inventory should be turned over every five to eight days. There may be some unusual items that will not be used that quickly, but that time frame should work.

- **Vendors.** All managers need to meet with their vendor sales reps from time to time. Schedule these meetings for a time that suits you.

- **Standing Orders.** Many times you can place a "standing order," especially when your sales are consistent. There were times when I had a standing order and made slight adjustments to accommodate special events.

- **Primary Vendor.** You will save additional work if you can use one primary vendor for most of the items you purchase. You will have fewer interruptions, deliveries, orders to place, possibilities of mistakes, invoices to handle, and no sales representatives to bother you. Being a larger customer will help you receive better service.

- **Trade Magazines and Web sites.** You may find rebates from specific manufacturers. You can also check **www.foodbuy.com** for more information.

- **Food Buying Groups.** One of these groups can be found at **www.foodservice.com**. They offer you pre-negotiated prices on over 10,000 food and food related items from over 125 suppliers. Some of the familiar companies involved include: Ecolab, General Mills, Sara Lee, and Sweetheart.

- **Buying Clubs.** There are many warehouse buying clubs. Some of the most common include Sam's Club **www.samsclub.com**, Costco **www.costco.com**, and Restaurant Depot **www.restaurantdepot.com**.

- **Cash.** Many vendors offer a small discount for early payments usually made within ten days or by the tenth of the month. Two percent may not seem like much, but if you purchase $500,000 a year, you will save $10,000.

- **Fresh versus Canned.** Take a close look at your recipes and see whether you can use canned fruits and vegetables instead of fresh. If you can make the substitution, you will save money. Remember to remove the word "fresh" from your menu if you used canned items.

These forms are beneficial if you prepare your order manually. There are several choices to allow you to find the one that works best for your facility. Sample purchase orders can be found at the end of this chapter.

ESTABLISH SPECIFICATIONS

Creating purchasing specifications enables you to control the number and quality of items you purchase and to maintain consistency in the products you order. Consistency makes it easier when more than one person places orders.

PURCHASING SPECIFICATIONS

These indicate the amount and quality of the items you purchase. They include:

- Product name.

- Quantity to be ordered – establish unit size.

- "Brand" or "grade" of the item if applicable.

- Find what unit was used to establish prices.

Here is some of the additional information you need:

- **Meats must be inspected by the USDA or another agency.** The federal or state inspection stamp should be on the packaging.

- **Eggs are assigned a grade by the USDA.** If you use frozen or dried eggs, they should be pasteurized.

- **The FDA has a list of Certified Shellfish Shippers for all your shellfish orders.** The supplier must have control tags available for live shellfish.

- **Record everything.** Your record sheet needs to be available for your employees to ensure they are ordering the correct items. You can also maintain the correct costs by using a record sheet.

Some people refer to specifications as the "heart of purchasing." When they are written, keep them short and simple. Anyone who reads them needs to be able to understand them. There are three main types of specifications: internal, external, and general.

Internal menu specifications name the item, provide portion sizes, cooking instructions, a serving image or photo, handling information, and possibly cost information. These specs give employees all the information they need to prepare, cook, and serve a satisfactory menu item. Most importantly, they aid in maintaining control over the product.

External pertains to the menu items but includes vendor specifics, details that enable the vendor to give accurate quotes on the right products for your facility. It is a good idea to make a permanent record of these item specifications for your vendors. You need not repeat these details every time you place an order because they should be in the vendor's file for your facility. Should any of your specifications change give the vendor verbal or written notification.

General includes delivery and food specifications included in purchasing for your facility such as delivery times, delivery practices and procedures, billing and payment, price quotes, and food specifications – brand, quality, grade, and similar details. Here are some of the ways that specifications are beneficial:

- Costs are lower.

- Quality is better.

- You have a written record of your orders.

- You save time.

- Verification of orders is simplified.

- You have more control.

- You have more consistent customer satisfaction.

- There should be fewer stock-outs (running out of items between deliveries).

- Trained employees can make decisions about delivery problems.

- You can negotiate for competitive prices and services.

- Misunderstandings between you and your vendors are fewer.

- Purchasing is organized.

Usually managers write these specifications, but it does not hurt to get input from others in the facility. The specifications will have an impact on everyone in the department, so ask for their feedback. You never know where a valuable idea will originate.

Other non-commercial food service managers could offer some great insights into which specifications to use. It would be helpful to see their lists, but these should only be used as a guide. Do not just copy them. No two facilities have the same needs and you need to customize your list to provide the best specifications for your facility.

As you work on the specifications, write down any ideas that come to mind and go back later to fine tune them. Some businesses choose to have an outsider write their specifications, but if you do, be sure the person has sufficient knowledge of your operation to make the specifications as beneficial as possible. When an outside person or company writes your specifications, they should be reviewed by you or someone else in the facility before they are finalized.

I have included some sample specifications to give you an idea of the information which should be included at the end of this chapter.

EVALUATE AND CHOOSE YOUR VENDORS

Your suppliers can make or break you. When you have trustworthy, timely suppliers, you can run a smooth operation and satisfy your customers. To select a vendor, consider cost, delivery, problem handling, promptness, quality, selection of products, and other services particular to your facility. There are four basic types of suppliers:

1. Full line suppliers

2. Local specialty wholesaler

3. National jobber

4. Supermarkets

Let us look at the advantages of these types of suppliers to help you determine what kind of suppliers you need.

Full Line Suppliers are also called one-stop or diversified suppliers. They handle large inventories and usually supply everything you need. If you can find one supplier for most of your needs, ordering and receiving will be simplified. They may offer fresh vegetables and fruits, frozen food, meat, fish, poultry, paper supplies, equipment, and chemicals, for example. Such a wide selection can save you time, paperwork, and money because one large delivery instead of several smaller orders costs less for delivery.

Local Specialty Wholesalers are suppliers who carry a limited selection, but their prices are often lower. They may carry only limited selections, but if they carry what you need at a better price, you should consider them a potential supplier.

National Jobbers will be especially useful for large operations, such as the military, school districts, and other similar operations. Some of these only sell full lot amounts while others sell only broken lots.

Supermarkets are better suited for small operations or the occasions when you run out of food. A small operation might not be able to attract the attention of larger suppliers. In this case the non-commercial food service facility may have to work with local grocery stores. If you have this problem, offer to pick up your orders from a supplier if you have suitable transportation.

When you evaluate suppliers, look for these characteristics: quality service and products and the best price. Each of these elements is important and you should consider each one individually and then make a decision based on all three plus the fact that suppliers offer many services for their customers beyond their products.

When you talk to potential suppliers, one of their most important qualities is dependability, including the time they deliver your supplies and the kind of supplies they offer. When your supplier does not have a set delivery time or schedule you will have untold problems and potential dissatisfaction from your customers. Some delivery methods are easier for you to process.

One consideration is the delay between the time you place your order and the time it is delivered to your door. What is their policy on billing and returns? Do they have the ability to provide the supplies you need? Do they have friendly, knowledgeable sales representatives who can answer your questions and make helpful suggestions? Consider which supplier will form a positive long-term relationship with you.

CREDIT

Not all vendors are willing to extend credit to their accounts, especially new ones. Paying for merchandise later can be risky business for them; therefore, they will require the facility to complete a credit application before they decide whether to extend credit.

Facilities need to create and maintain a good credit rating. A better rating will help you obtain favorable credit terms for a better overall relationship with your suppliers. When you have a good credit record with the supplier, they are more likely to work with you when money is short and you need to make payment arrangements. Be friendly with the credit managers and keep them informed of any problems or situations that develop. A copy of the sample credit application can be found at the end of this chapter.

PRODUCT QUALITY

It is important to offer a quality product to increase customer satisfaction. When determining the quality and items needed, start by listing the choices of menu items to be prepared such as fresh tomato sauce versus fresh sliced tomatoes. Quality could vary between these two items. In short, you need the right ingredients to make the right menu product.

The rule of thumb is that you do not always go with the lowest price. Instead, consider the quality of the product and the menu item to be prepared, as well as the price. These three factors determine what to purchase.

RICE

First-time decision makers may emphasize price and end up spending more money but not getting the best results. When considering price, also consider how many hands these items pass through. When you buy from a retailer, they purchase from a wholesaler and they purchase from another supplier. By the time it gets to you, several separate businesses have been paid. Can you work with companies that cut out the middle man?

Some facilities have few vendors to choose from because of their location or they must get supplies from a central commissary. In these situations, look at the overall picture and not just the price.

There are some managers who like to visit the supplier's facility to see how they are set up and to inspect cleanliness and sanitation practices. It is a good idea to check whether their trucks are refrigerated and in good working condition. Some may offer service, quality, and good prices, but an unsanitary facility might eliminate them from consideration. After you have made a list of vendors, you can use a Vendor Evaluation Form to determine which will be the best for your facility. This form is shown at the end of this chapter.

DEALING WITH SUPPLIERS

The way you deal with suppliers can make a big difference in your job. You want to establish and maintain a good relationship with vendors and sales representatives. Here are some tips:

- **Take the time to get to know the delivery driver and the person who takes your order.** Do not take this person for granted as he plays an important role in your success. It is also good to ask for the same person each time to help you establish a good working relationship.

- **Sometimes the vendor may have an overstocked item**. You can help them liquidate the inventory and negotiate a good price for your facility.

- **If you use the same items each week, the vendor might give you a small discount.**

- **Does your vendor have a Web site?** It can save you time and some sites even provide industry information that might be helpful. An example would be: **www.sysco.com**.

- **Keep an eye on prices.** Do you take time each month to check on prices with other vendors? When you find someone offering your items at a lower price, you can try to negotiate lower prices with your vendor.

THE CHANGING FACE OF DISTRIBUTORS

Distributors are expanding the products and services they offer to food service facilities. At one time they offered only food products, but now offer supplies and equipment, including recycled packaging for the good of the environment. Their additional services may include:

- Computerized services for clients.

- Information about new products, such as nutrition and food costs.

- Instruction, development, merchandising, and marketing services.

- Consultation services regarding design, layout, and equipment.

- Coordinating recycling efforts.

- Discounts for early invoice payment.

- Quantity purchasing discounts.

- Coupons and rebates for their customers.

These are some of the ways today's food service distributors strive to earn your business. Does your sales representative offer these services to you? Today the sales representative must be a consultant, problem solver — not just an order taker. They must offer additional information about products, packaging, economics, marketing suggestions, inventory control, product, and supply availability along with promotional and recipe ideas for your facility. Efficient sales representatives should have thorough and accurate knowledge of your needs and the product lines they represent. These company representatives can be valuable to a food service manager.

BUYER RESPONSIBILITIES

A buyer's responsibilities in non-commercial food service depend on the size of the facility. While large facilities may have a person dedicated to handling all buying, smaller facilities generally delegate this responsibility to the manager. The food buyer's responsibilities include:

- Evaluating and determining product equipment and service needs.

- Developing or selecting purchasing methods to be used.

- Evaluating and choosing vendors.

- Participating in awarding bids for contracts to vendors.

- Placing orders and following up with vendors or sales representatives.

- Fully training and supervising any staff members involved in receiving, storing, and issuing food and supplies.

- Establishing and maintaining proper, effective inventory control.

- Researching and evaluating new products.

- Establishing and maintaining effective relations with food vendors.

- Weighing cost-benefits of additional services offered by distributors.

- Researching and providing product information including cost and nutritional data in the department.

- Offering ways to track changes in the food market and economic conditions, attending trade and food shows, and staying abreast of trends by reading trade and professional magazines and publications.

- Learning to use technical advances to facilitate food procurement.

- Encouraging and demonstrating ways to keep communication lines open in the department and with others in the institution or facility.

Buyers who submit items for bids will find these forms helpful. They include the Bid Order Sheet and Bid Sheet to help you keep the specifics for each vendor organized to make an accurate decision.

STEPS IN THE BIDDING PROCESS

1. **New Products.** Identify any new products needed. All new product sales visits should be handled by the person or department who handles purchasing.

2. **Specifications.** Be specific about the amount, size, quantity, and quality that you need. Include all of the necessary information in your specifications.

3. **Usage Levels.** How much of each item will you need? It is critical when negotiating prices. Do not inflate your numbers, but give all details.

4. **Vendor List.** The food service manager and purchasing person need to compile a list of vendors who will be asked to place a bid.

5. **Bid Documentation and Distribution.** This documentation needs to be distributed in packets to all vendors who will bid. Include instructions, the deadline, and criteria to be used to award the bid and how questions will be handled. Include instructions about whom to contact and how questions should be submitted (in writing, by fax, or e-mail).

6. **Receiving Completed Bids.** Only the purchasing person or department should receive bids. Make that clear on the bid instructions.

7. **Analysis of Bids.** First, determine which bidders followed instructions. Eliminate any that did not. All suggested substitutions must be evaluated to determine if they are appropriate or if they should be approved. If items are not acceptable, the bidder must be eliminated.

8. **Awarding the Bids.** Purchasing recommends the winning bidder, but food service must review the recommendations. Objections and concerns need to be reviewed and handled. The actual decision to award the bid is handled by the administrators who sign contracts.

9. **Notify Vendors.** Purchasing is responsible for notifying winners and losers. Food service staff members are not to answer questions about the decisions that were made. Purchasing handles all inquiries.

10. **Verify Pricing.** Food service verifies that the items being delivered are in compliance with the bid details and needs to notify purchasing when there are discrepancies. Purchasing will take action on this information.

11. **Contract Dissolution.** If the vendor is unable or unwilling to provide items in compliance with the winning bid, the contract may be dissolved. The final decision is made by administration based on recommendations from the purchasing, food service, and legal departments.

BUYER QUALIFICATIONS

Buyer qualifications include food quality, background, product specifications, computer skills, marketing and distribution experience, accounting, business management, purchasing experience, soliciting and awarding bids, and contracts. A good buyer will also have personal attributes that serve him well in the non-commercial food service industry. An organized mind that pays attention to detail and accuracy is a must. New buyers and leaders who have a team mind set along with initiatives and good communication skills can be valuable in food service.

Good buyers keep an eye open at all times for ways to improve the department. This requires initiative and creativity along with the ability to develop and execute responsibilities. An effective manager must control costs while maintaining other food service responsibilities.

Each of these abilities enables the manager and buyer to control costs and eliminate waste. Keep in mind that you should always be on the watch for better products, equipment, and ways to provide better services for your customers while working within the financial constraints of the facility.

ALTERNATIVE PURCHASING SYSTEMS

If no one in the food service facility has the experience to handle purchasing, you may want to use an "indirect purchasing program." There are three main types of indirect purchasing programs:

1. **Programs that guarantee pricing, specific products, brands, and grades.** Delivery, payment arrangements, and problems are handled by the institution. Some purchasing departments handle negotiations and most purchasing for every department in the institution.

2. **Programs with guaranteed pricing and some management service** to include educational services, additional product knowledge, workshops and training for managers, marketing ideas, and assistance.

3. **Some other programs offer services for the manager, but no guaranteed prices.**

Would one of these services work for your facility? Determining which program would be most beneficial depends on the qualifications your staff members have and what additional services are needed. Each of these programs will cost the institution so you must decide whether the savings outweigh the costs incurred. If not, you can obtain additional training for personnel or hire someone with the proper skills.

PURCHASING KICKBACKS AND GIFTS

Some areas of the food service industry are well known for kickbacks. One of the downsides is that people who are not involved end up paying for these kickbacks with higher prices. Below are a few tips to keep kickbacks out of your facility.

- **Purchasing and receiving should be handled by two different people** to keep both people honest. One person places the order and another verifies that correct supplies were received.

- **Have a standard policy in your employee handbook stating that no employee can receive a kickback from a vendor** or a potential vendor. Also state the action to be taken if someone does receive a kickback.

- **You may need to have employees change jobs from time to time.** If you notice problems, job-changing can be a simple way to keep people honest.

- **Verify prices for expensive items yourself.** Anything out of the ordinary can be checked for your peace of mind. It does not hurt to let your team members know that you double check invoices and their work. They are accountable to do their jobs, and you are responsible for the facility.

BRANDS AND QUALITY

Well-known brands have first, second, and third quality products identified on their labels.

- **First quality.** Grade A for canned and frozen vegetables and frozen fruits; Grade B for canned fruits except when Grade B fruits are packaged with a conditional quality label.

- **Frosty Acres French Fries.** Package color indicates length of potato. Red = extra long, Brown = long, Blue = various lengths.

- **North American Buying Group.** Their "house" brand uses different colors and codes although they use the same quality standards.

- **Sysco.** The labeling system has been changed. Supreme Gold = rare items; Imperial Blue = fancy vegetables and choice fruits from prime growing areas; Classic Green = fancy vegetables and choice fruits from non-prime growing areas.

- **NIFDA.** Prime Pak = fancy vegetables and choice fruits from prime growing regions; Royal Pak = fancy vegetables and choice fruits from any region; Dandy Pak = fancy vegetables and choice fruits that meet the USDA standards.

Purchasing is a critical element in any food service organization. Once the food and supplies are ordered, you need an effective, thorough receiving procedure.

PAR ORDER SHEET

FOOD CATEGORY:		PURVEYOR:				
ITEM & DESCRIPTION	LOW-LEVEL PAR	DELIVERY DATES				

PAR AMOUNT REQUISITION

Date: _____   Req. #: _____

Time: _____   Department: _____

Prepared By: _____   Priced By: _____

Delivered By: _____   Received By: _____

Approved By: _____

Item Description	Par	On Hand	Order	Price	Extension
				Total $	

DAILY INVENTORY ORDER SHEET

VENDOR	ITEM	UNIT	Sunday			Monday			Tuesday			Wednesday			Thursday			Friday			Saturday		
			PAR	INV	BUY	PAR	INV	BUY	PAR	INV	BUY	PAR	INV	BUY	PAR	INV	BUY	PAR	INV	BUY	PAR	INV	BUY

WEEK OF:

PREPARED BY:

MISCELLANEOUS ORDER SHEET

DELIVERY DATE:	PURVEYOR:	
PRODUCT #	ORDER	ITEM & DESCRIPTION

PURCHASE ORDER

Company A:		PURCHASE ORDER #	
Company B:		Order Date:	
Company C:		Delivery Date:	

ITEM	QTY	COMPARE QUOTES			ITEM COST	ITEM TOTAL
		VENDOR A	VENDOR B	VENDOR C		

SPECIAL INSTRUCTIONS:		
	SUBTOTAL:	
	SHIPPING:	
	TAX:	
	TOTAL:	

NAME:	SIGNATURE OF AUTHORIZATION:

PURCHASE ORDER II

Vendor name:_____

Contact/Representative:_____

Address:_____

_____

_____

Phone:_____

Fax:_____

Required delivery date:_____

Ordered by:_____

Order date:_____

Ship to:_____

_____

_____

Delivery instructions:_____

_____

_____

ITEM PURCHASED	SPEC #	QTY ORDERED	QUOTED PRICE	EXT PRICE
			TOTAL $	

PURCHASE SPECIFICATION FORMAT

Product Name	
Product Use	Indicate product use clearly (such as pickle for garnish, chicken breast for deep-frying for fried chicken sandwich, etc.)
Product General Description	Provide general quality information about desired product. For example, pickle spears; to be juicy, firm, fresh, and crisp, not broken or spoiled. No more than 20 per jar; packed 10 jars per case.
Detailed Description	Purchaser should state additional factors that clearly identify the desired product. Examples of specific factors, which will vary, include: • Geographic origin • Grade • Size • Type • Density • Medium of pack • Style • Specific gravity • Brand Name • Variety • Container Size • Edible yield, trim • Portion size
Product Test Procedures	Test procedures occur when the product is received and as or after the product is prepared and used. For example, products to be at a specific temperature when delivered can be tested with a thermometer. Portion-cut chicken patties can be weighed. Pickles packed 10 jars per case can be counted.
Special Instructions and Requirements	Any other information needed to better indicate quality expectations can be added here. Examples include bidding procedures, if applicable, labeling and/or packaging requirements, and delivery and service requirements.
	Specification factors can include:
Meats	• Inspection (mandatory) • Fat limitations • Grading (if desired) • State of refrigeration • IMPS/MBG descriptions • Miscellaneous (tying, • Weight/thickness limitations boning, packaging, etc.)

Seafoods	• Type (fin fish or shellfish) • Quality requirements
	• Market form (whole, describe flesh, eyes, skin
	  eviscerated, etc.—fin fish; gills, etc.)
	  alive, whole, shucked, etc.— • Grade (if desired)
	  shellfish) • Inspection (voluntary)
	  • Processing requirements

Poultry	• Kind (chicken, turkey, • Style (whole, breasts, duck, goose) breasts w/ribs, etc.) • Class (typed by age) • Size (weight limitations) • Grading • State of refrigeration • Inspection (mandatory) • Grade (if desired)
Fresh Fruits and Vegetables	• Grade (if desired) • Type of pack • Variety • Count per container • Size • Growing area
Processed Fruits and Vegetables	• Grade (if desired) • Packing medium • Drained weight • Can (container) size

SAMPLE—CREDIT APPLICATION

Account No._____ Sales Representative _____ Terms Requested_____

Tax Certificate No._____

Ship To.   Bill To.

Corporate Name   Corporate Name
_____   _____

(dba) Trade Name   (dba) Trade Name
_____   _____

Address   Address
_____   _____

City, State, Zip   Phone   City, State, Zip   Phone

❑ Proprietorship   Length of time at present location_____years.

❑ Corporation   Contact:

❑ Partnership   _____   _____
                      Name   Title

Does operator own premises? ❑ Yes ❑ No   List any existing accounts under another name:
Name, Address and Phone No.   _____
   of Mortgagor:
_____   Name
_____   _____
_____   Account No.

If Leasing: Name and Address
   of Lessor:
_____   Is your Company responsible for purchases?_____
_____   Or is food service consigned to another?_____
_____   Name of food service consignees:
                                                _____

Bank Information

Bank Name
_____

Address
_____

City, State, Zip
_____

Account No
_____

List all corporate officers, partners, or an individual proprietor.

Name and Title   Name and Title
_____   _____

Home Address   Home Address
_____   _____

City, State, Zip   Phone   City, State, Zip   Phone
_____   _____

Social Security No.   Social Security No.
_____   _____

Name and Title   Name and Title
_____   _____

Home Address   Home Address
_____   _____

City, State, Zip   Phone   City, State, Zip   Phone
_____   _____

Social Security No.   Social Security No.

BID SHEET

Ordered By: _____ **Date:** _____

ITEM	QUANTITY	VENDORS (fill in names below)		

BID ORDER SHEET

Ordered By: _____

Date Ordered: _____   Delivery Date: _____

Vendors A: _____

Vendors B: _____

Vendors C: _____

ITEM	Quantity	Vendor A		Vendor B		Vendor C	
		Unit	Total	Unit	Total	Unit	Total
Individual Invoice Total:							

VENDOR EVALUATION FORM

Vendor:_____ Date:_____

Rate Scale: Excellent = 2, Satisfactory = 1, Poor = 0

Criterion		Rate Score
Product	Quality	
	Consistency	
	Price	
	Availability	
Service	Timely delivery	
	Delivery frequency	
	Condition of product upon delivery	
	Delivery accuracy	
	Complaint handling	
	Delivery personnel courtesy	
	Emergency deliveries	
Company	Size	
	Product selection	
	Financial stability	
	Location	
	Service orientation	
	Management policies	
	Invoicing accuracy	
	Credits/invoice adjustments handled in timely manner	
Sales Personnel	Knowledge of company policies and procedures	
	Product line knowledge	
	Interest in needs of operation	
	Willingness to provide information about products	
	Price quotes provided in an accurate and timely manner	
	Makes sales calls as frequently as needed by operation	
	Schedules sales calls	
	Complaints handled promptly	
	Total	

CHAPTER

INVENTORY, RECEIVING, AND STORAGE

RECEIVING

Receiving means checking your purchases to ensure the correct items have been sent. This task can be performed by the manager or delegated to a staff member. Even if you have a competent and well-trained staff member to receive your items, a supervisor needs to oversee the task because of quality and financial control issues. Also be aware that fewer deliveries help to control labor costs. The next page has a simple flow chart showing how the receiving process works.

Specific information must be checked when items are received into your inventory. Receipt practices should be kept simple while still maintaining complete records and accountability for your vendors. Basic equipment needs to be close at hand when deliveries are received, including scales, thermometers, dollies, conveyor belts, lift trucks or pallet jacks, and a laser gun scanner if you scan your PC labels.

Do you have a designated receiving clerk for your facility? When designating your receiving person, it is best to have another person serve as the storage and receiving clerk. It is helpful to have double checks in these areas and to involve different people in various stages of the process. For optimum benefit, your receiving person should not move items to storage but only verify the items, quantities, quality, and that the proper items were ordered and received.

Your receiving person should be intelligent, alert, and capable of checking the quantity and quality by doing necessary calculations and compiling reports. The person must understand the importance of doing the job properly. The receiver also needs to handle deliveries quickly while maintaining control over each step of the process. The delivery driver is on a tight schedule and delays in receiving can cause problems for the driver and your vendor.

There are a wide variety of receiving checklists and reports that are helpful for your receiving person. You can find a Receiving Checklist and Receiving Report at the end of this chapter.

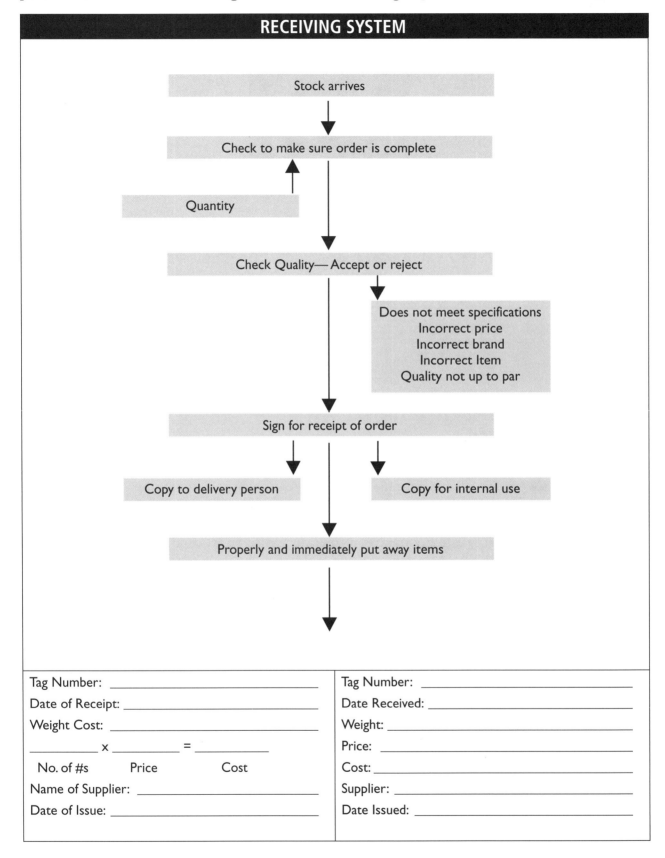

RECEIVING SYSTEM

Stock arrives

↓

Check to make sure order is complete

Quantity

↓

Check Quality—Accept or reject

Does not meet specifications
Incorrect price
Incorrect brand
Incorrect Item
Quality not up to par

↓

Sign for receipt of order

Copy to delivery person   Copy for internal use

↓

Properly and immediately put away items

Tag Number: _____

Date of Receipt: _____

Weight Cost: _____

_____ x _____ = _____
No. of #s   Price   Cost

Name of Supplier: _____

Date of Issue: _____

Tag Number: _____

Date Received: _____

Weight: _____

Price: _____

Cost: _____

Supplier: _____

Date Issued: _____

EFFECTIVE RECEIVING

As soon as the items are received, they need to be transferred to the proper storage facilities. There are three important elements of receiving: preparing to receive your order, inspecting the food when it arrives, and then verifying that you received everything you ordered. Your receiving person needs to be sure you are not being overcharged and that you are getting consistent quality. Here are some tips:

- **Your bookkeeper should never pay for an invoice not signed by an employee.** If no one feels confident signing for the delivery, you should not pay the bill. The bookkeeper should watch for unsigned invoices each day, giving you a chance to question on-duty staff members while the details are still fresh in their minds.

- **All employees need to understand they are responsible for any items on that invoice once they sign the paperwork.** If you discover a shortage in any of the delivered items, the employee who signed the invoice must explain the discrepancy.

- **Put the items away at once.** The longer the items are left out, the greater the chance of losing something or having it spoil. Try to schedule deliveries at a time when employees are available to receive the order and move it into storage.

- **The delivery person must sign for any missing or damaged items before he or she leaves your facility.** You will find it much harder to get credit if you contact someone later. Handle these problems immediately.

RECEIVING AND STORING SUPPLIES

Usually your deliveries will arrive at times that you have designated, between lunch and dinner. The manager should be responsible for receiving and storing your orders. When another person places the order, they should verify the right items were delivered.

Proper receiving and storage are critical. Anyone involved with these practices must be thoroughly trained because mistakes can be costly. These are the steps to process your orders:

1. Double check the delivery against the original order sheet.

2. Verify the quantity that was received.

3. Check the invoice to be sure the order you placed matches the items you received.

4. Verify the prices, totals, date, company name, and signatures on the invoice.

5. Weigh any items to confirm your order is correct.

6. When food items are received, date the containers, put the new items in back of older items, and store in the correct place right away.

7. Mark any discrepancies on the invoice. Call or fax to inform the vendor immediately of any overage or shortage. If the order was COD (cash on delivery), you need to take into account mistakes in your order before paying.

Many facilities have a box in the kitchen where all invoices and packing slips are placed during the day. At the end of the shift these are taken to the manager's office and filed in the designated place. Remember that any missing or incomplete invoices will make the bookkeeper's job difficult.

You can implement a receiving policy. It is easy to misplace products in the facility if no one is assigned to check in the orders. Sometimes, when someone moves things aside, the items cannot be located later to check the order.

ECEIVING TIPS

Here are important guidelines to follow as you prepare to receive your order.

- **Calibrate your scales and thermometers and store them in the right places.** Large scales should be near your delivery entrance. Smaller scales are placed in the work areas. Each cold or heated storage area should have thermometers. A large walk-in freezer should have more than one thermometer to ensure consistent temperatures.

- **Any carts you use to move food items should be sanitary.**

- **Clear sufficient storage area in the refrigerator and freezer** before the order arrives.

- **All items need to be dated when they are received.**

- **The receiving and delivery area should be clean and well lighted.**

- **As the order is moved to storage facilities, clear all empty containers and dispose of trash** as soon as possible.

- **The floor needs to be cleared of food particles and debris.**

- **Make it clear to the delivery personnel that you will verify your order before she leaves your facility.**

- **Do a quick inspection of the delivery truck when it arrives.** If you see conditions that concern you, take time to look closer.

- **Check the food immediately.**

- **Verify expiration dates for all perishable items.**

- **All frozen foods must be in airtight, moisture-proof containers.**

- **Any thawed or refrozen foods must be rejected.** Signs to look for are large crystals, solid areas of ice, or excessive ice on or in containers.

- **Any swollen cans or cans that have flawed seals and seams, dents, or rust should be rejected** right away.

- **Verify the temperature of any refrigerated or frozen foods – especially critical with eggs,** dairy products, fresh meat, fish, and poultry.

- **Keep your eyes open for damage or pest infestations.**

- **All dairy products delivered in dirty flats or crates need to be rejected.**

- **Meat, fish, and items shipped by the pound need to be weighed and marked.** Ensure all items are counted, weighed, and date stamped. This is not a suggestion; it is a necessity. Do not skip this step.

- **Double check your invoice for accuracy, including price, damage, brands, grades, quality, and quantity.** When items are incorrect, you need to make a notation and return these items to the driver. It is important that the driver sign the invoice to reflect any returns or corrections.

- **Delivery people should not enter storage areas.**

- **Remove any frozen items from ice before weighing them.**

- **Check fish and poultry for ice.**

- **Items can be placed on the shelves in the order they are inventoried, making inventory easier.**

- **Not all employees need access to your storage areas.**

- **Clear trash bags can be used as a way to discourage theft.**

- **The delivery entrance should be locked and well lighted.** It is also good to have an alarm on that door. A small peep hole is advisable to allow the employee who is receiving your delivery to verify who is outside before opening the door.

- **Keep storage specifications in a handy place for your employees.**

- **Note correct storage temperatures in convenient places.**

- **Are your staff members trained in your stock rotation policies?**

- **Any items that have questionable expiration dates should be refused or sent back on the truck.**

- **Calibrate your scales regularly to make sure they are accurate.** This should be done once a week and more often if needed.

- **Are your scales adequate to weigh the items being shipped?** If not, you should consider buying bigger scales. You can visit Scale World at **www.scaleworld.com** or Scale Man at **www.scaleman.com**.

Invoices are also an important part of the receiving process. The invoice will include:

- Company name and address
- Quantity to be delivered
- Quality of product to be delivered
- Price of each item
- Total price of each item shipped
- Total for each invoice

Your invoice is a written confirmation of what was ordered and shipped. The person who receives the order is responsible for confirming that your facility actually received all items listed on your invoice. The documentation should also show any back order, out of stock, or cancelled items. These items should be noted on the invoice and any discrepancies in your order should be mentioned to the driver immediately. The receiving person and driver should both sign and acknowledge any problems with the order. You can also use a discrepancy report or slip that may also be called the credit memo or a credit slip. Include all information identifying the problems in your deliveries. Your facility may also use a variety of general receiving reports. When you discover shortages on your order, complete a credit memo. Examples are the end of this chapter.

RECEIVING PROCEDURES

All your orders may not be received the same way. Here are some examples of different ways to receive products. The method that is right for someone else might not be right for your facility. You can gather thoughts from other restaurant managers, but make your decision based on the needs of your facility and staff.

Certified or Accepted Buying – Government agencies, large companies, or public schools may use certified or accepted buying. With this method, items are certified by an outside agent to guarantee quality and quantity. With accepted buying, federal inspectors have copies of your buying specifications and verify these requirements are met. After items are inspected, packages will be sealed and stamped to indicate approval. Below is an example of one of these stamps. Keep in mind there is a cost involved for these inspections to be paid by either the buyer or the seller. You need to know these details before deciding to use this method.

Blind Receiving – Some invoices are printed with the prices and quantity on black areas so they cannot be read by the receiver. With these invoices, each item must be checked for count, weight, or other measuring unit. These amounts are recorded on the invoice and receiving sheet. Prices are blanked out to keep them confidential.

No Inspection – In some situations the buyer and seller may agree not to inspect the quality or quantity when items are delivered. With this method the items are delivered, the invoices are signed, and the driver leaves. This method is normally used only when there is strong trust between the buyer and seller. It is advantageous to the seller and expedites faster delivery service. It could also be beneficial to the buyer since the items can be inspected later in a more accurate manner. However, when this method is used the seller agrees to accept any problems the buyer finds without question.

Night Drop Deliveries – Some vendors find it necessary to have their delivery trucks arrive during hours when your facility is not open. Night deliveries can be done quickly with less traffic on the roads, reducing labor costs. In this instance the delivery person may have a key to get into your facility and will leave the items. Obviously, this method requires strong trust between the vendor and the facility. When deliveries are made overnight or after hours, they are received and verified the following morning. Night deliveries require that refrigerated or frozen items be left in your freezer. Whenever this delivery is done, it is a good idea to arrive early to verify the delivery before starting the day's task.

Back Orders – Your invoice may indicate that an item is no longer available or is back ordered. These discrepancies need to be noted on the invoice which is attached to discrepancy reports to ensure proper credit for missing items.

After reports are properly received, the delivery area needs to be cleaned. In some instances the receiving area may need to be hosed down or swept. All delivery debris and trash should be disposed of. Each invoice should be placed in the assigned area of the kitchen or taken to the accounting office after all notations are complete.

FOOD STORAGE

There are several goals when storing food. These include maintaining safety and responsibility for the quality of the product. Any food or supply items in storage should be removed by authorized personnel. Securely organizing storage can discourage employee theft. When you enact controls over items, an effective manager can quickly detect theft.

I have already discussed how purchasing is affected by your inventory. The methods used to store your products have a bearing on your inventory practices and effectiveness. A disorganized storage area can make an accurate inventory nearly impossible. The other factor is maintaining the quality of your products while they are in storage.

TYPES OF STORAGE

There are four ways to store food safely. Dry storage is used for holding less perishable items liked canned goods. Refrigeration is short-term storage for perishable items like eggs, cheese, and milk. Deep chilling is for short-term storage. Freezers are used for long-term storage of perishable foods. There are specific safety and sanitation requirements for each type of storage.

DRY STORAGE

Many items can be stored in a sanitary storeroom. Dry storage areas must be kept clean and pest-free to avoid sanitary and safety concerns. Some of the items you can store there include baking supplies (salt, sugar, flour), canned goods, and grain items (rice or cereal).

Some fruits should be ripened at room temperature such as bananas, pears, and avocados. Vegetables such as onions, potatoes, and tomatoes should be stored in a dry place that is kept clean and organized. Ventilation, temperature, and humidity control are important in limiting mold and bacteria. Here are some tips to remember:

- **Chemical Contamination.** Cleaning supplies and chemicals should be stored in a separate room from food to avoid accidental contamination. Store all chemicals in a safe container that is labeled to avoid confusion.

- **Common storage.** This area is set aside for flour, sugar, canned items, shortening, and oils.

- **First In, First Out.** A simple way to ensure the freshness of your products is to use the first in, first out method. In an earlier chapter I discussed dating each product when it is received.

- **High Temperatures.** If the temperature in your storage area reaches 100 degrees Fahrenheit, the storage life of these items is cut in half.

- **Pest Control.** When you clean up all messes promptly, you can avoid pest infestations and contamination.

- **Raised Storage.** Supplies should never be stored on the floor including paper products. Your bottom shelf needs to be at least six inches off the floor.

- **Temperature.** Maximum shelf life requires 50 degrees Fahrenheit, but 60 to 70 degrees Fahreneheit is sufficient for most items.

- **Thermometers.** A wall thermometer will help you check the temperature to ensure the safest conditions. Atlantic Publishing at **www.atlantic-pub.com** offers a ThermaTwin Thermometer (Item TTT-03) and the Hanging Thermometer for your refrigerator or freezer (Item HTM-04).

REFRIGERATED STORAGE

Commercial refrigerators and walk-in units are usually equipped with mounted or built-in thermometers to let you see the interior temperature from outside the unit. Never trust just one thermometer. Keep at least one free standing thermometer inside the unit and two in a larger unit. If you have more than one, they need to be placed in different areas of the refrigerator to assure you that the unit is working properly and that the food is kept at the right temperature. Record the temperature each day on a chart kept on the outside of the unit. Keep in mind:

- **Circulation.** Keep a reasonable space between items in your refrigeration unit to allow air to circulate and keep foods uniformly cool.

- **Colder the better.** Cooler temperatures will slow bacterial growth.

- **Containers.** All containers need to be clean, non-absorbent, and covered.

- **Cross contamination.** Raw foods need to be separated from cooked and prepared foods.

- **Dates.** All items need to be dated and sealed properly.

- **Dairy products.** These foods must be stored away from food with strong odors such as onions, cabbage, and seafood.

- **Fresh items**. Fresh meat, poultry, dairy products, seafood, fruits and vegetables, and hot leftovers need to be stored below 40 degrees Fahrenheit.

- **Fresh fruits and vegetables.** Fresh vegetables should not be packed when they are put in storage. They need oxygen or they will turn dark and rot. Humidity around 75 to 85 percent is recommended to prevent dehydration. Some facilities moisten the items with a hose to keep them cool and moist. Be careful with this practice because some vegetables get too wet and rot. There is also the concern about a wet, slippery floor. It is a good practice to keep a close eye on fresh fruits and especially berries since they last only a few days.

- **Perishable items.** Perishable items must be kept below 40 degrees Fahrenheit to prevent food-borne illnesses. It is also important to remember that opening and closing the refrigerator door often can change your temperature so these items should be stored inside away from the door.

- **Raw Meats.** Fluids from raw meat, fish, and poultry must not touch other foods.

- **Ready to Eat.** Store these items above raw foods – never below.

- **Root Cellar Storage.** Some root vegetables can be stored in humidity below 60 to 70 percent. Items like potatoes need to be kept below 60 degrees Fahrenheit. Circulation is important for these items also, but sacks of potatoes can be stacked.

- **Shelves.** Refrigeration units need open slotted shelves to allow cool circulation around the food. Shelves should not be lined with foil or paper.

- **Stock Tags.** Fresh shellfish will arrive with a stocking tag. Keep this information on file for at least 90 days.

U.S. Cooler manufactures premium walk-in coolers, freezers, and combination units that are available at competitive prices. They are used for all types of cold storage. They also offer separate shelving, great for your walk-in freezer or storage room. Many accessories are available. For more information, visit **www.uscooler.com** or call 800-521-2665.

REQUIRED REFRIGERATOR SPACE

Your refrigerator space can be loosely determined by the number of meals you serve each day not counting beverages or frozen food.

MEALS SERVED DAILY AND CAPACITY	
Meals Served Daily	Recommended Capacity
75-150	20 Cubic Feet
150-250	45 Cubic Feet
250-350	60 Cubic Feet
350-500	90 Cubic Feet

If you will be serving more than 350 meals a day, it would be best to have a walk-in cooler. It is also advisable to have a reach-in refrigerator for small, frequently used items. Note that these capacity suggestions are minimums.

EEP CHILLING

Temperatures between 26 and 32 degrees Fahrenheit are considered deep chilling. These temperatures decrease bacterial growth and extend shelf life of some fresh foods, such as meat, poultry, seafood, and other protein products. Lower temperatures will not compromise their quality. You can use a special unit or lower your refrigerator temperature for this storage.

FROZEN STORAGE

Frozen meat, poultry, seafood, fruits, vegetables, and certain dairy items (ice cream) should be stored at 0 degrees Fahrenheit. The lower temperature will keep items fresher and maintain flavor and texture for a longer period. It is best to store foods to be frozen as soon as they arrive. Freezing perishable foods that have been refrigerated can diminish their quality.

Frozen foods should be put in the freezer immediately upon arrival at your facility. They can only be stored in a freezer for a limited time. When left in the freezer for too long, the chance of contamination and spoilage increases. When you store food in a freezer, you need to allow room for air to circulate around it. Follow these tips:

- **Cold Loss.** Freezer doors should be opened only when necessary; otherwise, the temperature will drop. A "cold curtain" seems like a nuisance, but it will help keep the temperature colder.

- **Moisture-Proof Containers.** Frozen foods need to be stored in moisture-proof containers to keep food from losing flavor and color and to avoid their drying out and absorbing odors from nearby foods.

- **Monitor Temperature.** Record the temperature each day and use more than one thermometer for a large freezer.

- **Frozen Food Storage Periods.** Here is the criteria for the length of time that some items can be frozen:

FOOD STORAGE LIFE	
Sausage, ground meat, and fish	1 – 3 months
Fresh pork (not ground)	3 – 6 months
Lamb and veal	6 – 9 months
Beef, poultry, and eggs	6 – 12 months
Fruits and vegetables	One growing season to the next

For a comprehensive list of frozen storage life and semi-perishable foods, see the following list.

FROZEN STORAGE LIFE	
Beef	Lasts the best
Cured or Smoked Meats	1-3 months
Ground Meat	3 months
Lamb	Lasts the best
Pork	Not as well, fat becomes rancid
Veal	Lasts well

LEANING PRODUCTS

Government requirements state that cleaning items and any hazardous materials must be stored separately from food items. Hazardous materials include poisons, pesticides, bleach, and strong chemicals. You may choose to store these items in a locked cabinet or in a separate section of your storeroom.

All chemicals need to be labeled properly. When a chemical is removed from its original container it must have a label and be stored in an appropriate container. Glass is usually your best option as many chemicals will eat through plastic. The label should include the chemical name and any mixing instructions, along with safety and emergency information. You may choose a storage area with hot and cold running water to mix the chemicals or for easy clean up.

ORGANIZE YOUR STORAGE AREAS

Each storage area needs to be organized with a place for each item. All items used often should be placed near the door. The door should be locked. You may consider having a separate unit to store more expensive items like cooking wine or exotic mushrooms, for example.

- **Aisles.** Each aisle in your storage areas needs to allow easy access to the items.

- **Five Gallon Bucket.** Dry goods like flour and sugar may be shipped in five-gallon buckets – wonderful storage containers that can be reused as they are designed for the best possible food protection. When they are empty, clean and re-label them, avoiding scraping the inside as bacteria will collect in the nicks.

- **Ice.** Some containers are specially designed for ice to avoid the risk of cross contamination if you are not careful. Saf-T-Ice Totes are a great way to handle this safety concern. They offer a stainless steel bucket that makes carrying and emptying easy. They meet Health Department standards and they can be cleaned in the dishwasher. Saf-T-Ice Totes (Item #SI-6000, $79.95 for two) are available from Atlantic Publishing at **www.atlantic-pub.com** or call 800-814-1132.

SAF-T-ICE Totes

- **Labels.** Each shelf should be labeled, making identification easier.

- **Shelving.** The best shelving units give you the option of adjusting the shelf height to save wasted space and make it simpler to find items you need.

- **Space.** Leave enough space for the quantity of the item that you plan to stock.

- **Stacking .** If you stack containers on top of each other, spills, breakage, and accidents are more likely. When you must stack containers, stack them in a way to make them easier to handle.

STORAGE SPOILAGE PREVENTION

Thorough records of all food spoilage are a must and should include date of spoilage, item description, and the reason for disposing of it. Make a note about whether too much was ordered or if there were equipment, cooling, or other storage problems. The information makes inventory adjustments easier.

At the correct temperatures, spices and sauces can be stored for a long time. Keep in mind the ingredients are in these sauces. If there is an ingredient that spoils easily, you can divide the sauces into small containers and freeze. When you need to use the items, defrost and serve.

Color codes, labels, and dates need to be on all food items. The first in, first out practice will ensure you use the older food before the newer food. This practice alone will help minimize waste from spoilage. Noting the arrival date will help employees know how long the item has been in storage. Water-dissolvable labels are the best option. Daymark Safety Systems offers a variety of biodegradable labels that dissolve in less than 30 seconds with no residue. They are FDA approved and are available at **www.daymarksafety.com** or call 800-847-0101.

- **Eggs**. If they are to be used in a few hours, they should sit at room temperature to prevent yoke breakage and cracking to cut down on waste. It is best to check with the local health department for their regulations about eggs, keeping in mind that eggs are perishable.

- **Refreezing.** If foods thaw, do not refreeze them because doing so affects the taste. It is better to keep foods refrigerated and use as soon as possible.

- **Spoilage Rate.** There are many variables in spoilage. Different qualities and brands of food spoil at different rates. Keep this in mind when you change suppliers or brands and watch the items for any variation in the spoilage rate. If there is a noticeable difference in spoilage rate, make a note on your inventory list for future reference.

- **Walk-Ins, Freezers.** Keep an eye on the temperature of your refrigerated units. You can also talk to your alarm company about a program that monitors your freezer and walk-in temperatures. One possibility is Food Watch at **www.foodwatch.com/foodwatch. htm.** These units accurately monitor the temperature and efficiency of your food cases, refrigerators, and walk-ins. They also offer a patent pending Compressor Watch sensor that attaches to the outside of the compressor motor and tracks how long it runs. Another interesting feature is that it monitors how long the walk-in door is open, an important feature to help save on electricity and maintain the quality of your food.

SAFE STORAGE

It is a good idea to create a periodic cleaning schedule for simple cleaning and for sanitizing to remove mold, bacteria, and any other microorganisms.

INVENTORY

There are various types of inventory providing varying degrees of protection and accountability. The types of inventory are periodic physical inventory and perpetual inventory. This is a simple formula to use to determine your inventory amounts.

Beginning Inventory + Deliveries = Food on Hand

Food on Hand – Final Inventory = Food Used

No matter how well your employees portion food and how well you keep records, there will be discrepancies in your inventory records resulting from food spoilage or theft. Physical inventories must be done from time to time. The frequency is determined by the number of problems the facility has. Do not allow the fact that you have few employees available prevent physical inventories from being done. The more organized your facility is, the easier a physical inventory is, and it also becomes easier with practice.

PERIODIC INVENTORY COUNT

A periodic physical inventory is the oldest form of inventory. At one time, people did a physical inventory at the end of the month or the quarter when they did all the other paperwork. However, many facilities want inventory details on a more regular basis. If there is a problem with inventory or usage, it is difficult to identify the cause of these problems weeks or months later.

There are several different rules of thumb about how often inventory should be done —weekly, monthly, or at the close of business each day. At one time, I had an assistant manager who was drastically overusing certain items. We walked through an abbreviated inventory at the end of his shifts. This is rarely done, but I needed to prove when the shortages were happening. The proof was indisputable after we did this for several days.

PERPETUAL INVENTORY

Perpetual inventory means checking your daily food and supply usage. It is important to track expensive items. An accurate perpetual inventory can guarantee that items are not being overused or stolen.

PERPETUAL ORDER FORM

All food items are listed on the Sign Out Sheet and Yield Form. The "Size" column includes the unit size used. The cook signs out food from the freezer or walk-in, noting the unit size and number of items. Each day of the month is listed across the top of the page. At the end of the day, enter the number of items remaining. This number must be subtracted from the "Amount Ordered." It is possible for an employee to hide a theft by removing items from a box and then re-sealing it, delaying discovery of the loss and making it difficult to determine the date of the theft.

How should you handle the situation if you discover theft? When you suspect theft, your first priority is to make a list of all employees who worked during the time items went missing. If you have additional theft, check to see which employees worked each of these shifts. Placing a note on the bulletin board that you are investigating suspected theft might be all you need. Include a statement that any employee who is caught stealing will be terminated.

DETERMINE INVENTORY LEVELS

When you prepare a food order, you must know the amount of food and supplies on hand. You can do this manually with an inventory sheet or use a computer program.

Take the printed sheet and work your way through the storage area marking how much of each item is "on hand" in that column. Remember to use the same unit of measure as your standard for inventory. The unit of measure should be on the inventory sheet to avoid confusion.

You need to find the "Build to Amount" or "Order Amount" (different worksheets will use different terms). To find the amount to be ordered, you need the time for scheduled deliveries and amounts needed between deliveries. It is good to add 15 percent to the amount you figure in case a delivery is late, you need more than usual, or an item is backordered. Try not to cut your order short.

It is good for your staff to know the following information. Place the buying schedule details on a bulletin board with easy access for staff members.

• When each order must be placed.

• When deliveries are scheduled to arrive.

• Which vendors deliver which items.

• Each sales representative's phone number and the company they represent.

• The quoted price for all items. You may prefer to keep the pricing information in your desk or a notebook in your office.

You can place a "Want Sheet" on a clipboard for staff members to list any items they need, including equipment, food, and supply items that are running low or used up. This sheet works well with items used infrequently. Simply train your staff to make a note on the "Want Sheet" when they use the last item or open the last box.

INVENTORY FORMS

There are many types of inventory forms. You will find a variety at the end of this chapter.

WEEKLY OR MONTHLY INVENTORY

It is good to assign teams of two people to work on inventory counts. One person should count the items while the other records the amounts. It works best when the recorder listens and records the numbers. No conversation is needed. Each team needs a list of the items in their area. It is best to list these items in the order they are assigned in the storeroom.

Inventory sheets should include a slot to write any items received or issued. Inventories should be conducted at a time of limited activity and no deliveries. It is important to recognize items when they are in different packaging.

ISSUING

Usage of any food or supply items is a critical part of the inventory and cost control process. Removing food from storage to use is called issuing. Below are some suggestions for issuing and using a sign out sheet.

- **Raw Food Items.** Issue these items on a daily basis. They include meat, fish, and poultry.

- **Signing Out.** When you remove bulk items from the walk-in or freezer.

- **Issuing.** Managers or kitchen managers should be the only ones to remove food from storage although in some facilities other people may be involved. It depends on the facility policies and the control that the manager has over the staff members.

The Sign Out sheet shows when each item was taken from storage to be used in the facility. Your daily usage for each menu item is determined using this information. It is also simple to verify whether food items are being over-used and to determine which items are not being controlled properly. An effective sign-out procedure can help eliminate theft.

RECEIVING CHECKLIST

Received By: _____ Date: _____

ITEM _____

_____

Actual Temp. _____ °F   Packaging Intact ❏ Yes ❏ No
Valid Use-By Date ❏ Yes ❏ No
❏ ACCEPTED   ❏ STORED   ❏ REJECTED

ITEM _____

_____

Actual Temp. _____ °F   Packaging Intact ❏ Yes ❏ No
Valid Use-By Date ❏ Yes ❏ No
❏ ACCEPTED   ❏ STORED   ❏ REJECTED

ITEM _____

_____

Actual Temp. _____ °F   Packaging Intact ❏ Yes ❏ No
Valid Use-By Date ❏ Yes ❏ No
❏ ACCEPTED   ❏ STORED   ❏ REJECTED

ITEM _____

_____

Actual Temp. _____ °F   Packaging Intact ❏ Yes ❏ No
Valid Use-By Date ❏ Yes ❏ No
❏ ACCEPTED   ❏ STORED   ❏ REJECTED

ITEM _____

_____

Actual Temp. _____ °F   Packaging Intact ❏ Yes ❏ No
Valid Use-By Date ❏ Yes ❏ No
❏ ACCEPTED   ❏ STORED   ❏ REJECTED

ITEM _____

_____

Actual Temp. _____ °F   Packaging Intact ❏ Yes ❏ No
Valid Use-By Date ❏ Yes ❏ No
❏ ACCEPTED   ❏ STORED   ❏ REJECTED

ITEM _____

_____

Actual Temp. _____ °F   Packaging Intact ❏ Yes ❏ No
Valid Use-By Date ❏ Yes ❏ No
❏ ACCEPTED   ❏ STORED   ❏ REJECTED

ITEM _____

_____

Actual Temp. _____ °F   Packaging Intact ❏ Yes ❏ No
Valid Use-By Date ❏ Yes ❏ No
❏ ACCEPTED   ❏ STORED   ❏ REJECTED

ITEM _____

_____

Actual Temp. _____ °F   Packaging Intact ❏ Yes ❏ No
Valid Use-By Date ❏ Yes ❏ No
❏ ACCEPTED   ❏ STORED   ❏ REJECTED

ITEM _____

_____

Actual Temp. _____ °F   Packaging Intact ❏ Yes ❏ No
Valid Use-By Date ❏ Yes ❏ No
❏ ACCEPTED   ❏ STORED   ❏ REJECTED

ITEM _____

_____

Actual Temp. _____ °F   Packaging Intact ❏ Yes ❏ No
Valid Use-By Date ❏ Yes ❏ No
❏ ACCEPTED   ❏ STORED   ❏ REJECTED

ITEM _____

_____

Actual Temp. _____ °F   Packaging Intact ❏ Yes ❏ No
Valid Use-By Date ❏ Yes ❏ No
❏ ACCEPTED   ❏ STORED   ❏ REJECTED

RECEIVING REPORT

Supplier: _____ Date: _____

Representative: _____ Delivery Date: _____

Item Description	Quantity	Notes	Unit Price

RECEIVING REPORT II

Received By: _____ Date: _____

Distribution Key: 1. _____ 2. _____

3. _____ 4. _____

Invoice #	Supplier	Item	Unit Price	# of Units	Total Cost	Distribution 1	2	3	4

GENERAL REQUISITION

Date: _____   Req. #: _____

Time: _____   Department: _____

Prepared By: _____   Priced By: _____

Delivered By: _____ Received By: _____

Approved By: _____

Item Description	Unit	Quantity	Price	Extension
	Total $			

FOOD REQUISITION FORM

Date: _____ Date Needed: _____ Requested By: _____

QTY Ordered	Ingredient #	Item Description	QTY Issed	Unit Cost	Unit Total
	Total $				

GENERAL RECEIVING REPORT

General Receiving Report
Month of _____ 20____

RECV. BY	DATE	P.O. #	COMPANY	INVOICE #	INVOICE IN	ITEM	TOTAL	DEPT.	CATEGORY	ACCRUAL $ AMOUNT	INV. ACT.

CREDIT MEMO

Credit Memo #: _____ Date Issued: _____

Vendors: _____ Vendor Invoice Number: _____

Vendor Representative: _____

Explanation: _____

_____

| ITEM | Quantity | Correction | | Price | Credit Amount |
		Short	Refused		

CREDIT MEMO II

Sold To: _____ Date: _____

Customer Number: _____

Invoice Number: _____ Invoice Date: _____

Instructions:
- ❏ Pickup Order Only
- ❏ Pickup and Credit Order
- ❏ Credit Only

ITEM	PRODUCT CODE	QUANTITY	PACKAGE	PRICE	AMOUNT

SIGNATURE OF AUTHORIZATION: DATE:

OPERATIONAL INVENTORY FORM

ITEM	SIZE	QUANTITY				TOTAL	COST	EXTENSION

PERPETUAL INVENTORY CHART

Location: _____

Item: _____ Unit: _____

Date	Beginning	Additions	Deletions	Ending	Unit Price	Extension	Initials

INVENTORY COUNT SHEET

Date Inventoried: _____ Month Of: _____

Item Description	Unit	Counts	Total	Cost	Total Value
				PAGE TOTAL $	

PAPER GOODS INVENTORY

Date: _____   Department: _____

Time: _____   Location: _____

Inventoried By: _____   Priced By: _____

Approved By: _____   Extended By: _____

Item Description	Unit	Quantity	Price	Extension
	Total $			

Notes:

CHINA & FLATWARE INVENTORY

Inventory Date: _____   Extended By: _____

Counted By: _____   Approved By: _____

ITEM	Par	Inventory					Total	+ or - Balance
		A	B	C	D	E		

EQUIPMENT INVENTORY

Inventory Date: _____   Department: _____

Counted By: _____   Approved By: _____

Item Description (Name & Serial #)	Unit Count	Office Count	Difference	Explanation

Notes:

INVENTORY VALUATION SHEET

Inventory Date: _____   Extended By: _____

Counted By: _____

Item	Item Amount	Item Value	Inventory Value
	Page Total		

CHAPTER

FOOD BUYING TECHNIQUES

This information will be valuable for people who place large orders. The first step is to determine whether large food orders are advantageous for you. Smaller orders have the advantages of offering:

- Lower storage cost for less risk, less inventory, less paperwork to maintain.

- Greater freshness for less risk of spoilage.

- Easier financial handling.

- Opportunity to take advantage of lower prices when they drop.

- Reduction in storage space.

- Greater flexibility in working with vendors.

- Less chance of theft due to having less inventory.

To make an educated decision, consider the advantages of placing large orders:

- Products can be purchased at a lower price when bought in quantity.

- There is less chance of running out of items.

- More stable prices mean more effective menu pricing.

- Buyer has more time to focus on other responsibilities.

- Lower labor cost to place, receive, and store orders.

Presented here are various items to be purchased, tips to find the best quality, and negotiating the best price for your facility.

EATS

Meat may be the most important food item for your facility. Usually one-third to one-half the food budget is spent on meat products because they are costly and most entrees contain meat. Red meats are more expensive because each cow produces only one offspring a year. In turn, a sow may produce several dozen pigs and a hen produces several hundred chicks. Another difference is the length of time it takes the animal to mature enough to go to market. Here are some of the differences:

ANIMAL MATURITY TO MARKET TIMETABLE	
Cattle	18 months
Chickens	12 weeks
Fish or Other Low Cost Seafood	Several weeks
Hogs	6 months
Veal or Lamb	3 months

These numbers show a drastic difference in the length of time from farm to market for beef compared to other meats.

Transporting animals to market is another costly factor. Most cattle are raised in grasslands far removed from large cities. The amount of food required to fatten cattle is significantly higher than for fish and poultry. It takes seven pounds of feed for cattle to gain one pound. Other ratios are: fish, 1:1; chickens, 2:1; and hogs, 4:1. Each of these factors pushes the price for the consumer and the restaurant manager.

Meat usually sets the tone for a meal, so the buyer needs to understand properties of meat, how to pick the best quality, and meat preparation that affects what cuts or parts should be purchased. If there are any questions, speak with the cook before making the final purchase or else the menus could fail.

PROPERTIES OF MEAT

Raw, unprocessed meat is made up of 45 to 72 percent moisture and the remainder is protein, bone, and fat. The muscle in meat is made up of long fibers bundled together with a threadlike appearance. Fibers that make up the muscle contain fats, flavor minerals, moisture, proteins, vitamins, and other compounds. Younger animals have fine fibers that become coarse with age. These fibers are moist without being sticky and they have a nice color with a soft sheen indicating a good quality and tenderness, an important characteristic directly related to the amount of connective tissue. Younger muscles are more tender, but the care and feed an animal is given also makes a difference. Animals confined and fed well are apt to be tender.

Meat that has slightly more collagen than elastin can be cooked to become more tender, but meat with high elastin will remain tough. The length of time meat is cooked makes a difference in the tenderness. Here are some specifics:

COOKING TYPES AND TENDERNESS	
Raw	Most tender
Rare	Less tender
Medium	Begins to toughen
Well Done	Tough

If you plan to cook meat until it is well done, you need to choose a tender meat to begin. As meat is heated, it begins to coagulate and shrink because juices are cooked out. You can control the amount of shrinkage by using lower heat. Low shrinkage allows the meat to retain more flavor and you get more servings from it; 15 to 20 percent shrinkage is low.

Bones increase weight and cost of meat although there is some added flavor to the meat near the bones. It is good to crack the bones and add some water to reach the marrow for added flavor. By adding a little acid to stock made with the bones, you can produce a soup richer in calcium than a glass of milk.

The trend to eat less saturated animal fat is expected to continue, so cattle is being raised to produce less fat and more fat is being trimmed from meats. Age and feed determine the amount of fat in meat. Younger cattle have less fat and well-fed cattle have a higher amount of fat. Higher grade contains more fat. There are three types of fat:

- **Body Cavity Fat:** Located inside the body, it starts on the kidneys and heart and spreads over time.

- **Finish Fat:** Located away from organs, it starts on the shoulders and rump and moves downward and forward with time.

- **Marbling:** Located in the muscles, fat appears as tiny flecks.

Fatty tissue contains 15 to 50 percent moisture, keeping the meat moist during dry cooking. Roasts are cooked upside down so the fatty juices can roll down over the meat. Turkeys are cooked backside up since that is where the fat is located. Another cooking tip is to cook lean meat in moist heat. When you try to sauté or broil lean meat, you often need to add some fat. Keep in mind that fat adds flavor and richness, but it also adds calories and cholesterol.

Myoglobin and hemoglobin make meat look red. When heat touches meat, they change to hematin, a gray pigment – the color of well-done meat. When oxygen combines with myoglobin, it creates oxymyoglobin which gives ground meat a bright red appearance on the outside but a darker color in the center. If you expose the center of ground meat to the air, it will become bright red too.

When meats are cured with nitrogen, it turns a pink color that we see in ham or corned beef brisket. Beware of brown meats: This means that the meat has deteriorated. When it is wet and slick, it has begun to spoil.

MEAT COOKING TEMPS	
Type	Temperature
Rare meat is red	115 – 140° F
Medium meat is pink	140 – 160° F
Well done meat is gray	160– 175° F

Heat builds on the outer surface of meat, so it is good to remove the meat from the heat before it reaches the desired core temperature.

THE MEAT MARKET

Meats have changed dramatically in the last 50 years because of improved breeding and production methods to produce more tender animals with higher meat yield. Research is being done to reduce the amount of fat animals develop. Meat is also being brought to the market younger. New scientific feeding practices promote faster growth on less feed to produce leaner animals. The practice of shipping animal carcasses has changed so that most meats are broken down and bones removed before shipping to cut shipping weight, size, and costs. All of these improvements provide a more valuable product.

Prices at all sorts of markets fluctuate, meaning that buyers need to adjust to trends and conditions. The USDA provides free daily information about market conditions, slaughter amounts, and current prices. Some of the publications you might want to check include:

- Urner Barry Publications, Inc., PO Box 399, Toms River, NJ 08754.

- *The National Provisioner Daily Market Service* ("yellow sheet").

- *The Hotel, Restaurant, Institutional Meat Price Report* ("green sheet").

- USDA Publications — **www.usda.gov**.

- *Market News Service Report.*

- *Meat Sheet for Boxed Meat Items.*

- Price Analysis Systems, Inc., P O Box 9626, Minneapolis, MN 55408.

- *Meat Price Relationships* — published every two years. The historic prices of 74 meat and poultry items are listed along with the seasonal charts. They also predict future prices that are useful for planning, budgeting, and projecting sales and promotions.

The federal government has prevailed over the meat market for almost 100 years. *The Jungle* by Sinclair Lewis, published in 1906, caused widespread concern, prompting President Theodore Roosevelt to create a panel inquiry into actual conditions. Congress passed the Meat Act in 1906 to control operating standards that meat processing plants must follow, allowing for a series of inspections to guarantee meat is "fit for human consumption." Federal inspectors stamp the meat when it has met requirements. When the meat does not pass inspection, they are stamped "condemned," "retained" for further inspection, or "suspect."

The stamp indicates the official establishment number that will help you determine where your meat actually originated. Check the number on the stamp against the federal list and you will know. Here are some samples.

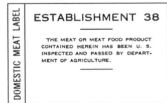

Inspections are required by law, but grading is voluntary. When a packager puts its own "brand" on the meat, they do not have to give it a grade. The grading process was established in 1927 and the company or buyers who request grading paid an additional cost which is passed along to the consumer. Grades have been established for beef, lamb, pork, and veal. Beef has a variety of grades since there are so many different cuts and types of animals. Grading was amended in 1967 by the Wholesome Food Act which tightened the standards and gave control to state and federal governments. Some states have more stringent rules than the federal government in which case they can inspect and stamp the meat.

FROZEN MEAT

Large ice crystals can form on frozen meat so fast freezing is recommended so that only small crystals form. Slow freezing also causes a loss of moisture, flavor, minerals, and vitamins. If you cook meat from a frozen state, you can prevent some of these losses, but doing so increases

the cooking time. Freezer burn is caused when the surface of the meat becomes dehydrated. It can be minimized by enclosing items tightly with moisture-proof wrap to eliminate air. Dry-paper cover toughens the meat and does not prevent freezer burn and flavor loss. You should also be sure to label all your frozen meat while in inventory to make sure it is used on a timely basis. DayMark Safety Systems offers CoolMark™ freezable labels which stick to all frozen surfaces. For more information call 800-847-0101 or visit **www.daymarksafety.com.**

You might want to consider the cost to store frozen meat compared to making smaller purchases of fresh meat. This chart shows how long meat can be frozen under good quality conditions.

FREEZING MEAT	
Beef	Lasts the best
Cured or Smoked Meats	1-3 months
Ground Meat	3 months
Lamb	Lasts the best
Pork	Not as well, fat becomes rancid
Veal	Lasts well

To be an effective meat buyer, you need to understand the classification and grading system used. Kinds of animals include beef, pork, sheep, and veal. There are additional classifications that include: cured meats, edible by-products, and sausage. Be aware of the prepared, canned, and substitute meat items available.

Two grading systems are used. One determines quality while the other is based on yield; age, maturity, and quality are all factors that determine the grade of beef. There are seven classifications that go from devoid (none) or slight to moderately abundant (heavy marbling).

The chart below shows how grades are determined based on the variables.

RELATIONSHIPS BETWEEN MARBLING, MATURITY, AND CARCASS QUALITY GRADE					
Degrees of Marbling	Young Animals		Older Animals		
	A^C	B	C	D	E
Abundant	PRIME				
Moderate			COMMERCIAL		
Some	CHOICE				
Little					
Very Little	SELECT		UTILITY		
Traces	STANDARD				
None		UTILITY		CUTTER	CANNER

Bones are graded based on their size, shape, ossification, amount of cartilage, and interior (marrow) color. These factors are indicators of the age of the animal. Younger animals have less ossification and more cartilage. The bones change shape as the animal matures. Interior bones have more red in younger animals than in older animals.

Flesh color is pink in young animals, but the color does redden with age. When you touch the flesh, it should be moist without being wet or slimy. Fibers in the meat should be silky with a soft sheen. These fibers are coarser in older animals.

Veal and calf grading are similar to beef grades although muscle structure is a factor. High grade veal and calves must have wide, thick carcasses with plump-muscled legs, shoulders, and breasts. Thin animals are graded lower.

In pork grading, age is the main factor based on body size, flesh color, and bone characteristics. Breaks in the bone indicate the animal's age. Younger animals have sharp and ragged breaks while older animals' breaks are smoother.

IDENTIFYING PORTIONS OF MEAT

You must know the differences between the cuts of meat and between the muscle and bone formations to recognize various cuts of meat. When you look at a porterhouse steak and a T-bone, the biggest difference is the size of the tenderloin muscle. In a T-bone, the muscle is smaller. I have always found the shape of the bone makes it easy to recognize a T-bone.

Remember that it takes practice to identify the various cuts. The buyer and receiver need to be familiar with these details. For a wealth of information on meat identification, see this Web site: **www.ffaunlimited.org/meevandte.html.** You can find many specifications at **www.ams.usda. gov/LSG/stand/imps.htm**. Some of the publications you can download include:

IMPS FILES FOR DOWNLOAD		
Series No.	**Name**	**File Size**
--	General Requirements – pdf file	62 Kb
--	Quality Assurance Provisions – pdf file	356 Kb
100	Fresh Beef – pdf file	582 Kb
100	Fresh Beef with Pictures – pdf file	2 Mb
200	Fresh Lamb and Mutton – pdf file	668 Kb
300	Fresh Veal and Calf – pdf file	218 Kb
400	Fresh Pork – pdf file	324 Kb
500	Cured, Cured and Smoked, Cooked Pork Products – pdf file	168 Kb
600	Cured, Dried and Smoked Beef Products – pdf file	982 Kb
700	Variety Meats and Edible By-Products – pdf file	45Kb
800	Sausage Products – pdf file	119 Kb
11	Fresh Goat – pdf file	970Kb

For copies and other information concerning the IMPS write:

USDA, AMS, LS, SB
1400 Independence Ave., SW, Stop 0254
Washington, D.C. 20250-0254

To contact them call 202-720-4486 or e-mail **Thavann.Un@usda.gov.**

Wholesale and **retail** cut charts can be helpful in identifying portions of beef, lamb, veal, and pork. See charts from the USDA at **www.usda.gov**.

PROCESSED MEAT

Processed meat can be restructured, smoked, or cooked to preserve the meat, give it more flavor, or reduce labor costs — processes that are monitored by the federal government.

Nitrites or nitrates can be added to bacon, ham, and sausage as a preservative. After 1979, meats cured without nitrites or nitrates have a label that reads, "not preserved; keep refrigerated below 40°F at all times." Large canned meats can contain the same label because of their size.

They may be considered fresh meats.

Cooked processed meats come in many varieties, including canned, frozen, and chilled. Some are refrigerated or frozen items which can be offered in bulk or portion packages. There is a greater chance of bacterial concerns with these products, so it is advisable to enforce bacterial standards. The federal government requires a minimum amount of meat in each of these products.

Cured meats are salted or smoked. Salting means soaked in brine or pumped with brine for preservation. Curing offers a better flavor, improved appearance, and a more tender product. These are some terms for cured meats and an explanation about what each term means:

- **"Country Cured".** Meat is given a dry cure (see below) with a combination of sugar, spices, and honey. (Beef cured like this is called "cured beef brisket.")

- **"Cured".** The finished weight is the same or less before curing.

- **"Cured, Water Added".** Finished product is 110 percent of weight before curing.

- **"Dry Cure".** 8 to 9 percent salt or preservatives are added to bring out the meat's juices, making brine that soaks into the meat, preserving it.

- **"Imitation".** More than 110 percent added weight after curing.

- **"Wet Brine Cure".** Meat is immersed in 55 to 70 percent salt and soaked enough to preserve the meat.

Bacon is the most popular cured meat. It looks pink and dry, but not greasy. It usually comes in eight to ten pound slabs. Ham is usually 12 to 14 pounds.

Edible meat by-products are less well-known but are still offered for consumption. Various types are classified as delicacies. These are some of the possibilities.

- **Brain.** Veal brains are common.

- **Heart.**

- **Kidneys.** Beef and lamb are commonly used.

- **Liver.** Calf and veal liver are the best. Lamb and pork liver are good. Beef liver is tough unless it is cooked quickly.

- **Oxtails.**

- **Stomachs.** First and second stomachs from cattle.

- **Honeycomb tripe** from the second stomach of cattle.

- **Sweetbreads.**

- **Tongue.** Beef tongue is the most common.

- **Sausage.** Ground meat combined with spices that vary depending on which type is being made. Nitrite is added to reduce bacterial risk. Most sausages must be refrigerated. See note below for ones that do not have to be refrigerated.

A number of ground meats are classified as sausage. These include:

- **Cured Sausage** – Good for 30 days, but fresh is good for one week.

- **Frankfurters** – Refrigerate.

- **Pepperoni** – Not refrigerated.

- **Salami** – Not refrigerated.

Canned meat can be a good alternative if fresh meats are not available. They are also a good choice when refrigerated or frozen storage is an issue. Some canned meats need to be refrigerated at 40 to 70 degrees Fahrenheit. Canned meat should not be kept for more than a year.

Some of the canned meat varieties include boned chicken or turkey, corned beef, luncheon meats, pork sausage, links, Vienna sausage, frankfurters, chili con carne, and canned ham.

OULTRY

Poultry and eggs are a huge industry that changed little until the last quarter of the 20th century. It changed dramatically because science enabled growers to raise heavier chickens in about half the time previously required.

Today thousands of chickens lay eggs in large henneries. A bit of chicken trivia—the average hen lays more than 260 eggs a year. Eggs are a wonderfully versatile and inexpensive food, but demand has decreased because they are high in cholesterol.

Turkey and chicken are high in protein and cost little so the demand grows. Both are incredibly versatile and low in cholesterol and unsaturated fats. In 1956 the government began to require that all poultry products be inspected. After an item passes inspection, it is stamped "Inspected and Passed." When poultry is processed, these are the steps needed: it is killed, bled, scalded, plucked, eviscerated, and inspected. Following are some details about the inspections performed to evaluate poultry products. Poultry items can be purchased cooked or raw.

SPECIFICATIONS

The specifications used to evaluate poultry include the following:

- **Kind–Poultry or Game Birds.** Poultry includes chickens, turkeys, ducks, geese, and pigeons. Game birds include pea fowl, swans, quail, wild ducks, geese, and pheasants. Rabbits are also classified as poultry.

- **Class.** This is based on the age and the sex of poultry.

- **Grade or Quality.** Standard poultry grades are A, B, and C. Grade is based on a list of characteristics and qualities. These include conformation, fleshing, fat coverage, and lack of feathers, tears, cuts and bruises, freezer burn, and disjointed and broken bones.

- **Packaging.** Frozen poultry is wrapped in polyethylene to eliminate or limit freezer burn. The number of items in each container is determined by the type of poultry item being packaged. Chicken is usually 12 to 24 per container. Turkey, duck, or geese are 2, 4, or 6 per container. Parts are 25, 30 or 50 pounds per container

- **Style.** Includes whole, halved, quarters, and parts. Parts are drumsticks, legs, thighs, legs with pelvic meat, wings, and breasts.

- **Size, Weight, and Portion.** Vary depending on the kind of poultry.

- **Transportation and Delivery Temperature.** Frozen core temperature of poultry items is 0 degrees Fahrenheit and the refrigerated temperature is 36 to 40 degrees Fahrenheit.

GGS

Every restaurant needs a reliable egg supplier. Be sure that your facility and your supplier refrigerate eggs right away. Eggs that are graded wrong can drive your price up unnecessarily. The longer they are exposed to room temperature, the lower the quality. Eggs can be purchased in these forms: in shells, as liquid, frozen, and dried. The type you need will depend on what you plan to prepare. I will discuss that in more detail shortly. Another interesting bit of egg trivia – the weight distribution of an egg is: white = 58 percent; yolk = 31 percent; and shell = 11 percent.

Shells are a factor in the grading process and are graded on soundness, cleanliness, shape, and texture. Scanners are used to see the interior of the egg for grading and they allow the inspector to see the centering of the yolk, the aqueous nature of the white, size of the air cell, blood spots, and any deficiencies. Remember that eggs will last for several weeks if they are refrigerated properly. Egg Standards are Grade AA, A, B, and C. This table shows how the grading process works.

U.S. STANDARDS FOR QUALITY OF SHELLED EGGS TO MEET QUALITY FACTORS			
Factor	**AA Quality**	**A Quality**	**B Quality**
Shell	Clean, unbroken, almost normal	Clean, unbroken, almost normal	Clean or slightly stained, slightly abnormal, may be bubbly
Air Cell	1/8" or less deep, almost regular	3/16" or less deep, almost regular	3/8" or less deep, free or bubbly
White	Clear and firm	Clear and reasonably firm	Clear, may be weak
Yolk	Outline is refined slightly, mostly free from defects	Outline fairly defined, mostly free from defects	Outline may be defined, slightly enlarged, flat, and may show defects although not serious

Processed eggs are frozen or dried and must be pasteurized. When you consider what type of eggs to use in your facility, evaluate what will be made with them. If they will only be used for cooking and baking, various cheaper options are available. The chart below will show you the egg equivalents to aid in your choice.

Frozen eggs are high quality eggs used for French toast, omelets, and scrambled eggs. Lower quality eggs can and are used for cooking and baking. Frozen eggs also tend to produce a tougher finished product.

Dried eggs whites are used for meringue. "Egg Beaters" are a common product used to eliminate the yolks and lower cholesterol. To prevent salmonella from fowl, keep eggs and poultry refrigerated below 45 degrees Fahreneheit and use safe, sanitary handling and cooking methods at all times.

THE MARKET

The poultry and egg market is volatile because of the quick turnaround time for producing poultry and eggs. Market reports are published daily. They help you to follow the poultry market when planning menus and to ensure your supplier's prices are in line. Market reports can be valuable if your facility uses a large quantity of eggs.

SELECTING FRESH PRODUCE

The fresh produce market is complex and it becomes more important as people want healthier foods. This chapter will walk you through the processes needed to buy fresh produce in the best way. An interesting tidbit is that the consumption of processed fruits and vegetables has decreased while fresh fruits and vegetable consumption has increased.

REGULATIONS

You should know the regulations that guide the produce market. Here are a few of the most important.

The Agricultural Commodities Act of 1938 requires that people in the produce business be licensed and use fair business practices. Market quality and procedures improved because of this act. The Agricultural Marketing Act of 1953 and 1957 created agencies that established standards and grades for foods. The Fresh Fruit and Vegetable Division established the 160 grading standards that we have today. The Food and Drug Act also provides standards that affect the plant operations, identification, labeling, and other processes affecting fresh produce. Since 1990 prepackaged items have been required to list nutrition information.

NUTRITION

People are demanding more fresh produce as they learn how healthy they are. They offer a high vitamin content – one serving can give a daily supply of Vitamin A and C. They provide calcium, iron, phosphorous, and potassium — and no cholesterol.

Complex carbohydrates, the healthiest kind, can be found in corn, legumes, potatoes, and squash. Some produce items also offer protein and fiber. It is recommended that people eat at least four servings of fruits and vegetables each day.

THE PRODUCE MARKET

The produce market can be affected overnight by a storm in California or a frost or hurricane in Florida. There are times when the market has too much of some items and not enough of others.

Science has had a profound effect on the produce market as advances help produce stay fresh longer. Flavor and freshness are much better with improved packaging and atmospheric control. We can create a better appearance and make produce tastier and more nutritious.

When produce is picked, it contains "field heat." The temperature needs to be raised to maintain freshness. The old way was to refrigerate produce, a slow process. Another process, hydrocooling, uses ice and water, but it is expensive. Vacucooling, a dry system, is the preferred method of cooling. A large amount of the item is pulled into a tightly sealed chamber which uses the heat in the items for evaporation. It is low cost and handles large quantities of produce quickly.

Improved shipping methods are changing the market. Items get to their destination much faster. Harvesting, cleaning, trimming, packaging, and weighing are done in the field. Produce is then cooled and transported to market on refrigerated trucks.

Packaging options have changed the produce market. Stronger packaging is being used to protect produce en route. Special wraps are used during shipment to ensure better appearance and a fresher flavor and bacteria static wraps are used to combat bacteria growth in items while they are being stored or shipped. Two terms for new wraps are CAP and MAP packaging, which stand for "controlled atmosphere packaging" and "modified atmosphere packaging."

Another factor that affects the market is the introduction of new varieties of produce including the number of tropical fruits that have been brought into the U.S. market and U.S. growers are raising these items as well. Kiwi is an example of a fruit that was once scarce. It was shipped from New Zealand in containerized compartments that were loaded directly onto trucks. Now kiwis are produced in California.

Prepared fruit is another option to consider. Some facilities have eliminated fresh raw fruits and vegetables and are using prepared produce to eliminate waste and reduce equipment, space, refrigerator space, and labor needed to prepare the items. As labor costs increase, prepared produce could become even more popular with food service managers.

The season of the year can make a difference in availability and price. Most fresh produce grown in the United States is available from spring through fall. Imported produce is ungraded and varies more than items grown in the United States. It is critical that the manager and buyer know what areas produce the best products.

PERISHABLE ITEMS

Fresh produce needs to be handled properly. If it is stored in elevated temperatures, quality is compromised. Every 18 degrees Fahrenheit elevation in temperature doubles deterioration.

Produce needs to "breathe," requiring cool temperatures and good ventilation. Here are items that should be stored separately because they emit high amounts of ethylene which accelerates deterioration of nearby produce:

- Apples
- Berries (not cranberries)
- Figs (not with apples)
- Peaches
- Persimmons
- Pomegranates
- Apricots
- Cherries
- Grapes
- Pears
- Plums and Prunes
- Quinces

Not being familiar with the times for deterioration can cause waste and soaring food costs. It is also important not to buy items that are already ripe unless you plan to use them right away.

PURCHASING PRODUCE

What if your supplier insists that you must order a specific amount of produce? An example would be if you want to order three and a half crates, but they require you to buy four crates, which is quite common. When this situation arises, check your menu and see where you can make adjustments to use the additional items. When produce is delivered, there are specific things you or your receiving person needs to confirm: amount, condition, damage, grade, net weight, packaging, rot, size, and pest infestation.

Standard grades for produce are U.S. No.1, No. 2, No. 3, Combination Grade, and Field Grade. U.S. No. 1 is the most desirable grade. Combination Grade is a combination of items which fall in each grade. Field Grade is the items as picked.

When you figure quantity, include item count, packaging, and net weight. With produce, a variety of packaging may be used, a reason for you to be specific about net weight in your specifications. Many times, the quantity will be whatever amount fits in a certain size container. Several packaging terms include.

- **"Loose pack".** Items are haphazardly placed in a package.

- **"Struck Full".** Items are packed just below the top and scraped off if needed to level the contents.

- **"Fill Equal to Facing".** The quality of the items on the top are equal to the quality of the products below the top and throughout the package.

It is important that you be familiar with the quantity of fresh produce to order so that you have enough to prepare food on your menus. A wonderful resource is the *Quantity to Order of Fresh Vegetables* in the USDA Agricultural Handbook. There is also extensive information in the book *Quantity Food Purchasing* by Lendal H Kotschevar and Richard Donnelly by Prentice Hall in Upper Saddle River, New Jersey 07458.

ROCESSED FOODS

The processed food market is complicated partly because many government regulations are in place to oversee it. Producers and manufacturers are a small indication of the number of people who are involved in the industry. Foods are produced in bulk and then passed on to consumers or food service facilities.

REGULATIONS

There are many regulations that affect processed foods, but there are several especially important to food service managers and buyers. One is the Pure Food, Drug, and Cosmetic Act which regulates what can and cannot be added to foods and sets acceptable labeling standards. The Agricultural Act gives the USDA authority to set quality standards for processed foods and should be taken seriously.

GRADING

Earlier we discussed the need to establish the grade, brand, and quality desired when you establish your order list with each vendor. At times a seller may buy a product and later determine the brand after evaluating the quality. It is good for a restaurant manager or buyer to be familiar with the usual quality of different brands to know which brands to avoid.

Surprisingly, sellers are not required to list product quality on their labels, another reason it is good to know which brands consistently offer a better quality product. The table below shows how an educated manager or buyer can identify the quality of the products from the label.

FEDERALLY APPROVED GRADES FOR FRUITS AND VEGETABLES					
	Word Terms		Letter Terms		
	Fruits	Vegetables	Fruits	Vegetables	Score
Top Grade	Fancy	Fancy	A	A	90-100
Second Grade	Choice	Extra Standard	B	B	80-89
Third Grade	Standard	Standard	C	C	70-79

The government does not recognize the word terms to indicate the produce quality, but the market has not caught up with the regulations. By including both techniques, you will be able to understand either designation.

Some items are rated "below standard," but they are not unusable. "Below standard" will be rated below 70. One example is canned peaches in small pieces. While they do not work as peach slices, they would be great for peach pie or peach cobbler.

LABELS

The Pure Food and Drug Division dictates the elements that must be included on produce labels. When items fall below standards, the label must explain discrepancies. The label must list the style pack, variety, any artificial colors, net contents, number of pieces in the package, package size, number of servings, and serving size. The picture on the label must be a real likeness to its contents.

STANDARDS OF IDENTITY

When the name is listed on the label it must be the proper name of the actual product in the package. An example would be sweet corn, sweet white corn, kernel corn, or cream corn.

SYRUP DENSITY

The label must list the syrup density in the container. Designations include light, medium, heavy, and extra heavy. Variations include lightly sweetened, water packed, or juice packed. Usually the higher grades contain heavier syrups although it is not guaranteed.

STANDARDS OF FILL

There are various standards of fill. A couple of these standards are:

- **Contents must fill 90 percent of the water capacity.**
- **"Filled as full as practical".** Without breakage or crushing.
- **"Below Standard Fill" or "Slack Fill".** The standard has not been met.
- **"Solid Pack".** No water has been added.
- **"Heavy Pack".** Water has been added.

METHODS TO PRESERVE PRODUCTS

There are many methods to preserve produce.

- **Canning.** Before items are canned, they must be washed, sized, graded, peeled, trimmed, and then loaded into the cans. People have found that it is more convenient to have canneries near the production locations. Some canneries are moved into the field to speed up the process. It is recommended that the produce be blanched to hold its color, improve flavor, destroy bacteria, and remove dirt and make rigid items easier to pack. Liquid is added to the cans; they are then closed, exhausted, and sealed. The filled, sealed containers are cooked in steam at a high pressure, and then rapidly cooled. In some cases the inside of the can is finished so the can will not react to the food.

- **Freezing.** The best way to maintain high quality is by freezing items soon after they are harvested. They can also be blanched to maintain color and destroy enzymes before freezing. When you review your product specifications with any supplier, indicate that you insist on "condition upon delivery should be the quality specified." The temperature in the transport trucks needs to be around -10 degrees Fahrenheit. If the temperature fluctuates, quality can suffer. If you suspect an item was not stored at the correct temperatures, check for refreezing and large patches of ice on the packages.

- **Drying.** Drying is the process of removing moisture from items. Once the moisture is removed, microorganisms cannot grow.

These are common drying methods:

- **Air Dried.** Natural drying and it is slow.

- **Sun Dried.** Just what it says, drying in the sun, and it is somewhat quicker. You can introduce heated, dry air to speed up the process.

- **Vacu-Drying.** Reduce air pressure and introduce heat.

- **Tunnel Drying.** Fast moving warm air or dry inert gases flow through a tunnel holding the produce.

- **Spray Drying.** Concentrated liquid is sprayed in a chamber and the moisture is extracted.

- **Drum Drying.** A drum rotates the item, lifts it, and dries it. The item is then scraped from the drum.

- **Freeze Drying.** Food is frozen and the moisture is pulled from the item with a vacuum.

CONVENIENCE FOODS

Convenience foods are classified as foods prepared for longer preservation at lower labor costs. There are many convenience foods and the list grows more every day. Some of them are high quality and can compete with products made fresh on site.

There are a variety of reasons to consider convenience foods. One would be a limit of skilled labor in your area. Another would be a way to reduce labor costs in a facility. Many facilities find that a combination of convenience foods and fresh foods works best for them. Here are some advantages to preparing items fresh on the premises:

- Overall operating expenses may be less.

- Patrons often place a higher value on homemade foods.

- Your food items can be unique.

- Nutritional value can be higher.

- Ability to limit the amount of additives used.

- More control over the food prepared.

- Less worry about downsizing.

- Convenience food instructions can be confusing or incomplete.

These are some advantages of convenience foods:

- They may be less expensive when you consider all relevant costs.

- It is simpler to track food usage.

- You can eliminate leftovers.

- Your staff requires fewer skills.

- Inventory, purchasing, receiving, and clean up are easier.

- Equipment usage could be less, but a thorough evaluation is needed.

- Menu options can easily be expanded.

- Foods are easy to fix in a short time.

- Product consistency should be guaranteed.

- It is easy to keep items on hand.

A thorough evaluation is needed before making a final decision on whether to buy or make items. Positives and negatives need to be considered based on the situation in each restaurant. Review all details before making a decision for your facility.

DAIRY PRODUCTS

We have all heard the recommendation to drink two- to eight-ounce glasses of milk every day because it is a great source of calcium, protein, and vitamins A and D. You can avoid milk fat by offering low fat and skim milk. Besides milk, dairy products include cheeses, sour cream, yogurt, ice cream, and butter.

REGULATION

The dairy industry is carefully regulated by the government because it is easy to contaminate milk products. It is produced every day and there is no effective way to shut off the market temporarily. Milk has a short shelf life, so it needs to be processed and moved to markets quickly.

PRICING

The Federal Milk Marketing Order Program establishes the pricing scale directly affecting more than 70 percent of the milk market and indirectly affecting the remainder. There are three price classifications for milk products:

1. **Class 1** – Liquid Milk Products (milk, skim, buttermilk).

2. **Class 2** – Soft Milk Products (cottage cheese, creams, ice cream, and yogurt).

3. **Class 3** – Hard Milk Products (cheese, butter, and powered milk).

Federal price setting has led to a stable market so that the supply is consistent. There is no "market destroying competition" and dairy prices are reasonable.

SANITATION

Your state and local government set sanitation standards and it is mandatory that they implement standards such as these.

- **Herds must be healthy.** USDA and public health officials inspect them.

- **Milk is obtained under sanitary conditions.**

- **Milk must be transported in modern, refrigerated, sanitized trucks.**

- **Milk is tested when it arrives** to ensure it meets all relevant standards, including: milk fat content, odor, sanitation, and taste.

- **When milk does not meet these criteria, it can be rejected.**

When the milk arrives at the dairy plant, it goes through an amazingly fast process. It is pasteurized, cooled, homogenized, and packaged in a few minutes. Pasteurizing can be done at various temperatures, but the highest temperature produces a cooked taste, although they are recommended for heavy milk products. The method of homogenizing milk forces it under pressures of 2,500 pounds per square inch or higher amounts, through tiny orifices which divide fat globules finely so that they are permanently suspended. The milk is packaged in non-returnable containers usually wax-coated or plasticized cardboard. The cardboard blocks any light that destroys the riboflavin in milk.

QUALITY STANDARDS

There are various state and federal standards which govern milk processing and production. Milk must be "fresh, clean cow's milk free from objectionable odors and flavors." Vitamins A and D are added to milk. Normal amounts are vitamin D – 400 units and vitamin A – 2,000 units per quart of extra dry milk solids. If you want detailed information, contact your local authorities.

TYPES OF MILK

Quality of milk is based on flavor, odor, quantity of milk fat, and milk solids. Bacterial content can also be used in the grading process.

- **Grade A** whole milk plate count must be less than 20,000 ml and less than 10 coli form. (Some states dictate no coli form.)

- **Certified Milk.** Raw milk with plate count over 10,000 ml with no coli form.

- **Cultured Milk.** Used for dietary purposes.

- **Filled Milk.** Non-milk fat is added (must be labeled "filled").

- **Flavored Milk.** Sweetener or flavoring is added.

- **Fortified Milk.** Has increased nutritional content, like vitamins A and C.

- **Low Sodium Milk.** Sodium is replaced with potassium.

- **Low-fat Milk.** 8.25 percent nonfat milk solids and 2 percent maximum milk fat.

- **Milk Drink.** Milk fat or milk solids have been altered.

- **Skim and Nonfat Milk.** 8.25 percent nonfat milk solids and 0 to ½ percent milk fat.

- **Soft Curd Milk.** Treated to be more digestible; used in baby formulas.

- **Soured Milk.** Buttermilk is the fluid left when butter is made. Today butter is made from whole, low fat, or skim milk and is soured with bacterial cultures. Some buttermilk products contain small bits of butter. It has 8 to 8½ percent milk fat content and the same milk solids as the milk used to produce it.

- **Yogurt.** A cultured product with a spoonable consistency. It has 2 to 3½ percent milk fat and 8 to 9 percent milk solids.

- **Low-fat and Nonfat Yogurt.** Yogurts can also be flavored with fruits or some other products.

CONCENTRATED MILKS

- **Evaporated Milk.** 7.9 percent milk fat and 18 percent nonfat milk solids. It can be homogenized and fortified with vitamin D. It is produced by boiling milk at 130 to 140 degrees Fahrenheit and using a vacuum to extract the moisture.

- **Nonfat Evaporated Milk.** Generally purchased by the case. You can add 2.2 times the water to evaporated milk to produce whole milk. A 14½ ounce can makes one quart of milk.

- **Condensed Whole Milk.** Contains no less than 19½ percent nonfat milk solids, 8½ percent milk fat, and enough sugar is added to prevent spoilage – about 45 percent

- **Nonfat Condensed Milk.** May be available in bulk but does not have to be sterilized in the cans

- **Concentrated Whole Fresh Milk.** Can be sold as a liquid or frozen product. There is a 10.5 percent milk fat content. The ratio used to create whole milk is three to one. When it is sterilized it has a three-month shelf life at room temperature or six months when refrigerated.

DIETARY MILKS

- **Dry and liquid diet foods produced with milk are available for sale.** They usually are high in milk solids and have been fortified with vitamins, minerals, and proteins. These can be used for dieting and are offered in various flavors. Baby formula is also offered as dry or liquid products. It is best to check the label to be sure what you are purchasing.

- **Dried Milks.** Milk solids with only 2 to 5 percent moisture. They must be stored in airtight containers to avoid quick deterioration.

- **Whole Dried Milk.** Does not contain less than 26 percent milk fat or less than 5 percent moisture.

- **Nonfat Dried Milk.** Does not contain more than 11 percent milk fat or less than 5 percent moisture. Some precautions – watch for stale taste, a cooked flavor, oxidation, tallowness, caramelization, and any other unusual flavors. Dry milk should be produced from pasteurized milk.

- **Spray Dried Milk.** The highest quality dried milk. Roller dried milk under a vacuum is also high quality.

- **Malted Milk.** This is a dried milk product with about 3½ percent moisture, 7½ percent milk fat, a mixture of 40-45 percent nonfat milk, and 55 to 60 percent malt extract.

The federal government's grades for dried milk are: U.S. Premium, U.S. Extra, and U.S. Standard. You should use only the first two. U.S. Premium has a sweet flavor and is good for bakery production. U.S. Extra has a good flavor and aroma.

CREAMS

Bacterial count of cream should not be over 60,000 per ml and not more than 20 coli form per ml.

- **Half and half.** Equal parts of whole milk (3¼ percent milk fat) and cream (18 percent). It is about 10½ percent milk fat.

- **Cultured half and half.** In addition to standard half and half, it has 2 percent acidity.

- **Table Cream.** Has 18 to 20 percent milk fat.

- **Sour Cream.** Similar to table cream but has 2 percent acidity.

- **Whipping Cream.** Light (30 to 34 percent milk fat) or heavy (34 to 36 percent milk fat). It is not homogenized and is ripened three days before it is marketed.

- **Filled Dairy Topping.** 18 percent fat and contains milk solids, but the fat is not milk fat.

- **Sour Cream Dressings.** 16 to 18 percent milk fat with 2 to 5 percent acidity

FROZEN DESSERTS

These frozen treats are pasteurized before they are frozen. The volume increase from whipping and freezing are: ice cream = 80 to 100 percent, sherbets = 40 percent, and ices = 25 percent. There are some states which forbid adding artificial flavors to frozen desserts.

CHEESE

There is a wide variety of cheeses on the market. It is important for a restaurant manager to know the quality factors of cheese. Various types depend on the type of milk used, bacterial cultures, milk fat content, processing method, aging process, and more. Quality depends on the ingredients being used, the age, and storage method. The grades are AA, U.S. Extra Grade, and Quality Approved.

Various types of milk can be used to produce cheese including, whole, partially defatted, or nonfat milk. Annatto, a yellow or orange color, can be used in cheese without being noted on the label. The milk must be pasteurized or cured for 60 days; either technique is acceptable. Interestingly, about 100 pounds of milk make ten pounds of cheese.

Clabbered milk curd is used to produce cheese. When milk is pasteurized and cooled, a starter is added to the milk to create lactic acid and to sour the milk creating a firm curd. The curd is cut into cubes and cooked. The temperature influences the cheese product. A higher temperature creates a firmer and harder cheese. Cheddar is cooked below 100 degrees Fahrenheit and Swiss is cooked below 110 degrees Fahrenheit.

The curd is stirred to release whey and remove it from the mix, leaving a rubbery substance. The mix is poured into each side of the trough in which it is made and it can be cut after it solidifies. This process is called cheddaring. Other types of cheese besides cheddar are made this way. The strips are ground, salted, and piled into hoops. Specific mold or bacteria can be added at this point. When cheese is cured or aged, it undergoes a change of texture from rubbery to a softer, waxy mixture. The flavor becomes sharper and smoother. Various types of cheese are handled in different manners to create the individual tastes and textures that we love.

For information about cheese visit **www.realcaliforniacheese.com**, which provides recipes to use cheese and information about which wines to serve with cheese. You can find all these answers and much more by clicking on "World of Cheese." This site is a great resource for any restaurant that serves cheeses. The information will be helpful when you experiment with recipes. You can e-mail them at ed@successfoods.com.

HARD CHEESES

There are many types of hard cheeses, but the most common are cheddar, American, Swiss, and Monterey jack.

Cheddar and American cheeses are the most common. Fine cheddars come from Oregon, Wisconsin, and New York. It is a hard cheese, cream to orange in color with a mild to sharp taste. The milk fat content must be below 50 percent and the moisture level below 39 percent. Grades are based on body, texture, aroma, taste, color, finish, and appearance. The grades for cheddar, curd cheddar, and Colby are AA (Extra), A (Standard), and B (Commercial). Aging is categorized with "current" (up to 60 days), "medium" (60 to 180 days), and "aged" (more than 180 days).

Swiss or emmental has a creamy, yellow, firm, smooth, sweet, nutty taste and large holes. Baby Swiss is the same but has smaller holes. This cheese is cooked at 125 to 130 degrees Fahrenheit to make it hard with a glossy appearance. The curing process for Swiss is tricky because the wrong humidity can cause mold or rinds. Federal grades for Swiss are AA, A, and B. The holes should be spaced and round or oval. Keep an eye out for sticky, dry cheese that is crumbly because the quality is poor. Swiss cheese becomes whiter as it ages. Aging is rated as "current" (60 to 90 days), "medium" (90 to 180 days), and "aged" (over 180 days).

Monterey Jack is creamy white, smooth, slightly firm, and mild flavored. It has 50 percent milk fat and is normally aged two to five weeks. Federal grades are AA, AS, and B. It has small holes and the surface is not shiny. Poor grades have large holes and a bitter taste.

SOFT CHEESES

- **Cottage or farm cheese** is made by setting milk into a curd and cooking at 90 degrees Fahrenheit. The curd is cut, the whey removed, and 1 percent salt is added. The curd size is determined by the size of the knife used. If the moisture is below 70 percent, it can become dry.

- **Ricotta Cheese** is a soft cottage cheese which originated in Italy.

- **Greek Feta** is a soft curd cheese used in Greek, Balkan, and Arabic dishes. It has a sharp and delicate flavor and is crumbly. The curd can be served with butter and seasonings.

SPECIFICATIONS FOR HARD AND SOFT CHEESES

- **Aging.** The time needed to create a specific kind of cheese.

- **Bacteria content.** This information is not required for all cheeses.

- **Fat Content.** There are some designations that address the amount of fat – "non fat" and "low fat."

- **Flavor.** Each kind of cheese has a distinctive flavor, but in some cases, spices, seasonings, or wines are added for a different flavor.

- **Grade, Brand, and Quality.** Only some cheeses have grades, but it is best to indicate the quality that you want.

- **Kind.** Use the common name for each item.

- **Kind of Milk.** Goat's milk cheese would be an example of this standard.

- **Moisture Content.** There are maximum moisture contents for each cheese to classify the type of cheese; for example, hard, soft, moderately hard, and very hard.

- **Origin.** Sometimes includes the area where it originated and other times it could be the manufacturer.

- **Size, Shape, or Packaging.** Some may be distributed in normal shapes and sizes. An example would be cheddar which can come in large or small rounds, bricks, and other shapes.

BUTTER

The federal government says that butter should not contain more than 80 percent milk fat. It might contain salt and food coloring, but unsalted butter is on the market. It takes about 100 pounds of milk fat to produce 120 to 125 pounds of butter. After the milk is pasteurized, its acidity can be increased or decreased and Annatto can be added for coloring. After butter and buttermilk are created, the buttermilk is drained. Then the remaining butter is washed, salted, and worked. Working is necessary to get the right consistency. If it is overworked, the butter will become sticky and greasy. Butter is graded AA, A, B, and C. Scores are based on body, color, flavor, packaging, and salt. Aroma is considered flavor. The federal government's standard for butter reads, "U.S. Grade of butter is determined on the basis of classifying first the flavor characteristics and then body, color, and salt. Flavor is the basic quality factor and is determined organoleptically by taste and smell."

MARGARINE

The federal government states that margarine is made from one or more various approved vegetable or animal fats combined with cream. It may also contain vitamins A and D, butter, salt, artificial flavoring, colors, and preservatives. Labels must list any of these additional items. Beef fat used to be a favorite, but now soy oils are used more often than others. Some other oils include cottonseed, corn, other vegetable oils, or a blend of animal and vegetable oils.

Margarine is evaluated with the same standards as butter. The color, body, and texture should be consistent throughout the product. Flavors are clean, sweet, and free of unpleasant or unusual odors. You notice inconsistent colors and tastes when margarine is warm.

CHAPTER

FOOD COST CONTROLS

I f you manage a food service operation, you have to buy food products; that is the reality. The largest expenditure for most food service operations is the cost of food. In this chapter we will show you many ways to reduce your food costs. Even a 3 percent reduction in food costs for a restaurant grossing $1,000,000 with food costs of $400,000 means an approximate savings of $12,000, which will go straight to your bottom line.

CONTROLLING FOOD COSTS: STRATEGIES AND TIPS

In order to control food costs effectively, there are four essential things that you need to do:

1. **Forecast** how much and what you are going to sell.

2. **Purchase, receive, and prepare** according to these forecasts.

3. **Portion effectively.**

4. **Control money, waste, and theft.**

Thankfully, improvements in technology and management techniques allow smart restaurant operators to keep food costs within the boundaries needed to generate a profit, while still providing their customers with the level of service that they need to generate repeat business. A restaurant manager must be prepared to develop and monitor cost-control programs, particularly food cost, to maintain profitability.

Unless you make changes, this book is of no use to you. You must begin to change your thinking and your methods. Take them one at a time, and make them a part of your business. Many of these tips will not only cut your food costs, but will also enhance your finished products. Better food brings more business, which brings more money. A reduction in your food costs means that you can keep more of that money. Armed with the information in this book, you will find actual tips that produce profitable results, without consuming all your time in unnecessary research or experiencing painful trial, risk, and error.

GETTING ORGANIZED

Organization is the easiest and cheapest manner of generating productivity and reducing food costs. The mere act of putting instructions on paper or giving your staff a checklist, instead of having to hold their hand through a process, can save your company thousands.

ORGANIZATIONAL AND STRUCTURE COMPONENT CHARTS

Use organizational charts to know and understand who does what in your restaurant on a daily, weekly, and monthly basis. How can this structure improve? Are jobs allocated in the most productive manner possible? Written job descriptions are good tools to use for this. You can find examples of job descriptions and a questionnaire for writing job descriptions at **www.hrnext.com**. Atlantic Publishing offers a complete set of restaurant job descriptions available on CD-ROM at **www.atlantic-pub.com**. Also from Atlantic Publishing is *The Encyclopedia of Restaurant Training: A Complete Ready-to-Use Training Program for All Positions in the Food Service Industry With Companion CD-ROM* (Item # ERT-02). This manual has job descriptions and other organizational tools that will help you train your employees and increase efficiency.

Use checklists for yourself. Create a checklist of tasks you perform every day and organize your time. Of course, variations from this checklist will always occur, but you will cover the basics a lot faster with a guide in hand, saving you and your staff time and confusion.

FOOD SALES AND COSTS SURVEY

Before you can determine the best ways to reduce food costs, look at sales and cost figures. Take a look at the following food sales and costs statistics. How does your operation compare?

WHAT DOES FOOD COST PERCENTAGE REALLY MEAN?

Johnny's steakhouse has a food cost of 38 percent; Sally's steakhouse has a food cost of 44 percent. Which is a more efficient operator? Which is more profitable? Your restaurant has a food cost in January of 38 percent; in February it is 32 percent. Did you operate more efficiently the second month? The answer to these questions is: You just do not know. There is not enough information to determine this from the figures; you need to know what the food-cost percentage should have been as well.

- **Importance of food cost percentages.** Do not become overly concerned over food-cost percentages; they are truly meaningless unless you know what your food-cost percentage should be for the given time in question. Remember, you get paid in and deposit dollars into the bank, not percentages.

- **Weighted food cost percentage.** Once your food cost is calculated, you must determine your weighted food-cost percentage. A weighted food-cost percentage will tell you what your food cost should have been over a given period of time if all procedures and controls in place operated at 100 percent efficiency. I will show you how to determine a weighted food cost in a later section.

RECONCILIATION

The key to controlling food cost is reconciliation. Every step or action in the cost-control process is checked and reconciled with another person. Once these systems are set up, management's responsibility is to monitor them with daily involvement. Should all the steps and procedures be adhered to, you will know exactly where every dollar and ounce of food went; there are no loopholes.

- **Teach them.** Management must be involved in the training and supervision of all employees. For any cost-control system to work, employees must be trained and know what actions are expected of them. It is management's responsibility to supervise employees and see that they receive this training.

- **Communicate.** Daily involvement and communication is needed in order to succeed. Employees must follow all procedures precisely. If they do not, they must be informed of their specific deviations from these procedures and correct them. It is a daily task that involves a hands-on management style.

- **Enforce.** Any control initiated is only as good as the manager who follows up and enforces it. The total amount of time a manager needs to complete all of the work that will be described in this section is less than one hour a day. There is no excuse for not completing each procedure every day. A deviation in your controls or involvement can only lead to a loss over the control of the restaurant's costs.

ESSENTIALS OF CONTROLLING FOOD COSTS

To control food costs effectively, there are four essentials that you need to do. First, forecast what and how much you are going to sell. Second, purchase and prepare according to these forecasts. Third, portion effectively. Finally, control waste and theft. Consider the following:

Standards. You must have standards to which you rigorously adhere. Here are several standards that will help you sustain quality, consistency and low cost.

- **Do not allow chefs to determine pricing.** The plates your chefs create are their pride and joy. But do not let them set prices. You have specific profit goals in mind; allowing a chef to set prices may mean your targets are not reached. Discuss menu pricing parameters and costs with your chefs so that they are dreaming of hamburgers instead of filet mignon, but keep the menu pricing a management function.

- **Standardized recipes.** Since the recipe is the basis for determining the cost of a menu item, standard recipes will ensure consistent quality and cost. Standardized recipes include ingredients, preparation methods, yield, equipment used, and plate presentation.

- **Standardized purchase specifications.** These are detailed descriptions of the ingredients used in your standardized recipes. Quality and price of all ingredients are known and agreed upon before purchases are made, making the recipe's cost consistent from unit to unit and week to week.

YIELD COSTS

Once you have standardized recipes in place, you can determine the per-plate cost of every dish. You need to know the basic ingredients' cost and the edible yield of those ingredients for each dish. There are a number of necessary terms for this process:

- **As-purchased (AP) Weight.** The weight of the product as delivered, including bones, trim, etc.

- **Edible-portion (EP) Weight.** The amount of weight or volume that is available to be portioned after carving or cooking.

- **Waste.** The amount of usable product that is lost due to processing, cooking, or portioning, as well as usable by-products that have no salable value.

- **Usable Trim.** Processing by-products that can be sold as other menu items. These recover a portion or all of their cost.

- **Yield.** The net weight or volume of food after processing but before portioning.

- **Standard Yield.** The yield generated by standardized recipes and portioning procedures—how much usable product remains after processing and cooking.

- **Standard Portion.** The size of the portion according to the standardized recipe. It is also the basis for determining the cost of the plated portion. With convenience foods, items where at least a portion of the preparation labor is done before delivery (pre-cut chicken, ready made dough), you simply count, weigh, or measure the portion size and determine how many portions there are. Then divide the number of servable portions into the AP price. Even with their pre-preparation, a small allowance for normal waste must be factored in, often as little as 2 percent per yield.

These factors allow you to calculate plate costs. The cost of convenience foods are higher than if you made them from scratch, but once you factor in labor, necessary equipment, inventories of ingredients, more complicated purchasing and storage, you may find that these foods offer considerable savings.

Costing items from scratch is a little more complex. Most menu items require processing that causes shrinkage of some kind. As a result, if the weight or volume of the cooked product is less than the AP weight, the EP cost will be higher than the AP price. It is a simple addition of the labor involved and the amount of salable product being reduced. Through this process, your buyer uses yields to determine quantities to purchase and your chef discovers optimum quantities to order that result in the highest yield and the least waste.

MENU SALES MIX

You begin to design a restaurant with the menu. If you have a specific menu idea, your restaurant's location must be carefully planned to ensure customer traffic will support your concept. Likewise, if you already have the location, design your menu around the customers you want to attract.

Consider the following basic requirements:

- **Functionality.** Once your concept is decided, your equipment and kitchen space requirements should be designed around the recipes on your menu. Once a kitchen has been built, there is, of course, some flexibility to menu changes, but new pieces of equipment may be impossible to add without high costs or renovations. To design correctly, you need to visualize delivery, processing, preparation, presentation, and washing. To do this, you must be intimately familiar with each menu item.

- **Fit for purpose.** When shopping for equipment, choose based on the best equipment for your needs, not price. Only when you have decided between a small non-vented fryer or an industrial one, two ovens or five, and which specific brand will meet your needs, should you begin to find the best price.

HE MENU

Your menu should not just be a list of the dishes you sell; it should positively affect the revenue and operational efficiency of your restaurant. Start by selecting dishes that reflect your customers' preferences and emphasize what your staff does well. Attempting to cater to everyone has you doing nothing particularly well and does not distinguish your restaurant. Your menu should be a major communicator of the concept and personality of your restaurant, as well as an important cost control.

An effective menu does five key things:

1. Emphasizes what customers want and what you do best.

2. Is an effective communication, merchandising, and cost-control tool.

3. Obtains the necessary check average for sales and profits.

4. Uses staff and equipment efficiently.

5. Makes forecasting sales more consistent and accurate for purchasing, preparation, and scheduling.

Bear in mind the following:

- **Menu item placement.** Where you place an item on your menu is important in determining whether or not the customer will order the item. Customers are most likely to remember the first and last things they read. By placing the items you want to sell (the items that yield the highest profits) first or last, you increase the chance of selling them.

- **Design.** A well-designed menu creates an accurate image of the restaurant in a customer's head, even before the customer has been inside. It also directs the attention to certain selections and increases the chances of them being ordered. Your menu also determines, depending upon its complexity and sophistication, how detailed your cost-control system needs to be.

- **Plan to have a menu that works for you.** The design of your menu will directly affect whether it achieves these goals. Certain practices can influence the choices your guests make. Instead of randomly placing items on the menu, single out and emphasize the items you want to sell. These will generally be dishes with low food cost and high profits that are easy to prepare. Once you have chosen these dishes, use design — print style, paper color, and graphic design — to direct the readers' attention to these items. A customer's eye will fall to the middle of the page first. It is an important factor; however, design elements used to draw a reader's eye to another part of the menu can be just as effective.

- **Print the menu in-house.** With today's desktop publishing technology, you can easily produce your own menus. All you need is a software program like Menu Pro, available at **www.atlantic-pub.com**. Choose from a selection of menu papers at **www.ideaart.com** or **www.armesco.com**.

- **Tell your story on the back of the menu.** People always want to know more. Use this chance to increase their perception of your restaurant quality. Tell them how your staff prepares fresh salad ingredients on a daily basis, never using pre-made items or canned goods. Let them know that you grind fresh gourmet coffee beans each morning before coffee is brewed. Tell your story and your guests will be impressed.

- **Provide clean, presentable menus.** Ensure that your menus are always clean and appear to be as good as new; otherwise throw them out. Greasy, sticky, soiled menus with bad creases, dog-ears, and stains are not very appealing to people who are preparing to dine. If a server hands a sticky, dirty menu to a customer, what kind of impression do you think that customer will have of your restaurant?

MENU "DO NOTS"

- **Do not charge extra for the small items.** Some restaurants will charge an additional $0.30 for a slice of cheese on their hamburger or $0.40 for blue cheese dressing. While it may cost you a bit extra for these items, you should cover the cost by averaging it in to the overall cost of the meal. When you break down charges, people get the impression that you are being petty.

- **Do not tell your guests that you have run out of a particular item.** You have sold out, not run out. Run out makes it sound as if the restaurant is poorly managed and unprepared. Selling out is a good thing, not a bad thing. It means business is good and food is fresh.

SETTING MENU PRICES

To follow are some important considerations when setting your menu prices.

For every dollar that you earn, you should aim for ten to 12 cents as a profit. Once you figure out your food cost, multiplying it by 3.3 will give you about a 10 percent profit per item, factoring in food cost, labor cost, and overhead. Do realize that some items will have to have a slightly higher cost structure and others will have a lower cost structure, giving you, overall, a 10 percent profit.

Keep in mind that factors other than direct costs will influence your menu prices. Indirect factors, such as how a customer perceives quality, your location, the restaurant's atmosphere, and the competition will also play a role in your menu-pricing decisions.

You can buy software that will facilitate the costing procedures. Atlantic Publishing offers once such program called NutraCoster. NutraCoster will calculate product cost (including labor, packaging, and overhead) and nutritional content. The program can be ordered online at **www.foodsoftware.com**.

Try to price your menu so that the food cost and labor cost of each meal is about 70 percent of the sales price. In other words, try to price your menu items so that direct expenses run about two-thirds of the sale price. If you can bring other expenses down and do a good job of up-selling to your customers, you should be able to make a good profit while providing your customers with great meals at a great price — a win-win situation. Up-selling can be accomplished in a number of ways. Coach your wait staff on suggestive selling. By having servers ask if a customer wants appetizers or desserts, the customer is more likely to order these extra items.

Change your menu to accommodate large price shifts. When the price of beef soars, consider raising your main menu prices to accommodate. Change your menu items to use pork, chicken, or another meat with an acceptable price level.

MENU COSTS

Use your menu as a means for reducing your operating costs. A menu sales analysis is a good tool to use to track what you are selling. Keeping track of this information will enable you to identify areas where you can reduce costs, such as labor, waste, rising food cost, or over-portioning. A menu sales analysis will tell you three things:

1. How much of a particular item was sold.

2. The cost of the item.

3. The profitability of the item.

Many restaurants have computerized cash registers, so getting a report on what items sold nightly, weekly, or monthly is easy. If your restaurant does not have a computerized register, you can track a period of time and get this information by pulling it off guest checks.

Pull all this information into a simple table so you can compare it easily. See the example below:

ITEM	POPULARITY*	COST	MENU PRICE	PROFIT MARGIN
Pork tenderloin	42/100	$0.62	$12.50	$4.88
Spaghetti & meatballs	12/100	$1.79	$8.25	$4.46
Shrimp scampi	46/100	$3.40	$15.95	$7.55

*42/100 means 42 tenderloins were sold out of a total of 100 entrées served in that time period.

What do you do with this information once you have it? What does this information tell you about how you can reduce costs? Looking at your table, you see that your pork tenderloin is almost as popular as your shrimp dinner, but it costs a good deal less to make. You can summarize that by focusing on such lower-cost items. You can also increase your profit margin by decreasing your food cost. Keep in mind that by only focusing on low-cost items, you will lower your guest check average and this will lower profits. To reduce costs and remain profitable, you should emphasize a mix of high- and low-cost food items on your menu.

There are many software packages available to help you with menu costing. CostGuard's Web site, **www.costguard.com**, offers a product called Menu/Sales Engineering that tracks your sales mix information and provides analysis of your most and least popular and profitable items. The product currently sells for $495. Calcmenu is another software product you can use for menu costing, inventory management, menu planning, and nutrition analysis. You can find Calcmenu at **www.calcmenu.com**. There are various versions that are priced between $580 and $950. The site also offers a free trial version.

CALCULATING FOOD AND DRINK COSTS

The following guidelines will help you calculate food costs for your restaurant:

- **Inventory.** Start by calculating the value of your beginning inventory. Then add your purchase costs over the course of the month. At the end of the month, subtract the value of your remaining inventory from that figure to produce your monthly food expenses. Divide this figure by food revenue for the month and you will know exactly the food-cost percentage of sales. Cost of sales is the cost of the food or beverage products sold.

- **Drinks.** Beverage cost of sales and operating supplies would be calculated in a similar manner. Wine and beer should also be separated into another cost of sales category.

STANDARDIZED RECIPES

Using standardized recipes helps control costs and ensures quality and consistency of menu items. By providing your cooks and bartenders with this necessary information, you can retain control over portioning. Keep these in the kitchen and bar so your kitchen and bar staff will use them. You can store them on index cards and in an index cardholder or use a three-ring binder with recipe sheets inserted into transparent envelopes that can be easily wiped clean. Information to include on your kitchen recipe form follows:

- **Name of item and recipe number.**

- **Yield.** The total quantity the recipe will prepare.

- **Portion size.** May be listed by weight or number of pieces. You may want to include what size of utensil to use for serving. For example, use the 6-oz. ladle for a cup of soup.

- **Ingredients.** Make sure to list quantities of ingredients used.

- **Preparation instructions.**

- **Garnish.** You may want to draw a diagram or include a photograph to show your staff how the item should look when it leaves the kitchen.

- **Finishing.** Describe any finish the product needs, such as brushing with oil or melted chocolate drizzled on top. Also include how to cool it and at what temperature the product should be held. Can it sit at room temperature or does it need to be refrigerated?

- **Cost.** Include every ingredient and every garnish for accuracy. You will need to look at product invoices to get unit prices, and then determine the ingredient cost from this. Total the cost of each ingredient for your total recipe cost. This figure can then be divided by the number of portions in order to arrive at a portion cost. You will find a sample standardized recipe below.

BLUE RIDGE JAMBALAYA		Recipe No. 126
Portion Size: 1.5 cups	Yields: 40 portions	COST PER PORTION: $0.90

INGREDIENTS	WEIGHT/MEASURE	COST
Chicken, boneless breast cut in 1-inch pieces	4 lbs	$8.00
Andouille sausage, sliced	2 lbs	$5.58
Celery, chopped	16 cups	$3.16
Red peppers, chopped	8 each	$6.00
Onions, chopped	4 each	$0.40
Garlic cloves, minced	8 each	$0.17
Short-grain brown rice, dry	6 cups	$4.74
Beer	32 oz	$3.50
Chicken stock	60 oz	$1.72
Canned diced tomato	60 oz	$2.12
Tabasco sauce	4 tsp	$0.03
Parsley (garnish)		$0.04
Corn bread (side)		$0.58
	TOTAL COST	$36.04

Directions: Trim chicken, and cut into 1-inch pieces. Heat vegetable oil in a large sauté pan. Add chicken and cook through. Add sausage and heat through.

In a large stockpot, sauté onion, garlic, celery and red pepper in oil. Add rice, and coat rice with oil. Turn heat down to low, add beer and broth a little at a time, allowing the rice to absorb the liquid before adding more. When rice has simmered about 15–20 minutes, add tomato, chicken and sausage. Continue cooking until done and rice is tender (about 1 hour). Add Tabasco, salt and pepper.

Portion out the jambalaya into smaller containers to cool. Can refrigerate or use immediately for service.

Serve: Serve in a dinner bowl with a piece of corn bread on the side. Top with parsley.

ECONOMIZE WITHOUT REDUCING QUALITY

Try the following food/ingredient cost-reducing tips. They could make a big difference to your overall expenditures.

- **Extend the life of oil or fat for the deep fryer.** By following these six simple steps, you can almost eliminate the need to discard old fry oil or fat.

    1. Thoroughly clean fryer baskets and the fryer elements with a mild detergent rinse at least once a week.

    2. Filter with the Fry-Saver, from **www.espressoplusmore.com**, one to three times per day or after each shift.

    3. After one week, remove 50 percent of the filtered oil or fat and store in a clean container to be used for daily "top off" oil.

    4. Refill fryer with 50 percent new oil and continue using.

    5. Add used, aged, filtered oil, or fat for upkeep to refill fryer back to fill line.

    6. Repeat steps on a regular schedule.

- **Use air pots for coffee.** They are sealed and insulated like a thermos and can hold temperature and coffee quality up to eight hours.

- **Bread baskets.** The potential for waste in bread baskets is large. Most of these come back from the table partially eaten at best. You may want to consider providing bread baskets only if requested or you may want to cut down on the amount served. You could also consider including packaged items since these can be reused. Some operators are now serving bread only by request and one roll or breadstick per guest served from a bread basket with tongs at a time.

- **Cut kitchen waste.** One of the major culprits in high food costs is waste. Put a new garbage can in the kitchen. This can is for wasted product only, such as wrong orders, dropped food, etc. By giving your kitchen staff this visual aid, you can reinforce the amount of money that gets spent on such product waste.

- **Substitute pre-made items for some items you have been making from scratch.** You do not have to sacrifice quality; many pre-made items are particularly high standard. You can also start with a pre-made item and add ingredients. You can buy a pre-made salad dressing and add blue cheese or fresh herbs. Using these items will lower your food and labor cost and you can still put out a quality item.

- **Use industry information.** Check out **www.restaurantnews.com/foodcost.html** for other restaurateurs' tips on how to lower food costs.

PORTION CONTROL

Ensure all employees adhere to portion standards. If the portions your staff are serving are just 10 percent more than you are budgeting for, you are losing a lot of money every month. Portion control holds true from the size of a slice of meat to the amount of salad and dressing served with each meal. Bear in mind the following:

- **Weights and measures.** Ensure your kitchen staff weighs all portions and ingredients before cooking them so as to meet recipe specifications on every meal. Often when you purchase from suppliers, you are paying by the pound, so if your portions are too large, you are losing money on every meal. Trim where necessary and maintain consistency wherever possible.

- **Established recipes.** Restaurant recipes have two purposes: to ensure consistency and control costs. Following these practices will keep food costs from getting out of control. Also, having a consistent quality for all your meals will enhance the way your establishment is perceived by customers.

- **No "free handing it."** Be sure your staff is using scales, measuring cups, measuring spoons, and appropriate ladles. Often cooks will "free hand it" after a while. Free handing usually results in over-portioning.

- **Does your staff use trim items from meal preparations in other meals?** Meat trimmings can be used for soups to great effect, celery leafs can be used as garnishes, and pastry off-cuts can be re-rolled and used.

- **Fixed menu.** Maintain a fixed menu for your business, one that allows you to keep a smaller inventory and a fairly simple price list for employees to remember. When you do offer daily specials, fashion them around whatever ingredients you managed to buy for a great price that week or items in your inventory that you would like to move. If you do use a seasonal menu, try to use local growers for lower produce prices and design seasonal menus that allow you to use ingredients in several dishes so you can order in bulk.

- **Side dishes.** Soups, breads, and salads have a far lower fixed per-plate cost than your entrée meals, so make your soups and salads available with a variety of meals and ensure they are of high quality. Your customers will notice how good these meals are and you can keep your entrée portions to a manageable size without leaving customers hungry.

- **Portion out all condiments, sauces, and breads according to the number of guests** at a table. If servers put more bread on the table than is needed, your patrons will inevitably eat more and order less. Similarly, if the bread is thrown away and not used, it is simply wasted money.

- **Plate size.** Be certain your kitchen staff uses the correct-sized dish for each menu item. If they are serving a salad on a dinner plate, they will probably serve too much since the prescribed portion will look small on a large dinner plate.

- **Train your staff.** Train all new employees and spend time retraining existing staff at regular intervals.

MANAGE COST—INCREASE SALES

Managing business costs such as inventory, supplies, labor, and other services takes focus and consistency, but there are also a few easy tips that can help you keep such costs to a minimum. Utilize existing resources, such as:

- **Expand sales without additional investment.** Provide a display case selling specialty items that can last for a few days or even weeks. Have your chef prepare these items during the slow hours. Many guests will love the idea of purchasing items "to go" that they cannot purchase in a store or anywhere else. Utilize existing resources and create additional sales on the side. Gourmet Display offers a wide array of food and beverage display equipment. Visit **www.gourmetdisplay.com** to see the wide selection. To capitalize on growing off-premise sales opportunities, package your desserts or carry-outs attractively. This three-tiered tray from Gourmet Display is an excellent way to display desserts or other items. Visit the Web site or call 800-767-4711 to order.

Sabert has many cost-effective disposable solutions. Sabert's elegant product styling makes food look great. Platters, bowls, and utensils are available in an extensive selection of styles and sizes. All products are food service tested for superior performance and designed with food service operators' needs in mind. Sabert's FastPac three-compartment tray is an excellent to-go solution. Available from **www.sabert.com** or call 800-SABERT1 or 800-722-3781 for more information.

- **Virgin drinks.** Offer a wide selection of virgin specialty drinks for children, nondrinkers, and designated drivers. Doing so saves you the expense of providing free refills on coffee, tea, and sodas.

- **Sell water.** Offer customers a choice of bottled water such as spring water, still water, sparkling water, or even flavored water, before you simply pour them a glass of ice water from a pitcher. You will be amazed at how much this simple act will increase your sales figures.

- **Reduce waste.** Remove all garbage cans from the kitchen and instead place plastic tubs throughout the prep area. At the end of each shift, the tubs' contents can be checked to ensure the proper procedures are being followed for preparation and trimming raw products. Make workers accountable for the quality of their work.

OTHER COST-SAVING TIPS

You may well have trimmed your inventory and staffing costs, but in a restaurant environment, many other possibilities exist for cost control.

- **Lease icemakers.** Icemakers are costly to purchase and repair. Rent or lease icemakers on an as-needed basis instead. If you already have an icemaker, be sure to install appropriate filters in the unit to enable it to last longer. Contact the following companies for leasing restaurant equipment and supplies:

  - Arctic Refrigeration and Equipment, **www.arcticfoodequip.com**, 866-528-8528.

  - Easy Lease Company, **www.easyleasecompany.com**, 800-514-4047.

  - Global Restaurant Equipment and Supplies, **www.globalrestaurantequip.com**, 800-666-8099.

- **Install electric hand dryers.** Not only do they save on costs, they are also better for sanitation purposes. Contact:

  - ASI Electric Dryer, **www.cescompany.com**, 707-664-9964.

  - Stielbel Eltron, **www.stiebel-eltron-usa.com**, 800-582-8423.

  - World Dryer, **www.worlddryer.com**, 800-323-0701.

- **Return pallets and crates to vendors.** Pallets and crates take up valuable space, as they are bulky items requiring labor to manage them. By making vendors responsible for taking pallets away and reusing them, the burden on your staff is reduced as well as the costs of waste management.

- **Save on table-top items.** To eliminate the use of individual wrapping, use straw and toothpick dispensers. Also consider using drink coasters that can be reused instead of cocktail napkins. Decorations do not have to be expensive. Consider browsing through online party and decoration sites such as 23 Party, **www.123party.com**, D and D Design, **www.ddchili.com** and Grab A Bargain, **www.grababargain.com**.

- **Offer discounts for mugs.** Offer discounts to customers who bring in reusable mugs for refills. Several restaurants have similar programs that encourage customers to reduce unnecessary waste. The incentive to bring in their own mug works when they receive beverages at reduced prices. Contact:

  - Advertising Magic, **www.advertisingmagic.com**, 800-862-4421.

  - Ceramic Mugs, **www.ceramic-mugs.com**, 305-593-0911.

  - DADEC Photo Mugs and Gifts, **www.dadec.com**, 866-853-3257.

  - Gift Mugs, **www.giftmugs.com**, 321-253-0012.

  - My Promo Store, **www.mypromostore.com**, 877-838-3700.

- **Use cleaning rags instead of paper towels.** Encourage staff to use cleaning rags instead of high-quality napkins and paper towels to mop up a spill. The purchase of disposable towels and napkins can be more expensive than laundry service.

- **Install thermal strips over cooler and freezer doors.** Keep cold air in and warm air out. Strips increase efficiency and reduce unnecessary electricity usage so that the compressor does not have to work as hard. Here are a few companies that provide seal-tight doors and replacement parts:

  - Arrow Restaurant Equipment, **www.arrowreste.com**, 909-621-7428.

  - Commercial Appliance, **www.commappl.com**, 800-481-7373.

- Loadmaster, **www.loadmaster.com**, 514-636-1243.

- **Separate hot and cold appliances.** Separate the locations of hot and cold appliances. It will increase efficiency and temperature regulation. Draw out an organizational diagram of your kitchen. The one-time effort will be worth it.

FOOD-COST PROBLEM AREAS

BEGINNING INVENTORY

The beginning inventory is the total dollar value of food supplies on hand at the beginning of the accounting period. This figure represents the starting point from which you can then compute total food cost each month.

Computing the beginning inventory is a simple calculation. If you are purchasing all new food products, simply total all your food purchases prior to opening day. This figure will be the beginning inventory.

Opening an old restaurant at a new location. If you are opening an existing restaurant and will be using some of the old supplies, first take an inventory of the old supplies. Add the dollar value of these supplies with all your new food purchases prior to opening day.

ENDING INVENTORY

An ending inventory is taken for a complete and accurate count of the food stock on hand at the end of an accounting period so that the remaining amount may be used in projecting the total cost for each category. When conducting the ending or physical inventory:

- **Use scales** for the most accurate determination.

- **Stocking order.** Place inventory sheets in the same order that the room is stocked.

- **Separate sheets.** Use a separate sheet for each area.

- **Include the following on the form: your inventory unit, units per case, pack or size, par, and vendor code.**

- **Use two people:** one to count (a manager) and one to record the figures (preferably an employee from a different area). For example, have the bar manager assist in the food inventory. One will count while the other writes. The person counting states each item, its unit, and its total amount. The other person enters the figure on the inventory sheet on the correct line.

- **Partial items.** If there is a partial item, such as half a case of tomatoes, estimate how much is remaining on a scale from 0.1 to 0.9 (0.5 being half of a container). Make sure there is a figure on either side of the decimal point (e.g., 0.5, 1.3).

- **Counting order.** Count shelves all the way across. Do not jump around.

- **Fill in all columns.** Put a zero (0) in columns where there is no item to be counted.

- **Use pound and unit costs.** Convert all items that are in prepared form into pound and unit costs. For example: 15 fish dinners at 12.5 oz = 11.72 lbs.

- **Multiples.** For items with multiple weights, such as different-sized cans of crushed tomatoes, use a separate pad for your addition and enter your total on the inventory form.

- **Double-check.** Make sure there is an entry for each item.

- **Be thorough.** Complete each area before moving on to a new one and check for blanks and possible mistakes.

- **Estimating.** When estimates must be made, they should be made with sound reasoning, not guessing.

FOOD COST PERCENTAGE

This basic ratio is often misinterpreted because it is calculated in so many different ways. Basically, it is food cost divided by food sales. Whether your food cost is determined by food sold or consumed is a crucial difference. For your food cost percentage to be accurate, a month-end inventory must be taken. Without this figure, your food cost statement is inaccurate and, therefore, basically useless because your inventory will vary month to month, even in the most stable environment.

Distinguishing between food sold and consumed is important. Food consumed includes all food used, sold, wasted, stolen, or given away to customers and employees. Food sold is determined by subtracting all food bought (at full price) from the total food consumed.

COST-CALCULATIONS — THE BASICS

MAXIMUM ALLOWABLE FOOD COST PERCENTAGE (MFC)

Maximum allowable food cost percentage (MFC) is the most food can cost for you to meet your profit goal. If your food cost percentage is over your maximum allowable percentage at the end of the month, you will not meet your profit expectations. To calculate it:

1. Write your dollar amounts of labor costs and overhead expenses (subtract food costs). Refer to past accounting periods and yearly averages to get realistic cost estimates.

2. Add your monthly profit goal as either a dollar amount or a percentage of sales.

3. Convert dollar values of expenses to percentages by dividing by food sales for the periods used for expenses. Generally, do not use your highest or lowest sales figures for calculating your operating expenses. Subtract the total of the percentages from 100 percent. The remainder is your maximum allowable food cost percentage (MFC).

100 – (monthly expenses – food costs) + monthly profit goal = MFC %

ACTUAL FOOD COST PERCENTAGE (AFC)

Actual food cost percentage (AFC) is the percentage at which you are actually operating. It is calculated by dividing food cost by food sales (only food sales, not total sales). If you are deducting employee meals from your income statement, then you are calculating cost of food sold. If there is no deduction of employee meals, which is true for most operations, then the food cost you are reading is food consumed; it is always a higher cost than food sold. If inventory is not being taken, the food cost on your income statement is just an estimate based on purchases and is not accurate.

POTENTIAL FOOD COST PERCENTAGE (PFC)

This cost is sometimes called the theoretical food cost. PFC is the lowest your food cost can be because it assumes that all food consumed is sold and that there is no waste at all. Calculate this cost by multiplying the number sold of each menu item by the ideal recipe cost.

STANDARD FOOD COST (SFC)

This is how you adjust for the unrealistically low PFC. The percentage includes unavoidable waste, employee meals, etc. This food-cost percentage is compared to the AFC and is the standard that management must meet.

THE PRIME COST

The prime cost includes the cost of direct labor with food cost. This cost includes labor incurred because the item is made from scratch (labor from baking pies and bread, trimming steaks, etc.). When the food cost is determined for these items, the cost of the labor needed to prepare them is added. This costing method is applied to every menu item needing extensive direct labor before it is served to the customer. Indirect labor cannot be attributed to any particular menu item and is overhead.

BEVERAGE EXCLUSIONS

Beverage sales should not include coffee, tea, milk, or juice, which are usually considered food. If you include soft drinks in your food costs, be aware that it will reduce the food cost, since the ratio of cost to selling price is so low.

RATIO OF FOOD TO BEVERAGE SALES.

Simply the ratio of the percentages of your total sales. In restaurants with a higher percentage of beverage than food sales, profits are generally higher because there is a greater profit margin on beverages.

SALES MIX

Sales mix is the number of each menu item sold. It is crucial to cost analysis because each item impacts food cost and food percentages differently.

DAILY FOOD COST ANALYSIS

Traditionally, food cost is calculated once a month. There is no reason, however, why you cannot compute a daily food cost and a daily weighted food cost to analyze problem areas. Much of the inventory counting can be eliminated by moving only the products used for production into the kitchen at the beginning of the shift. Doing so, you can pinpoint problem areas, problem employees or problem shifts. You can also calculate a separate food cost for breakfast or lunch.

WEIGHTED FOOD COST PERCENTAGE

Once your food cost is calculated, determine weighted food cost percentage. A weighted food-cost percentage will tell you what your food cost should have been had all procedures and controls operated at 100 percent efficiency. The schedule on the following page summarizes sales information from the restaurant's POS system or from other bookkeeping records. Basically, you are recreating the food cost for each item based on the standard recipe costs to determine what your food cost and, thus, food cost percentage should have been. For this example only four menu items are served in this restaurant. You can see that $7,000 of food costs have slipped away (assuming all calculations are accurate). The restaurant should have actually had a 34.28 percent weighted food cost percentage.

WEIGHTED FOOD-COST CHART			
Menu Item	Cost per Meal	# of Meals Served	Cost per Menu Item
Chicken Kiev	$5.00	2,000	$10,000.00
Steak Oscar	$8.00	4,000	$32,000.00
Stuffed Flounder	$9.00	1,000	$9,000.00
Hamburger Platter	$3.00	3,000	$9,000.00
Weighted Total Cost			$60,000.00
Actual Sales			$175,000.00
Weighted Food-Cost Percentage			34.28%
Variation Over Actual Food-Cost Percentage			4% or $7,000.00

RAISING PRICES

Want to immediately lower your food cost percentage? Raise your prices. At some point in your career as a food service manager, you have to deal with the issue of raising prices. Here are some tips:

- **Reasons for raising prices.** Make an overall review of your establishment. You may be experiencing higher food costs because food prices have risen significantly since your last price review. Perhaps you have just undergone major renovation and have upgraded the atmosphere of your restaurant. Competition may have changed since the last increase or you may have decided that you need to make a bigger profit in order for it to be worthwhile to stay in business. All of these are valid reasons for price increases. The way to implement increases should be considered carefully.

- **Target certain items first.** If you do an across-the-board price increase, you may scare off some customers. You may want to consider increasing the price on a certain number of key dishes and leaving other price increases for a later date.

- **Decide how to communicate these increases.** Should you print a new menu or devise a way to increase the price on existing copies of the menu? It is never a good idea to simply cross out the old price and write in the new, but many food service managers also feel that it is a bad idea to increase prices when you print new menus that have changes in the items being offered. Whatever you decide, do not alert customers to price increases.

- **Test market.** It may be best to reprint old menus with new prices and save any changes to the bill of fare until a later printing. This strategy will also let you "test market" the new prices. If you are not seeing the sales you need from the new prices, you can adjust them with a second printing.

CHAPTER

SUCCESSFUL KITCHEN MANAGEMENT AND CONTROL PROCEDURES

This chapter on kitchen management is divided into three separate sections: personnel, procedures, and controls. HACCP and food-safety sanitation practices are covered in Chapter 16.

The personnel section describes the duties, functions, and responsibilities of the various employees that are found in any restaurant. Every restaurant is unique in the way it operates. Some adaptation of these positions may be necessary in meet your own restaurant's needs. A list of specific job responsibilities provides details of some of the more critical positions.

The last part of the personnel section combines the functions into an organizational flowchart. This chart illustrates how kitchen employees unite their individual efforts and talents to present the final product to the customer.

The kitchen procedures section describes the basic day-to-day operational policies of the kitchen. Described are the procedures for purchasing, receiving, storing, rotating, and issuing all food items. Several sample forms are given at the end of this chapter, illustrating each of the procedures. These sample forms are also used in the control section and are an integral part of the control system.

Finally, the kitchen controls section combines all of the personnel and procedures previously described into a system of checks and balances. This section will enable the restaurant manager, through the use of the sample forms and simple procedures, to know exactly where every food item and every cent the restaurant business spent went.

The last few pages of this section consolidate all the personnel, procedures, and sample forms into a sequence of daily events to illustrate how every food item is controlled, from the initial purchasing stage to when the cashier rings up the sale.

Although Chapter 16 addresses HACCP food safety and sanitation, the kitchen controls section of this chapter describes basic sanitation practices with which every restaurant manager and every employee must be thoroughly familiar. This section is perhaps the most important. Improper handling of food items or disregarding sanitation procedures will undoubtedly lead to hazardous health conditions. There are numerous cases where restaurants have caused or were held responsible for the spread of severe sickness and infectious diseases that have even, in certain instances, led to death. There is no excuse for neglecting any health or sanitation procedure. It is the responsibility of the restaurant manager to guarantee the wholesomeness of the restaurant's product.

KITCHEN PERSONNEL

THE KITCHEN DIRECTOR — JOB DESCRIPTION

A kitchen director, head cook, or head chef position can usually be found in any medium- to large-volume restaurant. Although job descriptions differ among various establishments, the primary objective of the kitchen director is to establish the maximum operational efficiency and food quality of the kitchen. The director is responsible for all the kitchen personnel and their training. Her foremost responsibility is to ensure that all food products are of the highest quality obtainable. She must set an example to other employees through her work habits and mannerisms. The restaurant manager must have complete faith in the ability of the kitchen director. The kitchen director must possess the same goals and desires as that of the restaurant's manager: primarily a total dedication to serve only the finest food possible at the lowest cost.

Your kitchen director must be available during both the day and evening. During the day she must oversee the preparation cooks and ensure that all food products are ordered and accounted for. She would also be responsible for any breakfast, lunch, brunch, or catering functions. During the evening the director must make certain the kitchen is properly staffed and take any measures needed, including working in the kitchen behind the line to ensure positive results.

The restaurant manager cannot possibly spend the necessary time to supervise the kitchen and attend to all the minute details. Therefore it is highly recommended that a competent kitchen director be employed.

KITCHEN DIRECTOR'S AREAS OF RESPONSIBILITY

1. All personnel in the kitchen.
2. Food quality.
3. Controlling waste and food cost.
4. Ordering, receiving, storing, and issuing all food products.
5. Training of kitchen personnel.
6. Morale of the kitchen staff.
7. Health and safety regulation enforcement.

8. Communicating possible problem areas to the manager.

9. Scheduling all kitchen personnel.

10. Scheduling her own time.

11. Maintaining a clean and safe kitchen.

12. Holding kitchen staff meetings.

13. Filling out all forms for prescribed kitchen controls.

PREPARATION COOK — JOB DESCRIPTION

The preparation ("prep") cook's responsibility is to prepare all the food items in the restaurant in accordance with the preparation methods prescribed. The kitchen director trains, supervises, and is responsible for the preparation cooks. The preparation cooks are directly involved in determining the outcome and quality of the final food product. This area is where the greatest amount of waste occurs; the kitchen director must monitor preparation closely. Preparation cooks must follow the Recipe and Procedure Manual exactly as it is printed to ensure consistent products and food costs.

SOME RESPONSIBILITIES OF PREPARATION COOKS

1. Prepare all food products according to the prescribed methods.

2. Maintain the highest level of food quality obtainable.

3. Receive and store all products as prescribed.

4. Maintain a clean and safe kitchen.

5. Follow all health and safety regulations.

6. Follow all restaurant regulations.

7. Control waste.

8. Communicate all problems and ideas for improvement to management.

9. Communicate and work together with coworkers as a team.

10. Arrive on time and ready to work.

11. Attend all meetings.

12. Fill out all forms as prescribed.

13. Maintain all equipment and utensils.

14. Organize all areas of the kitchen.

15. Follow proper rotation procedures.

16. Label and date all products prepared. For resources visit **www.daymarksafety.com** or call 800-847-0101.

17. Follow management's instructions and suggestions.

COOKING STAFF — JOB DESCRIPTION

The cooking staff arrives one to two hours before the restaurant is open for business. Their primary responsibility is to cook the prepared food items in the prescribed method. The cooking staff may be made up of regular line cooks or highly skilled chefs, depending on the complexity of the menu. They must ensure that all food products have been prepared correctly before cooking. They are the last quality-control check before the food is presented to the wait staff and the public. It is imperative that the cooking staff work together as a team and communicate with one another. A group effort is needed to keep the kitchen operating at maximum efficiency.

SOME RESPONSIBILITIES OF THE COOKING STAFF

1. Arrive on time and ready to work.
2. Ensure that proper preparation procedures have been completed.
3. Prepare the cooking areas for the shift.
4. Maintain the highest level of food quality obtainable.
5. Communicate with coworkers, wait staff, and management.
6. Become aware of what is happening in the dining room (arrival of a large group).
7. Account for every food item used.
8. Maintain a clean and safe kitchen.
9. Follow all health and safety regulations prescribed.
10. Follow all the restaurant regulations prescribed.
11. Control and limit waste.
12. Communicate problems and ideas to management.
13. Attend all meetings.
14. Fill out all forms required.
15. Maintain all kitchen equipment and utensils.
16. Keep every area of the kitchen clean and organized.
17. Follow the proper rotation procedures.
18. Label and date all products used. For resources visit **www.daymarksafety.com** or call 800-847-0101.
19. Follow management's instructions and suggestions.

THE EXPEDITER — JOB DESCRIPTION

Sets the pace and flow in the kitchen. The expediter receives the order ticket from a waiter or waitress or from a printer in the kitchen and communicates which menu items need to be cooked to the cooking staff. Each cook performs a specific cooking function at his station, such as broiling, deep-frying, cooking pasta, sautéing, or carving. The expediter can regulate the pace in the kitchen by holding an order ticket for a few minutes before reading it to the cooking staff. Doing so is particularly useful when the cooks are bogged down in work.

The expediter is also responsible for lying out and garnishing all the plates. He makes certain that each member of the wait staff receives the correct plates with the correct items on them. As a double check, each wait staff member must check her order ticket against the actual prepared plates before taking them out of the kitchen. The expediter must make certain that every food item that leaves the kitchen has had an order ticket written for it. Under no circumstance is the expediter to instruct the cook to start the cooking of an item unless there is a written order ticket — it is crucial to the success of this control system. All order tickets are to be held by the expediter for reference at the end of the night.

SOME RESPONSIBILITIES OF THE EXPEDITER

1. Communicate with everyone in the kitchen.

2. Always get an order ticket from a waiter/waitress or kitchen printer.

3. Ensure all food leaving the kitchen is of the level of quality prescribed.

4. Make certain all plates are hot and garnished correctly.

5. Make certain that every food item is accounted for.

6. Safely store all food order tickets for later reference.

7. Fill out all required forms appropriately.

8. Maintain all equipment and utensils.

9. Keep own work area of the kitchen organized.

10. Follow all rotation procedures.

11. Label and date all products used. For resources visit **www.daymarksafety.com** or call 800-847-0101.

12. Follow management's instructions and suggestions.

SALAD PREPARER — JOB DESCRIPTION

The salad preparer fixes and portions salads from the ingredients prepared during the day. A salad preparer is used when the restaurant has salad table service. For better control, this person may also be assigned to issue desserts. A salad preparer can be a great aid in speeding up service and controlling food cost.

Smaller restaurants that cannot justify the employment of a salad preparer should use the wait staff or cooks to prepare the salads. In this case, all dessert tickets must go to the expediter before the desserts are issued.

DISHWASHER — JOB DESCRIPTION

The dishwasher position is unfortunately often thought of as an unimportant position that anyone can be trained to perform quickly and cheaply. However, a dishwasher is as important as any other employee in the restaurant. She is responsible for supplying spotless, sanitized dishes to the dining room and clean kitchen utensils to the cooks. A slowdown in the dishwashing process will send repercussions throughout the restaurant. Improperly cleaned china, glassware, or flatware can ruin an otherwise enjoyable dining experience. How many times have you sat at a table with a dirty fork or a glass with lipstick residue? The dishwasher handles thousands of dollars of china and glassware every day. Accidentally dropping a tray of dishes can erase a day's profits.

All glassware, china, flatware, and kitchen utensils have special washing requirements. The correct chemicals and dishwashing racks must be used in order to achieve the desired results. Your dishwasher chemical company can supply you with all the training. Your salesperson can set up a training session with your staff. He will instruct your staff on how to operate the dishwasher correctly, set up systems to alleviate breakage, use the chemicals correctly, and set up the proper daily maintenance needed on the machine.

KITCHEN PROCEDURES

PURCHASING

The goal of purchasing is to supply the restaurant with the best goods at the lowest possible cost. There are many ways to achieve lowest possible cost. The buyer must have favorable working relations with all suppliers and vendors. A large amount of time must be spent meeting with prospective sales representatives and companies. The buyer's responsibility is to evaluate and decide how to best make each of the purchases for the restaurant. Purchasing is a complex area that must be managed by someone who is completely familiar with all of the restaurant's needs. The kitchen director or manager would be the best choice to do the purchasing. It is preferable to have one or two people do all the purchasing for all areas of the restaurant. There are several advantages to this, such as greater buying power and better overall control.

Provided the buyer completes the necessary research and evaluates all of the possible purchasing options, she can easily recoup a large part of her salary from the savings made. The most critical element to grasp when purchasing is the overall picture. Price is not the top priority and is only one of the considerations in deciding how and where to place an order.

INVENTORY LEVELS

The first step in computing what item and how much of it to order is to determine the inventory level, or the amount needed on hand at all times. It is a simple procedure and requires that the order sheets are prepared properly. To determine the amount you need to order, you must first know the amount you have in inventory. Walk through the storage areas and mark in the "On Hand" column the amounts that are there. To determine the "Build-To Amount," you will need to know when regularly scheduled deliveries arrive for that item and the amount used in the period between deliveries. Add on about 25 percent to the average amount used; this will cover unexpected usage, a late delivery, or a backorder at the vendor. The amount you need to order is the difference between the Build-To Amount and the amount On Hand. Experience and food demand will reveal the amount an average order should contain. By purchasing too little, the restaurant may run out of supplies before the next delivery. Ordering too much will result in tying up money, putting a drain on the restaurant's cash flow. Buying up items in large amounts can save money, but you must consider the cash-flow costs. A buying schedule should be set up and adhered to. This schedule would consist of a calendar showing:

- Which day's orders need to be placed.

- When deliveries will be arriving.

- What items will be arriving from which company and when.

- Phone numbers of sales representatives to contact for each company.

- The price the sales representative quoted.

Post the buying schedule on the office wall. When a delivery does not arrive as scheduled, the buyer should place a phone call to the salesperson or company immediately. Do not wait until the end of the day when offices are closed.

A "Want Sheet" (see the example at the end of this chapter) may be placed on a clipboard in the kitchen. This sheet is made available for employees to write in any items they may need to do their jobs more efficiently. It is a very effective form of communication; employees should be encouraged to use it. The buyer should consult this sheet every day. A request might be as simple as a commercial-grade carrot peeler.

COOPERATIVE PURCHASING

Many restaurants have formed cooperative purchasing groups to increase their purchasing power. Many items are commonly used by all food service operators. By cooperatively joining together to place large orders, restaurants can usually get substantial price reductions. Some organizations even purchase their own trucks and warehouses and hire personnel to pick up deliveries. Doing so can be quite advantageous for restaurants that are in the proximity of a major supplier or shipping center. Many items, such as produce, dairy products, seafood, and meat, may be purchased this way. Chain-restaurant organizations have a centralized purchasing department and, often, large self-distribution centers.

RECEIVING AND STORING

Most deliveries will be arriving at the restaurant during the day. The preparation crew is normally responsible for receiving and storing all items (excluding liquor, beer, and wine). The buyer should also be present to ensure that each item is of the specification ordered.

Receiving and storing each product is a critical responsibility. Costly mistakes can come about from a staff member who was not properly trained in the correct procedures. Listed below are some policies and procedures for receiving and storing all deliveries. A slight inaccuracy in an invoice or improper storing of a perishable item could cost the restaurant hundreds of dollars.

Watch for a common area of internal theft. Collusion could develop between the delivery person and the employee receiving the products. Items checked as being received and accounted for may not have been delivered at all. The driver simply keeps the items. In an upcoming section I will discuss how to guard against internal theft.

All products delivered to the restaurant must:

1. Be checked against the actual order sheet.

2. Be the exact specification ordered (weight, size, quantity).

3. Be checked against the invoice.

4. Be accompanied by an invoice containing: current price, totals, date, company name, and receiver's signature.

5. Have their individual weights verified on the pound scale.

6. Be dated, rotated, and put in the proper storage area immediately. For resources visit **www.daymarksafety.com** or call 800-847-0101.

7. Be locked in their storage areas securely.

Credit slips must be issued or prices subtracted from the invoice when an error occurs. The delivery person must sign over the correction.

Keep an invoice box (a small mailbox) in the kitchen to store all invoices and packing slips received during the day. Mount the box on the wall, away from work areas. Prior to leaving for the day, the receiver must bring the invoices to the manager's office and place them in a designated spot. Extreme care must be taken to ensure that all invoices are handled correctly. A missing invoice will throw off the bookkeeping and financial records and statements.

ROTATION PROCEDURES

1. New items go to the back and on the bottom.

2. Older items move to the front and to the left.

3. In any part of the restaurant: the first item used should always be the oldest.

4. Date and label everything.

DayMark Safety Systems has offers a wide variety of labeling and food safety products. Their DissolveMark™ labels dissolve in 30 seconds and will not leave any sticky residue which can harbor harmful bacteria. The MoveMark™ labels with glow-in-the-dark technology perfect for dimly lit areas. They are FDA approved for indirect food contact. Standard MoveMark labels remove easily from plastic and metal containers. DuraMark™ permanent labels have aggressive adhesive that is moisture resistant and adheres to any surface. CoolMark™ labels are designed exclusively the freezer and are available in both hand-applied and machine-applied labels. To view DayMark's complete product line, visit **www.daymarksafety.com** or call 800-847-0101.

 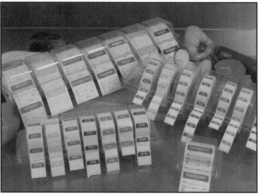 

Photos from left to right: DayMark CoolMark freezable labels. A selection of day-of-the-week labels in clear plastic dispensers. DayMark machine applied labels and marking gun.

TEMPERATURE RANGES FOR PERISHABLE ITEMS	
All frozen items	-10–0° F
Fresh meat and poultry	31–35° F
Produce	33–38° F
Fresh seafood	33–38° F
Dairy products	33–38° F
Beer	40–60° F
Wine (Chablis, rosé)	45–55° F
Wine (most reds)	55–65° F

ISSUING

All raw materials from which portionable entrees are prepared, such as meat, seafood, and poultry, must be issued on a daily basis. Whenever one of these bulk items is removed from a freezer or walk-in, it must be signed out. An example of a Sign Out Sheet may be found at the end of this chapter. When a part of a case or box is removed, the weight of the portion removed must be recorded in the "Amount" column. The Sign Out Sheet should be on a clipboard affixed to the walk-in or freezer. Once the item is signed out, the weight must be placed in the "Amount Ordered or Defrosted" column on the Preparation Form. An example of a Preparation Form may be found at the end of this chapter. This will show that the items signed out were actually used in the restaurant. From this information, the kitchen director can compute a daily yield on each item prepared. This yield will show that the portions were weighed out accurately and the bulk product that was used to prepare menu items. At any one of these steps pilferage can occur. The signing-out procedure will eliminate pilferage. Products such as dry goods or cleaning supplies may be issued in a similar manner. If these or other items were being stolen, the cost of each would show up in the cost projections at the end of the month.

KITCHEN CLEANLINESS

Kitchen cleanliness must always be of constant concern to both management and employees. A maintenance company should do little cleaning in the kitchen. They have not been trained in the cleaning procedures that must be used in the kitchen to maintain food safety requirements. A maintenance company should only be used for cleaning and washing the kitchen floor. The rest of the kitchen cleaning and maintenance is the responsibility of the staff.

All employees must be made aware that their daily cleanups are as critical as any of their other responsibilities — perhaps more so. A complete section on food safety can be found in the next chapter. Every employee must be completely familiar with its contents.

The most effective cleanup policy to institute is to make each employee responsible for his own area. Every workstation must have its own cleaning check-off sheet for the end of each shift. (See the example on the next page.) These sheets should be sealed in plastic, so that a grease pencil can be used to check off each completed item. Every employee must have his cleanup checked by a manager. You must inspect employee cleanup carefully and thoroughly. Once a precedent is set for each cleanup it must be maintained. At the end of a long shift some employees may need a little prodding to get the desired results.

CLEAN-UP SHEET FOR EACH COOK
Place a check mark on all completed items.

___1. Turn off all equipment and pilots.

___2. Take all pots, pans, and utensils to the dishwasher.

___3. Wrap, date, and rotate all leftover food.

___4. Clean out the refrigerator units.

___5. Clean all shelves.

___6. Wipe down all walls.

___7. Spot clean the exhaust hoods.

___8. Clean and polish all stainless steel in your area.

___9. Clean out all sinks.

___10. Take out all trash. Break down boxes to conserve space in dumpster.

___11. Sweep the floor in your area.

___12. Replace all clean pots, pans, and utensils.

___13. Check to see if your coworkers need assistance.

___14. Check out with the manager.

COOK	TIME OF LEAVING
MANAGER	

KITCHEN CONTROLS

The following section will present a system of kitchen controls. Combining these controls with the procedures and policies already set forth will enable you to establish an airtight food cost control system. The key to controlling food cost is reconciliation. Every step or action taken is checked and reconciled with another person. Management's responsibility is to monitor them with daily involvement. Should all the steps and procedures be adhered to, you will know exactly where every dollar and ounce of food went. There are no loopholes. Management must be involved in the training and supervision of all employees. Daily involvement and communication is needed in order to succeed. Employees must follow all procedures precisely. If they do not, they must be informed of their specific deviations from these procedures and correct them. Any control initiated is only as good as the manager who follows up and enforces it. The total amount of time a manager needs to complete all of the work that will be described in this section is less than one hour a day. There is no excuse for not completing each procedure every day. A deviation in your controls or involvement can only lead to a loss over the control of the restaurant's costs. *Please note:* Although a simple manual system is detailed here, many of these functions can be implemented into your computerized accounting system. Many of the basic purchasing and receiving functions are found in virtually all off-the-shelf accounting programs.

PREPARATION FORM

The Preparation Form is used by the preparation cooks. See the example form at the end of this chapter. It should be filled out as follows:

A. **The first procedure performed each morning by the preparation cook is counting the number of items on hand.** These are food items left from the previous night. The number of each item left is placed in the "Beginning Amount" column. Every item that needs to be prepared must be on this sheet: all entrees, side orders, desserts, salad items. This sheet will be used as a reference guide throughout the day to determine which items need to be prepared.

B. **List the minimum amount needed for the day from the Minimum Amount Needed Form.** This form sets the minimum amount you need to have prepared for the cooking staff. Each day will show a different amount, depending upon the amount of customers you anticipate serving. The minimum amount needed is computed by management based on the number of items previously sold on an average day in the past. Procedures for calculating the Minimum Amount Needed are discussed in the following section.

C. **Subtract the Beginning Amount from the Minimum Amount Needed.** This figure will be the amount that needs to be prepared for that particular item. Based on this figure you can then compute the amount of food that must be either ordered or removed from the freezer to defrost. All portion-controlled items must be signed out on the Sign Out Sheet before being removed from the freezer or walk-in.

D. **All items entered on the Sign Out Sheet must also be entered in the "Amount Ordered or Defrosted" column on the Preparation Form.** This information is entered here so that the kitchen director will be able to compute a yield on all the items prepared. This column will also be used by the manager to calculate the daily perpetual inventory, which will be discussed later in this chapter.

E. **As the day progresses, items will be prepared, dated, wrapped, rotated, and placed in the walk-in for use that night.** The number of portions prepared for each item is recorded in the "Amount Prepared" column.

F. **The Amount Prepared plus the Beginning Amount equals the starting total.** The starting total must be equal to or greater than the minimum amount needed. When all items are completed, the preparation sheet is placed in the manager's office.

MINIMUM AMOUNT NEEDED FORM

The purpose of the Minimum Amount Needed Form is to guide the preparation cook in determining the amount of food that will need to be prepared for each day. An example of the

Minimum Amount Needed Form can be found at the end of this chapter. The Minimum Amount Needed must be large enough so that the restaurant will not run out of any food during the next shift. However, too much prepared food will quickly lose its freshness and may spoil altogether.

To compute the Minimum Amount Needed of each item for each particular day, consult the Food Itemization Form, described in Chapter 35, "Internal Bookkeeping." This form will list the actual number of each menu item sold for every day of the past month. It will also indicate the percentage sold of that item in relation to the rest of the menu items for the month and for each day. Examine the last two months' product mixture figures. Based on this information you should get a relatively accurate depiction of the amount of each item sold on each particular day of the week. Based on the average amount sold each day and the percentage sold in relation to the total menu, you will be able to project the minimum amount needed for the following months.

EXAMPLE

According to the Food Itemization Form last month the restaurant sold between 20 and 25 shrimp dinners each Saturday night. The restaurant served between 200 and 300 dinners for each of these nights, so about 10 percent of the menu selections sold were shrimp dinners. To project next month's Minimum Amount Needed for an average Saturday evening, estimate the average number of dinners you expect to serve.

Let us assume 250 dinners will be sold on an average Saturday evening. Multiply this figure (250) by the average percentage of the menu sold (10 percent, or .10) — the answer (25) would be the approximate number of shrimp dinners you would sell on an average Saturday for the next month. It is only an educated guess; add 30 percent to the figure you projected to cover a busy night. In the example, this extra 30 percent is eight more dinners: 33 shrimp dinners is the minimum amount needed for Saturday night. Holidays and seasonal business changes need to be considered when setting minimum amounts.

DAILY YIELDS

Daily yields represent the actual usage of a product from its raw purchased form to the prepared menu item. The yield percentage is a measure of how efficiently this was accomplished or how effectively a preparation cook eliminated waste. The higher the yield percentage, the more usable material was obtained from that product.

All meat, seafood, and poultry products must have a yield percentage computed for each entree every day. Yields are extremely important when determining menu prices. They are also a very useful tool in controlling food cost. Daily yields should be computed by the kitchen director. An example of a Daily Yield Sheet can be found at the end of this chapter.

Yield sheets should be kept for several months: They may become useful in analyzing other problem areas. All the information to compute each yield can be obtained from the Daily Preparation Form.

TO COMPUTE THE YIELD PERCENTAGE:

1. **From the "Amount Ordered or Defrosted" column compute the total amount of**

ounces used. Verify the amount in this column against the Sign Out Sheet. This figure is the starting weight in ounces.

2. **The "Amount Prepared" column contains the number of portions yielded.** Enter this figure on the Yield Sheet.

3. **To compute the yield percentage, divide the Total Portion Weight (in ounces) by the Total Starting Weight (in ounces).**

Yields should be consistent regardless of who prepares the item. If there is a substantial variance in the yield percentages — 4 to 10 percent — consider these questions:

1. Are the preparation cooks carefully portioning all products? Over the months have they gotten lax in these methods?

2. Are you purchasing the same brands of the product? Different brands may have different yields.

3. Are all the items signed out on the Sign Out Sheet actually being used in preparing the menu items? Is it possible some of the product is being stolen after it is issued and before it is prepared? Do certain employees preparing the food items have consistently lower yields than others?

4. Is the staff properly trained in cutting, trimming, and butchering the raw products? Do they know all the points of eliminating waste?

Periodically compare the average yield percentage to the percentage used in projecting the menu costs. If the average yield has dropped, you may need to review the menu prices.

PERPETUAL INVENTORY

The perpetual inventory is a check on the daily usage of items from the freezers and walk-ins. This form is used in conjunction with the Sign Out Sheet. An example of the Perpetual Inventory Form may be found at the end of this chapter. When completed, the perpetual inventory will ensure that no bulk products have been stolen from the freezer or walk-ins. List all the food items that are listed on the Sign Out Sheet and Yield Sheet. In the "Size" column list the unit size that the item is packaged in. The contents of most cases of food are packed in units such as five pound boxes or two pound bags. Meat is usually packed by the number of pieces in a case and the case's weight. The size listed on the perpetual inventory must correspond to the size the preparation cooks are signing out of the freezer and walk-ins.

In the "Start" column, enter the number of each item listed. For example, if shrimp is packed in five pound boxes and you have two 50-pound cases, there are 20 boxes. Enter 20 in the "Start" column. Each number along the top corresponds to each day of the month. At the end of each day, count all the items on hand and enter this figure on the "=" line. Compare this figure to the "Amount Ordered or Defrosted" column on the Preparation Form; these amounts must be the same. Place the total number of each item on the "–" line. If there were any deliveries, place this total on the "+" line.

Check the invoices every day for the items delivered that are in your perpetual inventory. Ensure that all items signed off as being delivered are actually in the storage areas. Should there be a discrepancy, check with the employee that signed the invoice. The number of items you start with (20) plus the number you received in deliveries (five), minus the amount signed out by the preparation cooks (one), must equal the number on hand (24). If there is a discrepancy, you may have a thief.

Should you suspect a theft in the restaurant, record the names of all employees who worked that particular day. If thefts continue to occur, a pattern will develop among the employees who were working on all the days in question. Compute the perpetual inventory or other controls you are having a problem with at different times of the day, before and after each shift. Doing so will pinpoint the area and shift in which the theft is occurring. Sometimes placing a notice to all employees that you are aware of a theft problem in the restaurant will resolve the problem. Make it clear that any employee caught stealing will be terminated.

GUEST TICKETS AND THE CASHIER

There are various methods of controlling cash and guest tickets. The following section will describe an airtight system of checks and balances for controlling cash, tickets, and prepared food. Certain modifications may be needed to implement these controls in your own restaurant. Many of the cash registers and POS systems available on the market can eliminate most of the manual work and calculations. The systems described in this section are based on the simplest and least expensive cash register available. The register must have three separate subtotal keys for food, liquor and wine sales, and a grand-total key for the total guest check. Sales tax is then computed on this amount. The register used must also calculate the food, liquor, and wine totals for the shift. These are basic functions that most machines have. Guest tickets must be of the type that is divided into two parts. The first section is the heavy paper part listing the menu items. At the bottom is a space for the subtotals, grand total, tax, and a tear-away customer receipt. The second section is a carbon copy of the first. The carbon copy is given to the expediter, who then issues it to the cooks, who start the cooking process. Some restaurants utilize handheld ordering computers and/or the tickets may be printed in the kitchen at the time of entry into the POS system or register. Regardless, the expediter must receive a ticket in order to issue any food.

The tickets must have individual identification numbers printed in sequence on both parts and the tear-away receipt. They must also have a space for the waitperson's name, the date, table number, and the number of people at the table. This information will be used by the expediter and bookkeeper in tracking down lost tickets and/or food items. Each member of the wait staff is issued a certain number of tickets each shift. These tickets are in numbered sequence.

For example, a waiter may be issued 25 tickets from 007575 to 007600. At the end of the shift he must return to the cashier the same total number of tickets. No ticket should ever become lost; it is the responsibility of the wait staff to ensure this. Should there be a mistake on a ticket, the cashier must void out all parts. This ticket must be turned in with the others after being approved and signed by the manager. The manager should issue tickets to each individual waiter and waitress. An example of a Ticket Issuance Form can be found at the end of this chapter. In certain instances, the manager may approve of giving away menu items at no charge. The manager must also approve of the discarding of food that cannot be served. A ticket must be written to record all of these transactions. Listed below are some examples of these types of situations:

- **Manager food.** All food that is issued free of charge to managers, owners, and officers of the company.

- **Complimentary food.** All food issued to a customer compliments of the restaurant. This includes all food given away as part of a promotional campaign.

- **Housed food.** All food that is not servable, such as spoiled, burned, or incorrect orders.

All of these tickets should be filled out as usual, listing the items and the prices. The cashier should not ring up these tickets, but record them on the Cashier's Report Form. Write the word "manager," "complimentary," or "housed" over the top of the ticket.

The manager issues cash drawers, or "bank," to the cashier. The drawers are prepared by the bookkeeper. Inside the cashier drawer is the Cashier's Report itemizing the breakdown of the money it contains. An example of the Cashier's Report Form can be found at the end of this chapter. The accuracy of the Cashier's Report is the responsibility of both the cashier and the manager. Upon receiving the cash drawer, the cashier must count the money in the cash drawer with the manager to verify its contents. After verification, the cashier will be responsible for the cash register. The cashier should be the only employee allowed to operate it. Each member of the wait staff will bring his or her guest ticket to the cashier for totaling.

The cashier must examine the ticket to ensure:

- All items were charged for.
- All items have the correct price.
- All the bar and wine tabs are included.
- Subtotals and grand total are correct.
- Sales tax is entered correctly.

The cashier is responsible for filling out the charge-card forms and ensuring their accuracy. The cashier will return the customer's charge card and receipt to the appropriate member of the wait staff.

At the end of each shift, the cashier must cash out with the manager. List all the cash in the "Cash Out" columns. Enter the breakdown of sales into separate categories. Do not include sales tax. Enter all complimentary, housed, and manager amounts. Itemize all checks on the back. Itemize each ticket for total sales and total dinner count. Break down and enter all charged sales.

The total amount of cash taken in plus the charge sales must equal the total itemized ticket sales. Itemize all checks on the back of the Cashier's Report and stamp "FOR DEPOSIT ONLY:" the stamp should include the restaurant's bank name and account number.

Should a customer charge a tip, you may give the waiter or waitress a "cash paid out" from the register. When the payment comes in you can then deposit the whole amount into your account. Miscellaneous paid-outs are for any items that may need to be purchased throughout the shift. List all of them on the back and staple the receipts to the page.

When everything is checked out and balanced, the sheet must be signed by the cashier and manager. The manager should then deposit all tickets, register tapes, cash, charges, and forms into the safe for the bookkeeper the next morning. The cash on hand must equal the register receipt readings.

COOK'S FORM

The Cook's Form is used in conjunction with the Preparation Form. When both of these forms are completed, you will have complete accountability for all menu items. An example of the

Cook's Form can be found at the end of this chapter. In the "Item" column list all the entrees, side orders, and desserts. These items should be in the same sequence as in the Preparation Form for ease of comparison. In the "Start" column list all the items that were left over from the day before. Look at the dates to ensure that all the items used first are the oldest.

The "Additions" column contains the items that were prepared that day. The "Starting Balance" column contains the total of the Start amount plus the Additions. This figure represents the total number of starting items for the shift.

At the beginning of each cook's shift, the manager will compare the total starting figure on the Cook's Form to the total starting figures on the Preparation Form. All numbers must match. If any of the items do not match, the cook must go back and recount that item. You must be certain that both the Cook's Form and the Preparation Form are accurate. Recount the items yourself if necessary. Should there still be a discrepancy, you must consider whether there has been a theft sometime after the preparation cooks finished and before the cooking staff completed their form.

When the cooking shift is completed, the cooks will recount all the items not used. These figures are placed in the "Balance Ending" column. The difference between the Starting and the Balance Ending is the number sold. Once completed, the cooks will turn the sheet over to the expediter. The expediter will verify that the number of items sold equals the number of items cooked. To compare these two figures he must itemize the carbon copy part of the tickets that were given to him by the wait staff. An example of this Ticket Itemization Form can be found at the end of this chapter.

To itemize the tickets, place an "X" in the column next to the corresponding item. The total number of "X" marks equals the total number of tickets received for that item. Enter this figure in the "# Sold" column. The Total Sold from the Ticket Itemization Form must equal the total amount sold on the Cook's and Cashier's Report Forms. If there is a discrepancy:

- The expediter must re-itemize all tickets.

- The cooks must recount the ending balance.

- Make certain you considered all house, complimentary, and manager tickets.

Should there still be a discrepancy, the manager must recheck all the calculations and make certain all the tickets are accounted for. If the differences remain unresolved, you must consider that theft may be the reason. Either the item left the kitchen without a ticket or the item was taken without the cooking staff realizing it. The latter is unlikely, since the cooks are usually at their stations for the entire shift.

Once the Cook's Form is reconciled, return it to the office. All the Preparation, Cook's, and Ticket Itemization Forms should be kept in a loose-leaf binder for several weeks for reference.

Each morning the manager will compare the cook's Balance Ending figure with the preparation cook's Beginning Amount. Doing so will verify that all the items from last night are still there the following morning. This completes the daily cycle of checks and balances. The bookkeeper will further break down and analyze the forms, cash, and tickets.

SUMMARY

To enable you to envision precisely how the personnel procedures and controls combine to control the restaurant's food cost, a summary of the key points are listed in this section in sequence of events. In the example you will trace 25 pounds of shrimp through a typical day's operation, from the initial purchasing to the final product. The first column in each of the example forms are filled out so you will be able to see how they are used and why each one is a critical part in the overall control system. I would recommend that the manager put the following list in the form of a check-off sheet for his own organizational purposes.

SEQUENCE OF EVENTS

___1.   Determine the need to purchase shrimp.

___2.   Purchase the amount needed. An example: 25 pounds.

___3.   Shrimp is delivered. Follow the receiving and storing procedures.

___4.   Enter on the Perpetual Inventory Form the amount delivered. In example: five boxes of five pounds each.

___5.   Preparation cooks compute the opening counts. In example: 25 shrimp dinners is the beginning count.

___6.   Determine the Minimum Amount Needed: 33. The preparation cooks need to prepare eight more dinners for that night. They remove five pounds, or one box, of shrimp from the freezer.

___7.   Sign out the five pounds of shrimp on the Sign Out Sheet.

___8.   Place the amount, five pounds, in the "Amount Ordered or Defrosted" column on the Preparation Form.

___9.   Prepare the shrimp as prescribed in the Recipe and Procedure Manual.

___10.   The number of dinners prepared is nine; enter this figure in the "Amount Prepared" column. The starting total would be 34 (9 + 25). Enter these figures on the Preparation Form.

___11.   The Preparation Form is completed and given to the kitchen director. All storage areas are locked before leaving. The invoices are brought to the manager's office.

___12.   The kitchen director computes the yields.

___13.   The cooks enter and count all the items for the Starting Total.

___14.   The manager verifies that the Starting Total on the Preparation Form is the same as on the Cook's Form.

___15.   The manager issues the tickets to the wait staff. The manager issues the cashier drawer to the cashier and verifies the starting amount.

___16.   The manager checks the perpetual inventory.

___17.   The wait staff gives the order tickets to the expediter.

___18.   The expediter reads off the items to the cooks who start the cooking of the menu items.

___19.   When completed, the waiter/waitress takes the dinner to the customer.

___20.   The bill is totaled and given to the customer.

___21.   The cashier verifies the amount and collects the money or charge.

___22.   The cooks count the Balance Ending. In example: Starting Total is 34, and the ending balance is 21, leaving 13 as sold.

___23.   The expediter itemizes the carbon copies: 13 shrimp dinners sold.

___24.   The manager cashes out with the cashier. Ticket itemization: 13 sold.

___25.   All three figures verified: cooks to expediter to cashier.

___26.   The following morning the manager verifies the ending balance of the Cook's Form (21) to the Beginning Amount of the Preparation Form.

___27.   The bookkeeper rechecks and verifies all the transactions of the previous night.

DETAILED LAYOUT OF DISHROOM EQUIPMENT

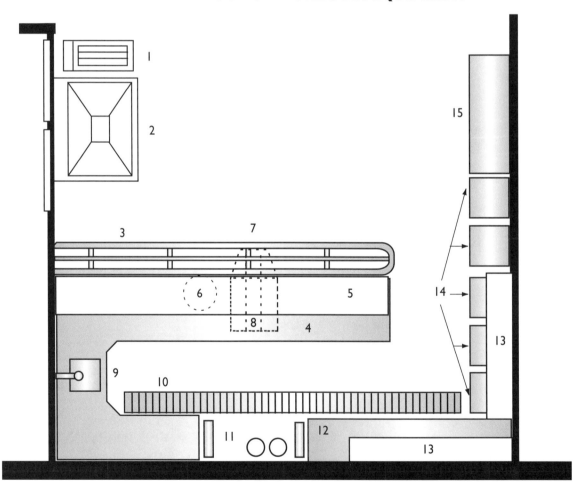

1. Silver burnisher
2. Linen hamper
3. Tray rail
4. Soiled-dish table
5. Glass rack overshelf
6. Disposal (3 h.p. hammermill type) and scrap chute
7. Silverware chute
8. Silverware soak tank
9. Prerinse sink with flexible spray arm
10. Dish-rack conveyor
11. Dish machine
12. Clean-dish table
13. Overshelves (two)
14. Dish-rack dollies (five)
15. Storage cabinet

DETAILED LAYOUT OF KITCHEN EQUIPMENT
IN A FAMILY RESTAURANT

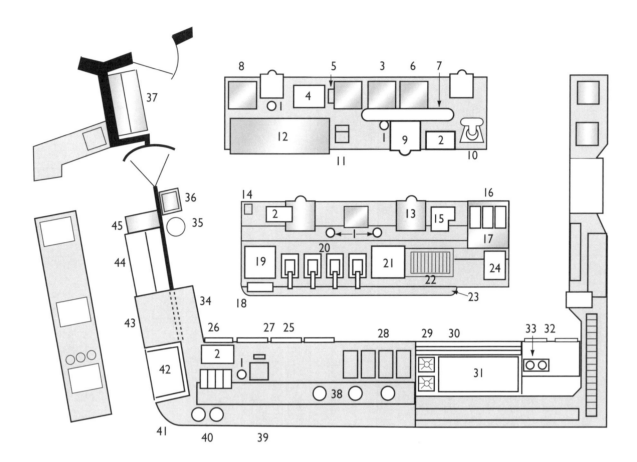

1. Knife wells (five)
2. Composition cutting boards (three)
3. Stainless-steel combination pot and pan washing table with three-compartment sink and meat and vegetable drawers (two)
4. Disposal (3 h.p. hammermill type)
5. Recirculating centrifugal pump
6. Flexible spray rinse arm
7. Overhead pot rack
8. Single-compartment sink
9. Stainless-steel salad preparation work table with undershelf
10. 12-quart mixer on mobile stand
11. Portion scale
12. Reach-in refrigerator
13. Stainless-steel meat and vegetable preparation worktable with angle-compartment sink, drawers (two), overshelf and undershelf

14. Can opener
15. Slicer
16. Closed-top range
17. Exhaust canopy
18. Wooden cutting board
19. Microwave oven
20. Deep fat fryers (four)
21. Griddle
22. Open-top broiler
23. Base cabinet refrigerator with overshelf
24. Steamer
25. Base cabinet refrigerator
26. Cold food wells (eight)
27. Sandwich grill
28. Hot food wells (four) and undercounter dish storage
29. Open-top burners (two)

30. Wooden cutting board
31. Griddle
32. Base cabinet refrigerator
33. Waffle grill
34. Pass-through window
35. Trash can
36. Wash basin
37. Ice machine
38. Heat lamps (two)
39. Waitstaff pickup counter
40. Soup wells (two)
41. Soup bowl lowerators
42. Reach-in refrigerator, sliding-door type
43. Customer takeout back counter
44. Fountain
45. Milkshake machine

PERPETUAL INVENTORY FORM

ITEM		1	2	3	4	5	6	7	8	9	10	11	12	13	14	15	16	17	18	19	20	21	22	23	24	25	26	27	28	29	30	31	I
Shrimp (20) (5 lbs.)	+	5																															
	–	1																															
	=	24																															

SIGN-OUT SHEET

ITEM	DATE	AMOUNT/WT.	EMPLOYEE
Shrimp-box	11-30	1 5-lb. box	Joe B.

DAILY PREPARATION FORM

ITEM	MINIMUM AMOUNT	AMOUNT DEF./ ORD.	BEGINNING AMOUNT	AMOUNT PREPPED	STARTING TOTAL
Shrimp	33	5 lbs.	25	9	34

MINIMUM AMOUNT NEEDED FORM

ITEM	MON	TUES	WED	THURS	FRI	SAT	SUN
Shrimp						33	

COOK'S FORM

ITEM	START	ADDITIONS	STARTING BALANCE	BALANCE ENDING	# SOLD
Shrimp dinners	25	9	34	21	13

THE RESTAURANT MANAGER'S HANDBOOK

DAILY YIELDS FORM

ITEM	STARTING WEIGHT (OZ.)	# OF PORTIONS	TOTAL PORTION WEIGHT (OZ.)	YIELD %	PREP/ COOK
Shrimp dinner	80.0	9	9 x 8.0 oz. = 72 oz.	90%	Bob S.

TICKET ISSUANCE FORM

WAITPERSON	INITIALS	TOTAL #	# THRU	RETURN # VERIFIED

TICKET ITEMIZATION FORM

ITEM	USE A ✓ MARK TO DESIGNATE ON SOLD	TOTALS
Shrimp dinners	✓ ✓ ✓ ✓ ✓ ✓ ✓ ✓ ✓ ✓	13

CASHIER'S REPORT FORM

Prepared By: _____

Date: _____ Day: _____ Shift: _____

		BAR REGISTER		SERVICE REGISTER		TOTAL
		Day	Night	Day	Night	All Shifts
1	**BANK DEPOSIT** Part I					
2	Currency					
3	Silver					
4	Checks					
5	**SUB TOTAL**					
6	**CREDIT CARDS:**					
7	MasterCard/Visa					
8	American Express					
9	Diner's Club					
10	Other					
11	**OTHER RECEIPTS:**					
12	**TOTAL BANK DEPOSIT**					
13	**CASH SUMMARY** Part II					
14	Sales per Register					
15	Sales Tax per Register					
16	**ADJUSTMENTS:**					
17	Over/Under Rings					
18	Other: Complimentaries					
19	Other					
20	**TOTAL ADJUSTMENTS**					
21	Sales to Be Accounted For					
22	Sales Tax to Be Acctd. For					
23	Accounts Collected					
24	Other Receipts:					
25						
26						
27	**TIPS CHARGED:**					
28	MasterCard/Visa					
29	American Express					
30	Diner's Club					
31	Other					
32	House Accounts-Tips					
33	**TOTAL RECEIPTS**					
34	**DEDUCT: PAID OUTS**					
35	Tips Paid Out					
36	House Charges					
37	Total Deductions					
38	**NET CASH RECEIPTS**					
39	**BANK DEPOSIT** (Line 12)					
40	**OVER or SHORT**					

CHAPTER

16

ESSENTIALS OF FOOD SAFETY, HACCP, AND SANITATION

Preparing and serving quality food in a safe environment is each employee's responsibility. In order to guarantee the quality and safety of your food, you must understand the basics of controlling food contamination. The definition of food contamination is the spread of infectious diseases.

Food safety is another issue that needs to be addressed in your employee training. Give them the know-how and necessary tools to allow them to establish and practice effective food-handling and sanitation procedures.

These are some things you must provide for your employees:

- **Give your employees hands-on training, reminders, and training manuals.**

- **Provide hair nets, uniforms, gloves, hand and nail brushes, germicidal hand soaps, and first-aid kits.**

- **Provide hand sinks at each workstation, sanitary employee bathrooms and lockers, scrub brushes, gloves, and disposable towels.**

- **Equipment and storage supplies should have dated labels and standard rotation procedures.** Give your employees color-coded utensils, test kits, and quality-control standards. These standards must be enforced.

Many types of bugs, animal pests, and bacteria can reside within your restaurant. These intruders search for food, water, and warmth. Since these unwanted creatures can be plentiful in your shop, make conditions unfavorable for them.

ACCP DEFINED

Hazard Analysis of Critical Control Points (HACCP) is a system to monitor food preparation to reduce the risk of food-borne illness. HACCP focuses on how food is processed – beginning with purchasing to how it is served. You and your staff need to understand the potential problems during each stage of preparation.

HACCP provides the necessary procedures to control food preparation in order to avoid the potential hazards. It helps you identify these critical control points (CCP). Each of these points can allow bacteria or harmful organisms to grow and contaminate food.

Atlantic Publishing offers a variety of HACCP products which can give you more in-depth information about HACCP regulations; a training kit, labels, and posters for employees, at **www.atlantic-pub.com/ HACCP_Main.htm**. You can order the items you need or they offer a HACCP kit which contains many items that you can use with your staff. The special sanitation package includes:

- *HACCP & Sanitation in Restaurants and Food Service Operations: A Practical Guide Based on the FDA Food Code: With Companion CD-ROM*

- A complete set of 20 Safety & Sanitation Labels (five each of four different labels)

- Sixteen sanitation and safety posters (pictured at right)

- Ten workplace safety posters

HY SHOULD YOU USE HACCP?

You are the owner of a restaurant and that means you are responsible for serving safe food to your customers. You must educate and motivate your employees to implement food safety procedures. These procedures must:

- Identify potential hazards.

- Implement safety procedures.

- Monitor how successful your safety system is on a consistent basis.

If the raw ingredients are safe and the process is safe, then the finished product is safe.

Using HACCP allows you to identify potentially hazardous foods and stages in the food preparation process where bacterial contamination, survival, and growth can occur.

IMPLEMENTING HACCP

These are the key steps to implementing HACCP:

STEP 1: ASSESS THE HAZARDS

- Have a system to track food from purchasing, receiving, preparation, serving, and reheating, if needed.

- Review your menu items. Identify the potentially hazardous foods and foods that could become contaminated.

- Risk can be reduced by removing very hazardous items from your menu.

- Review how you store, prep, cook, and serve items to identify any areas where contamination might occur.

- Rank the hazards based on whether they are severe or probable.

STEP 2: "CRITICAL CONTROL POINTS"

Identify areas in your process that can be controlled or prevented. Develop a step-by-step list that details the preparation of potentially hazardous foods. Then, identify ways to prevent, reduce, and eliminate recontamination at each step you listed.

These are ways food service workers can reduce the risk of food-borne illness:

- Practice good personal hygiene.

- Avoid cross-contamination.

- Use proper storage, cooking, and cooling procedures.

- Reduce the steps involved in preparing and serving.

Remember to review how your vendors handle your food, including being sure the food is transported and handled properly during delivery.

STEP 3: "CRITICAL LIMITS"

Part of this process requires that you establish the critical limits. These are standards that can be seen and measured. Include time and temperature rules.

- What is required to meet each standard? Avoid vague descriptions like "cook until done," and use "cook to internal temperature of 170 degrees within two hours."

- Your thermometers need to be calibrated on a regular basis.

- Your recipes need to include the end cooking, reheating, and hot-holding temperatures, along with thawing, cooking, and cooling times.

- Have sufficient staff at peak hours to ensure food is prepared and served safely.

STEP 4: MONITOR "CRITICAL CONTROL POINTS"

Step-by-step charts will show you potentially hazardous steps. Review your process and compare with the requirements to avoid potential problems in your process. Identify any problems and make the needed changes.

STEP 5: MAKE NEEDED CHANGES

Make changes as needed. Some reasons for change are:

- Food contaminated by hands or equipment must be rewashed or discarded.

- Food temperatures are not sufficient after cooking. Continue cooking to the required temperature.

- If food temperatures exceed 55 degrees Fahrenheit during prep or serving, discard it.

STEP 6: DEVELOP A RECORDKEEPING SYSTEM

Develop a system to document the HACCP process to monitor your results. Your employees can log their compliance. These records can provide proof that food-borne illnesses did not originate at your restaurant.

STEP 7: VERIFY YOUR SYSTEM IS EFFECTIVE

Verify that the HACCP process for your facility works. These are some ways you can do that:

- Note how often you need corrective actions. If frequent corrections are needed, evaluate the need to change, or fine-tune, your system. You may need to find time to retrain your employees.

- How can you test the strength of your sanitizing solution? Examine your records. Are employees entering actual valid data?

- Ensure your dishwashing and sanitizing equipment work properly. They need regular calibration and maintenance.

- The board of health can give you a non-biased assessment of whether or not your process is working.

 ACCP PROCEDURES

PURCHASING

When you purchase the food for your restaurant, you have several goals:

- To obtain safe and wholesome ingredients.

- Prepare food to meet your production and menu standards.

Carefully choose your vendors. They must meet the federal and state health standards. They should use the HACCP system in their operations and train their employees in sanitation. Delivery trucks need adequate refrigeration and freezer units. Foods should be packaged in protective, leak-proof, durable packaging.

Be clear with vendors, from the beginning, about what you expect from them. Include food safety standards in your purchase agreements. Ask to see the most recent board of health sanitation reports and tell them you will inspect their trucks quarterly or more often if warranted.

RECEIVING

The goals of receiving are:

- To ensure food is fresh and safe when it enters your facility.

- To transfer food to proper storage as quickly as possible.

These are the two important parts of receiving:

1. Preparing to receive food.

2. Inspecting the food when it arrives.

Keep these guidelines in mind, and complete these tasks when you receive food:

- Stock sanitary carts in your receiving area to transport goods.

- Prepare sufficient refrigerator and freezer space before deliveries arrive, especially during special events or high volume time periods.

- Label all deliveries with the date they arrived and a "use by" date.

- The designated receiving area needs to be well-lit and clean.

- All trash left after deliveries needs to be thrown into trash containers.

- Keep the floors free of food and debris.

- How does the delivery truck look when it arrives at your store? Is it clean and are the refrigerator units working properly?

Next inspect the food:

- Check expiration dates for all perishable items.

- Check that the shelf life dates have not expired.

- Check that frozen foods are airtight and moisture-proof.

- Check for any sign that food has been thawed and refrozen.

If there are any signs of refreezing, reject the items. Some signs include large crystals, solid areas of ice, or excessive ice in containers.

- Check cans for swollen areas, flawed seals or seams, dents, or rust. Also, reject cans that contain foamy or bad-smelling items.

- Check temperature of refrigerated and frozen foods, especially items that spoil quickly.

- Check for signs of insect infestations.

- Check for dirt on flats or crates that are dirty. If you find any, reject them.

STORAGE OPTIONS AND REQUIREMENTS

There are four ways to store food:

1. Dry storage is ideal for holding items longer and for less perishable items.

2. Refrigeration is for short-term and perishable items.

3. Deep chilling units are good for short-term storage.

4. Freezing is recommended for long-term storage of perishable foods.

You and your staff need to be familiar with safety and sanitation requirements for each type of storage.

DRY STORAGE

When you plan your storage areas, keep in mind that many items can be stored in a sanitary storeroom. You can store canned goods, baking supplies, grain, items like flour, and any other dry items. Some vegetables like onions, potatoes, and tomatoes should be stored in dry areas. It is best to have proper ventilation in this space and a temperature that will discourage bacteria and mold. Remember this:

- **Dry goods should be stored at 50 degrees, but 60 to 70 is adequate.**

- **Calibrate the wall thermometer to gauge the temperature in this area.**

- **Packages in this area should be in unopened cans or in tightly covered containers.** These items need to be rotated using the "first in, first out" (FIFO) system. To ensure accuracy, date the packages when they arrive and place new items behind older ones.

- **Clean all spills immediately and thoroughly to avoid pest infestation and cross-contamination.** Do not store trash or garbage cans in food areas.

- **No items should be placed on the floor.** The bottom shelf of your storage shelves must be six inches off of the ground. You can use pallets on the floor and store paper products on them.

- **Never use or store cleaning agents or other chemicals where they could contaminate foods.** Label all chemicals in a separate area and label all containers. Always store chemicals in their original containers.

REFRIGERATED STORAGE

Fresh meat, poultry, seafood, dairy products, most fresh fruits and vegetables, and hot leftovers should be stored in the refrigerator at temperatures below 40 degrees Fahrenheit. Keep in mind that food will not keep forever, even in a refrigerator. However, refrigeration does extend the shelf life and the cold keeps it safe from bacteria.

A refrigerator unit should have slotted shelves that allow air to circulate around the food. You should not line the shelves with foil or paper. Be careful not to overload the refrigerator or shelves. Empty space improves air circulation. Refrigerated food should also be dated and sealed.

Additional refrigerator tips:

- Use clean, nonabsorbent, covered containers for food storage.

- Dairy products are to be stored away from onions, cabbage, and seafood.

- Raw and uncooked food must be stored below prepared and ready-to-eat food to prevent cross contamination.

- Keep poultry, fish, and meat fluids away from other foods.

- The proper temperature for perishable items is critical to prevent food-borne illnesses. Check regularly to be sure the temperature stays below 40 degrees Fahrenheit. Each time the door opens and closes affects the inside temperature.

Have a backup thermometer for your refrigerator in addition to the built-in thermometers. Use several thermometers in different sections of the refrigerator, especially in a walk-in unit. Be sure you have a consistent temperature throughout and ensure no area is too warm.

DEEP CHILLING

Deep or super-chilling foods, at a temperature between 26 and 32 degrees Fahrenheit, decreases the growth of bacteria, extends the life of poultry, meat, and seafood without compromising their quality through freezing, and can be done in specially designed units or by lowering the refrigerator temperature.

FROZEN STORAGE

Frozen meats, poultry, seafood, fruits and vegetables, and some dairy products should be stored in a freezer at 0 degrees Fahrenheit to keep them fresh and safe for an extended period.

It is best to only freeze items that were shipped to you already frozen. When you freeze perishable foods, you can damage their quality. Storing food in the freezer for extended periods increases the chance of contamination and spoilage. Arrange your freezer to allow air to circulate through the shelves and around the food just like you do in your refrigerator.

Tips to maximize the efficiency of your freezer:

- Store frozen foods in moisture-proof containers to minimize loss of flavor, discoloration, dehydration, and odor absorption.

- Monitor the temperature using various thermometers to ensure consistent temperatures. Keep a written record of the temperatures of each freezer.

- Open freezer doors only when necessary and take multiple items each time. A "cold curtain" can guard against heat gain.

- Maintain the temperature by lowering the temperature of warm foods before storing.

- Use the first-in, first-out (FIFO) method to keep your inventory fresh.

- Date (with a freezer marker) "occasional-use" items. When anything has been in the freezer over the recommended time, it should be thrown out. The manufacturer or food vendor can give you their recommendations.

PREPARING FOOD

PREPPING

Most fruits and vegetables should be washed to remove dirt, sand, and insects. Soap and water should remove these and residual pesticides. You might use a food-safe disinfectant solution as a precaution for "high-risk" customers.

To prepare raw ingredients and to avoid contamination:

- Sanitize employees' hands and work surfaces before handling.

- Knives, choppers, and peelers should be sanitized between uses.

- Scrub produce before it is peeled or sliced to avoid transferring germs and chemicals.

When you prepare raw foods, it is necessary to do everything possible to avoid contamination. One way to do this is through the use of colored cutting boards. DayMark Safety Systems offers colored Cut-N-Carry cutting boards. The durable construction provides superior heat, chemical and warp resistance in commercial dishwashers. The tough surface won't dull knives and prevent unsafe cut-grooving where dirt and bacteria can hide. For more information, call 800-847-0101 or visit **www.daymarksafety.com**.

To prep many foods, you need the appropriate brushes. Some are used to clean the food items and others are used to clean your work area. Several types of brushes are shown at **www.tucel.com/cgi-bin/store/agora.cgi** within the prep food area. You can contact Tucel by phone at 800-558-8235 or via fax at 802-247-6826.

THAWING AND MARINATING

Freezing keeps bacteria from multiplying, but it does not kill them. Any bacteria, when food is removed from the freezer, will multiply rapidly when thawed at the wrong temperature. So it is critical to thaw foods below the temperature danger zone. Never thaw foods on a counter or in a non-refrigerated area.

Two of the best methods to thaw food:

1. Place a pan on the lowest shelf in a refrigerator below 40 degrees.

2. Place under drinkable running water at 70 degrees or less for no more than two hours or until the item is thawed.

MARINATING DO'S AND DON'TS

- Always marinate meat, fish, and poultry in the refrigerator.

- Never marinate at room temperature.

- Never save and reuse marinade.

- With all methods, be careful not to cross-contaminate.

COLD FOOD PRECAUTIONS

Preparing cold ingredients is a hazardous point in the process. These are the reasons:

- Cold food preparation is done at room temperature.

- Cold food is a common point of contamination and cross-contamination.

Be especially cautious of cold foods that will not be cooked. There is greater reason to properly clean and prepare these items. Chill the various ingredients and combine them while chilled.

Important precautions to remember:

- Do not prepare food too far in advance.

- Prepare small batches and place them in the refrigerator immediately.

- Store prepared cold foods below 40 degrees Fahrenheit.

- Wash all fresh fruits and vegetables with plain water to remove surface pesticide residues and other impurities.

- When you cut into thick-skinned produce, it can be contaminated.

- Scrub thick-skinned produce with a brush.

To avoid cross-contamination, you must:

- Sanitize hands before and after handling each item.

- Keep raw products away from prepared foods.

- Sanitize cutting boards, knives, and surfaces after each food item.

- Color-coded prep equipment can identify those used for produce, chicken, and other risky items.

- Discard leftover batter, breading, or marinade after it is used.

OOKING

Potentially hazardous foods can contain contaminates even when properly handled. Cooking to a proper internal temperature will kill bacteria. Keep in mind that conventional cooking procedures will not destroy bacteria.

Some "safe cooking" tips:

- Stir foods in deep pots frequently to mix and ensure thorough cooking.

- Consistent sizes make cooking time predictable and uniform.

- Do not interrupt the cooking process. Partially cooking poultry or meat can create conditions that encourage bacterial growth.

- Verify the accuracy of heating equipment by using thermometers.

- Use a thermometer to ensure food reaches the proper temperature. Use a sanitized metal-stemmed, a numerically scaled, or a digital thermometer.

- Check food temperature in several areas, including the thickest parts, to ensure it is thoroughly cooked.

- Always cook food to an internal temperature of 165 degrees Fahrenheit.

Ovens need to be cleaned. How you clean them depends on the type of oven you use. Deck ovens need to be scrubbed with an oven brush like the one that is sold by **www.tucel.com/cgi-bin/store/agora.cgi**. The products are listed in the Equipment Cleaning Supplies. You will need many types of brushes to keep your restaurant clean and many can be found in this section. You can contact Tucel at 800-558-8235 or by fax at 802-247-6826.

SERVING AND HOLDING

Food is not guaranteed to be safe because it has been cooked. If your holding temperature is too low, the food can be contaminated. To avoid this type of problem:

- Keep hot foods in hot-holding equipment above 140 degrees Fahrenheit.
- Keep cold foods in a refrigeration unit or below 40 degrees Fahrenheit.

Safe Serving and Holding:

- Use steam tables and hot food carts during service but not to reheat.

- Stir foods consistently to ensure even heating.

- Use a food thermometer to check temperatures every 30 minutes.

- Sanitize thermometers before each use or use a digital infrared thermometer that never touches the food.

- Cover hot-holding equipment to contain heat and prevent contamination.

- Monitor the temperature of hot-holding equipment.

- Discard food held in the "temperature danger zone" over four hours.

- Never add fresh food to a serving pan with food that has been served.

Important points:

- Wash hands with soap and warm water for at least 20 seconds before serving food.

- Use cleaned and sanitized long-handled ladles and spoons, so your bare hands do not touch food.

- Never touch parts of glasses, cups, plates, or tableware that come into contact with food.

- Never touch parts of dishes that come into contact with the customer's mouth.

- Wear gloves if serving food by hand.

- Cover cuts or infections with bandages or gloves.

- Discard gloves when they touch an unsanitary surface.

- Use tongs or wear gloves to distribute rolls and bread.

- Clean and sanitize equipment and utensils thoroughly after each use.

- Use lids and sneeze guards to protect food from contamination.

- Keep cash handling duties separate from food handling, when possible.

- Wash hands, utensils, and contact surfaces after contact with raw meat or poultry and before contact with cooked meat or poultry.

SANITARY SELF-SERVICE

Workers and customers can contaminate the food. Your customers are not trained in sanitation. Here are some things to watch for:

- Touching food and plastic ware with their hands.

- Touching the edges of utensils and equipment.

- Sneezing or coughing into food or self-serve displays.

- Touching salt and pepper shaker tops, sugar bowls, and condiment containers.

- Returning food items to avoid waste.

It is critical that you remove any food that could be contaminated as soon as you see something questionable. If you are unsure, throw it out. Some ways to protect your customers include:

- Serve sealed packages of crackers, breadsticks, and condiments.

- Pre-wrap, date, and label sandwiches, if possible.

Rosseto dispensers are a safe and sanitary way for customers to serve themselves and to help you control contamination. Toppings, cereal and other items are beautifully displayed and customers get measured portions. These items are ideal for salads, snacks, cereal, and ice cream. The design keeps your toppings fresh longer. The equipment is easy to use and easy to clean. Visit **www.rosseto.com** or call 847-491-9166 for more details.

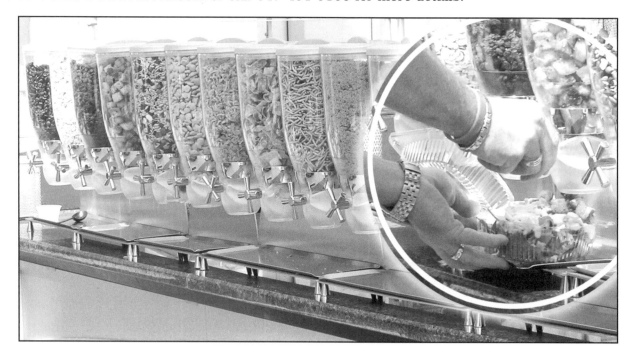

COOLING

There will be times when you will prepare foods in advance and use leftovers. Leftovers can lead to problems. It can be the number one cause of food-borne illnesses. Two key precautions to prevent these problems at this point are rapid cooling and protection from contamination.

CHILLING IT QUICKLY

Leftovers should be chilled to an internal temperature of below 40 degrees Fahrenheit. Quick chill any leftovers larger than a half a gallon or two pounds.

Simple Steps to Quick chill:

- **Reduce food mass.** Smaller amounts of food chill quicker than large amounts. Cut items into smaller pieces or divide into several containers.

- **Shallow, pre-chilled pans (no more than four inches deep).** Use stainless-steel containers because stainless-steel transfers heat better and cools faster than plastic.

- **Chill.** It is best to place food in an ice-water bath or quick-chill unit (26 to 32 degrees Fahrenheit) instead of a refrigerator. Water conducts better than air. Food cools quicker in an ice bath than in a refrigerator. Refrigeration units keep cold foods cold, rather than chilling hot foods. It can take too long to cool foods to safe temperatures.

- **Pre-chill foods in a freezer** for about 30 minutes and then refrigerate.

- **Separate items so air can flow around them.** Do not stack shallow pans. Never cool at room temperature.

- **Stir frequently.** Stirring accelerates cooling and gets cold air to all parts of the food.

- **Check temperature periodically.** Food should reach 70 degrees Fahrenheit within two hours and 40 degrees Fahrenheit within four hours. This time must be reduced if food spent time in the "temperature danger zone" during preparation and serving.

- **Tightly cover and label cooled foods.** List preparation date and time.

- **Store food on the upper shelves of the cooler and cover the container when they reach 45 degrees Fahrenheit.** Uncovered foods cool faster and have an increased risk for cross-contamination. Never store prepared foods beneath raw foods.

EHEATING

Remember that leftovers are not safe. During reheating and serving leftovers, be careful not to allow contamination. Tips to safely reheat and serve leftovers:

- Boil sauces, soups, and gravies and heat other foods to a minimum of 165 degrees Fahrenheit within two hours of taking food out of the refrigerator.

- Never reheat food in hot-holding equipment.

- Never mix a leftover food with fresh food.

- Never reheat food more than once.

Keeping the product warm and free from contamination makes a difference in how much you sell and how much you throw out. Heated holding cabinets from Henny Penny can make this difference for you. They provide floor or counter top units. They are energy efficient and built to last. For more information, visit **www.hennypenny.com/pd/pd1. phtml** or call 800-417-8417.

CLEAN VERSUS SANITARY

Heat or chemicals can reduce bacteria to acceptable levels. They can also combat other harmful microorganisms. Heat sanitizing requires exposing equipment to high heat for an adequate period of time. It can be done by placing equipment in 170 to 195 degrees Fahrenheit water for at least 30 seconds or in a dishwasher that washes at 150 degrees Fahrenheit and rinses at 180 degrees Fahrenheit. It is critical that you check water temperatures on a regular basis.

Equipment can be chemically sanitized by dipping or wiping it with bleach or sanitizing solution. Use a half ounce, or one tablespoon, of 5 percent bleach per gallon of water. Commercial cleaning agents contain manufacturers' instructions. These chemicals are regulated by the EPA.

Follow the instructions carefully. You can also use chemical test strips to test the strength of the sanitizing solution. Since exposure to air can dilute the strength of these agents test often.

Henny Penny has a full line of quality cleaning products that are formulated to sanitize Henny Penny equipment. These products are also useful for cleaning your food prep and serving areas. For more information, visit **www.hennypenny.com/pd/pd2.phtml?formTarget=cleaning**. Contact Henny Penny at 800-417-8417 or by fax at 800-417-8402.

SANITIZE PORTABLE EQUIPMENT

Properly cleaning and sanitizing portable equipment requires a sink with three separate compartments for cleaning, rinsing, and sanitizing. Have a separate area to scrape and rinse food and debris into the garbage or disposal before washing and another drain board for clean and soiled items.

The correct procedure to sanitize a piece of equipment:

1. Clean and sanitize sinks and work surfaces.

2. Scrape and rinse food into garbage or disposal. Pre-soak items like silverware.

3. First Sink – Immerse the equipment in a clean detergent solution at about 120 degrees. Use a brush or cloth to loosen and remove any remaining visible soil.

4. Second Sink – Use clear, clean water between 120 and 140 degrees Fahrenheit to remove all traces of food, debris, and detergent.

5. Third Sink – Sanitize items in hot water at 170 degrees Fahrenheit for 30 seconds or in a chemical sanitizing solution for one minute. Cover all surfaces of the equipment with hot water or sanitizing solution and keep them in it for the appropriate amount of time.

6. If soapsuds disappear in the first compartment or remain in the second, if the water temperature cools, or if water in any compartment becomes dirty and cloudy, empty the compartment and refill it.

7. Air dry. Drying with a towel can re-contaminate equipment and remove the sanitizing solution before it finishes working.

8. Let equipment dry before putting it into storage; moisture can foster bacterial growth.

SANITIZING IN-PLACE EQUIPMENT

Larger and immobile equipment must be washed, rinsed, and sanitized. Use this procedure:

1. Unplug electrically powered equipment.

2. Remove food particles and scraps.

3. Wash, rinse, and sanitize removable parts using the immersion method described in steps three through five of the previous section.

4. Wash the food-contact surfaces and rinse with clean water. Wipe with a chemical sanitizing solution, using the manufacturer's directions.

5. Wipe down non-food surfaces with a sanitized cloth and allow them to air-dry before reassembling. Sanitize cloth before and during sanitizing by rinsing it in sanitizing solution.

6. Re-sanitize external food-contact surfaces that were handled when reassembled.

7. Scrub wooden surfaces, like cutting boards, with a detergent solution and a stiff-bristled nylon brush. Then rinse in clear, clean water and wipe down with a sanitizing solution after every use.

A FIRST-RATE FACILITY

Safe and sanitary food service begins with a clean facility that is in good repair. The entire facility should be laid out for easy cleaning.

Eliminate and reorganize any areas that are hard to clean. You should also replace overloaded refrigerators or other equipment. The easier it is to clean an area, the more likely it will be cleaned.

FLOORS, WALLS, AND CEILINGS

Here are some tips to keep your floors, walls and ceilings in top condition:

*   Keep dirt and moisture away from floors, walls, and ceilings.

*   Clean walls by wiping down with a cleaning solution. Sweep floors and then clean with a spray method or by mopping.

*   Swab ceilings to keep from soaking lights and ceiling fans.

*   Do not ignore corners and other hard-to-reach areas.

With Sanifloor, the food goes in the floor, not on it. The potential for slip and fall accidents are dramatically reduced. It controls liquids, crumbs, and other items that are dropped on the floor, limiting the need to clean the floor during the work shift, allowing you to offer better customer service. The ability to flush the floor eliminates unpleasant smells and situations that attract pests. Visit the Web site for more information at **http://sanifloor.com**. For information on pricing or installing Sani-Floor units, call 760-345-7987 or e-mail info@sanifloor.com.

Various cleaning supplies are used to maintain a clean floor. Once source for these items is **www.tucel.com/cgi-bin/store/agora.cgi** in the Floor and Wall Clean section. These items include brooms, mops, and dust pans. They also offer mops to clean your walls. You can contact them at 800-558-8235, by fax at 802-247-6826, or by e-mailing info@tucel.com.

WORK AREAS

Choose nonporous materials in your work areas. These need to be able to withstand chemical and/or steam cleaning. You should also purchase tables and counters without seams or joints that are hard to clean. Worktables on wheels can be moved to useful areas during busy times.

VENTILATION

Ventilation is critical to a clean environment. Effective ventilation will remove smoke, steam, grease, and heat from your food-preparation area, improving air quality and reducing the possibility of fire from accumulated grease. Ventilation eliminates condensation and other airborne contaminants. In addition, it:

- Reduces the accumulation of dirt.
- Reduces odors, gases, and fumes.
- Reduces mold growth by reducing humidity.

Ensure good ventilation by:

- Using exhaust fans to remove odors and smoke.
- Using hoods over cooking areas and dishwashing equipment.
- Checking exhaust fans and hoods to make sure they operate properly.
- Cleaning hood filters according to the manufacturer's instructions.

RESTROOMS

Provide public and private restrooms that are convenient, sanitary, and adequately stocked with the following:

- Toilet paper.
- Antiseptic liquid soap.
- Disposable paper towels and/or air blowers.
- Covered trash receptacles with a foot pedal for the lid.

Someone needs to check public restrooms and clean them throughout the day. Provide nail brushes and sanitizing solution in employee restrooms.

CROSS-CONTAMINATION CONCERNS

Cross-contamination is a common cause of food-borne illness. It is the transfer of bacteria and viruses from food to food, hand to food, or equipment to food.

- **Food to food.** Raw, contaminated ingredients can be added to foods or fluids from raw foods may drip into foods that are not cooked. A common mistake is leaving meat on an upper refrigerator shelf where it can drip onto prepared foods stored below.

- **Hand to food.** Bacteria is located all over the body: in the hair, on the skin, in clothing, in the mouth, in the nose and throat, in the intestinal tract, and on scabs or scars from skin wounds. The bacteria can end up on hands where it can spread to food. People can transfer bacteria by touching raw food and transferring it to cooked or ready-to-eat food.

- **Equipment to food.** Bacteria can pass from equipment to food when the equipment touches contaminated food and is used to prepare other food without proper cleaning and sanitizing.

Plastic wrap can hold bacteria and transfer it to other containers and food. A can opener, boxes of wrap, or a food slicer can all create cross-contamination when they are not sanitized properly.

CONTRIBUTING TO FOODBORNE ILLNESS

The Centers for Disease Control (CDC) reveals the most common reason food-borne illness occurs is because of food mishandling. According the Center for Disease Control's Surveillance for Food-borne Disease Outbreaks (1988-1992) these are the major factors:

CAUSES OF FOODBORNE ILLNESSES	
Action	Percent Caused
Use of leftovers	4%
Improper Cleaning	7%
Cross-Contamination	7%
Contaminated raw food	7%
Inadequate reheating	12%
Improper hot storage	16%
Inadequate cooking	16%
Infected people touching food	20%
Time between preparing and serving	21%
Improper cooling of foods	40%

CONTROLLING BACTERIA

Some good ways to control bacteria are:

- Good personal hygiene.
- Monitoring time and temperature.
- Eliminating cross-contamination.
- Employing a sanitation program.

Your first step is to limit bacteria's access to the restaurant. All products need to be clean when they enter your restaurant. Following all the suggestions that have been discussed in this chapter is a great start.

TIME AND TEMPERATURE CONTROL

Controlling time and temperature can be a great way to avoid contamination. Most disease causing bacteria grows between 41 and 140 degrees. When food is cooked, reheated, and stored in the correct temperatures, the potential problems are reduced. Believe it or not, bacteria can double every 15 minutes, which will generate over 1,000,000 cells in just five hours. There can be enough bacteria within four hours in the temperature danger zone to cause food-borne illnesses. You can prevent food-borne illnesses by using correct storage practices.

There will be times when food has to be in risky temperatures. You must minimize those times. If you take a break, put the food back in the refrigerator briefly.

BACTERIA

Bacteria can be found everywhere: in the air, in your restaurant, and all over your body. Not all bacteria are bad and some are even beneficial. There are some types of bacteria that are added to foods. But a small amount will cause food to spoil and can generate food poisoning when eaten.

Bacteria are in a vegetative state and reproduce like any other living organism. There are types of bacteria that form spores which enable the bacteria to live in less than ideal situations, including cooking, high-salt environments, and freezing. These activities will not kill those bacteria. These spores must have the "ideal" conditions to multiply and cause illness.

These are the things bacteria need to reproduce:

- Food
- Temperature
- Oxygen

- Acid
- Time
- Moisture

FOOD

High protein or carbohydrate foods like meats, poultry, seafood, cooked potatoes, and diary products.

ACID

Most bacteria flourish in a neutral environment, but they are capable of growing in foods that have pH levels between 4.5 and 9.0. The "pH" is indicative of how acidic or alkaline a food is. pH ranges from 0.0 to 14.0, with 7.0 being neutral. High acid foods discourage the growth of bacteria. You can limit the hazard of lower pH foods by adding acidic ingredients to increase the pH level.

Temperature

Most disease-causing bacteria grow at between 41 to 140 degrees Fahrenheit. Listeria monocytogenes, the bacteria that causes food-borne illness related to processed luncheon meats, can grow below 41 degrees.

Time

Bacteria needs about four hours – the total time the food is in the temperature danger zone – to reproduce enough cells to cause a food-borne illness.

Oxygen

Aerobic and anaerobic bacteria have different oxygen requirements. Aerobic bacteria need oxygen to grow. Anaerobic bacteria do not. Anaerobic bacteria grow well in vacuum packed or canned items.

Moisture

The amount of water in a food to support bacterial growth is called water activity. It is measured on a scale of 0.0 and 1.0. The water activity must be greater than 0.85 to support bacterial growth.

The growth of bacteria is dependent on how favorable these conditions are. Bacteria prefer moisture-saturated foods. In turn, they will grow in dry conditions.

ANGEROUS BACTERIA

There is an estimated 76 million cases of food-borne diseases in the United States each year. Most of these are mild and do not last long. The CDC estimates 325,000 hospitalizations and 5,000 deaths are caused by food-borne diseases each year. The elderly and the young are the most at risk.

The most commonly recognized food-borne infections are those caused by the bacteria Campylobacter, Salmonella, E. coli O157:H7, and by a group of viruses known as the Norwalk and Norwalk-like viruses.

- **Campylobacter** causes fever, diarrhea, and abdominal cramps. Eating undercooked chicken or food contaminated with juices dripping from raw chicken is the most frequent source of this infection.

- **Salmonella** causes fever, diarrhea, and abdominal cramps. When this bacterium attacks a person with poor health, it can cause serious infections.

- **E. coli O157:H7** is usually caused by consuming water that is contaminated with microscopic amounts of cow feces, causing severe and bloody diarrhea and painful abdominal cramps without much fever. If the condition becomes more severe, it includes temporary anemia, profuse bleeding, and kidney failure.

- **Calicivirus**, or a Norwalk-like virus, causes an acute gastrointestinal illness, which is characterized with more vomiting than diarrhea and lasts about two days. It is usually spread from one infected person to another. Infected kitchen staff can contaminate cold foods during preparation.

More information can be found on the FDA's Web site at **www.cfsan.fda.gov/~mow/intro.html**.

ERSONAL HYGIENE

One of the best and easiest ways to stop bacteria is personal hygiene. Hands are a big source of contamination and need to be washed throughout the day. Any time you sneeze or scratch your head you expose your hands to bacteria and then pass those bacteria on to other things you touch. Some great things that help prevent the spread of bacteria are: nail brushes, disposable gloves, and anti-bacterial soaps. It is critical that you train your employees properly and follow up to ensure they are following these standards.

These are some basic ways to practice good basic hygiene:

- Short hair and/or use a hairnet.

- Clean shaven face.

- Clean clothes/uniforms.

- Clean hands and short nails.

- No unnecessary and large jewelry.

- A daily shower or bath.

- No smoking in or near the kitchen.

- Hand washing prior to work, periodically, and after handling foreign objects.

Many hand cleaning supplies are available to maintain the hygiene of your employees. These can be found at **www.tucel.com/cgi-bin/store/agora.cgi** in the Infection Control Clean section.

When employees are getting a cold or have a cut, they should not be at work. It is a way to spread bacteria. Some businesses require employees to take a complete medical exam with blood and urine tests, but the cost is prohibitive for others.

HAND WASHING

Hand washing is the most critical aspect of personal hygiene. Unless they are washing fruits and vegetables, employees should not touch ready-to-eat foods with their bare hands. Instead, they can use single use gloves, spatulas, tongs, or deli paper.

"Hand washing is the single most effective means of preventing the spread of disease," according to the Centers for Disease Control and Prevention. The Quik-Wash Hand Wash Faucet Control is an economical choice which can be better than the costly electronic faucets. The faucet offers automatic closing and hands-free positions. For additional information, visit **www.fmponline.com/featuredproduct.html**. You can contact FMP for more information by phone at 800-257-7737, by fax at 800-255-9866, or through e-mail at sales@fmponline.com.

Always wash your hands after these activities:

- Smoking
- Using the restroom
- Touching raw food
- Taking a break
- Coughing, sneezing, or blowing your nose

- Eating
- Handling money
- Touching or combing your hair
- Handling anything dirty

You should make sure all employees know and practice proper hand washing procedures. Posters are an excellent on-going reminder. Atlantic Publishing offers three different handwashing posters: "Wash Your Hands" (Item #FSP1-PS), "Step-By-Step Handwashing" (Item #FSP2-PS) and "Wash Your Hands After" (Item #FSP3-PS), Each brightly colored poster is in both Spanish and English and laminated with sealed edges. They are $8.95 each and available at **www.atlantic-pub.com** or by calling 800-814-1132.

  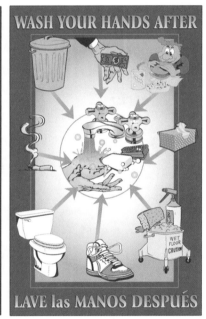

CLOTHING

Dirty clothes can hold bacteria, whether these are your work clothes or personal clothing. It is common to touch your clothing while working, transferring bacteria to the food. Another problem is that customers get a bad message when they see employees in dirty clothes.

Aprons, Etc provides a wide variety of apron options. There are washable and disposable choices. You have the opportunity to have your business name and logo printed on your aprons. Keep in mind that you will need a lot of aprons and will need to wash them. Some of the aprons available are displayed at **www.apronsetc.com/aprons.htm#1**.

Dickies Chef Aprons and Hats are high quality products. These items are functional and have the durability that Dickies is famous for. The aprons provide oversized pockets and are constructed to be comfortable for your staff. They are available with a soil resistant finish. Dickies has a wide selection of aprons, chef hats, shirts, pants, and vests. They can be seen at **www.dickieschef.com**. Call 866-262-6288 or fax 877-353-9044 for more information.

Royal Industries offers aprons, chef's coats, and chef's hats. These are all options for your cook staff. Royal Industries, Inc. is an innovative leader in the food service industry, serving a nationwide market of commercial products for the food service industry. Their Web site is **www.royalindustriesinc.com** and you can contact them by phone at 800-782-1200 or by fax at 800-321-3295.

EATING, DRINKING, OR USING TOBACCO

Some employees feel it is acceptable to eat in the food preparation area since they work in a restaurant: smoking, eating, and drinking need to be prohibited in the food preparation area. These activities increase the chance of spreading bacteria and other contaminants to the food.

EYES, NOSE, AND MOUTH

When you or your employees have a cold or even allergy problems, there will be sneezing and coughing, easily contaminating food, utensils, equipment, and linen. While employees are sick or sneezing, assign them to a duty where they do not come into contact with the food.

HAIR RESTRAINTS

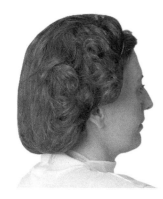

Customers are concerned about hair contamination in their food. Be aware of this common concern and be sure your employees use caps or hairnets. It is a simple way to keep hair out of the food that is being prepared. The food can also be contaminated when employees touch their hair and then continue working.

DayMark Safety Systems offers a complete line of personal safety equipment including hair nets and beard guards. You can view the complete line at **www.daymarksafety.com** or call 800-847-0101.

DISHWARE

Even though your employees have been trained to wash their hands correctly, they still need to use care when handling dishware. These tips will help your employees handle dishware without contaminating the portions that will touch the customers' food or mouth.

- Use tongs, scoops, or food grade rubber gloves to pick up food items.

- Pick up glasses from the outside and hold cups from the handle or the bottom to avoid touching the rims or inside.

- Pick up forks and spoons by the handles.

- Carry plates by the bottoms or edges. Do not stack dishes, cups, and saucers to carry more.

- Wash your hands after handling soiled dishes.

- Always wash your hands before putting on gloves. Those gloves can be contaminated if you do something else while wearing them. When your gloves are contaminated throw them away, wash your hands, and put on fresh gloves before returning to the food preparation.

• Do not use a utensil to taste more than one food item.

GLOVES

Multiuse gloves can be a breeding ground for pathogens. These gloves must be washed, sanitized, and rinsed between uses. Hands must also be washed before putting gloves on. When gloves are soiled or the inside is contaminated, they should be discarded. Do not use slash-resistant gloves with ready-to-eat foods because they cannot be cleaned and sanitized easily.

Disposable gloves are a great tool for keeping food safe from contamination. Vinyl gloves provide a safe and sanitary second skin to perform tasks requiring sensitivity and dexterity.

Food-handlers should change their gloves:

• As soon as they become soiled

• Before beginning a different task

• At least every 4 hours during continual use, more often when necessary

• After handling raw meats

The chart below outlines the features and benefits of the four common materials that disposable gloves are made from:

DISPOSABLE GLOVE CHARACTERISTICS				
	Nitrile	Vinyl	Poly	Latex (Rubber)
Barrier Protection	Excellent	Fair / Poor	Poor	Excellent
Strength & Durability	Excellent	Excellent	Poor	Fair
Elasticity	Good	Poor	Poor	Excellent
Puncture/Cut/Snag Resistance	Excellent	Poor	Poor	Good
Chemical Resistance	Excellent	Poor	None	Good
Fit and Comfort	Excellent (Loose)	Good	Poor	Excellent (Tight)
Protein Allergy	None	None	None	Possible

It is also important that gloves fit employees correctly. The next page has a sizing chart that can be used to determine the correct glove size, courtesy of DayMark Safety Systems. DayMark offers a wide variety of vinyl, poly, and nitrile disposable gloves. You can view the complete product line at **www.daymarksafety.com** or request a catalog by calling 800-847-010.

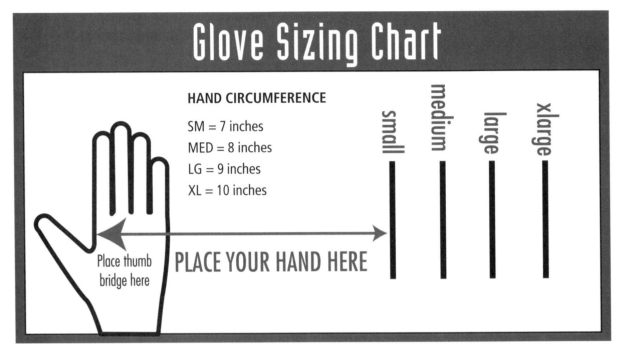

DayMark's gloves are sized using the traditional S, M, L, XL method. These alphabetical sizes are equal to the numerical sizing of 7, 8, 9, 10. The numerical number is the circumference of your hand, in inches. A person with a 7 inch circumference would wear a small glove.

SUMMARY

Each of these techniques is a way to protect your restaurant and your customers from bacteria and contamination. There are many sources for additional information. While these tips involve more work and training, they will help you protect your business and your customers.

CHAPTER

SAFETY AND RISK MANAGEMENT

S afety should be a primary concern for you as a business owner. This concern extends to your employees and customers. This chapter discusses things you can and should do to ensure a safe environment for staff and customers.

KITCHEN AND FOOD SAFETY

Ensuring your patrons and staff are not injured on the premises is more than a matter of caring for their well-being — it is an essential part of avoiding a business-threatening lawsuit and lengthy downtime. Labor savings, insurance savings, workers' compensation reductions, and sick pay savings, not to mention staying out of civil court, all come from putting safety procedures in place — and sticking to them. Here is how to do this:

- **Keep equipment in working order.** Make sure that equipment, tools, machinery, and substances are in safe condition.

- **Talk to your workers about safety in the workplace.** Encourage open discussion.

- **Hygiene.** Maintain safe and hygienic facilities including toilets, eating areas, and first aid.

- **Staff training.** Offer information, training, and supervision for all workers.

- **Involve your staff.** Implement processes to inform workers and involve them in decisions that may affect their health and safety at work.

- **Safety procedures.** Implement processes for identifying hazards and assessing and controlling risks.

- **Accident book.** Record work-related injuries and illnesses.

- **Be observant.** Pay attention to safe work. Your business will not only become more competitive, but you can help stop the pain and suffering from workplace injury or fatality.

- **Post safety signs.** Ensure safety signs, usually available for free from your local Department of Health or Labor or your appliance manufacturers, are posted about your kitchen. These will include details on how to safely lift heavy items, directions on proper signage for slippery floors, and dangerous equipment, as well as rules on who handles jobs like lighting gas pilots, changing light bulbs, and sharpening knives.

Atlantic Publishing offers a 10-poster set of workplace safety posters in both English and Spanish. Communicate important information to your employees by posting these colorful, four-color informative Safety and Human Resource posters throughout your workplace. Each poster is 11" x 17" and is laminated for long-term protection. Topics include: First Aid for Burns, First Aid for Cuts and Wounds, First Aid for Choking, Proper Lifting, Emergency Phone Numbers, Drug-Free Workplace, Fire Extinguisher Use, CPR Guidelines, Falling, and Sexual Harassment. To order visit **www.atlantic-pub.com** or call 800-814-1132 (Item # WPP-PS, $79.95).

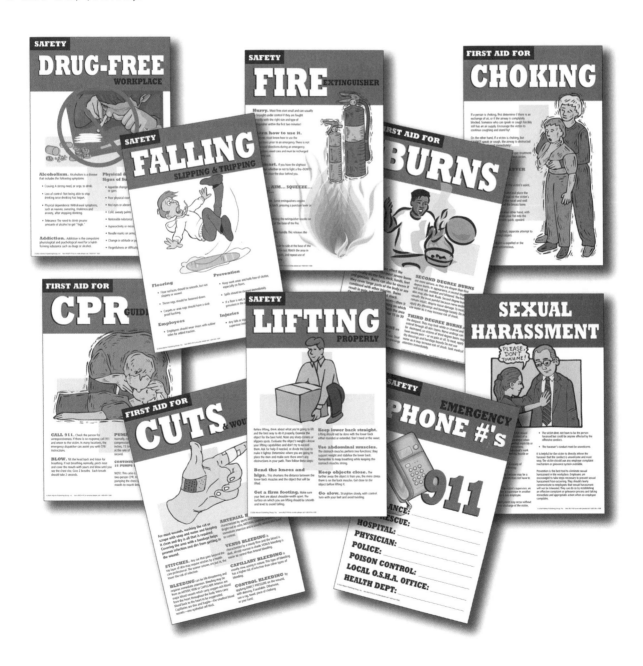

GENCIES

Below are some agencies that can come to your restaurant and offer various types of safety training.

- **Red Cross.** The Red Cross offers training in first aid, abdominal thrust, and CPR. They can be contacted through their Web site: **www.redcross.org**.

- **Fire department.** Your local fire department offers training for your employees on how to use fire extinguishers. Fires are more common in restaurants than other businesses, so everyone needs to understand how to operate fire extinguishers. Have fire extinguishers available throughout your restaurant. Place one in any location where fires are likely, especially near ovens and fryers. Your priority is making them accessible in case of an emergency. In addition, train employees how to avoid fires as well as how to handle a fire in case of an emergency. Include an evacuation plan for the staff and customers. All employees need to know your plan and how to help customers if there is a fire. Always call the fire department before using a fire extinguisher.

- **OSHA can also provide safety training information.** The Occupational Safety and Health Agency (OSHA) is the federal agency that oversees safety in the workplace. Be sure that you are in compliance with their regulations. Details about their requirements for food service establishments and training materials are available at **www.osha.gov**.

FIRST AID AND SAFETY

A restaurant with poorly trained employees can lead to hazardous conditions, another good reason to thoroughly train your employees. They need to be trained on how to handle first aid safety emergencies.

Have a safety plan in place and train your employees to implement the elements of this plan. Train them, so they can respond in a calm and quick manner. Safety training materials can be found on The Training Network's Web site at **www.safetytrainingnetwork.com.**.

You should be sure to have a comprehensive first aid kit in a prominent location in your facility. DayMark's patented first aid cabinet is stocked with OSHA compliant first aid products for those accidents that typically occur in the food service industry such as burns, cuts, sticks, and common workplace injuries. With the high risk of accidents in the food service industry, it's always challenging to maintain a first aid program that's both cost effective and up-to-date 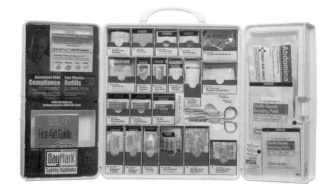 on current safety regulations. This process is easy and cost effective with the only first aid program with guaranteed OSHA compliance. For more information call 800-847-0101 or visit **www.daymarksafety.com**.

FIRE

Contact your local fire department for more information about their regulations and recommendations. You need fire extinguishers, fire alarms, carbon monoxide alarms, and smoke detectors. Place a note on your calendar to replace the batteries in your fire alarms every six months. When you consider fire extinguishers, there are several types, including:

- Dry chemical
- Halon
- Water and carbon dioxide

The type of fire extinguisher depends on the type of fire. The reason fire extinguishers are labeled:

- Class A – Ordinary combustibles
- Class B – Flammable liquids
- Class C – Electrical equipment

Many fire extinguishers are labeled with a graphic image that shows the type of fire. Once you have the fire extinguishers in your restaurant, they must be serviced once a year.

Part of your Fire Safety Plan should include an emergency number by all phones, along with evacuation plans around the kitchen, near the doors, and in the entryway and dining room area. There are interesting statistics and information on the NFPA Web site at **www.nfpa.org.**

ACCIDENTS AND SAFETY

Any person or business can have an accident, but you can reduce your risk. These are a few ways to do so:

- Ground your electrical outlets.
- Clean walkways and clear clutter.
- Shovel and salt walks and steps in the winter.
- Provide adequate outdoor lighting.
- Place rails along steps.
- Provide adequate interior lighting.
- Install solid doors.
- Put good locks on windows and doors.
- Have a quality security system installed.

These are only some of the possibilities. Assign someone to be your safety coordinator. She can plan and train employees about your evacuation plans, arrange training with local organizations, and be on the lookout for safety problems and concerns.

ITCHEN SAFETY

The restaurant business has many potential safety hazards. Knives, hot ovens, fryers, slicers, grinders, glass, and wet or greasy floors are only some of the hazards your staff faces every day. Many accidents can be prevented with good training.

HEAT AND BURNS

It is very easy for employees to get burns while they are working. They can be burned on grills, stoves, ovens, hot food and drinks, splatters, slashes, and spills These can be avoided if they are careful. To prevent burns:

- **Use thick, dry potholders** and stir food with long-handled spoons.

- **Use hot water carefully.** Wear insulated rubber gloves for hot rinse water. Follow operating instructions, especially with steam equipment. Expel all steam before opening the doors.

- **Lift lids and equipment away from yourself.**

- **Avoid splatters and splashes by not overfilling kettles.** Do not let food boil over.

- **Oil and water do not mix;** ensure food is dry before frying.

- **Point pan handles away from walkways**, but within reach, to avoid knocking over other pans.

- **Do not crowd hot pans.** Remove cooked foods from cooking surfaces.

- **Let oil cool and use caution when cleaning fryers.**

- **Wear insulated gloves or mitts when removing hot pans from the oven** and be certain no one is in your way.

- **Do not wear clothes that drape and could catch on fire.**

Kitchen Grips offer a great way to grab hot items safely up to 500°F. They are heat resistant, water repellent, and stain resistant. Visit their Web site for more information **www.kitchengrips.com**, call 800-785-4449, or fax 661-257-8123.

DayMark Safety Systems also offers a complete line of oven mitts and burn protection gloves which offer protection in temperatures up to 900°F. For more information call 800-847-0101 or visit **www.daymarksafety.com**.

TIPS FOR A BURN-FREE KITCHEN

Steam, oil and grease, boiling soups, hot grills, and ovens can all result in workplace burn injuries. The Burn Foundation has found that such injuries tend to occur when managers do not enforce safety rules or when workers themselves are careless about safety. The potential for accidents is also greater when workers are worn out, on drugs or alcohol, or are simply taking unnecessary risks. Every restaurant is fast-paced and generally congested, providing all the needed ingredients for a disaster. The following tips can make a big difference in maintaining a burn-free kitchen:

- **Mitts.** Wear protective gloves or mitts when handling hot pots or cooking with hot deep-frying oil.

- **Footwear.** Wear non-skid shoes to prevent slipping on wet or greasy tile floors.

- **Nip small fires in the bud.** Extinguish hot oil/grease fires by sliding a lid over the top of the container.

- **Avoid reaching over or across hot surfaces and burners.** Use barriers, guards, or enclosures to prevent contact with hot surfaces.

- **Equipment instructions.** Read and follow directions for proper use of electrical appliances.

- **First aid.** Keep first-aid kits readily available and make sure at least one person on each shift has first-aid training.

- **Keep fire extinguishers accessible and up-to-date.**

"AWARE." The National Restaurant Association's Educational Foundation offers an educational program called "AWARE: Employee and Customer Safety." The nine modules offered include sections on ensuring fire safety in the kitchen and preventing burns. The Educational Foundation also offers videos, along with interactive CD-ROMs, that promote workplace safety and focus on how to prevent on-the-job injuries.

CUTS

Another hazard for your workers is cuts, but knives are not the only potential problem. Some equipment has sharp edges. Broken glass is a problem. Opening boxes can be a hazard, too. Other hazards include nails, staples, and the edges of box tops. Take these precautions:

- **Use the proper tools to dispose of broken glass.** Place broken glass in a separate garbage container.

- **Cut rolls of kitchen wrap with the cutter.**

- **Watch the edges when opening cans.** Do not use a knife to open cans or to pry items loose.

- **Use a pusher to feed food into a grinder.**

- **Unplug slicers and grinders when removing food and cleaning.**

- **Utilize guards** when operating grinders and slicers.

- **Replace equipment blades when clean.** Do not let them sit around.

- **When you hire left-handed people, give them additional safety instruction** about slicers and similar equipment. The safety features on this equipment are designed for right-handed people.

Some Additional Tips:

- **Keep knives sharpened.** Dull blades cause more cuts.

- **Do not leave knives or blades in the bottom of a sink.**

- **Carry knives by the handle with the tip away from you.**

- **Never try to catch a falling knife.**

- **Cut away from yourself** on a cutting board.

- **Slice; do not hack.**

- **Use the proper knives for the project.**

- **Carefully store and clean knives and equipment.**

- **Store knives and sharp tools in separate areas.**

- **Wash glasses separately** to prevent them from being broken in the sink.

- **Do not stack glasses** and cups inside of each other.

- **Watch for nails, staples, and sharp edges while unpacking boxes.**

A good way to prevent cuts is to make sure all employees have proper equipment. DayMark Safety Systems offers a variety of gloves that prevent punctures, cuts and abrasions and are made specifically for food service. Here are some of their options:

- **DayMark's FingerArmor™ Cut Gloves** are made with highly cut resistant fabric, and protect food service workers from accidental cuts and pokes by shielding the most vulnerable parts of the hand—the middle finger, index finger, and thumb. Dual sided for superior protection, FingerArmor™ Cut Gloves can be worn under latex, vinyl, nitrile or poly gloves, making them ideal for food preparation. With their flexible fit, FingerArmor™ Cut Gloves give operators full range of motion, significantly reducing slippage. The gloves are machine washable and can be easily sanitized.

- **DayMark's 5 Finger HexArmor/Spectra Combination Cut Gloves** help employees feel safer and work faster. The traditional spectra cut glove with the DayMark Personal Safety touch. HexArmor fabric is added to the most often cut areas, the thumb and first finger.

- **DayMark's HexArmor® Oyster Gloves** protect operators' palms from cuts caused by sharp mussel shells and oyster shucking knives. Made with high cut, puncture and abrasion resistant fabric, the HexArmor Oyster Gloves provide superior protection on the palm and thumb crotch without limiting finger movement. The HexArmor Oyster Gloves are machine washable and can be easily sanitized.

- **DayMarks' Restaurant General Purpose Work Gloves** offer protection like none other in its class. It fits and feels like a mechanic's style glove, grips like a gel palm glove and protects like a cut and puncture resistant glove. Provides the highest level of cut protection based on the ISEA hand protection guidelines. Great for us in receiving, inventory rotation, pull thaw/slacking products, freezer/walk-in work, or kitchen organization and heavy restaurant maintenance.

For the complete glove product line or more information call 800-847-0101 or visit **www.daymarksafety.com**.

ELECTRICAL SHOCK

Many pieces of restaurant equipment are electrical, so shock is a concern. Some tips to prevent electrical shock are:

- **Ground electrical equipment.**

- **Replace worn or frayed electrical cords.**

- **Ensure employees can reach switches without touching or leaning against metal tables** or counters.

- **Unplug equipment before cleaning.**

- **Use electrical equipment with dry hands.**

- **Know locations of electrical switches and breakers for quick shutdown** in an emergency.

STRAINS

Your staff members can strain their arms, legs, or backs by carrying heavy food items or equipment. To prevent strains:

- Place heavy food items and equipment on low shelves.

- Use dollies or carts to move heavy objects.

- Use carts with rollers to move objects around the restaurant.

- Use a cart to carry excessive or heavy objects.

- Ask for help when lifting large or heavy objects.

- Bend from your knees, not with your back, when you lift heavy items.

SLIPPING AND FALLING

Anyone who slips and falls on a floor can be badly hurt. Implement practices and training to help avoid hazards that put workers at risk. Prevention:

- Clean spills immediately.

- Use signs or cones to let people know when floors are wet.

- Wear shoes with no-slip soles.

- Do not stack boxes too high; they can fall and cause people to trip.

- Keep boxes, ladders, step stools, and carts away from walkways.

Matrix Engineering offers Grip Rock and Super G floor mats. These are ideal for preventing slip and fall accidents which are a leading cause of injury in workplaces. They are durable, lightweight, and long lasting to make your wet, greasy, and hazardous areas safe for your staff. To contact Matrix call 800-926-0528, fax 772-461-7185, or e-mail griprock@gate.net. You can find more information on their Web site at **www.griprock.com**.

Grip Rock slip-resistant safety mat is:

- Slip-resistant in water, grease, and oil

- Extremely tough and durable

- Flexible even in freezing temperatures

- Lightweight and thin (⅛" thick; a 3' x 10' is only 25 lbs.)

- No installation needed

- Easy to handle, clean, and maintain

Dur-A-Flex flooring offers a variety of flooring options. Attractive, functional flooring systems are ideal for your facility. They are formed from heat resistant epoxy to withstand temperatures to 250°F and can be used to resurface floors in dining areas and restrooms. These floors resist penetration of grease or stains. Visit **www.dur-a-flex.com/ByIndustry/industries/restaurant.html** for the full line of food service facility flooring options or contact Dur-A-Flex at 800-253-3539 or by fax at 860-528-2802.

CHOKING

Restaurant safety means being aware of your customers. How to react:

- Hands on throat and unable to talk or cough equals choking.

- Do not pat a person's back if he can talk, cough, or breathe.

- Use the Heimlich Maneuver and call for help right away if the person cannot talk, cough, or breathe.

- All employees need to be trained in the Heimlich Maneuver. Post posters with Heimlich Maneuver instructions in employee areas.

EXPOSURE TO HAZARDOUS CHEMICALS

All cleaning chemicals, pesticides, and sanitizers can harm or poison people. Special precautions need to be taken to protect employees. The law requires that some of these steps be taken. OSHA requires a current inventory of all hazardous materials.

Manufacturers must properly label all hazardous chemicals and must supply a Material Safety Data Sheet (MSDS) to be kept on file in your restaurant. The MSDS provides the chemical name, the physical hazards, health hazards, and emergency procedures in case of exposure. This notebook must be up-to-date and handy in the case of emergency. Train all employees to use the MSDS. A sample MSDS is below.

MATERIAL SAFETY DATA SHEET		
CARBON KLEEN	Aerosol	#1016

Manufacturer's Name: Takeo Enterprises Corp. dba Diablo Products Phone # 1-800-548-1385
Address: P.O. Box 756, Fort Dodge, IA 50501

Section 1 - PRODUCT IDENTIFICATION

This Material Safety Data Sheet contains environmental, health, and toxicology information. It also contains information to help you meet community right to know emergency response reporting requirements under SARA TITLE III and many other laws.

D.O.T. PROPER SHIPPING NAME: ORM-D   CONSUMER COMMODITY
NFPA CODES: HEALTH – 2   FLAMMABILITY – 3   REACTIVITY – 0   SPECIAL - 0

Trade name: Carbon Kleen, Aerosol   Product Type: Carbon Stripper

Section 2 - Components

Chemical Name/Common Name	CASE NO.	PERCENT(Optional)	TLV(Source)
Dichloromethane	75-09-02	60-80	25ppm
Methanol	67-56-1	1-5	200ppm
2-butoxyethanol, glycol ether	111-76-2	1-5	25ppm
Toluene	108-88-3	1-5	200ppm
Propane	74-98-6	8	1000ppm
Butane	106-97-8	7	800ppm

No toxic chemicals subject to the reporting requirements of section313 of Title III and 40 CFR 372 are present.
This product may contain chemicals known to the State of California to cause cancer, birth defects or reproductive harm.

Section 3 – Physical Data

Boiling Point: (F) 104 deg   Freezing Point: <0 deg (F)   Specific Gravity: (H2O = 1.0) 1.01 pH: N/A
Vapor Pressure: (mmHg) 25 @ 20deg (C)   Vapor Density: 2.9
Solubility in water: Slight
Evaporation Rate (vs ether): 1
Appearance and Odor: Aerosol product

Section 4 – Fire and Explosion Hazard Data

Flash Point (T.C.C.): Level 2 Aerosol

Extinguishing Media: Foam, alcohol foam, CO2, dry chemical, water fog

Special Fire Fighting Procedures: Water may be ineffective. Water may be used to cool containers to prevent pressure build-up and explosion when exposed to extreme heat. If water used fog nozzles preferred. Wear goggles and SCBA

Unusual Fire and Explosion Hazards: Closed containers may explode from internal pressure build-up when exposed to extreme heat and discharge contents. Vapor accumulation can flash or explode if ignited. Over exposure to decomposition products may cause a health hazard. Symptoms may not be readily apparent. Obtain medical attention.

Section 5 – Reactive Data

Stability: Stable   Incompatibility: Strong oxidizing agents
Hazardous Decomposition Products: Phosgene & Muratic Acid when in contact with open flame.

Section 6 – Health Hazards

Threshold Limit Value – Product (see section 2 for ingredient TLV): 200ppm
Primary Routes of Exposure: Eyes – Yes Skin – Yes Inhalation – Yes Ingestion – Yes
Signs and Symptoms of Over-exposure (Acute): Irritation to the eyes and skin. Fatigue, numbness, weakness, tingling of the limbs, nausea.
Carcinogen or Suspect Carcinogen Ingredients:

Section 7 – Emergency and First Aid procedures

Eyes: Flush with water for at least 15 minutes, get medical attention.
Skin: Thoroughly wash exposed area with soap and cold water.
Ingestion: DO NOT INDUCE VOMITING. Get medical attention. If vomiting occurs spontaneously, prevent vomitus from entering the lungs by keeping victims head below hips.
Inhalation: Remove victim to fresh air. If breathing is difficult, administer oxygen. Get medical attention.

Section 8 – Special Protection Information

Respiratory Protection: none under normal use Ventilation Requirements: well ventilated area
Protective Gloves: Rubber   Eye Protection: Safety glasses

Section 9 – Spill or Leak Procedures.

Steps to be taken if Released or Spilled: Wear protective equipment including self contained breathing apparatus for large spills. Keep spilled material out of sewers, storm drains and soils.
Waste Disposal Methods: Consult state and local agencies to ascertain proper disposal procedures

Section 10 – Storage and Handling Information

Precautions to be taken in Handling and Storage: Store in a cool, dry, well ventilated area away from incompatible materials.

Section 11 – Disclaimer

The information contained herein is based on data considered accurate. However, no warranty is expressed r implied regarding the accuracy of the data or the results to be obtained from the use thereof. Because the information contained herein may be applied under conditions beyond our control, we assume no responsibility for its use.

Emergency Number:	1-800-255-3924

Here are some tips to prevent improper exposure to hazardous materials:

- Only trained workers can handle hazardous chemicals.

- Use safety equipment when working with hazardous chemicals.

- Wear nonporous gloves and goggles for sanitizing and cleaning agents.

Even accidental mishandling of food products or neglecting safety can lead to health problems or injury. To be successful you must build and maintain a reputation for offering quality food in a safe environment. If there is a question in your customers' minds about the quality of your product, you can quickly lose your hard-earned reputation. The sanitation and safety procedures described here are simple to initiate and they must be enforced.

GOOD ERGONOMICS

Ergonomics is "the study and engineering of human physical interaction with spaces and objects during activities." Any area that requires your workers to repeatedly stretch to reach the supplies they need is poor ergonomically.

Good ergonomics can positively affect your employee's well-being, safety, productivity, and comfort. Good ergonomics includes well-fitting tables and comfortable chairs to enhance your customers' experience. Below are tips to help you reorganize your restaurant to work well with people:

- Create mini-workstations with food, utensils, and prep space close.

- Rearrange your storage to minimize bending, lifting, and reaching.

- Provide stools or chairs that support the back and feet when sitting.

- Are your tools and equipment designed for men and women?

- Supply stable, heavy-duty ladders to access shelves and storage units.

- Purchase tools and utensils for left-handed employees.

- Consider how employees, customers, and vendors interact with your facility. Does the current layout make it easier or more difficult for employees to do their jobs or customers to enjoy dining?

- Choose fixtures and equipment that can be moved easily.

THE AIR WE BREATHE

Your restaurant needs healthy air, inside and out. "Poor air" can contribute to employee absenteeism and unhappy customers. Many communities have rigid air and work environment regulations that pertain to proper ventilation, grease, smoke, and wood burning. Any unpleasant odors contribute to "poor" air quality.

FRESH INDOOR AIR

Wood burning ovens, charbroilers, and fryers can create unhealthy or unpleasant air conditions. Flour can also be a concern. Bring in enough outdoor air to supply sufficient indoor air quality, by properly filtering, circulating, and redirecting airflow.

These are some ways to improve indoor air quality:

- **Smoking and non-smoking areas – Direct airflow away from nonsmoking tables.** Ban employee smoking in the kitchen and dining room.

- **Install an air cleaner/filtration system** that reduces airborne particles and dust.

- **Radon, mold, and biological dangers are possible when converting old or vacant buildings.**

- **Read EPA reports about air quality at www.epa.gov/iaq/pubs/insidest.html.**

- **Unhealthy emissions from carpet, paint, and cleaning products.** Sick Building Syndrome is explained at the National Safety Council site at **www.nsc.org/ehc/indoor/sbs.htm.**

- **Hire an HVAC contractor or engineer with restaurant experience.** Hire contractors to install new systems or to maintain existing systems.

OUTDOOR AIR QUALITY

Ovens, fryers, and other cooking equipment emit particulates, gases, grease, and odors that are regulated. Local and state standards vary greatly. The Federal Air Quality Standards may supersede these. You must pay close attention to the regulations because the penalties can be severe. Here are suggestions to meet emission regulations:

- **Hire an industrial air-cleaning firm to install emission-control systems** to handle grease, smoke, CO_2, and odors.

- **Inspect and repair exterior vents, hoods, and intake ducts.** Proper maintenance saves the air and your energy costs.

- **Install a catalytic oxidizer** that converts gases and smoke to water. Read the article at **www.pfonline.com/articles/010203.html.**

- **Contact your natural gas and electric company** and county or state environmental and health departments for air quality information, resources, and financial incentives.

- **Hire an air quality consultant** to help you comply with more complex emission issues and stringent regulations.

- **The Environmental Protection Agency's Web site, www.epa.gov, provides information on restaurant-specific regulations.**

A safe and healthy restaurant is important to your customers and their families. Your employees appreciate and deserve a safe and healthy work environment. Some of these elements are simple and some are more complicated, but all are needed to provide the atmosphere to support your customers and employees.

OTHER AVOIDABLE KITCHEN HAZARDS

However busy you are, you simply cannot afford to ignore the following danger zones:

- **Hot oil.** Transporting hot waste oil from the fryer is very dangerous. Serious accidents have occurred as the night crew changes the oil at the end of the shift. They are tired and want to go home and may be rushing. Consider purchasing Shortening Shuttles, **www.shortening-shuttle.com**, 800-533-5711. These inexpensive devices make hot-oil transfer safe and easy and virtually eliminate the dangers and liability of exposure to hot-oil burns.

- **Wet floors.** Ensure anyone mopping a floor area puts out ample signage to indicate the floor is wet and may be slippery. This does not mean a single yellow cone; it means enough signage so that a person has to make an effort just to get to the slippery floor. For a complete product line of wet floor signs, or more information call 800-847-0101 or visit **www.daymarksafety.com**.

- **Coolers.** Keep any heavy coolers or storage refrigerators located at or above waist level, wherever possible.

- **Keep your food supply safe.** Make sure your employees are trained in food service sanitation. Check with area community colleges for courses in food safety and sanitation. The National Restaurant Association also offers ServSafe certification courses through Atlantic Publishing at **www.atlantic-pub.com**.

REDUCING EMPLOYEE THEFT

Sometimes the best way to improve your bottom line does not include making cost reductions—it involves keeping a better eye on money you have already made. Theft reduction is an important area to keep an eye on, as one sticky-fingered employee can cost you big. Internal theft is an area of massive expense in many businesses. To keep employee theft to a minimum, you will need to concentrate on the following areas of your establishment:

- **Staff rotation.** Try to rotate your employees so that they are not working with the same people constantly, minimizing the opportunities to collude and steal from the business.

- **Routine inspections.** Using daily inspections makes it much more likely to spot an employee being dishonest or a system that is not working rather than waiting for a catastrophe to happen. Have management conduct regular surprise inspections throughout the facility.

- **Watch the bar area.** Reduce your bar expenses by keeping a watchful eye and performing spot register checks at unexpected times.

- **Are your bartenders or servers over-pouring drinks?** Implement portion-control pourers on your liquor bottles. Your pricing is based on a "per shot" basis. If your bartender or waitress is providing a "shot and a half" in every drink, they are in effect giving away one in every three bottles of liquor.

- **Are your employees failing to charge for add-on items**, such as coffee, tea, and extra sauces?

- **Do you monitor employee meals?** All employee meals should be paid for at the time of ordering, unless you offer them for free, in which case they should be signed for and noted by a manager.

- **If you wanted to serve a meal without ringing it up, how easy would it be?** Consider the ability of your servers to get food from the kitchen without recording sales.

REGISTER PRACTICES

Your earnings go through a number of steps before they make it into your checking account. The first of those steps is the journey it makes from the customer to the cash register. It is vital that you have rigorous register procedures in place and that all staff is fully aware of the importance of sticking to the rules. Here are a few essential guidelines:

- **Cashiers should never have access to the keys you use to display and print your end-of-day sales reports.** Any incident where a cash register is "rung off" should be noted and performed by a manager. A new cash drawer should be used from that point onwards.

- **Monitor all voids and over-rings.** If an employee makes a lot of "mistakes," she may be taking cash out of her drawer after a customer has paid and left the premises. The same goes for under-ringing of checks. Always watch and match your checks to your register rolls.

- **Ensure all guest checks are numbered and the numbers are kept on file alongside the server's name.** If checks do not match the total rung up on the register, you have hard evidence should you decide to terminate an employee.

- **Any guest check voided because of error still needs to be accounted for.**

GIVEAWAYS

Many establishments give food and drinks away to customers as part of their promotional expenses. A two-for-one deal or a free drink for every main course is a great incentive to get people through the door, but make sure you are not being ripped off in the process. Here is how:

- **Use a separate key.** If you occasionally give customers free drinks or meals, either as complimentary gifts or as part of a promotion, use a separate key on your register to ring up those giveaways and ensure a manager knows about every incident, either by signing for it or by receiving a voucher. Doing so tightens control on giveaways, maximizes your profits, and allows you to maintain incentives.

- **Monitor coupon usage.** Destroy all complimentary meal and discount coupons you receive to ensure that the same vouchers are not being used twice. Handing a used promotional voucher back to friends is a common ploy used by unreliable employees to defraud your establishment.

- **Employees often enjoy free or reduced meals while they are working.** You still need to account for these expenses in order to keep accurate tabs on your inventory and to be able to forecast your purchasing needs.

- **Are your employees consuming too many free drinks at the bar after work?** Many restaurants have a "one free drink" after-work policy, which may become a two- or three-drink policy without you realizing it. Consider implementing a rule whereby only management can dispense the free drink.

ECURITY

Inventory and supplies are an internal thief's "bread and butter" — a steak, a few knives and spoons, a bottle of champagne or two. Everything you own needs to be watched and secured. Safeguard the following vulnerable areas of your establishment:

- **Always be sure to lock your bar inventory when the bar is not open for service.** It deters employees and wandering customers from engaging in petty theft. It will also allow you to identify exactly when and where any losses occur.

- **Make sure you have locks on all of your storage areas.** Establish rules as to who can get their hands on the keys. Your local locksmith can help you not only with the locks, but also with more sophisticated measures, such as closed circuit cameras and card swipe systems.

- **Lock the office.** Limiting access to your office areas will prevent theft of valuables as well as valuable information.

- **Kitchen layout.** When designing or refitting a kitchen, locate your freezers and walk-in coolers as far from the back door as possible. Making it harder to sneak out high-cost items can only benefit your fight to avoid loss through theft.

- **Implement a robbery plan for your employees.** If the unthinkable should occur, you want to ensure that both your employees and customers are as safe as possible and that your cash is hard to get. Talk to a security expert and your local law enforcement officials to determine the best plan of action in the event of a robbery.

CORRECT CASH-HANDLING PROCEDURES

The correct handling of money is a skill in itself. It should never be left to chance.

- **Leaving the cash register unattended.** Unavoidably, there are times when employees have to leave their cash register unattended — a situation that invites dishonesty. Create a system where your staff does not have to leave the drawer unattended or they must log on with a pass code to open the drawer. Not only does it prevent theft, but it also allows you to instill confidence in your staff that any errors (or thefts) by someone else will not be attributed to them.

- **Ensure that your cashiers call out the total amount of a transaction and the amount tendered by a customer to reduce confusion.** Make certain your cashier does not put any notes into the cash drawer until after the transaction is complete.

- **Train employees to count aloud any change they are handing to the customer.** Count alouds ensure that the change is counted three times — once when your cashier takes it out of the drawer, once again when it is being handed to the customer, and finally, by the customer while it is being handed to her. Count alouds reduce the incidence of costly mistakes, misunderstandings, and employee theft.

- **Night drops.** If employees have to make night bank drops, make sure that they are accompanied by another employee.

- **Have all guest checks accounted for before an employee leaves.** Keeping strict control of the money within your business will significantly lower theft opportunities, not to mention man-hours spent trying to figure out shortages.

REDUCING CUSTOMER FRAUD

Your customers can also be a prime source of loss, especially if your employees are less than careful. Here are some common pitfalls:

- **"The letter scam."** The "customer is always right," yes, but use caution. This scam appears every few years. A letter arrives in the mail or over the fax telling you what a great evening they had at your restaurant. "Food, wine, service; everything was great. We cannot wait to come back." The zinger: "The only problem was, of course, when the busboy spilled some wine on my jacket, so enclosed is the bill for $30 for the cleaning."

- **Bad checks are a major source of customer theft.** Try to avoid accepting checks unless you know the customer well. If you absolutely must take a check, be sure to check the ID of the person signing it.

- **Credit cards.** When accepting credit cards, always have your employees check the signature on the card against the signature on the receipt. To ensure they do, have them write "verified" on the receipt afterwards.

- **Short-changed.** Occasionally, a customer will claim to have been given change for a smaller bill than they originally handed over. In this situation, if it is possible to "Z" the register and run a quick cash count to verify the cash drawer contents, then do so. If you are too busy to close a register, get the customer's name and phone number and tell her you will call her as soon as the drawer has been balanced and forward any overage to her at your own cost. Certainly, you do not want to lose a customer if you can help it, but being an easy target for fraud can do even more damage to your bottom line.

- **"Bundle" notes.** At various times throughout the night, under the supervision of the cashier involved, have your manager "bundle" any notes that number twelve or more in the cash drawer into bundles of ten. Move them to the safe, replacing them in the drawer with signed requisition slips. Bundling keeps the end-of-the-night count simple. It also keeps large cash amounts out of the place where it is most vulnerable.

- **Easy targets.** Do your table settings include expensive (or even inexpensive) centerpieces that customers may like to take home? Are these centerpieces easily slipped into a pocket or handbag? Consider using centerpieces that are large enough to be left on the table.

- **Walkouts.** In order to prevent customer walkouts, after presenting the bill, the server should return to the table promptly for payment. Having your cashier located at the only non-alarmed exit door will not prevent customers from leaving without paying, but it will certainly make such a move more risky for them. If your staff is alert and attentive, your customer walkouts should be cut to a minimum.

KEEPING YOUR OWN HOUSE IN CHECK

It is all well and good to keep an eye on everyone else, but you need to ensure that your own practices are as secure as everyone else's — put office procedures in place that will limit the chance of theft. The following practical procedures can make a big impact on reducing the operating costs of your restaurant:

- **Never make an outgoing check to "cash" and do not accept them either.** With a "cash" check, anyone could deposit the check as his own or worse; the receiver of the check could bank it and claim it never arrived. Your check is always your last chance for a receipt. Security of that check is paramount.

- **Keep all unused checks locked in a safe.**

- **Keep tabs on all check number successions.** Take immediate action if checks go missing. You always have the option of stopping payment if need be.

- **Limit all access to petty cash.** Petty cash is the number-one area of office fraud. Put your petty cash under lock and key.

- **The person who signs your company checks should also be the person that mails them.** Ensuring that your checks find their way to the company for which they are intended; it also makes certain you do not pay any "fake" invoices.

- **Double-check.** The manager responsible for writing deposit slips, counting money, and marking the deposit entry in your books should always be "seconded" by another person, especially with deposits, to ensure that nothing goes missing between the office and bank.

- **Reconcile all bank statements as quickly as possible.** If bank reconciliations are delayed and there is a major error in the checkbook, you could bounce checks. Do you need help in learning how to reconcile your bank statement? The following link provides ideas and tips in keeping your financials in order: Quick Books at **www.quickbooks. com/support/faqs/qbw2001/122131.html**.

ELECTRONIC SECURITY

In the restaurant industry, electronic security is a necessity. Consider the following essentials:

- **Back-door security.** Have your back door hooked up to a small buzzer so that anytime it is opened, a small noise sounds letting anyone in the kitchen and office know. Using this feature will also keep customers, inspectors, and even the competition from sneaking a peek into your kitchen. Also remember that a wide-open door invites bugs, rodents, and outside noise into your kitchen.

- **Utilize an employee login system into your POS wherever possible.** Make sure employees know that these numbers are for their own good and that sharing their numbers puts their safety in jeopardy. These systems not only let you keep track of who is opening a register, but also which employees are busiest, fastest, and make the least number of mistakes.

- **Install alarms on exit doors marked for "emergency use only"** to keep your clientele and employees from walking out when they are not supposed to, as well as keeping outsiders from sneaking into your establishment. For more information on door chimes and alarms, take a look at these online alarm retailers: Chime City at **www.chimecity.com** or Drive Alert at **www.drivealert.com**.

- **Visible cameras.** Security cameras, or at the very least, fake cameras, posted at exit doors and cash areas will keep your staff on their toes — and your customers from getting sneaky.

CHAPTER

SUCCESSFUL BAR LAYOUT, SET UP, AND LOCATION

Opening a bar is a daunting prospect, and should not be taken lightly. You have to plan and pay for the initial outlay of supplies and drinks, arrange the legal aspects of opening, and hire new employees, all time-consuming and potentially expensive tasks.

OPENING A BAR — AN OVERVIEW

When opening a new bar, there are a few advantages to look forward to:

- **The opening of a new bar will generate new interest and publicity on its own, especially in a place where no bar has been before**. Newspapers may report on the opening on their own volition, and customers are likely to drift in even with little advertising, merely to "try the new place."

- **You will also be dealing with employees who will still be excited with their jobs** and work hard to make a good impression on you.

Before opening a bar, you want to consider whether you will make a good bar manager. While the movies may make managing a bar seem simple, in real life successful bar owners and managers require a few specific traits:

- **Are you personable?** Bar management is largely about the people, not the drinks. If you want to operate a successful bar, you will do much better if you genuinely enjoy spending time with people (employees and patrons alike) or are willing to hire someone who will perform this function for you.

- **Can you get the startup money?** In addition to renting or buying a space for your establishment, you will need to budget for purchasing supplies and hiring your employees. You will also need to pay for a liquor license, advertising, and legal costs of starting a bar business.

- **Do you know what it will take to set up a bar in your area?** Spend some time looking at bars in your area with a critical eye. Talk to friends and family about their favorite establishments. Get a sense of why people go to bars and what sorts of bars are successful. What needs have yet to be filled by a bar or establishment in the area?

- **Can you take care of the legal and business aspects of running a bar?** Most governments closely control the running of a bar, but exact legalities differ from area to area. Contact your local municipality to find out which forms and licenses are needed to open an establishment.

MARKET RESEARCH

In market research, you will learn about your customers (or potential customers, if you have not yet opened for business) and your competition. Basically, you are trying to find out the answer to one question: What do my customers want?

Successful bar owners know who their customers are and focus their marketing and advertising on these customers to ensure a steady profit. Successful bars provide services and products more effectively than the competition.

WAYS TO CONDUCT MARKET RESEARCH

HIRE A MARKET RESEARCH COMPANY

In your local phone book, find companies that are willing to help you. The big advantage of hiring a market research and analysis group is that you will get professional market research results in a short amount of time. These companies use strategies such as customer polls, focus groups, online and in-person surveys, telephone surveys, and product testing to help you decide who your customers are (or who they could be) and what they want. The companies will interpret the results so that they are perfectly clear and understandable.

The major disadvantage is cost. These companies charge money for their services and this outlay of funds can seem very large. If you are unable to afford a market research company, consider saving up to hire one after you have been open for a while — the insight you can gain from a professional market analysis can be a big help in maximizing profits.

DO YOUR OWN CUSTOMER MARKET RESEARCH

If you cannot afford to hire professionals, you will have to invest your own time and effort into learning about your customers. You cannot skip this stage of planning a business. Without knowing your customer base, you simply will not have the information needed to make the right decisions about pricing, marketing, bar décor, and almost every other aspect of opening a bar.

What you learn in your market research will literally affect every aspect of your business and will make all parts of your business more profitable.

You can do your own customer market research by asking customers or potential customers questions. The easiest way is to have volunteers ask acquaintances or co-workers a few questions. Have questionnaires printed so the volunteers can record the answers. Keep questionnaires short and to the point. If you have not yet opened, ask questions such as the following:

- **When traveling, what was the best bar you visited like?** (This question will help you establish what people like and what they might like to see in their own hometown.)

- **When do you go to bars and pubs?**

- **How often do you go to bars and pubs?**

- **What do you like about bars and pubs?** (The answers here will give you a sense of what customers are looking for.)

- **What types of bars or pubs do you visit?**

- **What do you wish were different about bars and pubs?** (Listen closely to the answers to this question — the answers will give you some ideas about what the competition is missing.)

- **What sort of bar would you like to see open in the city?** (The answer to this question will give you ideas about niches that your bar could fill — and what the customer response might be.)

- **What is the best drink you ever had at a bar?**

- **Describe your best customer service experience at a bar.** (The answer will give you a sense of what your staff should be like to create enthusiastic customers.)

- **How much do you usually spend per drink and what sorts of drinks do you order on a night out?** (This question will give you an idea of what you need to offer and what prices you need to set to draw in customers.)

- **Name your three favorite bars. How did you find out about each?** (You get an idea of how to advertise to attract customers to the bar.)

- **Tell me a few things about you** (Note the sex and general age of each respondent. You want the basic demographics of each person to better analyze your market research.)

If you already have a bar, you still need to do market research. Offer your customers the chance to take a survey. You will get the best results if you offer a chance to win a prize in exchange for their participation. Have customers leave their first name and phone number on the survey and place each completed survey into a drawing for a nice prize. As an added bonus, you can also suggest customers provide their e-mail addresses for notification of upcoming events at your bar. For those customers who want this service, e-mail ads are a great and inexpensive way to promote your bar.

You want to do this type of market research occasionally once you are in business. Although going through the surveys is time consuming, it can tell you exactly what customers want and need. Better yet, regular surveys will let you know whether your customers (or their needs) are changing and whether you need to make changes in order to keep up.

On questionnaires for your existing customers, you want to ask similar questions asked of potential customers, but with a few differences:

- **Demographic information.** (Ask customers where they live, their age range, and their occupations. This information tells you who comes to your bar the most and who you need to target in ads and in the bar's appeal.)

- **What was your server like?** Were you satisfied with the service? What did you like/dislike about the way your server handled your order? (You find out how your employees are doing in making customers happy.)

- **Where did you first hear about us?** (You find out which of your marketing strategies is actually working.)

- **Would you come to this bar again?** (Lets you gauge customer satisfaction.)

- **How often do you come to this bar?** (Lets you see who your regulars are.)

- **How often do you visit establishments like this one?** (Lets you see how often the competition is getting business that could be yours.)

- **What would you like to see changed at this bar?** What would you like to see offered? (Here you get useful suggestions for changes or expansions.)

- **Are the hours of business convenient?** (If they are not, you may well be losing business.)

You cannot be shy about talking to others about bars. You do not need to announce that you are the owner of a new bar. Simply ask others about their bar experiences. Many people enjoy talking about themselves and will be glad to offer feedback. Talk to others, even to your competition's customers. You never know what you will find. There are other ways besides asking questions to find out who your potential customers may be, including the following:

- **What is around your bar?** If you are close to a college, you can expect college students to pop in and you can build a respectable business by creating a student-friendly atmosphere that will draw in students eager to unwind after a long day. If your bar will be located near a factory, find out about the drinking and eating habits of the workers there — many may be interested in dropping in after work for a pint. If there are businesses near your bar or pub, consider who might come into your establishment for a business lunch. Your bar's location can be an important clue as to who your potential clients may be.

- **What other establishments are in your area?** Chances are if there are other establishments in your area, they cater to a specific set of people. These same clients may be willing to come to your establishment. If your bar is located near boutiques that cater to women, setting up a cozy place where "the girls" can meet for a chat after shopping may be a savvy business strategy. If your bar is located near strip malls that sell auto parts to car enthusiasts and car mechanics, consider that these same clients may be willing to drop by your place for a quick drink and snack before heading home. If your bar will be located by several tourist traps, then a bar with plenty of local flavor may appeal to visitors eager to relax after sightseeing. The idea is that the stores and businesses near your bar's location are already marketing and drawing regular customers — you can attract these same clients simply by making your bar appealing to them. It is a very simple idea with a big profit potential.

- **How many bars are in the city and what are they like?** Researching your competitors is covered in detail in the next section of this book, but as you are researching your customers (or potential customers), be aware that they do not live in a vacuum. If they already have a sports bar that they frequent you may need to offer something different or better to draw loyalties away from the competition. Your customers are looking at other bars — and visiting them. Have an idea of where your customers are going and why they are going there. Get a sense of why they might come to your bar instead.

- **What was previously in your location and who frequented it?** If your establishment was a bar before (or a restaurant or other shop), find out who frequented it. You may find that the same groups of people are still willing to eat and drink at the "new" place.

- **What is not in your area?** Consider what types of bars are missing in your city or town. Is there no quiet bar that appeals to the artsy crowd? Is there no jazz bar? Is there no loud bar that is also a great place to dance? Research your customers well to make sure that there is a need. If you do see a need that is not met, jump at the chance. Being able to fill a need is a great way to ensure your bar's success.

- **Do not be afraid to ask people you know.** Acquaintances, friends, and family all have their own ideas about bars. Ask them where they go and tag along on a trip to the bar. Ask them what they like and dislike about their favorite bars.

Once your market research is complete, analyze your findings. Do not ignore the market research because your idea of the customers you want to attract is different. If your market shows that most of your paying customers are going to be blue-collar workers, it is best for you and your business to follow the market research rather than your own ideas of what will work.

At the same time, you should not make every change that customers want. Not only will it be a very expensive venture, it may make the bar too hectic. Instead, when you are looking at your market research, look for patterns:

- **Who are your customers?** What are their ages, sex, and occupation? Do you have a different crowd at lunch, a different one in the early afternoon, and a different one in the evening? If so, divide the surveys into these crowds to find what is needed at each "peak" hour.

- **What do your customers want?** Again, look for patterns. You may hear about everything from jukeboxes to bands. What your customers may be saying is more entertainment. Provide some of the customers' wants and always try to provide those things that do not cost extra (Friendlier atmosphere or wait staff, for example, often is demanded by customers and only costs the bar manager effort.).

- **Ask yourself what small changes could meet the most customers' demands — and then implement your changes.** A few small changes can have as much influence as a larger, more expensive change but at a smaller cost.

THE COMPETITION

Your competition is the other bars and restaurants with bars. Ignore your competition at your own peril, because as savvy bar managers know, what the competition is doing may have a big impact on your business. There are several things you will want to know about your competition:

- **Who are they?** Look in your phone directory at the bars and pubs in your area. Review ads to determine which bars are your most direct competitors (either because they are close to your establishment or because they seem to be appealing to the same customers who will be visiting your bar).

- **What are they like?** Try to get a sense of the selection, quality, service, and atmosphere of each competitor. Getting a sense of the competition gives you insight into what will lure customers your way.

- **Who visits them?** Which customers does your competition attract? College students? Businesspeople? Blue-collar workers?

- **How do they advertise?** Look at the ads your competition runs and analyze them. To whom are they appealing? How effective are they? Where does the competition advertise the most? Often bars that are successful have already done the market research that tells them which ads bring in the largest profits. You can learn a lot about a successful ad campaign by looking at a successful competitor.

- **What do they offer?** Which drinks does your competition overlook? Which drinks are hot sellers? What sort of menu or extras (gambling, live acts, jukeboxes) does the competition offer? Knowing what your competition offers lets you know what you need to offer. If every competitor offers local draft beer because it is a hot seller, then you need to offer it as well. From what the competition offers, you can also get a sense of what is missing. Do no bars in your area offer specialty coffees even though your market suggests some customers want it? Offering what your competition does not—and advertising exclusive availability at your bar—is often a good way to draw customers. You will know what to offer if you research both your customers and your competition.

- **What are they doing right?** Bars that draw plenty of customers are doing something right. If you can pinpoint what that something is, you will have learned a key lesson about what your bar needs to offer to draw customers. Is the competition able to offer many specialty drinks? A great atmosphere? Super service? A wonderful location? A view? Special events? You can learn a lot from a successful bar — and then tailor what you have learned to your own bar.

- **What are they doing wrong?** Try to figure out what the competition is not doing correctly — and then do it right at your bar. Is the hot bar in the city a beautiful place to drink but offers slow service? Offer speedy and friendly service as well as an attractive atmosphere and you will get plenty of customers to your bar. If you notice something wrong at a competing bar, chances are that customers notice too. They will be glad to visit a bar that offers a better experience. Look into bars that seem to be doing plenty wrong — the bars that seem to be empty every night. You can learn as much from these bars as from the successful ones. If you can pinpoint what the failing bars are doing wrong, you may be able to avoid their fate.

- **What are their busy nights?** What are the slow nights? Figure out what the "hot" nights are for the major competitors. You may want to hold your own big nights on other evenings to avoid the well-established competition. You may want to hold smaller specials on the big nights to draw those customers who cannot get into the crowded bars.

- **What are the prices?** Look at your competitors' prices; they are what they are for a specific reason. Can you under-price them (and if you can, will that draw customers)? Can you offer something more? Your prices should not be much higher or lower, but slight differences can make your bar successful.

There are several ways you can learn more about your competition:

- **Visit them.** The best way to see what your competitors are like is to visit them as a customer. Sit down at a competing bar, order a drink, and look around. What is the bar like? How are customers treated? Who is in the bar and how content do they look? What is the quality of the food and drink? What is the quality of the service like? Often the best research you can do on a competing bar is the research you do with your own senses. Visit as many bars as you can before you start to set up your own. There is nothing like being a customer to see what works and does not in nearby bars.

- **Talk to their customers.** Strike up conversations with your competition's customers. Talk to them about the bar and ask them what they like about it, where they heard about it, and what they think of it in general. Do not sound like an interrogator; simply strike up a conversation to find out how other customers see a particular bar.

- **Read their ads and press.** The competition spends plenty of time marketing and advertising. Read what they have to say about themselves; you can gauge what they offer and who they are trying to entice. Some bars use very good marketing strategies that you can incorporate into your own marketing and advertising. You will also see some costly advertising mistakes to avoid.

- **Read guidebooks and reviews.** Reviews online and in newspapers and guidebooks can give you a good sense of what others have to say about the competition. You can easily get another perspective on what a competitor is doing right or wrong. Use this information to do the same things right while avoiding the same mistakes. Reviews are a great way to see what is missing. If your top three competitors get poor reviews for service and great reviews for atmosphere, then you can provide excellent service. Even if you cannot hire the same expensive decorators, offering something that the competition does not can help ensure your bar's success.

BAR LAYOUT (NUTS AND BOLTS)

The nuts and bolts of your bar are the basic structures that are in place. If you are leasing or have bought a facility that was a bar before, you may not think about this aspect of your bar. Even if you had to build up your own bar and eating areas, you may not give much thought to the way your bar is set up. After all, a bar is just a bar, right? Wrong. The mechanics of your bar setup can affect your success because it can affect customer experience.

LAYOUT OF A TYPICAL BAR

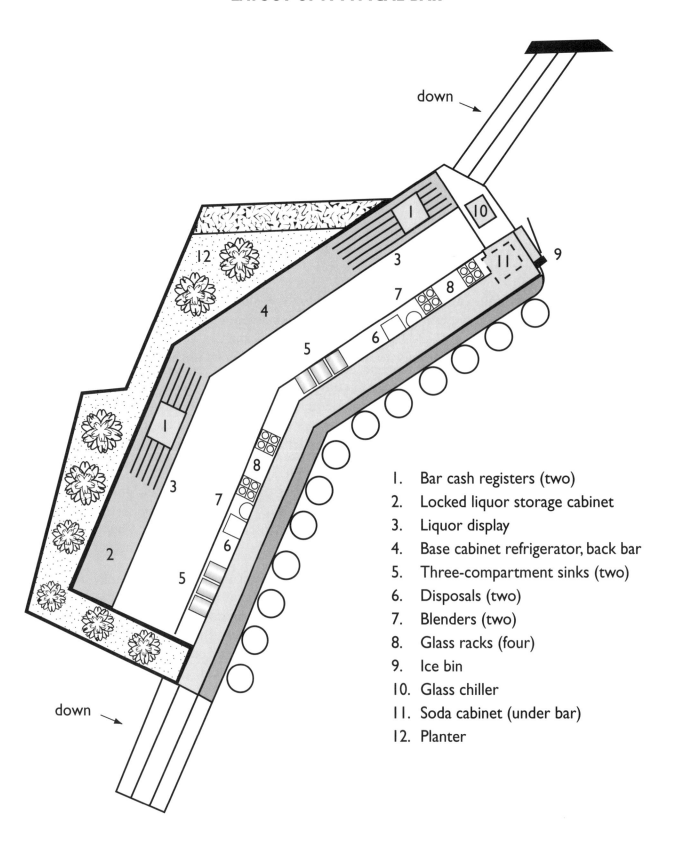

1. Bar cash registers (two)
2. Locked liquor storage cabinet
3. Liquor display
4. Base cabinet refrigerator, back bar
5. Three-compartment sinks (two)
6. Disposals (two)
7. Blenders (two)
8. Glass racks (four)
9. Ice bin
10. Glass chiller
11. Soda cabinet (under bar)
12. Planter

BAR HARDWARE

The way your bar operates depends on many factors, one being the machinery of the bar. Sometimes, the bar just is not set up to allow maximum productivity. Think about productivity and your staff before you think of décor. The look of your bar is important, but service is more important. If you set up your bar to allow for the best possible service, you will end up ahead of the competition.

A good bar allows staff to move around easily. A busy bar that allows only one bartender behind the bar at a time is sure to be a disaster, no matter how tastefully designed. A good bar also has plenty of room for supplies. If your staff has to keep running to the storage area for more drinks, they will get worn out and will serve fewer customers. Each drink will also take longer to make. Have enough space behind the bar for an extra refrigerator to store drinks. Here are some additional tips:

- **Make sure that the bar design is simple and easy to clean.** Too many details look garish and make cleaning difficult. Smooth surfaces not only look less cluttered, which is more attractive to customers, but they are easy to clean. A good bar should be impressive upon first glance. An expansive selection of spirits and liqueurs can be just as impressive. So, too, can a personable, neat, and tidy bartender in a well-pressed uniform, greeting the customers like an old friend. When a customer finds anything less than clean about a bar, the impression he or she takes home will be a bad one. A smart bar design can go a long way toward helping staff keep your establishment spotlessly clean.

- **Avoid tight corners.** Some surfaces are easier to keep clean than others. Tight corners collect "bar gunk." Your customers expect a comfortable level of cleanliness. Anything less is likely to draw their wrath, if not the attention of local health inspectors. Make sure your employees keep any tight corners as clean as they keep the flat surfaces. Do regular inspections to make sure.

- **Make it a habit to line all ice sinks with a plastic trash bag.** Whenever your staff needs to clean out the sink (either because of a broken glass or as part of regular bar cleaning) you can simply remove the bag — ice, water, and all. It is easy to replace, without inhibiting service.

- **Glass areas should be scrubbed several times a day.** These areas should always be out of the customers' field of vision. Your customers should never glimpse your bar's engine. Ensure that all boxes, empty glass racks, and dirty glasses are kept out of eyesight, either in "under-bar" sinks or out-of-view back-bar areas.

SEATING

A good bar is attractive and comfortable. The seats at the bar should be padded and comfortable. Tables should be heavy duty and beverage-friendly. If your bar décor or lack of bar comfort is sending away customers, then your bar design is costing you money.

For various high-quality products, check out Royal Industries, Inc. **www.royalindustriesinc. com**. They manufacture a full line of food service products and furniture including:

- **Restaurant seating.** Commercial restaurant and hospitality quality seating, durably constructed, and offered in hardwood, bistro style, metal stackable, and youth chairs.

- **Bar stools.** They offer metal bar stools in both standard (pictured at right) and bucket seat models.

- **Table tops and bases.** With heavy-duty reversible table tops, cast-iron table bases, and spiders, these tables are very durable products.

THE FRONT BAR

The front bar is essential to pleasing customers and ensuring a loyal clientele. Make sure that your front bar is not too wide. Many bar managers assume that a wider bar is better as it allows for more room, but a wide bar can crowd out a bar staff and make it quite hard for your staff and customers to chat and interact. If a customer has to yell over a wide bar to make his drink order heard, he is unlikely to return to your bar.

When designing your front bar, be sure that the space above the bar is not ignored. Traditionally, mirrors are placed behind and above the bar; it is a poor idea. They take a lot of time and money to clean and look foggy and dingy very quickly. Menu boards or artwork are better and less expensive options. Make sure that the area behind the bar is attractive and you will draw more customers. Keep a selection of inventory attractively displayed behind the front bar — it not only adds interest but can inspire customers to buy. Keeping menus or products before customers' eyes can tempt patrons and allow them to order easily, reducing the time your staff needs to explain the bar's offerings.

When well designed, your front bar should give patrons a clear idea of what is offered without interfering with their line of vision or distracting the bar staff. To get a sense of whether your bar is well designed, order a drink yourself and see how easy the staff moves to get your order prepared. Consider your own actions: Do you need to crane your neck to see a menu or to order? In a well-designed bar, both the customer and staff should be comfortable.

STREAMLINING SERVICE

When designing your service area, consider the necessary steps to prepare a drink and make these steps as few as possible. The fewer steps your bartender needs to get a clean glass, to scoop ice from the ice bins, to get drinks from the spirit dispenser, and to get the drinks from the soda guns, the easier each night's business will go. If your bartender has to walk to get each of these items, and then walk to yet another location to use the cash register, productivity will fall during the course of a night, even if each station is only a few steps away. If there is more than one bartender on duty, a bad setup can encourage spills and short tempers.

The service area should be large enough to handle more than one bartender comfortably. Everything needed to prepare drinks should be within easy reach. Since most people are right-handed, your bar should allow staff to pick up glasses with their left hand and bottles with their right. The floor of your bar should be uncluttered and contain no portable steps so that movement is not encumbered.

Consider keeping the most popular bottled beers in buckets of ice under the bar. That way, staff can easily produce these bottles when it is busy. During slower times, these buckets can easily be refilled with ice and beer, dramatically cutting down on unnecessary trips to the refrigerator.

THE UNDER-BAR

Your goal in designing your under-bar is to make it as productive as possible. The under-bar should have everything your staff needs to prepare most of their orders without walking away from the bar, ensuring fast service and allowing the bartender to strike up a quick conversation with the customer as the drink is being prepared.

FLOORING

When designing your bar area, do not overlook flooring. The customer area of the bar should be attractive and safe. Add anti-slip and anti-fatigue floor mats behind the bar area. These mats will help keep your staff comfortable during shifts and will prevent slips and glass breakage.

Grip Rock and Super G floor mats by Matrix Engineering are durable, long lasting, and lightweight. The Grip Rock safety mat was designed to be slip-resistant in wet, hazardous areas. This makes it especially useful behind the bar and in areas conducive to slips/falls. For more information, visit **www.griprock.com** or call 800-926-0528.

CLIMATE CONTROL

Body heat, cigarette smoke, sweat, outside temperature, and dance floor fog systems all affect the comfort-level of the bar. A too cold or muggy bar makes patrons feel like leaving. You can resolve this problem with a few handy devices and appliances:

- **A fresh-air exchange system.** An addition to your heating, ventilation, and air-conditioning system. It works by constantly bringing in fresh air from outside. Casinos use these systems to keep patrons from feeling sleepy. These systems can make any bar seem well-ventilated.

- **Fresh-air ducts.** These are especially useful over dance floors. It works by allowing you to bring in large bursts of fresh air from outside whenever you decide that conditions are too clammy.

- **A smoke extraction system.** This type of system can help remove smoke and purify the air.

- **Heating.** Whether you choose electric, gas, or a fireplace, make sure that your heating system is doing its job on cold nights by keeping your customers comfortable.

- **Air-conditioning.** Air-conditioning can help keep your bar nice and cool on hot days. It can also drive up your electricity bill. Many bars find that offering a patio and fans helps keep things cool as well.

CUSTOMER COMFORT

The longer customers stay, the more they order. Make chairs comfortable, ensure tables are not wobbly, lighting is comfortable, and music is at a good level. Install booths—they tend to make customers linger longer. Allow your customers to lean comfortably on the bar without getting cold elbows.

Do not overlook the bathrooms. Keep nice-smelling soap in the bathrooms and easy-to-access paper towels or dryers. Extra touches in the bathrooms, such as sofas or small mint candies by the sinks, can make customers feel pampered and more likely to come again.

COLOR SCHEMES

Research has shown that certain colors promote specific feelings in consumers; in restaurants decorated with reds and yellows, customers are more likely to experience hunger and may have a harder time settling down and relaxing — which may explain why so many fast-food places tend to use this color scheme. Researchers think that red and yellow may prompt a person who is already hungry to order more than they would if those colors were not present. Red and yellow are also likely to make a customer move on quickly once their money is spent, which is also ideal for the fast-food business.

Blues and greens, on the other hand, are likely to make customers settle down, according to researchers; thus, these are a better option for a bar that wants to encourage patrons to stay awhile.

BAR RECIPE AND PROCEDURE MANUAL

The purpose of the Bar Recipe and Procedure Manual is to ensure that the methods of preparing all cocktails are consistent among your bartenders. Drinks can be prepared in many different ways. It is imperative that all recipes and procedures are standardized to ensure that both the final product and cost is consistent. All recipes and procedures for preparing drinks should be written down and given to all staff members. Your bartenders should be tested to ensure that they know how each drink should be prepared. The Bar Recipe and Procedure Manual should be kept under the bar so that it can easily be referred to. It is an essential part of your bar's layout.

LIQUOR AND BEER ORDERING

Liquor ordering is not as involved as purchasing food items. There are fewer problem areas to contend with. Liquor has a long shelf life and will rarely turn bad, which enables it to be ordered in large quantities on a less frequent basis. Moreover, the quality is always consistent among distributors: They all carry the same products. It is far simpler to compare prices and terms knowing that each supplier has the same item. Once you establish which well and call brands you wish to serve, ordering should only involve projecting your needs and purchasing from the distributor with the best overall terms.

Each state has its own laws and regulations regarding the sale and distribution of alcoholic beverages. States may be divided into one of two classifications: those that permit private businesses to sell and distribute liquor and those that have a monopoly on the sale of liquor (usually excluding beer and wine) and sell through state-run stores. There are advantages and disadvantages to both situations.

SETTING BAR PRICES

Setting proper bar prices is an easier process than that of establishing menu prices. The procedures are basically the same; however, there are fewer cost factors to contend with in projecting liquor costs. The bar should operate at 18 to 25 percent cost of sales. Cost of sales is determined by dividing the total liquor cost by total liquor sales. This figure excludes wine, as it is considered a separate category and projected as such. As stated in Chapter 5, "Profitable Menu Planning," the cost of sales is the total cost over a given period of time, usually one month, divided by total sales. If the monthly total liquor cost was $10,000 and the total sales were $50,000, the cost percentage would be 20 percent.

To set the proper bar prices, it is necessary to calculate the cost of the cocktail. The cost refers to the liquor, mixers, and garnishes used to make the cocktail. Labor, ice, and glassware are not actual liquor costs and are computed in other categories. There are two cost factors to consider when computing the cost of a cocktail: 1) the cost of the shot of alcohol poured and 2) the cost of all the miscellaneous nonalcoholic ingredients.

To project the cost of each shot poured:

- Using the conversion chart convert the metric measurement of each bottle into ounces.

- Calculate the number of shots yielded from each bottle by dividing the bottle volume (in ounces) by the size (in ounces) of the average shot poured.

- Divide the cost of the bottle by the number of shots it should yield to compute the cost per shot.

To project the exact cost for each cocktail, it is necessary to calculate the cost of the nonalcoholic ingredients that are added. Since this computation would entail many hours, it is far simpler and nearly as precise to assess an average miscellaneous expense for all drinks. The average miscellaneous cost would account for the additional cost of juices, mixers, garnishes, and soda. This miscellaneous-expense figure would not be applied to beer or wine since there is no additional cost to the final product.

CONVERSION CHART FOR LIQUID MEASURES

Research shows that the average miscellaneous expense fluctuates between 5 and 20 percent of the cost of each shot poured. Of course, this figure will depend upon the type and number of drinks you serve. Blended drinks will have a high percentage of cost since they contain several different ingredients. To compensate for this additional cost, most restaurants pour a smaller shot (1⅛ to 1¼ ounces). Straight drinks and beer will help balance out this cost since they have no additional ingredients. Based upon this information it would be accurate enough to assess the miscellaneous expense at 10 percent of the shot cost. Thus, the cost of each shot plus the average miscellaneous expense will equal the estimated total cost of the drink.

To compute the charge for each drink, simply plug different prices into the formula listed below until you reach the desired liquor cost-of-sales percentage:

Total Drink Cost ÷ Price = 18–25% Liquor Cost of Sales

Certain expensive liquors, when priced out to get the desired cost-of-sales percentage, will be too expensive. Customers may not pay the price you would need to charge to reach the desired 18 to 25 percent.

Analyze what other restaurants in the area are charging for cocktails. When you first open, customers tend to be cautious. A reputation for overpriced drinks can be detrimental to your restaurant business. Should you have entertainment in the lounge, you may raise drink prices to offset the entertainment expense, a common and generally accepted practice.

Set as few different bar prices as possible. Bartenders and cocktail waitresses will have a difficult time remembering all the different prices and may inadvertently charge the wrong price. The ideal pricing structure is to have one price for each category of liquor: well items, call items, and cordials and liqueurs. Beer may also be grouped into three basic price categories: domestic, imported, and draft. Categorical prices may be set by averaging the high- and low-priced drinks and considering the number sold of each. The high-cost sale items will be offset by the sale of the lower-cost ones, resulting in the average cost-of-sales percentage desired.

Juice and soda prices should assimilate those set by area restaurants. These items are often compared by customers, as they are sold in all restaurants. Soda can be used as a promotional tool to attract teenagers and adults with children. Free soda with dinner and free refills are common inducements. The small cost factor involved in initiating these promotions makes them a good promotional vehicle.

The "Happy Hour," a period of time when drink prices are generally reduced, can be an effective means of increasing bar sales. To be substantiated, it must draw a large volume of customers. "Happy Hours" are often run prior to opening the dining room, usually between 4 and 6 p.m. Drinks are sold at half-price or at a substantial discount. Hors d'oeuvres and salty snacks, which will induce the customers' thirst, are often served.

To offset the increase in the cost of sales due to the lower drink prices, total liquor sales must be increased substantially. A restaurant that lowers all drink prices by 50 percent during "Happy Hour" will be doubling its cost of sales.

EGAL ADVICE

Legal issues will affect your business right from the start; bars are simply more closely regulated than other types of businesses. As a bar manager/owner, there are several types of laws that need your attention:

- Bylaws regarding signs and advertising

- Zoning bylaws

- Employee regulations and laws

- Fire regulations

- Safety regulations

Most bar owners worry about lawsuits — and with good reason. There have been many cases in recent years of bar owners/managers being sued as a result of a drunk patron's actions. Bar managers/owners can also be sued by employees if work conditions are unsafe. To legally protect your business, there are a few things you can do:

- Hire a good lawyer.

- Do all you can to make your bar a safe place.

- Get the very best insurance that you can.

A good lawyer is helpful. He can represent you in case of court action and in some cases can help avoid court action in the first place. Your lawyer can ensure that everything in your bar is legal. Do your research for a good business lawyer well before you ever need one. Choose a lawyer or law firm that you are confident in. You may require a lawyer to witness some of the forms you need to open your bar.

INTOXICATION

Make sure your bar staff know the signs of intoxication. It is the greatest concern for a bar. Intoxicated customers can create legal problems through their actions. Long before you open your bar's doors, you and your staff need to be prepared to deal with intoxication.

- **Develop an alcohol sales policy.** This type of policy generally includes a description of federal, state, and local laws that govern the sale of alcohol in your area. This information should be clearly and briefly written to make sure that your servers can understand and remember it. Your state department of alcohol and local chamber of commerce will have easy-to-understand legal information about alcohol sales. Your alcohol sales policy should also include the bar's own rules for servers. Basics such as not selling to minors and not selling to intoxicated customers should be part of these rules. You may want to put a policy into place that requires a server to notify the manager about any customer who has had more than four drinks. The manager can look at the situation and determine what to do. You may also want to set up a relationship with a local cab company in case you need to suggest a cab for a customer.

- **Make sure servers are aware of alcohol laws.** Test each server on her knowledge. Your state's department of alcohol regulation will generally have informational guides and even testing materials you can use.

- **Train your servers to serve alcohol responsibly.** MYou should have a documented alcohol service training program in place that covers the effects of alcohol, blood alcohol concentration levels, and alcohol's effects on the body. *The Responsible Serving of Alcoholic Beverages: A Complete Staff Training Course for Bars, Restaurants, and Caterers* is an excellent manual that covers all aspects of alcohol service in depth and has a comprehensive in-house training program that is easy to set up, customize, and implement. It comes with a CD-ROM that contains all forms and training materials discussed in the book. To order, contact Atlantic Publishing at 800-814-1132 or order online at **www.atlantic-pub.com** (Item # RSA-01, $49.95).

- **Make sure your rules are clear and are followed.** Make your employees fill out forms to keep track of customers' alcohol intake if there appears to be a potential problem. Have servers offer a menu to any customer who is only drinking or offer a free appetizer to a customer who has had a few drinks. Ensure that servers are checking IDs and that the amount of alcohol poured into each drink is measured.

- **Make sure your server gets management involved in any incident involving an intoxicated customer.** Document everything that occurs. The best way to ensure that you and your staff can handle an intoxicated customer is to make sure that everyone working at the bar knows what to do with an intoxicated customer.

SYMPTOMS *of* INTOXICATION

Know the symptons of intoxication! Intoxication is a legal term defining the level of alcohol in the blood.

Drinking Very Fast

Ordering More Than One Drink At A Time

Overly Friendly

Loud Behavior

Buying Drinks For Others

Lighting The Wrong End Of A Cigarette

Careless With Money

Use Of Foul Language

Concentration Problems

Mood Swings

Atlantic Publishing offers a series of ten posters that deal with alcohol awareness. Above is the Symptoms of Intoxication poster (Item # SIO-PS $9.95). To order call 800-814-1132 or online at www.atlantic-pub.com.

Many people think that alcohol stimulates. Certainly ads suggest that alcohol creates a fun time. Alcohol alters moods and affects the body functions — it acts as a depressant. As the bloodstream absorbs the alcohol that has been consumed, the body is affected. It is only when the liver removes the alcohol from the bloodstream by oxidizing it that the body returns to normal. It takes time for this process to take place. Folk remedies such as strong coffee or cool water will not help. A person needs to stop drinking alcohol entirely and allow the body to cope with the substance already in the system.

It is not always easy to tell when a person has over-indulged. In many cases, a person will sit quietly and keep drinking so that servers will not see visible signs. Each person can drink different amounts before being negatively affected. Larger men and frequent drinkers often have a higher tolerance and their bodies will be able to handle larger amounts of alcohol. Patrons who drink slowly and drink on a full stomach may also take longer to experience the ill effects of alcohol than patrons who drink quickly and on an empty stomach.

You do not want to "cut off" someone who is simply having a nice time. It is your legal responsibility to cut off any patron who is drunk. There are several ways that you and your staff can tell when a patron has had too much alcohol:

- **Patron will get louder and may become friendlier**, possibly accosting staff or other patrons with familiarity (this usually is thought of as the first stage of intoxication).

- **Patron may have motor skills affected by alcohol**, meaning speech will become slurred, walking will become unsteady, and may have a difficult time picking up change or a coaster. At this stage, usually called the second stage of intoxication, the patron may become more difficult, even aggressive. Patrons at this stage may also start swearing, complaining, or may become withdrawn. They will usually drink more at a faster pace and become careless with their money and their surroundings, dropping change or bumping into others.

If you see the above signs, you need to stop serving the patron. An intoxicated patron who makes a scene when not served can be a nuisance and a distraction to other customers. There are several ways to ensure that dealing with an intoxicated customer is less of a hassle:

- **Try to prevent a customer from becoming out of control in the first place by having the establishment's alcohol serving policies firmly in place.** Staff should refuse to serve any patron more than one drink at a time. Patrons should be offered a menu if they are drinking, as food in the stomach can slow down the speed in which alcohol is absorbed. Prevention is your best bet in avoiding problems associated with an intoxicated patron. Impairment begins with the first drink and the savvy bar staff will work hard to ensure that impairment does not turn into intoxication.

- **If a patron does get intoxicated, it is important that staff react while the patron is still at the first stage or early in the second stage of intoxication.** At this stage, the patron's drinks should be slowed down and the patron should be offered a menu.

- **Try to avoid direct confrontation with an intoxicated patron.** Staff who notice someone who has consumed too much should alert the manager and slow down service to that patron.

- **Staff and the manager should start paperwork as soon as they notice that a patron has had too much.** This paperwork should include a quick inventory of the date, a description of the patron, a listing of when the patron was served, a list of the drinks served, and a description of any events or conflicts that occurred. In case of legal trouble or a patron complaint, staff will have the information needed to show that the bar acted properly.

- **If avoiding serving the intoxicated patron does not help, the manager should be called.** The manager should treat the complaint as a regular service complaint, apologizing for the inconvenience but quietly and firmly noting that the bar cannot legally serve the patron. Many bar staff members shy away from this sort of direct confrontation, as they fear how such a conversation will look to other patrons. When handled firmly but politely, this sort of chat can help make other patrons more comfortable with the bar, as it shows other guests that the bar is serious about keeping customers safe.

- **Where appropriate, intoxicated patrons who have been refused service should be offered something else**, such as a free nonalcoholic beverage or a free snack, to keep the customer happy and to allow the customer time to "sober up."

- **The patron may continue to argue loudly.** If the patron becomes a problem or starts to distract other customers, she should be asked to leave. The manager will want to offer the patron a taxi cab, as it is important that the patron arrive home safely.

- **Do not worry if the patron threatens to never come back or to patronize another bar.** Be secure in the knowledge that you are protecting the patron, other customers at the bar, and your own business by refusing to serve someone who has had too much to drink. It is better to err on the side of caution and risk offending someone rather than continue serving someone who will be in an accident as a result of her intoxication. Most patrons will respect a bar for being firm with an intoxicated customer. These customers will continue to come to your bar.

M INORS CAN MEAN MAJOR LEGAL PROBLEMS

Serving alcohol or selling cigarettes to a minor is illegal. Unfortunately, many minors routinely try to get served. Minors can be quite a nuisance to bar managers. What is even more frustrating for the bar manager is that minors caught drinking will rarely find themselves in much legal trouble, but the bar that served the minors will generally face an entire array of legal problems and may be shut down. The problems will be worse if the minor is involved in another illegal activity or is hurt or injured after drinking. Every bar manager needs to make sure that no minors are served at the bar.

There are a number of ways that minors attempt to get served. The most popular method is by using fake IDs. Unfortunately, with scanners and high-quality printers available to almost every high school student, fake IDs are easier to make — and harder to spot.

Make sure that all employees check the ID of anyone who seems underage. Train your staff to spot fake IDs. Staff should first look at the type of ID being given to them. Acceptable forms of ID include driver's licenses or state identification for non-drivers, passports, and United States Uniformed Service Identification. The ID must contain a picture, the person's name and date of birth, a physical description, and a signature. The ID must be valid to be accepted at the bar.

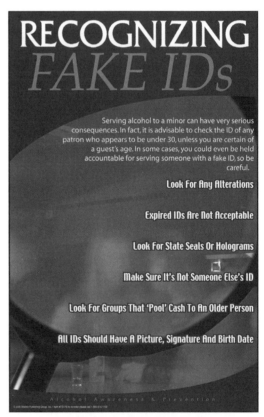

This poster will help employees recognizes fake IDs. To order, call 800-814-1132 or online at www.atlantic-pub.com (Item # FID-PS, $9.95).

Fake IDs can be spotted a number of ways. Marks or cuts around the date of birth or different fonts within an ID are often giveaways that it is fake. Valid IDs have protective holograms. Look for these features. You can help your staff by getting an ID checker, which uses the magnetized strips on IDs to check whether they are fake.

If you are unsure whether an ID is valid or fake, it is acceptable to ask for another piece of

ID. Many adults will have more than one piece of identification and will be happy to show it to you. Even other picture ID can show you whether the names and signatures on the various IDs match or not.

Some minors simply borrow valid ID from someone who looks like them but is older. Since the ID is valid, it is harder to detect. If you suspect that a minor is trying to get into the bar this way, you can ask the minor for a signature sample to compare to the ID. Many minors will get nervous and leave before signing.

Some minors will simply drop by a bar with drinking-age friends and drink the beer served to the friends. Many bars counter this problem by not allowing minors into the bar without parental supervision.

Some minors simply rely on looking older than they appear. With some makeup, older clothing, and the dim lighting of many bars, it is not difficult for a seventeen-year-old to appear several years older. One way to counter this problem is to simply ask all patrons under the age of thirty to show their IDs. Older patrons will actually be flattered to be mistaken for someone younger and few patrons will mind that you are taking such care to prevent underage drinking.

Some minors will even attempt to bribe your bartender or rely on friends that they have on staff to get served. The best way to prevent this problem is to make sure that your staff is reliable and trustworthy. Savvy bar managers always run background checks and will often send in an older teenager as a test to see how staff is able to detect and deal with the minor.

It is important to stress that you will never be angry about staff turning away someone who they think is underage. Tell your staff to trust their gut feelings and give them specific actions to take if they suspect that someone underage is trying to enter the bar or order a drink. Staff should fill out a denial-of-service form for turning away a minor, just as they would for turning away someone who is intoxicated. They should write down the time, date, a description of the person, and why they felt the person was a minor. In case of any problems, this paperwork will help your bar with any legal hassles.

OTHER FACTORS THAT MAY LEAD TO LEGAL PROBLEMS

SEXUAL CRIMES AND HARASSMENT

Where drinks and groups of people are involved, it is always possible that some person will try to grab or sexually assault another. Many cases of date rape or sexual assault involve alcohol. The best way to defend female customers and staff is to refuse alcohol to anyone who is intoxicated.

In some cases, a man may begin with leering or saying obscene things. He should be promptly evicted from the bar at this point and security staff should not let him in again. A zero-tolerance policy is best in these cases. A few men who seem to be following or crowding around a woman should also be approached. The woman in question should be asked if she needs a taxi cab called on her behalf.

One common problem today is date-rape drugs. These substances are often introduced into drinks at bars and parties. The victim loses consciousness or becomes unable to fight off her attackers. Ensure that only the bartender or qualified staff has access to drinks and mixing equipment. Servers should be alert for signs of intoxication or illness in someone who has not had much to drink. If it is suspected that a drug has been given to the customer, police should be called and the victim should be given medical attention.

Some additional problems may be:

- **Illegal workers.** It is important to ensure that all staff members you hire are legally allowed to work in your area. Immigration officers do check bars and restaurants, which tend to harbor disproportionate numbers of illegal workers.

- **Pickpockets and scam artists.** Bars are a heavy concentration of people and many of those people are focused on their drinks or the company they are with. Pickpockets and other scam artists view these bars as a haven. They may distract the wait staff or bartender with questions while stealing. By the time a customer realizes that a crime has taken place, the thief is usually long gone. The best defense here is often a sharp-eyed staff and a security camera that can catch the perpetrator on film. In many cases, women's purses, casually left on the back of a chair or empty seat make an ideal target. Offering a coat check or at least reminding customers to keep bags stowed can reduce the chances of robbery or theft.

- **Robbery.** Because of the expensive inventory of bars and the money that passes through such establishments, bars are very popular targets for burglars. Customers' purses, tip jars, cash, alcoholic beverages, and even cigarettes are all popular targets of burglars. In some cases, ex-employees who know the bar schedule or policy surrounding money take advantage of their knowledge. You should keep as little cash as possible on your premises. After closing, remove all cash from the premises and leave the till open so that would-be thieves can see that it is empty. You may want to change your money storage system every few months so that robbers cannot find an easy target. If you are robbed during business hours, your only priority is to ensure that no staff or customers are hurt. In case of an armed robbery, hand over all money and cooperate. Try to remember as many details about the robber and contact authorities as soon as it is safe to do so.

- **Assault.** If your bar gets a "reputation" as a place where this sort of activity occurs, you are likely to attract a clientele you may not want. Customers and bystanders can also get hurt in a fight. Refusing to serve intoxicated customers is one way to ensure that things do not get out of hand. Having at least some staff members large enough to intervene in case of an argument is another. If a fight breaks out, it should be stopped as quickly as possible. If weapons are involved, staff should be trained to take care that they are not hurt. Police should be called in such an incident, and other patrons of the bar should be moved to a safer place until help arrives.

- **Accidents.** Whether it is someone falling on an icy step, cutting themselves on glass, or an employee hurting herself on the industrial blender, accidents cause distress to everyone. You can help avoid accidents — and the legal and physical pain they cause — by keeping on top of spills and potential danger areas. All steps should be clearly indicated to prevent tripping. Staff should be properly trained to deal with bar equipment and with customers who may need help.

- **Zoning laws and licensing.** Some of the laws surrounding alcohol are straightforward, but there are many laws concerning who can sell alcohol where and at what time and how many miles alcohol has to be from the nearest school. Not knowing about a law is no excuse, so before you open your bar, review your local food and liquor laws. There are legal consultants who can help you sort out the laws. While such an expense may seem large when there are so many other things to pay for, paying a lawyer ahead of time to understand your local laws can help prevent legal hassles down the road.

- **Illness in the bar.** If someone becomes ill in your bar, you need to take swift action. An ill patron is your responsibility and you should train your staff to get help immediately.

- **Drugs.** Alcohol does not necessarily breed drugs, but drug peddlers do often try to sell their wares in bars, cafés, and dance clubs. Being on the front page as the location of a drug crack-down is certainly not the type of press you want for your establishment. Your staff should keep an eye out for suspicious activity and report it at once. Any person who has been selling drugs in or near your bar should be reported and refused future admission to your bar.

REDUCING THE CHANCES OF LEGAL TROUBLE

The longer you own a bar, the greater the chance that you will run into legal trouble of some sort. We live in a litigious society. There are a few ways to make your bar a safer place:

- **A great staff is your best defense against trouble.** An observant and experienced staff can often notice crooks and other trouble before it happens. Hire well and you will save yourself plenty of problems.

- **Good training.** Be sure to train your staff to observe customers and to help them when necessary. Your entire staff should know what to do in an emergency. Your bar has a fire-escape plan. Determine exactly what staff should do in case of a problem and review the procedures with them regularly.

- **Do not be afraid to refuse service — and do not be bullied into serving someone you should not.** It is illegal to refuse service without good reason. A drunken customer may try to talk their way into another drink and then threaten to sue if refused service.

- **Reduce temptation.** You can reduce temptation for robbers and other would-be thieves by eliminating large amounts of money in tip jars and by keeping as little money as possible on the premises. Some bars reduce temptation even more by proudly advertising that they offer free meals to police officers with police ID. Few criminals will be tempted to rob a bar where a police officer may be dining.

Make customers aware that you have the right to refuse service. To order, call 800-814-1132 or online at www.atlantic-pub.com (Item # RTR-PS, $9.95).

- **Hire security staff.** Security staff can add a touch of class to your bar and can also ensure that there is always a pair of eyes devoted to keeping your bar safe. Plus, if trouble does break out, security personnel are specially trained to handle the situation.

- **Keep things visible.** Bright lights outside the bar and easy access to full lights in the bar can help ensure full visibility the minute something happens. Being able to see can help stop a crime.

- **Keep things clear.** Reduce clutter and obstacles that can help criminals get away. The fewer shadowy places there are to hide, the less activity will be going on that you are not aware of.

- **Consider security systems — but do not rely on them.** Items such as buzzers, security cameras, and other devices may help after a crime, but these expensive systems are rarely as effective as a sharp-eyed security staff that can stop an incident before it occurs. Criminals aware of your security system will generally find ways to thwart it.

- **Lock up well and know who can get in.** Each night, be sure that the bar is locked up. Change locks after employees are fired or quit and control who has keys.

- **Know your customers.** Knowing who patronizes your bar, what their habits are, and what type of people they are may help you spot things out of the ordinary. If your clientele changes suddenly, you will be alert that something suspicious is going on.

No matter how careful you are, legal problems can occur. Get the very best insurance you can. Legal problems and crime can cost a fortune. If you have borrowed money to establish or expand a bar, you simply may not have the money for legal or rebuilding costs, so one problem could put you out of business for good. Bars should have excellent liability insurance, which protects in case someone sues the bar for injury or harm that befell them as a result of the bar. You will also want to invest in the best injury, fire, theft, employee, and property insurance you can so that any theft or accident will not cost you your establishment. Talk to a qualified insurance agent in your area, who can let you know what insurance types are available for bars in your area. Also, talk to other bar owners to get a sense of the types of insurance they have drawn on over the years. Whatever you do, though, do not scrimp on liability insurance, which is often what will protect your business financially in case of a lawsuit.

For more information about bar service, I would recommend the following books from Atlantic Publishing (**www.atlantic-pub.com**):

- *The Professional Bar & Beverage Manager's Handbook: How to Open and Operate a Financially Successful Bar, Tavern, and Nightclub—With Companion CD-ROM* (Item # PBB-01)

- *The Professional Bartender's Handbook: A Recipe for Every Drink Known — Including Tricks and Games to Impress Your Guests* (Item # PBH-01)

- *The Responsible Serving of Alcoholic Beverages: A Complete Staff Training Course for Bars, Restaurants, and Caterers—With Companion CD-ROM* (Item # RSA-01)

- *The Food Service Professional Guide To Controlling Liquor, Wine & Beverage Costs* (Item # FS8-01)

- *The Food Service Professional Guide To Bar & Beverage Operation: Ensuring Success & Maximum Profit* (Item # FS11-01)

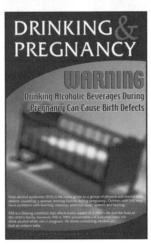

ALCOHOL AWARENESS POSTER SERIES

Pictured above are all of the alcohol awareness posters from Atlantic Publishing. This striking poster series covers ten fundamental topics and should be posted in any establishment that serves alcohol. Posters are laminated to reduce wear and tear and measure 11" x 17". Series of 10 Posters Item # AAP-PS for $89.95. You can also order each poster individually for $9.95 each: Right to Refuse Service Item # RTR-PS, One Drink Equals Item # ODE-PS, Spotting a Fake ID Item # FID-PS, Symptoms of Intoxication Item # SIO-PS, We Check IDs Item # CID-PS, Drinking & Pregnancy Item # D&P-PS, Blood Alcohol Content Chart—Female, Item # BACF-PS, Blood Alcohol Content Chart—Male Item # BACM-PS, Don't Drink & Drive Item # DDD-PS, Alcohol Slows Reaction Times Item # ASR-PS.

SERVICE REFUSAL FORM

If, at any time, you feel a patron is intoxicated and should not be served any more alcohol, notify your supervisor immediately. Then fill out the form below to the best of your ability.

Date: _____

Name of Employee Refusing Service: _____
_____

Please write a short description of why you felt the individual should not have been served alcohol or when the decision was made to discontinue further service. ____
_____
_____
_____
_____
_____

Did the patron exhibit signs of intoxication, such as the following? Check all that apply.

- ❑ Slurred speech
- ❑ Difficulty lighting a cigarette
- ❑ Arguing with or annoying other guests
- ❑ Tearfulness
- ❑ Drowsiness
- ❑ Difficulty focusing eyes
- ❑ Memory loss
- ❑ Spilling drinks
- ❑ Falling or stumbling
- ❑ Difficulty picking up change

Please provide specific information about the customer.

Customer's Name (if known): _____

Sex: ○ M ○ F Height: _____ Weight: _____

Hair: _____ Eyes: _____ Age: _____

Approximately how long was the customer on the premises? _____

Please list, if known, the time the customer entered, left and was denied service:

Arrival _____ a.m./p.m
Departure _____ a.m./p.m.
Time Service Denied _____ a.m./p.m.

How many drinks did the customer have on the premises?
○ 1-2 ○ 3-4 ○ 5-6 ○ 7-10 ○ _____

What was the customer drinking? _____
_____

How much money did the patron spend? _____
_____

What was the customer's reaction to being refused service? _____
_____
_____
_____
_____
_____
_____

Was a cab called for the customer? ○ Yes ○ No

Was an alternate method of transportation offered?
○ Yes (please list) _____ ○ No

Were the police called? ○ Yes ○ No

Did anyone witness the refusal of service? ○ Yes ○ No If so, please list their names.

_____
_____
_____
_____
_____
_____

_____ _____ _____
Signature of Employee **Print Name** **Position**

_____ _____
Signature of Manager on Duty **Print Name**

CHAPTER

BAR SERVICE, PRECAUTIONS, AND LEGALITIES

S erving beverages is the key function of bars. Any potential customer can walk into a liquor store, purchase his own beverage, and prepare it at home. Many people go to bars not only to spend time with friends, but also to experience the service that bars offer. You must be able to provide good service in order to get repeat customers.

When it comes to prepared beverages at bars, customers expect a few things:

- **Good service.** Customers not only want someone else to prepare a drink for them, but they want that drink prepared and served in a way that is friendly and kind.

- **Presentation.** Customers expect a drink that is presented nicely.

- **Atmosphere.** Bar patrons want to enjoy the ambience of a place outside their home. Lighting, colors, décor, and other customers all work together to create a pleasant atmosphere.

- **New experiences.** Customers rely on the expertise of bars, bartenders, and servers to offer drinks that are new to them.

The bar manager who can consistently deliver on these four aspects can usually create a loyal following and manage a successful bar that other patrons want to visit.

AR PERSONNEL

THE BARTENDER — JOB DESCRIPTION

A proficient bartender must be thoroughly familiar with all alcoholic beverages. He or she must prepare drinks in a polished, efficient, and relaxed manner. Aside from these traits he or she must at times borrow some of the qualities found in psychologists, policemen, and members of the clergy. Bartenders must know when to converse and when to be quiet and listen. No other position in the restaurant has more control over the final product than the bartender. They prepare the drinks from raw materials, make the final product, and often serve it themselves. No single employee carries so much financial responsibility as does the bartender.

RESPONSIBILITIES

1. Adhere to the basic procedures of personal hygiene.

2. Always greet customers with a smile and, if possible, by name. Recognizing new customers is critical; if you are busy, acknowledge them and indicate that you will be with them in a moment. Always place a cocktail napkin in front of a customer to show that she has been waited on.

3. When applicable, suggest the house specialty drinks and appetizers or offer the menu for perusing.

4. Be attentive to your customers. Clean ashtrays, light cigarettes, and keep the bar and stools neat and clean. Watch for empty glasses; politely ask customers if they would like another. Always ask before removing empty glasses.

5. Know how to operate the cash register correctly. You are responsible for accounting for every drink poured. Record all incorrect, manager, and complimentary cocktails accurately.

6. Make sure the cocktail waitresses'/waiters' tickets are accurate and complete. Do not fill any order until the prices are entered and totaled correctly.

7. Know all the bar prices.

8. Check questionable customer IDs to ensure they are of legal drinking age.

9. Communicate with coworkers throughout your shift.

10. Follow all the health and safety regulations prescribed.

11. Follow all the restaurant regulations prescribed.

12. Control and limit waste.

13. Communicate problems and ideas to management.

14. Attend all meetings.

15. Fill out all forms as prescribed.

16. Maintain all equipment and tools.

17. Follow all rotation procedures to ensure freshness of all products.

18. Follow management's instructions and suggestions.

COCKTAIL WAITRESSES/WAITERS — JOB DESCRIPTION

The primary function of the cocktail wait staff is to serve cocktails to the customers in the lounge and dining rooms. They also contribute other valuable services to the restaurant. Cocktail wait staff are usually the first service employees the customer meets, thus their approach, attitude, and appearance will set a tone in the customer's mind that will last throughout the evening. It is essential they be proficient, congenial, and able to put customers in a relaxed mood prior to going into the dining room. These points are all equal in importance to the quality of the cocktail served.

RESPONSIBILITIES

1. Maintain a neat, clean, and attractive appearance.

2. Ensure that all customers are relaxed and receptive prior to their meals.

3. Ensure that all customers are served quickly. Always greet customers with a smile and, if possible, by name. Always acknowledge new customers; if you are busy, indicate that you will be with them in a few moments. Place a cocktail napkin in front of each customer; it will indicate that the customer has been waited on.

4. When applicable, suggest the house specialty drinks and appetizers or offer the menu for perusing.

5. Know all bar prices.

6. Write tickets neatly and accurately. Fill in all prices and totals before issuing to the bartender. Make a notation to the bartender when wine is served.

7. Be attentive to your customers. Clean ashtrays and keep the tables and chairs neat and clean. Watch for empty glasses and politely suggest another drink. Always ask before removing empty glasses.

8. Ensure that all bar tabs are forwarded to the correct dinner check.

9. Always add the cost of cocktails served in the dining room onto the dinner check. It will undoubtedly be an annoyance to the customer to stop eating in order to pay for drinks.

10. Always count out change by repeating the total ticket amount, then "count up:" beginning with coins, name each denomination until you reach the amount received.

11. Assist the bartender in any way possible.

12. Check questionable customer IDs to ensure that they are of legal drinking age.

13. Communicate to coworkers throughout your shift.

14. Follow all health and safety regulations prescribed.

15. Follow all restaurant regulations prescribed.

16. Control and limit waste.

17. Communicate problems and ideas to management.

18. Attend all meetings.

19. Fill out all forms as prescribed.

20. Maintain all equipment and tools.

21. Follow all rotation procedures to ensure freshness of products.

22. Follow management's instructions and suggestions.

BAR OPERATIONS

State-operated liquor stores purchase their inventories in large quantities from distributors. Because they purchase vast amounts and eliminate most middlemen, their prices are often substantially less than that of privately owned stores. There are two distinct disadvantages for the wholesale user under this system.

The service provided cannot compare to that of a store in the private sector. Delivery arrangements and credit terms are difficult, if not impossible, to work out. No matter how efficiently its store is operated and how friendly the people working there, the state will not have the same interest in serving customers as would a private owner.

Price discounts are usually given on purchasing full cases, but there is often no discount allowed when purchasing several or more cases. Thus, you pay the same price for one case as you would for a hundred of the same.

In many of the states with private operations, liquor distributors may not have the right to sell some brands of liquor. This arrangement between the producer and the distributor is similar to a franchising agreement. You may have to purchase from many of the local distributors in order to stock all of the brands of liquor you wish to serve. It can be advantageous, as there will be a high level of competition among distributors for the common liquors each carry. If you spread your business out among several distributors, your individual account may not be very important to each supplier. Since you are not a prime customer you will probably not get the best terms, prices, or service from any one supplier.

Liquor salespeople are interested in obtaining a bar's well items for their accounts. Well liquor is poured at least five times as often as call items. Since the price you pay for liquor will depend directly upon the amount you use and purchase, it will be a very important consideration. Allow plenty of time for your selection of both the well brands and the distributor from whom you choose to purchase them.

In almost all states, beer is distributed by local suppliers, each of whom has a franchising agreement to sell a particular brewer's product. In most cases the distributor is only allowed to sell one manufacturer's products at a time. Each manufacturer usually produces several brands of beer under different labels.

Since each distributor sells only a few types of beer, you will probably need to use all of the suppliers in your area to stock all the different types you want. Since all distributors have different products, there is little or no competition among them regarding pricing. There is a high level of competition among distributors to get their manufacturer's products into your restaurant. So they are willing to install the restaurant's draft system for free in exchange for your exclusive use of their products.

The distributor you select to purchase the draft beer from will be your biggest supplier. Draft beer will outsell bottles and cans three to one. This large volume of keg beer will enable you to get considerable discounts on your supplier's other products.

A large part of your liquor order will be for nonalcoholic juices, garnishes, and mixers. Most liquor distributors and food-service suppliers can provide you with everything you will need; consider carefully from which supplier you will purchase these additional items. Juices and mixers must be of the best quality you can afford. It makes little sense to pour quality liquor into a cocktail made with a low-quality juice or mix. Juices must be 100 percent real — no substitutes added. Mixers can be of any brand that has the quality level you are striving for. It is often advantageous to use brand-name items even if they cost a little more. Customers who sit at the bar should see that you are using high-quality recognized liquors, juices, and mixers.

There will be a high level of competition among the various suppliers for this part of your business, due in part to the high profit margin of these products. When comparing prices, remember to look at the whole picture. Consider how much this extra business will mean to each supplier. Due to the increase in volume, how will it affect the prices of the other items you purchase from the supplier? Are the services and delivery arrangements to your satisfaction? What are the credit terms? What is the finance charge? How much is the overall purchase actually costing?

ESCRIPTION OF LIQUOR & ALCOHOLIC BEVERAGES

All liquor served in the restaurant can be divided into two basic categories: well items and call items. Some restaurants establish a three-tier system: well, call, and premium liquor. Premium liquor will have an additional surcharge.

Well items are the house liquors the restaurant serves. They are called well items because they are in a well speed rack in front of the bartender. Well liquors are used when a customer orders a particular drink without specifying a brand: a scotch and soda or a bourbon and water. For each major type of liquor, such as bourbon, gin, vodka, scotch, tequila, rum, brandy, and rye, you will need to select a well or house brand. The well liquor you select must be a popular and recognized brand which is moderately priced.

Call items are the more expensive, higher-quality types of liquor. These a customer orders by the particular brand name: a Cutty Sark scotch and soda or a Jack Daniel's bourbon and water. Call items are sometimes called back bar items because they are usually stored on the shelves behind the bar.

WHISKEY

All whiskeys are distilled from fermented grains. Commonly used grains are barley, rye, corn, and wheat. All whiskeys are aged in oak barrels. From this aging process they obtain their characteristic color, flavor, and aroma.

Most whiskey consumed in this country is produced in either the United States, Canada, Scotland, or Ireland. Each country produces its own distinctive whiskeys. Whiskey can be divided into two basic types: straight whiskey and blended whiskey.

Straight whiskey has never been mixed with other types of whiskey or with any neutral grain spirits. Straight whiskey itself has four major types, discussed below.

Blended whiskey is a blend of straight whiskeys and/or neutral grain spirits. It must contain at least 20 percent, by volume, of a straight whiskey and be bottled at no less than 80 proof.

STRAIGHT WHISKEY

Bourbon whiskey — Its name is derived from Bourbon County in Kentucky where the whiskey was originally produced. Bourbon must be distilled from grain mash containing at least 51 percent corn. (Suggested: one well bourbon and three to six call items.)

Rye whiskey — Rye has the similar amber color of bourbon, but the flavor and aroma are different. Rye whiskey must be distilled from a fermented mash of grain containing at least 51 percent rye. (Suggested: one well rye and one to two call items.)

Corn whiskey — Corn whiskey must be distilled from fermented mash of grain containing at least 80 percent corn. (Suggested: one call item only.)

Bottled-in-bond whiskey — Usually a rye or bourbon whiskey that is produced under the supervision of the United States Government. The government ensures the following:

- That the whiskey is aged at least four years.

- That it is bottled at 100 proof.

- That it is produced in one distilling by a single distiller.

- That it is bottled and stored under government supervision.

Since the government bonds these steps, the whiskey is referred to as "bottled in bond." The government does not guarantee the quality of the whiskey; it only ensures that these steps have been completed under its supervision. (Suggested: one to two call items.)

BLENDED WHISKEYS

Canadian whiskey — Canadian whiskey is a blend produced under the supervision of the Canadian Government. This whiskey is usually lighter bodied than most American whiskeys. (Suggested: one well and three to six call items.)

Scotch whiskey — Scotch whiskey is produced only in Scotland. All Scotch blends contain malt and grain whiskeys. The unique smoky flavor of Scotch is derived from drying malted barley over open peat fires. In recent years the popularity of single malt scotch and other whiskeys has grown phenomenally. Many bars have a vast selection of hard-to-find single malts and they are very expensive and profitable. Single malt whisky is the product from a single distillery and has not been blended with any other whiskies. Only water is added before it is bottled and, in the case of "cask strength" bottlings, not even that. There are bottlings with an alcohol-percentage of over 60 available. (Suggested: one well scotch and four to eight call items.)

Irish whiskey — Irish whiskey is produced only in Ireland. This whiskey is usually heavier and fuller bodied than most Scotch blends. The malted barley used in the distilling process is dried over coal-fired kilns. This drying process has little or no affect on the whiskey's taste. (Suggested: two to three call items.)

OTHER LIQUOR

VODKA

Vodka was originally produced in Russia from distilled potatoes. Now, produced in various countries, vodka is commonly made from a variety of grains, the most common of which are wheat and corn. It is bottled at no less than 80 and no higher than 110 proof. During the distillation process it is highly refined and filtered, usually through activated charcoal. Vodka is not aged. It is colorless, odorless, and virtually tasteless. Because of these traits, it is a very versatile liquor that can be mixed with almost anything. In addition, it can be served straight, chilled to taste. (Suggested: one well brand at 80 proof and one at 110 proof and two to three call items, one or two of which should be imported.)

GIN

Gin is distilled from a variety of grains and is bottled at 80 proof. Every gin manufactured has its own distinctive flavor and aroma. The aroma is derived from a recipe of juniper berries and other assorted plants. Gin is usually colorless and is most often used in making the popular martini cocktail. Vacuum-distilled gin is distilled in a glass-lined vacuum at lower than normal distilling temperature. This process tends to eliminate the bitterness found in some gins. (Suggested: one well and three to four call items, one or two of which should be imported.)

RUM

Rum is distilled from cane syrup, which is the fermented juice of sugarcane and molasses. It is bottled at no less than 80 proof. Most rums are a blend of many different types of aged rums. Dark rums often have caramel syrup added for color. Rums can be classified into two major types:

Light-bodied — Light-bodied rums are dry and light in color due to a lack of molasses. Among the light-bodied rums are two varieties, gold label and white label. The gold is often of slightly better quality and is darker and sweeter; the white is paler and slightly stronger in flavor. (Suggested: one well 80 proof and one to two call items.)

Heavy-bodied — Heavy-bodied rums have been distilled by a different and slower process. Because of this process, the rum contains more molasses, which makes the rum darker, sweeter, and richer. (Suggested: one well 80 proof, two to three call items and one to two high-proof items.)

BRANDY

Brandy is traditionally distilled from a mash of fermented grapes but may be produced from other fruits. There are many different types available.

Cognac — Cognac is perhaps the finest of distilled brandies. It is produced only in the Cognac region of France. Usually it is a blend of many different types of distilled Cognac of the region. Cognac may be aged for as long as 50 years.

Armagnac — This brandy is similar to Cognac but slightly drier in taste. It is produced only in the Armagnac region of France.

Apple Jack — This brandy is distilled from the cider of crushed apples. Calvados is produced only in Normandy, France. In the United States, Apple Jack is often bottled in bond.

Fruit-flavored brandies — These brandies have a distilled brandy base with a flavor ingredient added. These are commonly used in blended cocktails. A good selection of the more popular types will be needed.

TEQUILA

Tequila is usually produced in Mexico or the American Southwest. It is distilled from the fermented mash of the aqua or century plants, which are cacti. Tequila is usually clear, although some types may have a gold tint. The smell and taste are distinctive. Tequila is used primarily in making margarita cocktails. In recent years there has been a wide increase in the variety of "premium" tequilas. Tequila can also be chilled and served straight as a "shooter" with a beer chaser. (Suggested: one well and two to three imported call items.)

CORDIALS AND LIQUEURS

Cordials and liqueurs are created by the mixing or pre-distilling of neutral grain spirits with fruits, flowers, or plants to which sweeteners have been added. Cordials and liqueurs are all colorful and very sweet in taste, which is why they are usually served as after-dinner drinks. There are a wide variety of cordials and liqueurs available. A good selection of cordials and liqueurs would include 15 to 25 of these. There are approximately 10 to 12 different types that you must stock because of their popularity or because they are used in making certain cocktails. A list of the popular liqueurs for your area will be available from your local liquor distributor. (All cordials and liqueurs should be call items.)

VERMOUTH

Vermouth is not classified as liqueur or liquor at all, but is actually a wine flavored with roots, berries, or various types of plants. Vermouth is used almost exclusively in making martinis and Manhattans. There are two basic types:

Dry — Dry vermouth is usually produced in America or France. This variety has a clear to light goldish color. It is used primarily in martini cocktails. One good well item is all that is required.

Sweet — Sweet vermouth is a darker reddish wine with a richer, sweeter flavor. It is most often produced in Italy. Sweet vermouth is primarily used in making Manhattan cocktails. One good well item is all you will need.

BEER

Whether packaged in bottles or kegs, beer should be treated as a food product. It is a perishable commodity with a limited life span. To ensure the freshness and full flavor of bottled beer, it is essential to adhere to a few simple procedures. The two biggest enemies of beer are exposure to light and temperature extremes. The best way to combat them is to store beer in a dark, relatively cool place. There are five basic categories for the hundreds of brands of beer produced. They are: lagers, the most popular type produced today; ales, which contain more hops and are stronger in flavor; and porter, stout, and bock beers, which are all heavier, darker, richer, and sweeter than the first two.

Beer is available in bottles, cans, or on a draft keg system. Of the hundreds of brands available, fewer than a dozen are primarily demanded by customers. However, it should be noted that the popularity of "microbrewed" beers has come on very strong. There are many independent restaurants and at least two national chains that use a microbrewery in their own establishment as a marketing vehicle. It is suggested that your most popular beer be on draft—most customers prefer it that way and it is cheaper for you. Beer is a perishable item, so you will want to buy the other, less popular brands you will carry in bottles or cans to preserve their freshness. Most draft systems can handle three separate kegs; if your business warrants it, use all of them. If your restaurant serves ethnic or international food it is a nice touch to include some beer selections produced in that region or country.

Imported beers have gained popularity in recent years. Although they are 50 to 100 percent more expensive than domestic beers, customers still demand the more popular ones. There are three or four of these imported beers that you should always stock.

Light beer is produced with fewer calories than other beer and has developed a great demand within the past five years. One to two light beers should be included on your list.

LIQUOR STOCKING AND ORDERING

Once you establish which liquor, beer, mixer, and garnishes you will be using, transfer them onto the order sheets. List them alphabetically and by category on the order sheet. An example of a Liquor Order Form may be found at the end of this chapter. The liquor order form is filled out and used exactly the same way as the Food Ordering Form.

The storing, receiving, and rotating procedures described in the chapter for food items also pertains to liquor and all other items delivered to the restaurant. The manager and the person who placed the order should always be present when the delivery is received. Immediately after the order is checked for accuracy, it must be locked and secured in its separate room. The manager must be the only individual who has the key to the liquor storage room. Liquor may be stored at room temperature as long as the temperature remains relatively constant.

LIQUOR INVENTORY FORM — BEGINNING INVENTORY

The Liquor Inventory Form is used to count each item in the restaurant at the end of each month. You will find a sample at the end of this chapter. Based on this figure and others to be described in the upcoming chapters, you will be able to project operating costs for each area: food, liquor, wine, and operational supplies.

As with food items, transfer the contents of the completed order sheet to the inventory form. In the "Size" column list the size bottle each item comes in. The size listed on the inventory sheet must correspond to the size in inventory (Scotch 750 ml, Vodka 5th). An example of the Liquor Inventory Form may be found at the end of this chapter. The steps for calculating the beginning inventory for liquor are identical to those used for food. Again, the beginning inventory is the total dollar amount of a category's (liquor) supplies that are on hand opening day. This amount represents the starting point from which you may later determine what you have used and, therefore, the costs for the past month in that category.

To compute the beginning inventory for liquor, simply total all the liquor purchases prior to opening day. If you are opening an existing restaurant and will be using some of the old stock, add the dollar value of the old stock to that which you have purchased. To compute the value of the old stock you must first, of course, take an inventory of it to record the amount on hand.

POURING PROCEDURES

Liquor must be portioned in order to control costs and maintain consistency in the final product. Liquor is portioned not by weight but by volume. Volume is measured in shots or jiggers, which are liquid measurements ranging from ¾ to 2 ounces. Most restaurants pour between 1¼ and 1½ ounces per cocktail and slightly less — 1⅛ to 1¼ ounces — for blended drinks.

The first step in developing consistent pouring procedures is to determine the amount of liquor each drink will contain. It is suggested that you use the amount stated above for each shot. More than 1½ ounces of liquor in a cocktail will make it too strong and be dominated by the liquor's flavor, which many people do not care for. A cocktail containing less than 1⅛ ounces of liquor will be too weak and may give customers the impression that you are trying to cut corners.

There are two basic ways to portion-control liquor: a computerized bar gun and a free-pouring bartender. Both systems have advantages and disadvantages.

A computerized bar gun is by far the best way to control and account for every shot of liquor poured. Although there are many different types and models available, all basically operate the same. Each well item is hooked up to a hose that runs to the bar. The well items are hidden either underneath the bar or behind the back wall in an adjacent room. The hose at the bar is hooked into a gun which is similar to the one used for the soda canisters. Small buttons on the face of the gun indicate each of the well items.

When the bartender presses a button the exact measurement of liquor is dispensed. The number of shots and type of liquor poured is automatically recorded and written up with the correct price. A tape is simultaneously run showing the updated number and type of cocktails poured over the night. There are many variations on this system, but all can determine if there has been any loss of liquor or revenue. There are also liquor pour spouts available that are placed on the bottle and dispense only one shot at a time.

There are two distinct disadvantages to the computerized bar gun. The bar tends to lose its aesthetic value. Computerized bars may be applauded by accountants and restaurant owners, but they are generally frowned upon by the public. The restaurant and lounge should be a place where a person can go to get away from the hustle and bustle of the modern world. She should be able to get a cocktail made by a professional and enjoy it with her companions in a warm atmosphere and comfortable environment. The last thing most customers wish to see is some unknown liquor dribble out of a hose into a glass while a set of digital lights flash across the register. The art and showmanship of mixology is an important part of the atmosphere of a restaurant. A computerized bar may eliminate this integral part of the dining experience.

The second disadvantage is the substantial investment needed to purchase a system. Although it may pay for itself over a period of time, it is still an expensive start-up cost. Perhaps this reason is why bar guns are not universally used throughout the food-service industry.

These two disadvantages of the computerized bar are the primary advantages of the free pour system. The cost of operation is negligible: a few shot glasses and a pouring spout for each bottle is all that is required. The aesthetic value gained is immeasurable. It is impossible to put a value on atmosphere and taste. A good compromise is the use of the pour spouts that dispense an exact portion.

The main disadvantage to the free pour system is the lack of control and accountability for each shot poured. However, if bartenders are properly trained and supervised in the procedures described, there will be little problem in controlling the cost and the consistency of the product. Bartenders may become lax in using all the procedures. If a consistent, profitable operation is to be maintained, management must follow up, note, and review all procedures with each and every employee.

FREE-POURING PROCEDURES

There are two basic methods for free-pouring liquor. The first method is used primarily by beginners and inexperienced free-pour bartenders. This technique uses a fluted shot glass with a line drawn across the top of the glass at the level of the shot desired. The bartender simply places the shot glass on the bar or spill mat and pours until the liquid reaches the line. Then he pours the contents of the shot glass into the cocktail glass over the ice. This method is very accurate, but it is much slower and far less aesthetically pleasing than the second.

The second technique requires several weeks of full-time practice to master. Use an empty liquor bottle filled with water to practice pouring. This method gives the customer the impression that you have filled the shot glass once and then, after you have emptied the shot, continued to pour more liquor into the cocktail. In fact, what you did was measure out approximately ¾ ounce into the shot glass, emptied it into the cocktail, then made up the difference by pouring directly from the bottle into the drink, measuring by silently counting off, until you have reached the full shot.

To pour:

1. Grasp the bottle around the neck with your right hand (reverse if left-handed). Place your index finger around the pour spout.

2. Hold the ¾ ounce shot glass in your left hand above the cocktail glass and place the pour spout into the shot glass. Begin to pour. As you are pouring, angle the shot glass downward. When it nears capacity, spill the contents into the cocktail glass. Continue to point the pour spout into the glass while pouring. At this point you will have poured slightly less than ¾ of an ounce.

3. The difference will now be made up by pouring directly into the cocktail glass from the bottle. To measure the exact amount to pour directly into the cocktail glass, count to yourself while pouring. To determine the correct count for the remaining ½ to ¾ ounce, experiment by counting while pouring into a lined shot glass.

Bartenders should be tested periodically to ensure they are pouring the required number of shots from each bottle. This number directly determines the price of each drink. To compute the number of shots you should get from each bottle, divide the bottle volume in ounces by the size of the average shot poured. Bottle spouts are available in a variety of speeds: fast, medium, and slow; there is also a wide-mouthed juice spout. The speed at which the liquor flows is determined by the size of the air hole in the spout stopper. Partially covering this hole while pouring will regulate the flow. Fast-pour spouts should be used on liquors that are thick and syrupy, such as cordials. Medium pourers should be used on most bottles. Slow spouts may be used on any liquor that is poured in a shot containing less than 1 □ ounces. Some expensive brandies and cordials are often poured at only one ounce. A slow pourer will give the effect of a long pour.

Some hints on bar organization:

- Set up glasses and ice first.

- Make blended drinks next.

- Once you pick up the shot glass, do not put it down until everything is poured

- Once you pick up a bottle, pour into all the glasses needed.

- Allow at least ¼ inch of space at the top of each cocktail to allow for garnishes, straws, etc.

POURING DRAFT BEER

Draft beer should be poured so that it produces a head that rises just above the top of the glass or pitcher. The head will settle down to about ¾ inch in a few minutes. This head or foam has both great economical and aesthetic value.

The size of the head is controlled by the angle of the glass or mug to the spout when you begin to pour. Should the head be too small, you will be pouring more beer into each glass, leading to a lower than expected yield on each keg. Since the customer is swallowing the CO_2 gas that would normally escape from the head, the customer will probably drink less. A head that is too large may give the customer the impression that you are attempting to cut corners on quality.

It is important to serve beer in cold, spotless glasses or mugs. Glasses that appear clean may have a residual buildup of soap or grease. The slightest trace of these agents will break down the head and bubbles in the beer leaving a stale-looking product. Every glass used should be rinsed with cold fresh water before filling. Always use a new glass for each beer ordered.

The temperature at which beer is served is also crucial. To ensure that the proper flavor is released, all beer should be served at 40 degrees Fahrenheit. When beer is served below 38 degrees Fahrenheit, it loses its distinct taste and aroma. Beer served above 42 degrees Fahrenheit may turn cloudy and will lose its zest and flavor. Draft beer is not pasteurized, so it must always be held at a constant temperature. All beer coolers should be set at 38 degrees Fahrenheit to maintain the proper serving temperature.

Beer lines must be flushed out weekly, just as soda lines must. Beer is only as good as the lines it flows through. The service of a professional tap and line cleaner are needed weekly. Your beer distributor can recommend a reputable company.

TO POUR A PERFECT DRAFT

Pouring a perfect beer with every pull of the tap handle takes some skill, but can be easily mastered with practice. The following procedures offer some tips for maximizing draft beer service.

- **Start with a "beer clean" glass.**

- **The size of the head is determined by the angle at which the glass is held under the spout at the start of the draw** (never let the glass come in direct contact with the spout itself). If the glass is held at a sharp angle so that the beer flows down the side of the glass, there will be little or no head. Conversely, if the glass is held straight so that the beer splashes directly into the bottom of the glass, there will be a large head.

- **For flat-bottomed glassware (such as an hourglass): Open the tap all the way by grasping the handle at its base and pulling it quickly** (grasping at the top of the tap handle will result in too slow an open and the beer will come out overly foamy). Tilt the glass at about a 45 degree angle at the beginning of the pour and then straighten it up so that the beer splashes directly into the glass. The resulting head should be about ½ to 1 inch thick.

- **For wide-bottomed glassware (such as a schooner or goblet): Do not tilt the glass at all.** Open the tap as indicated above and allow the beer to pour directly into the bottom of the glass. The result should be a ½ to 1 inch head.

- **Note that unchilled glassware will have a warming effect on beer.** A thin, room-temperature glass will increase the temperature of the beer about 2 degrees Fahrenheit. An unchilled mug will raise the temperature of the beer about 4 to 6 degrees Fahrenheit.

BEER TROUBLESHOOTING	
Problem	**Reason**
Loose Foam (settles quickly)	• Beer line system/coils not as cold as beer in barrel • Pressure required does not correspond to beer temperature (unbalanced system) • Beer dispensed through small diameter tubing into large shanks and faucets
Flat Beer	• Glasses are not "beer clean" • Not enough CO_2 pressure • Pressure shut off at closing • Cooler or dispensing system too cold • Leak in pressure tubing or barrels • Loose tap or pressure connections • Defective pressure-check valve in tap • Sluggish pressure regulator • Obstruction in line near barrel • Compressor too small or inefficient • Oily air from compressor or kitchen • Long exposure to air instead of CO_2 gas pressure
Sour Beer	If the problem is sour beer, the difficulty is due to the temperature of the keg itself, either in the bar, at the distributor's warehouse, or en route. The beer should always be maintained at between 36 and 38 degrees Fahrenheit under normal operation. It should never be allowed to warm to 50 degrees Fahrenheit or more for any length of time, since it may begin a secondary fermentation.

BEER TROUBLESHOOTING

Problem	Reason
Unpalatable Beer	• Dirty faucets • Dirty beer system • Failure to leave water in beer • Failure to flush beer lines with water lines overnight after each empty barrel • Unsanitary conditions at bar • Coils not cleaned properly • Foul air or dirt in lines or air tank • Oily air from kitchen • Improper location or maintenance • Failure to purge condensation from and lubrication of air pump compressor storage tank • Temperature of beer in barrel too warm • Dry glasses • Failure to provide fresh air inlet for air pump

HOW MUCH BEER IN A KEG?

A barrel of beer contains 31 gallons, or the equivalent of 13.8 cases of 12-ounce bottles (24 bottles to a case). Each case contains approximately 2.25 gallons of beer. Typically, the kegs used at most on-premise establishments are actually half-barrels. Assuming a one-inch head, there are approximately 200 12-ounce servings per keg or about 150 16-ounce servings, varying slightly with the type of glass used.

BAR RECIPE AND PROCEDURE MANUAL

The purpose of the Bar Recipe and Procedure Manual is to ensure that the recipes and methods of preparing all cocktails are consistent among your bartenders. Drinks can be prepared in many different ways. Therefore, it is imperative that all recipes and procedures are standardized to ensure that both the final product and cost is consistent.

Of the hundreds of varieties of cocktails, less than 25 are ordered 90 percent of the time. To obtain consistency among them, a recipe and procedure manual should be developed. This manual should contain the following information: cocktail ingredients and amounts, which cocktail glass should be used, garnishes, pertinent serving instructions, and preparation procedures. An example of a Bar Recipe and Procedure Manual may be found at the end of this chapter.

There are several excellent bartender guides available that list all the various cocktails and how to prepare them. One of these books should be kept at the bar. Occasionally a customer will order a drink that you will not know, nor will it be listed in the book.

Usually the customer is pronouncing it wrong or it is some variation of another cocktail. Politely inform the customer that you are not familiar with the cocktail; many times she can tell you how to prepare it.

Twenty-five of the most commonly ordered cocktails:

- Screwdriver
- Piña Colada
- Gimlet
- Cosmopolitan
- Bloody Mary
- Collins drinks
- Sours
- Black Russian
- Long Island iced tea

- Sombrero
- Old Fashioned
- Margarita
- Manhattan
- Stingers
- Fizzes
- White Russian
- Gin and tonic

- Mai-Tai
- Tequila Sunrise
- Martini
- Gibson
- Coffee
- Daiquiris
- Black Russian
- Juice/punch drinks

The majority of drinks require no mixing, stirring, or blending. These cocktails are often made from a well or call item poured "on the rocks" or added to juice or a mixer.

SOME ENHANCING TOUCHES OF QUALITY

Sometimes the only element that separates successful restaurants from failures is the small professional touches of excellence. These extra touches imply that a tremendous effort has been made all around to attain the highest level of quality possible. These subtle signs of concern are most important in the bar and lounge area, where the product is prepared and served in the open under the watchful and interested eyes of the customer. Professional bartenders and courteous cocktail waitresses can be found in any well-managed restaurant. However, it is the small, undemanded touches and extra procedures that separate good lounges from superb ones. Described in this section are some simple, inexpensive suggestions that will give your bar and lounge the extra touches — the finesse — that will separate it from the rest.

HEATED SNIFTERS

Snifter glasses should be warmed prior to pouring brandy and certain cordials. Brandy heated in a warm glass has a stronger aroma and flavor that is preferred by most people. To heat the brandy snifter, pour near-boiling water into the bottom third of the glass. Let it sit for two to three minutes. Before using, wipe the entire glass dry with a clean bar towel. Coffee drink glasses and mugs should also be preheated to maintain the coffee's temperature. You may also preheat glasses by filling them with tap water and microwaving them for 15 to 30 seconds.

CHILLED COCKTAIL STRAIGHT-UP GLASSES

Chilled cocktail straight-up glasses must be kept ice-cold, as the cocktails themselves contain no ice. These glasses are used almost exclusively for straight-up martinis, Manhattans, Gibsons, and margaritas. If there is no cooler space available to keep a supply chilled, bury them stem-up in crushed ice. Glasses must be shaken dry before using.

FROSTED BEER MUGS

Beer mugs and glasses should be frosted prior to use. Aside from adding aesthetic value to the beer, chilled glasses help maintain the proper drinking temperature. Stock a supply of the mugs in a cooler set at 31 to 33 degrees Fahrenheit. When the mugs are removed from the cooler, condensation will occur, leaving the frosted glass with a thin layer of ice. Mugs must be dry when placed in the cooler. Should they contain droplets from a recent washing, this excess water will freeze onto the mug. The warmth of the beer will melt the ice, diluting the beer, and depriving the customer of its delicate flavor.

FLAMING LIQUOR

Certain cocktails are set aflame prior to serving. Extreme care must be used by employees and customers when handling these cocktails. Preheat the glass and warm the entire cocktail before attempting to ignite it. Remove a teaspoon of the cocktail and set it aflame. Pour the flaming liquid carefully back into the cocktail. Fire regulations in your area may prohibit any open flames, such as those from candles, flaming food, and flaming liquor. Contact the local Fire Department to learn of its restrictions.

FRESH FRUIT DAIQUIRIS

Fresh fruit daiquiris are incomparable in quality to daiquiris that are made from fruit-flavored liqueurs. Unfortunately, most bars prepare the latter. Aside from being a misrepresentation, substituting fruit-flavored liqueurs for real fruit is unnecessary. Fresh fruit is available in most places year-round. The small additional cost and bother is out-weighed by the resulting quality of the cocktail.

Glassware is an important consideration when promoting specialty drinks. The proper glass for each cocktail is essential. The appearance and the presentation are almost as important as the drink's taste. As a final touch, use a piece of freshly cut fruit to garnish the rim.

Fresh fruit daiquiris and other specialty drinks should be promoted; these cocktails are very popular and profitable items. Be creative: Develop some house specialties and give them exotic names. Employees must become enthusiastic about a promotion in order for it to become a success. Encourage them through monetary incentives to sell. Let them try the different specialty drinks; if they enjoy them they will promote them with vigor. Point out that the larger the average check, the larger the tip the employee will receive.

FLOATING CORDIALS — POUSSE CAFE

The most attractive cordial served uses a variety of liqueurs which are floating in layers, one on top of the other in the same glass. This presentation amazes customers and will bring praise to the bartender and restaurant. Although it appears complicated to create, the floating cordial is actually rather simple. Liqueurs and cordials have different densities, enabling liqueurs with lower densities to float atop those with higher densities. The trick is to pour the liqueur carefully on top of the preceding one. It is best accomplished by pouring each liqueur over an inverted spoon. The rounded bottom of the spoon will diffuse the liquid over the one below and no mixing will occur. Be certain that all ingredients given in the recipe are poured in the exact order listed.

GARNISHES

Garnishes sell drinks. Garnishes are part of the entertainment of drinking. There is nothing worse than a customer seeing less-than-fresh garnishes, left-over from the night before, laying in a tray about to go into her drink. They look bad and cost operators money in waste. Calculate how much is needed and cut just enough.

Heads turn when customers glimpse a pair of sunglasses or plastic animals hanging off a cocktail. Try using dry ice; a triple garnish of orange, lime, and lemon slices; a cluster of grapes for the glass of wine; a choice of olives, such as almond- or garlic-stuffed; a lemon twist wrapped around a coffee bean; a skewer of oversized cherries; or a pickled okra sprout. Garnishes add finesse and style and can become your trademark. Be creative: Review some food-garnishing books and let your inventive chef have a crack at some ideas.

CREATING THE PEACOCK EFFECT WITH NAPKINS

Undoubtedly you have seen stacks of cocktail napkins displayed like the feathers of a peacock, all jutting out in a different circular direction, in fancy bars. Although it appears to be a painstakingly difficult and time-consuming task, in actuality it is easily and quickly created. The bartender can prepare an entire night's napkins in less than five minutes.

Place a two-inch-high stack of cocktail napkins on the bar. Place a small highball glass on its side in the middle of the stack. Press down on the glass and rotate it two to three inches to the left. Move the glass around to each side until the napkins are all feathered out evenly. It is a simple procedure which results in elegant-looking napkins.

RECIPES

BLOODY MARY MIX RECIPE

Manufactured premixed Bloody Mary mix can be purchased from most liquor distributors and most restaurants do so. However, preparing your own mix can be less expensive and you will make a substantially better Bloody Mary if you do.

A bartender or preparation cook can concoct a batch of Bloody Mary mix in 15 minutes that will last for several days. The quality of the final product will outweigh the additional amount of time and cost needed to prepare the batch. Once the recipe is formulated, type it up and give a copy to all the employees responsible for preparing it. Enter a copy into the recipe and procedure manual. It will encourage proper and consistent preparation of all batches.

Some ingredients that may be used:

- Tomato or V-8 juice
- Tabasco or hot sauce
- Garlic salt
- Lime or lemon juice
- Celery salt
- Vegetable juices
- Minced onions

- Salt and pepper
- Worcestershire sauce
- Horseradish
- A.1. Steak sauce
- Celery seed
- Minced hot peppers
- Assorted spices

Experiment with different ingredients and develop your own unique recipe. Inform the cocktail waitresses and waiters that the bar is preparing its own unique mix; they can help promote it. Garnish Bloody Marys with a rim of celery salt, a lime or lemon wedge, and a celery stalk.

Some restaurants that serve Sunday brunch have set up a small "Bloody Mary Bar" where patrons can add their own ingredients.

SWEET AND SOUR BAR MIX

Sweet and sour bar mix is used in all sour drinks and some blended cocktails. This mix may be purchased in a premixed form or prepared from scratch. The easiest way to develop a recipe is to start with one of the commercially prepared powders or liquids as a base and then add your own ingredients.

Some of the ingredients that may be used:

- Sugar
- Honey
- Lime juice
- Lemon juice
- Mint flavoring

- Foam additive
- Water
- Orange juice
- Bitters
- Egg whites (to hold the mixture together)

REAL WHIPPED CREAM

All coffee drinks and many blended drinks use whipped cream as a topping or garnish. Real whipped cream is simple and inexpensive to prepare. The alternative to real whipped cream is the widely used aerosol can of whipped cream. Real whipped cream is superior to the canned variety. The taste, texture, and quality of the ingredients are, in my opinion, incomparable. Though there are many recipes, real whipped cream is made primarily with sugar, vanilla, and heavy or whipping cream. Real whipped cream is often used in the kitchen for topping desserts and other items. To prepare, whip these ingredients in a mixing bowl for several minutes. Care must be taken not to over whip. Real whipped cream can also be made by whipping the ingredients in the blender at the bar.

FRESHLY SQUEEZED JUICES

An impressive demonstration of quality is the use of freshly squeezed juices. Throughout the evening the bartender can extract fresh juice for cocktails that use the juice of oranges, grapefruits, lemons, and limes. The additional cost of using fresh juices is passed on to the customer through higher drink prices.

Advise your produce supplier of your intentions; make certain she can furnish the restaurant with fresh fruit year-round at an affordable price. The produce supplier should be able to get a discount on bruised or damaged fruit that, because of its appearance, cannot be sold as A-1 eating grade but may be used for juicing.

You can make your own juice with the Sunkist Commercial Juicer. It operates at 1,725 rpm, making it extremely easy for an operator to extract 10 to 12 gallons of juice per hour using precut citrus. It has a unique strainer that oscillates 3,450 times per minute to help separate the juice from the pulp. It's quiet yet heavy-duty motor is housed in gleaming chrome-plated steel and looks great with any décor. The Sunkist Commercial Juicer comes with three different-size extracting bulbs (one each for lemon/lime, orange, and grapefruit). Removable parts can go in a commercial dishwasher for quick and easy sanitizing.

The Sunkist Sectionizer will save you many hours in kitchen/bar prep time. It makes quick work of slicing, halving, and wedging a wide variety of fruits and vegetables. In addition to sectionizing citrus fruit, it can core and wedge apples and pears. It will also slice firm tomatoes and mushrooms for sandwiches and pizzas or wedge them for salads. The sectionizer can slice and/or wedge hardboiled eggs, kiwi fruit, small to medium potatoes, strawberries; just about any firm (not hard) fruit or vegetable without pits that will fit through the blade cup. It is as simple to use as pulling a handle and is much safer than cutting fruits and vegetables with a knife. The Sunkist Sectionizer has seven interchangeable blade cups to choose from, making it one of the most versatile manual food cutters on the market. Blade cups and plungers are commercial dishwasher safe.

Purchase Sunkist Foodservice Equipment from your dealer or order direct by calling the company toll free at 800-383-7141. More information can be found on the Sunkist Web site at **www.sunkistfs.com/equipment**.

BAR TAB PROCEDURES

To allow bar tabs or not is a policy debated from both sides with sound reasoning. Many restaurants have been victimized by customers who walk out and do not pay their bar tabs. A policy of no bar tabs will alleviate the initial problem, but it will certainly be inconvenient — and possibly insulting — to some customers.

A bar tab should always be run if the customer so desires. The lounge is a place where the customer may relax and enjoy a cocktail before dinner. He should not be inconvenienced by paying for each drink he orders as he goes along. Drinks should also be automatically added to the dinner bill unless the customer wishes otherwise.

A system must be established to ensure that the bar tabs get to the correct diners. There are a variety of ways to execute this; the best way depends upon the layout of the restaurant. Each bar tab should have the customer's name and table number written on the back so that misplaced tickets can be traced. Inevitably, some bar tabs will be lost and occasionally some unprincipled customer will sneak out before paying her bill. However, this loss in revenue and extra inconvenience is far outweighed by the benefits derived from having relaxed, unhurried, and completely comfortable customers.

BAR SECURITY

The first step in developing control over liquor cost is to ensure that it is received and stored properly. The manager must be present and take an active part in receiving the liquor delivery. Once verified the delivery must be placed immediately into the storage room. With the exception of wine, nothing but liquor should be stored in the liquor storage room. Again, the manager must be the only person (apart from the owner) with a key to the storage room; the control system described in this section is based upon this certainty. The door to the storage area must have nonremovable hinges and a sliding bolt lock.

Juices, mixers, and other bar items may be stored at the bar or in the food dry storage area. They cannot be kept in the liquor storage room, as the bartender will not have access to this room. The manager should not get into the habit of lending out her keys; if an article is needed from a locked storage room, she should retrieve it or accompany the employee retrieving it.

The bar itself needs to be as secure as the storage room. Every bottle must be locked up at the end of each shift. Many bars have sliding doors or removable panels that can be locked to cover the shelves of liquor. These are excellent devices, but make certain the hinges are nonremovable and on the inside. Locks and latches should be commercial grade and of tempered steel. Refrigerators and coolers usually have locks on the handles, but most of these are weak and can be jimmied with a knife blade: Replace them with latches and locks.

The walk-in where the beer and kegs are stored must be separated from the food area. If you do not have the room or capital to build a separate walk-in, divide off a section for the exclusive use of the bar. Screened partitions with lockable doors can be purchased from your food-service supplier or made locally by a welder. If the beer system does not already have one, install a cut-off valve in the walk-in. This valve enables the system to be shut off after each shift.

The number of bottles of liquor stored at the bar is an integral part of the control system. Each type of liquor and each brand must have only two bottles at the bar at any time. Should the bar run out of a particular bottle, the manager will have to go to the storage room to retrieve one.

BARTENDER'S PROCEDURES

Once an open bottle is exhausted, remove the pouring spout and place the spout on the backup bottle. Do not throw the empty bottle out. Store it in a box along with the others under the bar.

At the end of the shift, complete a Liquor Used and Restocked Form, an example of which you will find at the end of this chapter. List the exhausted bottles and the number of each under the appropriate columns. The "Restocked" column of this form will be completed by the manager. Double-check to be sure that the empty bottles correspond to the ones listed on the form. Give this form to the manager when closing out.

LIQUOR RESTOCKING

On a daily basis the manager must restock, from the storage room, all the liquor used the night before at the bar. First, compare the Liquor Used and Restocking Form completed by the bartender with the empty bottles at the bar. Each entry on the list must correspond to an empty bottle in the case. Doing so ensures that the bottle was actually used at the bar. After verification, the empty bottles may be thrown away or stored for the recycle center. Using the list completed by the bartender, restock the bottles needed from the storage room. Under the "Restocked" column of the form, fill in the number of bottles restocked. When the restocking is completed there should be two bottles for each type of liquor at the bar. Should there be fewer than two, either the bartender made an error or, more likely, a theft has occurred.

This system of restocking replaces every emptied bottle with a new one. Since the manager is doing the actual restocking, no bottle will ever become lost or stolen from storage. This system enables you to pinpoint areas that are cost problems. If the liquor cost-of-sales percentage is high at the end of the month, you can be certain that the bartender is responsible. He is either overpouring or not following some other procedure, which resulted in a cost increase. You can base this assumption on the fact that every bottle delivered to the bar was accounted for; only under the bartender's control did the cost problem arise.

ACCOUNTING FOR BAR SALES

There are many different ways to control or account for liquor sales. This section will outline some basic operating procedures that may be instituted in any restaurant. Liquor sales are derived from three sources:

1. Customers at the bar, which the bartender governs,

2. Orders from the lounge, which are usually handled by the cocktail waitress/waiter.

3. Customers in the dining room. The control system for accounting for each liquor sale will be similar to the one used in the dining room for food items. Substitute the cocktail waiter for the waitress and the cashier, the bartender for the cook and dishwasher, and it is exactly the same setup as food sales.

Only one person — the bartender — is responsible for operating and accounting for the cash register. The manager will issue the cash drawer, bar tickets, and bar keys to the bartender at the same time the cashier drawer and wait staff tickets are issued to the cashier. The bartender's report is similar to the cashier's report. It lists all the information necessary to account for all sales received at the register and to break them down into accountable terms for the bookkeeper. The cash drawer is prepared by the bookkeeper, and cash figures must be verified by the manager and bartender at the beginning and end of each shift. An example of the Bartender's Report may be found at the end of this chapter. At the bottom of this form, spaces for verifying and issuing the bar tickets are listed.

Liquor, wine, and food sales must be kept separate when entered into the register: Use a separate key for each. The sale of cigars and so forth may be recorded under the "Misc." Sales column; itemize each sale on the back of the report.

Bar tickets may be the same as those used in the dining room. They should consist of two parts, the first being the heavy paper copy on which the order and other pertinent information is written. The bottom section is the tear-away customer receipt. The second is a carbon copy of the first; the slip from which the bartender prepares the order. Before starting any order the bartender must make certain that the prices entered on the ticket are accurate and the bill is totaled.

Drink orders received at the bar by the bartender must be written like regular orders. The stiff paper copy of the ticket should be placed in front of the customer. Additional drinks may be written below the first one; doing so ensures that all drinks are recorded on a ticket. A common ploy used by dishonest bartenders is to not write the order on a ticket at all — when the tab is paid, the bartender pockets the money. Prevent this problem by making it a mandatory procedure to record every drink served on a ticket and to place the ticket in front of the customer. A periodic swing by the bar to make sure all customers have bar-tab tickets is all that is needed to enforce this policy.

The easiest system to account for sales in the lounge is to keep a running tab of each customer at the bar. When the customer is finished, the cocktail waiter will pick up the money and the tab and give them to the bartender, who will ring the sale into the register. This system is impressively accurate; there is no possible way a sale can become lost. The disadvantage to this arrangement is that it tends to slow the bartender down, as he will spend more time at the register.

Many busy restaurants resolve this problem by giving each cocktail waiter his own money bank. When a customer is finished, the cocktail waiter totals the tab and makes change from the bank on his tray. This system frees the bartender but will slow down the service in the lounge. More responsibility is given to the cocktail waiter under this system, as he must now account for his own money and fill out all the necessary paperwork. Additional bookkeeping hours will be required, as each bank must be audited after every shift. Remember that the simplest system is often the best: If applicable, use the first system described above.

As I stated in the beginning of this section, the best control you can establish in the bar is to have honest, concerned employees. All controls are effective to a point, but if an employee is determined to steal from you, he or she will. The employee with the greatest opportunity to steal and least chance of being discovered is the bartender. Many operators who have suspected a problem in the bar will hire spotters to sit at the bar and look over the bartender's procedures. If your bar control problem remains unsolved, you may find yourself forced to use this tactic. Aside from the habitually criminal employee, most employees steal from their employers as a way to get even for some injustice. Either they are unhappy with their pay scale or feel they are being treated unfairly. They compensate themselves by stealing. The easiest way to avoid this atmosphere of deceit and mistrust is to make certain that all employees are treated equally and fairly. Grievances should be aired before bad feelings can develop.

Get employees on your side by involving them in monthly inventories. Let them see what your costs are and that you are very concerned with what is taking place in the bar.

Monthly bonuses or other incentives for maintaining consistent cost-of-sales percentages will compel the bartenders to become involved and concerned with controlling costs.

INVENTORY CONTROLS

At the bar or in storage, an accurate liquor inventory is vital to control costs and maintain profitability. There are a number of computerized systems available that can help with this process. To follow are some examples:

- **AccuBar** is an excellent example of a computerized inventory system. Customers report 50 to 80 percent time savings when using the AccuBar system. It is easy to learn: Most users are up and running within 30 minutes. The patented technology eliminates the need to estimate levels; simply tap the fluid level on the bottle outline. Once you tap the bottle outline, data entry is complete. There is no further human intervention. Since no data entry or third party is involved, reports are generated immediately. It also provides a running perpetual inventory. Transfers between locations and returns of defective items are also covered. AccuBar also helps gauge which items are not selling, allowing you to consider stocking something else that might bring a better return. AccuBar also recommends what needs to be ordered from each supplier based on current perpetual, par, and reorder points. The order is totally customizable. When a shipment arrives, simply scan the items; any discrepancy from what was ordered is caught immediately. AccuBar can also track food, glassware, china, and other essentials. For more information, visit **www.accubar.com/Demo.asp**.

- **The Accardis liquor inventory system is another option to save time and money and eliminate over-pouring and theft.** The Accardis Cyclops Falcon Inventory System Overview: First, identify the product by scanning the bar code or using the find key. Next, weigh open bottles. Quantities are automatically controlling liquor sent to CYCLOPS with precise electronic accuracy. Third, enter quantity. Use the keypad inventory costs to enter full unit quantities or to estimate open bottles if scale not used. Finally, Accardis will generate reports and download data to a PC via the Falcon Docking Cradle. This alcohol inventory system has proven to be fast and accurate. It will lower your costs while increasing your profits. Most clients recover the cost of the liquor inventory system in only a few months. The Cyclops Falcon scans and weighs liquor bottles electronically and then downloads the data to the PACER 4.0 for Windows software. Pacer prints out all the management reports on a station-by-station basis. The liquor inventory system also tracks all purchases and requisitions and can be used for liquor, beer, wine, supplies, hats, T-shirts, etc. Cyclops Falcon gives the user complete control of beverages at a fraction of the cost of most other systems. For more information, contact Accardis Systems, Inc., 20061 Doolittle Street, Montgomery Village, MD 20886. Call 800-852-1992 or visit **www.accardis.com**.

CONTROLLING MIXED DRINKS

Drinks need to be closely controlled to keep profits and customer satisfaction high. Customers who feel they are getting less for their money are unlikely to return. On the other hand, if your bartender consistently over-pours, even by a small amount, then you are giving away free drinks. Controlling pours is a major concern for bar managers everywhere and a number of solutions have been put forth to help bars deal with this common problem.

In deciding how much liquor should be poured into each drink, try out several drinks and decide based on drink quality. In most bars, shots range from 1⅛ to 1½ ounces. Any more or less affects quality. In many bars, the standard is one ounce. In general, you should make pours consistent. If you make some of your mixed drinks with 1⅛ ounce shots, some with 1 ounce shots, some with 1½ ounce shots, and so on, you will create extra work for your bartender, as he will need to refer to your recipes for each drink, slowing down service and creating frustration all around.

CONTROLLING POURING

You want to give your bartender the tools needed to create drinks according to your specifications. By eliminating over-pour and spillage, bar owners and managers save money on every bottle served. If your bartender over-pours just ⅛ ounce per drink, your loss could be up to four drinks per bottle.

Use of technologically advanced portion-control systems is becoming increasingly commonplace in today's drinks industry. Liquor control systems (LCSs) are particularly effective at controlling liquor costs. They can eliminate employee theft. LCSs are marketed on the basis of a typical return on investment within 12 months. The following suppliers offer LCSs:

- Berg Company, **www.berg-controls.com**, 608-221-4281

- AzBar, **www.azbaramerica.com**, 214-361-2422

- Bristol BM, **www.bristolnf.com/liquor.htm**, 709-722-6669

- Easybar Beverage Management Systems, **www.easybar.com**, 503-624-6744

- Precision Pours, **www.precisionpours.com**, 800-549-4491

Easybar Beverage Management systems (**www.easybar.com**) has multiple solutions for beverage portion control. The Easybar CLCSII is a fully computerized beverage-dispensing system that controls beverage pour sizes and improves bartender speed. This system also prevents product loss by eliminating over-pouring, spillage, breakage, and theft. It accounts for all beverages dispensed through the system and boosts receipts by lowering costs and increasing accountability. Also available is the Easypour Controlled Spout System. This offers control for drinks that are dispensed directly from a bottle. The controlled pour spouts allow only preset portions to be dispensed and will not allow drinks to be dispensed without being recorded. Easybar's Cocktail Station (pictured at right) creates cocktails at the touch of a button. The cocktail tower can dispense up to 48 liquors plus any combination of ten juices or sodas. It mixes cocktails of up to five ingredients and ingredients dispense simultaneously to cut pour time. All ingredients dispense in accurate portions every time.

Precision Pours (**www.precisionpours.com**) manufactures measured liquor pours, gravity-feed portion control systems, and bar accessories. Precision Pours™ 3-ball liquor pours. Your customers want their favorite drinks to taste like their favorite drinks, neither underpoured nor overpoured. With Precision Pours, cocktails served in your bar will have the same great taste every time no matter who's pouring. At the same time, your profits will soar. Since Precision Pours eliminate overpour and spillage, you can expect to serve two to four additional drinks per bottle.

Precision Pours Rack & Pour™ units can mount on your wall, affix to your counters, or free-stand on your back bar. They offer measuring heads in five sizes, with or without counting meters. Some of their units accept 1.75 liter bottles, and they offer two styles of finish, chrome and gold. Available in a variety of styles.

FREE POURING

Modern technology has influenced free pouring as well. **BarVision** combines free pouring with wireless liquor inventory control. It allows you to track liquor inventory usage automatically in real-time. Every pour is transmitted to BarVision by a wireless liquor pour spout. Every empty liquor bottle is reconciled automatically — eliminating the need for manual inventory procedures. BarVision reports provide extensive flexibility, whether you need a usage summary for a quick grasp on your open liquor inventory or a journal detail for reconciling your POS/register receipts. It does not require extensive wiring or hardware installation.

Here is how it works:

1. Bartenders free-pour drinks.

2. The pour spouts transmit data about the pours to the receiver.

3. BarVision "talks" to the receiver and keeps a journal.

4. Managers print reports from BarVision's journal.

For more information, visit **www.barvision.com** or call 480-222-6000.

AUTOMATION

In the future, you may be able to do away with bar staff completely. Check out this automated option:

*   **Motoman's RoboBar** is a complete, self-contained robotic bar that serves mixed drinks, draft beer, wine, sodas, and juices, highlighting potential applications in the growing service sector. RoboBar features a UPJ dual-arm robot with a compact NXC100 controller housed in the base of the robot. The two manipulator arms on this unique robot each have five axes of motion and the base also rotates to provide an eleventh axis of motion. The end-of-arm tooling consists of simple parallel grippers. A safety enclosure is included. Programming is easy and the user interface is intuitive and graphics-based. The system is designed to use a magnetic card scanner to authorize drink service. After a valid card swipe, the customer uses a touch screen to choose a beverage. The Motoman UPJ dual-arm robot selects a cup and then fills it with the appropriate beverage(s) and ice, if desired. The robot then passes the drink to

the customer via an automatic turntable located at the side of the cell. "Robots are fascinating to watch, and the entertainment factor alone makes RoboBar a customer magnet," says Ron Potter, Motoman's Senior Director of Emerging Robot Markets. "But RoboBar not only out-draws the competition, it also out-pours and out-performs, while improving profits and pleasing customers—giving establishments a big advantage in the 'bar wars,'" he continues. "RoboBar doesn't take tips, so customers can spend more money on drinks. RoboBar is never late for work and doesn't get tired. Interaction with customers is always friendly. Plus, it does not drink on the job or dip into the till — and smoke does not bother the robot," he explains. For more information on Motoman products and services, visit the corporate Web site at **www.motoman.com**, call 937-847-6200, or write to Motoman Inc. at 805 Liberty Lane, West Carrollton, Ohio 45449.

POINT-OF-SALE SYSTEMS

The most widely used technology to help control costs in the food service and beverage industry is the touch-screen, or point-of-sale (POS), system. The POS system is basically an offshoot of the electronic cash register. Touch screen POS systems were introduced to the food and beverage industry in the mid-1980s and have penetrated 90 percent of establishments nationwide.

The touch screen is effortless. In fact, a child could be trained to use it in a few minutes. Such systems will pay for themselves. According to information published by the National Restaurant

Association, an operation averaging $1,000,000 in food-and-beverage sales can expect to see an estimated savings of $30,000 per year. Understanding the numbers collected by a POS system will give the operator more control over inventory, bar revenues, labor scheduling, overtime, customer traffic, and service. Understanding POS ultimately clarifies the bottom line, knocking guesswork out of the equation.

A POS system is comprised of two parts: the hardware, or equipment, and the software, the computer program that runs the system. This system allows wait staff to key in their orders as soon as the customers give them. Additional keys are available for particular options and specifications.

The order is sent through a cable to printers located throughout the establishment: at the bar and in the kitchen and office. All orders must be printed before they are prepared, thus ensuring good control. When a server has completed the ordering, a guest check can be printed and later presented. Most POS systems allow certain discounts and require manager control over others. Charge cards, cash, and checks can be processed separately and then reports can be generated by payment type. Some benefits of using a POS system:

- Increases sales and accounting information.
- Custom tracking.
- Reports wait staff's sales and performance.
- Reports menu-item performance.
- Reports inventory usage.
- Track credit card purchases.
- Accurate addition on guest checks.
- Prevents incorrect items from being ordered.
- Prevents confusion in the kitchen.
- Reports possible theft of money and inventory.
- Records employee timekeeping.
- Reports menu-sales breakdown for preparation and menu forecasting.
- Reduces time spent walking to kitchen and bar.

As the labor market continues to diminish, touch-screens POS systems will become necessary. Many POS systems have been greatly enhanced to include guest books, online reservations, and fully integrated systems with real-time inventory, integrated caller ID, accounting, labor scheduling, payroll, menu analysis, purchasing and receiving, cash management, and reports. Up-and-coming enhancements and add-ons include improved functionality across the Internet, centralized functionality enabling "alerts" to be issued to managers, and voice-recognition POS technology.

The following are some sources for POS systems:

- ExaDigm has taken a fresh new approach to POS connectivity with the launch of the Mate Plus point-of-sale terminal and in turn created a whole new way of doing business. With its unique modular format and interchangeable modems supporting IP (Ethernet), WiFi, cellular, and dial-up connections, the Mate Plus offers speed, portability, mobility, changeability, and universal connectivity.

Featuring a fully modular design and PC-based Linux operating system, merchants now only need to purchase a single terminal that offers multiple connectivity options, easy software upgrades, and simple configuration to adapt to new technologies. The Mate Plus terminal delivers a solution that is easier, faster, and ultimately cheaper—and that means a drastically streamlined product for both the merchant and those that support it. For more information, visit **www.exadigm.com**.

- InTouchPOS® is an advanced and user-friendly touchscreen point-of-sale system capable of handling every type of food service or beverage operation. Visit **www.intouchpos.com** or call 800-777-8202 for more information.

InTouchPOS

- Vital Link POS is another comprehensive and cost-effective point-of-sale system. With a robust set of integrated order, delivery, and management reporting features, Vital Link POS delivers efficient operations, increased profitability, and greater control. Spend less time worrying about business operations and more time spent improving the bottom line. Vital Link POS is specifically designed for easy order entry of complex menu choices. Vital Link POS offers your bar a comprehensive point-of-sale solution. For more information, visit **www.vitallinkpos.com** or call 877-448-5300.

CONTROLLING COMMUNICATIONS

Controlling communication is another important bar control. With multiple shifts and numerous employees, a communication system is essential. I recommend implementing a communication manual. You can set up your own to keep track of scheduling, employees, and bar information or invest in a pre-formatted system.

Vital Link POS Screen

- COMMLOG is a unique, fully customizable manager communication log. Created by hospitality professionals, COMMLOG's unique structure guides users through all parts of leaving a great note, improving communication and follow-up. COMMLOG utilizes a plastic coil binding so your log lays flat when open. It is available in either letter (8.5" x 11") or legal size (8.5" x 14"). COMMLOG covers all the important aspects of your business, with plenty of room for all your notes. COMMLOG is available in several formats or you can customize it to fit your needs at no charge. There are many variations available, including a manager log and bar log. For more information, visit **www.commlog.com** or call 800-962-6564.

CONTROLLING CLEANLINESS

Whether you hire a full-time cleaning staff or not, staff at every shift will need to ensure proper cleanliness before starting and after ending each shift, ensuring maximum cleanliness and hygiene for your bar. During each shift, you will want to adhere to the following cleaning practices:

Before each shift or day's work:

- Ensure that forms and paperwork are correctly filled out, filed, or sent to the proper persons. For example, restocking forms should be promptly delivered to suppliers to ensure that no important ingredient runs out.

- Ensure that tabletops are properly clean and set up with candles, ashtrays, and cutlery, as needed according to proper bar procedures.

- Ensure that side stands are clean.

- Look over the bar's general appearance — it should present a positive impression.

- Set lights to desired levels. Light candles, if used.

- Ensure that temperature is set to comfortable levels and there is adequate ventilation for pleasant dining.

- Ensure that walls are clean.

- Ensure that windows are clean and drapes or window treatments are either opened to let in light or closed to prevent glare (as is deemed best for customer comfort).

- Ensure that floors are clean and look nicely waxed.

- Ensure that furniture is properly arranged and looks polished. Tables and chairs should be checked to make sure that they do not totter.

- Look over glassware and cutlery to ensure that it is clean and ready to be used.

- Clean exterior of the bar, sweeping steps or shoveling the sidewalk if snow has fallen.

During each shift or day's work:

- Fill out and file forms as needed during work hours.

- Ensure that tabletops are properly clean and set up with candles, ashtrays, and cutlery, as needed according to proper bar procedures.

- Ensure that side stands are clean.

- Ensure that the bar's general appearance continues to present a positive impression.

- Set lights to desired levels. Relight candles as they burn out.

- Adjust temperature as needed to ensure that it stays at comfortable levels.

- Ensure that walls are clean.

- Ensure that windows remain clean and drapes or window treatments are either opened to let in light or closed to prevent glare.

- Clean floors of any spills or breakages that occur during the work shift.

- Ensure that furniture continues to be comfortable. Rearrange furniture in order to accommodate preferred customer seating or larger parties.

- Keep an eye on glassware and cutlery to ensure that it is clean and free of chips and breaks. Clean glassware and cutlery regularly to ensure that fresh items are available for customers.

- Greet and serve customers, following as many customer suggestions as possible to **ensure patron satisfaction.**

After the day's work/shift:

- Ensure that forms and paperwork are correctly filled out, filed, or sent to the proper persons.

- Wipe down and clean tabletops and set up as needed according to proper bar procedures.

- Clean side stands.

- Clean exterior of the bar — sweep steps or shovel snow.

- Look over the bar's general appearance — it should present a positive impression.

- Turn off lights after all employees have left.

- Tally the day's earnings and expenses and remove all money from the premises.

- Turn down temperature to minimal night levels.

- Ensure that walls are clean.

- Ensure that windows are clean and drapes or window treatments are clean. Close windows securely and draw drapes or blinds as well.

- Clean and wax floors.

- Clean work areas.

- Clean bar.

- Clean kitchen and bathroom thoroughly.

- Polish furniture and arrange properly. Most bars will place chairs on tables to allow for easier cleaning of the floors.

- Lock up safes, liquor cabinets, and other secure areas well.

- Clean all glassware and cutlery to ensure that it is ready to go for the next shift.

- Leave till open.

- Put up "closed" sign and lock up all windows and doors. Double-check that all is secure.

For more information about bar service, I recommend the following books from Atlantic Publishing (**www.atlantic-pub.com**):

- *The Professional Bar & Beverage Manager's Handbook: How to Open and Operate a Financially Successful Bar, Tavern, and Nightclub: With Companion CD-ROM (Item # PBB-01)*

- *The Professional Bartender's Handbook: A Recipe for Every Drink Known — Including Tricks and Games to Impress Your Guests (Item # PBH-01)*

- *The Responsible Serving of Alcoholic Beverages: A Complete Staff Training Course for Bars, Restaurants, and Caterers: With Companion CD-ROM (Item # RSA-01)*

- *The Food Service Professional Guide To Controlling Liquor, Wine, & Beverage Costs (Item # FS8-01)*

- *The Food Service Professional Guide To Bar & Beverage Operation: Ensuring Success & Maximum Profit (Item # FS11-01)*

BAR TERMINOLOGY

APERITIF A drink taken before a meal designed to stimulate the taste buds and appetite. It can be a liqueur, wine or cocktail. Sherry is an example of a popular aperitif.

BACK The companion drink, or a second cocktail, served in a second glass. "Bloody Mary with beer back" would be served in two glasses; one with the Bloody Mary and the other with beer. Referred to as a chaser.

BITTERS A very concentrated flavoring made from roots, barks, herbs and berries; used in an Old Fashioned cocktail.

CALL LIQUOR Any liquor other than well liquor. The term refers to "calling" the liquor brand by name, such as "Captain Morgan® and Coke" rather than "rum and coke."

CORDIAL A liquor (or liqueur) made by mixing or redistilling neutral spirits. Fruits, flowers, herbs, seeds, roots, plants or juices are used and a sweetening is added. Most cordials are sweet, colorful and highly concentrated. Many are made from secret recipes and processes.

CREME A cordial, such as Creme de Menthe, with a very high sugar content. Its cream-like consistency gives it its prefix.

DASH One-sixth of a teaspoon.

DRY "Dry" typically means "not sweet." A dry Manhattan means use dry vermouth instead of sweet vermouth. A dry martini refers to the use of dry vermouth.

DOUBLE Combining two drinks in one large glass. Double drinks may be stronger as there is less room for the mixer.

FLAG An orange slice and a cherry garnish held together by a fruit pick.

---

25 OF THE MOST COMMONLY ORDERED COCKTAILS:

- Screwdriver
- Sombrero
- Mai-Tai
- Piña Colada
- Old Fashioned
- Tequila Sunrise
- Gimlet
- Margarita
- Martini
- Cosmopolitan
- Manhattan
- Gibson
- Bloody Mary
- Stingers
- Coffee
- Collins Drinks
- Fizzes
- Daiquiri
- Sours
- White Russian
- Black Russian
- Alabama Slammer
- Gin and Tonic
- Juice/Punch Drinks
- Long Island Iced Tea

FRAPPES Several liqueurs combined and poured over shaved or crushed ice.

HIGHBALL A liquor served with ice, soda, plain water, ginger ale or other carbonated liquids.

JIGGER A jigger, or shot, is a small drinking glass-shaped container used to measure liquor.

LIQUEUR A sweet alcoholic beverage made from an infusion of flavoring ingredients and a spirit.

LIQUOR A distilled, alcoholic beverage made from a fermented mash of various ingredients.

MIST Crushed ice rather than cubed.

NEAT Liquor that is drank undiluted by ice, water or mixers.

ON THE ROCKS A beverage served over ice without adding water or other mixers.

PROOF The measure of the strength of the alcohol. One (degree) proof equals one-half of one percent of alcohol. For example, 100 proof equals 50% alcohol.

STRAIGHT UP Cocktails that are served up without ice.

TOP SHELF Expensive, high-quality brands such as Courvoisier®.

TWIST A lemon peel garnish. The peel is twisted over the drink, run around the rim and dropped in the drink.

VIRGIN A cocktail without alcohol.

WELL The standard "house" brand of liquors. Also the area where the drinks are made.

COMMONLY USED BAR MIXERS, JUICES, GARNISH GUIDELINES, AND BEVERAGE-SPECIFIC GARNISHES

Commonly Used Bar Mixers, Juices			
Juices	**Fresh Fruit**	**Soda & Water**	**Mixers, Misc.**
Orange juice	Oranges	Coke or Pepsi	Sweet-and-sour bar mix
Cranberry juice	Limes	Diet Coke or Diet Pepsi	Coconut cream concentrate
Pineapple juice	Bananas	Sprite or 7-Up	Grenadine
Grapefruit juice	Cherries	Ginger ale	Bitters
Tomato juice	Strawberries	Tonic water	Orgeat syrup
Lime juice	Lemon peels	Soda water	Worcestershire sauce
Lemon juice	Lemons	Sparkling or mineral water	Tabasco sauce
	Pineapple	Purified water	Sugar-saturated water

Garnish Guidelines

- For alcoholic beverages, one straw for every drink with ice.
- Kiddie Cocktails – an orange flag or two cherries.
- Three cocktail onions per sword – in drink.
- Two olives per sword – in drink.
- Cherries – no sword.
- Twist – lemon peel used to flavor rim of glass, then dropped in drink.

Drink Specific Garnishes

Drink Name	Garnish
Manhattans	cherry
Gibson	cocktail onions
Martini	olives or a twist (ask customer's preference)
Collins and Sours	orange speared with a cherry
Tonic Drinks	lime wedge
Rob Roy	cherry
Old Fashioned	cherry
Drinks with Bloody Mary Mix	lime wedge or wheel and celery or pickle
Coffee Drinks	whipped cream, cherry
All Coolers	lime wheel or wedge
Pineapple Juice Drinks	pineapple wedge speared with a cherry
Orange Juice Drinks	orange speared with a cherry
Margaritas/Daiquiris	lime wheel or wedge

UNIT BREAKDOWN OF LIQUOR

The following items are unit breakdowns of liquor that are useful in computing liquor cost percentages or markup percentages:

Size	Unit Breakdown
Keg of beer	15 ½ gallons
Keg of beer	1,984 ounces
1 gallon	128 ounces
1 fifth	750 milliliters
1 fifth	approx. 21.8 ounces
1 liter	approx. 33.8 ounces
½ gallon	64 ounces
½ gallon	1.9 liter
1 quart	32 ounces
1 quart	approx. 0.95 liters
1 pint	approx. 475 milliliters
1 pound	16 ounces
Miniature	50 milliliters
Miniature	1.6 ounces

Metric Size—Fluid Oz.	Number Of Drinks Sized In Ounces				
	1¾ oz.	1 oz.	1⅛ oz.	1¼ oz.	1½ oz.
1.75 Liter—59.2	78.9	59.2	52.6	47.4	39.5
1 Liter—33.8	45.1	33.8	30.0	27.0	22.5
750 Milliliters—25.4	33.9	25.4	22.6	20.3	16.9
500 Milliliters—16.9	22.5	16.9	15.0	13.5	11.3
200 Milliliters—6.8	9.1	6.8	6.0	5.4	4.5

COMPUTATION OF KEY PERCENTAGES

bar supplies ÷ bar sales = bar supplies cost percentage

beer cost ÷ beer sales = beer cost percentage

food cost ÷ food sales = food cost percentage

labor ÷ total sales = labor cost percentage

liquor cost ÷ liquor sales = liquor cost percentage

paper cost ÷ food sales = paper cost percentage

other ÷ total sales = other cost percentage

wine cost ÷ wine sales = wine cost percentage

SAMPLE MONTH LIQUOR PURCHASES BY BOTTLE

BRAND	COST	# PURCHASED	TOTAL COST	$ PER DRINK	# OF DRINKS EA	SALES BOTTLE VALUE/ SALES TOTAL VALUE
FRANGELICO	17.50	3	52.50	3.00	22.5	67.50 / 202.50
GALLIANO	12.55	1	12.55	2.50	22.5	56.25 / 56.25
BLUE CURACO	6.20	1	6.20	3.25	22.5	73.13 / 73.13
C BROS BRANDY	8.05	7	56.35	2.25	22.5	50.63 / 354.38
BL BER BRANDY	7.10	2	14.20	2.25	22.5	50.63 / 101.25
CHERRY BRANDY	7.10	1	7.10	2.25	22.5	50.63 / 50.63
CR DE CACAO DK	7.05	3	21.15	2.50	22.5	56.25 / 168.75
CR DE CACAO LT	7.05	1	7.05	2.50	22.5	56.25 / 56.25
TANQUERAY	13.80	10	138.00	3.00	22.5	67.50 / 675.00
BOMBAY SAPHIR	14.80	2	29.60	3.00	22.5	67.50 / 135.00
BEEFEATER	13.85	11	152.35	3.00	22.5	67.50 / 742.50
ABSOLUT	13.15	3	39.45	3.00	22.5	67.50 / 202.50
STOLICHNAYA	12.70	10	127.00	3.00	22.5	67.50 / 675.00
SO COMFORT	7.90	3	23.70	2.50	22.5	56.25 / 168.75
AMARETTO	8.65	5	43.25	2.75	22.5	61.88 / 309.38
VERMOUTH	6.20	1	6.20	2.25	22.5	50.63 / 50.63
BUSHMILLS	14.90	10	149.00	3.00	22.5	67.50 / 675.00
KAHLUA	14.75	22	324.50	2.75	22.5	61.88 / 1361.25
BAILEYS	17.85	13	232.05	3.25	22.5	73.13 / 950.63
PEACH SCHNPS	6.35	8	50.80	2.25	22.5	50.63 / 405.00
RASPBERRY	5.70	1	5.70	2.25	22.5	50.63 / 50.63
CROWN ROYAL	5.75	6	94.50	3.00	22.5	67.50 / 405.00
MALIBU	8.65	20	173.00	2.75	22.5	61.88 / 1237.50
QUERVO GOLD	10.70	13	139.10	2.75	22.5	61.88 / 804.38
CUTTY SARK	5.70	7	109.90	3.00	22.5	67.50 / 472.50
DEWARS WHITE	15.50	7	108.50	3.00	22.5	67.50 / 472.50
RED LABEL	5.05	1	5.05	3.00	22.5	67.50 / 67.50
BACARDI LT	8.00	6	48.00	2.75	22.5	61.88 / 371.25
BARCARDI DK	8.00	3	24.00	2.75	22.5	61.88 / 185.63
MYERS DK	10.95	5	54.75	2.75	22.5	61.88 / 309.38
YUKON JACK	10.30	4	41.20	2.75	22.5	61.88 / 247.50
RUMPLE MINZE	12.90	5	64.50	3.00	22.5	67.50 / 337.50
WILD TURKEY	13.50	1	13.50	3.00	22.5	67.50 / 67.50
JIM BEAM	7.35	1	7.35	2.50	22.5	56.25 / 56.25
EARLY TINES	7.05	1	7.05	2.50	22.5	56.25 / 56.25
JACK DANIELS	10.95	27	295.65	2.75	22.5	61.88 / 1670.63
CANADIAN CLUB	10.25	2	20.50	2.75	22.5	61.88 / 123.75
SEAGRAMS 7	7.75	3	23.25	2.75	22.5	61.88 / 185.63
SEAGRAMS VO	10.25	18	184.50	2.75	22.5	61.88 / 1113.75
CANADIAN MIST	7.25	9	65.25	2.75	22.5	61.88 / 556.88
MACNAUGHTON	6.75	11	74.25	2.75	22.5	61.88 / 680.63
BLACK VELVET	7.10	23	163.30	2.75	22.5	61.88 / 1423.13
RICH & RARE	7.05	3	21.15	3.75	22.5	84.38 / 253.13
GILBYS	6.25	51	318.75	2.25	22.5	50.63 / 2581.88
MONTEGO BAY	5.75	56	322.00	3.25	22.5	73.13 / 4095.00
KANCHATKA	5.10	143	729.30	2.50	22.5	56.25 / 8043.75
TRIPLE SEC	5.65	14	79.10	3.25	22.5	73.13 / 1023.75
ARANDAS	6.65	20	133.00	3.25	22.5	73.13 / 1462.50
USHERS	9.70	30	291.00	3.75	22.5	84.38 / 2531.25
CANAD'N HUNTER	6.70	40	268.06	3.75	22.5	84.38 / 3375.00
ARANDAS GAL	14.65	4	58.60	3.25	52.6	170.95 / 683.80
PEPPERMINT	6.10	6	36.60	2.25	22.5	50.63 / 303.75
GLENLVT SCOTCH	23.75	2	47.50	3.00	22.5	67.50 / 135.00
APR TRIPLE SEC	6.10	8	48.80	3.25	22.5	73.13 / 585.00
FLSMN ROYAL	5.10	13	66.30	2.50	22.5	56.25 / 731.25
ARR TRPE SF	3.70	4	14.80	3.25	22.5	73.13 / 292.50
CAN LTD	6.25	2	12.50	3.00	22.5	67.50 / 135.00

TOTALS 5,673.20 / 44,541.93

MARKUP FOR SAMPLE MONTH
SALES PRICE: $44,541.93
COST MARKUP: $5,673.20

BARTENDER'S REPORT

BARTENDER _____   BARTENDER _____
MANAGER _____   MANAGER _____
BOOKKEEPER _____   BOOKKEEPER _____

CASH IN

$100.00 _____		$1.00 _____
$50.00 _____		$0.50 _____
$20.00 _____		$0.25 _____
$10.00 _____		$0.10 _____
$5.00 _____		$0.05 _____
$1.00 _____		$0.01 _____
TOTAL		TOTAL

CASH OUT

$100.00 _____		$1.00 _____
$50.00 _____		$0.50 _____
$20.00 _____		$0.25 _____
$10.00 _____		$0.10 _____
$5.00 _____		$0.05 _____
$1.00 _____		$0.01 _____
TOTAL		TOTAL

CHARGES

1. _____
2. _____
3. _____
4. _____
5. _____
6. _____

TOTAL _____

SALES SUMMARY

LIQUOR SALES _____
FOOD SALES _____
WINE SALES _____
MISC. SALES _____

TOTAL _____

SALES TAX _____
VOID SALES _____

Note: Itemize checks separately on back.
Enter figure in sale and sales breakdown.

ITEM	LIQUOR	WINE
Housed	_____	_____
Manager	_____	_____
Comp	_____	_____

EMPLOYEE _____
Total # _____   #__# _____   Initial _____
Return _____   Verify _____

EMPLOYEE _____
Total # _____   #__# _____   Initial _____
Return _____   Verify _____

EMPLOYEE _____
Total # _____   #__# _____   Initial _____
Return _____   Verify _____

LIQUOR ORDER FORM

Item	Build to Amount	Date									

LIQUOR INVENTORY FORM

Item	Size	Quantity				Total	Cost	Extension

LIQUOR USED AND RESTOCKED FORM

Liquor	Used	Restocked

ITEM _____

INGREDIENTS:

_____
_____
_____
_____
_____
_____
_____
_____
_____
_____

PROCEDURE:

_____
_____
_____
_____
_____
_____
_____
_____
_____
_____

GLASS:

_____
_____
_____

GARNISH:

_____
_____
_____
_____

ITEM _____

INGREDIENTS:

_____
_____
_____
_____
_____
_____
_____
_____
_____
_____

PROCEDURE:

_____
_____
_____
_____
_____
_____
_____
_____
_____
_____

GLASS:

_____
_____
_____

GARNISH:

_____
_____
_____
_____

CHAPTER

Successful Wine Management

Wine is the most complicated drink to serve and one of the easiest to prepare. Since wine is delicate, it must be stored away from light, heat, and sudden movements before it is served. It should also be stored on its side or at an angle to keep the cork moist. If the bottle is stored upright, the cork will dry out and allow air to seep into the bottle, spoiling the wine's taste.

The taste of wine varies with temperature. Serve white and rosé wines at 46 to 50 degrees Fahrenheit, serve red wines at 62 to 68 degrees Fahrenheit, and serve champagnes and sparkling wines in an ice bucket at 42 to 48 degrees Fahrenheit. When serving wine, remember that there is a fair amount of snobbishness. Your goal should be a happy balance between making the customer feel comfortable in his knowledge of wine and giving the customer a chance to decide how he wants the wine served. Servers should ask the guest when he wants his wine served during the meal. If the customer seems unsure, it is acceptable for the server to make a gentle suggestion as to wine and the course to serve it with. The final decision rests with the customer.

SERVING WINE PROPERLY

There is a process in serving wine properly. Staff and servers should be taken through this process to ensure that the setting goes through without a hitch. Wine connoisseurs may not return to your bar if wine is not served according to accepted rules:

1. **If serving red wine, uncork the bottle as soon as it is at the table so that it can "breathe."**

2. **Place a napkin behind the bottle, with the label of the bottle facing the customer.** Ensure that you have a good grip on the bottle.

3. **Present the bottle, with label displayed, to the person who ordered the wine.** Wait

until the person has read the label to ensure that you have the bottle he requested. In most cases, a customer will nod slightly, make eye contact, or otherwise show approval of the wine. The cork should be slightly slanted toward the customer as well so that the customer can see any labeling or sealing on the cork.

4. **Using the knife blade of a corkscrew, cut around the foil and remove the foil and capsule.** Place these where the customer can reach them but out of the way of the other items on the table.

5. **Use the napkin to gently clean the bottle and the bottle neck.** A careful grip will ensure that the bottle does not slip.

6. **Hold the bottle and insert the corkscrew about two-thirds into the cork.** Place the bottle on the table and pull carefully on the cork. You do not want to jerk the bottle or push the corkscrew further into the bottle.

7. **Once the bottle is open, make sure that the cork is not dry. Place the cork on the table,** allowing the customer to see that the wine was stored correctly and that the bottle was opened properly. (No scarring on the underside means that the corkscrew was not punched in so far to cause floating cork bits in the wine.)

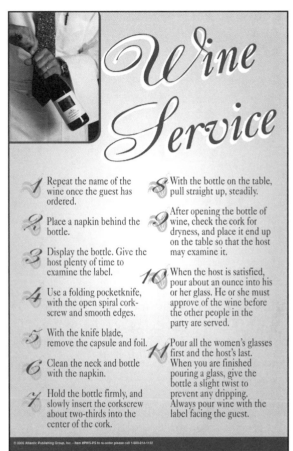

Wine Service

1 Repeat the name of the wine once the guest has ordered.

2 Place a napkin behind the bottle.

3 Display the bottle. Give the host plenty of time to examine the label.

4 Use a folding pocketknife, with the open spiral corkscrew and smooth edges.

5 With the knife blade, remove the capsule and foil.

6 Clean the neck and bottle with the napkin.

7 Hold the bottle firmly, and slowly insert the corkscrew about two-thirds into the center of the cork.

8 With the bottle on the table, pull straight up, steadily.

9 After opening the bottle of wine, check the cork for dryness, and place it end up on the table so that the host may examine it.

10 When the host is satisfied, pour about an ounce into his or her glass. He or she must approve of the wine before the other people in the party are served.

11 Pour all the women's glasses first and the host's last. When you are finished pouring a glass, give the bottle a slight twist to prevent any dripping. Always pour wine with the label facing the guest.

© 2005 Atlantic Publishing Group, Inc. – Item #PWS-PS to re-order please call 1-800-814-1132

8. **Pour a small amount of wine into the customer's glass.** To prevent drips, use the napkin at the neck of the bottle and give the bottle a slight twist as you finish pouring. Drips not only look unsightly, they indicate a waste of the customer's money. The customer may reject the bottle of wine if there is something wrong with it; he cannot simply reject it because of the taste. If a bottle is rejected due to spoiling, it should be brought to management for investigation. For newer bottles, vendors will generally replace the item. Older vintages are usually not refunded.

9. **Only once the customer has approved the wine should the others in the party be served.** Serve women first and then the men, always ending with the customer who ordered the wine. Fill each glass only two-thirds full so that wine can be slightly swirled in the glass to release full aroma and flavor.

10. **When a new bottle is ordered, new glasses should be brought and the process repeated.**

Continually remind your servers on how to properly serve wine. The above poster on wine service is part of a five-part wine poster series from Atlantic Publishing. It is full-color and laminated to reduce wear and tear. It is 11" x 17" and available for $9.95 (Item # PWS-PS). To order, call 800-814-1132 or visit **www.atlantic-pub.com**.

Although this process seems time consuming, proper wine service will favorably impress those who know about wine and will add a touch of class to the experience of those who enjoy wine but do not know much about it.

SERVING SPARKLING WINE AND CHAMPAGNE

Champagne and sparkling wine are served differently than wine. It is also important to stress proper serving of these drinks among your staff, as opening the corks on these bottles can be tricky and awkward. To follow are the steps for proper sparkling wine and champagne service:

1. **Bring the bottle to the table in an ice bucket.**

2. **Place a napkin behind the bottle. Show the bottle to the customer.**

3. **Using the knife implement, remove the foil from the bottle.** Carefully remove the wire muzzle using your fingers.

4. **Point the bottle away from the table and turn the bottle carefully and slowly.** The bottle should "steam," but no champagne should spill at all. The cork should be placed on the table.

5. **Carefully pour champagne into champagne flutes, using the same care as with wine not to spill any.** The process of tasting and approval is not necessary with champagne as the "fizz" of champagne shows the server that the champagne is not spoiled.

The Sparkling Wine poster pictured at right is also part of the five-part wine poster series from Atlantic Publishing. It is available for $9.95 (Item # SWC-PS). To order, call 800-814-1132 or visit **www.atlantic-pub.com**.

SERVING BY THE GLASS OR BY THE BOTTLE

Groups of bar customers will often order wine by the bottle or carafe. However, more and more bar customers are buying wine by the glass, even when they are meeting in groups and this makes selling wine by the glass an important marketing tool. Many of today's regular wine drinkers like wine-by-the-glass programs. This clientele may patronize your establishment if you offer such a program. Well-organized wine-by-the-glass programs can double wine profits.

With profit margins as high as 300 percent, premium wine by the glass can be as profitable as specialty drinks.

Some successful pubs, bars, and restaurants offer a wine-by-the-glass suggestion for certain appetizers and for every entrée to enhance each dish. Even customers not considering a glass of wine with their meal may be tempted to buy when it is suggested to them. You should not rely on the wait staff to recite the wine-by-the-glass list. The list is too long and the recitation may seem too intrusive or uninteresting to customers. A better idea is to use an attractive table tent or smaller menu design. Print the wine-by-the-glass list on a blackboard or sign that can be read from several areas of the dining room and bar. Even champagne sells better when sold by the glass. The fact is many patrons who would not consider buying wine or champagne by the bottle might consider buying a single glass, especially if the suggestion is presented to them in an appealing manner.

Every successful bar manager needs to decide how many wines-by-the-glass the bar should pour. It is not always an easy decision. You may select to offer as few as three wines or as many as 15 to 20. The numbers will depend on your marketing program and your customers. Be wary of offering more than 20 wines-by-the-glass because of potential losses from wine spoilage. Yet the average number of by-the-glass offerings in bars and restaurants has grown steadily. Many restaurants now pour at least 30 percent more wine than they did five years ago and their sales have benefited to a great extent.

There are various wine-by-the-glass dispensing systems available today that can assist with your program. These systems will keep uncorked wine fresh for up to six weeks, eliminating spoilage and waste. They are all temperature-controlled and use a nitrogen gas replacement system. The nitrogen gas instantly replaces the oxygen in a freshly opened bottle, thereby stopping the oxidation process that damages wine. There are a variety of manufacturers that now make these systems.

If you are offering wine-by-the glass programs — or are serving wine at all — you will need to consider wineglasses. The wineglass has a noticeable effect upon the taste of wine — the same wine will taste different in a fine crystal glass than in a cheap wineglass. Of course, crystal wineglasses are not very economical, especially since breakage can easily occur. Only the finest bars and restaurants can afford real crystal wineglasses. Nevertheless, you should purchase the best wineglasses that are affordable and you should never buy wineglasses without testing what wine tastes like in them.

You do not need to use a separate glass for reds, whites, and champagnes. You can save money by serving all wines in 10-ounce tulip-shaped glasses, which are quite suitable for any wine; buying these glasses in bulk leads to substantial savings. Invest in separate champagne glasses as soon as you can afford to; many people prefer the look for their champagne.

Buy glasses you can afford to break. In a bar, broken or missing glasses are quite common.

Simple, clear glasses that are not cut, faceted, etched, or colored are less expensive and easier to replace. Another advantage of simple glasses is that they actually allow you to see the wine more clearly. Always choose wineglasses with generous bowls that allow patrons to swirl the wine in the glass to release the wine's full flavor and aroma. A thin glass rim that tapers slightly inward will make the wine flow evenly and easily from the glass, also allowing the wine's aroma to be maximized. Finally, be sure that the base allows the wineglass to stand firmly whether the glass is full or empty.

HALF BOTTLES AND DECANTERS

For customers who want to purchase more than a glass of wine but less than a full bottle, half bottles and decanters make an attractive choice. Half bottles can save a bar money when used as part of a wine-by-the-glass program, as they offer less spoilage than full bottles. Half bottles are also favored by single diners and couples. Storing half bottles can be challenging as most storage racks are not designed to handle these bottles.

Decanters are used for older wines. Wines older than ten years have sediment in them. Pouring the wine into a carafe or decanter allows the sediment to be removed before serving.

To decant wine:

1. Place a candle on the table alongside the bottle and decanter.

2. As you pour, watch through the lit bottle for sediment to appear in the neck; when it does, stop pouring.

3. The remainder of the wine may be discarded or strained through cheese cloth in the kitchen.

WINE SERVICE INNOVATIONS

There are a number of innovative products that can help regulate wine service as well as store and preserve wine. You may be interested in:

- Winekeeper produces a line of dispensing and preserving systems for wine. Their use makes enjoying fine wine an extended and pleasurable experience. Winekeeper units consist of handcrafted, custom-quality cabinetry and employ proven nitrogen gas preservation technology. Single bottle units to larger commercial units are available. Custom applications, designs, and finishes are available. For more information, contact Winekeeper at 625 E. Haley Street, Santa Barbara, CA 93103, phone 805-963-3451, or visit **www.winekeeper.com**.

- OZ Winebars are another option for serving wine by the glass. OZ Winebars is a wine refrigerator designed specifically to store and dispense both red and white wine. OZ Winebars has an advanced commercial system for managing, refrigerating, preserving, and serving opened wines. OZ Winebars extends the serving life of your wines and provides your staff a clean, efficient vehicle for your wine service program in an exciting, authoritative ambience for your customers. For more information, contact OZEM Corp, 832 Harvard Drive, Holland, MI 49423, phone 866-617-3345, or visit **www.ozwinebars.com**.

WINE STORAGE AND PRESENTATION

If wine is an important part of your bar or nightclub, you may want to invest in a wine cellar, cabinet, or other wine accessories. There is a vast variety available for every type of service and décor. Following are just a few examples:

- Vinotemp offers a wide selection of wine cellars and wine cellar accessory equipment: storage systems, cooler systems, wine racks, wine storage cabinets, humidors, liquor cooler cabinets, wine cellar design, and wine storage. They have a wide design range of models, door styles, various woods, numerous finishes, and a variety of refrigerator and rack design options, as well as thousands of unique wine cellars and storage cabinets available, even custom-designed units. The 700 Monaco Modern by Vinotemp, pictured at right, features two decorative glass doors, special furniture trim design with fluorescent light, and individual redwood and aluminum racking. Dimensions: 59" W x 33" D x 92" H. Approximate bottle capacity: 550. For more information, visit www.**vinotemp.com** or call 800-777-VINO (8466).

CHOOSING TYPES OF WINE

Just a few years ago, many bars offered only two choices of wine: white or red. Today many bars now have extensive wine lists, with selections of wine from the common to the rare. This resurgence has to do with a renewed interest in wine. Wine tastings and wine classes are becoming more popular and knowledge of wines is now considered quite desirable. As a result, bar patrons are becoming more knowledgeable and curious about wines. Recent studies suggesting moderate wine consumption can be good for one's health are also adding to wine's popularity. As wine's popularity continues to grow, on-premise consumption grows.

Decide how much wine you want to keep in your bar. Some bars stock wine cellars with hundreds of bottles while others serve only a few or none at all. Wine always enhances meals and is still ordered by the glass at bars. The best way to determine which wines to stock is to look at your intended clientele and competition. If you decide to serve wine, develop a wine list to help determine which wines to keep in stock.

Certain wines go with certain foods. The smart bar manager will learn the rudiments of wine and ensure that his staff has a basic knowledge of wine. This knowledge will allow the bar staff to make suggestions to patrons.

Wine is a fermented grape juice that comes in three colors—white, red, and rosé. Three factors affect the quality of wine: the grape, the climate the grapes are raised in, and the preparers of the wine. Some bar patrons will ask for a wine by the type of grape used in its making not by brand (such as Chardonnay, Shiraz, Muscat, Cabernet Sauvignon, Cabernet, and others). Some patrons want wines from specific regions.

The human factor, or the special recipes and decisions of the winemakers, plays a big part in wine quality. Some patrons will ask for wines from specific brands or vineyards because they find that those wines offer the taste they desire.

The two posters pictured at right on red and white wine are good references for employees. Each has definitions and food pairings of the most common types of wines. Both are part of the five-part wine poster series from Atlantic Publishing. All five posters can be purchased for $39.95 (Item # WPS-PS). They can also be ordered individually for $9.95 each. To order, call 800-814-1132 or visit **www.atlantic-pub.com**.

Some patrons also want wines from specific years, as the climate or growing season of grapes may be more or less favorable from one year to the next. Many patrons will have no idea what sort of wine they wish to try and will turn to you or your servers for suggestions. Therefore, developing a wine list of wines that you are familiar with and can control and describe is an excellent idea. Some suggestions:

REDS

- **Light-bodied** is often served with red meat, roasted poultry, and oily fish (suggested: four).

- **Medium-bodied** is often served with game, veal, pork, and other red meats (suggested: four).

- **Full-bodied** is served with all red meats, lamb, and duck (suggested: four).

- **Semi-sweet** are served with dessert or after dinner, as they suppress appetite (suggested: two to three).

WHITES

After beer, white wines are most often ordered at bars, so keeping a good selection is well-advised:

- **Dry light-bodied** is often served with shellfish and seafood (suggested: two to four).

- **Semi-sweet** often accompanies a seafood meal (suggested: four).

- **Full-bodied** is often served with white meats and seafood (suggested: four).

- **Medium-bodied** is generally served with steak, roasted poultry, and fish such as salmon (suggested: two to four).

ROSÉ

- **Dry light-bodied** is generally served in place of dry white or red wines (suggested: one).

SPARKLING WINE

- **Dry** is served in place of dry white wines (suggested: one).

- **Semi-sweet** tends to be served in place of semi-sweet whites (suggested: one).

CHAMPAGNE

- **Dry** is served alone or with any food item (suggested: one).

- **Extra Dry (Brut)** is served alone or with any food item (suggested: one).

THE LANGUAGE OF WINE

Any bar manager who serves wine at his establishment quickly learns that wine comes with its own unique language. The successful bar manager will become familiar with this language. Being able to use the correct wine terms will make it easier to help customers who are confused about choices. Also, being able to use the language of wine will make the bar manager appear as an authoritative expert on the subject. There are a few basic wine terms that are useful for every bar manager and employee to know

WINE TERMINOLOGY	
Term	Definition
Aroma	Refers to the scent of a wine. Words such as "fruity" or "sweet" are often used to describe a wine's aroma. The smell of a wine is also referred to as its "nose."
Light	Refers to the wine's body and/or alcoholic content. Light wines have lower alcohol content.
Apertif	Usually a wine or fortified wine — served before meals.
Body	Refers to the fullness of the wine, its substantiality, which is described as light, medium, or full.
Color	Refers to the color of a wine. It is very useful to tell a customer about subtle variations in color. Details such as whether a white wine is a deeper yellow or a more clear color can often help a customer order.
Corked wine	Refers to wine that has been ruined due to an insufficient or flawed cork.
Dry	Refers to the lack of sweetness in the wine.
Semi-sweet	Refers to the underlying sweetness of a wine.
House wine	Refers to wine that is served by the carafe or the glass.
Jug wine	Refers to wine packaged and sold in large bottles or jugs. It is often less expensive than other types of wine.
Palate	Refers to the taste of a wine.

Ensure that every person on your staff can pronounce the different types of wines. Mispronunciation can affect the way customers see your bar. If a server cannot properly pronounce the name of a wine, it may confuse the customer. When hiring new staff, make sure that all new employees can pronounce the following most common wine types:

WINE PRONUNCIATION	
Term	Correct Pronunciation
Cabernet Sauvignon	Cah-bear-nay So-veen-yohn
Chardonnay	Shar-done-nay
Chenin Blanc	Chen-nahn Blohn
Fume Blanc	Foo-may Blohn
Johannisberg Riesling	Yo-han-iss-bairg Reez-ling
Merlot	Mare-low
Pinot noir	Pea-no Nwar
Sauvignon Blanc:	So-veen-yohn Blohn

You want to describe wine to customers in a way that is helpful and useful to them. There are several accepted terms to use when doing this:

Term	Definition
WINE TASTE CHARACTERISTICS DESCRIPTIONS	
Term	Definition
Bouquet	The complex fragrance that develops in a wine through fermentation and aging.
Buttery	Rich, creamy aroma and flavor. Some Chardonnays are described this way.
Finish	The flavor a wine leaves in the mouth after it is swallowed. You may talk about the main taste of the wine and then mention the finish for a more complete description of a wine.
Legs	When wine is swirled in its glass, it may leave a type of residue or some drops of wine on the sides of the glass. A wine with "good legs" leaves plenty of color on the sides of the glass as it is swirled.
Mature	Wine that is ready or aged enough to drink.
Bright	Fresh, fruity flavors.
Chewy	A wine that is heavy, tannic, and full-bodied.
Crisp	A wine that is noticeably acidic but pleasant. The acidity adds to the flavor.
Dense	A wine that is full-flavored or featuring a deep color.
Earthy	This word can suggest that a wine is clean and pleasant. In a negative sense, it can suggest a dirty wine that tastes funky. Because this word is vague, you may want to add other terms that clarify what you mean.
Fat	Full-bodied, high-alcohol.
Forward	Early maturing wine.
Fragrant	This word suggests that a wine has a floral aroma or bouquet.
Jammy	A sweet, concentrated fruit flavor.
Peppery	This word suggests a spicy, black pepper flavor.
Robust	Full-flavored, intense wine.
Round	Well-balanced, mellow, and full-bodied flavor.
Soft	Mellow and well balanced.
Aggressive	High tannins or acid taste. In many cases, this is a negative trait, but some customers prefer this taste.
Flat	This refers to an absence of flavor. Usually, flatness in wine is caused by lack of acidity.
Metallic	A wine with a tin-like flavor.
Off	A wine that is spoiled or faulty. It often clings to the teeth and may have an unpleasant vinegary or acidic taste.
Sharp	A wine with too much acid.

The wine merchant or salesperson will point out which wines will fit into various classifications. It is not crucial that you can taste the difference between each, but it is very useful for the bar manager to understand the basics about wine. It is also important that each group of wine is represented in your final list. As your bar expands, you may want to upgrade your selection to appeal to customers who are more knowledgeable about wines and more likely to order wines by the glass.

Wine is an interesting and fun hobby to pursue. If you are interested in learning more about it, there are a number of excellent books covering all phases of the subject. There are also a number of classes that can be taken to help you understand the basics of wine. Even going on a wine-tasting tour will help improve your general understanding of wines. At the very least, you will want to invest in a wine guide, which you can keep at your bar. You can refer to this guide to help you understand which wines to buy and distinguish which wines seem to be preferred by your customers.

A wine list must include wines of different prices and of different origins for each classification. There should be at least one moderate and one expensive bottle for each classification.

Although they have become increasingly popular, never use a wine that has a screw top. There is actually nothing wrong with the screw top itself, but it usually indicates a very cheap bottle of wine. The cork is traditionally used to allow the wine to "breathe" and it also imparts a specific flavor to the wine.

At least one domestic and one imported wine should be listed for each classification. Imported wines are usually more expensive. Wines from several different countries should be listed to give the customer the impression of a well-rounded list. Each of the wine-producing countries specializes in a particular wine variety. Your wine merchant or salesperson can point them out to you.

In addition to offering bottled wines, most bars/restaurants also sell a house or bulk wine, usually Chablis, Rosé, and/or Burgundy. Bulk wine may be purchased in gallon jugs or five-gallon casks. The wine is then portioned into and served from carafes. All the major California wineries produce a bulk wine. Because the wine is produced by a well-known winery and the price is often the lowest on the list, bulk wine tends to be a very popular item. House wine also seems like a good choice for many patrons who know little about wines but still wish to order wine from the menu.

 RDERING WINE

The procedures for ordering wine are identical to those used in purchasing liquor. These orders may be prepared at the same time, since the liquor distributor will likely carry most of the wines desired.

The computation of the beginning wine inventory is identical to that of liquor and food. The beginning inventory is the total dollar amount of the item prior to opening day. Based on this starting figure, you will then be able to project monthly wine costs.

When ordering wine, consider bottle size as well as type. Most wine comes in standard 750-mL bottles. It is also possible to order splits of wine, which come in bottles about half the size of a regular bottle — useful if you are offering a wine by the glass. Ordering some splits helps ensure that you can always offer customers a fresh and delicious glass of wine. Wines also come in larger bottles; it is economical to select these larger bottles when ordering your house wine.

PRICING WINE

Assessing the selling price of wines is similar to determining bar and menu prices. The first step is to compute a total portion cost for each item. Since wine is sold in the same unit as it is purchased, the total cost is the wholesale price at which each bottle was purchased. Although there are many other costs involved in serving wine — such as labor, wine books, glasses, corkscrews, carafes, decanters, utilities, and so forth — the only direct cost is the price of the bottle of wine. To compute the portion cost of bulk wine, simply multiply the cost per ounce by the portion size (glass or carafe).

A fair and customary markup for wine is 1.5 to 2.5 times the bottle cost or, on average, 40 percent of cost of sales. Price out each bottle using the formula.

Many diners assume that the price of the wine they order has been outrageously inflated. One issue in pricing wine is that the customer knows the retail price. If the perception is that your wine pricing is too high, customers may view all of your prices in that manner. To avoid the stigma of being over-priced, lower the prices on these bottles and make up the difference on other varieties and bulk wine.

Careful examination of market trends and conditions will help you purchase wine at substantial discounts. You can then pass on these discounts to your customers, while still maintaining the desired profit margin.

Wine is a good profit item; it will average approximately the same cost of sales as food, but the labor and operating costs needed to present it are substantially less. Therefore, a good representative wine list and a big effort on management's part to promote it is advocated.

CONTROLLING WINE

The manager must be present when a wine delivery is received to ensure it is accurate and accounted for. Wine must be locked away immediately after delivery. The manager must be the only person with the key to the storage area.

Wine should be issued by the bartender and restocked by the manager. Chilled wines may be stored in a cooler set at the proper temperature. Reds may be stored in a locked cabinet under the bar. Each serving area should be stocked with three of each type of white chilled wine and two types of each red.

When an order for wine is taken, the waiter goes to the bar and requests the bottle from the bartender. The bartender retrieves the bottle while the waiter fills out the ticket. The ticket should contain the following information: date, wine's name, table number, and the waiter's name. The bartender must check that information and price are correct before issuing the wine.

The hard paper part of the ticket remains with the bartender and will be used to verify the issuance. The carbon copy is attached to the customer's bill, ensuring that the wine will be charged for. If for some reason the waiter does not enter the amount on the customer's check, there will be a record of the bottle ordered from the bar.

The cashier will total the bill, ensuring that the price entered is correct. At the end of his shift, the bartender will deposit the ticket receipts with the liquor breakage form in a place designated by the manager.

The following morning, the bookkeeper will prepare and present to the manager an itemized list of the bottles sold, verified by the cashier. This list must match the receipts left by the bartender.

As the liquor is being restocked, the manager should also restock the wine used. After restocking is completed, there should be three chilled whites and two reds for every variety. Should this count not reconcile, recheck the itemization and the bartender's receipts. If everything reconciles, consider the possibility of theft.

Bulk wine may be issued by the gallon and portioned into carafes. The bartender will list the number of carafes prepared at the beginning of the shift and the number left at the end. This information may be recorded on the Liquor Used and Restocked Form. The carafes may then be treated as though they were full bottles.

For more information about bar and wine service, I would recommend the following books from Atlantic Publishing (**www.atlantic-pub.com**):

- *The Professional Bar & Beverage Manager's Handbook: How to Open and Operate a Financially Successful Bar, Tavern, and Nightclub: With Companion CD-ROM (Item # PBB-01).*

- *The Professional Bartender's Handbook: A Recipe for Every Drink Known — Including Tricks and Games to Impress Your Guests (Item # PBH-01).*

- *The Responsible Serving of Alcoholic Beverages: A Complete Staff Training Course for Bars, Restaurants, and Caterers: With Companion CD-ROM (Item # RSA-01).*

- *The Food Service Professional Guide To Controlling Liquor, Wine, & Beverage Costs (Item # FS8-01).*

- *The Food Service Professional Guide To Bar & Beverage Operation: Ensuring Success & Maximum Profit (Item # FS11-01).*

BIN CARD

Date: _____ Product: _____

Balance Brought Forward: _____ Bottle Size: _____

DATE	IN	OUT	TOTAL ON HAND

BIN CARD

Date: _____ Product: _____

Balance Brought Forward: _____ Bottle Size: _____

DATE	IN	OUT	TOTAL ON HAND

BIN CARD

Date: _____ Product: _____

Balance Brought Forward: _____ Bottle Size: _____

DATE	IN	OUT	TOTAL ON HAND

CHAPTER

MANAGEMENT OF
OPERATIONAL COSTS AND SUPPLIES

The preceding chapters described in detail only the costs that pertain directly to the product being sold. In computing the cost of menu items, only food costs were analyzed. When projecting the average cost of each cocktail, only the cost of the liquor poured and the miscellaneous expense were considered. The total wine cost was the wholesale price at which the bottle was purchased. Obviously, there are many other costs involved in presenting food, liquor, and wine products to the public. These additional costs are called operational costs. Operational costs are all of the non-food, non-liquor, and non-wine supplies that are used in preparing these items.

Labor and the cost of equipment are not considered direct operational expenses under this scenario. Labor is computed as a separate cost. Equipment is a capital expenditure and may be depreciated over several years. The operational supplies and costs considered here are only those products that must be continuously renewed each month as they are used up, lost, or broken.

Operational supplies and cost are divided into separate categories so that each may be broken down and analyzed. A cost for each operational category will be projected at the end of each month. Accurately setting up each category is crucial, as this information will be used in projecting budgets and profit and loss statements.

OPERATIONAL CATEGORIES

The following pages list each operational category and some examples of the type of supplies that belong to each. Based on the examples given, list on the Operational Order Form and the Operational Inventory Form all of the operational supplies the restaurant will need. An example of each form can be found at the end of this chapter. Separate each page by category and clearly label it in the space provided on the form.

Always keep the order and inventory forms up to date. Whenever a new product is ordered, enter the new item on both forms. When it comes time to do the weekly order and monthly inventory you will not miss anything. Certain items may fit into two categories because they are used in several areas of the restaurant. Place the item in the category where it is used the most. It will not affect the cost projection as long as the item is listed in only one category.

CHINA AND UTENSILS

All plates, coffee cups, saucers, silverware, etc.

WNA combines style, quality, and performance with the widest variety of single-service tableware. The company also offer cutlery, straws, and stirrers in some locations. And when you require custom products, WNA has the flexibility and knowledge to offer print and packaging solutions. From Concept to Completion®, WNA strives to enhance your brand image. Visit **www.wna-inc.com/products/custom/index.php** for the full line of disposable and one use products.

GLASSWARE

All bar glasses, wineglasses, water glasses, carafes, decanters, etc.

KITCHEN SUPPLIES

All of the non-food materials used in preparing food items, such as kitchen utensils, spatulas, scales, trays, measuring cups, skewers, foil, plastic wrap, fry-o-lator filter paper, etc.

BAR SUPPLIES

All of the miscellaneous supplies used at the bar, such as mixing spoons, straws, swords, napkins, pour spouts, corkscrews, etc.

DINING ROOM SUPPLIES

All of the miscellaneous supplies used in the dining room, such as candles, matches, menus, salt and pepper shakers, sugar bowls, tent-card holders, coffeepots, creamers, flower vases, etc.

Cal Mil Products offers a full line of dining room essentials for your restaurant. These items include display shelves, silver ware containers, salt and pepper shakers, and much more. Visit **www.calmil.com** for the full selection and for custom quotes.

Browne-Halco offers a wide selection of cookware and bakeware accessories. These products are invaluable in your recipe preparation. The full line of products can be seen at **www.halco.com** or you can call 888-289-1005.

CLEANING SUPPLIES

All of the miscellaneous cleaning supplies used by both the staff and the maintenance company, such as soap, paper towels, chemicals, vacuum bags, garbage bags, etc.

OFFICE SUPPLIES

All of the supplies used in the offices, such as tape, rubber bands, paper, stationery, etc.

UNIFORMS

Encompasses the cost of purchasing employee uniforms: aprons, smocks, hats, pants, dresses, etc.

Aprons Etc. offers a selection of aprons, chef, and dining room uniforms. Aprons, Etc. originally began as a manufacturer/supplier to retail outlets and expanded its business by adapting practices highly suited to the advertising specialty market. In the 19-plus years of operation, the major growth of the company has been through the development of strong relationships within the ad specialty trade and by growing a niche in the textile promotional market. The company's strengths are in their production time, creativity, quality well-priced promotional products, and professional and courteous customer service. Visit **www.apronsetc.com** for all the items Aprons Etc. offers.

Imagen offers a fine selection of restaurant uniforms. Their uniform selection can be seen at **http://anncarol.trustpass.alibaba.com/product/11285659/Restaurant_Uniforms.html**. Fully lined jackets and pants are available in a 55% polyester/45% wool blend or your selection of fabric composition and weight. Ask for price with your fabric selection. View more styles on the web site. They will make ten uniforms or tens of thousands for your restaurant needs.

LAUNDRY AND LINEN

It includes all napkins, tablecloths, kitchen towels, bar towels, and soap purchased by the restaurant from a laundry service or for an in-house system. It does not include the cost of services of a laundry company, as this is computed separately.

It is no coincidence that the Hilden Group is one of the world-leaders in the table linen industry. An in-depth understanding of the latest interior design trends has helped the company to develop a range of table linens to meet every individual need. Visit **www.hilden.co.uk** for more information.

ORDERING OPERATIONAL SUPPLIES

All of the procedures for storing, ordering, and receiving food, liquor, and wine also apply to operational supplies. Ordering operational supplies must be carefully thought out. Too large of an inventory (back-stock) will tie up capital at expensive interest rates. One careless bus person or waiter who drops a tray of glasses can destroy what little reserve you have, so there must be a large enough inventory to cover the unexpected. One to two cases of each item in the storeroom should suffice. Portion control items such as scales, scoops, and ladles are often difficult to obtain; when you find a supplier that has the size and type you desire, order several and keep them in reserve. A common excuse for not portion-controlling products is that the employee does not have access to the right type of utensil. It is management's responsibility to provide the employees with proper tools to do their jobs.

Allow a lead time of several weeks when ordering china. Your distributor probably does not stock all the types of china and must purchase specially from the manufacturer. Insufficient quantities of place settings will result in extra work, slow service, and a slow turnover in the dining room. Always maintain an adequate supply of stock out of the storeroom. The storeroom should be a separate room or closet and the manager must be the only person with a key. Do not create a situation where it is easier for an employee to run to the storeroom for a new case of water glasses than to help the dishwasher catch up.

BEGINNING INVENTORY

Computing beginning inventory is similar to computing the beginning amount for food, liquor, and wine. However, there is one difference. The beginning inventory amount for each operational category is the dollar amount that is in storage when the restaurant is totally set up, meaning that all the tables are set and there is plenty of stock in the kitchen and bar. The reason for this beginning inventory is that operational supplies are projected for each month. The cost of setting up the restaurant is considered a one-time start-up cost. Operational costs are measures of how well you controlled these costs following start-up. Separating this start-up cost may have some additional tax advantages. Your accountant will be able to advise you on this possibility.

OPERATIONAL ORDER FORM

Item	Build to Amount	Date										

OPERATIONAL INVENTORY FORM

Item	Size	Quantity				Total	Cost	Extension

CHAPTER

COMPUTERS AND
FOOD SERVICE OPERATIONS

Computers are here and integrated into every facet of the food-service industry: tracking sales and purchases, tracking inventory, comparing prices, maintaining ledgers and payrolls, developing menus, and minimizing food waste. According to a study commissioned by 13 U.S. and Canadian food-related associations, implementation of an efficient computer-based food-service response program could trim an estimated $14.3 billion in costs annually from the food-service industry in the two countries alone.

The resulting program, Efficient Foodservice Response, creates a paperless kitchen, linking buyers to distributors via the Internet. Food and supplies are ordered online and paid for by electronic transfer. Participating vendors tag goods with bar codes that are read by laser scanner. At the food-service operation, information is immediately stored in an in-house computer and the computer's inventory database is instantly updated. Benefits are across the board: precise inventory management, timely deliveries, reduced warehouse levels, and increased kitchen work space.

Let us take a closer look at how computer hardware and software will serve and benefit the food-service industry and glance at what options and features you might have.

The official definition of "PC" from **www.pcwebopedia.com**:

> *Short for personal computer or IBM PC. The first personal computer produced by IBM was called the PC and increasingly the term PC came to mean IBM or IBM-compatible personal computers, to the exclusion of other types of personal computers, such as Macintoshes.*

In recent years, the term PC has become more and more difficult to pin down. In general it applies to any personal computer based on an Intel microprocessor or on an Intel compatible microprocessor. For nearly every other component, including the operating system, there are several options, all of which fall under the rubric "PC."

Common questions are: What kind of computer should I get? How much RAM? How fast should the CPU be? Should I get Pentium or Athlon? What brand and what size monitor? What type of video card? Should I get a dial-up connection, DSL, or cable modem? What are the best accounting packages for the computer?

These are difficult questions and today's answer will be out of date in six months. The best advice on what type of computer system to purchase for your restaurant is, simply, to get the most powerful computer system that is within your budget. Here are some considerations:

- **CPU speed.** The CPU is the engine of your computer; the faster the engine, the greater its performance. I recommend a processor built for future growth capacity. The fastest your budget will allow is recommended.

- **RAM.** RAM is the temporary storage place for all information on your computer. The fastest RAM is the best to get and I recommend nothing less than 256 Megabytes (MB) on each computer; at least 512 MB RAM per workstation is preferable.

- **Operating system.** I recommend Microsoft Windows XP Professional Edition. This system provides stable operating platforms and superior networking capabilities.

- **Monitor.** I recommend 17" or bigger. (19" is my preferred standard.) You have a lot of choices in brands, as well as flat screen and LCD-screen varieties. I prefer 19" flat screen or 17" or larger LCD monitors.

- **Graphics card.** For business applications I recommend a graphics accelerator card with a minimum of 40 MB of RAM. There are dozens to choose from depending on the application, with chipsets from various manufacturers. My favorite for its great business and gaming performance is any card based on the Geforce Chipset.

- **Athlon vs. Pentium.** Both are world-class processors. There are die-hard fans of each.

- **Dial-up, DSL, or cable.** If you need high-speed connections, you want DSL or cable (if they are available in your area). Dial-up is the least costly but slowest type of connection. For the average Web browser, dial-up is usually sufficient. For power users, I recommend DSL or cable. Note: If you use a broadband connection, invest in a DSL/cable router or a good firewall software application.

- **Networking.** If you have more than one computer you will want to network your computers, allowing you to share programs, files, printers, Internet connections, and more. There are dozens of networking systems available, including standard wired networking, phone-line networks, and wireless networks. There are advantages to each. Standard wired networking is the fastest, but requires extensive cable installation in your building. Phone-line networks offer good performance, low cost, and use the existing phone lines in your restaurant to make network connections. Note: You can still talk on your phone while your network is being used. Wireless networking is the most costly, but highly versatile. It requires no cable installation and is very effective. The major advantage of wireless is you are not limited by phone lines or network cable. You can take your wireless laptop anywhere in your restaurant and maintain your network connection.

- **Platform.** Essentially Windows vs. Macintosh. A few years ago DOS-based systems would have been in the mix, but those software applications are antiquated by current industry standards. The choice is yours to make. Obviously, your hardware preference will select your software platform. In my opinion, the Windows-based operating systems and Windows' overall available software packages and long-term industry support make it the best choice.

F RONT-OF-THE-HOUSE COMPUTER SYSTEMS

POINT-OF-SALE SYSTEMS

The most widely used technology in the food-service industry is the touch screen, or POS (point-of-sale), system. The POS system is an offshoot of the electronic cash register. Touch screen POS systems were introduced to the food-service industry in the mid-1980s and have penetrated 90 percent of restaurants nationwide. From fine-dining establishments to fast-food, the touch screen is effortless. Understanding the numbers collected by a POS system will give the operator more control over inventory, bar revenues, labor scheduling, overtime, customer traffic, and service. Understanding POS ultimately clarifies the bottom line, knocking guesswork out of the equation.

A POS system is comprised of two parts: the hardware, or equipment, and the software — the computer program that runs the system. This system allows wait staff to key in their orders as soon as the customers give them. Additional keys are available for particular options and specifications — "rare," "medium-rare," and "well-done." Some systems prompt the wait staff to ask additional questions when the item is ordered, such as, "Would you like butter, sour cream, or chives with the baked potato?" Some will suggest a side dish or a compatible wine.

The order is sent through a cable to printers located throughout the restaurant: at the bar and in the kitchen and office. All orders must be printed before they are prepared, ensuring good control. When a server has completed the ordering, a guest check can be printed and later presented. Most POS systems allow certain discounts and require manager control over others. Charge cards, cash, and checks can be processed separately and then reports can be generated by payment type.

Some benefits of using a POS system:

- Increases sales and accounting information.
- Custom tracking.
- Reports wait staff's sales and performance.
- Reports menu-item performance.
- Reports inventory usage.
- Credit card purchases.
- Accurate addition on guest checks.
- Prevents incorrect items from being ordered.
- Prevents confusion in the kitchen.
- Reports possible theft of money and inventory.

- Records employee timekeeping.

- Reports menu-sales breakdown for preparation and menu forecasting.

- Reduces time spent walking to kitchen and bar.

As the labor market continues to diminish, touch screen POS systems will become necessary. It has been predicted that in the next few years customers may even place their own orders. Terminals will be simply turned around. During peak seasonal periods, ordering food may be like pumping your own gas; customers will key in their own selections and then slide their credit cards through to pay.

Many POS systems have been enhanced to include comprehensive home delivery, guest books, online reservations, frequent-diner modules, and fully integrated systems with real-time inventory, integrated caller ID, accounting, labor scheduling, payroll, menu analysis, purchasing and receiving, cash management, and reports. Up-and-coming enhancements and add-ons include improved functionality across the Internet, centralized functionality enabling "alerts" to be issued to managers, and voice-recognition POS technology.

$\mathbb{S}$ TAND-ALONE SOFTWARE APPLICATIONS

While there are literally dozens of software packages available to assist the restaurant manager, this discussion will concentrate on what I consider to be the current market leaders. It will provide some insight as to how they work, what they can do for your restaurant, and what benefits you will realize if you include them in your restaurant-management practices. These systems are what I refer to as "stand alone," as they are not part of a POS system:

CHEFTEC

ChefTec is an integrated software program with recipe and menu costing, inventory control, and nutritional analysis.

- **Recipe and menu costing.** Store, scale, and size an unlimited number of recipes. Write recipe procedures with culinary spell-checker. Instantly analyze recipe and menu costs by portion or yield. Update prices and change ingredients in every recipe with the touch of a button. Cost out bids for catering functions. Attach photos, diagrams, and videos to bids or add pictures of plate lay-out to recipes for consistency.

- **Nutritional analysis.** Preloaded with USDA information. Add your own items. Calculate nutritional value for recipes and menus. Provide accurate, legal information on "low-fat," "low-salt," etc. Print out "Nutrition Facts" labels. The nutritional-analysis module will get a quick and accurate analysis of nutritional values for up to 5,000 most-commonly-used ingredients. Allows you to add your own specialty items. Calculate nutritional values for your recipes and menu items. See at a glance which menu items are low-fat, low-calorie, etc.

- **Inventory control.** Preloaded inventory list of 1,900 commonly used ingredients with unlimited capacity for adding additional ingredients. Import purchases from online vendors' ordering systems. Track fluctuating food costs. Compare vendor pricing. See impact of price increases on recipes. Automate ordering with par values. Use handheld devices for inventory. Generate custom reports. The inventory control module allows you to track rising food costs automatically. Compare vendor pricing at the touch of a button, from purchases or bids. Enter invoices quickly using the "Auto-Populate" feature. Generate customized reports on purchases, price variances, bids and credits, physical inventory, and ordering and maintenance of par levels. Lists ingredients in different languages (Spanish, French, German and others).

- **ChefTec PDA is also available.** ChefTec is available from Atlantic Publishing Company (www.atlantic-pub.com or 800-814-1132, Item CTC-CS).

IPRO

IPro is a comprehensive restaurant inventory, recipe costing and food cost control software. Studies have shown that food service establishments using IPro reduce food cost by 5% to 10% of sales (i.e. from 35% to 30%). IPro has reduced food and liquor costs as much as 25%, doubled profits and saved businesses from going broke. This program was written by food service professionals for food service professionals, it features:

- Food and beverage cost control to help monitor and reduce food and beverage costs.

- Inventory tracking and reporting which can assist in detecting theft, overportioning and creeping vendor prices.

- Ordering and purchase history so help you reduce stock levels and order more accurately.

- Recipe costing, resizing and write-up which will assist in costing and re-costing recipes as ingredient costs change.

- Menu sales and profit analysis to determine menu item profit contribution and other sales analyses.

Here are some additional benefits of IPro:

- **Total Recall.** IPro stores all original details so you can report, compare, reconstruct and re-analyze any prior time period with total accuracy. See an entire year's figures or compare this New Year's to the last. Other software limits you to the current and prior period.

- **List Processing.** This is important because inventory control is almost nothing but working with lists for gathering data. IPro gives you complete control over worklists: their contents (which items), use (counting stock, sales, etc.) and order (alphabetical, numerical, etc.). You can copy, add and merge lists. You can fill them automatically with build-to-par quantities, on-hand counts from bar code readers and sales from cash registers. You can work on lists, put them away, get them out again, correct errors, update costs, post and unpost them.

- **Custom Reports.** IPro lets you customize and keep the settings for any number of new reports on file. You can retrieve reports by name.

- **Choice of Cost Systems.** Use either "Last Cost" for simplicity or "True Weighted Average Costs" for accuracy. IPro always uses correct values that reflect the mix of stock purchased at different costs. If your stock is from three shipments of different costs and quantities, that's fine. Other software can't do it right because they only use the last cost paid and can't be as accurate.

- **Custom measures.** IPro lets you define any and every measure: how you buy, count, use, make and sell items. Use pinches, slices, teaspoons, cups, globs and wedges. Give them weight, volume or unit values.

- **Inventory and recipes in one file.** IPro combines inventory and recipes into one file to effectively handle "batch recipes" such as sauces, dressings and soups. Batch recipes need to be recipe files and inventory files at the same time because making batches makes shelf stock that should be tracked.

IPro is available from Atlantic Publishing Company (**www.atlantic-pub.com** or 800-814-1132, Item IPR-02).

QUICKBOOKS

My favorite accounting package is QuickBooks by Intuit. QuickBooks is rich in features, including built-in remote-access capabilities and Web interfaces. QuickBooks is available at **www.quickbooks.com**. Another popular account package is Peachtree, available at **www.peachtree.com**.

DESKTOP PUBLISHING APPLICATIONS AND IDEAS

Desktop publishing applications allow you to print your own customer and/or employee newsletters, table tents, menus, business cards, employee-of-the-month certificates, customer gift certificates, advertising posters, employee manuals, wine lists, catering and banquet menus, office stationery, and newsletters. Some popular desktop publishing applications include: Adobe InDesign, Adobe Illustrator, QuarkXpress, and Microsoft Publisher 2007.

 # ONLINE RESERVATION SYSTEMS

An online reservation system can be simple or advanced. A fully functional online reservation system can be free. All you need is an active Web site and a reservation form. Your site visitor fills out the form requesting a reservation. You set up an auto-responder to respond to the site visitor stating that she will be confirmed within a reasonable amount of time, say two hours. You receive the reservation request by e-mail, confirm that you can accommodate the request, and then reply back to the person by e-mail or phone. Total cost: zero. Customer satisfaction: superior. That is the basic, no cost approach. There are dozens of reputable software packages and companies that can provide your on-line reservation system. These FRS (Foodline Reservations Systems) enable you to do the following:

- Accept reservations anytime — day or night.

- Track guests' preferences to provide enhanced customer service.

- Use the power of direct marketing to build guest traffic and offer premium services to your most frequent customers.

- Check reservation status from any Internet-connected computer.

- Network all computers and reservation systems in a restaurant group.

- Choose to manage all of your reservations or to put just a few of your tables online.

An Internet search will yield dozens of software packages and consultants who can assist you in finding the right one for your on-line reservation system.

THE FUTURE OF COMPUTERS IN FOOD-SERVICE

The food-service operation of the future will most likely resemble what it does today — with integrated software and hardware solutions to increase productivity, eliminate waste, and increase profits.

The POS computer will allow operators to closely monitor inventory and costs. Web-site reservations, marketing, and e-commerce will increase the return on investment in a Web presence, bringing in more guests than ever imaginable. Diners may enter their own menu selections into laptop POS systems right from their tables. Patrons will be able to pull up a screen showing all menu items, then select dishes with a push of a button. Consumers will also be able to customize meals and beverages — single malt scotch or blended, margarine or butter, salted or unsalted, medium-rare or well-done, spicy or mild. Ultimately, the restaurant will be a paperless operation.

THE EFFECTIVE USE OF E-MAIL

E-mail is a system that enables a computer user to exchange messages with other computer users within a communications network (Internet). To use e-mail, your computer must be linked to the Internet via a modem and phone line, cable modem, DSL connection, or other network connection. E-mail services are provided at no cost from your Internet service provider and they come with any domain names you purchase for Web sites. Careful consideration should be given to your choice of domain names and/or e-mail addresses, as these represent your company. For example, The Silvermine Tavern, a New England country inn and restaurant in Norwalk, Connecticut, purchased the domain name **www.silverminetavern.com**. Purchasing a domain name that directly represents your restaurant is an outstanding opportunity to gain the use of the corresponding e-mail addresses. In the case of The Silvermine Tavern, innkeeper@silverminetavern.com is one of their primary e-mail addresses, clearly stating to the casual observer that any e-mail sent to this address will be directed to the innkeeper of The Silvermine Tavern. I will discuss Web sites and why they are critical to every restaurant later in this chapter.

WHY USE E-MAIL INSTEAD OF THE POST OFFICE OR THE TELEPHONE

There are two reasons:

- **Convenience.** You send your message when it is convenient for you, and your recipient responds at his convenience.

- **Cost.** No more toll telephone calls. No more "telephone tag." You can send dozens of e-mails throughout the world, simultaneously; they will be delivered in mere seconds and they cost nothing. Communicate with all your purveyors or employees with one written message for free.

Sending e-mail is similar to sending mail through the U.S. Postal Service, but there are several important differences:

- E-mail is faster.

- E-mail is free.

- E-mail is simple to use.

- E-mail requires a password and is private. (Note: I highly recommend utilizing a virus-scanning program for all incoming and outgoing e-mails)

- E-mail is very fast, permanent, and unforgiving. Make sure you said what you wanted to say before you hit the send button. Once sent, it is too late to get it back.

- E-mail can be sent to many people at the same time.

To receive e-mail, as with postal letters, you must have an address (**sales@atlantic-pub.com**, for example). There are many Web sites that offer you free Web-based e-mail, such as **www.excite.com** or **www.yahoo.com**.

PROPER E-MAIL ETIQUETTE

- **Avoid flaming.** A flame is a nasty, personal attack on somebody for something he or she has written, said, or done.

- **Be unambiguous.** If you are responding to a message, include only the relevant part of the original message. Make sure you refer to the original message's contents. Always include a descriptive subject line for your message. If responding, your subject line should be the same as the original's, preceded by "RE:".

- **Write clearly and carefully.** Your words may come back to haunt you. Read carefully what you receive to make sure that you are not misunderstanding the message. Read carefully what you send, to make sure that your message will not be misunderstood. Avoid cluttering your messages with excessive emphasis. DO NOT USE ALL CAPS.

COMMON E-MAIL MISTAKES

- Typing the message in the subject line instead of in the body of the message.

- Forgetting that what you write, thinking it is funny or harmless, can be misinterpreted at the other end.

- Not signing off before leaving the computer (allowing others to send e-mail from your e-mail address).

- Not checking e-mail often, thus missing something important.

- Forgetting your password.

- Sending a message to the wrong e-mail address.

- Using "reply to all" which will send your message to everyone the sender sent the message to, rather than just the sender.

- Spam filters and quarantine features. While these features (typically a preference in your e-mail program) are very useful in blocking unwanted e-mail, they can also block important e-mail. Be sure to check your "junk-mail" folders periodically and use these features with care.

THE INTERNET AND THE WORLD WIDE WEB

The Internet is a global network of networks enabling computers of all kinds to directly and transparently communicate and share services throughout much of the world. Because the Internet is an enormously valuable, enabling capability for so many people and organizations, it also constitutes a shared global resource of information and knowledge and a means of collaboration and cooperation among countless diverse communities.

The Internet was originally conceived by the Advanced Research Projects Agency (ARPA) of the U.S. government in 1969 and was first known as the ARPANET. The original aim was to create a network that would allow users of a research computer at one university to "talk to" research computers at other universities. A side benefit of ARPANET's design was that, because messages could be routed or rerouted in more than one direction, the network could continue to function even if parts of it were destroyed in the event of a military attack or other disaster.

Today, the Internet is a public, cooperative, and self-sustaining facility accessible to hundreds of millions of people worldwide. Physically, the Internet uses a portion of the total resources of the currently existing public telecommunication networks. Technically, what distinguishes the Internet is its use of a set of protocols for the transmission of data.

For even the most novice Web users, e-mail has practically replaced the Postal Service as the primary means of communication between coworkers, family, friends, and business acquaintances. E-mail is the most widely used application on the Net.

You can also "stream" live video feeds from any computer with a Web cam, as well as utilize "Instant Messenger" and "chat" services. E-mail use is critical in the restaurant and hospitality industry. It is second only to the telephone as a means of communication between you and your potential customers and clients. I will talk later in the chapter about naming conventions in e-mail and the benefits of maintaining an active Web site to promote your business.

The most widely used part of the Internet is the World Wide Web. The unique, underlying language of the World Wide Web is hypertext, which is the language a Web browser reads then interprets into what you see in your browser window when you view a Web page. On most Web sites, certain words or phrases appear in text of a different color than the rest; often this text is also underlined. These are known as hyperlinks, or links.

When you click on one of these words or phrases, you will be transferred to the site or page that is relevant to the word or phrase. Sometimes there are buttons, images, or portions of images that are "clickable." If you move the pointer over a spot on a Web site and the pointer changes into a hand, it indicates that you can click and be transferred to another site, a "hot spot."

Using the Web, you have access to millions of pages of information. Web site viewing is done with a Web browser, the most popular of which are Microsoft Internet Explorer and Netscape Navigator.

DO YOU NEED A WEB SITE?

In a word, YES.

If your restaurant already has a Web site, you are already reaping the benefits of being online. Each day, the Internet reaches millions of people who use it for work, play, and research. The Web is the best marketing tool in the world; it allows your restaurant to be visible anywhere in the world. New services, such as digital cities, online city restaurant guides, and other food-service sites, will increase your Web site and restaurant visibility to levels unheard of. This type of free marketing promotions is available to Web-savvy restaurateurs. The Internet is a powerful tool, one that can be put to work for your restaurant.

Use the following checklist of potential advantages to see for yourself whether a Web site is right for you. Place a check mark next to each ability that would serve your business:

❑ Additional, global, sales, and marketing tool.

❑ Gather marketing information.

❑ Analyze and evaluate marketing information.

❑ Lower your phone expenses.

❑ Establish more frequent communications with customers.

❑ Establish more meaningful communications with customers.

❑ Reduce fax costs.

❑ Reduce courier costs.

❑ Deliver electronically encoded resources around the world.

❑ Supplement employee training through electronic updates and bulletins.

❑ Broadcast press releases.

❑ Communicate to people who are presently not available.

❑ Submit invoices and expenses more quickly.

❑ Reduce international communications costs and improve response time.

❑ Ease of collaboration with colleagues.

❑ Establish contact with potential "strategic partners" worldwide.

❑ Identify and solicit prospective employees.

❑ Provide immediate access to your catalog.

❑ Permit customers to place orders electronically.

❑ Reduce costs of goods sold through reduced personnel.

The Web is everywhere. You see Web sites promoted in the mass media — on commercials, on billboards, and in magazines. You even hear them on the radio. Web site addresses are the wave of the future — today. The Web is the most economical way to communicate with a worldwide audience. Can you think of any other tool that lets you advertise or sell products to a worldwide market, 24 hours a day, for a minimal monetary investment? The possibilities are endless — the return on investment, enormous.

Here is a brief list of reasons you need to have a presence on the World Wide Web:

- **It is the world's largest communications medium.** The World Wide Web provides maximum exposure and maximum potential to communicate with a worldwide audience, 24 hours a day. There are an estimated 285 million people online, from nearly every country. 48 percent of users use the Net one to four times a day; 39 percent use it more. One-in-five Web users use their browsers more than 35 hours a week.

- **Instantaneous access to information.** A Web site can be browsed at any time — day or night. Information can be downloaded, e-mails transmitted, supplies and services bought and sold.

- **Virtually unlimited potential.** There are no time, physical, or geographical limits in cyberspace and over 62 percent of Web users have bought something online.

- **The user is in control.** Web users may choose where they want to "go," when they want to go there, and stay for as little or as long as they choose.

- **Visual marketing.** Technology provides incredible ways to convey information about your business, products, and services.

WHAT TO PUT ON YOUR WEB SITE

The Silvermine Tavern (**www.silverminetavern.com**) had a Web site developed by Gizmo Graphics Web Design (**www.gizwebs.com**). The Silvermine went from no Web presence to a lively, active Web presence. What kind of information can a restaurant put on the Web? Here is a brief list of what the Silvermine Tavern has used their Web site for:

- **A picture is truly worth a thousand words.** The Silvermine Tavern has carefully selected high-quality images and photos to truly "sell" the beauty of their inn and restaurant.

- **News, events, and specials.** The opportunities are endless. The Silvermine Tavern promotes weekly jazz events, monthly Wine Dinners, and holiday dining specials. They have even developed Web-based distribution lists from their long list of loyal customers and use e-mail to promote the monthly and weekly events.

- **Menus.** These are not just basic menus, but menus with full-color photographs of each entrée.

- **Directions.** They have a link to **Mapquest.com** right on their site. You enter your address and you get door-to-door directions from your home to The Silvermine Tavern.

- **Products for sale.** The Silvermine Tavern operates a unique country store. They sell products from that store over the Web for a minimal investment and open up their store to millions more potential customers who visit the store "virtually" through the World Wide Web.

- **History.** Every restaurant has a history. Sometimes a history is truly unique — a story worth telling. Your Web site can do this for you. The Silvermine Tavern has gone a step further by not only giving you a rich history, but also a virtual walking tour through historic Norwalk, Connecticut.

- **Area attractions.** Sell your restaurant and your local community to the Web site visitor. The opportunities are endless. Be imaginative.

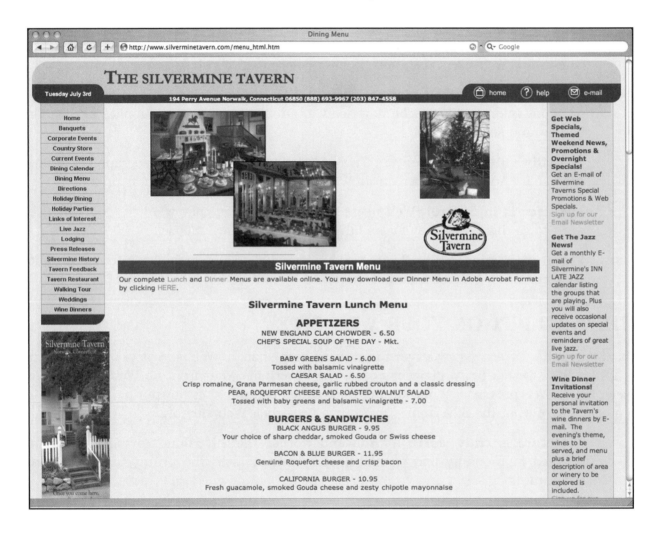

The browser window shows:

Current Events

http://www.silverminetavern.com/currentevents.htm

THE SILVERMINE TAVERN

Tuesday July 3rd

194 Perry Avenue Norwalk, Connecticut 06850 (888) 693-9967 (203) 847-4558

home | help | e-mail

Navigation menu:
Home
Banquets
Corporate Events
Country Store
Current Events
Dining Calendar
Dining Menu
Directions
Holiday Dining
Holiday Parties
Links of Interest
Live Jazz
Lodging
Press Releases
Silvermine History
Tavern Feedback
Tavern Restaurant
Walking Tour
Weddings
Wine Dinners

SILVERMINE TAVERN CURRENT EVENTS

Recent Happenings at the Tavern

Victor S. Navasky former editor of The Nation magazine with Clair Nathan of the Columbia University Alumni Club. Navasky, a journalism professor at Columbia, was speaking to the club at their June meeting about his new book, A Matter of Opinion.

Right sidebar:

Get Web Specials, Themed Weekend News, Promotions & Overnight Specials! Get an E-mail of Silvermine Taverns Special Promotions & Web Specials. Sign up for our Email Newsletter

Get The Jazz News! Get a monthly E-mail of Silvermine's INN LATE JAZZ calendar listing the groups that are playing. Plus you will also receive occasional updates on special events and reminders of great live jazz. Sign up for our Email Newsletter

Wine Dinner Invitations! Receive your personal invitation to the Tavern's wine dinners by E-mail. The evening's theme, wines to be served, and menu plus a brief description of area or winery to be explored is included.

HOW TO GET AN EFFECTIVE WEB SITE

The choice is entirely yours. There are thousands of Web development companies throughout the world. Consider companies specializing in the food-service and hospitality industries. I recommend Gizmo Graphics Web Design of Land O' Lakes, Florida (**www.gizwebs.com**). They have put together a solid, high-quality, low-cost package exclusively for restaurants. It offers a comprehensive cradle-to-grave cost approach, which includes all annual hosting fees, domain registrations, and annual support.

Some words of caution:

- **Do not overlook the little details.**

- **A Web site can be a significant investment.** Hire a professional if you want professional results.

- **Keep in mind the "hidden costs."** Most developers do not include Web site hosting, domain-name registration and renewal, support, and continued development services after site completion. (Note: The restaurant development package at Gizmo Graphics Web Design is all-inclusive.)

- **Make sure you promote your site.** A site is worthless if no one knows it exists. Search-engine registration is a critical part of a successful Web site. My favorite search engine is **Google.com**. If you navigate to **Google.com** and type in "Restaurants, Norwalk,

CT"—guess what the first listing is—the Silvermine Tavern. While they are certainly not the only restaurant in Norwalk, Connecticut, they have used search-engine ranking and effective Web-development services to promote themselves.

A Web site is an investment, not an expense. In the current marketplace, every restaurant must have a Web presence or it is missing the boat.

For additional computer usage information, I recommend the following books from Atlantic Publishing (**www.atlantic-pub.com/internet.htm**):

- *The Complete Guide to E-mail Marketing: How to Create Successful, Spam-Free Campaigns to Reach Your Target Audience and Increase Sales,* Item #GEM-01, $24.95.

- *How to Use the Internet to Advertise, Promote, and Market Your Business or Web Site —With Little or No Money,* Item # HIA-01, $24.95.

CHAPTER

MANAGING THE
DINING ROOM AND WAITSTAFF

I n many countries, waiting on tables is considered an honorable profession. There are even schools to educate people to become "professional" servers. In the United States for the most part, it is not the case. In many instances you will be interviewing a student, working mother, or someone else looking for part-time employment or in-between employment. Investing in training and education can reduce turnover and increase productivity. Technology is important in training, but getting through to your employees is even more important. The layout of the dining room and the type of food service affect the duties assigned to wait staff and the exact manner in which these duties are performed. However, certain fundamental duties that pertain to the serving of food are common to all food operations.

The precise dining-room procedures may differ between one food-service unit and another. A waitperson's efficiency is measured by the careful, complete manner their in which duties are performed — before meal service and customer's order, and after meal service and the customer has left the table.

PRE-SERVICE DUTIES

Generally each member of the wait staff is assigned to a group of tables. These sections are known as "stations." A waitperson may keep a reserve supply of silver, glasses, china, and linen at a side table and serve from it. Reserve supplies of condiments, ice, water, and butter are often kept on the table as well as a thermos of hot coffee. There is space for the serving tray either on the serving table or on a separate tray rack.

The waitperson should properly set tables with clean linen, polished silver, shining glassware, and spotless china before service is given. Tables should be promptly cleared after service and reset as needed. When a side table is used, the waitperson is responsible for having a supply of extra serving equipment and the required foods and stock supplies, arranged in an orderly manner on a clean surface.

The housekeeping duties of the waitperson at the serving station include dusting and cleaning chairs, tables, and window ledges, as well as cleaning spilled food and debris off the floor . In many establishments a bus person helps to keep the station in order and the side table supplied. The wait staff member should notify the bus person when supplies are needed and when her services are required.

 ETTING THE TABLE

THE COVER

The cover is the space — about 24 inches by 15 inches — where one place is set with china, silver, linen, and glass. An imaginary line may be drawn defining this area to assist in laying the cover (see FIGURE 1).

LINEN

FIGURE I

Linen is another item you can purchase or rent. While most rental companies do offer more unusual colors and patterns, for the most part these are more expensive and they have fewer in stock. If you expect that you will need these types of linens often, consider purchasing them. If you do purchase linens, you have to launder and iron them after every use.

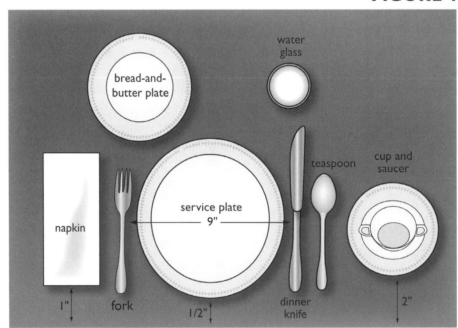

"Table Cover Setup" using 16" x 12" doily, showing space allowance for a 24" cover arrangement.

A silence pad, if used, should be placed evenly on the table so that the edges do not hang down below the tablecloth. The tablecloth is laid over the silence pad or undercover or directly over the table with the center fold up and equidistant from the edges of the table. All four corners should fall an even distance from the floor. The cloth should be free from wrinkles, holes, and stains.

Your tablecloths need to cover buffet and dining tables and have plenty of length to cover the sides. The following chart provides standard linen sizes.

CORRECT LINEN SIZES	
LINEN SIZE (INCHES)	TABLE SIZE
44 x 44	32 inch round
54 x 54	48 – 50 inch round
64 x 64	60 inch round
72 x 72	68 inch round
81 x 81	77 inch round
90 x 90	84 inch round
44 x 64	5 foot rectangle
54 x 72	5 foot rectangle
54 x 96	7 foot rectangle
54 x 120	8 foot rectangle
54 x 144	8 foot rectangle
72 x 144	10 foot rectangle

DINNER NAPKINS

Dinner napkins are 20 inches by 20 inches and lunch napkins are 18 inches by 18 inches. The colors most frequently used on buffet tables are white, pale yellow, pale pink, blue (medium and light), and red and bright colors such as yellow, green, and orange for informal events.

In addition to dining room linen, you will need kitchen cloth items. Make sure your cooks also have an ample supply of potholders, dish towels, hand towels, bar rags, and mop-up rags.

It is no coincidence that the Hilden Group is one of the world-leaders in the table linen industry. An in-depth understanding of the latest interior design trends has helped the company to develop a range of table linens to meet every individual need. Visit **www.hilden.co.uk** for more information.

When doily service is used, the doilies should be laid in the center of the cover, about one inch from the edge of the table. Silverware is placed on the doily. The folded napkin is placed, with open corners at the lower right, at the left of the fork and about one inch from the front edge of the table. For formal dinners when a service plate is used, the napkin may be folded and placed on the service plate.

SILVER

Knives and forks should be laid about nine inches apart, so that a dinner plate may be easily placed between them. The balance of the silverware is then placed to the right of the knife and to the left of the fork in the order in which it is to be used (placing the first-used at the outside and proceeding toward the plate). The handles of all silver should be perpendicular to the table edge and about an inch from it. Forks are placed at the left side of the cover, tines pointed up. Knives are placed at the right side of the cover with the cutting edge turned toward the plate.

Spoons are laid, bowls up, at the right of the knives. The butter spreader is placed across the top edge or on the right side of the bread-and-butter plate, with the handle either perpendicular or parallel to the edge of the table, the cutting edge turned toward the butter plate. The butter spreader is properly used only when butter is served and a bread-and-butter plate is provided. Sometimes when a sharp steel-bladed knife is used for the meat course, a small, straight knife for butter is laid at the right of the meat knife.

Oyster and cocktail forks are placed at the extreme right of the cover beyond the teaspoons or laid across the right side of the service plate underlying the cocktail glass or the oyster service.

FIGURE 2

Silver for dessert service — the iced teaspoon and the parfait or sundae spoon — are placed just before the respective course at the right side of the cover. The dessert fork is laid at the right side of the cover if it is placed just before the dessert is served.

Cover arrangement for main breakfast course.

Breakfast or luncheon forks, salad forks, and dessert forks are placed next to the plate in order of use; the spoons are arranged to the right of the forks, in order of use, beginning in each instance with the first course (on the outside) and working toward the center of the cover. When knives are not used in the cover, both the forks and spoons are placed to the right of the cover..

FIGURE 3

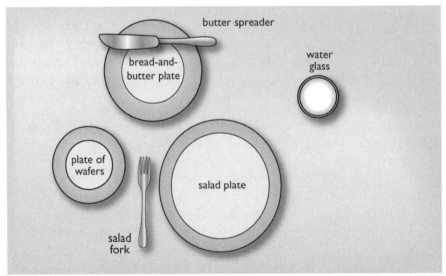

Cover arrangement when a dinner salad is served as separate course.

CHINA AND GLASSWARE

The bread-and-butter plate is placed at the left of the cover, directly above the tines of the meat fork. The water glass is placed at the right of the cover, immediately above the point of the dinner knife.

Wine, liquor, and beer glasses, if applicable, are placed to the right of the water glass. When a butter chip is used, it is placed to the left and on a line with the water glass, toward the center or left side of the cover. Sugar bowls and salt and pepper shakers are generally placed in the center of small tables. When wall tables for two are set, the sugar bowl and shakers usually are placed on the side nearest the wall or the side nearest the room rather than in the center of the table. When an open-topped sugar bowl is used, a sugar spoon is laid to the right of the bowl.

FIGURE 4

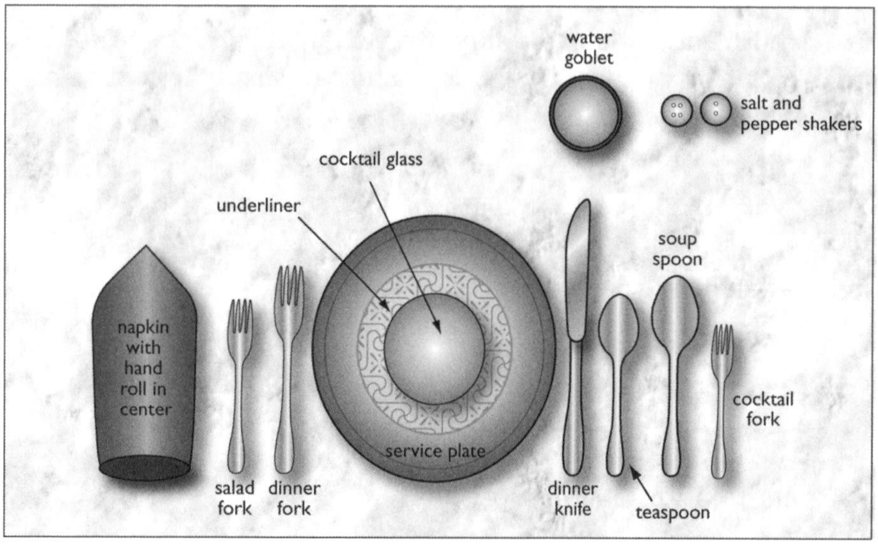

Cover arrangement for appetizer course of a formal dinner.

When a large table is being set up and several sets of sugars and creamers are needed, the cream pitchers and sugar bowls may be placed at equal distances down the center of the table. Guests can more conveniently handle them if the handles are turned toward the cover. When several sets of salt and pepper shakers are used on a large table, they may be placed between the covers on a line parallel with the bases of the water glasses.

FIGURE 5

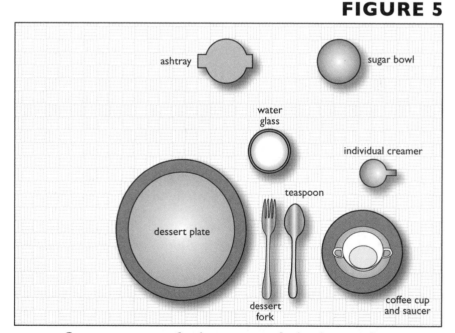

Cover arrangement for dessert course for luncheon or dinner.

IDE WORK DUTIES

Duties performed by the wait staff other than those related to the actual serving of food are commonly called "side work." This work takes considerable time and is scheduled so that each person is assigned certain duties. Side work is usually done during slack periods, before and after serving hours.

Sugar bowls should be kept spotlessly clean: emptied, washed, thoroughly dried, and refilled as often as necessary. Care should be taken to keep the sugar free from lumps and foreign material. If shaker-type containers are used, the screw tops should be securely fastened and the spout examined to see if it is clean and that the sugar flows freely.

Salt and pepper shakers should be washed with a bottle brush. A piece of wire or a toothpick may be used to unclog the holes in the lids before they are washed. Shakers should not be filled after washing until they are thoroughly dry. An empty saltbox with a spout may be refilled with pepper and used for filling pepper shakers.

There is a great invention for filling salt and pepper shakers called a "Posi-Fill Dispenser," which is about $20 and can be found at **www.atlantic-pub.com** or by calling 800-814-132 (Item PSF-03).

Syrup jugs and oil and vinegar containers should always be clean. The outside should be wiped carefully with a damp cloth after filling to remove any stickiness. Condiment bottles should be wiped with a clean, damp cloth. The top and inside of the cap may be wiped with a paper napkin to clean off gummy material. Mustard pots and condiment jars should be emptied and washed frequently. Clean paddles should be provided often.

Napkins should be folded carefully according to the style of the restaurant, with folds straight and edges even.

Menus must be replaced with new ones when they become soiled and torn.

Flowers should be arranged in containers appropriate in color, size, and shape.

Individual creamers should be washed and thoroughly cooled before being filled with cream. A container with a slender spout is used for filling if a cream dispenser is not available. Care should be taken not to fill creamers too full.

Ashtrays should be collected and cleaned frequently, especially during the serving period; a clean one should be provided each time newly arrived guests are seated at the table.

Serving trays should be kept clean and dry to protect both the waitperson's uniform and the serving-table surface. The top of the tray should be wiped clean before it is loaded, to prevent the bottoms of the dishes from being soiled.

Ice cubes or cracked ice should be clean and free of foreign matter; ice cubes should be handled with tongs and cracked ice with a special scoop or serving spoon. Ice should be transported in containers dedicated for ice only. Ice should be considered a food item.

Butter pots need to be chilled and a pan of ice made ready before serving.

Chairs should have crumbs dusted off after each guest has left. Backs, rounds, and legs of chairs should be dusted every day.

Silver or stainless should be cleaned according to the special directions of the restaurant. When a cream polish is used, it should be rubbed with a soft cloth or a small brush over the surface and well into the embossed pattern of the silverware. Then the silver should be thoroughly washed, rinsed, and polished with a dry cloth to remove all traces of the silver cream.

Polar Ware has a wide selection of food serving and dining room products. Visit **www.polarware.com** or call 800-237-3655 for more information.

CLOSING DUTIES

A waitperson should never go off-duty while guests are still seated at her station. When the serving period is over, tables should be stripped, soiled linen removed, and the tables reset for the next meal. If the tables are not to be reset, all unused tablecloths and napkins should be carefully folded and put in their proper places. Clean dishes and clean silver should be returned to their shelves, trays, or drawers; sugar bowls and salt and pepper shakers collected on trays for cleaning and refilling; and supplies, such as condiments, butter, and ice, stored in the proper places. The top of the side table should be washed clean and then wiped down with a dry cloth. Before the waitperson leaves her station, everything should be in order.

SERVICE DUTIES

HOSTING

Every employee in a restaurant is a host; the customer is your guest. Generally the host or hostess greets the customers as they enter the dining room and ushers them to tables. When the host is busy or the establishment does not have a host, it becomes the wait staff's responsibility to meet and seat customers. Whether guests form a favorable or unfavorable impression of the restaurant depends, to a considerable degree, upon the manner in which this service is performed.

Should there be a wait before a party's table is ready, there should be a system in place to monitor waiting times and tables. Electronic wait systems have become popular in recent years. This system consists of logging diners in and then issuing them a lighted coaster or vibrating pager. When their table is ready, the unit lights up or vibrates. At a recent restaurant show I saw a demonstration of a Web-enabled handheld device that allows customers to preview the menu, view promotions, check e-mail, and surf the Net. Another innovative system prints out tickets with estimated wait times based upon pre-programmed averages. The system also enables employees who seat guests to notify the front desk immediately if they view a party leaving a table or a bus person about to finish resetting a table. The wait and kitchen staffs also use many of these pager systems to communicate any problems or that food is ready to be delivered.

If a customer asks for information about the menu or suggestions about the food selection before deciding on his order, a well-informed and intelligent member of the wait staff can be of real service to the guest and, at the same time, merchandise food effectively for the restaurant. She has an opportunity to be more than an order-taker and server; she can be a successful salesperson as well.

TAKING THE ORDER

Customers like to have time to study the menu without feeling that their waitperson is waiting impatiently to take the order. The waiter should be ready to give prompt attention as soon as the guest has decided on her order. He stands at the left of the customer, close enough to hear her and to answer her questions. If the customer makes out a written order, the waiter should read it back to her and ask for any special instructions that may apply. When the waiter writes the order, his writing should be legible, the abbreviations correct, and the number of guests and table number indicated.

When a group is being served, the waiter should see if there is a host or hostesses for the group to whom he may go for instructions. While taking the order, he should ask for all the information he needs to serve the meal satisfactorily.

For example:

1. The food choices for each course.

2. How, for instance, the eggs are to be cooked.

3. Whether toast is to be dry or buttered.

4. Whether meat is preferred rare, medium, or well-done.

5. Whether a sandwich is to be served plain or toasted.

6. What kind of dressing is preferred for the salad.

7. Whether coffee is to be served with the main course or with the dessert.

8. Whether coffee is preferred hot or iced.

9. Whether black or green tea is desired.

10. Whether lemon or cream is preferred with tea.

Printed order forms, usually called "checks," are available in book form, numbered consecutively. When issued a book of checks, each wait staff member is responsible for the numbers he receives. Spoiled checks must not be destroyed; corrections should be made by drawing a line through the incorrect item — never by erasing it. The manager should approve these corrections. The check is issued as a means of recording the order, as the customer's bill, and as a source of information about the sale. Duplicate checks are used in filling orders in the kitchen. ACR Guest Checks and Register rolls by DayMark are an excellent source for all types of guest checks. With a wide variety of choices, from duplicate interleaving carbon to three part carbonless, they have the guest check to suit your needs. For more information or to order, call 800-599-8527.

MANUALLY GIVING AND COLLECTING ORDERS

The procedures used for giving and collecting orders in the kitchen vary somewhat with the organization, layout, and regulations of the restaurant. Certain general methods are applicable anywhere and help to determine the speed of the service as well as the condition and appearance of the food when it is placed before the customer. When the waiter is courteous and considerate in giving and assembling his order, he helps to maintain harmonious relations between the kitchen and dining room personnel.

The layout of the kitchen and the number of service stations will determine the routing the waitperson must follow in assembling an order. One new to the establishment must learn quickly the functions of each unit and what foods and supplies are available at each.

The waitperson gives an order by placing a written order on a spindle provided for the purpose or by giving it to the expediter to "call." Orders may also be sent to the kitchen from a POS system or "Wireless Waiter," as described below. When a written order is used, the waitperson uses his initials or number to identify it.

The wait staff should not make a habit of saying they are "in a hurry" for their orders; the cooks are probably doing their best to fill orders quickly and in rotation. When extra-fast service is really necessary, a waitperson may be justified in asking to be served rapidly or even out of turn.

TIMING THE ORDER

The waitperson should know when she will need a course and the time the meal will take to prepare in the kitchen, especially when foods are cooked to order.

ASSEMBLING THE ORDER

Food requiring the longest time to prepare should be ordered first. The waitperson should plan the assembling of the order so that she can pick up each item after it has been dished. Doing so ensures food is served when it is at the correct temperature and will prevent it from crowding the serving counters. The following general sequence is recommended:

1. **When the order is being filled, collect all the needed serving equipment and cold accompaniments** such as bread, crackers, relishes, butter, and cream.

2. **Pick up cold foods next,** taking care to keep them away from hot food on the tray.

3. **The hot food should be picked up last.** Cover soup to retain the heat. Cover the dinner plate with a hot cover when one is available.

4. **If hot breads are served, pick them up last** to serve them in their best condition.

5. **When bowl or platter service is used, provide heated plates for hot foods and chilled plates for salads and other cold foods.**

6. **Rinse tea and coffee pots with hot water before filling them with hot beverages.** Never pour iced drinks into warm glasses or place butter on a warm plate.

7. **Remember that the appearance and temperature of food that is perfectly prepared when it leaves the kitchen can be spoiled in the service by a waitperson** that is thoughtless, slow, or careless.

LOADING THE TRAY

When a waitperson loads his tray he puts the larger, heavier dinner plates and dishes in the center and the lighter pieces toward the edges. Cups are not placed on saucers. Hot and cold dishes do not touch. Tea and coffee pots are not filled so full that liquid will leak from the spouts. Pot spouts are turned in and away from plates or food. A tray should be loaded so that it is evenly balanced and the objects on it will neither slip nor spill while it is being carried. Among the precautions to take in loading a tray are the following:

1. **Be sure the tray is clean.**

2. **Before leaving a serving station, check the order to see that it is correct,** complete, properly cooked, the right quantity for serving, properly garnished, and attractively served, with no spilled food on the edges of dishes.

3. **Before leaving the kitchen check to see that all food and the necessary serving equipment** for the course are on the tray.

ELECTRONIC ORDERING SYSTEMS

In recent years many restaurants have switched to an "Electronic Guest Check System" or "Wireless Waiter." These systems use a mobile computer. The waitperson carries the mobile computer pad and places the order on the touch-screen display. As each dish is entered this information is transferred in real time to the kitchen where the order is printed out. The drink order is taken first and sent to the bar. The mobile computer is then notified by a beep or vibration when the order is ready for pickup or a "runner" delivers the meal.

Using a "Wireless Waiter," the wait staff can place multiple orders without ever walking into the kitchen or bar to check for previously placed orders or to pick up prepared orders. The wait staff in the dining area of the restaurant never leave the sight of their customers. The bill is calculated automatically, removing the risk of human error. Most systems have an optional snap-on credit card reader, which can be attached to the bottom of the handheld device. Customer credit cards are swiped through the handheld unit and processed. Under this system customers can feel confident that their credit cards are safe, as they are never out of sight. Because wait staff will always be visible in the dining area, customers will be able to get their waitperson's attention easily. Servers will be able to wait on six or seven tables at a time — twice as many as before. If more tables are waited on, more tables can be turned, providing the opportunity to increase sales volume. Utilizing this system you may need fewer waitpersons, since each one will be able to handle more customers, resulting in a reduction of labor costs.

TABLE SERVICE

The table service adopted by a food-service unit is developed to provide for the particular conditions of that establishment. Several methods of table service are considered acceptable and may be used appropriately. Restaurant managers strive to give commendable service to their guests. Good food service is achieved by adopting a suitable method of service, by training the sales force in it, and by requiring each wait staff member to follow the specified procedure This policy will result in a uniform standard of service.

AMERICAN SERVICE

American table service is "combination" service, which is a compromise of traditional forms of service that originated in other countries. If the soup course is served in a tureen and dipped into the soup plates at the table in the "English" fashion; if the main course is served on dinner plates from the kitchen or serving pantry in the "Russian" manner; and if the salad course is offered from a large bowl and served by the waitperson in the "French" style, three forms of service are combined in a single meal. The traditional forms of table service most commonly used in catering to the public are named for the countries in which the services originated: France, Russia, and England. Because these traditional methods have been adapted to American usage, it is interesting to consider briefly how they affect modern table service in the United States.

FRENCH SERVICE

The most elaborate form of table service is the "French" service used in some exclusive clubs, hotels, and restaurants. In the French service, the waitperson usually serves the guests from a food wagon or a side table. Attractive, tastefully arranged dishes of food are always presented to the guest for inspection before serving. The waiter then serves the individual plates from the platter, serving bowl, or chafing dish, as the case may be.

In a modification of French service called "platter service," the food is arranged attractively on serving dishes supplied with silver and offered to the guest so that he may serve himself. A single dish or the entire main course may be served in this way. In some restaurants, serving dishes of fresh-cooked vegetables are offered to each guest for selection; others serve attractive compartment trays of assorted relishes. Trays of assorted small cakes are sometimes offered after frozen desserts have been placed. French pastries frequently are offered to customers on a tray.

Another variation of the French service is the salad cart now popular in some restaurants and tearooms. Salads are placed on the cart and wheeled to tables so that the guests may make their selections. The waitperson arranges the individual servings at the cart and places them at each guest's cover. Another variation of French service is having the waitperson bring trays of assorted individual salads or assorted desserts from which to make a selection.

ENGLISH SERVICE

The "English" style of service is sometimes called "host service." When this service is used, the platters and serving dishes are placed before the host or hostess, who serves the individual plates. The waiter stands at the right of the host, receives the served plate from him and places it before each guest. Female guests are sometimes served first, then men; however, the usual procedure is to serve each guest in turn, beginning with the person seated to the right of the server. Commercial food-service units do not use English service for the main course except upon request in connection with private parties. A patron may ask for this type of service on some special occasion, such as a family dinner party or Thanksgiving Day, when, for instance, the host wishes to carve the turkey at the table and to serve the individual plates himself.

Occasionally the English style of service is used in serving the beverage course, perhaps at the tea hours. A tray containing the tea or after-dinner coffee service is placed before the hostess so that the hostess may serve her guests.

Special desserts and ice creams are sometimes served with host service. During the Christmas season a traditional "blazing plum pudding" may be brought to the table for guests to have the pleasure of watching the flames and seeing it served. A birthday cake may be set before the guest of honor, who is expected to "make a wish and blow out the candles," and cut the first slice or serve all of the guests. In each of these cases a particularly attractive dish is served at the table as an expression of hospitality on the part of the host or hostess. Variations of English service are frequently used in noncommercial operations, such as college dining halls.

RUSSIAN SERVICE

When the "Russian" form of service is followed, individual portions of food are placed on the plates in the kitchen or serving pantry, garnished, and ready to serve. The Russian method is used by most restaurants for serving meals as well as banquets.

BUFFET SERVICE

Buffets are used by some establishments for serving appetizer and salad courses. Occasionally an entire meal is served in buffet fashion. For buffet service, a table is attractively set with a variety of foods; each guest is given a large service plate, sometimes chilled or heated, and walks along the table, helping herself.

Under the usual procedure for restaurant buffet service, the waitperson serves breads, beverages, and desserts at each table. When hot foods are included, a cook or server carves the roast and helpers serve vegetables and other foods from casseroles, chafing dishes, and bowls.

The smorgasbord, used in many Swedish restaurants, is a form of buffet service. A large variety of typical Swedish appetizers, relishes, smoked meats, pickled fish, and salads are arranged on the table. The guest passes by this extensive array, helping himself. Usually the main and dessert courses are served later at the individual tables, but the buffet may be cleared and reset for the dessert and beverage service.

GENERAL RULES FOR TABLE SERVICE

Since there are several methods of table service, each food-service unit must follow the method appropriate to its particular conditions and each member of the wait staff must learn to follow the serving directions exactly so that service will be uniform throughout the unit. The following rules are approved by social custom:

1. **Place and remove all food from the left side of the guest.**

2. **Place and remove all beverages, including water, from the right of the guest.**

3. **Use the left hand to place and remove dishes when working at the left side of the guest and the right hand when working at the right side of the guest.** Doing so

provides free arm action for the server and avoids the danger of bumping against the guest's arm.

4. **Place each dish on the table, the four fingers of your left hand under the lower edge, and your thumb on the upper edge of the plate.**

5. **Never reach in front of the guest or across one person to serve another.**

6. **Present serving dishes from the left side**, in a position so that the guest can serve himself. Place serving silver on the right side of the dish with the handles turned toward the guest so that he may reach and handle them easily.

7. **Do not place soiled, chipped, or cracked glassware and china or bent or tarnished silverware before a guest.**

8. **Hold silverware by the handles when it is laid in place.** Be sure it is clean and spotless.

9. **Handle tumblers by their bases and goblets by their stems.**

10. **Do not lift water glasses from the table to fill or refill**; when they cannot be reached conveniently, draw them to a more convenient position.

11. **Set fruit-juice and cocktail glasses, cereal dishes, soup bowls, and dessert dishes on small plates before placing them in the center of the cover** between the knife and the fork.

12. **When it accompanies the main course, place the salad plate at the left of the forks,** about two inches from the edge of the table. When the salad is served as a separate course, place it directly in front of the guest.

13. **Place individual serving trays or bread and rolls above and to the left of the forks.** Place a tray or basket of bread for the use of several guests toward the center of the table.

14. **Place the cup and saucer at the right of the spoons**, about two inches from the edge of the table. Turn the handle of the cup to the right, either parallel to the edge of the table or at a slight angle toward the guest.

15. **Set tea and coffee pots on small plates and place above and slightly to the right of the beverage cup.** Set iced beverage glasses on coasters or small plates to protect tabletops and linen.

16. **Place individual creamers, syrup pitchers, and small lemon plates above and a little to the right of the cup and saucer.**

17. **Place a milk glass at the right of and below the water glass.**

18. **Serve butter, cheese, and cut lemon with a fork.** Serve relishes, pickles, and olives with a fork or spoon, not with the fingers.

More food-service operations are using booth- or banquet-type seating. It is extremely difficult to carry out proper table service in these situations. The general rules for booth service are:

- **Serve everything with the hand farthest from the guest**; use right hand to serve a guest at your left and your left hand to serve your guest to your right.

- **Remove soiled plates with the hand nearest your guest while substituting the next course with the hand farthest from your guest.**

BREAKFAST SERVICE

Good breakfast service is important because many customers are in a hurry; some have little appetite and others are "out of sorts" until they have had their coffee. A cheerful attitude on the part of the wait staff and prompt and efficient service will help customers "start the day right."

Breakfast is most palatable when freshly prepared and served at the correct temperature. The waitperson should serve breakfast in courses unless the customer requests otherwise. Cooked foods and hot beverages should be brought to the customer directly from the serving station. Under no circumstances should food remain on the serving stand to cool while the customer finishes a preceding course.

Order of service for breakfast:

1. When fresh fruit or fruit juice is ordered, serve it first; then, remove the soiled dishes before placing the toast and coffee.

2. When customers order a combination of cooked fruit, toast, and coffee, they may ask to have the whole order served at once. Place the fruit dish, set on an underliner, in the center of the cover, the plate of toast at the left of the forks and the coffee at the right of the teaspoons.

3. When the breakfast order includes a cereal and a hot dish, the service procedure may be as follows:

   A. Place the fruit course in the center of the cover.

   B. Remove the fruit service.

   C. Place the cereal bowl, set on an underliner, in the center of the cover. Cut individual boxes of cereal partway through the side near the top so the guest may open them easily.

   D. Remove the cereal service.

   E. Place the breakfast plate of eggs, meat, or other hot food in the center of the cover. Place the plate of toast at the left of the forks. Place the coffee service at the right of the spoons.

   F. Remove the breakfast plate and the bread plate.

   G. Place the finger bowl, filled one-third full of warm water. At times the finger bowl is placed after the fruit course when fruits that may soil the fingers have been served.

   H. Place the sales check, face down, at the right of the cover or present it on a clean change tray.

LUNCHEON SERVICE

Luncheon customers can be classified in two groups: business people who have a short lunch period wanting quick service, and casual diners wanting more leisurely service. The waitperson's duty is to avoid keeping customers in the first group waiting for service and to avoid making those in the second group feel they are being rushed.

Order of service for luncheon:

1. Fill the water glasses three-fourths full of ice water.

2. Place chilled butter on a cold bread-and-butter plate.

3. Place the appetizer in the center of the cover.

4. Remove the appetizer when the guest has finished.

5. Place the soup service in center of cover.

6. Remove the soup service.

7. Place entree plate in center of cover.

8. Place individual vegetable dishes (if used) above the cover.

9. If salad is served with main course, place salad at the left of the forks, about two inches from edge of table.

10. Place tray or basket of bread and rolls at left of salad plate.

11. Place hot beverages above and a little to the right of cup and saucer, with individual creamer above the cup.

12. Place an iced beverage or milk at the right and a little below the water glass.

13. Remove the main-course dishes.

14. Remove any extra silver not used for the main course.

15. Crumb the table, if necessary.

16. Place desert silver to the right of the cover, with fork nearest the dessert plate if fork and teaspoon are used. When several teaspoons are placed, the dessert fork may be laid on the left side to "balance the cover."

17. Place the dessert service in center of the cover.

18. Serve hot coffee if requested.

19. Remove dessert dishes and silver.

20. Place the finger bowl on the underliner (when one is used) in the center of the cover.

21. Present the check, face down.

DINNER SERVICE

Because dinner guests are seldom in a hurry, their waitperson is able to give them fastidious, leisurely service. Although guests should be given time to complete each course, long waits between courses should be avoided. The waitperson should observe the guests during the meal to serve the next course promptly and to comply with any guest requests.

Order of service for dinner:

1. From the left, place the appetizer or hors d'oeuvres service in the center of the cover. A tray of canapés and hors d'oeuvres is often offered to the guest. In this case, an empty plate should first be placed before the guest and the tray of hors d'oeuvres then offered to him.

2. Remove the first-course dishes.

3. Place the soup service in the center of the cover.

4. Remove the soup service.

5. When the entree is served on a platter, place it directly above the cover. Lay the serving silver at the right of the platter. Place the warm dinner plate in the center of the cover.

6. When plate, or "Russian," service is used, place the dinner plate in the center of the cover.

7. Place salad at the left of the forks when it is served with the main course.

8. Place beverages to the right of teaspoons.

9. Offer rolls or place them to the left of the salad plate.

10. Remove the main-course dishes when the guest has finished.

11. When salad is served as a separate course following the main course, place the salad fork at the left and the salad plate in the center of the cover.

12. Remove the salad service.

13. Crumb the table if necessary.

14. Place silver for the dessert course.

15. Place the dessert service in the center of the cover.

16. Serve hot coffee or place the demitasse.

Special attentions to observe when serving:

1. Serve hot food hot, on heated dishes.

2. Serve cold food chilled, on cold dishes.

3. Inquire how food is to be cooked:

   A. Eggs: fried or boiled; how many minutes.

   B. Steak: rare, medium, or well-done.

C. Toast: buttered or dry.

4. Refill water glasses whenever necessary during the meal.

5. Serve extra butter when needed.

6. Refill coffee on request and according to management policies. Bring more cream if necessary.

7. Serve granulated sugar with fresh fruit and unsweetened iced drinks.

8. Place silver necessary for a course just prior to serving.

   A. Soup spoons on extreme right of teaspoons.

   B. Cocktail fork to right of soup spoon.

9. Offer crackers, Melba toast, and other accompaniments or relishes with appetizer and soup courses, according to policies of management.

10. Provide iced teaspoons for ice drinks and place parfait spoons when a parfait is served. Place soda spoons and straws with malted milks, milkshakes, and ice cream sodas.

CLEARING THE TABLE

The following are standard procedures for clearing the table:

1. After any course, dishes should be removed from the left side, except the beverage service, which should be removed from the right.

2. Platters and other serving dishes should be removed first when clearing the table or they may be removed as soon as empty.

3. The main-course plate should be removed first, the salad plate next, followed by the bread-and-butter plate.

4. The empty milk or beverage glass is removed from the right after the main course.

5. The table should be crumbed by using a small plate and a clean, folded napkin, especially when hard rolls or crusty breads are served.

6. Hot tea and coffee service should be left on the table until the completion of the dessert course.

7. The water glass should remain on the table and be kept refilled as long as the guest is seated.

8. Replace soiled ashtrays with clean ones throughout the meal.

9. When a guest is seated at a table and it is necessary to change a soiled tablecloth, turn the soiled cloth halfway back, lay the clean cloth half open in front of the guest, and transfer the tableware to the clean cloth. The soiled cloth may then be drawn from the table and the clean one pulled smoothly into place. If this exchange of linen is accomplished skillfully, the guest need not be disturbed unduly during the procedure. Soiled linen should be properly disposed of immediately after it is removed from the table.

PRESENTING THE CHECK

The guest should not be kept waiting for her sales check. Present it immediately after the last course has been served or right after the guest has finished eating. The check should be accurately totaled and laid face down on the table to the right of the cover on a small change tray. When a group has been served, the check should be placed by the host's cover; if the host is not known and the order has been written on one check, the check should be placed toward the center of the table. When a man and woman are dining together, the check should generally be presented near to the man, unless separate orders have been written.

It is courteous to ask if any other service is desired before presenting the sales check and to thank the customer as the check is laid on the table. When a bill is received in payment, the waitperson should mention the denomination of the bill. When a credit card is presented, be sure to include a pen and the appropriate instruction, such as, "The top white copy is your copy and the bottom yellow copy is for the establishment." When tipping is sanctioned, the waitperson should leave the appropriate change, allowing the customer to leave a gratuity. Change should be placed on a change tray or tip tray, not on a china plate, as coins make unnecessary noise when handled on china. It is incorrect for the waitperson to indicate in any way that a tip is expected or that any certain amount is anticipated. It is also discourteous to show disappointment because the tip was less than is customarily received. When a guest leaves a gratuity, she indicates her desire to reward the waitperson for services rendered.

COURTESY TO DEPARTING CUSTOMERS

Guests should be shown small courtesies when departing. A waiter might draw out a woman's chair and assist with her wraps and packages. The waitperson should say goodbye to all customers and express the hope that they have enjoyed the meal or that they will come again. This sort of courtesy leaves customers feeling like truly welcomed guests.

SUPERVISING THE SERVICE

The primary function of the food-service host is to dispense hospitality as a representative of the management. When receiving customers, the host should greet them graciously and make them feel that they are welcome and will receive good service. A pleasant reception, careful service throughout the meal, and courteous treatment as they leave will impress customers with the excellence of the service — and make them feel that their patronage is appreciated. It is the feeling of being a valued patron that converts occasional customers into regular guests.

Food service is one of mankind's oldest forms of hospitality and is associated in one's mind with courtesy, cheerfulness, and goodwill. The host should realize that goodwill toward the establishment is created by courteous, interested service, just as it is lost by unwilling, indifferent service.

The host has working relations with all the individuals concerned with sales and service: the manager, the wait staff, and the guests. He must interpret management's policies and standards to the customers. He must convey the wishes of both the management and the guests to the sales staff. The skill with which he conducts himself in this pivotal position will determine the efficiency of the service and the satisfaction of the guests.

NATURE OF HOST WORK

The host reports recommendations, suggestions, and complaints from the customers and employees to management. Good judgment and tact on his part, are essential. When the restaurant is large and there are several dining rooms, more than one host will be necessary to receive guests and supervise service. In large food-service operations, the host usually has assistant hosts, captains, or head waitpersons who are responsible for supervising a section of the dining room or for the execution of specific duties involved in serving guests. It should be understood that the "duties of the host" discussed in this unit include all duties that may be executed by the host or by any of his assistants.

INSPECTING THE DINING ROOM

The host is responsible for the appearance, cleanliness, and order of the dining room during the service period. Before the meal service begins he should check to be sure that:

1. The main dining room, private rooms, booths, and counters are clean and in good order. Any disorder should be reported to the proper authority and remedied before the meal service begins.

2. Window curtains, Venetian blinds, and window roller-shades are adjusted to furnish satisfactory light.

3. The temperature and ventilation of the dining room are properly adjusted.

4. Tables are arranged properly and completely equipped.

5. Serving stands and side tables are properly arranged and have adequate supplies.

6. There are enough menu cards and they are distributed properly.

7. Order forms and sharpened pencils are provided.

8. Table reservations and "reserved" signs have been placed.

9. The tables arranged for special parties are ready and flowers, candles, and other decorations provided.

10. Flowers are fresh and attractively arranged. Plants should be inspected for proper care, pruning, and watering.

11. There is an adequate supply of tablecloths, table pads, doilies, napkins, and serving towels.

12. Necessary repairs have been made to furnishings and fixtures.

RECEIVING CUSTOMERS

The host should receive customers in a gracious yet dignified manner. With this in mind he may:

1. Stand near the entrance to the dining room to greet customers as they arrive and seat them promptly. This responsibility is often assigned to an assistant host when the host is charged with supervisory or service duties.

2. Greet the customers with a pleasant smile and nod, using the appropriate greeting—"Good morning," "Good afternoon," or "Good evening" — and greeting customers by name whenever possible.

3. When a checkroom is located near the entrance, suggest that guests check hats, wraps, umbrellas, and packages.

4. Ask how many are in each group and seat the group at a suitable table.

5. Ask the customers' preferences with regard to table location when the dining room is not too crowded.

6. Walk slightly ahead of the customers when escorting them to a table.

7. Seat couples at small tables or in booths. Place lame and elderly persons near the entrance so they will not be required to walk far.

8. Ask permission before seating strangers together, doing so only when the dining room is too crowded. First explain the wait time the guest will have and then ask if she would mind sharing a table with someone else. Avoid seating a man with a woman who is dining alone or taking a woman to a table where a man is already seated unless they are acquaintances and are willing to share a table.

9. Apportion the seating of customers to the several serving stations so no one section of the dining room will be overcrowded.

10. When customers must wait for tables, seat them where they are available or indicate a place to stand that is out of the way of traffic.

11. Have the table cleared of soiled dishes and reset before customers are seated.

12. Pull out the chair for a woman guest and help her arrange her wraps and packages.

13. Indicate a rack where a man may hang his hat and overcoat, if no checkroom is provided.

14. Provide a junior chair for small children and a highchair for infants in arms. Offer to help seat the child and arrange the napkin or bib if the mother wishes this service.

15. Place the opened menu before each guest, from the left side, or instruct the captain or waitperson to do so.

16. Fill the water glasses or instruct the bus person or waitperson to do so promptly.

HANDLING CUSTOMER COMPLAINTS

A difficult duty of the restaurant host is to receive complaints from customers and make satisfactory adjustments. When complaints are properly handled, the customer leaves the restaurant with a feeling of friendliness, rather than animosity toward the management. Customer complaints are an opportunity to turn the situation around and gain a lifelong customer. Complaints that are improperly handled make the customer disgruntled and may lead to the loss of her patronage and unfavorable advertising for the restaurant.

In adjusting complaints the host should:

1. Approach the customer in a friendly spirit and not allow her to be put on the defensive.

2. Listen attentively to the complaint and try to get the entire story.

3. Restate the gist of the complaint and have the customer confirm this summarized statement.

4. Express sincere regret for the occurrence.

5. Offer to exchange or substitute food that is unsatisfactory.

6. Cite the restaurant's policies when relevant.

7. When the refusal of a request is necessary, explain the reason clearly and tactfully.

8. When the restaurant is at fault, apologize and promise that an effort will be made to prevent a recurrence of the situation.

9. Thank the customer for making the complaint, saying, "I am glad you told me" or "Thank you for bringing this to my attention."

10. When the customer makes a return visit, see that the service is faultless and that she has no further cause for complaint.

11. Refer difficult and unreasonable complaints to the manager for settlement.

12. Report all serious complaints and those involving business policy and regulations to the management.

DEALING WITH DIFFICULT CUSTOMERS

Some customers are difficult to deal with because of their attitudes or special needs; they should be handled with intelligence, tact, and good judgment. Different types require different methods of treatment; here are some examples:

1. **The early customer.** Receive him courteously and explain when service will begin. Offer him a comfortable seat, possibly in the lounge, and give him a newspaper or magazine.

2. **The late customer.** Make her feel welcome. If the food selection is limited, explain that it is near closing time. Endeavor to provide good service without making her feel that she is being hurried.

3. **The hurried customer.** Recommend counter service when available. Tell him in advance approximately how long the service will take. Give the best service possible under the circumstances.

4. **The over familiar customer.** Be courteous but dignified with her. Avoid long conversations. Stay away from the table except when actual service is needed.

5. **The grouchy customer.** Meet him cheerfully and see that his waitperson treats him pleasantly. Do not argue with him. Listen to his complaints courteously, but do not encourage him. Do not be distressed by unreasonable complaints.

6. **The angry customer.** Listen to her, express regret at the occurrence that prompted her

complaint, thank her for calling it to your attention, and try to rectify the error.

7. **The troublemaker.** Be courteous and do not be drawn into arguments. Neither participate in criticisms of the management, nor make statements that may be construed as complaints about the restaurant. Warn other salespersons serving the troublemaker type to avoid antagonizing him.

8. **The tired customer.** Seat her at a quiet table. Assist her with wraps and packages. In cold weather, suggest a hot soup, a hot drink, and some particularly appetizing light food. On a hot day, suggest a chilled salad or a frosted drink and some cold food.

MAKING ARRANGEMENTS FOR SPECIAL PARTIES

Unless there is a supervisor in charge of catering, the host generally takes reservations for special parties. He may improve his ability to handle this business by following the regulations of the management concerning maximum and minimum size for special groups, minimum charges, number of courses, food choices allowed at a given price, time, and guarantee of number — and by obtaining the necessary information from the person making the reservation, including:

- Name, address, and telephone number of the person calling.
- The name of the organization, if one is involved.
- Day, date, and hour of reservation.
- Occasion.
- Probable number in the group and number of guests guaranteed.
- Preferences as to table location and dining room (main or private).
- Price or price range.
- Whether sample menus are to be mailed.
- Arrangements for flowers and decorations.
- Arrangements for payment of the sales check. Is the check to be paid in one amount or is the money to be collected individually?

When a table reservation is made, obtain the following information:

- Name of person reserving it.
- Number of persons included in reservation.
- Date and time.
- Preference of table location.
- Arrangements for flowers.
- Whether a special menu is desired or guests will make their selections from the regular menu.

SERVING SPECIAL PARTIES

The general responsibilities of the host for the service of a special party include such duties as:

1. Securing and assigning the extra wait staff and bus persons needed or service.

2. Rearranging the serving schedule to allow use of regular wait staff employees.

3. Making out the orders for liners and dishes.

4. Giving instructions for setting tables.

5. Checking set tables for completeness, arrangement, and appearance.

6. Checking to be sure that the correct number of places has been set.

7. Giving the necessary general instructions to individual servers.

8. Giving specific instructions to individual servers.

9. Notifying the kitchen staff of the time when the service will be required.

10. Notifying the kitchen staff when they should begin serving each course.

11 Signaling the head waitperson when it is time to begin placing each course.

12. Signaling the head waitperson when it is time to begin removing the dishes from each course.

13. Approving and supplying special services that may be requested by customers, such as tea instead of coffee, fish instead of meat, bread instead of rolls, and special foods for persons on special diets.

14. Providing supplies that may be requested, such as a pitcher of water for the speaker's place, a change tray for the person collecting the money at the table, change for the person selling tickets at the door, or an easel or blackboard for the speaker. Anticipate these requests in advance of the meal service, so that the proper provisions may be made. Otherwise, satisfy such requests to your best ability when they are made.

PERFORMING CLERICAL WORK

Some clerical duties are usually assigned to the host. The amount of these duties depends upon the organization of the restaurant, the size of the supervisory staff, and the number of office employees. From among the clerical duties, the host may:

- Before the service period, check printed menus with the kitchen menu to discover omissions, inaccuracies, or corrections. Change menus accordingly.

- Make out storeroom requisitions for supplies such as matches, paper doilies, paper inserts for metal dishes, candles, nuts, and condiments.

- Record reservations for tables and special parties; include all necessary information on a reservation form.

- Record the service hours of dining room employees on the daily time sheet, if a time clock is not used.

- Make out the linen report.

- Make out or assist with the sales analysis for the meal.

- Report to the manager, in writing, any important suggestions, serious complaints, or compliments from customers.

INFORMATION NEEDED BY THE HOST

The host needs both good background knowledge of correct procedures for serving food and a working knowledge of psychology. She should also be familiar with the policies and regulations of the business. Until the host has mastered this information she will not be thoroughly effective in supervising the service, dealing with customers, and assisting management to execute the business policies.

In their daily work the hosts should be familiar with the management's policy concerning the seating of customers, serving, filling orders in the kitchen, and party service. They should have answers to the following questions:

POLICY CONCERNING SEATING

- Is the customer permitted to designate a particular waitperson to serve him?

- Does the policy of the restaurant approve seating strangers at the same table?

- During what hours are reservations permitted? How long should tables be held?

POLICY CONCERNING SERVING

- What is the prescribed method for a table setup?

- What specific method of service is used for: table d'hôte meals, A la carte orders or special parties?

- What is the division of work between the wait staff and bus persons? What duties are each expected to perform independently? What duties are performed jointly?

- Are extra servings of hot bread offered? Are second cups of coffee allowed without extra charge?

- When and under what conditions may substitutions be made on a menu? Is there an extra charge when a guest requests a substitution?

POLICY CONCERNING FILLING ORDERS IN THE KITCHEN

- What foods does each kitchen station serve?

- What is the best routine for a waitperson to use in filling an order?

- To whom at each serving station should the waitperson give the order?

- Where are supplies of dishes, glassware, silver, and linen kept?

- Where may extra supplies of butter, cream, ice, crackers, and condiments be found?

- Are wait staff required to dish their own orders of desserts and ice cream?

- Are wait staff expected to make tea and coffee and fill orders for other beverages? Exactly what directions should be followed?

- Are "outs" and substitutions on the menu posted on a board in the kitchen? Should the menu cards be changed accordingly?

POLICY CONCERNING LARGE PARTY SERVICE

- What special rooms and dining room spaces may be reserved?

- What is the largest number of persons that can be accommodated? What is the smallest number for which any one room may be reserved?

- Is any leeway allowed on the guaranteed number of guests? What are the specific regulations concerning this matter?

- At what hours is party service provided? How late may a group remain?

- What is the minimum price for which a special group may be served? What is the usual price?

- What provisions are made for flowers and decorations?

- Is a portable stage available for the speaker's table and for entertainers?

- Are there electrical connections, extension cords, and screens available to use for the slide projector or video equipment?

- What is the policy with respect to gratuities?

- Is a special crew provided for party service? How are the members of these crews secured?

GENERAL POLICY

- Are guests permitted to use the dining-room or office telephones?

- Are menus provided as souvenirs without charge?

- Are pies, cakes, and rolls made to order? Other foods?

- Are lunches packed to order?

- Are tray meals sent out?

The service in your restaurant can make or break your operation. Numerous industry surveys show that wait staff service is often the deciding factor in returning to a restaurant or going to a competitor. Offering great food is not enough to stay competitive. It is up to you, the manager, to train, motivate, and supervise the staff to ensure your success and to keep customers coming back and spreading the word about your establishment.

RESERVATION PROCEDURES FORM

At some point, every employee will answer the phone, so everyone needs to know how to take a dining reservation. Any reservation of six or more should be brought to the manager's attention to be sure we have the proper staffing levels and that the kitchen is aware that the guests are coming.

There are six vital pieces of information needed to ensure we take care of our guests' reservation needs:

GUEST'S NAME (first and last).

PHONE NUMBER (home and work number if possible).

NUMBER of people reservation is for.

SMOKING PREFERENCE ("S" for smoking, "NS" for nonsmoking, or "E" for either/no preference).

TIME of arrival.

GROUPS of ten or more. Inquire if it will be separate checks or one check, and if the guest would like the gratuity added.

CHAPTER

INCREASE ORDER AMOUNT
AND YOUR BOTTOM LINE

As a restaurant manager, you want to increase the bottom line for your business. There are many effective ways to do so. This chapter will show you ways to increase the bottom line through increasing the order amount, menu add-ons, up-selling, adding additional services, and much more.

MAKE CHANGES TO YOUR MENU AND LAYOUT

DAILY SPECIALS

There are many ways to offer daily specials. In an earlier chapter, I mentioned using daily specials as a way to test new items. You do not have to offer them every day, but you can get feedback from your customers. If the feedback is good, you can consider adding them to your menu.

You can include a daily special card in your menu. Some restaurants offer the same daily specials week after week. Others list the specials on a special board. In some restaurants, the server lists the specials for customers.

A good thing about adding different specials is it allows you to use up leftovers or over ordered items. If you have left over vegetables you can offer soup. It is better to make less than to throw away spoiled food.

Specials also offer some diversity for your regular customers without having too many items on your menu. You can allow employees or customers to offer suggestions for specials, but you have the final approval after evaluating the costs involved.

MENU ADD-ONS

Some popular add-ons include personal pizzas, subs, appetizers, chicken, wings, pasta, soup, salads, and breadsticks or garlic bread.

APPETIZERS – TANTALIZERS

Appetizers are a great way to increase your average ticket price. They also give some variety and make great impulse purchases. Customers can munch on them while they wait for their order or on their drive home. Children love breadsticks and cheese sticks.

Chicken wings, mozzarella sticks, chicken tenders, and garlic bread are offered by LaRosa's in Cincinnati. Uno's offers pizza skins, which are a deep-dish pizza crust with mozzarella, whipped and buttered red bliss potatoes, bacon, cheddar cheese, and a dollop of sour cream. Bertucci's in Baltimore offers several seafood appetizers, including Mussels Caruso and shrimp scampi.

You and your employees need to tell customers about your appetizers. Add them to your menu board, menus, and add promo pieces around the public areas to promote them. All order takers need to be trained to up sell and add appetizers to their orders. I used to hold employee contests each month. The employee who sold the most of our selected items won a gift certificate or something similar.

Almost every country and culture enjoys some type of appetizer before the main course. Americans no longer think of appetizers as a salad, cocktail sausages, or cheese and crackers. Stuffed jalapeño peppers, kabobs, spinach dips, and chicken wings have all entered the appetizer market, making "appetizer savvy" a huge money-maker in restaurant sales. Appetizers are meant to whet the appetite of your customers and get them ready to enjoy the main course. Appetizers also serve as "tantalizers" before the main meal to help your guests relax with an accompanying cocktail, glass of wine, or other beverage of choice. The following ideas will increase your "appetizer savvy" and increase sales and profit — besides adding more tips for your wait staff:

- **The "eyes" have it.** Eye appeal of prepared food is 90 percent of the reason people try a new dish. Be sure that your side items are presented with "eye appeal" in mind – on the dish, pictured on the menu, or described by your wait staff.

- **Add flare to a meal with appetizers.** Appetizers can always add a distinctive flare to any restaurant's menu items. If you concentrate on serving appetizers with a flare, your sales will increase tenfold. Use garnishes to add color and spices to add zest. Make them look just as the name suggests – appetizing.

- **Tantalize your guests with vivid descriptions.** "How about a piece of our luscious cherry cream pie? It is made with fresh cherries and lots of whipped cream on top!"

- **Use catchy names for your appetizer menu items.** It is great to serve delicious, one-of-a-kind nachos at your restaurant, but rather than listing them on the menu as "nachos," a name like, "Jamaican Jerk Nachos," will paint a picture in your customer's mind of something special.

- **Specialty drinks or specially-priced drinks.** Be sure that each wait staff shift is aware of any specials on drinks that might not be on your menu. A customer will be more willing to try a new drink if it is presented first and sounds tantalizing.

- **Rethink the positioning of appetizers on your menu to make them more tantalizing.** If they are extremely popular and a great source of sales revenue, you want to increase their visibility on the menu. If you are thinking about making appetizers a bigger part of your sales, be sure to consider making them a special part of your menu. Use color and flare to make them appetizing.

PLACE SIDE ITEMS ON A PEDESTAL

Do not forget the side items in your quest to sell more entrées. Side items can increase your profit margin even more than a high-priced entrée. Do not disregard them in your menu-planning process. Plan promotions and displays that will appeal to your clientele. Consider the following possibilities:

- **Regale your sub-menu items to reap profits.** You can give your sub-menu items a special place on your menu by directing your wait staff to promote them or by setting up displays that are inviting and colorful. Promotions that feature special side items such as a mid-winter "Evening in the Tropics" served with Jamaican Rum Punch or Mango Sundaes can get your customers out of the winter doldrums.

- **If you have a "Happy Hour," be sure to offer samples of appetizers.** "Happy Hour" customers can also be "return" lunch or dinner customers. They will remember a delicious appetizer they sampled at "Happy Hour" and recommend it to their friends. "Happy Hour" can be an excellent promotional tool if you make it a memorable experience for your customers.

- **Do not forget the art of presentation.** No matter how delicious your sub-menu items are, presentation is the key to get them noticed.

"Scratch and sniff" your menu items. You can add scratch and sniff stickers to certain parts of your menu or table tents to attract patrons to the delectable smells of the ingredients you will be using. Order yours from Mello Smello at 800-328-4876, **www.mellosmello.com**.

PREPARATION AND PRESENTATION OF SIDE ITEMS PROMOTE SALES

Dare to be different in your food fare's preparation. Try a few of the following novel suggestions for enhancing your presentation of side items:

- **Prepare routine fare in an unusual way.** Even a plain potato can be prepared in ways other than mashing or baking. Grill them with some liquid smoke sprinkled on top or batter chicken fingers with a Cajun-spiced mixture for extra zing.

- **Enthusiastic descriptions.** Be sure your customers know that you put a great deal of effort into being different. How about the following description for your potatoes: "Our smoky, grilled potatoes have a hickory flavor that complements our grilled hamburgers."

- **Side item aromas can whet your customers' appetites.** Fresh herbs produce aromas that will appeal to your customers' sense of smell. Basil, tarragon, and rosemary are herbs that can be used in many side items to produce delicate, appealing scents. Fresh-baked bread is also a winner in the aroma department.

- **Prepare side items that will please your customers' palates.** Marinating ingredients is a wonderful way to make the ordinary dish stand out. Try soaking fresh vegetables in a marinade or experiment with layering flavors within the same dish; for example, grilled chicken fingers with a tomato-cream sauce topped with Bleu Cheese.

- **Flame the fires.** If someone orders Bananas Foster or fajitas for their meal or dessert, try to serve the dish while it is still on fire or sizzling. The special effect will bring attention to the order and increase sales.

- **Water has a calming effect.** If you are serving a beautiful side dish with edible flowers, you might consider bringing out a clear serving platter that showcases some water on the bottom and gives the effect of floating fare.

- **Use various cheeses as appetizers or to complement a main dish.** America is sold on cheese. With today's wide varieties of taste and color, you can create cheese appetizers that will appeal to your customers' sense of nutrition and taste. Try using cheeses as toppings on side dishes and desserts. You can learn all about the various uses of cheese at **www.cheese.com**.

- **Attractively displayed fruit can complement any meal.** Add fruit to a plate as a garnish. Its colorful appeal is a great alternative to parsley. Try something different. Rather than grapes, garnish a plate with a thin watermelon slice, an orange wedge, or a small bunch of cherries. And do not just cut it the standard way – make it pretty.

SPECIALTY ITEMS

Offering specialty items can set you apart from your competition. Finding ways to prepare menu items in a different way enables you to charge more for them. Promote these special items on your menu. You can also feature them on brochure menus and flyers.

Below are some great examples of what some pizza shops are offering to their customers. Even if you do not offer pizza, these ideas could inspire some unique new dishes for your restaurant.

ALTIERI'S PIZZA – STOW, OHIO	
Item	**Description**
Mexican Pizza	Refried beans and burrito meat topped with tortilla chips, provolone, cheddar, lettuce, black olives, and tomato
Ranch Pizza	Ranch dressing, bacon, mushrooms, red onion, tomato, and provolone
Potato Pizza	Sour cream, potato, pizza sauce, provolone, bacon, and red onion
Barkoukis Pizza	Roasted garlic oil, spinach, gyro meat, Kalamata olives, tomato, provolone, and feta
New Orleans Style Pizza	Spicy white cheese sauce, provolone, chorizo sausage, chicken, roasted peppers, red onion, sour cream, and Tabasco sauce

AL'S GOURMET PIZZA – WASHINGTON, DC	
Item	Description
Chicken Kabob Pizza	Marinated chicken, green peppers, onion, tomato, cherry hot peppers, mozzarella and feta cheese, and white garlic sauce
Surf and Turf Pizza	Marinated sirloin, baby shrimp, mushroom, onion, mozzarella and American cheese, and white garlic sauce
Jerk Chicken Pizza	Chicken marinated in jerk sauce and mozzarella cheese

COUNTERTOP DISPLAYS

Generate interest in your specialties or temporary specials with countertop displays. These are also great for impulse purchases like appetizers and desserts. It is important to keep it simple. Too many signs and displays are too busy and will not influence the customer in a positive way.

HEALTHY OPTIONS

In the United States, over 60 million people are classified as obese and this is a reason many restaurants are now offering healthy sections on their menus. It is almost a public service to offer a healthy menu, but it is also a way to increase the profits for your restaurant. You can ask for suggestions about what new items should be added to your menu.

The owner of Altieri's Pizza in Stow, Ohio, has a good friend who was allergic to gluten as a child. Altieri found one of his customer's was too, so he searched for a gluten-free crust. He now offers this choice and sells several each day.

LaRosa's, based in Cincinnati, has developed a "light pizza." Their Lite Topper has 60 percent less fat than a comparable deluxe pizza, with fresh mushrooms and green peppers, red onions, pepperoni, capocolla, and diced Roma tomatoes.

Healthy eating is a trend and it is worth your effort to offer healthy options. Reviewing the basics of nutrition will help you decide which items to include on your menu. The six basic nutrients include proteins, fats, carbohydrates, minerals, vitamins, and water. When you plan your menu, focus on carbohydrates and fats.

Carbohydrates include fiber, starches, and sugars. Carbohydrates provide an important source of energy for the body. Foods that contain carbohydrates include sugar, bread, potatoes, rice, pasta, and fruit. Vegetables contain lower levels of carbohydrates.

Fats provide concentrated energy and twice as many calories as carbohydrates and proteins. There are saturated and unsaturated fats which are differentiated by their chemical structure. Unsaturated fats are healthier. Sources of saturated fats include shortening and butter. Olive and canola oil contain unsaturated fats.

When you create a healthier menu, you can attract the portion of the population with heart disease or other chronic illnesses like diabetes. Ask customers to complete surveys for you. Find out what special needs they have. It will help you serve them better.

Customers with diabetes need to monitor their daily fat, carbohydrate, and protein intake. You can cater to their needs by offering low fat and low protein selections on your menu.

Some valuable resources to help you make these decisions include:

- American Institute of Cancer Research at **www.aicr.org**
- American Heart Association at **www.deliciousdescisions.org**
- American Diabetes Association at **www.diabetes.org**

Some good, healthy cookbooks include:

- *Vegetarian Cooking for Everyone* by Deborah Madison
- *The Joslin Diabetes Gourmet Cookbook* by Bonnie Sanders Polin, PhD, and Frances Towner Giedt
- *The French Culinary Institute's Salute to Healthy Cooking* by Alain Sailhac, Jacques Pepin, Andre Soltner, Jacques Torres, and the Faculty at the French Culinary Institute
- *Healthy Latin Cooking* by Steve Raichlen
- *Good Food Gourmet* by Jane Brody
- *Heart Healthy Cooking for All Seasons* by Marvin Moser, M.D., Larry Forgione, Jimmy Schmidt, and Julie Rubenstein
- *Moosewood Restaurant Low-Fat Favorites* by the Moosewood Collective
- *Canyon Ranch Cooking* by Jeanne Jones

It may be easier to make adjustments to your current recipes. These are some simple ways to tweak your existing menu to cater to additional customers:

- Offer a variety of vegetarian items.
- Offer reduced-fat/reduced-calorie salad dressings.
- Use olive or canola oil instead of butter or shortening.
- Offer whole grain bread options.
- Offer low-fat mayonnaise for sandwiches.
- Offer sorbet for dessert.
- Include a simple fruit dessert that is low in sugar and fat.
- Offer smaller portion sizes for some dishes.

Restaurants can consider adding a salad bar. Packaged salads are a good convenience item. In addition to salad ingredients, you will need to stock dressing packages, crackers, and other salad items. Salads are also a hit with your health conscious customers. Salads can help you target a new customer base.

Before you make a firm decision to add a salad bar, be sure that you have a good place for the bar. It needs to be convenient for customer flow in the dining room area. You also need enough refrigerated space for these ingredients. There is special equipment for the bar. Some are stainless steel and others are lightweight plastic, which are portable. When you price the bars, be sure that you include an attached sneeze guard, lighting, rails, and plate chillers. The units are four to six feet long and prices usually run from $3,000 to $8,000. You can also search used supply stores.

PROMOTING BEVERAGES

If you follow a plan to increase beverage sales in your restaurant, you can be assured of increasing your profits and tips for your wait staff! From suggesting a bottle, rather than a glass of wine – or a pitcher rather than a glass of beer – when you excel at putting beverages on the tab, you will excel at putting money in your pocket. You are in business to make money and if your guests do not enjoy their experience, they will not come back. Beverages and the service they require are a huge part of making sure that your clients leave refreshed and excited about your establishment. Focus on the following proven techniques for increasing your beverage sales:

- **Think media**. The media are always looking for new things to write about food service. Besides holiday events, try to think of new, creative angles about the beverages you serve that might just get a food service reporter excited enough to review and print. You may have a new and exclusive selection of Greek wines and want to have a wine-tasting event. Couple that with appetizers from regions such as "Dolmades" or Hummus served with pita bread. Spend a little on decorations that capture the feel of the region. Have a "media event." Send a press release to your local food editor and invite him in for the experience. You can get help crafting your own press release at **www.press-release-writing.com** or have a professional write it for you for only $100 at **www.writeconsultants.com**.

- **Billboards** or marquees can boost traffic in your business. Using billboards can be as easy as parking your company car out in the parking lot by the street and writing on it with shoe polish. Or you can use a marquee to attract customers and let them know your Cosmopolitans are $1 or top shelf liquors are half price.

- **You do not have to spend lots of money to promote beverages.** Attractive table tents, wine lists, and chalkboard specials can be valuable props to promoting beverages. Always feature selections that your greeters and wait staff can suggest as soon as the guests are seated. A number of suppliers will provide you with, free of charge, props that you can use to promote beverages in your restaurant. You can order them online at **www.artedesigngroup.com**.

- **Always suggest a "trade up" when it comes to beverages.** It is particularly effective for large groups of guests who are in "party mode" and likely to settle in for the evening. Be quick to recommend a "trade up:" perhaps bottles of wine rather than individual glasses or pitchers of draft beer rather than served by the glass. Not only can this practice increase your sales, it can also let your customers know that you are interested in providing them with the most cost-effective way to purchase their beverages.

- **Be known for something.** If you carry 130 different varieties of Scotch, then by all means, advertise it. Hang signs in the bar that say just that and make sure the local food editor gets wind of it too so that he can pass the word.

- **Always offer your guests a choice when they are ordering wine or champagne.** If your guests have not already ordered wine or champagne after you take their orders, take the opportunity to suggest one that would go with the food they ordered. Many people are shy when it comes to ordering a beverage to complement their order. A couple of suggestions on your part will help them to feel more confident with their choice.

- **Wine list.** Create an imaginative wine list with tasting notes to accompany each wine. Include a couple of unusual wines, such as the "new technology" Bordeaux reds. If you need more information about wine, its characteristics, and grape varieties, visit **www.demystifying-wine.com** or **www.grape-varieties.com.**

- **Advertise the fact that you have a comprehensive bar-food menu.** If you want to keep your customers at the bar, then you can develop a special menu that offers patrons a wider variety of bar fare than most of the other restaurants.

- **Happy Hour is a great opportunity to promote beverages.** If you sponsor a Happy Hour at your establishment, you can use this time to offer a variety of specialty drinks that your dinner customers might not otherwise try. It is fun for your customers; it is great advertising for you.

- **Do not forget to promote nonalcoholic drinks.** When you are thinking of promotions to sell wines, champagnes, and specialty drinks, do not forget to include some nonalcoholic beverages. Coffee, tea, and sodas can be a source of delight to your non-drinking guests and children too.

- **Children's drinks can increase your beverage sales.** If your restaurant caters to families with children, remember that children absolutely love fun drinks that they can slurp through a straw or one that comes in an unusual container.

- **After-dinner drinks present a great sales opportunity.** Many guests might order an after-dinner drink, such as an "Amaretto Coffee" instead of a dessert. Train your servers to know how to recommend an after-dinner drink and be sure they can make informative suggestions. These suggestions can result in a "double up-sell" when your wait staff can recommend desserts along with after-dinner drinks. If a guest orders a simple bowl of fruit for dessert, your server might suggest a "topping" of Grand Marnier or Chambord.

- **Train your wait staff to offer tempting appetizers with a guest's beverage order.** These two winners – appetizers and beverages – can be paired at a special price and used as a promotion to get your customers to try something different. It is also a good way to "off-load" slow movers or excess stock that is approaching its "sell-by" date.

- **Specials and promotions.** Do not simply depend on your servers to get the word out. Place colorful table tents on tables or at every other bar stool to advertise drink and appetizer specials.

- **Have an unforgettable promotion.** In many restaurants, you will see the wait staff wearing buttons that read, "FREE dessert if I forget to tell you about our daily specials." This promotion will keep your servers on their toes and ensure the customers are listening attentively to the delicious spiel being delivered. Order your custom-designed buttons at **www.buttonstore.com**.

- **Suggest trying something different from the "same-old" drink**. Your servers can suggest a Kir Royale rather than "only" a glass of champagne. It is a delectable drink made with champagne and a splash of crème de cassis. Blend the two and you have a sparkling, pink confection rather than "just" a glass of champagne.

- **Provide samples of a beverage if the customer is not sure of what she wants.** Providing samples of beverages often encourages customers to buy additional drinks. Samples also make guests feel special and promote goodwill. An excellent time to offer sample drinks is when guests have to wait for a table or as soon as they are seated.

- **Call on your vendors to help you with beverage promotions.** Most suppliers are only too ready to help you promote the beverages they sell. They will be pleased to help create promotions that will bring in new customers and try their products. And besides, they have a much greater marketing allowance than you. Demand their assistance to help increase your business. Call on your vendors to be present at special sales meetings with your wait staff. They can and will share valuable tips about their products to help your servers become confident in up-selling to their customers. It can only be a win-win situation for you and your suppliers.

MAKE NONALCOHOLIC BEVERAGES SELL

Nonalcoholic beverages are becoming increasing popular. There are many reasons for this including healthier lifestyles, stricter drunk-driving laws, and a general feeling that choosing nonalcoholic is "stylish." Provide what a growing number of customers want: a wide range of "smart" drinks. Here are a few tips for increasing your sales of nonalcoholic beverages:

- **Offer nonalcoholic specialty drinks to designated drivers.** Designated drivers need not be left out of the festivities. Create special drinks that look and taste appealing. For a list of nonalcoholic beverage suppliers, visit **www.allaboutpubs.com**. Also, try **www.nonalcoholicbeverages.com** to find distributors of nonalcoholic wines and beers.

- **Use garnishes to make nonalcoholic drinks look tempting.** Children love "Shirley Temples" made with 7-Up or Sprite and a splash of maraschino cherry juice to make it pink. Add a couple of cherries and you have a winner. Serving nonalcoholic drinks in clever containers (like coconuts) will also get your customers' attention. Garnish them with fresh, tropical fruits and you will soon reap the benefits in sales and profit.

- **Lessen your liability** by training bartenders and servers how to suggest nonalcoholic beverages.

- **Use herbs and spices to liven up nonalcoholic drinks**; add a sprig of mint to an iced-tea drink or sprinkle cinnamon or nutmeg on a milk-based hot or cold drink to make them more colorful and appealing to your guests. Experiment with recipes to find out what your guests like. The site **www.sasky.com** features great recipes for nonalcoholic beverages. Keep the ingredients for some of these drinks on hand. Train your servers how and when to suggest them.

- **Suggest nonalcoholic drinks to your lunch crowd.** Your lunch customers are prime targets to offer a variety of nonalcoholic beverages. Rather than simply "a glass of water," offer specialty waters such as Perrier. Teach your staff that a glass of water cuts profits for you and tips for them. By the time the glass for the "water, please" is ordered, inventoried, washed, and filled, you can run up to $1.08 in cost. And it is "free" to the customer. That means no profit for you and no addition to the tab.

- **Be sure the bartender uses some of his flamboyant drink tricks with nonalcoholic beverages.** If your bartender is skilled in the art of mixing cocktails, be sure he uses the same skills for mocktails. Your bartenders should also understand the basic types of flavors and know how the different combinations interact.

- **Feature nonalcoholic wines on your wine list.** You can also feature other nonalcoholic beverages on your table tents and menus. For a great list of nonalcoholic wines that you can order, or to simply educate yourself as to the unique flavors of nonalcoholic wines, visit the Web site **www.organicwines.com**.

- **If you have a wine tasting party, set up an area for nonalcoholic wines.** The customers who do not drink alcoholic beverages will appreciate your thoughtfulness. They will also see that you offer these wines and may order them when they come for dinner. Advertise that you serve nonalcoholic wines and beverages.

- **Visit Web sites such as www.probartender.com to learn about bartender software.** Some of these related sites offer recipes for nonalcoholic beverages that you may want to try in your restaurant. A nonalcoholic Black Cow can be made with Sarsaparilla (root beer) and vanilla ice cream. Great child pleaser – and you could feature it as "Black Calf" on your menu.

- **Stock your bar with items to help in nonalcoholic beverage sales.** Unique items such as fun-shaped, colored pitchers and cups and ice cubes that glow are all extras that you can use to promote alcoholic or nonalcoholic beverages. Make any drink fun for your customers and they will order more. See **www.barsrus.com** for a list of supplies, videos, bartending events, and links to other bartender sites.

UNIQUE NONALCOHOLIC BEVERAGES

You can also offer unique beverages. Some of these are offered by Jones Soda. The main categories are: soda, naturals, energy, and organics. Each category includes a wide variety of flavors. You can find complete details at **www.jonessoda.com**. You can contact them by phone at 800-656-6050. The company has an interesting background which can be read at: **www.jonessoda. com/files_new/about.html.**

An unusual healthy option is available. You can offer smoothies to your customers. Smoothies are a cool and refreshing treat for your patrons. The mission of Dr. Smoothie is to provide delicious, high quality beverage and food products that are good for your health, mind, and body. The explosive, full rich flavors of Dr. Smoothie will excite and tantalize your taste buds. Their special blends will amaze you taste after taste and are available in Original or 100 percent Crushed Fruit varieties. Dr. Smoothie offers the equipment and mixes you need to serve healthy and flavorful smoothies for your customers. Visit them on the web at **www.drsmoothie.com** or contact them at 888-466-9941.

FOOD ALLERGIES

Food allergies can be serious and life-threatening. Common allergies and intolerances include nuts, peanuts, eggs, shellfish, and wheat. It is advisable to ensure ingredient information is available to your customers. You can list these ingredients specifically on your menu. If they are not listed on the menu, your server must communicate these details to the customers.

I have all sorts of food allergies and intolerances. This condition is much more prevalent than most people realize. Even a small amount of an offending food can cause the person to become nauseous, vomit, develop hives, have trouble breathing, and anaphylaxis is even possible. It is critical that special order requests be taken seriously and that allergens are mentioned in person or on your menu.

You can obtain more information about food allergies from the International Food Information Council at 202-296-6540, or **www.ific.org**.

SERVICES TO IMPACT YOUR BOTTOM LINE

There are services that you can offer which will increase your bottom line and add convenient options for your customers. I will discuss some of these options below.

TAKE-AND-BAKE FOOD ITEMS

Another possibility is take-and-bake food items. A restaurant in the Shenandoah Valley offers a recipe book with the founder's recipes and offers prepared food items. These include entrees, side dishes, and their popular dessert items. The items are displayed in several large refrigerated units near their cash register, allowing customers to take items home or stop by to pick up items. Do you offer items that can be prepared as a take-and-bake or ready to cook item?

CARRYOUT

Carryout offers substantial profit and very little additional expense. It is a convenient option for your customers. They will enjoy your quality food items while eating at home. Carryout is a great add-on for lunch service. Many people like to order food from local businesses for their lunch break. There are some issues that are specific to a store that offers carryout, which I will discuss.

Creating a carryout business is easier than developing a dine-in business, but it does require additional skills and a different focus. Dine-in customers usually want to take their time. Carryout customers are in a hurry and your restaurant is just one of their stops. They want to be served quickly. Your counter staff needs to understand this concept and be efficient and attentive.

If you offer various services, distinguish which areas are for carryout, delivery, and dine-in. I have been in restaurants where the decoration and flooring are different in the various areas. It is a simple way to set areas apart. Signage is another good way to direct customers in the right direction. It is best to have a separate entrance for your carryout customers. You need a simple, easy to understand menu in the carryout area.

DELIVERY

Delivery can be a wonderful addition to your restaurant, but it is not for all food service businesses. Consider all the pros and cons before launching a delivery service. Operating expenses are less if you only offer carryout and delivery. It eliminates the need for all dine-in extras and your pizza shop will require less space, which could save money on your rent or lease. But a restaurant that only offers carryout and delivery will appeal to less people.

There are many expenses to consider before making the decision to deliver. They include:

- **Cars.** There are two options with delivery. You can supply company vehicles or your drivers use their vehicles. You will have the added expense for vehicles, gas, insurance, and maintenance.

- **Auto insurance.** Any company vehicle needs sufficient insurance. If your drivers use their vehicles, you must have a proof of insurance, proof of a valid driver's license, and proof of a good driving record.

- **Drivers.** You need drivers to deliver. Your drivers will make a minimal wage then receive tips and commissions for each delivery.

- **Liability Insurance for Delivery.** All businesses should carry liability insurance. Remember the saying, "Bad things happen to good people." That is true of your drivers. No matter how good their driving records, things happen when you are on the road. Talk to your insurance agent about delivery liability insurance.

There was a time when pizza shops offered free delivery. The current price of gas has made this offer difficult. It is becoming common to charge for delivery. The companies I spoke with are charging $1 for delivery. Pizza Hut, Domino's, and Papa John's are all charging a delivery fee at this time. Ironically, Papa John's has seen an increase in business. Even at $1 for delivery, it is still a deal.

WHAT TO DELIVER?

Many items travel well, so review your menu to see what you can deliver. Also consider how you will pack the items to ensure they get to the customer. Delivery containers will make a big difference in the items you can deliver. Most sandwiches and salads travel well, especially if you deliver the salad dressing separately. Prepackaged salad dressing is a great option. You can offer soup, if you find 100 percent leak proof containers. Many pasta dishes can be delivered. There are wonderful pans secured with cardboard lids. These are a great option.

Some of the companies which offer delivery containers include:

WNA products

WNA is a supplier of a very wide selection of quality plastic plates, cutlery, cups, serving ware, and you can choose custom packaging. View the products by category at **www.wnainc.com/products/selectCategory.php**. To find the customer service information for your area, check **www.wna-inc.com/company/contactus**.

Biocorp offers environmentally friendly products for your pizza and sub shop. They provide quality products at reasonable prices. They also supply a line of cutlery that is heat resistant and does not have an after taste or allergy concerns. Their full product line can be viewed at **www.biocorpaavc.com/index.asp**. Contact BioCorp at 866-348-8348.

Wes Pak's food service carriers are an affordable alternative for transporting food. They are one time use packages. The packages are quick and easy to use. Their lightweight design makes them an ideal choice. They can be used to cool drinks or store ice and hot foods. After the food is delivered, the packages can be thrown away. The selection can be viewed at **www.wespakinc.com/section. asp?secID=5**. Call 800-493-7725.

Wes Pak's food service carriers

TAKE CARE OF THE CHILDREN

Restaurant owners are realizing the importance of child-appeal. Children have a large influence on where the family dines. In a recent poll, over 55 percent of adults stated that their children have significant influence over which table-service restaurant they choose. Over 47 percent of adults said that the kids actually choose the restaurant. To gain the customer loyalty of children and their families you must create a child-friendly environment. Your servers play a big role in making an establishment child-friendly. Give your servers tools they can use to attain this goal. Here are some suggestions:

KEEP CHILDREN OCCUPIED

Have plenty of crayons or games on hand to keep the children occupied until the food is served. Two companies where you can find crayons, placemats, and table toys are:

- Binney & Smith, Inc: **www.binney-smith.com**

- Sherman Specialty Co., Inc: **www.shermanspecialty.com**

Besides the usual fare of coloring mats and crayons, your restaurant can set itself apart by offering small toys or books. If you are planning to offer toys with special promotions, do not offer junk; kids are smart and know the difference.

SPEEDY SERVICE

Make sure your staff serves children's drinks and something to munch on if it looks like the order may take a little while. Granted, your servers are not babysitters, but anything they can do to help the parents have a relaxing meal will be welcomed. Paying attention to children also helps your other customers, since an occupied child is less likely to be a screaming child.

If a server has a bad attitude towards children, the parents and the children will probably feel uncomfortable during the meal and — worst of all — will not come back. But, if you teach your servers to treat children as human beings and not merely something to be dealt with, you will surely attract more families to your place of business. Be sure that your servers point out the unique side items on the children's menu and perhaps offer a special treat, such as a balloon, at the end of a meal.

CHILDREN'S MEALS AND MENUS

Make sure your menu has a children's section or create a separate children's menu. It can be as simple as three or four items. Make sure it is simple and child-friendly with items like grilled cheese or macaroni and cheese.

Appetizers also make great children's meals. Children usually do not have enormous appetites, their attention span is minimal, and if something looks good, they will probably try it. That is where using side items to attract families comes into play. A small plate of appetizers, garnished with unusual veggie cutouts in the shape of animals, will get the children's attention — as will special beverages and fun desserts.

Make nutrition fun by offering healthy snacks, desserts, and drinks served in fun containers or carved into funny shapes and sizes. The parents will appreciate your efforts to help teach their children about healthy eating. Simple snacks, like veggie chips with a small serving of a popular dip or ketchup and a special drink served in fun containers with a "crazy" straw, are good items for keeping the children entertained.

INCLUDE YOUR WAIT STAFF IN MENU ITEM DECISIONS

Ask your wait staff what works. Your wait staff will know more about what pleases the customers. Ask for their input. If they know you take their advice seriously, they will pay closer attention to customers' feedback. The following tips will help you get your staff involved:

- **Make selling side items worth their while.** Promote the side items that will fatten the tab and make it more worth the wait staff's efforts by increasing the money in their pockets – and let them know what you are doing.

- **Have a contest.** Award a prize to the server who sells the most side items each month. It does not have to be an expensive prize; a lottery ticket or a special button to wear showing your appreciation are great recognition prizes. You can even give them an old-fashioned trophy engraved with their name. Order them online at **www.quicktrophy.com**.

- **Keep your wait staff informed about new side items.** Be sure to post any changes in your menu and also changes to ingredients or preparation of a side item. This tactic will avoid embarrassing your wait staff. It will also avoid frustration on the part of your customers if an item is not prepared as the menu states or the wait staff fails to mention a "new" item.

- **Include your greeters in promoting sub-menu items.** Your greeters can be a valuable part of your team if you include them in the selling process. They can always start the "thinking" process by suggesting beverages, appetizers, a special side dish, or even desserts before the guests are seated.

- **Show your wait staff the difference between a sample ticket that includes side items with resulting tips – and one that does not.** Nothing is as motivating as money – and once your wait staff sees the difference that side items play in increasing tips, they will be more inclined to suggest them to their customers.

- **Encourage your wait staff to make suggestions.** Have regular meetings with your wait staff and be sure to compliment them (or reward them) on any side item suggestions that become a success on your menu.

- **Get their attention.** Motivate your wait staff to recommend side items to their customers by grabbing their attention first. Money, recognition, and praise work. Set goals for them and then reward them when they reach those goals. Be sure that you praise them in front of other wait staff.

- **Schedule "kitchen" sessions to get your servers involved.** The more your wait staff knows about the ingredients in your menu items, the better their sales will be. Let them taste, cook, and make suggestions for new and tried-and-true items. Your servers should always know how a dish is prepared and what ingredients are involved. You may want to offer a written manual and a kitchen notebook so that they can take notes. Always be open to their suggestions.

- **Offer continuous training.** A stellar training program for your wait staff will not only increase their knowledge and performance, it will also attract a higher caliber of wait staff to your restaurant. A well-trained group of servers will feel more of a part of the operation and offer suggestions more freely. Keep in mind that your wait staff is your most valuable asset in running a restaurant business.

EXPLAINING THE MENU

The server should be thoroughly familiar with the menu contents, its arrangement, and its prices. To illustrate:

1. **Frequently a new customer is confused as to where to find certain items on the menu.** The server should be quick to sense this uncertainty and offer assistance.

2. **Sometimes the customer fails to notice specials or some other featured group of foods on the menu.** The server may tactfully indicate these to the customer.

3. **A foreign name or an unfamiliar term on the menu may be perplexing to the reader.** In response to an inquiry, a simple explanation of the contents of the dish will be appreciated. The server should give such explanations graciously with an attitude of helpfulness and never patronizingly or curtly.

4. **A customer with poor eyesight may have difficulty reading the menu.** The server could read the items to him and write his order.

THE ART OF SUGGESTING ACCOMPANIMENTS

Training your staff in the art of suggestion is an investment that you cannot afford to miss out on. It can mean the difference between a successful operation that boasts of regular customers and the failure of a restaurant to communicate with its customers. Try the following approach:

- **Do not make your customers have to ask about specials or side items.** Make providing information an ingrained part of your wait staff's service.

- **Encourage your wait staff to be attentive and diligent about providing necessary information to customers.** Sell more beverages by suggesting that your customers "trade up." If a party of four orders four glasses of beer, suggest that a pitcher will cost less and provide an extra round.

- **Discuss with your wait staff how to guide customers in their decision-making.** As a group, discuss items that your servers (and greeters) might suggest to customers. Also discuss ways to suggest those items to your guests. A greeter can make a number of suggestions to your guests before they are seated. They will appreciate the suggestion and might spend the "extra" money on an appetizer or dessert.

- **Have your servers point out menu tents that feature specialties or side items.** The best time to suggest most side items is when you first greet the customer and take her drink order.

- **Suggest items in pairs.** When suggesting a beer or cocktail, guide your customers toward an appetizer that would complement the drink. For example, "Our Gold Margaritas are on special today and they really hit the spot with our stuffed jalapeño peppers." When you return to the table, you can say, "Have you had time to decide on an appetizer?"

- **Have greeters recommend at least two appetizers** or mention any specialties you might have.

- **Be sure to suggest multiple appetizers to groups of four or more.** Groups of four or more present an excellent opportunity to suggest a variety of appetizers. Take advantage of this situation: Increase the tab and please your guests at the same time by making appetizer suggestions.

SUGGESTIONS AND SUGGESTIVE SELLING

Before a server can intelligently take an order, she must study the menu and be familiar with the day's specials and selective menu. When a foreign name or an uncommon term is used to describing a product, she should be able to pronounce the name correctly and know what it means in terms of preparation method or the manner of service. A guest is sure to ask for such information about the product. It is annoying to the guest if the server cannot answer promptly and must take time to ask someone else. The server should not only know how a product is prepared and served, but he should also know how it tastes. Many progressive restaurants demonstrate new dishes and specialties to their servers before the serving period begins, allowing them to taste as well as see the food before they sell it. When the server is asked if something is good, his reply will be much more effective if he can say truthfully: "Yes, I enjoyed it very much" or "I think it is delicious."

SUGGESTING SELECTIONS TO THE CUSTOMER

When a customer is unfamiliar with the restaurant, he is hesitant about his food choice, or confused about where to find certain items on the menu, the server has a real opportunity to be helpful by offering suitable suggestions. The server should be tactful in offering these suggestions and should use intelligence about their form and timing. The guest may be influenced to order more through suggestions made by the server. For example:

- **When the customer orders a sandwich or a salad, the server may ask, "Which do you prefer to drink: tea, coffee, or milk?"** thus influencing the customer to add a beverage to his original order.

- **When the customer orders a grilled food that must be cooked to order, the server may first tell the customer the time required and then ask if she would like an appetizer or a soup.**

- **When an a la carte order for a meat course has been served, the server may return to the table, present the opened menu and ask, "Would you like to select a dessert?"** Another form of suggestion is to name an attractive dessert such as, "The chocolate pie is very good" or "We have fresh peach ice cream today."

SUGGESTING ADDITIONAL ITEMS

The server may suggest additional items to the customer, which increase the size of the order. The purpose of such suggestions should be to help the customer make a satisfactory selection, and, at the same time, sell additional food. This type of suggestive selling may be used to advantage when the customer is ordering from an a la carte menu. For instance:

- **Suggest a beverage** with an order for a salad or dessert.

- **Suggest a sandwich** with an order for a soup or a milk shake.

- **Suggest a soup, cocktail, or some other "beginner"** with an order for grilled or fried food that must be cooked to order.

- **Suggest a vegetable or a salad with an order for meat and potatoes.**

- **A customer who has ordered a main course combination that does not include dessert may be encouraged to order dessert**; for example, "We have fresh Georgia peach shortcake today" or "The Colorado cantaloupe is very good." The presentation of the menu and the inquiry, "What would you like for dessert?" may initiate a sale, whereas the question, "Would you like something else?" probably will elicit a negative reply.

PROMOTING SPECIALS

Before you can suggest a special, you must be familiar with the special. Ask your chef or manager for a detailed description before the shift begins; perhaps they could offer a tasting so you can better describe the special to the customers. Restaurants offer specials for various reasons. Focus on these reasons when selling them to your customers:

- Specials are made from local ingredients.

- Specials are made from seasonal ingredients.

- Specials offer a better price value.

- Specials are smaller portions.

- Specials are items that are not usually on the menu.

- Specials are items the restaurant is trying out before putting on the menu.

SUGGESTING HIGHER-PRICED ITEMS

The food suggested by the server may be more expensive than the customer would have chosen. In this case, as when suggesting additional items, the server should consider the customer's desires and satisfaction more important than the amount of the sale. Higher-priced items may be suggested by the server when:

The customer is uncertain about his selection and remarks that a chicken sandwich is all he sees that appeals to him. The salesperson may suggest that the customer might enjoy a club sandwich made with chicken, describing how it is made.

DELICIOUS DESSERTS = BIG PROFITS!

Save room for dessert? Apparently, many diners are doing just that. If your restaurant has not already jumped on to the dessert bandwagon, it is time to do so. Recent statistics show that dessert sales in restaurants are on a rapid rise and show no signs of slowing down. Popular restaurant chains are developing desserts to sell pre-packaged to other restaurants, grocery stores, mail order, or directly to the customer from the restaurant. Refine your dessert menu now and reap the considerable profits that desserts can bring to your business. Here is how:

- **Consider going all out by hiring a pastry chef.** Pastry chefs are in demand, so you will pay dearly to employ a good one. Or you could buy pre-made, frozen dessert items from top brands like Marie Callender or The Cheesecake Factory.

- **Follow the trends.** Statistics point to the dessert boom continuing indefinitely. Technomics' Jackie Dulen says that more sophisticated consumers are one reason. These diners are willing to take "culinary chances." This fact has spurred a new crop of pastry chefs who are continually setting new trends in their work. Whether or not you can afford a pastry chef, go with the trend and be sure that your business offers the best desserts you can manage.

- **Be sure to offer low-calorie desserts such as fruit.** Low-calorie fruit and "sugarless" items are in great demand in restaurants. As people watch their diets more carefully or deal with health problems that prevent them from eating sugar or high-calorie foods, restaurants are coming up with creative ways to make these types of desserts appetizing. Using fresh fruit instead of canned is always a good idea — and sugarless sauces are easy to make and add another dimension to an otherwise bland choice.

- **Today's conveniences allow restaurants to serve high-quality desserts at a high profit.** Cheesecakes from The Cheesecake Factory or pies from Marie Callender can be sent to your restaurant in a minimal amount of time, thus increasing the quality and convenience of being able to offer signature desserts. There are also "thaw and bake" items that can be prepared quickly. Order some delectable treats at **www.dessertstodiefor.com**. You can add your own special touches so that the simplest of desserts becomes a much-talked-about item among your diners.

- **The "Grand Finale" is as important as "Fantastic Beginnings."** The "complete experience" for your diners definitely includes a top-rated dessert. You can strive to provide the best appetizers and entrées, but if your desserts fail to impress, the customers will leave disappointed. Pay attention to the quality of your desserts.

- **A great dessert will make a lasting impression on your customers.** More than likely, your customers will remember the last thing they eat at your restaurant. Think of desserts as a way to make lasting impressions on your diners and to increase your profits.

- **Give a classic dessert a special twist.** Even plain apple pie can be updated in new, trendy ways. Add nuts or raisins to the filling and a piece of melted cheese on top rather than ice cream. Think of new ways that you can give your tried-and-true desserts a "lift" and watch your dessert sales increase.

- **Simple is better when it comes to desserts.** Simply made and served desserts can always perk up your sales. If your restaurant is designed to appeal to families, try gelatin desserts or pudding. A beautifully molded dish of flan, swirled with caramel and served on a clear glass plate is a dish that will appeal to your customers' sense of taste and vision alike.

- **Smaller is better too.** For the more petite appetites, have your servers offer "half" helpings of your desserts. Even if you offer a discount for the smaller servings, your profit margin will increase on overall sales.

- **Experiment with textures – from lusciously creamy to crunchy.** Try adding various types of nuts to a creamy dessert. Experiment with your desserts so that you can offer a change from the norm. Ask your customers which they prefer.

- **Cheese can add a creative touch to many desserts.** Cheese has always been a mainstay for any meal, but when you add it in a creative way to desserts it becomes a taste sensation. Try adding various textures and tastes of cheeses to your desserts and have your wait staff try them and compare them to the "old" method of preparation.

PROMOTING DESSERTS

Profits on desserts can make up for losses on other menu items. A great dessert can make up for a mediocre meal. The ingredients are usually inexpensive; labor is where you incur the greatest cost. Nevertheless, desserts normally have a 0 percent food cost and can help cover more pricey items on the menu. Take every opportunity to promote your dessert selection; your efforts will pay dividends. Consider the following possibilities:

- **Implement a "dessert program" to increase sales.** A dessert program can be as simple as Boston Market's idea to offer a free dessert if the waitperson does not ask "Would you like dessert?" Another could be to offer a free appetizer or drink if you order a dessert at the beginning of the meal. Boston Market has seen a 10 percent increase in their dessert sales since they implemented the program.

- **Gentle suggestions can be big "nudges."** Your wait staff does not have to be a group of hard-core salespeople to push the dessert items on your menu.

- **Try offering desserts for two and watch your sales increase.** If your customers seem reluctant to order a dessert, try offering two spoons or forks with one dessert. It does not seem quite so indulgent when they are sharing.

- **Serve-yourself dessert bars are very popular.** Whether your restaurant is family-style and you offer a sundae bar with all the toppings or you offer a fine-dining experience, you can increase your profits by setting up "help-yourself" dessert bars. These are becoming as popular as salad bars throughout the country and your customers will appreciate being offered a variety of desserts from which to choose.

- **Suggest dessert "extras."** Dessert "extras," such as a scoop of vanilla bean ice cream on top of hot apple pie or a dollop of whipped cream on top of that strawberry shortcake, can be appealing suggestions to your guests. Be sure to have plenty of extras on hand and teach your wait staff how to suggest them.

- **"Your" personal favorite is a great selling tool.** People love a recommendation that comes from actually trying the product.

- **Ways to make your on-site desserts profitable.** If you decide to go all out and hire a pastry chef to make your own signature desserts, you can make them highly profitable by selling them to outside vendors and other restaurants. Selling whole desserts, such as cheesecakes, pies, and cakes, can greatly increase your profits while advertising your own restaurant's brand.

- **Suggest and serve desserts with lots of humor.** The meal is winding down and your diners are trying to decide which dessert to order. Fun remarks such as, "We've taken all the calories out of that hot fudge sundae." Or, "You only live once, don't live without dessert," can gather smiles from around the table and make your customers happier.

- **Offer whole desserts such as pies and cakes to go.** Many restaurants nationwide are offering whole desserts to take home or back to the office. Large parties may order a whole dessert to continue the party back home. It is a great profit-maker and also a great way to advertise your dessert.

- **Make your customers feel as if they deserve dessert.**

- **Display table tents that feature professional photos of your dessert items.**

- **After-dinner dessert accompaniments.** Some patrons may not want a real dessert, so be prepared to offer them a dessert coffee and, if you want to, include a small trinket of chocolate on the side of the saucer.

- **Dessert samplers make the sale.** One of your choices might be a dessert sampler—where guests get to try out a bite-sized taste of all of your various indulgences.

- **One dessert "made for two" will delight your guests.** Restaurants are taking advantage of the trend to "share" desserts and are actually advertising desserts "made-for-two." These special desserts can be a bit larger than a dessert offering for one and served on one plate with two forks or spoons. Even when sold at a discount, you will realize a profit from the sheer number you sell.

HOW TO SHOWCASE YOUR DESSERTS

A "ho-hum" attitude about desserts can ruin your dessert sale profits. When approached with enthusiasm, desserts can be a huge profit-maker for your business. The following tips will help you make the most of your desserts:

- **Draw a mental picture.** Use lots of adjectives. Using adjectives that whet the appetite is essential when suggesting dessert items. Luscious, creamy, rich, and crunchy are all great adjectives to use when describing dessert items.

- **Have meetings where your servers sample desserts.** Ask them to write down the adjectives that they would choose to describe the taste and texture. Encourage your staff to be enthusiastic when presenting them to your customers. Offer a prize for the most creative "wordsmith." Then, encourage your servers to go out and use those adjectives when describing desserts to your customers.

- **Keep your customers informed about special desserts.** Chalkboards at the entrance to your restaurant, table tents, and well-trained servers are all excellent ways to inform your customers about dessert offerings. If you advertise in the community, be sure to mention dessert specials or new desserts.

- **Offer plain vanilla ice cream with lots of toppings from which to choose.** You can even use alcoholic beverages such as brandy and whip up a thick and delightful "Brandy Ice" served in a brandy snifter or champagne glass to make a more sophisticated dessert item.

- **When you take your customers' entrée orders,** suggest that they leave room for dessert. One restaurant sells their hot blueberry and cherry cobbler specials by letting their customers know that they must order it when they place their entrée order because it is baked fresh and extra time must be allowed. Or, if you suggest a wonderful dessert before your diners order, they can be thinking of the dessert throughout the meal.

- **Whet appetites by describing the aroma of certain desserts.** Aromas wafting from the kitchen have sold many desserts. Your wait staff can also use aromas as a selling point for desserts by describing the aromas to your customers. Smells of vanilla bean and apple pie and cinnamon evoke memories of childhood and dining satisfaction.

- **Dabble in the sweet stuff.** Powdered sugar makes a great impression on guests when you dust the plate with it and then lay the actual dessert on top of it. You can also lay a cutout on the plate, and then dust it with powdered sugar. When you remove the cutout, you will have a wonderful design.

- **Serve chocolate-covered platters.** If you buy the old-fashioned ketchup and mustard squirt bottles, you will have your own chef's style decorating tool to create wonderful designs in chocolate right on the plate. It is best to lightly draw on the outer edge of the plate and make sure servers know to keep their thumbs out of the sauce.

- **Dazzle them with raspberry drizzle.** Raspberry sauce goes well with just about any dessert – even chocolate. You can use the same technique to design a beautiful reddish drawing on the dessert platters before you drizzle a bit of the sauce right on top of the actual dessert.

SPECIAL-OCCASION DESSERTS

You can offer frozen desserts that clients can take home to thaw and eat when wanted. Here are some other ideas for promoting your special dessert items:

- **Encourage your customers to order family-size "special occasion" desserts to take home.** Special-occasion desserts that can be picked up and taken home are growing in popularity as our nation becomes busier with work and home. People want quality and quantity for their hard-earned bucks. Offerings such as a "bucket of ice cream" with the order of a birthday cake is a great idea – and it might keep mom or dad from having to stop by yet another place to pick up ice cream to go along with the cake. Whether the occasion is a birthday, family reunion, or candlelit dinner for two, sending desserts home can be a great profit-maker for your restaurant.

- **Have a "Sundae Sunday" special.** Sunday dining at a restaurant is becoming as firm a tradition as a big Sunday dinner at home used to be in days gone by. A simple idea that will delight your guests and is easy to set up is a sundae bar.

- **Promote seasonal "special" desserts.** Holidays are perfect opportunities to offer seasonal desserts. Let your imagination soar; offer pumpkin cake with sage ice cream for Halloween or peppermint ice cream and a scrumptious Lane cake for Christmas. Go to the Web site **www.restauranthospitality.com** to find numerous recipes and articles about seasonal desserts.

- Be sure that you have specialty items on hand to go with your desserts. Always have items such as candles, syrups, sprinkles, berries, and nuts on hand for your desserts. Specialty dishes for sundaes and banana splits are great to show off your dessert items. If you cater to children, keep specialty items such as twisted straws and "character" spoons on hand to make them feel special.

- Christmas is a great time for special dessert offerings. Your customers will be in a more festive mood and more willing to "make room for dessert." Try something different from the norm, such as eggnog pudding or plum pudding, rather than the usual pumpkin pie or chocolate cake. You can file away some fabulous holiday finds at **www.christmasrecipe.com**.

- **Start a free birthday or anniversary club and offer a free dessert.** If you can get people to sign up for a birthday club, you get to capture their address, which means you will be able to mail out coupons and other offers to increase traffic to your establishment. About a week before their birthday, send them a coupon for a free birthday cake and then serve them a miniature-sized cake when they come in to celebrate.

- **Make your usual desserts festive at holidays by using garnishes.** Try twisting flexible, black licorice sticks into "scary" shapes for Halloween, or tint your whipped cream topping with food coloring. Use garnishes throughout the year to make your desserts memorable.

- **Offer "take home" desserts for holiday gatherings.** Holidays are especially hectic for families who work and try to shop and cook for holidays. It is a great time for you to really promote whole desserts for holiday gatherings and increase your dessert profits. Pies and cakes are easy to transport and will keep better than desserts such as ice cream or custard desserts. People want that "down home" taste, so if you make your own pie crust, for example, be sure to advertise the fact.

PRESENTING DESSERTS

Special cases and presentation trays can enhance the look of your desserts and make it impossible for customers pass them by. Here are some sources for presentation products:

- **Gourmet Display, www.gourmetdisplay.com**, offers a wide variety of presentation products including beverage housings, pastry cases. cubes and staircases, ice carving pedestals, juice dispensers, ornamental iron, tiers, epic edge trays, riser rim mirror trays, serving stone trays, and acrylic and mirror trays. Two examples are pictured below.

- **America - America Corporation** produces a line of elegant birch wood commercial servings trays that are totally dishwasher safe. They are exceptionally lightweight and handsome. They also dry faster than plastic trays and can support heavy loads. A variety of colored trays are also available or you can have them customized with your company's logo. For more information visit **www.america-americabirchtrays.com**.

For much more information on techniques to increase the bottom line, I recommend the books listed below from Atlantic Publishing (**www.atlantic-pub.com**).

- *The Food Service Professional Guide to Increasing Restaurant Sales (Item # FS15-01).*

- *The Food Service Professional Guide to Food Service Menus (Item # FS13-01).*

- *The Food Service Professional Guide to Building Restaurant Profits (Item # FS9-01).*

- *The Food Service Professional Guide to Restaurant Marketing and Advertising (Item # FS 3-01).*

- *The Food Service Professional Guide to Restaurant Promotion and Publicity (Item # FS4-01).*

- *The Food Service Professional Guide to Bar and Beverage Operation (Item # FS11-01).*

FINDING, RECRUITING, AND HIRING GREAT EMPLOYEES

TRAINING

The most serious problem facing labor relations in the restaurant industry today is the lack of trained personnel. New restaurant employees are often thrown into jobs with little or no formal . While on the job they must gather whatever information and skills, correct or not, they can. Blame for this situation lies with management. Managers regard training as a problem that must be dealt with — quickly and all at once — so that the new trainee can be brought up to full productivity as soon as possible.

Getting employees to do things right means taking the time to train them properly from the start, so that they understand: what needs to be done; how to do it; and why it should be done that way. Effective training involves more than simply providing information. Managers and supervisors at every level must realize that training is a continuous process — it must never stop.

Most managers and supervisors think of training as teaching new employees skills, such as dishwashing or bartending. Training needs to be far more than that; management must look beyond its own interests. You must start to consider the employee's interests, goals, needs, and desires, if you are to become successful.

Employees must know not only their jobs and how to perform them, but how their performance affects others in other parts of the restaurant. They must visualize their position as an integral part of an efficient machine, not as a separate, meaningless function. Take the plight of the dishwasher in most restaurants. Dishwashers are vitally important to the success of any restaurant and yet few managers, and virtually no other employees, are consciously aware of their importance. Rather than being treated with dignity and respect, they are considered, in most establishments, insignificant, menial laborers. They are often paid minimum wage with little or no benefits and expected to do all the dirty work: cleaning up after others and working in poor conditions while all the other employees shout orders and instructions. Many managers themselves do not fully realize the importance of this function or that it is far harder to find a good dishwasher than it is a good waitperson. I have always mandated that every new hire perform at least one shift in this position to fully understand its importance. Try giving the dishwashing staff an hour-long break one night and see the resulting chaos.

Telling an employee that his position and performance is crucial to the restaurant's success and showing him the reasons why are two entirely different things. The importance of performing his job in the manner in which he was trained must by physically demonstrated to the employee, as well as the ramifications of straying from these procedures. Using the example of the frustrated dishwasher, let us apply this philosophy with some practical, hands-on management.

Start the training program by having all of the dishwashers come into the restaurant for dinner, lunch, or a pre-shift meal with you. While the waitperson is performing her service, point out the importance of having clean, grease-free dishes and explain why silverware and wine glasses must be checked for spots. Show them why the wait staff needs their stock quickly and what happens if they do not get it.

Type out a list describing the cost of each plate, glass, and so forth in the restaurant for the dishwashers. It is the most effective way to show why they must be so concerned and careful about breakage. List the cost of the other articles that pertain to their job, such as the dishwashing machine, chemicals, soaps, pots, pans, and knives.

Show them that you are concerned with both them and their performance. Pay more than the other restaurants in the area so that you will attract the best people. Set up some small benefits such as a free meal and free soda per shift. A financial incentive is the most effective type of motivating force. Establish bonuses for the dishwashers, such as giving them three to five cents extra for each cover served that night. The small cost of these extras will be substantiated with lower turnover rates and higher production.

Apply this principle of demonstrating rather than lecturing to illustrate your points with all of your employees and you will have the basis for a good training program and good employee relations.

IRING TRAINABLE RESTAURANT EMPLOYEES

Your goal in hiring employees is to find the best possible fit for the job. As a service organization, you will be looking for employees with strong customer-service attitudes. By hiring the right person for the job, you save money and time on searching for, hiring, and training replacements. You will also save costs associated with additional FICA and unemployment insurance payments, overtime pay to cover unfilled positions, and fees for advertisements and employment agencies. You will also have fewer turnover and morale problems to worry about.

Like most management decisions, hiring the right employees requires planning. The first considerations are federal regulations concerning hiring employees. Make sure you know the rules before you start. The U.S. Department of Labor's Elaws, at **www.dol.gov/elaws**, provides business owners with interactive tools that supply information about federal employment laws.

Wages and compensation are always important to employees. Be aware of local, state, and federal laws governing pay rates. In 2004 the Department of Labor enacted a new rule regarding "white-collar" employees and overtime-pay requirements. Employers can obtain a copy of the regulations and other information about the new rules at **www.dol.gov/fairpay**. Other useful guides on human resources and making hiring decisions can be found at **www.uniformguidelines.com/uniformguidelines.html#3** (Uniform Guidelines on Selection Procedures) and The Council on Education in Management's Web site at **www.counciloned.com**.

RECRUITING SOURCES

So where do you find good employees? Running an advertisement in the local paper is always the first avenue that comes to mind, but may not be your best resource for employees. Consider the following alternatives as well:

- **Promoting from within.** It is an excellent source. Hosts and bus people are often eager to be promoted to serving staff because of the increase in income and prestige. Not only does this method motivate your current workers, it saves you money on training because these people already know a great deal about the establishment and position. It is much easier and cheaper to find bussers and hosts/ hostesses from the outside and train them than to recruit and train a new server.

- **Employee referrals.** Ask your employees if they have friends or relatives who are looking for work. Offer an incentive to employees for helping you recruit. You can offer an employee a $25 bonus for each referral; if the person works out and stays on for a year, give both the employee and new hire a cash bonus at the end of that year.

- **Open house.** Hold an open house to find new employees. This strategy is particularly effective if you are looking to fill several positions at once. These take more work than a regular interview, but it may be worth it. Get your managers or other employees to help. Make sure to advertise the open house.

- **Off-site recruiting.** Restaurant trade shows are excellent places to recruit. Consider using other events for recruitment purposes such as wine tastings, food festivals, and career fairs.

- **Customers.** Got a regular customer looking for employment? You know they already like your restaurant so they will probably make a good salesperson too.

- **Industry organizations and Web sites.** Many industry Web sites have pages for posting jobs and résumés. Check out the National Restaurant Association at **www.restaurant.org** or Nation's Restaurant News at **www.nrn.com**.

- **Area colleges.** Many college students are looking for a source of income and a schedule they can work around their classes. Many of these colleges also offer culinary arts or restaurant management programs such as Texas State Community College at **www.waco.tstc.edu.**

- **Culinary Schools.** Check out local and national culinary schools. They usually have a spot on their Web site for people to post résumés. Some examples include CIA at **www.ciachef.edu**, Sullivan's University in Louisville, KY at **www.sullivan.edu/programs/program2.htm**, New England Culinary Institute at **www.neculinary.com** and US Hospitality Schools at **www.restaurant.org/careers/schools.cfm**.

If you do run an ad, be sure to study other hospitality employment ads in the paper. How are they written? What types of information are important? You should also think about what type of information you want to emphasize about your organization and the position. Do you offer better benefits than most of your competitors? You want to highlight that in any recruitment ad to attract applicants. Do you emphasize a fun work environment? Do you need someone that already has some food service skills or do you prefer to train someone from the ground up so they do not come in with any preconceptions or bad habits? Make a list of all the information you feel is important to include in your ad, then start writing. Most papers charge by the word, so you want to get your ad across as succinctly as possible. Also remember that a classified ad is a marketing tool. You are trying to attract good applicants; use exciting language to make applicants want to work for you.

There are alternatives when placing classified ads. The local paper is just one option. Think about area college newspapers, local magazines, hospitality Web sites, and community bulletin boards as well.

HAT TO LOOK FOR IN POTENTIAL EMPLOYEES

Many managers fall into the "warm body" trap when hiring. This practice is widespread and causes many more problems than it solves. The manager will hire the first person that walks through the door to fill an empty space, which only leads to higher training and hiring costs because this person does not work out in the long run.

When hiring, take the time to carefully select your candidates. Here are some attributes to look for in this process:

- **Stability.** You do not want employees to leave in two months. Look at past employment-sheet records. Stability also refers to the applicant's emotional makeup.

- **Leadership qualities.** Employees must be those who are achievers and doers, not individuals who have to be led around by the hand. Look at past employment positions and growth rate.

- **Motivation.** Why is the applicant applying to this restaurant? Why the restaurant industry in general? Is the decision career-related or temporary? Does the applicant appear to receive motivation from within or by domineering others, such as a spouse or parent?

- **Independence.** Is the applicant on her own? Does she appear to be financially secure? At what age did she leave home? And for what reasons?

- **Maturity.** Is the individual mentally mature enough to work in a stressful environment? Will she be able to relate and communicate with other employees and customers who may be much older?

- **Determination.** Does the applicant seem to always finish what she starts? Does she seem to look for, or retreat from, challenges? Examine time at school and at the last job.

- **Work habits.** Is the applicant aware of the physical work involved in restaurant employment? Has the applicant done similar work? Does the applicant appear neat and organized? Look over the application. Is it filled out per the instructions? Neatly? In ink? Examine past jobs for number and rate of promotions and raises.

SCREENING POTENTIAL EMPLOYEES

Screening job applicants will enable you to reject those candidates who are obviously unsuitable before they are referred to a lengthy interview, saving the restaurant and the applicants time and money. The preliminary screening can be done by an assistant manager. Job candidates may then be referred to the manager for intensive interviews. All applicants should leave feeling they have been treated fairly and had an equal opportunity to present their case for getting the job. It is an important part of public relations; the applicant that just left may be your next customer.

THE APPLICATION

Always have job candidates fill out an application form. The application form gives you information about the person's skills and experience. The following tips will help you streamline your application process:

- **Application file.** You should keep applications on file for a year. It is a good source to use for potential employees the next time you have an opening. Rather than advertising, look at your application file first. Was there anyone who stood out that you did not have an opening for before?

- **References.** Make sure your application form has a spot for the candidate to list references. Then use this information. Many future problems can be avoided if you call two or three references. Ask the referee what job the candidate performed, what time period they worked for the referee, if the candidate got along with supervisors and coworkers, and if the referee would ever consider hiring her again.

- **Tests.** You may want to consider including job skills tests in your application process. Perhaps you could give the candidate a short math test or ask her to demonstrate how she would wait on a customer.

CRITERIA

Base your preliminary screening on the following criteria:

- **Experience.** Is the applicant qualified to do the job? Examine past job experience. Check all references.

- **Appearance.** Is the applicant neatly dressed? She will be dealing with the public; the way the applicant is dressed now is probably better than the way she will come to work.

- **Personality.** Does the applicant have a personality that will complement the other employees and impress customers? Is she outgoing but not overbearing?

- **Legality.** Does the applicant meet the legal requirements?

- **Availability.** Can the applicant work the hours needed? Commute easily?

- **Health and physical ability.** Is the applicant capable of doing the physical work required? All employees hired should be subject to approval only after a complete physical examination by a mutually approved doctor. Make certain the application is signed and dated.

APPLICANT CATEGORIES

All applicants at this point should be divided into one of the three following categories:

- **Refer applicant.** Refer applicant to manager for interview and, if feasible, to the department head where the job is open.

- **Reject.** Describe the reasons for rejection and place the application on file for future reference.

- **Prospective file.** Any applicant who is not qualified for this position but may be considered for other areas of the restaurant should be placed in a prospective applicant file.

INTERVIEWING

The application will give you some information about a potential employee, but the job interview will give you more. When interviewing, do not use a script; instead, have a conversation. Focus on what animates the candidate. Ask open-ended questions and look for thoughtful responses. Also have other employees participate in the interview process so that you can compare impressions. Look for new hires that will be amenable to cross-training and new opportunities. Ask how they feel about taking on new responsibilities and what other positions they would like to learn. Here are some guidelines that will help you through the interviewing process.

- **Be systematic.** Before you go into an interview, prepare a list of questions. Also, be sure to read the application before you sit down for the interview. Have the job description, expected work hours, pay information, and general restaurant policies in front of you. Discuss these details with the candidate. Inform the applicant of the time frame within which she will be notified about the position. Ask if the applicant has any questions before you finish the interview.

- **Take notes.** It will make it easier to compare potential candidates when you make your hiring decision.

- **Have a panel interview.** In restaurants, interviews are typically conducted by managers. Think about including others in the interview process. If you are hiring a new server, you may want the serving captain to interview with you. This person may think to ask important questions you would not. Do not include too many people or you are likely to make the candidate a bundle of nerves.

- **Develop a rapport.** Job interviews are stressful. Take a few moments at the beginning of interviews to chat and put the applicant at ease; let the person relax and the interview will be more successful.

- **Treat all applicants considerately and show a genuine interest in them**, even if they have little or no chance of obtaining the job. Every applicant should be treated as a potential customer because they are.

- **Be on time and ready to receive the applicant.** Arriving late or changing appointment dates at the last minute will give the applicant the impression that you are unorganized and that the restaurant is run in the same manner.

- **Know the job being offered.** You cannot possibly match someone's abilities with a job you do not know or understand completely.

- **Make the applicant feel at ease.** Have comfortable chairs and beverages available. Speak in a conversational, interested tone.

- **Applicants will be full of questions about the job, its duties, and the salary.** Newspaper advertisements tell only a little about the job and your company, so allow plenty of time for this important discussion.

- **Let the applicants speak whenever possible.** You can learn a great deal about them by the way they talk about themselves, past jobs, former supervisors, and school experiences. Watch for contradictions, excuses, and, especially, the applicant being on the defensive or speaking in a negative manner. Avoiding subjects is an obvious indication that there was some sort of problem there in the past; be persistent about getting the whole story, but do not be overbearing. Come back to it later if necessary.

- **Pay as much attention to the interviewee's appearance.** Notice if the applicant appears clean, well groomed, and appropriately dressed for the interview. Does the person have good posture? Is she chewing gum? Does the person smile frequently?

- **Never reveal that you may disapprove of something an applicant has done or said; always appear open-minded.** On the other hand, do not condone anything that is obviously in error.

- **Always ask a few questions they do not expect and are not prepared for**: What do they do to relax? What are their hobbies? What is the last book they read? Try to understand their attitudes, personalities, and energy levels.

- **Perhaps one of the most useful things you can ask when interviewing prospective employees is: What were your favorite parts of your previous job?** Look to see if the things they liked to do with previous employers fit with the things you will be asking them to do for you. It is important to cross-train employees to do as many jobs as possible and it helps employers know which of those jobs will be a good fit. Often in interviewing prospective food service employees, you will get two types of applicants: those who say they prefer the "people part" of the job (talking to guests, serving customers, running the cash register) and those who like the "food part" of the job (chef, salad prep, line cook). Most applicants will be fairly honest about what they like to do.

- **Be sure to ask at least one behavior-based question**; it will be very useful in getting at how an applicant responds in real-life work situations and how well she is able to handle them. For example: "What would you do if a customer complained that the soup just does not taste right?" or "What would you do if your seemingly happy patron did not leave any tip at all?"

WHERE TO INTERVIEW

Conduct interviews in a quiet place, such as a back table during a slow period. Most restaurant owners and managers like to hold interviews and accept applications in the mid-to late afternoon between lunch and dinner rushes. Be sure to eliminate distractions. Ask your staff not to interrupt you and turn off your cell phone and pager.

FIRST IMPRESSIONS

The interview is where you get your first impression of your potential employee. Notice what they are wearing. You can also get a feeling for their punctuality. Did they arrive on time? Better yet, did they arrive five minutes early? Do they seem organized? Do they have all the information they need to fill out the application?

INTERVIEW RED FLAGS

Watch out for individuals who show too much interest in hours, benefits, wages, and titles during the interview process. This interest can signal a person who is not too interested in work. Look for long lapses of time in the work history section of their application. Ask the person what they did during this time; they may simply have taken time out to raise children or it could signal a trouble spot.

WHAT TO LOOK FOR IN A PERSON YOU ARE HIRING AS A SERVER

Look for a passion for service. Often passion is more important than a lot of past experience. People with non-traditional backgrounds are often more flexible. Also remember that people skills are more important than technical skills; you can easily teach the technical skills. Does the candidate look you in the eye? Does he or she smile? Do they seem warm and friendly or aloof? What does their body language tell you? Someone who sits back with their arms folded sends a negative signal. Someone sitting forward signals interest and eagerness. Look for servers with outgoing personalities who will be good salespeople.

AVOIDING INTERVIEW-RELATED LAWSUITS

There are two basic types of interview problems: 1) interviewer deficiencies that can be improved with training and 2) discriminatory actions or impacts that may result in compliance actions or lawsuit. There is no way to guarantee that you will never be sued. However, employers can do several things that will minimize the risk. Employers should:

- Design questions carefully.

- Ask only pre-planned questions.

- Ask the same questions of every applicant.

- Carefully document responses.

- It is very important that the interview be documented in two ways: 1) notes taken during the interview and 2) recap documentation that supports a recommendation after the interview is over. Most employers provide forms and instructions to ensure that the record is carefully made and preserved.

- Be aware of bias. If you are aware that a manager is biased, do not allow that manager to interview. Managers who are biased will reflect those biases in the interview. The biased individual has a tendency to find traits and attitudes that fulfill preconceived beliefs.

- Treat every applicant with respect and dignity.

- Pay particular attention to your rejection methods. Although most applicants are rejected, ensure that the methods are professional, respectful, and kind.

- Consider rejected applicants' challenges. Provide an internal method for rejected applicants to challenge the rejection. Try to understand the applicant's perspective and, if there is error on the part of the company, rectify the error.

- Audit the process.

Do not wait for a third party to review your records and advise you that there is adverse impact in your selection rates. Do not only review the process annually for the affirmative action plan. Know what your selection rates are and, in the event there appears to be an adverse impact, fully investigate the matter. Advise management of risks and enlist managers in finding solutions.

UNLAWFUL PRE-EMPLOYMENT QUESTIONS

This section is not intended to serve on behalf of or as a substitute for legal counsel or even as an interpretation of the various federal and state laws regarding equal and fair employment practices. The purpose of this section is only to act as a guide to the type of questions that may be legally asked of a potential employee.

A thorough discussion of this subject with both the state and federal labor offices and with your lawyer would be in order. Standard employment applications may be purchased at your local office supply store. Before you use these forms, let your lawyer examine one to make certain that it does not contain questions that might be considered illegal.

The Federal Civil Rights Act of 1964 and other state and federal laws ensure that a job applicant will be treated fairly and on an equal basis, regardless of race, color, religious creed, age, sex, or national origin.

There is a fine line between what may and may not be asked of applicants. Use common sense in regard to the type of questions you ask. Avoid questions that are related to or might evoke an answer that infringes upon the applicant's civil rights. Beware of:

- **Age/date of birth.** Age is an area of great concern for establishments with liquor,

- **Wine, or beer licenses.** Age is a sensitive pre-employment question because the Age Discrimination in Employment Act (**www.eeoc.gov/policy/adea.html**) protects employees 40-years-old and above. It is permissible to ask an applicant to state his or her age if it is younger than 18 years.

- **Drugs, smoking.** It is permissible to ask an applicant if she uses drugs or smokes.

The application also affords an employer the opportunity to obtain the applicant's agreement to be bound by the employer's drug and smoking policies. The application also affords an employer an opportunity to obtain the applicant's agreement to submit to drug testing.

- **Other problem areas.** Questions concerning whether an applicant has friends or relatives working for the employer may be improper if the employer gives a preference to such applicants. Questions concerning credit rating or credit references have been ruled discriminatory against minorities and women. Questions concerning whether an applicant owns a home have been held to be discriminatory against minority members. While questions about military experience or training are permissible, questions concerning the type of discharge received by an applicant have been held to be improper because a high proportion of other-than-honorable discharges are given to minorities. The Americans with Disabilities Act prohibits general inquiries about disabilities, health Problems, and medical conditions.

A list of prohibited questions, some of which are obvious but used to illustrate the point:

- How tall are you, anyway?
- What color are your eyes?
- Do you work out at the gym regularly?
- Do you or anyone you know have HIV or AIDS?
- Did you get any workers' comp from your last employer?
- How old are you, anyway?
- Have you been in prison?
- Are you really a man?
- Do you rent or own your home?
- Have you ever declared bankruptcy?
- What part of the world are your parents from?
- Are you a minority?
- Is English your first language?
- I can't tell if you're Japanese or Chinese. Which is it?
- So which church do you go to?
- Who will take care of the kids if you get this job?
- Is this your second marriage, then?
- Just curious: Are you gay?
- Are you in a committed relationship right now?
- How does boyfriend feel about you working here?

QUESTIONS YOU WILL WANT TO ASK

Start out by reviewing the applicant's work history. You should also ask if anything would interfere with the person getting to work on time. You should ask specifics about experience. Has the candidate ever served wine? How many tables has she waited on at one time? Has she made salads before? You may also want to give the candidate hypothetical questions to answer to see how she would react in particular situations.

Ask the candidate, "If a customer sent back a freshly opened bottle of wine, what would you do?" or "It's a Saturday night. One of the other servers has called in sick and the salad person has just walked out. How would you react?" These types of questions can tell you about job knowledge and how well a person works under stress.

Some of the questions will only require a yes or no answer. You should also ask open-ended questions to give the applicant an opportunity to talk. A job applicant should do about 80 percent of the talking. You can ask an applicant to describe what she liked best about her previous job.

Here are some specific questions you may want to ask:

- What are your strengths?

- What are your weaknesses?

- How would your current (or previous) boss describe you?

- What were your boss's responsibilities? What is your opinion of him or her?

- How would your coworkers or subordinates describe you professionally?

- Why do you want to leave your present employer?

- Why should we hire you over the other applicants?

- What qualities or talents would you bring to the job?

- Tell me about your accomplishments.

- What is your most important contribution to your last (or current) employer?

- How do you perform under deadline pressure? Give me an example.

- How do you react to criticism?

- Describe a conflict or disagreement at work in which you were involved. How was it resolved?

- What are two of the biggest problems you have encountered at your job and how did you overcome them?

- Think of a major crisis you have faced at work and explain how you handled it.

- Give me an example of a risk that you took at your job (past or present) and how it turned out.

- What is your managerial style like?

- Have you ever hired employees? Have they lived up to your expectations?

- What type of performance problems have you encountered in people who report to you and how did you motivate them to improve?

- Describe a typical day at your present (or last) job.

- What do you see yourself doing five years from now?

SCENARIO QUESTIONS

You also want to ask scenario questions. These can be used to gain insight into an interviewee's service attitude:

- If you were serving a guest who appeared to have had too much to drink, what would you do?

- If a guest is served the wrong order or an improperly prepared order, how would you handle the situation?

- If a customer is on a restricted diet, what types of menu items would you suggest?

For more information about legal and appropriate interview strategies, visit **www.doi.gov/hrm/pmanager/st13c3.html**. The National Restaurant Association also offers a publication entitled *The Legal Problem Solver for Restaurant Operators*. You can order the publication online at **www.restaurant.org**.

RECRUITING FOR TEAMWORK

When hiring, you want to find people who are going to pitch in and help. You want people who can function well as part of a team. When recruiting, avoid superstars and seek both technical skills and evidence of being good with people. You may want to ask about teams they have been on (sports or other). Also ask how they may have handled conflict with fellow workers in the past.

There are four personality types that function well in a team environment. The best teams have a balance of all four members. Understand the different types and roles. Keep your eyes open for these types of individuals:

PERSONALITY TYPES ADVANTAGEOUS FOR TEAMWORK	
Personality Type	**Characteristics**
The contributor	Technically adept, task-oriented, born trainer. Excellent leader in kitchen or detail-oriented bus staff.
The collaborator	Goal-oriented, quick to help out. Excellent in front-of-the-house staff.
The communicator	Process-oriented, great floor manager, server, greeter, good trainer, attentive listening skills for problem-solving.
The challenger	Candor and openness, helps a team explore better ways of doing things, highly principled, willing to disagree, blow whistle.

THE FINAL SELECTION AND DECISION

Reaching the final selection is often a difficult choice. You may have many applicants who are qualified and would probably become excellent employees, but which one do you decide upon? Always base your choice on the total picture the applicants have painted of themselves through the interviews, résumés, and applications. Gather advice from those who interviewed or had contact with the individuals. Not only will it help you reach the correct decision but will also make the rest of your staff feel like a part of the management decision-making team. Whomever you select, she must be someone you feel good about having around, someone you will enjoy working with, and you feel will have a good chance of being successful at the job.

When you offer her the job, make certain the applicant fully understands the following items before accepting the position:

- **Salary.** Starting pay, salary range, expected growth rate, the day payroll is issued, company benefits, vacations, insurance, etc.

- **Job description.** List of job duties, hours, and expectations.

- **Procedures for first day of work.** Time and date of and to whom she will report on the first day of work.

REJECTING APPLICANTS

Rejecting applicants is an unpleasant, difficult task. The majority of the applications will be rejected immediately. Some applicants will ask the reason for rejection. Always be honest, but use tact in explaining the reasoning behind the decision. Avoid a confrontation, explaining only what is necessary to settle the applicant's questions. Usually it will be sufficient to say, "We accepted an applicant who was more experienced," or "...who is better qualified."

Some applications may be transferred into a "prospective file" for later reference. Inform the applicant of this action, but do not give the impression that she has a good chance of being hired, nor state a specific date when you will be looking for new employees.

PERSONNEL FILE

Once the applicant is hired, a personnel file should be set up. It should contain the following information:

- Application.
- Name, address, and phone number.
- Employment date.
- W-4 Form and Social Security number.
- Emergency phone number.
- Job title and pay rate.
- Signed form indicating receipt and acceptance of Employee Handbook/ Personnel Policy Manual.

You will continually add to the personnel file with items such as:

- Performance evaluations.
- Termination date and a detailed account of the reasons for termination.

EMPLOYEE HANDBOOK

One of the first training materials your new employees will see is an employee handbook. Federal law mandates that all employers, regardless of size, have written policy guidelines. Employee handbooks/policy manuals are used to familiarize new employees with company policies and procedures. They also serve as guides to management personnel. Formally writing down your policies can keep you out of court, prevent problems and misunderstandings, save time spent answering common questions, and look more professional to your employees. Explaining and documenting company policy to your employees has been proven to increase productivity, compliance, and retention.

Lack of communication, along with inadequate policies and guidelines, have been cited as major factors in workplace legal disputes. Failure to inform or notify employees of standard policies has resulted in the loss of millions of dollars in legal judgments. Simply not being aware that their actions violated company policy has been an effective defense for many terminated employees. Most important is to have the employee sign a document stating she has received, reviewed, understands, and intends to comply with all policies in the manual.

If you have ever written a policy document before, you know how time-consuming it can be. Even if you were a lawyer, it would likely take you 40 hours to research and write a comprehensive employee manual. To pay someone to draw one up can cost thousands of dollars. Atlantic Publishing has put together a standard employee handbook guide for the food service industry; all you have to do is edit the information. The template contains all of the most important company handbook sections and it is written in Microsoft Word so that customizing and printing your manual is easy. The program currently sells for around $70 and is available at **www.atlantic-pub.com**, or by calling 800-814-1132.

When writing your employee manual, keep these simple writing tips in mind:

- **Write for your audience.** Make sure the tone, style, and language reflect the audience for whom you are writing.

- **Organize your material before you begin writing.**

- **Make sure to revise and edit.** It is also a good idea to have someone else read your handbook. A second pair of eyes often catches mistakes you might have missed.

- **Use simple, direct language** and avoid wordiness.

- **Use the active voice.** Instead of saying, "The server was taking the drink order," say, "The server took the drink order." Active voice keeps your manual much more immediate and it emphasizes your subject (the employee or trainee) rather than the object.

- **Use gender-neutral language.**

For much more information about hiring, training and motivating restaurant employees, I recommend the following books by Atlantic Publishing (**www.atlantic-pub.com**). Some are general restaurant reference while others are topic specific for concerns that restaurant managers may need.

- *The Encyclopedia of Restaurant Training* (Item # ERT-02).

- *How to Hire, Train, and Keep The Best Employees* (Item # HTK-02).

- *The Food Service Manager's Guide to Creative Cost Cutting* (Item # CCC-01).

- *The Food Service Professional's Guide to Controlling Restaurant and Food Service Operating Costs* (Item # FS5-01).

- *The Food Service Professional's Guide to Controlling Restaurant and Food Service Labor Costs* (Item # FS7-01).

- *The Food Service Professional's Guide to Waiter & Waitress Training: How to Develop Your Staff For Maximum Service & Profit* (Item # FS10-01).

- *The Food Service Professional's Guide to Bar & Beverage Operation: Ensuring Success & Maximum Profit* (Item # FS11-01).

- *The Food Service Professional's Guide to Successful Catering: Managing The Catering Operation For Maximum Profit* (Item # FS12-01).

- *How to Communicate With Your Spanish and Asian Employees* (Item # CSA-02).

- *The Restaurant Manager's Success Chronicles* (Item # MSC-01).

- *Key Words Food Service Employee Translation Poster* (Item # KWF-PS).

- *The Professional Caterer's Handbook* (Item # PCH-01).

- *The Complete Guide to Successful Event Planning* (Item # SEP-01).

- *The Non Commercial Food Service Manager's Handbook* (Item # NCF-02).

- 8 Posters to Reinforce Good Service (Item # WSP-PS).

- *The Complete Wait Staff Training Course on Video or DVD* (English DVD: Item #CWS-ENDVD-02).

- *The Waiter and Waitress and Wait Staff Training Handbook* (Item # WWT-TH).

- *Design Your Own Effective Employee Handbook* (Item # GEH-02).

- *365 Ways to Motivate and reward Your Employees Every Day – With Little or No Money* (Item # 365-01).

- *199 Pre-Written Employee Performance Appraisals* (Item # EPP-02).

- *Superior Customer Service: How to Keep Customers Racing Back to Your Business-Time Tested Examples from Leading Companies* (Item # SCS-01).

SAMPLE EMPLOYEE HANDBOOK TABLE OF CONTENTS

EMPLOYEE HANDBOOK ACKNOWLEDGEMENT

I have received a copy of the Employee Handbook and acknowledge that I have reviewed, read and comprehend the contents. I understand that the handbook is an overview and summary of general policies and procedures in force at the time this handbook was written.

I also understand:

- that _____ policies, procedures and benefit programs are always being reviewed.

- that _____ reserves the right to modify, change, revise or rescind any policy or benefit.

- that I should always check with my manager for the most current information.

- that benefit plans are defined in legal documents such as _____ insurance policy and that should a question arise about the benefit, the legal language of the policy documents govern.

I also agree that both the Company and I, at any time, with or without cause, may terminate employment. This employment-at-will relationship will be in effect throughout employment with _____, unless it is changed by an agreement signed by me and _____ of the company.

_____

Employee Name (please print)   Date

_____

Employee Signature   Date

BEHAVIORAL EMPLOYMENT APPLICATION

Company Name: _____

Address: _____

City: _____ State: _____ Zip: _____

Phone Number: _____

PERSONAL INFORMATION	
Last Name:	First Name:
Address:	
City: State:	Zip Code:
Telephone (Home):	(Office):

DESIRED POSITION
Position Requested:
❑ Full-time ❑ Part-time ❑ Seasonal
❑ Day Shift ❑ Evening Shift ❑ Night Shift
Have you ever been employed by our company? If so, when?

EDUCATION			
Level	Date (Month/Year)	Grade/Years Completed	Diploma/Degree
High School:			
Name:	Starting:	9 10 11 12	Yes No
	Ending:		
College/University:			
Name:	Starting:		Yes No
Specialization:	Ending:		
Other Applicable Training			
Name:	Starting:		Yes No
Specialization:	Ending:		

EMPLOYMENT EXPERIENCE	
Company:	Type of enterprise:
Address:	Telephone:
Position:	Name of immediate supervisor:
Length of employment: Start: _____ End: _____ Salary: Start: ___ End: _____	
Reason for departure:	
Description of your tasks:	

Company:	Type of enterprise:
Address:	Telephone:
Position:	Name of immediate supervisor:
Length of employment: Start: _____ End: _____ Salary: Start: ___ End: _____	
Reason for departure:	
Description of your tasks:	

Company:	Type of enterprise:
Address:	Telephone:
Position:	Name of immediate supervisor:
Length of employment: Start: _____ End: _____ Salary: Start: ___ End: _____	
Reason for departure:	
Description of your tasks:	

In this section you are required to answer two behavioral-based questions. These questions are designed to get you to recall a specific event or accomplishment from your past. Be very specific and describe the incident accurately. If you can, include a reference. These references may be contacted so be sure it is someone who witnessed the incident or who can comment on your involvement in the situation. Use the following example to help you answer the two behavior questions:

Example: Organization "A" is committed to exceeding our customers' expectations. Please tell me about a time when you exceeded a customer's expectations.

When:	Explanation:
Situation:	
Action:	
Outcome:	
Frequency:	
Reference:	

Flexibility is important in this work environment. Please tell me about a time when you were most flexible in your job. Be very specific and describe one actual incident.

When:	
Situation: Describe the circumstance in detail.	
Action: Tell me what you did (be specific).	
Outcome: What was the end result?	
Frequency: How often do you do this?	
Reference: Who else was there? Did anyone comment?	

In our organization we expect employees to work cooperatively as team members. Please tell me about your best example of working cooperatively as a team member to accomplish an important goal.

When:	
Situation: Describe the circumstance in detail.	
Action: Tell me what you did (be specific).	
Outcome: What was the end result?	
Frequency: How often do you do this?	
Reference: Who else was there? Did anyone comment?	

REFERENCES

Please list the name and contact of a minimum of three references, excluding blood relations and/or personal friends, who can supply us with professional references concerning your work habits. These can be the same as those included with your answers for the behavior questions.

Name	Occupation	Company	Phone
Address			
Name	Occupation	Company	Phone
Address			
Name	Occupation	Company	Phone
Address			
Name	Occupation	Company	Phone
Address			

PLEASE READ CAREFULLY BEFORE SIGNING THIS DOCUMENT

I, the undersigned, do clarify that the information listed above on the present application is true and complete. I understand that any false declaration may result in the refusal of my application or the termination of my employment. I authorize (Company Name) to contact my former employer(s) and others listed here for references.

Signature: _____ Date: _____

APPLICATION REVIEW PROCESS

All applications for (Company Name) are reviewed and acknowledged within one month of receipt. The following standards apply:

Education: Grade 12 or equivalent (minimum). Work experience may be considered as an equivalency. (Company Name) is an equal opportunity employer that encourages a 50/50 male/female ratio.

Reference Check: References must be work-related. No personal references. Summer students will be allowed one personal reference due to lack of work experience.

EMPLOYMENT APPLICATION II

Notice to Applicant: We are an Equal Opportunity Employer and do not discriminate on the basis of applicant's race, color, religion, sex, national origin, citizenship, age, physical or mental disability or any other characteristic.

PERSONAL INFORMATION (please print)

Name: _____ Social Security Number: _____

Address: _____

_____

_____

City: _____ State: _____ Zip: _____

Phone Number: _____

POSITION INFORMATION

Position applied for (check all that apply):

❏ Executive Chef   ❏ Expediter   ❏ Assistant Manager
❏ Host/Hostess   ❏ Baker   ❏ Kitchen Manager
❏ Banquet Manager   ❏ Prep Cook   ❏ Bartender
❏ Pantry Cook   ❏ Beverage Manager   ❏ Server
❏ Bus Person   ❏ Cashier   ❏ Cocktail Server
❏ Cook   ❏ Counter Person   ❏ Dining Room Manager
❏ Other _____

Have you ever worked for this organization: ❏ Yes ❏ No

If yes, date(s): _____

Prior position: _____

Reason(s) for leaving: _____

_____

_____

EDUCATION (List from present to past)

School/Institution	Major or Area of Study	Degree or Number of Years

OTHER INFORMATION

Name of friends and/or relatives employed by this organization:_____

_____

Position(s) held: _____

_____

If you are eligible, are you interested in health insurance? ❑ Yes ❑ No

AWARDS/ACHIEVEMENTS

_____

_____

_____

_____

REFERENCES *(Please list at least three people who are not related to you)*

Name	Occupation	Phone Number

EMERGENCY CONTACT *In the event of an emergency, who should we contact?*

Name: _____ Relationship to applicant: _____

Address: _____

City:_____ State: _____ Zip: _____

Phone Number:_____

ACKNOWLEDGMENT *(please read carefully)*

I hereby certify that the information contained in this application form and in any attachments (hereafter made a part of this application) is true and correct to the best of my knowledge and agree to have any of the statements checked by the organization unless I have indicated to the contrary. I authorize the references listed above to provide the company any and all information concerning my previous employment and any pertinent information that they may have. Further, I release all parties and persons from any and all liability for any damages that may result from furnishing such information to the company as well as from the use or disclosure of such information by the organization or any of its agents, employees or representatives. I understand that any misrepresentation, falsification or material omission of information on this application may result in my failure to receive an offer or, if I am hired, in my dismissal from employment.

Applicant's Signature _____ **Date** _____

CONSENT FOR DRUG & ALCOHOL TESTING FORM

I, _____, freely give my consent for this drug and/or alcohol test. I have been fully informed of the reason for this urine test and I understand that the results will be forwarded to my supervisor.

If the test results are positive, I will be given the opportunity to explain the results before any action is taken.

Signature: _____

Date: _____

Employee Name: _____

Test Date: _____

Social Security Number: _____

Department: _____

Employee Start Date: _____

Supervisor: _____

SAMPLE RESUMÉ SCREENING WORKSHEET

Use this form to compare and rate top applicants for a position.

Company: _____

Position: _____

Date: _____ Time: _____

Rate each of the characteristics below according to the following scale:

0 = does not meet expectations   1 = meets some expectations

2 = meets expectations   3 = exceeds expectations

Name: _____

Education 0 1 2 3   Years of Experience 0 1 2 3

Food Service Knowledge 0 1 2 3   Professional Development 0 1 2 3

Demonstrated Skills   0 1 2 3

Other _____ 0 1 2 3

TOTAL SCORE _____

Name: _____

Education 0 1 2 3   Years of Experience 0 1 2 3

Food Service Knowledge 0 1 2 3   Professional Development 0 1 2 3

Demonstrated Skills   0 1 2 3

Other _____ 0 1 2 3

TOTAL SCORE _____

Name: _____

Education 0 1 2 3   Years of Experience 0 1 2 3

Food Service Knowledge 0 1 2 3   Professional Development 0 1 2 3

Demonstrated Skills   0 1 2 3

Other _____ 0 1 2 3

TOTAL SCORE _____

Name: _____

Education 0 1 2 3   Years of Experience 0 1 2 3

Food Service Knowledge 0 1 2 3   Professional Development 0 1 2 3

Demonstrated Skills   0 1 2 3

Other _____ 0 1 2 3

TOTAL SCORE _____

APPLICATION RESPONSE SAMPLE LETTERS

Dear _____:

Thank you very much for your interest in working for _____. We are not hiring at this time; however, your application will remain on file for 90 days.

Should a suitable opening become available during that time, we will call and advise you if you have been chosen to continue in our selection process.

Sincerely,

Manager

APPLICATION RESPONSE SAMPLE LETTERS

Dear _____:

This letter is to confirm the terms and conditions of your employment with _____.

Date of hire:

Position:

Wage:

Probationary period:

Union/Non-union:

Benefit eligibility:

Vacation entitlement:

For all other terms and conditions, please refer to the _____ Handbook or Collective Agreement.

Please sign this offer and return to (Name) if you are in agreement.

I HEREBY AGREE TO THE TERMS AND CONDITIONS OF MY EMPLOYMENT WITH _____ AS OUTLINED ABOVE.

Name:_____   Date:_____

Sincerely,

_____

EMPLOYMENT INTERVIEW: CANDIDATE ANALYSIS

Applicant: _____

Job Title: _____

Interviewer: _____ Title: _____

❑ 1st Interview ❑ 2nd Interview ❑ 3rd Interview

PERSONALITY TRAITS

Briefly list the personality traits the ideal candidate for this position would possess:

_____

_____

❑ Great for this position.   ❑ Acceptable for this position.

❑ Not very good for this position.   ❑ Not acceptable for this position.

Comments: _____

_____

EXPERIENCE

Briefly list the ideal type of experience and training the best candidate for this position would possess:

_____

❑ Above-average experience and background.   ❑ Average experience and background.

❑ Below-average experience and background.   ❑ No experience. Background not applicable.

Comments: _____

_____

JOB FAMILIARITY

❑ Exceptional familiarity; no training needed.   ❑ Above-average familiarity.

❑ Rudimentary familiarity, but able to meet job performance standards.

❑ Below-average familiarity; training needed.   ❑ Applicant has no familiarity in this field.

Comments: _____

_____

MOTIVATION

❑ High level of interest in job.   ❑ Basic desire to work.

❑ Interest in the position is minimal.   ❑ Little or no interest in the position.

Comments: _____

_____

AMBITION & ENTHUSIASM

❑ Positive drive to succeed.   ❑ Average goals.

❑ Lacks goals and enthusiasm   ❑ Relies on others; no goals or ambition.

Comments: _____

_____

WORK FIELD UNDERSTANDING

❑ Above-average knowledge and understanding. ❑ Average knowledge of this field.

❑ Below-average knowledge of this field. ❑ Poor knowledge and understanding in this field.

Comments: _____

_____

ORIGINALITY & APTITUDE

❑ Exceptional creativity; seems original and proposes new ideas.

❑ Above-average creativity. ❑ Average level of creativity.

❑ Few ideas or suggestions. ❑ Poor creativity; little or no suggestions.

Comments: _____

_____

POISE & COMPOSURE

❑ Very self-assured and capable. ❑ Able to handle problems well.

❑ Fair composure and control. ❑ Below-average composure.

Comments: _____

_____

APPEARANCE

❑ Neat and very well-groomed. ❑ Above-average personal appearance.

❑ Average personal appearance. ❑ Disheveled, disregard for appearance.

Comments: _____

_____

RATE THE APPLICANT:

❑ Excellent for this position. ❑ Highly possible for other position.

❑ A possible candidate. ❑ An unlikely candidate.

Carefully consider all factors in this evaluation. Then rate the candidate on a scale from 1 to 10, with 10 being the highest possible score.

1 2 3 4 5 6 7 8 9 10

Other position this applicant seems to have experience for: _____

Comments: _____

_____

_____

_____

EMPLOYMENT INTERVIEW QUESTIONS

Interviewer: _____ Title: _____

❑ 1st Interview   ❑ 2nd Interview   ❑ 3rd Interview

1. What are your strengths? _____

2. What are your weaknesses? _____

3. How would your current (or last) boss describe you?_____

4. What were your boss's responsibilities? _____

5. What's your opinion of him or her? _____

6. How would your coworkers or subordinates describe you professionally? _____
   _____

7. Why do you want to leave your present employer? _____

8. Why should we hire you over the other finalists? _____

9. What qualities or talents would you bring to the job? _____

10. Tell me about your accomplishments. _____
    _____

11. What is your most important contribution to your last (or current) employer? _____
    _____

12. How do you perform under deadline pressure? Give me an example. _____
    _____

13. How do you react to criticism? _____
    _____

14. Describe a conflict or disagreement at work in which you were involved. How was it resolved?
    _____
    _____

15. What are two of the biggest problems you've encountered at your last (or current) job and
    how did you overcome them? _____
    _____
    _____

16. Give me an example of a risk that you took at your last (or current) job and how it turned
    out. _____
    _____

17. Describe a typical day at your current (or last) job.
    _____

18. What do you see yourself doing five years from now? _____
    _____

REFERENCE CHECK GUIDE

1. How long have you known/supervised the candidate?

2. What was his/her position and job responsibilities?

3. Confirmation of employment dates.

4. What were his/her strengths?

5. Were there any areas that needed improvement?

6. How well did he/she get along with:

   Management   Good Fair Poor

   Coworkers   Good Fair Poor

   Clients/Customers Good Fair Poor

7. Would you describe this person as being people- or technologically oriented?

8. Describe his/her written and oral communication skills?

9. Did he/she require close supervision?

10. How satisfied were you with his/her time management skills?

11. How satisfied were you with his/her punctuality and attendance?

12. What would you say motivates this person to do a job well?

13. How was his/her attitude towards their work?

14. What kind of work environment and position would this person thrive in?

15. Why did he/she leave your company?

16. Was proper notice given?

17. Would this person be eligible for a rehire with your company?

EMPLOYEE REFERENCE CHECK

APPLICANT:_____

POSITION:_____

Reference: _____

Company:_____

Address:_____

_____

Phone: _____

Dates of Employment:_____

Job Title:_____

Duties: _____

_____

_____

Why did the applicant leave your employment?

_____

_____

What were the applicant's best job skills? _____

_____

_____

In what areas could the applicant improve? _____

_____

Did the applicant get along with supervisors? ❑ Yes   ❑ No   With peers? ❑ Yes   ❑ No

Following is a list of personal characteristics. Using a scale from 1 to 10 (with 10 being the highest), please rate the applicant, based on your experience working together.

Punctual	1	2	3	4	5	6	7	8	9	10	Pleasant	1	2	3	4	5	6	7	8	9	10
Honest	1	2	3	4	5	6	7	8	9	10	Flexible	1	2	3	4	5	6	7	8	9	10
Organized	1	2	3	4	5	6	7	8	9	10	Composed	1	2	3	4	5	6	7	8	9	10
Reliable	1	2	3	4	5	6	7	8	9	10	Competent	1	2	3	4	5	6	7	8	9	10
Professional	1	2	3	4	5	6	7	8	9	10	Team Player	1	2	3	4	5	6	7	8	9	10
Lazy	1	2	3	4	5	6	7	8	9	10	Inconsistent	1	2	3	4	5	6	7	8	9	10
Inattentive	1	2	3	4	5	6	7	8	9	10	Temperamental	1	2	3	4	5	6	7	8	9	10

Would you rehire this person? ❑ Yes   ❑ No   Why or why not? _____

_____

CHECKED BY: _____   DATE:_____

UNIFORM PURCHASE AGREEMENT

Employee: _____ Date: _____

ITEM	NO. PURCHASED	PRICE EA.	TOTAL
		TOTAL DUE	

❏ Items have been paid in full
❏ Cost of uniforms to be deducted from payroll check for the week ending _____

I agree to reimburse the company in full for the above items. In addition, I authorize my employer to withhold any salary due to me until all items have been paid for or returned.

_____

Employee's Signature   Date

_____

Manager's Signature   Date

WORK SCHEDULE

Employee	Sun	Mon	Tues	Wed	Thurs	Fri	Sat

TRAINING EMPLOYEES

MANAGEMENT'S ROLE IN TRAINING

As important as it is to hire qualified, trainable employees, the manager is also an important element in making any training program work.

YOU AS THE LEADER

As the restaurant owner/manager, you are the leader of your team of employees. Here are some tips that will help you to become a successful leader:

- **Leadership qualities.** What makes a good leader? Think back to bosses you had during your early years in food service. Who stands out and why? You probably remember the managers that respected employees, showed concern for their staff, and were not afraid to pitch in wherever needed. These are all qualities that make a good leader.

- **Do as I say and as I do.** If you do not want your staff to hang around the back booth chatting when business is slow, do not engage in this activity yourself. Show them how you want them to act as well as telling them. If management does not show concern for how the customer is treated, then employees are unlikely to perform any better.

- **Be on the floor during the dinner and lunch rushes.** As you walk through the dining room, if you see a plate that a customer has finished with, bus it. If water glasses need refilling, refill them. You will show your servers that you care about the customer enough to do these things and they will emulate your behavior.

- **Know yourself.** Know your own strengths and weaknesses; capitalize on the former and minimize the latter. If you have poor math skills, hire an accountant to compensate for this weakness. If your people skills are strong, make sure you spend a lot of time on the floor with your employees and customers.

- **Be part of the team.** Pitch in when someone is missing. Your employees will appreciate your effort and respect you for lending a hand rather than managing "from on high."

- **Always remember that your employees are individuals.** Accept the different styles of your employees, but always expect good performance. Be alert to the training and development needs of each individual employee. Meet those needs.

- **Be fair and consistent with policies and procedures.** Treat all your employees equally.

- **Do not show favoritism.** If you dock one employee's pay for an unexcused absence, do not look the other way when the next employee is a no-show with no excuse.

- **Reinforce positive behavior.** The saying "you catch more flies with honey" is true. You are more likely to get the behavior you want out of your employees if you reward them for acceptable behavior. While you always have to discipline for inappropriate behavior, let someone else know they did a good job and that you appreciate it.

- **Help your employees relate to the bigger picture.** Employees can easily get bogged down by detail and focus on one dish or one table, to the detriment of the rest of their duties. It can be difficult for them to step back and see how their behavior might affect the business and profits as a whole. Point out the benefits of good service: happier customers and more income for both the restaurant and themselves.

- **Encourage communication.** Encourage your staff to communicate with each other and yourself. Let them know that you want to know what they need and what they appreciate. By understanding their needs, you will make working together much easier.

- **Be careful not to assemble a team of "yes men."** Creative solutions to problems come from diverse points of view. Do not surround yourself with other management team members who think just like you do. Encourage those who disagree to speak up. You may want to consider rotating meeting leadership to make sure your own point of view is not the only one heard.

- **Be creative when looking for solutions.** In meetings, when you are looking for solutions, state your target/problem simply and clearly. Solutions are found within a range of possibilities with no single answer being right. Begin by brainstorming and appoint one or two "recorders" to keep track of all ideas. Halfway through, change recorders and also freshen the mix of the group. Encourage people to "play" and enjoy using their imaginations. Consider the suggestions logically and inventively.

- **Dealing with conflicts.** Conflict resolution is a tricky part of being a leader. Conflict is not always a negative thing and can often be useful. Encourage people to speak up about what bothers them. Engage in active listening when dealing with a conflict. Also be sure to set norms for politeness, good behavior, and honesty.

TEAMWORK

While you may be the leader in your food service organization, you cannot do everything. Consideration for colleagues and cooperation create a more productive environment, especially when circumstances are particularly demanding. Working and thinking as a team helps to create an environment of collaboration, which will help your restaurant's ability to make profits. Teamwork can increase your productivity, improve decision-making, maximize the use of your human resources, and make better use of your inventory. Make problem-solving an automatic function of daily work. Customer service also benefits from smooth teamwork. You can improve the bottom line — profitability — by efficient team-building.

WHAT IS A TEAM?

A team is a manageable number of people with similar or coordinated functions working together for the common goal of providing seamless service. Usually two to 25 people (ideally 10 to 15 people) make a manageable number of people. You can think of teams as front-of-the-house teams and back-of-the-house teams. If you have a large staff, one particular position could be a team or your teams could be organized by shift. The members of a team must have common goals, similar or complementary functions, and equal responsibility for team performance. Everyone should have the same definitions of "team" and "teamwork" for the teams to work.

To delegate some responsibility, you must choose team leaders. These people do not have to be the best performers, but they should be people who can motivate and train others and carry a full load. They will be the "naturals," the ones to whom others naturally look. Make sure you have more than one leader for each team so that changing schedules can be accommodated and no shift will be without a team leader.

Goals exclusively established by management will never be fully accepted by the group. Managers should encourage employees to share in the task of goal-setting and determining criteria to assess whether or not goals have been achieved. By allowing employees to participate in decision-making, managers help let the employees take ownership of their jobs and of the operation, When ownership occurs, employees are much more willing to go the extra mile and ensure performance standards are being maintained. If they have a stake in the decision-making, they have a stake in the outcomes.

In many ways, team leaders function as management. Team leaders should hold the team together and define individual member roles. Team leaders also guide and train team members. They also ensure open communication among team members and solicit solutions from within the team. Other functions team leaders can fulfill include monitoring performance, providing feedback, working as a liaison to other team leaders, and communicating and demonstrating that team success is the responsibility of each individual on the team. Team leaders can also act as spokespersons for presenting problems or ideas to management. You also can let them train team members and become part of your restaurant's overall training program.

TEAMBUILDING

Food service requires teamwork. Servers must have the cooperation of the kitchen staff and the kitchen staff must have the cooperation of the dining room staff. All employees must be able to work harmoniously with all other employees if they are to achieve good results.

COURTESY

Courteous behavior is as important in relationships with other employees as it is in dealing with the customer. It is hard to be courteous in the heat and hurry behind the scenes in the restaurant, but courtesy pays dividends. A courteous salesperson soon makes friends of fellow employees.

An employee can show courtesy to fellow workers by avoiding personal or slighting remarks about the appearance or actions of another person, avoiding whispering or laughing with one employee in the presence of others who may think that they are being ridiculed, being careful not to cross fellow workers' paths or to bump into them, using "please" and "thank you" when asking for and receiving favors from fellow workers, and being tolerant of the manner and working habits of others.

COOPERATION

Cooperation implies mutual helpfulness. It is reciprocal in character. One cannot receive cooperation from others unless he is also cooperative. One cannot expect to receive help unless he is also willing to give help.

Helping a fellow worker who needs assistance:

- Taking an order for another employee who may be delayed and then turning it over for him to serve.

- Helping another employee finish side-work when that employee has completed his own work.

- Keeping a serving stand, that is used jointly, cleared of an accumulation of soiled dishes.

- Letting bus people know when supplies and special services are needed far enough ahead that they may be able to keep supplies on hand.

- Helping to clear tables in his free time.

FRIENDLINESS

To secure the cooperation of other people, the employee must give them reason to like him. Courtesy, cooperativeness, and fair dealing are important factors in securing the friendship of others. The friendly employee will endeavor to maintain pleasant relations with fellow workers during working hours and will participate in group sociability outside of working hours. The employee will be polite, courteous, and friendly to every employee and avoid joining cliques or favoring certain individuals.

Engage in team-building behavior. A team falls apart easily if you fail to reinforce that they are a team working for a common goal. Let members get to know each other in a casual setting. Have a staff party, take instant photos of teams, and put them on bulletin boards in the back of the facility. You can also create a scrapbook that includes personal details, pets, family, and personal goals. Update it regularly.

If one member of a team does not perform, the whole team suffers and team trust is compromised. Be sure to reward good behavior, but also set conditions for poor behavior. Make sure everyone knows the standards. It is not useful simply to say, "Don't make mistakes" or "Don't have accidents." Find out why an employee is having problems and work together to find the cause and a solution.

Not all teams are the same. Kitchen team members are more specialized and less likely to switch functions. Front team members have primary but not fixed responsibilities and are more likely to interchange functions, covering for each other for smooth service. Make sure all team members understand the differences and what their own responsibilities are.

A slowdown in one function can upset the entire flow of service to all customers. The team leader can define and assign secondary task responsibilities during the daily meeting. Sometimes a buddy system works well to adjust front-of-the-house staff to shift away from the "not my job" syndrome. The server who is tipped according to service performance is affected in the long run by someone else's temporary work buildup.

If the same server has regular trouble, then consider additional training. Include answering the phone as one function that may need coverage.

TEAMWORK TRAINING

There are online sources available to help train your management and staff in teamwork. For training materials and information on teamwork training, visit:

*   **www.facilitationfactory.com/interstitial.html**
*   **www.temeculacreek.com/ball.htm**

BUILDING TRUST AND TEAM SPIRIT

Ask the dishwasher what he does. If he replies "I wash dishes," you have some work to do. If he replies, "I make sure that the restaurant can function properly by providing a constant supply of clean dishes," then you have succeeded. Every person in the organization is important and has a critical role. Ensure that employees know their roles in your organization. To get the best from your team, you need to build trust. Here is how to do so.

LEVELS OF TRUST

When working in a team environment, there are three levels of trust:

LEVELS OF TRUST	
Level	Typical Response
High	"I'm not concerned because I'm certain that others will not take advantage of me."
Low	"I need to see that I get my fair share and others don't take too much."
None	"I'll get them before they get me."

You can build trust many different ways. Try spending social time together. Make some jobs two-person jobs (for example: cleaning, napkin folding, etc.). Encourage discussion of problems and issues and let staff know that asking for help is okay. Improve communication and eliminate fear of ridicule or reprisal. Make room for the personal comments: "I feel," "I think," "What do you feel about...?" Provide positive reinforcement for helpful behavior and allow time for trust to grow.

BANISH UNTRUSTING BEHAVIORS

Make sure that no one on your staff or management team engages in the following behavior:

- Ignoring people.

- Embarrassing someone in front of others.

- Failing to keep confidences.

- Avoiding eye contact.

- Withholding credit where due.

- Interrupting others.

- Not helping when able.

- Taking over for someone who does not need help.

- Breaking a promise.

Lead by challenge and positive reinforcement. Set goals just ahead of expectations and reward employees when goals are reached. Try using scoreboards: 102 days since last accident; 2,453 meals served; 1,134 orders with no mistakes. Continually set new goals, but do not make goals too hard to achieve. Be sure that people understand the targets you have set for them; people feel secure in knowing what is expected.

Recognize, reinforce, and compensate outstanding performance. Recognition by itself is reinforcement and may not need compensation. A specific and timely "well done" often holds as much weight as monetary compensation, but monetary rewards have their place as well. Have a ready supply of movie passes and other "goodies" to distribute to the deserving. Even keep some in your pocket for any meritorious action you just happen to see in passing. Match the size of the reward to the size of the performance accomplishment. Have an annual "Academy Awards" ceremony with categories suited to your business (Biggest Helping Hand, Most Infectious Smile, Most Improved Performance) Make it a big deal, with invitations and a special menu. Let each employee bring guests. Set up a committee to select the winners.

Sales incentives. Start with the end result in mind and work backwards. Communicate specifically. Tell your staff you are looking for a particular percentage increase in dollar sales of some item, such as desserts. Break that down into how many desserts per day, per shift, per person need to be sold and be sure that it is a manageable goal for each team member. It is not a quota; it is a goal for the team. It allows for more than one "winner" while the whole team wins. It may also provide an opportunity to motivate the "slower" employees back into peak performance. Everyone should be in on both planning and carrying out incentives and the reward system for goals accomplished. Some rewards for good work include money, recognition, time off, a "piece of the action," getting favored assignments, promotion or advancement, freedom, personal growth, having fun, and prizes.

TRAINING OTHERS TO BE TRAINERS

You could do all the training for your organization, but it is not feasible. You will need to delegate some training activities. How do you determine who would make a good trainer?

- **Job competence.** Anyone you choose to train others must have job competence. Otherwise you are only going to teach new employees incorrect procedures and sloppy work habits.

- **The ability to know how to train.** Some people are natural teachers. Others are good at teaching but may need some guidance and instruction in proper teaching methods. Trainers should be taught the basic principles of adult learning and ways to organize and present training materials/topics.

- **Leadership qualities.** Trainers should have strong leadership qualities.

- **Professionalism.** Trainers must be professionals in their approach and attitude towards their jobs. They must consistently demonstrate high levels of performance standards and a commitment to excellence.

TRAIN MANAGEMENT FIRST

Before you start to train your wait staff, make sure that your management and team leaders are properly trained. Many people in restaurant management positions are promoted through the ranks and many of these people have no management experience. Get them that training so they can manage the rest of the staff effectively. If you do not, you will start seeing problems such as turnover and sloppy work. Consider the following training possibilities:

- **Training resources.** For a complete range of training resources, including books, videos, Software, and posters, see **www.atlantic-pub.com**. See a list of helpful titles at the end of the chapter.

- **Hospitality management courses.** Check with your area colleges and vocational schools. Many have hospitality management programs. It would be wise to enroll your new managers in one of these programs.

ONLINE COURSES

The number of online options available to the restaurant industry is growing. Check out the following Web sites for distance learning courses that can be useful to your managers:

- **www.ecornell.com**: Cornell University School of Hotel Administration's online courses include: "Managing People More Effectively" and other courses in hospitality marketing, management of hospitality, human resources, and hospitality accounting. You can register online or over the phone at 866-ecornell (866-326-7635).

- **www.ahma.com**: The American Hotel and Lodging Educational Institute also offers many hospitality and management courses online.

- **www.ciaprochef.com**: The Culinary Institute of America has recently introduced online courses.

- **www.atlantic-pub.com**: Atlantic Publishing offers ServeSafe® management certification programs and courses.

ROLE OF COMMUNICATION IN MANAGING YOUR STAFF

Communication between you and your staff is just as important as the communication between your servers and your customers.

There are four basic types of communication: speaking, writing, acting and listening.

SPEAKING

Effective speaking is critical in training. If you are planning to speak, you must be sure that your message is understood. When preparing to speak for a training session, make sure you prepare. Ensure that the message you are trying to get across is clear and focused. Spend some time practicing your speech. Ask your family and friends to listen to your practice sessions and ask for feedback on how to communicate more clearly. Practice in front of a mirror to get a sense of your "stage presence" and see what you can do to make yourself a more engaging and focused speaker.

Here are some things you should keep in mind when practicing and when speaking:

- **Make eye contact with your audience.** Do not just focus on the same two people if it is a large group — shift your focus to various parts of the room to engage your audience.

- **Control the speed of your voice.** When nervous, many of us tend to speak at a rapid pace and it will be difficult for your audience to focus on your message.

- **Make your voice varies when you speak.** Nothing will put people to sleep faster than a monotone speaker.

- **Be enthusiastic and sincere when speaking.** It will help you connect with your audience and help them to retain your message.

- **Move around when you speak.** If you stay planted in one spot, it will be easy to lose people's attention. If you move some, but not excessively, it will help keep your audience engaged.

- **Ask the audience if they understand.** If you feel that some of your concepts may be misunderstood, try restating them in different ways during the session.

- **Pay special attention to your opening and closing statements.** These should be attention-grabbers. You want a strong opening statement to ensure you have captured your audience's attention and you want a strong closing statement so they will take your message away with them and remember it later.

WRITING

Writing skills are also important to people in management positions. As a trainer you will write various training programs, job descriptions, and performances evaluations. When writing training materials, keep these following tips in mind:

- **Write in short, easily understandable phrases.** Your employees will come from a variety of backgrounds; make sure that your training materials can be understood by everyone.

- **Check your spelling and proofread material for errors.**

- **Use informal language that will not intimidate or bore employees.** You want them to read the materials you are providing.

There are a number of good writing and grammar references available:

- *The Elements of Grammar* by Margaret Shertzer
- *The Elements of Style* by William Strunck, Jr.
- *Roget's Thesaurus*
- *The Gregg Reference Manual* by William A. Sabin
- A dictionary

ACTING

We often forget that body language can communicate as much as the spoken or written word. Focus on your body language to make sure you are sending the right message. Learn to read others' body language so you can tell if you are getting your point across.

If a listener is engaged, she will have open arms (not folded across chest). She will lean forward. If she is bored, she will stare into space, tap her foot, doodle, or slump in her chair. If she is listening and reflecting, she will tilt her head, nod, blink frequently, and make a lot of eye contact. If your listener is combative and wants to speak, she will stare at you and tap her foot or a pencil.

LISTENING

Listening is one of the most important activities you will engage in as a manager/trainer. By listening to your employee you will get a sense of what is lacking in your organization and what type of training needs to take place.

Engage in active listening. How many times have you caught yourself daydreaming or planning when you were supposed to be listening to someone? It happens to us all at times. When communicating with your staff, engage in active listening. Make sure they know that you have heard them. As you are listening, nod, lean forward, and maintain eye contact. Using short verbalizations such as "I see" or "uh-huh" lets the person know you are actively following them. Verify that you understand by repeating. You can say, "I hear you saying ..." or "You seem disturbed by...." Make sure to ask open-ended questions, encouraging the other person to speak, such as "How did you feel when that happened?" Also be sure not to interrupt the speaker and seek clarification when points are not clear.

GENERAL COMMUNICATION TIPS

- **Eliminate negative speaking.** The words we choose have a major impact on how people hear what we are saying. Replace phrases such as "I can't," "I should have" and "What's wrong with..." with phrases like "I haven't yet," "Starting now, I will," and "How can we improve?"

- **Overcome cultural barriers and achieve diversity.** The restaurant industry has a very diverse employment base. Teach yourself and other employees tolerance and show respect for all race, gender, sexual preference, and religious differences. If you have a bilingual staff, you should also provide language assistance, including English for foreign speakers and foreign words/phrases for English speakers. (See **www.atlantic-pub.com** for simple food service communication guide books.) There are many sources for bilingual training. Berlitz Languages Centers can provide group training. For the center nearest you, call 800-457-7958 or log on to **www.berlitz.com**. Language Learning Enterprises also offers tutoring and training. They can be reached at **www.lle-inc.com**. The National Association for Bilingual Education tracks federal polices that can help employers. You can reach them at **www.nabe.org**. Worldwide Language Center is another training resource that can tailor instruction to a restaurant environment. Call them at 703-527-8666 or log on to **www.worldwide.edu**. You also might check with area colleges; you may be able to find a college graduate student willing to take on a freelance project. For cultural diversity training products, visit HR Press's Web site at **www.hrpress-diversity.com**.

- **Watch interactions amongst staff to identify those being excluded.** Ask those excluded what they feel would make them become part of the team. A good way to include loners is to get mixed groups together for "games" and coach them and involve all employees in decisions.

MAINTAINING PERFORMANCE STANDARDS

Once your training program is implemented, you want to continue monitoring employee performance to ensure performance levels stay within your high standards. People tend to forget and slack off after a period of time, so it is very important for you to closely supervise your employees and correct these slippages when they occur.

Management's job is not over when training is complete. You still need to give your employees feedback on how they are doing, letting them know if they are maintaining the performance standards you expect. One way is to develop a system to monitor employee performance and communicate how they are doing. There are two general ways to monitor employee performance informal and formal.

INFORMAL PERFORMANCE MONITORING

This type of monitoring is done on a day-to-day basis and includes actions on the manager's part such as observing employees at work, tasting food, and checking in with customers. Of course, it is only part of the informal monitoring process; you must also communicate with your employees. You must let them know when they are performing well and when they need to improve.

When communicating with employees about performance issues, you will be praising or criticizing. Many managers focus too heavily on criticizing employees for poor performance, thinking it is the best or only way to change behavior. Praise for work done well can be a strong reinforcement for the behavior you want to see. Employees need to know what they have done right as much as what they have done wrong. Praise motivates employees to do a good job by building confidence and pride. Constant criticism will only make an employee resentful rather than a good performer.

When criticizing an employee's performance, be respectful — give her the benefit of the doubt and always listen. Make sure you get all the facts before making a judgment. Criticism, when done constructively, is beneficial in improving employee performance and building skill level. Here are a few tips on making constructive criticism:

- **Criticize the action, not the person.** It is the action that is wrong, not the person doing the task. Do not criticize an employee's character or intelligence.

- **Do not focus on the trivial.** If it is one of the busiest nights of the year, do not focus on how messy the kitchen was during dinner rush — focus on how many meals were prepared correctly and on time. You will only gain your staff's frustration and ire by focusing on the trivial.

- **Be clear.** Make sure you are clear when explaining what the employee is doing incorrectly and explain the correct way to accomplish the task.

- **Do not get angry.** Anger will only provoke fear and cause a loss of motivation in your employees.

FORMAL PERFORMANCE MONITORING

Formal performance monitoring goes beyond the daily observing of employee behavior. In formal performance monitoring you will want to focus on particular aspects of job performance and you must develop specific ways to monitor these aspects. For these aspects you need to 1) set standards, 2) measure performance, and 3) provide employees with feedback on their performance.

SETTING STANDARDS

Your standards must be specific and clearly defined. They should also be achievable to prevent employee frustration. A standard may be for a cashier to come within $1 of balancing his cash drawer or a server to sell at least seven desserts.

MEASURING PERFORMANCE

Measurements must be fair and communicated to all employees.

PROVIDE FEEDBACK

People cannot change inappropriate or unwanted behavior if no one tells them to. Employees not meeting the standards need to be told so and corrective action must occur. Employees who are meeting or exceeding the standards also need to be praised and recognized for their efforts.

Remember, feedback should be given regularly. Here are some ways to measure performance:

- **Mystery shoppers.** Many restaurants hire people to dine anonymously at their establishments and then report back to management on the service they have received. These individuals can tell you how the food was presented, how they found the service, and how long they had to wait to be seated. You can find these services online at the following Web sites Secret Shopper at **www.secretshopnet.com**, Mystery Shopper at **www.mysteryshopperjobs.com** and Mystery Shop at **www.mysteryshop.com**

- **Comment cards.** Comment cards are a good source of information for measuring performance. Since they are anonymous, people are usually quite candid in their remarks.

- **Talking with guests.** Always make it a practice to walk around the restaurant and check in with the customers on how their meals were and how service was. Most people appreciate the attention and concern of management and many will be very honest in their comments.

ANNUAL PERFORMANCE REVIEWS

Performance reviews are another important way to give your staff feedback on how they are doing. These should never take the place of daily feedback; they should be used in conjunction with it. Nothing you say in a review should come as a surprise to your employee. Always give your staff regular feedback, both positive and negative. Performance reviews focus on how the employee is doing overall rather than focusing on specific tasks or job areas. Performance reviews usually consist of a manager filling out a performance form and a meeting between the manger and staff member to discuss the employee's performance. The purpose of the performance review is to maintain good performance and improve poor performance. It serves a purpose in your training program because it provides you with information on types of training the employee needs or wants. There is a sample evaluation form at the end of this chapter.

Remember, you are evaluating an employee's performance in relation to the standards you have set up. Refer to the job lists you developed when developing your performance review forms. Consider the following aspects of conducting performance reviews:

- **Intent of reviews.** The results of performance reviews are two-fold. First, the supervisor must use a review in order to judge how well the employee is doing her job and whether or not the employee is eligible for a wage increase. Additionally, and perhaps more importantly, reviews are used to set goals for employees.

- **Setting performance review goals.** When setting goals for improving performance, be sure to make them concrete. Give the server a quantifiable way of reaching her goal. Suggest that the server try to sell ten desserts per shift to increase her up-selling or maybe that the server who lacks customer interaction skills learns the names of two customers per shift.

TYPES OF REVIEWS

There are two kinds of performance reviews. One uses input just from the employee's supervisor.

The other type uses input from other staff members as well. Many companies have switched to a performance review system that involves other staff members. This type of review, called "360 degree feedback," involves the supervisor collecting information from staff members who work with the employee. The supervisor then takes this information and her assessment of the employee and uses this information during the evaluation interview. At no time are names used, so the other employees can feel comfortable giving honest feedback. The Web site **www.360-degreefeedback.com** has specific information pertaining to the "360 degree feedback" process. Additional sites with human resources information include the International Association for Human Resources Information at **www.ihrim.org, www.business.com/directory/human_resources/index.asp**, and The Society for Human Resource Management at **www.shrm.org.** You can download performance appraisal forms and related material for $39.95 at **www.performance-appraisal-form.com**.

REVIEW GUIDELINES

- **Be specific.** How do she need to improve? Does she need to be faster, more punctual, or friendlier towards guests? Give her specific behaviors you would like to see improved and tell her how to go about making positive changes. If she is doing great, tell her in what manner as well.

- **Be fair.** It is difficult to review someone, but be as fair and consistent as you possibly can.

- **Let the employee speak.** Performance reviews should be a dialogue, not a lecture. Let your employee talk about what she thinks she does well and where she might need improvement.

- **Discuss what the employee does well.** Do not just focus on the negative. Give praise where praise is due.

- **Maintain a review schedule.** Give your employees annual reviews. You may want to schedule all reviews during a month that is always slow. You could also schedule reviews for employees' anniversary dates. For new employees, schedule a review in the first couple of months to give them immediate feedback on their new job.

REVIEW QUESTIONS

Some of the behavior you want to find out about in reviews includes the person's relationship with others, her problem-solving skills, accountability, enthusiasm, and team spirit. Structure your questions accordingly. Focus questions on the following areas:

- Does the employee fulfill her job duties?
- Does the employee use sound judgment in keeping a safe work environment?
- Does the employee assist others with work?
- Is the employee responsible and punctual?

Use a rating system for the questions. Be sure to include an area for comments on the form as well; if someone is not performing their duties, you will want specific information on the problem areas.

REVIEW LOCATION

A performance review should always be conducted on neutral ground. Do not conduct them in your office; the person you are reviewing is likely to feel threatened. The review should not feel like a disciplinary interview; rather, it should be a dialogue between you and an employee with the goal of making the employee more productive. You may want to conduct the review off premises or you could go to the dining room. If you conduct the review in the dining room, pick a table rather than a booth and sit beside the person rather than facing them. This body language will help make the review feel non-confrontational. It is also very important that reviews be conducted in private, so if you use the dining room, do so when your establishment is closed and other employees and customers are not in the room.

REVIEW INTERVIEW

When you go into a review, the employee should not be blind-sided. If you have been having problems with an employee, the review is not the place she first hears about it. If that is the case, you need to look closely at your management practices and your disciplinary policy. Start the review on a positive note, then go into any problem areas, and end on a positive note. Summarize results and tell the employee what those results are, and then talk about future goals. Come to an agreement about what the goals will be and write the plan down. The employee should also have a chance to make comments on the review. Give the employee some time to reflect, and then ask that she make her comments in writing. These comments, as well as the review, should go into the employee's personnel file. Finally, after the review is over, continue to encourage the employee by providing praise after each step of improvement.

HANDLING DIFFICULT EMPLOYEES

Everyone is not going to be a model employee and you will have to deal with difficult employee situations. As a manger you have to address the issue and find a way to solve it. Difficult employees come in all shapes and sizes. Here are just a few of them:

- **The new employee.** A new employee is a difficult employee because she does not know what is expected and she needs training in order to reach the desired performance level.

- **The inconsistent employee.** This type of employee is difficult because he often performs well, but just as often he performs poorly. You know this particular person is capable of doing the job because he has shown you that on various occasions. Often, this employee requires much more feedback than other employees to get him on track.

- **The unbalanced employee.** These employees are often very good at one job task but only so-so at others. You may have a cook that is an excellent sous chef, but this same employee leaves the kitchen a wreck after the shift.

- **Mediocre employees.** These are employees that do just good enough. They show up on time and do their jobs, but they do not really produce high-quality work.

- **Less than mediocre employee.** These employees come just shy of doing their job. They often waste time and are rarely productive.

- **The bad employee.** These employees do little work, have a high absenteeism rate, and/or do little work correctly.

DIFFICULT EMPLOYEE WARNING SIGNS

- Poor work quality.
- Complains a great deal.
- Does not follow direction.
- Blames others for mistakes.
- Becomes defensive when approached about problems.
- Absenteeism is high.
- Shows little initiative.
- Does not cooperate.
- Does not interact well with coworkers.

DISCIPLINING DIFFICULT EMPLOYEES

Now that difficult employees have been identified, what do you do about them? Most organizations suggest using a progressive disciplinary policy when discipline is necessary.

- **Take corrective action.** Explain the problem to the employee. Identify the performance problem and talk about the reasons the problem is occurring. Make sure the employee understands the job performance expectations and talk about ways to correct the undesired behavior. The emphasis is on improvement, not punishment. Only after coaching and counseling has been tried several times should a manager move on to disciplinary action. Once disciplinary action does start, it should take place in several phases:

- **Oral warning.** The first step in a progressive disciplinary policy is usually an oral warning. The employee will be warned by the manager in a private conversation that covers: 1) what is expected of the employee, 2) the employee is allowed a chance to explain his behavior, 3) the manager making suggestions for correcting the actions, and 4) specify what further disciplinary action will occur if the actions continue. Even though this step is called "oral," the manager should make a written record of the warning and include it in the employee's personnel file.

- **Written warning.** If the employee repeats the offense, the manager will need to record it as a written warning and include it in the employee's personnel file. The manager should review the warning with the employee and the employee should sign it, indicating he has received the warning and understands.

- **Suspension or termination.** Some discipline policies allow for a suspension step between written warnings and termination and others do not. You will need to decide which type of policy best fits your operation. If you do include a suspension step, the seriousness of the offense should determine the length of time (all suspensions are without pay). Terminating an employee is a serious step to take. An employee can be terminated due to the frequency or serious nature of misconduct. Very serious offenses may be grounds for immediate termination without following the above progressive disciplinary steps. If you terminate an employee, you must include this paperwork in the employee's personnel file as well.

When you create a progressive discipline policy, keep the following in mind:

- **Be sure your policy is appropriate for your business and your employees.**

- **Specifically list what behaviors will be subject to the policy and which behaviors will result in immediate dismissal.** If an employee is chronically late, you may wish to use your progressive disciplinary policy. If an employee has been stealing, you may state that this type of behavior will result in immediate termination.

- **Advise all employees of the policy.** You can let new employees know in their orientation. If you need to communicate the information to current employees, include it on the agenda of a company meeting and make sure each employee receives a written handout of the policy.

- **Determine how you want to document the policy** (how you want to maintain a record of oral warnings, written warnings, and termination paperwork) and decide how long to keep the information on file.

For much more information about hiring, training, and motivating restaurant employees, I recommend the following books by Atlantic Publishing (**www.atlantic-pub.com**). Some are general restaurant reference while others are topic specific for concerns that restaurant managers may need.

- *The Encyclopedia of Restaurant Training* (Item # ERT-02).

- *How to Hire, Train, and Keep The Best Employees* (Item # HTK-02).

- *The Food Service Professional's Guide to Controlling Restaurant and Food Service Labor Costs* (Item # FS7-01).

- *The Food Service Professional's Guide to Waiter & Waitress Training: How to Develop Your Staff For Maximum Service & Profit* (Item # FS10-01).

- *How to Communicate With Your Spanish and Asian Employees* (Item # CSA-02).

- *The Restaurant Manager's Success Chronicles* (Item # MSC-01).

- *Key Words Food Service Employee Translation Poster* (Item # KWF-PS).

- *The Professional Caterer's Handbook* (Item # PCH-01).

- *The Complete Guide to Successful Event Planning* (Item # SEP-01).

- *The Non Commercial Food Service Manager's Handbook* (Item # NCF-02).

- 8 Posters to Reinforce Good Service (Item # WSP-PS).

- *The Complete Wait Staff Training Course on Video or DVD*

- *The Waiter and Waitress and Wait Staff Training Handbook* (Item # WWT-TH).

- *Design Your Own Effective Employee Handbook* (Item # GEH-02).

- *365 Ways to Motivate and reward Your Employees Every Day – With Little or No Money* (Item # 365-01).

- *199 Pre-Written Employee Performance Appraisals* (Item # EPP-02).

- *Superior Customer Service: How to Keep Customers Racing Back to Your Business-Time Tested Examples from Leading Companies* (Item # SCS-01).

EMPLOYEE PERFORMANCE EVALUATION FORM

Name: _____ Position: _____

Interviewer: _____ Date: _____

Last Evaluation Date: _____ Current Salary: _____

For each of the following categories, grade the employee's performance on a sliding scale of 1 to 10 (see scale below). The overall grade is the average of all scores plus the interviewer's comments.

1-2 poor   3-4 below average   5 average   6-7 above average   8-9 very good   10 exceptional

1. **KNOWLEDGE OF JOB** procedures, paperwork, skill, function   1 2 3 4 5 6 7 8 9 10
    Comments: _____
    _____

2. **QUALITY** up to specification, accuracy, consistency   1 2 3 4 5 6 7 8 9 10
    Comments: _____
    _____

3. **ATTITUDE** towards work, management, other employees, customers   1 2 3 4 5 6 7 8 9 10
    Comments: _____
    _____

4. **LEADERSHIP** ability to give direction   1 2 3 4 5 6 7 8 9 10
    Comments: _____
    _____

5. **RELIABILITY** dependable, on time, follows through on assignments   1 2 3 4 5 6 7 8 9 10
    Comments: _____
    _____

6. **PRODUCTIVITY** volume, utilization of time   1 2 3 4 5 6 7 8 9 10
    Comments: _____
    _____

7. **APPEARANCE** uniform, neat   1 2 3 4 5 6 7 8 9 10
    Comments: _____
    _____

8. **SERVICE** alert, fast   1 2 3 4 5 6 7 8 9 10
    Comments: _____
    _____

OVERALL RATING: _____ / 80

SALARY ADJUSTED: ❑ YES ❑ NO   **NEW SALARY:** _____

Signature of reviewer: _____

CUSTOMER COMMENT FORM

Prepared By: _____ Position: _____

Day: Sunday   Monday   Tuesday   Wednesday   Thursday   Friday   Saturday

Date: _____   Shift: _____   Manager: _____

SERVICE	FOOD	FACILITY
Comments heard:	Comments heard:	Comments heard:
Guest's name (if known):	Guest's name (if known):	Guest's name (if known):
Overall, comments were: ❏ positive ❏ negative ❏ neutral	Overall, comments were: ❏ positive ❏ negative ❏ neutral	Overall, comments were: ❏ positive ❏ negative ❏ neutral

CUSTOMER SATISFACTION SURVEY

Service

1. Were you greeted promptly upon entering the restaurant? ❑ Yes ❑ No
If no, how long did you wait to be greeted?

2. Was the host or hostess friendly and made you feel welcome? ❑ Yes ❑ No

3. How long did you have to wait to be seated?

4. Did you feel the wait was too long to be seated? ❑ Yes ❑ No

5. How would you rate the overall service provided by the waitperson who served you? On a scale from 1-10, with 1 being very poor and 10 being exceptional (circle one):
1 2 3 4 5 6 7 8 9 10

6. How would you rate the friendliness of all the staff?
1 2 3 4 5 6 7 8 9 10

7. Were you satisfied with the pace of the service? ❑ Yes ❑ No

Physical facilities

8. Please rate the cleanliness of the dining area:
1 2 3 4 5 6 7 8 9 10

9. Please rate the cleanliness of the restrooms, if used:
1 2 3 4 5 6 7 8 9 10

10. Was the lighting too bright? ❑ Yes ❑ No

11. Was the lighting too dim? ❑ Yes ❑ No

12. Was the temperature comfortable?
❑ Yes ❑ No

Appetizers

13. Did your server recommend any appetizers?
❑ Yes ❑ No

14. Please list any appetizers you ordered:

15. Were the hot appetizers served hot?
❑ Yes ❑ No

16. Were the cold appetizers served cold?
❑ Yes ❑ No

17. Please rate the flavor:
1 2 3 4 5 6 7 8 9 10

18. Please rate the overall quality:
1 2 3 4 5 6 7 8 9 10

Beverages

19. What beverages did you order?

20. Was there a wide selection of beverages from which to choose? ❑ Yes ❑ No

21. Are there other beverages you would like to see on our menu? ❑ Yes ❑ No
If yes, please list:

22. Did your server offer you refills in a timely fashion? ❑ Yes ❑ No

23. Were the beverages the proper temperature (hot drinks hot, cold drinks cold)? ❑ Yes ❑ No

24. Were the drinks served in conjunction with your meal? ❑ Yes ❑ No

25. Please rate overall quality:
1 2 3 4 5 6 7 8 9 10

Entrées

26. Did your server tell you the daily specials?
❑ Yes ❑ No

27. Was your server knowledgeable and able to answer your questions about the menu? ❑ Yes ❑ No

28. What did you order?

29. Were you pleased with the variety of food on the menu? ❑ Yes ❑ No
If no, please explain:

30. Are there items you would like to see added to the menu? ❑ Yes ❑ No
If yes, please list:

31. Were the cold entrées served on cold plates? ❑ Yes ❑ No

32. Were the cold entrées served cold? ❑ Yes ❑ No

33. Were the hot entrées served on hot plates? ❑ Yes ❑ No

34. Were the hot entrées served hot? ❑ Yes ❑ No

35. Please rate the flavor:
1 2 3 4 5 6 7 8 9 10

36. Please rate overall quality:
1 2 3 4 5 6 7 8 9 10

Side orders

37. What did you order?

38. Were you pleased with the side items offered? ❑ Yes ❑ No
If no, please explain:

39. Are there additional side orders you would like added to the menu? ❑ Yes ❑ No
If yes, please list:

40. Were the side items the proper temperature (hot items hot, cold items cold)? ❑ Yes ❑ No

41. Please rate the flavor:
1 2 3 4 5 6 7 8 9 10

42. Please rate overall quality:
1 2 3 4 5 6 7 8 9 10

Desserts

43. Did your server offer dessert or tell you about any dessert specialties? ❑ Yes ❑ No

44. What did you order?

45. Please rate the flavor:
1 2 3 4 5 6 7 8 9 10

46. Please rate overall quality:
1 2 3 4 5 6 7 8 9 10

Summary

47. Will you dine here again? ❑ Yes ❑ No
If no, please explain:

48. Would you recommend this restaurant to your friends? ❑ Yes ❑ No

49. Please rate overall quality:
1 2 3 4 5 6 7 8 9 10

Additional comments:

RESTAURANT SHOPPER'S REPORT

RESERVATION PROCESS

The telephone call to make the reservation was answered within three rings.
❏ Yes   ❏ No

The employee answering the phone was pleasant, identified himself/herself and the restaurant.
❏ Yes   ❏ No

The employee taking the reservation was courteous, repeated your reservation information and thanked you.
❏ Yes   ❏ No

The employee taking the reservation was knowledgeable, helpful and able to answer any questions (e.g., directions to restaurant).
❏ Yes   ❏ No

Additional Notes: _____
_____
_____
_____
_____

RESTAURANT EXTERIOR

The restaurant's sign was easily seen from a distance, easy to read, and in good condition.
❏ Yes   ❏ No

The restaurant's parking lot and grounds were free of debris and well-maintained.
❏ Yes   ❏ No

The area around the dining room was landscaped and well-lit.
❏ Yes   ❏ No

The restaurant had adequate parking.
❏ Yes   ❏ No

ARRIVAL & SEATING

You were greeted quickly upon entering.
❏ Yes   ❏ No

The host/hostess was appropriately dressed, smiling and pleasant.
❏ Yes   ❏ No

The host/hostess asked your smoking preference.
❏ Yes   ❏ No

You were seated within a reasonable time.
❏ Yes   ❏ No

The lounge was offered as an alternative if you had to wait for your table.
❏ Yes   ❏ No

The booths and tables were not crowded and easily accessible.
❏ Yes   ❏ No

The table or booth was comfortable and appropriate for your party.
❏ Yes   ❏ No

The host/hostess distributed menus for each guest and they were easily within reach.
❏ Yes   ❏ No

The host/hostess informed you of specials.
❏ Yes   ❏ No

The host/hostess told you the server's name.
❏ Yes   ❏ No

The host/hostess had a pleasant demeanor and treated you graciously.
❏ Yes   ❏ No

Additional Notes: _____
_____
_____

MENU

The menu was in good, clean condition.
❏ Yes ❏ No

The menu matched the restaurant's theme.
❏ Yes ❏ No

The menu size was physically easy to handle.
❏ Yes ❏ No

Available specials were listed prominently or separately.
❏ Yes ❏ No

The menu was well-organized, with selections grouped in an easy-to-read and easy-to-find manner.
❏ Yes ❏ No

The type on the menu was easy to read.
❏ Yes ❏ No

The number of selections was appropriate.
❏ Yes ❏ No

Appetizing descriptions were provided for menu items.
❏ Yes ❏ No

The menu had complete descriptions of side orders included or offered for each item.
❏ Yes ❏ No

The menu offered additional information as a marketing tool.
❏ Yes ❏ No

Vegetarian portions were offered.
❏ Yes ❏ No

Children's portions were offered.
❏ Yes ❏ No

Senior citizens' portions were offered.
❏ Yes ❏ No

Additional Notes: _____

_____

_____

WAITSTAFF

The waiter's or waitress's uniform was clean and attractive.
❏ Yes ❏ No

The waiter's or waitress's hands and fingernails were clean.
❏ Yes ❏ No

The waiter or waitress approached your table within three minutes after being seated.
❏ Yes ❏ No

The waiter or waitress greeted you pleasantly and introduced himself or herself.
❏ Yes ❏ No

The waiter or waitress smiled, was cordial, and created a genial atmosphere.
❏ Yes ❏ No

The waiter or waitress was familiar with menu items and able to answer questions.
❏ Yes ❏ No

The waiter or waitress used suggestive selling techniques, such as offering appetizers, in a friendly and non-offensive manner.
❏ Yes ❏ No

The waiter or waitress served beverage items promptly and from the left.
❏ Yes ❏ No

The waiter or waitress served food items in a timely manner and from the left.
❏ Yes ❏ No

The timing between courses was well-spaced.
❏ Yes ❏ No

The waiter or waitress knew each guest's selections and served them correctly.
❏ Yes ❏ No

The waiter or waitress returned to the table to check on satisfaction and provide additional service after the main course arrived.
❏ Yes ❏ No

WAITSTAFF (CONT.)

It was not necessary to summon the waiter or waitress during the meal.
❑ Yes   ❑ No

The waiter or waitress was attentive to guests' needs during the meal.
❑ Yes   ❑ No

The waiter or waitress seemed to enjoy their job.
❑ Yes   ❑ No

Overall, the waiter or waitress did a good job.
❑ Yes   ❑ No

Additional Notes: _____
_____
_____
_____
_____

BUS STAFF

The bus person provided water quickly after being seated.
❑ Yes   ❑ No

The bus person made sure water glasses were refilled promptly.
❑ Yes   ❑ No

The bus person was responsive to any service requests.
❑ Yes   ❑ No

The bus person removed dirty dishes quickly, so they were not left sitting on the table after being emptied.
❑ Yes   ❑ No

The bus person removed dirty dishes from the right.
❑ Yes   ❑ No

The bus person removed dirty ashtrays properly and replaced them quickly.
❑ Yes   ❑ No

The bus person was polite and courteous.
❑ Yes   ❑ No

The bus person was presentable, clean and well-groomed.
❑ Yes   ❑ No

The bus person's uniform was clean and attractive.
❑ Yes   ❑ No

The bus person did a good job, and service was not disruptive.
❑ Yes   ❑ No

Additional Notes: _____
_____
_____

FOOD

Food matched its menu description.
❑ Yes   ❑ No

All items ordered were available.
❑ Yes   ❑ No

Appetizer
Please list appetizer(s) ordered: _____
_____

Appetizing appearance	❑ Yes	❑ No
Proper temperature	❑ Yes	❑ No
(hot items hot, cold items cold)		
Tasted good	❑ Yes	❑ No

Please rate overall appetizer quality:
❑ Excellent   ❑ Good   ❑ Fair   ❑ Poor

Soup
Please list soup(s) ordered: _____
_____

Appetizing appearance	❑ Yes	❑ No
Proper temperature	❑ Yes	❑ No
(hot items hot, cold items cold)		
Tasted good	❑ Yes	❑ No

Please rate overall soup quality:
❑ Excellent   ❑ Good   ❑ Fair   ❑ Poor

Bread

Please list type of bread(s) ordered: _____

_____

Appetizing appearance	❏ Yes	❏ No
Proper temperature	❏ Yes	❏ No
(hot items hot, cold items cold)		
Tasted good	❏ Yes	❏ No

Please rate overall bread quality:
❏ Excellent ❏ Good ❏ Fair ❏ Poor

Salad

Please list type of salad(s) ordered: _____

_____

Appetizing appearance	❏ Yes	❏ No
Proper temperature	❏ Yes	❏ No
(hot items hot, cold items cold)		
Tasted good	❏ Yes	❏ No
Dressing choices adequate	❏ Yes	❏ No
Dressing amount correct	❏ Yes	❏ No

Please rate overall salad quality:
❏ Excellent ❏ Good ❏ Fair ❏ Poor

Entrée

Please list entrée(s) ordered: _____

_____

_____

Appetizing appearance	❏ Yes	❏ No
Proper temperature	❏ Yes	❏ No
(hot items hot, cold items cold)		
Tasted good	❏ Yes	❏ No
Portions appropriate	❏ Yes	❏ No

Please rate overall entrée quality:
❏ Excellent ❏ Good ❏ Fair ❏ Poor

Side Orders

Please list side order(s) ordered: _____

_____

_____

Appetizing appearance	❏ Yes	❏ No
Proper temperature	❏ Yes	❏ No
(hot items hot, cold items cold)		
Tasted good	❏ Yes	❏ No

Please rate overall side order quality:
❏ Excellent ❏ Good ❏ Fair ❏ Poor

Dessert

Please list dessert(s) ordered: _____

_____

_____

Appetizing appearance	❏ Yes	❏ No
Proper temperature	❏ Yes	❏ No
(hot items hot, cold items cold)		
Tasted good	❏ Yes	❏ No
Portions appropriate	❏ Yes	❏ No

Please rate overall dessert quality:
❏ Excellent ❏ Good ❏ Fair ❏ Poor

Additional Notes: _____

_____

_____

_____

_____

_____

_____

_____

_____

_____

_____

_____

DINING AMBIANCE

Noise level in dining room is not too loud.
❏ Yes ❏ No

Music pleasant, not too loud and not distracting.
❏ Yes ❏ No

Lighting in dining room is not too bright or dim.
❏ Yes ❏ No

Table decorations are clean and attractive.
❏ Yes ❏ No

DINING AMBIANCE (CONT.)

Table decorations are unobtrusive and do not block diners' view of each other.
❑ Yes   ❑ No

The restaurant presented a unified theme in décor, music, employee uniforms and overall atmosphere.
❑ Yes   ❑ No

Decor, furnishings and plants are in good physical condition and tastefully exhibited.
❑ Yes   ❑ No

Additional Notes: _____
_____
_____
_____
_____

FACILITY CLEANLINESS

The entrance, lounge, bar and dining room were clean.
❑ Yes   ❑ No

The dining table is clean, in good condition and has no food residue, crumbs or stains.
❑ Yes   ❑ No

Chairs and booths are clean, stain-free and stable.
❑ Yes   ❑ No

Glasses are clean and do not have water spots.
❑ Yes   ❑ No

Flatware is clean and does not have water spots.
❑ Yes   ❑ No

Dishes are clean and do not have water spots.
❑ Yes   ❑ No

Napkins are clean, not stained, and folded nicely.
❑ Yes   ❑ No

The ceiling is clean and in good condition.
❑ Yes   ❑ No

Lighting fixtures are working and clean.
❑ Yes   ❑ No

The walls and floors are clean and well-maintained.
❑ Yes   ❑ No

Additional Notes: _____
_____

RESTROOMS

Men's and women's restrooms clearly marked and in an easy-to-find location.
❑ Yes   ❑ No

The restroom door is clean and well-maintained.
❑ Yes   ❑ No

Overall, the restroom is clean and doesn't have any objectionable odors.
❑ Yes   ❑ No

The restroom lighting is in good working order and sufficiently bright.
❑ Yes   ❑ No

The restroom is adequately stocked with toiletries, soap and disposable paper towels (or a hot-air hand dryer).
❑ Yes   ❑ No

The restroom sink areas and fixtures are clean.
❑ Yes   ❑ No

The restroom mirrors are clean.
❑ Yes   ❑ No

The restroom walls, floors and windows are clean and well-maintained.
❑ Yes   ❑ No

An infant changing area is available, clean and in good condition.
❑ Yes   ❑ No

Additional Notes: _____
_____
_____

DEPARTURE

The check was presented in an appropriate and timely manner.
❑ Yes   ❑ No

The check was placed in a discreet location.
❑ Yes   ❑ No

The check is itemized, readable and easy to understand.
❑ Yes   ❑ No

The check is totalled correctly and reflects the items ordered.
❑ Yes   ❑ No

The waiter or waitress informs you that he or she will return for payment at your convenience.
❑ Yes   ❑ No

The waiter or waitress properly tabulated and processed credit card payment.
❑ Yes   ❑ No

The waiter or waitress brought your correct change directly from the cashier.
❑ Yes   ❑ No

The waiter or waitress thanked you upon receiving payment.
❑ Yes   ❑ No

The waiter or waitress thanked you for coming and said "It was a pleasure to server you," and "Please come again."
❑ Yes   ❑ No

Exits were well-lit and departure from dining room was free of obstacles.
❑ Yes   ❑ No

Additional Notes: _____

_____

_____

_____

_____

OVERALL RATINGS

Overall service quality was:
❑ Excellent   ❑ Good   ❑ Fair   ❑ Poor

Overall food quality was:
❑ Excellent   ❑ Good   ❑ Fair   ❑ Poor

Overall dining experience was:
❑ Excellent   ❑ Good   ❑ Fair   ❑ Poor

Please note any areas of service that could be improved:

_____

_____

_____

_____

_____

_____

_____

_____

_____

_____

Please note any areas of service that were exceptional or above ordinary:

_____

_____

_____

_____

_____

_____

_____

_____

_____

_____

_____

Additional Notes: _____

_____

_____

_____

_____

GROUNDS FOR IMMEDIATE DISMISSAL

- Misuse or abuse of property or equipment belonging to the restaurant.

- Theft of money, equipment, personal or restaurant property.

- Altering a guest's charge to add a gratuity without management approval.

- Requesting or approaching guest about a gratuity.

- Falsifying or changing a charge after the guest has signed it.

- Use of alcohol or illegal drugs during working hours or reporting to work under the influence of such.

- Missing a scheduled shift without prior management approval.

- Falsifying application information, paperwork or time cards.

- Threatening, attempting or doing bodily harm to another.

- Intentionally not charging for any food or liquor items.

- Animosity, rudeness or unkindness to a guest.

- Serving alcohol to a minor or an obviously intoxicated guest.

- Violating any safety procedures in food preparation or service.

- Disclosure or use of confidential information.

EMPLOYEE ATTENDANCE RECORD

Name: _____ Date of Employment: _____ Year: 20_____

Employee Number: _____ Department: _____

Mark each instance of missing work below with the reason for the absence.

| **S** = Sick **V** = Vacation **H** = Holiday **I** = Injury **D** = Death in the Family **J** = Jury Duty |
| **L** = Leave without Pay **U** = Unexcused **P** = Personal Time **F** = Maternity Leave/Family Leave Act |

	Jan	Feb	March	April	May	June	July	Aug	Sept	Oct	Nov	Dec
1												
2												
3												
4												
5												
6												
7												
8												
9												
10												
11												
12												
13												
14												
15												
16												
17												
18												
19												
20												
21												
22												
23												
24												
25												
26												
27												
28												
29												
30												
31												

Absence Summary

S _____   V _____   H _____   I _____   D _____

J _____   L _____   U _____   P _____   F _____

ABSENCE REPORT

Name: _____ Date of Employment: _____

First Date Absent: _____ Expected Return Date: _____

REASON FOR ABSENCE (circle one)	
Sick	Unexcused
Vacation	Personal Time
Holiday	Maternity Leave/Family Leave Act
Injury	Suspension
Death in the Family	Other (list)
Jury Duty	
Leave without Pay	

Explanation

ABSENCE DETAIL

This absence was:

Expected in Advance ❏ Yes ❏ No

Reported in Advance of Shift ❏ Yes ❏ No

Considered by Supervisor as ❏ Unexcused ❏ Excused

Manager's Signature

EMPLOYEE DEVELOPMENT & PERFORMANCE PLAN

The Employee Development & Performance Plan is a detailed, step-by-step program designed to improve communication between employees and supervisors, enhance customer service, increase overall productivity and boost company morale. It is divided into three sections: preview, preparation and feedback. Each section can be specifically tailored for any establishment by adding company-specific details.

STEP 1: PREVIEW SESSION

The first step of the Employee Development & Performance Plan (EDPP) is the Preview Session, where the supervisor schedules a time to discuss with the employee the program details. It is appropriate to schedule the Preview Session one week prior to the Feedback Session to allow the employee appropriate preparation for the EDPP.

The employee's immediate supervisor is designated the evaluator, unless the employee is a member of a self-managed work team and has no supervisor. In that case, an evaluator must be decided prior to the EDPP. Follow the steps below for the Preview Session:

1. Review all EDPP instructions carefully. Discuss each step of the process and answer any questions the employee may have. Next, incorporate any specific company evaluation policies into the EDPP.

2. Establish a timeline for the EDPP.

3. Review the employee's job description to make sure duties and responsibilities are accurate and up to date.

4. Review the employee's Personal Performance Standards. The Performance Standards should include particular behaviors, special assignments, specific goals or results, special training, etc., that relate directly to the employee.

5. Review the Performance Elements listed on the following page. Determine which are relevant to the employee's job and what may need to be added. Unlike Performance Standards (which are more personal), the Performance Elements should be used universally for all employees in that work unit to which they are applicable.

STEP 2: EDPP PREPARATION

The employee and the supervisor should each draft their own individual responses to Parts I through III of the EDPP. The responses should be based on performance of the employee's duties and responsibilities, Personal Performance Standards and the relevant Performance Elements. Both the employee and supervisor should demonstrate how the employee's job and performance standards relate to the organization's goals, values, objectives and quality improvement efforts. Finally, Part IV of the EDPP is completed by the employee only. This is the employee's opportunity to give the supervisor feedback on the supervisor's effectiveness, communication and leadership.

STEP 3: FEEDBACK SESSION

After completing Parts I through III of the EDPP, the employee and supervisor meet to discuss their individual responses. An open and constructive discussion is the main objective. This conversation should result in a clear understanding of the employee's past performance, future expectations and development objectives. Finally, the employee should present his or her review of the supervisor from Part IV. If the employee is uncomfortable doing this personally, it can be presented to the supervisor in writing after the Feedback Session.

If any problems or conflicts occur during the feedback session, another manager should function as a mediator at the request of either the supervisor or the employee.

Once the Feedback Session is complete, the supervisor compiles a final review form for the employee to review and sign. This form should contain all comments from Parts I through IV of the EDDP. The supervisor also signs the EDPP, and then gives the form to the reviewer whose signature indicates that the EDDP has been completed properly. The reviewer does not make changes or comments relative to the employee's performance. The supervisor gives the employee a copy and places the original in the employee's personnel file.

EMPLOYEE DEVELOPMENT & PERFORMANCE PLAN

The following "performance elements" should be considered, where applicable, in assessing employee performance (Part I) and determining future performance expectations and development needs (Parts II and III). Other performance elements may be added as needed.

PERFORMANCE ELEMENTS

PERSONAL MANAGEMENT TRAITS

- Using work time effectively.
- Possessing integrity and honesty.
- Following company rules and procedures.
- Absences, punctuality and attendance record.
- Being open to constructive feedback for self and others.
- Proper use of equipment and resources.
- Proper maintenance of equipment.
- Proper safety procedures.
- Seeking and fulfilling additional responsibilities as suitable.
- Treating others with respect and dignity.
- Focusing on the situation, problem or behavior rather than on the person.
- Other: _____

_____

TEAMWORK

- Communicating with others openly and honestly.
- Working with others towards the team and organization's goals.
- Realizing the benefits of teamwork.
- Offering assistance to others and recognizing the contributions of others.
- Viewing the organization's success more important than individual achievement.
- Working towards team cohesion and productivity.
- Sharing information internally and externally.
- Other: _____

_____

WORK PROCESSES & RESULTS

- Achieving results.
- Establishing and adhering to priorities.
- Using sound judgment.
- Meeting productivity standards and deadlines.
- Working accurately with minimal supervision.
- Providing products and services above or beyond the customers' needs and expectations.
- Being aware of customer satisfaction.
- Utilizing problem-solving to improve processes.
- Evaluating information to make informed decisions.
- Striving for efficiency in the use of resources.
- Informing supervisor of problems and offering solutions.
- Other: _____

_____

INNOVATION AND CHANGE

- Adapting willingly to new situations.
- Striving to be open to new ideas and explore different options.
- Avoiding being overly defensive.
- Seeking ways to improve work processes.
- Helping others adapt to changes.
- Other: _____
  _____

GROWTH & PROGRESSION

- Actively striving for ways to increase knowledge.
- Participating in opportunities that are offered by the organization to enhance skills.
- Developing or upgrading knowledge and skills independent of job position through self-initiative.
- Actively applying new skills acquired from developmental opportunities.
- Teaching others new processes or systems.
- Using technology effectively, when appropriate.
- Other: _____
  _____

COMMUNICATION

- Actively participating in meetings.
- Interacting with others in a cooperative and courteous manner.
- Competently communicating verbally in small groups and one-on-one.
- Writing clearly and concisely.
- Responding quickly and properly to other's verbal requests or e-mail, phone messages and mail.
- Other: _____
  _____

CUSTOMER SERVICE

- Being responsive to customers' needs.
- Striving to be accessible, timely and responsive to customers.
- Handling customer inquiries promptly and politely.
- Dealing with customer complaints courteously and in a non-judgmental manner.
- Expending extra effort to satisfy customer needs and expectations.
- Other: _____
  _____

SUPERVISORY PERFORMANCE

- Offering clear directions to staff and following through on instructions.
- Giving regular, ongoing feedback to staff.
- Clearly communicating organization's goals and mission to employees.
- Supporting staff's efforts to succeed.
- Facilitating and coaching employees.
- Recognizing individual and team efforts and performance.
- Supporting workplace diversity.
- Making appropriate decisions regarding employee selection and promotions.
- Other: _____
  _____

EMPLOYEE DEVELOPMENT AND PERFORMANCE PLAN

Name: _____ Date of Employment: _____

Job Position: _____ Date of Preview Session: _____

Evaluated By: _____ Evaluation Period: _____

Purpose of Evaluation: ❑ Annual Review ❑ Probationary Review ❑ Other

PART I: PERFORMANCE FEEDBACK

1. Assess the employee's overall performance in relation to carrying out job responsibilities and performance standards.
2. Evaluate the employee's contribution to helping the organization achieve its goals and be successful.
3. Review all Performance Elements and describe how well the employee has done in relation to each relevant area.

PART II: PERFORMANCE EXPECTATIONS

1. Review the employee's Personal Performance Standards in relation to job duties, special assignments and skills the employee needs to focus on in order to further his/her success and contribution to the organization.
2. Note any areas in which the employee could improve.

PART III: FUTURE TRAINING & DEVELOPMENT

1. Identify training and development opportunities that could improve and enhance the employee's existing skills and performance.

PART IV: ORGANIZATIONAL SUPPORT
(TO BE COMPLETED BY THE EMPLOYEE)

1. Please list at least five ways your supervisor, coworkers and company can support you in your present job and with future career goals.
2. What do you perceive as your supervisor's greatest strength?
3. Are there any areas in which your supervisor could improve?

PART V: COMMENTS AND SIGNATURES

By signing below, the evaluator agrees that this report is based on his or her judgment. By signing below, the employee agrees that he or she has had an opportunity to review and discuss this report.

Evaluator's Signature	Title	Date

Employee's Signature	Title	Date

I have reviewed this report and, in my judgment, the process has been properly followed.

Reviewer's Signature	Title	Date

Upon completion of this report and signatures of evaluator, employee and reviewers, a final copy should be provided to the employee and the original report placed in the employee's personnel file.

HUMAN RESOURCES AUDIT

Audit performed by: _____ Date: _____

MINIMUM WAGE LAW & WORKING CONDITIONS

Is there a regularly scheduled payday? ❏ Y ❏ N

Are minimum wage laws, both federal and state, upheld? ❏ Y ❏ N

Are payroll deductions made for Social Security, federal
and state income taxes and Medicare? ❏ Y ❏ N

Upon termination, are employees paid in a timely manner? ❏ Y ❏ N

If an employee works 6 hours or longer, is a 30-minute meal break given? ❏ Y ❏ N

For each 4-hour work period, do employees get to take 10-minute work breaks? ❏ Y ❏ N

Are 14- and 15-year-olds limited to working only 3 hours per school day? ❏ Y ❏ N

Are 14- and 15-year-olds limited to working only 8 hours on a non-school day? ❏ Y ❏ N

Are working hours for 14- and 15-year-olds limited to between
7 a.m. and 9 p.m.? ❏ Y ❏ N

Are 14- and 17-year-olds working with prohibited equipment, such as a slicer? ❏ Y ❏ N

Are working conditions for minors regarding breaks and meal
periods being met? ❏ Y ❏ N

Comments _____

_____

_____

OSHA

Is an OSHA information poster posted in a clear and visible area? ❏ Y ❏ N

Are MSDS forms for all chemicals used in the establishment available to
employees? ❏ Y ❏ N

Are all chemicals stored in proper containers and labeled correctly? ❏ Y ❏ N

Are pesticides stored in their original labeled container? ❏ Y ❏ N

Do suitable facilities (located within the work area for immediate emergency
use) exist for quick drenching or flushing of the eyes and body if exposure
to injurious corrosive material occurs? ❏ Y ❏ N

Do any potentially hazardous conditions exist? ❏ Y ❏ N

Have employees sustained serious injuries while working that results in
missed days of work? ❏ Y ❏ N

Have all workers been trained in and practice proper lifting procedures? ❏ Y ❏ N

Is personal protective equipment, such as gloves, eye goggles and special aprons, provided for employees? ❏ Y ❏ N

Do the facilities meet OSHA standards for safety? ❏ Y ❏ N

Comments _____

_____

AMERICANS WITH DISABILITIES ACT (ADA) COMPLIANCE

Have all employment tests been checked to make sure they are not discriminatory against disabled persons? ❏ Y ❏ N

Do job descriptions have reasonable accommodations for the disabled? ❏ Y ❏ N

Do physical facilities comply with ADA regulations? ❏ Y ❏ N

Have physical facilities been inspected by an ADA regulation specialist? ❏ Y ❏ N

Are health insurance considerations a reason for rejecting qualified potential employees with disabilities? ❏ Y ❏ N

Comments _____

_____

EQUAL EMPLOYMENT OPPORTUNITY COMMISSION (EEOC) CONSIDERATIONS

Are interview questions nondiscriminatory and legal? ❏ Y ❏ N

Are all pre-employment tests directly related to the job? ❏ Y ❏ N

Are employees of both genders hired? ❏ Y ❏ N

For corresponding work, are both genders paid equally? ❏ Y ❏ N

Are promotions awarded based upon job performance that is quantifiable and verifiable? ❏ Y ❏ N

Comments _____

_____

FAMILY AND MEDICAL LEAVE ACT

Does the employer/employee qualify for the Family and Medical Leave Act? (Employees are eligible to take FMLA leave if they have worked for their employer for at least 12 months, and have worked for at least 1,250 hours over the previous 12 months, and work at a location where at least 50 employees are employed by the employer within 75 miles.) ❏ Y ❏ N

Are employees allowed to take up to a total of 12 weeks of unpaid leave during any 12-month period? ❏ Y ❏ N

Upon returning to work, are employees returned to their previous position, or an equivalent position? ❏ Y ❏ N

During leave, are health care benefits continued? ❏ Y ❏ N

Comments _____

_____

IMMIGRATION REFORM ACT

Does employer possess, utilize and complete I-9 forms when needed? ❏ Y ❏ N

Does employer obtain verification of citizenship for I-9 forms? ❏ Y ❏ N

Does employer discriminate against people who are not citizens of the United States?❏ Y ❏ N

Comments _____

_____

SEXUAL HARASSMENT

Are all employees aware of what constitutes sexual harassment, including:
- *The victim or the harasser may be a woman or a man. The victim does not have to be of the opposite sex.*
- *The harasser can be the victim's supervisor, an agent of the employer, a supervisor in another area, a coworker or a non-employee.*
- *The victim does not have to be the person harassed but could be anyone affected by the offensive conduct.*
- *Unlawful sexual harassment may occur without economic injury to or discharge of the victim.*
- The harasser's conduct must be unwelcome. ❏ Y ❏ N

Were any sexual harassment claims made during the past year? ❏ Y ❏ N

If any sexual harassment claims were made, were they investigated immediately?❏ Y ❏ N

Was disciplinary action taken for any sexual harassment claims? ❏ Y ❏ N

Does establishment have a written procedure established for reporting
sexual harassment claims? ❏ Y ❏ N

Is the written sexual harassment policy posted for all employees? ❏ Y ❏ N

Comments _____

_____

TIP-REPORTING REQUIREMENTS

Is employer using Form 8027 for tip allocation? ❏ Y ❏ N

Does employer collect income tax, employee Social Security tax and employee
Medicare tax on tips reported by employees? ❏ Y ❏ N

Are employees using Form 4070A? ❏ Y ❏ N

Is a good-faith agreement being used? ❏ Y ❏ N

Are employees aware of IRS tip-reporting requirements and trained to
report all tips? ❏ Y ❏ N

Comments _____

_____

CHAPTER

HANDLING EMPLOYEES TIPS

When you pocket your tip change or deposit it into your checking account, have you ever stopped to think that you are participating in a multi-billion-dollar international economic system? Perhaps no other financial transaction is as commonplace or as confusing. Tipping is a paradox for the giver and the receiver — a voluntary transaction that has become compulsory and expected; a gift that is measured and taxed; an informal custom governed by formal government regulations; an interaction based on "social guilt" and an economic necessity; and a routine act filled with confusion and necessity. Tipping is a social puzzle for the giver.

- How much of a tip do I leave?

- Who should be tipped?

- Why should I tip?

Service employees and employers also struggle with questions like:

- Why should I pay taxes on a gift?

- Why should tips reduce my employer's responsibility to pay a "fair" wage?

- Why should I care how much tips my employees make?

This chapter will help demystify the psychology and economics behind tipping so you can understand why tipping is such a hot topic for food service personnel. You will learn about tipping attitudes, how to increase your tips, and why you should report your tip income.

WHO SHOULD READ THIS CHAPTER

These are some of the people in food service who regularly receive tips for services rendered:

- Waiter/Waitress
- Cocktail server

- Bartender
- Maitre d'
- Coatroom attendant

- Bus person
- Wine steward
- Valet parking attendant

May you discover the key to serving your customers with pride and reap the rewards daily.

HAT IS A TIP?

The dictionary defines a tip as a gift of money for a service, specifically an amount above what is owed. Also known as a gratuity. But that hardly covers the true definition of a tip which encompasses:

- A loosely regulated multi-billion-dollar economy.

- An economic necessity for millions of service industry employees worldwide.

- A practice based on historical customs, social norms, class status, and psychological distress.

TIPS ARE WAGES

Tips, like your hourly wage, are taxable income. The IRS and the federal court system have spent countless hours instituting tip laws and rulings that target tip earners and the employers who hire them.

TIPS ARE CONTROVERSIAL

Although anti-tipping laws are no longer on the books, many people would like to do away with tipping entirely.

Why not just pay everyone equitably and forget tipping? This question arises periodically when government entities review minimum wage or "living wage" laws. Politicians, business leaders and economists cannot agree on what would be fair for employers, employees, and their communities. Individual states (and even some cities) tackle the issue of minimum wage differently without addressing tipping.

A 1997 economic thesis suggests that raising minimum wages for tipped employees in the restaurant industry could actually increase employment. Trade associations, such as the National Restaurant Association, hold a different view, as noted in a 2004 position paper, "The National Restaurant Association strongly opposes federally-mandated increases in the starting wage. A dramatic increase in labor costs in a recovering economy will mean fewer jobs for entry-level workers, especially in labor intensive industries such as restaurants."

Eliminating tipping would also require a dramatic shift in thinking, along with minimum wage laws that alter wage structures dependent upon the generosity and "social guilt" of customers. Service companies, which currently are allowed tip credits, would have to increase posted prices or automatically add a service charge to cover the increased direct expense.

While in theory raising prices equal to the eliminated tips would not significantly alter the customers' final cost for dining out, the psychological changes would be difficult to absorb. The immediate reaction would be that increasing a $10 item by 15 percent ($11.50) would seem outrageous to customers. However, if they were to order the same $10 meal and leave greater than a 15 percent tip, they would actually be saving money.

Tipping is an emotion-based economic behavior. Changes that affect these behaviors are much more difficult to accomplish successfully.

WHY DO PEOPLE TIP?

Hospitality industry experts agree that isolating the why can be difficult because you are dealing with an emotionally based behavior that people may not want to reveal. The four most common reasons American's tip are:

- **Fear of being socially inappropriate** — the internal mechanism of guilt that causes us to tip (even when there are no social observers).

- **Economic awareness** — a genuine interest in supporting the lower paid "service class."

- **Reward for being helped** — gratitude for services rendered.

- **Status seekers** — using tipping as a way to "show off" or to point out "superior" social status.

MANNERS

Many adults were taught that tipping was a sign of good manners. Tipping is just something you do as a polite person. As children, we watched adult role models discreetly leave money on the table. Inquisitive, we asked why. In our fast food world, many of these dining- and entertainment-related manners have faded away.

GUILT

Guilt is used by parents, schools, and social institutions to regulate behavior. We are guided by guilt, often without even knowing it. Because you are "supposed" to tip the waitress or the bellman, our guilt causes us to act without giving it much thought beyond the mathematical calculation.

ECONOMIC AWARENESS

Closely related to guilty feelings, an awareness that the people who wait on us are among the lowest paid workers in our society drives many people to tip. Affluence does not guarantee this "share the wealth" attitude. Generosity seems more prevalent with "working class" customers—especially those who are or have been service employees.

THANKS

In the United States, tipping has become such an automatic response that the connection between tips and good service has dimmed for many tippers. Foreign visitors often mention their dismay as to why we would tip for good service, as good service should be the accepted standard. Only excellent or special service would warrant a tip in many countries.

However weak the association between rewarding actions and tipping amounts may be, many tippers cling firmly to the "TO INSURE PROMPT SERVICE" motto.

For some, tipping has become so automatic that they figure the tip replaces thanking the person who served them. For servers, a good way to minimize this response is to be an "active thanker." Take every opportunity to look the customer in the eye and thank him for the change in the tip jar, the extra dollars on the charge, or coins left beside a plate. Be present at the end of the customer-employee interaction and be thankful. You will feel better and be tipped better.

HAT? NO TIP?

You smiled and greeted everyone cheerfully, no complaints about the service, and everyone seems pleased. So, why no tip or a very small tip? Several researchers, including Michael Lynn, Ph.D. at Cornell's School of Hotel Administration, have repeatedly found that service quality has limited affect on tips. In Dr. Lynn's December 2003 report, he reviewed current studies and his own past reports to arrive at the same conclusion: restaurant tip percentages are only slightly affected by average service quality. (Employers should note that Dr. Lynn determined that restaurant turnover rates and even servers thinking about quitting negatively affected tips which fuels the cycle for dissatisfaction and turnover.)

So why should you care about good customer service? Because it is your job, your personal reputation, your integrity, and your responsibility to contribute to a civilized world. Good customer service is a vital part of a healthy economy and civilized culture.

Making your customers feel good makes you feel good and makes your community feel good. People do notice and will reward you for your excellent service. Remember, these studies are talking about averages mathematically calculated from a small sampling of situations. Your real life experience is what counts, so enjoy your job and your customers and earn great tips.

TIPPING SIGNALS

The 15 percent restaurant tip (while slowly inching up to 20 percent in many regions of the country) is so expected that leaving less is interpreted as a signal of poor service. While some studies show that the quality of service is not the primary reason for good tips, they also note that employers should not use tip size as the sole indicator of customer satisfaction.

WHY SOME PEOPLE DO NOT TIP

Tipping less than what is locally customary or even leaving no tip can be because the customer is:

- **Unaware of the average tip rate or other local custom.** (Remember, tipping behavior varies from region to region.)

- **Uninformed that tipping is common** when receiving this type of service.

- **Basing their tip on their perception of your service and products received.** Perceptions on service quality and customer expectations vary from region to region and from informal to formal establishments.

- **Using an internal "fairness" guide.** Was it harder to serve one inexpensive meal versus a costly one? Tips, when serving large groups, are especially affected — does he really deserve a $45 tip?

- **Rebelling against the concept of tipping.** Some people feel that the employer should be paying their employees and that tipping is an outmoded form of payment that has evolved to blackmail.

Poor tippers and non-tippers can be categorized into the uneducated, the rude, the righteous, and the social anarchist. You will probably only be able to influence and improve some tipping responses. Educating a customer would typically be considered rude and should be avoided; dealing with a rude customer, even if handled with tact and courtesy, probably will not result in a generous tip and you will have a hard time dissuading those rebelling against tipping to believe anything else. However, by concentrating on behaviors and attitudes (especially any relating to #3 above), can be worth the effort, both financially and emotionally.

ECEIVING TIPS

As a tip-earner, the issue of tips takes on new importance — your financial well-being. Being at the mercy of people who may not understand the nuances of tipping can be stressful. You must walk an invisible tightrope — do you risk offending someone or do you just hope for the best?

THE ETIQUETTE OF RECEIVING TIPS

Good manners are as important when you receive a tip as when you give one. Much is written for customers on proper tipping (although if you have been stiffed regularly, you are probably certain that no one ever reads Ms. Manners or other etiquette experts).

If a gratuity is a gift, then you are the gift recipient. The basic rules of etiquette are much like when you receive a birthday gift: be thankful. Even if you are not wild about the orange sweater with green polka-dots, good manners means that you acknowledge the gift, thank the giver, and appreciate the thought.

In many tipping encounters, you may not have the opportunity to thank someone directly. The key is not that you are to say, "Gee, thanks for the big tip." You are thanking them for giving you the opportunity to serve them. By simply acknowledging that you are glad they came in and glad you could assist them, you will be saying, "Thanks for the tip."

Kitchens and backrooms are filled with servers grousing that so and so stiffed them. While it helps to blow off steam, it also can become emotionally corrosive and affect your ability to enjoy your job.

As Mom says, "If you can't say something good about someone, don't say anything at all." Withholding service, or worse still, blasting someone about the lousy tip, just is not polite. Do you really think that your negative actions or words can change anything? Probably not and you may actually be making matters worse. Chalk it up to being part of a world filled with all kinds of people and concentrate on what you can control: a job well done and the resulting reward from appreciative customers.

TIP JARS

Tip jars were not invented by your local coffee shop. However, their reemergence as a not-so subtle way of asking for a tip really came about in the early 1990s. If tipping confuses people in sit-down restaurants, counter-service tipping can be even worse. So should you or should you not have a conveniently located tip jar in your establishment? Who should receive a share of the tips? The following pros and cons might help you make the right decision for you and your customers.

TIP JAR PROS AND CONS	
Con (No Tip Jar)	**Pro (Tip Jar)**
• Etiquette would say that tip jars are asking for a tip, which is considered to be rude behavior.	• Customers, who would like to tip unceremoniously, may appreciate the jar.
• Tip jars are meant to make customers feel guilty, and "guilt" is the emotional stimulus for tipping.	• A tip jar is a convenient way of gathering tips before dividing them amongst the shift personnel.
• Funny sayings about tipping karma don't make it "nicer."	• Funny sayings are a way for us to diffuse our own embarrassment about having to ask for tips, and customers like them.
• "If I felt like tipping, I would; I don't need a visual nag."	• Tipping etiquette and habits can be confusing. Our goal is to gently remind people that the custom is to tip us.
• Counter servers barely raise their head to wait on me or don't say a word other than "That will be $4.95."	• Many customers do not realize that service personnel (even trained baristas) receive only minimum wage or less.
• Why should counter servers get tips?	• Poor service = no tip.
• What's the difference between someone waiting on me at my favorite coffee shop and someone waiting on me at the pharmacy?	• You're right that many people are deserving of either tips or a "living wage." This is a question that probably doesn't have an answer that satisfies everyone.

If you choose to have a tip jar on the counter:

- **Create an attractive presentation.** A recycled pickle jar might not be the image you want to project.

- **Add a sign to the jar that fits your store and clientele.** Such as "Your tips are greatly appreciated. Thank you from the staff at Bill's Ice Cream Shop."

- **Make it easy to leave a tip** by including small bills when you return their change.

- **Smile** and look at people when they pay.

- **Pause and say, "Thank you!"**

EDUCATING CUSTOMERS

Educating your customers may be a solution. As many people still perceive tipping as a "gift," your good intentions may shout of rude behavior and backfire on you. The tip jar has an educational benefit; however, its use is limited to counter service. Imagine servers walking around with a tip jar.

Subtle reminders such as tip trays and tip lines printed on register tapes are perfectly acceptable. You might stock free tip cards next to the after-dinner mint bowl. Look for ways to make it easy for customers to tip and you will be reminding customers that it is customary.

Studies discussed in this book show that groups traditionally tip less than the local going rate. In response, companies have started to automatically add a service fee or "gratuity" to ensure a minimum tip level for serving groups or for a specific personalized service. This method may prove to be your best solution for dealing with "intense" work situations. The IRS does not consider these mandatory service charges tips. Employers will include the fees in their sales totals, divide the service charge among the appropriate personnel, and add it to their salary as a bonus.

To learn more about tipping etiquette, The Original Tipping Page at **www.tipping.org** provides a wealth of information on getting and giving tips. Denton Software offers a free tipping guide for Palm-based Personal Digital Assistants at **www.dentonsoftware.com/Products/Free/Tipper/Tipper.htm**.

 AYS TO INCREASE YOUR TIPS

PERCENTAGE OF SALES

There are only two ways to increase your tip income. The first is to increase your tip percentage. If you currently average 12 percent on products sold, one way to achieve greater income is to increase this percentage. Raising it to 15 percent means an extra $30 per $1,000 in sales. The second way is to sell more. If you write an additional $250 in dessert orders with your same 12 percent tip average, you earn an additional $30 per shift.

Increasing your average tip percentage can be as simple as introducing yourself. Enhancing your sales/service ability requires more training and effort; however, as you can see in the above example, the effort has a greater pay-off.

WHY DO SOME PEOPLE EARN BETTER TIPS?

Some service personnel simply earn more tips than others in their industry. Learning what makes peers successful tip earners is a great way to achieve your own goals.

As the saying goes for building a business: It is location, location, location. Where you work will affect your tip earning potential. No matter where you work you will discover some people simply earn more than their coworkers.

Studies show employees who rate their own service-providing skills higher than average earn more tips. Also those who are best able to assess the appropriateness of their behavior during work situations are better tip earners.

The reasons some people earn greater tips range from physical appearance and service ability to cheerfulness and attitude. Factors such as attractiveness do come into play for women. Women judged "attractive" earned larger tips. Studies show that a man's looks are not a significant factor for larger tips. You do not have to resort to plastic surgery to increase your tips; attitude and behavior are the most important reasons some people earn more in tips. A broad smile, good disposition, and some interpersonal skills can make all the difference.

LOOK IN THE MIRROR

You have taken the first step to earning larger tips by reading this chapter. The next step is to examine yourself — your physical appearance, your attitude, your behavior, and your skills. Look in the mirror and your heart to see what might be improved.

- **Physical appearance** — Are you making the most of your appearance? Do you dress appropriately?

- **Attitude** — Are you mentally and emotionally prepared for a great day? Do you get easily frustrated with customers or coworkers?

- **Behavior** — Are you aware of how your behavior affects others? Do you exhibit good manners at all times? Do you gossip or chat while customers wait?

- **Skills** — Are you performing as well as you could? Do you lack some skills? If your employer does not offer training programs, find a mentor, a book, or a program to help you grow.

LITTLE TIPS FOR BIGGER TIPS

Studies on tipping behavior have revealed some interesting ways you might increase your tip income. These, along with your own personal research, can be tested for effectiveness with your customers.

1. **Squat down for an eye-to-eye connection.** Cornell University studied this action and discovered that when a waiter in a Mexican restaurant squatted down when he introduced himself to his patrons, he increased his average tip from 14.9 percent to 17.5 percent of the bill. This scenario was repeated with a waitress in a Chinese restaurant who increased her tip from 12 percent to 15 percent of the bill by merely squatting down next to her tables. This demeanor would be suitable in a variety of casual restaurants.

2. **Tempt them with candy.** An experiment conducted randomly with two waiters and a waitress showed that giving diners a piece of candy at the end of the meal increased their tips. In the first experiment, diners were randomly given a single piece of candy

which raised tips from 15.1 percent to 17.8 percent of the bill. It seems that customers feel more obligated when they are given a sweet gift. The next experiment had diners randomly receiving no candy, one piece of candy per diner, two pieces of candy per diner, and one piece of candy per diner plus an "impulse offering" of another. Diners who received one candy tipped more than those who were not given any candy. Diners tipped even more when they were given two pieces of candy. The largest tips (23 percent) were given when the waitress offered a single piece of candy, and then before leaving offered another on "impulse." Large groups of diners were more affected when candy was offered.

3. **Touch your customer.** Placing your hand on a shoulder in a natural manner or shaking hands are powerful ways to connect with your customers. Research has shown that casual touching of one to two seconds has a significantly positive affect on customer happiness, shopping times, and tipping. Younger customers and women responded best to the touching experiment. The touching was part of the server's natural behavior, so it did not appear to be anything out of the ordinary. Tips during tests in a restaurant situation increased from an average 11.5 percent of the check to an average of 14.9 percent of the check. Employers who prohibit interpersonal touching for fear of inappropriate contact should review the studies and set "appropriate behavior" guidelines that incorporate casual server/customer touching. Studies show even prolonged touching (4 seconds or more) did not cause negative reactions. The benefits, beyond tipping, can be tremendous for your business as customers develop a bond with your staff. Note: Different cultures may interpret touching differently. To learn more about touching people with different heritages or foreign visitor, read *The Do's and Taboos of Hosting International Visitors* by Roger E. Axtell.

4. **Take a minute to explain things.** Cornell University studied a hotel bellman in a small upscale hotel. When the bellman gave the "normal" level of service, he received an average of $2.40 when escorting guests to their rooms. When he explained how the TV operated, how to adjust the thermostat, opened the drapes, and offered to bring them ice, he doubled his tip ($4.77 on average).

5. **Make a parent's life easier.** Dining or shopping with children can be tough. Pay special attention to children. Admire their hair or smile. Tell a silly joke. Quickly provide distractions for toddlers and above — things like crayons and coloring books. Ask if they would like you to bring some veggies or crackers for them to eat while the family is waiting. Ask whether drinks should be served early (children tend to fill up on beverages before the meal arrives). Note: Never touch an infant or small child without a parent's permission. Many parents have strong opinions about strangers touching their children and you may accidentally create a scene.

6. **Learn to read people.** Observe your customers' body language, listen to their tone of voice, and watch how they interact with others. It gives you the opportunity to "tailor" your interaction to suit the situation. Acting a bit silly, when a customer is obviously distressed, can backfire. Your intentions could be misinterpreted and leave you without any tip.

7. **Wear something unusual.** A flower in your hair, a silly tie, an elegant brooch, or a button with an intriguing saying are all great ice-breakers. Remember, religious, political, or other inflammatory sayings are a no-no.

8. **"My name is..."** While some people feel that introducing themselves seems pretentious,

studies show customers tip more if they feel that connection. Try different deliveries (casual, informal, and formal) until you feel comfortable and your customers respond well.

9. **Make them smile.** Share a smile, mention something silly or fun, discuss the sunny weather, or draw a smiley face on the check. These are all proactive ways, researchers have discovered, to increase tips.

10. **Do not just stand there — sell.** New customers, overwhelming menus, great daily specials are all reasons to sell more food and build bigger tips. Other service providers can also increase tips by providing consultive selling. Advise them on special services or extra benefits for buying something else. Buyers do not want to make a bad choice; they often select something "safe" because they are uncertain of the quality, taste, performance, or value of other choices. Tips are your rewards for helping people feel confident about their choices.

11. **Discuss delivery charges.** Order-takers should explain the added delivery charges and who gets these fees. Create a polite and informative explanation such as, "Our delivery fee covers a small portion of our delivery costs. Tipping your driver would go directly to them and be greatly appreciated."

12. **Repeat the order.** Not only can you avoid miscommunications, some people report that they receive better tips when they cheerfully repeat the order back. Some studies even assert that mimicking how the order was given word for word had a positive and significant affect on tips. This method is another that will require your ability to read people and the situation.

13. **Say their name.** Credit cards give you the customer's name. Make note of it and when asking for a signature say, "Thank you, Mr. Jones."

14. **Write on the check.** Write "thank you" on the back of their check to increase your tips. Other short messages can also have a positive effect on tips. To save time, write your message on your blank checks during a break. Happy faces or big grins also count.

15. **Give them tip change.** In the age of credit and ATM cards, people do not always have various denominations in their wallet. Because tipping has to do with social manners, not everyone feels comfortable about asking for tip-appropriate bills. Do not hand back a $10 bill — the return change should be a $5 and five singles. That way you know your customer can easily give you the right tip. Sometimes getting shortchanged on a tip is simply because they did not have the right amount handy.

DO YOUR OWN RESEARCH

Informal research on what motivates your customer base to tip can be quite beneficial and easy to implement. You must create some consistent factors and study your resulting tips. Because tips may vary from shift to shift, from day to day, and from month to month, you may have to repeat the test over a period of time. A good way to track your test is to make note of it in your daily tip logbook.

Try some of the suggestions based on the industry studies mentioned previously along with some of your very own:

1. **Makeup.** Some employers require makeup, others do not. Try wearing a little more

make up (or less) than you normally would. Concentrate on natural-looking makeup during daylight hours and a bit more glitter during evening hours. When practicing makeup application, use a makeup mirror that has lights similar to your workplace to get an idea how others will see your smiling face.

2. **Hair style.** Alter your hair style. If you have been wearing it pulled back from your face, try a looser style (watch out for stray hairs for sanitary reasons).

3. **Facial hair.** Beards or moustaches can alter your appearance significantly. Go without shaving during a vacation or shave yours off and see how your customers react. Just make certain that your facial hair meets your employer's dress code and that it is well maintained.

4. **Brighter colors**. If you are not required to wear a uniform or specific color schemes, try brighter colors. Even if you have to wear black slacks, try adding a bright tie or a blouse in a complementary color.

5. **Observe peers.** One of the best ways to increase your tips is to see what works for others in your establishment.

6. **Improve your attentiveness.** The key areas to focus on are your customers' convenience, comfort, time, privacy, and security. Learn to read signals and ask how you might help them.

   • Make it easier for them to do business with you or to dine with you.

   • Make them feel at home.

   • Create a unique, "better than at home" experience.

   • Do not waste their time if they are in a rush.

   • Help them relax and enjoy a leisurely pace.

   • Seat them near the play area so they can watch their children.

   • Seat them where conversations can be private.

   • Provide a discreet environment where people will not know that they are seeking your services.

   • Provide a secure environment for children or develop habits to protect customer information.

7. **Learn new skills.** There are plenty of ways you could increase your service (and tip income) with a new skill. It can be a great way to surprise regulars and treat new customers extra special. Learn:

   • How to elegantly wrap leftovers.

   • A few magic tricks to delight customers.

   • To greet foreign-speaking customers in their native tongue.

   • How to pour a drink dramatically.

8. **Increase your value.** Like learning new skills, the more you can do to help your customers the more valuable you will be. Valuable service providers are their customers' trusted solution and will bring people back again.

9. **Ask for advice.** Do not be afraid to ask your customer what you can do to serve them. Ask how they would like something or if they need something else. Anticipating their needs is part of superb service.

10. **Do not be afraid to say, "I don't know. Let me see what I can do for you."** Some customer requests may be out of the ordinary or even beyond your authority. Make the customer feel like you are doing everything you can to satisfy her needs. If you can handle the special request, you will be appreciated and, if the answer is no, you will still get points for willingness to try.

11. **Include peers in your tests.** Have other servers try out your ideas and see what results they get. Each person will have their own personal interpretation so you can observe what works for them also.

12. **Get management's support.** Having your supervisor behind you can be a powerful tool. He might have some ideas and can also help you fine-tune your findings. He may also appreciate knowing just why your hair style keeps changing every month.

To learn how to conduct your own tip research, visit The Center for Hospitality Research at Cornell University's Web site at **www.hotelschool.cornell.edu/chr** and download *Mega-Tips: Scientifically Tested Techniques to Increase Your Tips* by Michael Lynn, Ph.D.

TEAMWORK = BETTER TIPS

Unless you work alone, your service ability is directly related to the activities of others. Slow kitchen = poor tip. Inattentive receptionist = poor tip. It is in your best interest to learn how to work well with others and positively influence their performance. Learn how to partner and work with others by:

- **Participating in tip pools.** Sharing the wealth can be one way to support the behind-the-scenes personnel.

- **Concentrating on good communications.** Make certain people understand your needs and expectations.

- **Planning ahead.** Do not wait until you are in a panic to explain how you would like something done for you and your customers.

- **Get them to join you.** Tell people who work with you that you want them to help you be successful. People appreciate being valued and letting them know how important they are to your plan does that.

- **Recognizing greatness.** Be vocal when your peers and/or support personnel do something great. A small gift or recognition during a staff meeting will promote a repeat performance.

- **Saying "thank you."** It is amazing how powerful a few kind words can be in creating a partnership with coworkers.

If all else fails, report inferior performance to a supervisor. Sometimes the only solution is to inform management of situations that cannot be fixed without intervention. Just make certain that you have made a real effort to correct a problem before reporting it. There is a difference between tattling and seeking management support.

CHAPTER

MOTIVATE YOUR EMPLOYEES

CREATING JOB SATISFACTION

While it is important to attend to the training and support needs of your employees and to be actively involved in recruiting and hiring people who fit your organization, effective managers devote much of their time to motivating their employees to perform over and above the required minimums. A well-rounded motivation strategy integrates performance and satisfaction. Meaning that while it is important for employees to feel good about what they are doing and feel appreciated, it is still necessary to hold them accountable for results. The best companies have productive people who are satisfied with their work environment and who are committed to the company's success.

WHAT IS MOTIVATION?

In order to understand motivation, it must be broken down into three distinct and interrelated parts.

The first aspect of motivation involves satisfying one's needs: Motivation towards better performance depends on the satisfaction of needs for responsibility, achievement, recognition, and growth.

The second aspect of motivation is that needs are always changing: Needs are felt and their intensity varies from one person to another and from time to time, and so does the extent to which they are motivating.

Thirdly, motivated behavior can be reinforced: Behavior is learned and earned rewards encourage even better performance, thus reinforcing desired behavior.

Motivation is a very complex topic. If you know what people need and want, then you know what they will work for and if you reinforce them for their performance, they will continue to work well and achieve.

According to Maslow's Hierarchy of Needs theory, needs range from the most basic of physiological needs (food and shelter) to the need for self-fulfillment. When one chooses to work, he is doing it because he needs to earn money to survive, so working in and of itself satisfies a basic need. So, at a very deep level, one is motivated to work, period, but the contextual factors related to work environment provide further motivation to do a good job. These factors include the physical work environment (temperature, comfort, arrangement, noise, aesthetics, safety, etc.) and the employment conditions (salary, benefits, supervision, policies, job status, job security, etc.).

These "maintenance factors," as Hertberg calls them, are important and necessary to providing the kind of work environment that attracts employees in the first place. These factors can be viewed as base-line requirements for a healthy workplace and hopefully it has gotten to the point where most companies can offer a good base level of satisfaction. But a good or average base is not enough to keep the best people in your organization — they are looking for, and deserve, more from their work. To retain your top staff, you need to foster a culture and environment that values your employees and allows and encourages them to reach their potential.

This type of organization goes beyond basic needs and recognizes that people need to feel appreciated and recognized for their contributions and these are the types of social, ego, and self-fulfilling needs that have real motivating potential. The things that motivate on the job include:

- Achievement
- Work itself
- Responsibility

- Recognition
- Advancement
- Possibility of growth

EMPLOYEE MOTIVATION PROGRAM

To effect a successful motivation program, you must start with the following assumptions:

- **Employees start out motivated.** A lack of motivation is a learned response fostered by misunderstood or unrealistic expectations.

- **Management is responsible for creating a supportive, problem-solving work environment** in which necessary resources to perform a task are provided.

- **Rewards should encourage high personal performance** that is consistent with management objectives.

- **Motivation works best when it is based on self-governance.**

- **Employees need to be treated fairly and consistently.**

- **Employees deserve timely, honest feedback** on their work performance.

The onus is on managers to create a motivating environment and continuously monitor the situation to ensure it evolves and stays motivating.

RULES OF EMPLOYEE MOTIVATION

DEFINE EXPECTATIONS

The foundation of an effective motivation program is proper goal-setting. Do your employees understand their role in the organization? Do they see a connection between their daily duties and the bottom line? Unless the answer is yes to both of those questions, then they are simply showing up and collecting a paycheck.

It is very important for employees to feel ownership and empowerment. Ownership happens when they have goals to achieve that are tied to operational performance. These are called performance goals and the best way to achieve them is to make them SMART.

SMART goals are:

- **Specific:** Well-defined and clear to all parties.

- **Measurable:** You know if the goal is obtainable, how far away completion is, and when it has been achieved.

- **Achievable:** It should be something that is challenging but also within your ability to attain.

- **Realistic:** Within the availability of resources, knowledge, and time.

- **Time-framed:** Set a start and end date and leave enough time to achieve the goal within realistic parameters.

EXAMPLES OF SMART GOALS	
Reduce finished product defects by 15 percent next quarter.	Respond to employee suggestions within 48 hours of receipt.

Telling a person to take initiative or do their best is not motivating because these terms mean different things to different people. SMART goals are agreed upon and readily verifiable and quantifiable.

INCREASE THE VALUE OF WORK

To make something motivating, it is important to find out what is important to your employees. Most people think that money is the main motivator but that is actually not the case. Different people are motivated by different things at different times and the best way to find out what employees value is to ask them directly. Companies have spent thousands of dollars on recognition programs only to find out that the reward is a joke to the staff; instead of getting a company T-shirt, what they really wanted was a company picnic table out back. Here are some examples of things commonly considered valuable:

- **Flexible Schedules.** Options include employees working more hours on certain days and fewer on others, in fixed or variable schedules. Compressed work weeks offer employees the opportunity to bundle two full weeks of full-time work into a fixed schedule of eight or nine days. In all circumstances, the programs are structured to meet business objectives while recognizing individual needs.

- **Job Sharing.** Two or more people splitting position responsibilities is another way to acknowledge personal needs while bringing diversity of experience to a singular position. Individuals sharing jobs and working part-time may reduce benefit costs while retaining talent that may otherwise choose to retire or leave the company. Factors to consider are the need to communicate between position participants and the transferability of knowledge.

- **Telecommuting.** Employees with high motivation, self-discipline, necessary skills, and independent orientation are ideal candidates to work off-site. Loyalty and productivity may be enhanced in telecommuting situations; however, companies should have mechanisms in place to measure the success and contributions of telecommuting workers.

- **Paid Leave Banks.** A structured program that combines vacation, short-term sick leave, personal days, and emergency leave is a way to reward and motivate employees. Although the company retains the right to grant approval for leave, the employee can accrue more discretionary days than with some traditional programs. The costs remain the same for the company, while participants perceive greater control and are more likely to remain contented in the long run.

- **Phased Retirement.** By offering a combination of pension modification and staggered working periods, a program can be structured to reduce overall expenses, motivate and retain the employee, and help meet business objectives.

- **Developmental Opportunities and Career Planning.** Many individuals express frustration in performing the same responsibilities over and over. The ability of a company to structure career-planning programs, including job rotations, skills training, and project management assignments, are of interest to many employees. Providing opportunities to learn new technologies and methods and accomplish new achievements is significant in capturing prolonged interest from high-potential staff. Giving people the opportunity to gain exposure and implement new programs while building self-esteem and credibility is valuable for both the company and the employee. If an assignment increases his value on the job market, it is very motivating and ongoing training, especially in technological skills, is often a requirement for employment. Opportunity and recognition of accomplishments can prove to be a much more lucrative incentive than any financial considerations a company may offer.

- **Sabbaticals.** Providing a mid-career break to refresh and rejuvenate is exactly what some employees are looking for. Sabbaticals can be an effective means of energizing these workers.

- **Feedback.** People crave knowing what other people think of their work. Although autonomy is important, so is ready access to and abundant time with managers.

- **Tangible Rewards.** Small, immediate, concrete, tangible rewards, such as money, dinner certificates, and tickets to cultural events, are very motivating. The key is to find out what events or activities motivate the employee. Just because you like to watch the game from the corporate box seat does not mean that your accountant feels the same way.

- **Have Fun.** For well-balanced individuals, their personal lives are more important than their careers. Incentives and benefits that demonstrate an organization's support of a balance are attractive to them.

- **Pat People on the Back.** Few perks are cheaper, easier, or more effective than recognition. Recognition can take a variety of forms. The basic premise is to catch people doing something right and then tell them and others about it.

- **Share the Perks of Your Business.** Is there an aspect of your business that you could turn into an inexpensive employee benefit? Maybe you get merchandise or certificates from suppliers. Instead of keeping those for the managers, share them with your top performers. Let employees share in perks you provide to your clients.

- **Feed Employees' Bodies.** What is the easiest way to an employee's heart? Through the proverbial stomach. Provide monthly in-house luncheons, order pizza on a Friday afternoon, or bake a cake for each employee's birthday. These are fun events that encourage intermingling and foster loyalty.

- **Feed Employees' Souls.** Give employees time off to perform community service. Employees who do not have the time to volunteer at local schools or work with teens or canvas for a charity can do the work that gives back. Offer a wellness program where you reimburse employees, up to a certain amount, for anything that related to their spiritual, mental, or physical well-being.

- **Offer Advancement Opportunities.** One of the best incentives for ambitious people is opportunity. Fill management positions by promoting from within, ensuring that long-term employees have a chance to rise, and that new employees have an incentive to stay.

PROVIDE SUPPORT

For people to be motivated, you must set the groundwork by offering a supportive work environment. No amount of goal-setting or original rewards will work if your employees do not feel they are given the resources and materials necessary for success. You must ask yourself, "Do my employees feel it is possible to achieve this goal?" Support means providing resources, training, and encouragement; essentially, managers need to pave the way for success.

Take this concept beyond lip-service and commit to supporting your employees. Support comes back to the notion of validation; if an employee does not feel she has been given the tools necessary to succeed, then she will feel invalidated and unworthy. Nothing is less motivating than the feeling of helplessness and being sent out to sink or swim. From your first day of orientation to the employee's last day on the job, you must provide all the information, background, training, and encouragement necessary to be successful. Employees need to feel that management is working hard to help them achieve their performance goals.

GIVE FEEDBACK

Once a goal has been established and agreed upon, employees need access to how they are progressing. Once a year at performance review time is not enough, nor is it even remotely adequate. People need to know how they are doing — good and bad; by setting SMART goals, they have a tangible way to measure their progress. Spontaneous feedback is excellent and provides an immediate boost, but feedback also needs to be given formally. The process need not be overly time-consuming or overly rigid, it simply needs to take place at regular intervals.

Weekly or monthly progress reports are good ways to establish feedback controls. It ensures that timely praise is given and performance coaching can be done before the problem spins out of control. Brief, frequent, and highly visible feedback is the kind that motivates and managers should look for some opportunity to praise their employees every week. Study after study has shown that praise and recognition tend to build employee loyalty. People want to feel that what they do makes a difference and money alone does not do this; personal recognition does.

NO-COST WAYS TO RECOGNIZE EMPLOYEES

Here are some key no-cost ways to recognize employees:

- **Provide Information.** Information is power and employees want to be empowered with the information they need to know to do their jobs more effectively. And employees want to know how they are doing in their jobs and how the company is doing in its business. Open the channels of communication in your organization to allow employees to be informed, ask questions, and share information.

- **Encourage Involvement.** Managers today are faced with an incredible number of opportunities and problems and, as the speed of business continues to increase dramatically, the amount of time that they have to make decisions continues to decrease. Involving employees in decision-making, especially when the decisions affect them directly, is respectful and practical. Those closest to the problem typically have the best insight as to what to do. As you involve others, you increase their commitment and ease in implementing new ideas or change.

- **Foster Independence.** Few employees want their every action to be closely monitored. Most employees appreciate having the flexibility to do their jobs as they see fit. Giving people latitude increases the chance that they will perform as you desire — and bring additional initiative, ideas, and energy to their jobs.

- **Increase Visibility.** Everyone appreciates getting credit when it is due. Occasions to share the successes of employees with others are almost limitless. Giving employees new opportunities to perform, learn, and grow as a form of recognition and thanks is highly motivating for most people.

REWARD SUCCESS

Like feedback, rewards for success must be given in a timely manner. Rewards, even highly valuable ones, lose their motivating potential unless they are given at the correct time. It is the timing of reinforcements that lets employees know which behaviors are being encouraged. While it seems quite obvious, it is often not done — after going through all the administration required, their reward is sometimes not actually given for weeks after the fact. Delay between performance and feedback dilutes the effectiveness of the reward, so it is imperative that you be prepared with your system of motivation and plan ahead for the administrative aspects.

Reward success consistently and fairly. There is nothing more demotivating than a reward that is given under unfair circumstances or out of preferential treatment. Establish the parameters of your reward system and treat all employees with the same rules. Again, it seems obvious but it is very easy to reward Bob "just this one time" even though he was off his goal slightly. "After all, he is usually the top performer and he just had a bad month; we would not want to upset him or anything. The other guys will understand." The intent is honorable, but the effect can be devastating if the other guys do not understand. You have sacrificed many people for the sake of one.

Although this example may seem petty on the surface, it is this type of inconsistency in a workplace that festers and creates toxic work environments. Not to say that common sense and good judgment are thrown away for the sake of absolute fairness, but it does mean that you must think of all the ramifications of bending the rules ever so slightly.

MOTIVATION FACTORS	
Motivation Boosters	**Motivation Deflators**
Responsibility	Meaningless, repetitive work
Meaningful work	Confusion
Variety in assignments	Lack of trust
Measurable outputs	No input in decisions
Challenge	Not knowing what's going on
Solving problems	Not knowing how well you are doing
Trust	Someone solving problems for you
Participation in decisions	No time to solve problems
Ability to measure own performance	Across-the-board rules and regulations
Being listened to	Not getting credit for your ideas or efforts
Praise	Lack of resources, knowledge, skills and coaching
Recognition for contributions	Inconsistency

HOW TO MAINTAIN GOOD EMPLOYEE RELATIONS

Management attitudes create the culture of an organization. The following tips can be applied to create a culture that is satisfying to employees and productive for the organization. Here are some useful tips:

- **Be knowledgeable of employment laws.** Wages and compensation are always important to employees. Be aware of local, state, and federal laws governing pay rates. In 2004 the department of labor enacted new rules regarding "white-collar" employees and overtime-pay requirements. In July of 2007, the federal minimum wage was increased. Employers can obtain a copy of the regulations and other information about the new rules at **www.dol.gov/fairpay**. You should make sure to have employment laws posted in a prominent place. Atlantic publishing offers a laminated labor law poster with all current federal information (see the sample on the last page of this chapter). To order call 800-814-1132 or visit **www.atlantic-pub.com**.

- **Be available for discussion of employee problems.** Let employees know that they can go to management with problems and concerns. Ensure that management conduct creates an environment of trust and confidence. Managers must take concerns seriously and address them promptly. Do not put people off; they will not forget it.

- **Maintain confidentiality.** When employees discuss matters of concern to management, their confidences must be respected. When confidences must be shared to resolve the problem, the employee should be told.

- **Give uninterrupted attention to employees.** Do not allow visitors and phone calls when discussing an important matter with employees. Let your actions convey that the employee is important to you. Give employees the focused attention they deserve.

- **Conduct well-organized meetings.** Meetings should provide valuable information and solicit employee feedback. Avoid surprises in the agenda.

- **Do not criticize employees in public.** If an employee must be corrected, do so privately. Never point out an employee's mistakes to or in front of other employees.

- **Coach, rather than criticize.** When corrective action is necessary, be timely, clear, and accurate. Provide the employee with concrete examples to ensure that she understands the problem so that she can improve the performance.

- **Treat employees equally.** Perceptions of special treatment are damaging to morale and creates potential legal liability.

- **Remember the little things.** Consider celebrating birthdays, company anniversaries, and special events and give recognition when due.

- **Encourage staff input.** Share problems and challenges when appropriate and ask for suggestions on how to deal with them.

- **Delegate and develop.** Delegate new, challenging tasks to employees; provide opportunities for employees to develop new skills.

- **Welcome change.** Welcome change as a means for you, your employees, and the company to progress to a better future. Generate enthusiasm for change.

- **Support organizational goals.** Work as a team, ensuring there are no interdepartmental battlegrounds that are counterproductive.

- **Be human.** Enjoy your work and employees. Share your enthusiasm. Make yourself approachable and willing to listen.

For much more information about hiring, training, and motivating restaurant employees, I recommend the following books by Atlantic Publishing (**www.atlantic-pub.com**). Some are general restaurant reference while others are topic specific for concerns that restaurant managers may need.

- *How to Hire, Train, and Keep The Best Employees* (Item # HTK-02).

- *The Food Service Manager's Guide to Creative Cost Cutting* (Item # CCC-01).

- *The Food Service Professional's Guide to Controlling Restaurant and Food Service Operating Costs* (Item # FS5-01).

- *The Food Service Professional's Guide to Controlling Restaurant and Food Service Labor Costs* (Item # FS7-01).

- *The Food Service Professional's Guide to Waiter & Waitress Training: How to Develop Your Staff For Maximum Service & Profit* (Item # FS10-01).

- *The Food Service Professional's Guide to Bar & Beverage Operation: Ensuring Success & Maximum Profit* (Item # FS11-01).

- *The Food Service Professional's Guide to Successful Catering: Managing the Catering Operation For Maximum Profit* (Item # FS12-01).

- *How to Communicate With Your Spanish and Asian Employees* (Item # CSA-02).

- *The Restaurant Manager's Success Chronicles* (Item # MSC-01).

- *Key Words Food Service Employee Translation Poster* (Item # KWF-PS).

- *The Professional Caterer's Handbook* (Item # PCH-01).

- *The Complete Guide to Successful Event Planning* (Item # SEP-01).

- *The Non Commercial Food Service Manager's Handbook* (Item # NCF-02).

- *8 Posters to Reinforce Good Service* (Item # WSP-PS).

- *The Complete Wait Staff Training Course on Video or DVD.*

- *The Waiter and Waitress and Wait Staff Training Handbook* (Item # WWT-TH).

- *Design Your Own Effective Employee Handbook* (Item # GEH-02).

- *365 Ways to Motivate and reward Your Employees Every Day – With Little or No Money* (Item # 365-01).

- *199 Pre-Written Employee Performance Appraisals* (Item # EPP-02).

- *Superior Customer Service: How to Keep Customers Racing Back to Your Business-Time Tested Examples from Leading Companies* (Item # SCS-01).

2007-2009 THE LAW REQUIRES EMPLOYERS TO DISPLAY THIS POSTER WHERE EMPLOYEES AND JOB APPLICANTS CAN READILY SEE IT.

FEDERAL LABOR LAWS

Employee Polygraph Protection Act

The Employee Polygraph Protection Act prohibits most private employers from using lie detector tests for employment screening or during the course of employment

PROHIBITIONS
Employers are generally prohibited from requiring or requesting any employee or job applicant to take a lie detector test and from discharging, disciplining, or discriminating against an employee or prospective employee for refusing to take a test or for exercising other rights under the Act.

EXEMPTIONS*
Federal, state and local governments are not affected by the law. Also, the law does not apply to tests given by the federal government to certain private individuals engaged in national security-related activities.
The Act permits polygraph (a kind of lie detector) tests to be administered in the private sector, subject to restrictions, to certain prospective employees of security service firms (armored car, alarm, and guard) and of pharmaceutical manufacturers, distributors and dispensers.
The Act also permits polygraph testing, subject to restrictions, of certain employees of private firms who are reasonably suspected of involvement in a workplace incident (theft, embezzlement, etc.) that resulted in economic loss to the employer.

EXAMINEE RIGHTS
Where polygraph tests are permitted, they are subject to numerous strict standards concerning the conduct and length of the test. Examinees have a number of specific rights, including the right to a written notice before testing, the right to refuse or discontinue a test, and the right not to have test results disclosed to unauthorized persons.

ENFORCEMENT
The Secretary of Labor may bring court actions to restrain violations and assess civil penalties up to $10,000 against violators. Employees or job applicants may also bring their own court actions.

ADDITIONAL INFORMATION
Additional information may be obtained, and complaints of violations may be filed, at local offices of the Wage and Hour Division, which are listed in the telephone directory under U.S. Government, Department of Labor, Employment Standards Administration.

** The law does not preempt any provision of any state or local law or any collective bargaining agreement which is more restrictive with respect to lie detector tests.*

You Have a Right to a Safe and Healthful Workplace.

IT'S THE LAW!

- You have the right to notify your employer or OSHA about workplace hazards. You may ask OSHA to keep your name confidential.
- You have the right to request an OSHA inspection if you believe that there are unsafe and unhealthful conditions in your workplace. You or your representative may participate in the inspection.
- You can file a complaint with OSHA within 30 days of discrimination by your employer for making safety and health complaints or for exercising your rights under the OSH Act.
- You have a right to see OSHA citations issued to your employer. Your employer must post the citations at or near the place of the alleged violation.
- Your employer must correct workplace hazards by the date indicated on the citation and must certify that these hazards have been reduced or eliminated.
- You have the right to copies of your medical records or records of your exposure to toxic and harmful substances or conditions.
- Your employer must post this notice in your workplace.

The Occupational Safety and Health Act of 1970 (OSH Act), P.L. 91-596, assures safe and healthful working conditions for working men and women throughout the Nation. The Occupational Safety and Health Administration, in the U.S. Department of Labor, has the primary responsibility for administering the OSH Act. The rights listed here may vary depending on the particular circumstances. To file a complaint, report an emergency or seek OSHA advice, assistance or products, call 1-800-321-OSHA or your nearest OSHA office: • Atlanta (404) 562-2300 • Boston (617) 565-9860 • Chicago (312) 353-2220 • Dallas (214) 767-4731 • Denver (303) 844-1600 • Kansas City (816) 426-5861 • New York (212) 337-2378 • Philadelphia (215) 861-4900 • San Francisco (415) 975-4310 • Seattle (206) 553-5930. Teletypewriter (TTY) number is 1-877-889-5627. To file a complaint online or obtain more information on OSHA federal and state programs, visit OSHA's Web site at www.osha.gov. If your workplace is in a state operating under an OSHA-approved plan, your employer must post the required state equivalent of this poster.

1-800-321-OSHA • www.osha.gov

Fair Labor Standards Act Overtime Security Advisor

These regulations became effective August 23, 2004. The FLSA requires that covered employees in the United States be paid at least the federal minimum wage for each hour they work and overtime pay at one and one-half the employee's regular rate of pay for all hours worked over 40 in a workweek. If you are unsure about whether a particular employment situation is covered by the FLSA, you should review the FLSA Coverage and Employment Status Advisor. One particular exemption, FLSA section 13(a)(1), exempts from both minimum wage and overtime pay protections bona fide executive, administrative, professional and outside sales employees. FLSA sections 13(a)(1) and 13(a)(17) also exempt certain employees in computer-related occupations. The FLSA contains several other exemptions from the minimum wage and/or overtime pay protections which are not covered in this Advisor.

For the FLSA section 13(a)(1) exemptions to apply, an employee generally must be paid on a salary basis of no less than $455 per week and perform certain types of work that:

- is directly related to the management of his or her employer's business.
- is directly related to the general business operations of his or her employer or the employer's clients.
- requires specialized academic training for entry into a professional field.
- is in the computer field.
- is making sales away from his or her employer's place of business.
- is in a recognized field of artistic or creative endeavor.

FLSA Section 13(a)(17) exempts hourly paid employees who perform certain types of work in the computer field if they are paid at a rate of not less than $27.63 per hour.

Exemptions are determined based on each specific employment situation. Job titles alone do not determine the exempt or non-exempt status of any employee. Each determination is based on the specific job duties performed and compensation received. Therefore, you should run the Advisor for each specific employee or for each group of employees who perform essentially the same duties and receive essentially the same compensation package.

A number of states have also enacted minimum wage and overtime pay laws, some of which provide greater worker protections than those provided by FLSA. In those situations where an employee is covered by both federal and state wage laws, the employee is entitled to the greater benefit or more generous rights provided under the different parts of each law.

Your Rights Under the Family and Medical Leave Act of 1993

FMLA requires covered employers to provide up to 12 weeks of unpaid, job-protected leave to "eligible" employees for certain family and medical reasons. Employees are eligible if they have worked for their employer for at least one year, and for 1,250 hours over the previous 12 months, and if there are at least 50 employees within 75 miles. The FMLA permits employees to take leave on an intermittent basis or to work a reduced schedule under certain circumstances.

REASONS FOR TAKING LEAVE
Unpaid leave must be granted for any of the following reasons:

- To care for the employee's child after birth, or placement for adoption or foster care.
- To care for the employee's spouse, son or daughter, or parent who has a serious health condition.
- For a serious health condition that makes the employee unable to perform the employee's job.

At the employee's or employer's option, certain kinds of paid leave may be substituted for unpaid leave.

ADVANCE NOTICE & MEDICAL CERTIFICATION
The employee may be required to provide advance leave notice and medical certification. Taking of leave may be denied if requirements are not met.

- The employee ordinarily must provide 30 days advance notice when the leave is "foreseeable."
- An employer may require medical certification to support a request for leave because of a serious health condition, and may require second or third opinions (at the employer's expense) and a fitness for duty report to return to work.

JOB BENEFITS & PROTECTION

- For the duration of FMLA leave, the employer must maintain the employee's health coverage under any "group health plan."
- Upon return from FMLA leave, most employees must be restored to their original or equivalent positions with equivalent pay, benefits and other employment terms.
- The use of FMLA leave cannot result in the loss of any employment benefit that accrued prior to the start of an employee's leave.

UNLAWFUL ACTS BY EMPLOYERS
FMLA makes it unlawful for any employer to:

- Interfere with, restrain or deny the exercise of any right provided under FMLA.
- Discharge or discriminate against any person for opposing any practice made unlawful by FMLA or for involvement in any proceeding under or relating to FMLA.

ENFORCEMENT

- The U.S. Department of Labor is authorized to investigate and resolve complaints of violations.
- An eligible employee may bring a civil action against an employer for violations. FMLA does not affect any federal or state law prohibiting discrimination or supersede any state or local law or collective bargaining agreement which provides greater family or medical leave rights.

For additional information: If you have access to the Internet, visit our FMLA Web site: www.dol.gov/esa/whd/fmla. To [illegible] Wage-Hour toll-free information and help line at 1-866-4USWAGE (1-866-487-9243); a customer service representative is available to assist you with referral information from 8 a.m. to 5 p.m. in your time zone; or log onto our Web site www.wagehour.dol.gov.

Your Rights Under the Fair Labor Standards Act

Federal Minimum Wage

$5.85 per hour	$6.55 per hour	$7.25 per hour
beginning July 24, 2007	beginning July 24, 2008	beginning July 24, 2009

Employees under 20 years of age may be paid $4.25 per hour during their first 90 consecutive calendar days of employment with an employer. Certain full-time students, student learners, apprentices and workers with disabilities may be paid less than the minimum wage under special certificates issued by the Department of Labor.

Tip Credit
Employers of "tipped employees" must pay a cash wage of at least $2.13 per hour if they claim a tip credit against their minimum wage obligation. If an employee's tips combined with the employer's cash wage of at least $2.13 per hour do not equal the minimum hourly wage, the employer must make up the difference. Certain other conditions must also be met.

Overtime Pay
At least 1½ times your regular rate of pay for all hours worked over 40 in a workweek.

Child Labor
An employee must be at least 16 years old to work in most non-farm jobs and at least 18 to work in non-farm jobs declared hazardous by the Secretary of Labor. Youths 14 and 15 years old may work outside school hours in various non-manufacturing, non-mining, non-hazardous jobs under the following conditions:

- No more than 3 hours on a school day or 18 hours in a school week.
- 8 hours on a non-school day or 40 hours in a non-school week.

Also, work may not begin before 7 a.m. or end after 7 p.m., except from June 1 through Labor Day, when evening hours are extended to 9 p.m. Different rules apply in agricultural employment.

Enforcement
The Department of Labor may recover back wages, either administratively or through court action, for the employees that have been underpaid in violation of the law.

Violations may result in civil or criminal action. Fines of up to $10,000 per violation may be assessed against employers who violate the child labor provisions of the law and up to $1,000 per violation against employers who willfully or repeatedly violate the minimum wage or overtime pay provisions. This law prohibits discriminating against or discharging workers who file a complaint or participate in any proceedings under the Act.

- Certain occupations and establishments are exempt from the minimum wage and/or overtime pay provisions.
- Special provisions apply to workers in American Samoa.
- Where state law requires a higher minimum wage, the higher standard applies.

For additional information, contact the Wage and Hour Division office nearest you – listed in your telephone directory under United States Government, Labor Department.

YOUR RIGHTS UNDER USERRA

THE UNIFORMED SERVICES EMPLOYMENT AND REEMPLOYMENT RIGHTS ACT

USERRA protects the job rights of individuals who voluntarily or involuntarily leave employment positions to undertake military service. USERRA also prohibits employers from discriminating against past and present members of the uniformed services and applicants to the uniformed services.

REEMPLOYMENT RIGHTS
You have the right to be reemployed in your civilian job if you leave that job to perform service in the uniformed service and:

- You ensure that your employer receives advance written or verbal notice of your service.
- You have five years or less of cumulative service in the uniformed services while with that particular employer.
- You return to work or apply for reemployment in a timely manner after conclusion of service.
- You have not been separated from service with a disqualifying discharge or under other than honorable conditions.

If you are eligible to be reemployed, you must be restored to the job and benefits you would have attained if you had not been absent due to military service or, in some cases, a comparable job.

RIGHT TO BE FREE FROM DISCRIMINATION AND RETALIATION
If you:

- Are a past or present member of the uniformed service
- Have applied for membership in the uniformed service
- Are obligated to serve in the uniformed service

Then an employer may not deny you any of the following because of this status:

- Initial employment.
- Reemployment.
- Retention in employment.
- Promotion.
- Any benefit of employment.

In addition, an employer may not retaliate against anyone assisting in the enforcement of USERRA rights, including testifying or making a statement in connection with a proceeding under USERRA, even if that person has no service connection.

HEALTH INSURANCE PROTECTION

- If you leave your job to perform military service, you have the right to elect to continue your existing employer-based health plan coverage for you and your dependents for up to 24 months while in the military.
- Even if you don't elect to continue coverage during your military service, you have the right to be reinstated in your employer's health plan when you are reemployed, generally without any waiting periods or exclusions (e.g., pre-existing condition exclusions) except for service-connected illnesses or injuries.

ENFORCEMENT

- The U.S. Department of Labor, Veterans Employment and Training Service (VETS) is authorized to investigate and resolve complaints of USERRA violations.
- For assistance in filing a complaint, or for any other information on USERRA, contact VETS at 1-866-4-USA-DOL or visit its Web site at www.dol.gov/vets. An interactive online USERRA Advisor can be viewed at www.dol.gov/elaws/userra.htm.
- If you file a complaint with VETS and VETS is unable to resolve it, you may request that your case be referred to the Department of Justice or the Office of Special Counsel, depending on the employer, for representation.
- You may also bypass the VETS process and bring a civil action against an employer for violations of USERRA.

The rights listed here may vary depending on the circumstances. This notice was prepared by VETS, and may be viewed on the internet at this address: www.dol.gov/vets/programs/userra/poster.pdf. Federal law requires employers to notify employees of their rights under USERRA, and employers may meet this requirement by displaying this notice where they customarily place notices for employees.

U.S. Department of Labor
1-866-487-2365
Publication Date—February 2005

Employer Support of the Guard & Reserve
1-800-336-4590

Equal Employment Opportunity is the Law

EMPLOYERS HOLDING FEDERAL CONTRACTS OR SUBCONTRACTS

Applicants to and employees of companies with a federal government contract or subcontract are protected under the following federal authorities:

RACE, COLOR, RELIGION, SEX, NATIONAL ORIGIN
Executive Order 11246, as amended, prohibits job discrimination on the basis of race, color, religion, sex or national origin and requires affirmative action to ensure equality of opportunity in all aspects of employment.

INDIVIDUALS WITH DISABILITIES
Section 503 of the Rehabilitation Act of 1973, as amended, prohibits job discrimination because of disability and requires affirmative action to employ and advance in employment qualified individuals with disabilities who, with reasonable accommodation, can perform the essential functions of a job.

VIETNAM-ERA, SPECIAL DISABLED, RECENTLY SEPARATED, AND OTHER PROTECTED VETERANS
38 U.S.C. 4212 of the Vietnam Era Veterans' Readjustment Assistance Act of 1974, as amended, prohibits job discrimination and requires affirmative action to employ and advance in employment qualified Vietnam-era veterans, qualified special disabled veterans, recently separated veterans, and other protected veterans.

Any person who believes a contractor has violated its nondiscrimination or affirmative action obligations under the authorities above should contact:

The Office of Federal Contract Compliance Programs (OFCCP), Employment Standards Administration, U.S. Department of Labor, 200 Constitution Avenue, N.W., Washington, D.C. 20210, or call (202) 693-0101, or an OFCCP regional or district office, listed in most telephone directories under U.S. Government, Department of Labor.

PRIVATE EMPLOYMENT, STATE AND LOCAL GOVERNMENTS, EDUCATIONAL INSTITUTIONS

Applicants to and employees of most private employers, state and local governments, educational institutions, employment agencies and labor organizations are protected under the following federal laws:

RACE, COLOR, RELIGION, SEX, NATIONAL ORIGIN
Title VII of the Civil Rights Act of 1964, as amended, prohibits discrimination in hiring, promotion, discharge, pay, fringe benefits, job training, classification, referral, and other aspects of employment, on the basis of race, color, religion, sex or national origin.

SEX (WAGES)
In addition to sex discrimination prohibited by Title VII of the Civil Rights Act of 1964, as amended (see above), the Equal Pay Act of 1963, as amended, prohibits sex discrimination in payment of wages to women and men performing substantially equal work in the same establishment. Retaliation against a person who files a charge of discrimination, participates in an investigation, or opposes an unlawful employment practice is prohibited by all of these Federal laws.

DISABILITY
The Americans with Disabilities Act of 1990, as amended, protects qualified applicants and employees with disabilities from discrimination in hiring, promotion, discharge, pay, job training, fringe benefits, classification, referral, and other aspects of employment on the basis of disability. The law also requires that covered entities provide qualified applicants and employees with disabilities with reasonable accommodations that do not impose undue hardship.

AGE
The Age Discrimination in Employment Act of 1967, as amended, protects applicants and employees 40 years of age or older from discrimination on the basis of age in hiring, promotion, discharge, compensation, terms, conditions or privileges of employment. If you believe that you have been discriminated against under any of the above laws, you should contact:

The U.S. Equal Employment Opportunity Commission (EEOC), 1801 L Street, N.W., Washington, D.C. 20507 or an EEOC field office by calling toll free (800) 669-4000. For individuals with hearing impairments, EEOC's toll free TDD number is (800) 669-6820.

RACE, COLOR, RELIGION, NATIONAL ORIGIN, SEX
In addition to the protection of Title VII of the Civil Rights Act of 1964, as amended, Title VI of the Civil Rights Act prohibits discrimination on the basis of race, color or national origin in programs or activities receiving federal financial assistance. Employment discrimination is covered by Title VI if the primary objective of the financial assistance is provision of employment or where employment discrimination causes or may cause discrimination in providing services under such programs. Title IX of the Education Amendments of 1972 prohibits employment discrimination on the basis of sex in educational programs or activities which receive federal assistance.

INDIVIDUALS WITH DISABILITIES
Sections 501, 504 and 505 of the Rehabilitation Act of 1973, as amended, prohibits employment discrimination on the basis of disability in any program or activity which receives federal financial assistance in the federal government. Discrimination is prohibited in all aspects of employment against persons with disabilities who, with reasonable accommodation, can perform the essential functions of a job.

If you believe you have been discriminated against in a program of any institution which receives federal assistance, you should contact immediately the federal agency providing such assistance.

Above is the Federal Labor Laws poster from Atlantic Publishing. To order, call 800-814-1132 or online at www.atlantic-pub.com (Item # FLLEN-PS, $29.95). Available in both English and Spanish.

CHAPTER

DAILY LEADERSHIP AND TEAMBUILDING

It is often said employees do not leave the organization, they leave the manager. While it is invariably true that good leaders are crucial to staff retention, they are also much more. Good leaders are the fundamental ingredient to sustained organizational success. A number of factors affect staff retention. Organizations that hold onto employees create a work environment that is attractive to the people who are critical to organizational success. These companies do not think of employees as workers but treat them as associates or partners. Among the many factors that affect staff retention, the most fundamental component is the presence of people-centered leadership. The quality of leadership, especially in supervisory roles, impacts the quality of work life and improves the organization's ability to retain employees. It is great leadership that creates a supportive work environment, challenging work, recognition, and respect. When leaders focus on people, the organization will have competitive compensation and benefits programs. But quality leadership means much more than simply ensuring low staff turnover.

Successful leaders do not fit the popular media image of an ultra charismatic, larger-than-life character. Rather, organizations need leaders that can staff the organization with the right people, recognize the challenges and opportunities facing the organization, establish and implement an appropriate strategic direction, and drive the organization to continually innovate and succeed. Success depends on the ability to implement the strategic plan and circumstances require changes. Great leaders combine excellence in people management and strategic implementation. They create an environment that makes people want to stick around.

LEADERSHIP

A leader is a person you will follow to a place you would not go by yourself; a manager tells you where to go.

The qualities of a good leader have been studied and postulated to death and the list of attributes is very long. Regardless of their position or claim to leadership, there are a few key traits that true leaders demonstrate; these are traits they cultivate and demonstrate as a matter of choice, not title or job role.

MANAGER VS. LEADER	
The manager administers.	The leader innovates.
The manager has a short-range view.	The leader has a long-range perspective.
The manager asks how and when.	The leader asks what and why.
The manager has his eye on the bottom line.	The leader has his eye on the horizon.
The manager accepts the status quo.	The leader challenges it.

Leaders who are effective in the "little ways" strive for the following in their interactions and their work:

- **They are present.** Leaders pay attention to what they are doing at the moment or to whom they are speaking at the moment. Unlike those folks who are clearly "somewhere else" when you are talking with them, you do not feel unseen, unrecognized, or unheard in a leader's presence.

- **They listen.** Because they are present and paying attention, leaders do not just remember talking with you, they remember what you said. After talking with a leader, you do not think to yourself, "gee, I may have just as well spoken to the wall."

- **They speak mindfully.** Leaders are aware that their words have an effect on others, so they speak consciously. Unlike the stories of the unfortunate buffoons who scream and yell at executive meetings making people cower, leaders do not need to rely on such antics.

- **They encourage.** Leaders, being grounded and secure in themselves, find it easier to be encouraging of others. They encourage others to take risks, to pick themselves up after making mistakes, to take their skills to the next level, to pursue their dreams.

- **They are honest.** Real leaders strive to know themselves so that they have the inner resources to speak, live, and lead honestly. Leaders do not say one thing in public while doing something else more self-serving in private. Leaders do not have to make excuses about poor behavior; if it is unethical, they will find another way to do it.

- **They are humble.** Real leaders know the long-term costs of arrogance are high. Great leaders have always shown great humility, which allows them to cultivate the leadership traits that truly serve themselves and others.

- **They persevere.** Leaders know that failures and difficulties are not ends, but simply doors to pass through on the way to greater wisdom and skillfulness.

- **They are courageous.** Leaders know that everyone, themselves included, has fear at times. Leaders do not let their fears and uncertainties stop them from persevering and pursuing their dreams, from building their skills, or from speaking honestly.

- **They are thoughtful.** Leaders have the presence of mind to recognize others, whether when saying hello during the day or paying a compliment for work well-done. Being thoughtful of others, leaders are on time for meetings, are conscious of using time well, are organized, follow through on promises, and close the loop on communications.

- **They are respectful.** Leaders treat others respectfully and require that others are respectful in return. True leaders do not tolerate being spoken to or treated in a disrespectful manner and it is a rare occurrence for that to happen.

W HAT TYPE OF LEADER ARE YOU?

There are a variety of methods to discover what type of leader you are and a variety of names given to the various leadership types. Some models are based on personality traits, others are based on conflict resolution style, and others consider your behavioral style. The different types of leaders are endless: Leaders can be classified as supportive, directive, authentic, empathic, transformational, motivational, laissez-faire, autocratic, consultative, participative, or a whole host of other categories depending on the evaluation tool used. While the actual name of the leadership style you employ may be many different things, you determine the direction alone or let others participate in determining the direction. There are as many different theories about which type of leadership is the most effective as there are names for different leadership styles. What seems to be important to all of the discussions on leadership is the need to be flexible and adaptive when applying a leadership style to a certain situation or individual.

ADAPTIVE LEADERSHIP

Situational (adaptive) leadership was developed by Paul Hersey and Ken Blanchard and is based on the amount of direction and support a leader must provide given the situation and level of development of the employee in relation to the task. Development of the employee is based on his commitment level and competence. The four different types of leadership are: directing, influencing, collaborating, and delegating. Each situation requires awareness of the type of support and direction needed and then the appropriate leadership style is applied.

- **Directing.** Leader behavior is directive and is used when an employee is not ready to perform a task or set of tasks. The leader controls the process, teaches the basics, and uses a directive style.

- **Influencing.** Leader behavior is influential. While still closely managing the work that needs to be done, the leader coaches by counseling, mentoring, and tutoring the employee and inspiring and acknowledging the success the person is achieving.

- **Collaborating.** Leader behavior is consultative. The leader involves the employee in decision-making, invites ideas, or draws them out and focuses discussions. It is a team-oriented approach.

- **Delegating.** Leader behavior is trusting. The leader can let go, authorize, and determine "what" rather than "how" work gets done. Trust is also the highest form of motivation.

WORKPLACE ISSUES AND LEADERSHIP EXAMPLES

Situation	Leadership Strategy: Delegating
An employee has been with the company for three years and has mastered her work so well that she can teach it to new hires. Her motivation is slumping because she has little more to learn. What leadership approach best suits her situation?	This employee can and should be trusted to direct her own work. The leader is responsible for determining what needs to get done, and the rest is up to her. Because she knows the job so well, given a little trust and encouragement, she will probably come up with innovative (and cost-saving!) ways to get the job done and contribute more effectively to the company.
Situation	**Leadership Strategy: Influencing**
An employee, laid off from another organization was hired five months ago. His skill level is high, but he still hasn't grasped the company's ways of doing things. How do you lead him?	This employee does not need constant direction; what he needs is support to give him confidence in working within the policies and procedures of his new company. His leader needs to act as a mentor and coach; showing him the ropes and then letting him know when he is doing well or helping him to learn from his mistakes. With just enough support, this employee will become comfortable in his position and confident in his abilities.
Situation	**Leadership Strategy: Directing**
One of the most competent and dedicated employees asks for a transfer to a different job within the company in order to increase his versatility. From welding he goes to receiving. What style of management is appropriate for this person?	This employee is not ready to do the actual tasks of a receiver. In order for him not to get discouraged, he will need to be directed in his daily tasks until he has mastered them. Because his competence was so high in the welding department, if he is not given enough support and direction to learn his new job, he will come to see himself as a failure and his self-esteem, motivation and commitment will plummet.
Situation	**Leadership Strategy: Collaborating:**
An employee has been with the company for two years and does a modestly competent job in most tasks. She is not a star but a very dependable and capable worker. What style do you use I this situation?	While many mangers would be tempted to use an influencing style with this employee, she will not grow and realize her potential unless her manager collaborates with her. This participation will give her the confidence she needs to break out of the average rut and really earn praise and recognition. By including her in discussions and getting her input, the manager is saying that this employee is valued.

With a growing emphasis on tasks and results, supervisors have become less concerned with employee development. Unfortunately, this hard-pressure, results-oriented relationship between the supervisor and the employee tends to generate increasing levels of underperformance in the workplace. When employees are labeled underperformers, what really occurs in many cases is a mismatch between the manager's style of supervision and the employee's level of dependence or independence. What managers have to understand is that each employee relates to authority differently. Some workers need close supervision while others thrive when working on their own. Many people make the transition from dependence on authority to self-reliance without help, but still others are stuck at specific stages and need some catalyst to move to the next level of independent performance.

Managers need to understand that each employee relates to authority differently. The reality is that each employee can be effectively stimulated to perform better simply through the impact of the supervisor's leadership.

LEADERSHIP PROBLEMS AND SOLUTIONS EXAMPLE 1

Situation	Problem
An employee with limited skills was assigned the front desk reception function at a small company. The individual quickly earned the label of a "non-performer" because she did not find work on her own. Many assignments were not completed and those that were seemed to take forever, with results below expectations. She did manage the telephone reception really well, but that requirement was a limited portion of her job. The only training she received was based on self-help modules that she had to learn on her own.	It turns out that the supervisor was not providing this particular employee enough support.

Solution
The supervisor was given instructions on how to direct work during an assignment, help the individual decide what to do and how to do it, and review each assignment for effectiveness and improvement needed. With support, the non-performing employee began to understand what makes each assignment work well. Her assignments were increasingly successful, earning her recognition from each of the people assigning her. Today, this employee initiates, creates and completes work at a level that impresses her supervisors.

LEADERSHIP PROBLEMS AND SOLUTIONS EXAMPLE 2

Situation	Problem
An individual, who without much formal training, had learned to be a computer programmer. This employee was instructed and directed by a senior programmer who literally solved all problems. Recently, a change in the employee's behavior was observed. The individual began to complete work in his own time frame. He also began to show resentment toward the constant instruction from the supervising programmer. The greater the pressure from the supervisor, the more the employee backed away and seemed to work less. On the other hand, he was indicating that there were projects that he wanted to add to his workload, which always seemed to be in conflict with the supervisor's priorities.	This individual was outgrowing his supervisor's style of work. He wanted to become less dependent and take more initiative, but had not developed enough confidence to take on projects that were important enough to put him at risk and challenge his skills. At the same time, he was irritated by the constant overseeing of his work by his supervisor. The supervisor, focused as he was on tasks and results, had no awareness of his employee's growth and development and continued to insist that the individual conform to his style of direct supervision. It was later found that the employee was taking his work home to escape the constant overview. He was also becoming angry that he could not break from the patterns that were the preferred style of his supervisor.

Solution
The supervisor learned how to back away and supervise from a critical results path (Collaborating) instead of detailed analysis (Directing) of the employee's work. At the same time, the two had to learn how to inject creativity into the employee's projects.

Underperformance occurs at every level within a company, even in the most senior leadership roles. Underperformance is caused by a mismatch between the supervisor's expectations and the employee's stage of development. While there is a complex interaction between employees and supervisors, understanding the critical transition that occurs for every employee within a wide range of circumstances will better enable supervisors to draw out better levels of performance. The key factor is how the authority's and the employee's reaction can best be managed to help the employee develop independence. Improved performance results when managers learn adaptive leadership.

UTHENTICITY — THE NEW LEADERSHIP BUZZ WORD

Webster defines authentic as "*worthy of acceptance or belief, conforming to fact or reality, trustworthy, not imaginary, false or imitation.*" Our sense of people's authenticity has an enormous impact on how much we trust them, how comfortable we are with them, and how willing we are to follow them. It is clear, then, why authenticity is so important to be an effective leader.

What are the consequences when a leader is perceived as inauthentic? There is a significant impact on trust. People are less likely to volunteer ideas or information the leader needs to know. They are more likely to question the motives of the leader. They are less likely to give that leader their all. These undercurrents sap the energy of any team and trust and camaraderie are lost in this type of work environment.

What causes leaders to be inauthentic? Some people come across as guarded or secretive because they are naturally cautious or reserved. This tends to make people uncomfortable when that person is the formal leader because they wonder what she is thinking or feeling. Individuals in leadership positions, who have this kind of personality, must consider ways to reduce this uneasiness in others. Finding ways to communicate that are comfortable for all involved makes a significant positive impact, as can increasing the amount of communication, if it has previously been sparse.

Cultural conditioning from our hierarchical models can cause some leaders, especially those in formal management positions, to believe that to be genuine and vulnerable is a sign of weakness. Coupled with that is a belief that they must know, or at least look like they know, all the answers. But this is not the source of power of effective leaders. Ultimately, leadership is more about who you are than what you know.

TIPS FOR LEADERSHIP SUCCESS

To grow as leaders, we must constantly be growing ourselves. Some questions to ask yourself as you grow your leadership abilities:

- What are my beliefs about what it takes to be a good leader?

- What are my beliefs and expectations about myself as a leader?

- Am I willing and able to be open, authentic, and vulnerable?

- Do I have healthy self-esteem and self-confidence that allow me to be genuinely open to feedback and to the risk of making mistakes?

- Do my communication style and frequency clearly and honestly convey my views as leader?

Here are some additional tips:

- **Assume responsibility for your own actions.** If you are not successful, do not blame anyone else. Take it on the chin and learn from it.

- **Assume responsibility for your emotional reactions.** It is not what happens to you that matters; it is what it means to you that determines your reaction. Stand back and get perspective. Ask yourself, "What can we learn from this?" It is easier to control yourself.

- **Identify the potential in each of your subordinates.** Remember that people tend to live up to our expectations of them. Let your people know how terrific you think they are.

- **Make an inventory of the resources at your disposal and use those resources to help your staff perform better.** We live in a world of limited resources. Given that restraint, how can you optimize the results your department delivers?

- **Be optimistic.** Optimism is contagious; so is pessimism. If your team is going to develop a positive, can-do attitude, you will need to set the tone.

- **Develop a team vision for your department.** Define what the team will become—make it inspiring. It is powerful when you develop your vision as a team.

- **Set specific and measurable goals to make that vision come true.** Include time frames and resource requirements.

- **Treat others with empathy and respect — no matter what.** Gain the independence, power, and self-respect that come from doing the right thing, without regard to what others do.

- **Think less about your own needs and more about the needs of your team.** You will reap what you sow.

- **Set an example — be a high performer.** Work hard and smart; people will follow your example. Be honest with yourself and your team. Realize that people who work with you will know you for who you are. Be open to their criticism and learn from it.

- **Set a schedule for your own training and development — stick to it.** Keep yourself growing and motivated. You are worth it.

- **Model your leadership style after someone who inspires you.** It is hard work to cut a path through the woods; it is much simpler to walk in someone else's tracks.

- **Good input = good output.** Find and consistently use good sources of management guidance for reading, viewing, and listening.

TEAMWORK

Teamwork is the fuel that allows common people to attain uncommon results. What is a good leader without a team to lead? You want to develop leadership qualities to build a strong team that will accomplish more than your best individual effort. Teamwork has become an essential element of almost every job in today's labor market and it is important for business leaders to know how to develop and maintain a strong team culture.

PRINCIPLES OF EFFECTIVE TEAMS

- **Effective teams have independent members.** The productivity and efficiency of the unit is determined by the coordinated, interactive efforts of all its members.

- **Effective teams help members be more efficient working together than alone.** An effective team outperforms even the best individual's best effort.

- **Effective teams function so well that they create their own magnetism.** Team members desire to affiliate with a team because of the advantages of membership.

- **Effective teams do not always have the same leader.** Leadership responsibility is rotated among the highly skilled team members.

- **Effective teams have members who care for and nurture one another.** No team member is undervalued or under appreciated; all are treated as integral to the team's success.

- **Effective teams have members who cheer loudly for the leader.** Mutual encouragement is given and received freely.

- **Effective teams have a high level of trust among members.** Members are as interested in others' success as their own.

WHAT IS A TEAM?

A team is not just a group of people stuck together working on a project or task. A team is a group of people working together to achieve something bigger and better than any of the individual team members can accomplish.

GROUPS VS. TEAMS	
GROUPS	**TEAMS**
A set of individuals who rely on the sum of "individual bests" for their performance.	A small number of people with complementary skills who are committed to a common purpose, common performance goals and a common approach for which they hold themselves mutually accountable.
Little communication	Plenty of opportunity for discussion
No support	Plenty of support

Lack of vision	Process of discovery supported by openness and honesty
Exclusive cliques	Tactical and work groups combine easily into a single team
The whole is less than the sum of its parts	The whole is greater than the sum of its parts
Seeks to hide its identity	Seeks to discover its identity
Leaves new members to find their own way but insists on conformity	Welcomes new members by showing them existing norms and openness to change
Leader manipulates the team to own ends	Leader seeks team decisions by serving the team as a focus for two-way communication

EAMBUILDING

A team is not built overnight — it takes a concerted effort to transform a scraggly group of individuals into a true team. There are four stages of team building and each has its own challenges that demand different leadership skills. To build and lead an effective team, it is important to understand these stages and adapt your style to help the team through the transitions. Effective leadership requires helping the team through the early stages of development, when a team is struggling to become a coherent entity, to a more mature stage of development, where the team becomes a highly effective, smoothly functioning organization. The four stages are as follows:

STAGE 1: AWARENESS (FORMING)

This stage is when a group of people gets together and realizes that they have a common purpose. They make a commitment to achieve a certain outcome, and each team member accepts his responsibility in the process. In the initial stages of team development, the leader has to bring other members up to speed on the mission. The leader's job is to create cohesion amongst these individuals chosen for a team and the team members are likely uncertain about their role in the whole process. Very seldom do new team members want to question the leader for fear of appearing "out of the loop" and, likewise, they do not want to answer the leader's questions in case the answer is wrong.

At the beginning, it is all about self-protection, so the team leader has to deal head-on with the challenge, and that means taking charge and directing the process. There is plenty of opportunity for free, open discussion once the team is formed and comfortable, but now you must focus on direction, clarity, and structure.

Many teams fail to become effective: They get stuck in the forming stage and never really become a team; they remain a group in team clothing. You cannot rush the forming stage. It is imperative that the team members have time to explore and clarify the guidelines, boundaries and expectations, and reveal their uncertainties.

When the team leader successfully provides the necessary clarity and structure, the team can move on to the second stage.

ATTRIBUTES OF TEAM DEVELOPMENT WHILE FORMING			
Team Member Questions	Interpersonal Relationships	Task Issues	Effective Leader Behavior
Who are these other people?	Silence	Orient members	Make introductions
What is going to happen?	Self-consciousness	Become comfortable with team membership	Answer questions
What is expected of me?	Dependence	Establish trust	Establish a foundation of trust
Where are we headed and why?	Superficiality	Establish relationship with leaders	Model expected behaviors
What are our goals?	Reactivity	Establish clarity of purpose	Clarify goals, procedures, rules, expectations
How do I fit in?	Uncertainty	Deal with feelings of independence	Foster team spirit

STAGE 2: CONFLICT (STORMING)

At this stage, the team is formed and the members feel comfortable with one another: maybe too comfortable, because conflict surfaces. The team is suddenly dealing with issues of power, leadership, and decision-making. Team members are no longer uncertain of their roles and they all have committed to achieving the team's goals and contributing to its success. The individual team members will disagree on methods, actions, decisions, and opinions. Individual differences have been suppressed for the sake of the team, but this "honeymoon" stage does not last forever. The leader's role is to diffuse the conflict while validating all the arguments and mediating solutions.

The storming stage does not mean the team disintegrates into chaos and turmoil; it means effective ways to deal with conflict have to be developed and agreed upon. The team leader is responsible for spearheading this conflict resolution "charter" and fostering a win-win result.

Throughout this process, let your team know that this type of conflict is normal and it is not a sign of dysfunction. Many people have been socialized to avoid conflict so overtly let the team know that it is okay to voice their opinions and that the divergent thinking within a team is exactly what spurns teams on to greater efficiency.

The leader has a crucial role during the storming stage. The vision or goal that brought the team together in the first place must be emphasized and reinforced. The danger to avoid is the phenomenon of "groupthink," where preserving the team takes precedence over sound decision-making and suddenly there is very little conflict.

The storming stage is a good time to shake things up a bit, let other members lead certain projects, and encourage team members to cross-train and teach others. Emphasize the interdependence of the team members and reward the team for its accomplishments. It builds commitment and unity and prepares the team to get busy and get to work.

ATTRIBUTES OF TEAM DEVELOPMENT WHILE STORMING

Team Member Questions	Interpersonal Relationships	Task Issues	Effective Leader Behavior
How will we handle disagreements?	Polarization of team members	Manage conflict	Identify a common enemy and reinforce the vision
How will we communicate negative information?	Coalitions or cliques form	Legitimize productive expression of individuality	Generate a commitment among team members
Can the team be changed?	Competition	Overcome "groupthink"	Turn students into teachers
How can we make decisions amidst disagreement?	Disagreement with the leader	Examine key work processes of the team	Be an effective mediator
Do we really need this leader?	Challenging others' viewpoints	Turn counter dependence into inter-dependence	Provide individual and team recognition
Do I want to stay a part of the team?	Expressing individuality		Foster win-win thinking

STAGE 3: COOPERATION (NORMING)

Once teams emerge from the storming stage, they are very confident they can handle anything that is thrown at them.

The norming stage of team development is characterized by cohesiveness as team members discover they do have common interests with each other. They learn to appreciate their differences, work better together, and problem-solve together. Norming is also a time to sit back and assess just how much the team has accomplished.

Feedback is especially important at this stage, and the team should experience some successes to reinforce their commitment.

Norming can be a time of complacency, so the leader must continue to generate enthusiasm and spark team members' interest. The team is starting to look like a well-oiled machine and it is not the time to relax and ease up on proactive leadership. The way that teams continue to be successful is through constant effort and attention, so you will always need to keep the fire lit. Be supportive and complimentary, use humor and playfulness, and build strong coalitions within the team. These behaviors will confirm your involvement and commitment to the team and provide affirmation that the team is doing a good job.

ATTRIBUTES OF TEAM DEVELOPMENT WHILE NORMING

Team Member Questions	Interpersonal Relationships	Task Issues	Effective Leader Behavior
Will we be able to stay together?	Cooper-ativeness	Maintain unity and cohesion	Ensures the team experiences some success

ATTRIBUTES OF TEAM DEVELOPMENT WHILE NORMING

Team Member Questions	Interpersonal Relationships	Task Issues	Effective Leader Behavior
How can we be successful as a team?	Commitment to a team vision	Differentiate and clarify roles	Facilitate role differentiation
What is my relationship to the team leader and other team members?	Inter-dependence	Determine levels of personal investment	Show support to team members
What role do I play?	Supportive	Clarify the future	Provide feedback
How do we measure up to other teams?	Complacence	Decide on a level of commitment to the team's future	Articulate a vision for the team
Can we take this all the way?	Self-doubt	Deal with feelings of independence	Generate commitment to the vision

STAGE 4: PRODUCTIVITY (PERFORMING)

The team synergy takes off at this stage. It is apparent that the team is capable of setting and accomplishing innovative and progressive goals. The team is functioning as a highly effective unit because it has worked through all the issues embedded in the previous stages and can now focus on performance. The team members themselves also change their focus and look for ways to improve processes and find innovative solutions. Each team member is confident of the role he plays and he is self-sufficient, but his connection to the other team members ensures he is committed to learning, developing, and improving.

The team leader is now a delegator. In that role, you have to listen to your team members and bring their ideas forward for the team to evaluate. Support the team in their decisions and provide the resources necessary for success. The team leader is not the source of all the good ideas and, by enabling other team members' ideas, the whole team becomes more effective. Team leaders ensure that activities are coordinated and that innovative suggestions are introduced and fit into the team's plans. The team is now effectively self-managed and very competent. It is akin to a parent sending her child off to college; she will always be there for support and guidance, but she trusts that she has given her child the tools she needs to go out and be successful.

ATTRIBUTES OF TEAM DEVELOPMENT WHILE PERFORMING

Team Member Questions	Interpersonal Relationships	Task Issues	Effective Leader Behavior
How can we continuously improve?	High mutual trust	Capitalize on core competence	Foster innovative and continuous improvement at the same time

ATTRIBUTES OF TEAM DEVELOPMENT WHILE PERFORMING

Team Member Questions	Interpersonal Relationships	Task Issues	Effective Leader Behavior
How can we foster creativity?	Unconditional team commitment	Foster continuous improvement	Advance the quality culture of the team
How can we build on our core competence?	Multifaceted relationships among team members	Anticipate needs of customers and respond in advance of requests	Provide regular, ongoing feedback on team performance
What improvements can be made to our processes?	Mutual training and development	Enhance speed and timeliness	Champion team members ideas and provide additional resources
How can we maintain this high energy level?	Entrepreneur-ship	Encourage creative problem-solving	Help to avoid slipping back to previous stages

ATTRIBUTES OF TEAMBUILDING SUMMARY

TEAMBUILDING IS:	TEAMBUILDING IS NOT:
• A way of life. • The responsibility of every team member. • A continuous process. • About developing a clear and unique identity. • Focused on a clear and consistent set of goals. • Concerned with the needs and ambitions of each team member recognizing the unique contribution that each individual can make. • An awareness of the potential of the team as a unit. • Results oriented. • Enjoyable.	• A short term, flavor of the month. • Imposed without regard to peoples' feelings. • Spasmodic. • Reserved for only some members of the team. • An excuse for not meeting personal responsibilities. • A process where actions clearly contradict intentions. • Seen as a chore.

AN EFFECTIVE TEAM

An effective team is one that has worked through the various stages of team-building and emerged intact. Teams go through phases and even though the goal is to get to and remain in the performing stage, there are setbacks that occur. New direction, new team members, new leadership: These can all cause confusion within the team and threaten its stability, but if team members stay committed to the core characteristics of effective teams, then they should be able to withstand the pressures.

Successful, effective teams demonstrate high achievement in the following areas:

- **Appropriate leadership.** The leader has all the skills and desire to develop and use a team approach and is prepared to allocate time for team-building activities. He acts as a facilitator on the team. A leader is willing to develop a team approach and encourages team-building activities. He shares leadership responsibilities

- **Suitable membership.** Members are individually qualified and bring a mix of skills, experiences, and perspectives that provide a balanced group. A suitable member is socially or professional qualified to contribute to the team and helps to the team achieve its goals.

- **Commitment to the team's success.** Members are committed to the goals of the team and achieving them. They are willing to devote personal time to developing the team and supporting their fellow team members.

- **Positive climate.** People are relaxed, open, direct, and prepared to take risks.

- **Achievement focus.** Team goals are clear, considered worthwhile, require some "stretching," but are achievable. Performance is frequently reviewed to find ways to improve.

- **Relevant corporate rule.** The significance of the distinctive ways that the team contributes to the corporate goals and strategies are clear and understood. In effective teams, the team is included in corporate planning and is given or understands the "big picture."

- **Effective work methods.** There are systematic problem-solving methods, structured decision-making techniques, and skills for conducting productive meetings.

- **Role clarity.** Team roles are clearly defined and communication patterns are developed. Administrative procedures are in place that support a team approach.

- **Constructive criticism.** Feedback about team and individual errors and weaknesses are constructively and positively provided and used as a learning experience. Ineffective teams use soft critiquing: to not upset any team members, neither team nor individual errors are addressed directly and thoroughly enough to eliminate them.

- **Individual development.** The positive team climate and support helps members to achieve their personal potential. Effective teams have members who have developed the maturity and confidence needed to be assertive or deal with other members' strong personalities.

- **Creative strength.** The team encourages and generates new ideas from the interaction of members, rewards risk-taking, and puts good ideas into action.

- **Positive inter-group relations.** Members are encouraged to work with others for the common good. Relationships with other teams are systematically developed to identify opportunities for collaboration. Negative inter-group relations are characterized by competition and conflicting priorities.

An effective team is a high-performing unit whose members are actively interdependent and committed to working together for a common purpose. A team is a performance unit and the "acid test" is its ability to consistently achieve desired results. To do so, members of successful teams are committed to continuous quality improvement. They regularly review their experiences, assess the strengths and weaknesses of their process, and constructively criticize both individual and team performance. Team members identify blockages to effectiveness. They work together to clear the way for further success through team-development.

The theory of teams is great and all see how the team concept works. But, as much as you are committed to building a strong team, there are one or two employees who make the process difficult. Despite your best efforts and after reading every interpersonal relationship book ever written, there are still some participants who are disruptive and difficult.

This challenge is huge for team leaders. The way these difficult members are handled sets the tone and culture of the team. Does the team become intolerant and exclusionary or does it seek to support and collaborate with all of its members, using every available open communication and conflict-resolution technique known to man? Here are some suggestions for handling some of the typical examples of difficult team members.

Type	Behavior or Comments	Suggested Response
HANDLING DIFFICULT TEAM MEMBERS		
Hostile	"It'll never work." "That's a typical touchy-feely response."	"How do others here feel about this?" "It seems we have a different perspective on the details, but do we agree on the principles?"
Know-it-all	"I have an MBA from Harvard and…" "Let me tell ya, in my 30 years at this company…"	"Let's review the facts…" "Another noted authority has said…"
Loud-mouth	Constantly blurts out ideas and tries to dominate meetings and discussions.	Interrupt and ask, "Can you summarize your main point?" "I appreciate your comments, but we should also hear from Susan…"
Interrupter	Starts talking before others are finished.	"Wait a minute Carol, let's here what Stu was saying."
Interpreter	"What he's really trying to say is…" "Yeah, Mike's got a point. He's telling us that…"	"Let's let Mike speak for himself." "Mike, did Roy correctly understand what you were saying?"
Gossiper	"I heard the CFO say that…" "There's a new policy coming out that says…"	"Until we verify what was said, let's continue as planned." "Has anyone else heard about this new development?"
Silent Distracter	Reads, rolls eyes, shakes their head, crosses arms, etc.	Direct questions to them to determine their level of expertise and interest. Draw them into the discussion and try to build an alliance.

AN EFFECTIVE TEAM LEADER

Here are characteristics of an effective team leader:

- Communicates.

- Is open, honest, and fair.

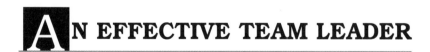

- Uses participative decision-making.

- Acts consistently.

- Gives all team members information necessary to do their job.

- Sets goals and emphasizes them.

- Keeps focused and follows-up regularly.

- Listens to feedback without defensiveness and ask questions.

- Shows loyalty.

- Creates an atmosphere of growth.

- Has wide visibility.

- Gives praise and recognition.

- Criticizes constructively and addresses problems directly.

- Develops plans.

- Displays tolerance and flexibility.

- Demonstrates assertiveness.

- Treats all members with respect.

- Accepts ownership for team decisions.

- Represents the team and stands up for its decisions and actions.

- Creates energy and excitement.

- Stimulates creativity in others.

- Acts as a sounding board, helping people think through their issues.

- Enforces standards (deals gently, promptly, but firmly with noncompliance).

It is critical for business leaders, managers, and supervisors to learn to function effectively within a team environment. A team culture means building a strong team and keeping the team operational and optimized. Not all groups are teams and using the word "team" in your organization does not necessarily mean your employees are actually functioning as one. Look at the effectiveness of your workplace and that will be your first clue as to whether you have a team environment.

Effective teams are highly productive so it is worth the time investigating and working toward your own team culture.

CONTROL LABOR COST WITHOUT SACRIFICING SERVICE OR QUALITY

From the parking attendant to the chef, the people who serve your customers are your restaurant. You can have a prime location, a beautiful dining room, and impeccably prepared food and have it all spoiled by a rude server, sloppy busperson, or an inattentive janitor. Your restaurant's success is based upon your ability to locate, hire, and solidify a group of people into your Customer Service Team.

The food service industry has long been plagued with an inadequate workforce and exceptionally high turnover rates. The increased demand for service workers and culture changes within the workforce means less educated recruits, more non-English speaking employees, and fewer younger people interested in restaurant work.

Whether you own a celebrity-filled, trendsetting establishment or a truck-stop diner, the situation is the same. Where do you find good employees? How do you keep good employees? How can you get your money's worth?

Labor costs typically run 25 to 35 percent of your budget. Depending upon your menu offerings, it can equal or exceed your food costs. Keeping your prime costs (food and payroll) in the 60 to 69 percent range is your profit-making goal. Simply cutting staff will not do it. Your aim should be to get the highest productivity possible for your money. But to save money without losing quality of service, you have to start at square one.

BUILDING YOUR TEAM — THE FOUNDATION OF SUCCESS

Good food and good service are the foundation of a successful restaurant. As a service industry, restaurant profit margins are notoriously slim. Your restaurant's profitability is a direct result of your ability to control your service costs without sacrificing your customers' needs and expectations.

SERVICE IS PARAMOUNT

Keep firmly in mind that service is paramount. Surveys show that 83 percent of customers will not return to a restaurant if they experienced poor service. Sixty-one percent mentioned slow service as a factor. However, we are not just talking about the front-of-the-house staff — every employee plays a vital role in good customer service. If your customer finds better service elsewhere, what do you lose? Just one customer, right? But if that customer spent $10 in your establishment twice a week: $10 x 2 = $20 x 52 weeks = $1,040 a year. What if you lose five customers or even ten? One server with a bad attitude can cost you her salary or more in lost revenue and permanently damage your reputation within the community. Good service is a combination of:

- **Strong commitment by management.** Standards and expectations backed by a respectful and partnership attitude.

- **Positive employee attitudes and motivation.** A desire and willingness to serve others and good communications.

- **Good training methods.** Top-notch employee skills and abilities.

- **Practical approaches and procedures.** To work together efficiently.

- **Labor-saving devices.** An environment filled with tools and equipment that promote good ergonomics and maximum productivity.

PROFITS ARE EVERYONE'S BUSINESS

As a restaurant owner you have a strong personal motive to be profitable — and so do your employees. Reducing your labor costs wisely and compassionately balances the needs of the organization with the needs of its team members. Reducing your labor costs requires:

- **Good hiring practices.** Search for the right person to fill the job. Look beyond the basic skills for a person that fits your restaurant's personality. Learn more about interviewing employees by reading *501+ Great Interview Questions for Employers and the Best Answers for Prospective Employees.* To order call 800-814-1132 or visit **www.atlantic-pub.com** (Item # 501-02, $24.95).

- **Balanced staffing levels.** Schedule ample people to get the job done and satisfy customers without wasting resources.

- **Greater employee productivity.** Teach them how to work smarter, not harder.

- **Excellent people skills.** Communicate well with managers, line supervisors, support staff, and customers. Loyal employees create loyal customers.

- **Sound financial decision making.** Analyze and invest in labor-savers. Research and utilize tax breaks and business support programs.

PEOPLE ARE ASSETS

You would not think too highly of someone who bought a beautiful automobile and then never bothered to clean it, change the oil, or tune it. Who would spend so much and not protect their investment? Well, employing one person can cost as much as a car and unless you are diligent, you, too, could be wasting your money.

Invest wisely. Every dollar you spend (directly and indirectly) to "purchase" and maintain an employee is an investment in your business. Protecting your human assets and securing your investment is integral to your labor-saving efforts. Are you investing wisely?

HIGH TURNOVER RATES

Employees leave after three months; why should I spend the money only to have them move to a competitor? Because the industry creates high turnover rates and you have a responsibility to your business to provide a solution. Exceptionally high food service turnover rates are deeply rooted in historical attitudes and a business model based upon spending as little as possible for workers and your "factory." By ignoring workers' physical and emotional needs, restaurant owners have created an industry filled with some of the "worst jobs."

- **Address problems.** Certainly you cannot solve these industry problems single-handedly; however, you can play an active role and reap the benefits of addressing such factors as low pay, excessive stress, inferior work conditions, limited career potential, poor economic security, and overwhelming physical demands.

- **Costs.** "I cannot afford to pay more!" But you already are. You are paying for it through costly recruiting and training, reduced productivity, increased food costs, inconsistent customer service, and larger overhead. By redirecting these dollars towards maintaining and enhancing your human assets, you will be investing in your business instead of just paying to keep the doors open.

- **Employee satisfaction.** Employee satisfaction is not just a touchy-feely goal — it is a key to your success. To learn more about building happy and productive employees, read:

  - *How to Hire, Train & Keep the Best Employees for Your Small Business* by Dianna Podmoroff, available at **www.atlantic-pub.com,** (Item # HTK-02, $29.95).

  - *365 Ways to Motivate and Reward Your Employees Every Day — With Little or No Money* by Dianna Podmoroff, available at **www.atlantic-pub.com,** (Item # 365-01, $24.95).

  - *Keeping Your Employees* at **www.keepemployees.com**.

  - *First, Break All the Rules: What the World's Greatest Managers Do Differently* by Marcus Buckingham and Curt Coffman.

  - *Follow This Path: How the World's Greatest Organizations Drive Growth by Unleashing Human Potential* by Curt Coffman and Gabriel Gonzalez-Molina.

REDUCING YOUR PEOPLE COSTS

Notice I said PEOPLE costs. Why? Because if you only think about cutting labor-hours, you will lose site of your objective: to please your customers and be rewarded with profits. Your business success is based upon your success at gathering together a group of workers with different skills and experiences to produce a quality product. Your most valuable assets — your employees — are filled with personal desires and expectations. You must tap into their need to be valued and respected. Here are three outstanding resources on people management, mentoring, and building partnerships with your employees:

- *The Encyclopedia of Restaurant Training* by Douglas Robert Brown, available from Atlantic Publishing (Item # ERT-02, $79.95). This restaurateur-written book offers excellent advice on hiring and leading employees. For more personnel and customer service advice, visit **www.atlantic-pub.com**.

- *Managers as Mentors* by Chip R. Bell, a nationally recognized customer service guru. This book explains creating strong employee relations; available on the Web at **www.chipbell.com**.

- **Restaurantowner.com**. This site provides extensive guidance for restaurant owners. A "Food for Thought" passage sums up their "people business" philosophy: "Your effectiveness as an owner or manager is directly related to your understanding of people and the quality of your interactions with your staff."

MANAGEMENT COMMITMENT

Your commitment to quality service is reflected in how you and your management staff conduct yourselves. Take a look at your behaviors and actions. Are they how you want your employees to act? Below are some thought-provoking questions on leadership. A "yes" answer to any of these means you should invoke the first rule of good leadership — leading by example.

- **Do you come to work grouchy?** Your employees will copy your mood. Greet your employees with a happy, friendly attitude — the way you want them to greet your customers.

- **Are you sloppy or careless in your work habits?** Are you late for appointments or forget to follow-up on requests?

- **Is your appearance unprofessional?** If you dress sloppily, your employees will resent having to meet higher standards and will slowly begin to ignore your dress code.

- **Do you disobey your own established standards?** If you pour doubles for your friends at the bar, your bartenders will start to do the same for their friends. If you ladle on extra portions, look for rising food costs because your kitchen staff will stop measuring too.

- **Do you avoid addressing problems when they arise?** When you see someone skirting established standards, promptly and tactfully remind them (but never in front of customers). If you let mistakes slide, soon your standards will be nothing but "hot air."

- **Do you ramble or lecture when answering questions or giving directions?**

- **Keep it short and simple** or your employees will "zone out" and miss the point. Always make sure they understand.

- **Mutual respect** plays an enormous role in good leadership. Respect is something you earn and not just because you sign the paychecks.

- **Do you share your goals with your employees?** Help reduce employee discontent by sharing your short- and long-term business goals. They will feel more valued and in greater control of their work.

- *Formal, written policies and procedures are very important* for setting standards. However, a large part of setting standards is done through leading by example.

IRING TEAM MEMBERS

Hiring is the start of a long-term relationship between employer and employee. Or at least it should be. Can you imagine hiring a full staff of qualified workers and having them stay with you for years? It is rare in the restaurant business, but it is not an unattainable goal. Hiring is more than just finding warm bodies to fill positions. You need to find competent, hard-working people who are a good fit for your restaurant personality.

YOUR CHALLENGE

Your challenge as a restaurateur is to balance your business needs with the needs of the people who will spend the majority of their day in the service of your customers. Perhaps your greatest challenges as an employer are the economic realities of a service industry where the majority of jobs are low paying with low social status. Federal reports show food prep and serving wages average $7.72 an hour and 75 percent make less than $8.50 an hour — the lowest wages among the major occupational groups studied. The result is a shortage of service workers and turnover rates of 250 percent for line staff and 100 percent for managers.

RESTAURANT EMPLOYEE CLASSIFICATIONS

Your mix of employees will include seasonal, part-time, full-time, and career-oriented employees. The list below is in pyramid order — with the top level being the smallest number within an organization and by highest to lowest salary.

- **Executive careers.** Comprehensive fiscal responsibility, college educated, may report to owner and/or stockholders (President or CFO).

- **Managerial careers.** Manages people and/or things, college educated (General Manager or Human Resources Director).

- **Artisans.** Creative talent may be self-taught based on natural abilities, on-the-job training, or career training (Lead Chef or Pastry Chef).

- **Skilled workers.** Valuable skills acquired from work experience or schooling (Bookkeeper, Wine Steward).

- **Semi-skilled workers.** More complex task with indirect supervision, some prior experience or training (Server or Baker).

- **Unskilled laborers.** Manual tasks with direct supervision, no special training (Janitor or Busperson).

THE RIGHT PERSON FOR THE JOB

Finding the right person for the job starts with a solid understanding of what your business team needs. As the saying goes, "You can't get what you want if you don't know what it is."

Before you start recruiting, you need to make some decisions that will become the basis for a written job description. The following sections will help you gather your thoughts and prepare you for the writing process.

CLARIFYING YOUR NEEDS

Whether you are hiring your first employee or adding to a staff of 75, there are five primary areas you should consider before you place that classified ad.

1. Tasks employee(s) must accomplish.

2. Skills and experience employee(s) must possess.

3. Training levels you must or are willing to provide.

4. Personality and attitude your customers expect.

5. Budget available for salary, taxes, and benefits.

TASKS

Identify the tasks (duties) that must be completed during the shift, week, month, and beyond. Categorize each activity by:

- **What will they do?** Detail action (clean, cut, and store salad ingredients; accept food delivery, compare to packing list, sort and store; or answer phone, accept, and schedule reservations).

- **Where will they do it?** Front- or back-of-the-house.

- **When will they do it?** Before, during, or after active serving times.

- **How often must they do it?** Daily, weekly, monthly, or other.

- **What is a success?** What is acceptable performance? What is award-winning performance?

SKILLS AND RESPONSIBILITIES

Classify each task by skills required and level of responsibility. Typically, the greater the skills and responsibility level required, the higher the salary you will pay. Identify areas where less costly labor can be used or whether you should reward someone for accepting more responsibility.

SKILLS AND RESPONSIBILITIES	
Skill Level	**Responsibility Level**
Management Skills • Dining room supervisor • Beverage manager	**Profit and Loss Responsibility** • Executive chef • Banquet manager
Prep Skills • Pastry chef • Sauce cook	**Reports "As Needed" To Superior** • Soup cook • Baker
Customer Service Skills • Server • Bartender	**Empowered To Act on Behalf of Restaurant** • Hostess • Dining room manager
Support Staff Skills • Busperson • Receiving clerk	**Direct Daily Supervision** • Server • Bartender
	No Significant Decision-making Duties • Dishwasher • Janitor

SKILL AND EXPERIENCE TRAINING EXPECTATIONS

All good companies train constantly. Learning is a never-ending process that enhances employee skills and your service quality.

Consider comprehensive training. Comprehensive job training programs and perhaps even life-skill training may be needed. New hires with little to no prior work experience or no food service history can be developed into loyal employees through in-house mentoring and training or work-study programs.

Some restaurant positions are, by nature, trainee jobs. In this case, your job description will also include an outline of the training program that the new hire must complete before moving beyond their probationary period.

Develop skilled workers. With restaurant owners nationwide routinely reporting a shortage of skilled workers, you may be forced to develop your own experienced workers. Many positions may have to be filled by trainees.

Above all, train your employees properly. *The Encyclopedia of Restaurant Training* (available at **www.atlantic-pub.com**) is an out-of-the box employee training program for all food service positions. From orientating the new employee to maintaining performance standards to detailed training outlines and checklists for all positions, this book will show you how to train your employees in all positions in the shortest amount of time. One of the best features of this book is the companion CD-ROM, which contains the training outline for all positions in MS Word, so you can easily customize the text. There are numerous training forms, checklists, and handouts. There are job descriptions for all positions including General Manager, Kitchen Manager,

Server, Dishwasher, Line Cook, Prep Cook, Bus Person, Host/Hostess, and Bartender.

Training videos are also a good investment. *The Complete Wait Staff Training Course Video* is a 53-minute, high-quality wait staff training video, where your staff learns how to consistently deliver quality service that makes customers come back and tell others about their memorable experience. Study guides and tests are included. Topics covered include: alcohol sales and wine service; preparing for service; taking beverage orders; hosting and greeting guests; correct service procedures; taking, placing, and picking up the order; serving food; and completing the service. Available at **www.atlantic-pub.com** or by calling 800-814-1132.

YOUR BUDGET

Employee wages are influenced in each community by the cost of living, available workforce, competition, and social status of the position. Your financial ability to pay for certain skills and training may limit your expectations for a position. Your compensation package (salary and benefits) must be appropriate for the duties and responsibility outlined in the job description.

Whether you have written several pages of job tasks or just scribbled some thoughts on a napkin, it is time to start writing an overview of the job you seek to fill.

WRITING JOB DESCRIPTIONS

A job description is a detailed definition of a job and a list of the specific tasks and duties the employee is responsible for daily, weekly, and monthly. The more complete the job description, the simpler the task of training. A good job description will help you and your staff to:

- Hire the best candidate for the job.

- Understand required job skills and expected responsibility levels.

- Develop and complete training programs.

- Create goals for employee growth and potential salary increases.

JOB DESCRIPTION TIPS AND RESOURCES

Below are some ideas and resources to help you create useful job descriptions.

- **Ask your staff. Their input can be invaluable.** You will also discover opportunities to redistribute duties and reward better employees with "prized" assignments.

- **Incorporate attitude standards.** Descriptions should include attitude standards such as, "Will answer phone with cheerful voice within three rings."

- **Hire a human resources expert.** Find expert help from the Human Resources Consultants Association (**www.hrca.com**) and the Society for Human Resources Management (**www.shrm.org**).

- **Have an attorney or human resources consultant review the description for legality.** Well- written job descriptions can help you defend yourself in wrongful termination or other employee litigation.

- **Review job descriptions posted on the internet.** Use keywords "restaurant job description" and "[insert job title] job description" to see how other restaurant owners explain the position.

- • **Buy a book.** Contact the National Restaurant Association at 800-482-9122 and request publication MG999, *Model Position Descriptions for the Restaurant Industry*.

- • Read about creating job descriptions. National Restaurant Association has helpful articles at **www.restaurant.org/business/ bb/2000_05.cfm** and **www.restaurant. org/rusa/magArticle.cfm?ArticleID=754**.

Y OUR EMPLOYEE PACKAGE

Employees are "paid" in a variety of ways: wages, tips, meals, profit sharing, bonuses, commissions, insurance coverage, vacations, tuition reimbursement, childcare assistance, transportation subsidies, retirement plans, and family leaves.

Paying minimum wage and offering no benefits is one way to keep your labor costs low, but rarely will you be hiring the best available and you will constantly be dealing with high turnover and employee dissatisfaction. Although money is not the only motivator, it certainly is an important factor in attracting and retaining quality employees. You have to think creatively and act aggressively to design a cost-effective yet valuable employee package.

WAGES

No other industry has such divergent wage standards between federal, state, and local jurisdictions. The Fair Labor Standards Act (FLSA) establishes federal work standards. However, these do not apply if state or local laws are more stringent.

Federal law requires that you pay the minimum wage ($5.85 per hour as of July 2007) for all hourly employees (except those who receive more than $30 a month in tips) and youth wages ($4.25 per hour as of 2006) for the first 90 days. Superseding laws may require that the prevailing minimum wage be paid even if the worker earns tips; others allow for a reduced hourly rate for tip earners. To learn more about wage regulations:

Visit the department of labor site at **www.dol.gov** for current wage and hour laws and links to state information or contact your local State Employment Division. State minimum wage rates can be found at **www.dol.gov/esa/minwage/america.htm**. Tipped employee wages by state are located at **www.dol.gov/esa/programs/whd/state/tipped.htm**. Read what the National Restaurant Association has to say about minimum wages at **www.restaurant.org/legal/law_ minwage.cfm**.

GRATUITIES

In recent years, IRS and court rulings have created a lot of headaches for the restaurant industry in regards to taxing tips. With ongoing litigation, your best bet is to read the current legal bulletins produced by state and national restaurant associations. The National Restaurant Association provides tip resources for employers and employees at **www.restaurant.org/legal/ tips/resources.cfm**. To protect your business from IRS audits and tax liabilities, encourage your employees to accurately report tips and hold employees responsible for tip income by having them read and sign a form that explains tipping rules.

You should also consider reading *The Complete Guide to Tips & Gratuities: A Guide for Employees Who Earn Tips & Employers Who Manage Tipped Employees and Their Accountants*. This book deals with all aspects of tips and gratuities. For the employee or self-employed, learn how to earn more tips and how to properly account for and pay taxes on them. For the employer, learn how to manage and properly account for the taxes on tipped employees. For the bookkeeper and accountant, get the latest on tax and withholding laws. Available at **www.atlantic-pub.com** or by calling 800-814-1132.

EMPLOYEE BENEFITS

Fringe benefits are an important part of compensating your employees. These are all voluntary rewards and enticements, as the law does not mandate them. Do not overlook the emotional impact (self-esteem, peace of mind, confidence, security, and safety) these have on employees when developing your package.

To learn more about employee benefits, visit BenefitNews at **www.benefitnews.com**, BenefitsNext at **www.benefitsnext.com**, or CCH Business Owner's Tool Kit at **www.toolkit. cch.com**.

- **Holidays.** Pay for closed holidays or offer comp time for open holidays.

- **Sick days.** Grant a set number of annual sick days. But to encourage attendance, offer a cash bonus for unused days. Allow staff to convert sick days to family leave or vacation days.

- **Vacations.** How employees take their vacation can create some unnecessary payroll costs. Learn about potential savings at **www.toolkit.cch.com/text/P05_4385.asp**.

- **Family leave.** Help reduce employee stress by offering family leave options. You might offer short leave periods for bereavement and funerals and extended leaves for maternity/paternity/adoption or long-term family care. For information on family leave under the Family and Medical Leave Act (FMLA), see the Department of Labor information at **www.dol.gov/elaws/fmla.htm**.

- **Other time off.** Jury duty, voting, and military leave may be required by law in your state.

- **Offer discounted meals for employees dining with immediate family members.** Thank workers and their families.

Costly but Valuable Benefits

Employers who provide the "costliest" benefits are providing employees peace of mind and security. Although these benefits can escalate your total payroll costs, their value can be significant. Many of these benefits would be financially unattainable without even limited employer support. By having these benefits, you will reduce turnover and the cost of benefits is usually less than turnover costs.

- **Invest in health insurance coverage.** Unless it is financially prohibitive, health insurance coverage should be your most touted benefit. Employer-paid premiums are rare, but sharing the cost and exploring partially self-insured plans can make it more affordable for everyone. It is the most desired benefit for job applicants.

- **Talk to your accountant and financial advisor about retirement plans.** Stock options, 401(k) plans, and IRAs can be created to attract career-minded individuals. Visit **www.dol.gov/ebsa/compliance_assistance.html** for information on federal pension plan law under the Employee Retirement Income Security Act of 1974 (ERISA).

- **Offer life and long-term care insurance.** Employees can benefit from tax-free life insurance coverage (up to $50,000) and long-term care insurance.

WHERE TO FIND YOUR NEXT EMPLOYEES

Searching for new employees can become a full-time job. Do not wait until you have a vacancy to develop contacts and personnel resources to draw from at a moment's notice. Building your team members requires a continuous proactive search effort. Overall, it is most cost effective for a business to hire a fully qualified and experienced employee. So how do you find one? Below I have outlined a variety of places and ways to find loyal, hardworking employees.

- **Employee referrals.** Personal referrals can be strong candidates, as your reliable employees will typically have good friends. Offer a referral bonus of $50 to $300 (perhaps even more for managerial hires).

- **Your competitors and peers.** If you encounter an experienced worker when dining out, discreetly give them your card and let them know you are hiring and thought she might be a good candidate.

- **Your customers.** Another reliable referral. Long-term customers have a good feel for your environment and are great "word-of-mouth" advertising.

- **Headhunters.** Top managerial and "talent" positions may require a headhunter. These employment specialists have connections and contacts within specific industries. Expect to pay up to 33 percent of the new hire's first year salary.

- **Employment agencies.** Semi-skilled workers can be found through employment agencies, but fees typically can outweigh benefits.

- **Trade organizations.** State and national hospitality and food service organizations offer employment services.

- **Employment open house.** Creating an open and friendly atmosphere puts potential employees at ease, builds great word of mouth, and establishes your business as a desirable workplace.

- **Job fairs.** Set up a booth at community job fairs. Sell your restaurant as a great place to work with great people.

- **Unions.** Many restaurateurs are "fearful" of unions, but quality employers who offer competitive compensation packages and good working conditions should not hesitate to take advantage of their job banks.

ADVERTISING FOR PEOPLE

"Help wanted" advertising is a common method for locating unskilled and semi-skilled food service employees. However, classified ads will not attract sufficient candidates for skilled, artisan, and managerial positions. The key is to select a medium (print or Web) and publication where your potential employees will be looking.

- **Classified ads.** Place text or display ads in print and electronic publications: local newspapers, school papers, and ethnic (native language) newspapers for your entry-level/trainee, unskilled, and semi-skilled positions.

- **Your Web site.** Include a link on your restaurant Web site to a "We are Hiring" page, detailing job opportunities and application procedures.

- **Trade associations.** Post jobs and search résumés at state and national restaurant associations' and hospitality associations' online job banks, newsletters, and magazines. Many hospitality and food service organizations also offer personalized recruitment services and training support.

- **Summer job sites.** Connect with students and recent graduates seeking summer jobs. Here are some sites to try are Work: A+ Summer Jobs at **www.aplus-summerjobs. com,** Seasonal Employment at **www.seasonalemployment.com/summer.html** and Summer Jobs at **www.summerjobs.com.**

PLACES TO FIND HELP

- **State employment divisions.** Every state maintains a job bank of potential workers. Some states work like a private employment agency (but with no costs to you) to actively match employees and employers.

- **Cable TV.** Cable advertising can be surprisingly inexpensive. Your initial ad development cost can be amortized over several ad campaigns. Your local cable company can assist with ad production.

- **At the movies.** On-screen advertising can be a great way to connect with potential employees as most moviegoers are in your targeted age group.

- **Billboards.** Although not inexpensive, billboards can potentially reach thousands every day with your "help wanted" message.

- **Radio.** Ask your best employees for their favorite radio stations to reach potential team members. Radio stations can handle everything in-house for you.

- **Résumé "archives" and rehires.** High turnover rates means workers are frequently shopping for another job. "Leftover" or rejected applicants may be the right match now. Former employees (providing they left in good standing) may have found "the grass isn't greener" elsewhere and be interested in returning.

- **Senior centers.** Need mature part-time support? Many active seniors are seeking to re-enter the workforce.

- **Foreign worker agencies.** Some service industries have discovered the benefits of hiring experienced foreign workers. More details on hiring foreign workers can be found at the Department of Labor at **www.workforcesecurity.doleta.gov/foreign/hiring. asp**. Also check human resource sites such as **www.safehr.com/hiring_foreign_ nationals_and_imm.htm**.

TRAINEES FOR HIRE

What do you do if you cannot find the right person for the job? Create one. Here are some ways to locate and develop people with potential:

- **High school and community college career centers.** Develop relationships with career counselors who can direct potential part- and full-time employees to you.

- **Trade schools (food service, hospitality, and restaurant management).** Work with guidance counselors to find students needing financial assistance. Participate in work-study programs.

- **Students. Start your outreach before the student graduates.** Offer tuition reimbursement or full sponsorship in exchange for guaranteed employment.

- **U.S. Armed Services.** Thousands of well-disciplined and dependable people leave active duty every year seeking civilian employment. See Corporate Gray Online at **www.corporategrayonline.com**, Transition Assistance Online at **www.taonline.com**, and Department of Defense at **www.dmdc.osd.mil/ot/linkpage.htm**.

- **Federal, state, and local full-employment programs.** Government, non-profit and faith-based programs offer employees a helping hand. Employers benefit from financial subsidies (reimbursement and tax credits), counseling, and off-site training.

- **Displacement, relocation, internship, and school-to-work programs.** Reach out to laid-off workers, rural areas (with typically higher unemployment), and high school and college students seeking a direct career path.

- **Special-needs labor pool.** Re-entry programs for the disabled, single mothers, welfare recipients, retirees, high-risk youth, Veterans, and non-English speakers.

- **Foreign-born (non-English speaking) job placement services.** English as a Second Language (ESL) training for workers and cultural advice for employers.

- **Ticket to Work and Work incentive improvement act (employing the disabled).** Department of Labor at **www.dol.gov/odep/pubs/ek00/ticket.htm**. Veteran employment. Department of Labor at **www.dol.gov/vets**.

- **Overlooked labor pools.** Thousands of people, every year, needing a second chance and "life saving" can be loyal and dependable workers, if given a chance. Like the "special-needs" work pool, there are numerous programs that provide financial, educational, and transition support for employers and employees. Contact such groups as United Way of America at **www.unitedway.org**.

OUTSOURCING, TEMPS, AND LEASING

Have an occasional need for a specialist? Need extra hands for a banquet or large event? Do not want to waste your time on personnel matters?

- **Seek out consultants** to provide you with decorating, floral arranging, bookkeeping, marketing, graphic design and other "as needed" activities. Check your local Yellow Pages, Business-to-Business Directory, Better Business Bureau membership roles, or restaurant association.

- **Explore independent contractors**. These freelancers are responsible for all of their employment taxes and workers' compensation insurance. Be aware of the regulations on using independent contracts by visiting Nolo Law for All at **www.nolo.com/lawcenter/index.cfm** or speaking with a legal advisor.

- **Borrow an employee.** In developing good relationships with other restaurant owners, you should explore referrals for workers who are looking to moonlight or pick up a few hours of extra work.

- **Lease an employee.** No hassles here as the leasing firm handles all human resources activities. This is not typically a cost-effective option, but circumstances may warrant it. Beware of "hiring" clauses that penalize you for direct hiring of placed individuals. For more information on employee leasing firms, also known as a Professional Employer Organization (PEO), visit PEO at **www.peo.com/peo** or the National Association of Professional Employer Organizations at **www.napeo.org,** 703-836-0466.

A DIVERSE WORKFORCE

When hiring and keeping food service employees turns into a full-time job, nurturing and growing dependable employees from diverse backgrounds becomes a necessity. Creating a diverse workforce is good for society and good for business. Below are some helpful suggestions and resources on creating a strong, diverse staff that includes the disabled, elderly, minorities, homosexuals, women, and people from various cultures and ethnic backgrounds.

- **Buy a book** such as *Workplace Diversity: A Manager's Guide to Solving Problems and Turning Diversity into a Competitive* by Katharine Esty, *The Diversity Toolkit: How You Can Build and Benefit from a Diverse Workforce* by William Sonnenschein. or *Peacock in the Land of Penguins* by B. J. Gallagher Hateley and Warren H. Schmidt.

- Take a class on diversity. Contact local universities and community colleges for management to learn how to smoothly transform a group of individuals into a cohesive team. For online classes visit **www.worldlearning.org/solutions/index.html**. Research videos on diversity from Newsreel at **www.newsreel.org/topics/diversity.htm**.

- **Take time to learn about other cultures.** Sometimes language is not the only barrier. Cultural differences may cause miscommunication, hard feelings, and work problems. Working with people from specific cultures and ethnic groups requires patience and a willingness to learn.

- **Search the Internet** and read articles using keywords like "diverse workforce," "diversity," and "equal opportunity." Look for articles like *Supervising Across Language Barriers* at **agecon.uwyo.edu/riskMgt/humanrisk/Supervisingacrosslanguagebarriers.pdf**.

- **Explore local minority-support organizations for English as a Second Language** (ESL) classes, diversity programs, and educational support.

- **Work with non-profit organizations** to develop equal opportunity and diversity programs. Good places to start are Goodwill Industries at **www.goodwill.org**, National Adult Literacy at **www.nala.ie**, American Association for Affirmative Action at **www.affirmativeaction.org**, and National Organization for Women at **www.now.org/issues/wfw/index.html**.

SELECTING THE RIGHT CANDIDATE

If you have done a good job attracting qualified candidates, you should have a stack of résumés and applications. Unlike other fields, well-qualified workers may struggle with the written word and have had multiple jobs. Below are some tips on how to select the best candidates for face-to-face interviews.

- **Read between the lines.** Does this person have the right experience? Spot-check references for red flags.

- **Why are they leaving their current position?** Applications should ask the reason for leaving. When checking references, verify why the employee left. Conflicting stories are not a reason to toss the application, but it is a red flag needing attention.

- **Is the application neat, legible, and filled out properly?** If they cannot fill out an application properly, how well will they do with writing guest checks, ringing up sales, or following recipe directions?

- **Are they a short-timer?** If they change jobs every few months, they will most likely do the same with you. If everything else looks good, you may want to interview them anyway, but keep it in mind and explore why they move around so much.

- **Conduct phone screenings.** You can learn a lot from a two-minute phone call. Always ask questions that require more than yes or no answers.

  - What are your career goals?

  - What income level do you expect?

  - What kind of career growth would you like?

  - Ask one to three questions that verify a person's knowledge and skills.

  - Ask about work history gaps.

- **Listen carefully and use your instincts.** Is the person articulate and friendly? Are they hard to reach? Be careful what you ask. Many traditional interview questions are no longer legal or wise.

GETTING READY TO INTERVIEW

Your next step is to schedule face-to-face interviews. Choose from three to six candidates. Set interview dates at least two days in advance for local applicants and two weeks in advance for out-of-state applicants. Explain when, where, and how long the interview will be, format of the interview, and what, if anything, they should bring with them. Tell them if you will be conducting tests.

Provide adequate directions along with a contact name and phone number.

Be prepared. Put together handouts and company introduction materials to present your restaurant as a great place to work. Create a quick tour to show off your facility and introduce candidates to key employees.

Improve your interview skills. There are plenty of good books, classes, videos, and Web sites to help. If you are nervous or inexperienced at conducting interviews, practice. Role-playing can be a great way to improve your interview skills. Rent tapes on learning how to improve interviewing skills. Job Interview (**www.job-interview.net/index.htm**) is a great site for interview advice or read one of these books:

- *501+ Great Interview Questions for Employers and the Best Answers for Prospective Employees* by Dianna Podmoroff. Available at **www.atlantic-pub.com** or by calling 800-814-1132.

- *High-Impact Hiring: How to Interview and Select Outstanding Employees* by Del J. Still (2001).

- *Hiring the Best: A Manager's Guide to Effective Interviewing* by Martin Yate (1993).

- *96 Great Interview Questions to Ask Before You Hire* by Paul Falcone.

THE INTERVIEW PROCESS

The interview process can be stressful and nerve-racking for everyone. Your job as an interviewer is to elicit information from an uncomfortable interviewee while being a mind reader, psychologist, and salesperson. You will be asking probing questions, listening intently, judging attitudes and appearances, and trusting your managerial instincts. Below are some helpful resources for interviewing and selecting qualified employees.

- **Web resources.** For restaurant-specific advice, visit consultant Simma Lieberman Associates at **www.simmalieberman.com/articles/interviewemp.html.** For hiring systems, visit Unicru at **www.unicru.com**.

- **Understand what characteristics, skills, and experience you need and what you can live without.** Refresh yourself by reading through the job description and preparatory notes.

- **Record your notes immediately.** Remember, just like the employee, you are under stress and your memory can falter. Also, do not take any notes that might appear to be discriminatory. These are all fair game for opposing attorneys.

- **Be prepared to answer the tough questions.** You should be able to answer salary, benefit, and advancement questions along with work expectations and your business stability.

- **Never over-promise.** Do not indicate there are advancement opportunities when none exist.

- **Create an interview team.** Include supervisors and team leaders in the interview process. They can help you select people who not only have the skills but also the attitude your restaurant needs.

ASK PROBING QUESTIONS

Be careful what you ask. Some questions are against the law, while others should be avoided to protect you and your business from discriminatory claims. For a list of illegal interview questions, visit Office.com at **www.office.com/templates/page1.asp?docid=34**.

- **Ask all your questions at once**, putting the burden on the interviewee. It will keep you from talking too much or leading the interviewee to the answers you want to hear.

- **Ask essay-style questions that cannot be answered with yes or no.** Use your own style of speaking, but ask questions such as:

  - What would your former employer or coworkers have to say about you?

  - Who was your best boss and why?

  - Describe your favorite job.

  - Was there anything at your last job that you did not get a chance to do or learn?

  - Describe a disagreement you had with a supervisor and how you resolved it.

  - If I were your boss, what would be the most important thing I could do to help you be successful?

- **Bring the interview to a close with, "We have about five more minutes."** When people know they are running low on time, they get down to what is really important to them. Often this last-minute exchange can cement your impression of the candidate—sometimes positively and sometimes negatively.

LISTEN INTENTLY

- **Watch the interviewee.** Do they fidget and constantly change position? If you are hiring for a high-energy position, she might be the right person. If what you are looking for is a calm, controlled employee, she may not be the best choice.

- **Improve your listening skills** with help from the International Listening Association at **www.listen.org**.

- **Learn to interpret body language.** Read about the signs in *Interview Body Language: It's Not What You Said* at MBA Jungle, **www.mbajungle.com**.

JUDGING ATTITUDES AND APPEARANCES

- **Did they show up on time?** Someone who is late for an interview has a good chance of being late for work. Of course, if they have a flat tire, be reasonable. How they handle being late is equally important.

- **How are they dressed?** You would not expect a prospective server to show up in a suit, unless you have a very high-class establishment. But a sloppy interviewee will surely be a sloppy employee. Are fingernails clean, hair washed, and clothes neat?

- **Do they look around and show interest during your tour?** If they have no interest in what may be their future place of employment, how much interest will they have if you hire them?

- **Does the interviewee respond in a friendly manner when introduced to other employees?** A friendly attitude and outgoing personality is vital for good customer service.

HIRING THE BEST PERSON FOR THE JOB

There is no exact science for making your final choice. You can improve your chances for success with good hiring practices. I have gathered some informative sources for tools and guidance to help you choose your next employee.

- **Research.** Read an excellent article on selecting the right employee at My Web (The Site for Small Business Owners) — Choosing Between Two Equally Qualified Candidates at **www.mywebca.com/infolibrary/staffing/staffing7.htm**.

- **Conduct multiple interviews if necessary.** First impressions can be deceiving and second interviews can reveal new facts. Use the second interview to bring in other interviewers and to discuss wages and benefits.

- **Check references thoroughly.** Failing to check references can be a costly mistake. You could be hiring a poor worker or someone with excessive absences. You could be risking a negligent hiring lawsuit where an employer can be held liable when they knew, or should have known, that an employee presented a foreseeable risk of harming others. **Monster.com** offers excellent advice to employers on reference checking at **http://hr.monster.com/archives/hiringprocess/reference**. Career Know-How, **www.careerknowhow.com/resumes/fibs.htm,** reports these job-seeker statistics:

  - 51 percent falsify length of past employment and salary.

  - 45 percent falsify criminal records (you can only ask about convictions, not arrests).

  - 33 percent lie about driving records.

- **Non-work-related references.** Entry-level workers, with little or no prior work experience, should provide teachers, pastors, Scoutmasters, or other responsible adults as references.

- **Hire a reference-checking company.** Companies like HRPlus, **www.hrplus.com**; Employment Screening Services, **www.employscreen.com**; and Info Link Screening, **www.infolinkscreening.com** can get the full scoop and save you hours of phone calls.

- **Do not tell all the candidates of your decision until your new employee starts.** You may find that the chosen candidate changes her mind at the last moment.

SAVING PAYROLL DOLLARS

Savvy entrepreneurs never overlook allowable tax deductions, credits, government programs, business subsidies, or other money-saving opportunities. Some will be easy to take advantage of, while others will require diligence and extensive paperwork. The direct and indirect savings can go a long way to balancing your budget. Below you will find some valuable resources and ideas on trimming payroll costs. The information provided here is for your educational benefit. Please consult with your accountant, tax advisor, or attorney for current information and applicability to your situation.

- **Pay employees with benefits.** The more cash wages you can move into exempt and pre-tax categories, the less payroll taxes you and your employees will pay.

- **Benefits fall into three categories: taxable, exempt, and pre-tax.** Taxable benefits are subject to federal income tax withholding, Social Security, Medicare, or federal unemployment tax. They are reported on Form W-2. Exempt benefits are excluded from employee withholdings and employer contributions (with some exceptions) and are not reported. Pre-tax benefits feature flexible benefit plans that allow employees to design and pay for customized benefit packages with nontaxable employer dollars. They can cover accident and health costs, adoptions, dependent care, and life insurance.

- **Create charts and employee guides to demonstrate how employers can "earn" more by saving tax dollars.** Use these tools during the hiring process and employee orientations to help employees understand the advantages of receiving benefits over a larger paycheck.

- **Properly calculate overtime pay for tipped workers.** The Department of Labor Web site at **www.dol.gov** offers up-to-date information on current and pending overtime laws.

- **Keep track of time.** Good recordkeeping can trim payroll costs up to 7 percent. Check out manual, electronic, and computer-based time clocks with thumbprint ID sign-in at Time Centre, **www.timecentre.net**; and Time Clock Plus, **www.timeclockplus.com**.

OFFER THE RIGHT BENEFITS PACKAGE

Employee compensation packages are comprised of taxable wages (employee and employer paid) and taxable (employee) and non-taxable benefits. Here are some tips on benefits:

- **Implement pre-tax benefit plans that save everyone money.** A variety of benefits can be packaged where deductions would be pre-tax (prior to withholding calculations). Retirement, commuting, dependent care, and medical savings plans can all be paid with pre-tax dollars, such as section 125 Plans ("cafeteria" or "flex" plans).

- **Explore benefits that cost almost nothing, but save you payroll dollars.** Although many employers contribute to benefit plans, you can set up 100 percent employee-paid plans where your only costs would be to administer the plan and file IRS Form 5500. See BenFlex, Inc. at **www.beneflexinc.com**; My Cafeteria Plan at **www.mycafeteria-plan.com**; U.S. Health Plans at **www.ushealthplans.com/medsavings.shtml**; or learn more about 401(k) plans at **www.401khelpcenter.com**.

- **Hire a benefit consultant.** Companies like Broad Reach Benefits, Inc., **www.brb1144.com/index.html**, can guide you through establishing voluntary benefit programs and expand your benefit choices.

- **Offer tax-exempt employee benefits.** Explore with your tax advisor the benefits of offering these fringe benefits (wage deduction figures given are per employee per year):

  - Achievement awards — personal property award up to $1,600 tax free.

  - Adoption assistance — $10,000.

  - Athletic facilities — value to employees.

  - Dependent care assistance — up to $5,000.

  - Education assistance — up to $5,250.

  - Employee discounts — formula based on cost.

  - Group-term life insurance — contact the IRS for current regulations.

  - Meals — up to 100 percent of costs. Read about de minimus (little value) meals and workplace meals at **www.5500accountant.com/meals-andlodging.htm** and in IRS Publication 15-B.

TAX DEDUCTIONS AND CREDITS

I have outlined some potential wage and tip tax-saving ideas that you should discuss with your business advisors.

- **Let an expert guide you.** Your first step to savings should be to hire a qualified CPA. Many payroll-related activities require strict compliance with court rulings and IRS opinions and state and federal laws change frequently.

- **Keep current on tip tax laws and court rulings.** The restaurant industry continues to tackle the issue of tips and their tax obligations. Recent rulings have been in the IRS's favor, but the discussion continues. Your local restaurant association can keep you and your accountant up to date. For current information and tip-reporting guides, visit the National Restaurant Association's tip reporting page at **www.restaurant.org/legal/tips;** call the IRS at 800-TAXFORM.

- **Protect yourself from an audit by agreeing to a standard tip calculation method.** The IRS agrees not to audit your tip records if you agree to and comply with either the Tip Rate Determination Agreement (TRDA) or the Tip Reporting Alternative Commitment (TRAC). For more information, visit the Restaurant Report at **www.restaurantreport.com/departments/ac_tiptactics.html**.

- **Take a 45(B) credit.** The IRS allows businesses to take a credit against Social Security and Medicare (FICA) taxes paid on tips. To learn more, read the National Restaurant Association's article at **www.restaurant.org/legal/law_fica.cfm**.

- **Claim wage credits and deductions for employees' meals.** Meals provided in your restaurant for your convenience are not taxable. If your staff must remain on-site during their shift, meals provided are not taxable as wages. Meals used as rewards or outside of the employees' scheduled work period are typically taxable. Meals provided at no charge may be credited against your employer's minimum wage obligation. Some states set specific values for meal credits while the Fair Labor Standards Act (FLSA) allows the "reasonable" cost as an offset.

- **Claim wage credits and pay exemptions for extended breaks.** Typically, rest periods longer than 30 minutes, where no work duties are required, are not compensable. Check the following Department of Labor links for information on your state's rules. For state laws on rest periods, see **www.dol.gov/esa/programs/whd/state/rest.htm**. For state laws on meal periods, see **www.dol.gov/esa/programs/whd/state/meal.htm**.

TAKE ADVANTAGE OF BENEFIT DISCOUNTS AND SUBSIDIES

- **Join trade, business, or community organizations to lower benefit costs.** Many offer reduced pricing on insurance, wellness programs, incentive plans, training, and retirement packages. Contact your state's restaurant association and the National Restaurant Association at **www.restaurant.org/join/services.cfm** to learn more about industry offerings. Small business organizations can provide reduced rates for members. Try one of these to reduce your employee benefit costs: National Business Association at **www.nationalbusiness.org** or Small Business Benefit Association at **www.sbba.com**.

- **Offer discounts for lifestyle and health needs** like prescriptions, vision, dental, and cosmetic surgery.

- **Create a carpool and ride-share program.** Employers' subsidies promote the reduction of urban traffic and energy usage. Information is available through federal, state, and local government energy and transportation departments.

- **Barter with local merchants for pizza, movie passes, theater tickets, and other items suitable for employee rewards.** Consult your tax advisor regarding your tax obligation and recordkeeping requirement.

- **Contact your bank for employee-banking services** including free checking, discounted loan services, and automatic payroll deposit.

- **Enroll your business with a credit union.** Credit unions offer employees excellent discounted financial services. Convenient on-site enrollments are available.

- **Set up a U.S. Savings bond program.** Funds are deducted from each paycheck, held until the purchase price is accumulated, and then the employee's bond is ordered. For information, visit **www.savingsbonds.gov**.

- **Offer no-cost life-skills classes.** Seek out bankers and investment counselors to provide free financial advice on savings, borrowing, investing, retiring, and owning a home. Nonprofit and government organizations are good sources for free classes on topics like parenting, choosing a child care provider, and health concerns.

GOVERNMENT EMPLOYMENT PROGRAMS

Government agencies frequently take active roles to help high-risk and disadvantaged people become employed by offering payroll subsidies, tax breaks, and training programs. There are also financial-support programs based on where your business is located and the type of benefits you offer.

- **Search out work programs, subsidies, and tax breaks** by contacting your local chamber of commerce, small business associations, State Departments of Welfare, Commerce, and Employment, and your accountant. Ask your state employment division about "empowerment or enterprise zone" tax credits.

- **Read IRS Publication 954 "Tax Incentives for Empowerment Zones and Other Distressed Communities"** to learn about federal wage (salary plus company-paid health insurance costs) credits.

  - Distressed communities (up to $3,000 per employee).

  - Native American employment credits (up to 20 percent credit).

  - Work opportunity credit for high unemployment groups; for example, felons, veterans, and food stamp recipients (up to $2,400 per employee/$1,200 summer youth employee).

  - Welfare-to-Work (up to $8,500 per employee).

- **Help the disadvantaged and your business.** Training programs and tax credits and deductions are available. CCH Inc. (**www.cch.com**) has an informative article on the four federal tax credits listed above at **taxguide.completetax.com/text/Q16_3214. asp**. Contact the U.S. Work Force at **www.usworkforce.org**, 877-US2-JOBS.

ISABLED WORKER PROGRAMS

The federal government defines "disability" as a physical or mental impairment that substantially limits one or more of the major life activities; walking, seeing, speaking, or hearing. Under the Americans with Disabilities Act (ADA), employers are to make "reasonable accommodation" to facilities, job duties, work schedule, equipment, and other accommodations. A "qualified individual with a disability" means an individual with a disability who, with or without reasonable accommodation, can perform the essential functions of the employment position that such individual holds or desires.

Learn more about the financial benefits of hiring the disabled under the Ticket to Work and Work Incentive Improvement Act (TWWIIA) at the Department of Labor, **www.dol.gov/odep/ pubs/ek00/ticket.htm**.

Improve your accommodations for disabled workers and accessibility for disabled employees and/or customers. The Disabled Access Credit (IRS Code Section 44) grants small businesses a tax credit (a 50 percent credit up to $5,000 annually).

OTHER HELPFUL TAX-SAVERS

- **Share credit card fee costs.** Before disbursing tips added to credit card charges, you may legitimately deduct the credit card company's processing fee on the tip portion. Be certain to verify if it is allowed in your state.

- **Hire family members to eliminate some tax obligations.** Many restaurants are unincorporated family businesses where everyone capable of working does.

- **If your children or spouse are not on the payroll and they can legitimately handle some type of work, you may be eligible for a variety of tax breaks.** Hire your under-18 child and do not pay Social Security or federal unemployment taxes. Speak with your tax consultant for specifics. Read the Motley Fool article at **www.fool.com/ taxes/2002/taxes020628.htm**.

- **Explore other tax deductions and credits related to benefits.** Many are tax-free to employees and all are legitimate business deductions. Below are a few tax-savers:

  - Up to 50 percent of employee pension plan set-up costs.

  - Up to $100 a month per employee for public transportation discounts or passes.

  - Up to $180 per month per employee for parking.

  - Clothing (uniforms, aprons, hats) imprinted with the name of your business can be considered an advertising expense.

HIDDEN PAYROLL EXPENSE SAVINGS

You will also have other costs associated with payroll. It takes time and money to maintain time slips, calculate taxes, write payroll checks, keep payroll records, administer benefit programs, and make tax deposits. To help you with the paperwork hassles and reduce these costs, I have compiled some practical ideas and useful resources.

- **Hire a local payroll service firm.** Even if you handle your own bookkeeping, outsourcing payroll can be a wise decision. You will not have to worry about the right tax table or when to deposit withholdings. One advantage of hiring a professional is that she frequently assumes all liability for filing errors and pays for all penalties or interest on late or inaccurate filings. Be certain to ask about liability issues.

- **Try online payroll services.** Search the Internet under the keyword "payroll service" for banks, national service firms, local consultants, and Web-based solutions. Ask about liability issues. See Wells Fargo Bank at **www.wellsfargo.com**; Paychex at **www.paychex.com**; or Automatic Data Processing at **www.adp.com**.

- **Buy payroll software and do it yourself.** Popular accounting packages have add-on modules and stand-alone software programs. Remember, you assume all liability for errors. See QuickBooks at **www.quickbooks.com/services/payroll**; Peachtree at **www.peachtree.com/epeachtree/payroll.cfm**; Pensoft (restaurant versions) at **www. pensoft.com**; or Restaurant Technology Inc. at **www.internetrti.com/productTours**.

- **Use human resources software, online services, and downloadable human resources forms.** See Trak It Solutions (HR software) at **www.trak-it.com/welcome. html**.

- **Find someone to do the human resources support and paperwork.** Human resource consultants and personnel service providers can handle every aspect from advertising to interviewing to overseeing your benefit plans. Eliminate writing payroll checks. Direct deposit paychecks into employee bank accounts. Some banks even offer free checking for employees needing to open a bank account associated with your direct deposit participation.

- **Consider lengthening your payroll periods.** You can reduce your payroll accounting costs (check writing, recordkeeping) by up to 70 percent by switching from weekly to monthly. If employees find the monthly cycle difficult, try offering a less costly procedure like a scheduled draw mid-month. To verify your state's pay period requirements, see the Department of Labor's chart at **www.dol.gov/esa/programs/whd/state/payday.htm**.

OTHER PAYROLLL RESOURCES

- Tax Tip Calculator at **www.paycheckcity.com/Tipcalc/tipcalculator.asp**.

- Time and attendance software listings at **www.hr-software.net/pages/211.htm**.

- Days off calculator at **www.daysoffcalculator.com/web.htm**.

- Pay raise calculator at **www.payraisecalculator.com**.

SAVE MONEY IN EMPLOYEE TRAINING

TEACHING SUCCESS

Accepting the responsibility for training is expensive, so your first choice should be to hire people with experience. Paying more than the prevailing wage and offering a comprehensive benefits package may cost you less in the long run. If you are lucky enough to have an ample, well-educated workforce in your community, your employee training may only consist of orienting new hires to your own procedures and establishing personal goals and employer expectations. However, if trained workers are not readily available, your only option may be to accept bringing their skills up to your standards.

INVEST IN TRAINING

Invest time and money in training to improve productivity, increase sales, and enhance quality. Allocate time to properly train employees. Their increased productivity will pay for your time and effort. A good job description = better training = more productivity.

Reasons for training:

- Unprepared employees are unhappy employees, resulting in high turnover.

- Unskilled or untrained employees will cost you more in low productivity, poor service, waste, and inefficiency.

- Lack of training creates employees with poor attitudes and bad work habits.

TRAIN THE TRAINER

If you did not hire someone for their training abilities, do not expect them to be a natural at it. Simply handing over a new employee to a coworker may work, but most often it does not. Your first step is to train the trainer.

- **Teach employees to be trainers** with help from Workforce.com at **www.workforce. com/section/11/article/23/24/25.html** and **www.atlantic-pub.com**.

- **Get food safety training tips and techniques** from Food Safety Training and Education Alliance at **www.fstea.org/resources/training.html**.

- **Find a "Train the Trainer" seminar.** Restaurant management-specific classes and seminars are available through your state's restaurant association.

YOUR TRAINING NEEDS

You pay for training, whether it is done right or wrong. Protect your investment by developing a program that meets the needs of your organization and brings you the greatest benefits.

- **Look at your current employees.** What natural talents do they have that need to be enhanced? What would they like to learn? Talk to them and review their current skills against their assigned job description. Which tasks are still as difficult for them as when they started their job? These tasks should move up higher on your training schedule.

- **Start cross-training.** Cross-training can be very valuable, especially to a smaller operation. Cross-trained employees can fill in when others are absent and jobs can be combined during slow economic times. Cross-training can also be used to prevent boredom for employees with routine jobs. Rotating positions can make the work more interesting.

SPECIFIC TRAINING AREAS

Below are some training areas from which your employees and restaurant might benefit:

- **Computer.** Personal computer hardware, computerized systems (sound and lighting systems), computerized equipment.

- **Software.** Point-of-sale systems, time management, scheduling, inventory control, reservation system.

- **Language.** English for immigrants or foreign languages to converse with non-English-speaking employees or customers.

- **Safety.** Food and alcohol, personal and workplace safety (accident prevention, injury, ergonomics), theft, and robbery.

- **Legal.** Discriminatory practices, sexual harassment.

- **Purchasing.** Inventory control, waste management.

- **Leadership.** Problem solving, motivational.

- **Personnel management.** Problem employees, disciplinary, hiring, firing, sexual harassment, discrimination prevention, diversity.

- **Time management.** Productivity improvements through time management.

- **Communication skills.** Peer-to-peer, employee-to-employer, customer contact, phone skills, grammar, vocabulary.

- **Customer service, sales techniques.** How to increase ticket sizes without offending customers, handling difficult customers, building customer relationships.

- **Etiquette.** Personal, phone, cultural differences.

SETTING GOALS AND EXPECTATIONS

Goals and expectations are benchmarks for future employee reviews, bonus systems, and salary increases. Here are some practical suggestions and resources to help you explain your performance standards and set success goals.

- **Read an eBook** from Restaurant Trainers at **www.restauranttrainers.com/html/goal_setting.html**.

- **Work with employees to discover their career path.** Goal setting is more than just stating someone must cover seven tables and serve 24 customers an hour or they will not get a raise. It is also working together to develop a career. Many food-service careers are based on advancing through the ranks and on-the-job training. You have a personal opportunity to transform a trainee into a talented chef or valuable manager.

- **Build in rewards and incentives.** Explain how their success relates to the success of their department and your operation. Employees that understand they can make a difference accept increased responsibility and think more often about the common good. Personnel motivators call this "owning" the job.

- **Establish schedules and deadlines whenever possible.** It is human nature to delay actions until the very last minute. By setting deadlines and regular performance reviews, you will keep the goals active.

- **Provide the tools and resources to reach goals.** It can be as simple as a book to read or as comprehensive as an educational subsidy.

- **Develop goals together and ask for a commitment.** Give employees a copy of agreed upon goals and expectations. Place a signed copy in their employee file.

ESTABLISHING QUALITY, PRODUCTIVITY, AND PERFORMANCE STANDARDS

For proper training and performance evaluation, you need to establish standards for each job description. These become your training, proficiency, and motivational guidelines.

- **Quality standards.** Quality standards can be difficult to express. Do your best to illustrate these in words (job descriptions) and demonstrations (on-the-job training). Show servers what the dinner salad should look like rather than just telling them.

- **Performance standards.** The information you gather becomes the basis for your training, motivational, and employee review efforts. These standards also take into account human factors. Only machines can be expected to consistently perform each task exactly the same way in the same amount of time.

- **Not a weapon.** Work standards should not be used as a weapon or threat but as a guideline. You cannot reduce a warm smile or a melt-in-your-mouth dessert to a standard.

- **Write them down.** These standards should all be in writing. Besides including them in operational manuals and job descriptions, create and display wall charts. Use performance improvements between employees or shifts as the basis for a contest or bonus program.

PRODUCTIVITY STANDARDS

In a single quick-service restaurant, 30 seconds can translate into thousands of dollars annually. To follow are some helpful tips on setting your restaurant's productivity standards.

- **Gather and analyze data.** The better your data, the more accurate your standards will be. Take time and elicit your staff's assistance in setting productivity standards.

- **Conduct studies using actual real-world situations.** Do time and motion studies. Review ergonomics and procedures for wasted time and motion.

- **Gather data from other sources.** A wide variety of data may already be available from credit card transaction time stamps, POS and inventory reports, equipment timers, usage calculators, and time clocks. Hosts/hostesses, servers, and cooks can gather information during their days.

- **Do not rely on "industry standards."** Food prepared and served, facility size, layout, and equipment factors are different for every operation.

- **Set realistic minimum activity levels.** Remember that trainees and experienced staff cannot be expected to perform at the same level. Everyone must be able to meet the minimum activity level.

- **Create tiered performance standards.** Start with your minimum standard level and then add an "experienced" level and an "expert" level. These additional levels can be used in incentive programs.

- **Use your most productive employees to set optimal standards.** No employee can perform at 100 percent capacity for 100 percent of the time. Depending on the task and employee experience, acceptable levels will range from 75 percent and up.

TRAINING PLANS

Take your standards and job descriptions and develop a training plan for each job. Make it clear to a new employee that the skills, tasks, and behaviors must be mastered by the end of their training period.

- **Analyze the job description.** Identify the specific duties to be done and the skills needed to do them. List the duties from the most basic to the most specific.

- **Use hands-on training and practice sessions.** The quickest way for an employee to learn new tasks is through on-the-job demonstrations and immediate practice.

- **Use role-playing for new employees who will be dealing with the public.** Make sure they understand their duties and can perform them before you send them out to take care of actual customers. Test employees on a few critical issues. Some food-handling and safety facts should be tested to ensure that your employees understand and can comply with regulations. As the cliché goes: Ignorance is no excuse, but it can be quite costly.

STARTING OFF RIGHT

Employee retention starts from day one. Do not just expect them to show up on Monday morning and be ready for work. You must be ready to start them off right.

- **Orientation is your first training session.** Do not just hand them a W-4 to complete and a policy manual. Good employer/employee communication starts here.

- **Tell them what you and your company stand for** and how important their success is to you and your team. Tell them what you are willing to do to make them a better employee and the benefits of building a future with your company.

- **Make it memorable.** Do not drone on and on. You can even break the orientation into segments to be held over several days.

- **Inject some humor.** Try this book for ideas: *The Big Book of Humorous Training Games: Dozens of Games for Popular Training Topics, From Customer Service to Time Management* by Doni Tamblyn and Sharyn Weiss.

- **Avoid technical words or jargon.** New employees are less likely to ask questions, so your point may be lost unless you keep it simple.

- **Demonstrate whenever possible.** Miscommunication can reduce productivity or create unsafe situations.

There are a number of questions that most new employees have. Here are a few that you should be sure to answer:

- **How do I get paid?** Make certain people understand how to complete and turn in time cards. Explain pay cycles, draws, and benefit deductions.

- **To whom do I report?** Clearly identify direct and indirect supervisors and explain the relationship.

- **Whom do I ask?** Tell new hires about each person's expertise and duties through personal introductions.

- **How do I work it?** Allow ample time for equipment training. Lack of training directly impacts employee and equipment productivity. Do not overlook common items such as phone systems and time clocks. Create cheat sheets and reminders for quick reference. Concentrate on ergonomics and safety training.

MEETINGS

A quick meeting before the shift gives you an opportunity to teach and listen. You can also use this time to recognize individual accomplishments and share personal updates, improve communications and reduce gossip, give pep talks and announce contests, and make everyone feel included. Feeling "in on things" is very important to employees.

- **Do not try to solve the world's problems.** Do listen to what your people have to say. You do not have to come up with a solution on the spot.

- **Make problem solving a team project.** Implement solutions to previously voiced problems during these meetings. When your employees know that you are listening and trying to make their job better, you may be amazed at the solutions they can suggest.

- **Create an atmosphere of trust.** If you ask for input but your people have nothing to say, then you do not have their trust. To be effective, listen to their complaints and suggestions with an open mind and to come up with a fair and reasonable solution.

CULINARY AND HOSPITALITY PROGRAMS

Building a relationship with one of the 1,700 culinary and hospitality trade schools nationwide can translate into a "first pick" from the most talented students. To follow are several resources for locating schools and programs dedicated to the culinary arts.

- **Trade schools.** National Restaurant Association at **www.restaurant.org/careers/schools.cfm**; Star Chefs at **www.starchefs.com/helpwanted.html**; Culinary Education at **www.culinaryed.com**; Cooking Culinary Arts Schools at **www.cooking-culinary-arts-schools.com**; CookingSchools.com at **www.cookingschools.com**; and Culinary Training at **www.culinary-training.com**.

- **Sponsor a student.** A CookingSchools.com article aimed at potential culinary students has some great ideas for potential employers. Go to **www.cookingschools.com/articles/scholarships** to learn more.

- **Learn about apprenticeship programs** from the American Culinary Federation at **www.acfchefs.org** or Hospitality Campus.com's online training at **www.culinaryconnect.com**.

IN-HOUSE TRAINING PROGRAMS

Below are resources and tools for enhancing your in-house training programs.

- *The Encyclopedia of Restaurant Training*, The Complete Wait Staff Training Course—Video and *The Waiter & Waitress and Wait Staff Training Handbook: A Complete Guide to the Proper Steps in Service for Food & Beverage Employees*. These are all available from Atlantic Publishing, **www.atlantic-pub.com**, along with other videos and training programs.

- *The Waiting Game: The Ultimate Guide to Waiting Tables* by Mike Kirkham.

- *The Restaurant Training Program: An Employee Training Guide for Managers* by Karen Eich Drummond and Karen A. Drummond.

- E-Learning and CD-ROM food service courses from Tap Series, **www.tapseries.com**.

ADULT EDUCATION

Adult illiteracy costs U.S. businesses an estimated $225 billion annually in lost productivity. Workplace literacy is not just an issue for non-English-speaking workers; American born-and-raised adults also lack the training to read written instructions, do basic math calculations, or complete a job application properly. Many restaurateurs have discovered the benefit of supporting, sponsoring, and offering adult education classes: greater productivity, fewer errors, and increased workplace safety. To support employer efforts, a variety of private and public funding, tax benefits, and wage subsidies are available.

- **Literacy.** Visit the National Institute for Literacy organization at **www.nifl.gov**. Watch an interactive presentation on adult literacy in the restaurant industry by the state of North Carolina at **www.ncrtec.org/pd/cw/rest/start.htm**. Develop a workplace literacy program. For information, visit the Adult Literacy Organization at **www.adultliteracy.org/wpl.html**.

- **The general educational development (GED) credential** was created as a solution for adults who have not graduated from high school.

- **English as a Second Language.** The goal of ESL instruction is English language (speaking, writing, reading, and comprehension) and literacy proficiency. Unlike general adult educational programs, ESL programs may be offered to highly educated learners who simply lack English proficiency. Read Communicating in a Melting Pot from Restaurants USA at **www.restaurant.org/rusa/magarticle.cfm?articleid=106**. Learn more from the National Association for Bilingual Education (NABE) at **www.nabe.org** or call 202-898-1829.

- **Life-skills training.** Life skills represent the knowledge and aptitudes necessary for a person to function independently and to keep a job. Workers lacking economic and educational opportunities may not have developed these basic skills and may struggle to meet employer expectations. Helping your workers develop life skills can be a wise investment. To learn more, Work Shops, Inc. has a manual online at **www.workshopsinc.com/manual/Toc.html**.

SCHEDULING YOUR STAFF

There are eight basic steps in the scheduling process:

1. **Developing work production standards.** Calculate the amount of work (covers, meals, place settings) that an individual employee with a specific job (server, cook, dishwasher) is expected to accomplish in a set time period.

2. **Plotting patterns of activity in various units of the operation.** Food service facilities usually have different patterns of activity during the day that requires different levels of scheduling.

3. **Forecasting levels of activity.** Shift, daily, weekly, and monthly customer/sales cycles should be factored in. These can be broken down into quarter, half, and hourly segments within each day.

4. **Determining the number of workers and/or hours needed.** Divide the work production standards into the anticipated number of covers (customers) and the number of personnel required can be calculated.

5. **Considering employee time and assignment requests.** Job assignments; skills, abilities and experience; scheduled absences; desired rotation; wage rates; and legal considerations such as hours for minors and overtime are all important considerations.

6. **Approval by management after the schedule is written.** Evaluate by criteria such as labor cost per hour, customers served per hour, or any other appropriate criteria.

7. **Distributing approved schedule to employees.** Employee handouts, break room and office postings, Web site postings, e-mail broadcast, and "call-in" systems are all ways to ensure staff members have ample notification of shift assignments.

8. **Recapping and reviewing the historical schedules by management** to discover problems, explore solutions, and improve processes.

SCHEDULING TRUISMS

Your goal is to complete all necessary work using the least number of labor hours possible while maintaining an outstanding level of service. Establish a baseline for a minimum acceptable service level. Then analyze how each additional worker impacts service quality and productivity. Employees appreciate getting more help but become irritated when they "lose" help.

Absenteeism will wreak havoc on your fine-tuned schedule on a regular basis. Controlling unplanned absences is critical to maintaining adequate productivity and service levels. See the section on "Absenteeism" for more information.

Good forecasting requires good data. Historical and current data must be accurately gathered and easily assessable. Outside factors are important forecasting issues, such as seasonal demands, weather conditions, special events, and competitive issues.

You must understand your team's capabilities and capacities. Consider individual skills and abilities to balance scheduling. Some servers cope with noisy children better, so schedule them during family times. Family needs create unplanned absences and distract workers. Whenever possible, you should consider these during scheduling.

Overworking (physically and emotionally) staff members can significantly lower productivity, increase absenteeism, and escalate turnover rates. Frazzled employees are potential customer-service nightmares. Inattentive service, inaccurate orders, spills, and angry encounters lower your service quality and chase away customers. Tired employees can cut corners — increasing food safety problems, food waste, equipment and dishware damage, accidents, and injuries.

Overstaffing does not just inflate your payroll; it can decrease your overall productivity. Congested serving and kitchen areas make everyone's job more difficult and lowers service quality.

You must balance quality and quantity. A fast cook who makes mistakes and turns out sloppy meals is not up to your quality standards. A slow cook who turns out perfect meals is not up to the quantity standards.

SCHEDULE TYPES AND PATTERNS

There are different types of schedules that can be used in a food service operation.

- **Scheduling by production requirements for individual items.** Determine what has to be produced for the meal, period, or day. You may include items that will be produced for future meals.

- **Scheduling by station production.** Items from the production schedule are assigned to a workstation (bakery, salads). Smaller operations may combine a production schedule and a station work guide.

- **Scheduling by staff coverage provides coverage for the various units within the operation.** Production schedules should be coordinated with individual scheduling. Dining room scheduling is based on the forecasted number of patrons divided by the work production standards of the dining room personnel.

There are three common scheduling patterns:

1. **Block or stacked schedule.** Everyone on a shift starts and stops working at the same time. It is easier to check that everyone is present and on time and share common information.

2. **Staggered arrivals and departures.** Employee schedules correspond to the work pattern and customer flow. It is more efficient than block scheduling, as the number of employees gradually increases during the peak volume periods and decreases towards the end of the day.

3. **Spanner shifts.** Provides overlapping coverage for a smooth transition between shift changes. Overlap times range from 30 to 60 minutes, depending upon the job category and duties. It eliminates staff working past scheduled departure times to "finish up."

OTHER POSSIBLE SCHEDULING METHODS

Forecasting can be difficult, especially for newer establishments without any historical data. Scheduling inaccuracies can inflate your labor costs or result in substandard service. You will find that unplanned events can directly impact your staffing requirements. There are other scheduling procedures to help you through unpredictable times. Below I will discuss six ways you might consider. Although federal wage and hour laws do not address these issues, you should be aware of union contracts, local labor practices, corporate policies, and state laws that may govern your use of flexible scheduling practices. Meal and rest periods may also be mandated by your state even if workers are on the clock for less than eight hours.

- **On-call scheduling.** Hourly employees remain at home until you call them into work. Quick response can be critical so employees can be given pagers or cell phones so they are not "trapped" at home. Employees can rotate being on-call to give them additional free time without significantly affecting their paycheck. On-call periods would be scheduled like any other work duty. Trainees and new hires can be used for on-call coverage during probationary periods. Minimum hours may be mandated by union contracts and other labor practices.

- **Send-home-early scheduling.** The reverse of on-call scheduling, employees are sent home when work slows. With good forecasting and intelligent scheduling, it would typically be used for unusual circumstances, such as bad weather. Employees can rotate, draw straws, or volunteer to go home early. Trainees and new hires can be chosen.

- **Part-timers.** Schedule part-timers for additional coverage during peak periods and seasonal influxes. Post a roster of workers interested in part-time or temporary work, a good choice for people seeking part-time work with flexibility.

- **Split shifts.** Similar to part-timers but where employees would work multiple, non-consecutive mini-shifts totaling up to 40 hours a week. Employees clock out between scheduled work periods. Workers would cover specific meal periods or required prep and clean-up times.

- **On-break schedules.** When it is not practical to send someone home, you can put them on an extended break. A 30-minute off-the-clock break and employer-provided meal means you can deduct the cost of the meal against the minimum wage requirement and save half an hour of pay.

- **Short-term overtime.** Overtime is costly but sometimes necessary when unforeseen emergencies arise and short-term coverage is required. Beware of burn-out and stress when employees are working extra hours to help out.

THE NEGATIVE IMPACTS OF UNDERSTAFFING

Unskilled managers can be too zealous in keeping labor costs low. A shortage of workers or relying primarily on inexperienced, lower-paid workers will initially reduce your costs. However, the long-term impact on service, morale, and productivity can mean a slow and painful death for your business. Below are some useful resources and ideas on how to measure whether your staffing levels are creating problems.

- **Tour the dining room throughout the meal and ask your customers.** Conduct customer service surveys. For information on surveys, visit The Business Research Lab at **www.busreslab.com/consult/restcslg.htm** or Mercantile Systems and Surveys at **www.mercsurveys.com**.

- **Hire a "mystery shopper."** Check the Mystery Shopping Providers Association at **www.mysteryshop.org** or call 972-406-1104 for a local consultant.

- **Employees suffer.** You risk losing your most productive employees, as they will probably be the ones working longer hours. Overworked employees can quickly become unhappy and unproductive employees. Some employees will not complain; they will just lose their incentive to work hard and leave. Others will develop a disruptive attitude before leaving.

- **Cumulative fatigue can become a financial burden.** A McDonald's restaurant was held responsible for $400,000 in personal injury damages after an employee, who had worked three consecutive shifts in 24 hours, fell asleep at the wheel causing a serious collision.

- **Business declines.** How long customers will wait varies from establishment to establishment. Customer expectations during a workday lunch are significantly different than at a leisurely resort. In our fast-food nation, waiting is a major issue for diners. Customers will only put up with slow service for so long.

THE NEGATIVE IMPACT OF OVERSTAFFING

Having too many people on hand can affect your bottom line in more ways than just wasting your payroll budget.

- **Poor work habits and attitudes will rise as employees slow down.** Employees will resist an increase in their workload after being overstaffed for a while. They will adapt their performance levels to a lower productivity standard. They will even feel overworked and find it difficult to "speed up."

- **Workers with idle time become distractions.** Water cooler chit-chat begins to interfere with customer needs. The atmosphere becomes too relaxed and service declines due to the resulting apathy.

- **Physical and mental fatigue becomes an issue because of boredom and time-wasting habits.** Morale drops because management must eventually reduce their labor costs. But before they do, tips will suffer, which also creates motivational problems.

COMPUTERIZED SCHEDULING

Restaurants of all sizes can successfully implement computerized employee-scheduling systems and software. Employee scheduling can be handled by a Web site, an uncomplicated Windows program, or linked directly to "time clocks." Below are a few sources for computerized scheduling:

- **Optimal Solutions at www.optimal-solutions.com.** They offer online solutions that run through your browser and desktop programs.

- **Schedule for restaurants at www.aschedule.com.** The program can automatically calculate your labor costs per cover and has an "Overtime Alert." Two versions are available for small or multi-store operations.

- **Asgard Systems Inc. at www.asgardsystems.com.** The "Time Tracker" system also keeps track of vacation time, sick time, etc. It can review past activity and prepare payroll data.

- **Restaurant Technology, Inc. at www.internetrti.com.** Management, scheduling, and accounting software for the food service industry.

- **Staff Schedule at www.staffscheduling.com** is a free Web-based scheduling program and can be accessed by management and employees from any Web-accessible computer to set and check work schedules.

- **Open Wave at www.open-wave.com** offers various Web- and PC-based programs.

SCHEDULING TIPS AND HINTS

Here are some final useful scheduling tips, hints, and resources:

- **Study your volume.** Schedule labor to match volume needs.

- **Study the level of activity breakdowns by area.**

- **Different work units have different patterns of activity throughout the day.** Normally, activity is highest in the kitchen before it is in the serving areas. The dishwashing unit activity peaks 15 to 45 minutes after the serving area peaks.

- **Schedule according to your customer flow.**

- **Plan for shift changes to minimize service disruptions.** Take into consideration the layout of your establishment and the total duties of each position.

- **Employees should be given enough flexibility to ensure that transitions are handled smoothly** and tasks completed to the customers' satisfaction. But set some limits to keep overtime in check.

THE PRODUCTIVE WORKPLACE

PRODUCTIVITY

To increase profits, you can increase sales or decrease costs. Your serving staff should all be trained to "sell" more — larger tickets lower your cost per cover. However, an extra $150 per shift does not increase profits by $150. After costs and taxes, you might be lucky to net $20. But saving $150 by operating more efficiently increases your bottom line by $150. Improved productivity can be defined as working smarter, not harder, to achieve more. To increase your staff's productivity, changes can be:

- **Simple.** Buying extra trash cans.

- **Complex.** Commissioning work-motion studies.

- **Free.** Overcoming poor work habits.
- **Costly.** Remodeling the entire kitchen.
- **Physical.** Building a facility with no stairs.
- **Psychological.** Creating an "ownership" attitude.

PRODUCTIVITY IS ALSO A QUALITY GOAL

If the quality of your food and customer service declines, you have hurt your business. The most important factor in improving productivity is smart management. Do not compromise your quality standards. A change that noticeably lowers your quality will also noticeably lower your sales. Beware of changes done for the sake of "efficiency" that cause employee morale to decline.

Invest in your business's productivity. Invest in training. Well-trained employees are happier, more productive, less prone to job stress, and less likely to be lured away by your competition. Or invest in equipment that pays for itself in labor-savings or in a worker-friendly building. Make it easier for your staff to do their jobs with proper ergonomics and well-designed rooms.

PRODUCTIVE PEOPLE

There are three basic ways to make employees more "cost effective." First, get more work from the employees you have in the same number of hours. Second, get the same amount of work from fewer employees in the same number of hours. Third, get the same amount of work from fewer employees in fewer hours. Here are some tips on productive people:

- **Being profitable is important to everyone.** Getting everyone to share this never-ending goal is your first step in directing people to be more efficient. Employees that see a direct correlation between their work performance, the customers' satisfaction, and your restaurant's success are going to work harder.

- **Do not waste a minute.** Have employee time cards initialed upon arrival and departure by the manager on duty. You will know exactly when the employees arrive and start to work and your manager can check the employees' appearance. If there are special instructions to be given to an employee, the manager does not have to go looking for anyone. At the end of each shift, the manager has an opportunity to thank the employee and privately address problems.

- **The quickest way to create unhappy employees is to "forget" to handle suggestions and complaints.** When asking for input, remember that it always requires some "output" by management. That does not mean you have to implement every suggestion or "solve" every complaint — it means that you take them seriously and act accordingly. Your actions tell your employees that their ideas and opinions have value.

- **Stimulate, but do not stifle.** Some employees are "naturally" productive. Their personal work ethic and positive attitude make them self-motivated and productive. Sometimes it can seem as if these are "problem" employees, as they tend to be more independent and headstrong. Your job is to harness and direct their energies without stifling them.

- **Make it easier.** Watch your employees at work. Silent observation can reveal inefficiencies in your system. Mentally break down their activities into small segments to see where you can add labor saving equipment, rearrange the work center, or save steps between work areas.

- **Unsupervised employees will not do their job quickly and accurately unless they clearly know what their job is.**

- **Reduce employee stress and fatigue.** Working people harder will increase productivity but only to a point. Employee burnout is 60 percent emotional and 40 percent physical.

- **Build in checks and balances to see that shortcuts are not being taken** that compromise your performance, quality, or safety standards. Assign team leaders to supervise implementation of productivity changes.

- **Create a follow-up plan** to verify that employees have not fallen back into old habits. Do not let turnover degrade good habits and efficient procedures.

STREAMLINED TASKS

Manufacturing productivity experts can spend hours analyzing what is the fastest and most efficient method for inserting Part A into Part B. You should be looking at your daily operations from the same point of view: How can you do it better? To follow are some suggestions to get you started in reviewing tasks and establishing better procedures and methods.

- **There is not just one right way to do something.**

- **It is easier to replace a bad habit with a good one than to try to break it.**

- **Target specific activities for time and performance studies one at a time.**

- **Do not overload yourself and your staff by trying to improve everything at once.**

- **Tackle the obvious first.** A few positive changes can stimulate your team to work together to find other areas for improvement.

- **Analyze production standards on a daily basis.** It takes some time and analysis to determine standards, but it is worth the effort.

- **Advance planning is the key to controlling costs.** Plan production activities in advance. Group together like activities in specific time frames to minimize cleanup.

- **Review your menu choices.** Are you selling enough of a specific item to warrant the labor required to prep, prepare, and serve it? Will altering a recipe allow you to do more advance prep? Does purchasing fully prepped ingredients or pre-processed entrées cost less than handling it in-house?

- **Provide less service.** If your restaurant style lends itself to self-serve salad bars, buffets, and self-bussing, you can cut your staffing needs and your labor costs. When reviewing the cost-benefit analysis, be certain to consider the cost of equipment, shrinkage/waste, and customer perception. Remember, many people eat out because they are waited on.

- **Make use of new, more efficient equipment.** Conveyer-style dishwashers can eliminate a part-time dishwasher.

WORK SMARTER, NOT HARDER

- **Read a book.** Atlantic Publishing offers several books for restaurant professionals, which are available at **www.atlantic-pub.com**.

- **Hire an efficiency consultant** like Peggy Duncan, **www.duncanresource.com**.

- **Learn how Pal's did it.** This Tennessee fast-food chain, **www.palsweb.com**, won the prestigious 2001 Malcolm Baldridge Quality Award, **www.nist.gov/public_affairs/pals.htm**.

- **Conduct memorable meetings.** Routine meetings become routine. Keep employees on their toes with humor, silly costumes, magicians, humorous training videos, and other attention-getters. To learn how to have fun meetings, see EffectiveMeetings.com at **www.effectivemeetings.com/meetingplanning/index.asp** or Patricia Fripp at **www.fripp.com/art.makefun1.html**. You can also read *Successful Meetings: How to Plan, Prepare, and Execute Top-Notch Business Meetings* from Atlantic Publishing at **www.atlantic-pub.com** (Item # SMS-01, $24.95).

- **Work ahead.** The more activities you can combine before serving times, the more prep labor you will save.

OTHER WAYS TO SAVE LABOR COSTS

- **Use disposables**. If the ecological concerns of disposables are not a concern, disposables can be a labor-saver when it comes to those nasty cleanups.

- **Label and color code.** Create a color-code system to quickly identify items at a glance. Colored labels can help people return items to their proper storage area or let them know if it needs to be refrigerated. See **www.daymarksafety.com**.

- **Use napkin rings.** Build wrapped napkin/silverware sets ahead of time to save table-setting time. You will reduce storage handling and rewashing. Add your restaurant logo for a personal touch. Bands are available from ColorKraft at **www.colorkraft.com**, 866-382-4730.

- **Use Griptite™ serving trays.** Available from local suppliers, these metal trays have a non-slip surface for easier carrying. The 31-inch oval tray can hold eight dinners!

- **Eliminate clutter.** Clutter is defined as anything that has no immediate use or value. Everything else should be tossed or properly stored. Hire an organizational expert to review your storage systems and suggest ways to reduce handling costs.

- **Eliminate pot and pan cleanup** with PanSaver, available at **www.atlantic-pub.com**. PanSaver is a high-temperature (400°F/204°C) material designed as a commercial pot and pan liner that keeps pans clean and can be used to store leftovers.

- **Use pre-prepared products**. Almost all ingredients come prepped, portion-controlled, or prepared for reheating. Not all are good candidates for your restaurant, but many can be incorporated into your food offerings, without any noticeable quality decline. Food that is eaten in its most natural state — washed, cut, and ready to serve, like fruit and vegetables — is an obvious choice. Bread products that are proof and bake- or brown-and-serve are another option. Tea and lemonade concentrates are very common and taste better than powdered versions.

CHAPTER 31

PUBLIC RELATIONS
FOR YOUR RESTAURANT

WHAT IS PUBLIC RELATIONS?

Public relations is the sum of its many definitions. It is a planned effort to build positive opinions about your business through actions and communications. Good PR sends a positive message to the public about your establishment.

PR should be part of your overall marketing communications program. It includes advertising, internal communications, sales promotion, speeches, contests, promotions, and personal appearances. It is who the public thinks you are and the nurturing of that opinion in a positive way.

WHAT PR DOES (AND DOES NOT DO) FOR YOU

The key to implementing an effective PR campaign is determining your business's image; what you want it to be and how best you can create that image in the eyes of the public. You need to clearly define your objectives and create a plan that will implement them. PR is not a way to gloss over a tarnished image or to keep the press at a safe distance; it is an organized and ongoing campaign to accentuate the positives of who you truly are.

THE MARRIAGE OF PR AND MARKETING

Public relations is one of marketing's tools. As a result, most restaurants keep these two departments close together. On a practical level, this close relationship obtains and retains customers, which is the obvious goal of any marketing plan. When management is communicating effectively with guests, employees, and community leaders, it is implementing an effective marketing plan.

HOW TO APPLY YOUR PR PLAN

Once you have established the objectives of your PR campaign and integrated them into your marketing plan, it is time to execute. These questions can help you do just that:

- **What is the right medium for this strategy?**

- **Who are the key contacts?**

- **Is this plan thorough?** Have you considered all the downside risks?

- **Are you prepared to deliver a package to the media?** This delivery package is an essential part of your plan. It contains descriptions, plots, contacts, phone numbers—all the pertinent information that will inform the media and direct them to you. The press may not use one word of your materials, but there is a greater likelihood they will describe you the way you want if you have given them the resources to do just that.

The following is a list of practical factors that will help you gain recognition:

- **Be honest.** The media wants credible, honest material and relationships. Your message should be genuine and factual. You do not have to reveal confidential data; it just means that your materials should be thorough and truthful.

- **Respond.** Do not lie, dodge, or cover up. If you do not have every answer to a question, do not say "no comment" or "that information is unavailable." Simply respond that you do not have that information, but will provide it as soon as humanly possible, and do so.

- **Give the facts and follow up.** If you supply the media with a printed handout of key facts, it lessens the chances of your getting misquoted. Make a concentrated effort to follow up and go over information with the media.

- **Be concise.** The media will burn you for what you say, not what you do not. Be deliberate about providing the facts without editorializing, exaggerating, or pulling things out of thin air.

- **Nurture relationships.** If you follow the above steps you are on your way to building a strong, lasting relationship with the press. These relationships can sour instantly if you are reactionary, hostile, aloof, hypersensitive, or argumentative in any way. No matter what you think of an interviewer, treat her with respect, courtesy, and professionalism. Causing negative reactions from the press will deny you print space and airtime. How you interact with the press is crucial, but it is only half the process. The content of your communications to them is the other side of press relations. The following list will help you identify your purpose and communicate it effectively to the press:

- **Identify your purpose.** Why do you want public exposure? What are you specifically trying to draw attention to? Are you selling your hotel's new lobby renovation? Then do not go on about its famous rose garden. Be sure you are conveying your purpose.

- **Identify your target.** Who are you targeting? Prospective customers? Your employees? The local business community? Civic leaders? Lay out whom you want to reach and then determine who in the media will speak to them most effectively.

- **Think as they are thinking.** Why would it be interesting to the media? Figure out how your interests can be packaged in a way that directly matches the interests of the press. Make your story one they want to print — i.e., one that will help them sell papers and gain listeners.

- **Customize your materials.** Once you have identified your purpose, who your target is, and the media's angle, tailor your materials to include all three. Give the press everything they need to tell the story — photos, copy — and be sure it is in the style and mediums they are using.

- **Know where to send your materials.** Is your story a news story or a feature story? Do you know the difference? A news story goes to a newspaper's city desk. Feature stories go to the appropriate editor: travel, lifestyle, etc. It is a very good idea to cultivate relationships with these editors beforehand so that when the time arises, they are thinking well of you and will want to help.

- **Make their job easy.** Do not ask the media for the ground rules for getting press and building relationships — learn these on your own and then meet them. Do as much of their work for them as possible: Give them something that is ready to go, that answers all their questions and is interesting. Be available immediately to answer questions.

B UILDING AND SUPPORTING STRONG MEDIA RELATIONS

Media relations are one of the most important aspects of PR because effective media relations generate publicity. Effective media relations open the channels for your public to receive the messages you want them to receive. Media relations are how you build your relationships with the press and determine how they respond when you want them to report on a story.

The first goal in building strong media relations is to determine who your target media is. News media are classified by the audiences they reach and the means they use to carry their messages. Your target media will change according to the type of message you wish to send and the type of audience you wish to reach. Your advertising agency can supply you with contact information for the newspapers, radio, and television stations in your area. In addition, you may want to target national media, as well as specialized trade and business publications. Hire a part-time PR consultant, a former reporter, or editor who can help you present your materials to the press. The following is a list of essentials for building a good relationship with the press:

- **Fact Sheet** — One of the most helpful items of media information, the fact sheet does most of the reporter's research for her. It also shortens the length of interviews by answering questions in advance. It should describe your property and what you are promoting. At a glance it tells where you are located, when you opened, your architectural style, capacity, and number of employees. It should also specify the types of facilities you have and the menu.

- **Staff Biographies** — You will need to write biographies for all of your key executives that include work experience, education, professional memberships, honors, and awards.

- **Good Photography** — Do not take chances with an amateur photographer. Space is limited in the print media and editors go through thousands of photographs to choose just a few. Do not give them reason to ignore your pictures; hire a pro. Ask for references and check them thoroughly. When the photos are done, write an explanatory caption for each picture in your collection. Doing so gives editors an easy understanding of what they are looking at. Before sending photos to the media, find out whether they prefer black and white, slides, or transparencies and send them in the desired format.

- **Press Kit Folder** — Put all of these materials into a single folder with your property's name and logo on the cover. Include brochures, rate cards, package flyers, and a brief on your involvement with local charities. Do not over stuff, but give the press a solid idea of what distinguishes you from the competition.

Before beginning your media campaign, invite the media — one at a time — to have a brief tour of your establishment and, perhaps, lunch. These relationship builders are not the time to sell them on doing a story. If the reporters trust you, they will help you and vice versa. They need article ideas as much as you need press.

Once you have built this relationship, you can begin your media campaign. Your relationship with the reporter will not get a boring story to press. Your story needs to be newsworthy on its own. Perhaps a reporter, who gets a story from an interview or news conference at your establishment, may mention your place in her story — free advertising that comes from developing strong relationships with the media and learning to think in their terms.

Many businesses go one step further and give the media contacts that are written in journalistic style. A news release describes the newsworthy development in your restaurant in a ready-to-print article. Editors can then change it or print it as is. These can be valuable for getting your message out there.

If writing journalistic articles is beyond your reach or budget, tip sheets can be very effective in getting your story across. A tip sheet gets the message to the media by outlining the who, what, when, where, why, and how of your story. It is an outline of the story the reporter will then write. Tip sheets give the spine of the story and, because they are so concise, often get more attention from busy editors.

Here are a few more tips on how to work effectively with the media:

- Earn a reputation for dealing with the facts and nothing else.

- Never ask to review a reporter's article before publication.

- Never ask after a visit or an interview if an article will appear.

- Follow up by phone to see if your fact sheet or press release has arrived, if the reporter is interested and if she needs anything else.

- Provide requested information — photos, plans, etc. — ASAP.

WHAT'S NEWS

Once you have identified your target media and begun your media relations program, you need to learn what makes news. Pick up the paper or turn on the TV; the media are looking for the strange, volatile, controversial, and unusual. It is not newsworthy that you run a nice restaurant that provides great food at a reasonable price. It is newsworthy when a customer gets food poisoning at your restaurant or when a group's convention reservations are cancelled. This news is not the type you want to make. Obviously, you want to be making great news. Take steps to avoid negative articles: making sure your reservations system works and your staff treats guests courteously.

Once you have taken these steps, you are ready to generate positive stories in the media. Here is a list of basic newsworthiness criteria:

- Is it local?
- Is it timely?
- Is it unique, unusual, strange?
- Does it involve and affect people?
- Will it provoke human emotion?

Think in terms of what sets your establishment apart from the competition and what is newsworthy about those qualities. When you have a story, be smart about who will be interested in writing about it and whose audience would love to read about it. Here is a short list of possibly newsworthy ideas:

- A new manager or chef.
- Visits by well-known politicians, entertainers, authors, or local heroes.
- Private parties, conventions, or meetings of unique organizations: antique car enthusiasts, baseball card collectors, scientific organizations.
- A new menu.
- Hosting a charitable event.
- Reduced rates, special menus, promotions, weekend specials.
- Personal stories about the staff: the waiter who returned a doctor's medical bag, helped a patron stop choking, returned a tip that was too big.

PR IS DIFFERENT FROM ADVERTISING

PR is not advertising; PR uses advertising as one of its tools. A good PR campaign is coordinated with advertising, but PR is not paid-for time and space. In advertising, clients pay the media to carry a message and the client has complete control over this message. With PR, the media receives no money. Your story about the medical dinner meeting with a noted speaker at your restaurant may end up on the five o'clock news, in the paper, or nowhere at all. The success of a PR story often depends on how timely it is or whether a newspaper editor feels it is worth reporting on. Furthermore, only a portion of your intended message may be used. The media may not even use your restaurant's name. Because they are choosing to write about your topic, the story could end up in a very different form than you initially presented or hoped.

With PR you have none of the control that you do with advertising in terms of the message being delivered. When done well, PR garners positive attention for your establishment, is hugely cost-effective, and is more credible than advertising. The public is getting its information from a third party — not directly from a business. Customers assume advertising to be self-serving, but a positive message delivered by a third party is authentic and trustworthy. Therefore, third-party messages are infinitely more persuasive than advertising. Also, the value of securing unpaid media space through PR is immeasurable.

LAUNCHING A CAMPAIGN

In a small restaurant the manager may be responsible for public relations. In a larger establishment the director of marketing or sales often plays this role. Regardless of who gets the job, the PR-buck stops with the general manager. Whoever takes on your PR function will be your liaison with the media. Having one person designated as media liaison makes it simple for the press to get their questions answered and makes it much easier for you to control the flow of information to them. This back-and-forth is a critical element in your PR campaign. Once this liaison is determined, notify your staff. Advise them not to talk with the press, but to refer all media inquiries to the liaison.

Remember when launching your campaign that you will be competing with professionals for a very limited amount of airtime and/or editorial space. Therefore, reading newspapers and trying to determine which pieces were inspired by PR people — and what about them made editors choose them — is a good discipline. Also, many colleges offer courses in public relations. The greater your knowledge, the more effective your campaign will be.

If your establishment is part of a chain, PR assistance may be available from the headquarters. If you manage an independent property, PR help may be available from your local Chamber of Commerce or Convention/Visitors' Bureau.

When contacting the media it is important to determine who will be the most useful to you. What type of customer are you seeking to attract? What is the size of your market area? Are you contacting the media who cater to those demographics? Your advertising agency can be helpful with statistical data and the interpretation of it.

Once you know who your target is, you begin building media lists. These include names of appropriate editors, reporters, news directors, assignment editors, media outlets, addresses, and contact numbers. From this list you contact and visit the media who are crucial to your campaign. If you want to mail fact sheets, press releases, or press kits, you can hire a company that sells media mailing lists and you can pay them or another firm to do your mailing for you. If that is beyond your budget, calling the editorial department of a newspaper or a newsroom will get you the contact numbers of the people you seek to reach and you can put your mailing together yourself. During your campaign, it is also important that you search for allies. Allies are businesses and organizations that have similar goals to yours. Your state's Tourism/Travel Promotion Office can be a great resource. This office is working year-round to bring business and leisure guests to your state. These, of course, are your prospective customers. Your state's travel promotion officials will be happy to give you advice on how to tie in with their advertising, PR, and other promotional programs.

Most states also have a Business/Economic Development Department that will be happy to help you, since their goal is to create new business in your state. Their mailing list will keep you informed of planned promotions. When meeting with state officials it is a good idea to volunteer to assist their promotional and PR programs. Doing so gets you "in the loop" and ahead of your competition because you will know about the programs your state is developing. Hotel and restaurant associations can also prove to be valuable allies, since they have PR people on staff or use national PR agencies.

There are a number of national travel industry organizations that work privately to generate travel in the United States. They are natural allies. Locally, your Chamber of Commerce may organize familiarization (fam) trips to your area. These are trips for travel writers and travel agents that showcase the attributes of your area. Let the organization arranging the "fam" trip know that you are willing to offer free accommodations or meals to the visiting journalists and travel agents. If you are selected, make sure time is allotted for a guided tour of your property, led by your most knowledgeable manager or salesperson. Present each guest with a press kit. Also mail press kits to the agents after the tour, since most of them prefer to travel light but accumulate tons of literature and souvenirs on their trips. Making a good impression with travel agents and writers is great for you because their third-party endorsement is the best kind of advertising.

When these agents and writers do visit, make sure that your establishment is in tip-top shape. Your visitors will probably be visiting numerous other hotels and restaurants and you want to stand out in every (positive) way. Only the most memorable hotels and restaurants will be on their "recommended" list and you want to be one of them.

Suppliers can also be a huge ally because the more business you do, the more orders you send them for their products or services. Airlines, tourist attractions, liquor distributors, wholesalers can all be allies. They often offer attractive packages of lower room rates, food costs, car rentals. Prices are usually deeply discounted to draw customers who would otherwise not use one of the packaged services. These packages are a great promotion and often garner notice from travel publications and consumer sections of newspapers eager to report a great deal. Also, airlines, car rental companies, and cruise lines have PR departments that can help design and implement your PR program.

SPECIAL EVENTS

Special events can be very effective in generating publicity and community interest. You may be opening a new property or celebrating a renovation or an anniversary. Any such occasions are opportunities to plan a special event that will support or improve your PR program. There are usually two kinds of special events: one-time and ongoing. Obviously you are not going to have a groundbreaking ceremony annually, but you might have a famous Fourth of July party every year.

The key question to ask when designing a special event is "why?" Clearly defining your objectives before you start is crucial. Is your goal to improve community opinion of your business? To present yourself as a good employer? To show off a renovation? Once these needs have been clearly defined, a timetable and schedule of events can be made. Ample time is necessary, since contractors, inspection agencies, and civil officials may be involved. If you are planning an anniversary celebration, research what events were going on in your community when you opened: Was there a huge fire? Had the civil war just ended? Did Dwight Eisenhower speak at the local college? Once you have this information, send it to the press. They will see your event as part of the historical landscape — as opposed to a commercial endeavor that benefits only you — and they will appreciate your community focus.

Special events require preparation to ensure everything is ready when the spotlight is turned on. Be certain the day you have chosen does not conflict with another, competing, event or fall on an inappropriate holiday. With a groundbreaking or opening of a new property, you should invite the developer, architect, interior designer, civic officials, and the media. You should prepare brief remarks and ask the architect to comment on the property. In your remarks, remind your listeners that the addition of your business does not boost school taxes or increase the need for police and fire protection; it adds new jobs and new tax revenues. If you are celebrating an opening, tours of the property are a must and should be led by your most personable employees. Refreshments should be served and, in many cases, lunch or dinner is provided. Whatever your occasion, you should provide press kits to the attending media and mail them to all media that were invited. Souvenirs are a good idea — they can be simple or elaborate, but should always be creative, fun, and useful to your guests.

THE VALUE OF LOYALTY

Obviously how you relate to your guests affects their opinion of you. That opinion then translates into potential loyalty and loyalty boosts your bottom line. In fact, a 5 percent improvement in customer retention translates into a 15 to 50 percent boost in profits.

Those are serious numbers. In common terms, that simply means getting your regular customers to return one more time per month. Furthermore, it costs about five times as much to attract a new customer as it does to retain an existing one. This is another huge benefit of loyalty to your bottom line and it comes through the overall commitment your establishment makes to its repeat customers. Focusing on your repeat customers — your most profitable clients — allows you to keep them coming back. Two things to focus on for retaining clients:

1. **Pay attention to your most profitable clients.** Listen. Keep in touch. Find out what they want and need and why they have chosen you.

2. **If they go to the competition, find out why.**

Brief, succinct comment cards where guests rate your service, facilities, etc., can be a great way to find out what they think of you. You can offer discounts or promotional items for the return of these cards. If you do use a comment card, the one question that must be there is, "Would you return to have dinner with us again?" If you get "no's," take immediate action to determine why and then fix the situation.

If your restaurant is located in a hotel, there are infinite ways for you to make your guests' stay more enjoyable and to show you appreciate them. Pamphlets describing local attractions in your community help guests plan their activities (and may entice them to extend their stay). First-aid kits, warm towels, water bottles with your logo on them — anything that makes things more convenient and enjoyable — will distinguish you from the competition. On a larger scale, whenever possible, provide upgrades; let customers know you appreciate them, inform them of services that may be useful to them, and go above and beyond what they expect from you. By doing this, you not only increase the chances of their returning, you increase the chances of them telling their friends about how well they were treated. This will bring in new and, if treated well, soon-to-be-loyal customers.

Many hotels and restaurants have established frequent-stay/diner plans that are similar to airline frequent-flyer plans. Customers accrue "points" or "dollars" towards food, merchandise, upgrades, or free rooms. Many hotels even have tie-ins with airlines that allow guests to earn frequent-flyer miles through their stay. These are great customer loyalty plans but are out of reach for many smaller operations. There are, however, many things smaller organizations can do to build loyalty. Here are a few:

- **Build a database** (or at least a mailing list) of your customers.

- **Track purchases and behavior**: food preferences, table preferences, entertainment needs, and special needs.

- **Constantly update your information** based on interactions with your customers.

- **Recognize birthdays, anniversaries, and special occasions.**

- **Show your appreciation** through holiday greetings, special discounts, and other forms of recognition.

- **Thank your customers** for their business.

- **Whenever you can, individualize your communications.**

- **Listen to and act on customer suggestions.**

- **Inform guests on new or improved services.**

- **Tell guests of potential inconveniences,** like renovations, and stress their future benefits.

- **Answer every inquiry**, including complaints.

- **Accommodate all reasonable requests** for meal substitutions, table changes, etc.

- **Empower employees to solve problems.**

- **Talk to your customers and employees** so you can let them know you are listening and find out what is going on.

This last point — the back and forth between guests and employees and you — is enormously important. Just as you need to focus on getting your message to your guests, you also need to focus on getting their messages to you. If they think their opinions are important to you, they will think they are important to you — and they will come back. People have more choices than ever about where to spend their money. If they know their individual needs will be met and that they will be taken care of, their choice will be to spend it with you.

EMPLOYEE RELATIONS IS ALSO PUBLIC RELATIONS

You cannot succeed in the hospitality industry if your employees do not deliver excellent service. They have the most daily contact with your customers and are therefore responsible for the opinion — positive or negative — people have of your establishment. Therefore, one of the most important "publics" that your public relations program should focus on is your staff.

Customers want to be taken care of and they judge a business as much on the quality of the service as the product. Basically, if a member of your wait staff is grumpy or tired, that is bad PR. Therefore; employee relations should be a main focus of your PR campaign. In order to do this you must have a well-trained staff that understands the technical ins and outs of their jobs and also believes in your organization's mission. Your employees need to know the high level of service your customers expect and they need to be empowered to deliver it. A staff that does this on an ongoing basis is one that generates repeat business through word-of-mouth referrals. And that is good PR.

Keeping your employees informed is a key way of making them feel involved and building positive feelings between staff and management. The following is a list of things to communicate to your staff:

1. **How your business is doing** and what you are planning.

2. **How the competition is doing** and what you are planning.

3. **What community issues** you are concerned about and taking a role in.

4. **Recent personnel changes.**

5. **Who is booked in the future**: private parties, conventions, social events, etc.

6. **Available training and job openings.**

7. **Staff weddings, birthdays, significant accomplishments, or happenings.**

Communicating this information gives employees the sense that you care and creates a unified work atmosphere where great service becomes a group responsibility. It also shows that you recognize the difference they make to your bottom line and that you are paying attention to them.

Opening the lines of communication between management and staff is the next step. No one knows the intimate ins and outs of your business like your staff. If they care about your business and know your ears are open, they can be your biggest resource in suggesting improvements and letting you know what is really going on. One-on-one meetings with supervisors, group meetings, employee newsletters, orientation/review sessions, and training meetings are all effective ways to open the channels of conversation between you and your employees. These sessions let them know you care and encourage them to make the biggest difference they can.

An ongoing employee appreciation program is a good idea. Create a structure that is a part of your daily operation: a large bulletin board in a high-traffic area or a monthly party where awards and prizes are given (cash, great parking spaces, etc.). Give employees something to wear (e.g., a recognition pin) that signifies acknowledgement of the services they provide. Be creative and find something that effectively and continuously supports the goals of both your employee relations program and your overall PR plan.

TALKING TO YOUR COMMUNITY

All business is local. This is especially true in the restaurant business. While you could make the argument that a large portion of your business comes from out of town, it is still your local community that needs to believe in the value of your business. Restaurants that are not accepted by their local communities disappear. Also, you will not find a prosperous restaurant in a depressed area. Your community and you are one and the same and it is crucial to remember this as you design your PR program.

Restaurants are often considered hubs of their communities. They offer facilities for meetings, banquets, conventions, and other important social/economic functions. Many decisions that affect the future of local economies take place in these facilities, so it is easy to see how and why a hotel or restaurant cannot be successful unless the local community accepts it.

So, what does that mean to the restaurant GM? It does not simply mean that you should help support good causes. It means your business needs to be a leader in its community. In practice this means building bridges between your company and your community to maintain and foster your environment in a way that benefits both you and the community. Basically, your goal is to make your immediate world a better place in which everybody can thrive. The following are a few ideas that can be part of an effective community relations program:

- **Fill a community need** — Create something that wasn't there before.

- **Remove something** that causes a community problem.

- **Include "have-nots"** in something that usually excludes them.

- **Share your space, equipment, or expertise.**

- **Offer tutoring** or otherwise mobilize your workforce as a helping hand.

- **Promote your community elsewhere.**

Being a good citizen is, of course, crucial, but you also need to convince your community of the value of your business. Most businesses provide jobs and pay taxes in their communities. Restaurants do these in spades because, despite technological advances, they are still labor-intensive businesses. Per dollar of income, they probably provide employment for more residents of your community than any other business. Also — and remind your community of this — hotels and restaurants not only attract visitors from all over the country and, perhaps, the world, but most hotel income is from money earned outside your community and is spent in it.

These are real benefits and they should be integrated into the message you send by being a good citizen. Designing this message is a straightforward but remarkably effective process:

1. **List the things your establishment brings to the community**: jobs, taxes, well-maintained architecture, etc.

2. **List what your business receives from its community**: employees, fire and police protection, trash removal, utilities, etc.

3. **List your business's complaints about your community**: high taxes, air pollution, noise pollution, narrow roads, etc.

Once you have outlined these items, look for ways your business can lead the way in improving what does not work. As you do this, consult with your local Chamber of Commerce or Visitors' Bureau. They may be able to integrate you into existing community betterment programs aimed at your objectives.

PLANNING FOR THE UNFORESEEN

If done well, your community relations program will create positive opinions in your community. In turn, this will cause local residents to recommend you as the place to eat when asked by tourists; it will encourage people to apply for jobs and may encourage suppliers to seek to do business with you. Also, if there is an emergency at your establishment, having a positive standing in the community will enable your property to be treated fairly.

An effective community relations program is a win-win situation because it gives you the opportunity to be a deep and abiding member of your community — improving the quality of life and opportunities around you — and, at the same time, contributes significantly to your bottom line.

Emergencies make bad news stories. Bad news stories are bad PR and they can destroy the image you have worked so hard to build. They can wipe away years of hard-won customer relations. There are numerous kinds of emergencies — earthquakes, fires, floods, political protests, crime, and more — and any of these events, if not managed properly, can destroy your public image. The law insists you have fire prevention programs and insurance, but there is no one forcing you to create a crisis–public relations program in case of emergency.

In order to meet a PR emergency, you must prepare now. If you have a strategy developed in advance, then when something bad does happen, you assure the most accurate, objective media coverage of the event. It is important that all your employees are aware of this plan and that they are reminded of it regularly. Since your employees generate a huge amount of your PR, it is crucial for them to know how to act and what to say — and not say — during a crisis. This simple detail can make all the difference in the world. Here are three basic aspects to an emergency press relations plan:

1. **Your general manager or owner should be the only spokesperson during the time of the emergency.** Make sure your employees know not to talk to the press and to refer all inquiries to the general manager or publicity coordinator. Make sure the GM is available at all times, day or night.

2. **Know the facts** of the situation before answering questions from the media.

3. **Initiate contact.**

Once the story is out, do not wait for the media to call you. This way you will ensure that they get accurate information. Plus, the media will appreciate your forthcoming attitude and your cooperation will reflect in their reporting.

The media will always ask the same who, what, when, where, why, and how questions. Knowing this and being prepared to anticipate their questions, you should be able to answer accurately. If you do not know the answer to a question, do not say, "No comment." Explain why you cannot comment: The police are investigating, for example, and you do not have enough information to answer now but you will try to find the answer and get back to them. Make a point to do as promised.

In times of crisis it is crucial to put a positive slant on the news. Try to focus press attention on the diligent efforts of management to handle the emergency or on employees whose compassion and assistance made a difference. If something happens in your establishment that is not your fault and your establishment handles it well, it is an opportunity to showcase your heart and responsiveness.

The importance of a crisis-PR plan cannot be overstated. When an employee is injured or killed in your establishment or a guest suffers from food poisoning, the public assumes you are guilty. Whether or not you are even mildly at fault, people assume you are. Therefore, how you handle public relations during this time means the difference between a temporary loss of public support or the permanent loss of a great deal of business.

One always hopes that a crisis-PR plan remains unnecessary. Unfortunately, given the amount of hotel and restaurant accidents, mishaps, and disasters every year, being prepared for the worst is the best policy. Furthermore, while the entire establishment suffers during an emergency, the general manager who was caught unprepared suffers the most. Therefore, after calling the police, fire department, etc., it is the GM's job to immediately find out what happened and take corrective actions. If the event warrants it, you should set up a room with a phone as a command post, then communicate to all your employees what you want them to do and not do. As part of your plan, your employees should know where flashlights are in case evacuation is necessary and they should be ready to guide guests to the nearest exits.

Next, the media must be contacted and the story disclosed, put into context, and told from your side. If the media gets all the information they need from you quickly, this increases the chances of the incident appearing as one story and not showing up again. If it is difficult for reporters to gather information and they need to seek other sources, the story may be spaced out over time, which will increase people's chances of seeing it. This is obviously not what you want.

Having built strong media relations pays off during an emergency. A reporter you have a good relationship with may report an incident at a "local restaurant," while one less acquainted with you — or downright hostile — will mention you specifically and push for the story to be on the front page. This is a crucial difference. It means that the person who will be the media liaison during an emergency should be building and nurturing good media relations now, in case anything does happen. And what have you got to lose? Strong media relations benefit you all the time.

All this is to say that if you do not guide the flow of information around your news event, somebody else will misguide it for you. With proper PR, a story that appears to the public, like a seafood restaurant that did not have any fresh seafood, can be authentically retold to show how the restaurant was the victim of a vendor's warehouse fire. You can shift the public from viewing you as incompetent to having more faith than ever in your establishment. Public opinion depends on how effectively you manage information and how well you get your story across.

For more information about promoting your restaurant I recommend the following books from Atlantic Publishing (**www.atlantic-pub.com**).

- *Superior Customer Service: How to Keep Customers Racing Back to Your Business – Time Tested Examples from Leading Companies* (Item # SCS-01).

- *Getting Clients and Keeping Clients for Your Service Business: A 30 Day Step by Step Plan for Building Your Business* (Item # GCK-01).

- *The Food Service Professional Guide to Building Restaurant Profits* (Item # FS9-01).

- *The Food Service Professional Guide to Restaurant Marketing and Advertising* (Item # FS3-01).

- *The Food Service Professional Guide to Restaurant Promotion and Publicity* (Item # FS4-01).

- *The Food Service Professional Guide to Increasing Restaurant Sales* (Item # FS15-01).

CHAPTER

HOW TO KEEP CUSTOMERS COMING BACK FOR MORE

Profitability is going to keep you in business. How and where you focus to become and stay profitable is the key. Are you crunching numbers and pushing your servers to raise their check averages or are you creating an environment that leaves patrons feeling served and eager to come back? Are you holding staff meetings that leave your crew energized or deflated? Are management, kitchen, and wait staffs working independently or as a team toward a common goal? This chapter will give you insights into how and where you can make changes to boost your sales volume 15 to 50 percent.

CUSTOMERS FOR LIFE

Take care of your guests and your sales will take care of themselves. "Customers for life" means that once guests come to your restaurant, they will never be satisfied with your competitors. Simple, right? It also means that the real work of building sales does not happen with your advertising schedule or marketing plan, but on the floor with your customers.

The key to building restaurant sales is to increase volume from your existing customer base. Think about it: If your customers return just one more time per month, that would increase sales volume 15 to 50 percent. These are people who already know about you, live within an acceptable travel distance, and will recommend you to their friends if you make them happy. These are the people you want to target in order to build a regular, loyal customer base — a customer base that shares the pleasures of your establishment with friends. Work on building loyalty, not the check average.

A WORD OF CAUTION

It is true: A bigger check is a bigger sale. However, selling techniques designed to boost check averages can be dangerous if customers feel they are being pressured. Guests come first. Your income comes from serving people, not food. Focusing only on the bottom line or a higher check average puts your customers second. If all who eat at your restaurant are so pleased that they cannot wait to come back with their friends, what will your sales be like? If eating with you was not a thrill, if they felt pressured to order something expensive or a dessert they did not want, the big check makes no difference when they do not come back.

KNOW WHAT YOUR PATRONS WANT

The type of restaurant that you manage dictates the types of side items that will appeal to your customers. An escargot appetizer plate will not appeal to your clients if you operate a family-style restaurant that features chicken-fried steak with mashed potatoes and gravy. But how do you figure out what your patrons want on the menu?

Here is how:

- **Experiment with your menu.** Discover what works by doing a monthly sales tally of every side item on your menu. Doing so will help weed out the items that are not being recognized. Highlight the "winning" items on your menu and advertise them wherever you can.

- **Learn from trends.** Always check out restaurant reviews in your local newspapers and magazines. Keep up to date on what is hot in restaurants across the country. Web sites such as **www.martinsnet.com/restaurantlinks.asp** are great sources of information about what is happening in the restaurant business.

- **Make them feel special.** Whenever you have a slow period, have a server take a cart around with a sampling of a new dish you are considering serving. Ask patrons to give their opinions on the items. They will appreciate the consideration — and the freebie.

- **Stimulate the appetite with sub-menu items.** Use glowing adjectives to describe side items: "Our Cokes are served in ice-cold frosty mugs." Place "menu tents" with colorful photos of your featured desserts on the table. These methods are sure to get your sub-menu items noticed. You can order table tents from **www.armsco.com** in a variety of styles — from acrylic to leather.

- **Advertise your specialty items.** Advertise (without spending a dime) with tactics like placing items such as desserts in a showcase at the entrance of your restaurant. You can have exact replicas made of your dishes from **www.trengovestudios.com** so that you do not have to keep restocking.

PAY ATTENTION AND DELIGHT CUSTOMERS

EXPECTATIONS

Satisfaction is not even close to good enough. It is an improvement on dissatisfaction, but in today's market, it will not keep people coming back. There is just too much competition. You need to exceed your guests' expectations every time. The food-service business is built on personal connections. You serve one person at a time, and the more personal that interaction, the more you will exceed his or her expectations — and the happier he or she will be.

Here is a list of basic guest expectations and some hints on how to meet and exceed them:

- **Guests expect hot food hot and cold food cold.** Serve cold food on a chilled — not frozen — plate. Try removing your heat lamps altogether: they do not keep food hot and they can cause your staff to delay in getting food to your guests.

- **From order to delivery, guests expect their drinks within two minutes, appetizers in five to ten, entrees in 15 to 25, and dessert in three to five minutes.** Check turnaround should take no more than two minutes. At the beginning and end of a meal guests are the least tolerant of delays. Make sure your staff does not keep customers waiting after they have been seated or when they are ready to leave.

- **Guests expect their servers to know the menu**, how dishes are prepared, and the wine list.

- **Guests expect restaurant staff to care.**

Do you know what your customers expect when they come through the door? Are you out to exceed those expectations and give each guest a memorable and delightful meal every time?

WAYS TO DELIGHT

Customers are delighted when you care — it is as simple as that. Doing things that demonstrate you care will make a difference. Part of the trick here is that there is no trick. You must be sincere. People know when they are being treated with sincerity or with a mechanical technique. Here is a list of practices that can make your guests feel valued and distinguish you from the competition:

- **Umbrellas when it rains.** Is it possible that, given the weather patterns in your area, your guests could arrive without an umbrella, only to find it raining as they are leaving? Offer them umbrellas to help them get to their cars or offices. It is a great incentive to have them come back at a later date to return the umbrella. Put your name and logo on the umbrella and maybe it is not the worst thing if they forget to bring it back.

- **Free stuff while they wait.** People tolerate a wait when they have a complimentary glass of wine or warm cider to keep them toasty or the local paper or magazine to read. They will appreciate you going the extra mile and this gives them something to tell their friends.

- **Free local calls with a portable phone**, a huge convenience to guests, allowing them to change travel plans or contact friends at almost no cost to you. Let customers know it is a service you offer.

- **Owner or manager on the floor.** People like to meet the person in charge. They appreciate that someone important is checking in on them.

- **Give people something for nothing.** Got some new menu items coming up next week? Why not give away free samples today to whet people's appetites? There is nothing customers like more than something for free — another great way to distinguish yourself from the competition.

- **Books, magazines, newspapers for single diners.** If you draw or want to draw single diners, have reading materials available — and a staff that knows how to offer them politely.

- **Free postcards and postage.** Do a lot of tourist business? If your guests are waiting— or even if they are not — why not give them stamped postcards (depicting your restaurant, of course) for sending their "Wish you were here" messages? It is a very low price to pay for advertising all over the world.

- **Fax directions to guests.** Have a clear map on hand when guests ask for directions to your restaurant. Offer to fax it to them. If they do not have a fax, have the directions on your Web site.

- **House camera.** If guests are celebrating but forgot a camera, have an instant camera or disposable on hand and snap a few shots for them to take home. Or, you can use a high quality digital camera and offer to e-mail guests their pictures. Not only will this please your guests, it will help you build a database of customers' e-mail addresses.

- **Armchairs for the elderly.** It is harder for the elderly to get in and out of their chairs. If you serve a lot of elderly customers, or even a few, have chairs with arms to make it easier for them to get in and out. Let them know you did it just for them. They will certainly appreciate it.

- **Guest book.** Make sure your guests fill in the guest book: You need a mailing list of your patrons to send them promotional material. Try to collect e-mail addresses, birth dates, and anniversaries for your database, as well.

WORD OF MOUTH

Positive word of mouth is the best advertising there is. But does it just come from serving great food? Yes and no. Do you have a deliberate, creative, and authentic plan to create great word of mouth? Guests will not talk about you unless they are thinking about you. You have to educate your guests on why they come to you. You must create points of difference between you and your competitors. Then people can tell their friends about why they eat at your restaurant.

An effective word-of-mouth program has five main goals:

1   Inform and educate your patrons.

2. Make the guest a salesperson for your restaurant.

3. Give guests reasons to return.

4 Make your service unique and personal.

5. Distinguish your business from the competition.

CREATING POINTS OF DIFFERENCE

You must distinguish yourself from the competition to get your guests to return one extra time a month and to tell their friends and family about you. You do that by creating "points of difference." What is different about your establishment, your concept, your type of food, and your combination of dishes? Do you guarantee your service?

Do you give free wine to waiting customers; have an organic vegetable garden in the back; put ice in your urinals and the sports page above them? What makes your place memorable and different from the competition? Here is a partial list of things that every restaurant offers and a few suggestions on how you can create points of difference with them:

- **Water.** Serve local spring water or imported bottled water or simply filter your tap water so it tastes good. Put a lemon slice or flower petal in the glass or carafe.

- **Soft drinks.** Serve bottled drinks instead of post mix. Have an extensive selection and offer free refills.

- **Salad.** Have unusual, local, and/or organic ingredients and dressings. Serve them in unique or oversized bowls. Serve chilled salads on chilled plates with chilled forks.

- **Restrooms.** Have twice as many restrooms for women. It tends to take them longer; why should they have to wait?

- **Beer.** Have a large microbrew menu, an extensive beer list, and local brews. Serve beer in exotic glassware, personalized mugs, or numerous bottles in a bucket of ice.

Certainly not all of these are appropriate for every restaurant, but finding a great way to distinguish yourself — often through a mishap or brilliantly ridiculous staff idea — is a great way to give your place a real identity and give your customers something to talk about.

EDUCATING GUESTS ON THE DIFFERENCES

Having a great idea in place is not enough; you have to inform your customers about it and give them the words they can then pass on. A customer telling his friends he had a great time is great. A customer telling his friends he had the best salad ever because you have an organic garden in the back and the lettuce was picked five minutes before his salad was prepared is worth his weight in gold. Details differentiate your product and make yours the place to go for something extraordinary.

How do you get this information across? Arm your staff with words they can comfortably work into a conversation. Do you offer a full menu until midnight? When guests call and ask how late you are open, say, "Dave's Café serves a full menu until midnight. We are the only place in town that does that." If a guest comes in at 11 p.m. wondering if you are still open, say, "Not only are we open, we serve a full menu until closing at midnight."

Over time your customers will be saying, "Dave's serves a full menu until midnight — let's go there."

An effective word-of-mouth program not only creates points of difference between you and the competition; it educates your guests on those distinctions. If you give your customers a great experience and the words to describe it, they will talk about it to their friends.

INCENTIVES

Incentives work because people are rewarded for what they are doing. It is as simple as that. Reward customers for coming back and they will. There are three basic ways to do this: discounts, promotions, and customer loyalty programs.

DISCOUNTS

An effective deal gives your guests a discount and generates more profit for you. How? By making a sale you would not have made otherwise. Is a customer buying a discounted lobster dinner that, even with the discount, has a 40 percent profit margin, instead of the salmon that she would have ordered that has a 30 percent profit margin? Then she is getting a deal and you are making more money. Are your business card drawings giving customers a chance to buy drinks at half price and bringing in more than twice the business? Are your drawings bringing people in right after work when they are hungry or making your bar the first place people think of to go for a drink after work?

Internal coupons can be a great way to increase repeat business. Three of the most widely used are:

1. **Courtesy coupons.** These are wallet-sized coupons that your staff carries. They can be issued to guests and used on return visits. They are great if a guest has a complaint or is put out somehow or they can be used to reward customers for their ongoing patronage.

2. **Cross-marketing coupons.** If you have very fast and very slow meal periods, why not offer a discount to customers if they return during the slower time? If you do a great lunch business, for instance, give people a free dessert if they come for dinner on a Tuesday.

3. **Companion coupons.** Encourage your regulars to bring a friend. You can offer a special group of dishes to be shared among four people, a free bottle of wine, or free appetizers for two or more.

PROMOTIONS

Five great promotional opportunities are birthdays, anniversaries, holidays, special events, and festivals.

BIRTHDAYS AND ANNIVERSARIES

Do you have an irresistible offer for patrons who celebrate their birthdays or anniversaries with you? You can get the dates of their special occasions when they sign up for your Frequent Diner Plan. With this information you can invite them to celebrate with you. Have your offer valid for the entire month of the actual date because people need some flexibility in planning their special events.

HOLIDAYS

The beauty of the holidays is that someone else advertises them. You do not have to tell your guests Thanksgiving is coming, but you could put a flyer in with their check that lets them know how fun it will be — and what a great deal they will get — if they spend it with you.

SPECIAL EVENTS

Special events can be a great way to promote business and goodwill. Have you thought of hosting a cigar dinner, a winemaker dinner, or a charity fundraiser? If a cigar event would fit your restaurant, it is a great way to combine high-priced cigars with fine wine and spirits. Hold a wine tasting early in the evening on a slow night of the week. You can showcase the knowledge of your sommelier or wine steward and afterwards guests can stay for dinner.

A CHARITY FUNDRAISER

A charity fundraiser can be a way to gain exposure for your restaurant that pays off for everyone. It will improve your image and distinguish you from competitors. It does not have to be a break-even venture either, because you only give a portion of the proceeds to the cause. Spirits distributors and other suppliers often give free or discounted products for such events, which could lower your costs and even bring heavy marketing muscle to your event. The charity will also promote you to its supporters, which can bring new people through your door who want to support your business.

FESTIVALS

Festivals are great reasons to invite guests to come back and they are great things for guests to talk about. They highlight specific cuisines or products and can be a great way to stir things up for staff and customers alike. You can run a festival on a specific night or for a specific time period — usually a week or two. Make sure that the festival you hold is right for your establishment and that it is run frequently enough to break up your routine, but infrequently enough to remain special. Do a memorable job and build a strong foundation for future events.

Highlighting regional cuisines is a great idea, with foods, wines, and recipes from another culture, as well as music, decorations, costumes, posters — you name it. You could have a guest chef from the celebrated country during your festival. Contact the country's embassy for ideas.

Product festivals usually coincide with seasonal items — raspberries, corn, etc. — when the items are abundant and cheaper. Off-season festivals can be great for word of mouth — if you can find the product. People will love a fresh strawberry festival in January. Regional food items like ribs, oysters, and lobster work great with various appetizers, salads, and soups and can make a dynamite festival.

T-shirts are a wonderful way to promote your event and business whether you give them to customers or have your staff members wear them. You could hold a drawing each week and award a t-shirt to one customer. It is a great way to get business cards from customers, or e-mail addresses for other promotional pieces. One business that offers custom t-shirts to include your logo or other information is **www.campuscollection.net/custom. php3** or call 800-BUY-T-SHIRTS (800-289-8744).

You may want to have special glasses for your event. Berry Plastics offers a wide selection of disposable plastic cups which are great if you have a self-serve beverage area. These cups offer high clarity, are crack resistant, decorative, and have a sleek design. The Web site is **www.berryplastics.com**.

CUSTOMER LOYALTY PROGRAMS

These programs can be a huge benefit to your business. Rewarding your customers for continued loyalty gives them added incentive to choose you over the competition. They come in variations of these three basic forms:

1. **Punch cards.** Punched every time guests purchase a product. When they purchase a certain number of items they receive something for free. The biggest plus of punch cards is their ease to produce. The biggest negative is the ease with which they can be altered. Keeping the guests' cards, or duplicate cards, on premises can help counter fraud.

2. **Point systems.** These are often dollar-for-point systems, in which a customer accrues points towards free food or merchandise. Point systems are a great way for guests to "eat their way" towards a free bicycle or dinner for four. A point system is more complicated to implement than a punch card system, often including outside vendors.

3. **Percentage-of-purchase programs.** The closest type to airline programs, with guests paying full price for items while accruing dollar credits for future meals. It gets people in the habit of thinking of their purchases as having a larger than normal value and keeps them coming to you.

These programs are all ways to monitor your guests' patronage, reward them for coming back, and increase your opportunities to delight them with your food and service..

PEOPLE, PEOPLE, PEOPLE

PRESENCE

The food-service business is about personal connection. People want to be treated as individuals; they will repeatedly do business in a place that makes this connection.

Multitasking, doing many things at once, has been accepted as effective in today's society. The same cannot be said of the restaurant business. If you are taking a phone reservation, putting tonight's specials on the board, and talking to your new waiter, how much real attention will any of those tasks get? Do you think the potential guest on the phone, or your waiter, will feel well treated? Will you have time to check the spelling on the specials board?

The truth is that you can only focus on one thing at a time. Drop distractions, handle each item individually, and then move on to the next. Presence is simply a lack of distraction. If you act distracted with your staff, they will keep asking the same questions or come to you with the same problems. If you are distracted around your guests, they will not come back. .

APPRECIATION

If you recognize your customers and make them feel important, it will draw them closer to your restaurant and further differentiate you in their eyes. The following list touches on a few tried-and-true examples. Many can be done at little or no cost.

- **Put your customers in your newsletter** (You can have either a print or an e-mail version).

- **Put them on a Wall of Fame** or "Outstanding Customer" plaques.

- **Give your regulars awards** and honor people in your community who make a difference through charitable work.

- **Name menu items after guests.** Customers love this and who knows what soon-to-be famous dishes are cooking in their minds?

- **Personalize booths or seats.**

- **Put guests' names up on your bulletin board.**

GETTING TO KNOW YOUR GUESTS

In a business that lives and dies on personal connection, getting to know your guests is crucial. Go beyond the procedures of service, and start thinking of your guests as individuals. There is a difference between serving 200 dinners and serving Steve and Mary Carson on their 30th wedding anniversary or doing a fundraiser for the Friends of the Museum of Science.

Numbers are important, but your relationship to your customers drives your business. Furthermore, the two easiest things to learn about your customers are also the most useful: who they are and what they like.

People love it when you remember who they are. It instantly makes them feel like insiders and makes them feel important in the eyes of their friends. Remember "Norm!" in Cheers? Norm felt pretty comfortable and he definitely came back. As a manager you probably know your regulars by name, but do you have a system in place that teaches your new staff who these important folks are? If you were a regular customer at a restaurant and a waitress you had never seen came up and greeted you by name, wouldn't you feel like a celebrity?

You can train your servers to write the guest's name on the back of the check so they can refer to it throughout the meal or you can have your greeter put guests' names on their checks when they arrive. However you do it, keeping servers using guests' names will help them remember the names in the future. It will continually remind wait staff that they are serving people — not anonymous mouths.

The next step is to find out what your customers want. You must ask them and remember what you have been told and what you have observed. If a customer is allergic to a certain ingredient, next visit offer to make a dish that is not on the menu. Remember the customer seated too close to the air conditioner; seat him away from it next time.

Small note cards kept about regular guests can make this possible. The cards hold information about customers' likes and dislikes, patterns, and desires — all the information necessary to treat them like royalty. You can even reward your servers for adding to the cards each time a guest dines. Throughout this process it is very important never to pry: Respect your customer's privacy. If a customer was reticent to share about his life, a savvy server would note on the biography card not to ask too many questions. In this case, you are serving your customer's preferences by leaving him alone. Either way, you are finding out what your guests want and giving it to them.

CLUBS

Clubs can be a great way of treating your regulars like individuals by giving them privileges or paraphernalia other customers do not have. If you sell draft beer, here are a few ideas for having a great and effective Mug Club:

1. **Keep the mugs or glasses on display**, so "Mug Clubbers" have to come in to use them.

2. **Make the mugs so distinctive** that other customers ask about them and the people with the mugs feel special.

3. **Put customers' names on their mugs.**

4. **Give them a deal: cheaper product**, more for the same price, or another incentive.

Do you sell oysters, ribs, or wings? Or anything else that could be a club that people would join? Through these clubs, customers can accrue points towards a prize. They could get a discount on appetizers and a free golf cap after they have eaten, say, 300 ribs. Clubs are a great way to distinguish your products, distinguish your guests, and give your guests a sense of belonging. The results will benefit your bottom line.

TAFF

Your food and staff keep your customers coming back. The quality of service your customers receive will determine their opinion of your restaurant. Your staff is who delights your guests or not, who gives them things to talk about, and who provides the crucial personal connection. Staff will: execute most of your sales promotions and programs; educate your customers about what makes your rib joint better than the one down the street; and give your guests information they can pass on to their friends.

It is in your wait staff's best interests to connect with customers, because through that connection their tip averages will go up. If you want your staff to be gracious, to listen, and to delight your guests, you have to do the same for them.

Take the pressure off your staff to get the check averages up. Instead, encourage them to commit to serving their customers' needs so they return one more time per month, thus increasing their monthly tips by 50 percent. Also, guests who know their wait persons usually leave higher tips. As your wait staff gets to know their customers, they will see increased revenue through repeat business. Here is a partial list of basic things your wait staff can do to make a personal connection and up their tip averages:

- **Greet guests within a minute.** Do not leave them waiting. Waiting negatively affects a customer's mood and her mood is going to directly affect the tip.

- **Make eye contact.** Do not stare at the table, the floor, or the artwork on the wall. Clear your head, smile, and pay attention. Make sure you are at the table when you are talking. Do not talk to your guests as you are flying by. It makes people feel unimportant.

- **Do not think about the tip.** Focus your energy on taking care of your guests, making them happy, doing little things that exceed their expectations and make their meals enjoyable.

- **Encourage your guests' food choices.** People can be strange about making decisions. Telling them that you have had what they are ordering and it is great can take away any anxiety they have about making a bad choice.

- **Tell the cooks good news.** Just as you need to be sensitive to the mood of your guests, be sensitive to the mood of the kitchen crew. The cooks do not want to hear about things just when they are wrong. Pass along good news to them and they will make it easier for you to take great care of your guests.

- **Notice lefties.** It is a small thing, but if your guest has moved his water glass and silverware to the other side of his plate, serve his drinks from there. He will appreciate it.

- **Make your movements invisible.** That means move with the speed of the room. Good service is invisible: Food and drinks simply arrive without a thought on the customer's part. If the room is quiet, do not buzz around in it. If it is more upbeat, move a little quicker. You will find fitting in with the atmosphere increases your guest's enjoyment.

- **Ask before refilling coffee.** Coffee drinkers can be very particular about the amount of cream and sugar they have in their coffee. Temperature also matters. Do not top off a cup they may have spent considerable time getting just right.

- **Tell guests about specific events at your restaurant and invite them.** It is more effective to invite guests to return for your rib special on Tuesdays than just to say, "Thanks, come again." While you are at it, invite them to sit at your station.

- **Show gratitude.** People are dealing with a lot in their lives and you have a chance to "make their day." Express gratitude in the tone of your voice when you thank them for their patronage or invite them to come back. Making them feel appreciated will make them remember you during tip time and when they are deciding where to eat next time.

- **Make personal recommendations.** Tell your guests what you like. It is not suggestive selling because it is sincere and will not alienate your guests. Your enthusiasm will be infectious, even if guests do not order what you recommend.

- **Remember: Guests leave good tips because they want to leave good tips.**

As a manager, you can make it easy for your servers to accomplish these goals. Have them taste everything on the menu. Ensure they know how every item is made so they can speak knowledgeably about it. As part of their training they could work in the preparation area for a day or two. If you want them to be able to recommend wines with dishes, they should taste the wines as well. Have a tasting party where everyone gets to know each other and gets an education. Then they will be able to make educated and sincere recommendations. Nothing is more persuasive than a waitperson who knows what he is talking about.

Also, let them use their own words to convey their enthusiasm. It is hard to make a personal recommendation using someone else's words. You want them sharing their enthusiasm, not a canned version of yours. Your crew will find their own way of expressing their enthusiasm. Letting them in on what you sell is the best way to give them something to be enthusiastic about.

A TRULY EFFECTIVE STAFF MEETING

How are you going to impart all this newfound wisdom and good spirit to your staff and how are you going to get them excited about delighting your customers? You need an effective staff meeting.

Most staff meetings are far from invigorating. In fact, they usually result in a drop in energy and a staff that feels like they are on management's bad side. An effective staff meeting is not just a gathering of bodies with one person giving out information; it is a meeting that generates positive feeling in the entire group. An effective staff meeting has three main goals: generating positive group feeling, starting a dialogue and training.

POSITIVE GROUP FEELING

Positive group feeling empowers your staff to discover what it has in common and to think in terms of working together, as opposed to strictly as individuals. Share good news in order to build good feeling. Staff meetings are not a good time to address individual or group shortcomings. Find the positive — even if you need to hunt for it — and talk about it. It builds a supportive feeling and gets people talking.

DIALOGUE

A good dialogue is a comfortable back-and-forth of ideas that gets people connected and leaves your staff feeling that they are a creative part of your restaurant. You learn from the staff and they learn from you. Allowing this flow of ideas reduces or eliminates the "Us vs. Them" mentality in your staff, putting everybody on the same team. Service improves and productivity and profits go up.

TRAINING

Good staff meetings are places to pass on ideas for better performance. Not having staff meetings passes the message that things are as good as they could possibly be. Staff meetings are your chance to effectively pass along tips to your staff and to have them learn from each other. Encouraging staff to share thoughts about work will turn meetings into a forum for discussing ideas. This atmosphere will increase their learning curve dramatically.

You should hold a staff meeting before every shift. If you frequently cancel staff meetings it sends the message that they are not important and that the staff's opinions are equally unimportant. An effective pre-shift meeting should last no longer than 15 minutes. If it is longer, you may lose people's attention — shorter, you will not get enough said. Pick a length, start, and finish on time. Include the kitchen staff as well. It is also a good time to let servers taste today's specials and have the kitchen staff tell the wait staff about them.

FORMAT FOR A 10 TO 15 MINUTE PRE-SHIFT MEETING

How your meeting will go depends on your state of mind. Are you looking at your staff as a group of dedicated people committed to doing a great job or a bunch of layabouts looking to milk the system?

Are you a coach on the playing field seeking to facilitate and encourage people's best performances or a judge looking to identify and punish people's mistakes? Whichever it is, your staff feels it and it will affect the work they do. Get committed to building on people's strengths and holding energizing staff meetings.

- **Good news (one to two minutes).** Acknowledge what works and create a good mood. Find something about the business that shows people doing a good job and making guests happy. Acknowledge the doer or bearer of the news with sincerity.

- **Daily news (two to three minutes).** Outline today's specials and upcoming events.

- **Ask your staff (five minutes).** The most important part of the meeting. It is your opportunity to find out what is really going on in your restaurant and what people are thinking. Listen, do not interrupt with your own thoughts, and do not judge people's comments. Create a safe space for people to sincerely share what is on their minds and to learn from each other. How well you listen directly affects how much they are willing to say. Since they are the restaurant, as well as your access to the nitty-gritty, get them talking. If they are shy, ask them questions: What is working for you guys? What is making things tough? Where have things broken down? What questions from customers have you been unable to answer? Once you get the ball rolling you may find it hard to stop. Good: That means people have things to say and you will benefit. Asking the rest of the staff if they feel the same way as the speaker is a great way to see if there is a group sentiment and to gauge the size of the issue being presented.

- **Training: the latest news (three to five minutes).** If staff comments run over, let it cut into this time. It is important that your staff learn from you, but it is more important for you to learn from them. Plus they will be open to learning from you if they know you are listening to them. Use this time to talk about a single point you want your staff to focus on during this shift, to give out specific knowledge about a product, or to train in another targeted way.

Becoming good at running staff meetings will translate into a feeling of camaraderie among your staff. They will give you true insights into how your business is being run; they will care about how to improve it because they know their suggestions count. You will be more effective because your staff will take weight off your shoulders, helping your restaurant run better.

The food-service business is about personal connection. Getting connected is the way to delight guests and bring them back. Bringing guests back just one time per month will give you a 15 to 50 percent increase in sales volume. If you dedicate your energies towards building an establishment where your servers are treated with respect and gratitude, they will treat you and your customers in the same way. Focus on building an environment that is friendly, helpful, informed, and welcoming and people will come back again and again. Everybody — especially customers — should feel they are on the same page.

Your job is to create a place that people think of first when deciding where to eat and when talking to their friends. You want them telling their friends why they eat there and get hungry for your specials in the process. Again:

- **Concentrate on building loyalty, not a higher check average.** A higher check average will come naturally when the customer has your loyalty. Dedicate your business to delighting your guests.

- **Give your guests something to tell their friends about.**

- **Give customers incentives to return.**

- **Get connected.** Your staff is your restaurant. Get connected with your staff and get them connecting with your guests.

For more information about promoting your restaurant I recommend the following books from Atlantic Publishing (**www.atlantic-pub.com**).

- *Superior Customer Service: How to Keep Customers Racing Back to Your Business – Time Tested Examples from Leading Companies* (Item # SCS-01).

- *Getting Clients and Keeping Clients for Your Service Business: A 30 Day Step-by-Step Plan for Building Your Business* (Item # GCK-01).

- *The Food Service Professional Guide to Building Restaurant Profits* (Item # FS9-01).

- *The Food Service Professional Guide to Restaurant Marketing and Advertising* (Item # FS3-01).

- *The Food Service Professional Guide to Restaurant Promotion and Publicity* (Item # FS4-01).

- *The Food Service Professional Guide to Increasing Restaurant Sales* (Item # FS15-01).

CHAPTER

PROMOTE YOUR RESTAURANT ON THE INTERNET

I n today's market, your restaurant needs a Web site. Every day there are millions of people using the Internet for work, play, shopping, and research. Even if you only want to be the best restaurant in your town or neighborhood, a Web site can be invaluable to you. Anyone can see your Web site, including people moving or traveling to the area. Your Web site can be an excellent tool to promote your restaurant, bring in customers, and even sell promotional items. This chapter will help you develop the most effective restaurant for your business.

Your Web site is a wonderful way to tell people:

- About your restaurant
- What you make
- Where you are located
- Why to buy from you

- Who you are
- Who you serve
- When you are open
- How to place special orders

Your site can also:

- **Be changed quickly.** You do not have to throw out items to make changes. You can also share mouth-watering pictures of your menu items.

- **Be a menu.**

- **Allow people to place orders.**

- **Be any size you want and need.**

- **Be interactive.** Give people a chance to respond to your information.

- **Build community spirit** and promote community and charity events.

- **Sell your specialties** to people around the globe through e-commerce.

Some businesses have password-protected sections to share information with their employees, to explain benefits, and to post work schedules.

You can reach local customers through online city guides and other community-oriented sites where you can place an advertisement, free directory listing, or link to your Web site. Chambers of Commerce, virtual travel guides, and guide sites, including About.com at **www.about.com**, offer chances to promote your business.

These are potential benefits for your business:

- Gather marketing information.
- Evaluate marketing information.
- Generate additional sales.
- Establish meaningful communication with customers and employees.
- Supplement employee training through updates and bulletins.
- Broadcast press releases.
- Submit invoices and expenses more quickly.
- Identify prospective employees.
- Provide immediate access to your menu.
- Permit customers to place orders online.

According to Nielsen ratings, 67.8 percent of the U.S. population uses the Internet. Many people go online to find information about your location and hours. Get listed in the online yellow pages and place ads on sites your customers visit. Include an obvious link to your menu online.

DEVELOP AN INTERNET PLAN

Before designing your Web site or hiring a some one to do it, you need to be prepared. There are three initial steps: research, legal matters, and domain name.

STEP ONE: RESEARCH

First, do some research. Go online and search restaurants in your area. Yahoo's Yellow pages can be a good place to start at **http://yp.yahoo.com**. Note what sites you like and why. Write down the addresses or print out the sites. You can also expand your search to national chains and restaurants outside your area. This will give you a good basis for meeting with a Web developer and serve as reference materials when developing your Web site content.

STEP TWO: LEGAL MATTERS

Have all the legal information needed to take your business online. Some of the legalities that need to be considered include:

- **Copyrights/Trademarks.** It may not seem like an important factor, but liability issues surrounding intellectual property are something that you will want to consider when you are doing business on the Internet. You can visit the U.S. Copyright Office for more information: **www.copyright.gov**.

- **Contracts and licenses.** Before signing any contract, fully understand it. By not paying attention to contracts and licenses, you could end up being liable for any number of things, such as Web hosting regulations. There are several contracts to sign, which include hiring a Web site designer, a programmer, and/or acquiring digital certification.

- **Internet legalities.** Understand all the legal issues of doing business on the Internet. I found a fantastic reference site sponsored by attorney Ivan Hoffman that contains a vast amount of information related to trademarks, domain names, and e-commerce, as well as articles for Web designers, Web site owners, and addresses of many other legal concerns surrounding the Internet. Mr. Hoffman's Web site is located at **www.ivanhoffman.com**.

STEP THREE: YOUR DOMAIN NAME

An important aspect of your Internet business is having your own domain name. A domain name is required to have your Web site hosted. It should uniquely identify your business. The rule of thumb is that the shorter the domain name, the better. It should be relevant to your restaurant. If you have an established corporate name or identity, you should base your domain name on that corporate identity, allowing customers to associate your company name with your domain name (i.e., Great Bear Steakhouse = www.greatbearsteakhouse.com). I recommend you secure any "similar"- sounding domain names, as in the example above, www.greatbearsteakhouse. net, www.greatbearsteakhouse.biz, www.greatbearsteaks.com. Your primary domain name should be the domain name that is "hosted," while others may be parked at no additional cost and pointed to the main domain name URL, allowing you to pay for only one hosted domain name while using many domain names on the Internet.

How do you find out if the domain name you would like is already in use? Visit GoDaddy (**www.godaddy.com**) and type the name you would like into the box "start a domain search". The site will do a search to see if the domain is available and suggest possible alternatives. You can also purchase and manage all of your domain names on Go Daddy. Some other sites that provide this service are **www.register.com** and **www.hostway.com**.

WHAT TO PUT ON YOUR WEB SITE

A Web site should reflect the personality and atmosphere of your restaurant. Use fonts, colors, and graphics that are consistent with your store. Here are some suggestions to include on your site:

- **Show what you have to offer.** What do your food items look like? What do customers see when they walk in your restaurant? How does the building look? Show the atmosphere in your shop. Show a picture of your friendly and cheerful staff. Show how you make your homemade bread or any specialty dishes.

- **Share the news.** You can develop a web-based newsletter to share information about your restaurant, employee news, and specials.

- **Menus.** Your Web site gives you a chance to include full color pictures with your online menu.

- **Directions.** You can include a link to **MapQuest.com** or **www.randmcnally.com.** Customers can enter their address and get directions to your door.

- **History.** Is there local or neighborhood history that Web site visitors would find interesting? Share the story. Have local individuals share some interesting stories.

- **Area attractions.** Promote your store and help new residents and visitors by adding information about what the local area has to offer. Include a local events page for tourists. All of these things make your site valuable.

- **Local sports teams.** A great addition would be information about local youth and sports teams.

You are only limited by your imagination. I really like to incorporate things in my sites that educate the visitors. It gives your site wider appeal. Give your visitors a reason to tell others about your site.

COUPONS

Do not underestimate the value of coupons in the food service business. Consumers love coupons. There are all sorts of coupons you can use. These include: a dollar amount discount, a percentage off, offer a free item with order, special price for multiple entrees, buy one get one free offers, and $5 off an order of $50 or more.

If you offer a printable coupon on your Web site, it will be a good tool to gauge how many people are visiting and using your site. Be sure to change the coupons regularly and put expiration dates and disclaimers on the coupons.

TESTIMONIALS

Using customer testimonials is a great way to promote the quality of your food, the speed of your service and the other amenities of your restaurant. It is an amazingly effective tactic. I highly recommend using audio and video testimonials, as well as printed quotes on your Web sites. You should include your customer's name, e-mail address, and Web address with each unsolicited testimonial to increase believability. A script which will rotate testimonials on your Web site is available from **www.willmaster.com**.

DO IT YOURSELF

If you attempt your own Web site design, I recommend using a professional Web design tool such as Macromedia Dreamweaver. Many Web hosting companies have online templates and will help you build your site step-by-step. Check out **www.hostway.com/smb/web-design/index.html** or **www.register.com/retail/product/website.rcmx**. These can be good solutions if you have a limited budget or little expertise. Beware, however, of a site that looks homemade or unprofessional—it can actually drive away customers.

HIRING A WEB DESIGNER

It is possible to achieve good results by designing a Web site yourself; however, it may be best to go with a professional design service. A professional Web site can cost $3,500 to $15,000. This money buys layout, design, copy writing, programming, and sometimes hosting. Keep these suggestions in mind if you decide to hire a web designer:

- **You can find a web designer online.** Search for "web design [your city name]" or "restaurant web design" for people with experience designing food service sites. Review designers' portfolios and samples. You should be able to view samples of sites they have designed to see if you like them.

- **Look at other restaurant sites.** Go back and review the sites from your initial research. When you find a design you like, contact the webmaster. The webmaster is usually listed at the bottom of the homepage.

One professional Web design firm I recommend is Gizmo Graphics Web Design (**www.gizwebs.com**). Gizmo Graphics Web Design has all-inclusive Web design packages for as low as $575, which includes site design, one year of Web site hosting, and free domain name registration.

PRECAUTIONS

If you decide to hire a Web design company, be sure to:

- Pay attention to the details.
- Invest time and money wisely.
- Make sure your site can grow with your restaurant
- Know all the "hidden" costs.

WEB DESIGN MISTAKES TO AVOID

Wether you design your site yourself or hire someone, be aware of these common pitfalls when designing your site.

- **The home page does not quickly tell you what the Web site is all about.** You should be able to visit the home page of any Web site and figure out what the site is about, what type of products it sells, or what it is advertising within five seconds.

- **The poor use of popup windows, splashy advertising, splash pages** (pages with neat animations and sound that you have to watch for five to ten seconds before you are taken to the real Web site), and other Web design features which draw interest away from your Web site, products, and services.

- **Poor Web site navigation.** Includes broken hyperlinks, hidden navigation, poor wording of navigational links, links that take you to pages with no links, and links from a page to the same Web page or no links back to the home page (always include a link back to the home page so that regardless of where a site visitor gets lost, he can find his way back home.).

- **Believing that because you have a Web site, you have a marketing campaign or overall marketing and advertising strategy.** You need to understand that your Web site is not your marketing strategy; your Web site is just part of your overall marketing strategy. Creating a Web site is great, but if it is not promoted and advertised, no one will ever find it. By passing out business cards with your Web site URL embossed on them, you are using a traditional marketing campaign to promote your Web site. If you offer a downloadable/printable coupon from your Web site, you are successfully using your Web site as part of your marketing strategy to meet your goal of increased restaurant sales.

- **Failure to attain Web site relevance and content updating.** There is nothing more dissatisfying to a Web customer than visiting a Web site that is grossly out of date. Incorrect pricing, products no longer available, dated content, and ancient advertising all signify to the Web site visitor that there is no devotion to your Web site. During an interview with Gizmo Graphics Web Design, they revealed that one client has not updated his Web site in more than three years. The site contains dated information (schedule of events, an outdated e-mail address, etc). Although the client is proud of his Web site and it looks great, it does not take a visitor long to realize that this site has not been updated since before the last presidential election and, typically, interest fades fast. Conversely, cramming your pages with non-relevant material will distract the visitor from getting the point of your Web site (the five-second rule mentioned earlier).

- **Avoid too many text effects.** Forget flashing, reversing, and gymnastic texts, or other eye-popping and dizzying effects, which do nothing more than annoy your site visitor. Do not create a "loud" Web site that contains so many blinking, flashing, twirling, and spinning icons, text, or graphics that visitors are overwhelmed by the effects and under-whelmed by the site content. Here is a great example of a Web site that is out of control: **http://arngren.net/**.

- **Limit the number of graphics on your Web site so that you do not overwhelm your site visitors with "graphics overload."** Do not use animated .gif images on your Web site. These were cool ten years ago, but in today's professional environment they are just another "loud," annoying distraction that site visitors do not want to see. Speaking of graphics, make sure you use the ALT = Attribute tag to display text descriptions of the images on your Web site.

- **Do not incorporate frames into Web site design.** The use of frames within a Web site will drive customers away faster than anything.

- **Do incorporate the proper Web site design elements to ensure that your Web site is ready to be found by search engines.**

EVALUATE YOUR WEB SITE

After the site has been designed and launched, spend some time on it. Ask customers, friends, and others for their feedback as well. Some important things to remember:

- **Professional looking site.** An amateurish site can reflect badly on your restaurant.

- **Does your site work?** I cannot stress this enough. Be sure visitors can navigate your site. Do all your links work? Are there links to all of your pages? Broken links give people a bad impression of you and your shop.

- **Search engine friendly.** Seventy-five percent of all online activity comes from search engines. Design your site with keywords that will bring targeted traffic to your Web site.

- **Content that promotes sales.** Is the content interesting? Check for basic things such as spelling and grammar.

- **Plan for updates and changes.** Once your site is live on the Web, do not assume your work is done. You want people to visit your site more than once, so give them reasons to come back. You can post regular updates or monthly coupons.

A quality Web site is an investment. Use the Web site with your other advertising strategies to maximize all of your marketing efforts.

WEB HOSTING

A Web host is the server that physically houses your Web site files. There are a variety of types of hosts around, each with their own web hosting plan and offers. Many Web design companies will take care of Web hosting for you. If you decide to choose your Web host yourself, look for a hosting company that will provide you with the following things:

- **Technical support that is available when you need it (24/7);**

- **A good "uptime" or "availability" history so that you know your Web site will be available to customers** (Web site availability should be in excess of 99 percent); it ensures that when you make changes to your Web site, the changes will go into effect as soon as possible.

- **A fast and reliable Internet connection** (Forget about dial-up service — go with high-speed broadband cable, DSL, or satellite).

- **Technicians and staff that understand all aspects of e-commerce, including shopping carts and SSL certification.**

- **Compatibility with other providers of e-commerce on the Internet.**

- **Compatibility with your selected shopping cart product**; many companies invest in expensive shopping cart software that is rendered useless by Web hosting companies that do not support essential features, such as server side includes, Web scripting, executable files, or other dynamic content.

Some of these features will only be used by Web sites that are more sophisticated and use e-commerce. However, you never know how you might want to expand your site in the future; don't let your host limit your options.

Take your time when looking for a Web hosting company. You will be entrusting a large part of the success of your Web site to this company. You want to choose a Web hosting company that has been in business for a long time since there are many start-up Web hosting companies on the Internet that come and go. One of the most costly things that you will be paying for when you do business on the Internet is your Web hosting service. You want to choose a company that is reliable and reputable. The following are several Web hosting companies that have reputations for being top in the field of hosting Web sites:

- **Readyhosting.** Ideal for the small- or medium-sized business, featuring one of the lowest costs around, with a feature-rich hosting package. **www.readyhosting.com**

- **Verio.** This company is great for medium- to large-sized companies. They also have a great Web hosting plan for small businesses that are just starting up on the Internet. **www.verio.com**

- **Rackspace.** Rackspace offers great Web hosting for small- to medium-sized businesses that are looking for a secure environment. **www.rackspace.com.**

- **Go Daddy.** Go Daddy offers a variety of options. **www.godaddy.com**.

When you are looking for a Web hosting company, there are several features you should also consider.

- **Guarantee.** Good Web hosting companies will offer you a money-back guarantee that shows their confidence in their ability to host your Web site at a high-reliability percentage.

- **Web hosting space.** Choose a Web host that offers you a large amount of hard drive space for your Web site to allow for future expansion. Most Web sites use a minimum of 10MB of hard drive space; however, large e-commerce-enabled sites may grow to more than 100MB in size. Readyhosting (**www.readyhosting.com**) offers 500MB of storage with superior reliability and low cost.

- **Data transfer.** Most Web hosting companies allow a certain amount of traffic to your site before charging you for any extra traffic because the more traffic to your Web site, the more their servers have to work. Look for Web hosting companies offering low cost for high traffic to your Web site. Readyhosting (**www.readyhosting.com**) offers unlimited data transfer. Other companies, such as Interland (**www.interland.net**), restrict your data transfer to as low as 25MB per month.

- **Security**. If you need a secure (encrypted) server space, you will pay an additional cost for the secure server certificate. If you are going to process personal data or credit card information on your Web site, you will need a secure certificate. It is important to note that if you use PayPal (**www.paypal.com**) or JustAddCommerce (**www.justaddcommerce.com**), a secure server certificate is included in these services. A digital certificate is used to protect any communication you have with your customers containing private information. You will need a digital certificate installed on your Web server to take credit card orders in a safe and secure manner.

- **Web site upload**. Find out what method is used to upload your Web site pages to the company server. Many Web hosting companies use FTP (file transfer protocol) for this upload. You want an FTP program that is compatible with your Web hosting company. Most Web hosting companies provide a free FTP application; however, I highly recommend you purchase IPSwitch's WS_FTP software (**www.ipswitch.com**).

- **Software.** Find out what software or built-in scripts the Web host offers. Some companies will not offer software tools, while others have several free tools that help you to operate your Web site easily and efficiently. Some of the software you may be offered includes: (a) auto-responders to send e-mail to your customers, (b) search engines so visitors can find your business Web site, (c) forms (guestbook, order forms, and questionnaires), (d) bulletin boards and chat room access, (e) file backup and recovery, (f) an e-commerce shopping cart, and (g) Web site management software.

- **Know what your Web host will support.** Several years ago, Gizmo Graphics Web Design utilized the PDG shopping cart successfully on one of its main accounts, a reputable hosting company. I had a successful e-commerce operation and the SSL certificate and shopping cart were operating perfectly. One day, the shopping cart stopped operating, and after much frantic research, Gizmo determined that its Web host provider changed their policy (overnight) about supporting the executable files that are required on the server to operate the PDG shopping cart on a Windows-based Web server due to "security concerns" and, subsequently, put Gizmo out of business with no advanced notice or warning. Despite Gizmo's attempts to convince them that its configuration was perfectly safe, the Web host provider flatly refused to support Gizmo's shopping cart and they were forced to change hosting companies at a significant expense. Needless to say, I do not recommend that particular Web hosting company. Know what hosting companies support and what their notification processes are to ensure a smooth operation of your Web site. Nothing hurts an online business more than starting an active marketing campaign, only to have your site rendered useless by your Web hosting company.

I strongly recommend that you thoroughly research all potential Web hosting companies to ensure they will support all of your needs. I have recommended the services of **Readyhosting.com** through this book; however, they do not support the PDG software shopping cart, which I also recommend and, therefore, they would not be the choice if I wanted a powerful e-commerce-enabled Web site. There are a variety of resources to review and compare Web hosting companies, including **www.findmyhosting.com**, **www.findmyhost.com**, **www.Websitehostdirectory.com** and **www.ratemyhost.com**. If you wish to combine Web hosting and Web design services with one reputable and highly respected company, I recommend Gizmo Graphics Web Design (**www.gizwebs.com**) of Land O' Lakes, Florida.

MARKETING YOUR WEB SITE

You will need to develop marketing plans to ensure that potential Web site visitors can find and navigate your Web site. Here are some basic things you can do to help people find your site:

- **Search engines.** List your business and Web site with at least 15 to 20 search engines.

- **Pay-per-click.** There may be circumstances where you need to implement a paid advertising campaign.

- **Keywords and meta tags.** Using keywords and properly formatted meta tags will generate more traffic to your Web site. Meta tags are special HTML (programming language) tags in the head section of an HTML document. The most important and commonly used meta Tags are the title, description and keywords tags. Search engines use meta tags to link to and index Web sites. The meta tag is used by search engines to accurately list your site in their indexes.

REPEAT CUSTOMERS

You can use your Web site to help create a solid customer database and harness repeat customers. A loyal customer base is the basis of a successful restaurant and continued profits. One way to achieve repeat customer sales is by having good service and establishing ongoing communication with your customers. Your Web site can be a great source of communication for your customers. Here are some tips:

- **Coupons for repeat customers.** We've already discussed having printable coupons on your Web site that you change monthly. Why not expand this idea? You can create targeted e-mail campaigns designed exclusively for your repeat customer base or through traditional mailings.

- **Contests in which your customers can participate.** Everyone loves a good contest (free dinner, discounts, gift certificates.). Online contests are a great way to keep people interested in your products and services and will drive them back to your Web site.

- **Newsletters that provide useful information.** The use of a well-designed, targeted newsletter (printed or online) is an effective marketing campaign. Make guest aware of menu changes or special events.

- **A program that features banners.** When done with class and style and in limited quantities, banner advertising is a great way to promote your Web site by placing banners on other Web sites that link back to your Web site. For example, you may want a banner on the local tourism site so visitors to the area know where to dine.

- **A program for discussion groups and forums.** Depending on your Web site, a discussion group or forum is a great addition (and is also free through **www.phpbb.com** or **www.ezboard.com**). Many restaurants are establishing discussion forums as a marketing tool to attract new clients, offer recipes and cooking techniques, or for patrons to discuss their dining experiences.

- **A chat room option for customers.** There are many free chat applications and a "live" session between customers and the business is often productive as customers can get immediate support and answers to their questions or concerns. You can find free chat rooms at **www.chat-avenue.com** and **www.parachat.com**.

- **Online reservations.** Many people like the convenience of making dinner reservations on-line. Visit Ruth's Chris Steak House's Web site to see an example at **www.ruthschris.com/reservations**. Over 7,000 restaurants use OpenTable Restaurant Management System for on-line reservations. Visit **www.opentable.com/info/restaurateurs.aspx?id=2** for more information.

- **Promote your business through e-mail.** It is fast, inexpensive, and many people check their e-mail more consistently than the mail box. Loyal Rewards offers options for clients who prefer e-mail or snail mail. Call 800-309-7228 or check **www.loyalrewards.com/merchant.asp** for more information about a program to promote your business through e-mail. They offer an interesting program and ways to build your mailing list.

ONLINE PUBLIC RELATIONS

Online public relations are easily marketable for several reasons:

1. **Accessibility.** Using SEO and search engines can give you the visibility to drive traffic to your Web site.

2. **Affordability.** By using free online press release services, you can work within the tightest budget. You can also select small, tightly targeted press releases within a niche or specific industry. Even though you are paying for the press release, you will not be blowing your budget by sending the release to non-qualified markets or media outlets.

3. **Internet speed.** The speed of the Internet lets you seize business opportunities immediately. Money can be made by tying your media events and campaigns to current events such as the World Series, the Super Bowl, and other themes. It is up to you to follow up on all customer sales and communication.

4. **Internet leverage.** The Internet deals with facts and information without focusing on the size or prestige of your company. Potential customers are using the Internet for research and obtaining helpful knowledge. Make yourself easy to find on the Internet.

ONLINE PRESS RELEASES TO GENERATE EXPOSURE

An online press release is part of the online medium of communication and online communication is all about timing. Your press release, whether printed and faxed or online, is one method of communicating with your customers and your industry. It is up to you to make the most of a press release so that it has as much impact as possible.

Most companies use press releases to alert the public about a new product or a new service they offer. These press releases, while informative, tend to be somewhat dry and consumers typically skim over them, sometimes even missing the key points. In fact, the bottom line is, "If it is not NEWS-worthy, then you will not be selected by the media for coverage." That said, a press release promoting specific events, specials, or newsworthy items can be very effective. The Silvermine Tavern (**www.silverminetavern.com**) has utilized effective press releases for years by publishing written press releases, which are printed in the newspaper. Additionally, they publish the press releases online and also disseminate highlights through their online newsletter promotional program, gaining maximum promotional potential at virtually no cost. As an alternative to a written press release, you could try a multimedia approach. If you are giving a live press release, you can incorporate the audio or video files onto your Web site, either to complement a written press release or replace it altogether. It is highly recommended that you have a media section on your Web site to serve reporters, columnists, producers, and editors with your latest press release information. Many people find listening to an audio clip or watching a video clip preferential to reading a written press release. There is so much written word on the Internet that trying another medium to get your message across could be just the boost your company needs. Think of other Web site owners as another media channel since everyone is looking for fresh content and expert advice.

Consider using an online press release service, such as **www.PRweb.com**, to generate successful media exposure for your restaurant business. This free service is another tool to distribute your press release information to thousands of potential new customers or clients. Keep in mind the value of using highly relevant keywords often within the content of your online press release in order to utilize the benefits of search engine optimization (SEO). Including live links within your online press release is another way for you to ensure increased media coverage. Linking to relevant Web sites increases the credibility and functionality of your online business. You may also do your own press release through your own e-zine or e-mail campaigns.

YOUR WEB SITE IS YOUR OWN MEDIA TOOL

Free media coverage is a great way to get your name out to the public and build your reputation. It is "free" if you do it yourself without hiring a media agency, but it does require an investment of your time, focus, and effort. There are several tactics you can employ to generate free media coverage. Paid advertisement may be important, but to the struggling small business, it is all about cheap or free media coverage. That said, paid advertising should still be considered as a feasible and desirable component of your overall online marketing portfolio if you can afford it. It is vital to use your advertising dollars wisely.

The Internet gives every individual a place where they can present their own media online. The Internet is a media channel and you have the power to own your own PBS — Personal Broadcasting System. There are many ways that you can increase the amount of traffic to your Web site and generate more business from your site. You want to drive as many potential customers to your Web site as possible, even if they do not become a customer. If you are operating a restaurant and your Web site is an online market and advertising tool for your restaurant, increasing the number of site visitors or page hits is considered a success as your goal is simple — to drive visitors to your site, which will, in turn, inspire them to dine at your establishment. You should advertise your "press releases," "product promotions," or other information venues in an opt-in form on your Web site. This form should be on the home page, easily found, and should capture each visitor's name and e-mail. Likewise, if you are engaging in face-to-face communications, you should ask for the customer's name, e-mail, and contact information, while starting a conversation that eventually leads to trust and that first purchase.

Your e-presence is not just about how good your Web site looks. You want to give your customers a reason to come to your Web site to do business with you instead of giving that business to your competitors. You need to pull out all the stops and build your e-presence via the media and Internet marketplace by providing quality content, unique experiences, ease and simplicity, savings, superior customer satisfaction, and other advantages. Building your online business comes back to earning the respect and trust of your customers with the combination of media, marketing, and relationship skills. There are many ways to improve your online marketing success.

INTERNET ADVERTISING

The Internet is significantly different from other marketing and advertising mediums is that it is full of multimedia content. The Internet is comprised of graphics, text, video, and audio. Some of the Internet marketing techniques that rely on multimedia include banner ads, interstitials, advertorials, 3-D visions, and advertisement.

If you are wondering how advertisers and Web promoters know how much traffic is on the Internet, all you have to do is look at the many surveys and tracking applications that monitor, record, and report Internet traffic and trends. These include the following:

- **Web-centric.** Internet tracking that uses log files to determine the number of Internet users that have visited the Web site. These log files are contained on a Web server. When you sign up for a Web hosting account at a reputable hosting company, you should have full access to a wide array of usage and visitor tracking reports.

- **User-centric.** Tracks Internet usage through software installed on the Web server and client workstation that automatically keeps track of the number of times a certain Web site is visited. The combination of this information with demographics and other user information creates what is called a "profile" of Web users.

You want to ensure that your Web hosting company provides you with access to detailed Web-centric statistical reports — the average number of site visitors per day; their length of stay; the type of Web browser used; Web pages visited; geographical location, and who referred them to your Web site. All these feature reports should be included in your Web hosting package at no additional cost.

ADVERTORIALS

Wikipedia (**www.wikipedia.org**) defines an advertorial as an advertisement written in the form of an objective opinion editorial and presented in a printed publication — usually designed to look like a legitimate and independent news story. The term "advertorial" is a portmanteau of "ad" and "editorial." Advertorials differ from publicity advertisements because the marketer must pay a fee to the media company for the ad placement, whereas publicity is placed without payment to the media company and with no control over the copy.

Most publications will not accept advertisements that look exactly like stories from the newspaper or magazine in which they are appearing. The differences may be subtle and disclaimers — such as the word "advertisement" — may or may not appear. Sometimes, euphemisms describing the advertorial as a "special promotional feature" or the like are used. The tone of an advertorial is usually closer to that of a press release than of an objective news story: Advertisers will not spend money to describe the flaws of their products.

Product placement is another form of non-obvious paid-for advertising. An advertorial is simply an endorsement or advertisement that is placed into the context of any Web site as information an designed to look like editorial content. The advertorial may seem to be part of the editorial text of the Web content but is actually a type of advertising message.

Although many businesses still use banner ads and other forms of advertising, the advertorial is becoming popular as people recognize its potential in successful marketing and for driving more traffic to a Web site. A sample advertorial may be viewed at **www.pdedit.com**/**images**/ **Shoreline.pdf**, courtesy of PDEdit (Paul Desmond Editorial Services). PDEdit produced this one-page advertorial on a Shoreline Communications IP voice customer for the July 8, 2002, issue of Network World.

Although advertorials may not generate as much Web traffic to a Web site as pay-per-click or search engine advertising, they do generate traffic that is better in terms of "quality" — more potential customers become actual customers. The customers that reach your Web site after reading an advertorial are arriving because they trust the resource that endorsed your product or service.

If you are going to use advertorials as part of your advertising and marketing campaign, make sure that you understand the importance of affiliates and endorsements and how they work hand in hand. An endorsement from a recognized industry professional is extremely valuable and typically conveys faith in the products advertised within the advertorial.

ADVERTAINMENTS

Advertainments are another form of new advertising on the Internet that is becoming popular. Advertainment is a form of advertising that is consumed and enjoyed by the consumer as if it were for entertainment purposes. Advertainments are advertisements disguised as entertainment.

Advertainments are targeted to consumers with an interest in the products advertised. Advertainments are extremely viral, meaning that they are easily shared and distributed as "entertainment" among peer to peer networks, among thousands of consumers, at no cost. Advertainments are very economical. Each year, billions of dollars in advertising are spent advertising to consumers who will probably never buy the particular product being advertised. Since an advertainment is targeted, it reduces costs by targeting selected marketing groups and increases the likelihood of sales.

Advertainments allow you to concentrate your efforts on your target audience and can save you thousands of dollars in advertising each year. The Budweiser beer commercials viewed during the Super Bowl are examples of advertainment, where the commercial advertisement is entertaining, while at the same time promoting the Budweiser product. No matter what form of advertising you use to promote your online business or brick and mortar business, you can be assured that advertising and marketing are going to be a big aspect of your business. *Source: Success Net* **http://www.bni.com/successnet/**.

EB SUMMARY

This chapter has given you an overview of creating a Web site, on-line promotion, Internet marketing and Internet advertising. For more detailed information, read *How to Use the Internet to Advertise, Promote and Market Your Business or Web Site — With Little or No Money* from Atlantic Publishing (**www.atlantic-pub.com**). For more information about promoting your restaurant I recommend the following books from Atlantic Publishing (**www.atlantic-pub. com**).

- *Superior Customer Service: How to Keep Customers Racing Back to Your Business – Time Tested Examples from Leading Companies* (Item # SCS-01).

- *Getting Clients and Keeping Clients for Your Service Business: A 30 Day Step by Step Plan for Building Your Business* (Item # GCK-01).

- *The Complete Guide to E-mail Marketing: How to Create Successful, Spam-Free Campaigns to Reach Your Target Audience and Increase Sales* (Item # GEM-01).

- *The Complete Guide to Google Advertising — Including Tips, Tricks, & Strategies to Create a Winning Advertising Plan* (Item # CGA-01).

- *Online Marketing Success Stories: Insider Secrets from the Experts Who Are Making Millions on the Internet Today* (Item # OMS-02).

CHAPTER

ADD CATERING
TO YOUR RESTAURANT

C atering has come a long way from the simple chicken and prime rib buffets of the past. "Customers today are looking for the catered experience to be more restaurant-like," says National Restaurant Association Chairman Denise Marie Fugo, who is also president and CEO of Sammy's in Cleveland, Ohio. Fugo and her husband, Ralph DiOrio, started doing small private banquets and off-premise catering in 1988. Sammy's catering became so successful that Fugo closed the restaurant to concentrate solely on catering.

According to the National Restaurant Association's Industry Forecast, social caterers are one of the fastest-growing segments of the restaurant industry. There are over 53,000 caters listed in the Yellow Pages across the United States. According to the online journal catersource®, **www.catersource.com**, the annual sales of these 53,000 caterers are between $7 and $8 billion. This figure includes off-premise and banquet facility caterers but not hotels.

No doubt, catering offers high income potential. Many people leave the worlds of business, law, and medicine, to name a few, to begin a second career in catering. While catering can be a lucrative career, it is important to keep all the aspects of the job in perspective. Catering is hard work and often the easiest part of the job is the cooking. When you are catering an off-premise wedding for 300 people, someone has to load, unload, and load up again the crates of china, silverware, and glasses — more often than not, that person is you.

Remember, too, that catering hours are long and the work is done when everyone else in the world is socializing. You do not just work the event; you work hard for many days, weeks, and even months before the event. And when you are working an event, chances are you are forgoing your own social events. For caterers, evenings, weekends, and lunchtime are bread and butter times, not down times.

With catering, timing is everything. You need to be able to multi-task, organize your time with military precision, and be prepared for the unexpected. Caterer Bev Goldberg recalls a time when she encountered the highly unexpected: She was getting ready for a cocktail party in a client's home and double checking her master list: linens, plates, glassware, soft drinks, garnishes, hors d'oeuvres, ice. Satisfied that everything she needed for the party was ready and loaded into the van, she and two of her staff left for the event location. Upon arrival, she discovered no host and no guests. "The person who had contracted for the party had apparently forgotten and was not at home," she says with a laugh. A veteran caterer with more than 30 years of experience, Goldberg, who co-owns Artistry Catering in Chantilly, Virginia, with her son, Randy, has become used to the frenetic pace and unexpected occurrences of this growing profession. "I love catering," she says. "People still think it is a glamorous job, but it is just plain hard work."

Not yet daunted? Okay, let us see if you have the skills to back up your enthusiasm.

SKILLS NEEDED IN THE CATERING BUSINESS

If you are an excellent cook, competent in artistic food presentation, possess some basic business knowledge, and love working with people, you have the basic prerequisites, but there are many skills and competencies that make for successful caterers.

COOKING AND FOOD PRESENTATION

Catered events, unlike restaurant meals, are usually centered around a special event such as a wedding, a product launch, or a special business meeting. As such, people expect more when attending a catered function. The food has to be outstanding and so does the presentation. For some venues and clients, you will be told that presentation is the most important factor, but always remember that no matter how artistically food is presented, if it does not taste good, it does not cut it. Make sure you and your staff are experienced with both aspects of food preparation.

PLANNING AND ORGANIZATION

Whether you cater off- or on-premise for business or social functions, you must have strong planning and organization skills. If you plan smartly, the physical work at the event goes much more smoothly. If you do not, you will find yourself in the middle of a hectic, unsuccessful event with unhappy clients.

Planning is especially important with off-premise catering because you cannot just run in the back and grab whatever it is you are missing. You need to plan for keeping hot food hot and cold food cold. You need to know what item gets served on which platter so you do not leave behind necessary serving dishes or serving ware. You need to ensure that the silverware has been counted and recounted: You do not want to be one fork short with no extra staff to round one up.

While 70 percent of a typical restaurant is food-oriented, with the rest going for service and organization, this figure flip-flops to 30 percent in the catering business. The rest is delivery, transporting the food, lining up rental equipment, and juggling personnel. In restaurants, every day is fairly similar. In the catering world, each day and event is different, making organizational skills vital.

EFFICIENCY AND CALM

As with any food industry business, efficiency is important. Ask yourself if you can work well under pressure. Because each event is unique, catering can be more stressful than many professions. It is not that most professions do not demand these skills, but in catering you not only have to deal with the stress, you have to make sure your customer never sees the stress. You need to be cool and remain smiling no matter what kind of chaos is tearing at your insides. You may have just finished putting out a fire in the oven after the praline topping for the French toast spilled over the side of the pan, but as soon as you come out to greet your client, you should have your chef jacket on, a smile on your face, and a cool, calm air that reassures your client that her event is going to be spectacular.

CRISIS MANAGEMENT

As a caterer a good deal of your time will be spent "putting out fires" — literal ones like above, as well as figurative. Expect problems to happen and be ready to solve them quickly and inventively. You need a great deal of crisis-management and problem-solving skills in catering, particularly with off-premise catering because you are dealing with so many unknown variables. You have to deal with event site problems, serving food at unfamiliar locations, and trying to find delivery entrances and parking spots. The event must go on, so you need to be creative. With catering you have to recognize that you are in the limelight and there are opportunities for error around every corner.

SALES AND MARKETING

Most likely, your restaurant has an established sales and marketing program. You can use this (and your good reputation) to build your catering business. However, you will also have more personal contact. You will be dealing with corporate executives, party planners, and nervous brides. You need to convince these prospective clients that you will not only provide a memorable feast, but it will be there on time, presented attractively, and served unobtrusively. You also need to come up with ways to retain business once you have been hired.

ASSESS YOUR SKILLS PROFILE

Even if you are a seasoned food service professional, adding catering to your food service establishment can be a daunting task. There are many factors to consider and much research to do— if you need additional space, additional staff, and what kind of food to serve. The most important factors to consider are you and your existing restaurant. Also consider these factors:

- Location
- Customer profile
- Restaurant style/concept

- Staffing capabilities
- Physical layout of building
- Cuisine and menu offerings

The proximity of your restaurant to other businesses will help determine where to focus your catering arm. In an area heavily populated with offices, universities, or hospitals, you may be able to incorporate business catering into your exiting business. If you are currently only open for dinner, it would be an excellent opportunity. You could cater corporate lunches and increase the earning power of your restaurant without worrying about interrupting existing business.

You can also consider social catering. Many restaurants close on Mondays and Tuesdays because these nights tend to be slow. Use those nights for catered events. For a small increase in food and labor cost, you can make a significant increase in sales for the week.

You may be able to get catering business from your existing customers. Let regular diners know about your catering service by using signs, table tents, and text within your menu.

When adding catering to your services consider the size of your facility and the type of food you serve. Is your building big enough to handle the extra production work? Do you have space for on-site catering? Do you serve formal dinners or lunch sandwiches? How much storage space is available for catering food prep and supplies?

Your space and menu may limit you in some areas but not others. Use what you have. If you do not have space for on-premise catering, you can try gourmet to-go dinners or another type of take-out service.

Before you sink your money into adding catering, ask yourself some questions to see if this really is the direction you want to take. The answers to these questions will help you determine whether you are ready to add a catering business and have the resources to do it or not.

- What are your goals in owning a catering operation?

- Will adding catering enhance your restaurant?

- What type of personality do you have? Are you an early riser or a night owl? Do you like interacting with people? Do you thrive on activity and crisis?

- Does your family support this decision and are they prepared to sacrifice time spent with you?

- Do your employees support this decision? Ask the opinions of your most trusted employees.

- Will your restaurant experience easily translate into catering? Can you apply the same management principles?

- How will you finance the operation? Will it jeopardize your existing restaurant?

ASSESS YOUR FINANCES

Take a good, hard look at your finances and determine if you really can afford to add catering—particularly if you are sole proprietor because your personal finances will come into play when you look for business financing.

How much of your own money can you afford to tie up in starting your catering business? When looking for financing you will have to demonstrate that you can finance a portion of it yourself. Do you have equity to invest and can you afford the monthly loan payments?

Check your personal credit before going out to find financing. To check on your personal credit record, call one of the three major credit unions:

- Equifax—800-685-1111

- Experian—888-397-3742
- TransUnion—800-888-4213

The Fair and Accurate Credit Transactions Act allows you to get one report from each of these three credit unions for free once per year.

While your current finances are very important, just as important are the potential profits your catering company can earn. You do not want to invest your money, or expect others to finance or invest, in a business that does not have a high likelihood of profitability.

TYPES OF CATERING

Many people start out by off-premise catering out of their own kitchen. Others are interested in joining a large hospitality company and will look for work in a major hotel or at a large restaurant. These types of organizations generally provide on-premise catering. Catering is also segmented by what type of event is being hosted. Caterers work for both business and social events. It is not necessary to specialize in any event type because they are usually scheduled differently. Social events are likely to occur at night and on weekends, while business events happen more often during regular business hours.

Many people who start catering businesses do so while they are still employed, so they limit their catering work to nights and weekends.

To get a good understanding of what is involved with the different types of catering, let us take a closer look at each one.

OFF-PREMISE CATERING

Off-premise catering refers to a business that has a central kitchen but no separate dining facilities. Off-premise caterers transport the food and various other items to different locations. They might provide service for events in people's homes, at kitchen-less banquet facilities, at parks for outdoor weddings, at offices for business meetings. In many ways, off-premise catering is more challenging than on-premise because each situation is new.

Many people start in off-premise catering because it takes less startup cash than on-premise catering. All you need to start is a kitchen facility — coined as a commissary — that will be used exclusively for preparation of foods to be served at other locations. Because of their low overhead, small off-premise caterers have the advantage of greater flexibility when it comes to price structures.

Off-premise catering has other advantages over on-premise catering as well. The experience can be more exciting and rewarding, especially if you are the type of caterer who enjoys the challenge of working in unusual, unique locations and dealing with new people.

One interesting specialization of off-premise catering is called mobile catering. Mobile catering specializes in feeding a basic menu to a large group of people, such as forest fire fighters, disaster relief workers, construction-site workers, and people taking camping trips or excursions. The caterer develops a seasonal menu and a picnic table concept on the back of a properly equipped truck. The fare is usually hot or cold sandwiches, beverages, soup, coffee, bagels, and burritos.

Certainly this type of work is less glamorous than catering a gala ball, but it is profitable just the same and provides a little less stress on a day-to-day basis. Regardless of the type of off-premise catering you do, there are several important considerations.

TEAMWORK

Build a strong team with strong leadership. The teamwork required in an off-premise catering operation can make your company stronger. Your staff will learn to handle just about everything that can go wrong and you will have the potential to make six-figure incomes, each year.

SUBCONTRACTORS

As the overall operating costs for off-premise catering are generally lower than for on-premise catering, you may find it within your budget to engage subcontractors for certain aspects of the event; for example, floral design, music, and entertainment. It can often prove more cost effective than doing it yourself. Many cities have agencies that provide these services; check the Yellow Pages under "entertainment" for such agencies. Often the best source of information is other caterers. Ask them which companies they use for flowers or music. Network with the people in your community to learn where to find sources of talent and expertise.

FIVE KEYS TO SUCCESS IN OFF-PREMISE CATERING

Here are five important things to look out for when involved with off-premise catering:

1. **Be ready for surprises.** There are literally thousands of potential sources for disaster that can ruin an otherwise successful affair. Always have a Plan B.

2. **Be prepared.** You need to be organized, plan ahead, and visualize in advance all of the aspects of a catered event. As a catering professional, you will find that you make many lists. Be sure to check these lists four times before an event, and then check them again. Have someone else check them as well; they may catch something you missed.

3. **Do a site visit.** Visit early in the planning stages and visit the site again as the day approaches. Compare what you see to your lists and make sure you bring everything you need to make the event a success.

4. **Be involved.** Understand that you can only be successful in off-site catering by running your company from the center of the action and getting involved in all of the details of the business. Ask for feedback from the client and guests. Oversee the catering staff to make sure that they are performing to required standards. Jump in and help out when a table needs to be bussed or coffee needs to be refilled.

5. **Keep cool.** The customer is screaming, the brioche is burning, and one of your staff members just cut himself. The result: stress. Learn how to deal with it. A step in the right direction is to manage your time effectively. Set realistic goals — for a lifetime, for five years, for each year, month, week, and day.

ON-PREMISE CATERING

It is estimated that on-premise catering accounts for about two-thirds of all catering sales in the United States. On-premise catering operations range from large profit-oriented and "not-for-profit" operations to smaller, start-up enterprises, but it generally takes place at hotels, clubs, and conference and convention centers. Some restaurants also have their own banquet facilities and engage in on-premise catering. Other restaurants choose to close their operations to the public for a night and rent the space for a private function.

On-premise catering often offers an advantage to clients because it is a type of "one-stop-shopping." Potential clients do not have the added stress of finding and securing a site to hold the function and typically the on-premise site is already nicely decorated and well laid-out for parties and events.

FOUR TIPS FOR ON-PREMISE CATERING

1. **Specialize**. If you are looking for a niche in the on-premise catering business, explore the possibility of catering weddings. Weddings can yield high profits, largely because of all the extra purchases that are incorporated into a single event. Be sure to include a bridal consultant on your staff. This person will help with all the nuances and expectations that brides have and are also versed in cultural differences and customs that you will encounter. Do not rely solely on your bridal consultant. You need to become familiar with the rituals of traditional weddings and the types of concerns bridal couples and their parents will have. There are many Web sites devoted to planning weddings; visit any of these to see the types of concerns couples will have. One such Web site is at **www.usabride.com**.

2. **Streamline.** Make sure that the layout of your premises works with you rather than against you. The convenience factor is important when you are working under pressure. The distinct advantage of catering on-premises is that everything can be positioned pretty much within reach.

3. **Comfort.** You need to know how many people can be comfortably seated in your facility. Are you able to provide entertainment? Can you prepare a wide variety of menu items at the last minute?

4. **Clubs.** If you run a private club, promote your catering services amongst your members. Offer special deals for private parties and celebrations. Country clubs are better off concentrating on catering for weddings and dances. City clubs are advised to target the business sector. Consider specializing in catering for corporate meetings, board luncheons, and civic events. There are many marketing opportunities to help develop this clientele. Join your local chamber of commerce and become involved. These alliances will provide you with rich networking opportunities and new business.

THE BEST OF BOTH WORLDS

Many restaurateurs cater on-premise special events and also pursue off-premise opportunities. Dual restaurant catering is advantageous because restaurateurs have invested in professional production equipment. By serving both markets you can lower the overall fixed costs of your operation while increasing, incrementally, gross sales. This increase in sales can be achieved without having to spend money on expanding the dining room or kitchen area. When in the pursuit of both types of business, aim to achieve the following:

- **Maximize on flexibility.** Take advantage of the flexibility offered by a combination of on-premise/off-premise catering. By blending both types of catering, dual restaurant-catering operations enjoy the freedom to prepare their foods within their own facility, while at the same time employing outside labor.

- **Maximize on expertise.** Because of the flexibility offered by dual catering operations, you can draw on a greater pool of specialized expertise. You will be in greater demand for a wider range of significant events.

- **Maximize on exclusivity.** Define your exclusive target market. Determine, in advance, the specific clientele for your business. Securing exclusive clients is a definite advantage for a caterer; it will give you a strategic advantage over many other caterers in the market. Work towards exceeding your clients' needs. It will bring you recognition and market dominance in an exclusive area of the catering trade.

- **Develop a seasonal niche.** The dual caterer should be aware of certain special annual events. These events involve preparation of the food on your own premises, while serving off-premises. The advantage of off-premise catering is that you can serve a greater number of people than at your own premises. Understand that the design of your kitchen will determine your capacity to cater off-premises.

Here are some suggestions for developing a catering business that serves up big profits:

- **Decide early whether your restaurant's catering operation will be in-house or off-premises.** An in-house operation will let you use your own kitchen and equipment but it also may limit the size of events. Off-premise catering offers an opportunity for greater exposure, multiple daily events, and more revenue, but you also will have to abide by the rules of each particular venue.

- **Staff smartly.** You can use a culinary-staffing service to supplement your restaurant's regular staff during catered events, but pull from your existing staff for smaller events. Your employees will appreciate making the extra money.

- **You do not have to create a whole new menu for catered events.** Look at what you have on your existing menu and see which items are cater-friendly. If you cater off premises, be sure to choose items that can hold their temperature during transport and can be partially cooked ahead of time.

- **Transporting food requires an even closer eye to food safety.** Train your staff on the additional guidelines they will need to handle transported food properly to prevent food-borne-illness outbreaks.

- **Unless you cater on a daily basis, you may want to rent equipment** for off-premise catering, such as stoves and hot boxes.

- **Create lists of food items, job duties, and equipment.**

- **Know when to say no.** Do not let your regular restaurant business suffer for your new catering business. If you try to do too much, quality will decrease and both businesses will suffer. Know your limits and live by them.

CATERING FOR BUSINESSES

Corporate sales make up approximately 75 percent of the total catering sales in the United States. Typical business events that require catering include the following:

- Meetings/Conventions
- New product introductions
- Recognition events
- Anniversaries
- Team meetings

- Incentive events
- Building openings
- Training sessions
- Annual meetings
- Employee appreciation events

The types of business events are quite varied and the corporate catering market is thus divided into three segments: shallow, mid-level, and deep.

The shallow market refers to the segment of low-budget functions such as employee-appreciation lunches. These events have limited budgets and resources and often do not include a great deal of lead-time. This segment usually includes businesses that are nonprofit, the educational sector, and the military sector. While these events may be less profitable than others, they do fill a certain niche for the caterer. These types of events can be used to fill in for lag time between larger, more resource-intensive events.

Some money coming in is better than no money at all. In addition, the number of resources required is limited, so the expense of catering such an event is limited as well.

The mid-level market includes clients such as local associations that host regular training meetings. Price is important in this sector, but the resources are not as limited as in the shallow market. Therefore, the client is willing to spend a little more to make the event more impressive. Business at this level often leads to repeat business and word-of-mouth advertising.

The deep market involves more elegant, upscale events such as university presidential inaugurations or board of director dinners. Cost is usually not a factor in this segment of the market. The client is interested in providing an excellent, memorable event and is willing to spend what is required.

SOCIAL EVENT CATERING

Individuals rather than businesses usually book social events. They are set up around occasions that take place in people's life cycle and include such events as:

- Weddings
- Anniversaries
- Bar/Bat mitzvahs
- Birthdays
- Holiday parties

- Births
- Reunions
- Graduations
- Fundraising events

Social catering is the first thing that comes to mind when people think of the catering business. Even though it is the smaller industry sector, caterers are drawn to this type of event because they are fun and lively and most everyone can relate to a birthday or anniversary as opposed to the launch of a new product or a building opening.

There are many different facets to the business of catering. It is up to you to decide which combination of catering segments most appeals to you and fits best with your skill set and objectives. Once you have a fairly clear idea of the direction you would like to take your catering career, it is time to get started and get into the business. The next sections detail how to start your own catering company.

MANAGING THE EVENT

Selling runs parallel to marketing and both are essential to the continued success of your catering operation. With your marketing plan in place, you know who your target customers are so now it is time to make your pitch.

If you are targeting several markets at once, it makes sense to segment your sales strategies and staff. Many firms divide their sales staff by corporate or private catering or even by specific types of functions, such as weddings, receptions, dinners, or special entertainment-related events. Develop specialized staff; let them focus on a specific area, thus gaining greater expertise and familiarity with all the particulars of their assignment.

Once you have determined the type of business you are after, you have to do just that: Go after it. Use lead referrals, advertising, and aggressive cold calling. Work your leads like your livelihood depended on it.

The most successful salespeople are the most persistent. Pay close attention to what conventions and groups are coming to town; gather the information as far in advance as you can.

One of the keys to developing leads is through networking your existing contacts. If the client is happy with your event, try to get a few good words of recommendation as well. Ask if you may use their words of reference in your sales catalogs or brochures. Be sure to add all influential attendees of your functions to your database.

Once you have a client that you are trying to win over, be sure to protect yourself. Many new caterers are hungry for those first few sales. Try to establish quickly and discreetly whether the client has sufficient funds to pay for your services. Aim to qualify them right away. If their budget still remains questionable, send them to your competition. Be suspicious when the promised deposits are not sent to you. If you already have a heavy commitment during the time of a proposed event, refuse, no matter how good a client is. Do not over-commit yourself and your staff.

HANDLING INQUIRIES

Most inquiries will be over the phone, so make sure you or your staff can answer the phone personally for as many hours as possible. Someone not getting a quick response will just move on to the next caterer on her list. If you are part of a large business, consider hiring someone full-time to man the phones. Ideally, you will have someone answering the phone and responding to inquires six days a week from 9 a.m. to 7 or 8 p.m.

The person answering the phone should be polite and knowledgeable. When someone calls in, the first step will be to check availability on the date the potential client needs services. Always have an updated day planner to give the potential client an immediate response on availability. If you have someone in the office handling calls, you can computerize this information on a banquet inquiry form. Make sure the person answering phones fills this form out completely.

The potential client is likely to be calling several area caterers, so you should follow up in a few days to see if there are any other questions you can answer and try to set up a meeting. Showing initiative can take you a long way in the competitive catering business.

MEETING WITH THE CLIENT

When meeting with your client, be professional and come prepared. Bring sample menus, photos of past parties, samples of dishware, a contract, notepaper, pens, and references. If you are an on-premise caterer, be sure to show the client the facility when you meet, including the dining and bar areas and parking. Take thorough notes so you can refer to this information when drawing up the contract and planning the event.

Make a question list to take with you to make sure you have covered every detail. Here is a sample list:

- When does the event start? When will the meal be served? What time will the event end?

- How many guests are you expecting?

- Is security needed?

- Do you need any signage?

- Should there be a checkroom available for guests' coats?

- What type of decorations does the client want? (Color of linens, flowers, balloons, etc.)

- Will someone be setting these up or will the caterer be responsible?

- When will the decorators need access to the room?

- What type of service does the client want?

- What type of china?

- Beverages?

- Will there be music? What times will the band be playing? Will there be dancing?

- Will the band be provided with dinner?

- Are there any audio-visual requirements?

- Is a photographer needed? Who will hire this person? When will photos be taken?

- What kind of room setup does the client want?

- Will there be a head table?

- Are there any programs or other printed material that need to be distributed to guests?

- Is there a formal seating chart?

- Are telephone or computer hookups necessary?

- Will there be a speaker?

- Any lighting requirements needed?

- Any special permits needed?

- How many cars will be expected? Will the client pay for parking or will the guests?

As you are listening to the client, try to pick what is most important. Part of your job is to figure out what is essential and what is not a priority in your client's mind. If the event is a wedding reception, the person may want to serve three different entrées — chicken, beef, and fish. On the other hand, the budget for the event may only allow for two entrée choices. Communicate this information to your client in a positive way. Everyone has budgetary limits. Rather than trying to force someone to spend more than they can afford and create potentially bad word-of-mouth advertising, try to adjust the client's expectations and still give her a memorable event.

SITE LIST

If you are an off-premise caterer, it is a good idea to hold one of your first meetings at the intended event location. You can see the equipment and storage and get an idea if you need to buy new equipment to make the party work. Bring your note pad, tape measure, and calculator on this trip. If the event is being planned far out in advance, it is also a good idea to take your camera. That way you will have a "memory jogger" when you get ready to work on the details at a later date. As you look at the facilities, ask yourself these questions:

- How will the tables be set up? Is there a buffet? Is there room for a separate dessert and appetizer buffet?

- Where will drinks be set up?

- How many ovens are there and how much cold storage do you have?

- Will you need to bring auxiliary equipment?

- Are there pots, pans, etc., to use or will you need to bring them?

- Where will the dirty dishes be bused to and washed?

- Where does the trash need to go?

- Are there adequate restroom facilities?

- What is the parking situation? Will there be valet parking?

- Does the room require any special decoration?

You also need to know the timing of the day's event. If you are working on a wedding reception, you should ask what time the ceremony is, when the guests will start arriving for the reception, and when appetizers and dinner should be served. Will there be toasts and bouquet tossing and at what times? What time should the event wrap up?

If you are an off-premise caterer, it is a good idea to make a site list to take to these meetings. One of the biggest challenges to an off-site caterer is how to deal with the variety of equipment and conditions you run into at various venues. It is easy to forget to check every detail in the beginning. A site list is a good way to make sure you bring all the equipment you need for the party. There is an example of a site list at the end of this chapter.

TYPES OF SERVICE

There are benefits and drawbacks to each type of service. You will want to keep these in mind while you are meeting with and negotiating with your client. The style of service will impact your event, the guests' interaction, and the quality of service you can give. The following table gives the advantages and disadvantages for various types of service.

TYPE OF SERVICE ADVANTAGES DISADVANTAGES		
Type of Service	Advantages	Disadvantages
Plated	You control portion sizes and establish the pace of the meal. It's easier to create dramatic plate presentations and a romantic or elegant ambiance.	Requires a lot of planning.
Family Style	Food is easy to assemble and won't get cold quickly because it is being served from large serving dishes. Good for casual events, creates a sense of camaraderie.	No plate presentation. Passing dishes among guests can be awkward.
Casual Buffet (guests serve themselves)	Most food will be in place before event begins. You can offer a variety of dishes, guests can help themselves, and you don't have to seat everyone at once to begin serving.	Serving size not controlled, will need to replenish buffet, and have considerable leftovers. Hot items can be difficult to keep hot.
Formal Buffet (servers are used)	Servers allow people to move through buffet line quicker and determine portion size, fewer problems with running out of food. Can serve a whole carved meat to add elegance to event. Hot dishes are easier to keep hot because servers are paying strict attention to these.	There is the added expense of servers.

Your job as the caterer is to navigate your client through the various options and possibilities to come up with an event that is outstanding yet still respects the client's budgetary limits.

QUOTES AND CONTRACTS

Never give a quote over the phone. Meet with the potential client and make sure of exactly what she wants before offering a quote or you may significantly underbid.

Write down every detail of what the client wants. Record food selections, number of servers, length of event, number of guests expected, linens desired, extra services, and bar specifics. Once you leave the meeting with the client, analyze the information and crunch numbers before calling back with a quote.

Everything affects the price you come up with, so think through all the details. What is the occasion? Will the event require a light lunch or a large, multi-course buffet? What are the logistics involved with the location if the event is off-site? Will you need to supply additional cooking or cold storage equipment? Will you be cooking on-site? If the event is on-premise, what is the typical room charge associated with a room that will hold the desired number of guests?

Once the client decides on food preferences, prepare an outline that includes the following tasks:

- Food shopping
- Travel time to and from event
- Setup time
- Serving time

- Food prep
- Loading and unloading time
- Reheating and arranging food
- Cleanup time

It will help you determine your time, start to finish, because even though the event may be from 7 p.m. to 10 p.m., you will be working long before and after the festivities. With this information and your pricing information, you will be able to develop a fair quote that will still ensure you make a profit.

WRITING A CONTRACT

Regardless of how well you know the person you are catering for or how nice he or she appears, you must have a written contract. Without a contract, you will be defenseless when attempting to collect from a non-paying customer. A contract is a binding agreement between two parties; the caterer is obligated to provide the food and service stated and the client is obligated to pay for this food and service.

Many caterers start small and their first clients are usually friends and family members. While it may seem uncomfortable to a friend or relative to sign a contract or give you a deposit, you should resist the temptation to skip these steps. Make sure all your agreements are committed in writing. In many states, only contracts in writing are enforceable. A written contract will encourage your client to ask for additional services to be provided during the initial phase of your negotiations. Think carefully about the tone of your contract. While you want to protect your business, you could alienate potential business with an aggressive tone. You can still convey the same information without being antagonistic. Templates and examples of contracts can be found at **www.catersource.com**.

Always ask for a deposit up front. Any time you do not receive a deposit, you are in danger of cancellation, even at the last minute. Deposit policies vary; some caterers ask for one-third when booking, another third one month prior to the event, and the remainder on the day of the event. Alternatively, a caterer may receive 10 percent on booking, up to 50 percent a month prior to the event, and the balance on the day of the event. Your terms will be dictated by your cash flow needs.

BASIC CONTRACT STIPULATIONS AND CONSIDERATIONS

The following list of stipulations and considerations is intended as a guideline only. It is by no means exclusive; it is intended to draw your attention to a few basic requirements. When developing your contract template, bear in mind the following:

- **Personal details.** When composing a contract, first include your name, address, phone and fax numbers. Next, enter the client's name, address, phone and fax numbers.

- **Dates and times.** After indicating the date of the contract, state the day and date of the event to be catered, as well as the starting and ending times for the party. The exact amount of time allocated to each activity is especially important; if the caterer runs into overtime, an overtime charge should be applied against the client.

- **Make sure to nail down the minimum number of guests.** Establish the exact number of people to be in attendance. If not possible, ascertain the minimum number of guests. Build in a clause that permits you to raise the price per person should you end up catering for less than the estimated minimum number of guests. You also should include a clause that you need final numbers by a particular date. Most caterers ask the client to give them a final guest count three days before the event. Doing so allows the caterer an appropriate amount of time to shop and prepare the correct amount of food.

- **Determine a method for tracking the number of guests.** Some common methods for tracking guest numbers include tickets, plates issued, bundled/rolled silverware with a napkin issued, and by a turnstile. Today, many events are preceded by invitations that request an RSVP. The RSVP allows you to have a more accurate guest count.

  Here is an easy formula to determine how many guests will actually show up at the event:

  Number of guests invited x 0.66 x 1.15 = number of guests to anticipate.

  For example: 300 invited guests x 0.66 x 1.15 = 228 anticipated guests.

  The 0.66 accounts for the number of no-shows and the 1.15 accounts for the uninvited guests that will arrive.

- **Guard your reputation.** Regardless of how you arrive at your number, remember that if the caterer runs out of food, it is the caterer's reputation at stake. The guests will not know that the host underestimated the count, nor will they care. They will just know that they are hungry, there is no food left, and it is the caterer's fault. Let the clients know that they are always welcome to take home any unused portions. Generally, caterers have a guarantee number as well as a real number for the guest count. This guarantee usually runs between 3 and 5 percent of the total. In other words, if the event is set for 200 people, the caterer will prepare food for 206 if their guarantee number is 3 percent.

- **Include a section in the contract that details the menu to be served.** Nothing should be left out and nothing should be assumed. If you need to make major changes to the menu, and you probably will, draw up a new contract.

- **Event price.** An event price is established at the same time the client is shopping for a caterer. The contract must state that the price is an estimate only. Include a clause that permits the caterer to adjust the price, based on unforeseen conditions. Large events are booked approximately six months in advance. Smaller events may happen on much shorter notice, but most caterers have guidelines for the latest date they can accept a job. For instance, a caterer may stipulate that she will book up to three days prior to a small event.

- **Payment policy.** According to the schedule agreed upon, include a clause stating unequivocally the method and time frame for the payments — in general, the larger and more expensive the event, the larger the deposit.

- **Staffing.** Include a section in the clause that states the number of staff to be provided, the hours they will work, as well as applicable charges for their services.

- **Define your policies regarding leftover food and alcohol.** It may be determined by the event. If you are catering a 40-person dinner party at a client's house, you are likely to box and leave the leftovers. If, on the other hand, you are catering a wedding reception for 150 at a rented hall, you will probably take the leftovers back with you and divide amongst the staff. You should also state your policy on serving alcoholic beverages to minors or those people who become intoxicated.

- **Cancellation/Refund policy.** Discuss in detail your policy regarding cancellations and refunds.

- **Caterer and client signatures.** Do not forget: Without the necessary signatures, the contract is not legally binding.

The sample contract at the end of this chapter may help you draw up your own catering contract agreement. Use it as a guideline only and consider obtaining professional legal advice.

CANCELLATIONS AND REFUNDS

In the event of a cancellation, should you refund some, all, or none of the deposit? In general, there are no clear-cut answers and you should determine it on a case-by-case basis. The timing of cancellations is crucial in determining your policy. If someone cancels months before the event, you probably can re-book the date. If, however, the client cancels a week ahead of time, you will probably not be able to re-book and you may lose deposits you made on rentals or money you have already spent on food purchases.

Many event locations, such as hotels, community halls, and convention centers, often have a step refund policy. If a client cancels three months before the event, the facility will refund the entire deposit. If the event is cancelled a month before the event, the facility will refund 50 percent of the deposit, and if the booking is cancelled a week to a month in advance, 35 percent of the deposit will be refunded. If the event is cancelled within the week of its occurrence, no refund is issued. This type of step policy helps to offset some of the costs the off-premise caterer may have already absorbed.

When deciding on the fairest course of action for your own cancellation/refund policy, consider the following issues:

- If the client cancels at least a month before the scheduled event, you may want to refund the full deposit. In fact, you can very well use this policy as a selling point when a client is trying to decide between you and another caterer.

- If the event is cancelled within a month of the scheduled event, discuss the matter with the client personally.

- If the cancellation happens at the last minute due to a tragedy involving one of the principals, it is best to wait a period of time before getting the client to discuss refunds.

When you are not sure how to handle the cancellation, postpone your decision; tell the client that you have to check your figures to see how much money and time has already been invested. Take this time to calculate a reasonable amount to pay for costs you have already made. Refund the rest.

CLIENT'S REFUSAL TO PAY

If you run into a situation where a client just will not pay, the first step is to send a personal letter requesting payment. It is very likely that your client simply forgot. Make sure to gently remind the client of the amount due and give the client a reasonable due date, such as 10 days, to pay the balance.

If this does not work, call the client. The next step would be to have your lawyer send a standard collection letter. While it may seem silly, people really do sit up and take notice when they receive a letter from a lawyer. While this tactic might result in payment, it is likely to cost you a lawyer fee as well.

If nothing else works, you can try small claims court. This process is time consuming but not very expensive. In most states, claims are usually limited to between $1,200 and $2,000. Nothing guarantees the judge will rule in your favor. And even if he does, you are not guaranteed immediate payment.

Another route to try for delinquent payments is a collection agency, but these agencies take a fairly large cut, so you may want to try all other alternatives first.

The best way to get the money you need to cover your costs is to prepare a solid refund and cancellation policy that addresses all of the issues discussed above.

PAPERWORK

Now it is time to get down to the nitty-gritty of event management. Once you have secured a contract, you will have many details to attend to and there is a good amount of paperwork that can help you keep track of all these details.

EVENT ORDER SHEETS

Prepare an event order sheet and give it to your service staff. This sheet will provide the information they need to make the function successful and it will work as a list so they can double check their equipment and food. Use and amend this sheet when you want to organize and plan for any special event. Make sure to record notes about the event; if it is a public event, write down anything such as weather and product and staffing issues and save it in your event book for future reference.

An example of an order sheet is at the end of this chapter. You can download a template of a worksheet from **www.restaurantbeast.com** and see another version of a similar worksheet on **www.wedoitallcatering.com**.

BANQUET EVENT ORDERS

Most large caterers or those associated with a hotel or restaurant use Banquet Event Orders (BEO) to record the bar and buffet layouts, table settings, and other pertinent setup information. Many of these also include a room diagram. Smaller caterers will benefit from using these orders as well because small or large, a caterer lives and dies by the details.

In hotels, BEOs are prepared for each meal or beverage function and circulated to the affected departments a week or so before the event. They are usually sequentially ordered to help keep track of them. A sample BEO can be found at the end of this chapter.

A typical BEO contains the following information:

- BEO number
- Type of event
- Person who booked the event
- Beginning and ending time of event
- Menus
- Room setup
- Billing information
- Name of person preparing BEO
- Special instructions (centerpieces, special accommodations, entertainment, etc.)

- Event date
- Client name and address
- Name of function room or event location
- Number of guests expected
- Style of service
- Prices charged
- Date BEO was prepared
- List of persons receiving a copy of the BEO

STAFFING

If you are only adding a small catering component to your restaurant, you will not need much additional staff. If you plan to expand, you may need to staff catering as a separate department. In a large catering facility, typical positions include:

CATERING STAFF

Title/Position	Job Duties
Director of Catering	Assigns and oversees all functions and marketing efforts. Interacts with clients, coordinates sales staff, creates menus in coordination with chef.
Assistant Catering Director	Services accounts, assists with marketing.
Catering Manager	Services accounts and maintains client contacts.
Catering Sales Manager	Oversees sales office and sales staff.
Catering Sales Representative	Handles outside and inside sales.
Convention/Conference Service Managers	Handles meeting and convention business and room setup (usually a position found in hotels).
Banquet Manager	Oversees captains, supervises all functions in progress, schedules front-of-the-house staff, acts as operations director.
Assistant Banquet Manager	Reports to Banquet Manager. Supervises table settings and décor.
Banquet Setup Manager	Supervises banquet setup crew, orders tables and chairs and other equipment, supervises tear down of the event.
Scheduler	Enters bookings in a master log, oversees timing of functions. Schedules meeting rooms and other meal function rooms, keeps appropriate records to ensure there is no overbooking or double booking, communicates information to relevant departments.
Maitre d'Hotel	The floor manager in charge of all service personnel and all aspects of guest service during the meal function.
Captain	Oversees the activity of a meal function and the service personnel.
Server	Food servers and cocktail servers work the event, handling and serving food and beverages to guests.
Bartender	Serves drinks during events and restocks bar inventory. May also need to keep track of drinks for pricing information for the event.
Sommelier	Wine steward.
Houseman	Physically set up the tables, chairs, dance floor, stage, etc., for an event.
Attendant	Refreshes meeting rooms. Does spot cleaning and trash removal.
Clerical Staff	Handles routine correspondence such as typing BEOs, contracts, and handling and routing phone messages.
Engineer	Provides utilities services and maintains catering equipment. May also handle audio-visual or lighting installation.
Cashier	Collects money at cash bars, sells drink tickets and meal tickets if event has them.
Ticket Taker	Collects tickets from guest before they are allowed to enter an event.
Steward	Delivers requisitioned china, flatware, linen, etc.
Cook/Food Handler	Prepares the finished food product according to the Banquet Event Order form (BEO).

You may need to hire temporary help for large events. Check with your staff or other area caterers. There is usually a large pool of people that work temporary catering jobs and they tend to work for several companies at once.

You will be paying your catering staff per event, even if some of the help comes from your regular employees. If your regular employees work an event they should be paid in the same fashion as temporary workers. Generally, for catered events, servers and bartenders are paid $95 to $120 for four hours (this does not include a tip the host or hostess might include). After four hours, the client is charged $15 to $20 per half hour. Kitchen staff is generally still paid a per-hour rate or flat rate per event. Per-hour rates generally fall between $15 and $25.

EQUIPMENT

Catering operations, much like restaurants, are production facilities. Unlike restaurants, which are designed to produce food in individual servings for individual diners, a catering kitchen must be able to serve many people the same food at the same time.

While you will already have most of the equipment you need, you will want to invest in additional flatware, china and linens, as well as the items listed in the "Equipment for Transporting Food" section of this handbook.

MENUS

When creating your catering menus, consider the following:

- Which items on your restaurant menu do well.

- What products you already order and have on hand.

- Which items on your menu would hold well.

- Which items can be mass produced easily.

- How much storage space you have available.

You do not have to start from scratch. If there are items you already sell that could hold and be produced in quantity, include these on your catering menus.

Use your menu sales analysis and sales history to determine popular, cost-effective recipes you may want to include in your catering operation.

Menu sales analyses, or menu scores, track each menu item that is sold. Many restaurants have computerized cash registers, so getting a report on what items sold nightly, weekly, or monthly is easy. If your restaurant does not have a computerized register, you can track a period of time (a month) and get this information from guest checks.

Cost can easily be pulled from your standardized recipes or cost sheets and your sales history can be pulled from a daily log that records customer counts, daily sales, daily costs.

A menu item's profit margin, what the item contributes to the overall profit of a restaurant, is the difference between the menu price and the item's food cost. To determine profit margin, you will need to look at monthly financial statements. Subtract your total food-costs from your total sales.

You should also consider creating catering menus that allow you to use products already on hand. When creating a catering menu, take the opportunity to include items that will allow you to use leftover inventory. For a complete discussion, see the "Menu Planning" section of the handbook.

MARKETING

Just like your restaurant, you will need to market your catering operation. Since you already have a customer base, you already have a leg up in marketing your catering business. Take advantage of your existing customer base and do some internal marketing.

Internal marketing refers to techniques used once the customer is inside your restaurant. This type of marketing tool can be a great way to build business for the catering side of your operation. Here are some internal marketing ideas:

- **The restaurant menu itself is an important internal marketing tool.** The menu and quality of food will help entice your customers to use your facility for special events.

- **Set up table tents or signs that let your customers know you cater.**

- **Provide carry-out catering menus at the cashier or hostess station,** as well as brochures and business cards.

- **Have one of your servers take a tray of appetizers you use for your catering menu into your front area and serve the customers waiting to be seated.**

- **Have people drop business cards into a fishbowl and hold a drawing once a week.** The winner receives a free catered lunch for himself and three friends.

- **Use these business cards to create an e-mail list.** Send out e-mails to promote your catering business.

- **Create T-shirts with your logo and catering information** and sell these at the hostess stand.

- **Give your servers buttons to wear that say "Ask me!"** When customers ask, the servers can tell the customer about your new catering business and give them a brochure. For external promotions, make sure you know exactly what needs promoting before spending your revenue on advertising. Advertising is expensive and there is no guarantee it will succeed. Do your homework before you spend your money.

Here are some ideas for external promotion of your catering arm:

- **Donate food to a local public radio fund drive.** It will give you free advertising on the station when they thank the people who donated food.

- **Visit your local chamber of commerce.** All cities have festivals, parades, and other events. See how you can involve your restaurant's catering operation.

- **If you have the advertising budget, place ads in newspapers, on the radio, or on television.**

- **Set up cooking demonstrations at a local mall.**

- **Talk to area schools about conducting a tour of your facility as a class field trip.**

- **Use a rubber stamp on outgoing mail saying "We cater!"**

- **Another possible marketing strategy is to offer cooking classes.** You may be interested in doing a class at your facility or just doing a demo at a mall kiosk to increase your public exposure.

ONCLUSION

Catering is a complex, exciting area within the food services industry. There are many factors to consider before deciding to add it to your restaurant. If you decide to take the plunge, the rewards can be considerable.

For much more information about running a catering business, whether in an established restaurant or a new catering operation, I recommend the following books, available from Atlantic Publishing (**www.atlantic-pub.com**).

• *The Professional Caterer's Handbook How to Open and Operate a Financially Successful Catering Business With Companion CD-ROM* (Item # PCH-01)

• *The Food Service Professional's Guide to Successful Catering: Managing The Catering Operation For Maximum Profit* (Item # FS12-01).

• *The Complete Guide to Successful Event Planning With Companion CD-ROM* (Item # SEP-01).

SITE LIST	
Client	
Client contact information	
Event date	
Event time	
Type of event	
Indoor/Outdoor	
Venue address	
Outside parking	
Area for catering staff to unload and park	
Lighting	
Accessibility	
Dining area tables (provided or need to be brought in?)	
Size of dining area	
Buffet tables	
Bar	
Gift table	
Decorations	
Electrical outlets	
Heating/Air-conditioning	
Extensions	
Microphone/Podium	
Dance floor	
Stage	

SITE LIST

KITCHEN	
Stove	
Oven dimensions	
Grill	
Refrigerator and freezer space	
Dishwashing area	
Microwave	
Access to pots, pans, utensils	
Sinks	
Cleanup equipment (brooms, mops, etc.)	
Electrical outlets	
Counter space	
Pantry/Storage	

Notes:

SAMPLE CATERING CONTRACT

DAPHNE'S CATERING

In consideration of the services to be performed by [insert Caterer's name here] ("Caterer") for the benefit of [insert Client's name here] ("Client") at the event scheduled for [insert event's date here], 200_, ("Event") as set forth in the attached invoice, Client agrees to the following terms and conditions:

1. In arranging for private functions, the attendance must be specified and communicated to Caterer by 12:00 p.m. (noon), at least seven (7) days in advance. If the actual number in attendance is greater than the amount confirmed, Caterer cannot guarantee that adequate food will be available for all persons attending. If the actual number is more than 20 percent less than the number confirmed, Caterer reserves the right to increase the price per person.

2. In order to reserve the date of the Event, Client must deliver a copy of this Agreement to Caterer along with a Deposit ("Deposit") of 50 percent of the invoice amount. The balance is due and payable no later than the day on which the Event is scheduled to be held.

3. If Client fails to make any payments when due, this Agreement may be cancelled or rejected by Caterer, and Client agrees that Caterer shall not thereafter be obligated to provide any services hereunder. Client agrees that Caterer may retain 50 percent of the Deposit, as liquidated damages and not as a penalty, which represents a reasonable estimation of fair compensation to Caterer for damages incurred by Caterer resulting from such failure to pay or cancellation by Client.

4. Menu requirements are to be followed as discussed and agreed upon with Client. All food and beverage is subject to __ percent sales tax and __ percent service charge. No beverages of any kind will be permitted to be brought into the premise by Client or any of the guests or invitees from the outside without the special permission of Caterer, and Caterer reserves the right to make a charge for the service of such beverages.

5. Performance of this Agreement is contingent upon the ability of Caterer to complete the same and is subject to labor troubles, disputes or strikes; accidents; government requisitions; restrictions upon travel; transportation; food; beverages; or supplies; and other causes beyond Caterer's control that may prevent or interfere with performance. In no event shall Caterer be liable for the loss of profit, or for other similar or dissimilar collateral or consequential damages, whether on breach of contract, warranty, or otherwise.

6. Client agrees to indemnify and hold harmless Caterer for any damage, theft, or loss of Caterer's property (including without limitation, equipment, plates, utensils, and motor vehicles) occurring at the Event that is caused by persons attending the Event.

EVENT ORDER

Customer:	Judith Jones
Contact:	Judith Jones
Phone:	555-555-5555
Event date:	12/14/07
Location:	J. Jones' house: 1516 Periwinkle Way
No. of guests:	60
Setup time:	5 p.m.
Event type:	Coworker Christmas dinner party

Schedule:

5 p.m.   Caterer arrives
6 p.m.   Guests arrive/serve appetizers/
            open bar
6:30 p.m. Serve dinner
7:45 p.m. Serve dessert
9 p.m.   Guests depart

Rentals:
- Six 60" round linens
- Six 10-ft rounds
- Two 5-ft banquet tables for buffet

Menu:
- **Smoked salmon mousse on endive**
- Fruit and cheese display with crackers
- New potatoes filled with sour cream and caviar
- Beef tenderloin glazed with reduced balsamic vinegar
- Wild mushroom cobbler
- Roasted green beans
- Bread and butter
- Individual chocolate soufflé cakes

CATERING AND EVENT CHECKLIST

Date of Event:		Time: : am/pm to : am/pm	
Private or Open Event?		Name of Party	

Description of Event

Approx. Covers Last Event*:		Sales Last Similar Event:	$
Number of Guests:		* Approx. "Cover" formula: # of Seats x # of Hours	

MENU

Entrée	Portion PP	Order Unit / Portion #	Estimated Servings	Amount to Order / Add to Pars
1.				
2.				
3.				'
Side Dishes				
Side 1				
Side 2				
Side 3				
Side 4				
Bread or Other				
1.				

CATERING AND EVENT CHECKLIST				
Dessert				
1.				
2.				
3.				
Beverages				
1.				
2.				
3.				
Other Ingredients/Items to Order Increase				
1.				
2.				
3.				
4.				
5.				
6.				
7.				
8.				
9.				
10.				
11.				
12.				
13.				
14.				

CATERING AND EVENT CHECKLIST				
KITCHEN SETUP	Time to Do	Person Responsible	Retrieve Item From	Place Item Where?
Product Prepping				
Prep Sheet Filled Out				
Prep Items Labeled				
Clean event area				
Equipment Setup				
Cooking Setup				
Tongs/#				
Spatulas/#				
Cold Side Dish Containers/ # plus backups				
Spoons for Cold Sides/ #				
Hot Dish Containers/ # plus backups				
Serving Spoons #				
Basting Brush				
Condiment Containers/ #				

CATERING AND EVENT CHECKLIST

Cold Holding Setup (40°)				
Aprons/#				
Food Handlers' Gloves				
Trash Cans Strategically Placed and Lined				
Kitchen/Staffing Person	POSITION	HOURS SCHEDULED	RATE	PRIVATE PARTY CHARGE?

CATERING AND EVENT CHECKLIST

SERVICE SET-UP	Time to Do	Person Responsible	Retrieve Item From	Place Item Where?
Table/Chairs Placement				
Tablecloths on Tables				
Condiments				
Beverages				
Cups				
Forks, Knives and Spoons				
Straws, Sugar, Cut Lemons				

GUEST BRINGING CAKE?

Plates				
Cake Cutter				
Candles				

FULL BAR OR WINE?	Cash 'n Carry	Host Bar	Cork Fee?	Cost PP	$NA
Set Up Bar					
Register					

NOTES:

CATERING AND EVENT CHECKLIST

SERVICE STAFFING FOR EVENT/ PERSON	POSITION	HOURS SCHEDULED	RATE	CHARGE TO PARTY?

THE MOVEABLE CHEF/ CATERERS BEO	
BEO #	16443
Date prepared:	6/2/05
Event date:	8/9/05
Event time:	6 p.m. – 10 p.m.
Contact name and number:	Joe Smith, 555-555-5555
Event site:	Botanical Gardens
Group/type of event:	Parents' 50th anniversary
Count:	100
Moveable Chef contact:	Julie Krach
Billing:	50% deposit paid on 5/8/07; 50% by check on day of event

BANQUET SETUP

Set up area for cocktail area and appetizer display. Dinner will be buffet with 10 dining table rounds. Client will provide table linens, floral arrangements for buffet, and dining tables and decorations. Room will be decorated and ready for caterer by 4:30 p.m. on day of event.

APPETIZERS

- Curried chicken salad in phyllo cups

- Cheese, fruit and cracker display with strawberries, grapes, brie, sharp cheddar, dill and Havarti, and assorted crackers

- Hummus and vegetables

- Smoked salmon and cream cheese rollups

DINNER

- Mixed green salad with champagne vinaigrette

- Smoked pork tenderloin with apple chutney

- Grilled chicken breast stuffed with leeks and mushrooms

- Roasted fingerling potatoes

- Haricot verts

DESSERT

- Client will provide anniversary cake. Servers to cut and serve with truffles and coffee.

SEATING

- There will be a head table with anniversary couple plus 8 other family members. Table to be round like other dining tables; place in front by stage.

ENTERTAINMENT

- Taped music for dinner (client will provide tape). A swing band will play after dinner.

CHAPTER

INTERNAL BOOKKEEPING

Internal bookkeeping is the area that ties all departments of the restaurant together into one efficient, airtight operation. Internal bookkeeping is the keystone from which all financial transactions may be monitored, analyzed, and reconciled. Management involvement in this department can never be enough.

The preceding chapters have introduced various means of controlling and securing specific areas of the operation. This chapter will cover:

1. The owner/manager's role in these controls systems.
2. Basic principles of accounting.
3. A system of checks and balances to ensure maximum efficiency and profit.

The internal bookkeeping procedures described in this chapter are simple. To ensure complete accuracy, a couple of hours each day must be devoted to them. It is recommended that a part-time bookkeeper be employed. The bookkeeper need not be highly trained or experienced but must be very accurate and thorough.

Since your bookkeeper will only be required for a few hours each morning, he must be well compensated for his efforts. The ideal candidate for this position might be a stay-at-home parent wishing to work a few hours each morning while children are at school or day care. Additional hours may be supplemented if the bookkeeper is able to assist with basic office and administrative functions such as taking reservations, booking private parties, or typing. A distinction must be made between the bookkeeper and an outside public accountant.

The bookkeeper's primary responsibility is to ensure that all sales and products are accurately recorded and balanced. An outside public accountant should be used from time to time to audit the records, prepare financial and tax statements, and lend management advisory services.

It is recommended that the bookkeeper not be used in any other capacity in the restaurant (other than office administrative duties), as he will be auditing the money and work of the other employees. The bookkeeper must understand and appreciate the confidential nature and importance of the work he is doing. It may be difficult finding a person suitable for this job.

Do not settle for just anyone in this crucial position. Once a competent person is located, make every effort to compensate and satisfy him, as he will be one of your most valuable employees.

This chapter on internal bookkeeping is divided into three separate sections. The first section, Accounts Payable, outlines a unique system for paying and accounting for purchases. The second section, Revenue Accounts and Reconciliation, explains in detail how to account for and reconcile the sales and products from the previous day. The third section describes the steps and procedures used in preparing the payroll.

ACCOUNTING SOFTWARE

As I described in previous chapters, I highly recommend the use of a basic accounting program, such as QuickBooks (**www.quickbooks.com**) or Peachtree (**www.peachtree.com**). These programs are inexpensive and easy to use and will save time, money, and countless errors. The procedures detailed below are for a manual system, but they can be easily (and wisely) brought into a computerized environment. Please note that the use of a POS system may also make some of these activities obsolete.

If you are just setting up your accounting program and decide to use QuickBooks, I recommend an add-on product called *"The Tasty Profits Guide to QuickBooks Software for Restaurants."* This helpful guide to QuickBooks enables you to save thousands of dollars doing your own accounting with its proven, easy-to-use system. Simply install the disc that is included with the "Tasty Profits Guide" directly onto your computer. You will download the pre-configured restaurant accounts and you are ready to go. You will have instant access to all your financial data; calculate accurate food and bar costs with ease; reconcile bank and credit-card statements; track and pay tips that are charged to credit cards; and calculate sales tax automatically. The program is available at **www.atlantic-pub.com** and by calling 800-814-1132, Item TP-01.

SECTION 1: ACCOUNTS PAYABLE

Accounts payable represents the money the restaurant owes its purveyors. Although there are various ways to record the restaurant's transactions, the procedures and systems described here will become an integral part of the restaurant's budgeting, controls, and financial management. Therefore, the adoption and use of these procedures is highly recommended.

INVOICES

The start of the accounts payable process begins when the invoices are brought to the manager's office at the end of each day. As I mentioned before, the employees handling the invoices must do so with the utmost of care and concern. Should an invoice become lost or mutilated, it will throw a "monkey wrench" into the bookkeeping records. Ideally, all invoices should be processed on a daily basis so that the transactions are still fresh in everyone's mind and can be easily referred to. The following are the suggested steps for invoice processing:

1. **Make certain the invoice is actually addressed to the restaurant.**

2. **Make certain the invoice is signed by one of your employees.** A signature ensures

that the items were received intact and accounted for.

3. **Verify the delivery date.**

4. **Check the price and quantity** to make certain the amount delivered was the amount ordered and at the price quoted.

5. **Check the extensions** on the invoice total for accuracy.

6. **If everything appears to be in order, stamp the invoice "Approved."**

CODING THE INVOICE

Every cost the restaurant incurs is assigned a code number. Coding each invoice is an integral part in setting up and establishing bookkeeping and budgeting procedures. Breaking down each invoice and cost into separate categories helps to analyze cost problems later and aids in preparing tax and financial statements. Following is a standard Chart of Accounts for restaurants, provided by the National Restaurant Association (**www.restaurant.org**), of every expenditure the restaurant will normally incur during monthly operations:

BALANCE SHEET OF ACCOUNTS	
ASSETS	**LIABILITIES & EQUITY**
Current Assets	**Current Liabilities**
Cash on Hand	Accounts Payable - Trade
Cash in Bank - General Checking	Accounts Payable - Other
Cash in Bank - High-Yield Checking	Gift Certificates Outstanding
Accounts Receivable - Trade	Deposits Held
Accounts Receivable - Owner/Employee	Sales Tax Payable
Accounts Receivable - Credit Cards	Payroll Taxes Payable
Food Inventory	Other Taxes Payable
Beverage Inventory	Accrued Insurance
Prepaid Taxes	Accrued Payroll
Prepaid Insurance	Accrued Rent
Prepaid Miscellaneous Expenses	Accrued Miscellaneous Expenses
Note Receivable - Current Portion	Note/Loan Payable - Current Portion
	Note/Loan Payable - Current Portion
Fixed Assets	
Leasehold Improvements	**Long Term Liabilities**
Accumulated Amortization - UH Imp	Note/Loan Payable - Long Term Portion
Furniture, Fixtures & Equipment	Note/Loan Payable - Long Term Portion
Accumulated Depreciation - FF&E	
China, Glass, Flatware Par	**Other Liabilities**
Small Equipment Par	Other Notes
	Shareholder Notes
Other Assets	
Deposits Paid	**Shareholders' Equity**
Liquor License	Capital Stock
Organizational Expenses	Retained Earnings - Prior Years
Logo/Artwork	Current Profit/Loss(-)
Note Receivable - Long Term Portion	

INCOME AND EXPENSE ACCOUNTS

Revenue
Food Sales
Liquor/Beer /Misc. Bar Sales
Wine Sales

Cost of Sales
Food Cost
Liquor/Beer /Misc, Bar Cost
Wine Cost

Salaries & Wages
Administrative Wages
Bar Wages
Kitchen Wages
Restaurant Wages
Bonuses & Incentives
Vacation Pay

Employee Benefits
Employer Payroll Tax Expense
Workers' Compensation Insurance
Medical & Dental Insurance
Employee Meals (cost)
Miscellaneous Employee Benefits

Direct Operating Expenses
Auto/Gas Expense - Operations
China/Glass/Flatware Replacement
Contract Cleaning/Janitorial Service
Decorations
Laundry/Linen
Licenses/Permits
Menus and Wine Lists
Supplies - Banquet/Catering
Supplies - Bar
Supplies - Cleaning/Janitorial
Supplies - Kitchen
Supplies - Restaurant
Uniforms

Occupancy Costs
Rent/Lease (Premises)
Equipment Lease
Property Taxes
Insurance - Property
Other Taxes

Repairs & Maintenance
Grounds/Gardening
Maintenance Contracts- Equipment
Repairs & Maintenance-Equipment
Repairs & Maintenance-Premises
Miscellaneous Repairs & Maintenance

Depreciation & Amortization
Depreciation Expense
Amortization Expense

Other (Income)/Expense
Interest Income
Room Rental Fees
Gifts/Novelties Sales
Gifts/Novelties Costs
Telephone Coin Box Commissions
Discounts Taken
Miscellaneous Income

Interest & Non-Operating Expense
Interest Expense
Officers' Salaries & Benefits
Corporate Office Expenses

Income Taxes
State Income Tax
Federal Income Tax

INCOME AND EXPENSE ACCOUNTS

Music & Entertainment

(see detail list)

Marketing

Complimentary Food & Beverage (cost)

Donations/Charities

Media Advertising

Other Promotional Expenses

Postage/Delivery (promo)

Photo/Printing/Graphics

Programs & Directories

Restaurant Research & Development

Signature Souvenirs

Telephone (promo)

Utility Service

Electricity

Natural Gas/Fuel

Scavenger/Waste Removal

Water & Sewage

Administrative & General

Auto/Mileage Allowance

Bad Debt Expense

Bank Charges

Cash Over/Short

Computer Supplies

Credit Card Discounts

Dues and Subscriptions

Educational Materials

Entertainment (Business Operation)

Forms/Paper Products/Printing (A&G)

Insurance- Liability/Umbrella

Insurance- Miscellaneous

Legal/Accounting Professional Services

Management Fees

Miscellaneous Expenses

Office Supplies

Outside Services

Personnel Expenses

Postage/Delivery (A&G)

Security/Alarm

Seminars/Conventions

Telephone/Communications

Travel Expenses

BALANCE SHEET FORMAT

ASSETS		LIABILITIES & EQUITY	
Current Assets		**Current Liabilities**	
Cash on Hand	XXX	Accounts Payable - Trade	XXX
Cash in Bank - General Checking	XXX	Accounts Payable - Other	XXX
Cash in Bank - High-Yield Checking	XXX	Gift Certificates Outstanding	XXX
Accounts Receivable - Trade	XXX	Deposits Held XXX	
Accounts Receivable - Owner/Employee	XXX	Sales Tax Payable	XXX
Accounts Receivable - Credit Cards	XXX	Payroll Taxes Payable	XXX
Food Inventory	XXX	Other Taxes Payable	XXX
Beverage Inventory	XXX	Accrued Insurance	XXX
Prepaid Taxes	XXX	Accrued Payroll XXX	
Prepaid Insurance	XXX	Accrued Rent XXX	
Prepaid Miscellaneous Expenses	XXX	Accrued Miscellaneous Expenses	XXX
Note Receivable - Current Portion	XXX	Note/Loan Payable - Current Portion	XXX
		Note/Loan Payable - Current Portion	XXX
TOTAL CURRENT ASSETS	XXX		
		TOTAL CURRENT LIABILITIES	XXX
Fixed Assets		**Long Term Liabilities**	
Leasehold Improvements	XXX	Note/Loan Payable - Long Term Portion	XXX
Accumulated Amortization - UH Imp	XXX	Note/Loan Payable - Long Term Portion	XXX
Furniture, Fixtures & Equipment	XXX		
Accumulated Depreciation - FF&E	XXX	**TOTAL LONG TERM LIABILITIES**	XXX
China, Glass, Flatware Par	XXX		
Small Equipment Par	XXX	Other Notes/Loans Payable	XXX
TOTAL FIXED ASSETS	XXX	**TOTAL LIABILITIES**	XXX
Other Assets		**Shareholders' Equity**	
Deposits Paid	XXX	Capital Stock	XXX
Liquor License	XXX	Retained Earnings - Prior Years	XXX
Organizational Expenses	XXX	Current Profit/Loss(-)	XXX
Logo/Artwork	XXX		
Note Receivable - Long Term Portion	XXX	**TOTAL SHAREHOLDERS' EQUITY**	XXX
TOTAL OTHER ASSETS	XXX	**TOTAL LIABILITIES AND**	
		SHAREHOLDERS' EQUITY	XXX
TOTAL OTHER ASSETS	XXX		

SUMMARY INCOME STATEMENT FORMAT	Current Period	% of Sales	Year-To-Date	% of Sales
Revenue				
Food Sales	XXX	XX	XXX	XX
Beverage Sales	XXX	XX	XXX	XX
Total Revenue	XXX	XX	XXX	XX
Cost of Sales				
Food Cost	XXX	XX	XXX	XX
Beverage Cost	XXX	XX	XXX	XX
Total Cost of Sales	XXX	XX	XXX	XX
Gross Profit	XXX	XX	XXX	XX
Operating Expenses				
Salaries & Wages	XXX	XX	XXX	XX
Employee Benefits	XXX	XX	XXX	XX
Direct Operating Expenses	XXX	XX	XXX	XX
Music & Entertainment	XXX	XX	XXX	XX
Marketing	XXX	XX	XXX	XX
Utility Services	XXX	XX	XXX	XX
Occupancy Costs	XXX	XX	XXX	XX
Repairs & Maintenance	XXX	XX	XXX	XX
Depreciation & Amortization	XXX	XX	XXX	XX
Other (Income)/Expense	XXX	XX	XXX	XX
General & Administrative	XXX	XX	XXX	XX
Total Operating Expenses	XXX	XX	XXX	XX
Income Before Interest & Non-Operating Expenses	XXX	XX	XXX	XX
Interest				
Interest Expense	XXX	XX	XXX	XX
Other Expenses	XXX	XX	XXX	XX
Total Interest & Non-Op Expenses	XXX	XX	XXX	XX
Income Before Income Taxes	XXX	XX	XXX	XX
Income Taxes	XXX	XX	XXX	XX
NET PROFIT (OR LOSS)	XXX	XX	XXX	XX

After approving each invoice, code the invoice to its appropriate category. A rubber stamp for processing invoices may be prepared at most office-supply stores. It should contain a space for the following information:

1. Date

2. Code

3. Amount due

4. Bookkeeper's initials

After stamping the invoice, simply fill in the appropriate blank with the required data. Some invoices may list purchases or costs that must be entered into the expenditure ledger under different codes. A food purveyor's invoice might list 50 pounds of flour and one case of pineapple juice. The cost of the flour would be coded to the cost of food and the cost of the pineapple juice would be coded to the cost of liquor. If you ask them, most purveyors that deliver products for more than one code will be glad to make out a separate invoice for each code.

Every invoice must be copied and filed according to its respective code number and purveyor's company name. Invoices containing two or more codes should have two or more copies prepared, one for each appropriate file. The original invoices should also be filed by code numbers and by the month in which the transaction occurred. Store the originals in a fireproof cabinet.

Most purveyors will issue a monthly statement itemizing all the invoices and the total amount due. Payment may then be made once a month on the total amount rather than with a separate check for each invoice received. Paying purveyors on a monthly-statement basis is advantageous. The restaurant's cash flow will be utilized more effectively and there will be less administrative work. Prior to issuing the check, be certain that the monthly statement is accurate by cross-checking the statement against the invoices in the file. Staple the received invoices to the monthly statement for future reference.

Accounts must be closed out on the last day of each month to accurately compute monthly profits and costs. Most monthly statements will not arrive until the fourth or fifth day of the following month. Thus, the bookkeeper must realize that, even though some bills may be paid in the following month, the cost of the goods and services will be applied to the month they were delivered to the restaurant. It will be a crucial point in the following two chapters when profits and costs will be computed.

To accurately record purchases delivered to the restaurant, you must record these expenditures in a separate ledger, called a Purchase Ledger. An example of a Purchase Ledger can be found at the end of this chapter. Use a loose-leaf binder to store all the Purchase Ledger pages. Separate Purchase Ledger pages are required for each of the following categories:

1. Food Costs

2. Liquor Costs

3. Wine Costs

4. Each operational category: Services, Utilities, etc.

5. Other Expenses

All invoices must be recorded in the Purchase Ledger under the date the items were delivered to the restaurant. (This is a hard-and-fast rule, regardless of whether goods and services are paid for in cash or by credit or other terms.) This process pertains to all expenses, regardless of whether or not you intend to use the items during that particular month.

In summation, this system will provide a record of expenses when they are paid. The Purchase Ledgers will record all invoices when they are received. The ending inventories, discussed in the following chapters, will make the necessary adjustments to determine the actual amount used over the month. It is necessary so that actual costs may be accurately projected. The crucial consideration now is to record every invoice in the Purchase Ledger under the correct expense category. It must be done on the date the material was received to ensure the cost projections calculated at the end of the month will be accurate.

To post the Purchase Ledger, simply determine which type of expense account it should be credited to and enter the invoice amount on the appropriate ledger page. Record the invoice number, amount, and the date received under the purveyor's column. "Paid Outs" are recorded as cash purchases even if recorded on the Cashier's or Bartender's Report. Determine which expense account the Paid Out should be credited to and record the transaction in the "Paid Out" column on the proper page.

TOTAL MONTHLY PURCHASES

To compute the total expenditure for each code over the month, simply add each expenditure column then each page total on the Purchase Ledger. Credits are subtracted out of the restaurant's total purchases on the monthly statement.

The cut-off time for each month is the close of business on the last day of the month. Transactions after midnight on the last day of the month are still to be included in the month's totals, as they are a part of the business for that previous month. (The measure of one day, for our purposes, is one complete business day or cycle.) To reiterate an important concept from the last section, costs are to be applied to the month the products were received at the restaurant, regardless of when they were paid for or used.

Some hints on preparing the Purchase Ledger:

- Enter all figures in pencil.

- Enter all credits in red and in parentheses.

- Have purveyors that deliver products for more than one code make out a separate invoice for each code.

MANAGING THE RESTAURANT'S CASH FLOW

Daily involvement and analyses of your financial records are necessary if the restaurant is to take full advantage of the credit terms and discounts offered by suppliers. Simply managing the restaurant's cash flow and utilizing its enormous purchasing power can acquire substantial savings.

After you have been operating for a few months, most purveyors will extend "30-day net" terms if you request them. This situation is advantageous; through proper management, the restaurant's inventory may be turned over as many as five or six times in a 30-day period. In effect, the purveyors will be financing your operations. Few businesses can turn their inventories over this quickly, so they are forced to pay interest or finance charges. Quick turnover is one of the blessings of the restaurant business. Careful planning and synchronization between the purchasing and bookkeeping departments is needed to obtain maximum utilization of the cash flow. The savings are well worth the additional effort.

Section 2: Revenue Accounts and Reconciliation

Revenue is the sales received for the restaurant's products: primarily food and beverages. The procedures in this section for setting up revenue accounts are the basis of the restaurant's controls. Every transaction will be checked and balanced. When the procedures are completed, there will be no margin for error and no loss of revenue.

PREPARING AND AUDITING SALES REPORTS

The procedures for preparing and auditing sales reports are listed below in numerical order— the order in which the bookkeeper should begin to record and reconcile the previous day's transactions. It is advisable to have the bookkeeper review the other control sections in the restaurant so that he will become familiar with how the controls fit together and how they work.

1. Remove the cash drawer, tickets, charge forms, Cook's Forms, and reports from the safe where the manager placed them at the close of the previous business day.

2. Separate the cashier and bartender drawers, tickets, and forms into their respective piles. Work in a closed, locked office while the cash is out of the safe.

3. Begin by verifying the Cashier's and Bartender's Reports. Count out and separate the cash by denomination. The total amount taken in must equal the difference between the new and old cash-register readings. These figures should all be in order, as the manager checked and verified the sales of the previous day with the cashier and bartender. Any discrepancies should be immediately brought to the manager's attention.

4. Using new Cashier's and Bartender's Report forms, enter the new register readings in the space provided on the reports.

5. Make up new cash drawers for each register. Enter the total and itemized amounts on the reports in the "Cash In" sections. Sign the reports and place them in the cash drawers. Place the drawers back into the safe. Return the remaining cash, charges, and checks to the safe. Later on you will need all these items to make up the daily deposit.

6. Using the Ticket Issuance Form and the bottom part of the Bartender's Report, verify that all tickets have been turned in. The total number issued must equal the amount used and returned. Should there be any tickets missing, determine which ticket number is missing and, using these two forms, you can determine which employee was issued the missing ticket. Notify the manager immediately. The manager should have verified that all tickets were turned in the previous day. This, again, is a double check.

7. From the unused tickets issue new cocktail and bar tickets. Issue the same number of tickets to each employee. Thirty is an average number for each shift. Using the employee schedule, write on the appropriate forms the name of each wait person and bartender working. Write in the total number of tickets issued and the number sequences of each

employee's tickets. Place a rubber band around each pile of tickets. On the top ticket write in the employee's name so that the manager knows to whom they should be issued. When completed, place everything in the safe.

8. Take the used tickets from the previous business day and separate wait staff and bar tickets. Starting with the wait staff tickets, check each for accuracy. Make certain that:

    A. The correct price was charged. (This is a double check on the cashier.)

    B. The ticket was added correctly and sales tax was computed and entered correctly. Wait staff and cashiers may be charged for these mistakes in some states. Regardless of the legality, they must be notified of their errors and correct them in the future. Write up all mistakes and post the sheet on the bulletin board at the completion of each day. Mistakes in writing tickets are caused by careless employees and can be a great expense to the restaurant. Management should use whatever action is necessary to resolve and limit the problem.

9. On the Food Itemization Format found at the end of this chapter, place an "X" in the appropriate column for each menu item sold. Using the Wine Itemization Form, itemize any wine sold from the tickets. List any housed, managerial, or complimentary product in the itemization, but also list them separately on the back of the form in their respective categories; this information will be used later.

10. Check the wait staff, bar and, if utilized, cocktail tickets for accuracy. Any wine or food item listed on these tickets must also be added to the Food and Wine Itemization Forms. Cocktails and liquor are not itemized.

11. Take the credit-card sales drafts and separate them into piles by company. Each employee is responsible for her own credit-card charges, but they should be double-checked by the cashier. Verify the accuracy of each charge:

    A. Make sure the charge slip is signed.

    B. If the card was imprinted manually, make sure the slip was imprinted clearly, the right charge form was used, the expiration date is good, the slip is dated correctly and the total amount was added correctly.

    C. If the tip was charged, a "Cash Paid Out" from the cashier or bartender should have been given to the employee. The Cash Paid Out is not a purchase because, when the charge goes through, the restaurant will be reimbursed. Set up a cash reserve or special account and reimburse the cash drawer for this Cash Paid Out. When the check or electronic deposit from the credit card company comes in, put the Paid Out amount back into the reserve or special account.

    D. Be sure an approval code is on the charge, in case the floor limit of the charge card was exceeded.

12. Separate and examine for accuracy any checks received. The manager should have approved personal checks. The customer's driver's license number and telephone number should be listed on the back. Also, only the manager should approve traveler's checks. The manager must witness the second signature and compare it to the first.

13. Total and verify all the charge and check amounts on both reports.

14. Total the Food and Wine Itemization Forms. Multiply the total number sold by the selling price (without sales tax).

15. Compare the itemized number of menu items sold against the daily Cook's Form and the Ticket Itemization Form. It will ensure that every food item is now accounted and paid for. Should there be a discrepancy, recheck both your figures and the cook's calculations. If everything still appears to be in order, refigure the Cook's Form using the carbon-copy tickets. It is possible a ticket may have been changed after the carbon copy was given to the cook.

16. Total the food sales on the Food Itemization Form. This figure must match the total food sales entered on the Cashier's and Bartender's Reports.

17. Total the wine sales on the Wine Itemization Form. This figure must match the total wine sales entered on the Bartender's and Cashier's Reports.

18. Add the itemized wine and food sales together.

19. The difference between the total itemized food and wine sales and the total sales taken in must equal the liquor sales.

20. The total sales multiplied by the percentage of sales tax must equal the total sales tax taken in. After this step, all sales will be completely checked and balanced by three different individuals and against every other transaction that occurred in the restaurant. There is no possible way items or money could be stolen, undetected, unless every single employee — including the manager — was in collusion.

21. Send the Wine Itemization Form to the manager so that he may reconcile and restock the wine for the next day.

22. Make up the daily deposit. Use indelible ink and prepare two copies of the deposit form. Stamp all checks with the restaurant's account number and "For Deposit Only." Put the appropriate employee's name on the back of each check so that, if it is returned, the manager can go back to the employee who accepted it.

23. Sort the bills and wrap as many of the coins as possible. Charge card sales receipts can usually be deposited along with your cash deposit or electronically, direct from the terminal. If your bank does not offer this service, you will have to mail the receipts directly to the credit card company. The manager should personally bring the deposit to the bank every day. Change or small bills needed for the following day should be picked up at this time.

24. Never let two days' worth of receipts sit in the safe. Make certain the deposit receipt is returned and filed in a fireproof box. Check the duplicate deposit stub against the deposit receipt to make sure the correct amount was deposited. Enter the deposit amount, date, and source onto the check register. Enter the verified figures for the day on the Daily Sales Report Form (see example at the end of this chapter).

To compute individual category percentages, divide the category sales by the total daily sales. "Actual Month-to-Date Sales" is a tally of the daily sales. The budget sections will be explained in detail in the next chapter. "Dinner Count" refers to the number of daily customers served. "Cash, Over/Short" refers to any mistakes made at the register. Complimentary, house, and manager figures are recorded from when you itemized the food and bar tickets in Step 9. Break down the food, liquor, and wine sales for each category and enter at full price.

This concludes the reconciliation part of the revenue accounts. Every item and sale is accounted for and reconciled against every other transaction in the restaurant. Keep all of these forms for at least five years in a fireproof storage file. All forms used during the month may be kept in loose-leaf binders in the bookkeeper's office. The Daily Sales Report should be left at the manager's desk at the end of the day. Remember that all this information is strictly confidential and should never be the subject of idle conversation.

SECTION 3: PAYROLL

As stated earlier, preparing the payroll is best left to a computerized payroll program, such as QuickBooks® or Peachtree® or to a payroll service.

TAXES AND TIPS

One of the biggest challenges facing restaurant owners and managers in regard to payroll is getting employees to report and pay taxes on their tips, as required by the IRS. Complying with the intricacies of the tip reporting and allocation rules can be difficult and confusing. Tip tax laws are constantly changing. There are at least five legal suits involving tip regulations that are currently pending. You must use extreme caution in this area; get assistance from your accountant, attorney, state restaurant association, or the National Restaurant Association (**www.restaurant.org**).

U.S. SUPREME COURT DECIDES TIP-REPORTING CASE

United States v. Fior d'Italia Inc., 01-463: The Internal Revenue Service can use estimates to make sure it is collecting enough taxes on cash restaurant tips, the Supreme Court said Monday, June 17, 2002. The ruling is a defeat for the estimated 350,000 restaurants with tipped workers. The court said the IRS can estimate the amount of cash tips given to employees based on tips shown on credit card receipts. The estimate is used to determine taxes. This case pitted one of the nation's oldest Italian restaurants against U.S. tax collectors. The restaurant contends the IRS formula does not take into account stingy cash tips, take-out meals, or tip-sharing among hostesses and other staff.

Justice Stephen Breyer, writing for the 6-3 court, said, while the practice is not illegal, "we recognize that Fior d'Italia remains free to make its policy-related arguments to Congress." The ruling is a follow-up to the Supreme Court's 1973 decision that the IRS can make an educated guess about employees' tip taxes when records are inadequate. Fior d'Italia, operating in San Francisco for 116 years, had challenged an extra $22,000+ bill that was calculated with estimates. Using credit card receipts, the IRS had calculated that workers were tipped about 14 percent on meals. The San Francisco-based 9th U.S. Circuit Court of Appeals said the IRS could not prove that people who paid with cash tipped 14 percent and that the IRS therefore should stop using the estimates.

OTHER TIP TAX CASES

Since the IRS first began pursuing employer-only and employer-first restaurant audits in the mid-1990s to collect taxes from employers on tips employees allegedly failed to report, the restaurant industry has mounted several major court challenges. Several of these challenges have made it to the federal appeals court level. In the Fior d'Italia case, the 9th Circuit (San Francisco) ruled in the restaurant's favor. Three other federal appeals courts have sided with the IRS.

Get more details on all the rulings:

- 9th Circuit (California), in Fior d'Italia, Inc. v. United States (March 2001);

- 11th Circuit (Florida), in Quietwater Entertainment, Inc. v. United States (June 2000; no published opinion);

- 11th Circuit (Alabama), in Morrison Restaurants, Inc. v. United States of America (August 1997); and

- Federal Circuit (Washington, DC): Bubble Room, Inc. v. United States (Pending).

TIPPED EMPLOYEES

The Supreme Court ruling of June 25, 2002, states that the Internal Revenue Service can use aggregate tip estimates to ensure that the employer is paying enough FICA taxes on allegedly unreported tips. This essentially means the IRS can look at the restaurant's records, come up with a total amount of tips it thinks employees should have reported, and bill the restaurant business for the employer's share of FICA taxes (currently 7.65%) on any allegedly unreported tips. Under the new ruling, the IRS does not need to examine individual employees' records or credit employer FICA tax payments to individual employees' Social Security accounts. It is permissible for the IRS to estimate the amount of cash tips given to employees based on tips included on credit card receipts.

Potentially, a restaurant could face a tax bill for FICA taxes on allegedly unreported tips going as far back as 1988, when Congress first began requiring employees to pay FICA taxes on all tips. As an employer of tipped employees you are essentially being forced to protect yourself from IRS audits and aggregate FICA tax assessments.

So what is the restaurant owner to do? In 2000, the IRS announced it was lifting a five-year moratorium on its employer-only audits. We recommend restaurant owners at least consider signing the Tip Reporting Alternative Commitment (TRAC) with the IRS.

Through the TRAC (under a more customized employer-created approach, EmTRAC), a restaurant business agrees to assume greater responsibility for training, educating, and getting employees to report their tips. In exchange, the IRS agrees that it will not bill the restaurant for FICA taxes on allegedly unreported tips unless it has first examined which employees had not reported tips accurately. The TRAC program essentially allows you a release from employer-only assessments if you comply with the program. This is the only remedy, albeit a partial one, unless Congress acts on the subject. The National Restaurant Association, as well as other trade group associations, has vowed to take the fight over tip reporting to Congress. In the meantime, you must govern yourself accordingly and seek the advice of your CPA.

THE TIP RATE DETERMINATION AND EDUCATION PROGRAM

The Tip Rate Determination and Education Program was developed by the Internal Revenue Service in 1993 to address the concern of widespread underreporting of tip income in the food-

and-beverage industry. The goal was to involve employers in monitoring their employees' tip-reporting practices.

There are two different IRS programs available: the Tip Rate Determination Agreement (TRDA) and the Tip Reporting Alternative Commitment (TRAC). Participation in one of these programs is voluntary and the restaurant may only enter into one of the agreements at a time. Please note that 1998 tax legislation specifies that IRS agents cannot threaten to audit you in order to convince you to sign a TRAC or TRDA agreement.

The benefit for you as an employer is that you will not be subject to unplanned tax liabilities. Those who sign a TRAC or TRDA agreement receive a commitment from the IRS that the agency will not examine the owner's books to search for withheld or underpaid payroll taxes on tip income. There are benefits to employees, also, including increases in their Social Security, unemployment compensation, retirement plan, and workers' compensation benefits.

Under TRDA, the IRS works with you to arrive at a tip rate for your employees. Then, at least 75 percent of your tipped workers must agree in writing to report tips at the agreed-upon rate. If they fail to do so, you are required to turn them in to the IRS. If you do not comply, the agreement is terminated and your business becomes subject to IRS auditing.

The TRAC is less strict but requires more work on your part. There is no established tip rate, but you are required to work with employees to make sure they understand their tip-reporting obligations. You must set up a process to receive employees' cash tip reports and they must be informed of the tips you are recording from credit card receipts.

TIP CREDITS FOR EMPLOYERS ARE POSSIBLE

As an employer, you may also be eligible for credit for taxes paid on certain employee tips (IRS Form 8846). The credit is generally equal to the employer's portion of Social Security and Medicare taxes paid on tips received by employees. You will not get credit for your part of Social Security and Medicare taxes on those tips that are used to meet the federal minimum wage rate applicable to the employee under the Fair Labor Standards Act (as detailed later in this chapter). This is also subject to state laws. You must also increase the amount of your taxable income by the amount of the tip credit. Note the following changes to this credit:

1. The credit is effective for your part of Social Security and Medicare taxes paid after 1993, regardless of whether your employees reported the tips to you or when your employees performed the services.

2. Effective for services performed after 1996, the credit applies to the taxes on tips your employees receive from customers in connection with providing, delivering, or serving food or beverages, regardless of whether the customers consume the food or beverages on your business premises.

EMPLOYEE TIP REPORTING "FREQUENTLY ASKED QUESTIONS"

Because you are an employee, the tip income you receive — whether it is cash or included in a charge — is taxable income. As income, these tips are subject to federal income tax and Social Security and Medicare taxes and may be subject to state income tax as well.

EMPLOYEE TIP REPORTING FREQUENTLY ASKED QUESTIONS

QUESTION	ANSWER
What tips do I have to report?	If you received $20 or more in tips in any one month you should report all your tips to your employer so that federal income tax, Social Security and Medicare taxes — maybe state income tax, too — can be withheld.
Do I have to report all my tips on my tax return?	Yes. All tips are income and should be reported on your tax return.
Is it true that only 8 percent of my total sales must be reported as tips?	No. You must report to your employer all (100 percent) of your tips except for the tips totaling less than $20 in any month. The 8-percent rule applies to employers.
Do I need to report tips from other employees?	Yes. Employees who are indirectly tipped by other employees are required to report "tip-outs." This could apply to bus persons, for instance.
Do I have to report tip-outs that I pay to indirectly tipped employees?	If you are a directly tipped employee, you should report to your employer only the amount of tips you retain. Maintain records of tip-outs with your other tip income (cash tips, charged tips, split tips, tip pool).
What records do I need to keep?	You must keep a running daily log of all your tip income.
What can happen if I do not keep a record of my tips?	Underreporting could result in owing substantial taxes, penalties, and interest to the IRS and, possibly, other agencies.
If I report all my tips to my employer, do I still have to keep records?	Yes. You should keep a daily log of your tips so that, in case of an examination, you can substantiate the actual amount of tips received.
Why should I report my tips to my employer?	When you report your tip income to your employer, the employer is required to withhold federal income tax, Social Security and Medicare taxes, and, maybe, state income tax. Tip reporting may increase your Social Security credits, resulting in greater Social Security benefits when you retire. Tip reporting may also increase other benefits to which you may become entitled, such as unemployment or retirement benefits. Additionally, a greater income may improve financing approval for mortgages, car loans, and other loans.
I forgot to report my tip income to my employer, but I remembered to record it on my federal income tax return. Will that present a problem?	If you do not report your tip income to your employer, but you do report the tip income on your federal income tax return, you may owe a 50 percent Social Security and Medicare tax penalty and be subject to a negligence penalty and, possibly, an estimated tax penalty.
What about indirectly tipped employees?	You are required to report all your tips to your employer.

EMPLOYEE TIP REPORTING FREQUENTLY ASKED QUESTIONS

QUESTION	ANSWER
What is my responsibility as an employee under the Tip Rate Determination Agreement (TRDA)?	You are required to file your federal tax returns. You must sign a Tipped Employee Participation Agreement proclaiming that you are participating in the program. To stay a participating employee, you must report tips at or above the tip rate determined by the agreement.
What can happen if I do not report my tips to the IRS?	If the IRS determines through an examination that you underreported your tips, you could be subject to additional federal income tax, Social Security and Medicare taxes and, possibly, state income tax. You will also be charged a penalty of 50 percent of the additional Social Security and Medicare taxes and a negligence penalty of 20 percent of the additional income tax, plus any interest that may apply.
If I report all my tips, but my taxes on the tips are greater than my pay from my employer, how do I pay the remaining taxes?	You can either pay the tax when you file your federal income tax return or you can reach into your tip money and give some to your employer to be applied to those owed taxes.
What is my responsibility as an employee under the Tip Reporting Alternative Commitment (TRAC)?	Directly tipped employee: Your employer will furnish you with a written statement (at least monthly) reflecting your charged tips: 1. You are to verify or correct this statement. 2. You are to indicate the amount of cash tips received. 3. When reporting your cash tips, keep in mind that there is a correlation between charged tips and cash tips. 4. You may be asked to provide the name and amount of any tip-outs you have given to indirectly tipped employees.

EMPLOYER'S TIP RECORDS

It is in your company's best interest to insist that all employees accurately report their income from tips. The IRS will hold you responsible. Establishments that do not comply are subject to IRS audit and possible tax liabilities, penalties, and interest payments. As a precaution, if you have any employees who customarily receive tips from customers, patrons, or other third parties, we recommend you keep the following additional information about tipped employees:

1. **Indicate on the pay records** — by a symbol, letter, or other notation placed next to his or her name — each tipped employee.

2. **Weekly or monthly amount of tips reported by each employee.**

3. **The amount by which the wages of each tipped employee have been increased by tips.**

4. **The hours worked each workday in any occupation in which the employee does not receive tips** and the total daily or weekly earnings for those times.

5. **The hours worked each workday in any occupation in which the employee receives tips** and the total daily or weekly straight-time earnings for those times.

Large Food or Beverage Establishments Need to File Form 8027 with the IRS. You may meet the definition of a "large food or beverage establishment" if you employ more than 10 employees. If you do, the law requires that you file Form 8027, Employer's Annual Information Return of Tip Income and Allocated Tips, with the IRS. If you meet the definition, the law requires that you report certain tip information to the IRS on an annual basis. You should use Form 8027 to report information such as total charged tips, charged receipts, total reported tips by employees, and gross receipts from food-and-beverage operations. Also, employers must allocate tips to certain directly tipped employees and include the allocation on their employees' W-2 forms when the total of reported tips is less than 8 percent.

The IRS offers a program that business owners can enter into to help them educate their employees about tip reporting and tax obligations. This is the "Tip Rate Determination and Education Program." There are two arrangements under the program that a food- and-beverage employer can enter into: TRDA, the Tip Rate Determination Agreement, or TRAC, Tip Reporting Alternative Commitment.

To find out more about these programs and about whether you should be filing Form 8027, contact the Tip Coordinator of your local IRS office. Check your telephone directory for the IRS office in your area. They can provide the mailing address and phone number for the Tip Coordinator.

You can get a copy of Form 8027 and its instructions by calling 800-TAX-FORM (800-829-3676). You can also get copies of most forms by dialing 703-368-9694 from your fax machine.

FOR MORE INFORMATION ON TIP REPORTING

The following IRS forms and publications relating to tip income reporting can be downloaded directly from the government Web site **www.irs.gov/forms_pubs/index.html**. Look under the heading "Forms and Publications by Number."

- Pub 505 — Tax Withholding and Estimated Tax
- Pub 531 — Reporting Tip Income
- Form 941 — Employer's Quarterly Federal Tax Return
- Form 4137 — Social Security and Medicare Tax on Unreported Tip Income
- Form 8027 — Employer's Annual Information on Tip Income and Allocated Tips

"THE IRS TIP AGREEMENTS REALLY HELP EMPLOYERS AND WORKERS" FROM THE IRS

The IRS is continuing its emphasis on a multiyear strategy to increase tax compliance by tipped employees. Originally developed for the Food and Beverage industry, this program has now been extended to the Gaming (casino) and Hairstyling industries.

There are two arrangements under this program that, depending on their business, employers in specific industries can agree to enter into: The Tip Rate Determination Agreement (TRDA), which is available to the Gaming and the Food and Beverage industries, and the Tip Reporting Alternative Commitment (TRAC), which is available to the Food and Beverage and the Hairstyling industries.

First introduced in 1993, the TRDA set the stage for a new way of doing business at the IRS. This arrangement emphasizes future compliance by tipped employees in the Food and Beverage industry by utilizing the tip rates individually calculated for each restaurant. In addition, as long as the participants comply with the terms of the agreement and accurately report their tip income, the IRS agrees not to initiate any examinations during the period the TRDA is in effect. When TRDA was first introduced in 1993, initial response from the industry was mixed. Today the TRDA is a viable option for many restaurants.

The second arrangement, TRAC, grew out of a collaborative effort between the IRS and a coalition of restaurant industry representatives. It was first introduced in June 1995.

TRAC emphasizes educating both employers and employees to ensure compliance with the tax laws relating to tip income reporting. Employees are provided tip reports detailing the correlation that exists between an employee's charged tip rate and the cash tip rate. In general, the District Director will not initiate any examinations on either the employer or employees while the agreement is in effect if participants comply with the provisions of the agreement.

The overall response to TRDA and TRAC has been very positive among employers who seek to foster compliance by their employees in a manner that is relatively simple and that makes good business sense. In addition, there are benefits for both the employer and the employees.

Employer Benefits — After Congress passed a law in 1988 requiring employers to match and pay assessments made against employees, the IRS performed significant amounts of tip audits. The IRS expended a significant amount of resources to conduct these examinations. Some employers found themselves in a financial crisis, having to come up with the tax being assessed against them when there had not been any financial planning for this. Employees were being hit just as hard. Under the Tip Rate Determination Agreement (TRDA), the IRS agrees not to perform any tip audits while either a Tip Rate Determination Agreement or a Tip Reporting Alternative Commitment is in effect. The employer is granted a credit allowance (Code Section 45B) for Social Security taxes paid on tips in excess of minimum wage reported by employees. The employer is then in compliance with the law.

Employee Benefits — The employee receives several benefits. Greater Social Security benefits accrue based on the tip earnings reported. Increased tip earnings translates to increased proof of income when applying for mortgage, car, and other loans. There is an increase in unemployment benefits, retirement plan contributions (if applicable), and to workers' compensation. There will not be any subsequent tip examinations of the employee's tax returns as long as the terms of the arrangement have been met and all tips have been reported.

As of June 30, 1998, the IRS has received more than 8,000 TRAC agreements representing over 25,000 establishments nationwide. The number of TRDAs is nearly 1,100, representing over 2,400 establishments. Please note many of the agreements encompass multiple unit locations. The IRS is continuing its efforts to raise the compliance level in this industry and to promote consistency across the country. IRS employees have been receiving updated training in this area.

As part of an outreach effort, IRS employees will be making field calls to businesses where tipping is customary, explaining both arrangements and providing business owners with copies of written material to aid them in educating themselves and their workers. But you do not have to wait for an IRS representative to visit you to get more information about TRDA or TRAC. Information is available through the Tip Coordinator at your local IRS office and the IRS's "Tips on Tips" brochures (employer and employee versions). These and other publications relating to tip income can be ordered by calling the IRS at 800-829-3676.

PAYROLL ACCOUNTING

Although you may decide to use an outside payroll service or a software program, your bookkeeper must still be involved in the computation of the daily labor costs. After each pay period, the bookkeeper will need to compute each employee's time card and call the information to the payroll service company or key the information into the accounting software. There are time clocks available that can link employee scheduling, time clock administration, and accounting all into one foolproof system. Described in this section are the procedures used to compute and analyze by manual system daily and monthly labor costs. On a daily basis the bookkeeper should:

1. Gather all of the employees' time cards.

2. Using the posted schedule, ensure that each employee punched in at the scheduled time.

3. Compute the number and fraction of hours worked.

4. Enter hours worked on the time card and on the Daily Payroll Form. An example of this form can be found at the end of this chapter. Any overtime should be written in red on a separate line. Notify the manager of any overtime or of any employee who is approaching overtime status. She may be able to rearrange the schedule to avoid paying overtime.

5. Fill in the hourly rate of pay. If the employee performs more than one job, make sure the rate of pay corresponds to the job performed.

6. Extend the gross amount to be paid.

7. Divide each salaried employee's total monthly salary by the number of days in the month. Enter this figure in the "Gross Paid" column for each day. Although the employee will be paid the same each week, the salary is broken down this way so that labor may be analyzed and budgeted accurately.

8. The manager and owner's salaries should be listed separately at the bottom of the Daily Payroll Form. These costs are separated, as they will be budgeted differently in an upcoming chapter. Also, by separating them out you may get some additional tax advantages.

9. Total the gross amount payable for each day at the bottom of the form. When the week is completed (seven days) total each employee's hours worked and total gross pay. Check your calculations by cross-checking all of the figures against each other.

10. Enter the daily sales and labor costs on the Labor Analysis Form. An example of this form can be found at the end of this chapter. Remember that manager and owner salaries are computed separately and are not in the total labor cost computations. The Labor Analysis Form is divided into two sections: the daily payroll and the month-to-date payroll. These are computed by adding each day's transactions to the previous day's balance. Budget figures will be explained in the next chapter.

The month-to-date payroll percentage is computed by dividing month-to-date sales by the month-to-date actual payroll costs. The budget figures are the budgeted total labor costs divided by the number of days in the month. The month-to-date payroll column is the prorated budgeted amount.

The following pages contain various excerpts pertaining to withholding procedures for restaurants, courtesy of the Internal Revenue Service and the U.S. Department of Labor.

TIPPED EMPLOYEES UNDER THE FAIR LABOR STANDARDS ACT (FLSA)

This fact sheet provides general information concerning the application of the FLSA to employees who receive tips. Use caution: This document was last revised in November 2001; unless otherwise stated, the information reflects requirements that were in effect, or would take effect, as of January 1, 2002.

CHARACTERISTICS

Tipped employees are those who customarily and regularly receive more than $30 a month in tips. Tips actually received by tipped employees may be counted as wages for purposes of the FLSA, but the employer must pay not less than $2.13 an hour in direct wages.

REQUIREMENTS

If an employer elects to use the tip credit provision the employer must:

1. Inform each tipped employee about the tip credit allowance (including amount to be credited) before the credit is utilized.

2. Be able to show that the employee receives at least the minimum wage when direct wages and the tip credit allowance are combined.

3. Allow the tipped employee to retain all tips, whether or not the employer elects to take a tip credit for tips received, except to the extent the employee participates in a valid tip pooling arrangement. If an employee's tips combined with the employer's direct wages of at least $2.13 an hour do not equal the minimum hourly wage — $4.75 an hour effective 10/1/96; $5.15 an hour effective 9/1/97 — the employer must make up the difference.

Youth Minimum Wage

The 1996 Amendments to the FLSA allow employers to pay a youth minimum wage of not less that $4.25 an hour to employees who are under 20 years of age during the first 90 consecutive calendar days after initial employment by their employer. The law contains certain protections for employees that prohibit employers from displacing any employee in order to hire someone at the youth minimum wage.

Dual Jobs

When an employee is employed concurrently in both a tipped and a non-tipped occupation, the tip credit is available only for the hours spent in the tipped occupation. The Act permits an employer to take the tip credit for time spent in duties related to the tipped occupation, even though such duties are not by themselves directed toward producing tips, provided such duties are incidental to the regular duties and are generally assigned to such occupations. Where tipped employees are routinely assigned to maintenance, or where tipped employees spend a substantial amount of time (in excess of 20 percent) performing general preparation work or maintenance, no tip credit may be taken for the time spent in such duties.

Retention of Tips:

The law forbids any arrangement between the employer and the tipped employee whereby any part of the tip received becomes the property of the employer. A tip is the sole property of the tipped employee. Where an employer does not strictly observe the tip credit provisions of the Act, no tip credit may be claimed and the employees are entitled to receive the full cash minimum wage, in addition to retaining tips they may/should have received.

Service Charges:

A compulsory charge for service, for example, 15 percent of the bill, is not a tip. Such charges are part of the employer's gross receipts. Where service charges are imposed and the employee receives no tips, the employer must pay the entire minimum wage and overtime required by the Act.

Tip Pooling:

The requirement that an employee must retain all tips does not preclude tip splitting or pooling arrangements among employees who customarily and regularly receive tips, such as waiters, waitresses, bellhops, counter personnel (who serve customers), busboys/girls, and service bartenders. Tipped employees may not be required to share their tips with employees who have not customarily and regularly participated in tip pooling arrangements, such as dishwashers, cooks, chefs, and janitors. Only those tips that are in excess of tips used for the tip credit may be taken for a pool. Tipped employees cannot be required to contribute a greater percentage of their tips than is customary and reasonable.

Credit Cards:

Where tips are charged on a credit card and the employer must pay the credit card company a percentage on each sale, then the employer may pay the employee the tip, less that percentage. This charge on the tip may not reduce the employee's wage below the required minimum wage. The amount due the employee must be paid no later than the regular payday and may not be held while the employer is awaiting reimbursement from the credit card company.

TYPICAL PROBLEMS

Minimum Wage Problems:

Employee does not qualify as a "tipped employee;" tips are not sufficient to make up difference between employer's direct wage obligation and the minimum wage; employee receives tips only — so the full minimum wage is owed; illegal deductions for walk-outs, breakages and cash register shortages; and invalid tip pools.

Overtime Problems:

Failure to pay overtime on the full minimum wage; failure to pay overtime on the regular rate including all service charges, commissions, bonuses, and other remuneration.

WHERE TO OBTAIN ADDITIONAL INFORMATION

This publication is for general information and is not to be considered in the same light as official statements of position contained in the regulations. Copies of Wage and Hour publications may be obtained by contacting the nearest office of the Wage and Hour Division listed in most telephone directories under U.S. Government, Department of Labor Employment Standards Administration/Wage and Hour Division.

MINIMUM HOURLY CASH WAGES FOR TIPPED EMPLOYEES UNDER MINIMUM WAGE LAWS

The Department of Labor is providing this information as a public service to enhance public access to information relating to state wage and hour laws that supplement the federal wage and hour laws administered by the Department of Labor. This is a service that is continually under development. The user should be aware that, while we try to keep the information timely and accurate, there might be a delay between the date when a change in state law takes place and the modification of these pages to reflect the change. Therefore, we make no express or implied guarantees. We will make every effort to correct errors brought to our attention.

The statutes, regulations, and court and administrative decisions of each of the states should be relied upon as the official statement of a state's law. In some instances, county or municipal law also may affect wage and hour standards applicable to employers, employees, and other persons.

Some documents on the Department's Web site contain hypertext pointers to information created and maintained by other public and private organizations. Please be aware that we do not control or guarantee the accuracy, relevance, timeliness, or completeness of this outside information. Further, the inclusion of pointers to particular items in hypertext is not intended to reflect their importance, nor is it intended to endorse any views expressed or products or services offered by the author of the reference to the organization operating the server on which the reference is maintained.

This document was last revised in November 2001; unless otherwise stated, the information reflects requirements that were in effect, or would take effect, as of January 1, 2002.

Use Caution: Regulations and laws on tips and tip reporting are constantly changing.

DAILY PAYROLL FORM

Date	Month		Year					H = Hours	G = Gross						
Employee	Rate	H	G	H	G	H	G	H	G	H	G	H	G	H	G	Total

LABOR ANALYSIS FORM

	Day	Date	Daily Sales	Daily Payroll			% Month to Date	Month to Date	Month-to-Date Payroll			
				Budget	Act.	Ov/Un			Budget	Act.	Ov/Un	%
1												
2												
3												
4												
5												
6												
7 Day Total:												
8												
9												
10												
11												
12												
13												
14 Day Total:												
15												
16												
17												
18												
19												
20												
21 Day Total:												
22												
23												
24												
25												
26												
27												
28 Day Total:												
29												
30												
31												
TOTAL												

DAILY SALES REPORT FORM

	Day	Date	FOOD SALES		LIQUOR SALES		WINE SALES		TOTAL SALES	MONTH-TO-DATE	
			AMT $	INV #	AMT $	INV #	AMT $	INV #		ACT.	BUDG.
1											
2											
3											
4											
5											
6											
7 Day Total:											
8											
9											
10											
11											
12											
13											
14 Day Total:											
15											
16											
17											
18											
19											
20											
21 Day Total:											
22											
23											
24											
25											
26											
27											
28 Day Total:											
29											
30											
31											
TOTAL											

DAILY SALES REPORT FORM (CONTINUED)

OVER UNDER	# DINERS	PER HEAD	CASH O/UN	MANAGERIAL			HOUSED			COMPLIMENTARY		
				FOOD	LIQ.	WINE	FOOD	LIQ.	WINE	FOOD	LIQ.	WINE

WINE ITEMIZATION FORM

Item	Use a ✓ mark to designate one sold	Totals

FOOD ITEMIZATION FORM

Item	Use a ✓ mark to designate one sold	Totals

PURCHASE LEDGER

Company						Month		
Date	INV #	AMT $	INV #	AMT $	INV #	AMT $	Paid Outs
						TOTAL	

Department of the Treasury
Internal Revenue Service

Publication 1244

(Rev. August 2005)

Employee's Daily Record of Tips and Report to Employer

This publication contains:

Form 4070A, Employee's Daily Record of Tips

Form 4070, Employee's Report of Tips to Employer

For the period

beginning _____ , _____ and

ending _____ , _____

Name and address of employee

Instructions

You must keep sufficient proof to show the amount of your tip income for the year. A daily record of your tip income is considered sufficient proof. Keep a daily record for each workday showing the amount of cash and credit card tips received directly from customers or other employees. Also keep a record of the amount of tips, if any, you paid to other employees through tip sharing, tip pooling or other arrangements, and the names of employees to whom you paid tips. Show the date that each entry is made. This date should be on or near the date you received the tip income. You may use Form 4070A, Employee's Daily Record of Tips, or any other daily record to record your tips.

Reporting tips to your employer. If you receive tips that total $20 or more for any month while working for one employer, you must report the tips to your employer. Tips include cash left by customers, tips customers add to debit or credit card charges, and tips you receive from other employees. You must report your tips for any one month by the 10th of the month after the month you receive the tips. If the 10th day falls on a Saturday, Sunday, or legal holiday, you may give the report to your employer on the next business day that is not a Saturday, Sunday, or legal holiday.

You must report tips that total $20 or more every month regardless of your total wages and tips for the year. You may use Form 4070, Employee's Report of Tips to Employer, to report your tips to your employer. See the instructions on the back of Form 4070.

You must include all tips, including tips not reported to your employer, as wages on your income tax return. You may use the last page of this publication to total your tips for the year.

Your employer must withhold income, social security, and Medicare (or railroad retirement) taxes on tips you report. Your employer usually deducts the withholding due on tips from your regular wages.

Unreported Tips. If you received tips of $20 or more for any month while working for one employer but did not report them to your employer, you must figure and pay social security and Medicare taxes on the unreported tips when you file your tax return. If you have unreported tips, you must use Form 1040 and Form 4137, Social Security and Medicare Tax on Unreported Tip Income, to report them. You may not use Form 1040A or 1040EZ. Employees subject to the Railroad Retirement Tax Act cannot use Form 4137 to pay railroad retirement tax on unreported tips. To get railroad retirement credit, you must report tips to your employer.

If you do not report tips to your employer as required, you may be charged a penalty of 50% of the social security and Medicare taxes (or railroad retirement tax) due on the unreported tips unless there was reasonable cause for not reporting them.

Additional Information. Get Pub. 531, Reporting Tip Income, and Form 4137 for more information on tips. If you are an employee of certain large food or beverage establishments, see Pub. 531 for tip allocation rules.

Recordkeeping. If you do not keep a daily record of tips, you must keep other reliable proof of the tip income you received. This proof includes copies of restaurant bills and credit card charges that show amounts customers added as tips. Keep your tip income records for as long as the information on them may be needed in the administration of any Internal Revenue law.

Form **4070A** (Rev. August 2005) Department of the Treasury Internal Revenue Service	**Employee's Daily Record of Tips** This is a voluntary form provided for your convenience. See instructions for records you must keep.	OMB No. 1545-0074

Employee's name and address	Employer's name	Month and year
	Establishment name (if different)	

Date tips rec'd	Date of entry	**a.** Tips received directly from customers and other employees	**b.** Credit and debit card tips received	**c.** Tips paid out to other employees	**d.** Names of employees to whom you paid tips
1					
2					
3					
4					
5					
Subtotals					

For Paperwork Reduction Act Notice, see Instructions on the back of Form 4070.   Page 1

Date tips rec'd	Date of entry	a. Tips received directly from customers and other employees	b. Credit and debit card tips received	c. Tips paid out to other employees	d. Names of employees to whom you paid tips
6					
7					
8					
9					
10					
11					
12					
13					
14					
15					
Subtotals					

Date tips rec'd	Date of entry	a. Tips received directly from customers and other employees	b. Credit and debit card tips received	c. Tips paid out to other employees	d. Names of employees to whom you paid tips
16					
17					
18					
19					
20					
21					
22					
23					
24					
25					
Subtotals					

Date tips rec'd	Date of entry	a. Tips received directly from customers and other employees	b. Credit and debit card tips received	c. Tips paid out to other employees	d. Names of employees to whom you paid tips
26					
27					
28					
29					
30					
31					
Subtotals from pages 1, 2, and 3					
Totals					

1. Report total cash tips (col. **a**) on Form 4070, line **1**.
2. Report total credit and debit card tips (col. **b**) on Form 4070, line **2**.
3. Report total tips paid out (col. **c**) on Form 4070, line **3**.

Form **4070** (Rev. August 2005) Department of the Treasury Internal Revenue Service	**Employee's Report of Tips to Employer**	OMB No. 1545-0074

Employee's name and address	Social security number
	⋮　　⋮

Employer's name and address (include establishment name, if different)	**1** Cash tips received
	2 Credit and debit card tips received
	3 Tips paid out

Month or shorter period in which tips were received from _____ , _____ , to _____ ,	**4** Net tips (lines **1** + **2** - **3**)
Signature	Date

For Paperwork Reduction Act Notice, see the instructions on the back of this form.　　Cat. No. 41320P　　Form **4070** (Rev. 8-2005)

Purpose. Use this form to report tips you receive to your employer. This includes cash tips, tips you receive from other employees, and debit and credit card tips. You must report tips every month regardless of your total wages and tips for the year. However, you do not have to report tips to your employer for any month you received less than $20 in tips while working for that employer.

Report tips by the 10th day of the month following the month that you receive them. If the 10th day is a Saturday, Sunday, or legal holiday, report tips by the next day that is not a Saturday, Sunday, or legal holiday.

See Pub. 531, Reporting Tip Income, for more details.

You can get additional copies of Pub. 1244, Employee's Daily Record of Tips and Report to Employer, which contains both Forms 4070A and 4070, by calling 1-800-TAX-FORM (1-800-829-3676) or by downloading the pub from the IRS website at *www.irs.gov*.

Paperwork Reduction Act Notice. We ask for the information on these forms to carry out the Internal Revenue laws of the United States. You are required to give us the information. We need it to ensure that you are complying with these laws and to allow us to figure and collect the right amount of tax.

You are not required to provide the information requested on a form that is subject to the Paperwork Reduction Act unless the form displays a valid OMB control number. Books or records relating to a form or its instructions must be retained as long as their contents may become material in the administration of any Internal Revenue law. Generally, tax returns and return information are confidential, as required by Code section 6103.

The average time and expenses required to complete and file this form will vary depending on individual circumstances. For the estimated averages, see the instructions for your income tax return.

If you have suggestions for making this form simpler, we would be happy to hear from you. See the instructions for your income tax return.

Employer's Annual Information Return of Tip Income and Allocated Tips

▶ See separate instructions.

OMB No. 1545-0714

2006

⌐ Name of establishment ¬	Type of establishment (check only one box)
Number and street (see instructions) Employer identification number	☐ 1 Evening meals only
City or town, state, and ZIP code	☐ 2 Evening and other meals
L ⌐	☐ 3 Meals other than evening meals
	☐ 4 Alcoholic beverages

Employer's name (same name as on Form 941)

Establishment number (see instructions)

Number and street (P.O. box, if applicable)   Apt. or suite no.

City, state, and ZIP code (if a foreign address, see instructions)

Does this establishment accept credit cards, debit cards, or other charges?
☐ Yes (lines 1 and 2 **must** be completed)
☐ No

Check **if:** Amended Return ☐
Final Return ☐

Attributed Tip Income Program (ATIP). See Revenue Procedure 2006-30 . . . . ▶ ☐

1	Total charged tips for calendar year 2006.	**1**	
2	Total charge receipts showing charged tips (see instructions)	**2**	
3	Total amount of service charges of less than 10% paid as wages to employees. . . .	**3**	
4a	Total tips reported by indirectly tipped employees	**4a**	
b	Total tips reported by directly tipped employees	**4b**	
	Note. Complete the **Employer's Optional Worksheet for Tipped Employees** on page 6 of the instructions to determine potential unreported tips of your employees.		
c	Total tips reported (add lines 4a and 4b)	**4c**	
5	Gross receipts from food or beverage operations (not less than line 2—see instructions) .	**5**	
6	Multiply line 5 by 8% (.08) or the lower rate shown here ▶_____ granted by the IRS. (Attach a copy of the IRS determination letter to this return.)	**6**	
	Note. If you have allocated tips using other than the calendar year (semimonthly, biweekly, quarterly, etc.), mark an **"X"** on line 6 and enter the amount of allocated tips from your records on line 7.		
7	Allocation of tips. If line 6 is more than line 4c, enter the excess here	**7**	

▶ This amount must be allocated as tips to tipped employees working in this establishment. Check the box below that shows the method used for the allocation. (Show the portion, if any, attributable to each employee in box 8 of the employee's Form W-2.)

a Allocation based on hours-worked method (see instructions for restriction) . . . ☐
Note. If you marked the checkbox in line 7a, enter the average number of employee hours worked per business day during the payroll period. (see instructions) _____

b Allocation based on gross receipts method . . . . ☐

c Allocation based on good-faith agreement (Attach a copy of the agreement.). . . ☐

8 Enter the total number of directly tipped employees at this establishment during 2006 ▶

Under penalties of perjury, I declare that I have examined this return, including accompanying schedules and statements, and to the best of my knowledge and belief, it is true, correct, and complete.

Signature ▶   Title ▶   Date ▶

For Privacy Act and Paperwork Reduction Act Notice, see page 6 of the separate instructions.   Cat. No. 49989U   Form **8027** (2006)

CHAPTER

SUCCESSFUL BUDGETING
AND PROFIT PLANNING

All restaurants are in business to make a profit. To plan financially you must first set up a long-range plan detailing how much money you want the restaurant to return and when. This financial plan is the restaurant's budget. This chapter will detail the steps for setting up a budget. The following chapter will describe the procedures for projecting actual operating costs, as well as how to recognize, analyze, and resolve cost problems.

Aside from being the restaurant's financial plan, the budget is also used to control costs and account for sales and products. Budgeting is an accounting record and a tool used to evaluate how effectively the restaurant, management, and employees operated during the month. Based on this information, management can then recognize cost problem areas and act accordingly to correct them. Although many businesses maintain a yearly or quarterly budget, restaurants, because of their fluctuating operating performances, should use a monthly budget. The annual budget and profit and loss statement can then be easily computed by totaling all 12 monthly budgets. Monthly budgeting is the system described in this book. Once set up and operating, about four hours each month is all that will be required to compute the old budget and project a new one. Although the restaurant may be only in the pre-opening stage, it is imperative that you start to develop an operating budget now. As soon as the budget is prepared, you will possess the control for guiding the business towards your financial goal.

Initially the proposed budget may be under- or over-inflated. You may have overruns, but at least you will be starting to gain control over the organization, rather than the organization controlling you. After a few months you will have past operating budgets to guide you in projecting new ones. The budgeting process will become easier and more accurate as time goes by.

There are many other benefits to preparing and adhering to a monthly operational budget. Supervisors and key employees will develop increased awareness and concern about the restaurant and controlling its costs. This involvement will invariably rub off on the other employees. A well-structured, defined budget and orderly financial records will aid you in obtaining loans and will develop an important store of information should you decide to expand or sell in the future. Cost problems can be easily pinpointed once the expense categories are broken down. Last, you will become a better manager. Your financial decisions and forecasts will become increasingly consistent and accurate, as more information will be available to you. Financial problems may be seen approaching down the road rather than suddenly cropping up and forcing you to act quickly when you are uninformed. Management all too often reacts to a problem's symptoms, instead of curing the disease. Budgeting will give you the tool for an accurate diagnosis

PROJECTING THE OPERATIONAL BUDGET

This section describes in detail all of the operational costs listed on the Operational Budget (which can be found at the end of this chapter), as well as how to accurately project each expenditure and revenue for the following month.

TOTAL SALES

Projecting total sales is the most crucial and difficult aspect of budgeting. The fact that it is impossible to know how business will be from day to day makes budgeting total sales a perplexing task. Most costs are either variable or semi-variable, which means they will fluctuate directly in relation to the total monthly sales. Thus, accurately projecting these costs depends largely upon using an accurate total sales figure. Projecting total sales, at first, will be difficult — and most likely inaccurate — but after several months of operation, your projections will be right on target. You will be surprised at how consistent sales and customer counts are and how easy it will be to consistently budget accurately.

The initial budgets may be unrealistic expectations. Sales will probably be low, as you will not have been able to build a substantial clientele or reputation. Operating costs will be higher than normal. It will take a couple of months to streamline and build an efficient restaurant even with the best-laid plans. Labor and material costs will be extremely high, as there will be a lot of training, low productivity, and housed food, liquor, and wine. All of these costs are normal and should be anticipated. Profit margins will be small and possibly nonexistent.

This period of time (four to 12 weeks) should be used to ensure that your product is perfected and all the bugs are worked out of the systems. This period is no time to cut back on costs. Your intention is to be in business for a long time. Allocate sufficient funds now to make sure the business gets off on the right foot and profits will be guaranteed for many years. Schedule a full staff every night to make certain all details will be covered. Discontinue those items that are passable but not of the quality level desired. Slow, clumsy service and average food will never build sales. Strive for A-1 quality products and service. Constantly reiterate to employees this primary concern and before long they will self-monitor the quality. Once you develop a clientele and a solid reputation for serving consistent, quality products, the budget and profits will fall into place. There are eight basic steps for projecting total sales:

1. If possible, use last year's customer count. This information can be found in last year's Daily Sales Report Form. Projections for the first year can be based upon prior months' reports and educated estimates.

2. Using the Sales Projection Form (which can be found at the end of this chapter) and a calendar, calculate the number of days in the month. Enter this figure in the first column. From the information in #1, calculate the average number of covers served each day. Enter this figure in the second column. Compute the average number of covers served on any holidays that may be in the month; include scheduled functions, banquets, and large parties in this total.

3. Multiply the number of days in the month by the average number of covers served for that day; enter the result in the "Subtotal" column. Add the eight "Subtotal" columns to arrive at the grand total.

4. Review and analyze the growth in customer counts during the past year, current year, and current month. Based upon past customer counts determine the percentage of growth or decline in growth anticipated in the coming month. Percentage of growth or decline can be computed by subtracting the most recent period of customer counts by the past period of customer counts. The difference is then divided by the actual number of dinners served during the past period of time. A negative percentage figure shows a drop in customer counts. A positive figure indicates the percentage of increase.

   When computing and analyzing these computations, keep in mind that each period of time must have the same number and type of days. In other words, you can only accurately compare months that have the same number of Mondays, Tuesdays, and so forth, since sales are different for each day; otherwise the results and analysis would be inaccurate. The most accurate way to analyze the percentage of growth or loss is to compare the previous month to the same month last year and then compare the percentage to the current month. Remember to only examine actual cover counts as indicators of growth; changes in sales may be the result of a price change.

5. Multiply the percentage of gross or loss by the grand total. Add the result to the grand total to compute the projected volume, or number of dinners. Subtract this figure instead if you are multiplying by a negative percentage figure that indicates a loss in customer counts.

6. Multiply the projected volume by the average check of the past month. The average check amount may be located on the Daily Sales Report Form. Adjust this figure if a price increase will be occurring during the month. Breakfast, lunch, and dinner sales may all be projected together unless the percentage of growth or loss is suspected in one area and not in the other two. A separate chart for each category should then be used to project each sales amount; simply add all three figures together to compute grand total of sales.

7. Compute individual food, liquor, and wine sales by simply dividing total sales by the average percentage of sales on last month's Daily Sales Report Form. A restaurant budgeted at $25,000 in sales that has a division of sales at 70 percent food, 20 percent liquor, and 10 percent wine would have a breakdown of $17,500 food, $5,000 liquor and $2,500 wine sales.

8. The final step in budgeting sales is to enter the budgeted amount for each day on the Daily Sales Report Form. To compute the budgeted amount for each day, divide the total projected sales by the number of days in the month. This amount is the budgeted sales for one day. Enter this figure on line one of the first day of the month. Add this same amount to itself to compute the budgeted sales for day two and continue adding

this same amount to itself until you have computed the sales for each day. Double-check your calculations by running a tape on the sales. The total must equal the total budgeted sales projections. Breaking down sales this way will enable the manager to see exactly where actual sales are in relation to budgeted sales. On a daily basis, enter the amount over or under budget in sales in the appropriate column (Use parentheses and/or a red pencil to enter sales that are under budget.).

MATERIAL COSTS

Material costs will fluctuate directly with the sales variance. More food, liquor, or wine sales will result in higher material costs. In budgeting material costs, the important figure to analyze is not the actual cost but the percentage of cost, or the cost-of-sales percentage, as it is more commonly known. Compute the cost-of-sales percentage by dividing the actual cost of the category by the category's total sales. The result will be a percentage figure. This formula will present an accurate indication of the category's costs, as the cost of sales are proportionate to each other.

The cost-of-sales percentages for each category — food, liquor, and wine — were projected in the previous chapters when determining the selling price of each item. Food cost was projected at between 35 and 40 percent, liquor, 18 to 25 percent, and wine, approximately 40 percent cost of sales. Enter the percentage figure used in the previous sections in the "Budgeting Percentage" column. This percentage figure can be used initially in order to project the first month's budget. After several months of operation, the actual figure can be substituted.

Multiply the individual material costs by each respective budgeted percentage; the results are the budgeted cost amounts. If food sales were budgeted at $100,000, and the food cost percentage was estimated at 40 percent, the budgeted food cost would be $40,000. Increases in product costs will raise the actual cost-of-sales amount; adjust the budgeted amount accordingly. However, be certain that if an increase is anticipated, the increase will affect the following month, which is what is being budgeted. Items purchased at a higher price and then stored in inventory will have no effect upon the following month's actual cost of sales, as the product will not have been used. Add all three budgeted costs to compute the total budgeted material costs. Subtract the total gross costs from the total sales to compute the gross profit dollar amount. Divide gross profit by total sales to calculate the gross profit percentage.

LABOR

MANAGER SALARY

Manager salaries should be a fixed monthly cost. Total all the manager salaries for one year; divide this figure by the number of days in the year, and multiply this cost by the number of days in one month. Salary changes during the year will require adjustments. When owners take an active part in the management of the restaurant, or when the company is incorporated, the owners should have their salary amount included in this category.

EMPLOYEE SALARY

The employee salary expense is a semi-variable cost that will fluctuate directly with total sales. Employee labor costs have a breakeven point, the point where the labor cost is covered by the profit from sales. As this point is reached and total sales increase, the labor cost percentage will decrease, increasing net profit. Thus, the cost of labor is determined by its efficiency and by the volume of sales it produces. Multiply the projected total sales by the average labor cost percentage to arrive at the anticipated labor cost dollar amount. Adjust this figure in relation to the amount of employee training anticipated for the month.

OVERTIME

Overtime should be nonexistent — or at least kept to an absolute minimum. No amount should be budgeted for overtime. Money spent on overtime usually indicates poor management and inefficiency. Bookkeepers should be on the lookout for employees approaching 40 hours of work near the end of the week. Carefully prepared schedules will eliminate 98 percent of all overtime work and pay. Employees who wish to switch their schedules around should only be allowed to do so after approval from the manager.

CONTROLLABLE OPERATIONAL COSTS

CONTROLLABLE OPERATIONAL COSTS: SUPPLIES	
China and Utensils	**Glassware**
Cost of china and utensils bought should be a consistent amount and percentage of sales for each month. Review Chapter 10, "Successful Management of Operational Costs and Supplies."	Same as china and utensils.
Bar Supplies	**Dining Room Supplies**
Same as china and utensils.	Same as china and utensils.
Uniforms	**Laundry and Linen**
The uniform expense will depend upon the state in which the restaurant is located and individual management policies. Some states allow the company to charge the employees for uniforms; others do not. Many restaurants that do charge employees for uniforms do so at cost, which, if done correctly, should cost the restaurant nothing but administrative time.	Laundry and linen buying should be a consistent monthly expenditure, as laundry and linen is usually purchased once or twice a year, in bulk. This expenditure column is for the purchase price only; cleaning is computed in a separate column, under "Services".
Office Supplies	**Kitchen Supplies**
Cost of office supplies should be a fixed dollar amount each month. Capital expenditures must be depreciated.	Same as china and utensils. Capital expenditures for equipment with utility for more than one year generally must be depreciated over the item's anticipated life span.

CONTROLLABLE OPERATIONAL COSTS: SERVICES

Laundry Cleaning	Protection
Cleaning of laundry is a variable expense directly related to total sales. Multiply last month's percentage of cost by budgeted sales. Adjust the figure for price increases.	Protection should be a consistent, fixed monthly expenditure. Service-call charges should be coded to "Equipment Repairs" under "General Operating Costs".

Legal	Accounting
Legal services are a variable expense that can fluctuate greatly. Estimates for most legal work can be obtained, but it is best to budget a little each month to cover periodically large legal fees.	A semi-fixed expense depending upon the amount and the type of accounting services used. Once set up and operating, the accounting expense should be a consistent monthly charge except for an annual tax-preparation and year-end audit fee.

Freight
This expense may not be applicable to all restaurants. Freight is the expense incurred shipping material via rail, truck, or other method to the restaurant for exclusive use in the restaurant. Freight charges are usually incurred only by businesses in remote areas or when the restaurant purchases a product and then has an independent company deliver it.

Maintenance	Payroll
Maintenance should be a fixed monthly expenditure if you are using a maintenance service company with contract service.	A semi-fixed expense fluctuating directly with the number of employees on the payroll. Restaurants not utilizing a computerized payroll service will not have a payroll preparation expense. The wages paid to the bookkeeper are included in the employee labor expenditure.

CONTROLLABLE OPERATIONAL COSTS: UTILITIES

Water	Heat
Water should be a semi-variable expense.	Heat includes the cost of any heating material used but not listed above, such as coal, wood, and oil.

Telephone
Telephone service should be a relatively consistent monthly expense. All long-distance phone calls should be recorded in a notebook (Your local office-supply store has a specially designed book for this purpose.). The itemized phone bill should be compared against the recorded phone calls to justify each one.

Gas	Electricity
Gas may be a variable or semi-variable expense depending upon the type of equipment it operates. Gas used in heating will be a variable expense, because more will be used during the winter months than in the summer.	Electricity may be a variable or semi-variable expense depending upon the type of equipment it operates. Electricity bills are normally higher during the summer months, as this is when the air-conditioning units are used.

FIXED OPERATING COSTS

FIXED OPERATING COSTS	
RENT	**INSURANCE**
The monthly amount of rent or, if the building is leased, the monthly lease. Certain business-rental and lease agreements also include payment of a percentage of the total sales or per-tax profit amount. Should this be the situation, use the budgeted total sales figure and project the anticipated amount due. Enter this amount and the total rent amount in the "Budgeted" column.	Total all insurance premium amounts (fire, theft, liability, workers' compensation, etc.) and divide by 12. This figure will equal the average monthly insurance expense.
PROPERTY TAXES	**DEPRECIATION**
If applicable, divide the annual property tax amount by 12. This figure will equal the average monthly property tax amount.	Depreciation will be discussed in detail below

DEPRECIATION

Depreciation may be defined as the expense derived from the expiration of a capital asset's quantity of usefulness over the life of the property. Capital assets are those assets that have utility of more than one year. Since a capital asset will provide utility over several years, the deductible cost of the asset must be spread out over its useful life — over a specified recovery period. Each year a portion of the asset's cost may be deducted as an expense.

Some examples of depreciable items commonly found in a restaurant include: office equipment, kitchen and dining room equipment, the building (if owned), machinery, display cases, and any intangible property which has a useful life of more than one year. Thus, items such as light bulbs, china, stationery, and merchandise inventories may not be depreciated. The cost of franchise rights is usually a depreciable expense.

The Depreciation Worksheet and Record at the end of the chapter will be a great aid in computing depreciation amounts, regardless of the methods used. Record the purchase of all depreciable items right away and you will keep on top of this complex and time-consuming area. The IRS publishes guidelines for the number of years to be used for computing an asset's useful life.

GENERAL OPERATING COSTS

GENERAL OPERATING COSTS: TAXES	
Payroll and Labor Taxes	**Other Taxes**
The tax amount the employer is required to contribute to the state and federal government. A separate tax account should be set up with your bank to keep all the tax money separate. Labor taxes include: Social Security, Medicare tax, federal unemployment tax, and state unemployment tax.	Includes all miscellaneous taxes, such as local taxes, sales tax paid on purchases. This column is for any tax the restaurant pays for goods and services. It is not for sales tax or other taxes the restaurant collects, as they are not expenditures. Federal income tax is not a deductible expenditure and should not be listed here, either.

GENERAL OPERATING COSTS

REPAIRS AND MAINTENANCE: EQUIPMENT	REPAIRS AND MAINTENANCE: BUILDING
Includes the cost of scheduled and emergency repairs and maintenance to all equipment. Always budget a base amount for normal service. Adjust this figure if major repairs or overhauls are anticipated.	Includes the cost of minor scheduled repairs and emergency repairs and maintenance to the building. Always budget a base amount for repairs/maintenance. Large remodeling or rebuilding projects should be budgeted as a separate expenditure and depreciated.
ENTERTAINMENT	**ADVERTISING**
Entertainment includes bands, music, entertainers, and so forth.	Advertising includes all the costs of advertising the restaurant, including television, radio, mailing circulars, newspapers, etc.
PROMOTIONAL EXPENSE	**EQUIPMENT RENTAL**
The expense of promotional items: key chains, calendars, pens, free dinners, T-shirts, sponsorship of events, etc.	This cost is the expense of either short- or long-term renting of pieces of equipment or machinery.
POSTAGE	**CONTRIBUTIONS**
Postage paid for business purposes.	These are all contributions paid to recognized charitable organizations.
TRADE DUES, ETC.	**LICENSES**
Includes dues paid to professional organizations such as the National Restaurant Association. Trade magazine subscriptions should also be entered in this category. This expense should be divided by 12 to apportion the cost from the month in which it occurs.	The expense of all business and government licenses: operating licenses, a health permit, liquor licenses, etc. This expense should also be divided by 12 to apportion the cost from the month in which it occurs.
CREDIT CARD EXPENSE	**TRAVEL**
Credit card expense can be computed by multiplying the service-charge cost-of-sales percentage by the total projected credit-card sales volume.	Travel includes the expense of ordinary and necessary travel for business purposes for yourself and your employees.
BAD DEBT	
This expense should be nonexistent if the proper procedures for handling credit cards and checks are enforced. Normally, the full amount of a bad debt is a tax-deductible expense. However, you must prove the debt is worthless and uncollectible. In some states, the employee who handled the transaction may be held legally liable for the unpaid amount.	

TOTAL EXPENDITURES

Add the total budgeted expenditures from both pages and enter the figure in this column.

TOTAL NET PROFIT

Subtract Total Budgeted Expenditures from Total Sales. The result is the total net profit (or loss). Divide the Total Net Projected Profit by projected Total Sales to compute the projected Pre-Tax Net Profit Percentage. Total projected sales minus total material costs will equal the gross profit amount.

DEPRECIATION WORKSHEET AND RECORD

Date	Description	Meth	Life	New/ Used	AC RS%	Cost	Salvage	Addit. 1st Year

DEPRECIATION WORKSHEET AND RECORD (CONTINUED)

Balance	Depreciation 20	Balance	Depreciation 20	Balance

OPERATIONAL BUDGET

Item	Budgeted	%	Actual	%
SALES				
Food				
Liquor				
Wine				
TOTAL SALES				
MATERIALS				
Food Costs				
Liquor Costs				
Wine Costs				
TOTAL COSTS				
GROSS PROFIT				
LABOR				
Manager Salary				
Employee				
Overtime				
TOTAL LABOR COST				
Controller Oper. Costs				
China & Utensils				
Glassware				
Kitchen Supplies				
Bar Supplies				
Dining Room Supplies				
Uniforms				
Laundry/Linen				
Services				
Trash Pick-Up				
Laundry Cleaning				
Protection				
Freight				
Accounting				
Maintenance				
Payroll				
TOTAL THIS PAGE				

OPERATIONAL BUDGET (CONTINUED)

Item	Budgeted	%	Actual	%
UTILITIES				
Phone				
Water				
Gas				
Electricity				
Heat				
FIXED OPERATING COSTS				
Rent				
Insurance				
Property Taxes				
Depreciation				
GENERAL OPERATING COSTS				
Labor Taxes				
Other Taxes				
Repairs—Equipment				
Repairs—Building				
Entertainment				
Advertising				
Promotion				
Equipment Rental				
Postage				
Contributions				
Trade Dues, ect.				
Licenses				
Credit Card Expense				
Travel				
Bad Debt				
TOTAL THIS PAGE				
TOTAL EXPENDITURES				
TOTAL NET PROFIT				

SALES PROJECTION FORM

Date	# of Each	Avg # of Dinners	Subtotal	
Mon				**BREAKFAST TOTAL**_____
Tues				
Wed				**LUNCH TOTAL** _____
Thurs				
Fri				**DINNER TOTAL**_____
Sat				
Sun				**GRAND TOTAL** _____
Holidays				

Grand Total x % Growth/Loss = Projected Volume x Check Avg. = Projected Sales

DIVISION OF SALES

	TOTAL PROJECTED SALES x	% SALES DIVISION	= SALES DIVISION
Food			
Liquor			
Wine			

HOLIDAYS THAT MUST BE CONSIDERED:

- Washington's Birthday
- Memorial Day
- Thanksgiving
- New Year's Eve
- Valentine's Day

- Easter
- Fourth of July
- Christmas Eve
- New Year's Day
- Graduation Day

- Mother's Day
- Labor Day
- Christmas
- Halloween

DEPRECIATION WORKSHEET

Description of Property:

Date Placed in Service:	Cost or Other Basis	Business/Investment Use %	Section 179 Deduction and Special Allowance	Depreciation Prior Years
Basis for Depreciation	Method/Convention	Recovery Period	Rate Table or %	Depreciation Deduction

Description of Property:

Date Placed in Service:	Cost or Other Basis	Business/Investment Use %	Section 179 Deduction and Special Allowance	Depreciation Prior Years
Basis for Depreciation	Method/Convention	Recovery Period	Rate Table or %	Depreciation Deduction

Description of Property:

Date Placed in Service:	Cost or Other Basis	Business/Investment Use %	Section 179 Deduction and Special Allowance	Depreciation Prior Years
Basis for Depreciation	Method/Convention	Recovery Period	Rate Table or %	Depreciation Deduction

Description of Property:

Date Placed in Service:	Cost or Other Basis	Business/Investment Use %	Section 179 Deduction and Special Allowance	Depreciation Prior Years
Basis for Depreciation	Method/Convention	Recovery Period	Rate Table or %	Depreciation Deduction

Form **4562**	**Depreciation and Amortization**	OMB No. 1545-0172
Department of the Treasury Internal Revenue Service	**(Including Information on Listed Property)** ▶ See separate instructions. ▶ Attach to your tax return.	**20**06 Attachment Sequence No. **67**

Name(s) shown on return	Business or activity to which this form relates	Identifying number

Part I **Election To Expense Certain Property Under Section 179**
Note: *If you have any listed property, complete Part V before you complete Part I.*

1	Maximum amount. See the instructions for a higher limit for certain businesses	**1**	$108,000
2	Total cost of section 179 property placed in service (see instructions)	**2**	
3	Threshold cost of section 179 property before reduction in limitation	**3**	$430,000
4	Reduction in limitation. Subtract line 3 from line 2. If zero or less, enter -0-	**4**	
5	Dollar limitation for tax year. Subtract line 4 from line 1. If zero or less, enter -0-. If married filing separately, see instructions	**5**	

(a) Description of property	(b) Cost (business use only)	(c) Elected cost	
6			

7	Listed property. Enter the amount from line 29 . . . . **7**		
8	Total elected cost of section 179 property. Add amounts in column (c), lines 6 and 7	**8**	
9	Tentative deduction. Enter the **smaller** of line 5 or line 8.	**9**	
10	Carryover of disallowed deduction from line 13 of your 2005 Form 4562	**10**	
11	Business income limitation. Enter the smaller of business income (not less than zero) or line 5 (see instructions)	**11**	
12	Section 179 expense deduction. Add lines 9 and 10, but do not enter more than line 11. . .	**12**	
13	Carryover of disallowed deduction to 2007. Add lines 9 and 10, less line 12 ▶ **13**		

Note: *Do not use Part II or Part III below for listed property. Instead, use Part V.*

Part II **Special Depreciation Allowance and Other Depreciation (Do not** include listed property.) (See instructions.)

14	Special allowance for qualified New York Liberty or Gulf Opportunity Zone property (other than listed property) placed in service during the tax year (see instructions)	**14**	
15	Property subject to section 168(f)(1) election	**15**	
16	Other depreciation (including ACRS)	**16**	

Part III **MACRS Depreciation (Do not** include listed property.) (See instructions.)

Section A

17	MACRS deductions for assets placed in service in tax years beginning before 2006	**17**	
18	If you are electing to group any assets placed in service during the tax year into one or more general asset accounts, check here . . . . ▶ ☐		

Section B—Assets Placed in Service During 2006 Tax Year Using the General Depreciation System

(a) Classification of property	(b) Month and year placed in service	(c) Basis for depreciation (business/investment use only—see instructions)	(d) Recovery period	(e) Convention	(f) Method	(g) Depreciation deduction
19a 3-year property						
b 5-year property						
c 7-year property						
d 10-year property						
e 15-year property						
f 20-year property						
g 25-year property			25 yrs.		S/L	
h Residential rental property			27.5 yrs.	MM	S/L	
			27.5 yrs.	MM	S/L	
i Nonresidential real property			39 yrs.	MM	S/L	
				MM	S/L	

Section C—Assets Placed in Service During 2006 Tax Year Using the Alternative Depreciation System

20a Class life					S/L	
b 12-year			12 yrs.		S/L	
c 40-year			40 yrs.	MM	S/L	

Part IV **Summary** (see instructions)

21	Listed property. Enter amount from line 28	**21**	
22	**Total.** Add amounts from line 12, lines 14 through 17, lines 19 and 20 in column (g), and line 21. Enter here and on the appropriate lines of your return. Partnerships and S corporations—see instr.	**22**	
23	For assets shown above and placed in service during the current year, enter the portion of the basis attributable to section 263A costs . . **23**		

For Paperwork Reduction Act Notice, see separate instructions.   Cat. No. 12906N   Form **4562** (2006)

Part V | **Listed Property** (Include automobiles, certain other vehicles, cellular telephones, certain computers, and property used for entertainment, recreation, or amusement.)

Note: *For any vehicle for which you are using the standard mileage rate or deducting lease expense, complete **only** 24a, 24b, columns (a) through (c) of Section A, all of Section B, and Section C if applicable.*

Section A—Depreciation and Other Information (Caution: *See the instructions for limits for passenger automobiles.*)

24a Do you have evidence to support the business/investment use claimed? ☐ Yes ☐ No   **24b** If "Yes," is the evidence written? ☐ Yes ☐ No

(a) Type of property (list vehicles first)	(b) Date placed in service	(c) Business/ investment use percentage	(d) Cost or other basis	(e) Basis for depreciation (business/investment use only)	(f) Recovery period	(g) Method/ Convention	(h) Depreciation deduction	(i) Elected section 179 cost
25 Special allowance for qualified New York Liberty or Gulf Opportunity Zone property placed in service during the tax year and used more than 50% in a qualified business use (see instructions) **25**								
26 Property used more than 50% in a qualified business use:								
		%						
		%						
		%						
27 Property used 50% or less in a qualified business use:								
		%			S/L –			
		%			S/L –			
		%			S/L –			

28 Add amounts in column (h), lines 25 through 27. Enter here and on line 21, page 1. . **28**

29 Add amounts in column (i), line 26. Enter here and on line 7, page 1. . . . . **29**

Section B—Information on Use of Vehicles

Complete this section for vehicles used by a sole proprietor, partner, or other "more than 5% owner," or related person.

If you provided vehicles to your employees, first answer the questions in Section C to see if you meet an exception to completing this section for those vehicles.

		(a) Vehicle 1		(b) Vehicle 2		(c) Vehicle 3		(d) Vehicle 4		(e) Vehicle 5		(f) Vehicle 6	
30	Total business/investment miles driven during the year (**do not** include commuting miles)												
31	Total commuting miles driven during the year												
32	Total other personal (noncommuting) miles driven												
33	Total miles driven during the year. Add lines 30 through 32												
		Yes	No	Yes	No	Yes	No	Yes	No	Yes	No	Yes	No
34	Was the vehicle available for personal use during off-duty hours?												
35	Was the vehicle used primarily by a more than 5% owner or related person?												
36	Is another vehicle available for personal use?												

Section C—Questions for Employers Who Provide Vehicles for Use by Their Employees

Answer these questions to determine if you meet an exception to completing Section B for vehicles used by employees who **are not** more than 5% owners or related persons (see instructions).

		Yes	No
37	Do you maintain a written policy statement that prohibits all personal use of vehicles, including commuting, by your employees?		
38	Do you maintain a written policy statement that prohibits personal use of vehicles, except commuting, by your employees? See the instructions for vehicles used by corporate officers, directors, or 1% or more owners		
39	Do you treat all use of vehicles by employees as personal use?		
40	Do you provide more than five vehicles to your employees, obtain information from your employees about the use of the vehicles, and retain the information received?		
41	Do you meet the requirements concerning qualified automobile demonstration use? (See instructions.)		

Note: *If your answer to 37, 38, 39, 40, or 41 is "Yes," do not complete Section B for the covered vehicles.*

Part VI | **Amortization**

(a) Description of costs	(b) Date amortization begins	(c) Amortizable amount	(d) Code section	(e) Amortization period or percentage	(f) Amortization for this year
42 Amortization of costs that begins during your 2006 tax year (see instructions):					
43 Amortization of costs that began before your 2006 tax year. **43**					
44 **Total.** Add amounts in column (f). See the instructions for where to report. **44**					

Form **4562** (2006)

CHAPTER

HOW TO PREPARE THE MONTHLY AUDIT AND COST PROJECTIONS

The following sections will prepare the restaurant manager for closing, projecting, and analyzing the expenditure and sales records established during the month. The preceding chapters have described in detail how to set up, operate, and manage a profitable restaurant. This chapter will go through the procedures for projecting the actual costs for each category so that the budget may be completed and analyzed for possible cost problem areas. The completed budget and abbreviated profit and loss statement will be a measure of how effectively management operated the restaurant during the month.

The procedures described in the following sections are fundamental accounting procedures. Although the procedures are fundamental in nature, great care must be taken when compiling and processing the information to ensure complete accuracy. Management will be basing its decisions upon the statistics provided in these reports. Inaccurate information will ultimately result in faulty decisions.

The individuals collecting and utilizing the various data should be familiar with the restaurant's operations and the various internal control systems. All calculations should be double-checked by another employee prior to being used in the cost projections. Calculators with printed tapes should always be used so that column totals may be verified.

The general manager must take an active part in the end-of-the-month closeout. His participation will serve two purposes:

1. It will ensure that the closeout procedures are correctly carried out.

2. The computations will be much easier for the manager to recall and hold more meaning in the day-to-day operations.

The most common error made in the end-of-month closeout is carelessness. Attention to detail and proper management involvement will eliminate most errors. Countless hours of extra work for the internal bookkeeper, manager, and public accountant can easily be avoided simply by taking a little more time to ensure all business and accounting papers are handled correctly.

For the purposes described in this book, the accounting period, or cycle, begins on the first day of each month and ends on the last day, regardless of the actual number of days in the month. At the end of the month all the sales and expense accounts will be closed out and balanced. The ending inventory, the computation of which will be described in an upcoming section, will be taken on the last day of the month after the close of business. This month's ending inventory will be the new beginning inventory for next month.

DEFINING THE ACCOUNTING PERIOD

As noted in Chapter 35, "Internal Bookkeeping," it is imperative that all expenses be entered into the Purchase Ledger for the month in which they were received. The expenses must be entered in this manner regardless of when the restaurant was billed for the items.

Adjustments will be necessary to accurately record prepaid accounts — such as insurances and magazine subscriptions — to ensure the expense is entered into the budget during the month the expense is incurred. Most of these adjustments may be computed during the budgeting process.

Certain expenditures — such as the telephone and utilities bills — might not be received until five to six working days after the end of the month. Since the bank statement and suppliers' monthly statements will arrive during the first week of the month, it is recommended that the final profit and loss statement not be prepared until the 7th or 15th of the following month. It allows time for the bank statement to be reconciled, unrecorded expenses to be entered into the Purchase Ledger, and any necessary final adjustments to be included. Although the profit and loss statement will not be published until the middle of the next month, the ending inventories and most costs will be projected on the first of the month.

MONTHLY AUDIT PROCEDURES

On the last day of the month:

1. Gather the completed inventory forms for food, liquor, wine, and operational supplies.

2. Using current invoices and past inventories, cost out the Inventory Form. The unit cost (or price) entered on the Inventory Form must correspond to the item and unit in the actual inventory. Correct prices are ensured by continual evaluation of invoices and/or contact with the suppliers. Review the section on the beginning inventory in Chapter 8, "Profitable Menu Planning."

3. Ensure that the employees organize and clean the storage areas and walk-ins, so that the ending inventory may easily be taken the following morning. Combine all containers and bottles. Organize and label all shelves.

4. Schedule the bookkeeper and the employees involved in taking the physical inventory— the assistant manager, kitchen director, bar manager, and general manager — to arrive prior to the start of business on the first of the month.

5. Schedule the preparation cooks to arrive an hour after the inventory crew so that you may inventory the food areas without disturbing them.

On the following morning, the first of the month:

6. The bookkeeper should arrive as early as possible in order to complete all of his work prior to management's completion of the inventory:

    A. Reconcile and record all the transactions from the previous day, as usual.

    B. Enter the information on the Daily Sales Report Form. Total, double-check, and verify all the columns.

    C. From the employee time cards complete, total, double-check, and verify the Labor Analysis Form.

    D. Ensure that all purchases are recorded in the Purchase Ledger. Complete, total, double-check, and verify the Purchase Ledger for each company. Total the purchases in each expenditure category: food, liquor, wine, and each individual operational category.

        Ensure that all paid-outs entered on the Cashier's and Bartender's Reports have been posted into the appropriate Purchase Ledger categories. Total the cash paid-outs. Add this figure into the purchase total for each expense category.

COMPUTING THE ENDING INVENTORY

PURPOSE

An ending inventory is taken for a complete and accurate count of the stock and materials on hand for each cost category (food, liquor, wine, and operational supplies) so that the unused amount may be used in projecting the total cost for each category.

PROCEDURE

1. Use pencils, scales, scratch pads, and a clipboard and be accurate. Liquor should be weighed on a liquor scale.

2. Two people should take the inventory. One will count while the other writes. The person counting states each item, its unit, and its total amount. The other employee enters the figure on the inventory sheet on the correct line. If there is only a part of the item, estimate how much on a scale from 0.1 to 0.9 (0.5 being half of a container). Make sure there is a figure on either side of the decimal point (e.g., 0.5, 3.0).

3. Count shelves all the way across. Do not jump around.

4. Put a zero in columns where there is no item to be counted.

5. Convert all items that are in prepared form into pound and unit costs. Example: 15 fish dinners at 12.5 oz. = 11.72 lbs.

6. For multiple weights or numbers of items, use a separate pad and double-check the entries.

7. Make sure there is an entry for every item.

8. Complete each area before moving on to a new one. Check for blanks and possible mistakes.

9. When estimates must be made, they should be made with sound reasoning, not idle guessing.

EXTENDING THE INVENTORY

1. Add the amount of each item counted and enter the figure in the "Total" column.

2. Multiply each item total by the unit price to compute the extended total. Double-check the figures. Add the total amount of the extended column to compute the page total. Double-check every figure.

3. Add the page totals to compute the total for each category. Exchange papers with each other to double-check all figures again. Save the calculator tapes and staple them onto the front of the inventories.

4. All extension columns should have a figure or a zero to ensure the item was considered.

PROJECTING COSTS

From the previous sections you will need:

A. The completed Daily Sales Reports.

B. The completed Purchase Ledgers.

C. The beginning inventory amounts.

D. From the inventory just completed, the total ending inventory amounts.

E. The Operational Supplies Cost Projection Forms.

STEP 1. FROM THE DAILY SALES REPORT:

1. Enter total food sales less tax on the "Food Sales" line of the Materials Cost Projection Form.

2. Enter total wine sales less tax on the "Wine Sales" line of the Materials Cost Projection Form.

3. Enter total liquor sales less tax on the "Liquor Sales" line of the Materials Cost Projection Form.

4. Enter total sales (food plus liquor plus wine sales less tax) on each sales line of the Operational Supplies Cost Projection Form.

5. Double-check the complimentary and manager charge columns for food, liquor, and wine. Multiply the food total by .50 and place this figure on the "Food Comp/Manager" line on the Materials Cost Projection Form.

6. Multiply the wine comp/manager total by 0.40 and place this figure on the "Wine Comp/Manager" line on the Materials Cost Projection Form.

7. Multiply the liquor comp/manager total by 0.25 and place this figure on the "Liquor Comp/Manager" line on the Materials Cost Projection Form.

In essence, through these actions (5, 6, and 7) you are taking a credit in the cost projections for products that you have received no revenue, even though the items were perfectly acceptable to be sold. The products were given away to promote business or as a benefit to the manager and owners. Multiplying the total comp/manager sales recorded by the estimated cost percentage results in an estimated cost for these benefits. It will more than cover the costs if the food cost averages 40 percent; wine, 33 percent; and liquor, 22 percent. There is no credit taken for housed products — items that were improperly handled and, therefore, had to be discarded.

STEP 2. FROM THE PURCHASE LEDGER:

Enter the total purchases including cash paid-outs for each category on the Materials Cost Projection Form. Enter the purchases for each operational supply category in the appropriate "Projection" column on the Operational Supplies Cost Projection Form. Keep in mind that each expense category must be projected separately. For each operational supply category to have a separate "Projection" column, additional Operational Supplies Cost Projection Forms will need to be copied. There is a space provided above each projection for the category's name and code number.

STEP 3.

Enter the beginning inventory dollar amount (last month's ending inventory) for each category on the appropriate line of the cost projection sheets. For new restaurants, the first month's beginning inventory amounts would have been computed when the inventory sheets were initially set up. Once the original beginning inventory is computed, it need not be calculated again since the previous month's ending inventory amount will be the following month's beginning inventory amount.

STEP 4.

Enter the ending inventory amount (just computed by taking the inventory) for each category on the "Ending Inventory Amount" line on both cost projection forms.

COMPUTING THE COST AND PERCENTAGE FIGURE FOR EACH CATEGORY

Add: beginning inventory (+) purchases and paid-outs (+)

Subtract: comp/manager (–) ending inventory (–)

This will equal the cost of sales for each category.

Cost of sales, divided by sales, equals the percentage of cost.

If the figure seems incorrect:

- Check mathematics on projection sheet.
- Check ending inventory for mistakes (counting, extending).
- Check all mathematics from the beginning.

If costs seem too high:

- Go over Purchase Ledger, sales, invoices, credits, and totals.
- Check purchases recorded but not inventoried.
- Check for incorrect beginning inventory.

If costs seem too low:

- Check items inventoried but not on the Purchase Ledger.
- Check for incorrect beginning inventory.

COMPLETING THE BUDGET

Once the cost projections are computed, the operating budget may be completed and the net pre-tax profit calculated.

1. Enter the total sales and sales breakdown in the "Actual" column of the operating budget.

2. From the cost projection forms, enter the actual cost of each category onto the budget.

3. Subtract the total material costs from the total sales to determine gross profit.

4. From the Labor Analysis Form, enter the total labor costs and cost breakdowns.

5. Office supplies may be actually projected, but will require a lengthy inventory, so an estimate may be used.

6. The uniform expense will vary depending upon the state in which you reside. Some states require the restaurant to provide uniforms, whereas others allow the restaurant to charge the employees for them.

7. "Service Expenses" is the total amount recorded in the Purchase Ledger plus any additional invoices.

8. The fixed operating expenses should remain constant. The monthly accumulated depreciation may vary when new assets are purchased during the month and the depreciation expense is prorated.

9. General operating costs. Labor taxes may be computed by multiplying the total labor cost for the month by the sum of:

   A. The current employer's Social Security contribution, plus

   B. The state unemployment compensation rate, plus

C.   The federal unemployment compensation rate, plus

D.   Any miscellaneous payroll taxes. Sales tax collected is not an expense and should not appear on the budget. In essence, the proprietor is acting as an agent for the state — providing a collection service.

10. Other general operating expenses may be computed by totaling the Purchase Ledger for each category plus any additional invoices.

11. Total all expenses and enter this figure in the "Total Expenditure" column. The total net pre-tax profit is computed by subtracting total expenditures from total sales.

NALYZING THE COMPLETED BUDGET

A comparison analysis of the current budget against past operating budgets is the best way to identify cost problem areas. The goal of management is for the restaurant to operate consistently in all ways: consistent food products, service and cost percentages, and net profits. When striving to identify cost over-runs, examine the operating budget's costs against those of previous months and past years for the same month. The important figure to regard when computing the budget is not the actual dollar amount at cost, but the percentage of cost in relation to sales.

Examine budgeted and actual sales closely. Is the sales level as high as anticipated and needed? Are customer counts increasing or decreasing when compared to previous months and last year? Why? Without a sufficient level of sales, the restaurant will ultimately fail, as sales will eventually not meet the fixed costs necessary to maintain the operation.

Concentrate all efforts on increasing sales. Advertise, develop promotional programs, make menu changes, do whatever is required to locate the problem, resolve it, and increase sales. Before looking to the outside for answers to this problem, take a good, hard look at the entire operation. Make certain all areas of the restaurant are operating properly and that all internal controls previously described throughout this book are enforced, being adhered to, and working.

ARIATIONS IN GROSS PROFIT

Changes in gross profit from month to month may be due to any one, or a combination, of the following variables:

•   Changes in sales caused by a change in selling price.

•   Changes in cost of goods sold caused by changes in materials costs and/or changes in volume of goods sold.

•   Sales volume changes, which may be further analyzed into a change in the final sales volume.

For an illustration of this point, consider the following example:

Assume a restaurant serves only two products:

1. Shrimp, with a total food cost of $5 and a selling price of $10.

2. Chicken breast, with a total food cost of $2.50 and a selling price of $8.50.

MONTH 1 (1,000 Entrees Sold)

900 Shrimp Dinners

Sales (900 X $10)	= $9,000
Cost of Sales (900 X $5)	= $4,500

100 Chicken Breasts

Sales (100 X $8.50)	= $850
Cost of Sales (100 X $2.50)	= $250

Total Items Sold	= 1,000
Total Sales	= $9,850
Total Cost of Sales	= $4,750
$4,750 ÷ $9,850 X 100	**= 48% Food Cost**

Now examine the second month with the reverse sales mix:

MONTH 2 (1,000 Entrees Sold)

900 Chicken Breasts

Sales (900 X $8.50)	= $7,650
Cost of Sales (900 X $2.50)	= $2,250

100 Shrimp Dinners

Sales (100 X $10)	= $1,000
Cost of Sales (100 X $5)	= $500

Total Items Sold	= 1,000
Total Sales	= $8,650
Total Cost of Sales	= $2,750
$2,750 ÷ $8,650 X 100	**= 32% Food Cost**

In this simplified example, you can clearly see the effect the weighted average sales have on food cost percentages. This example will also apply to liquor and wine cost percentages under similar circumstances.

POSSIBLE FOOD COST PROBLEM AREAS

1. No balance of high- and low-cost items on the menu.

2 No consideration of locally obtainable products.

3 No competitive purchasing plan.

4. Theft in any form.

5. Purchasing more than needed (spoilage).

6. No daily check of invoices, quality, and prices.

7. Improper rotation procedures.

8. No perpetual inventory.

9. No controls on issuing items from storage areas.

10. Low yields on products.

11. Over-preparing (waste, spoilage).

12. Not using or following exact recipes.

13 Not following exact portion sizes.

14. Improper handling (wrapping, rotating, storing).

15. No reconciliation of dinners sold versus dinners consumed.

16. Employee theft.

COMPUTING THE ACTUAL YIELD OVER A SPECIFIED PERIOD OF TIME

Add: beginning inventory (lbs.) (+) purchases for period (lbs.) (+)

Subtract: ending inventory (lbs.) (–)

Multiply the total by 16. This is the total ounces used.

From the itemized cooks sheets, compute the number of dinners sold using this particular product.

Multiply the number of dinners sold by portion size to compute ounces sold.

Divide ounces used by ounces sold, giving the actual yield percentage. It is a check of the yields projected by the kitchen director and shows the actual yield percentage of raw products sold.

FOOD COST PERCENTAGE

This basic ratio is often misinterpreted because it is calculated in so many different ways. It is food cost divided by food sales. Whether your food cost is determined by food sold or consumed is a crucial difference. Also, for your food cost percentage to be accurate, a month-end inventory must be taken. Without this figure, your food cost statement is inaccurate and basically useless because inventory will vary month-to-month — even in the most stable environment.

Food cost of sales calculation

Beginning Inventory +	$5,000.00
Purchases +	100,000.00
Total =	$105,000.00
Ending Inventory -	35,000.00
Food Used =	70,000.00
* Employee meals, comp food, manager	– 3,000.00
Cost of Food	**$67,000.00**

Divide the cost of food by the Food Sales.

Food Sales	**$175,000.00**
Food Cost Percentage	**38.28%**

* Employee meals, complimentary food, and manager-consumed food are removed from the food cost equation as these costs should be reclassified on the P&L. Employee meals are an employee benefit, complimentary meals are considered promotional costs, and manager meals are a management benefit.

Distinguishing between food sold and consumed is important. All food consumed is not sold. Food consumed includes all food used, sold, wasted, stolen, or given away to customers and employees. Food sold is determined by subtracting all food bought (at full price) from the total food consumed. See the above example.

WEIGHTED FOOD COST PERCENTAGE

Once your food cost is calculated, a weighted food cost percentage must be determined. A weighted food cost percentage will tell you what your food cost should have been had all procedures and controls in place operated at 100 percent efficiency.

On the following page, I have summarized sales information from the restaurant's POS system or from other bookkeeping records. What you are doing is recreating the food cost for each item based on the standard recipe costs to determine what your food cost and food cost percentage should have been. For this example assume that only four menu items are served in this restaurant. From this example you can see that $7,000 in food costs have slipped away (assuming all calculations are accurate). The restaurant should have had a 34.28 food cost percentage.

MENU ITEM	COST PER MEAL	# OF MEALS SERVED	COST PER MENU ITEM
Chicken Kiev	$5.00	2,000	$10,000.00
Steak Oscar	$8.00	4,000	$32,000.00
Stuffed Flounder	$9.00	1,000	$9,000.00
Hamburger Platter	$3.00	3,000	$9,000.00

Weighted Total Cost **$60,000.00**

Actual Sales $175,000.00

Weighted Food Cost Percentage 34.28%

Variation Over Actual Food Cost Percentage .... 4% (or $7,000.00)

DAILY FOOD COST ANALYSIS

Traditionally, the food cost of sales is calculated once a month. Yet, you can compute a daily food cost and a daily weighted food cost to analyze problem areas. Much of the inventory counting can be eliminated by moving only the products used for production into the kitchen at the beginning of the shift to pinpoint problem areas or possible problem employees or shifts. You can also calculate a separate food cost for breakfast or lunch.

BUDGETING & PROFIT PLANNING

BREAKEVEN ANALYSIS

Breakeven analysis is a simple and useful accounting tool for the restaurant manager. An understanding of breakeven analysis will aid the restaurant manager in budgeting, profit planning, expansion decisions, and pricing decisions. The breakeven point is the point where the total sales minus the total costs equals zero. Total sales may also be regarded as the customer count times the average check amount.

All costs may be broken down into three major categories:

1. **Fixed Costs.** The costs that remain the same regardless of a change in sales or production. Fixed costs remain constant at all possible levels of sales. Examples of fixed costs are: depreciation, insurance, and property taxes.

2. **Variable Costs.** The costs that change in direct proportion to a change in the level of sales or production. Examples of variable costs are: food, liquor, and wine material costs.

3. **Semi-variable costs.** The costs that contain properties of fixed and variable costs. An example of semi-variable cost is telephone expense. A fixed monthly service charge

will be billed to the restaurant regardless of use. When sales are increased, more long distance phone calls will be made to suppliers. This additional use of the telephone for toll charges is the variable cost.

The first step in computing the break-even point is to separate the semi-variable cost into its two components. Using the Breakeven Cost Analysis Form and the completed budget, break up each semi-variable cost into its variable and fixed amounts. Enter the full amounts of each of these expenditures in the appropriate column. Some semi-variable costs may be difficult to precisely break down into either a fixed or variable amount. If so, estimate the figures.

Although the total expense must remain the same, using the telephone expenditure example, the monthly service charge would be entered in the fixed column and toll charges would be entered in the variable column. The total bill remains the same. To better visualize the concept of breakeven analysis, view the graph at the end of this chapter. Note that the fixed costs are $40,000, total sales are $100,000, and the variable cost per customer is $7.20. The breakeven point occurs at $8,333. The average sale per customer is $12.

$$\$100,000 - \$40,000 = \$60,000 / \$7.20 = \$8,333$$

Total Sales - Fixed Costs = Variable Costs divided by the Variable Cost per Customer.

Total Sales = Customer Count x Average per Head Sales.

Note that as sales increase, the profit margin percentage will substantially increase once the break-even point is realized. The restaurant manager should also note that once sales fall below the break-even point, losses will be incurred proportionately.

Once the graph is set up and drawn, it is interesting to note how changes in the level of sales affect the profit margin. The profit or loss at any customer count level may be easily determined by the difference between the total sales line and cost line.

Suppose sales were increased to $120,000 (an additional 10,000 customers served). At this level of sales, total costs are $112,000. $40,000 fixed costs + ($7.20 variable cost per customer x 10,000 the number of customers served), which shows a profit of $8,000 or a 40 percent profit on the additional $20,000 in total sales. Thus, once the break-even point is reached, it is accurate to assume that each additional dollar in sales will result in 40 percent profit.

Thoroughly understanding break-even analysis will aid the restaurant manager in the following situations:

1. Determining the amount of customers needed in a specific time period (usually one month) before a profit is realized.

2. Analyzing remodeling or rebuilding plans for length and cost to project the additional customers needed to make the project profitable.

3. Evaluating menu prices and net pre-tax profit margins to determine the additional profits realized from a menu price increase.

The three situations just described will be resolved using break-even analysis. For ease in understanding the major concepts, the information used in the graphic representation will remain the same in the following problems.

SITUATION 1

Situation number one is the number of customers that must be served to reach the break-even point rather than the level of total sales. The following formula will resolve this problem:

The break-even point = Fixed Costs

The average check amount	**Variable cost per customer**
$40,000 = $40,000	= 8,333 customers
$12.00 - $7.20 = $4.80	

SITUATION 2

Situation number two requires some additional information before the problem may be solved. The cost of the remodeling or rebuilding is required and the recovery time is also needed. For example, we shall estimate the renovation amount at $50,000. The owner wants to recover this amount in two years. Thus, $25,000 in additional profits must be recovered each year. The following formula will resolve this problem:

The number of additional customers needed per year = The increase in Fixed Costs

The average check amount	**Variable cost per customer**
$25,000 = $25,000	= 5,208 additional customers
$12.00 - $7.20 = $4.80	

SITUATION 3

Situation number three requires an additional assumption; the desired additional monthly pre-tax profit of $5,000. The following formula will resolve this problem: The variable cost per customer + (fixed costs + the desired additional profit/customer count). Computations surrounded by parentheses must be calculated first.

$7.20 + ($40,000 + $5,000 / 10,000) = $7.20 + $4.50 = $11.70

This formula will also be helpful in determining the prices that must be charged in order to reach the break-even point. Assume a particular number of customers sold and a constant cost structure in these calculations. Whenever computing a break-even formula it is always a good idea to check your answers.

Check: Sales - fixed costs - variable costs = 0

Using the above situation, the check is computed below:

Sales $11.70 x 10,000 customers = $117,000

Variable costs $7.20 x 10,000 customers = 72,000 fixed costs = $40,000

Desired additional profit $5,000

There are certain assumptions made in projecting breakeven analysis that may not always hold true and should be pointed out. The most common assumption is that the menu or selling price and costs will remain constant over a long period of time, which may not be the case, as no one can accurately foresee the future. A change in the product mix (the portion of each individual menu item to the total number of menu items sold), may drastically change, thus affecting the breakeven point.

Breakeven analysis provides the restaurant manager with a valuable tool in analyzing the relationships between volume, selling prices, and expenses. Furthermore, breakeven analysis enables the restaurant manager to effectively prepare long range budgets and provide essential information relating to price levels, expansion possibilities, and past operational performances. The graphic representation of this data provides an easy-to-read-and-interpret report containing information from several financial statements from which the restaurant manager may then make decisions based upon accurate relevant information.

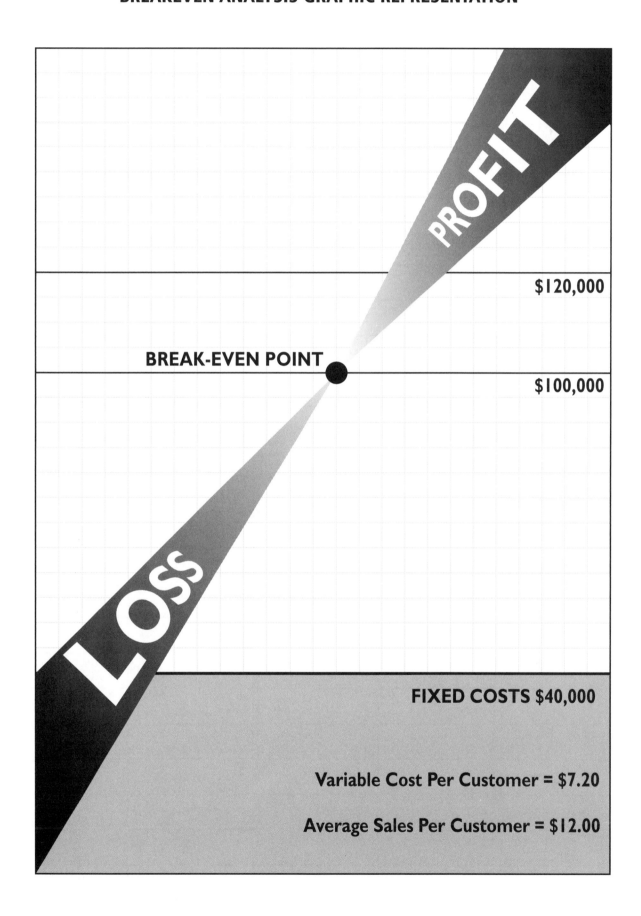

BREAKEVEN COST ANALYSIS

COST	TYPE	FIXED	VARIABLE	TOTAL

MATERIALS COST PROJECTION FORM

MONTH:	
FOOD	
Beginning Inventory	
Purchases	
Comp/Manager	
Ending Inventory	
Cost	
Sales	
TOTAL FOOD COST PERCENTAGE	
WINE	
Beginning Inventory	
Purchases	
Comp/Manager	
Ending Inventory	
Cost	
Sales	
TOTAL WINE COST PERCENTAGE	
LIQUOR	
Beginning Inventory	
Purchases	
Comp/Manager	
Ending Inventory	
Cost	
Sales	
TOTAL LIQUOR COST PERCENTAGE	

OPERATIONAL SUPPLIES COST PROJECTION FORM

PAGE _____ MONTH_____

CATEGORY	#
Beginning Inventory	
Purchases	
Ending Inventory	
Cost	
Sales	
TOTAL COST PERCENTAGE	

CATEGORY	#
Beginning Inventory	
Purchases	
Ending Inventory	
Cost	
Sales	
TOTAL COST PERCENTAGE	

CATEGORY	#
Beginning Inventory	
Purchases	
Ending Inventory	
Cost	
Sales	
TOTAL COST PERCENTAGE	

CATEGORY	#
Beginning Inventory	
Purchases	
Ending Inventory	
Cost	
Sales	
TOTAL COST PERCENTAGE	

CHAPTER

PERFORM AN INTERNAL AUDIT ON RESTAURANT AND BAR OPERATIONS

The purpose of this chapter is to demonstrate methods of auditing your restaurant or bar operation. These methods are helpful in locating and understanding cost control problems. These investigative methods are also useful when considering purchasing a restaurant operation. Many of these methods are utilized by IRS examiners as well as national restaurant chains. For this chapter, audit procedures will utilize liquor costs and liquor sales. These procedures also apply to food and wine.

PRE-AUDIT PLAN

An analysis of the tax return should be conducted to determine potential issues. One form of analytical review, comparing balance sheets and income statements, will give meaning to the changes that took place between the years; the individual figures are relatively meaningless. Large percentage changes not standard for the industry can be highlighted as potential issues for the initial interview focus. An important ratio computed on the comparative income statement is the gross profit ratio. It is computed from the following:

gross sales – cost of goods sold = gross profit

GROSS SALES RATIO

This ratio tells approximately how much of an item's sale price represents gross profit and how much is a recovery of the cost of the item. During the initial interview, the manager/owner should be asked the markup percentage on the goods sold. The percentage obtained from the interview can be compared to the computed ratio to see if it is similar. If not, it is an indication that cost of goods may be overstated or revenues understated. An analysis of these accounts should be performed to determine if either is the case.

THIRD-PARTY SOURCES OF INFORMATION

The following represent possible third-party sources of information that can aid you in examining your bar or restaurant. The information may not be organized in the same way in your state; also, additional information may be available in your state. You should research your state to obtain the needed information.

- **Alcohol Beverage Control.** Demands that holders of on-premises licenses maintain available records of all purchases for three years.

- **State Liquor Dispensary.** Maintains records of all purchases by liquor license number. Does not maintain the details of the purchases. Maintains records of the liquor costs for most periods of time.

- **Local beer/wine distributor.** Maintains records of purchases made by customers. Maintains the records of the costs of the products. Permits required by the state.

- **Building permits.** Give cost of building. Also may contain blueprints of the building.

- **Health Department Permit.**

- **Bank statement.**

- **Bank reconciliation.**

- **Paid-out recaps (by account classification).**

- **Unpaid bills recap** (vendor and account classification).

- **Equipment purchases** (include copy of invoice).

- **Payroll summary.**

- **Accrued payroll.**

- **Monthly and/or quarterly tax returns.**

- **Copies of daily and weekly profit and loss statements.**

QUESTIONS PREPARED FOR THE INTERVIEW OF THE OWNER

1. Who runs the business? Is it family-operated or management-operated?

2. What are the duties of those who run the business?

3. What amount of time does each individual spend at the business?

4. What types of reports (tip reports, daily sales reports) are prepared for the business and who prepares them?

5. How much of the bookkeeping is done or kept at the business site?

6. Does the owner have an accountant or bookkeeper who maintains the bookkeeping system?

7. Who else has managerial control over the employees at the restaurant?

8. Does the management have any prior experience in the industry?

9. What are the days and hours of normal business operations?

10. What type of restaurant is it?

11. What type of clientele frequents the restaurant?

12. What is the customer capacity of the restaurant?

13. What are the average number of dinners sold on the weekdays and weekends?

14. What type of payment is accepted (cash only, credit cards, checks)?

15. What is the average cost of a meal?

16. Who determines the price of the meal?

17. What type of entertainment, if any, is offered?

18. Is there a cover charge for the bar or any entertainment at some time during the evening?

19. How are the entertainers paid?

20. Are banquet facilities available?

21. Is there a set fee for banquets or is the charge determined on an individual basis?

22. Is there a "Happy Hour?"

23. Are food specials offered daily?

24. What is the average number of employees on the payroll?

25. How many people are working on day, afternoon, or night shifts for the various areas of the restaurant?

26. What type of shifts do the employees work (day, afternoon, evening)?

27. How are employees paid: weekly, biweekly, or monthly?

28. Are any individuals working at the restaurant considered independent contractors?

29. How is time kept for the employees: sign-in or time clock?

30. What type of side duties, if any, do the employees have on a daily, weekly, or monthly basis?

31. Who calculates tips for each server?

INTERVIEW QUESTIONS

MANAGEMENT AND/OR OWNER INTERVIEW

1. On what days is the restaurant open?

2. What are the restaurant's hours of operation?

3. How many shifts are there?

4. What is the average number of employees on each shift: Captains? Wait persons? Bus persons? Others?

5. Does an employee work the same shift on a regular basis?

6. If not, how are shifts rotated? How are different shifts recorded?

7. Who sets up the room?

8. What is the average setup time?

9. How is setup time rotated?

10. If stations are not rotated, how are they assigned?

11. What is the seating capacity of the restaurant?

12. Are tips pooled and split among wait persons?

13. How are tips split?

14. If tips are not split, who gets tipped out and what percent of the tips do they get?

15. Where do customers pay for their meals? That is, do they pay the wait person or a cashier on the way out?

16. How do the employees receive their charge tips?

17. Do you have the following types of sales: Charge sales? Banquets? Complimentary sales? Ticket/Tour sales?

    A. Approximately what percentage of sales does each of these types bring in?

    B. How do the employees receive any non-cash tips for these types of sales?

18. Are wait persons required to pay for customers who leave without paying?

19. Does the average cash customer tip better or worse than the average charge customer? If so, by how much?

19. Do customers tip differently according to the time they eat?

20. Are there any unusual factors that affect tipping in your establishment?

21. Other Comments:

EMPLOYEE INTERVIEW

1. Who is your manager?

2. How many shifts are there that you might be scheduled for in a given day?

3. How many hours are there in each shift?

4. Do all wait persons work setup and breakdown?

5. If not, who does and how long does it take?

6. Do you have a steady schedule?

7. Are shifts rotated?

8. How are they rotated?

9. How are stations assigned?

10. Are stations rotated?

11. How are they rotated?

12. What is the average number of tables per station?

13. What is the average number of chairs per station?

14. How many tables, on the average, do you serve per shift?

15. How many checks, on the average, do you write per shift?

16. Who assigns workstations?

17. Who assigns work shifts?

18. Does the average cash customer tip better or worse than the average charge customer? By how much?

19. Do you have to pay for walkouts? If yes, how often does this happen?

20. What is your position?

21. What are your duties?

22. How long have you worked at this establishment?

23. Have you worked in any other position at this establishment?

24. As a food server, do you consider yourself above average, average, or below average?

25. Is there a reason why a determination of average sales and tips would be unfair to you?

26. Other Comments:

INTERNAL CONTROLS: QUESTIONS FOR THE OWNER AND/ OR MANAGER

INVENTORY

1. Who are the primary suppliers of the business? What do they supply?

2. When are the purchases recorded (daily, weekly)?

3. Who is responsible for making the purchases?

4. Are the purchases recorded from checks or invoices?

5. What types of records are available for purchases? For example, is there a purchase journal?

6. Are there any records available for the number and size of bottles of alcohol purchased?

7. Are purchase discounts available? Were they taken?

8. Do the suppliers offer kickbacks or rebates? How are they recorded?

9. How many ounces of liquor are in each mixed drink? What are the prices of the mixed drinks?

10. Is the inventory of alcohol and food stored in a locked storeroom?

11. Who has access to the storeroom?

12. Who restocks the bar from the storeroom inventory and at what intervals?

13. What type of record is maintained of stock being removed from the storeroom?

14. Does the bartender have to turn in an empty bottle before receiving a new bottle?

15. Who checks in incoming merchandise to the storeroom?

16. Are the contents of incoming cases verified?

17. Are automatic liquor-dispensing devices used?

18. What is the price per beer for imported beer? Domestic?

19. If draft beer is available, how many ounces are in a glass? A pitcher?

20. Is there a price list of drinks available?

    A. Do you have wine for sale? By the glass and/or bottle?

    B. How many ounces are in a glass? Carafe?

    C. What are their prices?

21. What is the price of the wine coolers sold?

22. How many glasses of wine are served from each bottle?

23. What is the normal markup on mixed drinks? Beer? Wine? Wine coolers?

24. Do you compute spillage?

25. At what intervals are physical inventories of merchandise taken and who is responsible for it?

26. Is beginning bar inventory plus storeroom withdrawals less ending inventory periodically extended to retail prices and compared to receipts?

27. Who checks incoming inventory for the kitchen?

28. Are incoming shipments weighed?

29. Once the incoming inventory has been accounted for, what happens to the receiving document?

30. Do the employees eat on the premises? Are they given the meals at a discount?

31. Are written records maintained for complimentary and employee-consumed meals and drinks?

INTERNAL CONTROLS — CASH

1. How are sales by the wait staff controlled?

2. Are prenumbered meal tickets used for each customer and/or table? If so, how are they issued to each server?

3. How is each server responsible for his or her numbered meal tickets?

4. What happens to voided meal tickets?

5. Does someone in management verify voided tickets?

6. Are cash registers used for the restaurant and/or bar?

    A.   Where are they maintained?

    B.   Are they preset for the individual menu or drink items?

7. Who has access to the cash registers?

8. Are cash-register drawers closed after each sale?

9. Do the cash registers print sales tickets?

10. How are over-rings handled?

11. Are sales tickets given to the customers?

12. Is access to the register tapes restricted? To whom?

13. Are the registers closed out at the end of each shift? By whom?

14. Are beginning and ending cash-register transaction numbers compared?

15. If two or more bartenders and/or hosts, etc. work simultaneously, do they use the same or different cash registers?

16. Are cash-register readings taken during each cashier's shift?

17. Is the cash reconciled to the register tapes and deposited in the bank intact? If so, at what intervals and by whom?

18. How are expenses for the business paid?

19. Are any expenses paid in cash? If so, are these amounts accounted for?

20. What types of controls are placed on the cash?

21. Who has access to the cash receipts?

OTHER INFORMATION

1. Who determines the prices of the meals offered?

2. How are portions controlled?

3. Do you have valet parking?

4. What happens to the money received for valet parking?

5. What type of advertising is used?

6. Are there any promotions used?

7. What happens to the used grease?

8. Are there any coin-operated machines in the restaurant/bar?

9. What is the age and condition of the equipment?

10. What is the employee turnover?

BALANCE SHEET EXAMINATION

An examination of the balance sheet can be advantageous for detecting items not found through the examination of the income statement. This section provides a correlation between the balance sheet and the income statement. By properly planning an examination, one can eliminate a duplication of effort and conduct a thorough examination. The following information can be used to conduct the examination:

- A detailed examination of accounts receivable can eliminate the sales cutoff procedures of the income statement.

- An analysis of the bad-debt reserves on the balance sheet will determine if the provision to the bad-debt reserve is reasonable.

- An analysis of the debits of the prepaid assets will verify what items are being amortized or expensed.

- A detailed examination of the fixed assets and the accumulated depreciation would eliminate the need to verify depreciation expense.

- Examining accounts payable can eliminate the need to audit the accrued amounts that were expensed on the income statement. Similarly, examining loans payable will eliminate the need to verify interest expense.

The first step in examining the balance sheet is to prepare a comparative balance-sheet analysis. A minimum of three years will be involved: the assigned year and the prior and subsequent years. These three years will provide four years of "end-of-year" balances.

The primary emphasis in this examination of the balance sheet is placed on the last year.

It eliminates the duplication of efforts for each year examined because of "rollovers". Rollovers are items that would affect the subsequent years if they were adjusted. It is at the agent's discretion whether prior years' balances are to be adjusted just for the interest due to the government.

Cash in the bank should be reconciled between book balances and the bank statements. Generally the taxpayer's accountant will have bank reconciliations available to inspect or examine. The bank reconciliation(s) should then be reconciled to the tax return.

UNREPORTED INCOME

Normal audit procedures, tracing gross receipts to bank deposits, doing a bank deposit analysis on the business bank accounts, should be performed. Restaurants and bars are cash driven establishments. Cash can be hard to tie down in a bank deposit analysis if the cash is not being deposited into the bank accounts. Therefore, it is important to tie down the cash that is collected as gross receipts from every source and the cash that is paid out as expenditures. In the income statement section an indirect method is presented on how to audit the gross receipts from a bar or restaurant; however, consider the following techniques in auditing the cash on the balance sheet.

INTERNAL AUDIT TECHNIQUES

- Obtain the year-end reconciliation and compare it to the books. Outstanding checks should be considered income.

- Likewise, the most recent outstanding checks should be examined to determine if the taxpayer engages in drawing checks but not issuing them promptly. This practice is usually applicable to cash-basis taxpayers. If you believe this practice exists, observe the dates checks were paid, as stamped by the bank on the cancelled checks. Another way is to look for a credit balance in the cash account indicating checks drawn but not issued until later.

- Using cancelled checks, test one month's returned checks in the following manner: Compare the name of the payee with that of the endorser. If they do not agree, or if the name of any officer, partner, or shareholder appears as secondary endorser, determine why. The cash disbursement book should be open to the appropriate month while this is being done. If the payees of any checks are the officers, or if the checks are drawn to "bearer" or "cash," look at the cashbook to see if the payee described is the same one named on the check itself.

- Review the cash disbursements journal for a selected period. Note any missing check numbers and large or unusual items. Determine the propriety of these items by comparing with vouchers and other records.

- Determine if voided checks have been properly handled.

- Review the cash receipts journal for items identified as ordinary business sales and be alert for items such as sale of an asset or prepaid income.

- Review entries in the general ledger under "Cash Accounts" for unusual items that do not originate from the cash receipts or disbursements journal. These entries may indicate unauthorized withdrawals or expenditures, sales of capital assets, or omitted income.

- Determine whether the taxpayer has included interest income from time deposit accounts.

- Verify that any method of inventory valuation conforms:

    A. Compare inventory balances in the return with the balances for the prior and subsequent years' returns and verify.

    B. Check for unauthorized changes from cost to cost or market.

C.   Check for gross profit percentage variations.

D.   Determine meaning and significance of any notes or qualifying statements on financial reports prepared by independent accounting firms.

E.   Determine that all direct and indirect overhead and burden expenses are in the overhead pool that is used in the computation of overhead rates where applicable.

F.   Analyze unusual entries to cost-of-sales account for labor, material, and burden charges not directly related to sales or transfers of finished goods, if applicable.

G.   Confirm that year-end purchases were included in closing inventory.

H.   Determine whether there have been write-downs for "excess" inventory at below cost. Verify the method of inventory valuation for "excess" inventory.

DISCRETIONARY AUDIT PROCEDURES

1. Compare prior year's closing inventory with current year's opening inventory.

2. Determine whether a consistent and acceptable pricing method has been used.

3. Review manner in which overhead has been applied to inventories.

4. Review all inventory adjustments to ensure that no premature write-downs or reserve of anticipated losses have been included therein.

5. Where obsolescence adjustments have been made, review usage for prior, current, and subsequent years.

6. Where a standard cost system is used, review the factors composing the standard frequency of updating and disposition of variances.

7. Test end-of-year purchases and accruals to ensure inclusion of these items in inventory.

LOANS TO SHAREHOLDERS — AUDIT TECHNIQUES

Most bar and restaurant corporate returns will be organized as closely held corporations. Many of these will have loans to the shareholders. The following information will provide the general audit techniques to use when addressing this issue.

Obtain copies of any notes or evidence of indebtedness. Test them to see if the terms of the note are being followed. Is interest being accrued as income? Does the loan call for monthly payments or is it payable on demand? Does the note have a fixed maturity date? Does it have an interest rate? Is the interest rate near market? The absence of one or all of the above may indicate the loan was made at less than an arm's length transaction or below the prevailing market rate and may be construed as a constructive dividend (or, in an alternative position, interest income).

DISCRETIONARY AUDIT PROCEDURES

1. Analyze the composition of the account balance.

2. Trace the source of repayments.

3. Determine whether or not a bona fide debtor-creditor relationship exists.

4. Ascertain whether the current year's increase represents dividends.

5. Confirm that interest income has been properly recorded.

FIXED ASSETS

The initial investment for starting a restaurant or bar is quite high. Capital is required for the purchase of the property, leasehold improvements, equipment and furnishings, possible franchise fees, licenses, permits, taxes, liquor licenses, utilities, insurance, food inventory, advertising, and payroll. The basic fixed assets that will be found in any bar or restaurant are as follows:

A. **Kitchen equipment.** Stove, grill, fryer, walk-in freezers, walk-in refrigerators, ovens, dishwashers, and storage equipment.

B. **Office equipment.** Desk, computer, and telephone.

C. **Property.** Fencing, building, and outside seating.

D. **Dining room.** Tables, chairs, music (stereo/speakers), jukebox, cash register, floor coverings, salad bar, coffee makers, soda fountains, silverware, glassware, and dishes.

E. **Bar.** Refrigerators, cash register, sinks, bar, glassware, ice machine, ice bin, draft beer dispensers, alcohol dispensers, telephone, and coin-operated machines.

AUDIT PROCEDURES

1. Review the acquisitions to confirm that they have been properly recorded.

2. Where the acquisition consideration is other than cash, fully review the manner of arriving at basis.

3. Does the basis include all expenditures required to place the asset in readiness for operating use?

4. Allocations should be reviewed where a lump-sum purchase price is involved.

5. If there is an allocation in the contract between buyer and seller, verify that the allocation is consistent with the agreement. Also, verify that the allocation reflects economic reality.

PROFIT AND LOSS STATEMENT EXAMINATION

Examining the profit and loss statement may be the quickest and easiest way to perform an audit on a bar or restaurant. This approach is limited, however, when examining the gross receipts of the establishment. Since these establishments deal largely in cash, you will need to determine if the internal controls in place are adequate to ensure that the cash is being deposited into the bank accounts. Because of this uncertainty, an indirect method — besides a bank deposit analysis — may be warranted.

AUDIT TECHNIQUE

The first step in examining the profit or loss statement is to prepare a comparative analysis. Generally, a minimum of two years will be involved: the assigned year and the subsequent year. Based on the analysis, unusual or significant fluctuations in account balances can be selected for a more detailed examination.

The primary emphasis of an examination of the profit or loss statement is placed on "permanent" types of issues. Permanent types of issues are contrary to the "rollover" types of issues and do not affect the subsequent year: travel and entertainment, political contributions, investment tax credit, and investment tax credit recapture.

NOTE: Not all classifications of income or expenses are included in this package, which does not imply that the other items are correct or should not be audited.

SALES

The sales generated by a bar or restaurant are generated from the following sources: food, receipts, beverages (alcoholic and nonalcoholic), and coin-operated machines. The sales generated from these sources are hard to trace, since income is being generated by every customer. Also, the level of sophistication of the books may be poor. To gauge the daily, weekly, or monthly performance of sales, you will have to rely heavily on the information obtained in the initial interview, such as the number of meals sold in a typical day, average price of a meal, and markup percentages on food and alcohol.

If you can obtain accurate information in these areas, you will be able to accurately estimate the sales for a specific period. This estimate will enable you to determine if unreported sales are possible. If it is discovered that underreporting exists, further detailed analysis of the information gathered will ensure that the underreporting can be adjusted in the examiner's report.

Since the bar/restaurant business is largely cash based, the use of the indirect methods discussed in this section may only uncover that an understatement of income exists; it may be difficult or impossible to detect how the understatement came about.

The taxpayer may only be reporting income from one cash register when two are used. The only possible way to uncover this deceit is to ask a lot of questions and keep your eyes open during the tour of the business. Another helpful technique would be to visit the operation during its normal business hours and observe how the transactions are handled or send in a secret shopping service.

INCOME FROM THE SALE OF FOOD

The formula below can provide a reasonable estimation of annual sales for you to compare to figures on the tax return. The numbers used should be derived from the initial interview. Any large discrepancy between the income derived from these numbers and those reported on the tax return may indicate unreported income or inflated expenses. You should then look closely at the pertinent accounts (such as food/beverage purchases, monthly sales) in the books and records.

possible daily volume x average check per seat = daily sales

The possible daily volume is the number of seats in the establishment multiplied by how many times in a day they are occupied. The possible daily volume can be broken down into time periods — breakfast, lunch, or dinner — to get a more accurate tally.

The average check per seat can be obtained from the initial interview or past records. The daily sales can be extended to weekly and yearly sales based on the days open in a week and the weeks open in a year.

daily sales x days open in a week = weekly sales

weekly sales x weeks open in a year = yearly sales

These estimates can be accurate if consideration is made for vacant seats and people who walk out before paying their bills. During the initial interview ask enough pertinent questions to determine if these or any other situations should be considered.

Normal audit procedures should be performed. Consider the interview responses received concerning internal controls. Does the same person who counts the daily receipts also make the bank deposit? Are the meal orders taken on numbered tickets or is it easy to not ring up a sale on the cash register for some orders? Look closely at the supervision habits in the restaurant to evaluate how sales might be understated or how easily theft may occur and by whom.

The advertising account should be examined to test the accuracy of reported income. Are specials advertised? How often? Specials may refer to certain menu items or discounted prices or both. Are the times during which specials are offered (such as Happy Hour, breakfast hours) reflected in the daily receipts ledger?

CASH TRANSACTION ANALYSIS, NET WORTH, AND OTHER INDIRECT METHODS

A cash transaction analysis, net worth, or other indirect method may be used to determine an understatement. One way to further support your suspicions of an understatement is this indirect method: Inspect the supply invoices to find the name of the printer of the guest checks. This printer can provide the number of guest checks purchased by the restaurant in a year. A projected income can then be determined from the average guest-check dollar amount multiplied by the number of checks. If these indirect methods are used in combination, they strengthen the case.

Even in states where the distribution of liquor is carefully regulated, the bar owner may remove cash from his drawer; purchase liquor off the shelf at a store; sell the drinks in his establishment; and return the amount of cash to the drawer, while pocketing the profits. In such a case there usually will be no indication in the books that anything is wrong, as neither the invoice nor the income touches the books. An indirect method may uncover this subterfuge.

INCOME FROM THE BAR

The auditing techniques used depend on the quality and quantity of the books and records maintained by the taxpayer. If the examination consists of a larger bar — where there are inventory records maintained that detail the daily and/or monthly purchases and quantities sold — then the liquor cost percentage can be computed and applied to total purchases to determine the gross receipts and gross profit of the taxpayer. If the examination is of a smaller, "Mom and Pop" bar chances are it is going to be time- consuming and difficult to determine the purchases for one day or one month. In this situation it might be better to rely partly on third-party information to verify purchases and compute the markup on cost. The markup can then be applied to total purchases to determine the gross receipts and gross profit.

USING THE LIQUOR COST PERCENTAGE TO COMPUTE GROSS RECEIPTS

To compute gross receipts using the liquor cost percentage, the following steps should be followed:

1. Determine the cost of some of the more popular brands of liquor.

2. Determine the sales value of the bottles if all liquor out of these bottles was sold.

3. Divide the sales value into the cost to get the potential pouring cost.

EXAMPLE 1

1. **Determine the cost of liquor.** Verify from third-party sources that the cost per quart (bottle) is, in fact, $4.48.

2. **Determine the sales value of the bottle.** A quart has 32 ounces in it. If there are one and one fourth ounces per drink, there are 25.60 drinks per bottle. (32 ÷ 1.25 = 25.60). If drinks go for $1.10, then the sales value per bottle — less sales tax of $1.97 — would be $26.19. (25.60 X $1.10 = $28.16 – $1.97 = $26.19)

3. **Compute the liquor cost percentage.** Divide the sales value into the cost, giving you the potential pouring cost.

   The sales value per bottle is $26.19 and the cost is $4.48, so the liquor cost percentage would be 17.1 percent. **$4.48 ÷ $26.19 = 17.1%**

Conclusion: 17.1 percent of $26.19 is the cost. The rest is the markup. If this percentage is applied to total purchases of $5,000, the gross receipts should be $29,239.77. **($5,000 ÷ 17.1% = $29,239.77)**

Gross receipts (100%)	**29,239.77**
Less: purchases (17.1%)	**–$5,000.00**
Equals: gross profit (82.9%)	**$24,239.77**

The computations done with the formula discussed above can be used to calculate the total sales value of all bottles sold in a week, a month, or a year.

USING THE MARKUP ON COST TO COMPUTE GROSS RECEIPTS

If it is difficult to determine daily and monthly purchases by an establishment, the markup on cost may be used to compute gross receipts and gross profit. This method works closely with the liquor cost percentage method; however, different percentages will be determined.

As with the cost percentage method, the cost and sales value of the various items need to be computed. Then the markup on cost can be computed. Markup on cost is the amount of the sales price over the cost of an item.

EXAMPLE 2 (SIMPLIFIED)

price ($10) – cost ($5) = gross profit ($5)

sales price ($10) ÷ cost ($5) = percentage markup (200%)

The following steps should be followed to compute gross receipts based on markup on cost:

1. **Determine the markup of the various alcoholic items sold.** The markup should be determined in the initial interview. If the manager/owner does not know the markup of the bar items, you must compute it based on the sales price of drinks and the cost of the drinks.

2. **Determine the purchases made.** You can get this information off the invoices provided, if available and accurate. If not, you should request in the initial interview the names of all the vendors used. Send letters to the vendors requesting records of all purchases made.

3. Apply the markup to the purchases of the various types of alcohol. Using the figures from Example 2:

    purchases and total costs ($5) x markup (200%)

    = projected sales ($10.00)

The steps discussed above do not take into account amounts for spillage or Happy Hour prices. This information must be determined in the initial interview so that these amounts can be adjusted in determining the correct gross receipts.

OTHER INCOME

INCOME FROM COIN-OPERATED ACTIVITIES

Another important area of income to audit is the receipts generated by the coin-operated machines located in a bar. Coin-operated machines include jukeboxes, cigarette machines, pool tables, and dartboards. These machines can be owned or leased from another party. If the machines are leased, the general rule is that the income generated from the machines is split based on some percentage determined by the owner of the machine. Income generated from coin-operated activities is very difficult to determine accurately. Therefore, it is important to

---

ask a lot of pertinent questions in the initial interview regarding the operation of and income generated from these machines.

OTHER ACTIVITIES

Other areas of income in a bar or restaurant are the sale of lottery tickets, check-cashing, cover charges, and gaming pools. Scrutinize these areas in the initial interview. Ask pertinent questions to determine if the business engages in these areas and how the cash is handled and reported on the tax return.

COST OF GOODS SOLD

The cost of goods sold can be one of the largest expenses on the return. Be aware that the purchase figure reported might be a "plug" figure in order to balance the cost-of-goods-sold computation.

PURCHASES

1. Review the cutoff date. Confirm that year-end purchases were recorded in the proper accounting period.

2. Determine whether the owners consume or withdraw merchandise for personal use, such as food, liquor, appliances. If so, proper reductions should be made to purchases or cost of sales.

3. Scan "Purchases" column in the cash disbursements journal and voucher register for items unusual in amount and to payee or vendors not generally associated with the products or services utilized.

4. Review entries in the general ledger control account. Note and verify entries that originate from other than usual sources (general journal entries, debit, and credit memos).

5. Test check the recorded purchases for a representative period with vendor's invoices and cancelled checks. Be alert to such items as personal expenditures and capital expenditures.

6. If purchases are made from related or controlled foreign entities, review a representative number of such transactions to determine if the following are present:

    A. Prices in excess of fair market value.

    B. Excessive rebates and allowances.

    C. Goods or services not received.

7. Ascertain if merchandise, prizes, trips, etc. were received from suppliers as a result of volume purchases.

BASICS OF SELLING A RESTAURANT

STRATEGIES FOR SELLING

A strategy of clearly stated sales objectives will ensure that an acceptable sale is made. Sellers need to prioritize their sales objectives and consider what trade-offs may help achieve them. Deciding what is most important to hold onto and the ability to be flexible in other areas will support your overall selling goals. If a high asking price is important, being flexible on the down payment is a likely trade-off and vice versa. The following is a list of typical sales objectives:

- **Selling quickly.** Once an owner decides to sell, his enthusiasm for the business can fade and hurt his bottom line. Most restaurant sales take eight to 15 months to complete. Most of the attention a restaurant gets when it goes on the market is in the first three to four weeks, so it is important that the business be attractively priced to capitalize on this initial attention. Sellers should also be ready to respond to offers from the moment the restaurant goes on sale. Chances of selling are not good if buyers are interested but the seller does not have a well-prepared sales solicitation ready.

- **Best present-value sales price.** The sales price needs to be incorporated in the terms and conditions. Otherwise you will not have a business that is representing its present value. You may sell quickly at a very high price if your terms and conditions are favorable. Price, terms, and conditions are interrelated. If one changes the others do as well. Sellers must determine the price, terms, and conditions that must be met so that they can have a baseline to operate from. It is particularly important because different buyers will want different prices, terms, and conditions. The seller who has determined variable scenarios of what he absolutely requires for his price and from the terms and conditions is preparing himself well for negotiations.

- **Large down payment.** The bigger the down payment the lower the probability the seller will need to foreclose on the new operation. Investors who have put in large amounts of equity are less likely to abandon an investment if troubles arise. Thus, sellers are often willing to reduce sales prices by as much as 50 percent if the buyer will make a large down payment.

LOOKING FOR THE RIGHT BUYER

Sellers should look for buyers who will manage the restaurant well. The only way a seller should sell his business to a new restaurateur is if the buyer cashes out the seller. A seller wants a competent buyer who will run the business and prevent the need for repossession. Sellers want their business to stay sold.

Sellers should learn as much as possible about potential buyers. Reference checks are helpful in determining if a buyer is seriously interested, but they do not tell you what their motivations are. Sellers should understand what is motivating the buyers and these factors should be highlighted in negotiations.

Are they looking for the property only? Do they want the prestige of owning a restaurant right in town? Are they looking for a consistent return on their investment? Savvy sellers answer these questions and then push the appropriate attributes of the business.

Sellers should develop a professional property information package that will entice buyers. This package should contain just enough information for buyers to see if the business meets their investment requirements. If a buyer wants more information, she is expected to prepare an offer and pay an earnest money deposit before the seller will provide it.

This brochure is often an investor's first view of the property and is a crucial tool for the seller. Sellers should devote considerable time and effort to its preparation. An effective brochure does not reveal more than the seller wants to divulge, while enticing buyers. It should be printed on high-quality card stock and have the following data:

- **Pictures of the restaurant.**

- **Confidential inquiries.** Seller's name and contact information and other sources such as broker, answering service.

- **Description of the restaurant.** Concept, theme, hours of operation, square footage.

- **Map/Description of neighborhood.** Types of businesses, attractions, residential makeup. The map should be easy to read and the business's location should be highlighted.

- **Real estate description.** Property's legal description, common description, and the tax assessor's most recent valuation figure — unless it contrasts with the seller's estimate.

- **Summary of leasehold improvements.** China, glass, and utensils. Original cost, current book value, and estimated replacement cost of these assets.

- **Income analysis.** Monthly profit and loss statements from the previous 12 months.

- **Real-property lease review.** Remaining term, monthly base rent, percentage-rent clause, common-area maintenance fees, insurance requirements, options, and rate adjustments.

- **Personal-property lease review.** Remaining term, monthly base rent, maintenance costs, insurance requirements, options, and amount of final payment that must be made if lease is rent-to-own.

- **Financing availability.** Amount, interest rate, terms, and conditions of both assumable and seller financing.

- **Market survey.** Summary data on the restaurant's target area.

- **Competition survey.** Summary data on the restaurant's current and pending direct competition.

- **Initial investment summary.** Includes estimate of the initial investment required to buy and manage the restaurant.

- **Summary of seller's solicitation.** Asking price and down payment. Should also highlight the assets included in the sale and the availability of assumable and seller financing.

Sellers can be contacted directly or through an intermediary. Most sellers prefer to use an intermediary to keep a professional distance and attract buyers through an established system. Intermediaries also help to distinguish the serious investors from the suspect. A good broker protects the seller's privacy and knows how to sell a business. There are drawbacks to intermediaries. Brokers need to be paid — as much as 10 percent of the restaurant's sales price — and conflicts of interest can arise. Due diligence in selecting a broker is recommended.

PASS YOUR BUSINESS ON

Millions of businesses are owned and operated by family members. Some of these are passed down through the generations and some family members continue the family legacy. Another option is to have business partners or employees run your business.

If you plan to leave the business to your family, consider the tax implications. These issues and concerns include inheritance tax, trusts, and tax-free gifts. Each of these options is complicated and you should let the experts handle them. Talk with your banker, accountant, lawyer, and your estate planner. These professionals can ensure a smooth transition and minimize the tax burdens on your family.

- The U.S. Chamber of Commerce offers advice on passing your business on at **www.uschamber.com.**

- CCH Business Owner's Toolkit has helpful articles at **www.toolkit.cch.com**.

GROOM YOUR REPLACEMENT

Depending on your plan, someone else may take over your position and responsibilities within the company. It is time consuming to groom a replacement. When you hire people, you can consider whether they would be a good successor to you. Also consider whether they would keep the best interests of your family in mind. When you are at this point, talk to the person you are considering. Share your vision for the future and develop a plan. Develop a plan to:

- Train him on the aspects of the business he does not understand.

- Increase his responsibilities to learn new aspects of the business.

- Review his decision-making abilities and skills.

- Listen to his needs and ideas and discuss ways to make them work.

- Share money-management goals and how you accomplish them.

- Set a timeline for transfer and stick to it unless there are major problems.

- Implement transition stages to lessen your duties and increase his.

- Set benchmarks and goals for each stage in the process.

- Examine and improve "problem" issues.

- Physically and mentally prepare yourself to leave the business.

SELLING YOUR BUSINESS TO YOUR EMPLOYEES

If your family is not interested in being involved without you, there is the option to sell to an employee or a group of employees. If you plan to sell to employees or friends, it is best to have your accountant or attorney act as a go-between to keep the transaction professional.

It is very easy to hurt one another in this situation. The potential buyers will likely have ideas about how to change "your business" and "your way of doing things." You may also find it difficult to haggle over money with your friends.

Suggest that your employees talk to a professional to clearly understand what they are getting into. Business Law at **www.businesslaw.gov** discusses Employee-Owned Stock Plans (EOSP) as a way to transfer the business to your employees. You can also find advice from The National Center for Employee Ownership at **www.nceo.org** and the Beyster Institute for Entrepreneurial Employee Ownership at **www.fed.org.**

Transferring your business to a worker co-op offers some advantages for everyone. Worker co-op structures are discussed at the National Cooperative Business Association at **www.ncba.org**. Transferring your ownership to employees (similar to family inheritance) can also be done. Talk with professionals to ensure you have covered all the bases and things are being done in the best interest of the people involved. Talk to professionals you trust.

Bear in mind that an employee often makes an excellent owner. The chef who has dreamed for years of owning her own restaurant and the head waiter who just got married and wants more out of his life are examples of good candidates. It also provides a way for you to make a real profit out of the place as well as keep your restaurant heritage alive. Consider selling to an employee under one of the following plans:

- **Management Buy Out (MBO)** - It involves your management team guaranteeing a loan for the employee to purchase the company from you. Because the financing for such an arrangement is based on the financial performance of the company, it will only work if the restaurant can support the loan needed to make the transaction. Because the manager (or management team) is arranging the financing, she will normally be awarded about 30 percent of the company's equity when the deal is finished. It is considered a type of "commission" payment.

- **Leveraged Buy Out (LBO)** - Similar to an MBO, but with a different financier. In this type of arrangement, a third party arranges the financing and splits the commission with the management team. In this arrangement, management will end up with no more than 10 percent commission.

- **Employee Stock Option Plan (ESOP)** - With this type of agreement, your employees buy your stock as part of their retirement plan. ESOP can be a good plan in that employees are more apt to work hard for a company that they "own." However, because ESOP invests the employees' money almost entirely in the stock of this one restaurant or business, the employees take a great risk. If the stock takes a downturn, they could very well lose their profits.

Realistically, the ESOP route will only work for restaurants with very large payrolls. If you decide to go this route, there could be great tax incentives for you: If your company cannot be traded publicly; if you use the proceeds to buy securities in American companies; if you have had the stock three years or longer; and if you have sold between 30 and 100 percent of shares to the ESOP, you may be eligible for a tax-free transaction. There are a few more requirements for such a perk, so check with your tax professional to see how you can qualify.

DECIDING NOT TO SELL

One option that every seller needs to keep open is the option not to sell (as with the buyer who does not have to proceed with the purchase). It is far better to suffer the embarrassment of pulling out than to end up in a really bad situation. The seller has the right and option to stop the process at any time. Bear in mind the following:

- **Get a realistic view of your asking price.** One discouragement to sellers is when they get offers that are way below their asking price. You should find out if your price is too high. Have a professional evaluate your asking price. If you did set it high, are you willing to accept less? If not, you better roll up your sleeves; you have a restaurant to run. If you are willing to accept less, work with the professional to set a more realistic price.

- **Find out why buyers are not biting.** If the price seems right and all seems in order to you, you are obviously missing something — especially if you have had more than one interested buyer who did not bite. Think about a buyer you developed rapport with; take that buyer out to lunch. Find out the reasons why she did not buy. The best person to find out from is the one who got away.

- **Let bygones be bygones.** During the sale process, you probably let a lot of worms out of the can. Let those worms go. Many restaurant owners worry about how much they disclosed to potential buyers or key employees during the process. If anyone has a problem with the sale phases you went through, talk her through it honestly. If the buyer who got away uses information to hurt your business, outsmart her. But do not become obsessed with the process that did not work. Get back to business as usual. The survival of your restaurant depends on it.

- **Put your employees at ease.** You must consider that they have dealt with stress, too, if they knew about your plans to sell. It is not easy thinking that you will have a new boss, not knowing if you will be kept on by the new owner, and so on. Your employees will not be feeling super-confident right now. It is your job to win their trust again.

- **Do not lose your customer base.** The restaurant owner has a great advantage over owners of businesses in other industries when it comes to taking the business off the market. Many customers of a food service establishment will actually be glad to hear you are not leaving, especially if you have a high goodwill rating with the community and your customer base. But while most will be relieved that you will still be there laughing and giving them specials on their anniversary, you may have some customers who are leery about your commitment to them and the business. Whatever you do, do not talk to them too much about the details of the failed sale. It is none of their business. Instead, work very hard to provide them with incredible service and extra perks during this period.

- **Watch for changes in relationships with vendors.** Some vendors, especially smaller companies, may be hesitant to offer you such lenient payment and credit terms as they once did. Simply stated, they do not want you to close up shop for good and leave them holding the bag. Make sure your bills are paid ahead of time and your dealings with them are iced in integrity. You can win their trust again. Their business depends on you.

- **Considering liquidation.** If you realize that the right buyer did not come along but you still want out of the restaurant, you will need to prepare yourself for liquidation of your company. It cannot happen overnight. You must develop a "game plan" to make the closing of your business as profitable for you as possible and fair for your employees.

CLOSING YOUR DOORS FOR GOOD?

Sometimes, closing down and liquidating is the right choice. Sometimes it is not. Never make a hasty decision about anything. It is not good business. When reaching any decision regarding a total closeout, consider the following:

- **Motives.** Look at why you want out. Examine and reexamine your motives for wanting to get away from it all.

- **Hire a manager.** The food service industry is unique with regard to the hours that one must work to be successful. If you love your restaurant and the revenues it brings in but are simply tired of the hours, consider hiring a manager. The additional salary will cut into your profits, but it may save your restaurant.

- **Take a vacation.** Maybe you do not need to change your schedule permanently. Maybe you just have not had a vacation in the last five years. Take a long vacation. Leave someone very capable in charge and go. A vacation may be all you need to get pumped about your business again.

- **Learn to delegate.** Owning a restaurant can be a very high-stress, high-pressure job. The problem may not be that you need a manager or a vacation, but that you need to delegate to employees who are already on the payroll. Make a list of your job responsibilities. Now write down everything for which your key employees are responsible. Honestly evaluate these lists. Do you have trouble delegating? If so, make the decision to begin delegating immediately. It may provide the relief you need to really enjoy your restaurant once again.

DO NOT MAKE A DECISION OUT OF EMBARRASSMENT– CONSIDER ALTERNATIVES

Too many business owners get embarrassed once their business has been on the market and failed to sell. Some see it as a reflection on them personally as a successful businessperson. If that is how you feel, get over it. Do not totally close the doors because of your pride.

- **Challenge yourself.** Think back to your original idea to sell the restaurant. Did it have anything to do with being restless and wanting a job change? It is natural to get bored with any job. The great thing about owning your own business is that you can change just about anything you want unless you are tied to a franchiser. If you do not have a controlling entity like a franchise, make changes that challenge you and your staff. Make changes that create a new, fun atmosphere to work and dine in. Basically, everything you have ever thought about doing, do it. Chances are, the business will profit from the changes and your creative juices will begin to flow again. Go for it.

- **Create something totally different.** If you wanted to sell because the profit margin of your restaurant is just not sufficient enough to keep the doors open, consider rolling everything over into a new business venture. There is a simple way to do this. Change the business address to your home address or a post office box (if your state will allow a P.O. box) so that the restaurant is still considered an existing business. Liquidate all the assets of the business and invest this cash in a high-interest bearing account. When you are ready to start over again, it will serve as start-up funds for your new business or restaurant venture. Check with your legal and accounting professionals to ensure that you are complying with all the laws in your state that refer to this type of situation.

- **Give it away.** If you have a child or other heir who has shown interest in your restaurant at any time, consider giving it to her now as a part of her inheritance. Closing up for good is not as easy as it sounds. Many business owners say that they have "grieved" over a closed business. If you think closing up would be hard for you, it might be easier to stomach if the restaurant continued on in your family. Do not think that just because she has not shown interest that she does not want it. Some kids feel like they cannot ask for something that is not theirs. If you have an instinct she might be interested, talk to her about it. Let her know it is okay if she is not interested, but give her the chance.

So, YOU STILL WANT OUT?

If, after all the considerations about selling your restaurant, you still want out, do it right so that there are no regrets in the future. Take time to develop a plan. You did not expect to sell your restaurant overnight and you should not expect to close it overnight. Many think of closing a business as a split-second decision that takes effect quickly. You need to develop a plan that will allow you the most return on your investment dollars. You want to use up as much food and beverage inventory as possible and you want to develop a closeout plan that is fair for your employees. You should know up front that it usually takes months — sometimes years — to totally close up and liquidate a business. As you close the doors on your restaurant for good, consider the following:

- **Make a list of all liens.** Make a list of all the assets your restaurant has that have liens attached to them. You will need to sell them at a price that will cover the amount you owe your creditors.

- **Consider a liquidating professional if you are not concerned with price.** An estate buyer (someone who buys entire estates for the purpose of selling the items and making a profit) can offer you one price for everything. Pro: It gets everything sold and out of your restaurant quickly. Con: She will not offer you the best price. Her bid will be lower than what you could get out of the assets if you sold them yourself.

- **Develop a garage-sale mentality.** That probably sounds terrible to the person who has poured her life into a restaurant. The same kinds of "profits" can be expected when you begin liquidating your restaurant's assets.

- **Have a private sale for employees.** You may have one or two employees who are saving up to start their own restaurant one day. They will pay more than garage-sale prices to begin stockpiling the equipment needed for when they are ready to become restaurant owners.

- **Check with creditors to see if they will let you turn in assets for credit.** Some creditors and vendors will actually allow you to return assets for a partial credit. They may be open to this idea if they deal in used equipment that they can turn around and sell or lease to another restaurant.

- **Going-out-of-business sale.** A serious and humbling last-ditch effort to sell your business and provide continuing employment for your staff. After you have developed your liquidation plan and know the dollar figure you are expecting to get out of the liquidation process, make a phone call to one of the potential buyers you were in negotiations with earlier. He may be willing to by the whole restaurant; lock, stock, and barrel, now that the price has been so drastically reduced. It provides a way for you to get out quickly and not affect your employees. You can select this option if you are a very confident person who can swallow your pride.

- **File all proper tax and legal documents.** There are tax responsibilities involved even when you liquidate your business. Actually, these tax documents might be good for you. But whether a gain or a loss is posted, do not forget to take care of any IRS business that is left undone after the closing of your restaurant. There may also be state, federal, or local documents to file, depending on where your business is located. Do not forget to tie up these loose ends.

- **Close the business legally.** When you are filing documents and filling out IRS papers, be sure to officially and legally file the documents that will close the restaurant in the eyes of the legal system. If you have no intention of opening this business or another business in this name in the future, then there is no reason to keep the restaurant open, legally speaking. If you do, the business continues to be open to all sorts of problems including different kinds of litigation. If it is closed in your mind, make sure it is also closed in the minds of the IRS and government officials in your area.

LEAVING YOUR BUSINESS

No matter how much you enjoy your business, at some point in time, you will probably try to sell it. The alternatives are to go out of business or pass it on to your heirs. There is no way to know what will prompt you to sell. At that time, you will realize how important it was to build a saleable business to increase your return on investment. Since you are reading this book, you will know in the beginning that it is good to build your business with a possible sale in mind.

A profitable restaurant with a loyal customer base and effective business systems can generate top dollar when you are ready to sell. This profit is a reward for those long, hard hours that went into developing the business.

Start building a valuable and profitable business from the start and it will provide you with an excellent income. The right building blocks and a solid foundation will provide you with a valuable asset that can be sold in the future.

Atlantic Publishing offers a book titled *How to Buy and or Sell a Small Business for Maximum Profit – A Step-by-Step Guide With Companion CD-ROM* (**www.atlantic-pub.com**, Item # HBS-01). This one book offers many tips on how you can get the best price for your business when you are ready to sell. It explains the piles of paperwork and the laws that affect you when you sell or buy a business. You should not begin the sales process before you read this book.

YOUR EXIT PLAN

You need to develop an exit plan. It does not need to be as detailed as your business plan, but you should review it annually to make any necessary changes. These changes are based on the condition of your business and your goals.

Your plan should cover:

- **Best-case scenario** – When do you want to retire? Will you sell the business outright or will your family manage it?

- **Current value** – What could you get if you liquidated or sold it?

- **Enhance business value** – Are there changes that would make the business more appealing to a buyer? Are there changes you did not want to make, but that would increase the value? It is time to consider those.

- **Worst-case scenario** – What can be done in an emergency?

- **Prepare for the sale** – What are the tax implications of selling?

- **Bowing out** – How can you leave your business to others? How do you dissolve partnerships or corporations?

- **Secure your family's financial health** – Prepare your will.

Can your family run the business without you? Do they have instructions for what to do if you are incapacitated? You should meet with your attorney and accountant for valuable advice about how to create your plan. You can see some examples of exit plans at:

- **Principal Financial Group** – www.principal.com/bizprotection/exitplan.htm

- **Family Business Experts** – www.family-business-experts.com/exit-planning.html

- **American Express Small Business** – www.americanexpress.com/smallbusiness

SAY GOODBYE

Saying goodbye to your restaurant, the long hours, and your dreams can be difficult. No matter how much you want to retire or to leave, actually leaving is hard. It is easier to say that final goodbye when you have planned for it. Knowing that your business will be taken care of will help you make the adjustments and changes that are necessary. You sacrificed and struggled to build a profitable and successful restaurant — it is also your responsibility to preserve it.

ALI AMUNDSON

COMPANY: *Uncorked—The Unpretentious Wine Bar*

POSITION: *Owner/Managing Member Operator*

ADDRESS: *16427 N. Scottsdale Rd. Ste.130 Scottsdale, AZ 85254*

WEB: *www.uncorkedwinebar.com*

PHONE: *480-699-9230*

FAX: *480-699-9239*

BACKGROUND

Ali Amundson has been in the restaurant industry for 20 years and in restaurant management for 7 years. She worked in many other restaurants before the restaurant she owns, Uncorked—The Unpretentious Wine Bar. Her first job in the hospitality industry was as a salad bar stocker and cashier at a Sizzler Steak House when she was a junior in high school. She decided to become a restaurant manager because of her personal and professional drive to move up in companies. Uncorked opened in October 2005, a year after she married her husband Tim.

Although opening a restaurant in your first year of marriage is not recommended, it helps to have an understanding husband like Tim!

CAREER

Ali now owns her own restaurant, Uncorked—The Unpretentious Wine Bar where she manages seven employees. Her ideal employee possesses the ability to be on time, has an outstanding work ethic, and a pride in what they do. She believes being able to multitask and delegate responsibilities is what it takes to be a good manager. Her qualities that help in her management career are being very hands on and setting a good example by doing everything that she asks of her employees. Her specific management style is to watch and observe and then make suggestions that will help correct situations. Something unique she does when managing is to work with her employees instead of them only working for her.

The toughest lesson Ali has learned so far in her management career is that when you are on salary rather than hourly pay, you end up working way over 45 hours every week. When she first started in management, she wishes someone had told her not to be a pushover or let her employees walk all over her. She wasn't really given any advice when she started in management.

Ali is very proud of her wine bar which she managed to open at the age of 38 after six years of planning. Her estimated sales from 2006 were $320,000. Her goal for the next five or ten years is to have her wine bar be successful financially as well as being able to expand or sell her business.

RESTAURANT INFORMATION

Their busiest hour varies everyday and every week. Reservations are accepted but they do not have valet parking available. They serve wine, beer, and non-alcoholic beverages (soda, coffee, tea, and bottled water to name a few). They also offer the full menu to go and catering.

According to Ali, the cozy atmosphere and great service are what set the restaurant apart to draw in clientele. She says it is like being in your own living room. They also offer one television in the restaurant. The age group that seems to recommend the restaurant is 25 to 55.

All of the restaurant's food arrives fresh on a daily basis and Ali hand picks the produce from local groceries. Pricing has never had to be adjusted

Uncorked—The Unpretentious Wine Bar serves bistro type food that goes well with wine. The restaurant is open Monday through Wednesday from 11 a.m. to 10 a.m., Thursday from 11 a.m. to 11 p.m., Friday and Saturday from 11 a.m. to midnight, and closed on Sunday.

due to competition and their customer checks do not include a gratuity. She has found the best way to keep costs down is by weekly inventory control and keeping food and wine spoil and waste sheets.

When it comes to her staff, the most important trait Ali looks for is a superstar work ethic. She has had to step in for her staff before. Being a small establishment she does it all. There is not an official host or hostess on staff, but everyone who is working greets each person who walks through the door. Bouncers are not needed for the restaurant. The staff is required to follow a dress code of black tops and black pants or jeans. Men are not required to wear ties.

Outside companies are hired to do accounting and payroll for the restaurant. They use a P.O.S. (Point of Sale) system to print the reports of daily records. Dishes are cleaned with a high temperature under-counter dishwasher.

Although they do not reward frequent diners, they will sometimes give their regular customers a percent off their bill. Coupons are offered in advertising (the Savvy Shopper).

Ali says that Uncorked—The Unpretentious Wine Bar has fulfilled her dream of what it should be, even though she would like it to be twice as busy! When asked if she would do it all over again if she had the chance, Ali said yes, but only if she had more money in the beginning to work with.

ADVICE TIDBITS

I don't know about managers, but for potential restaurant owners, I would say don't even entertain the fact of opening your own place unless you do years of research and know a lot about the business, preferably working in it for several years! It is so much more than investing a lot of money, hiring employees, and opening the doors.

It is also best to concentrate a large part of your efforts on constantly coming up with new ways to build your business and keep increasing sales. It is very important to keep your "regulars" coming back-they are what will "make or break" your business.

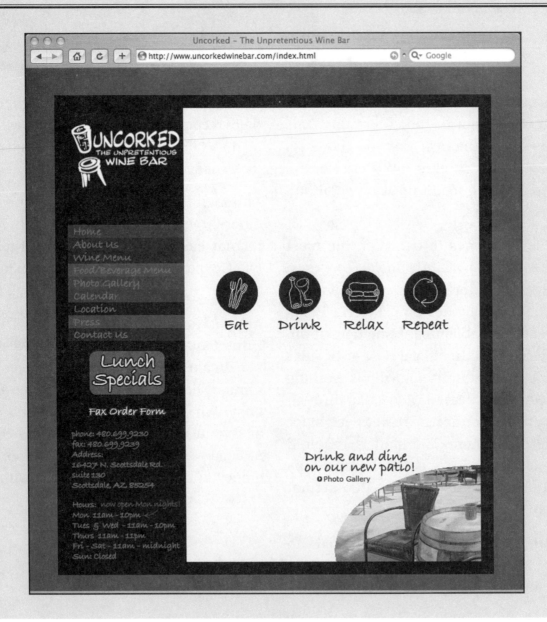

JAY JOHNSON

COMPANY: *Bubba's Roadhouse & Saloon*

POSITION: *Owner*

ADDRESS: *2121 SW Pine Island Road Cape Coral, FL 33991*

E-MAIL: *bubbasroadhouse@excite.com*

WEB: *www.bubbasroadhouse.net*

PHONE: *239-282-5520*

FAX: *239-282-5523*

BACKGROUND

Jay Johnson has been in the restaurant industry for 27 years and in management for 20 of those years. Besides Bubba's Roadhouse & Saloon, Jay has also worked at Brown Derby, McDonalds, and Sheraton Hotels. His first job in the hospitality field was as a dishwasher at Brown Derby in Cleveland, Ohio. He decided to become a restaurant manager because it was a family tradition. He graduated the University of Denver with a major in Hotel and Restaurant Management. He worked for ITT Sheraton in Hawaii, Seattle, Miami, Orlando, Chicago, Los Angeles, and Tucson. He left being the hotel manager at Sheraton to move to Florida and start his own business.

CAREER

Jay now owns his own restaurant, Bubba's Roadhouse & Saloon, where he manages 50 employees. He says the qualities his ideal employee possesses are a willingness to please the customer, quick thinking, a willingness to work hard, and a nice personality.

He believes it takes many things to be a good manager including: a firmness while being fair, an ability to adjust to any situation, an understanding of accounting and how every area of business interacts with each other (marketing, human resources, and finance), and being able to treat people as individuals knowing that what works with one person may not work with another.

Understanding and the ability to adapt to each situation are the qualities he possesses that help him in his management career. His specific management style is to be very open and honest. He treats his employees as he would like to be treated himself.

The toughest lesson Jay has learned in management has been to approach each situation with an open mind. When he first started in management he wishes he had been told to treat his employees right because they would take care of him and to take time for himself. His best piece of advice he was given when first starting was to listen to his employees.

Jay's goal for the next few years is to continue to build the business. His estimated 2006 sales were $2 million. Something he is very proud of is that Bubba's Roadhouse & Saloon hosted President Carter and his family for dinner in 2005.

RESTAURANT INFORMATION

Bubba's Roadhouse & Saloon is a steakhouse that serves hand-cut steaks, barbeque ribs, chicken, and seafood. The restaurant is open from 11:30 a.m. to 11 p.m. and their busiest hour is 5 p.m. They do accept reservations but do not offer valet parking. Alcohol is served and is considered an important aspect to the business. They also do catering. Jay says being a local roadhouse with fresh food and drink sets them apart to draw in their clientele. They also have live music on Friday and Saturday nights. They are a member of their local Chamber of Commerce.

The age group that seems to prefer Bubba's Roadhouse & Saloon is the 40 and up group. Customer checks do not include the gratuity. They do not reward their frequent diners nor do they offer coupons in their advertising.

About 5 percent of the foods arriving at Bubba's are frozen and 95 percent arrives fresh. They do not buy their fresh foods locally. Jay says they have never had to adjust their pricing due to their competition and that the best way to keep costs down is to order smart and keep waste to a minimum.

The most important traits Jay looks for in his wait staff are a good smile and friendliness. He has had to step in for members of his staff before. They do have a host/ hostess, but they do not have managerial duties over the other staff members. They do not require bouncers. The staff does have to follow a dress code of a Bubba's Roadhouse & Saloon shirt, jeans, and black non-slip shoes but the men are not required to wear ties. He does use flex scheduling. He evaluates his wait staff by their demeanor with the guests and fellow co-workers, knowledge of the menu, and sales ability.

Outside companies are hired to wash the towels and sharpen the knives for the restaurant. A computer is used to keep the daily records. The kitchen has all the equipment needed and no make-do is required. A machine is used to wash the dishes. To reduce accidents in the restaurant, all staff members are required to wear non-slip shoes.

When asked if he had to do it all over again, Jay responded he would in a heartbeat.

ROY B. ASSAD

COMPANY: *Leila Restaurant*

POSITION: *Managing Partner (Owner)*

ADDRESS: *120 S. Dixie Highway*
West Palm Beach, FL 33401

E-MAIL: *roy@leilawpb.com*

WEB: *www.leilawpb.com*

PHONE: *561-659-7373*

FAX: *561-833-9417*

BACKGROUND

Roy B. Assad has been in management for 15 years, in the restaurant industry for three years, and in restaurant management for all three years. Besides Leila, Roy also owned and operated L'Opera Brasserie. He decided to become a restaurant manager because he owned the restaurant.

Roy is a professional advisor, motivational speaker, and executive coach. With nearly 30 years experience in an award-winning sales career, he has mastered the arts of networking, negotiation, and bridge-building. These skills have enhanced his effectiveness in the coaching of executives and entrepreneurs.

In 1990, Roy formed Rainmaker Strategies, a motivational speaking firm. Today he is a partner in the Human Capital Group, a four member executive coaching and consulting firm, and a managing partner/ owner in Leila Restaurant, both of which are located in West Palm Beach, Florida. He also participates in numerous boards and committees and holds positions in some of them. These include: Board Chairman, Downtown Development

P 561 659 7373   F 561 659 5484
120 S Dixie Highway West Palm Beach FL 33401
www.leilawpb.com

Authority of West Palm Beach; Board of Directors, Conventions & Visitors Bureau; and Board Member, Cystic Fibrosis Foundation.

His areas of expertise are personal development, leadership training, effective networking, art of negotiation, emotional intelligence, communication skills, financial coaching, sales training, keynote addresses, and strategic thinking.

CAREER

At Leila Restaurant, Roy manages 20 employees. His ideal employee possesses awareness and presence. He believes a good manager should possess leadership qualities. His experience in motivating people and helping them see the value of the role they play are what make him a good manager. His specific management style includes inspiring and continually educating his staff. Something unique he does is consider his employees his most valuable asset.

The toughest lesson Roy learned was that it is just not that easy. The one thing he wished he had been told when he started in management was to have plenty of cash on the side. The best piece of advice that he was given was to find quality people and then hold on to them.

Leila's won many awards its first year in business and turned a profit the second year. In the next five to ten years, Roy wants to make sure they grow their people to the next level and to create a restaurant that can be duplicated.

Roy was named one of 55 Most Fascinating People in Palm Beach County by Palm Beach Illustrated and was also named one of the most powerful people by South Florida CEO.

A change that they implemented at Leila's was changing the management and it coming out successful. They are currently in the process of changing their head chef.

Leila's 2006 estimated sales were $1.4 million.

RESTAURANT INFORMATION

Leila Restaurant serves Middle Eastern cuisine. They are members of their local Chamber of Commerce as well as many of local organizations. They are open for lunch from 11:30 p.m. till 2:30 p.m. and dinner from 5:30 p.m. to 11 p.m. every day. Their busiest hour starts at 7 p.m. and they do accept reservations. The do not require bouncers nor do they have valet parking. They serve beer and wine, but Roy doesn't believe alcohol is an important aspect to the business.

The ambiance, cuisine, and culture are what set Leila's apart to draw in its clientele. In the evenings they have a belly dancer performance. They occasionally will cater.

All of the food at the restaurant arrives fresh and they do purchase some of it from local vendors.

Roy describes the cuisine as fresh and healthy. His markup is 3 times. He says he has never had to adjust prices because of competition, but has found the best way to keep costs down is to be present often.

When a customer is unsatisfied with the service, food, or atmosphere of Leila Restaurant, Roy will comp their meal with no questions asked. There is not really a specific age group that prefers the restaurant. Frequent diners are recognized, but they do not offer any coupons in their advertising. Customer checks do not include a gratuity.

When it comes to his wait staff, the most important trait Roy looks for is cleanliness and a great attitude. Roy has had to help his wait staff before, but has never had to step in for a chef. They do have a host/ hostess and to some degree that staff member does have certain managerial duties over other employees. The staff is required

to follow a dress code but they do not require the men to wear ties. Roy does not use flex scheduling. To handle staff arguments Roy works on preventing them from even happening. The chef is responsible for evaluating the kitchen staff and the wait staff is evaluated through a system that measures attendance, timeliness, and results.

Roy uses a computer to keep up with the daily records of the Leila Restaurant. He contracts many outside professional services. The kitchen has all the equipment needed and dishes are cleaned by machine. To reduce accidents they have instituted many maintenance measures.

Roy believes Leila Restaurant has reached his goal of what he wanted it to be and when asked if he would do this all over again if he had the chance he said for sure, over and over.

ADVICE TIDBITS

Everyone in the organization must be respected and appreciated from the dishwasher to the executive chef; if that is the culture people stay.

STEPHANIE MORLEY

COMPANY: *Ninety-Nine Restaurant*

POSITION: *Assistant Manager*

ADDRESS: *20 MacArthur Blvd. Coventry, RI 02816*

E-MAIL: *Smorin11@cox.net*

PHONE: *401-615-1673*

BACKGROUND

Stephanie Morley has been in the restaurant industry for 12 years. She has been in management for nine of those years. Currently, she is assistant manager for Ninety-Nine Restaurant. She's been the assistant manager there for two years. Besides the Ninety-Nine, she has also work at Appetite's Family Restaurant and TGI Fridays. Her first job in the hospitality field was at Appetite's Family Restaurant as a cashier and waitress. The reason she got into management is that she loved the pace of the restaurant and dealing with customers and knew there was a great potential for advancement.

CAREER

Stephanie does not own her own restaurant, but as assistant manager at the

Ninety-Nine, she manages around 65 employees. Her ideal employee is hardworking and energetic and cares about the guests. She believes patience, understanding, consistency, and accountability are what it takes to be a good manager. Stephanie says she is a very hard worker who cares about her guests and employees. She enjoys working around food and loves teaching others new things. She says all these things are what make her a good manager.

I am tough and expect a lot from my employees but as long as they are doing the right thing, I like to have fun too.

Something unique Stephanie does when it comes to managing her employees is playing games and having contests on a daily basis. The toughest lesson she has learned while in management has been that everyone is different.

> *You have to handle each person in a different way while still being consistent across the board.*

Something Stephanie has done in her management career so far that she is proud of is the long way she has come in dealing with employee relations and how she has learned through doing. She recently implemented some new policies involving the handling of guest complaints. She also has helped in many changes with the organization of the management staff.

In the next five to ten years Stephanie would like to become a general manager of a Ninety-Nine Restaurant (there are currently 122 locations). She would eventually like to be a training general manager and run a successful store.

RESTAURANT INFORMATION

Ninety-Nine Restaurant serves American food—mainly steaks and seafood—and they are famous for their boneless buffalo wings. Their estimated 2006 sales are about $1,600,000. There are currently 122 locations of the Ninety-Nine Restaurant throughout New England, New York, Pennsylvania, and New Jersey. Stephanie's store is open on Monday, Tuesday, and Wednesday from 11:30 a.m. to 11 p.m. On Thursday, Friday, and Saturday they are open from 11:30 a.m. to midnight. On Sundays, they are open from 11:30 a.m. to 10 pm. Their busiest hour is from 5:30 to 6:30.

They do serve alcohol and it is important to their business as it is currently 19 percent of sales. Their goal is to bring it up to 22 percent of their sales. Stephanie says that their family atmosphere and the huge variety of their great food is what

sets their restaurant apart and draws clients in. Although they do not cater, they do offer platters for takeout. They do not take reservations, but do accept call-ahead seating. The age group that seems to prefer the restaurant is 30 to 45 year olds.

Stephanie describes the Ninety-Nine Restaurant cuisine as American steaks, seafood, chicken, pasta dishes—just a little bit of everything. Most of the food arrives frozen; the ribeye and haddock arrive fresh. Not much of the fresh food is bought locally, most come from the Ninety-Nine Commissary. Their markup is 66 percent on most of their food items.

They have not really adjusted prices because of competition. This is because the prices are done on the corporate level. They do some price tiers based on different regions. Stephanie says the best way for them to keep their costs down is by following a declining balance budget.

Customers of the Ninety-Nine Restaurant sometimes receive coupons in advertising. The advertising is mailed to homes in area twice a year. They do not reward frequent diners. When it comes to customers being dissatisfied with their service, food, or atmosphere, Stephanie says they do the following to satisfy them.

Get them what they want as far as food and if they cannot be satisfied then we don't let them pay for their meal. As far as service, ensure that you apologize and make it a point to give them a gift card or free appetizer card to return on a future visit and have them ask for you (or another manager) when they come back in—and be sure they have a wonderful visit. As far as atmosphere, change the television station or the air conditioning to make them happy unless it is not feasible.

When it comes to her employees, Stephanie the most important trait she looks for in her wait staff is friendliness, a nice smile, and a good attitude. The managers in her store are required to cook at least one shift every two weeks to keep them up on the specs and help keep a good relationship with the kitchen staff. They do have a host/hostess, but they do not have any managerial duties over the other staff. Stephanie says they are the most inexperienced in the restaurant. The employees are required to wear a uniform shirt and black or khaki pants. They do not require the men to wear ties.

To evaluate the kitchen staff, they have semi-annual reviews that allow the managers to choose a specific measurement of specific categories of performance (for example, needs improvement, meets expectations, or exceeds expectation). The wait staff is also reviewed in the same manner, but with daily and weekly audits done as well.

To reduce accidents, they follow the safety procedures as well as they have a safety committee. When there are staff arguments or troubles, management will mediate between the parties involved and make decisions, trying to squash the problem before it goes too far.

They do hire outside help for things like laundry, cleaning, baking, and accounting. They do use a computer to keep their records. The system polls automatically overnight. The kitchen does have 99 percent of all the equipment it needs, unless something happens to break. They wash dishes using a machine with industrial strength sanitizers.

Stephanie says Ninety-Nine is getting there as far as fulfilling the dream of where it should be. If she had to do it all over again, she said she would.

JAIME MILLER

COMPANY: *Remember That Chef, In Home Dining & Personal Chef Services*

POSITION: *Chef/Owner*

ADDRESS: *40 Grandville Ave. Ste, 1510 Hamilton Ontario L8E 1J7*

E-MAIL: *Jaime@rememberthatchef.ca*

WEB: *www.rememberthatchef.ca*

PHONE: 905-560-6924

FAX: 905-560-9795

CLASSIFIED CASE STUDIES

directly from the experts

BACKGROUND

Jaime Miller is the chef and owner of Remember That Chef in Canada. It is an in-home dining and personal chef service (catering). He has been in the restaurant industry for over 20 years and in management for six years so far. Besides his current restaurant, he has also worked at Bo Chins, Royal York Hotel, Holiday Inn, Liuna Gardens Banquet Center, Kelsey's Road House, Good Sheppard, Stinson House Bistro, La Boheme Bistro, and Emma's Back Porch Bar and Grill. His first job in the hospitality field was at Bo Chins Chinese as a prep cook where he says he learned how not to cut his fingers with a cleaver! He decided to become a manager because of the ability to take charge and to be able to do food the way he felt it should be done.

Many places I've watched them just plate food with no consistency or it looks unappealing when it goes out. People pay good money for their food. I'd take the extra five minutes and plate it right. Also I want them to remember us and come again.

CAREER

Jaime manages 10 to 15 employees at Remember That Chef. The qualities his ideal employee possesses are honesty, being on time and dressed in uniform when arriving to work, being approachable, and having a willingness to learn.

He believes a sense of humor, willingness to teach, patience, understanding, and respect are what it takes to be a good manager. He says the qualities he has that help him in his management career are: understanding, listening, teaching, respect, and the ability to admit he is wrong. His management style is being straightforward. Something he does that is unique in his management is having fun and working as a team.

The toughest lesson Jaime has had to learn while in management is taking orders from people who really didn't know what they were talking about. When he first started in management the advice he wishes he was given was to not talk back even if he was right.

When I was the chef at the Good Sheppard after a year and a half it felt like the more I did the more they wanted. When told that one person didn't like liver, I was told to take it off the menu. The other 30 tenants still ate the liver. Three months later my boss asked me why there was no liver. I told her that she had requested not to serve it again. Her response was NO I never said that, but start serving it again. So I put it back on the menu and had to serve another meat for the ones that didn't like liver. After three years there they let me go. Why? Because I wasn't putting up with their politics and they said I had a bad attitude toward some tenants.

His best piece of advice he was given when he first started was to treat the tenants like they were normal people. The place he worked in, The Good Sheppard, was for people who had disabilities. These people were almost to the point they could go live out on their own, but still needed consulting which they provided 24 hours a day.

While Jaime was at The Good Sheppard, he was acknowledged for his clean kitchen always passing inspection and for the food. So far at Remember That Chef, the clients are raving about the food. He has testimonials from his clients acknowledging the food (you can see some of these on his Web site). Something he has accomplished so far in his career and that is he proud of has been opening his own business while other people laughed at him and told him he was wasting his money and time. He did it anyway.

Slowly I'm building my business and learning from my mistakes.

Jaime's goal for the coming years is to expand his Remember That

Chef business so that it becomes a household word.

RESTAURANT INFORMATION

Remember That Chef's hours are based on when their client's events take place. They are usually busiest during 3 and 7 p.m. The menus are tailored to their customer's likes and dislikes. They go their clients home and prepare their meal. Alcohol is served if the client provides it, and any activity such as musicians or clowns are provided if the client would like. Most of their clients are 30 years old and over. Remember That Chef is a member of the Burlington Chamber of Commerce and are members of the Canadian Personal Chef Alliance.

Jaime describes the cuisine they serve as bistro to fine dining. All of the foods used to prepare the dishes are bought fresh the day of the event. They have local suppliers.

Our fruit and vegetables are purchased from organic and local farms in the area. (Farm Fresh) Meats are from Nardni's Specialty and the seafood is from Dave's Fish Market.

To keep costs down, Jaime shops at the Bulk Barn and purchases food from local suppliers. He has reduced his prices to compete with competition before.

I'm very flexible with prices. I try and work with the customer.

Although he has not had any customers unhappy with their service or food, Jaime says if they did, he would offer them a dinner for free. He rewards a client after five bookings with him by giving them a free dinner for two. They do not yet offer coupons in advertising.

The most important traits Jaime looks for in his wait staff is being able to work independently, friendliness, and dependability. His servers and bartenders are required to wear white dress shirt, black dress pants, and a bow tie or black tie. The chefs are required to wear a chef jacket and black or design-patterned pants. Jaime has had to step in for an employee before.

One time I was doing a wedding for 25 people in their home. I arrived at 1 p.m. to start the preparation of the food. My server was to be there at 3 p.m. to start with the hor'dourves. At 3:30 I called her thinking she might have gotten lost or was running behind. Her boyfriend said he would pass the message on and have her call me. No reply! She never showed up so I also become the host. Thankfully, some of the guests that attended their wedding helped out in the kitchen and helped clean up! I received an unbelievable testimonial from them. To view their testimonials visit my Web site www.rememberthatchef.ca under testimonial from Diane.

Jaime evaluates his kitchen staff by their knowledge of the food, how well they work and clean (an example is whether they wipe food from the table onto the floor instead of into the trash), and by any comments he receives from clients on their performance. For his wait staff he evaluates their cleaning and from the comments received from clients on their performance. To handle staff squabbles, he will ask the parties involved to go get a cup of coffee and then meet him in his office so they can sit down and talk.

There are always three sides to a story. I'll listen to both sides of their story and then give my opinion. Most of the time we all end up laughing at the problem.

To wash the dishes most times he uses the dishwasher of the client, unless they do not have one. As for his equipment, he says most of the time the clients have the pots and pans on hand to use. Occasionally he has had to bring along a cuisiart.

I always bring my bag of herbs and spices, knives, vinegars and oils, meat terminator, and other kitchen gadgets. My bag weighs about 25 to 30 pounds. You never know what to expect going into someone's home.

When asked if his business had fulfilled everything he felt it should be, Jaime said since he is everything from the bookkeeper to the chef, he

doesn't believe so because there is still a lot of learning for him to do. Finally, when Jaime was asked if he had to do it all over again would he, he replied yes.

Owning your own business is the way to go. Mind you I would have learned not to make so many mistakes in the beginning.

ADVICE TIDBITS

Do not yell at someone in public. If there's a problem take them back into the office. Many times I have been myself and seen others being yelled at in the restaurant or in the kitchen in front of the public or staff. Never do it in the restaurant! What are your customers going to think? In the kitchen why embarrass them? If the manager has something to say do it behind doors. No one likes being yelled at especially in view of customers or staff.

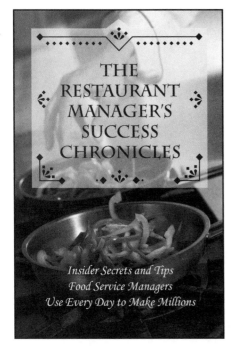

GLOSSARY OF TERMS

A

A LA CARTE Items are prepared to order and each one is priced separately.

ACCOUNTANT A person skilled in keeping and adjusting financial records.

ACCOUNTS PAYABLE Money owed for purchases.

ACCOUNTS RECEIVABLE Money owed by the customers.

ACTUAL-PRICING METHOD All costs plus the desired profits are included to determine a menu selling price.

ADVERSE IMPACT Impact of employer practices that result in higher percentages of employees from minorities and other protected groups.

ADVERTISING Purchase of space, time or printed matter for the purpose of increasing sales.

AFFIRMATIVE ACTION Steps to eliminate the present effects of past discrimination.

AGE DISCRIMINATION IN EMPLOYMENT

ACT OF 1967 Protects individuals over 40 years old.

AMBIANCE Sounds, sights, smells and attitude of an operation.

AMERICANS WITH DISABILITIES ACT (ADA) Prohibits discrimination against disabled persons.

ANNUAL Happening once in 12 months.

ANNUAL BONUS Monetary incentive tied to company profitability and designed to encourage continuous improvement in employee performance.

ANNUITY Promise of a definite payment for a specific period.

AP WEIGHT As-purchased weight.

APPLICATION FORM A form that, when filled out by a potential employee, gives information on education, prior work record and skills.

ARBITRATION Third-party intervention, in which the arbitrator has the power to determine and dictate the terms.

AS PURCHASED (AP) Item as purchased or received from the supplier.

AS SERVED (AS) Weight, size or condition of a product as served or sold after processing or cooking.

ASSESSOR Someone who estimates the value of property for the purpose of taxation.

ASSETS Anything of value; all property of a person, company or estate that can be used to pay debts.

AUTOMATION Automatic control of production by electronic devices.

B

BALANCE The amount that represents the difference between debit and credit sides of an account.

BALANCE SHEET Written statement that shows the financial condition of a person or business. Exhibits assets, liabilities or debts, profit and loss, and net worth.

BANK NOTE A note issued by a bank that must be paid back upon demand. Used as money.

BASELINE BUDGET Based on a past budget and adjusted for current conditions.

BASIC MARKETING MOVES Basic moves that an operation should use to increase its sales volume.

BATCH PREP RECIPE Lists prices per ingredient for a detailed recipe for the purpose of obtaining a total cost for one batch of a meal.

BATCHING Adjusting recipes for equipment or recipe size constraints.

BEGINNING INVENTORY The quantity and value of beverage and food products or operational supplies in stock at the beginning of an accounting period.

BEHAVIOR MODELING A training technique. Trainees are shown good management techniques by role-play or viewing a film. Trainees are then asked to play roles in a simulated situation, and supervisors give feedback.

BEHAVIORISTIC APPROACH TO CONTROL Control through workers' desire to perform for the best interests of the organization.

BENCHMARK JOB The job that is used to secure the employer's pay scale and around which other jobs are systematized in order of relative worth.

BENCHMARKING Analyzing operation features in comparison to the best of its competitors in the industry.

BENEFITS Indirect payments given to employees. These may include paid vacation time, pension, health and life insurance, education plans and/or rebates on company products.

BID SHEET A sheet that is used in comparing item prices from different vendors.

BLIND RECEIVING When there are no quantities or weights printed on packages. The receiver must count or weigh items.

BLOCK SCHEDULING Workers begin and end work at the same time on a specified shift.

BONA FIDE OCCUPATIONAL QUALIFICATION (BFOQ) Requirement that an employee be of a certain religion, sex or national origin where this is reasonably necessary to the organization's normal operation. Specified by the 1964 Civil Rights Act.

BOTTLE MARK A label or ink stamp with information that identifies bottled products as company property.

BOTTOM UP BUDGET Secondary employees prepare a budget and then send it to upper management for approval and combining.

BOUNCEBACK CERTIFICATE OR COUPON A coupon good for a product upon a return visit. The customer is "bounced back" to the business.

BREADING The process of placing an item in flour, egg wash (egg and milk), then bread crumbs before frying or baking.

BREAKEVEN ANALYSIS A computative method used to find the sales amount needed for a food-service operation to break even.

BREAKEVEN CHART A chart that shows the relationship between the volume of business and the sales income, expenditures and profits or losses.

BREAKEVEN POINT The association between the amount of business and the resulting sales income, expenditures and profits or losses. When income and costs are equal.

BUDGET A plan for a specific period that estimates activity and income and determines expenses and other adjustments of funds. Planning the company's expenditures of money, time, etc.

BUDGET CALENDAR The dates/time that a budget should be finished.

BURNOUT Depletion of physical and mental capabilities usually caused by setting and attempting unrealistic goals.

BUSINESS INTERRUPTION INSURANCE Insurance that covers specific costs when a business cannot operate as normal.

BUSINESS PLAN Defines the business image, clarifies goals, calculates markets and competition and determines costs and capital needs.

BUTCHER AND YIELD TESTS Testing of products to determine usable amounts after preparation.

BY-PRODUCT Item or items that are made in the course of producing or preparing other items.

C

CALCULATE Compute or estimate an amount.

CALENDAR YEAR Consisting of 365 days. The period that begins on January 1 and ends on December 31.

CALL BRAND The brand (of a type of liquor) asked for by customers.

CALL DRINK A drink made with brand-name liquor.

CAPACITY The volume limit.

CAPACITY MANAGEMENT The use of an operation's resources to serve the greatest number of guests.

CAPITAL Financial assets.

CAPITAL ACCUMULATION PROGRAMS Long-term incentives. Plans include stock options, stock appreciation rights, performance achievement plans, restricted stock plans, phantom stock plans and book value plans.

CAPITAL BUDGET Equipment, building and other fixed assets.

CARRYOVER Amount left over.

CASE STUDY METHOD Method in which the manager is given a written description of an organizational problem to diagnose and solve.

CASH BUDGET The amount of money received, the amount of money disbursed, and the resulting cash position.

CASH FLOW Profit plus depreciation allowances.

CASH ON DELIVERY (COD) Merchandise must be paid for on delivery or prior to delivery.

CASH OR CASH OUTLAY FOR PROJECT Annual net income (or savings) from project before depreciation but after taxes.

CASHBOOK A book containing records of all income and expenses of a business operation.

CELSIUS A unit used to measure temperature in the metric system, divided into 100 equal parts called degrees; previously called centigrade.

CENTIGRADE See Celsius.

CENTIMETER One hundredth part of a meter.

CENTRAL TENDENCY The disposition to rate all employees the same way, such as rating them all average.

CERTIFICATE Authorizing document issued by a bank indicating that a specific amount of money is set aside and not subject to withdrawal except on surrender of the certificate.

CHAIN OF COMMAND A top authority and a clear line of authority from that top to each person in the organization. Also called the scalar principle.

CIPHER Zero.

CITATIONS SUMMONS Informs employers and employees of regulations and standards that have been violated.

CIVIL RIGHTS ACT Law that makes it illegal to discriminate in employment on the basis of race, color, religion, sex or national origin.

CIVIL RIGHTS ACT OF 1991 (CRA 1991) Places the burden of proof back on employers and permits compensatory and punitive damages.

CLASSES Groupings of jobs based on a set of rules for each grouping. Classes usually contain similar jobs.

CLASSICAL PRINCIPLES (OR THEORY) OF ORGANIZATION Focuses on enterprise structure and work allocation.

CLASSIFICATION (OR GRADING) METHOD Categorizing jobs into groups.

CLASSIFICATION RANKING SYSTEM Constitutes grades and categories to rank various jobs.

COLLECTIVE BARGAINING Representatives of management and the union meet to negotiate the labor agreement.

COMMISSION An individual's pay based on the amount of sales personally derived.

COMMITTED ITEM A product that is scheduled for production between the time it is ordered and the time it is received.

COMMON SIZE ANALYSIS Analysis of financial statements by dividing each item on two or more statements by the total revenue for the period.

COMPARATIVE ANALYSIS Analysis of displaying the difference of line items on financial statements for two or more financial periods or two or more financial dates along with the percentage changes.

COMPENSABLE FACTOR A fundamental, compensable element of a job, such as skills, effort, responsibility and working conditions.

COMPENSATION Something given in return for a service or a value.

COMPETITIVE ADVANTAGE The elements that allow an organization to distinguish its product or service from those of its competitors.

COMPOUND Composed of more than one part.

COMPUTERIZED By means of a computer or computers.

CONFIGURATION An arrangement.

CONFRONTATION MEETINGS The method of explaining and bringing up intergroup misconceptions and problems so that they can be resolved.

CONSIGNMENT PRODUCTS Items provided to a company by a vendor who charges for them after they are used.

CONSUMER ORIENTATION The needs of consumers determine management decisions.

CONTRIBUTION RATE The contribution margin, in dollars, divided by sales.

CONTROL To have charge of.

COOK/CHILL SYSTEM Cooking food item to "almost done" state, packaging it (above pasteurization temperature) and chilling it rapidly.

CO-OP BUYING A group of similar operations working together to secure pricing through mass purchasing at quantity discount prices.

CORPORATION A group of people who obtain a charter giving them (as a group) certain legal rights and privileges distinct from those of the individual members of the group.

COST The amount paid to acquire or produce an item.

COST ALLOCATION The process of distributing costs among departments.

COST CONTROLLER The person or persons whose responsibilities include analyzing expenses, revenues and staffing levels.

COST FACTOR Cost calculated by dividing the cost per servable pound by the purchase price per pound.

COST LEADERSHIP Being the low-cost leader in an industry.

COST OF SALES Food and beverage cost for menu items in relation to the sales attained by these items during a specific period.

COST PER PORTION The cost of one serving calculated by total recipe cost divided by the number of portions.

COST PER SERVABLE POUND The cost calculated by multiplying the purchase price by the cost factor.

COST-BENEFIT ANALYSIS Determining the cost, in monetary terms, of producing a unit within a program.

COST-EFFECTIVENESS ANALYSIS Identifying the cost, in nonmonetary terms, of producing a unit.

COST-PLUS Paying vendors cost plus a percentage.

COUNT The number of units or items.

CPA (CERTIFIED PUBLIC ACCOUNTANT) An accountant who has fulfilled certain requirements and abides to rules and regulations prescribed by the American Institute of Certified Public Accountants.

CPP (COST PER POINT) BUDGETING Method used to obtain an advertising level at a predetermined cost.

CRITERION VALIDITY Validity is based on showing that scores on a test are related to job performance.

CULTURAL CHANGE Changes in a company's shared values and aims.

CURRENT LIABILITY A debt or obligation that will become due within a year.

CURRENT RATIO Current assets divided by current liabilities.

CUTTING LOSS Weight lost from a product during fabrication.

CVP The relationship between cost, volume and profit.

D

DAILY PRODUCTION REPORT A list of items and quantities produced during a specific shift or day.

DEAD STOCK ITEM Item no longer offered.

DEBIT Showing something owed or due.

DECIMAL A system of counting by tens and powers of ten.

DECIMETER Equal to one tenth of a meter.

DEDUCTION A value that may be subtracted from taxable income.

DEFAULT Failure to pay when due.

DEFERRED PROFIT-SHARING PLAN A plan in which a certain amount of profits are credited to an employee's account. May be payable at retirement, termination or death.

DEFINED BENEFIT PENSION PLAN A formula for determining retirement benefits.

DEFINED-CONTRIBUTION PLAN The employer makes specific contributions to an employee's pension but does not guarantee the amount.

DEGREE DAY The difference between outside temperature and 65° F.

DECAMETER Equal to 10 meters.

DELEGATION Distribution of authority and responsibility downward in the chain of command.

DEMOGRAPHIC SEGMENTATION Segmentation based on human population variables such as age, gender and family size.

DENOMINATOR Common trait or standard.

DEPOSIT To put in a place, especially a bank, for safekeeping.

DEPRECIATION Lessening or lowering in value.

DESIGNATE Point out; indicate definitely.

DIFFERENTIAL (BEVERAGE) Difference of the sales value of a drink from the standard sales value of beverages used.

DIFFERENTIATE To distinguish a product or service from similar products or services.

DIFFERENTIATION Trying to be unique within an industry with dimensions that are valued by buyers.

DIRECT COSTS (FOOD) The costs associated with direct purchases.

DIRECT ISSUE Items that are directly delivered and charged to a food-and-beverage outlet—not stored in a central storeroom.

DIRECT LABOR Labor used directly in the preparation of a food item.

DIRECT PURCHASES Food delivered directly into the kitchen and charged as a food cost on that day.

DIRECTING Showing and explaining to others what needs to be done and helping them do it.

DISCIPLINE A correction or action towards a subordinate when a rule or procedure has been violated.

DISMISSAL Involuntary termination of employment.

DIVIDEND An owner's share of the surplus when a company shows a profit at the end of a period.

DIVISOR A number by which another (the dividend) is divided.

DOWNSIZING The process of reducing the size of an operation.

E

EP WEIGHT Edible portion weight. The usable portion after processing.

EARNINGS PER SHARE Earnings of a company divided by the number of its stock shares outstanding.

EARNINGS RATIO The net profit before taxes divided by net sales.

ECONOMIC ORDER QUANTITY (EOQ) Determines a purchase quantity that does the best of minimizing purchases and inventory costs.

ECONOMIC STRIKE A strike resulting from a failure to agree about terms of a contract that involve wages, benefits and other employment conditions.

EDIBLE PORTIONS (EP) The actual yield available for processing a food item.

ELASTICITY OF DEMAND How demand for a product can fluctuate in response to other factors.

ELASTICITY OF SUPPLY The response of output to changes in price. Quantity supplied divided by the percentage change in the price.

ELECTRONIC DATA INTERCHANGE (EDI) Allows a food-service operator to receive prices electronically and generate an order form to send back.

ELECTRONIC SPREADSHEET Computerized worksheet with vertical and horizontal columns that are easily manipulated.

EMBEZZLEMENT Taking of property by someone to whose care it has been entrusted.

EMPLOYEE ADVOCACY Human Resources takes responsibility for defining how management should treat employees and represent the interests of employees within the framework of its obligation to senior management.

EMPLOYEE ASSISTANCE PROGRAM (EAP) Program employers promote to help employees overcome employee assistance program, usually in regard to alcoholism, drug abuse,

EMPLOYEE COMPENSATION Any form of pay or reward an employee gets from his or her employment.

EMPLOYEE ORIENTATION Introduction of basic company background information to new employees.

EMPLOYEE RETIREMENT INCOME SECURITY ACT (ERISA) The law that provides government protection of pensions for all employees with pension plans.

EMPLOYEE STOCK OWNERSHIP PLAN (ESOP) A company contributes shares of its own stock to a trust to which additional contributions are made annually. Upon retirement or separation from service the trust distributes the stock to employees.

EMPOWERMENT Giving lower-level employees the opportunity, responsibility and authority to solve problems.

ENDING INVENTORY The quantity and value of items on hand at the end of a period.

ENTREE The main dish of a meal.

ENTROPY Lack of useful input causing a system to solidify or run down.

EQUAL EMPLOYMENT OPPORTUNITY COMMISSION (EEOC) The commission, created by Title VII, empowered to investigate job discrimination complaints and sue on behalf of complainants.

EQUAL PAY ACT OF 1963 An amendment to the Fair Labor Standards Act designed to require equal pay for women doing the same work as men.

EQUIPMENT Machines or major tools necessary to complete a given task.

EQUITY FINANCING Financing by owners of the organization or company.

EQUIVALENT Equal in value or power.

ESTIMATE Judgment or guess determining the size, value, etc., of an item.

EVALUATE To find the value or amount of.

EXCEPTION PRINCIPLE Recurring decisions are handled in the normal manner and specific ones are referred upward for appropriate action.

EXPECTANCY CHART Shows the relationship between test scores and job performance.

EXPENDITURE Amount spent.

EXPIRATION The date on which a food or beverage product ceases to be usable.

EXPLODED RECIPE Changing recipe quantities to create the number of portions required.

EXTENSION To equate out, lengthen or widen.

EXTRA INDUSTRY Comparison of your practices with other industries.

F

FABRICATED Made or made up.

FABRICATED PRODUCT The item after trimming, boning, portioning, etc.

FABRICATED YIELD PERCENTAGE The yield, or edible portion, of an item shown as a percentage of the item as purchased.

FACTOR One of two or more quantities, multiplied.

FACTOR SYSTEM Raw food cost is multiplied by a factor to determine a menu selling price.

FAIR LABOR STANDARDS ACT Passed in 1936 to provide for minimum wages, maximum hours, overtime pay and child labor protection.

FINANCES Funds, money or revenue; financial condition.

FINANCIAL POSITION The status of a company's assets, liabilities and equity.

FINANCIAL STATEMENTS Used in a business operation to inform management of its exact financial position.

FINISHED GOODS Menu items that are prepared and ready to serve.

FIRM PRICE The price agreed to by the purchaser and vendor.

FISCAL YEAR The time between one yearly settlement of financial accounts and another.

FIXED BUDGET Budget figures based on a definite level of activity.

FIXED EMPLOYEES Employees who are necessary no matter the volume of business.

FLEX PLAN A plan giving employees choices regarding benefits.

FLEXIBLE BUDGET Projected revenue and expenditures based on production.

FLEXIBLE CAPACITY STRATEGY Handling varying volumes of business without having high overhead costs.

FLEXTIME A system that allows employees build their workdays around a core of midday hours.

FLIGHT The period of an advertiser's campaign.

FLUCTUATE Change continually.

FOOD COST The cost of food items purchased for resale.

FOOD INGREDIENT DATABASE Contains basic information about each food item. Name, cost, purchase units, inventory units, issue units, vendors and conversion factors are included.

FOOD ITEM DATA FILE (FIDF) NUMBER The number assigned to a food item in a database.

FOOD COST PERCENTAGE Cost of food divided by sales from that food.

FORECAST A prediction.

FORECASTING Estimating future revenue and expense.

FORMAT Refers to size, shape and general arrangement of a book, magazine, etc.

FORMULA A recipe or equation.

FOUR Cs OF CREDIT Character, capital, collateral and the capacity to repay.

FOUR-DAY WORKWEEK An arrangement that allows employees to work four ten-hour days instead of the more usual five eight-hour days.

FRACTION One or more of the equal parts of a whole.

FRANCHISE A franchise grants the right to use a name, methods and product in return for franchise fees.

FRANCHISEE The person or organization acquiring the franchise.

FRANCHISOR The person or company selling the franchise.

FREEZER BURN Fat under the surface of food having become rancid and possibly having caused a brown deterioration.

FTE, OR FULL-TIME EQUIVALENT A method of measuring labor costs with use of overtime pay.

FUNDAMENTAL EQUATION ASSETS Liabilities plus equity.

G

GARNISH To decorate.

GELATIN A tasteless, odorless substance that dissolves easily in hot water and is used in making jellied desserts and salads.

GENERAL LEDGER (GL) A ledger containing all financial statement accounts.

GOURMET A lover of fine foods.

GRADUATED Arranged in regular steps, stages or degrees.

GRAM Twenty-eight grams are equal to one ounce.

GRATUITY/TIP A gift or money given in return for a service.

GRAZING When employees consume food, unauthorized.

GRIEVANCE A complaint against the employer that may include factors involving wages, hours or conditions of employment.

GROSS The overall total.

GROSS COST The total cost of food consumed.

GROSS MARGIN Sales minus the cost of food.

GROSS PAY Money earned before deductions are subtracted.

H

HARD WATER Water containing excessive calcium and magnesium.

HEALTH MAINTENANCE ORGANIZATION (HMO) Health-care providers that use their own physicians and facilities.

HECTOMETER Equal to 100 meters.

HEDGING A contract on a future price entered into to secure a fixed price.

HOMOGENEOUS ASSIGNMENT A form of specialization that assigns an employee to one job or limits the employee to a related specific task.

HORIZONTALLY On the same level.

HOST/HOSTESS The person who receives guests.

HOUSE BRAND The brand of liquor normally served by a given bar.

HVAC Heating, ventilation and air-conditioning.

HYPOTHETICAL Assumed or supposed.

I

IMPERIAL SYSTEM A measurement system using pounds and ounces for weights and pints for volume.

INDICATOR That which points out.

INGREDIENT One part of a mixture.

INGREDIENT ROOM Where non-cooking personnel prepare food before it is sent to cooking personnel.

INSTALLMENT Part of a sum of money or debt to be paid at regular times.

INSUBORDINATION Willful disobedience or disregard of a boss's authority.

INSURANCE Trading the possibility of a loss for the certainty of reimbursement. Paid by small premiums.

INTEGRATED BEVERAGE CONTROL SYSTEM An automatic beverage dispensing system integrated with a computer or point-of-sale register.

INTEREST Money paid for the use of borrowed money.

INTERNAL CONTROL The methods and measures within a business to safeguard assets, check the accuracy and reliability of accounting data and promote operational efficiency.

INVENTORY A list of items with their estimated value and the quantity of each.

INVENTORY CONTROL System used for maintaining inventories.

INVENTORY CONTROL METHOD (BEVERAGE) Method in which the beverage amount used is determined from guest checks and then reconciled with replacement requisitions.

INVENTORY TURNOVER The amount of times inventory turns over during a specific period.

INVENTORY VARIANCE ACCOUNTING The amount of sales of an item is compared with the number used from inventory records, and the variance is noted.

INVERT Turn upside down.

INVOICE Shows prices and amounts of goods sent to a purchaser.

ITEMIZE To state by item.

J

JIGGER Used to serve a volume predetermined of a beverage.

JOB ANALYSIS Job description and specifications.

JOB DESCRIPTION A description of tasks and duties required on a job.

JOB SHARING Allowing two or more people to share a single full-time job.

JOB SPECIFICATIONS The qualifications needed to hold a job. Includes educational, physical, mental and age requirements.

K

KILOGRAM Equal to 1,000 grams.

KILOMETER Equal to 1,000 meters.

KLEPTOMANIA The persistent impulse to steal.

L

LAPPING A type of embezzlement when funds are taken from an account then covered with later receipts.

LEAST SQUARES ANALYSIS In-depth method of calculating an average of variable or fixed costs.

LEGUMES Vegetables, especially beans and peas; technically, plants in the pea family, or the fruits and seeds of such plants.

LEVERAGING Using borrowed money to acquire assets to make money.

LIABILITY Being under obligation or debt.

LINE MANAGER The manager who is authorized to direct work and is responsible for accomplishing the company's goals.

LINE OF IMPLEMENTATION Division of planning and organizing activities from "doing" activities.

LIQUIDITY RATIOS Ratios that show the ability to meet short-term obligations.

LIQUOR COST Amount paid for liquor after discounts.

LIQUOR COST PERCENT The portion cost divided by the selling price.

LITER Metric system measure of volume.

LOCKOUT When an employer refuses to provide opportunities to work.

LOGO Trademark.

LONG-TERM DEBT Fixed liabilities.

LOSS CONTROL Attempting to prevent losses.

M

MAITRE D' Person in charge of dining room service.

MANAGEMENT BY OBJECTIVES (MBO) Setting measurable goals with employees and periodically reviewing their progress.

MANAGEMENT PROCESS Five basic functions of planning, organizing, staffing, leading and controlling.

MANAGEMENT PROFICIENCY RATIO Net profit after taxes divided by total assets.

MANUAL Done by hand.

MARGIN The difference between the cost and the selling price.

MARGINAL COST The amount of output by which aggregate costs are changed if the volume of output is increased or decreased by one unit.

MARKET Groups with similar characteristics, wants, needs, buying power and willingness to spend for dining or drinking out.

MARKET PRICE INDEX Used to show the change in the cost of raw foods.

MARKET SHARE The share of a market that a business has for its products or services.

MARKETING Means by which an outlet is exposed to the public.

MARKETING OBJECTIVES Measurable and achievable goals that marketing efforts are intended to accomplish.

MARKETING PERSPECTIVE Consumer satisfaction is placed first in all planning, objectives, policies and operations.

MARKETING POLICY A course of action to be followed as long as conditions exist.

MARKETING SEGMENTATION Dividing the market into smaller sub-markets or segments.

MARKETING STRATEGY Overall plan of action that enables the outlet to reach an objective.

MARKUP Amount by which a higher price is set.

MBWA Management by walking around.

MEASURE A lineal measure equal to a thousandth of a meter.

MEAT TAG Used for identification and verification.

MEDIA Various types of advertising, such as television, radio and newspapers.

MEDIATION Intervention using a neutral third party to help reach an agreement.

MEDICARE A federal health insurance program for people 65 or older and certain disabled people.

MENU A list of dishes served at a meal.

MENU ENGINEERING Technique that is used for analyzing menu profitability and popularity.

MENU MIX Menu popularity calculation.

MENU PREFERENCE FORECASTING Predicts how various items will sell when in competition with other items.

MENU PRICE The amount that will be charged for an item.

METRIC Pertains to the meter or to the system of weights and measures based on the meter and the kilogram.

MILL When dealing with monetary numbers, the third place to the right of the decimal.

MILLIGRAM One thousandth part of a gram.

MILLILITER One thousandth part of a liter.

MILLIMETER One thousandth part of a meter.

MISSION STATEMENT A statement giving the reason why the organization exists and what makes it different from other organizations.

MODEM ORGANIZATION THEORY A behavioral approach to organization.

MODULE A discrete and identifiable program.

MONETARY To do with money or coinage.

MOVING AVERAGE The total of demand in previous periods divided by the number of periods.

MUNICIPAL SOLID WASTE (MSW) Waste products that are deposited in landfills.

N

NATIONAL EMERGENCY STRIKES Strikes that might "imperil the national health and safety."

NET The remaining amount after deducting all expenses.

NET PRESENT VALUE (NPV) The present value of future returns discounted at the appropriate cost of capital minus the cost of the investment.

NET PROFIT Profit after all product costs, operating expenses and promotional expenses have been deducted from net sales.

NET PURCHASE PRICE The price paid by the company for one unit.

NET WORTH Excess value of resources over liabilities.

NORRIS-LAGUARDIA ACT This law marked the era of strong encouragement of unions and guaranteed each employee the right to bargain collectively "free from interference, restraint or coercion."

NUMERAL Symbol for a number.

O

OCCUPATIONAL MARKET CONDITIONS Published projections of labor supply and demand for various occupations by the Bureau of Labor Statistics of the U.S. Department of Labor.

OCCUPATIONAL SAFETY AND HEALTH ACT Law passed by Congress in 1970 assuring every working man and woman in the nation safe and healthful working conditions to preserve our human resources.

OCCUPATIONAL SAFETY AND HEALTH ADMINISTRATION (OSHA) The agency created within the Department of Labor to set safety and health standards for all workers in the United States.

ON-THE-JOB TRAINING (OJT) Training to learn a job while working it.

OPEN BAR Practice at banquet functions whereby customers are not charged individually for the drinks they consume. The host pays for banquet-goers' consumption.

OPEN DEPARTMENT REGISTER KEYS Keys that break down sales by categories.

OPEN MARKET BUYING Food purchasing method where competitive bids are secured for various items.

OPERATING BUDGET Detailed revenue and expense plan for a determined period.

OPERATING RATIO Net profit divided by net sales.

ORGANIZATIONAL CHART Shows the relationships of jobs to each other with lines of authority, responsibility and communication.

ORGANIZATIONAL DEVELOPMENT INTERVENTIONS Techniques aimed at changing employees' attitudes, values and behavior.

OUTPUT The end product.

OUTSOURCING Calling upon other companies help supply your products.

OVERHEAD-CONTRIBUTION METHOD All non-food cost percentages are subtracted from 100. The resulting figure is divided into 100 and that figure times the raw food cost equals the menu selling price.

OVERTIME Time exceeding regular hours.

P

P AND L SHEET A profit and loss statement.

PAR STOCK Stock levels established by management for individual inventory items in varying locations.

PARKINSON'S LAW Workers adjust pace to the work available.

PAYBACK PERIOD Period of time required to recover an expenditure.

PAYROLL A list of employees and amounts to pay them, as well as records pertaining to these payments.

PENSION BENEFITS GUARANTEE CORPORATION (PBGC) Established under ERISA to ensure that pensions meet vesting obligations and to insure pensions should a plan terminate without sufficient funds to meet its vested obligation.

PENSION PLANS Plans that provide a fixed sum when employees reach a predetermined retirement age or when they no longer work due to disability.

PERCENTAGE CONTROL SYSTEM Wherein the cost of food or beverage is divided by sales to provide a percentage.

PERCEPTION OF VALUE A consumer's perception of what a product is worth.

PERPETUAL Continuous, endless.

PERPETUAL INVENTORY Accounting for inventory changes. Beginning and ending inventory figures are changed along with any sales or purchases.

PHYSICAL INVENTORY A count of all items on hand.

PIECEWORK The system of pay based on the number of items produced by each individual worker.

POINT-OF-SALE (POS) SYSTEM A sales transaction register and processor.

POPULARITY INDEX Total sales of an item divided by total number of that item sold.

PORTION One serving.

PORTION CONTROL Ensures that the correct amount is being served each time.

PORTION COST The cost of one serving.

PORTION SERVED The amount served to a customer.

PORTION SIZE A specific portion amount.

POSITION REPLACEMENT CARD A card prepared for each position in a company. Shows possible replacement candidates and their qualifications.

POTENTIAL COST Calculating what the expected cost of an item should be.

PPBSE Planning, programming, budgeting, staffing and evaluating.

PRE-CHECKING SYSTEM Independent record of what is ordered from a kitchen.

PRE-COST/PRE-CONTROL Accounting system that determines what the food cost should be, compares it with the actual food cost, and includes sales analysis.

PREFERRED PROVIDER ORGANIZATIONS (PPOS) Groups of health-care providers that contract with employers, insurance companies or third-party payers to provide medical care services at a reduced fee.

PREP YIELD PERCENTAGE The ratio of product yield after preparation to the quantity of product as purchased.

PRICE ELASTICITY The change in the rate of sales due to the change in price.

PRICE INDEXING Measures the effect of product price changes.

PRICE LOOK-UP (PLU) Assigned menu item numbers in POS systems.

PRIMAL CUT Primary division for cutting meat into smaller cuts.

PRIME COST The cost of a product after calculating and adding in labor.

PRINCIPAL Sum of money on which interest is paid.

PRIVILEGE CONTROL SYSTEM A system that permits or denies access to restricted areas.

PRO FORMA Statement prepared on the basis of anticipated results.

PROCEDURE The method of doing a task.

PRODUCT SPECIFICATION A listing of quality and service requirements necessary for products to be purchased from a vendor.

PRODUCTION SCHEDULE The items and quantities that must be produced for a specific meal, day, etc.

PROFILE Data creating an outline of significant features.

PROFIT Gain.

PROPORTION The relationship between one thing and another with regard to size, number or amount.

PROPRIETORSHIP Ownership.

PSYCHOGRAPHIC SEGMENTATION Segmentation based on lifestyles.

PURCHASE SPECIFICATIONS Standard requirements established for procuring items from suppliers.

PURVEYOR One who supplies provisions or food.

Q

QUALITY CONTROL Assuring the execution of tasks and responsibilities according to established standards.

QUANTITATIVE FORECASTING Forecasting based on past and present numerical data.

QUANTITATIVE METHODS Using numbers to help make decisions.

QUANTITY The amount; how much.

QUICK RATIO Current assets less inventory value divided by current liabilities.

R

RANDOM WALK Assuming a present period of sales will be the same as a past period.

RANKING METHOD Ranks each job relative to all other jobs.

RATIO The ratio between two quantities is the number of times one contains the other.

RATIO ANALYSIS A technique for determining staff needs by using ratios between sales volume and the number of employees needed.

REACH Percentage of people in a target audience who will see or hear a specific advertising message.

RECEIPT A written statement that something has been received.

RECEIVING REPORT A report that indicates the value and quantity of items received.

RECIPE Directions used for preparing a menu item.

RECIPE COST The total cost of all ingredients in a recipe.

RECIPE YIELD The weight, count or volume of food that a recipe will produce.

RECONSTITUTE Put back into original form, especially by rehydration.

RED-LINING Placing a red mark on a guest check so it cannot be used again.

REENGINEERING To change an enterprise to be more customer oriented or more efficient.

REPORT An account of facts used to give or get information.

REQUISITION To apply for something needed.

RESIDUAL INCOME ANALYSIS (RIA) Comparing the return on an investment to the cost of invested capital.

RETURN ON INVESTMENT A ratio found by dividing profit by investment.

REVENUE Income.

REVENUE CENTER Outlet or department that produces revenue.

RFP Request for proposal.

ROI (RETURN ON INVESTMENT) Incremental sales dollars divided by total costs.

ROP (RUN OF PAPER/RUN OF PRESS) Placement of advertisement anywhere within a publication that the publisher elects.

ROTATING MENU A menu that alternates in a series. Usually set up on a yearly basis.

S

SALARY A regular payment for services rendered.

SALES MIX The number of sales of individual menu items.

SALES REVENUE Money from the sale of certain items.

SCATTER PLOT Helps identify the relationship between two variables.

SEAT TURNOVER The number of times a seat is occupied during a meal period. Calculate by dividing the number of guests seated by the number of available seats.

SENSIBLE HEAT Heat measured by a thermometer.

SERVER BANKING When the server or bartender also does the cashier duties.

SHRINKAGE The amount of food lost due to cooking, dehydration or theft.

SHRINKAGE (INVENTORY) The difference between what is on hand and what should be on hand.

SIMPLE RANKING SYSTEM Ranking jobs in order of difficulty or importance.

SIMPLIFY To make easier to understand or carry out.

SMART CARD A credit card with a computer chip that holds data.

SOCIAL APPROACH TO MANAGEMENT Considers management's responsibilities to employees, customers and community as well as to its stockholders.

SOLO INSERT Usually printed on different stock than that used by the publication, this page is printed by the advertiser and inserted into a magazine or newspaper by the publisher.

SOLVENCY RATIOS Ratios that show an organization can meet its long-term debt obligations.

SPECIFICATION A detailed statement of the particulars of an item.

SPILLAGE The alcohol lost during the drink making process.

SPOILAGE Loss due to poor food handling.

STAFF MANAGER The manager who assists and advises line managers.

STAGGERED SCHEDULING Scheduling employees to start and stop at different times according to the work pattern.

STAGGERED STAFFING Employees are staffed according to business volume.

STANDARD HOUR PLAN An employee is paid a basic hourly rate and an extra percentage of his or her base rate for production exceeding the standard.

STANDARD RECIPE Producing a particular food or drink item by a definite formula.

STANDARD-COST METHOD (BEVERAGE) Determines the cost of beverages from the number of each beverage sold then compares it to the cost of beverage requisitions.

STANDARDIZE To make the same in size, shape, weight, quality, quantity, etc.

STANDARDIZED RECIPE Directions describing the way an establishment prepares a particular dish.

STANDARD-SALES METHOD (BEVERAGE) Comparing actual beverage sales with the sales value of the beverage.

STANDING ORDER An order for delivery that is automatic.

STATEMENT OF INCOME Shows whether an operation has made or lost money.

STATIC MENU A menu that rarely changes.

STEPPED COSTS Costs which increase in elongated steps but at regular intervals.

STOCK OPTION The right to purchase a stated number of shares in a company at today's price at a future time.

STOCKHOLDER The owner of stocks or shares in a company.

STOREROOM PURCHASES Items are placed into storage rather than sent to the kitchen.

STORES (FOOD COST) The value of food that is in storage.

STRAIGHT LINE METHOD Used when figuring depreciation on an item.

STRATEGIC CHANGE A change in a company's strategy, mission or vision.

SUMMARIZE Briefly express, stating the main points.

SUNK COSTS Costs already incurred that cannot be recouped.

SYSTEM Components working together in the most efficient way.

T

TABLE D'HOTE A complete meal at a set price.

TARGET FOOD COST The amount a company hopes to spend for a particular menu item.

TENDER KEYS Cash register keys that break down sales by payment method.

THERM 100,000 Btu.

TIE-INS Joint venture promotions involving your company and another.

TIME AND MOTION STUDY A study done to establish a standard time for each job.

TIPPING FEE The cost of disposing of waste at a landfill.

TITLE VII OF THE 1964 CIVIL RIGHTS ACT States that an employer cannot discriminate on the basis of race, color, religion, sex or national origin.

TOP DOWN BUDGET A budget prepared by upper management and "passed on" to operating units.

TOTAL QUALITY MANAGEMENT (TQM) A program aimed at maximizing customer satisfaction through continuous improvements.

TRAINING Teaching new employees the basic skills needed to perform their jobs.

TREND ANALYSIS Study of a company's past employment needs over a time period of years to predict future needs.

TRIM The part or quantity of a product removed during preparation.

TRIPLICATE Three identical copies.

TUMBLE CHILL SYSTEM Pumpable foods prepared with steam kettles and then rapidly chilled.

U

U.S. SYSTEM The system of measurement used in the United States, whereby weight is measured in pounds and ounces, and volume is measured in cups and gallons.

UNIFORM PRODUCT CODE (UPC) A computer readable code on a package.

UNIT Refers to the number or amount in a package.

UNIT COST The purchase price divided by the applicable unit.

USABLE PORTION The part of a fabricated product that has value.

USAGE METHOD (OF FOOD PURCHASING) Purchasing food based on past consumption.

V

VARIABLE COST The production cost that changes in direct proportion to sales volume.

VARIABLE EMPLOYEES Employees whose time requirements change with changes in business volume.

VARIABLE RATE Variable costs divided by sales.

VARIATION The extent to which a thing changes, or the change itself.

VENDOR The person or company who sells.

VERBALLY Expressed in words.

VERSATILE Easily changing or turning from one action to another.

VERTICAL Straight up and down.

VOLUME Calculated as length times width times height.

VOUCHER Evidence of payment in written form such as a receipt.

W

WAGES The amount paid or received for work.

WEIGHT The measurement of mass or heaviness of an item.

WELL DRINK A drink not made with name-brand liquor.

WITHHOLDING TAX The deduction from a person's paycheck for the purpose of paying income taxes.

WORK SAMPLES Job tasks used in testing an applicant's performance.

WORK SIMPLIFICATION Finding the easiest and most productive way to perform a job or task.

WORKING CAPITAL The difference between current assets and current liabilities.

X

X MODE Allows reports to be produced on the POS register without resetting totals.

Y

YIELD The total created or the amount remaining after fabrication. The usable portion of a product.

YIELD CONVERSION FACTORS A factor that when multiplied by the gross weight amount of an item purchased shows how much will be available.

YIELD PERCENTAGE/YIELD FACTOR The ratio of the usable amount to the amount purchased.

Z

Z MODE Produces final reports and clears information from a POS register.

ZERO-BASED BUDGET A budget prepared without previous budget figures.

MANUFACTURERS REFERENCE

The following manufacturers submitted photos and information to be used as references in *The Restaurant Manager's Handbook*.

Accardis Systems, Inc.
20061 Doolittle Street
Montgomery Village, MD 20886
800-852-1992
www.accardis.com

Accubar
9457 S University Blvd #261
Highlands Ranch, CO 80126
800-806-3922
www.accubar.com

Amana Commercial Products
2800 220th Trail
Amana, IA 52204
888-262-6271
www.amanacommercial.com

America Corporation
P.O. Box 91
13686 Red Arrow Highway
Harbert, MI 49115
800-621-5075
www.america-americabirchtrays.com

Aprons, Etc.
P.O. Box 1132
9 Ellwood Court
Mauldin, SC 29662
800-460-7836
www.apronsetc.com

Belson Outdoors, Inc
111 North River Rd
North Aurora, IL 60542
630-897-8489
www.belson.com

Big John Grills & Rotisseries
770 W College Ave
Pleasant Gap, PA 16823
800-326-9575
www.bigjohngrills.com

Biocorp
15301 140th Ave
Becker, MN 55308
866-348-8348
www.biocorpaavc.com

Blodgett
44 Lakeside Avenue
Burlington, VT 05401
800-331-5842
www.blodgett.com

Browne-Halco, Inc.
2840 Morris Ave
Union, NJ 07083
888-289-1005
www.halco.com

Buffet Enhancements International
P.O. Box 1000
Point Clear, AL 36564
800-990-0990
www.buffetenhancements.com

Caterease Software
1020 Goodlette Road N
Naples, FL 34102
800-863-1616
www.caterease.com

Chillin' Products, Inc.
1039 Railroad Street
Rockdale, IL 60436
866-932-4455
www.chillinproducts.com

CommLog
2509 E Darrel Rd
Phoenix, AZ 85042
800-962-6564
www.commlog.com

Cookshack, Inc.
2304 N Ash St
Ponca City, OK 74601
800-423-0698
www.cookshack.com

DayMark Food Safety Systems
12830 South Dixie Highway
Bowling Green, OH 43402
800-847-0101
www.daymarksafety.com

Duncan Industries
P.O. Box 802822
Santa Clarita, CA 91380
800-785-4449
www.kitchengrips.com

EasyBar Beverage Management Systems
19799 SW 95th Ave, Suite A
Tualatin, OR 97062
503-624-6744
www.easybar.com

Franklin Machine Products
101 Mt. Holly Bypass
Lumberton, NJ 08048
800-257-7737
www.fmponline.com

General Espresso Equipment Corporation
7912 Industrial Village Road
Greensboro, NC 27409
336-393-0224
www.geec.com

Genpak
P.O. Box 727
Glen Falls, NY 12801
518-798-9511
www.genpak.com

Gourmet Display
6040 South 194th, Ste #102
Kent, WA 98032
206-767-4711
www.gourmetdisplay.com

Henny Penny Corporation
1219 U.S. 35 West
Eaton, OH 45320
800-417-8417
www.hennypenny.com

Holstein Manufacturing
5368 110th St
Holstein, IA 51025
800-368-4342
www.holsteinmfg.com

iSi North America, Inc.
175 Rt 46 West
Fairfield, NJ 07004
800-447-2426
www.isinorthamerica.com

Motoman Inc.
805 Liberty Lane
West Carrollton, OH 45449
937-847-6200
www.motoman.com

OZEM Corp.
832 Harvard Dr
Holland, MI 49423
866-617-3345
www.ozwinebars.com

Polar Ware Company
2806 North 15th St
Sheboygan, WI 53083
800-237-3655
www.polarware.com

Precision Pours, Inc.
12837 Industrial Park Blvd
Plymouth, MN 55441
800-549-4491
www.precisionpours.com

Regal Ware, Inc.
1675 Reigle Dr
Kewaskum, WI 53040
262-626-2121
www.regalwarefoodservice.com

Sabert
879-899 Main St
Sayreville, NJ 08872
800-722-3781
www.sabert.com

Satellite Cooling
308 Washington Blvd, Ste A-105
Mundelein, IL 60060
888-356-2665
www.satellitecool.com

Scannabar
101 Federal Street, Suite 1900
Boston, MA 02110
888-666-0736
www.scannabar.com

Sitram USA
4081 Calle Tesoro, Ste G
Camarillo, CA 93012
800-515-8585
www.sitramcookware.com

Slecta Corp dba Dickies Chef
13780 Benchmark Dr.
Farmers Branch, TX 75234
866-262-6288
www.dickiechef.com

Sunkist Foodservice Eq.
720 E Sunkist St
Ontario, CA 91761
800-383-7141
www.sunkistfs.com/equipment

Tucel Industries
2014 Forestdale Road
Forestdale, VT 05745
800-558-8235
www.tucel.com

Vinotemp International
17621 S Susanna Rd
Rancho Dominguez, CA 90221
310-886-3332
www.vinotemp.com

Wes-Pak, Inc.
9100 Frazier Pike
Little Rock, AR 72206
800-493-7725
www.wespakinc.com

Winekeeper
625 E Haley St
Santa Barbabra, CA 93103
805-963-3451
www.winekeeper.com

WNA Comet
6 Stuart Road
Chelmsford, MA 01824
888-962-2877
www.wna-inc.com

Zing Zang Inc
950 Milwaukee Ave
Glenview, IL 60025
888-891-7489
www.zingzang.com

Zojirushi America Corp
6259 Bandini Blvd
Commerce, CA 90040
800-733-6270
www.zojirushi.com

STATE RESTAURANT ASSOCIATIONS

Offices outside of the U.S are located at the end of the list.

ALABAMA

Alabama Restaurant Association
PO Box 241413
Montgomery, AL 36124-1413
Phone: 334-244-1320
www.stayandplayalabama.com

ALASKA

Alaska Cabaret, Hotel and Restaurant Association
1111 E 80th Ave Ste 3
Anchorage, AK 99518-3312
Phone: 907-274-8133
www.alaskacharr.com

ARIZONA

Arizona Restaurant & Hospitality Association
2400 N Central Ave Ste 109
Phoenix, AZ 85004-1300
Phone: 602-307-9134
www.azrestaurant.org

ARKANSAS

Arkansas Hospitality Association
PO Box 3866
Little Rock, AR 72203-3866
Phone: 501-376-2323
www.arhospitality.org

CALIFORNIA

California Restaurant Association
1011 10th St
Sacramento, CA 95814-3501
Phone: 916-447-5793
www.calrest.org

COLORADO

Colorado Restaurant Association
430 E 7th Ave
Denver, CO 80203-3605
Phone: 303-830-2972
www.coloradorestaurant.com

CONNECTICUT

Connecticut Restaurant Association
100 Roscommon Dr Ste 320
Middletown, CT 06457-7559
Phone: 860-635-3334
www.ctrestaurant.org

DELAWARE

Delaware Restaurant Association
PO Box 8004
Newarkde19714-8004
Phone: 302-738-2545
www.dineoutdelaware.com

DISTRICT OF COLUMBIA

Restaurant Association of Metropolitan Washington
1200 17th St Nw Ste 100
Washington, DC 20036-3010
Phone: 202-331-5990
www.ramw.org

FLORIDA

Florida Restaurant & Lodging Association
PO Box 1779
Tallahassee, FL 32302-1779
Phone: 850-224-2250
www.flra.com

GEORGIA

Georgia Restaurant Association
480 E Paces Ferry Rd Ne Ste 7
Atlanta, GA 30305-3324
Phone: 404-467-9000
www.garestaurants.org

Georgia Hospitality and Travel Association
600 W Peachtree St Nw Ste 1500
Atlanta, GA 30308-3630
Phone: 404-771-2996
www.ghla.net

HAWAII

Hawaii Restaurant Association
1451 S King St Ste 503
Honolulu, HI 96814-2509
Phone: 808-944-9105
www.hawaiirestaurant.com

IDAHO

Idaho Lodging & Restaurant Association
PO Box 1822
Boise, ID 83701-1822
Phone: 208-342-0010

ILLINOIS

Illinois Restaurant Association
33 W Monroe St Ste 250
Chicago, IL 60603-5300
Phone: 312-787-4000
www.illinoisrestaura

INDIANA

Restaurant and Hospitality Association of Indiana
200 S Meridian St Ste 350
Indianapolis, IN 46225-1076
Phone: 317-673-4211
www.indianarestaurants.com

IOWA

Iowa Restaurant Association
8525 Douglas Ave Ste 47
Des Moines, IA 50322-2929
Phone: 515-276-1454
www.iowahospitality.com

KANSAS

Kansas Restaurant and Hospitality Association
3500 N Rock Rd Bldg 1300
Wichita, KS 67226-1335
Phone: 316-267-8383
www.krha.org

KENTUCKY

Kentucky Restaurant Association
133 N Evergreen Rd Ste 201
Louisville, KY 40243-1484
Phone: 502-896-0464
www.kyra.org

LOUISIANA

Louisiana Restaurant Association
2700 N Arnoult Rd
Metairie, LA 70002-5916
Phone: 504-454-2277
www.lra.org

MAINE

Maine Restaurant Association
PO Box 5060
Augusta, ME 04332-5060
Phone: 207-623-2178
www.mainerestaurant.com

MARYLAND

Restaurant Association of Maryland
6301 Hillside Ct
Columbia, MD 21046-1048
Phone: 410-290-6800
www.marylandrestaurants.com

MASSACHUSETTS

Massachusetts Restaurant Association
333 Turnpike Rd Ste 102
Southborough Technology Park
Southborough, MA 01772-1775
Phone: 508-303-9905
www.marestaurantassoc.org

MICHIGAN

Michigan Restaurant Association
225 W Washtenaw St
Lansing, MI 48933-1533
Phone: 517-482-5244
www.michiganrestaurant.com

MINNESOTA

Minnesota Restaurant Association
305 Roselawn Ave E
Saint Paul, MN 55117-2031
Phone: 651-778-2400
www.hospitalitymn.com

MISSISSIPPI

Mississippi Hospitality & Restaurant Association
130 Riverview Dr Ste A
Flowood, MS 39232-8921
Phone: 601-420-4210
www.msra.org

MISSOURI

Missouri Restaurant Association
1810 Craig Rd Ste 225
Saint Louis, MO 63146-4761
Phone: 314-576-2777
www.morestaurants.org

MONTANA

Montana Restaurant Association
1645 Parkhill Dr Ste 6
Billings, Mt 59102-3067
Phone: 406-256-1005
www.mtretail.com

NEBRASKA

Nebraska Restaurant Association & Hospitality Education
1610 S 70th St Ste 101
Lincoln, NE 68506-1565
Phone: 402-488-3999
www.nebraska-dining.

NEVADA

Nevada Restaurant Association
1500 E Tropicana Ave Ste 114a
Las Vegas, NV 89119-6516
Phone: 702-878-2313
www.nvrestaurants.com

NEW HAMPSHIRE

New Hampshire Lodging and Restaurant Association
PO Box 1175
Concord, NH 03302-1175
Phone: 603-228-9585
www.nhlra.com

NEW JERSEY

New Jersey Restaurant Association
126 W State St
Trenton, NJ 08608-1102
Phone: 609-599-3316
www.njra.org

NEW MEXICO

New Mexico Restaurant Association
9201 Montgomery Blvd Ne Ste 602
Albuquerque, NM 87111-2470
Phone: 505-343-9848
www.nmrestaurants.org

NEW YORK

New York State Restaurant Association
409 New Karner Rd
Albany, NY 12205-3883
Phone: 518-452-4222
www.nysra.org

NORTH CAROLINA

North Carolina Restaurant Association
6036 Six Forks Rd
Raleigh, NC 27609-3899
Phone: 919-844-0098
www.ncra.org

NORTH DAKOTA

North Dakota State Hospitality Association
804 E Main Ave
Bismarck, ND 58501-4526
Phone: 701-223-3313
www.ndhospitality.com

OHIO

Ohio Restaurant Association
1525 Bethel Rd Ste 301
Columbus, OH 43220-2054
Phone: 614-442-3535
www.ohiorestaurant.org

OKLAHOMA

Oklahoma Restaurant Association
3800 N Portland Ave
Oklahoma City, OK 73112-2994
Phone: 405-942-8181
www.okrestaurants.com

OREGON

Oregon Restaurant Association
 8565 SW Salish Ln Ste 120
Wilsonville, OR 97070-9633
Phone: 503-682-4422
www.ora.org

PENNSYLVANIA

Pennsylvania Restaurant Association
100 State St
Harrisburg, PA 17101-1024
Phone: 717-232-4433
www.parestaurant.org

RHODE ISLAND

Rhode Island Hospitality & Tourism Association
94 Sabra St
Cranston, RI 02910-1031
Phone: 401-223-1120
ww.rihospitality.org

SOUTH CAROLINA

South Carolina Restaurant Association
PO Box 7577
1005 Gervais St
Columbia, SC 29202-7577
Phone: 803-765-9000
www.schospitality.org

SOUTH DAKOTA

South Dakota Retailers Association Restaurant Div.
PO Box 638
Pierre, SD 57501-0638
Phone: 605-224-5050
www.sdra.org

TENNESSEE

Tennessee Restaurant Association
PO Box 681207
Franklin, TN 7068-1207
Phone: 615-771-7056
www.thetra.com

TEXAS

Texas Restaurant Association
PO Box 1429
Austin, TX 78767-1429
Phone: 512-457-4100
www.restaurantville.com

UTAH

Utah Restaurant Association
515 S 700 E Ste 3d
Salt Lake City, UT 84102-2801
Phone: 801-322-0123
www.utahdineout.com

VERMONT

Vermont Lodging and Restaurant Association
PO Box 37
Montpelier, VT 05601-0037
Phone: 802-223-2636
www.vlra.com

VIRGINIA

Virginia Hospitality & Travel Association
2101 Libbie Ave
Richmond, VA 23230-2621
Phone: 804-288-3065
www.vhta.org

WASHINGTON

Restaurant Association of the State of Washington, Inc.
510 Plum St SE Ste 200
Olympia, WW 98501-1587
Phone: 360-956-7279
www.wrahome.com

WEST VIRGINIA

West Virginia Hospitality and Travel Association
PO Box 2391
Charleston, WV 25328-2391
Phone: 304-342-6511
www.wvhta.com

WISCONSIN

Wisconsin Restaurant Association
2801 Fish Hatchery Rd
Fitchburg, WI 53713-3120
Phone: 608-270-9950
www.wirestaurant.org

WYOMING

Wyoming Lodging & Restaurant Association
PO Box 1003
Cheyenne, WY 82003-1003
Phone: 307-634-8816
www.wlra.org

OUTSIDE OF U.S.

CANADA
Canadian Restaurant & Foodservices Association
316 Bloor Street W
Toronto, Ontario Canada
M5S 1W5
Phone: 416-923-1450
FAX: 416-923-1450

Ontario Restaurant Association
121 Richmond St. W Ste 1201
Toronto, Ontario Canada
M6S 2P2
Phone: 416-359-0533
FAX: 416-359-0531

U.S. VIRGIN ISLANDS
Saint John Hotel & Tourism Association
PO Box 2300
St Thomas, VI 00803-0300
Phone: 340-774-6835
sttstjhta.com

PUERTO RICO
Puerto Rico Hotel and Tourism Association
165 Ave Ponce De Leon Ste 301
San Juan, PR 00917-1235
Phone: 787-758-8001
www.Prhta.org

JOURNALS & TRADE PUBLICATIONS

Bar & Beverage Business Magazine
Mercury Publications
1740 Wellington Ave..
Winnipeg, Manitoba R3H 0E8

Bartender Magazine
Foley Publishing Corporation
P.O. Box 158
Liberty Corner, NJ 07938-0158

Beverage Dynamics
Adams Business Media
833 West Jackson, 7th Floor
Chicago, IL 60607

Beverage World
Ideal Media, LLC
90 Broad Street, Ste. 402
New York, NY 10004

Cheers
Adams Business Media
833 West Jackson, 7th Floor
Chicago, IL 60607

Chef
Talcott Communication Corp.
20 W Kinzie, Ste. 1200
Chicago, IL 60610

Coffee Talk
HNCT, Inc.
23712 49th Ave. SW
Vashon, WA 98070

The Consultant
Foodservice Consultants Society
International
304 W Liberty Street, Ste. 201
Louisville, KY 40202-3011

Cooking For Profit
CP Publishing, Inc.
P.O. Box 267
Fond du Lac, WI 54936-0267

Council on Hotel, Restaurant & Institutional Education Communique
Council on Hotel, Restaurant &
Institutional Education
2810 North Parham, Ste. 230
Richmond, VA 23294-3006

Culinary Trends
Culinary Trends Publications
6285 Spring Street, #107
Long Beach, CA 90808-4000

Dairy Foods
BNP Media
1050 IL Route 83, Ste. 200
Bensenville, IL 60106

El Restaurante Mexicano
Maiden Name Press
P.O. Box 2249
Oak Park, IL 60303-2249

Fancy Foods & Culinary Products
Talcott Communication Corp.
20 W Kinzie, Ste. 1200
Chicago, IL 60610

FEDA News & Views
Foodservice Equipment
Distributors Association
2250 Point Blvd., Ste. 200
Elgin, IL 60123

Food & Beverage News
Saffron Media Private Limited
5th Floor, Manek Mahal,
90, Veer Nariman Road,
Churchgate, Mumbia 400020
India

Food Arts Magazine
M Shanken Communications, Inc.
387 Park Avenue South
New York, NY 10016-8872

Food Channel
Noble & Associates
515 N State Street, 29th Floor
Chicago, IL 60610-4325

Food Management
Penton Media, Inc.
1300 E 9th Street
Cleveland, OH 44114-1503

Foodservice and Hospitality
Kostuch Publication Limited
101-23 Lesmill Road
Toronto, Ontario M3B 3P6

Foodservice Equipment and Supplies
Reed Business Information
360 Park Avenue South
New York, NY 10010

Fresh Cup Magazine
P.O. Box 14827
Portland, OR 97293-0827

Journal of Food Distribution
Food Distribution Research
Society, Inc.
P.O. Box 5187
Mississippi State, MS 39762

Journal of Food Protection
International Association for
Food Protection
6200 Aurora Avenue, Ste 200W
Des Moines, IA 50322-2863

**Journal of Foodservice
Business Research**
The Haworth Press, Inc.
10 Alice Street
Binghamton, NY 13904

Midwest Food Network
Plus Publications, Inc.
57 South Third Street
Newark, OH 43058

National Culinary Review
American Culinary Federation
180 Center Place Way
St. Augustine, FL 32095

The National Dipper
1028 W Devon Ave.
Elk Grove Village, IL 60007

Nation's Restaurant News
Lebhar Friedman, Inc.
425 Park Avenue, 6th Floor
New York, NY 10022

Nightclub & Bar Magazine
Oxford Publishing
307 W Jackson Avenue
Oxford, MS 38655

On Campus Hospitality
Executive Business Media
825 Old Country Road
Westbury, NY 11590

Onboard Services
International Publishing
Company of America, Inc.
664 La Villa Drive
Miami, FL 33166-6095

Pizza Today
Mcfadden Protech LLC
908 S 8th St., Ste. 200
P.O. Box 1347
Louisville, KY 40203

Prepared Foods
BNP Media
1050 IL Route 83, Ste. 200
Bensenville, IL 60106

Restaurant Business
Ideal Media LLC
90 Broad St., Ste. 402
New York, NY 10004

Restaurant Hospitality
Penton Media
1300 East 9th Street
Cleveland, OH 44114-1503

Restaurant Wine
TasteTour Productions
P.O. Box 222
Napa, CA 94559-0222

Restaurants & Institutions
Reed Business Information
860 Park Ave South
New York, NY 10010

Restaurants USA (Online Only)
National Restaurant Association
1200 17th Street NW
Washington, D.C. 20036-3006

Southern Beverage Journal
Beverage Media Group
116 John St, 23rd Floor
New York, NY 10038

Specialty Food Magazine
National Association for the
Specialty Food Trade, Inc.
120 Wall Street, 27th Floor
New York, NY 10005-40001

Yankee Food Service
Griffin Publishing Company
P.O. Box 2826
Duxbury, MA 02331

INDEX

D

G

H

I

J

K

N

O

P

Q

R

S

T

Y

Z

DID YOU BORROW THIS COPY?

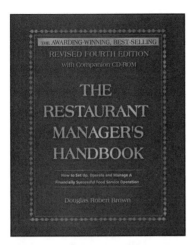

Have you been borrowing a copy of *The Restaurant Manager's Handbook: How to Set Up, Operate and Manage a Financially Successful Food Service Operation With Companion CD-ROM* from a friend, colleague, or library? Wouldn't you like your own copy for quick and easy reference? To order, photocopy the form below and send to:

Atlantic Publishing Company • 1405 SW 6th Ave. Ocala, FL 34471-7014

HACCP & Sanitation in Restaurants and Food Service Operations:
A Practical Guide Based on the FDA Food Code

According to the FDA, it is estimated that up to 76 million people get a food-borne illness each year. Since people don't go to the doctor for mild symptoms, the actual number of illnesses can't be known, but 5,000 people a year die from food-borne illness in the United States, and many others suffer long-term effects.

Most all of this sickness and death could have been prevented with the proper procedures that are taught in this comprehensive book. If these numbers don't upset you, realize that a food-borne outbreak in your establishment can put you out of business, and if the business survives, it will certainly be severely damaged; this, of course, after the lawsuits are resolved. If you do not have proper sanitation methods and a HACCP program in place, you need them today.

This book is based on the FDA Food Code and will teach the food service manager and employees every aspect of food safety, HACCP and sanitation, from purchasing and receiving food to properly washing dishes. They will learn:

- Time and temperature abuses

- Cross-contamination

-   Personal hygiene practices

- Biological, chemical and physical hazards

- Proper cleaning and sanitizing

- Waste and pest management

- Basic principles of HACCP

- Bacteria, viruses, fungi and parasites

- Various food-borne illnesses

- Safe food-handling techniques

- Purchasing, receiving and food storage

- Food preparation and serving

- Sanitary equipment and facilities

- Explain what safe food is and how to provide it facilities

- Accident prevention and crisis management

- Food safety and sanitation laws

The companion CD-ROM contains all the forms needed to establish your HACCP and food-safety program.

Item # HSR-02 $79.95
600 Pages Hardbound
ISBN 0910627-35-5

This series from the editors of *The Food Service Professional Magazine* are the best and most comprehensive books for serious food service operators available. Step-by-step guides on specific management subjects that are easy to read and understand. The information is "boiled down" to the essence. They are filled to the brim with up-to-date and pertinent information. These books cover all the bases, providing clear explanations and helpful, specific information. All titles in the series include the phone numbers and Web sites of all companies discussed. Each book is 144 pages and **$19.95 each**.

1-800-814-1132 Call toll-free 24 hours a day, 7 days a week. Or fax completed form to: **1-352-622-1875.**
Order Online!   Just go to **www.atlantic-pub.com** for fast, easy, secure ordering.

Qty	Order Code	Book Title	Qty	Order Code	Book Title
	Item # FS1-01	Restaurant Site Location		Item # FS9-01	Building Restaurant Profits
	Item # FS2-01	Buying & Selling a Restaurant		Item # FS10-01	Waiter & Waitress Training
	Item # FS3-01	Restaurant Marketing & Advertising		Item # FS11-01	Bar & Beverage Operation
	Item # FS4-01	Restaurant Promotion & Publicity		Item # FS12-01	Successful Catering
	Item # FS5-01	Controlling Operating Costs		Item # FS13-01	Food Service Menus
	Item # FS6-01	Controlling Food Costs		Item # FS14-01	Restaurant Design
	Item # FS7-01	Controlling Labor Costs		Item # FS15-01	Increasing Restaurant Sales
	Item # FS8-01	Controlling Liquor & Beverage Costs		Item # FSALL-01	**Entire 15-Book Series for $199.95**
Subtotal		Shipping	Sales Tax		**TOTAL DUE**

SHIP TO:

Name_____ Phone(____) _____

Company Name_____

Mailing Address _____ City _____ State _____ Zip

FAX _____ E-mail _____

❑ My check or money order is enclosed   ❑ Please send my order COD   ❑ My authorized purchase order is attached

❑ Please charge my: ❑ Mastercard ❑ VISA ❑ American Express ❑ Discover

Card # ☐☐☐☐ – ☐☐☐☐ – ☐☐☐☐ – ☐☐☐☐   Expires ☐☐☐☐

Please make checks payable to: **Atlantic Publishing Company** • 1405 SW 6th Ave. • Ocala, FL 34471-7014   USPS Shipping/Handling: add
$5.00 first item and $2.50 each additional or $15.00 for the whole set. Florida residents PLEASE add the appropriate sales tax for your county.